CONTENTS

- Along the Route 2
- Internet Site 12
- Because You Need To Know 13
- Legend 14
- Index 15
- Locomotives 27
- Train Sets 53
- Passenger Cars 61
- Freight Cars 69
- Decals 95
- Couplers-Trucks 105
- Track & Accessories 109
- Signals, Detection Units & Signs 123
- Scenery 139
- Structures 185
- Magic Of Model Railroading 279
- Figures 301
- Vehicles 313
- Z Scale 325
- Lighting-Electrical-Motors 355
- Power Supplies-Sound-Smoke Systems 371
- Command Control 377
- Adhesives-Cleaners-Lubricants 387
- Paint & Paint Supplies 393
- Tools 409
- Scratch Building Supplies 421
- Super Detailing Parts 431
- Books-Videos-Railroadiana 447

ON THE COVER

"There's daylight in the swamps!"

Down through the years, many a lumberjack started his day with that rousing shout from the foreman. Back then, iron men spent long days in the woods cutting timber or driving teams that dragged fresh-cut logs to the railhead. From there, rugged engines gingerly coaxed their heavy trains over rough tracks to the sawmills. Millions of feet of board lumber rolled out of these mills and into box cars, where mainline railroads hauled it to customers around the country.

The workday still starts early, but it's horsepower not horses that get the timber to market now. Old-time lumberjacks would stand in awe of the modern machines that harvest and move timber. And while the engines and cars have changed, they'd still recognize the role modern railroads play in handling forest products.

Steel, lumber, coal, grain, petroleum — virtually any industry you can think of relies on railroads. Most are huge operations, but with its smaller size and an ever-growing selection of models, N Scale makes the perfect choice for re-creating these and many other heavy industries in miniature.

Kits like the Mountain Lumber Company Sawmill (#933-3236) are a great starting point to create a theme for a new layout or module, or to add authentic industry to your current operations. Add motive power like the new PROTO N GP38-2 diesels from Life-Like and hard-working cars like Walthers 45' Logging Flats (#932-8857 series) and GSC 54' Flat Cars (932-8207 series), and you'll be able to have your new industry up and running.

You can see these models and many, many more inside *Walthers 2007 N&Z Scale 75th Anniversary Reference Book*.

ON THE BACK COVER

Any trip downtown was a special one, but if we happened to go on a Saturday, Dad would always make it a point to drive past the yards. I'd hang so far out the window of our Desoto that Dad would always have to laugh and ask me to be sure not to fall out! But what 10-year-old railfan wouldn't be excited! Every trip brought something new from Alco, EMD or F-M. Sure, some buyers still liked "basic black," but it's those flashy new paint schemes that I still remember to this day.

As railroads large and small made the change to diesel power, competition between the major builders grew more and more intense. Like the auto industry, buyers were faced with a wide range of choices and could basically custom-build a loco to meet their every need.

And, finding the perfect motive power for your N Scale empire has never been easier, with a wide selection of everything from classic steam to modern diesels. Our back cover showcases many releases from Life-Like, including the ALCO PA, F-M "C-Liner," and EMD E8/9 units.

The shop complex also features the Modern 130' Turntable (#933-2613), Modern Roundhouse (#933-3260), and an assortment of buildings constructed from Cornerstone Modulars™, all shown against a photographic background.

WALTHERS 75TH ANNIVERSARY EDITION 2007 N&Z MODEL RAILROAD REFERENCE BOOK

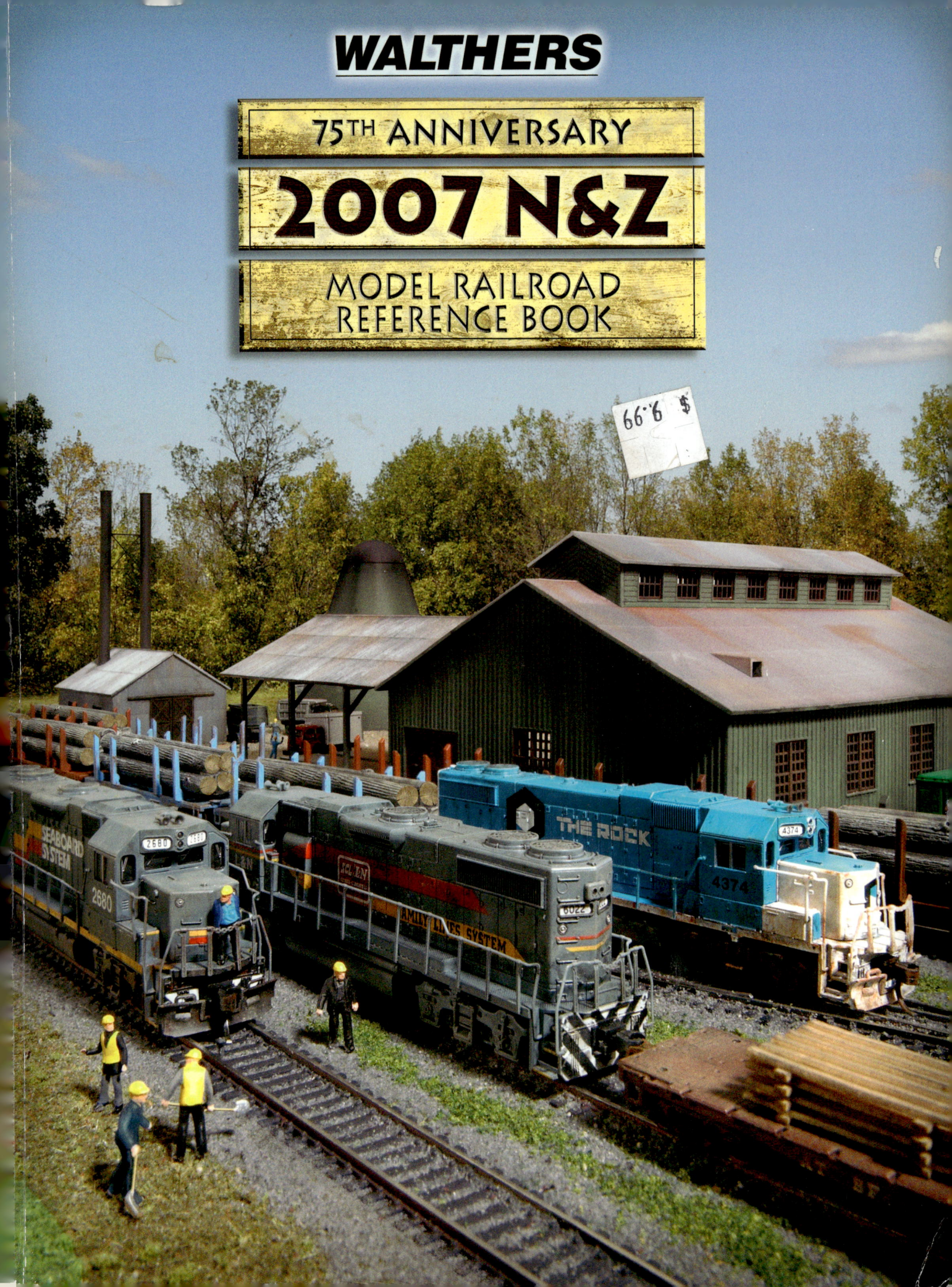

WELCOME TO WALTHERS 75TH ANNIVERSARY N&Z REFERENCE BOOK

The car man gives us thumbs up – all brakes inspected and released. Down the line, signals at the yard throat flash from red to green.

"2100 to the helper… Rich, we're ready when you are… over."

"Roger 2100… we're starting our shove now…."

Nearly two miles back in the autumn twilight, an SD40-2 digs in and starts pushing. As the slack bunches along the train, you open your throttle in the lead EMD and begin to creep forward.

Just outside of town, you'll be fighting gravity for 20 miles. It's uphill all the way and while the grade doesn't look all that tough, you'll be some 400 feet higher at the summit then you are in the yards. Getting to the top is never easy. You know what can happen if you're not careful. Run too fast and the wheels may slip and damage the rail — or if it's really bad, you might stall the entire train. Run too slow and the slack may start to run in and out as the helper tries to keep up. That's an easy way to break an air hose, forcing the train into an emergency stop, or worse yet, breaking a coupler knuckle or drawbar. Leaving town, the EMDs are howling in run 8, and straining to make track speed as the climb begins.

Part of the fun of model railroading is that there are always new challenges. Sometimes though, overcoming those hurdles requires a little extra help to get you over the top and on your way.

This year, we're looking back at our own first days of operation as 2007 marks our 75th year of helping you reach your modeling goals. It's almost unimaginable what Bill Walthers faced when he turned his hobby into a full-time business in 1932. But one thing that hasn't changed is our commitment to sharing information and ideas with you.

What began with the "Signal and Control Manual for Miniature Trains" (which Bill wrote, illustrated and printed himself in 1932) keeps growing in the Reference Book you're holding today. Like those first publications, your new Book will help you find the newest products, photos and prices, along with modeling information and inspiration. We've done a lot of work behind the scenes to get this special edition ready, updating each listing and creating some new features.

Our history section has a brand-new feature called "Along the Route," which provides a fun timeline of facts covering model, prototype and Walthers history. There's also a new article on the company, and that's just the beginning!

Many of you have let us know how much you enjoy the free sign sets in each new edition of our Books. For 2007, we have a special set of vintage and contemporary signs you can use to customize structures and scenes in various modeling eras. And, it can easily be removed without damaging your Book.

For many years, it has been our privilege to share the work of modelers and photographers from around the world in the "Magic of Model Railroading." It's always a pleasure to see how kits and supplies are transformed into amazing works of layout art. These great shots appear on the first page of each section through the Book, and in their own "Magic" section. Information Station articles appear in every section too. These fun-to-read features cover all sorts of modeling and prototype topics, and provide some great tips and ideas for your own projects.

We're also working hard on our Web site at walthers.com, where we bring you the latest new product announcements, photos, industry news and more. You'll also find the site is your best on-line resource for finding must-have products. Hobby shops, where you can see items in person as well as ask questions and place special orders, are listed by state (and in other countries). You can also check our entire inventory of over 100,000+ items to see what's in stock and our Product Locator™ can put you in touch with dealers that have ordered scarce items from us in the past and may have them available for immediate delivery.

As always, your comments and suggestions for improvements are welcome. And if you are in the Milwaukee area during this special year, we hope you'll drop in to say hello.

Happy Modeling

Phil Walthers

WALTHERS
P.O. Box 3039
Milwaukee, WI 53201-3039
(414) 527-0770
www.walthers.com

ISBN
0-941952-77-0

Printed in the USA

Copyright Notice
The actual parts illustrated herein, as well as the reference itself, are protected by the 1977 copyright law.
©2006 Wm. K. Walthers, Inc.
All rights reserved

If you purchased this book without a cover you should be aware that this book is stolen property. It was reported as "unsold and destroyed" to the publisher. The publisher has not received any payment for this "stripped book".

ISBN 0-941952-77-0

Along the Route

New Year's Eve 1899 was a pivotal time in seven year-old Kearney Walthers life. (William Kearney Walthers was called by his middle name – a family tradition – until he was married and his wife insisted he be called Bill). Kearney had just received his first wind-up toy train as a Christmas present. He was fascinated by the new toy—so much so that he wound it up so many times he got blisters on his thumb! This great gift was the catalyst for his lifelong interest in trains of all kinds. Since little Kearney received that train on the dawn of the 20th Century, model and real railroading have both experienced enormous changes.

Leaps in technology have spurred improvements and refinements to railroads large and small. The introduction of small electric motors to model railroading revolutionized the industry; electric trains replaced wind-up toy trains. Over time, detailed plastic models have taken the place of stamped metal and wood models. Prototype railroads have seen the progression from steam to diesel, wooden cars to steel, and the loss of most passenger traffic to the automobile, but they have never been more important for moving the nation's freight. Many non-modelers think trains are dead because they don't ride them, but, in truth, trains are more important than ever for moving goods to market in the global economy.

Walthers, as a model railroad company, has undergone tremendous change over the years. Bill Walthers was a railroad hobbyist. He started Walthers as a manufacturing business to share his modeling ideas and inventions with others. It was the Depression and his main business, the Findex Company, was in bankruptcy, so he used his time to share his ideas and fulfill a thirty-year ambition. If he could feed his family in the process, so much the better. $500 for the first year's sales was a lot back then!

When Bill's son, Bruce, took the reins of the company, his goal was to make sure that every hobbyist would have a chance to buy the products he needed and wanted. Because model railroad items were typically sold in low volumes, toy distributors were reluctant to carry the product line. That's why Bruce turned Walthers into a successful specialty hobby distributor, a wholesaler that would carry each manufacturer's full line and promote it in a catalog — a revolutionary idea at the time.

Phil Walthers took the throttle of a progressive model railroad distributor and manufacturer in 1984. Under his leadership, the Walthers product line has undergone many changes.

Walthers entered the N Scale market with decal sets in the early 1970s. Through early partnerships with Arnold and Roco, the 80s saw the introduction of N Scale North American-prototype train sets. Beginning in 1989, Cornerstone Series® kits in both HO and N Scales made their debut. Today, N Scale products are among the most important components of the business.

As with real railroad companies, mergers and takeovers in the model railroad industry have changed the business. Since its founding in 1932, Walthers has acquired a number of companies including Ulrich, Magnuson, Train Miniature and HO West to name a few.

Most recently, the acquisition of Life-Like, has positioned the company for growth in the HO and N Scale arenas. Through Life-Like products, Walthers now offers train and road race sets to beginners through mass market outlets where many potential modelers have their first exposure to the hobby. Life-Like SceneMaster™ scenery ground cover and trees are usable in any scale from Z to O. Trainline® sets and accessories appeal to intermediate railroaders looking for hobby quality items. Walthers and PROTO™ series HO and N locos and rolling stock appeal to serious model railroaders concerned with detail and authenticity.

Of course, as the real railroad industry has changed, Walthers has kept up the pace by offering models of new prototype trains along with those from the early days.

So, as Walthers celebrates its 75th anniversary, let's take a look at events along the way that have shaped model railroading since Bill received his first train in 1899.

1899

Bill Walthers makes an early career move and gets into model railroading. He receives his first wind-up train set for Christmas at age 7.

1902

NYC 20th Century Limited makes first run.

1903

Wright Brothers first flight at Kitty Hawk, NC. While many ups and downs were to come, airliners would eventually eclipse rail passenger traffic. But, don't forget — steel rails, not the friendly skies, built this country!

1906

American Flyer predecessor Edmonds-Metzel Hardware Company founded. AF name introduced in 1910.

1900

Lionel® founded in New York.

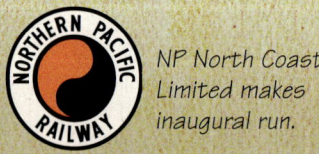

NP North Coast Limited makes inaugural run.

1912
PRR Broadway Limited makes first run. Luxury travel from New York to Chicago was now even better.

1915
Canadian Government to the rescue: Canadian Government Railways formed to control the Intercolonial and National Transcontinental railways.

1918
First United States Railway Administration design locomotive constructed, becomes B&O #4500.

1919
Marx Trains founded.

Canadian Government Railways becomes Canadian National Railway.

1922
Smaller is better! OO Gauge trains introduced in England by Bing.

1923
GE/Ingersoll Rand build first standardized 60-ton boxcab diesel-electric.

H.L. Hamilton's Electro-Motive Engineering Corporation begins building gas-electric "Doodlebug" self-propelled railcars in Cleveland.
Collection of Bob Gallegos

1930
Electro-Motive Corporation purchased by General Motors.

B&O gives passengers a cool ride — introduces first successful air conditioned car, a diner named Martha Washington.

1913

The Dan Patch line in Minnesota tries something new — a GE oil-electric box cab — the first commercially successful internal-combustion loco in the U.S. While not a diesel, it proved that internal combustion had a place in railroading.
Photo by Dennis Pehoski

1917

U.S. enters World War I.

United States Railway Administration (USRA) takes charge of U.S. railroad network. Its mission is standardization to keep railroads running reliably during the War.

GE builds first diesel-electric loco. The 225-horsepower experiment never made it past the gate; it lived at the company's Erie Works laboratory, but was a test bed for the propulsion systems that led to modern locos.

1925
Small switcher success! Alco/GE/Ingersoll Rand diesel-electric unit delivered to CNJ; operates on Bronx line until 1957.

1928
The Canadians were first! Diesel-electric passenger loco built by Canadian Locomotive Company, Baldwin and Commonwealth Steel speeds passengers at up to 63m.p.h.

1929
GN "Empire Builder," named for GN founder James J. Hill, makes first run. The Builder makes it easy to "See America First!". The Great Northern Railroad built Glacier Park to provide a vacation destination.

1932

Bill Walthers starts his business. His first ad in the May, 1932 issue of Model Maker magazine offers signaling and electrical products so modelers could improve their "toy" railroads. His first catalog was 24 pages and sold for 15¢. $500 sales in first year. Bill also offered his first book, the Signal & Control Manual; it sold for $3.00.

Walthers first catalog is published in 1932.

1934

Model Railroader Magazine publishes first issue.

First diesel-electric streamliner in the U.S., CB&Q's Pioneer Zephyr dedicated. Screams across the prairies from Denver to Chicago on a record-breaking, nonstop run in May. Collection of Bob Gallegos

UP M-10000, first U.S. distillate-powered streamliner dedicated. Barnstorms the U.S. with 12,625-mile exhibition trip. 1.2 million see it.

Milwaukee Road constructs first practical, light-weight, streamlined standard passenger car.

Electro-Motive Division of General Motors opens first plant in LaGrange, IL.

Pennsy begins construction of first streamlined electric locomotive—the legendary GG1.

1933

Railroad Model Craftsman magazine publishes first issue.

Look at the little trains! Century of Progress Exposition at the Chicago World's Fair puts model railroading before the public eye.

1935

B&M/MEC Flying Yankee enters service.

National Model Railroad Association founded in Milwaukee.

Bill Walthers, Al Kalmbach and soon-to-be Milwaukee Mayor Frank Zeidler are key founding members.

First streamlined "Hiawatha" passenger trains operated by the Milwaukee Road.

Collection of Bob Gallegos

EMC constructs #511 & 512, first self-contained diesel passenger locomotives in the U.S.

Bill Walthers is given a wild project! Popular Science Magazine commissioned him to design, build, photograph and prepare an article on how to build a model of UP's M-10001 streamliner—in only five days! It's done on time.

1937

ATSF "Super Chief" hits the high iron between Chicago and L.A.

1939

Beginning of the end for steam locomotives: EMD Builds FT Demo Set — the first mass-produced diesel-electric road freight locomotive.

Walthers moves to bigger quarters — 241 E. Erie St., Milwaukee. This was the "Terminal Building" from which Terminal Hobby Shop took its name. The business is incorporated as Wm. K. Walthers, Inc.

SP "Daylight" zips up the California coast for the first time. Photo by Bob Gallegos

New York World's Fair "Railroads on Parade." By this time a well-respected businessman in the model railroad field, Bill Walthers is asked to produce cars for the huge O Scale layout display. They become the basis for the streamlined passenger car line.

Somewhere in between HO and O: S Scale trains introduced by A.C. Gilbert/American Flyer.

Walthers Crestline News kept modelers informed of new releases in O and HO.

1936

CN steam-powered streamliner makes 112.5mph run.

UP/CNW/SP City of San Francisco inaugurated.

N&W receives first Class A 2-6-6-4.

1938

AC Gilbert purchases American Flyer, introduces line of HO Scale.

Walthers Crestline O and HO cars feature metal sides, a wood core and cast-metal details.

Mid-1930s

The company that eventually became Life-Like founded by Sol and Lou Kramer.

Walthers starts HO Scale line. Wartime restrictions delay further development until after the war.

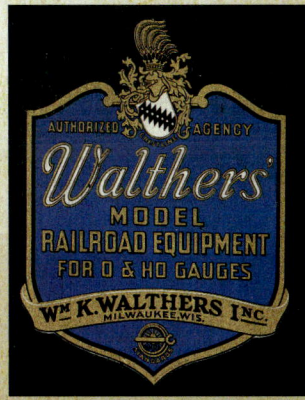

Dealers who carried Walthers kits and parts displayed these window stickers beginning in the 40s.

1940
Walthers "Polydrive" for locomotives patented. MP begins running "Eagle" streamliners.

Biggest of the big steam locos delivered: UP receives Alco "Big Boy" 4-8-8-4s.

Baldwin M-3 "Yellowstone" 2-8-8-4 delivered to Duluth, Missabe & Iron Range.

"Willie" first appeared at Walthers in the early 40s.

First Lima "Allegheny" 2-6-6-6 delivered to C&O. Photo courtesy of Railfan & Railroad Magazine

1945
Last Shay locomotive built - WM #6

1946
Bruce Walthers joins his father's company. He had spent the last three years in the U.S. Navy and knew relatively little about what was happening in the postwar model railroad market.

Life-Like started producing paper maché train tunnels.

1950s
Life-Like produces first foam model railroad tunnels and grass mats.

1951
Booming business: GN re-equips "Empire Builder" with state-of-the-art streamlined cars.

1953

ATSF re-equips Super Chief with new cars.

The beginning of the end for steam: Southern Railway is the first major railroad to completely dieselize.

1941

Last Heisler geared steam locomotive constructed.

U.S. Enters World War II - Walthers scraped the bottom of the barrel for materials because of wartime restrictions. Most companies switched to war production work. Walthers was one of a few that continued to make model kits. Bill sought war work, but his equipment was not suitable for volume production. It was tough. Materials were rationed, prices controlled and all of the experienced employees either enlisted or left for war production work, but Bill had rent to pay and a family to feed, so he kept at it. His wartime ads helped build morale and sustained interest in the hobby during what would otherwise have been a bleak period. Both of Bill's sons and one of two daughters served in the armed forces and returned safely.

1944

Fairbanks-Morse of Beloit, Wisconsin, begins locomotive production. Collection of Bob Gallegos

NKP receives S-2 Class 2-8-4 "Berkshire" locos from Lima. Collection of Bob Gallegos

1947
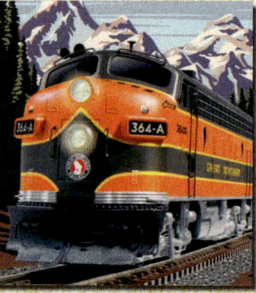

Postwar passenger premier: GN inaugurates streamlined "Empire Builder".

First American Freedom Train tours U.S. behind new Alco PA loco. Cars loaded with historical displays make patriotic journey.

Bill Walthers had hoped to continue with his prewar plans to expand O Scale, but the market moved off in a different direction with the development of plastics, HO Scale and ever easier-to-build kits. Old-time modelers kidded, "all you have to do is shake the box", but it wasn't much of a joke. Walthers barely survived, until a competitor unknowingly came to the rescue.

1949
California Zephyr makes first run Chicago-Oakland.

1957

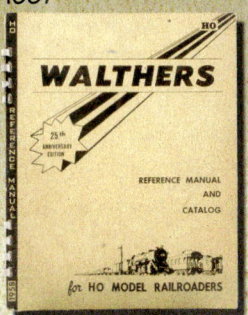

Walthers celebrates 25th Anniversary.

Walthers, producing HO but still emphasizing O gauge is struggling in the post-war market. The turning point came when Athearn produced unlettered HO cars and locos. Walthers decals became the second hottest thing on the market. Profits earned selling decals for these cars and locos provided the capital for Walthers expansion into the wholesale business.

1960

Walthers becomes a full-line model railroad distributor. Toy distributors weren't interested in low-volume hobby products, so Bruce decided to make the company a distributor of specialty hobby products, to make sure every modeler could buy the things he wants and needs. Profits from sale of decals for Athearn's unlettered plastic cars and locomotives make this possible.

Models get even smaller: N Scale introduced in Germany by Arnold.

GE introduces U25B – first of its "Universal" series of mainline diesel-electric locos. Photo by Bob Gallegos

So long steam! GTW operates last scheduled steam-powered passenger train from Durand to Detroit, MI. In the U.S. a few mainline roads were still running steam in freight service, but not on a regular basis. Shortlines, a few Canadian lines and the National Railways of Mexico still boasted regular operations, but these were on the way out.

1963

FM delivers its final H16-44 roadswitchers to Mexico.

1966

Toy Train Operating Society organized.

1967

The beginning of the end: U.S. Post Office pulls most railroad mail contracts, railroads begin discontinuing passenger trains en masse.

Model Railroad Industry Association founded.

N Scale growth spurt: Atlas, Con-Cor, Arnold and Model Power introduce detailed, North American-prototype models.

1968

Set up for failure: NYC and PRR merge to form Penn Central. Overbuilt, under-trafficked and subject to company infighting, the road declares bankruptcy by 1970.

1954

Walthers purchases Hobsco (the Hobby Supply Co. – manufacturer of a power truck).

Train Collectors Association formed.

1955

GN Empire Builder at its zenith: luxury train receives dome coaches and dome lounge. This is the prototype for the train introduced by Walthers in 2006.

Montreal-Vancouver passenger trains get a streamlined look: CP's "Canadian" and CN's "Super Continental" hit the rails.

1956

Baldwin exits locomotive business; last models built were S-12 and RS-12 roadswitchers.

1958

Bill Walthers retires, hands throttle to Bruce Walthers.

Walthers moves into its own building: 1245-47 N. Water Street, Milwaukee.

1961

Chihuahua al Pacifico completes last Mexican mainline between Chihuahua and the port of Topolombampo. Originally, the line was to connect with Kansas City.

1962

B&O merged into C&O. This merger signals the beginning of a trend in the railroad industry that leads to many favorite lines becoming "fallen flags."

N Scale introduced in U.S.

1969

Walthers moves to 4050 N. 34th St. Milwaukee, doubles its space, expands the wholesale business.

Bigger and better: UP purchases DDA40X "Centennial," the largest, most powerful diesel ever built on a single frame. Named for Golden Spike 100th anniversary. Photo by Bob Gallegos

1970s
Instant Horizons™
Walthers purchases HO West, renamed Instant Horizons™.

1970

The largest merger to date: Burlington Northern gobbles up GN, NP, CB&Q, SP&S and Pacific Coast RR.

Congress passes Rail Passenger Service Act creating the National Rail Passenger Corporation—Amtrak®.

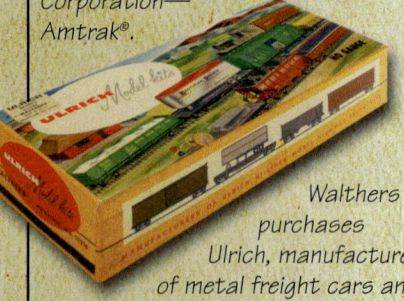

Walthers purchases Ulrich, manufacturer of metal freight cars and vehicles.

1973
Walthers HO Catalog reaches 200 pages.
Walthers offers its first N Scale decals.

1975
American Freedom Train begins two-year tour for U.S. Bicentennial celebration.

1976

Walthers moves to 5601 W. Florist Ave. With nearly two and a half acres under roof, the wholesale business is greatly expanded. What had started out as a Walthers Catalog is rapidly becoming a Reference Book for the industry. U.S. government-created Conrail (Consolidated Rail Corporation) rises from the ashes of bankrupt PC, EL, RDG, LV, L&HR, CNJ and other northeastern roads.

1980s
Walthers purchases Train-Miniature.

1980
Congress passes Staggers Act deregulating rail rates and allowing railroads to act as businesses.

Rock Island liquidated.

1982
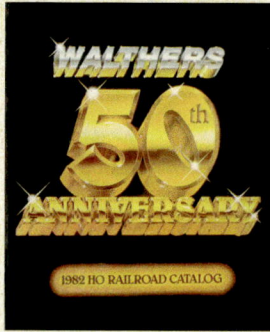

Walthers celebrates 50 years in business.
Walthers Catalog reaches 576 pages.

Purchases Magnuson Models.

1988
CP opens 9.1-mile Mount MacDonald Tunnel in British Columbia - longest in the Americas.

GE introduces Dash 8-40B.

1971
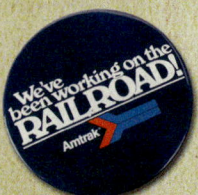
Amtrak takes over U.S. intercity passenger service on May 1st.

1972
Phil Walthers joins his family's business.

More flags fall: Previously merged C&O/B&O system (now including WM) is officially renamed Chessie System.

Marklin introduces Z Scale. At 1/220 Scale, these are the smallest commercially available model trains.

EMD introduces GP38-2 roadswitcher.

1977
Milwaukee Road bankrupt.

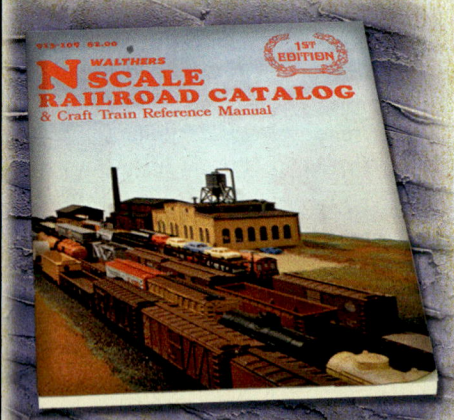

Walthers publishes first N Scale Catalog.

1979
Montreal Locomotive Works (MLW) acquired by Bombardier.

märklin®
Marklin, the premier European manufacturer selects Walthers as its U.S. marketing partner. Other European firms follow and the Walthers catalog is expanded with many new imported lines.

1983
UP merges MP, WP into system.

1984

Bruce hands throttle to Phil Walthers.

1985
Walthers HO Code 83 track system introduced.
Cabooseless operation takes hold in U.S.

1989

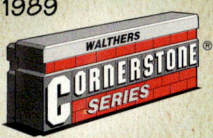

Walthers introduces its revolutionary, easy-to-build Cornerstone Series® injection-molded plastic structures.

Bombardier acquired by GE.

Life-Like introduces first PROTO 2000® HO locomotive, the EMD BL2.

First cabooseless trains run in Canada.

Life-Like produces its first HO racing sets.

1992

Life-Like starts making NASCAR® licensed racing sets.

1993

First Walthers Trainline® train sets introduced.

Mexico begins privatizing railroad system.

1998

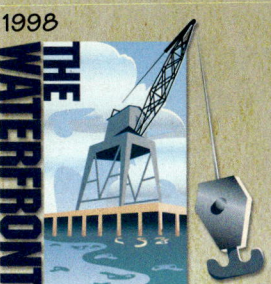

Walthers introduces its popular "Great Circus Train" series. With these detailed kits, modelers could build a complete circus train based on actual equipment at the Circus World Museum in Baraboo, Wisconsin.

Rails meet water: Cornerstone Series® "Waterfront" rail-marine series introduced.

1999

Gold Ribbon Series™ multi-colored kits introduced. Detailed models offer snap-together main pieces; siding and trim colors are molded into a single part.

Cornerstone Series® "America's Driving Force" brings the auto industry to HO.

2005

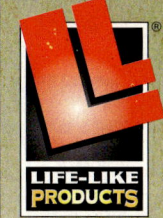

Division of Wm. K. Walthers, Inc.

Walthers acquires Life-Like Products. The acquisition of Life-Like complements Walthers product offerings.

PROTO™ series locos and cars appeal to serious model railroaders, Life-Like train sets (and other products) place Walthers products in mass market stores where beginners get their first taste of the hobby. Life-Like also places Walthers solidly in the N Scale market. Outside of model railroading, Walthers reaches kids of all ages through Life-Like Racing™, Darda™ Toys and Bolz™ Tops.

PROTO 2000 SERIES™ From Walthers

1995

Merger mania: BN/ATSF merger forms Burlington Northern & Santa Fe Railway Company.

UP takes over C&NW.

1996

Big steel on a small scale: Cornerstone Series® "The Works" steel works series debuts.

1997

Modern logging and paper mills: Cornerstone Series® "Trees & Trains" forest products series offered.

Life-Like introduces EMD SW9/1200, its first N locos with modern split-frame drive and intricate detailing. Precursors to PROTO N models.

2001

Ultimate detail: Life-Like introduces first HO PROTO 2000 Heritage Steam collection loco, the 2-8-8-2.

2002

More detail in N: first N Scale PROTO 2000 Heritage Steam collection loco, the 2-8-8-2, hits the rails.

2003

Walthers introduces complete ATSF "Super Chief" train in HO Scale. Photo by V. S. Roseman

2004

The best gets even better: Life-Like releases PROTO 2000 Heritage 2-8-8-2 with factory-installed Quantum® sound and DCC.

Amtrak celebrates the Empire Builder's 75th anniversary.

Walthers Senior Management Team (left to right) John Sanheim, Vice President, Marketing & Sales; J. Philip Walthers, President; Bruce J. Walthers, Chairman of the Board; Paul Rotzenberg, Vice President, Finance & Operations

Walthers owes its success to its employees who keep things on-track. These are the 157 folks who are poised to take Walthers into its next 75 years.

The Milwaukee Crew (above)

The Baltimore Crew (left)

Walthers.com *is the most comprehensive source of model railroading product information on the Internet.*

Only at walthers.com will you find the kind of information you want:
- Current stock information on over 100,000 items in a searchable online catalog
- Daily updates to your Walthers Model Railroad Reference Books
- Online ordering from your favorite participating dealer
- Product Locator™ for hard-to-find products
- Nearly 40,000 product photos
- Breaking news on new product releases
- Current retail prices

Find Out More About Walthers
Everything from company history to the most frequently asked questions about Walthers can be found on the Web site.

Product Pix And Write-ups!
Walthers Web site offers more color product photos than we could possibly print in the Reference Book. Along with more product information and up-to-date availability and pricing, walthers.com is a great tool for keeping your Model Railroad Reference Books current all year long!

Product Locator™ Service
Find it even if it's already sold out!

The Web site can show you where to look for limited-run and hard-to-find products. The search page checks to see which participating dealers purchased the item from Walthers and lists them for you to contact.

Online Hobby Shops
Walthers.com includes an online gathering of Walthers dealers from which you can order through our Web site. Each participating dealer has a storefront, and all you have to do is select which dealer you want to order from. Your shopping cart order goes directly to the dealer.

Contests
Get all the info about the annual Walthers "Magic of Model Railroading" photo contest. Prize-winning photos are published each year in the "Magic of Model Railroading" section of each Reference Book. Check out the entry rules, deadlines and a few fantastic photos on the site.

Again this year, we have a contest for Cornerstone Modulars™ buildings! Show us how you created a custom structure for your layout and you could win a great prize! We'll showcase the winners in next year's N&Z Reference Book and other Walthers promotions. Complete rules and entering information are available on-line.

Keep Your Model Railroad Reference Book Current
The Walthers Web site is the best way to update the information in your Model Railroad Reference Books. With the click of your mouse you can keep track of constantly changing availability and pricing. You'll also be in the know about new products introduced between Reference Books. With all the information updated on the site each day, you'll want to keep walthers.com bookmarked and check it often!

Hobby Shop Locator
Find the top Walthers dealers from around the world with our Dealer Locator. Use this service to find a nearby store or to find stores along your travel and vacation routes!

Who Makes What?
Our Manufacturer List is a great way to learn a little more about your favorite manufacturers. Selected manufacturer listings tell about the history of the vendor and the products they produce.

We're Taking Suggestions
Have an idea for a new product you would like us to produce? Please take a few minutes to fill out a customer suggestion form. It'll be mailed directly to our marketing department. We read 'em all, so your suggestions and ideas for new products really count!

Online Customer Service
Have a question about a Walthers product? Contact our customer service department with a click of your mouse.

Get The Latest Scoop!
Get the most current information on what's hot and what's new. The site is updated daily, so you'll always know what's in stock. Just try the search page — it covers every item we have on hand and more. Check availability on the Web site, along with your Reference Book, when putting together your shopping list before visiting your favorite hobby shop! You might just find some products you didn't know existed!

Walthers.com is your greatest resource for finding the products you need!

walthers.com

BECAUSE YOU NEED TO KNOW

FREQUENTLY ASKED QUESTIONS

WHAT DOES WALTHERS DO?
We're a manufacturer of passenger cars, freight cars, locomotives, Trainline® Models, Cornerstone Series® buildings and other kits.

We're also a wholesaler, distributing products from over 300 manufacturers to hobby shops worldwide.

And we're an importer, bringing you products from around the world.

Combined as one operation, we're the world's largest distributor of model railroad products, offering over 100,000 items so you and your dealer have the best possible selection.

DOES WALTHERS HAVE A WORLD WIDE WEB SITE?
Yes, **www.walthers.com** is the quickest and easiest way to contact Walthers.

HOW DOES THIS REFERENCE BOOK HELP ME AND MY DEALER?
This is a comprehensive listing of merchandise that's available or will be delivered shortly.

All manufacturers have reviewed and updated their listings. Based on this, Walthers lists items we believe will be available during the life of this book.

HOW DO I PURCHASE ITEMS SHOWN IN THIS REFERENCE BOOK?
Walthers is a wholesaler and sells to approved hobby shops who are committed to helping you enjoy the hobby and supplying products from this book. Please support your local shop by purchasing materials and supplies there.

If your dealer has Walthers EXPRES™ III, he or she can find out almost instantly if we have the product you want in stock and the current price. We can usually ship it the next day.

THE PRODUCT I WANT IS LISTED IN THE REFERENCE BOOK AND ON THE WEB SITE, BUT WALTHERS DOESN'T HAVE IT IN STOCK. HOW CAN I GET IT?
With the Product Locator™ service on our Web site, we can help you find any item that's out of stock or has been discontinued. This search page draws upon the purchase history of dealers to see who ordered the item from us in the past. Even though Walthers may no longer have the item, the Product Locator™ will be able to lead you to dealers that may still have it in stock.

HOW DO I FIND A HOBBY SHOP IN MY AREA?
Simply send Walthers a SASE and we will send you a list of dealers in your area. Please send to:

Walthers—DEALER LIST
5601 W. Florist Ave.
P.O. Box 3039
Milwaukee, WI 53201-3039

Walthers.com also has a dealer locator that lists quality hobby shops around the world.

WHAT IF MY DEALER DOESN'T HAVE THE ITEM I WANT?
There are more products than your dealer can possibly have in stock. If you don't find what you want, ask to place a special order.

THE ITEM IS OUT OF STOCK - WHAT DOES THAT MEAN?
We try to stock these products at all times, but some manufacturers' products run out and are temporarily unavailable. Ask your dealer to place it on backorder.

I RECEIVED THE ITEM, BUT I'M NOT HAPPY - WHO CAN HELP?
We try to describe each item in this Reference Book accurately. If it's not what you expected, your dealer can return it. If the kit is too difficult, it can be returned BEFORE starting construction. We cannot accept returns of items that have been worked on or are partially assembled.

I STILL DON'T HAVE MY ORDER - WHY NOT?
Most manufacturers make every effort to ship products on schedule, but many are small businesses with limited resources. They may rely on outside suppliers for parts, packaging, use of a molding machine, etc., which they can't always get. This means items may be temporarily out of stock, or in extreme cases, may never go into production.

Some manufacturers use "batch production," making just enough product to satisfy current demand. Orders are then allowed to accumulate to a specific level before another batch is made. With slow-moving items, there can be long delays (sometimes several years) until enough orders are received.

WHY ARE SOME LISTINGS PRINTED IN BLUE INK?
This is Walthers way of letting you know we haven't received these products for quite some time, and they may not be in stock. They haven't been discontinued, but you may not be able to get them right away. We expect delivery sometime this year and suggest you backorder them with your dealer.

HOW CAN I KEEP THIS REFERENCE BOOK UPDATED?
Visit www.walthers.com. You'll find new product and new arrival information updated daily. Or, if you don't have on-line access, ask your dealer about the latest arrivals and product announcements.

WHO SHOULD I CONTACT WITH A QUESTION ABOUT A PRODUCT?
We do our best to describe each item in this Reference Book accurately. We are happy to answer all questions sent to us with a SASE or on-line.

For questions about techniques or materials, see your dealer. There are many "how-to" books and videos available that may have the answers you need. Your dealer probably knows several experienced modelers who visit the shop and can answer your questions.

There may also be a club in your area where you can visit their layout. You can ask questions, watch trains and see how things are done.

A membership in the National Model Railroad Association (NMRA) will put you in touch with thousands of modelers worldwide. A monthly magazine, "Scale Rails," provides listings of clubs, special interest groups and helpful articles.

(An application for membership is printed in this Reference Book; please see the index listing under NMRA for the page.)

If you are looking for information on an actual car, locomotive or rail line, consider joining a railroad historical society. These addresses are listed in some hobby magazines. Members are dedicated to studying and preserving the history and equipment of their favorite lines. Most issue a newsletter or magazine and can answer in-depth questions.

WALTHERS REFERENCE BOOK POLICY/ WARRANTY INFORMATION

WALTHERS REFERENCE BOOK POLICY
We realize there are more products listed in this book than the average hobby shop can stock at one time. Therefore, we try to describe every item accurately so you can special order them with confidence. However, if the item is not as you expected, your dealer can return it to us. If it is clearly our mistake, we will pay return transportation; otherwise your dealer must pay the return transportation, plus restock fees.

PRICES
All prices are subject to change without notice. All items are invoiced at the prices in effect at the time of shipment.

IMPORTANT
There are certain things beyond Walthers control, therefore: 1) All items offered are subject to availability at the time of shipment. 2) We reserve the right to correct errors, change prices and modify designs without notice and without obligation to previous purchasers. If you do not like the change or correction, the item may be returned by your dealer.

ABOUT WARRANTIES
As a prospective buyer of materials offered in this book, you benefit from three separate warranties:

1) The warranty offered by the manufacturer
2) The warranty we extend to our dealers
3) The warranty offered by the dealer to you, the purchaser

Some warranties are better than others; we suggest you ask before you buy.

WALTHERS LIMITED WARRANTY
We will replace any part of a Walthers kit that's defective at the time of purchase or was lost or damaged during assembly. We reserve the right to ask you to send the damaged or defective part back to Walthers; however, DO NOT send it back until we ask for it, as we will not be responsible for this shipping cost. If the part was defective, we'll pay the transportation costs to send you a new one. If you are asking for a replacement because the part was lost or damaged during assembly, please include $5.00 service fee payment (in U.S. funds), payable to Wm. K. Walthers, Inc. This warranty applies to the original purchaser only, with a time limit of 90 days.

Walthers reserves the right to request proof of purchase. To save time, write to Walthers directly regarding replacement or repair and DO NOT RETURN THE MERCHANDISE UNLESS REQUESTED. Since Walthers designs are subject to change, Walthers reserves the right to make reasonable substitution if the item requested is no longer available. Remember, Walthers warranties apply ONLY to merchandise purchased through authorized retail establishments.

OTHER MANUFACTURERS' WARRANTIES
Manufacturers establish their own policies. Detailed information may be included with the product, or may be obtained by contacting the company. Most require that parts be returned to them with proof of purchase. Under Federal regulations, this is defined as a limited warranty. Your rights on warranty repairs vary depending on which state you live in. If you have problems with another manufacturer's warranty, Walthers will try to help, but again, DON'T SEND MERCHANDISE UNLESS WALTHERS ASKS FOR IT.

DEALER WARRANTIES AND POLICIES
Dealers set their own policies for returns, refunds, credits or exchanges. Ask before you buy, as some are unable or unwilling to return merchandise. Walthers can't accept responsibility or issue refunds for merchandise sent without authorization.

KITS VS ASSEMBLY
Unless stated otherwise, the merchandise offered is in kit form, for assembly by you. If you feel that you are unable to put it together, this is a reason for return under Walthers policy, but please do this BEFORE starting construction. Walthers normally will not accept the return of items that have been worked on or are otherwise in unsellable condition. Please note that Walthers does not have an assembly service.

PUT "SAFETY FIRST" ON YOUR RAILROAD
Working on a real railroad can be dangerous. The "Safety First" message on equipment reminds employees to work carefully, think about what they're doing and follow proper procedures.

"Safety First" is a good message for model railroaders, too. Properly used, hobby products provide hours of enjoyment. But you must understand and appreciate the tools and materials. That's especially important if younger members of the family are going to help.

The items in this Reference Book are NOT toys, and should only be used by children with adult supervision. You can set a good example by working carefully and taking the time to read and follow directions.

The use of hazardous substances in hobby products is declining, but you can be exposed to TOXIC, MECHANICAL (including heat) and ELECTRICAL hazards.

SAFETY IS HABIT FORMING
By paying attention, reading instructions and using common sense, you can safely use a variety of materials. Model railroading is fun, and by making safety a habit, you can keep it that way!

LEGEND & TRADEMARK INFORMATION

NORTH AMERICAN ROADNAME ABBREVIATION KEY

AA Ann Arbor
A&WP Atlanta & West Point
ACL Atlantic Coast Line
ACY Akron, Canton & Youngstown
ART American Refrigerator Transit
ATSF Santa Fe (Actual = Atchison, Topeka & Santa Fe)
B&M Boston & Maine
B&O Baltimore & Ohio
BCOL British Columbia Railway
BCIT BC Rail
BN Burlington Northern
BNSF Burlington Northern Santa Fe (1996 Merger)
BS Birmingham Southern
C&G Columbus & Greenville
C&O Chesapeake & Ohio
C&S Colorado & Southern (CB&Q Subsidiary)
CB&Q Chicago, Burlington & Quincy
CG Central of Georgia
CN Canadian National
CNJ Central Railroad of New Jersey/Jersey Central
CNW Chicago & North Western
CP Canadian Pacific
CR Conrail
CRR Clinchfield (Actual = Carolina, Clinchfield & Ohio)
CSX CSX Transportation
D&H Delaware & Hudson
DL&W Delaware, Lackawanna & Western (a.k.a. Lackawanna)
DT&I Detroit, Toledo & Ironton
DMIR Duluth, Missabe & Iron Range (a.k.a. Missabe Road)
DRGW Rio Grande (Actual = Denver & Rio Grande Western)
EL Erie-Lackawanna
FEC Florida East Coast
FGE Fruit Growers Express
FNM Ferrocarriles Nacionales de Mexico (Actual = Mexican National Railways)
GF Georgia & Florida
GM&O Gulf, Mobile & Ohio
GN Great Northern
GTW Grand Trunk Western
IC Illinois Central
KCS Kansas City Southern
KCSM Kansas City Southern de Mexico
L&N Louisville & Nashville
LS&I Lake Superior & Ishpeming
LV Lehigh Valley
MEC Maine Central
MILW Milwaukee Road (Actual = Chicago, Milwaukee, St. Paul & Pacific)
MKT Katy (Actual = Missouri-Kansas-Texas)
MN&S Minneapolis, Northfield & Southern
MON Monon (Actual = Chicago, Indianapolis & Louisville)
MOW Maintenance-Of-Way
MP Missouri Pacific
NdeM National Railways of Mexico
NH New Haven (Actual = New York, New Haven & Hartford)
NKP Nickel Plate Road (Actual = New York, Chicago & St. Louis)
NP Northern Pacific
NS Norfolk Southern
N&W Norfolk & Western
NYC New York Central
PC Penn Central
PFE Pacific Fruit Express
PRR Pennsylvania Railroad (Also "Pennsy")
RDG Reading
RI Rock Island (Actual = Chicago, Rock Island & Pacific)
RUT Rutland
SAL Seaboard Air Line (a.k.a. "Seaboard")
SCL Seaboard Coast Line
SLSF St. Louis-San Francisco "Frisco"
SOO Soo Line (Actual = Minneapolis, St. Paul & Sault Ste. Marie)
SOU Southern Railway
SP Southern Pacific
SP&S Spokane, Portland & Seattle
SSW Cotton Belt (Actual = St. Louis-Southwestern)
UP Union Pacific
TFM Transportacion Ferroviaria Mexicano
TTX TTX Corporation
W of A Western Railway of Alabama
WC Wisconsin Central Limited
WM Western Maryland
WP Western Pacific

SYMBOLS

NEW - Identifies a brand new item appearing for the first time in this book.

Items listed below are available by Special Order (see Legend Page). These items are currently available, but are not stocked in the Walthers warehouse. Walthers orders them directly from the manufacturer and ships them to you as soon as received.

NEW SUPPLIER - Identifies an all-new line of products making their first appearance in this book.

Blue Line Items
When an item is listed in blue, it's because the manufacturer has not been able to deliver them regularly. The item was out of stock when the catalog was printed and delivery was not known. All "blue line" items CAN still be placed on backorder. Ask your dealer or check our Web site at www.walthers.com for current delivery information.

Limited Quantity Available
When a product appears under this heading, it means we are running out of the item and unable to order more. The item may have been discontinued by the manufacturer, or is produced on an irregular schedule and will not be available again for quite some time.

PACKAGE QUANTITY - pkg(#) - Indicates the number of items included in the package. Some items used in pairs (trucks, diaphragms) are listed as 1 Pair, 2 Pair, etc.

RETIRED MODEL - Indicates a Walthers product which has been taken out of production. Supplies are limited to the remaining inventory at your dealer or in our warehouse. A future production run may be scheduled.

TRADEMARK INFORMATION

Wm. K. Walthers, Inc. is an authorized Amtrak supplier. Amtrak is a registered service mark of the National Railroad Passenger Association.

CSX Proprietary Marks Used By Permission of CSX Transportation, Inc.

Wm. K. Walthers, Inc., is a licensed supplier of products bearing Union Pacific Trademarks.

LICENSING INFORMATION

Dr Pepper and 7 UP are trademarks of Dr Pepper/Seven Up, Inc. used by Wm. K. Walthers under license.

©2005 Good Humor-Breyers Ice Cream. All Rights Reserved. Trademark used under license. Licensed by Broad Street Licensing Group, LLC

©1929, 1956, 1958 SEP: Licensed by Curtis Publishing, Indianapolis, IN. All rights reserved. www.curtispublishing.com

©2005 King Features Syndicate, Inc./Fleischer Studios, Inc.™ Hearst Holdings, Inc./Fleischer Studios, Inc. www.bettyboop.com

Moon Mullins®, Brenda Starr®, Little Orphan Annie®, Dick Tracy® & ©2005 Tribune Media Services, Inc.

LIFE is a registered trademark of Time Inc. Used under license.

Joe Nemechek Name and Likeness Licensed by ©2006 MB2 Motorsports, LLC/NEMCO Motorsports. Permission to use these insignia, marks or logos in no way implies endorsement of products, services, events or organizations by the Department of the Army or any other component of the Department of Defense. ©2006 U.S. Army. BMW designs and trademarks used with permission of BMW AG. Dave Blaney and Bill Davis Racing trademarks and likenesses are used under license from Caterpillar Inc. CAT, CATERPILLAR and their design marks are registered trademarks of Caterpillar Inc. ©2006 Caterpillar Inc. General Motors trademarks used under license to Wm. K. Walthers, Inc. The yellow/black color scheme is a trademark for DEWALT® Power Tools and Accessories. The DEWALT® trademarks, Roush Racing and Matt Kenseth's name and/or likeness used by authority of Roush Racing, Livonia, MI. ©2006 Evernham Motorsports, LLC. The stylized E with checkered flag® and 19® are registered trademarks and service marks of Evernham Motorsports, LLC. used under license. Jeremy Mayfield® likeness and signature are trademarks of Mayfield Motorsports licensed by Evernham Motorsports, LLC. Dodge® is a registered trademark of DaimlerChrysler Corporation. ©2006 Evernham Motorsports, LLC. The stylized E with checkered flag® and 9® are registered trademarks and service marks of Evernham Motorsports, LLC, used under license. Kasey Kahne™ likeness and signature are trademarks of Kasey Kahne Inc. licensed by Evernham Motorsports, LLC. Dodge® is a registered trademark of DaimlerChrysler Corporation. Dodge is a trademark of DaimlerChrysler Corporation. Dodge Charger and its trade dress are used under license by Wm. K. Walthers, Inc. ©DaimlerChrysler Corporation 2006. ©2006 HGL, LLC. The name, likeness and signature of Jeff Gordon and the likeness of the #24 DuPont Chevrolet are used under license granted by HGL, LLC. 'Ford,' 'Mustang' and 'Fusion' trademarks used under license from Ford Motor Company. Goodyear is a trademark of The Goodyear Tire & Rubber Company used under license to Wm. K. Walthers, Inc. "Tony Stewart®," "#20®," and "The Home Depot®" licensed under authority of Joe Gibbs Racing, Huntersville, NC. "J.J. Yeley®," "#18®," and "Interstate® Batteries" licensed under authority of Joe Gibbs Racing, Huntersville, NC.® Unless otherwise indicated, all trademarks are owned by Newell Rubbermaid, Inc. or its subsidiaries, and are used by permission. All rights reserved. Roush Racing's and Jamie McMurray's name and/or likeness used by authority of Roush Racing, Livonia, MI. TM, ® Kellogg Company in/dans Canada. TM, ® Kellogg North America Company elsewhere/partout ailleurs/en otros paises. ©2006 Kellogg North America Company. Used under license/utilze sous license/bajo licencia. ® #5 design, ® Hendrick Motorsports. Used under license/utilze sous license/bajo licencia. ©2006 HGL, LLC. The name, likeness and signature of Kyle Busch and the likeness of the #5 Kellogg's Chevrolet are used under license granted by HGL, LLC. ©2006 HGL, LLC. The name, likeness and signature of Jimmie Johnson and the likeness of the #48 Lowe's Chevrolet are used under license granted by HGL, LLC. ®/TM M&M's®, the letter M and the M&M's Brand Characters are trademarks of MARS, Incorporated and its affiliates. Manufactured and distributed under license by Wm. K. Walthers, Inc., 5601 W. Florist Ave., Milwaukee, WI 53218. 1-800-773-9350. ©Mars, Incorporated 2006. www.mms.com. Elliott Sadler and Robert Yates Racing are used under license. TM/® PEDIGREE and the ROSETTE DESIGN are trademarks of Kal Kan Foods, Inc. ©Mars, Inc. National Guard used by permission of the National Guard Bureau. Roush Racing and Greg Biffle name and/or likeness used by authority of Roush Racing, Livonia, Michigan. NASCAR® is a registered trademark of The National Association for Stock Car Auto Racing, Inc. The name Office Depot and the Office Depot logo are registered trademarks of Office Depot. The Roush Racing trademarks and Carl Edwards name or likeness used by authority of Roush Racing, Livonia, MI. Porsche, the Porsche shield and distinctive design of Porsche cars are trademarks and trade dress of Porsche AG. Permissions granted. Copyright ®2006. Travis Kvapil Name and Likeness licensed by Travis Kvapil Racing LLC. All rights reserved. Tide, the Bullseye Design and the Downy Design are trademarks used under license from The Procter & Gamble Co. PPI, PPI MOTORSPORTS and the stylized numeral 32 are trademarks of PPI Motorsports, L.L.C., and are used under license. UPS, the UPS Shield, the color Brown, and the UPS Racing Logo are registered trademarks of United Parcel Service of America, Inc. used under license. Dale Jarrett and Robert Yates Racing trademarks are used under license. ©2006 Valvoline Evernham Racing, LLC. The VER logo and stylized No. 10 are trademarks and service marks of Valvoline Evernham Racing, LLC and Evernham Motorsports, LLC respectively. Scott Riggs likeness and signature are trademarks of Scott Riggs Enterprises licensed by Valvoline Evernham Racing, LLC. V® and Valvoline, used under License and are registered trademarks of Ashland. Stanley and Stanley in a notched rectangle design are registered trademarks of Stanley Logistics, Inc., or its affiliates.

INDEX

A

A-LINE

Hobby-Tote High Side Storage Container 73
Hobby-Tote Low Side Storage Container 73
Hobby-Tote System Accessories 73
Storage Containers 73

A-WEST

Blacken-It 143
Patina-It 143
Weather-It 143
Adhesive Applicators 389
Weathering Solutions 143

A.I.M. PRODUCTS
Scenery 145

A.J. FRICKO COMPANY
Cleaners 389
Pinhole Camera Lenses 410

Abrasives
Guns 396
Sheets 410
Track Cleaners 110, 388, 390
Abutments, Bridges 145, 148, 162, 277

Acela
Locomotive Set 58, 63
Passenger Cars 58, 63
Power Car 58, 63
Train Set 58

ACME
Track & Accessories 114

Acrylic
Paint 398, 399, 406
Actuators, Signal 128, 136, 137

ADAIR SHOPS
Adhesives 432
Rite-Wey Weight Upgrade Kits 432
Steel Plate Loads 77

Adapters 362
Track Power 362
AC 381

Adhesives
All-Purpose 388-390, 423, 432
Aluminum Foil 97
Applicators 388, 389, 410
Clear Parts/Canopies 97
Container 82
Cyanoacrylate (CA) 391
Epoxies 410
Foam 168
Instant 391, 419
Plastic 388, 389, 391, 400
Scenery 142, 152, 160, 166, 168, 175, 180, 182, 392
Wood 391
ADHESIVES - CLEANERS - LUBRICANTS SECTION 387-392
Advertising Signs 96, 162, 360

Air
Abrasive Guns 396
Air Conditioners 433, 435, 443
Compressors & Accessories 394, 395, 407, 408
Filters 396
Horns 435, 438, 446
Hoses 396, 401, 434, 442

Airbrushes
Accessories 394-396, 401, 407, 408, 410
Airbrushes 394, 395, 401, 407
DVDs 453
How-To Books 396, 448, 451, 455
Recommended Air Pressures & Thinning Ratios 400
Sets 394, 395
Videos 448

Aircraft
Books 455
Airplanes 321

ALEXANDER SCALE MODELS
Super Detailing Parts 432

Alignment Tools 121

ALPINE DIVISION SCALE MODELS
Scratch Building Supplies 423

Aluminum
Foil Adhesive 97
Paper 423

AM MODELS
Scenery 144

AMACO
Molding Materials 144

AMBROID
Adhesives 388

Ambulances 314, 317, 320, 324
American Flags 103

AMERICAN LIMITED MODELS
Diaphragms 37, 62
Passenger Trucks 106
Tank Containers 73

AMERICAN MODEL BUILDERS

Alton Elevator 226
Crossroads Church 226
Hinkle Mill 226
Structures 226, 227
Super Detailing Parts 432

AMERICAN PLASTICS
Terrain For Trains 163

AMI INSTANT ROADBED

Instant Roadbed (black) 110
Instant Roadbed (gray) 110
Insta Base 110
Instant Roadbed 110

Amp Meters 383

Amtrak
Acela Cars 45
Acela Express 58
Decals 97
Locomotives 45
Passenger Cars 58, 63, 65
Train Sets 58
Work Cars 90
Animals 302-305, 310, 311, 441
Antennas 229, 433, 436-438, 446

AMACO
Molding Materials 144

Applicators
Adhesives 388-390, 410
Bottles 418
Decals 417
Grass 155, 160
Paint 397
Arc Welders 360, 362
Arcades 149, 152, 158, 161, 164, 220, 225
Arched Bridges 225, 244, 250, 268
Armatures, Tree 169

ARNOLD/RIVAROSSI
Freight Cars 77
Electric Locomotives 37
Lighting-Electrical-Motors 356
Passenger Cars 62

Asphalt Top Coat 168, 403
Atlas Master DCC System 378

ATLAS MODEL RAILROAD CO., INC.

NEW Fantastic Layouts Booklet 448
Barb's Bungalow 228
Right Track Power Pack 372
Books 448
Cleaners & Lubricants 388
Command Control 378
Freight Cars 74-77
Lighting-Electrical-Motors 356
Locomotives 38-41
Mill Lumber 432
Power Pack 372
Scenic Ridge Track Pack 113
Signals System & Accessories 124
Snap Saw 410
Structures 228, 229
Telephone Poles 143
Track & Accessories 112, 113
TRAINMAN Freight Cars 94
Trucks & Accessories 106
Vehicles 314
Wheelsets 106

Auto Reverse Units 378, 381, 384
Automobiles 314-321, 324
Automotive Paint 404, 405

B

BACHMANN INDUSTRIES

NEW Diesel Locomotives 43
NEW Yard Boss Train Set 56
Silver Series® Amfleet® Passenger Cars 63
Adhesives 389
Catalogs 448
Command Control 378
Dummy Knuckle Couplers 106
Electrical Accessories 356
Figures 303
Freight Cars 78, 79
Locomotives 42, 43
Passenger Cars 63
Power Packs 372
Signals 124
Smoke Fluid 372
Spectrum Locomotives 43-45
Spectrum Train Sets 58
Spectrum Acela Express 63
Structures 230
Track & Accessories 111
Train Sets 56-58
Trolley Cars 43

Background Buildings 214, 236
Backgrounds
CD-ROMs 147
Scenery 140, 141, 145, 147, 148, 153, 156, 164

BADGER AIR-BRUSH CO.
Airbrushes & Accessories 394-396
Books 396
Books & Videos 448
Catalogs 397
Decal Accessories 397
Paint 396, 397

Baggage Carts 155, 319, 440, 444
Ballast
Ballast 117, 142, 151, 155, 182, 247
Loads 77
Tapes 110

15

INDEX

BAR MILLS

Laser-Cut Wood
 Billboards 124
Mooney's Plumbing
 Emporium 231
  Highway Signs 124
  Structures 231, 232

Barn Decals & Signs 260
Barns 223, 226, 227, 235,
 242, 246, 248, 257, 260,
 267, 272, 274
Barrels 432, 440, 443
Barren Trees 169, 170
Batteries
 Batteries 369
 Holders 362
Bells
 Bells 433, 435, 438
 Sounds 129, 363
 Towers 221
Benches 157, 158, 221,
 435, 440, 444
Bending Tools 416
Bi-Level Passenger Cars 66
Bicycles 320, 321, 436
Billboards 96,124, 125,
 130-136, 437, 444
Binocular Magnifiers 411,
 415

BK ENTERPRISES
Track 115

BL HOBBY PRODUCTS
Lighting-Electrical-Motors
 356
Railroadiana 448
Signals & Accessories
 124

Blades
 Knives 168, 413, 417, 419
 Saws 413

BLAIR LINE

Graffiti Decals 96
Laser-Cut Wood Grade
 Crossings 144
Laser-Cut Structures 236,
 237
 Billboards 125
 Decals 96
 Scenery 144
 Signs 125, 126
 Structures 236, 237

BLMA
Signals 127
Structures 229
Super Detailing Parts 433
Z Scale Scenery 329
Z Scale Signals 329
Z Scale Super Detailing
 Parts 329

Block Detectors 382, 386
Block Signals 124, 126,
 135-137
Blowers 415
Boats
 Boats 316, 319-322
 Docks 237, 272
 Parts 445
Body Mount Couplers 107
Bolster Pins 107
Books
 Airbrushing 396, 448, 451,
  455
 Aircraft 455
 Bridges 452, 454
 Children's 450, 459, 463
 Coloring 463
 DCC 451, 452
 Dioramas 455
 Figures 455
 How-To 396, 448-453,
  455
 Layouts 448, 453, 455
 Military 455
 Model Railroading 448,
  450-452, 454
 Prototype Railroads 450,
  453, 456-459, 461-463
 Reference 449-451, 460
 Scenery 145, 150, 167,
  183, 450, 451-453, 464
 Structures 450, 451, 454
 Styrene Modeling 425,
  449, 460
 Track Planning 451, 453-
  455
 Wiring 453-455
 Z Scale 339
BOOKS, VIDEOS,
 RAILROADIANA
 SECTION 447-464
Boosters, DCC 378, 381,
 383, 385
Booths
 Spray 395, 408
Bottles
 Applicator 418
 Paint Mixing 400
Boxes 434

BRANCHLINE TRAINS
Structures 233-235

BRASS CAR SIDES
Passenger Cars 62

BRAWA

NEW Pin-Socket Street
 Lamps 357
NEW Railroad Yard Lamps
 357
Catalog 448
Lighting-Electrical-Motors
 357-359
Scenery 143
Scratch Building Supplies
 423
Signals 126, 127
Structures 229
Z Scale Lighting 329
Z Scale Signals, Detection
 Units & Signs 329

Bricks
 Sheets 151, 423, 426,
  427, 430
 Walls 161
Bridge Rectifiers 358, 368
Bridges
 Abutments 145, 148, 162,
  277
 Arched 225, 244, 250, 268
 Books 452, 454
 Covered 242, 267
 Fishbellied 216
 Foot 217, 224, 250
 Girder 116, 117, 218, 219,
  225, 229, 244, 245,
  250, 259, 268, 276
 Highway 203, 271
 Motorized 222
 Parts 229, 246, 271
 Piers 111, 117, 148, 149,
  219, 224, 225, 229,
  244, 271, 277
 Railroad 219, 221, 225,
  230, 237, 262, 268, 277
 Signal 127, 135-137
 Track 118
 Trestle 156, 207, 231,
  237, 243, 244, 254,
  268
 Truss 117, 207, 229, 244,
  259, 262, 277
*Bright Boy Abrasive
 Track Cleaner* 110, 388
Brushes
 Dusting 410, 416
 Paint 400, 406, 407
 Wire 415
Budd Cars 65, 66
Buffing Paint 406
Buildings
 Building Materials 164
 Details 232, 253, 254,
  270, 276
 Lights 356, 358, 360, 366
 Modular Systems 189-
  191, 238
 Sets 178
 Bulbs, Light 68, 356, 358,
  359-361, 363, 366, 368,
  369
Bumpers, Track 111, 113,
 116, 119, 156, 193
Burnishers 413

BUSCH

Building Lights 360
Roadway Street 147
Tree Assortments 146
 Catalogs 448
 Decals 127
 Lighting-Electrical-Motors
  360
 Scenery 146-148
 Signals 127
 Sound Systems 373
 Tower 127
 Track Accessories 110
 Vehicles 314
 Z Scale Scenery 328
 Z Scale Signals 328

Buses
 Buses 316, 320, 321
Bushes 150, 175
Business Signs 103, 125,
 126, 130-134, 136-138,
 360, 436, 444
Businesses 202, 205, 208,
 214, 215, 217, 218, 220,
 222-227, 230, 231, 233-
 237, 239-247, 252, 253,
 257-260, 267-272, 273,
 275-277

CA Adhesives &
 Accelerators 391
Cableways 229

CABOOSE INDUSTRIES
Operating Ground
 Throws 111

Cabooses
 Bay Window 71, 90
 Cupola 73, 76, 84, 89
 Narrow Gauge 88
 NE-6 77
 Northeastern Style 73
 Rib Side 79
 Standard 89
 Steel 87, 89
 Wide Vision 76, 79
 Wood 88

CAL-FREIGHT
Structures 237
Super Detailing Parts 434
Vehicles 316

Calendars 451

CALUMET TRAINS
Traction Tire Tool 106
Traction Tires 106

Cameras
 Accessories 375
 Lenses, Pinhole 410
 Night Vision 375
 Systems 375
 Wireless 375

CAMPBELL SCALE MODELS
Structures 237
Track Test Light 110
Wooden Barrels 432

Campers 319, 320
Campgrounds 157
Can Motors 363
Canadian Flags 103
Cap Tiles 430
Capacitive Discharge Units
 365
Capacitors 368
Caps, Railroad 456
*Car System Vehicles &
 Accessories 318*
Carnival
 Booths 225
 Rides 223-225, 243
 Cases, Display 46, 83
 Casting Compounds 144,
  150, 153
 Castles 217, 220, 222
Catalogs
 Bachmann 448
 Badger Air-Brush 397
 Brawa 448
 Busch 448
 Circuitron 362
 Design Preservation
  Models 449
 Faller 450
 Kibri 450
 Mascot Precision Tools
  415
 Microscale 97
 Miller Engineering 254
 Miniatronics 366
 Peco 121
 Period Miniatures 270
 Precision Craft 51
 Precision Scale Co. 460
 Preiser 308, 460
 Tomar Industries 68
 Vollmer 460
 Woodland Scenics 183
Catenary 117, 122, 247
CD-ROMs 147, 460
Cell Phone Towers 229
Cement
 All-Purpose 388-390, 423,
  432
 Applicators 388, 389, 410
 Aluminum Foil 97
 Applicators 388, 389
 Clear Parts/Canopies 388
 Container 82
 Cyanoacrylate (CA)
  Adhesives 391
 Epoxies 410
 Foam 168, 419
 Instant 391
 Plastic 388, 389, 391, 400
 Scenery 142, 152, 160,
  166, 168, 175, 180,
  182, 392
 Wood 391

INDEX

Centering Springs 108
Chains 438
Chairs 436, 437, 440
Chase Lights 134, 361, 369
Children
  Books 450, 459, 463
  Figures 303-307, 311
Chimneys 156, 254, 432, 437, 441, 443
Chisels 416

CHOOCH ENTERPRISES
Loads 79
Scenery 148

Chopper, The 417
Christmas
  Decals 104
  Freight Cars 83, 87, 340
  Ornaments 87, 88, 341
  Train Sets 56, 59, 255
  Trees 146
  Villages & Accessories 255
Churches 215, 217, 220, 224, 226, 230, 234, 236, 245, 246, 248, 250, 258, 276
Circuit Breakers 383, 385, 386

CIRCUITRON

Mitey Lites™ 361
NEW Slow Motion Switch Machine 118
Tortoise Switch Machine 118
  Catalog 362
  Lighting-Electrical-Motors 361, 362
  Mitey Lites 361
  Opto-Sensors 361
  Signal Accessories 128, 129
  Slow Motion Switch Machine 118
  Tortoise Switch Machine 118
  Track & Accessories 118
Circus
  Tents 275
City
  Accessories 232
  Scenes 145, 148
  Structures 204, 214-225, 230, 239, 240, 244, 246, 248-250, 252, 253, 257-259, 265, 267, 269, 270, 273, 274-277

CITY CLASSICS
Structures 237

Clamps 362, 363, 414

CLASSIC METAL WORKS

NEW White WC Delivery Vans 315
NEW White WC Tractor/Trailer Sets 315
32' Covered Wagon Trailer 316
Vehicles 315, 316

Clean Machine Track Cleaning Car 73
Cleaners
  Airbrushes 395, 410
  Anti-Static 46
  Kits 410
  Locomotives 416
  Paint 397, 398, 406, 408
  Plastic 83, 400
  Track 110, 389-391, 415
  Track Cleaning Cars 73, 77

CLEAR CASE

Acrylic Cleaner 46
Car Display Cases 46
Train Display Cases 46
  Anti-Static Cleaner 46
  Display Cases 46

Clocks 127, 135, 440

CM SHOPS
Coal Loads 73
Mugs 449

CMX
Clean Machine Track Cleaning Car 73

Coal
  Coal 151, 155, 182
  Facilities 201, 213, 216, 218, 222, 230, 244, 257, 259, 265-267, 270, 273
  Loads 73, 77, 91
  Trestles 156, 254
Code 40 Track 115, 118
Code 55 Track 112, 113, 115, 118, 120
Code 60 Track 120
Code 70 Track 115, 118, 122
Code 80 Track 112, 113, 120
Coil Cars 93
Coloring Books 463
COMMAND CONTROL SECTION 377-386
Command Stations, DCC 378, 379, 384-386
Compressors, Air 394, 395, 407, 408

Computers
  Interfaces 379, 381, 385
  Software 129, 460
CON-COR
  Freight Cars 83
  Locomotives 47, 48, 49
  Passenger Cars 64-66
Concrete
  Top Coat 168, 403
  Walls 145
Conductive Lubricants 389
Conductive Paint 360
Conifers - See Evergreen Trees
Connectors 114, 359, 362, 365, 368, 369, 378
Constant Lighting Kits 369
Construction
  Signs 126, 127
  Vehicles 317, 318, 321, 324
Containers
  20' Box Type 82, 90
  20' Tank 73, 82
  40' Box Type 72, 82, 83
  40' Chassis 82
  40' Hi-Cube 82
  40' Reefer 82
  45' Box Type 82, 83
  48' Box Type 72, 83
  48' Reefer 82
  48' Smoothside 82
  53' Box Type 82, 83
  Bulktainer 73
  Cranes 72, 244, 275
  Glue 82
  Storage 73, 82
  Terminals 229
Contests
  Cornerstone Modulars 188
  Magic of Model Railroading 279
Control Units, DCC 378, 383, 384, 386
Conversion Kits, Couplers 107
Converters 117
Conveyors 275
Cork Roadbed 110, 114, 119
Cornerstone Built-ups 192, 193, 200

CORNERSTONE MODULARS™

NEW Sterling Dairy Complex 190
NEW 3-IN-1 Building #2 190
3-in-1 Building #2 190
Contests 186-188
Modulars 189-191
Sterling Dairy Complex 190

CORNERSTONE® SERIES

CORNERSTONE – BUILT-UPS
NEW Sunrise Feed Mill 192
CORNERSTONE – KITS
NEW State Line Farm Supply 202
NEW Electric Furnace 202
NEW Santa Fe Style Brick Depot & Freight House 202
NEW Art Deco Highway Underpass 203
NEW Van Dyke Farm Windmill 203
NEW Coke Ovens 203
  Art Deco Highway Underpass 203
  Background Buildings 214
  Building Replacement Bulb 356
  Coke Ovens 203
  Electric Furnace 202
  Santa Fe-Style Brick Depot & Freight House 202
  State Line Farm Supply 202
  Structures 201- 214
  Van Dyke Farm Windmill 203
Corrugated Metal Sheets 423, 424, 426
Couplers
  Accessories 416
  Body Mount 107
  Conversion Kits 107
  Dummy 106
  Height Gauges 416
  Parts 107, 108
  Starter Kits 107
  Truck Mount 107
COUPLERS & TRUCKS SECTION 105-108
Covered Bridges 242, 267
Cows 303-305, 310, 311, 441
Cranes
  Construction 317
  Container 72, 244, 275
  Gantry 220, 223, 258
  Overhead 274
  Railroad 79, 90, 94

CREATIONS UNLIMITED
Tools 410

CREATIVE MODEL ASSOCIATES
Super Detailing Parts 432

CREST

Conductive Lubricants 389
Lube Oil 389
Smoke Fluid & Track 389
  Cleaners & Lubricants 389
  Power Packs 372
  Train Engineer 372

Crossbucks 124, 126, 134, 136, 137
Crossing Towers 241, 242, 245
Crossings
  Flashers 128, 136, 137
  Gates 124, 127, 129, 136
  Grade 110, 111, 121, 144, 222, 224, 225. 434, 437
  Signals 124, 127, 134, 136, 363
  Track 111, 113, 115, 116

CTT, INC.

CTT, Inc.

N Scale Template 115
N Scale Ruler 115
Track Accessories 115

Culverts 156, 162, 181, 434
Curved Track 110, 111, 113, 115-117, 119, 120, 441
Cutters
  Cutters 417
  Disks 412
  Foam 168, 416, 419
  Rail 118
  Sets 417
Cyanoacrylates (CA)
  Accelerators 391
  Adhesives 391
  Debonders 391

D

Dams 156
DC Control Modules 383
DCC - Digital Command Control Items
  Accessories 378, 382-385
  Books 451, 452
  Boosters 378, 381, 383, 384
  Control Systems 378
  Decoders 379, 380, 382-386
  Generators 378
  Locomotives 38-41, 43, 45, 47, 49, 50, 52
  Power Supplies 381, 383, 385
  Signaling Systems 379
  Starter Sets 378, 379, 384, 385
  Throttles 380, 381, 384, 385
  Train Sets 58
  Translators 382

17

INDEX

DCC SPECIALTIES
Command Control 383

DCC Starter Sets 378, 379, 385
Debonders, CA 391
Decal Starter Kits 104
Decals
Adhesives 104
Alphabets 97
Applicators 417
Blank Paper 97, 104
Christmas 104
Dry Transfers 127, 138
Films 97, 397
Flags, American 103
Graffiti 96, 97, 127
Military 103
Numbers 97
Railroad 97-103, 127, 138
Removers 400
Sets 97
Setting Solutions 97, 391, 397, 400, 405, 406, 423
Signs 96, 103, 136
Vehicles 102, 104
Z Scale 342
DECALS SECTION 95-104
Deciduous Trees 142, 146, 149, 154, 155, 157-159, 165, 169-172
Decoders
DCC 379, 380, 382-385, 386
Owner's Manuals 376
Signal 379, 382, 385, 386
Sound 376, 379, 386
Stationary 380, 383
Switch Machines 385
Test Kits 376, 386
Deer 302, 303-305, 311
Delivery Vans & Trucks 315-317, 320, 321, 324

DELUXE INNOVATIONS
Freight Cars 80-82
Structures 241
Super Detailing Parts 432
Vehicles 316

Dental Probes 415
Depots 192, 202, 207, 216, 220-223, 225-228, 230, 231, 233, 236, 241-244, 246, 249, 250, 257, 258, 268-270, 272

DEPOTS BY JOHN
Structures 241

Derailers 120

DESIGN PRESERVATION MODELS

N Scale Gold Kits 240
N Scale Modular Systems 238
N Scale Building Kits 239, 240
Catalog 449
Structures 238, 239, 240

DETAIL ASSOCIATES
Background Scenes 145
Super Detailing Parts 435
Vehicles 316

Detection Units
Current Sensing 128
Grade Crossing 128
Occupancy 124, 128
Optical 128
Rolling Stock 128
Detectors 382, 386
Diaphragms 37, 62
Diesel
Locomotives 29-45, 47, 48-52
Sounds 376
Train Sets 54-59
Digital Command Control Items
Accessories 378, 382-385
Books 451, 452
Boosters 378, 381, 383, 384
Control Systems 378
Decoders 379, 380, 382-386
Generators 378
Locomotives 38-41, 43, 45, 47, 49, 50, 52
Power Supplies 381, 383, 385
Signaling Systems 379
Starter Sets 378, 379, 384, 385
Throttles 380, 381, 384, 385
Translators 382
Train Sets 58

DIGITRAX

NEW Plug'n Play Decoders 379
NEW Sound FX Decoders 379
Plug'n Play Signaling 379
Command Control 379-382
Diodes 359-362, 365, 369

Display
Cases 46, 83
Domes 403
Ditch Lights 446
Docks, Boat 237, 272
Domes, Display 403

DONEGAN OPTICAL COMPANY
Optical Accessories 411

Doors
Freight Cars 439
Locomotives 433
Passenger Cars 437
Structures 427, 434, 437, 439, 442, 443

DPA-LTA ENTERPRISES
Books 449

DR. MIKE'S MODEL N' CRAFTER'S GLUE
Glue 389

Drills
Accessories 422
Bits 422
Drills 414
Sets 414, 422
Driver Sets 106
Drop Cloths 417
Dropping Resistors 361
Drumheads 41, 68
Drums, Oil 435, 439, 440, 443, 444
Dry Transfer Signs 127, 138
Dullcote 406
Dummy Couplers 106

DURANGO PRESS
Fairmont Speeder 82

Dusting Brushes 410, 416
DVDs
Airbrushing 453
How-To 464
Prototype Railroading 463
Scenery 183, 453, 464
Dwarf Signals 126, 136, 137
Dyes 153

E

E-O-Ts 68, 137, 369
E-Z Streets 135
E-Z TRACK Products 111
E-Z Water 179
Electrak Track Cleaning Unit 365
Electric Locomotives 37, 43, 45
Electrical
Meters 383
Switches 137, 356, 358, 360
Wire 356, 359, 362, 363, 366, 367
Electroluminescent Wire 134

Emergency
Vehicles 314, 315, 317, 319-321, 324
Enamels 404-406
End-Of-Train Devices 68, 137, 369
Engine Terminal Building Article 194-199

ENVIRONMENTAL TECHNOLOGY
Molding Materials 153

Epoxies 410

EASTERN SEABOARD MODELS
Passenger Cars 63

ESU
LokSound Decoders 386

Etch Mate 416
Etched Brass Car Sides 62
European Equipment 77

EVAN DESIGNS
Building Software 232
Inkjet Decal Paper 104
Sign Software 129

EVERGREEN SCALE MODELS
Books 449
Scratch Building Supplies 424, 425

Evergreen Trees 142, 146, 149, 150, 154, 155, 157-159, 165, 169-172

F

FALLER

NEW Burning Tax Office 216
NEW Nordex Wind Generator 217
NEW Motorized Lawn Mower 169
Adhesives & Lubricants 389
Books 450
Cork Roadbed 114
Crossing Gates 129
Figures 302
Lighting-Electrical-Motors 363
Paint & Paint Supplies 397
Scenery 149-153
Sidewalk Tiles 425
Station Voice Announcer 373
Structures 216-225
Tools 416
Vehicles 318
Z Scale Figures 326, 328
Z Scale Scenery 326, 328
Z Scale Structures 326, 327

Fans 433, 434, 438
Farm
Machinery 317, 318, 320, 321, 324
Structures 221-223, 226, 230, 235, 236, 242, 245, 246, 248, 257, 258, 265
Fences 130, 144, 146, 153, 155-161, 162, 164, 232, 247, 253, 427, 436, 440, 442, 443
Ferris Wheels 223, 243
Fiber Optics 356, 362, 369
Fields 146, 147, 158, 162
Figures
Animals 302-305, 310, 311, 441
Assortments 303, 308, 309
Books 455
Children 303-307, 311
Firefighters 302, 306, 308, 310
Glues 309
Musicians 308, 309
Paint 405
Passengers 304, 311
Pedestrians 302-306, 309-311, 440
Police Officers 302, 306, 309
Railroad 302-304, 306, 309, 310
Religious 303, 305, 307
Sports & Recreation 302, 304, 306, 307, 309-311
Travelers 302, 303, 305, 307, 308, 311
Unpainted 308
Working People 302-305, 307-311
Z Scale 326, 328, 349, 350, 352
FIGURES SECTION 301-312
Files 410, 413, 416, 417
Filler Material 152
Films
Decal 397
Masking 396
Filters, Air 396
Finishes
Flat 97, 397, 402, 405, 406
Gloss 97, 397, 400, 402, 405, 406
Satin 97, 397, 405
Fire
Alarm Boxes 435
Escapes 254, 436
Extinguishers 434, 445
Fighters (Figures) 302, 306, 308, 310
Hydrants 435, 440
Simulated 360, 365
Stations 215, 227, 244, 252, 257, 268, 273, 275, 277
Vehicles 314, 315, 317, 319-321, 324
Flagpoles 435
Flags 103
Flames 360, 365

INDEX

Flashers/Blinkers 68, 128, 134, 136, 137, 360, 361, 363, 366, 367, 369
Flat Finishes 97, 397, 402, 405, 406
Flatbed Trucks & Trailers 315, 316, 320, 324
Flex Paste 176
Flex-I-File 410
Flexible
  Track 113, 118-120, 122
  Light Bands 360
  Wire 359, 366
Flocking 146, 147, 150, 158, 160, 173
Flooring 423, 430

FLOQUIL

NEW Polly Scale Acrylic Weathering Markers 398
Brushes 400
Polly Scale Paint 398-400
  Paint & Paint Supplies 398-400

Flowers 146, 155, 158
Fluid, Smoke 372, 373, 376, 389
Fluorescent Lamps 134, 359
Foam
  Cutters 168, 416, 419
  Glue 168, 419
  Ground Covers 142, 147
  Knives 168, 419
  Nails 168
  Pencils 168
  Putty 168
  Risers 167
  Sheets 167
Foliage 158, 159, 172-175, 440
Footbridges 217, 224, 250
Footings 156
Forklifts 320, 321, 443
Fountains 152
FRED 68, 137, 369
Freight
  Car Details 432-434, 436, 438, 439, 442, 446
  Car Trucks 106, 108
  Cars, Z Scale 334, 335, 340-342
  Houses 192, 202, 207, 220, 222, 230, 243, 244, 265, 267, 268, 275
  Train Sets 54-59
FREIGHT CARS SECTION 69-94
Fruit Trees 142, 146, 149, 154, 158, 159, 165
Fuel Tanks 250, 258
Funicular Sets 229

G

G-Guns 389
Galleries 152
Gantry Cranes 220, 223, 258
Garages 237, 252, 261, 264, 275
Garbage Cans 254, 435
Gas Pumps 435, 439, 444
Gates, Crossing 124, 127, 129, 136
Gauges
  Track 118
Gazebos 252

GB ENGINEERING
Work Holder 400

GC LASER
Scratch Building Supplies 423
Structures 242, 243
Super Detailing Parts 437
Z Scale Scenery 340
Z Scale Structures 340
Z Scale Super Detailing Parts 340

Gearboxes 363
Gears
  Lubricants 388-390
  Pullers 415
Generators
  DCC 378
  Smoke 216, 373
  Steam 373
Gentle Grips 309

GHQ
Depressed Center Flat Cars 77
Vehicles 317

Girder Bridges 116, 117, 218, 219, 225, 229, 244, 245, 250, 259, 268, 276
Girders 439
Glass 427
Gloss Finishes 97, 397, 400, 402, 405, 406
Glosscote 406
Glow-in-The Dark Decals 97
Glue
  All-Purpose 388-390, 423, 432
  Aluminum Foil 97
  Applicators 388, 389, 410
  Container 82
  Cyanoacrylate (CA) Adhesives 391
  Epoxies 410
  Foam 168, 419
  Guns 419
  Instant 391
  Plastic 388, 389, 391, 400
  Scenery 142, 152, 160, 166, 175, 180, 182, 392
  Wood 391

GOLD MEDAL MODELS
Super Detailing Parts 436, 437

GOO 388, 423
Grabhandler, The 416
Grab Irons 433, 436, 438
Grade Crossings 110, 111, 121, 144, 222, 224, 225, 434, 437
Graffiti Decals 96, 97, 127
Grain
  Structures 205, 211, 226, 227, 233, 237, 245, 271, 273
  Grain-of-Rice Bulbs 356, 363, 366
  Grain-of-Sand Bulbs 366
  Grain-of-Wheat Bulbs 356, 359, 363, 366, 368

GRAND CENTRAL GEMS
Scenery 154
Structures 246

GRANDT LINE
Structures 243
Super Detailing Parts 437

Gras-Master 160
Grass
  Applicators 155, 160
  Flocking 147, 150
  Grass 158, 159, 173, 174
  Mats 142, 143, 147, 151, 158, 160, 180
  Static 155, 160, 173
Grease 389
Ground Covers 142, 146, 147, 150, 151, 155, 157-160, 166, 173-175, 180, 182

H

Hacksaws 413
Hammers 415
Hand Cars 319, 444
Handheld Throttles 378, 385
Handrails 430
Hardware 422, 426
Hare Stationary Decoder 383
Headlights 356, 364, 366, 368, 434, 435, 446
Heat Shrink Tubing 362, 365, 368-370
Heat Tools 180
Heavyweight Passenger Cars 62, 67
Hedges 150, 159

HEICO MODELL

N Scale Freight Car Loads 90
Z Scale Freight Car Loads 342
Freight Car Loads 90
Z Scale Freight Car Loads 342

Height Gauges, Couplers 416

HEKI
Trees 155

HELJAN
Structures 244, 245
Telephone Poles 129

Hemostats 415

HIGHBALL PRODUCTS
Ground Covers 155
Z Scale Ballast 329

Highway
  Bridges 203, 271
  Signs 124, 126, 129, 134, 135
Hob-E-Lube 392
Hob-e-Tac 175
Hobby-Tote System Storage Containers 73
Holders
  Batteries 362
  Light Bulbs 434
  Tools 410, 412
  Wire 358, 362, 363
  Work 400, 414, 419, 422, 434
Holiday
  Train Sets 56, 59
  Trees 146
  Villages & Accessories 255, 256
Hook-Up Wire 356, 362, 363
Horse-Drawn Vehicles 319, 320, 321, 346
Horses 302-305, 310
Hoses, Air 396, 401, 434
Houses 216-220, 222, 223, 226-228, 230, 233, 234, 236, 237, 243, 245, 246, 248, 250, 251, 257-261, 271-277
How-To
  Books 396, 448-453, 455
  DVDs 464
  Videos 464
Hydrocal 176

I

Incline Sets 167
Industrial Structures 190, 191, 202-204, 208-210, 212, 213, 216-220, 222, 225, 226, 230, 236, 239, 240, 242-245, 249, 250, 253, 254, 257-259, 261, 262, 265-267, 269, 270
Information Stations 129, 134, 144, 162, 215, 259, 268, 323, 345, 349, 360, 378, 390, 397, 427, 456
Infrared Timing Circuits 360
Inspection Pits 120
Instant Horizons 140, 141
Instant Roadbed 110
Interiors
  Details 434, 435
  Lights 356, 358, 360, 363, 364
Interlocking Towers 226, 241, 246, 266

INTERNATIONAL HOBBY CORP.
Books 450
Lighting-Electrical-Motors 362
Structures 243

ITTY BITTY LINES

N Scale Multi-Track Yard Pads 115
Z Scale Catenary Mast Cork Base 342
Z Scale Multi-Track Yard Pads 342
Display Cases 83, 342
Roadbed 114
Wire Management Products 363
Z Scale Track Accessories 342

IWATA
Airbrushes & Accessories 401

J

JAEGER
Bulkhead Flat Car Loads 77

Jeweler's Tools 413, 414

JL INNOVATIVE DESIGN
Signs 130
Structures 241

INDEX

JNJ TRAINS
Freight Cars 79
Locomotive Shells 41
Passenger Cars 67
Super Detailing Parts 438

Joiners, Rail 113, 114, 117-120

JR MINIATURES
Structures 246

Jumper Cables 363
Junk
 Assortments 311
 Loads 77
 Piles 157
 Yards 157, 269

JV MODELS
Structures 243

K

KALMBACH PUBLISHING CO.

NEW DCC Projects & Applications 451
NEW The Model Railroader's Guide to Coal Railroading 451
NEW The Model Railroader's Guide to Passenger Equipment & Operations 451
Books DVDs & Videos 451-456
Calendars 451

KAPPLER
Scale Lumber 426

KATO

Locomotives 45
Power Pack 116, 373
UniTrack 116, 117
 California Zephyr Train Set 59
 Figures 303
 Freight Cars 84
 Lighting-Electrical-Motors 360
 Locomotives 45
 Passenger Cars 67
 Power Pack 373
 Structures 247
 Track & Accessories 116, 117
 Vehicles 318

KIBRI

Gottwald GS 100.06-Ton Railroad Crane 318
NEW Railway Station 248
Z Scale Tunnel Portals 331
 Catalogs 450
 Scenery 155
 Scratch Building Supplies 426
 Structures 248-250
 Vehicles 318
 Z Scale Scenery 331
 Z Scale Scratch Building Supplies 331
 Z Scale Structures 330, 331
 Z Scale Super Detailing Parts 331
 Z Scale Vehicles 331

Knives
 Blades 168, 413, 417, 419
 Foam 168, 419
 Knives 413, 417
 Sets 413

KRAUSE PUBLICATIONS
Books 450

Kristal Kleer 97

KROMER CAP CO.
Railroad Caps 456

L

LABELLE INDUSTRIES
Burma Shave Signs 130
Figures 304
Lighting & Electrical 363
Lubricants 390

Ladders 427, 430, 433, 436-438, 440, 441, 443, 444
Lake Construction Kits 152
Lamps 68
 Cable 360
 Fluorescent 134, 359
 Incandescent 364
 Lamps 361, 443
 Lampshades 368
 Magnifying 366
 Marker 435, 442, 446
 Posts 357, 364
 Shades 364
 Street 435
Landscape Kits 169, 175, 180
Latex Rubber 144, 153, 176
Lawn Mowers 440
Layouts
 Books 448, 453, 455
 Modules 163, 177, 178
 Systems 167

LBF COMPANY
Freight Cars 85, 86

Leaves 159
LED Lenses 124
LEDs 356, 359-362, 365, 367, 369, 386
Lenses, Camera 410
Levels 415
Lichen 142, 150, 160, 173

LIFE-LIKE TRAINS FROM WALTHERS

Freight King Second Edition Train Set 54
SceneMaster™ Grass Mats 143
SceneMaster™ Trees 142
 Books 448
 Cleaners 388
 Diesel Locomotives 37
 Freight Cars 73
 Lighting-Electrical-Motors 356
 Maintenance Kit 388
 SceneMaster Scenery 142
 Scenery 142, 143
 Smoke Fluid 372
 Spotlights 124
 Steam Locomotives 37
 Structures 215
 Track & Accessories 110
 Train Sets 54, 55

Lighthouses 250
Lighting & Electrical
 Z Scale 329, 338, 344, 345
 LIGHTING - ELECTRICAL - MOTORS SECTION 355-370
Lighting - See Lights
Lighting Effects Modules 367
Lights
 Buildings 356, 358, 360, 363, 366
 Bulbs 68, 356, 358-361, 363, 368, 369
 Chase 361, 369
 Dual Filament 368
 Emitting Diodes 359-362, 365, 367, 369
 Flood 357, 364
 Fluorescent 134
 Interior 356, 358, 360, 363, 366
 Kits 356, 360, 361, 369
 Marker 435, 442, 446
 Panel 356, 359
 Passenger Cars 360
 Platform 357
 Spotlights 357, 364
 Street 135-137, 435
 Streets 357, 364
 Strobe 361, 365, 369
 Traffic 127, 135, 137
 Tubular 359, 368

Liquids
 Decal Film 97
 Masking 97, 397, 423
 Smoke 372, 373, 376, 389
Loading Ramps 156, 157, 218, 237, 242, 254, 268, 269
Loads
 Aluminum Bales 91
 Ballast 77
 Cable Reels 79
 Coal 73, 77, 91
 Coils 79, 94
 Crates 79, 90
 Junk 77
 Lumber 77, 90, 243
 Machinery 77, 79
 Ore 91
 Pipe 90
 Scrap 77
 Scrap Metal 91
 Steel Plate 77
 Sugar Beets 77, 91
 Woodchips 91
Locomotives
 Body Shells 432
 Cleaners 416
 DCC Equipped 38-41, 43, 45, 47, 49, 50, 52
 Details 432, 433, 435-438, 442, 444, 446
 Diaphragms 37
 Diesel 29-45, 47-52
 Electric 37, 43, 45
 Shells 41
 Steam 28, 37, 38, 42-44, 47, 48, 50-52
 Z Scale 332, 333, 340
LOCOMOTIVES SECTION 27-52
Logging
 Cars 70
 Logs 439
LokSound Decoders 386
Lubricants 388, 389, 390
Lumber 428
 Loads 77, 90, 243
 Lumber 432, 434, 437, 441
 Scale 426, 428

M

M-Trak System 441
Magic Masker 397, 423
Magic Photos 27, 53, 69, 105, 109, 123, 139, 185, 279- 301, 313, 325, 355, 371, 377, 387, 393, 409, 421, 431
MAGIC SECTION 279-300
Magic Water 164
Magne-Matic Couplers 107
Magnetic Uncouplers 107, 108
Magnets 358, 362
Magnifiers 366, 411, 414, 415
Mailboxes 440, 446
Maintenance-Of-Way Equipment 70, 75, 77, 79, 82, 90, 94, 321, 322
Mallets 415
Manhole Covers 144

Marine Paint 397
Marker Lights 435, 442, 446
Markers
 Paint 397, 406
 Weathering 398

MARKLIN

NEW Steam Locomotive 332
NEW "Metronom" Commuter Train Set 333
Wire Stripper 416
Z Scale Catalog 332
Z Scale Freight Cars 334, 335
Z Scale Lighting & Electrical 338
Z Scale Locomotives 332, 333
Z Scale Passenger Cars 334-336
Z Scale Power 339
Z Scale Scenery 339
Z Scale Signals, Detection Units & Signs 337
Z Scale Structures 338, 339
Z Scale Track 337
Z Scale Vehicles 339

MASCOT PRECISION TOOLS
Adhesives 390
Catalog 415
Tools 412-415

Masking
 Films 396
 Liquids 97, 397, 423
 Tape 408
Material Handling Cars 65
Mats
 Grass 142, 143, 147, 151, 158, 160, 180
 Ground Covers 151
Membership Application, NMRA 464
Mesh 430
Metal
 Sheets 144, 423, 424, 426, 430

METAL MINIATURES
Vehicles 318

Metallic Paint 397, 403, 404, 406
Meters, Electrical 383
Mi-Jack Cranes 72
Micro Bulbs 356, 361, 363, 368
Micro Coat Clear Finishes 97

INDEX

MICRO ENGINEERING COMPANY

NEW Building Kits 257
Structures & Bridges 257-259
Track & Accessories 118
  Adhesives 390
  Fences 156
  Structures 245
  Super Detailing Parts 439
  Track & Accessories 118
Micro LEDs 367
Micro Liquitape 97
Micro Mask Masking Liquid 97
Micro Metal Foil Adhesive 97
Micro Set 97
Micro Sol 97
Micro Switch 121
Micro-Mesh 430
Micro-Seasons Holiday Village & Accessories 255-256

MICRO-TRAINS LINE

NEW Micro-Seasons 255, 256
NEW Narrow Gauge 30' Box Cars 88
NEW State Series Cars 87
Christmas Ornaments 87, 88, 341
Couplers 107, 108
Freight Cars 87, 88
Locomotives 41
Micro-Seasons 255, 256
Super Detailing Parts 439
Tools 416
Train Sets 59, 340
Trucks 108
Uncouplers 107
Wheelsets 108
Z Scale Freight Cars 340
Z Scale Locomotives 340
Z Scale Micro-Track™ 341
Z Scale Train Sets 340

MICRON ART
Scratch Building Supplies 427
Signs 134
Structures 246
Super Detailing Parts 439
Vehicles 319
Z Scale Scratch Building Supplies 347
Z Scale Signals, Detection Units & Signs 346
Z Scale Structures 346, 347
Z Scale Super Detailing Parts 346, 347
Z Scale Track & Accessories 346
Z Scale Vehicles 347

MICROSCALE
Decals 97-104
Railroadiana 456

Mikro Tip Glue Tips 388
Military
  Commemorative Cars 80
  Decals 103
  Modeling Books 455
  Paint 396, 399, 400, 404, 405, 406
  Structures 258
  Vehicles 314, 320, 323
  Milk Cans 441, 443, 446

MILLER ENGINEERING
Catalog 254
Lighted Sign Kits 131-134
Structures 251-254
Z Scale Scenery 345
Z Scale Structures 343-345
Z Scale Super Detailing Parts 345

Mills 192, 202, 208-210, 217, 218, 220, 223, 224, 226, 233, 235, 243, 244, 257, 266, 277
Mines
  Cars 435, 439, 441
  Facilities 259, 265, 266, 269, 435
  Structures 213, 221, 236, 237, 243, 245
  Track 441

MINI HIGHWAYS

Straight Passing Zone 148
Railroad Crossing Intersection 148
Curved Roadway 148
  Roadways 148

Mini Metals Vehicles 315, 316
Mini-Scenes 403

MINIATRONICS
Catalog 366
Lighting-Electrical-Motors 364-366
Miniature
  Bulbs 356, 359, 361, 364
  Lighting Effects Modules 367
  Scenes 146, 149, 161, 304
  Switches 362, 365, 367, 369
  Tools 435, 439
  Mirrors 415

MISSION MODELS
Tools 416

Miter Boxes 413
Mixing Bottles, Cups & Dishes 153, 400, 419

MLR MANUFACTURING
Track Tools 115

Mobile Homes 263, 264
Mod-U-Rail System 177
Model Builder Software 232
Model Building & Finishing Kits 406
Model Master Paints 404-406

MODEL POWER

Freight Cars 89
Structures 257-259
Train Sets 59
  Cleaners & Lubricants 390
  Detail Sets 440
  Figures 303
  Freight Cars 89, 90
  Lighting & Electrical 366
  Loco Driver Sets 106
  Locomotives 50
  Passenger Cars 67
  Power Packs 373
  Scenery 157
  Signals & Signs 135
  Smoke Fluid 373
  Structures 257, 259
  Track & Accessories 119
  Train Sets 59
  Trucks 106

Model Railroading Books 448, 450-452, 454

MODEL RAILSTUFF
Freight Car Loads 91
Scenery 156
Structures 254, 258
Track Accessories 119

MODEL RECTIFIER CORP. (MRC)

Prodigy Express System 384
NEW Symphony 77 Sound System 375
Tech 4 Power Pack 374
  Command Control 384
  Sound Systems 375

MODELflex Paint 396
Modulars
  Building Systems 189, 190, 191, 238
  Contest 188
  Contest Winners 186, 187
  Parts Packages 189, 238
  Planning Packets 238
  Molding Materials 144, 147, 150, 153
  Molds, Rocks 154, 176

MONROE MODELS
Scenery 157
Structures 268

Moon Lighting Kits 356

MORNING SUN BOOKS
Books 457-459

Mortar 147
Motorcycles 320, 321
Motors
  Cableways 229
  Motors 362, 363
  Structures 212, 223

MOUNTAINEER PRECISION PRODUCTS
Structures 260
Z Scale Decals 342
Z Scale Structures 342

Mountains
  Building Kits 144
  Paper 142
  MU Hoses/Stands 433, 435, 446
  Mugs, Railroad 449
  Multi Tools 416
  Musicians 308, 309

N

N SCALE ARCHITECT
Model Builders Supply Line 427
Nansen Street Models 348, 349
Scratch Building Supplies 427
Structures 265, 266
Super Detailing Parts 441
Vehicles 320
Z Scale Figures 349
Z Scale Structures 348, 349
Z Scale Vehicles 349

N.J. INTERNATIONAL
Signals 136
Structures 245
Switch Stands 119

Nails
  Foam 168
  Track 110, 114, 119
Nano LEDs 367
Narrow Gauge
  Freight Cars 88
  Track 441

NATIONAL MODEL RAILROAD ASSOCIATION (NMRA)
Membership Application 464
Standards Gauge 418

NCE
Command Control 385, 386

NEAL'S N GAUGING TRAINS
Figures 304
Signals 137
Structures 261
Super Detailing Parts 440
Vehicles 320
Z Scale Scenery 349
Z Scale Signals 349
Z Scale Structures 349
Z Scale Super Detailing Parts 349
Z Scale Vehicles 349

NEW LONDON INDUSTRIES
Scenery 156

NEW RAIL MODELS
Blue Point Turnout Controller 121
Scenery 157
Structures 261
Throttle Pockets 383
Turnout Controllers 121

NGINEERING
Lighting & Electrical 367, 368
Scratch Building Supplies 427
Solder 390
Tools 417

NOCH
Boats 319
Fences 158, 161
Field Grass 158
  Books & DVDs 459
  Figures 304
  Lighting-Electrical-Motors 362
  Paint Rollers 400
  Scenery 158-161
  Scenic Accessories 304
  Sign Assortment 135
  Track Cleaners 390
  Vehicles 319
  Z Scale Figures 352
  Z Scale Scenery 351, 352
  Z Scale Vehicles 352

NORTHEASTERN SCALE LUMBER CO.
Scratch Building Supplies 428, 429

NORTHEASTERN SCALE MODELS
Structures 267, 268

INDEX

NORTHWEST SHORT LINE
Motors & Gearboxes 363
Tools 417
Wheelsets 106

NU-LINE STRUCTURES
Structures 262
Super Detailing Parts 442

NUCOMP MINIATURES
Scenery 157
Structures 263, 264
Vehicles 319

Number Boards 435, 438, 446
Nuts 422, 426

Occupancy Detectors 382
Oil
 Drums 435, 439, 440, 443, 444
 Lubricants 389, 392
 Structures 212
 Tanks 156, 221, 230, 254, 257, 262, 272, 443
Oilers 389, 390
Operating Ground Throws 111
Optical Aids 411
OptiVISOR 411
Opto-Sensors 361, 365

OSO PUBLISHING
Books 459

Outhouses 157, 229, 243, 245, 444
Overhead Cranes 274

P.I. ENGINEERING
Railroadiana 460

PACER TECHNOLOGY & RESOURCES
Adhesives 391

Paint
 Acrylic 398, 399, 406
 Applicators 397
 Automotive 404, 405
 Bottles 400
 Brushes 400, 406, 407
 Buffing 406
 Cleaners 397, 398, 406, 408
 Conductive 360
 Enamels 404-406
 Extenders 397
 Figure Colors 405
 Marine 397
 Markers 397, 406
 Metallic 397, 403, 404, 406
 Military 396, 399, 400, 404-406
 Mixing Bottles 400
 Patina 397, 403
 Pens 397
 Pigments 179, 403
 Primers 398
 Railroad Colors 398, 399, 402
 Removers 400, 402
 Rollers 400
 Scenery 153, 165, 166
 Sets 396, 403, 406
 Shakers 400
 Spray 398, 402, 404-406
 Thinners 398, 400, 402, 405, 406
 Undercoats 403
 Water Based 396, 403
PAINT & PAINT SUPPLIES SECTION 393-408

PALACE CAR COMPANY
Passenger Car Interior Details 67

Pallet Jacks 321
Pallets & Skids 437, 439, 441, 444
Palm Trees 154, 159, 162, 170
Panel Lights 356, 359
Paper
 Aluminum 423
 Decaling 97, 104
 Mountain 142
 Paper Mache 144
 Scenery 161, 164
Parking Lots 147, 152, 160
Passenger Vans 314, 317
Passenger Cars
 Acela 45, 58, 63
 Bi-Level 66
 Details 62, 67, 68, 438, 439
 Heavyweight 67
 Lighting 68, 360
 Rail Diesel Cars 45
 Sides 67
 Streamlined 47-49, 63-65, 67
 Train Sets 56-59
 Trucks 106, 108
 Z Scale 334-336
PASSENGER CARS SECTION 61-68
Passengers 304, 311

PASTIME HOBBIES & MINIATURES
Signal Bridge Kit 135

Patina Finishes 397, 403

PECO
PECO
Catalog 121
Flex-Track 120
Turnouts 120
 Catalog 121
 Lubricants 390
 Track & Accessories 120, 121

Pedestrians 302-306, 309-311, 440

PEERLESS INDUSTRIES
Track & Accessories 119

Pencils, Foam 168
Pens, Paint 397

PERIOD MINIATURES
Catalog 270
Freight Car Loads 77
Scenery 162
Structures 269, 270
Super Detailing Parts 443, 444
Vehicles 321

Phone
 Poles 124, 129, 134, 135
Phosphor Bronze
 Wire 432
 Sheets 369
Pickup Trucks 314, 316, 317, 320
Piers, Bridges 111, 117, 148, 149, 219, 224, 225, 229, 244, 271, 277
Pigments 179, 403

PIKESTUFF
Culverts 162
Dome Window Insert 439
Scratch Building Supplies 430
Structures 270

Pilings 156
Pillars 152
Pin Vises 414, 417, 422
Pink Sound Bond Glue 432

PIRATE MODELS
Vehicles 321

Planning Templates, Track 113, 115

PLANO
Super Detailing Parts 444

Plaster
 Cloth 144, 151, 167, 168, 176
 Plaster 168, 176
 Spackling 158
Plastic
 Adhesives 388, 389, 391, 400
 Cleaners 400
 Polishing Kit 83
 Rods 425
 Shapes 425, 430
 Sheets 423, 424, 426, 427
 Siding 424, 426
 Strips 424, 425
 Tubing 425

PLASTRUCT
Building Sheets 162
Figures 304
Lights & Signs 136
Scratch Building Supplies 430
Structures 262
Super Detailing Parts 444
Vehicles 321
Z Scale Figures 349

Platforms 143, 204, 216, 217, 219, 221, 224, 228, 229, 230, 242-245, 247, 249, 261, 266, 274, 275
Pliers 412, 418
Plows, Snow - Railroad 435, 438, 446
Plug 'N Play Signaling 379
Plug-N-Play Decoders 380, 385
Plugs 358
Poles, Utility 124, 129, 134, 135, 143, 445
Police
 Officers 302, 306, 309
 Stations 215, 258, 273, 274
 Vehicles 314, 315, 317, 320, 324
Polishers 410
POLLY Scale Paint Products 398-400
Polymer Coatings 153
Portals, Tunnel 145, 148, 151, 155, 156, 158, 161, 162, 164, 181, 259
Pourable Metal 422
Powders, Weathering 145
Power
 Accessories 375
 Management Equipment 381
 Packs 116, 119, 372, 373, 374
 Supplies 362, 366, 367, 374, 376, 381, 383, 385
 Z Scale 339
Power Distribution Blocks 358, 365
Power-Loc Track System 110
POWER-SOUND-SMOKE SECTION 371-376
Powered Vehicles
 Accessories 318
 Starter Sets 318
 Vehicles 318

PRE-SIZE MODEL SPECIALTIES
Scenery 162
Z Scale Scenery 352

PRECISION CRAFT MODELS
Catalog 51
DC Command Control 383
Freight Cars 91
Locomotives 51, 52

PRECISION SCALE CO.
Books 460
Catalogs 442, 460
Lighting 368
Scratch Building Supplies 430
Sideframes 106
Super Detailing Parts 442

PREISER

NEW Paramedics 305
NEW People Waiting on the Platform 305
NEW Seated Passengers 305
Catalogs 308, 460
Figures 305-308
Scenery 162
Super Detailing Parts 444
Vehicles 321
Z Scale Figures 350

Press Tools 417
Primers 398
Prodigy Command Control 384
Profile Boards 167

PROTO 2000 HERITAGE™ STEAM COLLECTION

From Walthers
NEW 2-8-4 Berkshire Steam Locomotive 28
2-8-4 Berkshire 28

PROTO N SERIES
HOBBY QUALITY
From Walthers
NEW EMD GP38-2 Locomotives 29
NEW EMD E8/9 Locomotives 30
NEW F-M C-Liner Locomotives 31
NEW ALCO DL-109 Locomotives 32
NEW EMD SW8/9/600 Locomotives 33
NEW ALCO PA Locomotives 34
NEW EMD GP20 35
NEW EMD GP18 36
ALCO DL-109 Diesels 32
ALCO PA Diesels 34
EMD E8/9 Diesels 30
EMD GP18 Diesels 36
EMD GP20 Diesels 35
EMD GP38-2 Diesels 29
EMD SW8/9/600 Diesels 33
F-M C-Liner 31

Puller, The 417
Pumps, Water 153, 356
Punches 415
Push-Button Switches 137, 358, 365, 369
Putty 168

INDEX

Q
Quick Dry 402
Quonset Huts 271

R
Radio Control Systems 379, 381, 385
Radio Towers 229, 272
Rail
 Code 40 118
 Code 55 118
 Code 70 118
 Code 80 114
 Cutters 118
 Gauges 118, 418
 Joiners 113, 114, 117-120
 Weathering Solutions 118
Rail Diesel Cars 45
Rail Zip Track Cleaner 391
Rail-It Rerailer 121
Railbuses 47

RAILDRIVER
Railroadiana 460

Railings 153, 164, 436, 440, 443

RAILNET SOLUTIONS
Command Control 382

Railroad
 Books 450, 453, 456-463
 Calendars 451
 Caps 456
 Cranes 79, 90, 94
 Decals 97-103, 127, 138
 DVDs 463
 Figures 302-304, 306, 309, 310
 Mugs 449
 Paint 398, 399, 402
 Signs 103, 124, 126, 129, 130, 134, 135, 137, 138, 456
 Stickers 456

RAILROAD AVENUE ENTERPRISES
Books 461

RAILROAD PRESS

ALCO Reference #1 Railroading Book 462
Children's Coloring & Activity Book 463
CFT Locomotives Reference Book 462
Delaware & Hudson Thunder & Lightning Stripes Reference Book 462
Hawaiian Railways WW II Album Softcover Series 462
NEW New York Central Steam Softcover Series 462
Passenger Cars of New England Softcover Series 462
PRR Lines West Hardcover Series 463
NEW Railroading in Downtown Chicago 1958-1969 462
Books 462, 463

RAILWAY EXPRESS MINIATURES
Vehicles 322

RAMPMETER Digital Volt Meter 383
Rasps 414
ReadyGrass 180
Reamers 413
Receivers 381

RED CABOOSE

RED CABOOSE

NEW Bi-Level Auto Racks 92
NEW 73' Centerbeam Flat Car 93
Couplers 106
Freight Car Parts 445
Freight Cars 92, 93

Reed Switches 137, 358, 362, 365, 369
Reference Books 449-451, 460
Relays 114, 358
Religious Figures 303, 305, 307
Remote Switches 113
Removers, Paint 400, 402
Rerailers 110, 113, 117, 119, 121, 416
Resistors 124, 356, 358, 359, 361, 368
Respirators 396
Retaining Walls 143, 145, 148, 156, 158, 161, 181, 237
Reversing Units 365, 381, 382

RIBBONRAIL
Alignment Gauges 121
Track Cleaner 390
Work Cradle 419

Rides, Carnival 223-225, 243

RIVAROSSI/ARNOLD
Freight Cars 77
Electric Locomotives 37
Lighting-Electrical-Motors 356
Passenger Cars 62

RIX PRODUCTS
Structures 271
Track Accessories 121
Uncoupling Tool 108

RK PUBLISHING
DVDs 463

Roadbed
 Cork 110, 114, 119
 Instant 110
 Track-Bed 168
Roads
 Barricades 144
 Details 144, 145, 153
 Kits 180
 Roadways 135, 147, 148, 152, 153, 160, 164
 Systems 168, 175

ROBART
Paint Shaker 400

Rock Rite 165
Rocks
 Coloring System 165
 Ground Covers 151
 Molds 154, 176
 Rocks 144, 145, 155, 161, 175, 182
Rods
 Brass 423
 Styrene 425
 Rollers, Paint 400
Roofs
 Roofing 164, 425, 426, 430, 432
 Shingles 157, 162, 423, 426, 430, 432
 Roofwalks 436, 439
 Rotary Beacons 432, 446
Rotary Tools
 Accessories 412
 Roundhouses 201, 206, 223, 228
 Rulers 415
Rural
 Scenes 140, 141, 145, 146, 148, 153, 164
 Structures 211, 215, 217, 218, 220-224, 226, 227, 230, 231, 235-237, 240, 242, 245-248, 258, 261, 265, 269, 271-275, 277

S

S&S HOBBY PRODUCTS
Coloring Books 463
Signs & Streets 135
Z-Scale 352

Sacks 434, 441
Sand Houses & Towers 222, 243, 244, 260, 272, 275
Sand, Modeler's 147

SANDIA SOFTWARE
Cadrail 463
DVDs 463

Sanding
 Tools 410, 412, 417
Sandpaper 417
Satin Finishes 97, 397, 405
Saws
 Blades 413
 Hacksaws 413
 Hobby 410, 413
 Jeweler's 413

SCALE SCENICS

Flat Wire 430
Gears 430
Micro-Mesh 430
Scratch Building Supplies 430
Solder 391

SCALE SHOPS
Lighting-Electrical-Motors 369
Switch Machines 122
Voltrollers 376

SCALECOAT
Paint & Paint Supplies 402

Scalpels 413
Scatter Material 147, 150, 160
Scene Details 145, 149, 153, 155, 157, 158, 220-222, 224, 225, 232, 241, 254, 274, 304, 309, 311, 444
SceneMaster Scenery 142, 143

Scenery
 Accessories 168, 175
 Adhesives 142, 152, 160, 166, 168, 175, 180, 182, 392
 Assortments 150, 155, 157
 Backgrounds 140, 141, 145, 147, 148, 153, 156, 164
 Base Materials 161
 Books 145, 150, 167, 183, 450-455, 464
 Coloring 165, 166, 179
 DVDs 183, 453, 464
 Kits 175, 178, 179, 183
 Modules 177, 178
 Paint 153, 165, 166
 Paper 161, 164
 Solutions 145
 Terrain 167
 Videos 156, 167, 183, 453, 464
 Z Scale 326, 328, 329, 331, 339, 340, 345, 348, 349, 351, 352
SCENERY SECTION 139-184
Scenic Accents By Woodland Scenics 309
Scenic Accents Glue 309
Scissors 415, 418
Scrapers 413
Scratch Building Supplies, Z-Scale 331
SCRATCH BUILDING SUPPLIES SECTION 421-430
Screwdrivers
 Screwdrivers 415
 Sets 415
 Sharpeners 415
Screws
 Machine 422, 426
 Multi-Purpose 439
 Nylon 422
 Track 110
 Wood 422
Scribers 410, 413
Sculptamold 144
Sealants 388, 402

SEAPORT MODEL WORKS
Boats 322
Super Detailing Parts 445

Seasonal Trees 142, 146, 149, 154, 157-159, 165, 170-172
Semi Tractors 314-317, 321
Semaphore Signals 126, 136
Setting Solutions, Decal 97, 391, 397, 400, 405, 406, 423

SEUTHE
Smoke & Steam Units 373

Shaker Bottles 182
Shakers, Paint 400
Shears 418

INDEX

Sheets
- Abrasive 410
- Brick 151, 423, 427
- Building 162, 423, 424, 426, 427, 430
- Corrugated Metal 423, 424, 426
- Flooring 423
- Foam 167
- Metal 144, 423, 424, 426, 430
- Phosphor Bronze 369
- Plastic 423, 424, 426, 427
- Roofing 425, 426, 430
- Siding 424, 430
- Stone 151, 423, 427
- Styrene 423, 424, 426, 427
- Trackbed 168
- Tunnel Walls 151
- Water 147, 155, 160

Shells, Locomotive 41
Shingles 157, 162, 423, 426, 430, 432

SHINOHARA
Track 122

SHOWCASE MINIATURES
Structures 272
Vehicles 321

Shrubs 150
Sideframes, Trucks 106
Sidewalks 147, 153, 155, 162, 423, 425, 442, 444

Siding
- Board & Batten 424, 429, 430
- Brick 423
- Clapboard 424, 429
- Concrete 429
- Corrugated 423, 424, 426, 429, 430
- Novelty 424
- Scribed 429
- Steel 429, 430
- Styrene 424
- Tin 423

Signals
- Actuators 128, 136, 137
- Automatic 116
- Block 124, 126, 135-137
- Bridges 127, 135-137
- Control Board 124
- Crossing 124, 127, 135, 136, 363
- Decoders 379, 382, 385, 386
- Dwarf 126, 136, 137
- Heads 127, 136
- Semaphore 126, 136
- Switch Control 127
- Towers 216, 219, 221, 225, 228, 248, 249, 273, 275
- Traffic 127, 135, 137
- Wig Wag 136, 446
- Z Scale 328, 329, 337, 346, 349, 352

SIGNALS, DETECTION UNITS & SIGNS SECTION 123-138

Signs
- Advertising 96, 162, 360
- Animated 131-134
- Billboards 96, 124, 125, 130-136, 437, 444
- Business 103, 125, 126, 130-134, 136-138, 360, 436, 444
- Construction 126, 127
- Decals 96, 136, 138
- Dry Transfers 127, 138
- Highway 124, 126, 129, 134, 135
- Railroad 103, 124, 126, 129, 130, 134, 135, 137, 138, 456
- Software 129
- Street 124, 126, 129, 134, 135
- Traffic 124, 126, 129, 134, 135, 153

SJT ENTERPRISES
Camera Systems 375

Skylights 442
Slide Switches 365, 369
Slip Switches 120
Slow Motion Switch Machine 118

SMAIL Slow Motion Activator 118

Smoke
- Accessories 373
- Fluid 372, 373, 376, 389
- Jacks 443
- Generators 216, 373, 376
- Stacks 443

Snow
- Plows 435, 438, 446
- Powder 147, 160, 175

Sockets
- Bulbs 356, 358
- Sockets 358

Soda Machines 444
Software, Computers 129, 232, 460

Solder
- Soldering Accessories 359
- Solder 391
- Soldering Tools 415
- Solutions, Decal Setting 97, 391, 397, 400, 405, 406, 423

Solvaset 397

Sounds
- Bells 129, 363
- Decoders 376, 379, 386
- Diesel 376
- Steam 376
- Systems 373, 375, 376

SOUNDTRAXX
Lighting-Electrical-Motors 368
Sound Decoders 376
Speakers 376

Spark Arrestors 435, 438, 446
Speakers 366, 376

Spectrum by Bachmann
- Locomotives 43-45
- Train Sets 58

Spikes 110, 118
Sport Utility Vehicles 314, 320
Sports & Recreation Figures 302, 304, 306, 307, 309- 311
Spotlights 357, 364

Spray
- Booths 395, 408
- Paint 398, 402, 404-406
- Sprayers 182
- Sprue Cutters 408, 412, 417

Stairs 232, 436, 444
Stake Bed Trucks 317, 319
Standards Gauge 418
Stars Lighting Set 356
Starter Sets, DCC 378, 379, 384, 385
State Line Farm Supply 202

STATE TOOL & DIE CO.
Glue & Mixing Dishes 419
Wire Ties 368

Stations
- Fire 215, 227, 244, 252, 257, 268, 273, 275, 277
- Police 215, 258, 273, 274
- Train 204, 207, 216, 218, 219-223, 225, 227, 228, 230, 231, 233, 236, 241-244, 246-249, 257, 260, 262, 265, 266, 270, 272, 274-276

Steam
- Accessories 373
- Generators 216, 373, 376
- Locomotives 28, 37, 38, 42-44, 47, 48, 50-52
- Sounds 376
- Train Sets 55-59

Stencils
- Tank Car 97

Steps 430, 435, 438-441, 445
Sterling Dairy Complex 190

STEWART PRODUCTS
Freight Cars 94
Structures 272
Super Detailing Parts 445

Stickers, Railroad 456

Stone
- Sheets 151
- Stone 161
- Walls 143, 145, 148, 156, 158, 162

Storage
- Containers 73, 82, 439, 445
- Tanks 221, 222, 269, 272, 274

Storm Drains 144
Streamlined Passenger Cars 47-49, 63-65, 67

Streets
- Lights 135, 136, 137, 357, 364, 435
- Signs 124, 126, 129, 134, 135
- Streets/Roads 135, 147, 148, 152, 153, 160, 164

Strippers
- Paint 400, 402
- Wire 416, 418

Strips
- Styrene 424, 425
- Wood 426, 428, 429

Strobe Flashers 361, 365, 369
Structural Shapes 423, 429

Structures
- Books 450, 451, 454
- Details 232, 253, 254, 270, 276, 427, 432, 434, 437, 439, 440-444
- Interiors 434, 435, 437
- Lights 356, 358, 360, 363, 364, 366
- Sheds 434, 438, 440
- Z Scale 326, 327, 330, 331, 338-340, 342-346, 348, 349, 352, 353

STRUCTURES SECTION 185-278

Styrene
- Modeling Books 425, 449, 460
- Rods 425
- Sheets 424, 425, 427, 430
- Strips 424, 425
- Structural Shapes 425, 430
- Tubing 425

SubTerrain System 167
Sunrise Feed Mill 192

SUNRISE ENTERPRISES
Signals 137
Structures 271
Super Detailing Parts 446

Sunshades 433, 435, 438, 446
SUPER DETAILING PARTS SECTION 431-446
SUVs - See Sport Utility Vehicles
Swimming Pools 444
Switch Towers 275

Switches
- Electrical 114, 117, 121, 137, 356, 360, 369
- Machines 113, 114, 118, 376
- Miniature 362, 365, 367, 369
- Panels 114
- Push-Button 137, 358, 365, 369
- Random 360
- Reed 137, 358, 362, 365, 369
- Rotary 365
- Slide 365, 369
- Stands 118, 119, 435
- Toggle 358, 362, 365, 367, 369
- Wye 114

Syringes 417

T

Tables 157, 437, 440, 444
Talus 182
Tanker Trucks 321

Tanks
- Fuel 250, 258
- Oil 156, 221, 230, 254, 257, 262, 272, 443
- Propane 446
- Storage 221, 222, 269, 272, 274
- Water 193, 218, 219, 221, 223, 230, 243, 246, 248, 262, 269, 272

Tapes
- Ballast 110
- Masking 408
- Paving 168

Taps & Dies 416, 422, 426
Taxis 314, 315, 317

Telephones
- Booths 229, 437
- Poles 124, 129, 134, 135, 143

Temp-Low 422
Templates, Track Planning 113, 115

TENAX-7R

Space Age Construction Kit 391
Tenax-7R 391
- Adhesives 391

Tents 157, 275
Terminal Strips 358, 359, 363, 365
Terminals, Container 229
Terrain For Trains 163
Terrain, Scenery 163, 167, 179
Test Leads 363

INDEX

TESTORS

Airbrush w/Compressor & Paint 407
Aztek Airbrushes 407
Model Master 406-408
  Adhesives 391
  Airbrushes & Accessories 407, 408
  Paint & Paint Supplies 404-407
  Tools 408

The 1-Kit 232
Thinners, Paint 398, 400, 402, 405, 406
Throttles
  DCC 380, 381, 384, 385
  Kits 376
  Pockets 383
  Systems 372
  Walk-Around 378, 384
Ties 118
Tiles 423, 426, 430

TIMBERLINE SCENERY
Scenery 165, 166

Timers 360

TL MARSHALL CO.
Foam Cutters 416

Toggle Switches 358, 362, 365, 367, 369

TOMAR INDUSTRIES
Catalog 68
Drumheads 41, 68
Lighting 369
Signals 137
Track Accessories 122

Tools
  Holders 410, 412
  Jeweler's 413, 414
  Sets 144, 414, 416, 418
  Traction Tire Tools 106
TOOLS SECTION 409-420
Torquemaster Switch Motors 122
Tortoise Switch Machine 118
Towers 364
  Bell 221
  Cell Phone 229
  Coaling 201, 244
  Crossing 241, 242, 245
  Interlocking 226, 241, 246, 266
  Radio 229, 272
  Sand 222, 243, 244, 260, 272, 275
  Signal 216, 219, 221, 225, 228, 248, 249, 273, 275
  Switch 275
  Transmitter 126, 127
  TV Broadcast 126
  Watch 267
  Water 193, 218, 219, 221, 223, 230, 243, 248, 262, 264, 274

Track
  Alignment Tools 121
  Ballast Tapes 110
  Beds 168
  Bridges 118
  Bumpers 111, 113, 116, 119, 156, 193
  Cleaners, Car 73, 77
  Cleaners 110, 388-391, 415
  Code 40 115, 118
  Code 55 112, 113, 115, 118, 120
  Code 60 120
  Code 70 115, 118, 122
  Code 80 112, 113, 120
  Crossings 111, 113, 115, 116
  Curved 110, 111, 113, 115-117, 119, 120, 441
  Cutters 118
  Flexible 113, 118-120, 122
  Gauges 118, 418
  Joiners 113, 114, 117, 120
  Maintenance Packs 388
  Mine 441
  Nails 110, 114, 119
  Narrow Gauge 441
  Planning Books 451, 453-455
  Planning Templates 113, 115
  Power Adapters 362
  Roadbed 110, 114, 119, 168
  Screws 110
  Sets 113, 116
  Straight 110, 111, 116
  Test Lights 110, 119, 366
  Tools 115
  Track 229
  Turnouts 110, 111, 113, 115, 116, 118-120, 122, 441
  Weathered 118
  Weathering Solutions 118
  Z Scale 337, 341, 342, 346, 351
TRACK & ACCESSORIES SECTION 109-122
Track-Bed Roadbed 168
Trackside
  Accessories 221
  Details 275, 434, 439
  Structures 192, 193, 201, 205, 207, 210, 211, 213, 216, 218, 219, 222, 223, 226, 227, 229, 230, 233, 235-237, 239, 241-246, 248, 249, 257, 260-262, 266, 267-270, 272, 273, 275

TRACKSIDE TREASURES
Vehicles 323

Traction
  Tire Tools 106
  Tires 50, 106
  Trolleys 43
Tractor/Trailers 315, 319, 321

Tractors
  Farm 317, 320, 321
  Semis 314-317, 321
Traffic
  Light Controllers 361
  Lights 127, 135, 137
  Signs 124, 126, 129, 134, 135, 153
Trailer Parks 263
Trailers
  24' 77
  40' 77
  Camping 319, 320
  Flatbed 316
  Highway 316
  Hitch Covers 460
  RoadRailer 81
  Semi 77, 316
  Utility 316, 317

TRAIN AMERICA STUDIOS
Torquemaster Switch Motors 122

Train Control Circuits 128, 137
Train Engineer 372
Train Sets
  Amtrak 58
  Birthday 59
  Christmas 56, 59
  DCC 58
  Diesel 54-59
  Freight 54-59
  Holiday 56, 59
  Passenger 56-59
  Steam 55-59
  Z Scale 332-334, 340
TRAIN SETS SECTION 53-60
Train Stations 204, 207, 216, 218-223, 225, 227, 228, 230, 231, 233, 236, 241-244, 246-249, 257, 260, 262, 265, 266, 270, 272, 274-276

TRAIN TRONICS
Lighting-Electrical-Motors 369
Signal Accessories 137
Sound Systems 376
Switch Power Unit 376

Train Whistles 460

TRAINMAN BY ATLAS

NEW 70-Ton Ore Cars 94
NEW 50' Double Door Box Cars 94
NEW Hoppers 94
  Freight Cars 94

Trains, Reversing Units 365
Transformers 366
Translators 382
Transmission Towers 127, 364

Transponding Devices 380, 382
Travelers (Figures) 302-305, 307, 308-311
Treadplate 430, 436, 440
Trees
  Armatures 169
  Assortments 146, 150, 155, 158, 159, 171, 172
  Barren 169, 170
  Deciduous 142, 146, 149, 154, 155, 157-159, 165, 169, 170-172
  Evergreen 142, 146, 149, 150, 154, 155, 157-159, 165, 169-172
  Fruit 142, 146, 149, 154, 158, 159, 165
  Holiday Village 255
  Kits 169, 172, 175, 180
  Palms 154, 159, 162, 170
  Seasonal 142, 146, 149, 154, 157-159, 165, 170-172
  Stumps 156, 157, 169, 175, 434
Trestles 156, 207, 231, 237, 243, 244, 254, 268
Trolleys 43
Truck Mount Couplers 107
Trucks
  Accessories 106
  Assortments 318
  Delivery 315, 319-321
  Flatbed 315, 316, 319, 320, 324
  Freight Cars 106, 108
  Parts 108
  Passenger Cars 106, 108
  Pickups 314, 316, 317, 320
  Semis 315, 321
  Sideframes 106
  Stake Bed 317, 319
  Tankers 321
Truss Bridges 117, 207, 229, 244, 259, 262, 277
Tubing
  Brass 423
  Heat Shrink 362, 365, 368-370
  Hexagon 423
  Square 423
  Stainless Steel 427
  Styrene 425
Tunnels
  Liner Forms 179
  Portals 145, 148, 151, 155, 156, 158, 161, 162, 164, 181, 259
  Tunnels 142, 152, 161
  Wall Sheets 151
Turf 173, 174
Turnout Control Switches 117, 121
Turnouts
  Curved 115
  Kits 115
  Turnouts 110, 111, 113, 115, 116, 118-120, 122, 441
  Wye 115, 120
Turntable Drives 206, 228
Turntables 121, 200, 206, 228
TV Broadcast Towers 126
Tweezers 309, 412, 413, 416-418

U

Uncouplers 107, 108
Underbrush 175
UNITRACK Track System 116
Unpainted Figures 308

UNREAL DETAILS
Magic Water 164

US Flags 103

UTAH PACIFIC
Lighting 369

Utility
  Poles 124, 129, 134, 135, 143, 445
  Trailers 316

V

Vans
  Delivery 315-317, 321, 324
  Passenger 314, 317
Vehicles
  Decals 102, 104
  Detail Sets 322
  Lighting Kits 365
  Trailers 77
  Z Scale 331, 339, 346, 347, 349, 352
VEHICLES SECTION 313-324
Vents 434, 435, 439, 441-443
Viaducts 116, 117, 161, 221, 224, 225, 245, 250, 265, 274, 277
Videos
  Airbrushing 453
  How-To 464
  Scenery 156, 167, 183, 453, 464
  Viewliner Passenger Cars 66
Village Sets 223
Vines 150
Vises 414

VITACHROME GRAPHICS
Decals 104

VOLLMER

VOLLMER

NEW Eichenreid Station 273
NEW House Kit 272
NEW Shanty Kit 272
Catalog 460
Catenary 122
Figures 304
Lighting 369
Scenery 164
Smoke Unit 376
Structures 272-277
Z Scale Structures 352, 353

Voltrollers 376

INDEX

W

Wagons 317, 320
Walkways 436, 438, 444
Walls
  Bricks 161
  City 220
  Concrete 145
  Modulars 238
  Retaining 143, 145, 148, 156, 158, 161, 181, 237
  Stone 143, 145, 148, 156, 158, 162
  Tunnels 151
  Walls 161, 162, 219

WALTHERS

NEW Logging Flat Cars 70
NEW Difco Dump Cars 70
NEW GSC "Commonwealth" 54' Flat Car 70

CORNERSTONE – MODULARS
NEW Sterling Dairy Complex 190
NEW 3-IN-1 Building #2 190

CORNERSTONE – BUILT-UPS
NEW Sunrise Feed Mill 192

CORNERSTONE – KITS
NEW State Line Farm Supply 202
NEW Electric Furnace 202
NEW Santa Fe Style Brick Depot & Freight House 202
NEW Art Deco Highway Underpass 203
NEW Van Dyke Farm Windmill 203
NEW Coke Ovens 203

Adhesives & Cleaners 388
Blank Decal Paper 97
Cornerstone Series Built-ups 192, 193, 200
Cornerstone Modulars 189-191
Cornerstone Series 201-214
Decal Setting Solution 397
Freight Cars 70-72
GOO 423
Instant Horizons 140, 141
Life-Like 73, 215, 356
Lighting-Electrical-Motors 356
Magic Masker 423
Masking Liquid 397
PROTO 2000 Steam Locomotives 28
PROTO N Diesel Locomotives 29-36
Scratch Building Supplies 422, 423
Solvaset 97, 423
Temp-Low 422
Track Cleaner 110

Washers 426
Watch Towers 267
Water
  Columns 222, 441, 446
  Effects 174, 175
  Fountains 152
  Lakes 152
  Pumps 153, 356
  Sheets 147, 155, 160
  Tanks & Towers 193, 218, 219, 221, 223, 230, 243, 246, 248, 262, 269, 274
  Water 146, 158, 160, 164, 174, 179, 180
Waterfront Structures 267
Weather-Rite 166
Weathering
  Powders 145
  Sets 398
  Solutions 118, 143, 166
Web Site Directory/Address/Information 12
Weight Bond Glue 432
Weight Upgrade Kit 432
Weights 82, 432
Welders, Arc 360, 362

WESTERN RAIL PRODUCTS

Lighting 369

Wheelsets 106, 108

WHISTLES UNLIMITED

Train Whistles 460

Wig-Wag Signals 136, 446

WIKING

Automobile Assortments 324
European Construction Equipment 324
Farm Machinery 324
Vehicles 324

Wind Turbines 217
Windmills 203, 223, 248, 257
Window Designer Software 232
Windows
  Buildings 427
  Cabooses 439
  Locomotives 437, 438
  Structures 432, 437, 442, 443
Windshield Wipers 438

Wire
  Brass 435
  Brushes 415
  DCC 378, 382, 385, 386
  Electrical 356, 359, 362, 363, 366, 367
  Electroluminescent 134
  Etched Screen 440
  Flat 366, 435
  Flexible 359, 362, 366, 367
  Holders 358, 362, 363
  Hook-Up 356, 359, 362, 363
  Magnet 367
  Mesh 152, 161
  Multi-Conductor 356, 359, 363, 366, 370
  Phosphor Bronze 432
  Ribbon 356
  Strippers 416, 418
  Test Lead Sets 363
  Ties 358, 362, 363, 368
  Wrap 363

WIRE WORKS

Wire 370

Wireform Modeling Mesh 144
Wireless DCC Systems 379, 381, 385
Wiring
  Books 453-455
Wood
  Mouldings 429
  Shapes 429
  Sheets 429
  Strips 426, 428, 429
  Woodworking Tools 413, 414

WOODLAND SCENICS®

ReadyGrass Vinyl Mat 180
Mod-U-Rail 170
N Scale Scenic Accents 309-311
  Adhesives & Lubricants 392
  Books, DVDs & Videos 464
  Catalog 183
  Dry Transfer Decals 138
  Figures 309, 310, 311
  Hob-Bits Miniature Hardware 426
  Paint & Paint Supplies 403
  Scenery 167-183
  Scenic Accents Figures 309-311
  Tools 419
  Track-Bed 122

Work
  Holders 400, 414, 415, 419, 422
  Work Train Cars 70, 75, 77, 79, 82, 90, 94, 321, 322
  Working People 302-305, 308-311
  Wrenches 415, 422, 426
  Wye Turnouts 115, 120

X

XURON CORP.

Tools 418

Y

Yard Equipment & Facilities 200, 201, 206, 218, 219, 222, 223, 225, 227, 233, 237, 244-246, 248, 249, 257, 258, 260, 261, 265, 267, 269, 270, 272, 273, 275

Z

Z Scale
  Books 339
  Decals 342
  Figures 326, 328, 349, 350, 352
  Freight Cars & Accessories 334, 335, 340-342
  Lighting 329, 338, 344, 345
  Locomotives 332, 333, 340
  Passenger Cars 334-336
  Power 339
  Scenery 326, 328, 329, 331, 339, 340, 345, 348, 349, 351, 352
  Signals, Detection Units & Signs 328, 329, 337, 346, 349, 352
  Structures 326, 327, 330, 331, 338-340, 342-346, 348, 349, 352, 353
  Super Detailing Parts 329, 331, 340, 345-347, 349
  Track & Accessories 337, 341, 342, 346, 351
  Train Sets 332-334, 340
  Vehicles 331, 339, 346, 347, 349, 352
Z SCALE SECTION 325-354

Models and Photo by Bernard Kempinski, Alexandria, Virginia

LOCOMOTIVES

From Toledo to the Virginia Tidewater, the Chesapeake & Ohio ran a busy railroad. Double track over much of the route, this heavily built line was the railroad's artery for hauling coal—lots of it! Huge 2-10-4s and articulated 2-6-6-2 "H" class and Allegheny 2-6-6-6 locos handled endless trains of coal hoppers day in and day out. But the C&O also handled plenty of conventional freight. For these duties, fleet-footed power like 2-8-4 Berkshires sped long trains on fast schedules.

C&O #2740 coasts around a banked curve on the high iron somewhere in the Virginia foothills. This late in the steam era, improved highways have reached the hinterlands; a refrigerated delivery van cruises across a modern concrete overpass as the train rumbles underneath. In less than three years, diesels will replace #2740 and her sisters across the railroad.

On most layouts, modeling era is defined by the locomotives. Early steam, late steam, steam-to-diesel transition, early diesel and modern diesel locos set the stage for the rest of the layout. Here, a brass 2-8-4 heads up a freight as a Classic Metal Works truck rolls over a Rix modified vintage overpass. With plenty of steam, diesel and electric locos available from a variety of makers, find your railroad's defining power in the Locomotives Section.

LOCOMOTIVES N SCALE

Proto 2000 Heritage Steam Collection
From Walthers

2-8-4 "Berkshire"

Introduced in 1924, the 2-8-4 ushered in the super-power era. Its larger firebox and other improvements produced a combination of speed and power that was ideal for many railroads.

Among these were C&O, Nickel Plate and Pere Marquette, which were controlled by the Van Sweringen brothers. In 1929, management pooled the talents of the road's engineering departments to create the "Advisory Mechanical Committee" that would oversee future locomotive developments, including new 2-8-4s.

The Committee's first 2-8-4s were delivered to the Nickel Plate in 1934 and these speed demons worked fast freights between Bellevue, Ohio, and Buffalo, as well as Bellevue and Frankfort, Indiana. Building on this success, a new series was designed for Pere Marquette in 1937, followed by additional classes delivered in 1941 and 1944. During the war years when production was limited to existing designs, C&O ordered 40 2-8-4s based on these earlier locos, but with numerous mechanical improvements and other changes to match C&O practices. Between 1945 and 1947, 50 more were ordered by the C&O; the PM was absorbed in to the C&O in 1947 and some of its 2-8-4s remained in use there until 1953. Five near-copies of the C&O locos were delivered to the Virginian (though it was never a Van Sweringen-controlled road) in 1946.

Several Van Sweringen Berkshires were preserved, with three restored to operation.

Order Now! Limited Availability
Please Note: All Proto Series manufacturer numbers have changed from 433 to 920.

2-8-4 Berkshire
195.00 ea

- Over 50 Hand-Applied Parts
- Roadname-Specific Detailing
- Blackened Nickel-Silver RP-25 Wheels
- Driver & Tender Electrical Pickup
- Working Knuckle Couplers Front & Rear
- LED Headlight & Backup Light
- Powerful, Flywheel-Equipped Five-Pole Motor w/Skew-Wound Armature
- Runs on Code 55 Track
- Handles 9-3/4" Radii

C&O

NEW 920-90050 #2744

NEW 920-90051 #2759

Second Release
920-7875 #2768
920-7876 #2779

First Release
Limited Quantity Available

920-7465 #2724
920-7466 #2736

NKP

NEW 920-90052 #776

NEW 920-90053 #779

Second Release
920-7879 #740
920-7899 #765

First Release
Limited Quantity Available
920-7470 #738

Pere Marquette

NEW 920-90054 #1235

NEW 920-90055 #1239

Limited Quantity Available
920-7467 #1202
920-7468 #1209

Unlettered

NEW 920-90056

Second Release
920-7902 Black

Virginian

920-7877 #505
920-7878 #508

LOCOMOTIVES N SCALE

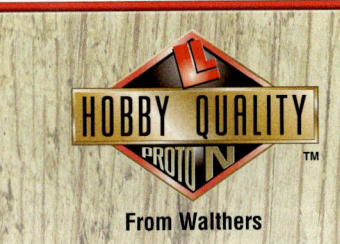

From Walthers

EMD GP38-2

EMD changed the face of railroading in 1972 with its Dash 2 series, which was based on existing designs, but equipped with new electrical systems and other improvements. Of these, the GP38-2 became the standard medium-sized diesel in the line and one of the most successful EMD designs ever built, with over 2200 constructed through 1987.

These reliable, non-turbocharged 2,000-horsepower units proved ideal for all kinds of road and switching chores. Hundreds are still in use by railroads of all sizes including all Class I lines down to shortlines and industrial lines. As with most EMD production, there were numerous owner-specified changes resulting in some variations including high, short hood models for Southern and N&W as well as steam-boiler passenger units for the National Railways of Mexico. Federal requirements to make engine cabs safer led to the introduction of a slightly larger 88" nose (81" had been standard) in 1977.

EMD GP38-2 w/88" Nose
99.98 ea

First Release

BNSF

NEW 920-75000 #2371   NEW 920-75001 #2373

Clinchfield - Family Lines

NEW 920-75002 #6001   NEW 920-75003 #6003

L&N - Family Lines

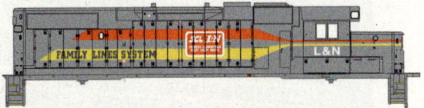

NEW 920-75004 #6022   NEW 920-75005 #6043

NS

NEW 920-75006 #5334   NEW 920-75007 #5385

Pittsburgh & Lake Erie

NEW 920-75008 #2051   NEW 920-75009 #2053

Rock Island

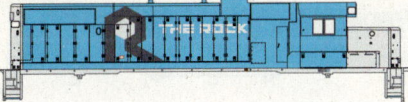

NEW 920-75010 #4374   NEW 920-75011 #4379

Seaboard System

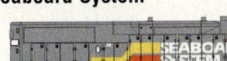

NEW 920-75012 #2680   NEW 920-75013 #2690

Soo Line

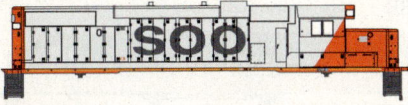

NEW 920-75014 #4400   NEW 920-75015 #4436

Undecorated
NEW 920-75016

Second Release - January 2007

ATSF

NEW 920-75017 #3563   NEW 920-75018 #3570

See What's Available at
www.walthers.com

BN

NEW 920-75019 #2151   NEW 920-75020 #2154

CNW

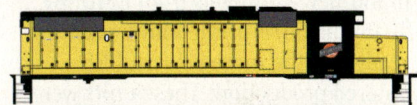

NEW 920-75021 #4629   NEW 920-75022 #4632

CR

NEW 920-75023 #8206   NEW 920-75024 #8227

CSX

NEW 920-75025 #2764   NEW 920-75026 #2771

Long Island Railroad

NEW 920-75027 #257   NEW 920-75028 #271

Missouri Pacific

NEW 920-75029 #2138   NEW 920-75030 #2164

SP

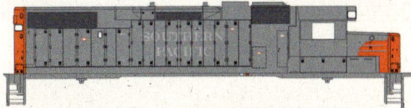

NEW 920-75031 #4810   NEW 920-75032 #4827

UP

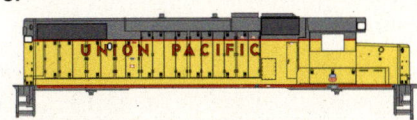

NEW 920-75033 #2139   NEW 920-75034 #2142

Undecorated
NEW 920-75035

LOCOMOTIVES N SCALE

Hobby Quality PROTO N From Walthers

EMD E8/9

As America's railroads rebuilt their passenger service following World War II, premiere trains received new equipment from engine to observation car. And once production resumed in 1945, many were led by brand-new E7 diesels from EMD. By 1948, the 567B prime mover was ready and the more powerful E8 entered production. These units were built through 1954, when the virtually identical E9 with its 567C prime movers was introduced. Speedy, powerful and economical, E8s and their kin proved to be an excellent choice for long-distance name trains. Despite the many changes in passenger service over the years, E8s were among the first diesels to serve Amtrak® when operations began in 1971; others ended their days in commuter service a few years later.

EMD E8/9

A Units Only 95.00 ea

Atlantic Coast Line 
NEW 920-34072 #545
NEW 920-34073 #546

Erie 
NEW 920-34074 #821
NEW 920-34075 #822

NYC 
NEW 920-34076 #4088
NEW 920-34077 #4089

PRR 
NEW 920-34078 #5700
NEW 920-34079 #5765

Rock Island 
NEW 920-34080 #644
NEW 920-34081 #645

Seaboard Air Line 
NEW 920-34082 #3053
NEW 920-34083 #3054

SP 
NEW 920-34084 #6018
NEW 920-34085 #6050

Undecorated
NEW 920-34086

A-B Sets 195.00 ea

Baltimore & Ohio
NEW 920-34099 A #1433; B #2414
NEW 920-34100 A #1435; B #2415

Illinois Central

NEW 920-34101 A #4020; B #2100
NEW 920-34102 A #4027; B #4108

UP

NEW 920-34103 900 & 900B
NEW 920-34104 930 & 930B

Undecorated
NEW 920-34105

LOCOMOTIVES N SCALE

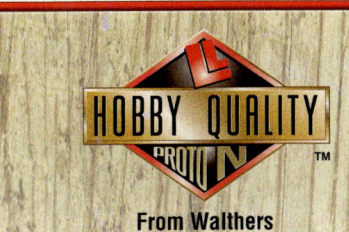

From Walthers

F-M C-Liner

EMD's F-series had introduced American railroads to the cab unit diesel in 1939. But World War II prevented other builder's from introducing competing designs until the late 40s. ALCO rolled out its FAs, Baldwin introduced its "sharks" and newcomer Fairbanks-Morse (F-M) unveiled its new Consolidation Line or "C-Liners" in 1948. To go the competition one better, F-M marketed its new cab units much like automobiles, offering several options among 14 different models. Buyers could choose from three freight or four passenger versions, each in A or B units. Three different prime movers were available, along with a variety of gear ratios for power or speed as needed, and additional equipment such as steam generators and water tanks could also be added. First built in 1950, the C-Liners performed well, but appeared just as cab units began losing favor to hood unit diesels. Orphans in a sea of EMD and ALCO power on most roads, F-Ms were quickly retired by the late 1960s, but a handful of C-Liners remained in use in Canada into the mid-70s.

Order Now! Limited Availability
Please Note: All Proto Series manufacturer numbers have changed from 433 to 920.

F-M C-Liner

A-B Sets 99.98 ea

A Units Only 59.98 ea
- Now with Powered B Units
- Redesigned Split Frame
- Now DCC-Friendly with Isolated Motor
- Clip-Fit Printed Circuit Board - Easily Replaceable for DCC Conversions
- Directional LED Headlight in A Units
- 8-Wheel Electrical Pick-Up
- Heavy Metal Chassis
- Five-Pole, Skew Wound Armature Motor
- Dual Machined Flywheels
- Outstanding Slow Speed Operation
- AccuMate® Knuckle Couplers Included
- Fully-Assembled, Ready for Service

MILW

A-B Sets
NEW 920-34087 24A-24B
NEW 920-34088 28A-28B

A Unit Only
NEW 920-34093 24C
NEW 920-34094 28C

NYC

A-B Sets
NEW 920-34089 #6601/#6900
NEW 920-34090 #5006/#6902

A Unit Only
NEW 920-34095 #6603
NEW 920-34096 #6604

PRR

A-B Sets
NEW 920-34091 #9450 & #9450B
NEW 920-34092 #9448 & #9448B

A Unit Only
NEW 920-34097 #9451
NEW 920-34098 #9497

Get the Scoop!
Get the Skinny!
Get the Score!
Check Out Walthers
Web site at

www.walthers.com

LOCOMOTIVES N SCALE

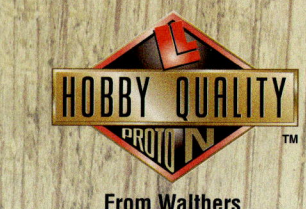

From Walthers

ALCO DL-109

As a member of the Alco-GE "DL100 Project" introduced in 1940, the DL-109 was among the American Locomotive Company's (Alco) early entries into the passenger diesel market. Alco hired noted industrial designer Otto Kuhler to design its distinctive carbody. With its sleek lines, knife-edged nose, three-panel windshield and long wheelbase, it was ideally suited for high-speed service. The 2,000-horsepower DL-109 was powered by twin McIntosh & Seymour 539 prime movers, the same engine that powered the popular RS-1 roadswitcher.

While designed as a passenger locomotive, the DL-109 could also handle high-speed freight with ease. In fact, its dual-service capabilities allowed its very construction; Alco was permitted to build 60 units for the New Haven in the face of wartime restrictions on passenger-only locos. The units performed admirably round the clock, handling passengers during the day and freight trains at night. Using lessons learned with the DL-109, it was succeeded by the famous PA-1 in 1946.

ALCO DL-109

105.00 ea

These detailed, ready-to-run models are ready for service on your railroad. Each features
- Powerful Motor w/Skew-Wound Armature & Dual Flywheels
- Working Headlights
- Split Frame Mechanism
- 8-Wheel Drive & All-Wheel Electrical Pick-Up
- AccuMate Operating Couplers (Unless Noted)

CNW

920-7704 #5007A (green, yellow)

Gulf, Mobile & Ohio

920-7706 #270 (maroon, red)
920-7707 #271 (maroon, red)

MILW

920-7716 #14A (orange, gray "Hiawatha")
920-7727 #14B (orange, gray "Hiawatha")

NH

920-7729 #0704 (green, yellow)
920-7737 #0709 (green, yellow)

Rock Island

920-7738 #621 (silver, red, black "Rocket")
920-7741 #623 (silver, red, black "Rocket")

SOU

920-7743 #6400 (green, aluminum)
920-7756 #6401 (green, aluminum)

Undecorated

920-7757

For Daily Product Updates Point Your Browser to
www.walthers.com

LOCOMOTIVES N SCALE

Order Now! Limited Availability
Please Note: All Proto Series manufacturer numbers have changed from 433 to 920.

HOBBY QUALITY
From Walthers

EMD SW8/9/600

Switchers had been an important part of EMD production from the early 1930s on. The SC (cast frames) and SW (welded frames) models were first introduced in 1936 and paved the way for many future models. The later development of improved power plants and other equipment led to a succession of higher horsepower units.

Introduced by EMD in 1950, the SW8 offered railroads and industry a rugged and reliable unit for switching chores, replacing the last of steam or earlier diesel switchers still in service. Powered by the famed 567B, the engines delivered 800 horsepower. In 1954, industry demand for a more powerful switcher led EMD to introduce the SW900, producing 100 additional horsepower from the 567C prime mover. Outwardly, these units (and the SW600 of which only 15 were built) were virtually identical. Production ended in late 1965 with a combined total of 743 engines. Well into the 1980s, these early switchers served railroads large and small and some remain in service today.

EMD SW8

75.00 ea

Atlantic Coast Line

920-7000 #50 (purple, silver)
920-7100 #59 (purple, silver)

ATSF

920-7300 #650 ("Zebra Stripes")
920-7377 #652 ("Zebra Stripes")

Boston & Maine

920-7378 #804 (maroon, yellow)
920-7379 #806 (maroon, yellow)

BN

920-7382 #98 (Cascade Green, white)
920-7384 #101 (Cascade Green, white)

Chessie System (B&O)

920-7385 #9401 (yellow, orange, blue)
920-7386 #9412 (yellow, orange, blue)

IC

920-7387 #800 (black, white)
920-7388 #801 (black, white)

Lehigh Valley

920-7389 #275 (Tuscan, black)
920-7399 #276 (Tuscan, black)

Penn Central

920-7597 #8638 (black)
920-7598 #8642 (black)

Texas & Pacific

920-7599 #812 (Swamp Holly Orange, black)
920-7699 #817 (Swamp Holly Orange, black)

Undecorated
920-7700

33

LOCOMOTIVES N SCALE

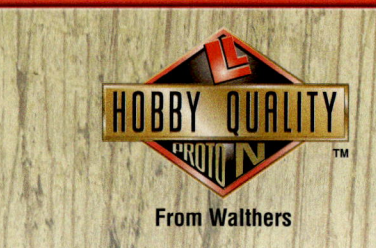

From Walthers

ALCO PA

As World War II drew to a close, American railroads began planning, promoting and ordering equipment for all-new streamlined trains. In addition to new cars, these much-publicized "trains of tomorrow" demanded equally stylish motive power, and in 1946, many buyers found exactly what they wanted in the American Locomotive Company's (ALCo.) PA diesel.

With its long nose and sleek, square body, the PA projected strength and power whether flying along the mainline or waiting for departure. Under the hood was a turbocharged 16-cylinder 244 prime mover that generated an amazing 2000 horsepower. For buyers who needed additional pulling power, a cabless B unit was also available. Finished in a rainbow of color schemes, PAs could soon be found at the head of many flagship trains. Production of the first series, designated PA-1, continued until 1950 when the more powerful but outwardly identical PA-2 was introduced. With the decline of passenger traffic in the 50s and 60s, some PAs were bumped into freight service. Most reached the end of the line in the late 60s. Today, a handful of survivors remain, including one being restored to operating condition.

Order Now! Limited Availability
Please Note: All Proto Series manufacturer numbers have changed from 433 to 920.

ALCO PA-1 & PB-1
Powered PA-PB Sets 210.00

DRGW

920-7547 #6001 & #6002 A-B Set
920-7550 #6013 & #6012 A-B Set

UP

920-7572 #602 & #604B A-B Set
920-7583 #607 & #607B A-B Set

Alco Demonstrator

920-7584 #8375 & #8375B A-B Set

Undecorated
920-7585 A-B Set

Powered A Unit Only 105.00 ea

Gulf, Mobile & Ohio

920-7551 #290
920-7554 #291

MP

920-7557 #44
920-7564 #49

NH

920-7566 #0760
920-7570 #0767

ALCO FA-1 & FB-1
- Rapido-Type Couplers
- Dummy Knuckle Front-Pilot Coupler on A Unit

Powered FA-FB Sets 87.50

GN
920-7445 #310A & 310B (green, Omaha Orange As-Delivered Scheme)
920-7446 #276A & 276B (green, Omaha Orange As-Delivered Scheme)

LV
920-7447 #530 & 531 (Cornell Red, black)
920-7448 #548 & 549 (Cornell Red, black)

NH
920-7449 #0408 & 0458 (Script Herald)
920-7450 #0424 & 0464 (Script Herald)

PRR
920-7451 #9603 & 9603B (Brunswick Green, Single Stripe)
920-7452 #9605 & 9605B (Brunswick Green, Single Stripe)

RDG
920-7453 #300 & 300B (black, green, As-Delivered Scheme)
920-7454 #304 & 304B (black, green, As-Delivered Scheme)

Seaboard Air Line
920-7455 #4200 & 4300 (green, yellow, As-Delivered Scheme)
920-7456 #4202 & 4302 (green, yellow, As-Delivered Scheme)

St. Louis-San Francisco "Frisco"
920-7457 #5200 & 5300 (black, yellow)
920-7458 #5215 & 5315 (black, yellow)

Undecorated
920-7431

LOCOMOTIVES N SCALE

From Walthers

EMD GP20

By the mid 50s, increasing pressure from long-haul trucks, declining passenger revenues and mounting costs forced western railroads to find new ways to improve service. Faced with expensive overhauls of early cab and hood unit diesels, many began looking at new equipment as well as ways to improve existing motive power. In 1955 Union Pacific equipped several GP9s with turbochargers as an experiment. Their success inspired EMD to create its own turbocharger for the 567 prime mover, leading to the introduction of the six-axle SD24 in 1958. Further experiments in 1959 created a four-axle version, dubbed the GP20. The first GP20s, which were built for GN and WP, were delivered with high, short hoods, and were the only units so equipped as later buyers favored the improved visibility of the short nose. Early in their careers, GP20s were typically assigned priority freights that demanded higher speeds. With the arrival of newer power, they were gradually bumped into secondary runs, and eventually spent their last years in local and yard service. Following their retirement, a few went to work for shortline operators.

EMD GP20
97.00 ea

ATSF

920-7764 #3149
920-7769 #3154

BN

920-7772 #2042
920-7774 #2064

CB&Q

920-7777 #928
920-7789 #932

NYC

920-7790 #2109
920-7791 #2112

SP

920-7794 #7234
920-7796 #7235

UP

920-7808 #476
920-7809 #493

Penn Central

920-7871 #2102
920-7872 #2105

ATSF (SPSF Merger Scheme)

920-7873 #3058
920-7874 #3073

Undecorated
920-7823

Hot New Products
Announced Daily! Visit
Walthers Web site at
www.walthers.com

LOCOMOTIVES N SCALE

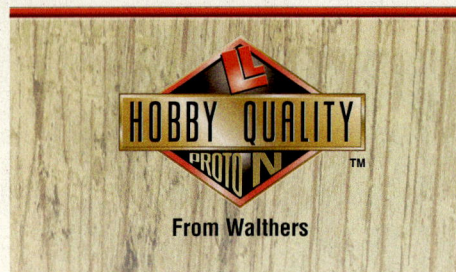

From Walthers

EMD GP18

Although EMD had been the last major builder to introduce a hood unit diesel, its GP7 proved to be exactly what many railroads were looking for. In turn, the GP7 was replaced by the more powerful GP9, and in 1959, the 1800-horsepower GP18 took its place. All three models shared the same basic and boxy but practical styling. The two 48" radiator fans found on late production GP9s were carried over to the roof of the GP18, but these new models had metal grids over the air intakes, replacing the so-called "chicken wire" screens used on the GP7 and 9. By this time the market was beginning to move in two directions and EMD responded with two models, the GP18, and the 2000-horsepower GP20 for roads that wanted faster and stronger units for important mainline service. The GP18 remained in production until 1963 when it was replaced by the GP28 with its completely restyled "35-Line" body.

Order Now! Limited Availability
Please Note: All Proto Series manufacturer numbers have changed from 433 to 920.

EMD GP18
90.00 ea

Illinois Central Gulf

920-7814 #9405 (orange, white)
920-7815 #9410 (orange, white)

LV

920-7816 #302 (Tuscan w/single yellow stripe)
920-7817 #303 (Tuscan w/single yellow stripe)

N&W

920-7818 #943 (black w/Large "NW" logo)
920-7819 #956 (black w/Large "NW" logo)

Limited Quantity Available
920-7117 #954 (blue w/"Hamburger" Herald)
920-7118 #958 (blue w/"Hamburger" Herald)

Seaboard Coast Line

920-7820 #1056 (black, yellow)
920-7821 #1057 (black, yellow)

SOU

Limited Quantity Available
920-7124 #176 ("Tuxedo" Scheme)

Undecorated

920-7822 With Dynamic Brakes

Limited Quantity Available
920-7131 No Dynamic Brakes

LOCOMOTIVES N SCALE

LIFE-LIKE TRAINS
Division of Wm. K. Walthers, Inc.

DIESEL LOCOMOTIVES

FM C-Liner A-B Set Powered 130.00 ea

433-7224 NYC #5008 & #5102 (Lightning Stripe)

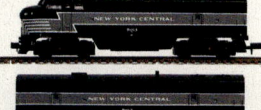

433-7225 NYC #5013 & #5103 (Lightning Stripe)

433-7226 PRR #9448A & #9448B (dark green)

433-7227 PRR #9493A & #9493B (dark green)

433-7229 Undecorated

Limited Quantity Available
433-7223 MILW #26C & #26B (orange, maroon, black)

EMD F40PH

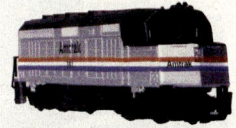

433-7641 Amtrak (silver) **51.00**
Introduced in 1976, these specially designed passenger service locos are in use by Amtrak and several regional commuter operations.

EMD F7

Limited Quantity Available
433-7752 UP (yellow) **47.00**

EMD GP38-2 51.00 ea

433-7841 BN (Cascade Green)

433-7842 CSX (gray)

433-7843 ATSF (blue, yellow)

433-7846 CR (blue)

EMD SD7/9
Models feature eight-wheel drive, twelve-wheel electrical pick-up, dual machined brass flywheels and five-pole, skew-wound armature motor for optimum pulling power, realistic speed, low noise level and body-mounted coupler pockets.
433-7708 B&O #762 **70.00**

Limited Quantity Available
433-7763 GN #566 **70.00**

433-7775 UP #776 **65.00**

FM C-Liner A-B Set
Roadnumbers Shown Not Available

SD7/9 B&O #762 433-7708

SD7/9 GN #566 433-7763

GP38 CSX 433-7842

EMD GP18 Hi-Nose 70.00 ea
Without Dynamic Brakes

433-7110 Rock Island #1347

With Dynamic Brakes
433-7115 NP #378

Info, Images, Inspiration! Get It All at
www.walthers.com

STEAM LOCOMOTIVES
0-6-0 Saddle Tank

433-7781 ATSF (black) **38.00**

AMERICAN LIMITED

Superdetail your motive power with these easy-to-assemble, injection-molded plastic diaphragms. For A-B-A sets (four diaphragms). Kits include complete instructions. 12" minimum radius.

Diaphragms 5.45 ea
For Kato E & F Units

Kato F units require Micro-Trains® #1128 couplers; E units use standard Kato couplers.
147-8800 Gray
147-8810 Black

For Con-Cor Alco PA & PB Locos

Require Micro-Trains #1101/1102 for powered models, or #1129 for unpowered models.
147-8900 Gray
147-8910 Black

ARNOLD/RIVAROSSI

Arnold/Rivarossi locomotives feature highly detailed plastic bodies dressed in authentic railroad colors and logos. Powerful German-made can motors have been combined with new transmissions to give a smoother ride.

Limited Quantity Available On All Items

EUROPEAN EQUIPMENT

These ready-to run locos feature prepainted and lettered plastic bodies and a variety of details.

Electric Locomotive

125-2353 C-C DB Class 103 (red) **229.99**

Control Trailer
125-15300 2nd Class DB Control Trailer (green, silver) **49.99**

37

LOCOMOTIVES N SCALE

Atlas® ready-to-run locomotives feature detailed plastic bodies (many with roadname-specific details), realistic paint schemes, powerful five-pole ScaleSpeed™ motors with twin flywheels (in diesel models), and heavy diecast metal chassis. Handrails are made of flexible engineering plastic and many models include additional applied details. Most models are also equipped with directional LED headlights and AccuMate® knuckle couplers. AccuMate couplers are made under license from Accurail. New models and roadnames are released on a monthly basis; visit www.walthers.com for the latest updates.

Limited Quantities Available on All Items Except Undecorated Models

NEW PRODUCTS

Steam Locomotives
Different roadnumbers shown for some models.

Two-Truck Shay
Favorites of logging and mining railroads, these locos could lug incredible loads over rough track. Units feature directional headlights, all-wheel electrical pickup and drive, detailed metal boiler and applied details.

Standard DC 199.95 ea
NEW 150-41628 Bloedel Stewart & Welch Ltd. #9 (black, white)
NEW 150-41629 Eufaula Company #3 (black, white)
NEW 150-41630 Federal Valley Railroad Company #10 (black, white)
NEW 150-41631 Frost-Johnson Lumber Company #112 (black, white)

NEW 150-41632 Lima Locomotive Works #2 (black, white)
NEW 150-41633 Potlatch Lumber Company #10 (black, white)
NEW 150-41627 Unlettered (black, white)

Diesel Locomotives
Different roadnumbers shown for some models.

Alco C-628 Phase 2B
These heavy-haul road freight units were part of the American Locomotive Company's (Alco) Century Locomotive Line. 185 units were built between 1963 and 1968.

Standard DC 104.95 ea
NEW 150-54067 CR #6722 (blue, white)

NEW 150-54068 CR #6742 (blue, white)

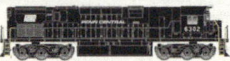

NEW 150-54069 PC #6302 (black, white)
NEW 150-54070 PC #6304 (black, white)
NEW 150-54071 PC #6313 (black, white)
NEW 150-54072 NdeM #8305 (green, red, yellow, silver)
NEW 150-54073 NdeM #8322 (green, red, yellow, silver)

NEW 150-54074 NdeM #8324 (green, red, yellow, silver)
NEW 150-54075 SP #3114 (gray, scarlet)
NEW 150-54076 SP #3118 (gray, scarlet)
NEW 150-54077 SP #3121 (gray, scarlet)

DCC Decoder Equipped 134.95 ea
NEW 150-54164 CR #6722 (blue, white)
NEW 150-54165 CR #6742 (blue, white)
NEW 150-54166 PC #6302 (black, white)
NEW 150-54167 PC #6304 (black, white)
NEW 150-54168 NdeM #8305 (green, red, yellow, silver)
NEW 150-54169 NdeM #8322 (green, red, yellow, silver)
NEW 150-54170 SP #3114 (gray, scarlet)
NEW 150-54171 SP #3118 (gray, scarlet)

Alco C-630
Produced beginning in 1965, these units incorporated an advanced GE a.c. traction alternator which boosted the horsepower rating to 3,000. The main spotting feature is the large aftercooler radiator housing extending above the roofline. The C-630 also featured a cab with more interior space for the crew.

Standard DC 104.95 ea
NEW 150-54232 CN #2017 (red, black, white)
NEW 150-54233 CN #2023 (red, black, white)
NEW 150-54234 CN #2029 (red, black, white)
NEW 150-54235 CP #4500 (red w/Multi Mark)

NEW 150-54236 CP #4503 (red w/Multi Mark)
NEW 150-54237 CP #4507 (red w/Multi Mark)
NEW 150-54238 Quebec Cartier Mining #30 (red, black)
NEW 150-54239 Quebec Cartier Mining #34 (red, black)

NEW 150-54240 Quebec Cartier Mining #37 (red, black)

DCC Decoder Equipped 134.95 ea
NEW 150-54320 CN #2017 (red, black, white)
NEW 150-54321 CN #2023 (red, black, white)
NEW 150-54322 CP #4500 (red w/Multi Mark)
NEW 150-54323 CP #4503 (red w/Multi Mark)
NEW 150-54324 Quebec Cartier Mining #30 (red, black)
NEW 150-54325 Quebec Cartier Mining #34 (red, black)

Alco RS-11 Classic
The RS-11 was Alco's answer to EMD's very successful GP9. The turbocharged RS-11 accelerated faster, had a higher tractive effort rating and typically used less fuel than the competition. It was also at home in heavy-haul freight as well as passenger service. A few units still serve shortlines in 2006.

Standard DC 99.95 ea
NEW 150-42624 BN #4181 (Cascade Green)

NEW 150-42625 BN #4185 (Cascade Green)

NEW Two-Truck Shay Bloedel Stewart & Welch Ltd. #9 150-41628

NEW Alco C-630 CN #2023 150-54233

NEW Alco RS-11 Classic Central Vermont #3611 150-42628

NEW 150-42626 BN #4191 (Cascade Green)
NEW 150-42627 Central Vermont #3603 (green, yellow)
NEW 150-42628 Central Vermont #3611 (green, yellow)
NEW 150-42629 LV #7640 (red, yellow)

NEW 150-42630 LV #7643 (red, yellow)
NEW 150-42631 L&N #954 (gray)
NEW 150-42632 L&N #959 (gray)
NEW 150-42633 NH #1402 (black, orange)
NEW 150-42634 NH #1409 (black, orange)

NEW 150-42635 NH #1414 (black, orange)

NEW 150-42636 NKP #852 (black)
NEW 150-42637 NKP #861 (black)
NEW 150-42638 PRR #8618 (Brunswick Green)

NEW 150-42639 PRR #8622 (Brunswick Green)
NEW 150-42640 PRR #8625 (Brunswick Green)

DCC Decoder Equipped 134.95 ea
NEW 150-42714 BN #4181 (Cascade Green)
NEW 150-42715 BN #4185 (Cascade Green)
NEW 150-42716 Central Vermont #3603 (green, yellow)
NEW 150-42717 Central Vermont #3611 (green, yellow)
NEW 150-42718 LV #7640 (red, yellow)
NEW 150-42719 LV #7643 (red, yellow)
NEW 150-42720 L&N #954 (gray, yellow)
NEW 150-42721 L&N #959 (gray, yellow)
NEW 150-42722 NH #1402 (black, orange)
NEW 150-42723 NH #1409 (black, orange)
NEW 150-42724 NKP #852 (black)
NEW 150-42725 NKP #861 (black)
NEW 150-42726 PRR #8618 (Brunswick Green)
NEW 150-42727 PRR #8622 (Brunswick Green)

LOCOMOTIVES N SCALE

EMD GP7 Phase I
Introduced in 1949, the 1500-horsepower EMD GP7 was essentially an F7 with a hood-type carbody that offered high visibility and easy engine access. The GP-7 was used in pulling every conceivable type of train and was sometimes substituted for part of a set of cab units.

Powered 94.95 ea (Unless Noted)
NEW 150-48071 Chessie/C&O #5705 (yellow, vermillion, blue)

NEW 150-48072 Chessie/C&O #5713 (yellow, vermillion, blue)
NEW 150-48073 Chessie/C&O #5717 (yellow, vermillion, blue)

NEW 150-48074 Chicago Great Western #120 (maroon, red, yellow)
NEW 150-48075 Chicago Great Western #121 (maroon, red, yellow)
NEW 150-48080 ATSF #2662 (blue, yellow)

NEW 150-48081 ATSF #2684 (blue, yellow)
NEW 150-48082 ATSF #2692 (blue, yellow)
NEW 150-48083 SSW #320 ("Daylight," red, orange, black, white) 104.95

DCC Decoder Equipped 129.95 ea
NEW 150-50800 Chessie/C&O #5705 (yellow, vermillion, blue)
NEW 150-50801 Chessie/C&O #5713 (yellow, vermillion, blue)
NEW 150-50802 Chicago Great Western #120 (maroon, red, yellow)
NEW 150-50803 Chicago Great Western #121 (maroon, red, yellow)
NEW 150-50805 Grand Trunk Western #6049 (blue, red)
NEW 150-50806 Guilford #14 (gray, orange)
NEW 150-50807 Guilford #16 (gray, orange)
NEW 150-50808 ATSF #2662 (blue, yellow)
NEW 150-50809 ATSF #2684 (blue, yellow)
NEW 150-50810 SSW #320 ("Daylight")

EMD GP9 Phase II
Visually similar to the GP7, the 1,750-horsepower GP9 was its successor. Like the GP7, these units were extremely popular in all kinds of service and many still serve railroads across the continent.

Powered 94.95 ea (Unless Noted)
NEW 150-48350 BNSF #1604 (orange, green)
NEW 150-48351 BNSF #1633 (orange, green)

NEW 150-48352 N&W #724 (black, white "NW")
NEW 150-48353 N&W #740 (black, white "NW")
NEW 150-48354 N&W #753 (black, white "NW")
NEW 150-48355 PRR #7002 (Brunswick Green)
NEW 150-48356 PRR #7006 (Brunswick Green)

NEW 150-48357 PRR #7019 (Brunswick Green)
NEW 150-48358 SOO #403 (maroon, yellow)

NEW 150-48359 SOO #406 (maroon, yellow)
NEW 150-48360 SP #3498 (gray, red "Bloody Nose")

NEW 150-48361 SP #3509 (gray, red "Bloody Nose")
NEW 150-48362 SP #3518 (gray, red "Bloody Nose")

DCC Decoder Equipped 129.95 ea
NEW 150-50850 BNSF #1604 (orange, green)
NEW 150-50851 BNSF #1633 (orange, green)
NEW 150-50852 N&W #724 (black, white "NW")
NEW 150-50853 N&W #740 (black, white "NW")
NEW 150-50854 PRR #7002 (Brunswick Green)
NEW 150-50855 PRR #7006 (Brunswick Green)
NEW 150-50856 SOO #403 (maroon, yellow, black)
NEW 150-50857 SOO #406 (maroon, yellow, black)
NEW 150-50858 SP #3498 (gray, red "Bloody Nose")
NEW 150-50859 SP #3509 (gray, red "Bloody Nose")

EMD GP38
GP38s are workhorse units that are equally at home on the road or handling switching and wayfreight assignments. Constructed beginning in the mid 60s, many of these units still work for railroads of all sizes.

Standard DC w/Low Hood 99.95 ea

NEW 150-49861 GMTX #2619 (blue, white)
NEW 150-49862 GMTX #2622 (blue, white)
NEW 150-49863 GMTX #2624 (blue, white)
NEW 150-49864 Providence & Worcester #2010 (brown, orange, white)

NEW 150-49865 Providence & Worcester #2011 (brown, orange, white)
NEW 150-49866 Wisconsin & Southern #3803 (red, gray)

NEW EMD GP7 Phase I SSW #320 150-48083

NEW 150-49867 Wisconsin & Southern #3806 (red, gray)
NEW 150-49868 Wisconsin & Southern #3807 (red, gray)

DCC Decoder Equipped 129.95 ea
NEW 150-53462 GMTX #2619 (blue, white)
NEW 150-53463 GMTX #2622 (blue, white)
NEW 150-53464 Providence & Worcester #2010 (brown, orange, white)
NEW 150-53465 Providence & Worcester #2011 (brown, orange, white)
NEW 150-53466 Wisconsin & Southern #3803 (red, gray)
NEW 150-53467 Wisconsin & Southern #3806 (red, gray)

EMD GP40
GP40s were popular for lines needing high-horsepower road locos for fast freights. Many roads later operated them in secondary freight service and on locals. Still others have been rebuilt for continued service on shortlines, commuter railroads and even Amtrak leased a small fleet for use in passenger and work train service. Many of these 60s-era units are still at work.

Standard DC w/Low Hood 99.95 ea
NEW 150-53907 Amtrak #657 (silver, black)

NEW 150-53908 Amtrak #658 (silver, black)
NEW 150-53909 Amtrak #660 (silver, black)
NEW 150-53910 FEC #401 (blue)

NEW 150-53911 FEC #405 (blue)
NEW 150-53912 FEC #408 (blue)

NEW 150-53913 Vermont Railway #301 (red)

NEW 150-53914 Green Mountain #305 (green, yellow)

NEW 150-53915 DRGW #3082 (black, Large Logo)
NEW 150-53916 DRGW #3084 (black, Large Logo)
NEW 150-53917 DRGW #3087 (black, Large Logo)

NEW 150-53918 New York, Susquehanna & Western #3040 (black, yellow)

Low Hood w/DCC Decoder 129.95 ea
NEW 150-48596 Amtrak Phase III #657
NEW 150-48597 Amtrak Phase III #658
NEW 150-48598 FEC #401 (blue)
NEW 150-48599 FEC #405 (blue)
NEW 150-53495 Vermont Railway #301 (red)
NEW 150-53496 Green Mountain #305 (green, yellow)
NEW 150-53497 DRGW #3082 (black, Large Logo)
NEW 150-53498 DRGW #3084 (black, Large Logo)
NEW 150-53499 New York, Susquehanna & Western #3040 (black, yellow)

Daily New Product Announcements! Visit Walthers Web site at www.walthers.com

LOCOMOTIVES N SCALE

EMD GP40-2
Like GP40s, these 70s and 80s-built units featured more modern electronics. Many are still at work in all kinds of service.

Standard DC w/Low Hood 99.95 ea
NEW 150-48645 Alaska Railroad #3008 (black)

NEW 150-48646 Alaska Railroad #3311 (black)

NEW 150-48647 Alaska Railroad #3007 (black)

NEW 150-48648 CSX/B&O #6344 (gray, blue)
NEW 150-48649 CSX/SBD #6382 (gray, blue)
NEW 150-48650 Indiana Harbor Belt #4012 (orange)
NEW 150-48651 Indiana Harbor Belt #4015 (orange)
NEW 150-48652 Indiana Harbor Belt #4018 (orange)

Low Hood w/DCC Decoder 129.95 ea
NEW 150-48695 Alaska Railroad #3008 (black, gold)
NEW 150-48696 Alaska Railroad #3311 (black, gold)
NEW 150-48697 CSX/B&O #6344 (gray, blue)
NEW 150-48698 CSX/SBD #6382 (gray, blue)
NEW 150-48699 Indiana Harbor Belt #4012 (orange)
NEW 150-49799 Indiana Harbor Belt #4015 (orange)

EMD SD35
EMD introduced the 2,500-horsepower SD-35 in the early 60s as the successor to the SD24. Essentially a six-axle version of the GP35, these 567-engined units were ideally suited for heavy drag freight service where tractive effort was paramount. In service, they lasted in rough service into the 80s, and a few still operate on regional lines.

Standard DC 94.95 ea

Low Nose
NEW 150-49667 C&O #7420 (blue, yellow)
NEW 150-49668 C&O #7424 (blue, yellow)

NEW 150-49669 C&O #7431 (blue, yellow)
NEW 150-49670 Family Lines/L&N #4513 (gray, red, yellow)
NEW 150-49671 Family Lines/L&N #4523 (gray, red, yellow)

NEW 150-49672 Guilford (Springfield Terminal) #614 (gray, orange)
NEW 150-49673 CNJ #2506 (green, gold)

NEW 150-49674 CNJ #2512 (green, gold)
NEW 150-49675 PRR #6008 (Brunswick Green)

NEW 150-49676 PRR #6021 (Brunswick Green)
NEW 150-49677 PRR #6034 (Brunswick Green)

High Nose

NEW 150-49572 SOU #3031 (black, imitation aluminum)
NEW 150-49573 SOU #3088 (black, imitation aluminum)
NEW 150-49574 SOU #3096 (black, imitation aluminum)

DCC Decoder Equipped 129.95 ea

Low Nose
NEW 150-49681 C&O #7420 (blue, yellow)
NEW 150-49682 C&O #7424 (blue, yellow)
NEW 150-49683 Family Lines/L&N #4513 (gray, red, yellow)
NEW 150-49684 Family Lines/L&N #4523 (gray, red, yellow)
NEW 150-49685 Guilford (Springfield Terminal) #614 (gray, orange)
NEW 150-49686 CNJ #2506 (green, gold)
NEW 150-49687 CNJ #2512 (green, gold)
NEW 150-49688 PRR #6008 (Brunswick Green)
NEW 150-49689 PRR #6021 (Brunswick Green)
NEW 150-49690 SP #6910 (gray, scarlet)
NEW 150-49691 SP #6912 (gray, scarlet)

High Nose
NEW 150-49692 SOU #3031 (black, imitation aluminum, gold)
NEW 150-49693 SOU #3088 (black, imitation aluminum, gold)

EMD SD50
EMD introduced the 3,500-horsepower SD-50 in the early 1980s. With improved tractive effort and wheel slip monitoring, these units were ideal for heavy road freight service. Many of these units are still in service, and some are on their second and third owners.

Standard DC 99.95 ea

NEW 150-49335 Chessie System #8569 (blue, vermillion, yellow)
NEW 150-49336 Chessie System #8571 (blue, vermillion, yellow)
NEW 150-49337 Chessie System #8630 (blue, vermillion, yellow)
NEW 150-49338 CNW #7003 (Zito Yellow, green)
NEW 150-49339 CNW #7022 (Zito Yellow, green)
NEW 150-49340 CNW #7028 (Zito Yellow, green)

DCC Decoder Equipped 134.95 ea
NEW 150-49374 Chessie System #8569 (blue, vermillion, yellow)
NEW 150-49375 Chessie System #8571 (blue, vermillion, yellow)
NEW 150-49376 CNW #7003 (Zito Yellow, green)
NEW 150-49377 CNW #7022 (Zito Yellow, green)

NEW EMD SD35 Family Lines/L&N #4523 150-49671

NEW EMD GP40-2 Indiana Harbor Belt #4012 150-48650

NEW EMD SD50 CNW #7003 150-49338

EMD SD60
In 1984 the SD60 was introduced as the successor to the SD50. Boasting 3,800 horsepower, these powerful units are powered by the 710G prime mover, while SD50s had incorporated the older 645 design. The two locomotives can be distinguished by the door panels; the SD-50 features four latched doors in six door panels and the SD-60 has six latched doors in eight panels.

Standard DC 99.95 ea

NEW 150-49034 CR #6848 (blue)
NEW 150-49035 CR #6856 (blue)
NEW 150-49036 CR #6861 (blue)
NEW 150-49037 Oakway Leasing #9008 (blue, white)

NEW 150-49038 Oakway Leasing #9046 (blue, white)
NEW 150-49039 Oakway Leasing #9073 (blue, white)

NEW 150-49040 Helm Leasing #5966 (blue, white, black)
NEW 150-49041 Helm Leasing #5992 (blue, white, black)
NEW 150-49042 Helm Leasing #5998 (blue, white, black)

NEW 150-49043 KCS #728 (gray)
NEW 150-49044 KCS #731 (gray)
NEW 150-49045 KCS #732 (gray)
NEW 150-49046 NS "Horsehead" #6596 (black)

NEW 150-49047 NS "Horsehead" #6709 (black)
NEW 150-49048 NS "Horsehead" #6714 (black)

DCC Decoder Equipped 134.95 ea
NEW 150-49125 CR #6848 (blue)
NEW 150-49126 CR #6856 (blue)
NEW 150-49127 Oakway Leasing #9008 (blue, white)
NEW 150-49128 Oakway Leasing #9046 (blue, white)
NEW 150-49129 Helm Leasing #5966 (blue, white, black)
NEW 150-49130 Helm Leasing #5992 (blue, white, black)
NEW 150-49131 KCS #728 (gray)
NEW 150-49132 KCS #731 (gray)
NEW 150-49133 NS "Horsehead" #6596 (black)
NEW 150-49134 NS "Horsehead" #6709 (black)

LOCOMOTIVES N SCALE

EMD SD60M w/3 Window Cab

First offered as an option on U.S. locos in 1988, UP received the first safety-cab units in 1989. These units are models of the early three-window versions.

Standard DC 99.95 ea

NEW **150-49216** BN #9220 (Cascade Green)
NEW **150-49217** BN #9222 (Cascade Green)
NEW **150-49218** BN #9230 (Cascade Green)

NEW **150-49219** UP #2280 (yellow, gray w/yellow Sill Stripe)
NEW **150-49220** UP #2354 (yellow, gray w/yellow Sill Stripe)
NEW **150-49221** UP #2374 (yellow, gray w/yellow Sill Stripe)

DCC Decoder Equipped 134.95 ea

NEW **150-49241** BN #9220 (Cascade Green)
NEW **150-49242** BN #9222 (Cascade Green)
NEW **150-49243** UP #2280 (yellow, gray w/yellow Sill Stripe)
NEW **150-49244** UP #2354 (yellow, gray w/yellow Sill Stripe)

GE U23B

The 2250 h.p. U23B was GE's competitive answer to EMD's GP38. Produced from 1968 through the 1977, a total of 481 units were built, making it the second best selling "U Boat." Primary spotting features include a stepped-out radiator section and two sets of three tall engine access doors near the center of the long hood. During production, U23Bs were built with a variety of trucks from trade-ins of older units. A handful of these versatile units still work for shortlines and regionals across the continent. Models feature roadname-appropriate truck and body details.

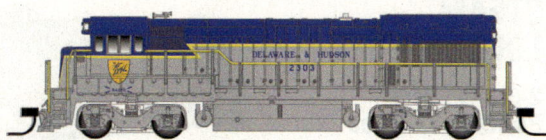

NEW GE U23B D&H #2303 150-45913

Standard DC 104.95 ea
NEW **150-45910** C&O #2319 (blue)
NEW **150-45911** C&O #2325 (blue)
NEW **150-45912** C&O #2327 (blue)
NEW **150-45913** D&H #2303 ("Lighting Stripe")
NEW **150-45914** D&H #2310 ("Lighting Stripe")
NEW **150-45915** D&H #2316 ("Lighting Stripe")

NEW **150-45916** LV #505 (Cornell Red)
NEW **150-45917** LV #510 (Cornell Red)
NEW **150-45918** LV #512 (Cornell Red)

NEW **150-45919** MILW #5000 (orange, black)
NEW **150-45920** MILW #5002 (orange, black)
NEW **150-45921** MILW #5003 (orange, black)
NEW **150-45922** MP #4512 (blue)
NEW **150-45923** MP #4525 (blue)

NEW **150-45924** MP #4530 (blue)
NEW **150-45925** ATSF #6324 Pre-1972 Scheme (blue, yellow)
NEW **150-45926** ATSF #6330 Pre-1972 Scheme (blue, yellow)

NEW **150-45927** ATSF #6346 Pre-1972 Scheme (blue, yellow)
NEW **150-45928** WP #2252 (green, orange)

NEW **150-45929** WP #2258 (green, orange)
NEW **150-45930** WP #2260 (green, orange)
NEW **150-45900** Undecorated w/Low-Nose Headlight & AAR Type B Trucks
NEW **150-45901** Undecorated No Low-Nose Headlight & FB-2 Trucks
NEW **150-45902** Undecorated w/Low-Nose Headlight & FB-2 Trucks
NEW **150-45903** Undecorated, No Low Nose Headlight & Blomberg

DCC Decoder Equipped 139.95 ea
NEW **150-47900** C&O #2319 (blue)
NEW **150-47901** C&O #2325 (blue)
NEW **150-47902** D&H #2303 ("Lighting Stripe")
NEW **150-47903** D&H #2310 ("Lighting Stripe")
NEW **150-47904** LV #505 (Cornell Red)
NEW **150-47905** LV #510 (Cornell Red)
NEW **150-47906** MILW #5000 (orange, black)
NEW **150-47907** MILW #5002 (orange, black)
NEW **150-47908** MP #4512 (blue)
NEW **150-47909** MP #4525 (blue)
NEW **150-47910** ATSF #6324 Pre-1972 Scheme (blue, yellow)
NEW **150-47911** ATSF #6330 Pre-1972 Scheme (blue, yellow)
NEW **150-47912** WP #2252 (green, orange)
NEW **150-47913** WP #2258 (green, orange)

For Up-To-Date Information and News Bookmark Walthers Web site at
www.walthers.com

JNJ TRAINS

Locomotive Shells 22.00 ea (Unless Noted)
All shells are undecorated.
344-4302 E3/6 A/B 44.00
344-4305 Alco DL109/110 44.00
344-4427 EMD F45 w/Plow (Fits Kato Chassis)
344-4429 FP45
344-4476 GP60 SP/DRGW

MICRO-TRAINS®

NEW PRODUCTS
Life-Like EMD GP20

NEW **489-98500206** Happy Birthday **109.95**

DIESEL LOCOMOTIVES
EMD FT

A Unit Only
489-98701511 12 Days of Christmas **97.85**

A-B Set

489-99200152 Seaboard Coast Line #4019, #4119 "Citrus Scheme" **229.90**

TOMAR INDUSTRIES

Tomar N Scale Drumhead kits are complete with cast and machined drum housing, 1.5V micro-miniature lamp, full-color train sign, light diffuser, four diodes and hookup wire, plus complete instructions with illustrations.

DRUMHEADS
12.00 ea

81-51500   81-51501   81-51502

81-51500 Sacramento Northern, Comet (HW round)
81-51501 Sacramento Northern, Meteor (HW round)
81-51502 Sacramento Northern, Sacramento Valley (HW round)

81-51510   81-51525

81-51510 Illinois Traction System, The Owl (round)
81-51525 Illinois Terminal Railroad Company (rectangular)

81-51535   81-51536

81-51535 Cincinnati & Lake Erie, Fleeting Sun
81-51536 Cincinnati & Lake Erie, Valley Queen

Items listed below are available by Special Order (see Legend Page).

81-51505   81-51506   81-51511

81-51505 Sacramento Comet (round)
81-51506 Sacramento Northern, Meteor (round)
81-51511 Illinois Traction System, St. Louis/Peoria Ltd. (round)
81-51515 North Shore Line, Gold Coast Ltd. (round)
81-51516 North Shore Line, The Eastern Ltd. (round)
81-51517 North Shore Line, Prairie State Special (round)

81-51530   81-51540   81-51550

81-51530 Milwaukee Electric Railway & Light Company, Land O' Lakes Ltd.
81-51540 Chicago South Shore & South Bend, Herald (round)
81-51550 LV Transit, Liberty Bell Route (round)

LOCOMOTIVES N SCALE

Ready-to-run locos feature prepainted and lettered plastic bodies.

GE B23-7/B30-7 MP 160-61355

FM H16-44 Virginian 160-61454

NEW PRODUCTS
Diesel Locomotives

GE B23-7/B30-7 50.00 ea
Assembled models feature directional headlights. HO models shown.

NEW 160-61351 ATSF

NEW 160-61352 CR

NEW 160-61353 Chessie System

NEW 160-61354 BN
NEW 160-61355 MP

NEW 160-61356 CSX

FM H16-44 55.00 ea
Assembled models feature directional headlights. HO models shown.

NEW 160-61451 ATSF

NEW 160-61452 B&O

NEW 160-61453 CP
NEW 160-61454 Virginian

NEW 160-61455 NH

NEW 160-61456 SOU

Get the Scoop!
Get the Skinny!
Get the Score!
Check Out Walthers
Web site at
www.walthers.com

STEAM LOCOMOTIVES

2-6-2 "Prairie" Powered 63.00 ea

NEW 160-51551 UP

NEW 160-51562 B&O
160-51570 NYC
160-51598 Painted, Unlettered (black)

Northern 4-8-4 98.00 ea
Each engine features an operating headlight.
160-58052 ATSF w/52' Tender
160-58066 Burlington w/52' Tender

160-58157 SP w/Vanderbilt Tender

160-58161 GN w/Vanderbilt Tender

4-4-0 American 63.00 ea
Perfect for operation, or as collectibles, these locomotives feature detailed, colorful paint schemes, and metal handrails.
160-11751 B&O
160-11752 CB&Q

160-11753 PRR
160-51151 UP #119
160-51174 CP "Jupiter"

0-6-0 USRA Switcher w/Slope Tender 48.00 ea
160-50552 ATSF

160-50564 PRR

NEW 160-50570 NYC

160-50598 Painted, Unlettered (black)

2-6-2 "Prairie" Powered NYC 160-51570

Northern 4-8-4 ATSF 160-58052

4-4-0 American CB&Q 160-11752

0-6-0 USRA Switcher w/Slope Tender ATSF 160-50552

EMD GP40 Powered Alaska Railroad HO Version Shown

DIESEL LOCOMOTIVES

MDT Plymouth 30.00 ea

160-60052 ATSF

160-60066 CB&Q

160-60089 Industrial (yellow w/black stripes)

160-60090 Industrial (red w/yellow stripes)

EMD GP40 Powered 33.00 ea
160-63552 ATSF
160-63556 CR
160-63587 WM
160-63598 Alaska Railroad

LOCOMOTIVES N SCALE

GP50 33.00 ea
Powered w/8-wheel drive & flywheels.
160-61251 UP
160-61252 ATSF
160-61254 SOU
160-61291 NS

U36B 33.00 ea
Powered loco features flywheels and eight wheel drive for smooth operation.
160-64052 ATSF
160-64053 BN
160-64068 CSX

Powered GP50 NS 160-61291
HO Version Shown

Powered U36B ATSF 160-64052

TROLLEY CARS
Lighted
PCC Streamline 34.00 ea

160-62989 Yellow PCC No. 7407
160-62995 Philadelphia Transportation Co.

Brill 32.00 ea
160-61090 Main Street

160-61098 Yellow No. 36

Brill Trolley Main Street 160-61090

Spectrum®

N&W Class J 4-8-4 #611 160-82153

N&W Class Auxillary Water Tender N&W "Railfan" Excursion Scheme 160-89952

2-8-0 Steam Locomotive Boston & Maine 160-81158

NEW PRODUCTS
Steam Locomotives

N&W Class J 4-8-4 150.00 ea (Unless Noted)
Replicas of some of the last mainline steam locos to run in the U.S., these detailed, DCC-ready models feature a precision motor and diecast boiler, underframe, tender frame and spoked driver centers. Other features include applied details and front and rear dummy knuckle couplers.

Different Roadnumber Shown
NEW 160-82152 #608 (50s-60s Scheme)
NEW 160-82153 #611 (50s-60s Scheme)
NEW 160-82154 With Auxillary Tender #611 (80s-90s "Railfan" Excursion Scheme) **180.00**
NEW 160-82155 #601 (Passenger Scheme)

N&W Class Auxillary Water Tender 30.00 ea
From the 30s to the 50s "canteen" or "water bottle" cars carried extra water so freights could bypass water stops. Cars feature directional headlights, dummy knuckle couplers and NMRA wheel profile. Ideal for use with N&W Class J 4-8-4 locos. HO models shown.

NEW 160-89952 N&W "Railfan" Excursion Scheme

NEW 160-89953 N&W

NEW 160-89951 Painted, Unlettered

STEAM LOCOMOTIVES

Spectrum® 2-8-0 Steam 145.00 ea (Unless Noted)
These DCC-ready engines feature a precision motor, driver axle bearings, operating headlight, gear drive, metal wheels, detailed cab interior, separate detail parts and sanding lines, builder's plate, front and rear couplers, and diecast driver spokes

160-81154 B&O
160-81158 Boston & Maine

160-81160 MP
160-81169 UP #723
160-81170 WM "Fireball" #761
160-81171 ATSF #2516
160-81172 Rock Island #2118

160-81173 Seaboard #914
160-81174 NH #151
NEW 160-81175 C&O

160-81152 Painted, Unlettered

Limited Quantity Available

160-81165 Rock Island

160-81167 Nashville, Chattanooga & St. Louis **140.00**

Spectrum® USRA 4-8-2 Light Mountain 175.00 ea
These DCC-ready engines feature a precision metal motor, operating headlight, hidden drive train, gear drive, metal tender wheels and pickup, dummy knuckle coupler, detailed cab interior, separate sanding lines and separate detail parts.

160-81660 SOU #1454

160-81661 UP #7012

43

LOCOMOTIVES N SCALE

160-81662 Nashville, Chattanooga & St. Louis #1454
160-81663 NH #3303
160-81664 SP #4308
160-81665 New York, Ontario & Western #404
160-81651 Painted, Unlettered

Limited Quantity Available
160-81654 Nashville, Chattanooga & St. Louis #556

160-81658 New York, Ontario & Western

Spectrum® USRA 2-6-6-2 Articulated Powered 275.00 ea

These DCC-ready locomotives feature a five-pole skew-wound motor, tender pickup, amber LED headlight, detailed cab interior, separate detail parts and finescale driver spokes.

160-82652 C&O H-5 #1522
160-82653 C&O H-5 #1524
160-82654 NKP #941
160-82655 NKP #942
160-82656 Wheeling & Lake Erie #8003
160-82657 Wheeling & Lake Erie #8007
160-82651 Painted, Unlettered

DIESEL LOCOMOTIVES

Baldwin RF-16 "Sharknose" Powered A-B Sets 125.00

In 1948, Baldwin Locomotive Works introduced the RF-16 locomotive. With its modern streamlined styling and distinctive snout, the locos became instant classics among railfans. Railroads liked them because of their power and performance—they were great for hauling heavy tonnage trains like ore and coal drags. These detailed DCC-ready models feature a diecast chassis, a powerful skew-wound five-pole motor with dual flywheels, all-wheel drive and electrical pickup, reversing LED headlight and Rapido-type couplers. Units come in powered A-B sets.

160-81352 PRR #2004
160-81353 PRR #2001
160-81354 PRR #2000
160-81355 PRR #2002
160-81356 NYC #3806 & 3706

160-81357 NYC #3807 & 3707
160-81358 B&O #855 & 855X

160-81359 B&O #857 & 857X
160-81360 Monongahela Railway #1205 & 3708

160-81361 Monongahela Railway #1210 & 3709

Spectrum EMD SD45 90.00 ea

Features all-wheel pickup, white LED lighting and NMRA wheel flange profile

160-82759 RDG #7606
160-82760 PRR #6116
160-82761 BN #6474
160-82762 CR #6146
160-82763 UP #17
160-82764 ATSF "Warbonnet" (blue, yellow) #5416
160-82751 Undecorated

Limited Quantity Available

160-82754 PRR

160-82756 CR

160-82758 ATSF (Warbonnet)

Spectrum GE Dash 8-40C 135.00 ea

Features all-wheel pickup, white LED lighting and NMRA wheel flange profile

160-85053 UP #9218
160-85055 NS #8654
160-85056 CR
160-85059 CSX #7592
160-85063 CNW
160-85051 Undecorated

Limited Quantity Available
160-85054 NS
160-85058 CSX

Spectrum GE Dash 8-40CW 135.00 ea

Extra features include a precision balanced motor and flywheel assembly, directional lighting and RP25 wheels.

160-86052 CR
160-86054 CSX

160-86058 ATSF
160-86060 UP
160-86066 CR "Quality"
160-86075 BNSF

160-86076 LMS/Lease
160-86051 Undecorated

Spectrum EMD F7A & B Powered 90.00 ea

Models include a five-pole skew-wound motor, pillow block bearing in gear towers, new gear mechanism, accurate nose contour, operating headlight in the A unit, teardrop windows, diecast chassis, all-wheel pickup and blackened wheels with NMRA wheel profile.

160-81255 EL (gray, maroon)

160-81258 PRR (Single Stripe)

Different Roadnumber Shown
160-81259 ATSF "Warbonnet" #307 & 316B
160-81260 SP "Black Widow" #6442 & 8291

Limited Quantity Available

160-81253 B&O

160-81254 NYC Lightning Stripe
160-81257 GN

Hot New Products Announced Daily! Visit Walthers Web site at
www.walthers.com

USRA 4-8-2 Light Mountain Nashville, Chattanooga & St. Louis 160-81662

Spectrum USRA 2-6-6-2 Articulated Powered NKP #941 160-82654

Spectrum USRA 2-6-6-2 Articulated Powered Wheeling & Lake Erie #8003 160-82656

Spectrum USRA 2-6-6-2 Articulated Powered Painted, Unlettered 160-82651

Baldwin RF-16 "Sharknose" PRR 160-81352

EMD SD45 BN Roadnumber Shown Not Available

GE Dash 8-40C UP 160-85052

GE Dash 8-4CW UP 160-86060

EMD F7A & B Powered GN 160-81257

LOCOMOTIVES N SCALE

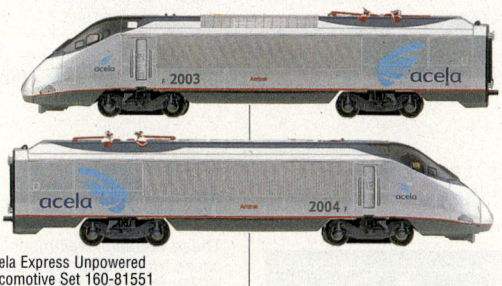
Acela Express Unpowered Locomotive Set 160-81551

Café Acela Power Car 160-89971

Acela Express First Class Passenger Car 160-88972

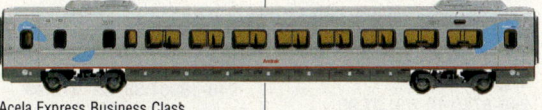
Acela Express Business Class Passenger Car 160-88973

Acela Express End Business Class Passenger Car 160-88974

ELECTRIC LOCOMOTIVES

Amtrak® HHP-8 171.00
DCC ON BOARD Constructed by Bombardier/Alsthom for Amtrak, these modern, powerful electrics power Amtrak Acela℠ regional trains of Amfleet® cars in the northeastern U.S. These detailed replicas feature a smooth-running, flywheel-equipped mechanism with a five-pole skew-wound motor and a factory-installed DCC decoder for utmost speed control and lighting effects. each is decorated in Amtrak's Acela scheme.

Prototype Photo Shown

160-83053 #655
160-83054 #650
160-83055 #664

Acela Express Equipment

Unpowered Locomotive Set
Features DCC lighting functions and movable pantographs.
160-81551 103.00

Café Acela Power Car
DCC ON BOARD This detailed model incorporates the drive system for an entire Acela train set. The model features a smooth-running mechanism and factory-installed DCC decoder.
160-89971 147.00

Acela Express Passenger Cars 55.00 ea
160-89972 First Class
160-89973 Business Class
160-89974 End Business Class

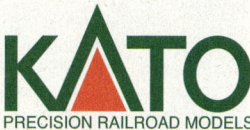

Kato models are masterful reproductions of the prototype, exhibiting meticulous detail and accurate recreation of the roadname lettering and paint scheme. A powerful five-pole motor with dual brass flywheels delivers smooth and reliable operating performance.

DIESEL LOCOMOTIVES

EMD F3 Phase II A Unit
381-1761301 CB&Q 85.00

EMD SD70M w/Phase II Cab & Flared Radiators

381-1767501 NS #2591 **105.00**

381-1767504 UP #3972 **110.00**

GE P42 "Genesis"
Perfect for handling consists of Superliner® passenger cars, these modern diesels are Amtrak's standard road units.

Powered 2-Unit Set
381-1066103 Amtrak Phase V #123 & 134 **210.00**

Powered Single Units, 98.00 ea (Unless Noted)
381-1766004 Amtrak Phase V #62 **105.00**

381-1766005 Amtrak Phase IV #22
381-1766006 Amtrak Phase IV #121

EMD SD70MAC

381-1766503 BNSF #9647 (cream, green "Warbonnet" Merger Scheme) **105.00**

EMD SD80MAC

381-1765504 CSX #801 **105.00**

GE P42 "Genesis" Powered Single Unit Amtrak® Phase V #62 381-1766004

Rail Diesel Car CP 381-1660002

Rail Diesel Cars NYC RDC-2 #381-166016 & RDC-3 #381-1660206; Both Sold Separately

Budd Demonstrator RDC-1 (Single Unit) 381-1660001

GE AC4400CW 104.99 ea (Unless Noted)
Boasting 4400 horsepower, these modern units have become favorites for moving tonnage over the road.
381-1767002 CEFX #1021
381-1767213 CP #9516
381-1767214 CP #9532
381-1767000 Undecorated

RAIL DIESEL CARS

Single Cars 80.00 ea
These motorized models feature a "golden glow" LED directional headlight and body-mounted, fully automatic knuckle couplers

RDC-1 - Coach
NEW 381-1660001 Budd Demonstrator
NEW 381-1660002 CP
NEW 381-1660003 CN
NEW 381-1660004 NH
NEW 381-1660005 CNW
NEW 381-1660006 CNJ #551
NEW 381-1660007 CNJ #552

RDC-2 - Coach/Baggage
NEW 381-1660101 CP
NEW 381-1660102 CN
NEW 381-1660103 NH
NEW 381-1660104 CNW
NEW 381-1660105 NYC
NEW 381-1660106 NP
NEW 381-1660107 WP #375
NEW 381-1660108 WP #376
NEW 381-1660109 Alaska Railroad #711
NEW 381-1660110 Alaska Railroad #712
NEW 381-1660100 Unlettered

RDC-3 - Coach/Baggage/Railway Post Office
NEW 381-1660201 CP
NEW 381-1660202 CN
NEW 381-1660203 NH
NEW 381-1660206 NYC
NEW 381-1660207 NP
NEW 381-1660208 Rock Island #9002
NEW 381-1660209 Rock Island #9003
NEW 381-1660200 Unlettered

RDC-4 - Railway Post Office Only
NEW 381-1660301 CP
NEW 381-1660302 CN
NEW 381-1660302 NH
NEW 381-1660300 Unlettered

LOCOMOTIVES N SCALE

Clear Case

Protect your investment in your favorite models with Clear Case display cases. These handmade cases are constructed of rich-grain solid oak or walnut, with a mitered edge to ensure a dust-free enclosure and felt pad feet to protect your furniture. The cover is crystal clear optical grade acrylic. The result is a display case that makes your model look like a museum masterpiece.

Note: Clear Case displays can be ordered in other sizes that are more appropriate for G, O, N and Z Scale models. See your Walthers dealer for more information.

Train Display Case 248-8722

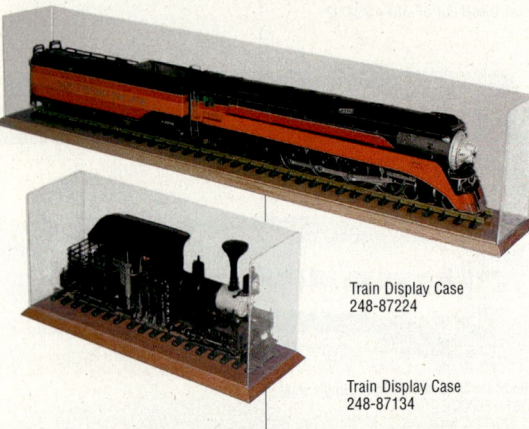
Train Display Case 248-87224
Train Display Case 248-87134

Train Display Case 248-87133

Multi-Shelf Display Case 248-18223

SPORTS DISPLAY CASES

Show off your sports memorabilia in these handcrafted Medium Oak display cases. Though not all shown here, Clear Case offers a variety of sports display cases, sized appropriately for holding everything from baseballs to basketballs. See your Walthers dealer for more information.

248-1615 Football Case **75.99**
248-1620 Football Helmet Case **114.99**

MODEL CAR CASES

Though not all listed here, Clear Case displays to protect your scale model automobiles are available in 12 different sizes. Contact your Walthers dealer for more information.

6" Long x 2-3/4" Wide x 2-1/2" High
248-1230 Light Oak **28.99**
248-12303 Medium Oak **28.99**
248-12301 Dark Oak **28.99**
248-12302 Black Walnut **29.99**

10" Long x 3-3/4" Wide x 5-1/2" High
248-1245 Light Oak **44.99**
248-12453 Medium Oak **44.99**
248-12451 Dark Oak **44.99**
248-12452 Black Walnut **46.99**

13" Long x 5" Wide x 4" High
248-1253 Light Oak **53.99**

248-12533 Medium Oak **53.99**
248-12531 Dark Oak **53.99**
248-12532 Black Walnut **57.99**

TRAIN DISPLAY CASES

Interior dimensions of covers are 2-3/4" wide by 3-1/4" high. Dimension shown with part number is interior length.

Light Oak
248-8710 10-5/8" **37.99**
248-8713 13" **46.99**
248-8716 16-1/2" **54.99**
248-8722 22" **61.99**

Medium Oak
248-87103 10-5/8" **37.99**
248-87133 13" **46.99**
248-87163 16-1/2" **54.99**
248-87223 22" **61.99**

Dark Oak
248-87101 10-5/8" **37.99**
248-87131 13" **46.99**
248-87161 16-1/2" **54.99**
248-87221 22" **61.99**

Black Walnut
248-87102 10-5/8" **39.99**
248-87132 13" **49.99**
248-87162 16-1/2" **57.99**
248-87222 22" **70.99**

Rosewood Finish
248-87104 10-5/8" **39.99**
248-87134 13" **49.99**
248-87164 16-1/2" **57.99**
248-87224 22" **70.99**

MULTI-SHELF DISPLAY CASES

These beautiful wall-mounted cases are ideal for displaying HO Scale trains and 1:43 Scale model cars. Each case is 27-1/2" tall and 5" deep; there are 8 shelves per case. Dimension shown with part number is case width.

Light Oak
248-1822 24-1/2" **251.99**
248-1836 38-1/2" **375.99**

Medium Oak
248-18223 24-1/2" **251.99**
248-18363 38-1/2" **375.99**

Dark Oak
248-18221 24-1/2" **251.99**
248-18361 38-1/2" **375.99**

ANTI-STATIC CLEANER

248-500 Spray Cleaner 4oz **6.59**
Spray cleaner for plastic and acrylics: the perfect way to keep your Clear Case display covers crystal clear and sparkling like new. Polishes, repels dust and resists fingerprints.

Get Your Daily Dose of Product News at
www.walthers.com

LOCOMOTIVES N SCALE

Galloping Goose Railbus Rio Grande Southern #5 223-4171

NEW PRODUCTS

Galloping Goose Railbuses

PLEASE NOTE: Due to the small size of this model, the circuit board will not include a DCC socket; watch our Website for details on a new second series of Galloping Goose Railbuses that will include a factory-installed DCC decoder.

179.98 ea
NEW 223-4171 Rio Grande Southern #5
NEW 223-4172 DRGW
NEW 223-4173 ATSF
NEW 223-4174 PRR
NEW 223-4175 GN
NEW 223-4176 UP
NEW 223-4177 SP
NEW 223-4178 NYC
NEW 223-4179 MOW
NEW 223-4170 Undecorated (silver, no lettering)

STEAM LOCOMOTIVES

USRA Heavy 2-10-2
329.98 ea (Unless Noted)

Designed to haul heavy freight, the USRA Heavy 2-10-2 was copied by many other railroads. Models feature factory mounted Micro-Trains® couplers, tender-mounted, DCC-ready PC board and flywheel drive.

PRR

223-3901 #1
223-3911 #2

IC
223-3902 #1
223-3912 #2

CB&Q
223-3903 #1
223-3913 #2

Bessemer & Lake Erie

223-3904 #1
223-3914 #2

Erie
223-3905 #1
223-3915 #2

Central of Georgia
223-3906 #1
223-3916 #2

MP
223-3907 #1

223-3917 #2

Atlantic Coast Line
223-3908 #1
223-3918 #2

UP
223-3909 #1
223-3919 #2

SP

223-3910 #1
223-3920 #2 **298.98**

Undecorated
223-3900 Black

Second Release 298.98 ea

223-13921 PRR #9634 w/Doghouse Brakeman's Cabin
223-13922 PRR #8952 ("Pennsylvania Lines" w/U.S.)
223-13923 C&O #2001 w/Dual Airpumps
223-13924 C&O #2003 w/Dual Airpumps (Dulux Gold)

"This Train will save an Industry" declared a New York Central advertisement in 1956. With passenger traffic declining in the mid-1950s due to the rapid expansion of the Interstate Highway system, railroads were looking for ways to attract more ridership. Many, including the Pennsy, NYC, UP and others hoped the AeroTrain would do just that. Featuring a wraparound windshield, multiple headlights, a low center of gravity and new air suspension, EMD's stylish AeroTrain debuted in 1955 at the GM Powerama. Modelers can easily recreate the original 10-car introductory set with two add-on three-car sets.

Introductory Four Car Set $429.98 Each
Includes engine, two coaches and observation car.
223-8761 GM Demonstrator
223-8762 PRR
223-8763 NYC
223-8764 UP
273-8765 ATSF
223-8766 RI
223-8760 Undecorated

Add-on Three Car Coach Set TBA Each
223-8771 GM Demonstrator
223-8772 PRR
223-8773 NYC
223-8774 UP
233-8775 ATSF
223-8776 RI
223-8770 Undecorated

223-13925 GN #2108 w/Dual Airpumps
223-13926 GN #2112 w/Dual Airpumps (large GN goat herald, red cab roof)
223-13927 ATSF #3817 w/Dual Airpumps

223-13928 ATSF #3835 w/Dual Airpumps
223-13929 N&W #2309 w/Doghouse Brakeman's Cabin
223-13930 N&W #2355 w/Doghouse Brakeman's Cabin (Dulux Gold)
223-13931 Unlettered w/Dual Airpumps & Doghouse Brakeman's Cabin

"GS-4" 4-8-4

Wartime GS-4 298.98 ea
During World War II the shrouding was removed and the locomotives were painted black. Models include DCC-friendly printed circuit board with the NMRA 6-pin DCC connector for ease in adding a DCC decoder of your choice.
223-3876 SP #4430
223-3877 SP #4435

223-3880 Western Pacific #485
223-3875 Undecorated

Limited Quantity Available
223-3881 Western Pacific #486

GS-4 Adaptations 298.98 ea

The 4-8-4 "Northern Class" wheel arrangement was one of the most popular among the major railroads as it proved to be very efficient. But, of course, every railroad had its own idea about what was the ideal wheel arrangement and cosmetic look of the locomotive. The following locos feature some adaptations to the basic 4-8-4 mechanism to make the models look cosmetically more like the individual railroad's version of the 4-8-4.

All models except the Pennsy version include a coal bunker tender, new smoke box door on the front of the boiler that features a center-mounted headlight and a bell mounted at the top of the smoke box.

The Pennsy version has a coal bunker tender, new smoke box door on the front of the boiler that features a top-mounted headlight and a PRR Keystone logo in the middle of the smoke box door.

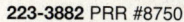
223-3882 PRR #8750

223-3883 PRR #8752
223-3884 PRR #8755
223-3885 UP #832
223-3886 UP #837
223-3887 UP #TBA

223-3888 ATSF #3776
223-3889 ATSF #3778
223-3890 ATSF #3782

223-3891 NP #2654
223-3892 NP #2655
223-3893 NP #2656

223-3894 DRGW #1801
223-3895 DRGW #1803
223-3896 DRGW #1804

American Freedom Train GS-4

223-3863   298.98

LOCOMOTIVES N SCALE

Streamlined 4-6-4 Hudson
Steam Locomotive 223-1003077

4-6-4 Hudson "Blue Goose" Nose Style
Streamliner ATSF "Blue Goose"
223-1003061

4-6-4 Bullet Nose Scullin Driver
Streamliner NYC "20th Century"
223-1003052

THE 1934 PIONEER ZEPHYR

Prototype Photo Shown

The *Pioneer Zephyr* is a name that has become synonymous with the word "Streamliner". Almost all railfans the world over instantly recognize the name.

The train was already famous when it made its record breaking 1015-mile run on May 26th from Denver to Chicago, but it gained even more attention later on. It was one of the biggest attractions at the *Century of Progress Exposition* in Chicago during the summer of 1934. Before it went into regular service in the fall of 1934, it was taken on tour. During 1934 it traveled to over 220 different American cities and was toured by over two million people.

So even if you are not a Burlington Route Fan, it is quite possible that the *Zephyr* visited your city and you could run it on your layout as a white flagged special, just like the real train did during its travels in 1934 over many different railroads in the East, Midwest and Western USA.

These models will be of the original 3-car *Pioneer Zephyr*.

This model is fully ready to run, and comes with a factory-installed, standard 8-pin, "DCC Ready board" plus two extra pins for speaker mounting meeting NMRA standards so it will be easy to install the DCC decoder of your choice.

HO Scale Versions $399.00 Each
223-8720 Undecorated (silver, no lettering)
223-8721 Pioneer Zephyr Lettering
223-8723 Add-On Car **$139.98**

N Scale Versions $399.00 Each
223-8730 Undecorated (silver, no lettering)
223-8731 Pioneer Zephyr Lettering
223-8733 Add-On Car **$139.98**

4-6-4 Hudson

One of the finest and fastest steam locos ever built, 4-6-4 "Hudsons" could be found on the point of some of America's most important passenger trains. Introduced in the late 1920s, the engines were equipped with a larger firebox and huge (some as tall as 84"!) drivers. Built for speed and power, they could easily race trains of heavyweight cars across country. When streamlining became the rage, both older and brand-new engines were fitted with metal shrouds designed to match the new lightweight trains.

Like the prototype, these models incorporate the latest ideas, resulting in one of the most reliable, detailed models available today. Originally based on the famous New York Central J3a, the ready-to-run models now sport five different boiler configurations and are available in over 30 paint schemes.

Nonstreamlined 179.98 ea (Unless Noted)
223-1003002 ATSF (black, white)
223-1003003 GN (Glacier Green, black) **189.98**
223-1003004 SP "Daylight" **189.98**
223-1003005 PRR (black, white)
223-1003006 NYC (black, white)
223-1003007 B&O "Royal Blue" (blue color scheme) **189.98**
223-1003008 UP (black, white)
223-1003009 SOU "Crescent" (green) **189.98**
223-1003010 MILW "Hiawatha" (older gray & maroon colors) **189.98**
223-1003011 PRR (Brunswick Green)
223-1003012 UP "Greyhound" (gray scheme) **189.98**
223-1003016 D&H (blue, gray scheme) **189.98**
223-1003018 CNW (black w/3-color herald)
223-1003019 DRGW (black w/graphite smoke box)
223-1003021 GN (black w/3-color herald)
223-1003022 Lackawanna (black w/graphite smokebox)
223-1003023 NKP (black w/Dulux Gold lettering)
223-1003001 Undecorated
Item listed below is available by Special Order (see Legend Page).
223-1003015 CB&Q (black w/3-color herald)

"Blue Goose" Nose Style Streamliners 189.98 ea
223-1003061 ATSF "Blue Goose" (blue, silver)
Item listed below is available by Special Order (see Legend Page).
223-1003060 Undecorated

Bullet Nose Streamliners 189.98 ea (Unless Noted)
223-1003071 PRR (Brunswick Green, gold lettering)
223-1003072 SP "Daylight"
223-1003073 GN (Glacier Green)
223-1003075 SOU "Tennessean" (green, gold)
223-1003076 N&W
223-1003077 UP "49er"

Standard Drivers
223-1003051 NYC (gray)
223-1003050 Undecorated **179.98**

Scullin Drivers
223-1003052 NYC "20th Century" (gray)
Item listed below is available by Special Order (see Legend Page).
223-1003053 Undecorated

"Hiawatha" Streamlined Hudson w/Tender 199.98 ea
223-1003091 Cab #1
223-1003092 Cab #2
223-1003093 Cab #3

Shovel Nose Style Streamliners 189.98 ea (Unless Noted)
223-1003082 CB&Q
223-1003083 NYC "Commodore Vanderbilt"
Item listed below is available by Special Order (see Legend Page).
223-1003081 Undecorated **179.98**

4-8-4 GS-4 Engine w/Tender Powered 298.98 ea

The introduction of the Daylight 4-8-4 GS-4 engines with their matching train sets in the late 1930s was perhaps the zenith of rail passenger travel in the United States. Features a powerful five-pole skewed armature motor, fine handrails and lots of factory added detail parts. Also included is a matching tender with correct tender trucks and numerous fine details.

Daylight Colors w/Logo On Skirt & "Southern Pacific" Tender

223-3854 SP #4449
223-3855 SP #4432

GS-4 Daylight Set
223-8523 **459.98**
Set features loco, SP tender and seven Budd cars that include an RPO, Parlor Car, Diner, Observation and three coaches.

4-6-4 J3a Hudson Tenders 29.98 ea

Ideal for use with other engines. Retired tenders were also converted to various kinds of work train cars. See the Passenger Cars section of this Reference Book for cars to match these tenders.

223-1003000 J3a Regular, Undecorated
223-1003070 J3a Streamlined, Undecorated

DIESEL LOCOMOTIVES

MP-15 Switcher 72.98 ea

First introduced in 1974 and produced into the mid-1980s, the MP15 offered railroads a versatile locomotive that was at home in the yard and, because of its Blomberg roadswitcher trucks, could also pinch hit on the road. Featuring a new dual-flywheel-equipped drive, factory-installed Micro-Trains® couplers and detailed plastic shells, these new models are perfect for heading up your switchers and wayfreights.

ATSF
Red/silver
223-2301 #1212
223-2302 #1215

48

LOCOMOTIVES N SCALE

MP-15 Switcher B&O Chessie System
#5311 223-2305

UP
Yellow/gray w/red lettering
223-2303 #1004
223-2304 #1007

B&O Chessie System
Black/yellow/red w/blue lettering
223-2305 #5311
223-2306 #5316

CSX
Gray/blue/yellow

223-2307 #1141
223-2308 #1146

CB&Q Burlington Route
Black/white
223-2309 #576
223-2310 #580

Amtrak

223-2311 #531 (white w/black)
223-2312 #536 (silver w/black)

SOU
Green w/white
223-2313 #2349
223-2314 #2375

BN
Green/black w/white

223-2315 #1000
223-2316 #1003

BNSF
Green/orange
223-2317 #4002
223-2318 #4003

CR Quality
Blue w/white
223-2319 #9627
223-2320 #9630

SP w/Speed Lettering
Gray/scarlet
223-2321 #2695
223-2322 #2698

PRR
Black
223-2323 #296
223-2324 #298

Undecorated
223-2300

Powered PA-1 89.98 ea
Feature factory installed Micro-Trains® couplers.
223-202002 ATSF "Warbonnet"
223-202003 Pennsy (Maroon 5-stripe)
223-202004 GN (orange, green)

223-202005 SP "Daylight"
223-202008 UP
223-202011 D&H
223-202012 NKP
223-202013 B&O
223-202014 NH (McGinnis scheme)
223-202015 Erie
223-202019 Amtrak®
223-202020 SOU "Crescent"
223-202021 EL
223-202022 DRGW
223-202023 MP
223-202024 NYC
223-202001 Undecorated (gray)

Non-Powered PB-1 Dummy 27.98 ea
223-202042 ATSF "Warbonnet"

UNION PACIFIC M-10000

Union Pacific won the race to place a modern streamlined high-speed train into service. Their M-10000 streamliner hit the rails in February 1934, two months before the rival Pioneer Zephyr. Although the Zephyr received far more publicity, UP's M-10000 was exhibited across the U.S. on a coast-to-coast tour. Over one million people climbed aboard for a look at the beautiful interior and each received a souvenir coin made of the same aluminum material as the M-10000 body.

These models are based on the original three-car train as delivered in 1934. Each three-car set includes a replica souvenir coin. A Pullman built for the M-10001 was tested for several months on the M-10000. This Pullman fourth car will be available separately as an add-on car.

HO M-10000 3-Car Train Set $429.98 Each
223-8781 UP (brown & yellow paint scheme)
223-8780 Undecorated (silver, no lettering)
223-8782 Pullman 4th Car **$139.98**

N M-10000 3-Car Train Set $429.98 Each
223-8791 UP (brown & yellow paint scheme)
223-8790 Undecorated (silver, no lettering)
223-8792 Pullman 4th Car **$139.98**

223-202043 Pennsy (Maroon 5-stripe)
223-202044 GN (orange, green)
223-202045 SP "Daylight"
223-202048 UP
223-202051 D&H
223-202052 NKP
223-202053 B&O
223-202054 NH (McGinnis scheme)
223-202055 Erie
223-202059 Amtrak
223-202060 SOU "Crescent"
223-202061 EL
223-202062 DRGW
223-202063 MP
223-202064 NYC
223-202041 Undecorated (gray)

Non-Powered PA-1 w/Light 29.98 ea
Feature factory installed Micro-Trains couplers.

223-202102 ATSF "Warbonnet"
223-202103 Pennsy (Maroon 5-stripe)

223-202104 GN (orange, green)
223-202105 SP "Daylight"
223-202108 UP
223-202111 D&H
223-202112 NKP
223-202113 B&O
223-202114 NH (McGinnis scheme)
223-202115 Erie
223-202119 Amtrak
223-202120 SOU "Crescent"
223-202121 EL
223-202122 DRGW
223-202123 MP
223-202124 NYC
223-202101 Undecorated

PB-1 w/Built-In DCC Sound Unit 199.98 ea
Complete programmable Soundtraxx brand sound decoder built in, including speaker. DCC module can be programmed to run in "consist format" with DCC module in PA-1. Sound decoder features air horn, bell, engine exhaust through eight notches and dynamic brakes. Feature factory installed Micro-Trains couplers.

223-202202 ATSF "Warbonnet"
223-202203 Pennsy (Maroon 5-stripe)
223-202204 GN (orange, green)

223-202205 SP "Daylight"
223-202208 UP
223-202211 D&H
223-202212 NKP
223-202213 B&O
223-202214 NH (McGinnis scheme)
223-202215 Erie
223-202219 Amtrak
223-202220 SOU "Crescent"
223-202221 EL
223-202222 DRGW
223-202223 MP
223-202224 NYC
223-202201 Undecorated

PA-1/PB-1 Set
223-8524 American Freedom Train **298.98**
Includes powered PA-1 with factory-mounted DCC decoder in A unit and factory-mounted DCC sound unit in B unit. Features factory-installed Micro-Trains couplers.

223-8526 American Freedom Train **129.98**
Includes one powered A unit and one dummy B unit. Less DCC sound unit. Features factory installed Micro-Trains couplers.

LOCOMOTIVES N SCALE

2-6-0 "Mogul" NYC 490-7607
Prototype Photo Shown

4-4-0 "American" Type
Minneapolis & St. Louis 490-7628
Prototype Photo Shown

STEAM LOCOMOTIVES

2-6-0 "Mogul" 145.00 ea

Larger, a bit heavier and more powerful than a 4-4-0, the 2-6-0 was a perfect choice for all types of assignments. These locos could be found handling commuter trains, short freights on branchlines and as switchers, and many were in use well into the 1950s.

- 490-7601 Boston & Maine
- 490-7602 B&O
- 490-7603 CB&Q
- 490-7604 GN
- 490-7605 Minneapolis & St. Louis
- 490-7606 NP
- 490-7607 NYC
- 490-7608 PRR
- 490-7609 SP
- 490-7610 SOU
- 490-7611 ATSF
- 490-7612 CP
- 490-7613 CN
- **NEW** 490-7614 Long Island Railroad
- 490-7600 Undecorated

4-4-0 "American" Type 145.00 ea

Used by virtually every American railroad, the 4-4-0 was tailor-made for rough track and equally at home in freight or passenger service. In later years, many were rebuilt for secondary assignments, especially on branchlines where the lightweight engines were often the only locos that track and bridges could support!

- 490-7621 ACL
- 490-7622 Boston & Maine
- 490-7623 B&O
- 490-7624 CB&Q
- 490-7625 CNW
- 490-7626 GN
- 490-7627 L&N
- 490-7628 Minneapolis & St. Louis
- 490-7629 NP
- 490-7630 NYC
- 490-7631 PRR
- 490-7632 SP
- 490-7633 SOU
- 490-7634 ATSF
- 490-7635 CP
- 490-7636 CN
- **NEW** 490-7637 Long Island Railroad
- 490-7620 Undecorated

USRA Light 2-8-2 Mikado

Features include a metal boiler, super detailing, brass gear-driven wheels, eight-wheel pickup on boiler, motor with flywheel drive, and all-axle pickup on the tender.

With Standard Tender 145.00 ea (Unless Noted)

490-7571 PRR

490-7572 ATSF

490-7573 SOU

490-7574 CNW 155.00

490-7575 DRGW 155.00

490-7570 Undecorated

Limited Quantity Available

490-7576 CN

490-7577 CP

With Vandy Tender 155.00 ea (Unless Noted)

- 490-7591 B&O
- 490-7592 UP

490-7593 SP 165.00
490-7594 GN
490-7595 C&O
490-7590 Undecorated

4-6-2 Powered

These highly detailed, all-metal engines feature all-new tooling, a detailed metal boiler, gear-driven wheels, all-wheel pick-up on the locomotive and tender, flywheel drive with a skewed can motor, and state-of-the-art running and detailing. Each unit is also DCC compatible for further modeling excitement.

With Standard Tender 145.00 ea (Unless Noted)

These locomotives are the second release in new roadnumbers.

490-7400 ATSF
490-7401 PRR

490-7402 B&O (blue)
490-7403 SP 155.00
490-7404 NP
490-7405 SOO
490-7406 CN
490-7407 CP
490-7408 SOU (green)

490-7409 L&N
490-7410 NYC
490-7412 CNW 155.00
490-7413 NH
490-7414 CB&Q
490-7415 MKT 155.00
490-7416 Rock Island
490-7417 ACL

490-7399 Undecorated

With Semi-Streamline Pacific - Standard Tender 155.00 ea (Unless Noted)

490-7421 ATSF
490-7422 B&O
490-7423 C&O
490-7424 UP Greyhound
490-7425 PRR
490-7426 DL&W
490-7427 CN
490-7428 CP
490-7429 SP "Daylight" 165.00
490-7430 NP
490-7431 Minneapolis & St. Louis
490-7420 Undecorated

With Vandy Tender 155.00 ea (Unless Noted)

490-7471 B&O
490-7472 UP

490-7473 GN
490-7474 SP 165.00
490-7470 Undecorated

Tender Only 43.98 ea (Unless Noted)

490-7481 B&O

490-7482 UP

490-7483 SP 46.49
490-7480 Undecorated

STEAM ADD-ONS

Driver Set w/Traction Tire (Retro-Kit) 6.98 ea

490-7398 73" Diameter for 4-6-2 Pacific
490-7569 63" Diameter for 2-8-2 Mikado

TRAILING TRUCK

490-7397 Delta Type w/Wheels & Mounting Screw 6.98

DIESEL LOCOMOTIVES

Model Power is in the process of upgrading these locos with can motors, flywheels and metal chassis. Ask your dealer for current information as to availability and price.

Alco C-420 32.98 ea

490-7512 CR (blue)
490-7518 SOU (green, white, black)

FP7 Generation 2-Dual Drive 65.98 ea (Unless Noted)

Engines feature all-new tooling, an all-metal body, dual flywheels and skewed drive. Cars are DCC compatible and can be outfitted with a magnetic coupler.

Phase I

490-7440 ATSF
490-7442 CP
490-7444 SOU
490-7446 WP 69.98

Phase II

490-7441 PRR
490-7443 CN

490-7445 UP 69.98
490-7447 C&O
490-7448 CP
409-7450 Amtrak
490-7451 NP
490-7452 SOO

DCC Decoder Equipped TBA ea

Phase I
490-9442 CP
490-9444 SOU
490-9446 WP
490-9448 CP (Action Red)

Phase II
490-9440 ATSF
490-9441 PRR
490-9443 CN
490-9445 UP
490-9447 C&O
490-9450 Amtrak
490-9451 NP
490-9452 SOO

LOCOMOTIVES N SCALE

Alco PA2 Powered DRGW California Zephyr
HO Scale Model Shown

EMD E8A Powered IC
HO Scale Model Shown

Pennsylvania Class M1a 4-8-2 Powered Limited Run #6720 588-9

NEW PRODUCTS

Diesel Locomotives

These beautifully detailed models feature authentic design, paint and color schemes, diecast chassis, five-pole can motor with skewed armature and dual flywheels, operating sprung diaphragms, directional lighting, strobing Mars light, lighted number boards and many separately applied details. Sound equipped models feature LokSound and operate on DC or DCC. Units without sound function only in DC and can be upgraded with installation of NMRA compliant DCC decoder (not included).

Alco PA1

PRR Five-Stripe Tuscan w/Train Phone Antenna

PA1/PA1 Powered A Units
NEW 588-455 #5754A & 5759A w/Sound **429.99**

NEW 588-475 #5754A & 5759A No Sound **219.99**

PA1/PB1 Powered A, Unpowered B
NEW 588-456 #5755A & 5756B w/Sound **299.99**

NEW 588-476 #5755A & 5756B No Sound **199.99**

PA1 Powered
NEW 588-457 #5756A w/Sound **249.99**

NEW 588-477 #5756A No Sound **109.99**

PB1 Unpowered
NEW 588-458 #5754B **79.99**

Undecorated

PA1 Powered w/LokSound
NEW 588-465 No Antenna **199.99**

NEW 588-466 With Antenna **209.99**

PA1 Powered, No Sound
NEW 588-484 No Antenna **99.99**

NEW 588-485 With Antenna **109.99**

PB1 Unpowered
NEW 588-486 **79.99**

Alco PA2

DRGW California Zephyr

A-B-A Sets With Sound **499.99 ea**
Two powered A units, unpowered B.

NEW 588-451 #600

NEW 588-452 #601

See What's Available at
www.walthers.com

A-B-A Sets No Sound **299.99 ea**
Two powered A units, unpowered B.

NEW 588-471 #600

NEW 588-472 #601

PA2 Powered
NEW 588-453 #600 w/Sound **239.99**

NEW 588-473 #601 No Sound **99.99**

PB2 Unpowered **79.99 ea**
NEW 588-454 #600

NEW 588-474 #601

ATSF Warbonnet

PA2/PB2 With Sound **299.99 ea**
Powered A unit, unpowered B unit.

NEW 588-447 #53L & 53A

NEW 588-448 #59L & 59A

PA2/PB2 No Sound **199.99 ea**
NEW 588-467 #53L & 53A

NEW 588-468 #59L & 59A

PA2 Powered
NEW 588-449 #59L w/Sound **239.99**

NEW 588-469 #59L No Sound **99.99**

PB2 Unpowered
NEW 588-450 #59A **79.99**

Delaware & Hudson Blue Warbonnet

PA2 Powered With Sound **239.99 ea**
NEW 588-463 #16

NEW 588-464 #19

PA2 Powered No Sound **99.99 ea**
NEW 588-482 #16

NEW 588-483 #19

Alco PA3

SP Daylight

PA3 A-B-A Sets With Sound **499.99 ea**
Two powered A units, unpowered B.

NEW 588-459 #6023, 5922 & 6025

NEW 588-460 #6033, 5924 & 6030

PA3 A-B-A Sets No Sound **299.99 ea**
Two powered A units, unpowered B.

NEW 588-479 #6023, 5920 & 6025

NEW 588-480 #6033, 5924 & 6030

PA3 powered w/LokSound, DC/DCC
NEW 588-461 #6033 w/Sound **239.99**

NEW 588-481 #6033 No Sound **99.99**

PB3 Unpowered
NEW 588-462 SP #6007 Daylight **79.99**

Alco PB Chassis Only

Powered.
NEW 588-470 With Sound **149.99**

NEW 588-478 No Sound **49.99**

EMD E8/9

Models feature diecast chassis, five-pole can motor with skewed armature and dual flywheels, directional lighting, Micro-Trains® couplers, authentic paint and color schemes and many separately applied details. Sound equipped models operate on DC or DCC. Units without sound function only in DC and can be upgraded with installation of NMRA compliant DCC decoder (not included).

E8A-B Sets

Powered A, unpowered B.
NEW 588-524 IC #4026 & 4104 w/Sound **299.99**

NEW 588-775 IC #4026 & 4104 No Sound **179.99**

E8A Powered

With Sound **239.99 ea**
NEW 588-510 UP #929 w/Snow Shields

NEW 588-511 UP #930 w/Snow Shields

NEW 588-525 IC #4027

NEW 588-526 L&N #785

NEW 588-527 L&N #788

NEW 588-528 NYC #4036

NEW 588-529 NYC #4037

NEW 588-534 SOU #2925

NEW 588-535 SOU #2926

No Sound **129.99 ea**
NEW 588-760 UP #929 w/Snow Shields

NEW 588-761 UP #930 w/Snow Shields

NEW 588-776 IC #1027

NEW 588-777 L&N #785

NEW 588-778 L&N #788

NEW 588-779 NYC #4036

NEW 588-780 NYC #4037

NEW 588-785 SOU #2925

NEW 588-786 SOU #2926

E8B Powered

UP With SnowShields & Horizontal Grilles

NEW 588-512 #929B w/Sound **229.99**

NEW 588-513 #930B w/Sound **229.99**

NEW 588-762 #929B No Sound **119.99**

NEW 588-763 #930B No Sound **119.99**

E8B Unpowered

UP w/SnowShields & Horizontal Grilles

NEW 588-764 UP #928B No Sound **74.99**

E8A Powered With Horizontal Grilles

With Sound **239.99 ea**
NEW 588-536 Undecorated w/Mars Light

NEW 588-537 Undecorated No Mars Light

No Sound **129.99 ea**
NEW 588-787 Undecorated w/Mars Light

NEW 588-788 Undecorated No Mars Light

E8B Powered With Horizontal Grilles

NEW 588-540 Undecorated w/Sound **229.99**

NEW 588-791 Undecorated No Sound **119.99**

EMD E9 With Vertical Grilles

E9A Powered

With Sound **239.99 ea**
NEW 588-538 Undecorated w/Mars Light

NEW 588-539 Undecorated No Mars Light

No Sound **129.99 ea**
NEW 588-789 Undecorated w/Mars Light

NEW 588-790 Undecorated No Mars Light

E9B Powered

NEW 588-541 Undecorated w/Sound **229.99**

NEW 588-792 Undecorated No Sound **119.99**

Catalog

NEW 588-1002 Precision Craft 2006 Product Flyer NC

STEAM LOCOMOTIVES

Pennsylvania Class M1a 4-8-2 Powered Limited Run

w/LokSound **349.99 ea**
588-1 #6743
588-2 #6720
588-3 #6798
588-5 #6704
588-6 #6716
588-4 Unlettered
588-7 Unlettered

No Sound **249.99 ea**
588-8 #6743
588-9 #6720

588-10 #6798
588-12 #6704

LOCOMOTIVES N SCALE

588-13 #6716
588-11 Unlettered
588-14 Unlettered

DIESEL LOCOMOTIVES

EMD E7A Assembled
Powered w/Quantum™ Sound DC & DCC 239.99 ea

588-600 NYC #4000
588-601 NYC #4007

588-606 UP #986
588-607 UP #999

588-612 GN #512
588-613 GN #500
588-618 CB&Q #9918A
588-619 CB&Q #9926A
588-624 SP #6004
588-625 SP #6002
588-629 PRR #5841A (Tuscan Red)
588-630 PRR #5843A (Tuscan Red)
588-635 B&O #64
588-636 B&O #72
588-641 Undecorated w/Small Number Boards
588-644 Undecorated w/Large Number Boards

Powered No Sound DC & DCC Socket Equipped 129.99 ea
588-602 NYC #4001
588-603 NYC #4005
588-608 UP #990

588-609 UP #988
588-614 GN #502
588-615 GN #505

588-620 CB&Q #9926B
588-621 CB&Q #9921A
588-626 SP #6001
588-627 SP #6003
588-631 PRR #5842A (Tuscan Red)

588-632 PRR #5844A (Tuscan Red)
588-637 B&O #76A
588-638 B&O #68
588-642 Undecorated w/Small Number Boards
588-645 Undecorated w/Large Number Boards

Dummy No Sound 79.99 ea
588-604 NYC #4002
588-605 NYC #4004
588-610 UP #998
588-611 UP #989
588-616 GN #510
588-617 GN #506
588-622 CB&Q #9922A
588-623 CB&Q #9924A
588-628 SP #6000
588-633 PRR #5853A (Tuscan Red)
588-634 PRR #5847A (Tuscan Red)
588-639 B&O #72A
588-640 B&O #80A
588-643 Undecorated w/Small Number Boards
588-646 Undecorated w/Large Number Boards

EMD E7B Assembled
Powered w/Quantum Sound, DC, DCC 229.99 ea
588-647 NYC #4100

588-648 NYC #4107
588-653 UP #986B
588-654 UP #996B

588-659 PRR #5840B (Tuscan Red)
588-660 PRR #5854B (Tuscan Red)

588-665 SP #5900
588-666 SP #5906
588-671 Undecorated

Powered DC, DCC Socket Equipped, No Sound 119.99 ea
588-649 NYC #4101
588-650 NYC #4105
588-655 UP #990B
588-656 UP #988B
588-661 PRR #5842B
588-662 PRR #5844B
588-667 SP #5901
588-668 SP #5905
588-672 Undecorated

Dummy No Sound 74.99 ea
588-651 NYC #4102
588-652 NYC #4104
588-657 UP #998B
588-658 UP #986C
588-663 PRR #5852B (Tuscan Red)
588-664 PRR #5846B (Tuscan Red)
588-669 SP #5909
588-670 SP #5907
588-673 Undecorated

EMD E7A Assembled NYC #4005 588-603

EMD E7A Assembled SP #6002 588-625

EMD E7A Assembled B&O #64 588-635

EMD E7A Assembled PRR #5842A 588-631

EMD E7B Assembled UP #996B 588-654

EMD E7B Assembled NYC #4105 588-650

Models & Photo by Dudley Ross, Montgomery, Alabama

It's a crisp fall day in Alleghany, Virginia. The mountains are covered with a dusting of red, yellow, orange and burgundy. Soon the green will be gone, the leaves will fall and winter will set in. But for now, the residents are enjoying the color show as the local freight train passes through on its way down the mountain to Clifton Forge. Nestled at the southern tip of the Shenandoah Valley, Clifton Forge was a major C&O maintenance facility for steam locomotives. Nearly 2,000 people were employed there before diesels took over and maintenance was moved to West Virginia. Today the Chesapeake and Ohio Historical Society makes its home in Clifton Forge.

Dudley Ross scratch-built all of the structures of basswood or styrene. The cross arms are by Depots by John and the strung wires are from Berkshire Junction.

Growing up in a railroad town is just one of many routes to becoming a model railroader. Another great way to get started in the hobby is with a train set. From the track to the train, everything comes in one package. Choose from vintage steam, classic diesels or modern passenger trains in the Train Sets Section.

TRAIN SETS N SCALE

Division of Wm. K. Walthers, Inc.

TRAIN SETS

Yard Master Second Edition 89.99 ea
Yard Master N Scale Train Sets feature a reliable EMD SW9/1200 switcher with a heavy split-frame chassis, five-pole motor with dual flywheels and working headlight. This authentic model hauls a train with a 50' double-door box car, 50' single-door box car, three-dome tank car and offset-cupola caboose, around an easy-to-assemble 20-1/2 x 30" oval of Power-Loc™ track. For extra realism, this set also includes roadway signs and power poles, hotel structure kit, trees, a power pack and complete instructions.

433-34001 Chessie System/C&O
433-34002 SOU
433-34003 EL

Diesel Transport Second Edition 109.99 ea
Diesel Transport Second Edition sets include a powerful Alco FA-1 locomotive with a heavy split-frame chassis, five-pole motor with dual flywheels and working headlight. This road freight includes a 50' plug-door box car, 50' double-door box car, 40' stock car, three-bay hopper and center-cupola caboose. The mainline is a big 21 x 30-1/2" oval of nickel silver Power-Loc track, controlled by a UL-listed power pack with forward and reverse. Accessories include operating dual crossing gates, roadway signs and power poles, police station and fire station structure kits, trees, power pack and complete instructions.

433-34004 LV
433-34005 NH
433-34006 GN

Freight King Second Edition 129.99 ea
Freight King sets include a high-performance FM C-Liner locomotive with realistic paint scheme, rugged diecast split-frame chassis, five-pole motor with dual flywheels and working headlight, 50' mechanical refrigerator car, three-dome tank car, three-bay hopper, 50' box car and center-cupola caboose. Run your freight around a huge 21 x 27-1/2" double oval of easy setup Power-Loc nickel silver track, two manual turnouts. Control your train with the power pack; complete instructions are also included. Finally, decorating your set is easy using the included roadway signs and power poles, country store and chapel structure kits and trees.

433-34007 MILW
433-34008 NYC
433-34009 PRR

Yard Master Second Edition
433-34001

Diesel Transport Second Edition
433-34004

Freight King Second Edition
433-34007

TRAIN SETS N SCALE

Division of Wm. K. Walthers, Inc.

Freight King 433-7523

Diesel Charger 433-7558

Little Joe 433-7549

Yard Master 433-7574

Freight Flyer 433-7535

Diesel Transport 433-7567

Freight Flyer
433-7535 89.99
This train set contains a GP18 hi-nose diesel locomotive with working headlight, seven railroad cars including an eight-wheel caboose, country store building kit, a nickel-silver track oval with rerailer, road signs, a UL-listed power pack, hook-up wires and illustrated instructions.

Freight King 129.99 ea
Each set includes a GP20 diesel locomotive with working headlight, five multi-colored cars, right- and left-hand manual switch tracks, four handcrafted shade trees, rural chapel building kit, 36 signs, 21 x 27-1/2" double-oval of Power-Loc track with terminal rerailer, UL-listed power pack, hook-up wires and illustrated instructions.

433-7523 UP
433-7524 NYC

Diesel Transport 109.99 ea
Included with each set are one SD7 diesel locomotive with working headlight, five multi-colored cars, four handcrafted shade trees, operating dual crossing gate, police station building kit, fire house building kit, 36 signs, a 30-1/2 x 21" oval of Power-Loc track with terminal rerailer, UL-listed power pack, hook-up wires and illustrated instructions.

433-7567 CB&Q

Limited Quantity Available
433-7568 UP

Little Joe
433-7549 59.99
Includes 0-6-0 saddle tank loco, two freight cars and caboose, two building kits, trees, railroad signs and telephone poles.

Diesel Charger
433-7558 79.99
With powered and unpowered Conrail GP38-2 diesel locos, three freight cars and caboose, operating crossing gate, railroad signs and telephone poles.

Yard Master 89.99 ea
Comes with SW9 diesel locomotive with working headlight, four multi-colored freight cars (including an eight-wheel matching caboose), four handcrafted shade trees, downtown hotel building kit, 36 signs, a 30-1/2 x 21" oval of Power-Loc track with terminal rerailer, UL-listed power pack, hook-up wires and illustrated instructions.

433-7574 Florida East Coast
433-7576 CNW

See What's Available at
www.walthers.com

TRAIN SETS N SCALE

TRAIN SETS FEATURING E-Z TRACK®

All train sets feature Bachmann E-Z Track, the snap-fit track system that can be set up almost anywhere in minutes. There's no need for boards, nails, screws or tools. E-Z Track combines track and roadbed together into one track section, so you can get your trains up and running in minutes. Track sections are designed with a special snap-fit locking feature that holds the pieces securely together for smooth and trouble-free action. All train sets include a plug-in terminal and a power pack.

McKinley Explorer 160-24010

White Christmas 160-24016

NEW PRODUCTS

Yard Boss
NEW 160-24014 105.00
Includes an 0-6-0 steam locomotive, box car, quad hopper and Wide-Vision Caboose, 24" circle of nickel silver E-Z Track, power pack, speed controller and illustrated instructions.

White Christmas
NEW 160-24016 130.00
Perfect for under-the-tree fun, this festively decorated set includes an 0-6-0 steam locomotive, box car, gondola and old-time combine, 24 x 34" oval of nickel silver E-Z Track, power pack, speed controller and illustrated instructions.

Iron Duke
160-24005 136.00
The Iron Duke is headed by an 0-6-0 steam locomotive with slope back tender, a single-dome tank car, covered hopper, box car, off-center-cupola caboose, 34 x 24" oval of E-Z Track including plug-in rerailer, UL-listed power pack and illustrated instruction manual.

McKinley Explorer
160-24010 120.00
The prototype for this set runs through the Alaskan wilderness carrying passengers through the Denali National Park en route from Anchorage to Fairbanks. The set includes one powered EMD F9 diesel locomotive, one unpowered EMD F9 unit, three full-dome passenger cars (named after Alaskan rivers), 34 x 24" oval of E-Z Track, power pack and instruction manual.

Yard Boss 160-24014

Iron Duke Train Set 160-24005

TRAIN SETS N SCALE

Thunder Valley Train Set 160-24013
Explorer Train Set 160-24008
Empire Builder Train Set 160-24009
Centennial Train Set 160-24007
Frontiersman Train Set 160-24006
Prairie Flyer Train Set 160-24004

Prairie Flyer
160-24004   128.00
This old-time favorite includes an American 4-4-0 steam locomotive and tender, old-time combine, two old-time coaches, a 34 x 24" oval of E-Z Track® and instruction manual.

Frontiersman
160-24006   136.00
Includes an American 4-4-0 steam locomotive and tender, old-time water tank car, old-time box car, old-time gondola, old-time flat car, old-time bobber caboose, a 34 x 24" oval of E-Z Track including a plug-in rerailer, a UL-listed power pack and illustrated instruction manual.

Centennial
160-24007   129.00
Run your own modern passenger train with The Centennial, sleekly styled after the Amtrak Amfleet passenger trains. Includes an E60CP electric locomotive with diode directional headlights, dual pantographs and full Lustra Chrome, three Amfleet coach cars, a 34 x 24" oval of E-Z Track including a plug-in rerailer, a UL-listed power pack and illustrated instruction manual.

Explorer
160-24008   125.00
The Explorer Train Set is a great way to get started in the model railroading hobby. The modern train is hauled by an EMD F9 diesel locomotive with operating headlight and Lustra Chrome finish, along with an unpowered "A-unit." Also included is a single-dome tank car, reefer car, covered hopper, plug-door box car, flat car with containers, off-center cupola caboose, a 34 x 24" oval of E-Z Track including a plug-in rerailer, 12 telephone poles, 24 railroad and street signs, UL-listed power pack and illustrated instruction manual.

Empire Builder
160-24009   200.00
Create your own empire with the Empire Builder Train Set. This incredible starter set includes a Northern 4-8-4 steam locomotive with operating headlight and tender, wood reefer, single-dome tank car, centerflow hopper, plug-door box car, wood stock car, wood-braced gondola, open quad offset hopper, off-center cupola caboose, a 44 x 24" oval of E-Z Track including a plug-in rerailer, 12 telephone poles, 24 railroad and street signs, UL-listed power pack and illustrated instruction manual.

Thunder Valley
160-24013   82.00
Hauling freight to destinations far and wide, this set includes a 24" circle of E-Z Track, powerful EMD GP40 Locomotive, steel reefer, three-dome tank car, wide-vision caboose, power pack and speed controller and complete instructions in English and Spanish.

TRAIN SETS N SCALE

NEW PRODUCTS

Acela℠ Express
160-24130   450.00

DCC ON BOARD Capture the excitement of Amtrak's flagship service with this detailed replica of America's revolutionary high-speed passenger train. Designed in cooperation with Amtrak, this train set comes equipped with DCC for added control and realistic, reliable and simple operation. Set includes dual non-powered locomotives, one powered Café Acela car, one first class and one business class car, all with detailed, lighted interiors and tinted windows. Also includes 59 x 39" oval of nickel-silver E-Z Track, power pack, speed controller and instructional DVD video.

Acela Express Accessories

Unpowered Locomotive Set
160-81551   103.00
Features DCC lighting functions and movable pantographs.

Café Acela Power Car
160-89971   147.00
DCC ON BOARD This very detailed model incorporates the drive system for an entire Acela train set. The model features a smooth-running mechanism and factory-installed DCC decoder.

Acela Express Passenger Cars 55.00 ea
160-88972 First Class
160-88973 Business Class
160-88974 End Business Class

Spectrum® Electric Train Sets
Each set comes with a Spectrum GE Dash 8-40CW diesel locomotive with diode directional headlights, gondola, plug-door box car, ACF covered centerflow hopper, reefer, PS2 covered hopper, wide-vision caboose, a 39 x 24" oval of nickel-silver E-Z Track (including 11 pieces of curved track and six pieces of straight track) and VHS video with assembly instructions.

160-24105 BNSF 165.00

Spectrum "Station Master" Train Sets
Dedicated to those who hold the title of station masters, ensuring the smooth operation of the nation's freight yards, these train sets feature a DCC-ready Baldwin 2-8-0 steam locomotive with operating headlight and tender, box car, quad hopper, single-dome tank car, PS-2 covered hopper, wide-vision caboose, 39 x 24" oval of E-Z Track, power pack and instructional video.

160-24122 ATSF 203.00

Acela Express 160-24130

Acela Express Unpowered Locomotive Set 160-81551

Café Acela Power Car 160-89971

Acela First Class Passenger Car 160-88972

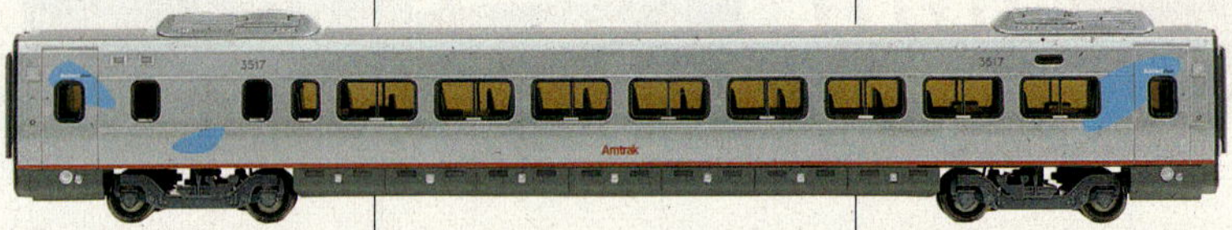

Acela Business Class Passenger Car 160-88973

Acela End Business Class Passenger Car 160-88974

Spectrum "Station Master" 160-24122

Spectrum® Train Set BNSF 160-24105

TRAIN SETS N SCALE

MICRO-TRAINS LINE

NEW PRODUCTS
Train Sets
149.95 ea

North Pole Central

NEW 489-99321731
Finished in festive holiday silver red and green, this set includes a powered Life-Like GP20 Diesel, Toy Factory Transfer Car, Egg Nog Delivery Tank Car, Sugar & Spice Cookie Car and a Letters to Santa Mail Car.

Booville & Beyond Railroad

NEW 489-99321040
This spooky set is filled with Halloween fun with its glow-in-the-dark cars and gleaming blue ghosts, plus a load of ghosts in one of the cars! Comes complete with powered Micro-Trains FT Diesel, B&BRR "Moving Freight for the Afterworld" car with ghost load, B&BRR Flying Banshee Box Car and B&BR Phantom Caboose.

Liberty Railroad

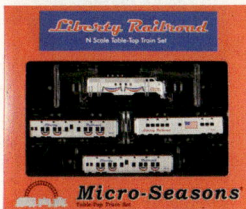

NEW 489-99321030
Decorated in red, white and blue this patriotic passenger train features two Liberty Railroad Sleepers and a Liberty Railroad Kitchen Car (all former troop cars) pulled by a Micro-Trains FT Diesel.

Happy Birthday Train Set

NEW 489-99321020
Celebrate your special day every day with this great N Scale set! Includes a powered Life-Like GP20 Diesel, three Happy Birthday Box Cars and a Caboose, all in bright colors with balloon graphics.

KATO

California Zephyr

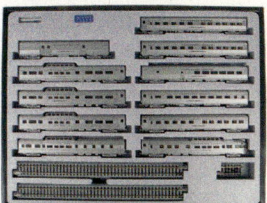

381-106055 250.00
The California Zephyr, one of the most famous passenger trains in North American railroading, offered service between Chicago and San Francisco from 1949 until 1970. Traveling more than 2,500 miles in just over two days, passengers of the CZ enjoyed breathtaking scenery and excellent service. With newly tooled cars, this set recreates the first-year consist of the CZ with eight different car types. Each car features a silver corrugated-side body, accurate lettering, blackened metal wheels and Kato semi-automatic knuckle couplers. The Observation car features lighted tail lights, marker light and tail sign. As an added bonus, this 11-car set includes enough N scale Unitrack for presentation on a desk or shelf when not in operation on a layout. Optional lighting kits #s 381-11204, 381-11206, 381-11209 and 381-11210 (each sold separately) are available.

New Arrivals Updated Every Day! Visit Walthers Web site at
www.walthers.com

model power

These train sets feature ready-to-run all-metal F7 locomotives with flywheel drive, and rolling stock decorated in authentic colors. Each set includes a power pack and a 24-piece sign and pole set. Sets include track and transformer.

TRAIN SETS

Silver Eagle
490-1150   110.00
This dynamic train set allows for twice the fun in half the space. Each set comes with a lighted all-metal F7 eight-wheel diesel locomotive. The set also includes four freight cars: a Hudson's Bay Oil and Gas tanker, a Soo Line hopper, an Ontario Northland box car and an ATSF caboose. Also includes a 14-piece oval of track, power pack, hook-up wire and instructions.

Continental Express
490-1151   121.00
This 44-piece train set is led by a lighted, gear-driven, all-metal, eight-wheel F7 diesel locomotive. Following behind are three streamline passenger cars. Cars ride on a 12-piece circle of track. Package includes hook-up wire, power pack and instructions.

The Presidential Special
490-1159   220.00
Includes a lighted 4-6-2 Pacific locomotive with coal-hauling tender and three passenger cars.

Double Diesel
490-1166   154.00
Set includes lighted powered ATSF F7 all-metal diesel, matching lighted dummy, four freight cars (including caboose), signal bridge, tunnel, oval of track, and 40-piece pop-out buildings.

Golden Rail Train Set
490-1185   220.00
A 4-6-2 Pacific leads the way with its churning side rods and blazing headlight. The loco features all-wheel drive and electrical pick-up, plus a husky motor for great performance. Three freight cars follow behind, capped off by the traditional red caboose. Hook-up wire and complete instructions are also included.

Silver Eagle 490-1150

Continental Express 490-1151

The Presidential Special 490-1159

Double Diesel 490-1166

Golden Rail Train Set 490-1185

TRAIN SETS N SCALE

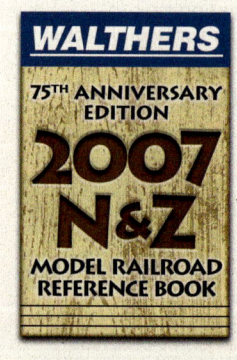

Models and Photo by Lee Edgar, Wye Mills, Maryland

PASSENGER CARS

Where the mighty Mississippi meets the Wisconsin shore, travelers on Burlington's Chicago-Twin Cities mainline are treated to spectacular scenery "Where nature smiles for 300 miles!" For the railfan in search of unique shots, there are plenty of great locations where you can shoot the daily parade of fast freights or important trains like the "Twin Zephyrs" and the "Empire Builder." But on occasion, something happens along the nearby Milwaukee or North Western, and detours offer a chance for some rare shots.

No word on what caused the problem, but we're just in time – barely — to see the Milwaukee Road's "Olympian Hiawatha" speeding north of La Crosse. Based on the La Crosse Division circa 1957-1961 in the area of milepost 320.6, this handsome diorama is the work of Lee Edgar from Wye Mills, Maryland. Natural materials and Woodland Scenics products were combined to capture the look of the Mississippi Palisades and the diorama was photographed outdoors for authentic lighting. Waiting in the siding, the pair of "Q" motors on the freight are superdetailed Life-Like units. The classic Milwaukee Sky Top is a brass model from Railway Classics.

From the early days to Modern Amtrak, passenger service is easy to model with the great selection of items you'll find in this section!

PASSENGER CARS N SCALE

From the glory days of steam to the first post-war streamliners, it's easy to model a complete passenger train with these sets. Each includes different cars, but all are painted in the same scheme. By mixing and matching sets, you can build a train of any length. (Sorry, individual cars are not available.) Cars are ready-to-run with appropriate four- or six-wheel trucks and Rapido couplers.

Limited Quantity Available On All Items

EUROPEAN EQUIPMENT

Ready-to-run cars are prepainted and lettered and include a variety of details.

German State Railways (DR 1945-85)
Former East German Lines.

Urban Railway Of Berlin pkg(2)
125-190 German State Railways-DRG **109.99**

German Federal Railways (DB 1945-85)
Former West German Lines.

Advertising Baggage Cars
Painted in colorful billboard schemes, found on the head-end of many trains.
125-3882 Eckart/Fürth **47.49**
125-3885 Knorr-Meese Express **39.99**

Hobby Assortment Coach
125-3208 86' D4um Baggage (blue) **44.99**

Intercity (IC) Cars

Latest Red & White 41.99 ea
Finished in latest red & white scheme.
125-3874 1st Class Coach
125-3879 Diner

2nd Class Compartment Coaches 41.99 ea
125-3877 Turquoise & White

Austrian Federal Railways

2nd Class Uic "x" Type Coaches 39.99 ea
125-3829 Ivory, Red

DIAPHRAGMS

Operating passenger car diaphragms are accurate models of specific prototypes and realistically fill the gap between cars. Easy-to-build kits feature injection-molded plastic parts and will not interfere with operation of most couplers. All kits include complete instructions and are available in single pair (one car) or 12-pair (six cars) sets.

Heavyweight Passenger Cars

For Rivarossi and Con-Cor heavyweight passenger cars with Micro-Trains® 1129 or standard couplers and a minimum curve of 15 inches.
147-8400 Black pkg(2) **4.95**
147-8406 Black pkg(6) **12.95**

Streamline Passenger Cars

Fits Kato, Con-Cor and Rivarossi cars with popular coupler conversions.
147-8500 Gray pkg(2) **4.95**
147-8506 Gray pkg(6) **12.95**
147-8510 Black pkg(2) **4.95**
147-8516 Black pkg(6) **12.95**

Con-Cor Superliners

Designed especially for these modern bi-level cars.
147-8300 Gray pkg(2) **4.95**
147-8306 Gray pkg(6) **12.95**

BASIC PASSENGER CAR KITS

All kits include roof, floor and detailed ends for streamlined passenger cars, along with operating diaphragms, metal weight and underbody equipment including typical air conditioning, electrical, brake, water equipment and roof details. Instructions include a section designed to help identify visible underbody equipment from prototype photos. All you need are sides to complete a car.

With Outside Swing Hanger Trucks 12.95 ea

147-8010 Gray
147-8020 Black

Without Trucks 10.95 ea
147-8030 Gray
147-8040 Black

Core Kits w/Commonwealth Trucks 12.95 ea
147-8015 Gray
147-8025 Black

ROOF & UNDERFRAME ACCESSORIES

147-8050 **3.95**
Underbody parts from the core kits for superdetailing existing streamlined plastic and brass cars. Includes five types of battery boxes, five air conditioning systems, brake reservoirs and valves, water tanks, generator, and roof vents and stacks. Instructions are designed to help identify visible underbody equipment from prototype photos.

Get the Scoop!
Get the Skinny!
Get the Score!
Check Out Walthers Web site at
www.walthers.com

BRASS CAR SIDES

Customize your streamliner fleet with these car sides. Made from photo-etched brass, each side already has window openings and grab iron holes or dimples, plus additional surface features. Non-dome sides are designed to be used with American Ltd. Models core kits. Dome sides are designed for specified Con-Cor, Bachmann, or Kato plastic cars. (Some trimming of plastic around windows may be needed.) All kits include instructions and are undecorated. Since the same car plans were used by several railroads, additional roadnames are listed where appropriate. See our Web site at www.walthers.com for illustrations of each item.

Chicago & North Western
NEW 173-506 16-3-1 "Northern" Sleeper **19.75**

Great Northern/ Chicago, Burlington & Quincy/Spokane, Portland & Seattle "Empire Builder" 19.75 ea

173-510 "Ranch" Coffee Shop GN 1240-1245.

173-511 GN "River" 7-4-3-1 Sleeper
PS Plan 4181, GN 1260-74, SP&S 702, CB&Q 1266, -69, -73.

173-513 "Pass" Series Sleeper GN 1370-1384, Spokane, Portland & Seattle 701.

173-514 GN ACF 60-Seat Coach
GN 1209-14, CB&Q 1211, BN.

173-527 "View" Great Dome Lounge
GN 1390-95, Bachmann Dome Overlay.

Illinois Central
173-542 "B" Series 11-Bedroom Plan 4168A PS Sleeper **19.75**

Milwaukee Road 19.75 ea (Unless Noted)

173-502 52-Seat 1948 Hiawatha Coach
MILW 480-497, 535-551, 600-series.

173-503 "Valley" Parlor Car 1948 Hiawatha 190-197.

173-552 RPO Express 1208-30, with integral doors.

173-553 Lunch/Tap Lounge 162-67, 172-73.

173-554 75' Express 1317-1329 w/Integral Doors.

173-555 Diner
For 1947-48 "Olympian" and "Twin Cities Hiawatha."

173-557 Baggage-Dorm 1309-14 w/Integral Doors

173-558 "Touralux" 14-Section P-S Sleeper "Mountain"

NEW 173-559 60' Postal Car #2152-53 w/Integral Doors

NEW 173-560 Café Parlor Car #180-185 "Grove" w/Integral Doors

Northern Pacific/ Chicago, Burlington & Quincy/Spokane, Portland & Seattle "North Coast Limited" 19.75 ea

173-519 "Travelers Rest" Lounge
NP 494-99.

173-524 Budd Dome Sleeper NP 307-314, CB&Q 304-305, Spokane, Portland & Seattle 306. Con-Cor Budd dome coach overlay.

173-550 Mail-Dorm
NP 425-429, CB&Q 430.

173-556 Water-Baggage
NP 400-404, CB&Q 405.

Pennsylvania
173-533 "Rapids" 10-6 4140 PS Sleeper, N&W, L&N. **19.75**

Pullman Sleepers 19.75 ea

173-516 "Imperial" Plan 4069 4-4-2
NYC, PRR, UP, SP, CNW, Rock Island, IC and CN.

173-517 "Cascade" Series Plan 4072 10-5
NYC, PRR, B&O, SP, ATSF and CP.

Union Pacific 19.75 ea

173-522 Dome Diner 8000-9 Kato Dome Overlay

173-536 Dome Observation Lounge One-Piece Kato Overlay

PASSENGER CARS N SCALE

PASSENGER CARS

Silver Series® Amfleet® I Passenger Cars 31.00 ea
These sleek passenger cars are based on cars built by Budd in the late 70s and 80s for Amtrak®. Cars feature detailed plastic bodies, lighted interiors and Rapido-type couplers.

Coach
HO models shown.

160-14156 Amtrak Phase II

160-14157 Amtrak Phase III

160-14158 Amtrak Phase IV

160-14156 Acela℠ Regional
NEW 160-14164 Amtrak Phase IV
NEW 160-14166 Amtrak Phase V

Café (Diner)
HO models shown.

160-14160 Amtrak Phase II

160-14161 Amtrak Phase III

160-14162 Amtrak Phase IV

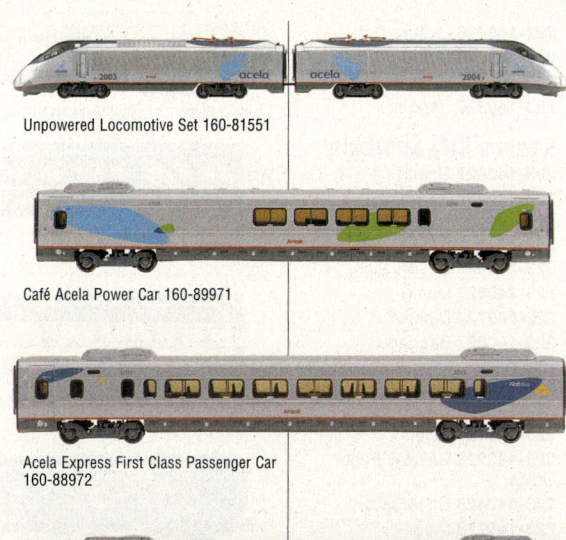
160-14163 Acela Regional
NEW 160-14165 Amtrak Phase IV
NEW 160-14167 Amtrak Phase V

Unpowered Locomotive Set 160-81551
Café Acela Power Car 160-89971
Acela Express First Class Passenger Car 160-88972
Acela Express Business Class Passenger Car 160-88973
Acela Express End Business Class Passenger Car 160-88974

Streamlined Cars
Ready-to-run passenger cars feature molded plastic bodies, which are prepainted and lettered. Complete with trucks and Rapido couplers.

Full-Length Dome 13.00 ea

160-74352 ATSF
160-74355 Amtrak

Acela Express Equipment

Unpowered Locomotive Set
160-81551 103.00
Features DCC lighting functions and movable pantographs.

Café Acela Power Car
DCC ON BOARD
160-89971
147.00
This detailed model incorporates the drive system for an entire Acela train set. The model features a smooth-running mechanism and factory-installed DCC decoder.

Acela Express Passenger Cars 55.00 ea
HO models shown.
160-88972 First Class
160-88973 Business Class
160-88974 End Business Class

The great streamliners are rolling again with these conversion body sides for N Scale passenger cars. Based on actual equipment used by eastern roads, the sides come prepainted and lettered. Depending on the size of the car, the injection molded plastic sides are designed for use with the American Limited Models core kit (#147-8020 sold separately), and can be fitted with separate grab irons if desired, also sold separately.

NEW PRODUCTS

14-4 Sleeper Sides (Pullman Plan #4159)

NH 1949 Dumaine-Era Scheme 22.95 ea

Different Name Shown

NEW 263-312001 #503 "City Point"
NEW 263-312002 #514 "Monomoy Point"
NEW 263-312003 #515 "Morgan Point"
NEW 263-312004 #519 "Quonset Point"

NH 1954 McGinnis-Era Scheme 23.95 ea
NEW 263-312101 "Allyns Point"
NEW 263-312102 "Lords Point"
NEW 263-312103 "Goshen Point"
NEW 263-312104 "India Point"

Penn Central Scheme 23.95 ea
NEW 263-312301 "Lookout Point"
NEW 263-312302 "Mishaum Point"
NEW 263-312303 "North Point"
NEW 263-312304 "Shippan Point"

Information STATION

Who Owns That Passenger Car?

Back in the days of fancy streamliners and premier trains, many railroads worked with connecting railroads to offer long-distance service. Participating lines supplied equipment, often painted to match specific consists.

For example, the "Empire Builder" was GN's premier train between Chicago and Seattle/Portland. The GN did not reach Portland, Oregon, from the east and it's tracks only reached St. Paul, Minnesota. The train was jointly operated by GN and its affiliates Spokane, Portland & Seattle (SP&S) and Chicago, Burlington & Quincy (CB&Q). The entire train wore GN's colors and the letterboards above the windows said "Empire Builder", but at the ends of the letterboards very small lettering indicated who owned each car. GN-owned cars carried "Great Northern;" SP&S and CB&Q initials appeared on their cars.

Other trains that carried sublettered cars included IC's "City of Miami" with C of G cars; UP's "City of San Francisco," hauled cars from PRR, CNW, SP, N&W, MILW and Wabash at times; and the WP/DRGW/ CB&Q "California Zephyr," carried cars from its three participants plus a through sleeper from the Pennsy. And don't forget, many streamlined sleepers were painted to match specific trains but said Pullman on the letterboards. Upon their sale to the railroads, Pullman became the sublettering on some road's cars.

Sublettering is easy to model on your passenger fleet. Cars often come with number and name decals, and many include sublettering too. Some decal makers also include appropriate sublettering on some of their sets.

PASSENGER CARS N SCALE

85' STREAMLINED CARS 15.98 ea

Amtrak Phase II Paint
223-1400110 Coach
223-1401110 Pullman
223-1402110 Railway Post Office
223-1404110 Observation
223-1406110 Dome
223-1407110 Diner
223-1408110 Baggage

Atchison, Topeka & Santa Fe
Regular
223-140017 Coach
223-140117 Pullman
223-140217 Railway Post Office
223-140417 Observation
223-140617 Dome
223-140717 Diner
223-140817 Baggage

"Scout"
223-140023 Coach
223-140123 Pullman
223-140223 Railway Post Office
223-140423 Observation
223-140623 Dome
223-140723 Diner
223-140823 Baggage

"Blue Goose"
Two-Tone Blue with silver roof and letterboard.
223-1400210 Coach
223-1401210 Pullman
223-1402210 Railway Post Office
223-1404210 Observation
223-1406210 Dome
223-1407210 Diner
223-1408210 Baggage

Baltimore & Ohio
223-400123 Coach
223-401123 Pullman
223-402123 Railway Post Office
223-404123 Observation
223-406123 Dome
223-407123 Diner
223-408123 Baggage

Burlington Northern
223-140018 Coach
223-140118 Pullman
223-140218 Railway Post Office
223-140418 Observation
223-140618 Dome
223-140718 Diner
223-140818 Baggage

Canadian National
223-1400119 Coach
223-1401119 Pullman
223-1402119 Railway Post Office
223-1404119 Observation
223-1406119 Dome
223-1407119 Diner
223-1408119 Baggage

Chesapeake & Ohio
223-1400124 Coach
223-1401124 Pullman
223-1402124 Railway Post Office
223-1404124 Observation
223-1406124 Dome
223-1407124 Diner
223-1408124 Baggage

Chicago & North Western
223-1400120 Coach
223-1401120 Pullman
223-1402120 Railway Post Office
223-1404120 Observation
223-1406120 Dome
223-1407120 Diner
223-1408120 Baggage

Erie
223-140025 Coach
223-140125 Pullman
223-140225 Railway Post Office
223-140425 Observation
223-140625 Dome
223-140725 Diner
223-140825 Baggage

Erie Lackawanna
223-400111 Coach
223-401111 Pullman
223-402111 Railway Post Office
223-404111 Observation
223-406111 Dome
223-407111 Diner
223-1408111 Baggage

Great Northern
223-140014 Coach
223-140114 Pullman
223-140214 Railway Post Office
223-140414 Observation
223-140614 Dome
223-140714 Diner
223-140814 Baggage

Illinois Central
223-140026 Coach
223-140126 Pullman
223-140226 Railway Post Office
223-140426 Observation
223-140626 Dome
223-140726 Diner
223-140826 Baggage

Kansas City Southern
223-140027 Coach
223-140127 Pullman
223-140227 Railway Post Office
223-140427 Observation
223-140627 Dome
223-140727 Diner
223-140827 Baggage

Lackawanna
223-140028 Coach
223-140128 Sleeper
223-140228 Railway Post Office
223-140428 Observation
223-140728 Diner
223-140828 Baggage

Louisville & Nashville
223-1400212 Coach
223-1401212 Pullman
223-1402212 Railway Post Office
223-1404212 Observation
223-1406212 Dome
223-1407212 Diner
223-1408212 Baggage

Milwaukee Road
223-1400125 Coach
223-1401125 Pullman
223-1402125 Railway Post Office
223-1404125 Observation
223-1406125 Dome
223-1407125 Diner
223-1408125 Baggage

"Hiawatha" Passenger Car Sets 169.98 ea (Unless Noted)
223-41011 Set #1
Includes seven passenger cars and one 50' express box car.
223-41012 Set #2
Includes seven passenger cars and one 50' express freight box car.
223-41206 50' Double-Door Express Box Car 9.98

Missouri Pacific
223-1400211 Coach
223-1401211 Pullman
223-1402211 Railway Post Office
223-1404211 Observation
223-1406211 Dome
223-1407211 Diner
223-1408211 Baggage

New York Central
223-1400117 Coach
223-1401117 Pullman
223-1402117 Railway Post Office
223-1404117 Observation
223-1406117 Dome
223-1407117 Diner
223-1408117 Baggage

Nickel Plate Road
223-400126 Coach
223-401126 Pullman
223-402126 Railway Post Office
223-404126 Observation
223-406126 Dome
223-407126 Diner
223-408126 Baggage

Norfolk & Western
223-140012 Coach
223-140112 Pullman
223-140212 Railway Post Office
223-140412 Observation
223-140612 Dome
223-140712 Diner
223-140812 Baggage

Norfolk Southern
223-140021 Coach
223-140121 Pullman
223-140221 Railway Post Office
223-140421 Observation
223-140621 Dome
223-140721 Diner
223-140821 Baggage

Northern Pacific
223-1400213 Coach
223-1401213 Pullman
223-1402213 Railway Post Office
223-1404213 Observation
223-1406213 Dome
223-1407213 Diner
223-1408213 Baggage

Pennsylvania
223-140011 Coach
223-140111 Pullman
223-140211 Railway Post Office
223-140411 Observation
223-140611 Dome
223-140711 Diner
223-140811 Baggage

"Senator"
223-1400121 Coach
223-1401121 Pullman
223-1402121 Railway Post Office
223-1404121 Observation
223-1406121 Dome
223-1407121 Diner
223-1408121 Baggage

Amtrak Phase II Coach 223-1400110

Baltimore & Ohio Observation 223-404123

Chicago & North Western Observation 223-1404120

Erie Lackawanna Pullman 223-401111

Lackawanna Railway Post Office 223-140228

Nickel Plate Road Coach 223-400126

Pennsylvania "Senator" Diner 223-1407121

PASSENGER CARS N SCALE

Rio Grande
223-1400114 Coach
223-1401114 Pullman
223-1402114 Railway Post Office
223-1404114 Observation
223-1406114 Dome
223-1407114 Diner
223-1408114 Baggage

Royal American Shows
223-140013 Coach
223-140113 Pullman
223-140213 Railway Post Office
223-140413 Observation
223-140613 Dome
223-140713 Diner
223-140813 Baggage

Southern
223-1400112 Coach
223-1401112 Pullman
223-1402112 Railway Post Office
223-1404112 Observation
223-1406112 Dome
223-1407112 Diner
223-1408112 Baggage

Southern Pacific
"Daylight"
223-140016 Coach
223-140116 Pullman
223-140216 Railway Post Office
223-140416 Observation
223-140616 Dome
223-140716 Diner
223-140816 Baggage

"Golden State"
223-1400214 Coach
223-1401214 Pullman
223-1402214 Railway Post Office
223-1404214 Observation
223-1406214 Dome
223-1407214 Diner
223-1408214 Baggage

"San Joaquin" (silver)
223-1400113 Coach
223-1401113 Pullman
223-1402113 Railway Post Office
223-1404113 Observation
223-1406113 Dome
223-1407113 Diner
223-1408113 Baggage

Union Pacific
223-140015 Coach
223-140115 Pullman
223-140215 Railway Post Office
223-140415 Observation
223-140615 Dome
223-140715 Diner
223-140815 Baggage

"Overland"
223-140024 Coach
223-140124 Pullman
223-140224 Railway Post Office
223-140424 Observation
223-140624 Dome
223-140724 Diner
223-140824 Baggage

VIA Rail
223-140022 Coach
223-140122 Pullman
223-140222 Railway Post Office
223-140422 Observation
223-140622 Dome
223-140722 Diner
223-140822 Baggage

Undecorated
223-1400130 Coach
223-1401130 Pullman
223-1402130 Railway Post Office
223-1404130 Observation
223-1406130 Dome
223-1407130 Diner
223-1408130 Baggage

Car Set
223-40050 Set of 8 **127.84**
Includes two each; Coach, Pullman, Baggage and Observation.

SUPERLINERS®

Amtrak® 19.98 ea (Unless Noted)

Phase II
223-4601 Coach
223-4611 Dining Car
223-4621 Coach/Baggage
223-4631 Sleeper
223-4641 Lounge Cafe
223-4651 5-Car Set **99.90**

Phase III
223-4602 Coach
223-4612 Dining Car
223-4622 Coach/Baggage
223-4632 Sleeper
223-4642 Lounge Cafe
223-4652 5-Car Set **99.90**

Phase IV
223-4603 Coach
223-4613 Dining Car
223-4623 Coach/Baggage
223-4633 Sleeper
223-4643 Lounge Cafe
223-4653 5-Car Set **99.90**

MATERIAL HANDLING CARS

223-4683 Amtrak® – US Post Office Logo **16.98**
223-4681 Amtrak Phase III **15.98**
223-4685 Amtrak Phase IV **16.98**
223-4686 Amtrak Phase IV pkg(3) **53.89**
223-4680 Undecorated **17.98**

SMOOTHSIDE STREAMLINED 5-CAR SETS
79.90 ea
Include one each of coach, sleeper, baggage, observation, dome and diner cars.
223-4009 SOU
223-4017 MILW
223-4018 Lackawanna
223-4020 B&O
223-4023 EL
223-4024 IC
223-4025 Kansas City Southern
223-4029 ATSF "Blue Goose" #1
223-14030 MP

BUDD PASSENGER CARS
24.98 ea (Unless Noted)
Ready-to-run cars.

Amtrak® Phase III
223-420109 Coach
223-421109 10/6 Sleeper
223-422109 Slumber Coach
223-423109 72' Baggage
223-424109 Dome **29.98**
223-425109 Dome/Observation **32.98**
223-426109 Parlor
223-427109 Railway Post Office
223-428109 Diner **27.98**
223-429109 Twin Window
223-430109 Round End Observation **32.98**
223-450109 Pullman - Standard Pleasure Dome **27.98**

Amtrak Phase IV
223-420111 Coach
223-421111 10/6 Sleeper
223-422111 Slumber Coach
223-423111 72' Baggage
223-424111 Dome **29.98**
223-425111 Dome/Observation **32.98**
223-426111 Parlor
223-427111 Railway Post Office
223-428111 Diner **27.98**
223-429111 Twin Window
223-430111 Round End Observation **32.98**
223-450111 Pullman - Standard Pleasure Dome **27.98**

Atlantic Coast Line
223-420107 Coach
223-421107 10/6 Sleeper
223-422107 Slumber Coach
223-423107 72' Baggage
223-424107 Dome **29.98**
223-425107 Dome/Observation **32.98**
223-426107 Parlor
223-427107 Railway Post Office
223-428107 Diner **27.98**
223-429107 Twin Window
223-430107 Round End Observation **32.98**
223-450107 Pullman - Standard Pleasure Dome **27.98**

Baltimore & Ohio
223-420106 Coach
223-421106 10/6 Sleeper
223-422106 Slumber Coach
223-423106 72' Baggage
223-424106 Dome **29.98**
223-425106 Dome/Observation **32.98**
223-426106 Parlor
223-427106 Railway Post Office
223-428106 Diner **27.98**
223-429106 Twin Window
223-430106 Round End Observation **32.98**
223-450106 Pullman - Standard Pleasure Dome **27.98**

California Zephyr
223-420112 Coach
223-421112 10/6 Sleeper
223-422112 Slumber Coach
223-423112 72' Baggage
223-424112 Dome **29.98**
223-425112 Dome/Observation **32.98**
223-426112 Parlor
223-427112 Railway Post Office
223-428112 Diner **27.98**
223-429112 Twin Window
223-430112 Round End Observation **32.98**
223-450112 Pullman - Standard Pleasure Dome **27.98**

Royal American Show Carnival Baggage 223-140813

Rio Grande Dome 223-1406114

Southern Pacific "San Joaquin" RPO 223-1402113

Amtrak Phase IV 10/6 Sleeper 223-421111

For Up-To-Date Information and News Bookmark Walthers Web site at
www.walthers.com

PASSENGER CARS N SCALE

Canadian Pacific
223-420110 Coach
223-421110 10/6 Sleeper
223-422110 Slumber Coach
223-423110 72' Baggage
223-424110 Dome **29.98**
223-425110 Dome/Observation **32.98**
223-426110 Parlor
223-427110 Railway Post Office
223-428110 Diner **27.98**
223-429110 Twin Window
223-430110 Round End Observation **32.98**
223-450110 Pullman - Standard Pleasure Dome **27.98**

Chicago, Burlington & Quincy
223-420105 Coach
223-421105 10/6 Sleeper
223-422105 Slumber Coach
223-423105 72' Baggage
223-424105 Dome **29.98**
223-425105 Dome/Observation **32.98**
223-426105 Parlor
223-427105 Railway Post Office
223-428105 Diner **27.98**
223-429105 Twin Window
223-430105 Round End Observation **32.98**
223-450105 Pullman - Standard Pleasure Dome **27.98**

Florida East Coast
223-420108 Coach
223-421108 10/6 Sleeper
223-422108 Slumber Coach
223-423108 72' Baggage
223-424108 Dome **29.98**
223-425108 Dome/Observation **32.98**
223-426108 Parlor
223-427108 Railway Post Office
223-428108 Diner **27.98**
223-429108 Twin Window
223-430108 Round End Observation **32.98**
223-450108 Pullman - Standard Pleasure Dome **27.98**

New York Central
223-420102 Coach
223-421102 10/6 Sleeper
223-422102 Slumber Coach
223-423102 72' Baggage
223-424102 Dome **29.98**
223-425102 Dome/Observation **32.98**
223-426102 Parlor

223-427102 Railway Post Office
223-428102 Diner **27.98**
223-429102 Twin Window
223-430102 Round End Observation **32.98**
223-450102 Pullman - Standard Pleasure Dome **27.98**

Pennsylvania
223-420103 Coach
223-421103 10/6 Sleeper
223-422103 Slumber Coach
223-423103 72' Baggage
223-424103 Dome **29.98**
223-425103 Dome/Observation **32.98**
223-426103 Parlor
223-427103 Railway Post Office
223-428103 Diner **27.98**
223-429103 Twin Window
223-430103 Round End Observation **32.98**
223-450103 Pullman - Standard Pleasure Dome **27.98**

Santa Fe
223-420101 Coach
223-421101 10/6 Sleeper
223-422101 Slumber Coach
223-423101 72' Baggage
223-424101 Dome **29.98**
223-425101 Dome/Observation **32.98**
223-426101 Parlor
223-427101 Railway Post Office
223-428101 Diner **27.98**
223-429101 Twin Window
223-430101 Round End Observation **32.98**
223-450101 Pullman - Standard Pleasure Dome **27.98**

Southern "Crescent"
223-420115 Coach
223-421115 10/6 Sleeper
223-422115 Slumber Coach
223-423115 72' Baggage
223-424115 Dome **29.98**
223-425115 Dome/Observation **32.98**
223-426115 Parlor
223-427115 Railway Post Office
223-428115 Diner **27.98**
223-429115 Twin Window
223-430115 Round End Observation **32.98**
223-450115 Pullman - Standard Pleasure Dome **27.98**

Southern Railway
223-420104 Coach
223-421104 10/6 Sleeper
223-422104 Slumber Coach
223-423104 72' Baggage
223-424104 Dome **29.98**
223-425104 Dome/Observation **32.98**
223-426104 Parlor

223-427104 Railway Post Office
223-428104 Diner **27.98**
223-429104 Twin Window
223-430104 Round End Observation **32.98**
223-450104 Pullman - Standard Pleasure Dome **27.98**

Southern Pacific "Daylight"
223-420116 Coach
223-421116 10/6 Sleeper
223-422116 Slumber Coach
223-423116 72' Baggage
223-424116 Dome **29.98**
223-425116 Dome/Observation **32.98**
223-426116 Parlor
223-427116 Railway Post Office
223-428116 Diner **27.98**
223-429116 Twin Window
223-430116 Round End Observation **32.98**
223-450116 Pullman - Standard Pleasure Dome **27.98**

Union Pacific
223-420114 Coach
223-421114 10/6 Sleeper
223-422114 Slumber Coach
223-423114 72' Baggage
223-424114 Dome **29.98**
223-425114 Dome/Observation **32.98**
223-426114 Parlor
223-427114 Railway Post Office
223-428114 Diner **27.98**
223-429114 Twin Window
223-430114 Round End Observation **32.98**
223-450114 Pullman - Standard Pleasure Dome **27.98**

VIA Rail
223-420113 Coach
223-421113 10/6 Sleeper
223-422113 Slumber Coach
223-423113 72' Baggage
223-424113 Dome **29.98**
223-425113 Dome/Observation **32.98**
223-426113 Parlor
223-427113 Railway Post Office
223-428113 Diner **27.98**
223-429113 Twin Window
223-430113 Round End Observation **32.98**
223-450113 Pullman - Standard Pleasure Dome **27.98**

Undecorated
223-420100 Coach
223-421100 10/6 Sleeper
223-422100 Slumber Coach
223-423100 72' Baggage
223-424100 Dome **29.98**

Corrugated Bi-Levels at left, Smoothside Bi-Levels at right Assorted Roadnames Shown

Viewliners Amtrak Phase III Sleeper (#223-4661) & Diner/Lounge (#223-4671)

Southern Railway "Crescent Limited" RPO Car Shown Not Available

223-425100 Dome/Observation **32.98**
223-426100 Parlor
223-427100 Railway Post Office
223-428100 Diner **27.98**
223-429100 Twin Window
223-430100 Round End Observation **32.98**
223-450100 Pullman - Standard Pleasure Dome **27.98**

BI-LEVELS

Corrugated 19.98 ea

Amtrak
223-4436 Cab Unit
223-4426 Coach

Burlington
223-4434 Cab Unit
223-4424 Coach

Burlington Northern Santa Fe
223-4438 Cab Unit
223-4428 Coach

METRA
223-4437 Cab Unit
223-4427 Coach

Milwaukee Road
223-4431 Cab Unit
223-4421 Coach

Rock Island
223-4433 Cab Unit
223-4423 Coach

Southern Pacific
223-4432 Cab Unit
223-4422 Coach

Undecorated
223-4430 Cab Unit
223-4420 Coach

Smoothside 19.98 ea

Amtrak
223-4417 Cab Unit
223-4407 Coach

Rock Island
223-4414 Cab Unit
223-4404 Coach

METRA
223-4416 Cab Unit
223-4406 Coach

Milwaukee Road
223-4411 Cab Unit
223-4401 Coach

Rock Island
223-4413 Cab Unit
223-4403 Coach

Southern Pacific
223-4412 Cab Unit
223-4402 Coach

Undecorated
223-4410 Cab Unit
223-4400 Coach

VIEWLINERS
19.98 ea

Amtrak Phase III
223-4661 Sleeper
223-4671 Diner/Lounge

Amtrak Phase IV
223-4662 Sleeper
223-4672 Diner/Lounge

Undecorated
223-4660 Sleeper
223-4670 Diner/Lounge

PASSENGER CARS N SCALE

Please visit Walthers Web site at www.walthers.com for a complete listing of all available items.

DETAIL KITS

Items listed below are available by Special Order (see Legend Page).
344-3100 For "California Zephyr" Cars **7.00**
344-3103 Photo-Etched Brass Kit For 1939 "Hiawatha" 9 Car **4.25**

ETCHED BRASS CAR SIDES

Harriman Style Cars 14.00 ea
344-3450 60' RPO
344-3460 60' Baggage Without Skirts

Pullman-Standard Cars
Santa Fe 17.50 ea
344-3435 10/3/2 Sleeper w/Skirts

Item listed below is available by Special Order (see Legend Page).
344-3490 Baggage/Dorm w/Skirts

Southern Pacific 19.00 ea (Unless Noted)
344-3442 Fluted Tavern - Plated
344-3448 Pullman 3 Car Articulated Diner/Kitchen/Coffee Shop **45.00**

1939 MILWAUKEE ROAD "HIAWATHA" PASSENGER CARS & ACCESSORIES

Individual Cars 23.00 ea
Items listed below are available by Special Order (see Legend Page).
344-3003A 60' Railway Post Office
344-3003B Express Tap
344-3003CD 1939 Hiawatha 80' Parlor Less Trucks
344-3003EH 80' Coach
344-3003I 1939 Hiawatha Diner Less Trucks
344-3003J 1939 Hiawatha 80' Observation Less Trucks

NEW PRODUCTS

Smooth-Side GN Passenger Cars

Re-create the famous trains of the Great Northern Railway on your layout with these sets and individual cars. Models come fully assembled and finished in orange and green. Interior LED lighting is easily added with kit #381-11209 for a single car or #381-11210 for six cars (both sold separately) - complete details can be found in the Lighting-Electrical-Motors section of this Reference Book.

4-Car Sets 100.00 ea
NEW 381-1061051 Set A: Sleeper, Dome, Diner & Observation
NEW 381-1061052 Set B: Railway Post Office, Baggage, Coach & Diner
NEW 381-1061053 Set C: Coach, Dome, 2 Sleepers

Single Cars 25.00 ea
NEW 381-1560701 Dome Car
NEW 381-1560702 Coach
NEW 381-1560703 Sleeper

BUSINESS CARS

29.98 ea
Let the world know you've made it big with your own private business car! Perfect for touring any railroad, business or pleasure trips will be more fun aboard these N Scale models. Based on a Burlington prototype built by Budd, the cars are highly detailed with corrugated sides and an open rear platform. Cars are finished in silver with black lettering. For additional realism, LED interior lighting can be added with #381-11209, sold separately.

381-1560817 SP "SP 150"
381-1560818 Southern Pacific "SSW Cottonland"

HEAVYWEIGHTS

Coaches 15.98 ea
490-8614 Circus
490-8619 CN
490-8620 ATSF
490-8621 PRR
490-8623 Amtrak®
490-8624 SOU
490-8615 Undecorated

Combines 15.98 ea
490-8617 NYC
490-8625 ATSF
490-8626 PRR
490-8627 Amtrak
490-8628 SOU
490-8629 CN
490-8622 Undecorated

Observation Cars 15.98 ea
490-8618 NYC
490-8630 ATSF
490-8631 PRR
490-8633 Amtrak
490-8634 SOU
490-8635 CN
490-8636 Circus
490-8632 Undecorated

Heavyweight Coach 480-8616

75' Streamlined Coach 480-3037

Heavyweight Combine 480-8626

Heavyweight Observation Car 480-8630

75' Streamlined Observation Car 480-3043

75' STREAMLINED

Coaches 15.98 ea (Unless Noted)
490-3031 UP
490-3032 ATSF
490-3033 Amtrak
490-3035 CN
490-3036 CP
490-3037 BN
490-3038 PRR
490-3039 SP **16.98**
490-3030 Undecorated

Vista Domes 15.98 ea (Unless Noted)

490-3052

490-3051 UP
490-3052 ATSF
490-3055 CN
490-3056 CP
490-3057 BN
490-3058 PRR
490-3059 SP **16.98**
490-3050 Undecorated

Observation Cars 15.98 ea (Unless Noted)
490-3041 UP
490-3042 ATSF
490-3043 Amtrak
490-3045 CN
490-3046 CP
490-3047 BN
490-3048 PRR
490-3049 SP **16.98**
490-3040 Undecorated

PALACE CAR COMPANY

Modernize and detail passenger car interiors quickly and easily with these one-piece parts. Easily painted and installed in ready-to-run cars, kits or scratchbuilt models, parts are typical of seating found in many types of cars.

NEW PRODUCTS

Passenger Car Interior Details

Coach Seats 7.95 ea

NEW 548-5042 Coach Seats - 76 Passenger

NEW 548-5050 Superliner Coach Interior

New Arrivals Updated Every Day! Visit Walthers Web site at
www.walthers.com

67

PASSENGER CARS N SCALE

TOMAR INDUSTRIES

Drumhead kits include illustrated instructions, cast and machined housing, 1.5V micro-miniature lamp, full-color sign, light diffuser and constant lighting components (four diodes, ballast lamp and hookup wire) which operate from track power. (Cars may require modification to provide electrical pick-up.) Kits can also be battery powered using #81-812, sold separately. Single kits are $11.45, while double kits (parts for one car with two tailsigns) are $18.45 each. For a complete listing, visit walthers Web site at www.walthers.com.

LIGHTED DRUMHEAD KITS

Typical Applications
Rectangular housing mounted on streamlined observation car. Round drumhead mounted on heavyweight observation platform railings. (Some may use rectangular housing).

Housing Styles & Shapes
- Pennsy Keystone
- Square
- Round
- Rectangular

Roadnames
- Alaska
- Algoma Central
- Amtrak
- Atchison, Topeka & Santa Fe
- Atlantic Coast Line
- Baltimore & Ohio
- Boston & Maine
- Canadian National
- Canadian Pacific
- Central New Jersey
- Chesapeake & Ohio
- Chicago & Alton
- Chicago, Burlington & Quincy
- Chicago & Eastern Illinois
- Chicago Great Western
- Chicago, Indianapolis & Louisville (Monon)
- Chicago & North Western
- Chicago, Rock Island & Pacific
- CMSTP&P (MILW)
- Colorado Midland
- Cotton Belt
- Delaware & Hudson
- Delaware, Lackawanna & Western
- Denver & Rio Grande
- Duluth, Missabe & Iron Range
- East Broad Top
- Erie
- Florida East Coast
- Grand Trunk Western
- Great Northern
- Green Bay & Western
- Gulf, Mobile & Northern
- Gulf, Mobile & Ohio
- Illinois Central
- Kansas City Southern
- Lake Erie, Franklin & Clarion
- Lehigh & New England
- Lehigh Valley
- Long Island
- Louisiana & Arkansas
- Louisville & Nashville
- Michigan Central
- Missouri-Kansas-Texas
- Missouri Kansas
- Missouri Pacific
- NdeM
- New York, New Haven & Hartford
- New York Central
- Nickel Plate Road
- Norfolk & Western
- Northern Pacific
- Northwestern Pacific
- Ontario Northland
- Pennsylvania
- Pere Marquette
- Reading
- Richmond, Fredericksburg & Potomac
- Rutland
- San Diego & Arizona
- Seaboard Air Line
- Seaboard Coast Line
- Sierra
- Soo Line
- Southern
- Southern Pacific
- Spokane, Portland & Seattle
- St Louis - San Francisco
- Texas & Pacific
- Texas State
- Union Pacific
- VIA
- Virginia & Truckee
- Wabash
- Western Maryland
- Western Pacific
- White Pass & Yukon

Catalog
For a copy of the latest Catalog, send $5.00 (US funds) to:
Tomar
9520 E. Napier Ave.
Benton Harbor, MI 49022

ACCESSORIES

End-Of-Train Devices 16.50 ea
Fully assembled and painted, includes metal casting with permanent lens, 1.5V lamp, electronic flasher unit, AA battery holder (less battery) and instructions. Choose from red or amber lens to match prototype practice.
- 81-5806 Amber
- 81-5822 Red

Lamps
81-819 1.5V pkg(2) **5.20**
Replacement bulbs for EOTs #5806 or #5822, each sold separately.
81-820 1.5V Axialight Replacement Bulb pkg(2) **3.60**
Replacement lamps for N Scale drumheads.

Flasher Unit
81-5823 **9.95**
Flasher unit with N cell battery holder. Matches unit in End-Of-Train devices.

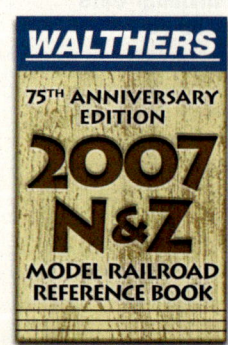

Models and Photo by Jim Berling, University Place, Washington

FREIGHT CARS

Paper is big business for many railroads. Pulpwood and wood chips arrive at paper mills by rail, often in solid trains of pulpwood cars or in huge wood chip hoppers. Chemicals like chlorine for bleaching and clay slurry for making glossy stock arrive in tank cars, other additives come in covered hoppers. A few mills receive coal or oil for firing the boilers; these fuels arrive in hoppers or tank cars, respectively. Finished paper and byproducts are shipped out in box cars and trucks. At the plant, switchers shuttle cars between holding yards and sidings 24 hours per day.

On Jim Berling's layout on-line paper mills generate plenty of traffic. BNSF switches the mills with a pair of Geeps. Over the course of the day, the units will spot loads at the wood chip unloader, tanks at the clay siding and box cars inside the mill buildings. The paper mill buildings are several Cornerstone Series® kits combined into a single complex, locos in the scene are PROTO N from Walthers and Atlas. Vehicles are from Atlas, GHQ and Con-Cor. Freight cars are from several of the manufacturers listed in the Freight Cars Section including Atlas, Red Caboose, Micro-Trains®, Red Caboose and others.

FREIGHT CARS N SCALE

WALTHERS

Walthers N Scale freight cars make it easy to add colorful equipment to your layout. Each car comes fully assembled, with a prepainted body in an authentic scheme, plus trucks and couplers.

NEW PRODUCTS

45' Logging Flat Car
December 2006
- Revised Tooling
- AccuMate® Magnetic Knuckle Couplers
- New Roadnumbers

Single Cars 19.98 ea
- NEW 932-8857 MILW
- NEW 932-8858 BN
- NEW 932-8859 Georgia-Pacific
- NEW 932-8860 UP
- NEW 932-8861 SP
- NEW 932-8862 Chehalis Western

Limited-Run 2-Packs 37.98 ea
- NEW 932-28857 MILW
- NEW 932-28858 BN
- NEW 932-28859 Georgia-Pacific
- NEW 932-28860 UP
- NEW 932-28861 SP
- NEW 932-28862 Chehalis Western

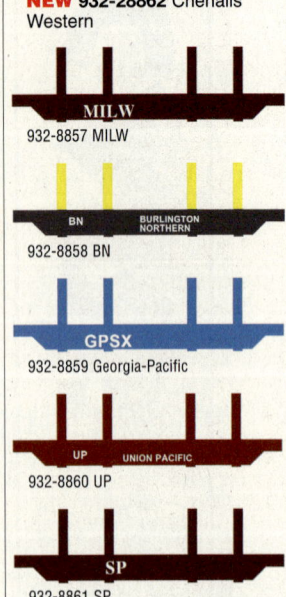

932-8857 MILW
932-8858 BN
932-8859 Georgia-Pacific
932-8860 UP
932-8861 SP
932-8862 Chehalis Western

Difco Dump Car
February 2007
- All-New Tooling
- AccuMate Magnetic Knuckle Couplers
- Great for Work Trains & Rock Service

Single Cars 19.98 ea
- NEW 932-8601 UP
- NEW 932-8602 DMIR
- NEW 932-8603 ATSF
- NEW 932-8604 BNSF
- NEW 932-8605 CSX
- NEW 932-8606 MOW
- NEW 932-8607 SP
- NEW 932-8608 NS
- NEW 932-8609 DRGW
- NEW 932-8610 MILW
- NEW 932-8611 Amtrak
- NEW 932-8612 CP
- NEW 932-8600 Undecorated

Limited-Run 3-Packs 36.98 ea
- NEW 932-38601 UP
- NEW 932-38602 DMIR
- NEW 932-38603 ATSF
- NEW 932-38604 BNSF
- NEW 932-38605 CSX
- NEW 932-38606 MOW
- NEW 932-38607 SP
- NEW 932-38608 NS
- NEW 932-38609 DRGW
- NEW 932-38610 MILW
- NEW 932-38611 Amtrak
- NEW 932-38612 CP

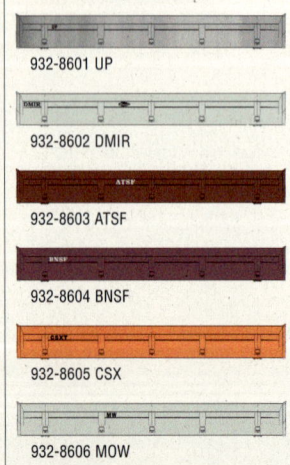

932-8601 UP
932-8602 DMIR
932-8603 ATSF
932-8604 BNSF
932-8605 CSX
932-8606 MOW
932-8607 SP
932-8608 NS
932-8609 DRGW
932-8610 MILW
932-8611 Amtrak
932-8612 CP

GSC "Commonwealth" 54' Flat Car
January 2007
- Revised Tooling
- Bulkheads as Appropriate
- AccuMate Magnetic Knuckle Couplers
- New Roadnames

Single Cars 19.98 ea
- NEW 932-8207 SOO
- NEW 932-8208 PRR
- NEW 932-8209 UP
- NEW 932-8210 ATSF
- NEW 932-8211 BN
- NEW 932-8212 CR
- NEW 932-8213 SP
- NEW 932-8214 NP

Limited-Run Two-Packs 37.98 ea
- NEW 932-28207 SOO
- NEW 932-28208 PRR
- NEW 932-28209 UP
- NEW 932-28210 ATSF
- NEW 932-28211 BN
- NEW 932-28212 CR
- NEW 932-28213 SP
- NEW 932-28214 NP

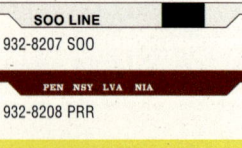

932-8207 SOO
932-8208 PRR
932-8209 UP
932-8210 ATSF
932-8211 BN
932-8212 CR
932-8213 SP
932-8214 NP

45' Logging Flat Car MILW 932-8857

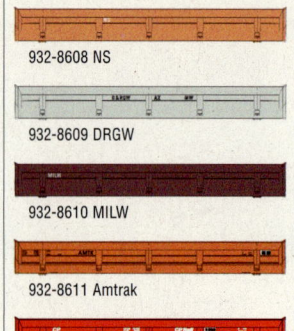

Difco Dump Car CSX 932-8605

GSC "Commonwealth" 54' Flat Car ATSF 932-8210

See What's Available at
www.walthers.com

FREIGHT CARS N SCALE

WALTHERS

WELL CARS

Five-Unit Articulated Well Car 39.98 ea

Thrall introduced a five-unit articulated well car in 1983, equipped with interbox connectors (IBCs) to lock containers on the car using the four corner castings. By the late 1980s, longer 45 and 48' containers were in service, and the design was again reworked to accommodate these heavier loads in the middle wells. The prototype for this model has additional reinforcements and IBCs to carry everything from a pair of 20' containers up to a single 48' container in any of the wells. These ready-to-run models feature authentically painted diecast metal bodies for maximum weight and performance.

932-8108 TTX #72855
932-8109 TTX #72403

Stand-Alone Well Cars

Stand-Alone Well Cars entered service in the early 1990s as larger and heavier containers came into use. With a truck at each end, they have a larger carrying capacity and are easier to maintain than the articulated cars. Some owners run them connected with drawbars as three, four or five "unit cars."

This detailed car has a diecast metal body for maximum weight and superb on-track performance. The cars are ready to run and finished in a variety of colorful schemes.

Single Cars 9.98 ea
932-8051 TTX Scheme
932-8055 CN (blue)
932-8056 CP (orange)
932-8050 Undecorated

Multiple-Unit Cars
932-8053 3-Unit Set - TTX Scheme 27.98
932-8054 4-Unit Set - TTX Scheme 36.98

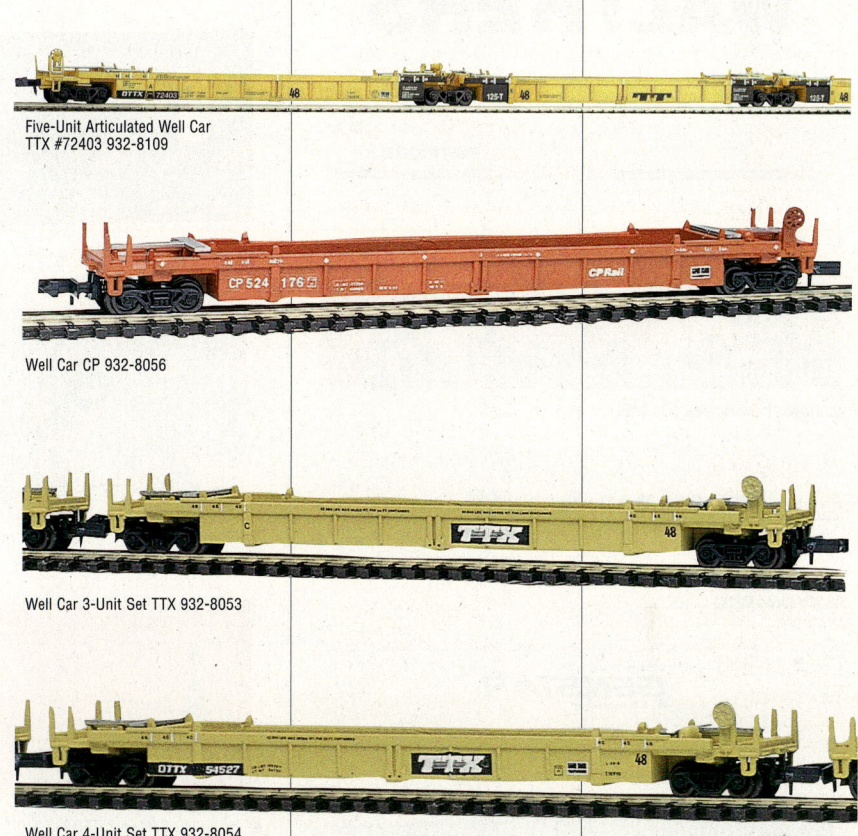

Five-Unit Articulated Well Car TTX #72403 932-8109

Well Car CP 932-8056

Well Car 3-Unit Set TTX 932-8053

Well Car 4-Unit Set TTX 932-8054

BOX CARS

Limited Quantity Available On All Items

50' North American Outside-Braced Insulated Box Car DRGW 932-8802

50' North American Outside-Braced Insulated Box Cars 9.98 ea

Introduced in 1964, these insulated box cars carried loads which required a constant temperature, but didn't need to be refrigerated in transit. This included cereal, beer, canned goods and chocolate, as well as a variety of lubricants and chemicals. Just over 1300 roamed the rails and a few remain in use today.

Individual Cars 9.98 ea
932-8801 CNW
932-8803 Green Bay & Western

932-8804 Nestles (TNCX)

932-8805 Western Pacific
932-8806 Quaker Oats (QOCX)
932-8808 Johnson Wax (JWAX)

CABOOSES

Limited Quantity Available On All Items

Bay Window Caboose BN 932-8754

Bay Window Caboose CR 932-8762

Bay Window Caboose 12.98 ea

Serving as office, lookout, restaurant and hotel to crews on the road, no other piece of rolling stock may be as much a part of railroading as the caboose. Each features finely detailed plastic bodies with appropriate bay windows for each prototype.

932-8754 BN

932-8757 N&W
932-8762 CR

71

FREIGHT CARS N SCALE

WALTHERS

48' Ribbed Container CN 933-3452

48' Ribbed Container APC 933-3456

48' Ribbed Container CR Mercury 933-3457

48' Ribbed Container Genstar 933-3458

40' High-Cube Container Maersk 933-3401

40' High-Cube Container K-Line 933-3404

40' High-Cube Container Hapag-Lloyd 933-3405

40' High-Cube Container Cast 933-3408

40' High-Cube Container APL 933-3402

40' High-Cube Container Mitsui OSK 933-3406

40' High-Cube Container ITEL 933-3407

CONTAINERS

These colorful containers make great loads for the Stand-Alone Well Cars, or as details in your intermodal terminal. The all-plastic containers come ready to use and are prepainted in many different schemes.

40' High-Cube Container 3.98 ea
- 933-3401 Maersk
- 933-3402 APL
- 933-3403 Evergreen
- 933-3404 K-Line
- 933-3405 Hapag-Lloyd
- 933-3406 Mitsui OSK
- 933-3407 ITEL
- 933-3408 Cast
- 933-3400 Undecorated

48' Ribbed Container 3.98 ea
- 933-3451 BN America
- 933-3452 CN
- 933-3453 NS Triple Crown
- 933-3454 JB Hunt
- 933-3455 ATSF
- 933-3456 APC
- 933-3457 CR Mercury
- 933-3458 Genstar
- 933-3450 Undecorated

CONTAINER CRANE

Mi-Jack Translift Intermodal Crane

933-3222   26.98
This kit will be the star of your intermodal terminal! The Translift Crane is a dual-purpose machine, used by many railroads, that can lift trailers or containers. It's wide enough to straddle two rows of trailers or containers parked side by side, making short work of loading or unloading. Many parts of the model are positionable to simulate a working crane. Magnets are included to hold containers securely without gluing. Decals and complete instructions are included. Measures 4 x 3-1/8 x 3".

FREIGHT CARS N SCALE

Division of Wm. K. Walthers, Inc.

FREIGHT CAR ASSORTMENT

Elgin, Joliet & Eastern Box Car

Wabash Box Car

Chessie Hopper

PRR Hopper

Atlantic Coast Line Box Car

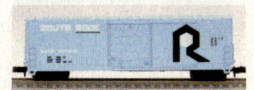
Route Rock Box Car

C&O Reefer

Maine Central Reefer

DRGW Stock Car

GN Stock Car

SHPX Gustafson Bros. Tank Car

SHPX Shipper's Line Corp. Tank Car

433-7600 pkg(24) **210.00**
Includes two each of the following: Elgin, Joliet & Eastern 70-Ton Hi-Cube Box Car, Wabash 70-Ton Hi-Cube Box Car, Chessie 100-Ton Hopper, PRR 100-Ton Hopper, Atlantic Coast Line Evans 50' Box Car, Route Rock Evans 50' Box Car, C&O Reefer, Maine Central Reefer, DRGW Stock Car, GN Stock Car, SHPX Gustafson Brothers Three-Dome Tank Car and SHPX Shipper's Car Line Corp. Three-Dome Tank Car.

CABOOSES

Northeastern-Style Center-Cupola Cabooses 9.75 ea

Limited Quantity Available

433-7723 CNW #10809

433-7971 Chessie/WM #1828

433-7985 New York, Susquehanna & Western

Offset-Cupola Cabooses 9.75 ea

Limited Quantity Available

433-7713 ATSF

433-7720 Florida East Coast

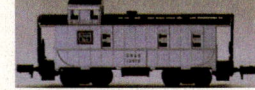
433-7726 CB&Q

AMERICAN LIMITED

Tank Container Kits pkg(2) 7.95 ea

Injection-molded in color, complete with decals.

147-7110 UP Bulktainer (blue w/white tank)
147-7115 UP Bulktainer
147-7120 UP Bulktainer (blue w/silver tank)

147-7130 Alaska West Express (blue w/silver tank)

147-7140 Stolt-Neilsen Leasing (red w/white tank)

CM SHOPS

Coal Loads
12-3111 For Micro-Trains® Twin Hoppers pkg(3) **4.50**

CMX

Track Cleaning Cars

226-CMXN Clean Machine Track Cleaning Car (Brass) w/10 Cleaning Pads **124.95**
226-CMXNPADS Clean Machine Track Cleaning Car Replacement Pads - pkg(20) **5.00**

Get Daily Info, Photos and News at
www.walthers.com

A division of PROTO POWER WEST

HOBBY-TOTE SYSTEM™

Hobby-Tote Storage Containers

Protect your valuable model railroad equipment with these versatile and economical storage containers. For club members or anyone who stores and/or transports model railroad equipment, Hobby-Tote storage containers are a must. They are also handy for storing modeling materials such as styrene, stripwood, wire, detail parts, etc. Hobby-Tote storage containers will last indefinitely with normal use. Hobby-Tote containers are designed to fit into the Hobby-Tote nylon carrying case for easy transport.

Innovative storage container features:
- Tray lids ensure dust-free storage and maximum protection during transport
- Removable chip board dividers
- Made from heavy-duty 250lb test, double-wall corrugated cardboard
- Easy assembly; instructions included
- Clean white exterior
- Additional foam spacers available to provide additional cushioning for the ends of models.

High-Side Containers

High-Side Container 116-19258

Inside dimensions of container: 27" long x 7" wide x 2-3/4" high; four containers fit into nylon case. Each container can hold 98 40' box cars on two internal trays.
116-19257 pkg(2) **45.00**
116-19258 pkg(4) **75.00**
116-19259 Complete System: Case, 4 Containers & Foam Spacers (holds a total of 392 40' cars) **122.00**

Low-Side Containers

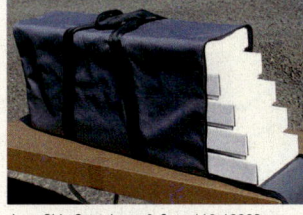

Low-Side Containers & Case 116-19262

Inside dimensions of container: 27" long x 7" wide x 2-1/4" high; five containers fit into nylon case. Each tray can hold 49 40' box cars. These containers are perfect for tall cars like bi-level passenger cars, auto racks and loaded double-stack cars.

116-19260 pkg(2) **34.00**
116-19261 pkg(5) **64.00**
116-19262 Complete System: Case, 4 Containers & Foam Spacers (holds a total of 245 40' cars) **113.00**

Hobby-Tote System Accessories

116-19250 Hobby-Tote Nylon Carrying Case **47.50**
Accommodates up to four hi-side or five low-side storage containers and can be used to transport virtually any scale models and/or supplies. Made from tough, heavy cordura fabric. Features a heavy-duty double zipper closure and strong, comfortable, integral carrying straps.

116-19300 Foam Spacers pkg(24) **3.75**
Foam is placed between ends of cars to protect and separate equipment while in trays.

NEW **116-19301** Foam Liner Material **5.95**
2' Wide x 10' Long x 3/32" Thick
Use this strong, lightweight foam liner material to make a "cradle" to lift equipment in and out of the storage containers. This material provides for even less handling of models, extra protection from damage to painted finish and details, and no more bent locomotive handrails. Foam Liner material is virtually crushproof, lint free, non-abrasive, and chemically inert.

FREIGHT CARS N SCALE

New models and roadnames are released on a monthly basis; visit www.walthers.com for the latest updates.

Limited Quantities Available on All Items Except Undecorated Models

Box Cars

USRA Double-Sheathed Box Cars 13.95 ea (Unless Noted)

All cars are Box Car Red with appropriate markings unless noted.

NEW 150-45710 B&M #70039

NEW 150-45711 B&M #70115
NEW 150-45712 CB&Q #120801

NEW 150-45713 CB&Q #120857

NEW 150-45714 GN #23555 15.95
NEW 150-45715 GN #23715 15.95
NEW 150-45716 EL #44029
NEW 150-45717 EL #44157

NEW 150-45718 Minneapolis & St. Louis #22513
NEW 150-45719 Minneapolis & St. Louis #25108

NEW 150-45720 NYC #14024
NEW 150-45721 NYC #14029
NEW 150-45722 ATSF #38749
NEW 150-45723 ATSF #38850

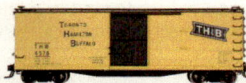

NEW 150-45724 Toronto, Hamilton & Buffalo #4576 15.95
NEW 150-45a725 Toronto, Hamilton & Buffalo #4795 15.95
NEW 150-45700 Undecorated 9.95

USRA 40' Rebuilt Steel Box Car 14.95 ea (Unless Noted)

All cars are Box Car Red with appropriate markings unless noted.

NEW 150-45810 CNW #1672 (green, yellow) 16.95

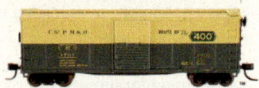

NEW 150-45811 CNW #1701 (green, yellow) 16.95
NEW 150-45812 Elgin, Joliet & Eastern #7621 (green, orange)

NEW 150-45813 Elgin, Joliet & Eastern #7627 (green, orange)

NEW 150-45814 PRR #104287
NEW 150-45815 PRR #105200
NEW 150-45816 ATSF #148850 ("The Chief")

NEW 150-45817 ATSF #148888 ("The Chief")
NEW 150-45818 ATSF #149005 ("The Grand Canyon")
NEW 150-45819 ATSF #149014 ("The Grand Canyon")

NEW 150-45820 Texas & Pacific #80282
NEW 150-45821 Texas & Pacific #81142

NEW 150-45822 UP #181580
NEW 150-45823 UP #181586

NEW 150-45824 Vermont Railway #505 (green, white)
NEW 150-45825 Vermont Railway #524 (green, white)
NEW 150-45800 Undecorated 12.95
NEW 150-45801 Undecorated w/Vertical Brake Wheel 12.95

Hoppers

90-Ton 3-Bay Hopper w/Load 8.50 ea (Unless Noted)

NEW 150-32616 CB&Q #163218 (silver, red)
NEW 150-32626 CB&Q #172503 (red, white)
NEW 150-32636 UP #18431 (Box Car Red, white)
NEW 150-32646 N&W #12569 (black, white)
NEW 150-32655 WM #85014 (gray, black)
NEW 150-32666 WM #63705 (Oxide Red, gray)

NEW 150-32675 MKT #15000 (red, yellow) 8.95
NEW 150-32676 MKT #15334 (red, yellow) 8.95
NEW 150-32685 ATSF #179308 (Mineral Red, white)
NEW 150-32695 Ontario Northland #6008 (green, white)
NEW 150-32706 EL #33637 (black, white)
NEW 150-32715 D&H #1132 (yellow, blue)
NEW 150-32717 SLSF #87820 (black, white)
NEW 150-32726 SOU #360561 (Box Car Red, White)
NEW 150-32736 DRGW #14922 (black, white)
NEW 150-32746 RDG #41764 (black, white) w/Speed Lettering
NEW 150-32756 CRR #54430 (black, white)
NEW 150-32766 PRR #180400 (black, white)

NEW 150-32775 CR #490448 (Box Car Red, white)

NEW 150-32786 C&O #82516 (black, white)

90-Ton 3-Bay Hopper w/Load CSX-CSXT 3-Pack 150-5539

NEW 150-32796 NYC #904940 (black, white)

NEW 150-32806 BN #521420 (black, white)

NEW 150-32817 SLSF #87820 (black, white)
NEW 150-32818 SLSF #88611 (black, white)

NEW 150-32825 Lake Erie, Franklin & Clarion (black, yellow) 8.95
NEW 150-32836 NS #144148 (black, white)

NEW 150-32856 CN #111309 (black, white) 8.95

NEW 150-32865 SOO #60218 (Box Car Red, white)

NEW 150-32875 B&O #186866 (black, yellow) 8.95

NEW 150-32886 C&O #183045 (black, yellow) 8.95

NEW 150-32896 WM #832359 (black, yellow) 8.95

NEW 150-32906 PRR #669112 (black, white)

NEW 150-32916 CSX #811270 (black, yellow) 8.95

NEW 150-32925 PC #480572 (black, white) 8.95

NEW 150-32935 CNW #135838 (green, yellow) 9.50

NEW 150-32944 BN #542000 (black, white) 8.95

NEW 150-32954 L&N #191074 (orange, white) 8.95
NEW 150-32964 Pittsburgh & Lake Erie (black, white, yellow) 9.50
NEW 150-32983 RDG #483863 (black, white) w/Block Lettering 8.95

NEW 150-32993 Seaboard System #341490 (black, red, yellow) 10.50
NEW 150-40411 CSX #806339 (black, yellow) 9.50

NEW 150-40431 SP #481000 (Box Car Red, white) 9.50
NEW 150-40432 SP #481087 (Box Car Red, white) 9.50
NEW 150-32601 Dimensional Data (black)
NEW 150-32602 Dimensional Data (brown)

Three-Packs

NEW 150-5539 CSX-CSXT #808971, 811464 & 814577 (black, yellow) 34.95

FREIGHT CARS N SCALE

70-Ton Hart Ballast Car 18.95 ea (Unless Noted)

All cars are Box Car Red/Mineral Red/brown with appropriate markings unless noted.

NEW 150-34777 CB&Q
NEW 150-34778 CNW
NEW 150-34779 CW
NEW 150-34780 MP (black, white)
NEW 150-34781 SP&S
NEW 150-34782 WC (black, white)

NEW 150-347771 CB&Q #221000
NEW 150-347772 CB&Q #221020
NEW 150-347773 CB&Q #221052
NEW 150-347774 CB&Q #221055
NEW 150-347775 CB&Q #221060
NEW 150-347776 CB&Q #221062
NEW 150-347781 CNW #13501
NEW 150-347782 CNW #13507
NEW 150-347783 CNW #13511
NEW 150-347784 CNW #13523
NEW 150-347785 CNW #13555
NEW 150-347786 CNW #13559

NEW 150-347791 Colorado & Wyoming #14001
NEW 150-347792 Colorado & Wyoming #14007
NEW 150-347793 Colorado & Wyoming #14010
NEW 150-347794 Colorado & Wyoming #14017
NEW 150-347795 Colorado & Wyoming #14022
NEW 150-347796 Colorado & Wyoming #14030
NEW 150-347801 MP #7000 (black, white)
NEW 150-347802 MP #7055 (black, white)
NEW 150-347803 MP #7075 (black, white)

NEW 150-347804 MP #7090 (black, white)
NEW 150-347805 MP #7093 (black, white)
NEW 150-347806 MP #7099 (black, white)
NEW 150-347811 SP&S #21001
NEW 150-347812 SP&S #21004

NEW 150-347813 SP&S #21010
NEW 150-347814 SP&S #21012
NEW 150-347815 SP&S #21020
NEW 150-347816 SP&S #21024
NEW 150-347821 WC #112
NEW 150-347822 WC #125

NEW 150-347823 WC #131
NEW 150-347824 WC #111
NEW 150-347825 WC #122
NEW 150-347826 WC #129
150-34770 Undecorated 14.95

Flat Cars

Pulpwood Flat Car w/Load 15.95 ea (Unless Noted)

NEW 150-38355 ATSF #92900 (Mineral Red)
NEW 150-38356 ATSF #92989 (Mineral Red)
NEW 150-38365 WM #402 (Box Car Red)

NEW 150-38366 WM #406 (Box Car Red)

NEW 150-38413 D&H #8000
NEW 150-38414 D&H #8059

NEW 150-38423 L&N #20553 (Box Car Red)
NEW 150-38424 L&N #20572 (Box Car Red)
NEW 150-38451 Illinois Central Gulf #101367 (orange, black)

NEW 150-38452 Illinois Central Gulf #101371 (orange, black)

NEW 150-38461 St. Louis, Brownsville & Mexico #1050 (black)
150-38300 Undecorated w/Open Ends 10.95
150-38301 Undecorated w/Closed Ends 10.95

Tank Cars

ACF 17,360-Gallon Insulated General-Service Tank Cars 16.95 ea (Unless Noted)

All cars are black with appropriate markings unless noted.

NEW 150-40603 SHPX #240282
NEW 150-40604 SHPX #240381
NEW 150-40611 ACFX Hooker Chemicals #85437

NEW 150-40612 ACFX Hooker Chemicals #85440

NEW 150-40621 GATX #35647 (white w/black center band)
NEW 150-40622 GATX #36376 (white w/black center band)
NEW 150-40631 GATX #35690

NEW 150-40632 GATX #35695
NEW 150-40641 HOKX #132503

70-Ton Hart Ballast Car CNW #13501 150-347781

ACF 11,000-Gallon Tank Car with Platform Hooker Chemicals (SHPX) #1285 150-43772

NEW 150-40642 HOKX #132589
NEW 150-40651 PPGX #1742

NEW 150-40652 PPGX #1866
150-40500 Undecorated 11.95

ACF 11,000-Gallon Tank Cars 16.95 ea (Unless Noted)

All cars are black with appropriate markings unless noted.

Without Platform

NEW 150-43323 Warren (WRNX) #12306 (light gray, black)
NEW 150-43324 Warren (WRNX) #12366 (light gray, black)
NEW 150-43351 Anchor Petroleum (ANPX) #120 (silver, black)

NEW 150-43352 Anchor Petroleum (ANPX) #122 (silver, black)
150-43300 Undecorated 13.95

With Platform

NEW 150-43613 Gulf Oil Corp. (SHPX) #5774 (black, silver, orange, white)
NEW 150-43614 Gulf Oil Corp. (SHPX) #5776 (black, silver, orange, white)

NEW 150-43673 Union Tank Car (ULTX) #96263 (black, yellow)
NEW 150-43674 Union Tank Car (ULTX) #96272 (black, yellow)

NEW 150-43761 Adirondack Bottled Gas (Homgas) Arlington Siding, NY #189

NEW 150-43762 Adirondack Bottled Gas (Homgas) Saranac Lake, NY #431

NEW 150-43763 Adirondack Bottled Gas (Homgas) Hudson Falls, NY #5645

NEW 150-43771 Hooker Chemicals (SHPX) #1284 (black)

NEW 150-43772 Hooker Chemicals (SHPX) #1285 (orange, black)

FREIGHT CARS N SCALE

NEW 150-43781 Mallard Transportation Co. (MTCX) #2005 (black)

NEW 150-43782 Mallard Transportation Co. (MTCX) #2018 (black)

NEW 150-43791 Republic Car Line (RTCX) #8500 (black)

NEW 150-43792 Republic Car Line (RTCX) #8507 (black)

NEW 150-43901 Texas Natural Gasoline Corp. (RTCX) #5252 (black)

NEW 150-43902 Texas Natural Gasoline Corp. (RTCX) #5256 (black)

NEW 150-43911 Wyandotte Chemicals (SHPX) #3715 (silver, black, yellow)

NEW 150-43912 Wyandotte Chemicals (SHPX) #3722 (silver, black, yellow)

150-43600 Undecorated **13.95**

Cabooses

Extended-Vision Cupola Cabooses

With Micro-Trains® Couplers

NEW 150-30218 BN #10586 (green, yellow) **24.95**

NEW 150-30237 Chessie/C&O #C-3188 (yellow, vermillion, blue) **24.95**

NEW 150-30238 Chessie/C&O #C-3190 (yellow, vermillion, blue) **24.95**

NEW 150-30257 SSW #40 (brown, orange) **19.95**

NEW 150-30258 SSW #45 (brown, orange) **19.95**

NEW 150-30267 D&H #35794 (red, yellow, black) **21.95**

NEW 150-30268 D&H #35797 (red, yellow, black) **21.95**

NEW 150-30558 Chessie Safety #6 #903246 (blue, white, silver) **27.95**

NEW 150-30638 Detroit & Toledo Shore Line #130 (red, white) **25.95**

NEW 150-30639 Detroit & Toledo Shore Line #132 (red, white) **25.95**

NEW 150-30648 Housatonic #654 (yellow, green) **24.95**

NEW 150-30649 Duluth, Winnipeg & Pacific #53101 (red, blue, white) **35.95**

NEW 150-30658 Family Lines/CRR #1090 (orange, black) **27.95**

NEW 150-30659 Family Lines/CRR #1091 (orange, black) **27.95**

NEW 150-30668 Illinois Central Gulf #199044 (orange, black, white) **22.95**

NEW 150-30669 Illinois Central Gulf #199045 (orange, black, white) **22.95**

150-30528 No Roofwalk Undecorated **17.95**

150-30529 With Roofwalk Undecorated **17.95**

With Rapido Couplers

NEW 150-30214 BN #10586 (green, yellow) **18.95**

NEW 150-30233 Chessie/C&O #C-3188 (yellow, vermillion, blue) **18.95**

NEW 150-30234 Chessie/C&O #C-3190 (yellow, vermillion, blue) **18.95**

NEW 150-30252 SSW #40 (brown, orange) **13.95**

NEW 150-30253 SSW #45 (brown, orange) **13.95**

NEW 150-30262 D&H #35794 (red, yellow, black) **15.95**

NEW 150-30263 D&H #35797 (red, yellow, black) **15.95**

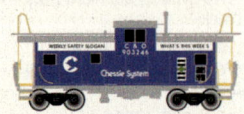

NEW 150-30552 Chessie Safety #6 #903246 (blue, white, silver) **21.95**

NEW 150-30631 Detroit & Toledo Shore Line #130 (red, white) **19.95**

NEW 150-30632 Detroit & Toledo Shore Line #132 (red, white) **19.95**

NEW 150-30641 Duluth, Winnipeg & Pacific #53101 (red, blue, white) **29.95**

NEW 150-30642 Housatonic #654 (yellow, green) **18.95**

NEW 150-30651 Family Lines/CRR #1090 (orange, black) **21.95**

NEW 150-30652 Family Lines/CRR #1091 (orange, black) **21.95**

NEW 150-30661 Illinois Central Gulf #199044 (orange, black, white) **16.95**

NEW 150-30662 Illinois Central Gulf #199045 (orange, black, white) **16.95**

150-30200 No Roofwalk Undecorated **11.95**

150-30520 With Roofwalk Undecorated **11.95**

International Standard-Cupola Cabooses

Details include endrails, window glazing, roofwalks, open smokestack, and separate cylinder, triple valve and reservoir.

With Micro-Trains® Couplers

NEW 150-43006 GN #X39 (red, white, black) **24.95**

NEW 150-43007 GN #X74 (red, white, black) **24.95**

NEW 150-43096 NS "Research Car" #49 (gray, black) **21.95**

NEW 150-43097 NS "Research Car" #51 (gray, black) **21.95**

NEW 150-43098 NS "Horse Head Logo" #555074 (red) **21.95**

NEW 150-43099 NS "Horse Head Logo" #555518 (red) **21.95**

With Rapido Couplers

NEW 150-43003 GN #X39 (red) **18.95**

NEW 150-43004 GN #X74 (red) **18.95**

NEW 150-43091 NS "Research Car" #49 (gray, black) **15.95**

NEW 150-43092 NS "Research Car" #51 (gray, black) **15.95**

NEW 150-43093 NS "Horse Head Logo" #555074 (red) **21.95**

NEW 150-43094 NS "Horse Head Logo" #555518 (red) **21.95**

150-43000 Undecorated **11.95**

BOX CARS

USRA Single-Sheathed Box Cars

Extended-Vision Cupola Caboose with Rapido Couplers Detroit & Toledo Shore Line #132 150-30632

Modeled after the World War I-era cars designed by the United States Railway Administration, these cars, and thousands of copies built after the war, were common on every railroad in North America. Cars feature two different styles of ends as appropriate for each roadname.

150-41700 Undecorated, 7-8 Rib Ends **8.95**

ACF 50' Single-Door Precision-Design Box Car Roadname Shown Not Available

150-41701 Undecorated, 5-5-5 Rib Ends **8.95**

ACF 50' Single-Door Precision-Design Box Cars

150-45000 Smooth Side Undecorated **12.95**

REEFERS

40' Ice-Cooled Wood Reefers

Based on cars built by Pullman for the Northern Refrigerator Car Co. in 1930. Thousands of similar cars took to the rails during this era, many wearing colorful billboard schemes.

150-41400 Undecorated **9.95**

GONDOLAS

Coalveyor Bathub Gondolas

150-43800 Undecorated **10.95**

ARTICULATED AUTO CARRIERS

These partially-assembled models are complete with prototypical painting and lettering, diecast chassis, end door detail, articulated diaphragm, 70-ton roller-bearing trucks and AccuMate knuckle couplers. The halves of these models are easily connected together following the manufacturer's directions. Because of their size, a minimum radius of 9-3/4" is recommended. All cars wear TTX yellow with appropriate heralds.

150-40900 Undecorated **29.95**

FREIGHT CARS N SCALE

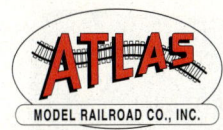

ATLAS MODEL RAILROAD CO., INC.

TANK CARS

Kaolin Tank Car
150-34800 Undecorated **10.95**

33,000-Gallon Tank Cars
150-37000 Undecorated **13.95**

Trinity 17,600-Gallon Corn Syrup Tank Cars
Constructed between 1994 and 1998, over 7,000 of these cars were built, and many still ply the continent's rails. Like the prototypes, the cars feature three different top platform/handrail styles as appropriate for each roadname.

150-40200 Undecorated, ADM/MCP Style **12.95**

150-40201 Undecorated, Cargill Style **12.95**

150-40202 Undecorated, Corn Products Style **12.95**

CABOOSES

International Car Company NE-6 Cabooses
Based on cars used by a variety of northeastern and midwestern railroads, these distinctive steel-sided cabooses will look perfect on your transition and diesel-era freights. Cars have appropriate window placement as appropriate for each roadname.

150-33400 Undecorated, NH Style (Windows Closer to Cupola) **12.95**

150-33401 Undecorated, NKP Style (Windows Farther from Cupola) **12.95**

INTERMODAL TRAILERS

24' Trailers pkg(2) 9.95 (Unless Noted)
150-2931 B&O (blue, orange)

150-2932 CN
150-2933 CP (green, yellow)
150-2934 GN (green, orange)
150-2935 M&M (red, yellow)
150-2936 NYC Pacemaker (red, gray)
150-2937 PRR (Tuscan Red)
150-2938 REA Leasing (silver, black)
150-2939 SP (silver)
150-2998 Minneapolis & St. Louis (red, white)
150-2930 Undecorated **8.50**

40' Trailers pkg(2) 11.95 (Unless Noted)
150-2952 CNW (yellow, green)
150-2953 PRR (Tuscan Red)
150-2954 ATSF (red, silver)
150-2955 PFE (silver, orange, black)
150-2956 NKP (silver, blue)
150-2957 B&O (silver, blue, yellow)
150-2958 BC Rail (green)
150-2959 EL (silver, maroon)
150-2999 Rock Island (silver, red, white)
150-2951 Undecorated **10.95**

MAINTENANCE-OF-WAY

Track Cleaning Car 65.95 ea
Keep trains running smoothly on clean track. Each car includes three dry-type cleaning discs, three moist-type cleaning discs, vacuum fan disc (installed), disc changing tool, brush and sponge. Car comes equipped with Rapido-type couplers only. Cleaning fluid sold separately (any commercially available track cleaning fluid may be used according to manufacturer's directions).

150-32550 Atlas #1949 (yellow, black, red, white)

150-32551 MOW No Number (gray, black, yellow)
150-32554 MOW No Number (orange, black)
150-32555 MOW No Number (yellow, black)

ADAIR SHOPS

NEW PRODUCTS
Freight Car Loads

Rite-Wey™ Steel Plate Loads w/Spacers
Measurements in scale feet.

Flat Cars
Thick
NEW 143-7030 8 x 20' **3.20**
NEW 143-7031 8 x 30' **3.60**
NEW 143-7032 10 x 20' **3.20**
NEW 143-7033 10 x 25' **4.10**
NEW 143-7034 10 x 30' **3.60**

Gondolas
Thick
NEW 143-7039 6 x 45' **3.60**
NEW 143-7040 6 x 60' **3.80**
NEW 143-7041 6 x 45' **3.60**
NEW 143-7042 6 x 60' **3.80**

FREIGHT CAR LOADS

Rite-Wey™ Steel Plate Loads with Spacers
(measurements in scale feet)

Flat Cars
143-7020 6 x 20' **3.60**
143-7021 5 x 20' **3.60**
143-7022 4 x 20' **4.10**

Gondola Cars
143-7023 6 x 20' **2.70**
143-7024 5 x 20' **2.70**
143-7025 4 x 20' **3.20**
NEW 143-7029 6 x 30' **3.60**

GHQ

90-Ton Depressed Center Flat Car Twinpack

284-50006 Undecorated Kit Less Trucks & Couplers pkg(2) **17.95**

See What's New and Exciting at
www.walthers.com

ARNOLD/RIVAROSSI

EUROPEAN EQUIPMENT
These N Scale ready-to-run cars feature prepainted and lettered plastic bodies and a variety of details as noted.

Limited Quantity Available On All Items

Box Cars
46' Box Car
125-4457 DB Internal US **33.99**

Gondolas
Type E Gondola

Roadname Shown Not Available
125-4795 BLS **22.99**

33' Gondola

125-4672 SNCF Ommr 33 **24.99**

Tank Cars
52' Modern Tank Car
125-4384 OBB OMV **35.99**
125-4396 Class GmbH "Intern Oil" **33.99**

Jaeger

Bulkhead Flat Car Loads pkg(2) 15.00 ea
Protected building product loads are assembled and will fit Micro-Trains® 61-1/2' bulkhead flat car.

347-3
347-1 Evans Products
347-2 Gold Bond Products
347-3 Johns-Manville
347-4 Masonite
347-5 Plum Creek
347-6 US Gypsum
347-7 Georgia-Pacific
347-8 Lignum
347-9 Louisiana-Pacific

PM Period Miniatures

These freight car loads are resin and can be used with Bachmann, Micro-Trains®, Con-Cor, Atlas, Dimi Trains or Roundhouse N Scale cars.

FREIGHT CAR LOADS

Flat Car Loads
555-825 Lumber Load pkg(8) **10.45**
555-826 Machinery Load, Crated pkg(12) **10.95**

Scrap Loads pkg(2) 7.15 ea
555-850 Dimi Trains 40' Gondola
555-853 Micro-Trains 50' Gondola
555-858 Con-Cor 50' Gondola
555-868 Roundhouse 50' Gondola

Junk Loads pkg(2) 7.15 ea (Unless Noted)
555-851 Dimi Trains 40' Gondola
555-854 Micro-Trains 50' Gondola **7.50**
555-859 Con-Cor 50' Gondola
555-865 Bachmann/Atlas 42' Gondola
555-869 Roundhouse 50' Gondola

Coal Loads pkg(2) 5.45 ea
555-857 Micro-Trains Hopper
555-862 Con-Cor 40' Steel Hopper
555-866 Bachmann 41' Hopper
555-870 Roundhouse Thrall Gondola
555-872 Con-Cor 3-Bay Hopper

Ballast Loads pkg(2) 5.45 ea
555-861 Con-Cor Wood 3-Bay Hopper
555-863 Con-Cor 40' Steel Hopper
555-864 Bachmann/Atlas 42' Hopper
555-867 Bachmann 41' Hopper
555-871 Roundhouse Thrall Gondola

Sugar Beet Load
555-852 Dimi Trains Gondola pkg(2) **5.45**

77

FREIGHT CARS N SCALE

These N Scale cars are prepainted, lettered and ready to run. Trucks and standard N couplers are included.

40' Box Car 160-70060

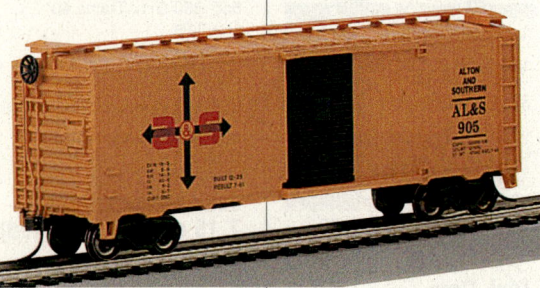
40' Box Car 160-70084

Hi-Cube Box Car 160-71251

50' Steel Reefer 160-70952

"SILVER SERIES" FREIGHT CARS

Box Cars 9.00 ea
40' Box Cars
160-70060 RDG "Bee Line"
160-70084 Alton & Southern
160-70086 Green Bay & Western
160-70088 Bangor & Aroostook
160-70089 DRGW "Cookie Box"

50' Plug-Door Box Cars
160-71059 Chessie
160-71060 RDG
160-71067 MILW
160-71075 Frisco
160-71078 EL

Hi-Cube Box Cars
160-71251 UP
160-71266 CB&Q
160-71270 NYC
160-71289 DRGW

50' Steel Reefers 9.00 ea
160-70951 UP
160-70952 ATSF
160-70963 CN
160-70977 LV
160-70997 Tropicana
160-70998 PFE

Hoppers 9.00 ea
56' Centerflow Hoppers
160-70552 ATSF (orange)
160-70558 Rock Island
160-70577 LV
NEW 160-70582 ACF "Cannonaide"
160-70584 Shell
160-70594 Enjay

40' Quad Hoppers
NEW 160-73360 RDG
160-73368 CSX
160-73372 C&O
NEW 160-73390 Seaboard
160-73392 N&W
160-73396 Minneapolis & St. Louis

PS2 Covered Hoppers
160-73861 GN
160-73862 B&O
160-73893 Kopper's Plastic
160-73897 Wabash

40' Stock Car 160-71561

NEW 56' Centerflow Hopper 160-70582

NEW 40' Quad Hopper 160-73390

PS2 Covered Hopper 160-73861

40' Gondola 160-73654

40' Gondolas 9.00 ea
160-73651 UP
160-73654 SOU
160-73659 Chessie
160-73664 PRR
160-73666 CB&Q

40' Stock Cars 9.00 ea
160-71551 UP
160-71561 GN
160-71582 ATSF (brown)
160-71591 CNW

FREIGHT CARS N SCALE

52' Depressed-Center Flat Cars
160-71391 With Missile **14.00**
160-71398 With Transformer **11.00**

160-71399 No Load **10.00**

89' Tri-Level Car Transporter
160-46502 ATSF (Caboose Red, white) **16.00**
This transporter comes with 15 autos.

40' Tank Cars 9.00 ea
3-Dome
160-70184 Shell
160-70186 Pennsalt
160-70187 Quaker State
160-70188 Exxon
160-70190 Phillips 66

Single-Dome
160-73484 Shell
160-73486 Pennsalt
160-73487 Quaker State
160-73488 Exxon
160-73490 Phillips 66

36' Wide-Vision Cabooses 9.00 ea
160-70751 UP
160-70752 ATSF
160-70753 BN
160-70768 CSX
160-70778 EL
160-70792 N&W

250-Ton Operating Crane & Boom Car 19.00 ea
160-46611 UP (yellow, black)
160-46612 ATSF

52' Center-Depressed Flat Car w/Missile 160-71391

40' 3-Dome Tank Car 160-70188

40' Single Dome Tank Car 160-73484

36' Wide-Vision Caboose 160-70792

250-Ton Operating Crane & Boom Car 160-46612

89' Tri-Level Car Transporter 160-46502

These realistically handpainted and weathered resin castings are suitable for use in HO, TT and N Scale.

NEW PRODUCTS

Freight Car Loads
Steam Equipment

NEW 214-7280 40-Ton Steam Boiler Equipment **13.99**
Fits in N Scale gondolas and flat cars. Also great for vehicle loads. Comes with two boilers (3/4" diameter each), two gears and one flywheel.

Heavy Equipment

NEW 214-7277 40-Ton Rock Crusher & Pulley **14.99**
Fits N and HO Scales. Comes with one rock crusher, one pulley, three open crates and one sealed crate.

Industrial

NEW 214-7283 10-Ton Driveshaft Bearing & Hydraulic Pulley w/Gearbox **13.99**

LOADS
Wood Sheathed Crates

214-7265 Small pkg(4) **13.99**
4 different-sized crates w/largest being 3-5/8 x 5/8"

Steel Ribbed Cable Reels

214-7268 Small pkg(6) **13.99**
1/2" reel diameter 3 pieces of 2 different sizes

Single Palleted Coils

214-7271 Small pkg(6) **13.99**
5/8" coil diameter

20 Ton Structural Beams

214-7274 Small pkg(2) **10.99**
3-1/2 x 3/4"

JNJ TRAINS

40' Horizontal-Rib Box Car
344-1277 Undecorated, MILW Prototype, Less Trucks **23.50**

50' Horizontal-Rib Box Car
344-1278 50' Undecorated **23.50**

Caboose w/Horizontal Side Ribs
344-1279 Undecorated, MILW Prototype, Less Trucks **23.50**

Get the Scoop!
Get the Skinny!
Get the Score!
Check Out Walthers Web site at
www.walthers.com

FREIGHT CARS N SCALE

Ready-to-run freight cars feature detailed plastic or diecast metal bodies with etched metal detail where appropriate, and magnetic knuckle couplers. Most cars are available in multi-packs with different road numbers. "Orphans" are cars originally offered in multi-packs, but are now individually packaged; numbers duplicate those found in multi-pack sets.

BOX CARS
Models feature etched metal details.

1944 40' AAR Cars
Individual Cars
238-140011 Data Only - Brown **13.75**
238-140021 Data Only - Black **13.75**
238-141601 PRR (Orphans) **13.95**

238-141901 Vesuvius Crucible **14.15**
238-142101 GTW **14.15**

238-142201 Gulf, Mobile & Ohio **14.15**

238-142601 Erie Lackawanna **14.35**

238-142701 D&H **14.35**

238-142801 NYC **18.35**
238-142901 GN (Vermillion) **19.75**
NEW 238-143101 Rock Island (Billboard) **19.95**

NEW 238-143201 IC ("Mainline of Mid-America") **19.95**
NEW 238-143301 CB&Q (green; "100,000th Car") **20.95**
NEW 238-143401 PRR (Circle Keystone) **TBA**
238-140001 Undecorated **13.25**

2-Packs
238-141602 PRR **27.90**
238-141902 Vesuvius Crucible **28.30**
238-142102 GTW **28.30**
238-142202 Gulf, Mobile & Ohio **28.30**
238-142602 Erie Lackawanna (brown) **28.70**
238-142702 D&H **28.70**
238-142802 NYC (green, small logo) **36.70**
NEW 238-143102 Rock Island (Billboard) **39.90**
NEW 238-143202 IC ("Mainline of Mid-America") **39.90**
NEW 238-143301 CB&Q (green; "100,000th Car") **20.95**
238-143402 PRR (Circle Keystone) **TBA**

3-Packs
238-142903 GN (Vermillion) **59.25**

40' AAR - No Roofwalk
Individual Cars

238-130101 BN **15.95**

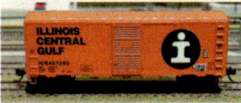
238-130201 ICG **17.45**

238-130301 PC **19.95**

238-130401 Chicago & Eastern Illinois "Buzzsaw" **19.95**
238-130601 B&O **TBA**
238-130701 CB&Q (gold) **TBA**
238-130801 L&N **TBA**

2-Packs
238-130102 BN **31.90**
238-130202 ICG **34.90**
238-130302 PC **39.90**
238-130402 Chicago & Eastern Illinois "Buzzsaw" **39.90**
238-130602 B&O **TBA**
NEW 238-130702 CB&Q (gold) **TBA**
NEW 238-130802 L&N **TBA**

3-Packs
238-130103 BN **47.85**
238-130303 PC **59.85**

COVERED HOPPERS
Individual Cars

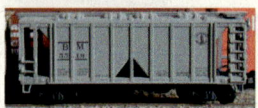
238-7060 Boston & Maine **9.95**
238-7110 C&O **9.95**

238-7130 D&H **9.95**
238-71211 GE Mazda Lamps **10.55**
238-72801 IC (Split Rail) **10.55**
238-72901 M&StL - Misspelled "Minneapo St. Lolis & uis" **10.55**
238-73101 Spokane International **TBA**
238-73201 Wabash **TBA**
238-70001 Undecorated **10.98**

2-Packs
238-71002 Southwest Portland Cement **19.90**

238-71602 Missouri Portland **19.90**
238-71902 SOO **19.90**

238-73002 Toxic Transport (Glow-in-the-Dark Car) **26.95**
238-73102 Spokane International **TBA**

3-Packs
238-70603 Boston & Maine **29.85**
238-71303 D&H **29.85**
238-72703 N&W **31.65**
238-73203 Wabash **TBA**

AMERICA'S HONOR COLLECTION
This collection of cars honors all who served in the armed forces of the USA. The Military Honors Series features insignias from the armed forces. The Liberty Squadron Series features nose art from actual combat aircraft. The American Home Front Series features poster and mural art from a nation at war. A portion of the proceeds from the sale of these cars is donated to the following: US War Survivor Foundation, National Military Family Association, AmVets National Service Foundation and Save Our Ladies Foundation for the Preservation of Original Nose Art.

Military Honors Series 29.95 ea
238-240311 Army 1st Armored Division
238-240231 Air Force 49th Fighter Wing

NEW 238-240251 Coast Guard 5th District
NEW 238-240321 Navy 7th Fleet
NEW 238-240331 Air Force Special Operations Command
NEW 238-240411 POW/MIA You Are Not Forgotten

Liberty Squadron Series

238-240361 "5 by 5" **26.95**
238-240461 "Surprise Attack" **29.95**

FLAT CARS
AAR Standard 53'6" w/Loads 23.95 ea
238-190701 Monon w/Limestone Block #1
238-190711 Monon w/Limestone Block #2
238-190801 Elgin, Joliet & Eastern w/Steel Slab #1
238-190811 Elgin, Joliet & Eastern w/Steel Slab #2

TWIN TUB COAL GONDOLAS
238-120011 Data Only - Black **13.45**
238-120021 Data Only - Silver **13.45**

238-120121 NS **13.95**
238-120711 CN (Orphans) **13.25**

NEW 238-240561 "Sack Time" **29.95**

Limited Quantity Available
238-240261 "Moonshine Raiders" **27.95**

American Home Front Series 29.95 ea
238-240171 B&O "Uncle Sam"

238-240271 ATSF "Keep 'em Flying"

238-240371 Akron, Canton & Youngstown "Save Rubber"

NEW 238-240471 MILW "Quiet"

238-121011 BN - Second Run (black) **14.95**
238-122101 DETX Detroit Edison (Orphans) **13.25**
238-122301 BethGon Demonstrator **18.95**

238-122501 DAPX Dairyland Power **14.95**
238-120001 Undecorated **10.55**

2-Packs
238-122502 DAPX Dairyland Power **29.90**

3-Packs
238-120123 NS **41.85**
238-121013 BN - Second Run (black) **44.85**
238-122103 DETX Detroit Edison (Orphans) **39.75**
238-122403 UP **43.35**
238-122503 DAPX Dairyland Power **44.85**

FREIGHT CARS N SCALE

6-Packs
238-120126 NS **83.70**
238-121016 BN - Second Run (black) **89.70**
238-122506 DAPX Dairyland Power **89.70**

Limited Quantity Available
238-120716 CN **83.70**

10-Packs
238-120120 NS **139.50**

COVERED TWIN-TUB "COAL PORTER" GONDOLAS

These GATX coke service train gondolas are used to carry petroleum coke from oil refineries to steel mills. Blocks of these cars operate in regular freight trains or in complete unit trains.

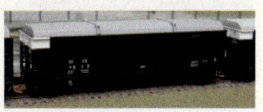

238-122801 GCCX Single (Orphans) **19.95**
238-122802 GCCX pkg(2) **39.90**
238-122803 GCCX pkg(3) **59.85**
238-122804 GCCX pkg(4) **119.70**

WOODCHIP CARS

Deep Rib Cars
Individual Cars
238-100021 Data Only - Black **10.85**

NEW 238-105111 NP - 2nd Run **TBA**
NEW 238-105201 Columbia & Cowlitz **TBA**
NEW 238-105501 NS **TBA**

NEW 238-105601 Seaboard Coast Line **TBA**
NEW 238-105701 CSX; Ex-SCL **TBA**
238-100001 Undecorated **10.55**

3-Packs
NEW 238-105113 NP - 2nd Run **TBA**
NEW 238-105203 Columbia & Cowlitz **TBA**
NEW 238-105503 NS **TBA**
NEW 238-105603 Seaboard Coast Line **TBA**
NEW 238-105703 CSX; Ex-SCL **TBA**

Shallow Rib Cars
Individual Cars
238-160301 Williamette & Pacific **19.75**
238-160401 Golden West w/Graffiti **22.45**
238-160001 Undecorated **10.35**

Limited Quantity Available
238-160211 Montana Rail Link - 2nd Run **17.25**

238-160701 Chattahoochee Industrial **19.65**

2-Packs
Limited Quantity Available
238-160212 Montana Rail Link - 2nd Run **34.50**

3-Packs
238-160303 Williamette & Pacific **59.25**
238-160403 Golden West w/Graffiti **73.45**

Limited Quantity Available
238-160213 Montana Rail Link - 2nd Run **51.75**
238-160703 Chattahoochee Industrial **58.95**

Flat-Side Cars
Individual Cars

238-170301 SP **13.75**

238-170701 Golden West GVSR **13.15**
238-170001 Undecorated **10.35**

3-Packs
238-170703 Golden West GVSR **39.45**

6-Packs
238-170106 ATSF **65.70**
238-170306 SP **82.50**
238-170406 SP w/UP Shield **82.50**

ROADRAILER®

RoadRailer trailers back onto special rail bogies and connect into strings, creating a trailer train without flat cars!

PlateWall Design
Single Units
238-180000 CouplerMate **7.95**
238-180001 Undecorated **13.15**
238-180011 Data Only **13.35**

238-180701 Swift WNC (Orphans) **14.75**

238-180901 TMM Logistics (Orphans) **14.95**

Triple Crown
Triple Crown RoadRailer trains have run on NS, Conrail, UP, BNSF (Santa Fe), CN and CP.
238-180201 Scheme II w/Large Logo (Orphans) **14.75**

3-Packs
238-180903 TMM Logistics **44.85**

5-Packs 89.95 ea
Includes two CouplerMates

238-180605 ATSF

238-180805 Amtrak Mail-Express/Flag

6-Packs
238-180906 TMM Logistics (Orphans) **89.70**

10-Packs
238-180120 Triple Crown 2nd Run #1 **148.75**
238-180130 Triple Crown 2nd Run #2 **148.75**
238-180700 Swift WNC #1 **154.75**
238-180710 Swift WNC #2 **154.75**

DuraPlate Designs
Single Units

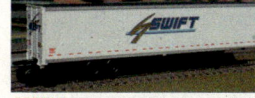

NEW 238-290301 Swift **TBA**

NEW 238-290401 Triple Crown; Tan, ex-CN **TBA**
NEW 238-290501 Triple Crown; ex-Amtrak Trailer #10000 **TBA**

Six-Packs
NEW 238-290306 Swift **TBA**
NEW 238-290406 Triple Crown; Tan & White Mixed **TBA**

J/A 5-UNIT SPINE CARS

These five-unit, articulated "all-purpose" spine cars are used to carry containers and trailers.

NEW 238-220101 TTX Set #1 **TBA**
NEW 238-220111 TTX Set #2 **TBA**

TWINSTACK

5-Unit Container Cars 79.95 ea (Unless Noted)
238-151011 Soo Distribution #2

238-151401 BNSF (green, old lettering)
238-151411 BNSF (green, BN Covered Up)
238-150001 Undecorated **74.95**

LO-PAC 2000

5-Unit Container Cars

NEW 238-110021 BRAN Pacer Stacktrain; ex-APL **TBA**

MAXI-STACK III

5-Unit Container Cars 94.95 ea
NEW 238-210121 TTX 2nd Run #1
NEW 238-210131 TTX 2nd Run #2

NEW 238-210501 American President Lines #1
NEW 238-210511 American President Lines #2

Hot New Products Announced Daily! Visit Walthers Web site at
www.walthers.com

238-210601 Trailer Train #1
238-210611 Trailer Train #2

238-210701 BNSF #1
238-210711 BNSF #2
NEW 238-210801 ATSF #1
NEW 238-210811 ATSF #2

MAXI-STACK IV

3-Unit Container Cars with 53' Wells TBA ea
NEW 238-250101 TTX #1
NEW 238-250111 TTX #2
NEW 238-250201 BNSF #1
NEW 238-250211 BNSF #2
NEW 238-250301 AOK III Transportation #1
NEW 238-250311 AOK III Transportation #2
NEW 238-250401 BRAN Pacer Stacktrain #1
NEW 238-250411 BRAN Pacer Stacktrain #2
NEW 238-250501 Mass Central #1
NEW 238-250511 Mass Central #2

MAXI-STACK III - SHORT-STACK

TTX shortened the wells of these five-unit cars from 48' to 40'.

NEW 238-360101 TTX #1 **TBA**
NEW 238-360111 TTX #2 **TBA**

TRIPLE-57 SPINE CARS

TBA ea

These three-unit, articulated "all-purpose" spine cars are used to carry containers and trailers.

NEW 238-370101 TTX #1
NEW 238-370111 TTX #2
NEW 238-370201 FEC #1
NEW 238-370211 FEC #2
NEW 238-370301 Tomahawk Railway #1
NEW 238-370311 Tomahawk Railway #2

FREIGHT CARS N SCALE

CONTAINERS

20' Wrinkle Side 2-Packs

238-3190 Alianca **13.95**

238-3200 YM Line **11.35**

238-3220 Bridgehead **9.95**

238-3230 Genstar **12.75**
238-3240 Contship **12.25**
NEW 238-3250 "K" Line **TBA**
NEW 238-3260 Safmarine **TBA**

Limited Quantity Available
238-3180 NOL Neptune Orient Line **9.95**

20' TankTainer 2-Packs

238-25010 Cronos **19.35**
238-25020 Agmark **19.65**
238-25030 Tiphook **TBA**

40' Wrinkle Side 2-Packs

238-5011 Data Only - Brown **8.75**
238-5021 Data Only - Red **8.75**
238-5250 Trasatlantica **9.95**
238-5260 Linea Mexicana (billboard) **10.25**
238-5290 Cronos **TBA**

238-5300 NYK (green) **12.15**

238-5310 Sea Train **9.95**

238-5320 APL (silver) **11.25**

238-5340 AJCL **8.75**

238-5350 Italia Line **10.25**

238-5360 YS Line **9.95**
NEW 238-5370 Atlantic Container Line **TBA**
NEW 238-5380 "K" Line (gray) **TBA**
NEW 238-5390 Showa Line **TBA**

40' Reefer 2-Packs
238-4011 Data Only - Silver **8.75**
238-4021 Data Only - White **8.75**

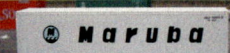
238-4270 Maruba **8.95**

238-4300 Florens **9.25**
238-4280 Mitsui OSK **TBA**
238-4310 Transamerica (Billboard) **10.95**

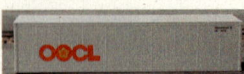
238-4320 OOCL (2-Color Logo) **9.95**

238-4330 Horizon Lines Transamerica **13.25**
238-4340 Sea Land (Large Logo) **TBA**
238-4350 Crowley Marine Transport **TBA**

Limited Quantity Available
238-4001 Undecorated **8.45**

45' Wrinkle Side 2-Packs
238-6011 Data Only - Red **8.85**
238-6021 Data Only - Blue **8.85**

238-6070 NYK (blue) **13.65**
238-6100 CPI **11.95**

238-6110 Seaco **12.45**
238-6120 P&O Nedlloyd **TBA**
238-6130 Hanjin **TBA**
238-6140 CMA GGM **TBA**
NEW 238-6150 Sinotrans **TBA**
NEW 238-6160 MOL (green) **TBA**

Limited Quantity Available
238-6080 "K" Line **13.95**

40' Hi-Cube 2-Packs

238-20020 Cronos **11.25**

238-20040 Senator Line (blue) **10.85**
NEW 238-20050 NYK Logistics & Mega-Carrier **10.85**

NEW 238-20060 COSCO **10.85**
NEW 238-20070 Evergreen **TBA**
NEW 238-20080 Maersk Sealand **TBA**

48' Smoothside 2-Packs
238-8011 Data Only - Silver **8.85**
238-8021 Data Only - White **8.85**

238-8032 SP - 3rd Run **10.55**
238-8190 ITEL **10.95**

238-8260 APC **11.95**
238-8270 NACS - ex-Genstar **13.75**

238-8001 Undecorated **8.55**

48' Container w/Reefer Unit

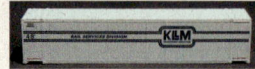
238-9050 KLLM **11.95**

NEW 238-9070 CH Robinson "Top Position Only" **13.35**

53' Corrugated 2-Packs

238-13020 CSX Intermodal **11.95**

238-13030 STAX **12.95**
NEW 238-13040 NACS **12.55**

NEW 238-13050 Alaska Marine Lines **13.65**
NEW 238-13060 Crowley (1 Each Blue, Brown) **12.85**

NEW 238-13070 APL **TBA**

NEW 238-13080 Hub Group **13.95**

NEW 238-13090 Swift Intermodal **TBA**

NEW 238-13100 CN **TBA**

53' Exterior Post 2-Packs

NEW 238-15010 EMP **TBA**
NEW 238-15020 STAX **TBA**
NEW 238-15030 BNSF - Hub Group **TBA**

40' Chassis 2-Packs

238-1010 Flexi Van **16.45**

238-1020 Trac Lease **16.45**

PARTS
238-990101 Removable Container Glue - For Double Stacking **3.95**
238-990502 Interior Brace Kit for Twin-Tub Coal Gons **2.15** Includes parts for two cars.
238-990612 Brass Stirrups pkg(12) **5.25**

Container Weights
238-990202 Set of 2 **1.45**
238-990204 Set of 4 **2.25**

Storage Boxes **9.45 ea**
Includes foam inserts.
238-990700 UnitPak 14-Slot

238-990750 PassengerPak 9-Slot

DURANGO PRESS

Fairmont Speeder

HO Scale Model Shown

254-150 pkg(2) **4.95**
Rush your maintenance crew to the repair site aboard this speeder kit made from plastic and metal parts.

FREIGHT CARS N SCALE

These ready-to-run N Scale freight cars are prepainted and include trucks and couplers.

89' Flat Car w/Trailers BNSF
223-120603

125-Ton Husky Stack Car 223-603108

89' Flat Car w/2 Containers
Trailer Train Flat 223-120602

INTERMODAL

40' Sea Containers pkg(2) 9.98 ea
223-4005201 Sealand (silver)
223-4005202 Evergreen (green)
223-4005203 Hanjin (blue)
223-4005204 NOL (silver)
223-4005205 Y.M. Line (silver, orange, yellow)
223-4005206 Genstar (orange, blue)
223-4005207 Hyundai (orange)

45' Sea Containers pkg(2) 9.98 ea
223-4005231 Maersk (silver, light blue)
223-4005232 NYK Version #1 (blue)
223-4005233 NYK Version #2 (silver, blue)
223-4005234 K-Line Version #1 (red)
223-4005235 K-Line Version #2 (silver, red)
223-4005236 APL Version #1 (silver, blue)
223-4005237 APL Version #2 (silver)
223-4005238 CP Rail Intermodal (white, red)
223-4005239 ATSF (white)

48' Containers pkg(2)
223-48009 ITEL Leasing 6.98
223-48013 Pacer StackTrain 9.98
223-48014 BNSF 9.98
223-48015 American Presidents Line #2 (blue) 9.98

53' Containers pkg(2)
223-53008 Pacer StackTrain 9.98
223-53009 BNSF 9.98
223-53010 American Presidents Line #2 (blue) 9.98

125-Ton Husky Stack Car 22.98 ea
223-603101 TTX
223-603102 SP
223-603103 CSX
223-603104 BN
223-603105 Sealand
223-603106 ATSF w/JB Hunt Conatiners
223-603107 Maersk
223-603108 Pacer Stack Trains w/48 & 53' Pacer StackTrain Containers
223-603109 Southwind w/48 & 53' NS Containers
223-603110 BNSF w/48 & 53' BNSF Containers
223-603111 UP ("We Can Handle It" logo) w/48 & 53' Containers
223-603112 Rail Bridge w/2 45' K-Line Containers
223-603113 Trailer Train w/2 48' EMP Containers
223-603100 Undecorated

FLAT CARS

89' Flat Car w/Trailers 19.98 ea
223-120603 BNSF w/2 BNSF 45' Trailers
223-120605 UP w/2 TransAmerica 45' Trailers

89' Flat Car w/2 Containers 19.98 ea
223-120601 Trailer Train Flat (older logo) w/2 Pacer StackTrain 45' Containers
223-120602 Trailer Train Flat (newer logo) w/2 Barber Blue Sea 45' Containers
223-120604 SP Flat (flying SP logo) w/2 EMP 45' Containers
223-120606 CR Flat w/2 Conrail Mercury Containers

CHRISTMAS BOX CARS
223-10000514 2005 Eight Maids A Milking 15.98
NEW 223-100006 2006 Nine Ladies Dancing 17.98

New Arrivals Updated Every Day! Visit Walthers Web site at
www.walthers.com

357-1740

357-1330

Wood Display Cases
Great for displaying Z, N, TT and HO Narrow Gauge equipment, these cases feature a solid Red Oak frame and shelves, white plastic back and plastic sliding doors. Mounting hardware and self-sticking door handles also included.

30 x 13 x 2-1/2"
357-1330 124.95

47 x 17 x 2-1/2"
357-1740 199.95

Riser Blocks
Items listed below are available by Special Order (see Legend Page) Riser blocks double shelf capacity.

357-1335 pkg(10) 23.95
For use with #1330 wood display case, Z Scale rolling stock only.

357-1745 pkg(14) 46.95
For use with #1740 wood display case, Z Scale rolling stock only.

Plastic Polishing Kit

357-1339 Plastic Polish/Anti-Static Cleaning Solution 2oz 6.95
A handy kit containing a pump spray and polishing cloth. Use on display case doors or any other hard shiny surface. Cleaned surface resists dust and fingerprints. Kit comes in re-sealable poly bag with hang hole for easy storage.

FREIGHT CARS N SCALE

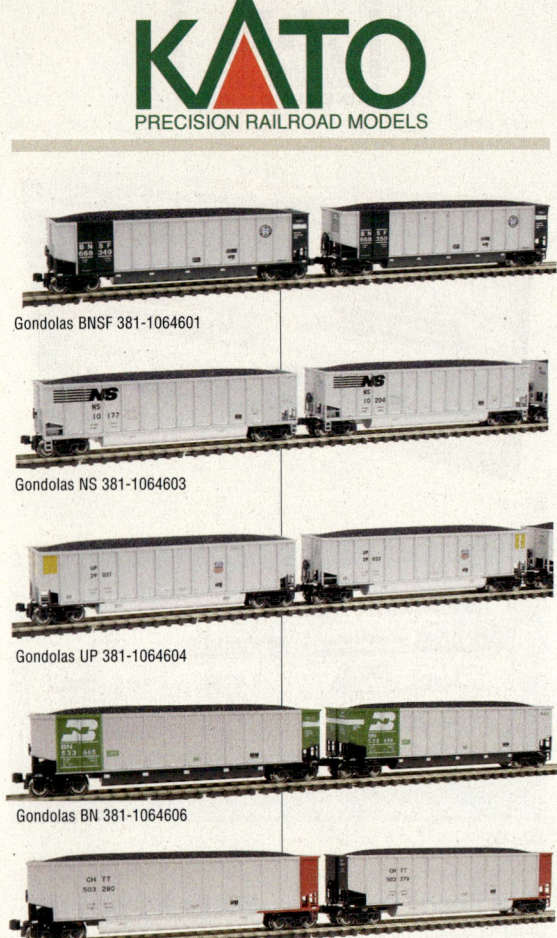

Gondolas BNSF 381-1064601
Gondolas NS 381-1064603
Gondolas UP 381-1064604
Gondolas BN 381-1064606
Gondolas CHTT 381-1064607

NEW Gondolas UP 381-1064609

NEW Gondolas WEE 381-1064610

GONDOLAS

The BethGon Coalporter™ aluminum gondola is a favorite for coal-hauling duty. With thousands of cars in service, these rotary-dump cars can be seen across the continent in long unit trains. You'll be able to model a unit train in minutes with these ready-to-run eight packs. Cars feature detailed plastic bodies, removable coal loads, appropriate trucks and Kato knuckle couplers.

8-Car Sets, 105.00 (Unless Noted)

381-1064601 BNSF
381-1064603 NS
381-1064604 UP 109.00
381-1064606 BN (aluminum, Cascade Green)
381-1064607 CHTT (aluminum, red)
381-1064608 BNSF (green, silver)
381-1064609 UP "Building America" 109.00
381-1064610 Wisconsin Electric Energies (silver, yellow)
381-1064611 CSX (silver, yellow)

EL #21019 & 21035 381-1860201

MILW #99142 & 99099 381-1860204

Nickel Plate Road #91034 & 91085
381-1860205

Seaboard Air Line #8100 & 8247
381-1860209

SP #90602 & 90801 381-1860210

HOPPERS

AC&F 70-Ton Closed-Side Covered Hopper 2-Car Sets 29.00 ea

Precision craftsmanship and fine details make Kato models a premium addition to your rolling stock roster.

These hoppers are based on the American Car & Foundry units introduced in the 1940s to haul granular bulk commodities. Many are still in service today as MOW cars.

These models feature Kato's highly detailed ASF "Ride Control" trucks with blackened metal wheels. Two styles of brake wheels are provided for modeler installation according to preference. The semi-automatic knuckle coupler mates with all other brands. (Rapido couplers also included in package.)

Different numbered cars lets you operate multiple units without duplication of roadnumbers.

Limited Quantity Available On All Items

381-1860201 EL #21019 & 21035
381-1860202 EL #21028 & 21047
381-1860203 MILW #99073 & 99208
381-1860204 MILW #99142 & 99099
381-1860205 Nickel Plate Road #91034 & 91085
381-1860209 Seaboard Air Line #8100 & 8247
381-1860210 SP #90602 & 90801
381-1860211 SP #90735 & 90798
381-1860212 SP #90654 & 90785

CABOOSES

Cupola Cabooses 24.98 ea

These cabooses feature a Kato fully automatic magnetic knuckle coupler, and fine detailing on the roof walkway, end platforms, railings and truck sideframes. Interiors can be lighted with Lighting Kit #381-11204, sold separately in the Lighting-Electric-Motors section of this Reference Book.

381-1860302 BN #11433

381-1860303 C&O #900920
381-1860304 WM #901828

381-1860305 CNW w/Chicago Great Western Reporting Marks #606
381-1860306 CNW w/Chicago Great Western Reporting Marks #10507

381-1860308 PRR #478124

381-1860309 ATSF #1785R
381-1860310 ATSF #1910R

For Up-To-Date Information and News Bookmark Walthers Web site at

www.walthers.com

FREIGHT CARS N SCALE

LBF Company

Add color and variety to your freight car fleet with this line of unique Railroad Ready™ models. Each equipped with free-rolling trucks and working knuckle couplers.

NEW PRODUCTS

Gondolas

52'6" Mill Gondola w/Cast Load 20.95 ea

- NEW 414-6401 SP ("Old")
- NEW 414-6402 CP
- NEW 414-6403 CN
- NEW 414-6404 CR
- NEW 414-6405 DRGW
- NEW 414-6406 Elgin, Joliet & Eastern
- NEW 414-6407 P&LE
- NEW 414-6408 WC
- NEW 414-6409 Oregon Steel Mills
- NEW 414-6410 Coe Rail Inc.
- NEW 414-6411 SLSF "Frisco"
- NEW 414-6412 SOU
- NEW 414-6413 BN (Cascade Green)
- NEW 414-6414 UP
- NEW 414-6415 CSX (black)
- NEW 414-6416 ATSF (brown)
- NEW 414-6400 Undecorated

BOX CARS

Gunderson 50' 6" High Cube Box Car 17.95 ea (Unless Noted)

414-5502 Chicago Heights Terminal Transfer/UP

414-5503 AG Stone Container

414-5504 CSX Transportation Big Blue **19.95**

414-5505 IC

414-5506 WC

414-5510 Canadian American

414-5513 Upper Marion & Plymouth

414-5514 Chicago Heights Terminal Transfer

414-5515 Quebec Gatineau Railway

414-5517 CN (blue, no logo)

414-5518 NOKL

414-5519 Louisville & Wadley (blue)

414-5520 Bangor & Aroostook/ Canadian American

414-5521 CP

414-5523 FBOX TTX **21.95**

Gunderson 50' Double Plug Door Box Car 19.95 ea

414-5551 Columbia & Cowlitz

414-5552 Minnesota, Dakota & Western

414-5553 Montana Rail Link

414-5554 BN (original logo)

414-5555 Golden West Service

414-5556 UP (tuscan)

414-5557 BNSF

414-5558 BN (new logo)

414-5559 Oregon, California & Eastern

414-5562 ATSF (brown)

414-5563 UP (yellow, silver)

414-5564 ATSF (red, large emblem)

414-5565 MILW/CP Rail (red)

414-5550 Undecorated

Gunderson High Cube Box Car Chicago Heights Terminal Transfer/UP 414-5502

Gunderson 50' Double Plug Door Box Car Montana Rail Link 414-5553

Gunderson 60' Hi Cube Box Car NS 414-6004

National Steel Hi Cube Box Car FBOX 414-6201

National Steel 60' Hi Cube Box Car w/Double Plug Door Louisville & Wadley 414-5902

Gunderson 60' Hi Cube Box Car 21.95 ea

414-6001 CHTT/UP

414-6002 BNSF
414-6004 NS
414-6005 UP

National Steel 50'6" Hi Cube Box Car 21.95 ea

414-6201 FBOX

414-6203 Southern Railway of British Columbia (brown)

414-6204 Southern Railway of British Columbia (MRL Blue)

National Steel 60' Hi Cube Box Car w/Double Plug Door 19.95 ea (Unless Noted)

414-5901 CP Rail (Beaver, red) **21.95**

414-5902 Louisville & Wadley

414-5903 Southern Railway of British Columbia

414-5900 Undecorated

FREIGHT CARS N SCALE

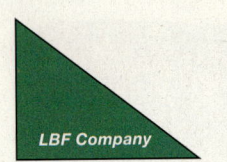

LBF Company

GONDOLAS

63' Woodchip Gondola

414-5001 SP **19.95**

414-5002 Golden West **19.95**
414-5004 Central Oregon & Pacific **19.95**

414-5005 Oregon State University "Beavers" **25.00**

414-5006 University of Oregon "Ducks" **25.00**
414-5000 Undecorated, FMC Welded Side **17.95**

65' Mill Gondola 16.95 ea

Corrugated Side

414-5351 BN
414-5352 CNW
414-5354 L&N
414-5355 MP
414-5356 ATSF

414-5357 SP

Smooth Side
414-5361 BN

414-5363 SP

NEW 414-5365 CSX
414-5366 North Star Steel
414-5367 Oregon Steel Mill

414-5368 Gondola Connection

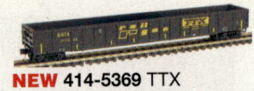
NEW 414-5369 TTX

NEW 414-5370 BNSF

48' Johnstown America Corp Bethgon

Single Car
414-5401 CR **18.95**
414-5403 NS **17.95**
414-5409 CSX Transportation (gray) **21.95**
414-5415 WEPX (silver) **16.95**

414-5418 CSX Transportation (Aluminum) **21.95**

414-5419 GPEX **16.95**
414-5431 UP New Danville **18.95**
414-5438 NS Top Gon **17.95**

NEW 414-5445 BNSF **22.95**

414-54100 BN Double Rotary (black, green) **31.95**
414-54170 BNSF Double Rotary (green, silver) **26.95**

NEW 414-54190 GPEX Double Rotary **31.95**

6-Pack 109.95 ea (Unless Noted)
Items listed below are available by Special Order (see Legend Page).
414-5401X CR
414-5402X CSX Transportation, 13 Panel **119.95**
414-5403X NS
414-5409X CSX Transportation (gray)
414-5410X BN (black, green) **131.95**
414-5411X BNSF **131.95**
414-5418X CSX Transportation (Aluminum)
414-5430X CR/NYC
414-5431X UP New Danville
414-5438X NS Top Gon **104.95**
414-5442X UP/CMPO **131.95**

Trinity "Aluminator" Coal Gondola

Single Car
414-5702 UP **18.95**
414-5706 Demonstrator TIMX **27.95**
414-57030 CN Double Rotary **26.95**

6-Pack
Items listed below are available by Special Order (see Legend Page).
414-5702X UP **109.95**
414-5703X CN **131.95**

Johnstown American Corporation AeroFlo™

Single Car 18.95 ea (Unless Noted)
414-5802 CN

414-5804 LUSX Luscar of Canada

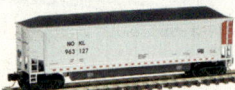
414-5806 NOKL
414-5807 CWEX

414-58040 LUSX Luscar of Canada Double Rotary **26.95**
414-58050 BNSF Double Rotary **26.95**
414-58060 NOKL Double Rotary **26.95**

6-Pack 109.95 ea
Items listed below are available by Special Order (see Legend Page).
414-5802X CN
414-5804X LUSX Luscar of Canada
414-5806X NOKL
414-5807X CWEX

SKYBOX-EQUIPPED FLAT CARS

Tuscan Skybox Hood 22.95 ea
414-56011 SP

414-56021 GN

414-56031 BN
414-56041 ATSF

414-56091 CR
414-56101 TTX

Classic Boeing 747 Skybox Hood 24.95 ea
414-56012 SP
414-56022 GN
414-56032 BN

414-56042 ATSF

Boeing Tuscan Skybox Hood 24.95 ea
414-56016 SP
414-56026 GN

414-56036 BN
414-56046 ATSF

Mill Gondola ATSF 414-5356

Mill Gondola Smooth Side North Star Steel 414-5366

48' Johnstown America Corp Bethgon NS 414-5403

Trinity "Aluminator" Coal Gondola Demonstrator TIMX 414-5706

Johnstown American Corporation AeroFlo™ CWEX 414-5807

Southern Pacific Skybox Hood
414-56053 SP **24.95**

General Dynamics Skybox Hood

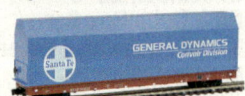
414-56064 ATSF **24.95**

Lockheed Skybox Hood 24.95 ea

414-56075 SP

414-56085 ATSF Shock Control

FREIGHT CARS N SCALE

Micro-Trains® ready-to-run cars feature prepainted and lettered, injection-molded styrene bodies. Models include free-rolling trucks with contoured axles, truck-mounted Magne-Matic® couplers and die cast metal underframes. Box cars have thin profile roofwalks, foot stirrups, brake wheels and working sliding doors.

Micro-Trains offers a wide variety of freight car body styles. New releases arrive on a monthly basis; for current availability, check the Walthers Web site at www.walthers.com.

50' Plug Door Box Car - No Roofwalk
USS Missouri BB-63, Iowa Class
Battleship "The Mighty Mo" 489-3800401

50' Plug Door Box Car - No Roofwalk
Quebec #QC 1867 #2 in Series
489-7700152

40' Plug Door Box Car #4
"Four Calling Birds" 489-2100504

BOX CARS

40' Single Door
489-2000376 Ontario Northland #90235 **14.05**
NEW 489-2000726 Spokane, Portland & Seattle #950194 **13.45**

NEW 489-2000730 National Railways of Mexico #63317 **14.85**

Chicago & Eastern Illinois 18.90 ea

489-2000704 #4
489-2000705 #5

40' w/Single Youngstown Door, No Roofwalk
489-2400280 CN #446220 **16.35**

40' Plug Door

NEW 489-2100170 Northern Pacific #98524 **18.75**
489-2100500 Happy Birthday 2005 **24.95**
Cars feature ends painted in yellow, blue, orange or purple and are shipped at random so they're sure to be a birthday surprise! Also includes confetti.

See What's New and Exciting at
www.walthers.com

50 State Series 19.85 ea
NEW 489-2100399 Hawaii #1959 - #35 in Series
NEW 489-2100401 Mississippi #1817 - #37 in Series
NEW 489-2100402 Vermont #1791 - #38 in Series
NEW 489-2100403 Indiana #1816 - #39 in Series

NEW 489-2100404 New Hampshire #1788 - #40 in Series

NEW 489-2100405 North Dakota #1889 - #41 in Series

40' Plug Door – No Roofwalk
NEW 489-7400010 CP #165181 **21.35**

40' Standard Double-Door
NEW 489-2300170 Grand Trunk Western #585883 **14.80**

40' X29 w/Overlapping Flat Panel Roof
NEW 489-12000720 PRR #92420 Merchandise Service **21.45**

50' Rib Side
With Single FMC Door, No Roofwalk
NEW 489-2500440 Maine Central #20081 **19.75**
With Single Door, No Roofwalk
NEW 489-2500570 Wisconsin & Southern #101541 **16.55**

NEW 489-2500580 Apalachicola Northern #5508 **19.15**

50' Single Door

NEW 489-3100170 MKT #1422 **19.10**

NEW 489-3100210 Container Corporation of America #TLDX 20 **23.75**

50' Plug Door
NEW 489-3200190 New Haven #40600 (Simplified Alpert Scheme) **19.95**

NEW 489-3200420 MILW #2635 **22.15**

50' w/Plug & Sliding Door
489-3300170 Atlantic Coast Line #15394 **16.80**
NEW 489-7600080 DRGW #63293 **23.45**

50' Plug Door - No Roofwalk

NEW 489-3800320 Chessie System/WM #36008 **20.95**
NEW 489-3800370 IC #11579 **14.15**

NEW 489-3800380 Seaboard Air Line #593491 - FGE **19.55**
NEW 489-3800390 Bangor & Aroostook #501 **15.95**

U.S. Navy Series 18.95 ea
NEW 489-3800401 USS Missouri BB-63, Iowa Class Battleship "The Mighty Mo"

NEW 489-3800402 USS Hornet CV-12, Essex Class Carrier

Canadian Province & Territory Series
NEW 489-7700152 Quebec #QC 1867 #2 in Series **18.25**

50' Double Plug Door - No Roofwalk

NEW 489-7500140 Evans Products Company #180 **20.55**

50' Double-Door

NEW 489-3400190 MP #90257 **15.25**

50' PS-1 w/Plug & Sliding Doors
NEW 489-7600070 Rock Island #63290 **19.15**

50' w/Single Youngstown Door, No Roofwalk
NEW 489-7700110 Penn Central #160252 **13.95**

NEW 489-7700150 ATSF #12002 **15.55**

12 DAYS OF CHRISTMAS SERIES

40' Plug Door Box Car 19.15 ea
489-21501 #1 "A Partridge in a Pear Tree"
489-21502 #2 "Two Turtle Doves"
489-21503 #3 "Three French Hens"
489-2100504 #4 "Four Calling Birds"

489-2100505 #5 "Five Golden Rings"

489-2100506 #6 "Six Geese a'Laying"
489-2100507 #7 "Seven Swans a'Swimming"
489-2100508 #8 "Eight Maids a'Milking"
489-2100509 #9 "Nine Ladies Dancing"

Steel Caboose
489-5100250 **22.90**

Ornaments 9.99 ea
Full-size holiday decorations for display on your tree.
489-96060001 #1 "A Partridge in a Pear Tree"
489-96060002 #2 "Two Turtle Doves"
489-96060003 #3 "Three French Hens"

NEW 489-96060004 #4 "Four Calling Birds"

FREIGHT CARS N SCALE

MICRO-TRAINS LINE

NEW 489-96060005 #5 "Five Golden Rings"

NEW 489-96060006 #6 "Six Geese a'Laying"
NEW 489-96060007 #7 "Seven Swans a'Swimming"
NEW 489-96060008 #8 "Eight Maids a'Milking"
NEW 489-96060009 #9 "Nine Ladies Dancing"

SMOKEY BEAR FOREST FIRE PREVENTION SERIES

This series salutes Smokey Bear and his tireless efforts to protect America's woodlands for over 40 years.

50' Plug Door Box Cars 18.35 ea

Cars are finished in Charcoal Gray and feature a full-color reproduction of an historic fire prevention poster, plus the "Remember - Only You can Prevent Forest Fires" slogan.

489-3200401 #1; 1953 "Please... help people be more careful!"

489-3200402 #2; 1959 "Why?"

489-3200403 #3; 1953 "This Shameful Waste Weakens America!"

NEW 489-3200404 #4; 1980 "Remember, You're Among Friends"

NEW 489-3200405 #5; 1983 "Think Before You Strike"

NEW 489-3200406 #6; 1982 "Think...Thanks"

Steel Caboose
NEW 489-10000260 "Please Help Prevent Forest Fires" 22.20

REEFERS

40' Double-Sheathed Wood Reefer
End-Mounted Brake Wheel
489-4700080 New York Despatch Refrigerator Line #8050 16.60

Vertical Brake Wheel
NEW 489-4900390 Union Refrigerator Transit Co #24058 18.95

40' Steel Ice Cooled

489-5900140 Needham Packing Company Inc. 21.25

51' 3-3/4 Rivet Side Mechanical
NEW 489-6900180 CN #231031 17.25

HOPPERS

33' H-5 Class 2-Bay Rib Side Hopper
NEW 489-5600110 WM #10011 18.20

2-Bay ACF Center Flow Covered Hopper w/4 Round Hatches

NEW 489-9200200 ROCK #512093 24.65

NEW 489-9200220 Canadian National D&TS #2630 23.15

3-Bay Ortner Rapid Discharge Hopper

NEW 489-12500052 Chessie System/C&O #45088 21.70

100-Ton 3-Bay Open

NEW 489-10800170 St. Louis-San Francisco #88470 15.35

GONDOLAS

50' Steel 14-Panel, Fixed End
Open

NEW 489-10500130 Golden West Service #327013 16.05
NEW 489-10500530 St. Louis-San Francisco #51523 13.65

Covered

NEW 489-10600020 UP #229609 15.85

50' Steel 15 Panel Covered
NEW 489-10600240 CB&Q #83107 (Chinese Red) 17.80

FLAT CARS

60'8" Thrall Centerbeam
NEW 489-5300061 WP #1401 25.95
NEW 489-5300062 WP #1403 25.95

TANK CARS

39' Single Dome Tank Car

NEW 489-6500200 SP #6066 18.50
NEW 489-6500290 CNJ #95206 18.75

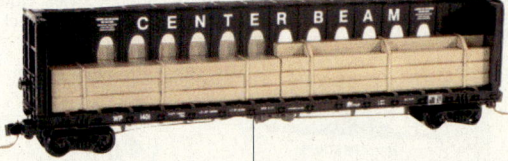
50' Plug Door Box Car #4; 1980 "Remember, You're Among Friends" 489-3200404

60'8" Thrall Centerbeam Flat Car WP #1401 489-5300061

58' General Service Tank Car Procor #23303 489-11000090

58' General Service Tank Car
NEW 489-11000090 Procor #23303

CABOOSES

34' Wood-Sheathed w/Straight Cupola

489-5100020 Seaboard Air Line #5458 19.50

Steel
NEW 489-10000270 Happy Birthday 26.35

NARROW GAUGE CARS

30' Box Car
NEW 489-15106 Colorado & Southern #8202 15.65

NEW 489-80000130 Rio Grande Southern #8506 13.65

NEW 489-80000140 Austin & North Western #7047 14.05

NEW 489-80000170 Denver, South Park & Pacific #889 14.05

Caboose with Two Window Cupola

NEW 489-81600020 Cumbres & Toltec Scenic #0503 23.60

For Daily Product Updates Point Your Browser to

www.walthers.com

FREIGHT CARS N SCALE

These N Scale freight cars are assembled and ready to run. Models are prepainted, prelettered and include trucks and Rapido-type couplers. Cars may be packaged with a Model Power or Minitrix label on the box.

BOX CARS

40' Box Car 8.98 ea (Unless Noted)

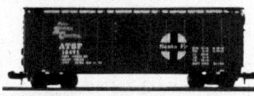

490-3438

490-3433 SP **9.49**
490-3435 CN (brown)
490-3436 CP Rail (red)
490-3437 UP (yellow) **9.49**
490-3439 CR (light brown)
490-3440 Maine Central
490-3708 Algoma Central
490-3709 British Columbia Rail
490-3710 CP (brown)
490-3711 CN (silver)
490-3712 Grand Trunk Western
490-3713 Ontario Northland
490-3714 Toronto, Hamilton & Buffalo
490-3432 Undecorated

Limited Quantity Available
490-3438 ATSF (red)

40' Box Car - Deluxe w/Metal Wheels 9.98 ea (Unless Noted)

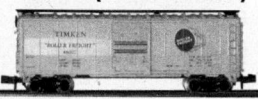

490-3704

490-3701 B&O (silver, blue)
490-3702 GN (green, orange)
490-3703 Central of Georgia (purple, silver)
490-3704 Timken (yellow)
490-3706 SP "Overnight" **10.49**
490-3707 PRR

50' Box Car 8.90 ea (Unless Noted)

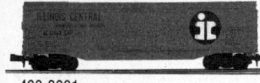

490-3091

490-3088 CR (rust)
490-3089 DRGW **9.49**
490-3090 Western Pacific **9.49**
490-3091 IC
490-4032 Duluth, Winnipeg & Pacific
490-4033 CP
490-4035 GE

REEFERS

40' Reefer 8.98 ea (Unless Noted)

490-3381 BN
490-3382 GN (Big Sky Blue)
490-3383 ATSF
490-3384 UP Freight **9.49**
490-3385 Central Vermont
490-3390 Railway Express Agency
490-3395 CP
490-3401 CN

40' Reefer - Deluxe w/Metal Wheels 9.98 ea

Roadname Not Available

490-3716 Apple Car
490-3717 A&P Company
490-3718 Banana Car
490-3719 Maine Potatoes
490-3720 Tropicana
490-3721 Heinz (orange, Tuscan)
490-3722 Pabst
490-3723 PFE (orange, silver)
490-3724 Schlitz
490-3726 Tropicana (orange, green)

40' Chemical Tank Car 9.98 ea (Unless Noted)

490-3750 DRGW **10.49**
490-3753 SP (silver) **10.49**
490-3754 Roma
490-3755 Union 76

Limited Quantity Available
490-3758 Brea Chemical

50' Reefer 8.98 ea

490-4029

490-4028 Thermice
490-4030 SOO
490-4031 Alaska

STOCK CARS

40' Stock Car 8.98 ea (Unless Noted)

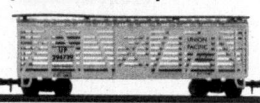

490-3441 BN (Cascade Green)
490-3442 UP (yellow)
490-3446 MKT
490-3447 ATSF
490-3449 DRGW **9.49**
490-3450 GN

Limited Quantity Available
490-3445 CN (Tuscan)

50' Stock Car 8.98 ea (Unless Noted)

490-3077

490-3075 MKT (yellow)
490-3076 Atlantic Coast Line (white)
490-3077 GN
490-3078 N&W (black) **9.49**

HOPPERS

4-Bay Hopper 8.98 ea (Unless Noted)

490-3220 Peabody (yellow) 8.98
490-3221 SOU
490-3222 Illinois Central Gulf (orange)
490-3223 CN (orange)
490-3224 CP
490-3226 Domino Sugar (white)

55' Canada Grain Hopper 10.98 ea

490-3488 Canada (red, black)
490-3489 Government of Canada (silver, yellow)
490-3490 Heritage Fund (blue)
490-3491 Saskatchewan (Tuscan, orange)
490-3492 Canada (Tuscan, yellow)

55' ACF Hopper 10.98 ea (Unless Noted)

490-3469

490-3465 ATSF (gray)
490-3466 C&O Chessie
490-3467 Missabe
490-3468 BN (Cascade Green)
490-3469 SOO
490-3470 Roacor
490-3471 Arco
490-3472 Chemplex Plastics (white)
490-3473 N&W
490-3474 DRGW (orange) **11.49**
490-3475 Undecorated

GONDOLAS

50' Gondola 8.98 ea (Unless Noted)

490-3061

490-3060 CR
490-3061 SOU
490-3062 DRGW (black) **9.49**

50' Gondola w/Coal Load 8.98 ea

490-4018

490-4015 SOU
490-4016 Ontario Northland
490-4017 ATSF
490-4018 CN

FLAT CARS

40' Depressed Center Flat Car w/2 Reels, Figures & Metal Wheels 10.98 ea

490-4110

490-4110 ATSF
490-4111 PRR
490-4112 CN

Flat Car w/Two 20' Containers 9.98 ea (Unless Noted)

490-4003

490-4001 CP Ships
490-4002 SeaLand
490-4003 Evergreen
490-4004 Atlantic Coast Line

With Metal Wheels
490-4050 Maine Casket
490-4054 DRGW (50' Car) **10.49**

Flat Car w/Autos 8.98 ea

490-4010

490-4010 ATSF
490-4011 PRR

Flat Car w/Cables 8.98 ea

490-4042

490-4041 GN
490-4042 PRR

TANK CARS

40' Chemical Tank Car 8.98 ea

490-3455 Shell
490-3456 Texaco (silver, black)
490-3458 DOW
490-3459 Michigan Alkali Company
490-3760 Champion Oils
490-3761 Dominion Sugar
490-3762 Imperial Oil Limited

40' 3-Dome Tank Car 8.98 ea

490-3411 Exxon (silver)
490-3413 Baby Ruth
490-3415 Hudson Bay (orange)
400-3416 Shell (yellow)
490-3417 Tank Train (black)
490-3418 Hercules
490-3419 Lion

CABOOSES

Standard Caboose 8.98 ea

490-3105

490-3101 ATSF (Box Car Red)
490-3102 Transfer (Box Car Red)
490-3103 Chessie
490-3104 CR
490-3105 BN (Cascade Green, black)
490-3106 UP (orange)
490-3107 CN

89

FREIGHT CARS N SCALE

Bay Window Caboose
8.98 ea (Unless Noted)

490-3128

- 490-3120 BN (Cascade Green)
- 490-3121 Chessie (yellow)
- 490-3122 SOU (red) **9.49**
- 490-3123 CR (blue)
- 490-3124 UP (orange)
- 490-3125 PRR (Tuscan)
- 490-3126 ATSF (Caboose Red)
- 490-3127 Transfer (Caboose Red, black)
- 490-3128 CP Rail
- 490-3129 Amtrak (orange, black)
- 490-3130 CN
- 490-3131 SP Special **9.49**

MAINTENANCE-OF-WAY

Work Crane w/Car
27.98 ea
- 490-3162 ATSF
- 490-3163 Amtrak
- 490-3164 SOU
- 490-3165 PRR
- 490-3166 CN

Searchlight Car w/Figures

490-4100 **10.98**
All metal.

CIGAR CARS
9.98 ea (Unless Noted)

- 490-3608 Cigar Reefer Car Assortment pkg(4) **39.98** Includes one each Dutch Masters, Muriel, El Producto and Antonio & Cleopatra.
- 490-3728 El Producto
- 490-3729 Antonio & Cleopatra
- 490-3730 Dutch Masters
- 490-3731 Muriel

ASSORTMENTS

20' Containers pkg(4)
9.98 ea
Assembled models are precolored plastic.

- 490-1360 Evergreen, Sealand, CP Ships, American President Lines
- 490-1361 Consolidated Freightways, K&N, CR, ACL
- 490-1362 ATSF, BN, Hanjin, SP

HEICO MODELL
IMPORTED FROM GERMANY BY WALTHERS

FREIGHT CAR LOADS

Fully assembled, one-piece loads are complete with real wood bracing and are ideal for use with various flat cars and gondolas. Simply set in place for loads-in/empties out operation, or glue down for permanent detail. Can be used to model finished products stacked for loading or unloading alongside industries. Short loads may be kitbashed for use with trucks. Dimension shown is overall length. All photos shown are HO Scale loads. Freight cars shown in photos are not included.

335-16011 Construction Steel Matting 2-3/4" 7cm **16.99**

335-16043 Banded Steel Plates 3" 7.5cm **14.99**

335-16122 Ingot Molds For Steel Works 2-1/8" 5.5cm **25.99**

335-16125 Large Drive Gears 2-1/8" 5.5cm **18.99**

335-16131 Lattice Steel Pylon 2-3/4" 7cm **21.99**

335-16205 Broken Concrete, Long 3" 7.7cm **12.99**
335-16311 Concrete Sewer/Water Pipe 2" 5cm **18.99**
335-16314 Reinforced Concrete "Betomax" 2-3/4" 7cm **27.99**

335-16406 Old Railroad Ties 2-3/4" 7cm **17.99**
335-16416 Building Lumber "Trinkl" **34.99**

335-16425 Square Wood Beams (Large & Small - 2 Piles) 4-3/8" 11cm **18.99**

335-16426 Round Wooden Poles/Beams 4-3/8" 11cm **19.99**
335-16502 Large Plastic Pipes 4-3/8" 11cm **18.99**

335-16503 Banded Aluminum Pipes 3" 7.5cm **14.99**
335-16504 Banded Water Pipes Small (blue) 2-1/8" 5.5cm Each pkg(2) **18.99**
335-16506 Banded Gas Pipes w/Fitting Flanges Small (yellow) 2-3/8" 6cm **18.99**

335-16512 Aluminum Pipe "Alusuisse" Long 4-3/8" 11cm **20.99**

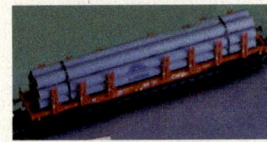

335-16812 Industrial Pressure Tank 2" 5cm **16.99**

335-16821 Overseas Shipping Crate 2-1/4" 5.8cm **20.99**
335-16832 Bridge Sections "Betomax" **31.99**
335-16833 Air Conditioner & Duct Piping 2-7/8" 7.3cm **20.99**

335-16837 Canvas-Covered Electrical Generator 2" 5cm **21.99**

335-16873 Heat Exchanger 2" 5cm **14.99**

335-16931 Large Wooden Machinery Crate Siemens 2" 5cm **17.99**
335-16934 Transport Crates **32.99**

FREIGHT CARS N SCALE

Here's a quick and easy way to make almost any car look and run better! Highly detailed one-piece loads capture the appearance of various bulk cargoes, making passing freights more fun to watch. Plus, the added weight of the plaster castings improves car performance without a lot of extra work. Each is hand-cast from a very strong gypsum material that picks up fine details much like dental plaster. Loads are then hand-painted to bring out the many details. Loads are custom measured to fit specific models as shown. (All cars shown in photos are HO Scale Models; all cars are sold separately.)

FREIGHT CAR LOADS

Coal Loads pkg(3) 7.02 ea
Keep coal revenues climbing on your railroad with these affordable loads, sculpted to capture the gleaming, faceted appearance of the real thing. Made for exact fit in the car shown, this is a quick and easy way to add the extra weight that hoppers and gondolas so often need to be good runners.

506-880 For Micro-Trains 33' 2-Bay Hoppers

506-1040 For Precision Masters 5-Bay Hoppers

506-1050 For Atlas 3-Bay Hoppers

506-1060 For Con-Cor 3-Bay Hoppers

506-1070 For Roco 4-Bay Hoppers

506-1300 For Roundhouse (MDC) Thrall Gondolas

506-1710 For Roco 2-Bay Hoppers

506-1750 For Model Power 4-Bay Hoppers

506-1770 For Atlas Ore Cars

506-2170 For E&C Shops Coal Porter Gondolas

Crushed Aluminum Bales 8.10 ea

506-1100 For Micro-Trains 50' Gondolas

506-1110 For Atlas 42' Gondolas

506-1120 For MDC 50' Gondolas

506-1130 For Con-Cor 50' Gondolas

Ore Loads
506-910 For Atlas 70-Ton Ore Cars pkg(3) 5.99

Pulpwood Loads
7.55 ea (Unless Noted)
506-1550 For Atlas 42' Flat Cars

506-1560 For Atlas Bulkhead Flat Cars - Lengthwise Logs

506-1561 For Atlas Bulkhead Flat Cars - 8' Logs

506-1570 For Micro-Trains Bulkhead Flat Car - Lengthwise Logs

506-1571 For Micro-Trains Bulkhead Flat Car - 8' Logs

506-1740 For Con-Cor Bulkhead Flat Car - Lengthwise Logs 6.99

506-1741 For Con-Cor Bulkhead Flat Car For 8' Logs 6.99

Scrap Metal Loads pkg(3) 6.47 ea
506-1140 For Micro-Trains 50' Gondolas

506-1150 For Atlas 42' Gondolas

506-1160 For Roundhouse (MDC) 50' Gondolas

506-1170 For Con-Cor 50' Gondolas

Sugar Beet Load
506-1720 For Dimi Trains Sugar Beet Gondola 7.55

Tarp Covered Loads
506-890 For Micro-Trains 50' Gondolas pkg(3) 7.29

506-900 For Atlas 42' Gondolas pkg(3) 7.29

506-1080 For MDC 50' Gondolas pkg(3) 8.10

506-1090 For Con-Cor 50' Woodchip Load Gondolas pkg(3) 8.10

Woodchip Load
506-1760 For Deluxe Innovations Gunderson Hoppers 6.47

Coal Load

Coal Load

Crushed Aluminum Load

Ore Load

Pulpwood Load

Tarp Covered Load

PRECISION CRAFT MODELS

HOPPERS

N&W H2a Hoppers Limited Run 6-Packs 129.99 ea

w/24" Lettering

HO Scale Sample Model Shown

588-800 Set #A
588-801 Set #B
588-802 Set #C
588-803 Set #D
588-816 Unnumbered

w/17" Lettering
588-804 Set #A
588-805 Set #B
588-806 Set #C
588-807 Set #D
588-817 Unnumbered

w/PRR Lettering
588-808 Set #A
588-809 Set #B
588-810 Set #C
588-811 Set #D
588-818 Unnumbered

w/B&O Lettering
588-812 Set #A
588-813 Set #B
588-814 Set #C
588-815 Set #D
588-819 Unnumbered

Info, Images, Inspiration! Get It All at
www.walthers.com

FREIGHT CARS N SCALE

RED CABOOSE

Model colorful freights in your favorite eras with these cars. All decorated models are supplied fully assembled, ready for use on your layout. For more variety, most are offered in multiple car sets, which feature individual car numbers. Undecorated cars are easy-to-build kits and are complete with trucks, couplers and weights.

New models and roadnames are released regularly: visit Walthers.com for the latest updates.

Items listed in blue ink may not be available at all times (see Legend Page).

Bi-Level Auto Rack
Roadname Shown Not Available

NEW PRODUCTS

Bi-Level Auto Racks 36.95 ea
NEW **629-19000** Undecorated w/Anti-Vandalism Panels
NEW **629-19100** Undecorated w/No Anti-Vandalism Panels

BOX CARS

Ready-to-run cars feature detailed plastic bodies and Micro-Trains® knuckle couplers.

62' PC&F 10' 6" Door Box Cars

Individual Cars 20.49 ea (Unless Noted)
629-172196 Western Pacific w/Feather Emblem **21.49**
629-17200 Undecorated **15.49**

Items listed below are available by Special Order (see Legend Page).
629-17205 DRGW
629-17207 Golden West Service
629-17209 ATSF (Indian Red)
629-17213 SP
629-17215 Tropicana
629-17221 UP w/Shield (Union Pacific Red)
629-17223 Golden West Service (blue)
629-17225 Tropicana (white)
629-17227 Manufacturers Railway

Three-Packs 61.47 ea (Unless Noted)
Items listed below are available by Special Order (see Legend Page).
629-17208 Golden West Service
629-17210 ATSF (Indian Red)
629-17214 SP
629-17216 Tropicana
629-17222 UP w/Shield (Union Pacific Red)
629-17224 Golden West Service (blue)
629-17226 Tropicana (white)
629-17228 Manufacturers Railway

62' PC&F 12' Door Box Cars

Individual Cars 20.49 ea (Unless Noted)
629-17293 Lamb Weston (white)
629-17297 ATSF Q for Quality

Items listed below are available by Special Order (see Legend Page).
629-17281 BN (Cascade green)
629-17285 MP
629-17289 CR
629-17291 BN (Cascade Green, small BN herald)
629-17295 ATSF (Mineral Brown)
629-17280 Undecorated **15.49**

Three-Packs 61.47 ea
Items listed below are available by Special Order (see Legend Page).
629-17282 BN (green)
629-17290 CR
629-17292 BN (Cascade Green, small BN herald)
629-17294 Lamb Weston
629-17296 ATSF

Thrall All-Door Box Cars

Cars include Micro-Trains trucks and couplers.

Individual Cars 20.49 ea (Unless Noted)
629-17408 St. Regis Paper
629-17422 Bennett Lumber (blue)
629-17427 Celotex
629-17430 St. Regis

629-17435 NOKL (Freight Car Red)

Items listed below are available by Special Order (see Legend Page).
629-17402 Georgia-Pacific
629-17403 Sacramento Valley Moulding
629-17404 Armstrong **20.95**
629-17405 Ashley, Drew & Northern
629-17410 Masonite Corporation **19.95**
629-17411 Brooks Scanlon
629-17413 Minneapolis, Northfield & Southern
629-17414 Seaboard Coast Line
629-17420 Canfor (gold)
629-17423 Thrall Demonstrator (red)
629-17424 Canfor (red & white) **20.95**
629-17425 MacMillan Bloedel (red & white) **20.95**
629-17426 Green Bay & Western (yellow & black) **20.95**
629-17428 Simpson
629-17400 Undecorated **16.49**

Three-Packs 61.47 ea (Unless Noted)
Items listed below are available by Special Order (see Legend Page).
629-17502 Georgia Pacific
629-17503 Sacramento Valley Moulding
629-17504 Armstrong
629-17505 Ashley, Drew & Northern
629-17508 St Regis Paper (blue)
629-17510 Masonite Corporation **62.85**
629-17511 Brooks Scanlon
629-17513 Minneapolis, Northfield & Southern
629-17514 Seaboard Coast Line
629-17515 British Columbia Railway **59.85**
629-17520 Canfor (gold)
629-17522 Bennett Lumber (blue)
629-17524 Canfor (red & white) **59.85**
629-17525 MacMillan Bloedel (red & white) **62.85**
629-17526 Green Bay & Western (yellow & black) **62.85**
629-17527 Celotex
629-17528 Simpson
629-17530 St. Regis

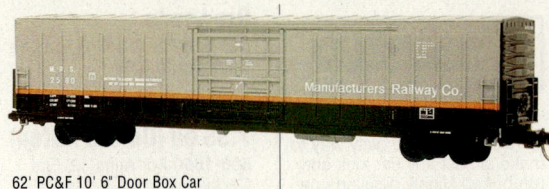

62' PC&F 10' 6" Door Box Car Manufacturers Railway 629-17227

3000 Cubic Foot 2-Bay Covered Hopper BNSF 629-25022

REEFERS

Ready-to-run (unless noted). Cars now come with Micro-Trains trucks and couplers.

57' Mechanical Reefer 20.49 ea
629-18603 SPFE (white) w/Hydra Cushion Underframe
629-18653 UPFE #2
629-18655 UP - Fruit Express
629-18809 Western Fruit Express (Mineral Brown, white roof)
629-18811 Maine Central
629-18815 NP (silver)
629-18817 ART - MP/N&W
629-18819 Erie

Items listed below are available by Special Order (see Legend Page).
629-18601 PFE - SP Version w/Hydra Cushion Underframe
629-18605 SPFE #1
629-18651 PFE - UP Version w/Keystone Underframe
629-18801 BNFE - Western Fruit Express "Safety is a Way of Life" (BN Green, white roof)

629-18803 BNFE - Western Fruit Express "Safety is the Future" (BN Green, white roof)
629-18813 Bangor & Aroostook

3-Packs 61.47 ea
629-18818 ART - MP/N&W

Items listed below are available by Special Order (see Legend Page).
629-18602 PFE - SP Version w/Hydra Cushion Underframe
629-18604 SPFE (white) w/Hydra Cushion Underframe
629-18606 SPFE #1
629-18652 PFE - UP Version w/Keystone Underframe
629-18654 UPFE #2
629-18656 UP - Fruit Express

629-18802 Western Fruit Express "Safety is a Way of Life" (BN Green, white roof)
629-18804 BNFE - Western Fruit Express "Safety is the Future" (BN Green, white roof)
629-18810 Western Fruit Express (Mineral Brown, white roof)
629-18814 Bangor & Aroostook
629-18816 NP
629-18820 Erie

COVERED HOPPERS

Ready-to-run (unless noted). Cars now come with Micro-Trains trucks and couplers.

3000 Cubic-Foot 2-Bay

Individual Cars 20.49 ea (Unless Noted)
629-25020 CNW
629-25000 Undecorated **15.49**

Items listed below are available by Special Order (see Legend Page).
629-25014 BNSF (green)
629-25018 Dakota, Minnesota & Eastern
629-25022 BNSF (Mineral Brown)

Three-Packs 61.47 ea
Items listed below are available by Special Order (see Legend Page).
629-25005 BN
629-25019 Dakota, Minnesota & Eastern
629-25023 BNSF

4700 Cubic-Foot FMC 3-Bay

Individual Cars
Items listed below are available by Special Order (see Legend Page).
629-25208 Western Pacific (gray) **20.49**
629-25200 Undecorated **15.49**

Three-Packs 59.85 ea
Item listed below is available by Special Order (see Legend Page).
629-25203 BNSF

FREIGHT CARS N SCALE

RED CABOOSE

4740 Cubic-Foot Pullman-Standard PS-2CD 3-Bay

Individual Cars 20.49 ea (Unless Noted)
629-25410 GN
629-25426 MP "Buzz Saw" Herald (gray)
629-25400 Undecorated 15.49

Three-Packs 61.47 ea
Item listed below is available by Special Order (see Legend Page).
629-25411 GN

4750 Cubic-Foot Pullman-Standard PS-2CD 3-Bay

Individual Cars 20.49 ea (Unless Noted)
629-25622 ATSF "Q" Herald (Mineral Brown) 21.49
629-25600 Undecorated 15.49

Items listed below are available by Special Order (see Legend Page).
629-25604 MKT
629-25624 Frisco
629-25626 D&H

Three-Packs 61.47 ea
629-25617 BN

Items listed below are available by Special Order (see Legend Page).
629-25623 ATSF "Q" Herald (Mineral Brown) 64.47
629-25625 Frisco
629-25627 D&H

OPEN HOPPERS

Ortner 5-Bay Rapid-Discharge
With Micro-Trains® Trucks and Couplers
629-25818 UP (black) 21.49

Items listed below are available by Special Order (see Legend Page).
629-25819 UP (black) pkg(3) 64.47
629-25800 Undecorated 15.49

100-TON EVANS COIL CARS

Models include Micro-Trains trucks and couplers. For extra covers and coils, please see the Red Caboose listing in the Parts section.

Ready-to-Run
Ready-to-run cars feature coil covers glued in place (some cover details will need to be added by modeler). Coils are not included.

Latest New Product News Daily! Visit Walthers Web site at
www.walthers.com

Individual Cars 21.49 ea (Unless Noted)
Items listed below are available by Special Order (see Legend Page).
629-17605 RDG
629-17607 SOU
629-17615 Grand Trunk Western
629-17617 N&W
629-17625 MILW
629-17627 CNW #1
629-17629 MP (Freight Car Red)
629-17633 Indiana Harbor Belt (black)
629-17637 IC #1 (black)
629-17643 CNW #2
629-17675 Illinois Central Gulf (orange, black) 22.49
629-17600 Undecorated 18.49

Three-Packs 64.47 ea (Unless Noted)
629-17630 MP (Freight Car Red)

Items listed below are available by Special Order (see Legend Page).
629-17606 RDG
629-17608 SOU
629-17616 Grand Trunk Western
629-17618 N&W
629-17628 CNW #1
629-17634 Indiana Harbor Belt (black)
629-17638 IC #1 (black)

Kits
Kits come unassembled so that modelers can arrange covers and coils how they want.

Individual Cars 20.49 ea (Unless Noted)
629-17707 SOU
629-17717 N&W

Items listed below are available by Special Order (see Legend Page).
629-17705 RDG
629-17715 Grand Trunk Western
629-17727 CNW #1
629-17729 MP (Freight Car Red)
629-17731 Rock Island (black)
629-17733 Indiana Harbor Belt (black)
629-17737 IC #1 (black)
629-17700 Undecorated 17.49

Three-Packs 61.47 ea (Unless Noted)
629-17730 MP (Freight Car Red)
629-17732 Rock Island (black)
629-17734 Indiana Harbor Belt (black)

Items listed below are available by Special Order (see Legend Page).
629-17706 RDG
629-17708 SOU
629-17716 Grand Trunk Western
629-17718 N&W
629-17728 CNW
629-17738 IC #1 (black)

FLAT CARS

42' Fish Belly Side Sill
Ready-to-run cars feature detailed plastic bodies and Micro-Trains trucks and couplers (unless noted).

Individual Cars pkg(2) 27.95 ea (Unless Noted)
Items listed below are available by Special Order (see Legend Page).
629-26002 SP
629-26006 C&O
629-26014 NH
629-26016 CB&Q
629-26024 PRR

Six-Packs 83.85 ea (Unless Noted)
Items listed below are available by Special Order (see Legend Page).
629-26007 C&O
629-26015 NH
629-26017 CB&Q
629-26025 PRR

73' Centerbeam Flat Car - Standard
Ready-to-run cars come equipped with Micro-Trains trucks and couplers.

Individual Cars
NEW 629-16501 TTX 22.49
629-16519 Plum Creek 21.49

3-Packs
NEW 629-16502 TTX 67.47
629-16516 BNSF (Mineral Brown) 62.85
629-16520 Plum Creek 59.85

73' Centerbeam Flat Car - Opera Window

Individual Cars 21.49 ea (Unless Noted)
629-16601 CSX 22.49
629-16603 UP w/Shield (UP Red)
629-16605 BC Rail
629-16607 MidSouth
629-16609 CN (yellow)
629-16611 Cascade Warehouse 22.49
629-16625 Tree Source (red, black) 22.49
629-16627 Atlanta & St. Andrews Bay (green)
629-16629 Centex (gray)

Items listed below are available by Special Order (see Legend Page).
629-16621 Tri-Con (blue)
629-16631 TTZX (yellow)
629-16633 BC Rail (BCR Green)

3-Packs 64.47 ea (Unless Noted)
629-16602 CSX 67.47
629-16606 BC Rail
629-16608 MidSouth
629-16628 Atlanta & St. Andrews Bay (green)

Items listed below are available by Special Order (see Legend Page).
629-16604 UP w/Shield (UP Red)
629-16610 CN (yellow)
629-16612 Cascade Warehouse 67.47
629-16622 Tri-Con (blue)
629-16626 Tree Source (red, black) 67.47

629-16630 Centex (gray)
629-16632 TTZX (yellow)
629-16634 BC Rail (BCR Green)

73' Center Beam Flat Car w/Open Panel

Individual Cars 21.49 ea
629-16803 Burlington Northern Santa Fe (Mineral Brown)

Item listed below is available by Special Order (see Legend Page).
629-16801 TTZX (red)

Three Packs 64.47 ea
Items listed below are available by Special Order (see Legend Page).
629-16802 TTZX (red)
629-16804 BNSF (Mineral Brown)

4750 Cubic Foot Pullman-Standard PS-2CD 3-Bay Covered Hopper Different Roadname Shown

Ortner 5-Bay Rapid Discharge Open Hopper UP 629-25818

100-Ton Evans Coil Car ICG 629-17675

42' Fish Belly Side Sill Flat Car Different Roadname Shown

73' Centerbeam Flat Car - Standard Different Roadname Shown

FREIGHT CARS N SCALE

Whether you're just starting out or you're a seasoned modeler, Atlas Trainman rolling stock is great for building your fleet. Ready-to-run cars feature injection-molded bodies, accurate painting and printing, free-rolling trucks with realistic brown plastic wheelsets and Accumate® knuckle couplers. Accumate couplers are made under license from Accurail, Inc. Different roadnumbers shown for some products.

NEW PRODUCTS

Ore Cars

70-Ton Ore Cars 7.95 ea (Unless Noted)
Cars are Box Car Red with appropriate markings unless noted.

NEW **751-39960A** BN #95901 (Cascade Green)
NEW **751-39961A** BN #95915 (Cascade Green)

NEW **751-39962A** CN #343002
NEW **751-39963A** CN #343018

NEW **751-39964A** CP #377200 (red w/"Multimark")
NEW **751-39965A** CP #377241 (red w/"Multimark")

NEW **751-39966A** GN #94140
NEW **751-39967A** GN #94157

NEW **751-39968A** DMIR #32807
NEW **751-39969A** DMIR #32811

NEW **751-39970A** UP #26420 (silver)
NEW **751-39971A** UP #26449 (silver)
NEW **751-3200** Undecorated **6.95**

Hoppers

ACF® 3560 Centerflow Covered Hoppers 9.95 ea (Unless Noted)
Cars are gray with appropriate markings unless noted.

NEW **751-39901A** C&O #601388 (gray, black)

NEW **751-39902A** C&O #601398 (gray, black)

NEW **751-39903A** Corn Products #80010 (yellow)
NEW **751-39904A** Corn Products #80012 (yellow)
NEW **751-39905A** DMIR #5020

NEW **751-39906A** DMIR #5025

NEW **751-39907A** Stauffer Chemical #63853
NEW **751-39908A** Stauffer Chemical #6385

NEW **751-39900** Undecorated **7.95**

GATX Airslide Covered Hoppers 9.95 ea (Unless Noted)
Cars are gray with appropriate markings unless noted.

NEW **751-38751A** KCS #5120 (red)

NEW **751-38752A** KCS #5129 (red)

NEW **751-38761A** RI #8510

NEW **751-38762A** RI #8521
NEW **751-38771A** PC #878841 (Jade Green)

NEW **751-38772A** PC #878842 (Jade Green)
NEW **751-38523A** SP (GACX) #42917

NEW **751-38524A** SP (GACX) #42918

NEW **751-38593A** UP #20013 (silver, red)
NEW **751-38594A** UP #20049 (silver, red)
NEW **751-38723A** GACX #45295

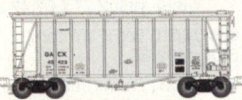
NEW **751-38724A** GACX #45429
NEW **751-3850** Undecorated **7.95**

Box Cars

ACF® 50'6" Box Cars 9.95 ea (Unless Noted)

NEW **751-39931A** Atlanta & St. Andrews Bay #7111 (green, yellow)
NEW **751-39932A** Atlanta & St. Andrews Bay #7141 (green, yellow)
NEW **751-39933A** CSX #136026 (blue)

NEW **751-39934A** CSX #136036 (blue)

NEW **751-39935A** St. Marys Railroad #4202 (white)
NEW **751-39936A** St. Marys Railroad #4240 (white)
NEW **751-39937A** Railbox #33604 (yellow)

NEW **751-39938A** Railbox #33677 (yellow)
NEW **751-39930** Undecorated **7.95**

50' Double Door Box Cars 9.95 ea (Unless Noted)
Cars are Box Car Red with appropriate markings unless noted.

NEW **751-36403A** Burlington Route #47065 (red)
NEW **751-36404A** Burlington Route #47099 (red)

NEW **751-36405A** C&O #6054 (black, white)
NEW **751-36406A** C&O #6055 (black, white)
NEW **751-36407A** NH #40506 (orange, black, white)

NEW **751-36408A** NH #40507 (orange, black, white)

NEW **751-36409A** ATSF "El Capitan" #10348
NEW **751-36410A** ATSF "Grand Canyon" #10237
NEW **751-36411A** SOU #44363
NEW **751-36412A** SOU #44365
NEW **751-36413A** UP w/"Automated Railway" Slogan #554001 (logo)
NEW **751-36414A** UP w/"Automated Railway" Slogan #554066 (logo)
NEW **751-3600** Undecorated **7.95**

STEWART PRODUCTS

Electric Loco Crane Kit

683-1200 25-Ton Diesel **36.95**
This kit is an American Hoist & Derrick Company prototype. The all-metal kit includes isometric drawings, detail parts and Atlas trucks and couplers.

Flat Car Loads

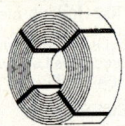

683-1210 Strip Steel Coils pkg(6) **5.95**
683-1225 Steel Mill Ingots pkg(6) **5.95**
683-1229 Ingot Molds & Stools pkg(3) **7.95**

Heavy Duty Ingot Flat Car Kit

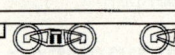

683-1230 Ingot Flat Car w/Atlas Trucks **12.95**

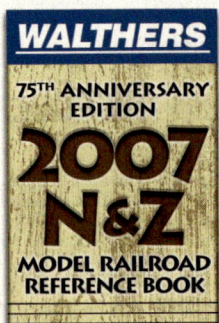

Models and Photo by Marc Pitanza, Old Bridge, New Jersey

DECALS

When you're in the business of moving rail freight to the largest city in North America, your switch crews keep busy round the clock. But back in 1953 when the hurricane hit, the Staten Island Rapid transit found itself working double duty handling its regular traffic bound for carfloats plus construction materials for repairing storm damage. This switch job on the South Beach Branch is led by one of the road's hardy Alco S-2s; it's pulling an LV gondola heaped with power poles to replace those damaged in the storm. They'll be unloaded on the siding at Wentworth Ave. by this afternoon.

When Marc decided to model the SIRT, he knew that there are no commercially available locos or cars decorated for the road. He custom painted the Arnold locomotive and lettered it with decals.

If there's a railroad you want to model, chances are that there are products in the Decals Section that will help make it easy to decorate your favorite equipment.

DECALS N SCALE

Blair Line LLC
PRODUCTS FOR MODEL RAILROADERS

All decals are reproductions of graffiti found on real railroad cars. Use on freight and passenger cars, buildings, walls, bridges and everywhere. Decals are not shown actual size.

BARN/WALL SIGN DECALS

4.00 ea

For many years, the sides of barns, silos and outbuildings were used as a convenient place for roadside advertising. These decals harken to that bygone era and can add realism to your layout. The prototypes for these signs were found on farm structures and barns.

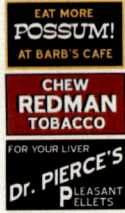
184-1250 Set #1 - Eat More Possum, Chew Redman, Dr. Pierce

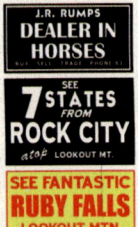
184-1251 Set #2 - Dealer In Horses, See Ruby Falls, See Rock City

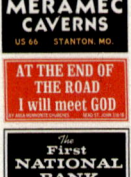
184-1252 Set #3 - Meramac Caverns, Will Meet God, First National Bank

184-1253 Set #4 - Meramac Caverns, Except Ye Repent, Kentucky Club

184-1254 Set #5 - Melo Crown Stogies, Mail Pouch, One Nation

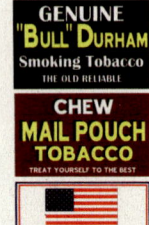
184-1255 Set #6 - Chew Mail Pouch, United We Stand, Bull Durham

Decal Set 184-602201 (shown on rolling stock, not included)

MODERN "TAGGER" GRAFFITI DECAL SETS 2.50 ea

184-1221 PAYDIRT

184-1222 ELVIS/SUSI

184-1223 CHOOCHOO/FACE

184-1224 KROS/SENIK

184-1225 HEATSEVER/RTZ

184-1226 PETROCK/BOUS

184-1227 DEBT/EMIR/OREC

184-1228 DOS

184-1229 HEAT/TCI

184-1230 PHAME/DEVA

184-1231 JOKER/MASK/NOEL

184-1232 KING/RESA

184-1233 ASIC/TAKO

184-1234 FAME/RKRE

184-1235 HALLOWEEN/BATUI

184-1236 ISRAEL/NEXT

184-1237 WONE/BULL/TVC

184-1238 JASE/SKETCH

184-1239 GISK/VEEGEE

184-1240 TATTOO NOMADS

184-1241 GODZILLA

184-1242 MUSE

184-602201 APEX/ZOOM

184-602202 PEASER/QUISP

184-602203 XYDE/QUASHE

184-602204 MONK/HOTWAX

Decal Set 184-602210 (shown on rolling stock, not included)

184-602205 AZTEK X2

184-602206 HEK/JUNK

184-602207 APART/TCI

184-602208 FUSE/GLIOTW

184-602209 ZOOM/PRAE

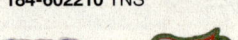
184-602210 TNS

184-602211 ANVL/JAIT

184-602212 SMOG/MBER/NISE

184-602213 WILD/BUG

184-602214 DRANE/FROG

184-602215 JESO/HM

184-602216 DISKO/CROME

184-602217 WEVER/AHUE

184-602218 NEZ/HOAX

184-602219 ONOROK/INCA

184-602220 MONK/MUZE

Mega Sets 4.00 ea

Each set has multiple decals per package

184-1244 Set #1 pkg(8) **4.00**

184-1245 Set #2 pkg(9)

184-1246 Set #3 pkg(8)

184-1247 Set #4 pkg(3)

184-1248 Set #5 pkg(8)

184-1249 Set #6 pkg(9)

DECALS N SCALE

WALTHERS

BLANK DECAL PAPER

Create custom decals for any kind of models with these blank sheets. Same high quality paper used in Walthers decals, ready to use. Choose from the standard 9 x 6" sheets, or larger 8-1/2 x 11" sheets (ideal for use with most photocopiers) in flat or gloss finish.

9 x 6" 22.5 x 15cm Sheets pkg(4) 3.98 ea
934-706820 Flat (Dull) Finish
934-706823 Gloss (Shiny) Finish

8-1/2 x 11" 21.2 x 27.5cm Sheets pkg(4) 7.98 ea
934-706821 Flat (Dull) Finish
934-706822 Gloss (Shiny) Finish

SOLVASET DECAL SETTING SOLUTION

904-470 Two Ounce Bottle **2.98**
For the most realistic models, decals should look like they're painted on. Getting professional results is easy with Solvaset. It actually softens the decal film so it snuggles down to the surface and stretches over details, such as rivets, without hiding them. Also eliminates air bubbles, white spots, draping and silvering. Just brush it on and Solvaset does the rest!

Daily New Arrival Updates! Visit Walthers Web site at
www.walthers.com

MICROSCALE

For a complete listing of Microscale decals, visit Walthers web site at www.walthers.com.

DECAL ACCESSORIES

460-50 Microscale System Pack **24.75**
Complete starter kit with one bottle each: Micro Set, Micro Sol, Micro Coat Flat, Satin and Gloss finishes, Micro Mask, Kristal Kleer, Micro Metal Foil Adhesive, Micro Weld Cement, Micro Liquitape and Micro Liquid Decal Film.

Adhesives 1oz (30ml) 2.50 ea

460-114 Kristal Kleer
Perfect for attaching window glass, aircraft canopies, headlights and other clear parts to models. Dries completely clear, or tint with food coloring to make light lenses, stained glass or other special applications. Can be used to model window glass by applying in a thin layer to window openings. Cleans up with water; waterproof when dry.

460-115 Micro Liquitape
Make any part removable with this special formula. Holds parts firmly, but gentle finger pressure will loosen them. Works over and over. Great for test fitting parts, or for showing off "hidden" features, such as interior detail.

460-116 Micro Metal Foil Adhesive
Give models the look of real aluminum with this adhesive. Works with thin metallic foils, (including common aluminum foil) to simulate stainless steel, chrome plating, or natural metal finishes.

Decal Setting Solutions 1oz (30ml) 2.50 ea

Setting solutions soften decal film, allowing it to stretch over details for the best appearance. Prevents air bubbles and results in an invisible carrier film, reducing silvering. Formulated especially for Micro Scale decals, can be used with most other brands.

460-104 Micro Set
Brush over area where decal is to be applied. Special wetting agents cut oils in new paint and strengthen adhesive on decal.

460-105 Micro Sol
A stronger formula, for use on larger details or stubborn areas. Just brush on and let it work, actually makes decal part of the paint.

Clear Finish 2.50 ea

Water clear, non-yellowing, acrylic resins adhere strongly to paint and plastics and hide decal film. Can be applied with a brush, or airbrushed (40lbs pressure), cleans-up with water.

460-103 Micro Coat Flat
Dead-flat for dirty, weathered or camouflaged look.

460-106 Micro Coat Satin
Semi-gloss, for a less shiny or slightly dirty look.

460-108 Micro Coat Gloss
Provides a smooth surface for decaling and produces a high-gloss, "wet look" when dry.

Liquid Decal Film

460-117 Micro Liquid Decal Film 1oz (30ml) **2.50**
Create your own decals or save old ones. To make your own, brush film on a flat clean surface, allow to dry and draw or paint on your image. When brushed over an old decal, film seals and provides a new surface.

Masking Liquid

460-110 Micro Mask 1oz (30ml) **2.50**
Works like masking tape in a bottle! Just brush on surface and allow to dry. Can be cut with sharp hobby knife to create special effects. For use with solvent based paints. (Micro Mask is water soluble.)

Decal Catalog

460-300 General Purpose **4.00**
Sets for larger models, including alphabets, signs, Pinewood Derby Cars, military equipment, dollhouses and more.

ACCESSORY DECAL SETS

Trim Film 1.75 ea

Solid sheets of a single color for all kinds of special effects, backgrounds, or custom art.
460-1 White
460-2 Black
460-3 Metallic Gold
460-4 Metallic Silver
460-5 Red
460-6 Yellow
460-7 Dark Blue
460-8 Dulux Gold
460-9 Dark Green
460-10 SP "Daylight" Orange
460-11 Guilford Gray
460-12 UP/Amtrak® Blue
460-13 Brown
460-14 Bright Blue
460-15 Gray Green
460-16 Boston & Maine Gray
460-17 Emerald Green
460-18 Maroon
460-19 Light Blue
460-20 DRGW Orange
460-21 NYC Gray
460-22 Royal Blue
460-23 CR Blue
460-24 Box Car Red
460-25 Caboose Red
460-26 Pullman Green
460-27 Stainless Steel
460-38 Flat Black
460-39 Dark Dulux Gold
460-40 "Micro-Glo" Glow-in-the-Dark Material
Great for signs, signals, special effects and much more on your layout. Lots of fun for Halloween and other craft projects too.
460-100 Clear

8-1/2 x 11" Sheets 2.00 ea

Create custom decals for any model using your own artwork or computer-generated designs. Correct size for most printers and copiers. Comes in clear, or white (most printers/copiers can not print white) for background color.
460-200 Clear
460-210 White

ALPHABETS & NUMBERS

Graffiti
Simulates spray-painted or hand-drawn lettering and numbers.
460-70211 White
460-70212 Black
460-70214 Silver
460-70215 Red

Stencils
460-601236 Tank Car Lading **4.40**

Union Pacific Style
NEW 460-70162 Black; No Outline
NEW 460-70165 Red; No Outline
NEW 460-70175 Red w/Black Outline

RAILROAD SETS 4.80 ea (Unless Noted)

Aberdeen & Rockfish
460-601245 Diesel Hood Units 1947+

Alaska Railroad
460-60256 Freight Cars 1960-70
460-60280 Diesels 1960-80
460-60480 Hood & Alco Cab Unit Diesels 1980+
460-604094 High Cube Box Car 1993+

American Freedom Train
460-601065 Alco PA Diesel & Cars 1947-49
460-601066 Alco PA Diesel & Car Stripes 1947-49

Amtrak®
460-60868 Superliner Phase IV Stripes 1994+
460-601244 Station Signs 1971+ (black lettering)
NEW 460-601267 GE P40/42 Diesels, Late
460-604314 "Pacific Parlour" Passenger Cars

Apache Railway
NEW 460-604323 Woodchip Cars

Baltimore & Ohio
460-6055 50' Double-Door Box Car 1970
460-6083 Steam Locos Medium 1930-50
460-601224 "Time Saver Service" Box Cars

Bangor & Aroostook
460-601187 Diesels 1970-95

BC Rail/British Columbia Railway
460-60783 British Columbia Railway Diesels 1990+

Boston & Maine
460-60176 Cab Unit Diesels 1960-1970
460-601014 Passenger Cars, Gold Lettering-60
460-601193 Bicentennial Diesels 1976+

Box Cars
460-6055 Spokane, Portland & Seattle, Chessie/B&O, Savannah & Atlanta, MP, DRGW
460-60218 Hutchinson Northern, Sabine River & Northern 50' Single Door 1970
460-604064 Tropicana 60' Insulated 1990
460-604388 Cotton Belt - SSW-40' & 50' Boxcars (blue streak)

Burlington Northern
460-6025 Diesels 1970-80
460-6070 SD60M Diesels 1990+
460-60251 Freight Cars 1970-80 (white lettering)
460-60292 40' Trailers 1970-80
460-60332 50' Gondola 1970-80
460-60340 62' Bulkhead Flat Car 1970-80
460-60364 Diesel Nose Stripes
460-60436 Bulkhead Centerbeam Flat Cars
460-60458 45' Trailers 1980
460-60459 Bicentennial Hood Unit Diesels 1970s
460-60477 5- & 10-Unit Piggy Back Flat Cars 1980
460-60484 Experimental Scheme for SD40, GP50, SD60 Diesels 1985
460-60492 Fuel Tenders & Loco Data
460-60515 50' Airslide Hopper 1980
460-60549 Diesels 1989

DECALS N SCALE

MICROSCALE®

460-60559 48' Container 1988
460-60569 45' Trailers 1989
460-60576 Cryogenic Box Car, Temp-Lok & 57' Mechanical Reefers 1970s
460-60621 SD60M Diesels #1991 "Desert Storm" 1991-2000
460-60631 20th Anniversary GP38 Diesel 1991
460-60649 Freight Cars 1990 Scheme w/Logo
460-60669 Husky Stack Container Cars 1991+
460-60674 48' Container America Special 1991
460-60695 Executive Train F Unit Diesels 1992
460-60711 Auto Racks
460-60716 Diesel Data 1980+
460-60723 48' Container & Chassis 1990+
460-60760 SD60M Diesels 1990+
460-60779 Passenger Cars & E Unit Diesels 1989+
460-60780 SD70MAC Diesel 1994+
460-60803 SD70MAC Diesels 1994+
460-60826 Maxi III Double Stack Cars 1990+
460-60842 Cabooses 1970+
460-604055 Natural Gas Powered SD40-2 Diesels & Tenders 1991
460-604069 Caboose-Freedom 1991
460-604072 EMD SD60MAC Demonstrator Diesels 1991+
460-604085 Commuter E Unit Diesels 1975-92
460-604097 Thrall Double-Stack Car 1986+
460-604106 BN/Western Fruit Express 57' Mechanical Reefers 1993+
460-604119 59' Tank Cars 1994+
460-604135 SD45 Diesels 1973-85
460-604157 67' Composite Box Car 1995+
460-604256 GP38M #1524 "Operation Lifesaver" Diesel

Limited Quantity Available
460-60252 Freight Cars 1970-80 (black lettering)

Burlington Northern Santa Fe
460-60943 "Warbonnet" SD75M Diesels 1996+
460-60944 SD70MAC Diesels-First Scheme (green, cream) 1996+
460-60968 Dash 9-44CW Diesels 1996+
460-60979 Dash-8 Diesels 1996+
460-601008 Dash 9-44CW Red & Silver Diesels 1997+
460-601009 Dash 9-44CW Red & Silver Diesels w/Nose Logo 1997+
460-601023 Repainted Diesels 1996+
460-601024 Dash 9-44CW Orange & Green Diesels 1997+
460-601035 Renumbered Diesels 1997+
460-601037 Center Flow Covered Hoppers 1996+
460-601038 3-Unit Double-Stack Cars 1997+
460-601044 SD70MAC "Premium Heritage" Hood Unit Diesels w/"Cigar-Band" Nose Herald
460-601071 "Warbonnet" SD75I Diesels 1997+
460-601235 82' Mechanical Reefers 2002+
NEW 460-601255 GE ES44DC Diesels 2005
NEW 460-601263 Standard Cab Hood Unit Repaints - 2005+
460-604148 SD70MAC Diesel #9647 (Early green & cream "Warbonnet") 1995+
460-604178 Gondolas 1996+
460-604254 Diesel "Patches" 1997+
460-604258 48' Trailer or Container 1997
460-604366 Dash 9-44CW #4723 w/Microsoft Train Simulator Logo
NEW 460-604380 ACF Center Flow Covered Hoppers
NEW 460-604383 Switchers & Slugs; Wedge Logo 2006+

B.C. HYDRO
NEW 460-601256 SW9, MP15 & SD38-2 Diesels 1961-88

Canadian National
460-60234 Freight Cars & Cabooses 1970-80
460-60567 Modern Diesels 1990+
460-60568 Diesel Stripes 1990+
460-60641 Switchers 1990+
460-60664 Intermodal/Trailers, Containers, Truck Cabs 1991
460-60707 4-Bay Cylindrical Hoppers 1976+
460-60720 Auto Racks 1980+
460-60746 CN North American Diesels 1992+
460-60804 48' Refrigerated Containers 1993+
460-60829 5-Unit Double Stack Cars 1990+
460-60849 48' Trailer & Tractor 1970+
460-60939 Diesels 1995+
460-60947 Cab Unit Diesels 1953-60
460-60948 Hood Unit Diesels 1953-60
460-601033 Wooden Cabooses 1920-61
460-601226 Expo "86" Diesels
460-604086 40' Box Cars 1985-95
460-604121 Gondolas 1980+
460-604227 Cabooses 1970+
460-604228 Center Flow Covered Hoppers 1995+

Limited Quantity Available
460-60957 Alco & F-M RS-3 1953-60 Diesels; H16-44, H24-66

Canadian Pacific
460-6038 40' Single-Door Box Cars 1950-60
460-6060 Maroon & Gray Cab Unit Diesels 1950-60
460-6087 Maroon & Gray Cab Diesels
460-6092 Maroon & Gray Hood Unit Diesels 1950-60
460-60221 Freight Cars 1970-80
460-60339 62' Bulkhead Flat Cars 1970-80
460-60671 48' Container 1991
460-60706 Cylindrical Covered Hopper 1976+
460-60721 Auto Racks 1985+
460-60733 Diesels 1969+
460-60737 Multimarks for Diesels 1970+
460-60738 CP Rail 8" Loco Stripes 1970+
460-60754 Diesels 1993+
460-60844 Bathtub Gondolas 1985+
460-60974 CP Rail System AC-4400CW Diesels 1995+
460-601073 SD70I Diesels 1997+
460-601131 Diesel Nose Stripes - 5" 1969-75
460-601152 Hood Diesels 1998+
460-601226 Expo "86" Diesels
460-604115 SD40-2 Diesels 1994+
460-604137 Covered Hoppers 1994+
460-604217 St. Lawrence & Hudson Diesels 1996+
460-604339 Cabooses 1969+
460-601052 "Golden Beaver" Modern Hood Unit Diesels 1997+

Central California Traction Company
NEW 460-604334 SW1500 Diesels; 100th Anniversary 2005+

Central of New Jersey
460-60231 Diesels 1950-65
460-60232 Diesels 1965-70
460-604361 Cabooses 1965-76
460-604367 Cabooses 1942-65

Central Vermont
460-60846 Diesels & Cabooses 1989+
460-60990 Hood Unit Diesels RS-3/GP7 1956-60
460-601020 Steam Locos 1931-60
460-601031 Wooden Cabooses 1920-61
460-601039 Black & Orange Diesels 1963-77
460-601040 Green & Yellow "Larson Scheme" Diesels 1977-95
460-604378 Bicentennial GP9 1976

Chesapeake & Ohio
460-6076 Steam Locos-Medium 1940-50
460-6095 Berkshire (2-8-4) Steam Locos 1940-50
460-60401 Hood Unit Diesels 1970
460-60875 Hood Unit Diesels & Switchers 1950-60
460-601042 E7A Diesel 1948-55
460-601045 Open Top Coal Hoppers w/Roman Lettering 1935-56
460-604245 Piggyback Flat Cars 1959-70

Chessie System
460-60308 40' Trailer 1970-80
460-60356 52' Gondola, 50' Flat Car 1970-80
460-60400 Hood Unit Diesels 1970-80
460-60790 Cabooses WM Safety 1976-89
460-60952 Cabooses C&O Safety 1976-89
460-604257 50th Anniversary EMD Diesel 1972
NEW 460-604325 2,600 Cubic-Foot HC-44 Class Centerflow Covered Hopper

Limited Quantity Available
460-601228 Covered Hoppers #1 - ACF & P-S Cars (1972-1989)

Chicago, Burlington & Quincy
460-6015 Hood Unit Diesels 1950-70
460-60108 California Zephyr Passenger Cars 1950-70
460-60752 Passenger Cars 1940-70
460-601110 California Zephyr Cars

Limited Quantity Available
460-6098 E Unit Diesels 1950-70

Chicago & North Western
460-6051 E Unit Diesels 1950-60
460-6089 Steam Locos 1930-50
460-60276 40' Trailer 1970-80
460-60290 SD40-2 Diesels 1970-80
460-60370 GP50 Diesels 1980
460-60515 50' Airslide® Hopper 1980
460-60541 C40-8, SD60 Diesels 1988
460-60560 F Unit Diesels 1949-75
460-60561 Diesel Cab Striping 1950s
460-60562 Coal Gondolas & Hoppers
460-60692 Auto Rack 1980+
460-60735 40' Wood Fowler Patent Box Cars 1914-59
460-60742 50' Coil Steel Cars 1969+
460-60781 Diesels 1990+
460-60845 Freight Cars 1992+
460-60859 Passenger Cars 1940+
460-60928 AC-4400-CW & Dash-9 Diesels 1995+
460-60963 Diesel Stripes 1948-60
460-601006 40' Box Cars w/Slogan 1937-58
460-601167 Cabooses
460-604006 Dash 9-44CW Diesels 1993+
460-604047 GE C40-8 Diesels 1990+
460-604054 Dash-8 40C Diesels 1991+

460-604113 Coal Hoppers 1994+
460-604166 Steam Loco Class RS-1 1944-55
460-604229 40' Box Cars-No Slogan 1944-62
460-604230 40' Box Cars Yellow Lettering 1963-69

Conrail
460-60157 Diesels 1976-80
460-60332 50' Gondola 1976-80
460-60339 62' Bulkhead Flat Cars 1976-80
460-60614 GE Diesels 1976-92
460-60627 Hood Unit Diesels 1976-91
460-60628 Diesel Data & Stripes 1991
460-60684 48' Containers 1992
460-60685 48' Trailer & 53' Container 1992
460-60709 Auto Racks
460-60740 Diesels 1992+
460-60742 50' Coil Steel Cars 1976+
460-60856 Hoppers 1985+
460-60862 "Quality" Freight Cars 1992+
460-60899 Coal Hoppers 1992+
460-60960 Hood Unit Diesels 1995+
460-60987 "Quality" Repaints 1995+
460-60994 SD80MAC Diesels 1996+
460-601034 United Way/Savings Bonds Diesels
460-601046 Assorted 50' Box Cars 1976+
Includes PRR and NYC reporting marks to show cars going to CSX or NS.
460-601051 SD70MAC Hood Unit Diesels (blue, white matches SD80MAC)
460-604049 SD50 #6707-Desert Storm Scheme 1991
460-604065 57' Mechanical Reefer 1989
460-604070 SD40-2 #6373 & SD50 #6726 US Olympic Cycling Special 1992
460-604223 Operation Lifesaver Diesels 1997+
460-604255 "Keep It Moving with Conrail" B23-7 Diesel 1980
460-604271 Engine Numbers Only for SD70/80MAC Diesels

Covered Hoppers
460-6023 Chemplex, Hercules, El Rexene, Ethyl 54' Center Flow 1970
460-60244 Kerr-McGee 30 & 45' 3-Bay ACF 1950-80
460-60301 Arco, Amoco, Gulf 55' 4-Bay Center Flow 1970-80
460-60314 Stauffer Chemical, Fort Worth & Denver, Continental Grain 54' ACF 3-Bay Center Flow 1960-80
460-60331 ADM, Norchem, Aurora Co-Op 54' Pullman-Standard 1970-80
460-60342 FMC Chemicals 55' ACF 4-Bay Center Flow 1970-80
460-60351 Pillsbury 54' 3-Bay Cylindrical 1970-80
460-60352 North American, American Hoechst Plastics 55' ACF 4-Bay 1970-80

98

DECALS N SCALE

MICROSCALE

460-60355 Dupont, Carlon 54' Pullman-Standard 4-Bay 1970-80
460-60410 W.R. Grace, Rexall, Plaskon Products 55' ACF 4-Bay 1970-80
460-60429 Englehard, Amoco, Shell Chemicals 55' ACF 4-Bay Center Flow 1970-80
460-60432 American, Reynolds Metals, Sinclair-Koppers 55' ACF Center Flow 1970-80
460-60660 Private Owner Names (gray, aluminum) 70-Ton 1939-75
460-60661 Private Owner Names (black) 70-Ton 1939-70
460-60690 NAAS Foods, Wonder-Bread, Engelhard North American Pressure Differential 1990s
460-60727 Corn Products 4-Bay ACF 1980+
460-60730 Penford, Goodyear, Amaizo ACF 4-Bay Center Flow 1975+
460-60739 North American Chemical 1992+
460-60744 Dupont, Saskatchewan Minerals Center Flow 2- & 3-Bay 1966+
460-60749 Private Owners 40' Airslide 1967+
460-60765 CO-OP Standard & Cylindrical Cars 1973+
460-60809 Canadian Potash Cylindrical & ACF Cars 1979+
460-60900 ADM 3- & 4-Bay ACF 1980+
460-604036 POLYSAR Resins ACF 4-Bay Center Flow 1989
460-604103 Holly Sugar Rapid Discharge 1990+
460-604123 Minnesota Corn Processors, Trinity Power Flow, ACF Pressure Aid 1994+
460-604259 Grain Train (Washington DOT) P-S/Trinity
460-604260 Grain Train (Washington DOT) Center Flow
460-604267 Kodak/Eastman Chemical ACF 4-Bay Centerflow 1960s Scheme
460-604275 AGP Grain Trinity 3-Bay
460-604276 ConAgra Pullman-Standard 4750 3-Bay 1973+
460-604277 Southdown Cement Co. 2-Bay 1998+
460-604291 Producers Grain 1970+
460-604296 Hostess/Wonder Bread ACF 4-Bay Covered Hopper Special US Bicentennial Scheme 1974+
460-604313 Farmland — For 5,161 Cubic-Foot Covered Hoppers 1996+

Limited Quantity Available
460-6024 Cosden, Equity, Cargill, Commodity Traders Pullman-Standard 1950-70

CSX
460-60497 Diesels 1986
460-60504 Freight Cars 1986
460-60508 45' Trailer 1986
460-60536 Diesels 1989
460-60575 Diesels 1990

460-60647 48' Container XTRA 1990
460-60682 Cabooses - Special 1991+
460-60697 Auto Racks 1990
460-60915 Wide Cab Diesels 1990+
460-60988 Freight Car Data 1985+
460-601180 Blue Scheme Diesels 2002+
460-601213 Box Cars - 50' Wood Packer, 50' Hi-Cube, 51' PC&F RBL
460-604082 Dash 8-40CW Diesels 1992+
460-604141 Diesels & Cabooses 1995+
460-604145 Coal Hoppers 1995+
460-604162 Diesel Data 1990+
460-604200 Aluminum Coal Gondolas-Coal Porter 1995+
460-604212 Grain Express Hoppers 1996+
460-604248 Switchers 1990+
NEW 460-604324 Diesel Names & "Spirit of..." Lettering

Data
460-601 Roman for Freight Car (black, white) 1940-70
460-602 Gothic for Freight Car (black, white)1940-70
460-6048 Diesels (black, white) 1950-80
460-60134 Diesels Builder's Plates (yellow & red) 1950-80
460-60193 Freight Car Capacity (black, white) 1970-80
460-60205 Diesel Number-boards Current
460-60228 Placards & Graffiti Freight Cars 1970s
460-60236 Tank Cars - Yellow & Black Lettering
460-60243 Graffiti Freight Cars 1970s
460-60260 Freight Large Capacity (black, white) 1960-80
460-60286 Box Car Door Markings 1930-40
460-60460 Freight Gothic (red, yellow) 1940-70
460-60462 For Freight Car (red, yellow)
460-60463 Freight Car Capacity (red, yellow) 1970-80
460-60527 EMD & GE Diesels 1988
460-60793 Data & Number Boards-E & F Units 1944+
460-60794 Data & Number Boards-FT Units 1939+
460-60852 Trailer & Containers 1965+
NEW 460-60925 General Electric Dash 9 & AC4400
460-601012 MOW Markings-Gothic 1950+
460-601013 MOW Markings-Roman 1950+
460-601122 Box Car Door Markings (black)
460-601123 Box Car Door Markings (yellow)
460-601168 Steam Loco Striping & Decorations 1860+
460-604117 International Containers 20, 40, 45' 1980+
460-604126 Consolidated Lube Plates 1985+
460-604161 EMD Diesels 1990+
460-604204 Trailer 1980+
460-604280 Automatic Car Identification ACI "Kartrack" Computer ID Plates 1967-77
460-604306 Steam Locomotive Data & Numberboards - Railroad Roman (white)
460-604309 Builder's Plates & Logos
460-604343 Diesel Model Number Plates (silver & black) 1939+
460-604353 Steam Locomotive Data & Numberboards - Railroad Roman (silver)
460-604355 Steam Locomotive Data & Numberboards – Gothic (white)
460-604356 Steam Locomotive Data & Numberboards – Gothic (Dulux Gold)
460-604357 Steam Locomotive Data & Numberboards - Gothic (silver)
460-604362 Steam Locomotive Numberboards & Data – Roman (gold)
460-604363 Steam Locomotive Numberboards & Data – Gothic (gold)

Delaware & Hudson
460-6031 Diesels & Cabooses 1970
460-6038 40' Single-Door Box Car 1960-70
460-60587 Blue & Gray "Lightning Stripe" Diesels 1970s-1980
460-604010 Baldwin "Shark" Diesels 1950
460-604061 Alco PA Diesels 1960-1980
460-604384 50' Box Car "I Love NY" 1982
460-604385 40' Boxcars

Detroit, Toledo & Ironton
460-604268 50' Outside-Post "Railbox" Box Car 1973+
460-604302 Diesels 1951-55
460-604303 Diesels 1962-77
460-604304 Diesels 1977-80
460-604305 Diesels 1980-83
460-604329 Bicentennial GP38-2 1975-80

Durham & Southern
460-601189 Diesel Hood Units

Elgin, Joliet & Eastern - EJ&E
NEW 460-601259 EMD SD38-2 #668 Bicentennial Scheme - 1976

EMD-Electro-Motive Division of General Motors
460-60141 E, F & SD45 Demonstrators 1950-70
460-60524 GP59 & GP60 Demonstrators & Oakway Leasing
460-60602 Lease Fleet Diesels
460-60603 SW1001 & 1500 Switchers
460-60613 FT Diesel Demonstrators 1939-89
460-60858 Demonstrators 1950 & Test Car 1959-63
460-60904 Numberboards 1985+
460-601003 GP7 & BL-1 Demonstrators 1949-53
460-604130 Numberboard Numbers, Round Style 1950+
460-604131 Numberboard Numbers, Square Style 1960+
460-604161 Diesel Data 1990+
460-604232 SD90MAC Demonstrator 1997+

EMD
NEW 460-604326 BL-20-2 Demonstrator Unit

Erie
460-6091 Steam Locos 1930-50
460-60606 Hood Units & Diesel Switchers 1945-60
460-60876 Hood Units & Switchers 1945-60

Erie Lackawanna
460-605 40' Trailer 1960-70
460-6016 Diesels 1960-70
460-60327 65' Gondola 1970
460-60573 Stripes for Passenger E, F & PA Diesels 1960-75

Florida East Coast
460-60140 Modern Diesels 1960-80
460-60142 Early Hood Unit Diesels 1970-80
460-60556 Diesels 1980s
460-60767 E & F Unit Diesels 1939-60
460-604244 Ortner Hoppers 1996+
460-601157 Ex-UP SD40-2 Diesels 2002
460-601158 Diesels 2002+

Fruit Growers Express
460-604238 Mechanical Reefers & Insulated Box Cars
460-604450 Mechanical Reefer 1980
460-604450 Insulated Box Cars
460-604022 57' Mechanical Reefers 1986

General American (GATX)
460-60557 Lease Fleet Diesels 1989
460-60601 Capital Corp. Lease Fleet Diesels 1990
460-60625 Tank Cars 1980s
460-60736 50' Tank Car 20-30,000 Gallon 1970+
460-60770 Covered Hoppers; 50' Airslide & 4-Bay Cars 1970+
460-604076 LPG Tank Car 66' & 63' 1990+
460-604058 Capital Corp. Lease Fleet Ex-UP SD40-2 Diesels 1991
460-604146 Cryogenic Box Cars 1995+

General Electric - GE
460-60532 GE Leasing B40-8 Diesel
460-60607 Dash-8 Diesel Demonstrators 1988-91
460-60834 Dash 9-44CW Diesel 1994+
460-60904 Numberboards 1985+
460-604056 Diesel Builders Plates 1950-91
460-604125 U25B Diesel Demonstrator Units 1962
460-604129 Numberboard Numbers 1960+

Golden West Service
460-60658 Assorted Freight Cars 1990
460-60693 62' Bulkhead Flat Car 1992
460-60693 Ballast Hopper 1992
460-60693 89' Flat Car 1992
460-60693 60' Woodchip Car 1992
460-60694 57' Mechanical Reefer 1992
460-60694 60' Cryogenic Box Car 1992

Gondolas
460-604332 Southwestern Electric Power Company (SEPX) 50' Coal Gondola 1979+
460-604335 Northwestern Oklahoma Railroad Co. - NOKL 50' Coal Gondola 1999+

Government of Canada 4-Bay Cylindrical Hoppers
460-60710 Alberta
460-60714 Saskatchewan 4-Bay Cylindrical
460-60717 Government of Canada (green) 1973+
460-60718 Canadian Wheat Board (green) 1973+
460-60724 Government of Canada 1982+
460-60725 Alberta 1976+
460-60729 Government of Canada 1970+

Grand Trunk Western
460-60650 Blue & Red Diesels
460-604350 50' Box Cars

Limited Quantity Available
460-60306 50' Single-Door Box Car 1970-80

Great Northern
460-6045 Cab Unit Diesels 1950-70
460-6086 Switchers 1940-60
460-60153 "Empire Builder" Passenger Cars 1950-60
460-60185 40' Single-Door Box Cars 1950-60
460-60268 Big Sky Blue 40 & 50' Box Cars, 3-Bay Open & Covered Hoppers
460-60417 Gray 70-Ton Airslide® Hopper
460-60571 40' Express Box Cars 1945-55
460-60815 Hood Unit Diesels 1950-67
NEW 460-601261 Steam Locos - Silver & White Lettering

Illinois Central
460-60348 E7 & E8 Diesels 1960-70
460-60528 Diesels (black & white) 1988+
460-60655 Diesel & Passenger Car Stripes 1980+
460-60895 Ice-Cooled Reefers 1960-73
460-604002 EMD Switchers
460-604029 45' Trailer 1988
460-604144 Executive E Unit Diesels 1995+

DECALS N SCALE

MICROSCALE

460-604210 Operation Lifesaver Locos 1993+

Illinois Central Gulf
460-60411 40' Single-Door Box Car 1970

Intermodal
460-60295 K-Line 40' Container 1970
460-60311 APL 20', Sea Land 40', Japan Lines 20 & 40' Container 1970-80
460-60731 Sea Land 40 & 45' Containers 1989+
460-60784 K-Line 20-45' Containers 1970+
460-60805 Mitsui (MOL) Lines 20-45' Containers 1980+
460-60877 Evergreen 20 & 40' Standard & Refrigerated Containers 1980+
460-604263 EMP 48' Box Containers
460-604286 Intermodal Equipment — Strick Lease 48' Trailers & Railtrailer
460-604331 Stone Container Corp. 48' Or 53' Trailer & Tractor (1996+)
460-604410 North American Container System (NACS) 53' Containers
460-604411 North American Container System (NACS) 53' Container Logos
460-604341 American President Lines 53' Containers

Lehigh Valley
460-60775 Cornell Red & Black Diesels 1940-60
460-60776 Cornell Red & Black Diesel Stripes 1940-60
460-60855 Late Cornell Red Diesels 1970-76
460-60922 Cabooses 1932-80

Locomotives - Miscellaneous
460-608 Logging Steam Locos 1930-50
460-6032 Interstate Diesels 1950-70
460-6044 New York, Ontario & Western Cab Unit Diesels & Cabooses 1950-70
460-60120 Virginian Steam Locos 1920-50
460-60147 Erie Mining Co. Diesels 1960-70
460-60187 Tidewater Southern RS-1 Diesels 1970+
460-60209 Kaiser Steel U30C Diesels 1970-80
460-60211 Tidewater Southern Diesel Switchers 1950-80
460-60440 Dark Blue & Black Anti-Glare Panels
460-60449 Light Blue & Maroon Anti-Glare Panels
460-60451 Red & Orange Anti-Glare Panels
460-60520 LMX B39-8 Diesels 1988
460-60524 Oakway Leasing SD60 Diesels

460-60545 Middletown & New Jersey and Middletown-Unionville Diesels & Freight Cars
460-60563 Pacific Electric Interurban Cars 1911-61
460-60570 Washington Central Diesels & Caboose
460-60586 Monongahela Railroad Hood Unit Diesels 1970-90
460-60598 Kyle Diesels
460-60668 Utah Railway SD40 Diesels 1992
460-60681 Alco Diesel Demonstrators 1965
460-60696 Chicago, Missouri & Western, Gateway Western Diesels 1987+
460-60701 St. Louis Short Lines Diesel Switchers 1954+
460-60755 Georgia North-Eastern GP7/9/18 Diesels 1988+
460-60782 Indiana Harbor Belt Diesels 1950+
460-60785 Belt Railway of Chicago Diesels 1950+
460-60820 Dakota, Minnesota & Eastern Diesels 1990+
460-60825 California Northern Diesels 1992+
460-60827 Willamette & Pacific Diesels 1993+
460-60860 Lake Superior & Ishpeming Diesels 1950+
460-60882 Lehigh & New England Diesels 1948-61
460-60886 Arkansas & Missouri Diesels 1989+
460-60951 Springfield Terminal Diesels 1995+
460-60955 Buffalo & Pittsburgh, Rochester & Southern Diesels 1989+
460-60985 Wheeling and Lake Erie Diesels 1991+
460-60985 Portland Terminal Switchers 1950-90
460-601027 I&M, Rail Link Diesels 1997+
460-601117 First Union Rail (FURX) Leasing Diesels
460-601173 Western & Atlantic Steam Locos 1860-66
460-601174 Western & Atlantic Freight & Passenger Cars 1860-66
460-601219 Central of Georgia Cabooses
460-601233 Seatrain Lines 40' Containers
460-601237 CWFX Lease SD40-2M Diesels (yellow, gray)
460-601240 Florida Tri-Rail F40PH, F40PH-2C, F40PH-2 Diesels 2000+
460-601250 Locomotive Leasing Partners, LLPX-Diesel Hoods & Switchers 2000+
460-604008 Gateway Eastern/Western Diesels 1993+
460-604018 McCloud River SD38 Diesels
460-604030 Chicago Central & Pacific Diesels 1985
460-604059 PLM SD40 Diesels 1991
460-604090 Midsouth GP7/9/18 Diesels 1988+
460-604092 Twin Cities & Western Diesels 1989+
460-604108 Blue Mountain Diesels 1993+

460-604110 Spokane International RS-1 Diesels 1962-67
460-604114 South Shore GP38-2 Diesels 1989+
460-604116 Red River Valley & Western Hood Unit Diesels
460-604127 Indiana Southern Diesels 1990+
460-604132 Cape Breton & Central Nova Scotia Diesels 1993+
460-604140 New England Central Diesels 1995+
460-604153 Central Oregon & Pacific Diesels 1995+
460-604154 LMS Dash-8 40CW Diesels 1994+
460-604156 TransKentucky Transportation Railroad Diesels 1985+
460-604158 Finger Lakes Railway Locomotives, Hoods 1995+
460-604167 Reading Blue Mountain & Northern Diesels 1991+
460-604175 Arkansas Midland Diesels 1992+
460-604176 Bay Colony Railroad Diesels 1994+
460-604177 Cape Cod Railroad Diesels 1993+
460-604179 Minneapolis, Northfield & Southern Hood Unit Diesels 1950-90
460-604182 Masscentral Diesels 1990+
460-604185 Reading & Northern Diesels 1992+
460-604187 Algoma Central FP9 Diesels 1995+
460-604188 Northwestern Pacific Diesels 1996+
460-604193 Georgia Group 1940-70
460-604216 Canadian American Diesels 1996+
460-604225 Clarendon & Pittsford Diesel Hoods 1985+
460-604249 Vermont Northern Diesels 1996+
460-604252 Quebec Southern Diesels 1996+
460-604252 Green Mountain Diesels 1965-87
460-604261 Allegheny Railroad Diesels 1990+
460-604287 Central California Traction GP7, GP18, Cabooses 1976+
460-604294 Yreka Western 50' Box Cars
460-604310 Evergreen Freight Car Corp. 50' Insulated Box Cars 1966-79
460-604312 Minnesota Soybean Processors 5,461 Cubic Foot Covered Hoppers 2004+
460-604365 Chattahoochee Industrial Railway 50' Box Cars
460-604370 ADM Corporation Tank Cars (New Logo)

Limited Quantity Available
460-60889 Georgia Group Railroads Diesels 1948-76
460-60901 Nashville, Chattanooga & St. Louis Diesels 1949-63

Louisville & Nashville
460-605 40' Trailer 1960-70
460-6038 40' Single-Door Box Car 1960-70

460-60817 Diesels (gray & yellow) 1963-80
460-60823 Diesels (gray & yellow) 1970-80
460-60824 Diesel Stripes (gray & yellow) 1963-70
460-60917 Diesels (solid blue or black) 1958-62
460-604105 Cabooses 1963-80
460-604295 50' Double-Door Box Cars 1978+
460-604387 Louisville & Nashville - L&N — 40" Boxcars

Maine Central
460-6081 50' Outside-Braced Plug-Door Box Car 1970-80
460-60218 50' Single-Door Box Car 1970

US Military Railroad Equipment
460-604278 US Army Diesels 1990s
460-604391 US Army Transportation Corps Diesels 1940+
460-601172 US Military Freight & Passenger Cars 1861-65

Milwaukee Road
460-6053 E & F Unit Diesels 1950-60
460-60389 E9A/B Diesels 1960-70
460-60441 Diesels w/Modern Hiawatha Logo 1980
460-60514 50' Box Cars 1970
460-60789 Diesels (orange & black) 1960-87
460-601004 "Hiawatha" Passenger Cars 1939-46
460-601113 Bicentennial SD40-2 Diesel

Missouri Pacific
460-605 40' Trailer 1960-70
460-6055 40' Single-Door Box Car 1960
460-6074 Hood Unit Diesels 1960-70
460-60113 Hood Unit Diesels 1970-80

Missouri-Kansas-Texas ("Katy")
460-601112 Cabooses
460-601124 Airslide Covered Hoppers

National Railway Equipment - NREX
NEW 460-601266 Lease Diesel Locos (Ex- BNSF, CP, SP, UP etc.)

National Railways of Mexico NdeM
NEW 460-604337 Box Cars 3.60

New Haven (New York, New Haven & Hartford)
460-6068 Hood Unit Diesels 1954-68
460-601060 Early Green & Yellow Diesel Lettering Only (use #601061 for stripes, sold separately) 1941-74
460-601061 Stripes Only- Green & Yellow Diesels & Electrics (use #601060 for lettering, sold separately)

460-601062 Electric Locos - Green & Yellow Scheme 1947-65

New York Central
460-6049 Cab Unit Diesels 1950-60
460-6058 40 & 50' Box Cars 1960-68
460-6078 Steam Locos- Medium 1900-57
460-6088 Cab Unit Diesels 1960-68
460-60618 Hood Unit Diesels 1950s
460-60932 General Service Passenger Cars 1939-68

Nickel Plate Road
460-6041 Diesels 1950-60

Norfolk & Western
460-6022 Hood Unit Diesels 1950-70
460-60106 Steam Locos 1930-80
460-60482 Cabooses (red, white) 1940-80

Norfolk Southern
460-60435 GE & EMD Hood Unit Diesels 1980
460-60574 Hoppers, 50 & 60' Box Cars 1988
460-60591 Freight Cars 1988+
460-60597 Road Railers
460-60945 Dash-8 & Dash-9 Diesels 1984+
460-604057 GP60 Diesels 1991
460-604270 48' Semi Trailer w/NS Herald 1996+
460-604392 GP59 Diesels: #4610 in Southern Railway Colors & #4611 in TRANSCAER Scheme

Northern Pacific
460-60037 40, 50 & 60' Box Car 1958-70
460-60046 Freight Service Cab Unit Diesels 1950-70
460-60118 Steam Locos 1889-1958
460-60132 Hood Unit Diesels - Gothic Lettering 1960-70
460-60133 Hood Unit Diesels 1950-70
460-60143 Switchers 1950-70
460-60184 Cabooses 1960-70
460-60208 Passenger Cars 1953-70
460-60404 50' Single-Door Box Car Pre-1970
460-60417 70-Ton Airslide® Hopper
460-60488 40' Ice-Cooled Reefers 1930-60
460-60511 50' Airslide Hoppers
460-60530 Passenger Service F Unit Diesels 1950s
460-60555 40, 50 & 57' Mechanical Reefers Pre-1970
460-60584 Freight Service F Unit Diesel Stripes 1950
460-60777 Assorted Freight Cars 1940-70
460-60786 Passenger Cars (Two-Tone Green) 1946-54
460-60787 Passenger Car Stripes Two-Tone Green Scheme 1946-54
460-60837 2- & 3-Bay Covered Hoppers 1964-70

DECALS N SCALE

MICROSCALE

460-60843 40 & 50' Box Cars 1942-70
460-601011 Maintenance-of-Way Equipment 1920-69
460-604109 40' Box Car w/Plug or Sliding Doors 1958-70

Pacific Fruit Express
460-6017 Mechanical Reefers 1960-70
460-60250 40, 50 & 57' Reefer 1960-80
460-60297 40' Trailer 1970
460-60407 50 & 57' Mechanical Reefers 1980
460-60408 SPFE 57' Outside-Braced Mechanical Reefers (white cars) 1980
460-60409 SPFE 57' Outside-Braced Mechanical Reefers (orange cars) 1980
460-60414 Ice-Cooled 40' Reefers 1946-52
460-60501 40' Mechanical Reefers 1949-60
460-604021 Ice-Cooled Reefer 1960

Limited Quantity Available
460-604240 Early Ice-Cooled Reefers 1920-42

Penn Central
460-605 40' Trailer 1968
460-6084 Diesels 1968
460-601094 Box Cars w/PRR-Style Numbers 1968-76
460-601096 Box Cars w/PC-Style Lettering 1968-76
460-601098 Box Car Esoterica - TOC, P&E Lettering, Black & Multicolor PC Logos

Pennsylvania
460-6021 Hood Unit Diesels 1937-68
460-6038 40' Single-Door Box Car 1960
460-6039 Cab Unit Diesels & Electrics 1950-60
460-6066 Steam Locos
460-6067 Cab Unit Diesels & Electrics 1955-68
460-60108 Passenger Cars-California Zephyr 1950-70
460-60677 Diesel & Electric Locos-5-Stripe (gold) 1939-52
460-60810 E Unit Diesels w/Single Stripe 1953-68
460-60891 Passenger Cars (Tuscan Red) 1947-68
460-60892 Passenger Car Stripes 1947-68
460-60893 Lightweight Passenger Car Names 1949-68
460-60894 Heavyweight Passenger Car Names 1945-68
460-60972 Merchandise Service Box Cars 1947-57
460-601141 Heavyweight Passenger Cars Pre-1945
460-601142 Heavyweight Passenger Car Striping Pre-1935
460-601143 Heavyweight Passenger Car Names Pre-1945
460-601166 Dulux Gold Lettering for Steam Locos 1948-60
460-601200 40' Box Cars Classes X26A, X26C, X28A, X29, X29A, X29B 1954-60
460-601201 40' Box Cars Classes X29D, X31A, X37, X37A, X37B, X43A 1954-60
460-601202 40' Box Cars Classes X43B, X43C, X46, X46A, X48 Series 1954-60
460-601210 Cabin Cars (Cabooses) 1927-68
NEW 460-601262 Class F30 (F30a, D & E) Flat Cars

Pittsburgh & Lake Erie
460-601248 NYC Flexi-Van

Pere Marquette
460-6047 Cab Unit Diesels
460-6095 Steam Locos-2-8-4 Berkshires
460-601042 E7A Diesels 1948-55

Rail Box
460-60160 50' Single-Door Outside-Braced Box Car 1960-80
460-60217 50' Single-Door Box Car 1970-80
460-60316 50' Single & Plug-Door Box Cars & 52' Gon 1970-80
460-604173 50' Repainted Box Cars 1992+

Reading
460-60125 Cab Unit Diesels 1950-60
460-60144 50' Plug-Door Box Car 1970
460-60379 50' Outside-Braced Box Car 1970
460-60686 Diesels, 1962-73
460-60691 RS-3 GP9, GP40-2 Diesels 1947-73
460-60708 Diesel Barricade Stripes 1947-73
460-60883 Cabooses 1924-76
460-604138 2-Bay Open-Top Hoppers 1944-76

Reefers
460-60144 Armor, Dubuque 40'
460-60150 Hormel 50'
460-60167 Land O' Lakes, White Rock, Wescott & Winks 40' Billboard
460-60172 Jelke Margarine, Wilson Milk, Puritan Malt 40' Billboard 1910-30
460-60173 Hygrade Food Products, Red Top Milk, Raths Packing Co., Southern Starr 40' Billboard 1910-30
460-60174 Wescott & Winks 40' Billboard
460-60890 Merchants Despatch Transportation Co. 1930-68
460-601010 Railway Express Agency 50' Cars 1929-67
460-601030 GPEX Milk Cars 1920-70
460-601111 Palace Cars Scrolls, Names & Numbers 1880-1910 (gold) UP, ATSF, Rock Island, CB&Q, GN, Tonopah & Tidewater
460-604107 Americold Cryogenic Box Car 1993+

Reflective Conspicuity Markings 2005+ (Reflector Stripes)
Now being applied to new and older equipment; mounted vertically on tank cars, horizontally or vertically on all other types of cars and locos.
NEW 460-604389 Yellow
NEW 460-604390 White

Rio Grande (DRGW)
460-605 40' Trailer 1960-70
460-6028 Hood Unit Diesels 1960-80
460-6040 Cab Unit Diesels 1950-60
460-6055 55' ACF 4-Bay Covered Hopper 1975
460-6056 F, PA & PB Cab Unit Diesels 1950
460-6060 Narrow Gauge Steam Locos & Cabooses 1920-70
460-6073 Narrow Gauge Freight Cars 1930-70
460-6082 50' Single Double-Door Box Cars 1954-72
460-6096 Early Hood Unit Diesels
460-60108 Passenger Cars-California Zephyr 1950-70
460-60199 Caboose 1970-80
460-60271 EMD Hood Unit Diesel Stripes 1960-80
460-60356 52' Gondola 1970-80
460-60411 40' Single-Door Box Car 1970-80
460-60456 45' Trailers 1980
460-60515 50' Airslide Hopper 1980
460-60542 Standard Gauge Steam Loco 1930s
460-60577 Ski Train & Business Cars 1986
460-60660 Auto Racks 1980s
460-60816 12-Panel, 4-Bay Hoppers 1970+
460-601047 Pullman PS2CD 4427 Covered Hoppers
460-601110 California Zephyr Cars
460-601128 Hood Diesels 1962-84
460-601129 Hood Diesel End Stripes
460-604311 40' Hi-Cube 1967
460-604408 40' Airslide Covered Hoppers 1960+

Rio Grande Southern
460-6059 Narrow Gauge Steam Locos & Caboose 1930-40
460-60170 Narrow Gauge Passenger Cars - Narrow Gauge 1920-40
460-60179 Narrow Gauge Freight Cars & Cabooses 1920-40

Rock Island
460-6018 Diesels 1960-70
460-6019 Box Cars & Hoppers 1960-70
460-6020 Box Cars & Hoppers 1960-70
460-60218 50' Single-Door Box Car 1960
460-60229 Freight Cars - ROCK 1970
460-60230 Diesel Hoods - ROCK 1970
460-60233 40' Trailer 1970
460-60259 (Last) Freight Cars - Fallen Flag 1970-80
460-60351 54' Pullman-Standard 3-Bay Covered Hopper 1970
460-60361 F Unit Diesels 1940-60
460-60956 E & F Unit Diesels 1943-60
460-60989 GP7 & RS-3 Diesels 1950-60
460-601132 Steam Locos 1915-37
460-601133 Steam Locos 1937-54
460-601229 Cabooses Part I; Wood & Early Steel Cars
460-601230 Cabooses Part II; Late Steel & Transfer Cars
460-604104 Passenger Sleeping Cars 1947-60

Santa Fe (ATSF)
460-609 Box Cars & Reefers 1960-70
NEW 460-879 Box Cars
460-6012 Diesels 1950-70
460-6029 Diesels 1972
460-6030 Box Cars, Hoppers & Reefers 1972
460-6064 Steam Locos-Silver Lettering 1930-50
460-6072 Passenger Service Cab Unit Diesels 1940-60
460-6077 Freight Service Cab Unit Diesels 1940-70
460-6079 Maintenance-of-Way Cars 1940-80
460-60101 Passenger Service Cab Unit E8, F7, DL-109 Diesels 1950-70
460-60112 Express Box Cars w/Maps 1950-60
460-60114 "Super Chief" Passenger Cars 1950-70
460-60121 Cabooses 1940-80
460-60127 "Scout" Passenger 1950-60
460-60128 Tank Cars 1950-80
460-60136 40' Reefer w/Map 1940-50
460-60168 Gas Electric 1929-68
460-60188 Red & Silver Warbonnet U28CG & U30CG Diesels
460-60215 50' Box Cars w/Map 1950-60
460-60216 50' Box Cars w/Map 1950-60
460-60233 40' Trailer 1970
460-60247 Switchers w/Silver Zebra Stripes
460-60248 Hood Unit Diesels (silver) 1950-60
460-60255 Mechanical Reefers 1960-80
460-60261 50' Single-Door Box Car 1970
460-60263 50' Double-Door Box Car 1960
460-60264 50' Insulated Box Cars 1960-80
460-60267 Food & 60' Auto Parts Box Cars 1960-70
460-60288 70-Ton ACF 2-Bay Covered Hoppers 1950-80
460-60291 40' Trailers Blue & Red 1960-70
460-60332 50' Gondola 1970-80
460-60356 52' Gondola 1970-80
460-60363 Steam-Tender Data 1920-50
460-60369 SD40-2 "Snoot" Diesels 1980
460-60383 Heavyweight Passenger Cars 1920-50
460-60390 Passenger Car Stripes 1940+
460-60444 54' Pullman-Standard 3- & 4-Bay Covered Hopper 1970
460-60469 SD45 Pre-Merger 1985
460-60470 10-Pack Piggyback Flat Cars 1970-80
460-60475 ATSF Warbonnet (Solid blue panels w/curves, for blue & yellow hood unit diesels)
460-60476 SFSP Warbonnet Merger Scheme (Solid red panels w/curves, for red & yellow hood unit diesels)
460-60483 Bicentennial SD45-2 Diesel 1976
460-60496 ATSF Warbonnet Merger Scheme 1986
460-60498 40' Box Cars w/Straight Line Map 1940-47
460-60503 50' 100-Ton Airslide Hopper 1985
460-60505 All 40-50' Box Cars 1947-59
460-60506 All 40-50' Box Cars 40' All 1947-59
460-60509 40' Ice-Cooled Reefers 1940
460-60510 50' Mechanical Reefers 1950
460-60516 40' Box Cars w/Curved Line Map 1940
460-60517 40' Ice-Cooled Reefers w/Curved Map 1930-40
460-60548 Alco Hood Unit Diesels 1960
460-60585 GP60M Diesel 1990
460-60599 FP45 Diesel 1970-90
460-60619 Hood Unit Diesels 1990
460-60637 GE Dash 8-40BW/CW & 9-44CW Diesels 1991
460-60638 Containers & Chassis 1990+
460-60647 48' Container XTRA 1990
460-60676 GP60B Diesel 1991
460-60688 Auto Racks 1980s+
460-60699 F Unit Diesels 1940-52
460-60772 5-Unit Double Stack Cars 1989+
460-60791 Covered Hoppers 1990+
460-60800 Box Cars 1990+
460-60831 Alco, F-M Erie-Built & Baldwin DL-109 Diesels 1941-63
460-60832 Sleeping Cars 1940-65
460-60914 Cabooses Ce-1 to Ce-13 1979+
460-60961 Sleeping Cars 1939-70
460-601067 Extra Numbers for Diesels (use w/#8729, 87369, 87619, all sold separately) 1972-95
460-601072 E3 & E6 Diesels 1939-68

DECALS N SCALE

MICROSCALE®

460-601161 Hood Diesels w/White "Zebra Stripes" 1934-61
460-601164 Steam Locos w/White Lettering & "Blue Goose"
460-601188 Passenger F-Unit Striping 1946-75
460-601234 Selective Ballast Hopper 1940-96
460-601243 Shadow-Line Passenger Cars 1996+
460-601254 SK Class Stock Cars; Sk-Q, R, S, T, U, Z, 2, 3, 4, & 5
NEW 460-601265 40' Ice Reefer Car Numbers for Ends, Roof & Ice Hatches
460-604003 Rebuilt EMD SSB1200 Diesel Switchers (yellow "Warbonnet") 1974-85
460-604025 50' Steel Coil Cars 1988
460-604037 25' Van & Tractor 1970s
460-604042 ATSF/J.B. Hunt 48' Trailer - Quantum 1989
460-604128 Woodchip Cars 1985+
460-604174 High Level Passenger Cars 1956-70
460-604190 General Service Passenger Cars 1939-70
460-604281 "SFTT" 40' Trailer (blue, white) 1979+
460-604346 ACF Center Flow Covered Hoppers
460-604401 Way Cars (Cabooses) 1910-1971

Seaboard Air Line
460-6096 40 & 50' Box Cars 1950-65
460-60104 Cab Unit Diesels Diesel Cabs 1950-60
460-60151 Cabooses 1950-60
460-60152 Diesel Switchers 1950s-60s
460-60307 50' Single-Door Box Car 1950-70
460-60439 E Unit Diesels 1950-60
460-60565 Freight Service Diesels 1950s
460-60566 Freight Service Diesel Stripes 1950s
460-601007 Covered Hoppers 1947-63

Seaboard Coast Line
460-605 40' Trailer 1960-70
460-606 Freight Cars 1960-70
460-60896 Diesels 1967-72
460-601238 "Split Image" Diesels

Limited Quantity Available
460-60398 Hood Unit Diesels 1980

Soo Line
460-60116 Diesels Yellow & Maroon 1950-60
460-60117 Diesels Red & White 1970-80
460-60119 Switchers 1950-61
460-60327 50' Gondola 1970-80

460-60418 57' Mechanical Reefer 1970-80
460-60553 Diesels 1989
460-60692 Auto Rack 1980+
460-60965 40 & 50' Box Cars 1950-65
460-60998 Early Piggyback Trailers 1955-63
460-60999 Late Piggyback Trailers 1963-80
460-601048 40 & 50' Box Cars 1950s+
460-601114 50' Box Car 1960s-80s
460-601115 50' Box Cars "Colormark" 1963-79
460-601116 Box Cars "Colormark" Variations
460-601136 Steam Locomotives 1920-55
NEW 460-601215 Steel Cabooses 1966-97
460-604215 Flat Cars 1961-90

SRY Rail Link
NEW 460-601258 Diesel Hood Units & Switchers

Southern Pacific
460-603 Freight Cars 1950-70
460-6011 Diesels 1960-70
460-6033 "Daylight" Steam Loco 1940-50
460-6034 "Daylight" Passenger Cars 1940-60
460-6050 "Daylight" Cab Unit Diesels 1950-60
460-6065 Steam Locos Medium 1920-50
460-6071 Early Diesel Switchers "Tiger Stripes" 1950-60
460-6075 Steam Locos Heavy 1940-50
460-60105 Steam Locos Light 1930-50
460-60107 Passenger Cars - Gray Letters 1960-80
460-60122 "Golden State" Passenger Cars 1950-60
460-60126 Passenger Cars 1950-60
460-60155 Maintenance-of-Way Equipment 1940-80
460-60177 Diesels 1960-80
460-60178 "Sunset Limited" Passenger Car Stripes 1960-80
460-60186 Diesels-Experimental "Daylight" Scheme (orange, red) 1970
460-60194 Ore Cars 1960-80
460-60201 "Black Widow" Diesels 1940-50
460-60204 "Sunset Limited" Passenger Cars 1950-60
460-60227 Cabooses 1940-80
460-60239 Covered Hoppers
460-60241 Heavyweight Passenger Cars (gold, Dulux)
460-60857 "Speed Lettering" 1994+
460-60258 Loading Symbols 1970-80
460-60261 57' Mechanical Reefer 1970
460-60262 "Daylight" Passenger Car Stripes 1950-60
460-60270 Pullman-Standard 70-Ton 2-Bay Covered Hoppers 1960-80

460-60390 Passenger Car Stripes 1940+
460-60403 45' Trailer 1980
460-60419 70-Ton Airslide Hopper 1970-80
460-60447 Hood Unit Diesels 1980
460-60464 SD40 Diesel & 45' Trailer Los Angeles Olympics Scheme 1980s
460-60469 SPSF SD45 Diesel Pre-Merger "Kodachrome" 1985
460-60472 4-Pack Piggyback Flat Cars 1980
460-60495 40' Trailer 1980
460-60496 SPSF Hood Unit Diesels-Proposed Merger "Kodachrome" 1986
460-60500 40' Trailer 1984-85
460-60503 50' 100-Ton Airslide Hopper 1985
460-60529 57' Mechanical Reefers 1960
460-60611 Company Police Cabooses & Passenger Cars
460-60612 Red Names & Numbers for Hood Unit Diesels (Use with #60447) 1989
460-60617 Red Wings for Diesels 1950s
460-60620 GP40 Diesels in Merger Scheme Speed Lettering 1991
460-60646 GP60 Diesels 1991
460-60657 48' Container 1990
460-60660 Auto Racks 1980s
460-60745 Gunderson Maxi Stack 1990+
460-60761 Passenger Car Emblems 1937-70
460-60835 Bicentennial Diesels 1975-80
460-60857 Modern SD70, Dash 9 Diesels 1994+
460-60911 Wood Box Cars 1923-62
460-60923 "Overnight" Box Cars 1946-59
460-601055 "Shasta Daylight" & "Coast Daylight" Passenger Cars 1947-58
460-601057 "Shasta Daylight" E7A/B Cab Unit Diesels 1947-49
460-601069 SP/SSW Extra Diesel Numbers & Nose Heralds
460-601148 Bridge Lettering 1959+
460-601214 100-Ton Open Hoppers
460-601251 86' Hi-Cube Auto Parts Box Cars; Classes B-100-19, 1968-96
460-601252 86' Hi-Cube Auto Parts Box Cars w/Gray Striping & Arrows 1968-96
460-601253 SP/SSW — ACF 4,650 Cubic Feet Centerflow Covered Hoppers 1966-1996
NEW 460-601260 Diesel Hood Numbers (Lettering Gray)
460-604001 "Black Widow" GP9 Diesels 1950-60
460-604027 25' Trailer & Tractor 1950
460-604044 Tank Car 12,500-Gallon 1950
460-604101 Woodchip Cars 1975+
460-604136 Silver Trailer Flat Service Cabooses 1951-65
460-604160 50' Box Cars w/Speed Lettering 1995+

460-604273 SFSP Cabooses 1986+
460-604298 89' Enclosed Autoracks w/Speed Lettering 1991-96
460-604400 Diesels w/San-Serif Lettering 1958+
NEW 460-604381 "Overnight" Box Car Number Set **3.60**
NEW 460-604382 Speed Lettering for GP38-2 Diesels **3.60**

Southern Railway
460-6013 Box Cars & Hoppers 1960-70
460-6014 40, 50 & 86' Box Cars 1960-70
460-6032 Hood Unit Diesels 1950-70
460-6062 Diesel Cab E & F Units 1950-80
460-60297 40' Trailer 1960-70
460-60308 40' Trailer 1970-80
460-60419 70-Ton Airslide Hopper 1970-80
460-60461 45' Trailer 1980
460-60539 Diesels 1971
460-60540 Diesel Stripes 1971
460-60608 Diesels 1940-60
460-60878 Early Hood Units & Switchers, Green Scheme 1940-60
460-60879 Diesel Cabs 1940-60
460-604084 Bay Window Cabooses 1960
460-604196 Coil Steel Car 1974-85

Southern Railway of British Columbia
NEW 460-601257 EMD MP15 & SD38 Diesels

Spokane, Portland & Seattle
460-60102 E, F & FA Diesels 1950-70
460-60196 Switchers (black) 1950-60
460-601026 40 & 50' Steel Box Cars 1946-68
460-604016 EMD or Alco Cab Unit Diesels 1950

STAX
460-601249 Containers

Tank Cars
460-60413 Tank Train 50' Cars 1980
460-60502 Corn Products, Amaizo, Hubinger, Trusweet 50' Cars 1985
460-60615 Staley 1975-91
460-60645 Cargill 1970-91
460-60689 ADM 1990s
460-60727 Corn Products Tank Car 40' 1980+
460-60796 Assorted Private Names 1970+
460-60828 Engelhard, SCM Chemicals, Thiele 40' Cars 1975+
460-60986 10,000-Gallon CB&Q, CNW, Frisco, Indian Refining, Kansas City Southern, Southwestern Refining, Texas Co., Western Pacific 1910-50
460-601016 Assorted ACFX 6,000 & 8,000-Gallon 1910-50
460-604118 Occidental Chemical 1994+

460-604124 Minnesota Corn Processors 40 & 50' Cars 1994+
460-604236 ACFX 33,000-Gallon 1979
460-604264 Richmond Tank Car Co. 65' Propane Gas Tank Car
460-604345 40' Box Cars

Texas-Mexican
460-604373 Diesels 1950-58

Toledo, Peoria & Western
460-60129 Hood Unit Diesels 1950-70
460-60648 "Lightning Stripe" Diesels 1991
460-601063 SW1500 Diesel Switchers (orange, white) 1968-83

Trailer Train/TTX
460-60339 62' Bulkhead Flat Cars 1970-80
460-60471 5-Unit Piggyback Flat Car 1980
460-60552 50, 60, 68, 85 & 89' Flat Cars
460-60578 50, 60, 68 & 85' Flat Cars 1970+
460-60670 Husky Stack Container Cars 1991+
460-60722 Thrall Double Stack Car 1991+
460-60732 TTX Thrall Double Stack 1991+
460-60747 89' Long Runner Flat Car 1990+
460-60750 4-Unit Double Stack 1990+
460-60788 Articulated Double Stack Car 1989+
460-60822 All-Purpose Spine Car 1990+
NEW 460-604386 NTTX Container Spine Cars (Trailer-Train, TTX & Santa Fe)

Limited Quantity Available
460-60579 89' & Long Runner Flat Car

Trucks & Vehicles
460-604087 Sunkist 40' Trailers & Tractors
460-604163 Trans Western Express Trailers & Tractors
460-604369 Haslam Septic Co. Tank Truck

Union Pacific
460-607 Freight Cars 1960-70
460-6010 40 & 50' Box Cars 1950-70
460-6035 Diesels & Turbines 1960-70
460-6036 Diesels 1960-80
460-6063 Steam Locos 1930-80
460-6097 Cabooses w/Safety Slogan 1970
460-60109 Passenger Service Cab Unit Diesels 1950-80
460-60169 Diesel Hoods 1979
460-60222 Bathtub Gondolas 1970-80
460-60223 Cabooses CA11 1970-80
460-60242 57' Mechanical Reefer 1970-80
460-60254 Maintenance-of-Way Equipment 1960-70

DECALS N SCALE

MICROSCALE®

460-60257 Caboose Safety Slogans 1970-80
460-60265 100-Ton Pullman-Standard Covered Hoppers 1960-80
460-60321 50' Plug-Door Box Car 1970-80
460-60340 62' Bulkhead Flat Cars 1970-80
460-60343 40' Trailer 1960-70
460-60354 Hood Unit Diesels (gray & yellow) 1970-80
460-60356 52' Gondola 1970-80
460-60373 Switchers 1980
460-60390 Passenger Car Stripes 1940+
460-60392 Passenger Cars 1950
460-60417 70-Ton Airslide® Hopper 1970-80
460-60431 UP Gray Anti-Glare Panels
460-60437 Bulkhead Centerbeam Flat Car
460-60453 SD40-2 Diesels w/Slogans
460-60465 50' Plug-Door Box Car
460-60466 40, 50 & 86' Box Cars 1980
460-60467 50' Plug-Sliding Door Box Cars 1980
460-60468 50 & 86' Plug-Sliding Door Box Cars 1980
460-60489 40-50' Box Cars 1939-50
460-60490 Semi Tractors & 30, 40 & 45' Trailers 1980
460-60494 40 & 50' Box Cars 1952-59
460-60499 40' Box Car 1926-39
460-60507 50' 100-Ton Airslide® Hopper 1980
460-60512 Stock Car 5-40-10, 11 & 12
460-60522 GP40, SD40, B23-7 & GP15-1 Diesels
460-60523 C40-8, SD60 Diesels
460-60580 Coal Turbine #8080
460-60616 Passenger Cars 1947-89
460-60622 E Unit Diesels 1950s
460-60623 E Unit Diesels 1950s
460-60624 E Unit Diesels 1950-60
460-60630 Passenger Cars 1947-89
460-60635 Lightweight Passenger Cars 1947-71
460-60636 Heavyweight/Business Passenger Cars 1947-91
460-60653 Loco E Unit Diesels 1950s
460-60679 Auto Racks 1990
460-60683 40' Express Box Car 1960+
460-60833 Passenger Cars 1942-53
460-60841 Early Piggyback Trailers 1947-60
460-60847 60' Insulated Beer Service Box Cars 1977+

460-60850 4750 Cubic Foot Covered Hoppers 1976+
460-60851 Diesel SD40-2 1994
460-60905 Early Cabooses 1941-77

460-60977 Diesels 1996+
460-60997 SD90MAC Diesels 1996+ (Includes "We Will Deliver" Slogans)
460-601053 1996 Olympic Torch Relay SD40-2 Diesel
460-601054 1996 Olympic Torch Relay Passenger Cars
460-601056 Business/Excursion Passenger Cars 1996+
460-601068 Extra Numbers for Diesels (red) Use with 60523, 60977, 60997, 604028 or 604120, all sold separately.
460-601080 "Challenger" Passenger Cars (green scheme)
460-601085 Chair Cars & Coaches - Gold Lettering (1920-1938)
460-601087 Diner, Lounge & Observation Cars - Gold Lettering (1920-1938)
460-601089 Heavyweight Pullman Sleepers Gold Lettering #1 1928-47
460-601091 Heavyweight Pullman Sleepers Gold Lettering #2 1928-47
460-601090 Pullman Assigned Sleepers #1 - Dulux Lettering 1938+
460-601091 Pullman Assigned Heavyweight Sleepers #2 1928-1947 w/Gold Lettering
460-601092 Pullman Assigned Sleepers #2 - Dulux Lettering 1938+
460-601103 SD70M Diesels w/Winged Shield 2000+
460-601125 Diesels w/Small Winged Shield 2001+
460-601145 SD70M Diesels 4526-4528 "Building America" w/Flag 2001+
460-601147 Dash 9-44CW/AC4400CW Diesels w/Winged Shield 2000+
460-601150 SD70M Diesels "Building America" w/Flags 2002+
NEW 460-601247 Steam Locos; 2-Tone "Gray Hound"
460-604048 SD40-2 #3593 "Desert Storm"
460-604009 Yard Switchers 1950
460-604028 SD40-2 Diesels 1988
460-604077 Mechanical Reefers 1988+
460-604079 Tank Cars 12,500-Gallon 1937-55
460-604080 Tank Car 12,500-Gallon 1955+
460-604120 SD40-2 Diesels 1994
460-604180 Hoppers 1996+
460-604285 40' Trailers "We Can Handle It" Slogan 1980+
460-604328 Renumbered Diesels 2000+

460-604402 "Chilled Express" Refrigerator Car 2002+
460-604403 57' Mechanical Reefers "Building America"

VIA Rail Canada
460-60667 Diesels 1979-92
460-60672 Passenger Cars 1990+
460-60673 Passenger Car Stripes 1990+
460-60678 Passenger Cars 1990+
460-601153 P42DC Diesels 2001+

Wabash
460-60434 70-Ton Airslide Hopper 1960-70
460-60644 Diesel Stripes 1949-64
460-60698 Diesels 1960-64

Limited Quantity Available
460-60306 40' Single-Door Box Car 1950-60

Western Maryland
460-605 40' Trailer 1960-70
460-60130 Hood Unit Diesels 1950-70
460-60700 Cabooses 1936-80
460-60916 40, 50 & 60' Box Cars 1953-70
460-601005 Diesels-Fireball Scheme 1947-54

Western Pacific
460-6026 Diesels 1950-70
460-60108 Passenger Cars-California Zephyr 1950-70
460-60160 F7 & Hood Unit Diesels 1970
460-60211 Diesel Switchers 1950-80
460-60212 Bay Window Cabooses 1950-80
460-60220 White Freight Cars 1970-80
460-60253 Freight Cars 1960-70
460-60272 Freight Cars-New Image 1980
460-60274 Diesels 1970-80
460-60404 50' Single-Door Box Car 1950-70
460-60433 40' Single-Door Box Car 1950-60
460-60436 Bulkhead Centerbeam Flat Cars
460-60438 40 & 50' Box Cars 1950-60
460-60445 Cabooses UP Scheme 1980
460-60448 Cabooses & GP40 Diesels UP Scheme 1985
460-60456 45' Trailers 1980
460-60491 40' Ice-Cooled Wood Reefers 1920-40
460-60507 50' 100-Ton Airslide Hopper 1980
460-60601 Insulated Beer Service Box Cars 1969+
460-60802 FT Cab Unit Diesels 1940-65
460-60818 Freight Cars 1970
460-601077 Black Diesel Stripes
460-601110 California Zephyr Cars
460-601151 Heavyweight Passenger Cars 1910+

460-601240 89' Piggyback Flats (Includes DRGW & Kansas City Southern Re-Stencil)
460-604266 50' Single-Sheathed Automobile Service Box Cars - Original White Lettering
460-604274 Bicentennial GP40 Diesel 1976-79
460-604338 EMD GP40 Diesel #3532 in UP Colors 1983-84
460-604349 50' Box Car w/Metric Data
460-604409 50' Berwick Forge Box Cars

Wisconsin & Calumet
460-60654 Diesels/Passenger Cars 1980+
460-60655 Diesel & Passenger Car Stripes 1980+

Wisconsin & Southern
460-60762 Diesels 1985+
460-60763 Diesel Stripes 1985+

Wisconsin Central
460-60533 GP35, GP38, SD45 Diesels 1988
460-60534 30" Wide Yellow Stripes for All Locos 1988
460-60543 Switchers 1988
460-60546 Box Cars 1989
460-60547 Hoppers, Gondolas 1989
460-60712 Diesel GP40 1991+
460-60921 F45 Diesels 1995+
460-601074 Operation Lifesaver SD45 #7638 1999
460-601241 Operation Lifesaver SD45 #7525 2000+
460-601242 50' Pullman-Standard Box Cars
460-604102 Model Railroader Anniversary Box Car 1993+

MILITARY VEHICLES
460-604279 US Army Vehicles 1940s+

SIGNS 4.80 ea

Flags
460-604201 US 48 Star 1912-59
460-604202 US 50 Star 1960+
460-604371 Canadian Flags 1870-1965
460-604372 Canadian Flags 1965+
460-601176 Confederate Flags 1861-65

Gas Stations
460-60604 Texaco & Flying A 1949-60
460-60853 Detail Signs 1945+
460-60902 Gulf 1936-63
460-60938 Mobil 1940-66
460-60959 Esso 1946-65
460-60969 Sinclair 1935-60
460-60993 Shell 1935-60
460-601002 Ashland & Pepper 1924-60
460-601017 Atlantic Refining 1935-60

Business & Commercial
460-60162 Western Cowtown 1850
460-60163 Small Rural Town 1850
460-60164 Western Town 1850
460-60165 Industrial Town & City 1850
460-60166 Rural Farming 1850
460-60197 Early-20th Century 1900
460-60198 Mid-20th Century 1950-80
460-60206 Railroad Right-of-Way-Current
460-60228 Signs & Placards Freight Cars 1970s
460-60260 Market Windows 1930-40
460-60273 Industrial 1960-80
460-60275 City Streets & Buildings 1950-80
460-60287 1930s-Era Posters & Window Signs
460-60289 Industrial Names 1960-80
460-60420 Commercial 1930-40
460-60421 Commercial 1930-40
460-60422 Commercial 1930-40
460-60771 Sunkist Fruit Packing House 1955+
460-60795 Farm Community 1960+
460-60806 Packing House & Cold Storage #1 1970+
460-60807 Packing House & Cold Storage #2 1970+
460-60811 Farm Community 1960+
460-60840 Hazardous Placards 1984+
460-60866 Canadian Grain Elevators #1 1980+
460-60870 Canadian Grain Elevators #2 1985+
460-60898 Canadian Grain Elevators #3 1980+
460-60924 Industrial Safety & Warning 1985+
460-60941 Suburban & Superior Propane Vehicles & Terminal 1985+
460-60982 Diners #1 1950+
460-60983 Diners #2 1950+
460-601049 Commercial Buildings/Stores Late 1950s - Mid 1960s

TRUCK & VEHICLE SETS 4.80 ea

460-604 Transcon, Republic, Navajo, Dixie Ohio Express, Consolidated Freight, Pacific-Intermountain-Express 40' Trailer 1960-70
460-605 Monon 40' Trailer 1960-70
460-60233 Cooperative Shippers, Extra, Preferred Pool 40' Trailer 1970
460-60237 Brillion & Forest Junction, Bekins, Budd Leasing, Cooperative Shippers 40' Trailers 1970-80

DECALS N SCALE

MICROSCALE

460-60246 Consolidated Freight, Digby's Golden Arrow, ICX, Leeway Trailers & Tractors 1960-80
460-60282 Matson Lines 40' Trailer 1970-80
460-60292 Crab Orchard & Egyptian, Texas-Mexican 40' Trailers 1970
460-60308 Chief Freight Lines 40' Trailer 1970-80
460-60343 Brae Corp., TransAmerica 40' Trailer 1970-80
460-60344 Nevada Northern, Brae Corp., The Fresh Approach, Intermodal Systems, IMEX 40' Trailer 1970-80
460-60345 Cornucopia, International Nu-Way Shippers 40' Trailer 1970-80
460-60346 Agricultural Express of America, MSA Lamda 40' Trailer 1970-80
460-60347 Clipper Express, Columbus & Greenville, Metro Shippers Inc. 40' Trailer 1970-80
460-60385 Peninsula Creamery, Jag's Diesel Inc., Langendorf Bread, Svenhard's Bakery Delivery Van 1970-80
460-60387 Kilpatrick's Bread Delivery Van 1970-80
460-60403 Superior Freight 40 & 45' & KLM 40' Trailer 1970-80
460-60454 Preferred Pool 45' Trailers 1980
460-60464 TransAmerica 45' Trailer Los Angeles Olympic 1980s
460-60495 Interstate, Rail Services 40' Trailer 1980
460-60500 Union Ice Tractor & 40' Trailer, PMT Tractor 1982
460-60508 XTRA, US Mail, Seaboard System Trailer 45' 1985
460-60513 Valvoline, Pennzoil Tractors & 40 & 45' Trailers 1986
460-60521 Castrol, Quaker State Trailers & Tractors 40' 1986
460-60665 Chicago Central, Minnesota, Dakota & Western, Kankakee, Beaverville & Southern 45' Trailers 1990
460-60703 Transamerican 45' & 48' Trailers 1992
460-60723 Western Fruit Express Tractor 1990+
460-60814 Schneider National 48 & 53' Trailers & Tractors 1980+
460-60872 May Trucking Trailer 28 & 53' 1989+
460-60873 May Trucking Tractors & Striping 1989+
460-60941 Superior, Suburban Propane Trucks 1985+
460-604051 J.B. Hunt Tractor & 45 & 48' Trailer 1990
460-60461 Clarendon & Pittsford 40' Trailer 1980
460-604122 Safety Striping Trailer 1993+
460-604149 License Plates Vehicle 1975-85
460-604150 Markings Vehicle, Emergency 1970+
460-604159 Yellow Freight Tractors & Trailers 1975+
460-604168 Commercial Vehicle License Plates 1970-95
460-604169 Overnite Transportation Co. Trailers & Tractors 1990+
460-604172 XTRA 45' Trailers 1990+
460-604192 England Tractor & Trailers 1990+
460-604199 Nations Way Tractors & Trailers 1990+
460-604203 Viking Freight Tractors & Trailers 1990+
460-604211 Old Dominion Tractors & Trailers, 28' 1994+
460-604219 Bullocks Express Tractors & 28' Trailers 1994+
460-604224 GI Trucking Co. Tractors & 28' Trailers 1980+
460-604234 Interstate Distribution Co. Tractors & Trailers 1990+
460-604242 Preston 151 Line Tractors & Trailers 1990+
460-604282 Gelco Leasing 40' Trailer (blue, green)
460-604283 Western Express 40' Trailer (white, red) 1978+
460-604322 Bekins Moving & Storage Tractor/Trailer 1970-80
NEW 460-604330 Roads West 53' Trailer & Tractor 1997+ **4.80**

Limited Quantity Available
460-604171 Martrac Refrigerated Trailers 1985+

CHRISTMAS
460-601118 Greetings of the Season
460-601119 Candy Canes, Snowflakes & Holly
460-601120 Snowmen Scenes

EVAN DESIGNS

INKJET DECAL PAPER

266-P7 HobbyCal 8-1/2 x 11" Decal Paper White pkg(5) **15.00**
Create great decals with ANY inkjet printer. Ink is absorbed into the special coating on the decal paper. No oversprays required. Simply print, water slip and apply to any surface. Thin decals easily conform to smooth or irregular surfaces. Matte finish. Background dries white, can be made clear. Instructions included. Customize your layout!

VITACHROME GRAPHICS

Express your creativity while customizing your locomotives and rolling stock by creating your own decals. Vitachrome Graphics provides kits and individual products that allow modelers to design their own easy-to-apply decals. By using your existing inkjet printer (paper compatible with most printers), the options are limitless in creating unique and imaginative semi-permanent designs.

Decal Paper 768-5000

Clear Sealer Spray 786-5050

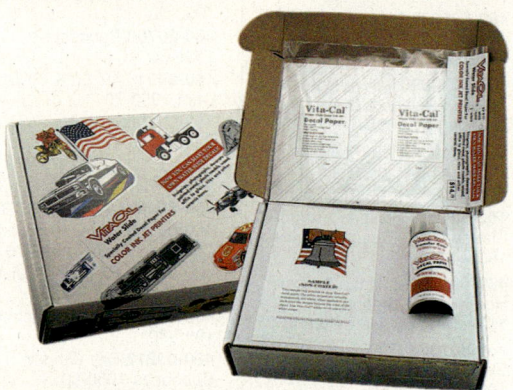
Inkjet Decal Starter Kit 768-5070

DECAL PAPER
Create your own decals using VitaCal™ decal paper. Compatible with most inkjet printers, decal paper has a high-gloss finish. Paper is easy to apply and adheres to most hard, smooth surfaces. Sheets measure 8-1/2 x 11" 20 x 27.5cm. Color indicated reflects background color.

768-5000 White pkg(5) **24.95**
768-5020 Clear pkg(5) **24.95**
768-5030 White pkg(100) **350.00**
768-5040 Clear pkg(100) **350.00**

CLEAR SEALER SPRAY
768-5050 4oz **10.95**
Sealer for use with decal paper. Childproof packaging.

DECAL STARTER KIT
768-5070 **26.95**
Use your inkjet printer to create decals right away. Includes two sheets each of clear and white VitaCal decal paper, each sheet measuring 8-1/2 x 11" 20 x 27.5cm. Also includes one can of 4oz Clear Sealer spray.

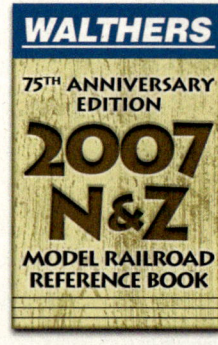

Scenery by Ian Millar, Model and Photo by BJ Davis, Elk Grove, Illinois

COUPLERS

A loud rumble fills the canyon as California Zephyr Train 27 rushes over the trestle on its way to Oakland, California. A BNSF freight coming off the highline from Oregon will follow Amtrak through trackage rights on the Union Pacific, which now owns the Feather River route. This scene was photographed on the Midwest N Pioneer Model Railroad Club layout in Illinois.

Arriving in California in the early 1860s, Scottish-born Arthur W. Keddie began exploring the north fork of the Feather River. A trained land surveyor, he felt the easy grades and light winter snows would make it the best route for the transcontinental railway. He sold his dream to several important investors and formed the Oroville and Virginia Railroad Company in 1867. Although construction was soon abandoned, Keddie held onto his dream. After many attempts by various companies to develop the route, the Western Pacific Railway Company finally completed the line when east met west on the steel trestle over Spanish Creek in November 1909. But the Keddie wasn't actually a wye until 1931 when the highline extension north to Bieber, California was completed to form the triangle called Keddie Wye.

Keeping both trains on track and running smoothly through the wye are couplers and trucks like the ones you'll find in the Couplers & Trucks Section.

COUPLERS - TRUCKS N SCALE

ATLAS Model Railroad Co., Inc.

TRUCKS & ACCESSORIES

150-22055 & 22050

- **150-22003** Plastic King Pins pkg(12) **9.00**
- **150-22050** Friction Bearing Trucks 1 Pair **2.95**
- **150-22051** Friction Bearing Trucks w/Accumate® Couplers 1 Pair **3.85**
- **150-22055** Roller Bearing Trucks 1 Pair **2.95**
- **150-22056** 70-Ton Roller Bearing Trucks w/Accumate Couplers 1 Pair **3.85**
- **150-22060** Roller Bearing Caboose Trucks 1 Pair **2.95**
- **150-22070** 100-Ton Roller Bearing Trucks 1 Pair **2.95**
- **150-22071** 100-Ton Roller Bearing Trucks w/Accumate Couplers 1 Pair **3.85**
- **150-22081** 70-Ton Roller Bearing Trucks w/Accumate Couplers & Extended Bolster 1 Pair **3.85**

WHEELSETS

Free rolling, blackened metal wheels.

- **150-22020** 33" pkg(12) **7.25**
- **150-22036** 36" pkg(12) **7.50**
- **150-22133** 33" For Micro Trains® Trucks pkg(12) **7.25**

Low Profile

Plastic 33"-diameter wheelsets fit Micro-Trains trucks, allowing operation on Code 55 or larger rail.

- **150-22134** pkg(24) **6.50**
- **150-22135** pkg(48) **11.95**
- **150-22136** pkg(100) **18.65**

AMERICAN LIMITED

4-Wheel Passenger Trucks 1 Pair 4.95 ea

Easy-to-assemble, injection-molded plastic trucks for streamline passenger car conversions. Correct for Kato UP cars and many other prototypes. Comes with wheelsets and mounting screws. Also has adjustable coupler position and fits Micro-Trains® 1023 or 1025 couplers.

147-8100 Outside Swing Hanger

147-8150 Commonwealth Streamline

147-8190 PRR 2D-P5 Passenger Car Trucks 1 Pair **5.95**

BACHMANNN

NEW PRODUCTS

Dummy Knuckle Couplers

NEW 160-42531 Variety Pack **1.67**
Includes three pairs of couplers per set, one pair each for rolling stock, standard Bachmann locomotives and Spectrum® locomotives. Dealers MUST order in multiples of 12.

NEW 160-42532 Rolling Stock Couplers Only 1 Pair **.60**
Dealers MUST order in multiples of 25.

NEW 160-42533 Freight Trucks w/Coupler 1 Pair **1.67**
Less wheels. Dealers MUST order in multiples of 12.

Get the Scoop!
Get the Skinny!
Get the Score!
Check Out Walthers
Web site at
www.walthers.com

CALUMET TRAINS

Traction Tire Tool

192-1504 **11.95**
For easy application of diesel traction tires. Comes with 10 traction tires.

Vinyl Super Traction Tires 6.95 ea

These vinyl tires increase pulling power and give a smoother ride with less bounce. These tires can only be used on wheels that had traction tires on the original. Wheels must have grooves to accept the tires.

- **192-2505** Diesel pkg(20)
- **192-1513** Steam pkg(18)

MODEL POWER

Trucks

Freight Trucks
- **490-3512** With Metal Wheels **3.00**
- **490-36012** With Plastic Wheels **2.25**

Passenger Trucks w/Metal Wheels
- **490-3029** 4-Wheel **3.25**
- **490-8612** 6-Wheel **4.25**

Steam Loco Driver Set w/Traction Wheels

Retro-fit kits.
- **490-7398** 73" Diameter for 4-6-2 Pacific **6.98**
- **490-7569** 63" for 2-8-2 Mikado **8.98**

Truck Accessories

- **490-36242** King Pins **1.25**

NorthWest Short Line

These precision, all-metal wheelsets are made in the United States.

72 TREAD NICKEL-SILVER WHEELSETS

For Code 40 and 55 rail.

N Gauge Pointed Axle pkg(4) 7.95 ea

.540" Pointed Axle For Micro Trains, MDC, Most Atlas, Others
- **53-374154** 28"/72
- **53-374174** 33"/72
- **53-374184** 36"/72

.560" Pointed Axle For Con-Cor, Bachmann, Some Atlas
- **53-374654** 28"/72
- **53-374674** 33"/72
- **53-374684** 36"/72

HOn30 Shoulder Axle
- **53-374504** For Grandt Line pkg(4) **7.95**

64 TREAD SEMI-FINESCALE NICKEL-SILVER WHEELSETS

For Code 40 and 55 rail.

N Gauge Pointed Axle pkg(4) 7.95 ea

.540" Pointed Axle For Micro Trains, MDC, Most Atlas, Others
- **53-375154** 28"/64
- **53-375174** 33"/64
- **53-375184** 36"/64

.560" Pointed Axle For Con-Cor, Bachmann, Some Atlas
- **53-375654** 28"/64
- **53-375674** 33"/64
- **53-375684** 36"/64

HOn2-1/2 Flush Axle pkg(4) 7.95 ea
- **53-375254** 28"
- **53-375294** 40"

HOn30 Axles

Shouldered
- **53-375504** 20" For Grandt Line pkg(4) **7.95**

Pointed .615"
- **53-375534** 20" For Joe Works pkg(4) **7.95**

Pointed .580"
- **53-375564** 20" For Sango pkg(4) **7.95**

50 TREAD FINESCALE NICKEL-SILVER WHEELSETS

N Gauge Pointed Axle pkg(4)

.540" Pointed Axle For Micro Trains, MDC, Atlas, Others
- **53-575174** 33"/50 **8.95**
- **53-575184** 36"/50 **8.95**

PRECISION SCALE CO.

Six-Wheel Truck Sideframes

Sideframes are available as lost wax brass castings or plastic parts.

EMD First Generation Flexicoil

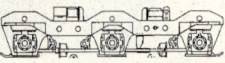

- **585-6700** Brass pkg(4) **6.00**
- **585-6701** Plastic pkg(4) **4.00**

E8 Diesel
- **585-6702** Brass pkg(4) **6.00**
- **585-6703** Plastic pkg(4) **4.00**

RED CABOOSE

Nonoperating plastic knuckle couplers; will couple with most N Scale knuckle couplers including Micro-Trains® and Precision Masters.

Couplers 2.50 ea
- **629-51000** Short Shank (black)
- **629-51010** Medium Shank (black)
- **629-51020** Long Shank (black)
- **629-51060** Body-Mount Couplers (black) pkg(8)
- **629-51064** Body-Mount Coupler Bracket (black) pkg(8)

COUPLERS - TRUCKS N SCALE

Micro-Trains® Magne-Matic® delayed-action couplers automatically uncouple when stopped over a magnetic uncoupler (see illustrations below).

THE MAGNE-MATIC COUPLING & UNCOUPLING SYSTEM

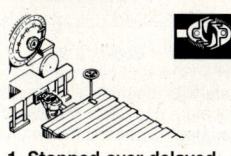
1. Stopped over delayed magnetic uncoupler, knuckles have opened.

2. Back up slightly to unhook couplers. Magnetic force draws couplers off center.

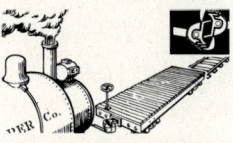
3. Forward again, couplers now in delayed position. Push car to desired track.

4. Back up again, couplers snap back to normal position.

Micro-Trains is a Registered Trademark.
Magne-Matic is a Registered Trademark.

BODY MOUNT COUPLERS
With draft gear boxes.

489-102008 TOFC 2 Pair **5.35**
489-102009 Assembled 2 Pair **6.70**
489-102011 Kit 2 Pair **3.90**

Wide Angle Short Shank (.312")

489-102000 Kit 3 Pair **5.60**
Revised with reverse draft angle pulling face for maximum coupling and pulling performance, body-mount design with snap-together assembly. Includes two pair of short shank (.312") and one pair of medium shank (.375") style couplers.

489-102003 Assembled 2 Pair **9.40**

Flat Cars & Gondolas
489-102013 Flats/Gondolas **5.85**
For flat cars, gondolas, 57' 6" TOFCs and similar underbodies.

Short Shank

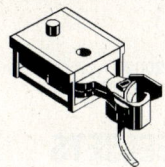

489-102014 2 Pair **4.50**
With draft gear boxes.

Low/Short Profile
489-102021 2 Pair **7.90**
For locos and cars with limited mounting area, including Life-Like E8 pilot and Bachmann 4-8-4 pilot.

TRUCK MOUNT COUPLERS

Bachmann

489-133020 F7 Loco 2 Pair **5.95**
One A and one B unit front and rear, or two B units front and rear.

489-133030 Short Coupler 2 Pair **5.95**
Newer locos and cars equipped with 9722 short coupler and 9723 draft gear box.

489-133031 Long Coupler 2 Pair **5.95**
Newer locos and cars equipped with 9722-1 long coupler and 9723 draft gear box.

Life-Like® from Walthers
489-142000 Fits F/GPs 2 Pair **5.95**
For F7, GP38, F40PH and other diesels with same Blomberg truck sideframes.

"T" Shank 2 Pair 5.50 ea
With adapter; for converting Kato, Con-Cor, AHM and other equipment with split single one-piece draft gear box.
489-130012 .225" (short)
489-130013 .275" (medium)
489-130014 .345" (long)

UNCOUPLERS
489-98800172 Magnet Uncoupler, Less Track pkg(2) **7.55**
489-98800173 Magnet Uncoupler **9.75** Mounted in section of Atlas type Code 80 track.
489-98800171 Permanent Magnet **5.05** Mount under track.

COUPLER CONVERSIONS
The following kits will adapt the most popular N Scale locomotives to Micro-Trains Magne-Matic couplers. You can install Micro-Trains conversion kits with a few simple hand tools, and in most cases, little or no modification is necessary.

AHM 5.50 ea
489-130004 Fits FA-1 Powered
489-130005 Fits 0-6-0T Saddle Tank Switcher

Arnold
489-130003 Fits S2 Switcher **5.50**

Atlas 12.90 ea (Unless Noted)
489-130003 Fits GP9, GP30, F9A, E7A Powered or Davenport & Saddletank 0-6-0 Switchers **5.50**
489-130009 Fits Industrial Diesel Switcher **5.50**
489-132000 Fits EMD E8 **5.50**
489-132010 Fits Fairbanks-Morse Diesel **5.50**
489-130008 Fits EMD SD45, Alco RSC2 **5.50**
489-130004 Fits GP40 **5.50**
489-132020 Fits Plymouth Switcher **5.50**
489-132030 Fits RS-11
489-132040 Fits RS-3
489-132050 Fits RSD-4/5
489-132060 Fits RSD-12
489-132110 Fits GP7/GP9
489-132100 Fits FA-1
489-132070 Fits RS-1
489-132080 Fits U25B
489-132090 Fits SD7/SD9

Bachmann 12.90 ea (Unless Noted)
489-133000 Fits EMD F9 A or B Unit **5.50**
Fits older model with metal gearbox.
489-133010 Fits 0-6-0 USRA Switcher w/Tender **5.50**
489-133040 Fits Dash 8-40C (black pilot)
489-133050 Fits SD40-2
489-133060 Pilot Conversion Kit For Bachmann 8-40CW (Dash 8)

Con-Cor 5.50 ea (Unless Noted)
489-130002 Fits 2-8-8-2 Mallet **6.10**
489-130003 Fits U50 Gas Turbine Without Tender
489-135000 Fits PA-1 Powered
489-135010 Fits PB-1 Powered
489-130008 Fits Alco 636
489-130004 Fits EF70, SD45
489-130007 Fits Con-Cor/Dimi Trains SW1500 Cow or Calf

Kato 12.90 ea (Unless Noted)
489-141000 Fits GP38-2
489-141010 Fits GP50
489-141030 Fits U30C
489-141040 Fits E8/E9 **6.20**
489-102050 Fits Japanese ED-79 Electric, Shorty Caboose & C44-9W, SD40 **6.20**
489-141060 Fits 2-8-2 Mikado **6.70**
489-102051 Fits Dash 9 **6.25**
489-102052 Fits SD40-2 w/Underslung Short Shank Couplers **9.45**

489-102006 Fits SD40, Medium Shank-Assembled **9.40**

Life-Like from Walthers 12.90 ea (Unless Noted)
Conversions are for non-split-frame mechanism locos.
489-130004 Fits GP40, SD45 **5.50**
489-130005 Fits 0-6-0T Side Tank Switcher **5.50**
489-142010 Fits BL-2
489-142020 Fits FA-2
489-142030 For GP18

Minitrix 5.50 ea
489-130003 Fits Fairbanks-Morse H12-44
489-144000 Fits EMD F9
489-130009 Fits 2-10-0 Tender, U30CG, GE U28
489-144010 Fits 0-6-0T Donkey

Model Power 5.50 ea
489-130004 Fits RSD-15, Century 420
489-130006 Fits FP45

MRC
489-147000 Fits 2-8-4 **9.35**
489-130002 Fits 2-8-8-2 **6.11**
489-130004 Fits Alco C420, RSD-15 **5.50**
489-130008 Fits Alco FA-1/FA-2 **5.50**

Rivarossi
489-130011 Fits 4-6-2 USRA Pacific, 2-8-2 USRA **16.80**

COUPLER ACCESSORIES

Coupler Starter Kit
489-98800081 Starter Kit **40.05**
Everything needed to convert rolling stock to Magne-Matic® couplers. Includes #102000, 102009 and 130012 couplers, coupler tweezers, Greas-em, coupler assembly jig, tap and drill set, coupler height gauge, trip pin height gauge and #98800173 uncoupler.

COUPLER PARTS

Bolster Pins 3.25 ea
489-312030 Atlas-Type Conversion Bolster Pins pkg(24)
489-312031 For Roundhouse (MDC) pkg(24)

COUPLERS - TRUCKS N SCALE

MICRO-TRAINS LINE

Centering Springs pkg(12) 1.65 ea

489-112001 Centering Springs For #1023/25 Couplers pkg(12)

489-112003 Centering Springs pkg(12) For "T" Shank couplers (3/32" or .098" thick shank) and some conversion kits.

489-112004 Centering Springs pkg(12) For "T" Shank couplers (5/64" or .075" thick shank), some conversion kits and #130012, 130013 and 130014 couplers.

Parts Packet
489-312040 Small Parts Packet #1025 **5.15**
00-90 screws, bolster pins, bushings and washers.

TRUCKS

Allied Full Cushion
489-302121 With Short Extension Couplers 1 Pair **5.40**

Andrews

489-302010 Less Couplers 1 Pair **3.60**
489-310010 Less Couplers 10 Pair **29.80**
489-302011 With Short Extended Couplers 1 Pair **5.40**
489-302012 With Medium Extended Couplers 1 Pair **5.40**
489-302015 With Low Profile Wheels **3.60**
489-302016 With Short Extension Coupler & Low Profile Wheels **5.45**

Arch Bar

489-302001 With Couplers 1 Pair **5.40**
489-310001 With Couplers 10 Pair **47.15**
489-302004 With Extended Couplers 1 Pair **5.40**
489-302000 Less Couplers 1 Pair **3.60**
489-322000 Brown Less Couplers 1 Pair **3.60**
489-302005 Less Couplers, w/Low Profile Wheels 1 Pair **3.60**

489-322025 Brown Less Couplers, w/Low Profile Wheels 1 Pair **3.60**
489-322005 Brown Less Couplers 1 Pair **3.60**
489-310000 Less Couplers 10 Pair **31.30**

Barber Roller Bearing
489-302043 With Medium+ Extension Couplers 1 Pair **5.40** Shank length is just slightly longer than standard medium-length coupler. Features reverse draft angle pulling face.

489-302041 With Couplers 1 Pair **5.40**
489-302046 With Low Profile Wheels & Short Extension Couplers 1 Pair **5.40**
489-310041 With Couplers 10 Pair **47.15**
489-302044 With Extended Couplers 1 Pair **5.40**
489-310044 With Extended Couplers 10 Pair **47.15**
489-302042 With Medium Extended Couplers 1 Pair **5.40**
489-302047 With Medium Extension Couplers & Low Profile Wheels 1 Pair **5.40**
489-302040 Less Couplers 1 Pair **3.60**
489-302045 Less Couplers, w/Low Profile Wheels 1 Pair **3.60**
489-310040 Less Couplers 10 Pair **31.30**

Bettendorf
489-302021 With Couplers 1 Pair **5.40**
489-310021 With Couplers 10 Pair **47.15**
489-302024 With Couplers, Extended Bolster 1 Pair **5.15**
483-302022 With Couplers, Medium Extended Bolster 1 Pair **5.40**
489-302020 Less Couplers 1 Pair **3.60**
489-322020 Brown Less Couplers 1 Pair **3.60**
489-310020 Less Couplers 10 Pair **31.30**
489-302025 Less Couplers, w/Low Profile Wheels 1 Pair **3.60**
489-322025 Brown Less Couplers, w/Low Profile Wheels 1 Pair **3.60**
489-310025 Less Couplers w/Low Profile Wheels 10 Pair **31.30**
489-302026 With Short Extension Couplers & Low Profile Wheels 1 Pair **5.40**
489-302140 Swing-Motion w/Standard Wheels **3.60**
489-302145 Swing-Motion w/Low-Profile Wheels **3.60**

489-304021 With Rapido Style Couplers 1 Pair **4.70**

Dalman

489-302162 With Couplers & Standard Wheels Pair **5.40**

REA Express Reefer Style Trucks
489-302090 No Couplers **3.60**
489-302093 With Medium Extension Couplers **5.40**

Buckeye
489-302112 With Medium Extended Couplers 1 Pair **7.10**

Coil-Elliptic 5.40 ea
489-302071 With Short Extension Couplers
489-302072 With Medium Extension Couplers

Commonwealth
489-302132 6-Wheel Freight w/Medium Extended Couplers 1 Pair **7.10**

National B-1

489-302151 With Couplers & Standard Wheels Pair **5.40**

Nn3 Barber Coleman Arch Bar
489-402410 Less Couplers 1 Pair **3.95**

Nn3 Diamond Arch Bar
489-402400 Less Couplers 1 Pair **3.95**

Passenger Car 9.50 ea
489-302051 4-Wheel Passenger Car Trucks w/Couplers 1 Pair
489-302061 6-Wheel Passenger Car Trucks w/Adjustable Couplers 1 Pair
489-342051 4-Wheel Passenger Car w/Couplers (silver) 1 Pair
489-342061 6-Wheel Passenger Car w/Couplers (silver) 1 Pair

Roller Bearing

489-302031 With Couplers 1 Pair **5.40**
489-310031 With Couplers 10 Pair **47.15**
489-302034 With Extended Couplers 1 Pair **5.40**
489-302032 With Medium Extended Couplers 1 Pair **5.40**
489-310032 With Medium Extended Coupler 10 Pair **47.15**
489-302030 Less Couplers 1 Pair **3.60**
489-322030 Brown Less Couplers 1 Pair **3.60**
489-310030 Less Couplers 10 Pair **31.30**
489-302035 Less Couplers, w/Low Profile Wheels 1 Pair **3.60**
480-302037 Barber w/Medium Extension Couplers & Low-Profile wheelsets **5.40**
489-322035 Brown Less Couplers, w/Low Profile Wheels 1 Pair **3.60**
489-302039 With Long Extension Couplers & Low Profile Wheels 1 Pair **5.40**

TRUCK PARTS
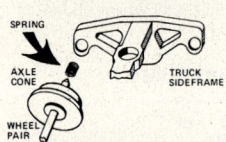

489-112002 Truck Restraining Springs pkg(12) **1.65**

WHEELSETS
Micro-Trains nonmagnetic wheelsets are made of slippery engineering plastic and feature needlepoint axles. Use them as replacements in Micro-Trains and most other manufacturers' trucks.

Standard Flanges

489-312000 Black pkg(12) **5.10**
For use on Code 70 or larger rail.

Low-Profile Flanges
These wheelsets are designed with realism in mind. They feature a smaller flange that allows smooth operation on track with scale-sized Code 40 or larger rail.

489-312010 Black pkg(12) **5.20**
489-312011 Black pkg(48) **16.50**

489-312013 Brown pkg(48) **16.50**
489-312014 Black pkg(100) **28.05**
489-312015 Brown pkg(100) **28.05**

Nn3
Item listed below is available by Special Order (see Legend Page).
489-412001 26" Diameter Freight pkg(12) **6.30**

RIX PRODUCTS

Uncoupling Tool
628-24 Rix Sticker **2.99**
When inserted between two cars with magnetically actuated couplers, the tool will cause the couplers to open immediately.

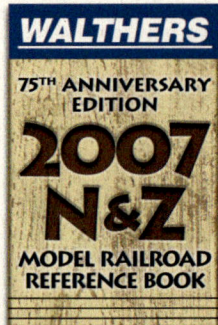

Models by Jim Kelly, Photo by Tim Wickerham, Milwaukee, WI

Like the tendrils of a vine, industrial spurs wrap themselves around buildings and loading facilities at industrial complexes of all kinds. In areas where several industries are adjacent to one another, switch crews can keep busy for hours spotting empties and pulling loads. A puzzle of turnouts awaits the crew of this Santa Fe local working the industries in Edison. This produce warehouse is just one of the businesses with sidings here; there is also a winery, a team track and a packing shed on the other side of the mainline. The volume of traffic at this important location requires the track be in good shape to minimize derailments. From curvy, misaligned industrial spurs that slice between tall brick warehouses to 70mph triple-track mainlines across the heartland, track is the element that ties railroads on the continent together. It's also what makes model railroads interesting. The Peco track in this scene can connect to thousands of N Trak modules around the globe; like prototype track, it shares common standards. On your pike, good track is the key to making trains run reliably; you'll find the products you need for your railroad in the Track Section.

TRACK & ACCESSORIES N SCALE

WALTHERS

Bright Boy Track Cleaner

949-521 Bright Boy (2 x 1 x 1/4") **5.98**
Easy-to-use Bright Boy track cleaning block keeps rails and wheels clean and bright. Just run Bright Boy over rails for clean track with better conductivity.

BUSCH

IMPORTED FROM GERMANY BY WALTHERS

Track Ballast Tape

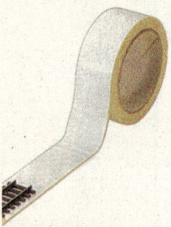

189-7120 Ballast Tape **6.99**
10 feet long, 7/8" wide.

Cork Roadbed
189-7505 Strip **9.99**
Measures 1/8" x 6' 3mm x 2m.
189-7506 Sheet **7.99**
Measures 12 x 8" 30 x 20cm.

CAMPBELL SCALE MODELS

Track Test Light

200-550 **9.20**
When set on track, test light shines if power is on. Works with any gauge.

Division of Wm. K. Walthers, Inc.

POWER-LOC™ TRACK SYSTEM

Finally, an easy-to-use track system ideal for beginners or experienced railroad builders! Everything from a basic oval to a complete layout is quick and easy to assemble with these components. Each section has a special plastic roadbed with built-in clips in place of difficult-to-use rail joiners. Simply connect the sections to match your track plan. Sets up in minutes; a complete oval can even be picked up and hung on the wall for storage! Perfect for temporary or seasonal layouts, as well as long-term operations. Features nickel-silver rail for best electrical performance and gray roadbed for utmost realism.

Straight Track

433-7802 5" pkg(4) **5.75**

433-7807 Power Link Short Adapter Track pkg(2) **3.75**

Terminal Rerailer
433-7806 **4.00**

Curved Track

433-7803 9-3/4" Radius pkg(4) **5.75**

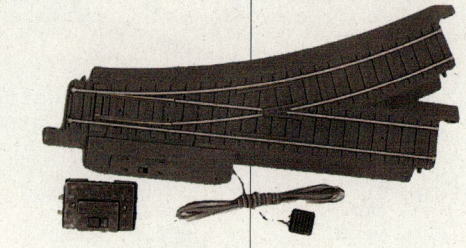

Left Hand Remote Switch 433-7811

Dual Crossing Gate 433-7210

Dual Crossing Gate 433-7209

Remote Switches 14.50 ea
433-7810 Right Hand
433-7811 Left Hand

Dual Crossing Gate
433-7210 **16.75**
Keep cars and trucks moving safely. Gates drop as train passes, rise automatically after train clears. For use with Power-Loc track only.

STANDARD TRACK

N Scale nickel-silver track, Code 80 rail.

Remote Switches 11.00 ea
Limited Quantity Available
433-7804 Right Hand
433-7805 Left Hand

Dual Crossing Gate
433-7209 **14.75**

Screws
433-1401 1/2" pkg(24) **4.75**

Nails 4.75

433-1402 1/2" (20g)
433-1411 For Cork Roadbed (20g)

Spikes

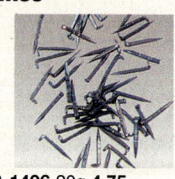

433-1406 20g **4.75**

Got a Mouse? Click Walthers Web Site at
www.walthers.com

Instant Roadbed

Just press realistic appearing Instant Roadbed onto a clean surface, then press track into it to complete layout. Made of uncured butyl rubber. Easily cut and formed. Sound deadening, self-adhesive, nontoxic. Can be used with any scale.

Also makes it easy to model very realistic asphalt, concrete, bricks and other material for sidewalks, cobblestone streets, highways and more.

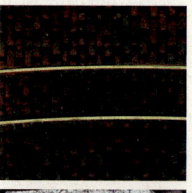

128-25 Black **19.95**
1" x 1/8" x 30' roll. Perfect for N scale. Easily cut in half for perfect Z Scale roadbed.
128-30 Black **22.95**
2" x 1/8" x 30' roll. Easily cut for N and Z Scale.
128-45 Black **29.95**
3" x 1/8" x 30' roll. Perfect for O Scale.
128-130 Gray **22.95**
2" x 1/8" x 30' roll. Easily cut for N and Z Scale.
Dealer: MUST order dealer pack of 8 rolls.

Insta Base
128-18 **11.95**
May be used under switches and yards, as parking lots, etc. Same material as instant roadbed but in sheets. 8-1/2 x 11 x 1/8" 21.5 x 27.5 x .3cm

TRACK & ACCESSORIES N SCALE

E-Z TRACK® SYSTEM

Whether you're building your first or your 50th layout, Bachmann E-Z Track will have your railroad up and running in no time. Each piece is complete with plastic roadbed, where special locking clips replace those hard-to-handle rail joiners. Simply click the track sections together, hook up your power pack and run trains. It's that simple! Perfect for first-time builders, display layouts or long-term operation. Each section features nickel-silver rail for the best electrical performance. The roadbed is molded in gray to make your finished track look more realistic without extra work.

NEW PRODUCTS

45° Crossing

NEW 160-44843 **13.50**

Hayes Bumpers

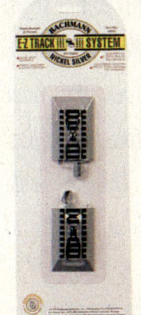

NEW 160-44891 pkg(2) **11.00**

Curved Track

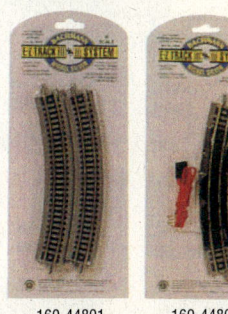

160-44801   160-44802

160-44801 11-3/4" Radius Sections pkg(6) **9.50**
160-44802 11-3/4" Radius Terminal Rerailer w/Wire **5.00**
160-44804 19" Radius pkg(6) **13.00**

Straight Track

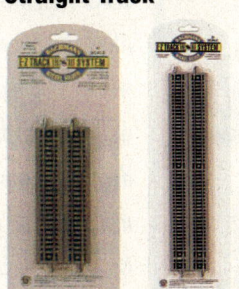

160-44811   160-44815

160-44811 5" pkg(6) **9.50**
160-44815 10" pkg(6) **16.50**
160-44820 10" Terminal Rerailer w/Wire **6.50**
160-44887 30" pkg(25) **211.00**

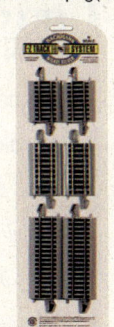

160-44829 Assorted Straight Sections pkg(4) **16.50**

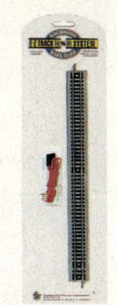

160-44897 10" Terminal w/Under-Track Power Feed **6.50**

Crossing Gate 160-44879

Remote Control Turnouts

160-44861 Left Hand **17.00**
160-44862 Right Hand **17.00**

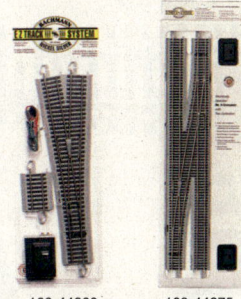

160-44869   160-44875

160-44869 #6 Wye **37.50**
160-44875 #6 Single Crossover Left Hand **66.50**

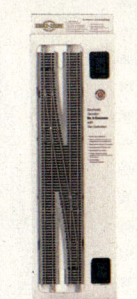

160-44876 #6 Single Crossover Right Hand **66.50**

Bulk Track

160-44880 11-1/4" Radius Curved pkg(50) **70.00**
160-44881 5" Straight pkg(50) **71.00**
160-44882 10" Straight pkg(50) **119.00**
160-44884 19" Radius Curved pkg(50) **119.00**

Track Bumpers

160-44890 End of Track Bumpers pkg(2) **6.00**

Crossings 13.50 ea

160-44840   160-44841

160-44840 30°
160-44841 90°

160-44842 60°

Pier Sets

160-44871 16 Pieces **13.50**

160-44872 Tall pkg(8) **11.00**

Crossing Gate

160-44879   **22.50**

CABOOSE INDUSTRIES

OPERATING GROUND THROWS

Strong, self-lubricating, black Delrin® ground throws with external cam for strength and maximum throw. Molded-on pin for direct mounting. All 100 series (Rigid) stands require modelers to fabricate a spring connecting link between the stand and the turnout. All 200 series stands have internal springs so they can be connected directly to the turnout throwbar.

.135" Travel
97-105 Rigid **3.03**
97-206 Sprung **3.20**

.165" Travel w/Selectable End Fittings

Operating ground throws including five different connectors: flat blade for Roco, small diameter pin for Micro Engineering, .083" hole for Peco, 90° slender shaft for Atlas, and large pin for most other turnouts. Also includes shim plate to raise the stand to tie height if needed.

97-117 Rigid **3.03**
97-218 Sprung **3.20**
97-222 Sprung For Atlas Code 55 Turnouts w/.135" Travel **3.25**

.165" Travel w/SPDT Contacts

With parts to assemble one low-current SPDT contact set.

97-119 Rigid **4.83**
97-220 Sprung **5.10**
97-224 Sprung For Atlas Code 55 Turnouts w/.135" Travel **5.20**

TRACK & ACCESSORIES N SCALE

YOU'RE ON THE RIGHT TRACK... WITH ATLAS®!

Atlas Model Railroad Company has two different N scale track lines to suit the needs of all model railroaders! On the following pages you will find a complete listing of all Atlas N Scale track available. Below is some information that may help you determine which track is best for your layout.

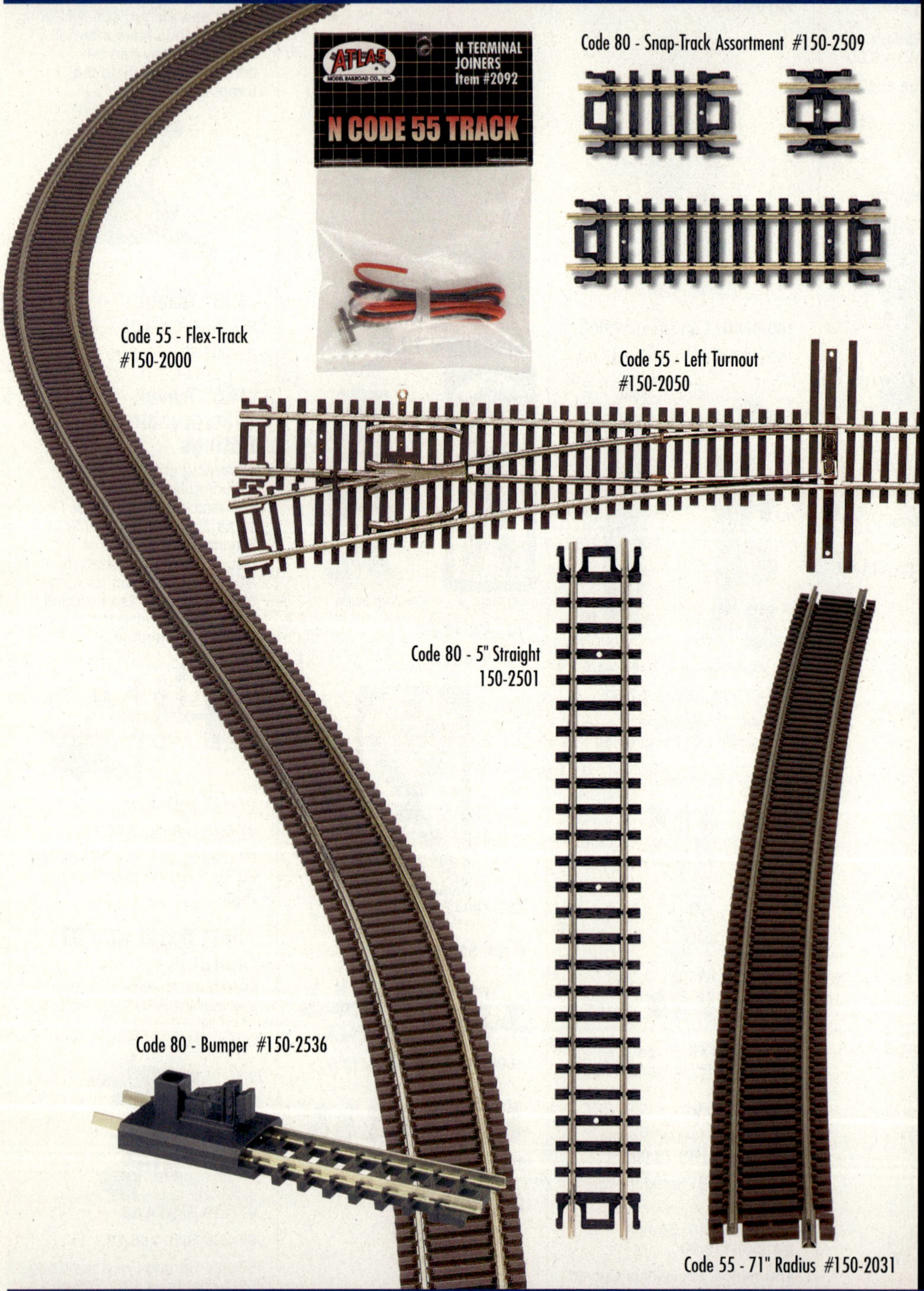

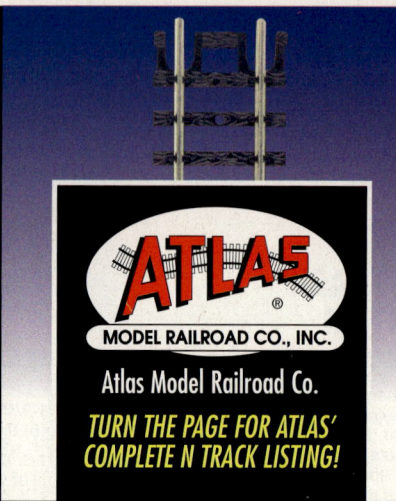

Atlas Model Railroad Co.

TURN THE PAGE FOR ATLAS' COMPLETE N TRACK LISTING!

ATLAS N CODE 80 TRACK
BLACK TIES/NICKEL SILVER RAIL

Atlas' traditional line of Code 80 track was started over 30 years ago, and it is well known for its high quality and durability. Made with black injection-molded plastic ties and nickel silver rail, it is sturdy, reliable and looks great on any layout. The Code 80 line is very extensive and includes Super-Flex® Track, Snap-Track, switches and accessories.

ATLAS N CODE 55 TRACK
BROWN TIES/NICKEL SILVER RAIL

Designed with precision and sophisticated technology, the N Scale Code 55 track (with nickel-silver rail) has the same reliability and durability as our popular Code 80 track, but with some slight differences that make it more prototypical. Code 55 track has finer brown ties and smaller rail than Atlas' traditional N Scale track. This fine-scale track will quickly become a favorite of N scalers.

Code 55 - Flex-Track #150-2000

N TERMINAL JOINERS Item #2092

N CODE 55 TRACK

Code 80 - Snap-Track Assortment #150-2509

Code 55 - Left Turnout #150-2050

Code 80 - 5" Straight 150-2501

Code 80 - Bumper #150-2536

Code 55 - 71" Radius #150-2031

Planning a layout? Download our Right Track Software at www.atlasrr.com - It's FREE!

TRACK & ACCESSORIES N SCALE

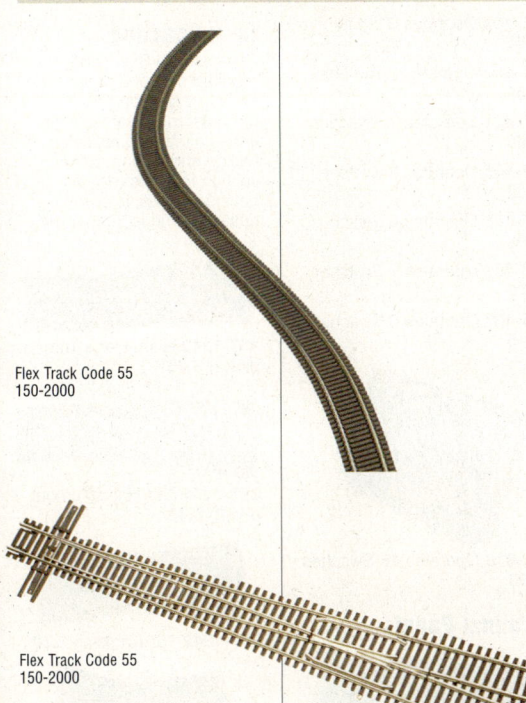

Flex Track Code 55
150-2000

TRACK

Code 55 Track
Features the same reliability and durability as Atlas' Code 80 track, but with some slight differences to make it more prototypical. Code 55 track has nickel-silver rail, finer brown ties and smaller rail than traditional N Scale Atlas track.

Flex Track
150-2000 **3.50**

Straight Pieces
150-2002 6" **4.75**
150-2003 4-1/4" **4.25**
150-2004 3" **3.50**
150-2005 2" **3.50**
150-2006 1-1/4" **2.95**
150-2007 1" **2.95**
150-2008 3/4" **2.95**

Curved Pieces pkg(4)
150-2010 10" Radius **4.75**
150-2011 10" Radius, Half **3.50**
150-2012 11-1/4" Radius **4.75**
150-2013 11-1/4" Radius, Half **3.50**
150-2014 12-1/2" Radius **4.75**
150-2015 12-1/2" Radius, Half **3.50**
150-2016 13-3/4" Radius **4.75**
150-2017 13-3/4" Radius, Half **3.50**
150-2018 15" Radius **4.75**
150-2019 15" Radius, Half **3.50**
150-2020 16-1/4" Radius **4.75**
150-2021 16-1/4" Radius, Half **3.50**
150-2022 17-1/2" Radius **4.95**
150-2023 17-1/2" Radius, Half **3.50**
150-2024 18-3/4" Radius **4.95**
150-2025 18-3/4" Radius, Half **3.50**
150-2026 20" Radius **5.35**
150-2027 20" Radius, Half **3.85**
150-2028 21-1/4" Radius **5.35**
150-2029 21-1/4" Radius, Half **3.85**
150-2030 30.6" Radius **4.75**
150-2031 71" Radius **6.50**

Crossings 7.75 ea
150-2040 11.25°
150-2041 22.5°
NEW 150-2042 30°
150-2043 45°
NEW 150-2044 60°
150-2045 90°

Turnouts 11.75 ea (Unless Noted)

150-2050 #5 Left Hand
150-2051 #5 Right Hand
150-2052 #7 Left Hand
150-2053 #7 Right Hand
NEW 150-2054 #10 Left Hand **13.95**
NEW 150-2055 #10 Right Hand **13.95**
150-2056 #2-1/2 Wye **12.95**

NEW 150-2057 3.5 Wye **12.95**

Accessories
150-2065 Under Table Switch Machine **15.25**
150-2090 Metal Rail Joiners pkg(24) **2.65**
150-2091 Insulated Rail Joiners pkg(24) **1.50**
150-2092 Terminal Joiners 1 Pair **2.95**

Code 80 Track
Atlas' popular and traditional Code 80 N Scale track features nickel-silver rail on black plastic ties. Switches feature refined and narrow flangeways at the frog and guard rails, and positive mechanical attachment of points. The difference between Standard and #6 switches is the angle at which the curved piece of track splits from the straight piece. Because the rails of Standard switches split at a sharper angle than #6 switches, they create a sharper curve and work better in smaller spaces.

Super-Flex Track®

150-2500 Black Ties **3.25** 29-1/2" long sections.

Bulk Snap-Track® Case 40.00 ea
Items must be purchased in cases of 100.
150-2513 5" Straight
150-2514 9-3/4" Radius
150-2515 11" Radius
150-2516 19" Radius

Straight Snap-Track

150-2501 5" Black Ties pkg(6) **2.95**

150-2509 Assorted, Black Ties **3.50**
Contains two 2-1/2", four each of 1-1/4" and 5/8" track sections.

Track Planning Template
150-360 **3.65**

Rerailer

150-2517 Black Ties **.65**
150-2532 Black Ties pkg(3) **2.35**

Scenic Ridge Track Pack

150-2588 **65.95**
For Woodland Scenics Scenic Ridge Layout Kit (#785-1482), sold separately.

Bumper

150-2536 Black Ties pkg(2) **2.35**
2-3/8" length.

Curved Snap-Track

150-2520
150-2510 9-3/4" Radius, Black Ties pkg(6) **2.95**
150-2511 Half 9-3/4" Radius, Black Ties pkg(6) **2.35**
150-2520 11" Radius, Black Ties pkg(6) **2.95**
150-2521 Half 11" Radius, Black Ties pkg(6) **2.35**
150-2526 19" Radius, Black Ties pkg(6) **2.95**

Crossings 7.25 ea
150-2564 15°, Black Ties
150-2565 20°, Black Ties
150-2566 30°, Black Ties
150-2567 45°, Black Ties
150-2568 60°, Black Ties
150-2569 90°, Black Ties

Standard Line Manual Switches 11.50 ea
Manual switches can be converted to remote control with Switch Machines.
150-2702 Left Hand Standard, Black Ties

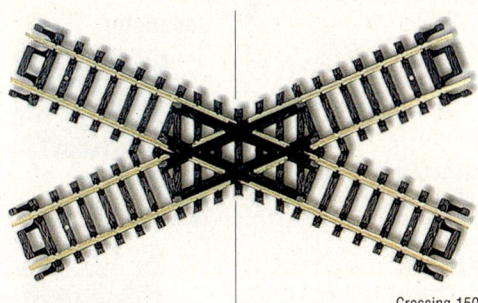

Crossing 150-2568

150-2703 Right Hand Standard, Black Ties

Standard Line Remote Switches 17.50 ea
Remote control switches include #150-56 Switch Control Box.

150-2700 Left Hand Standard, Black Ties
150-2701 Right Hand Standard, Black Ties

#6 Manual Switches 11.50 ea
150-2706 Left Hand, Black Ties

150-2707 Right Hand, Black Ties

#6 Remote Switches 17.50 ea
150-2704 Left Hand, Black Ties
150-2705 Right Hand, Black Ties

Wye Switches
NEW 150-2708 Remote w/Black Ties **17.50**
NEW 150-2709 Manual w/Black Ties **11.50**

Custom Line Switches 10.50 ea
Custom Line switches are made to be used with the Atlas Under-Table Switch Machine #150-65 or a ground throw. Switches feature full length ties and a double-ended throwbar, allowing placement of the under-table switch machine on either side of the switch.

150-2750 Left Hand, Black Ties
150-2751 Right Hand, Black Ties

TRACK & ACCESSORIES N SCALE

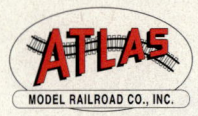

Custom Line #6 Switches 10.50 ea
150-2752 Left Hand, Black Ties
150-2753 Right Hand, Black Ties

Wye Switch
NEW 150-2754 With Black Ties 10.50

Rail Joiners
150-2535 pkg(48) 2.35

150-2538 Plastic pkg(24) 1.25
Dealers MUST order rail joiners by card (card is 6 packages).
150-2539 Terminal Joiners 2.75
Dealers MUST order box of 24 packages.

Remote Control Switch Machines 8.25 ea
Convert Atlas Standard or #6 switches to remote control. All twin-coil switch machines must be controlled by a normally off momentary contact switch to prevent burnouts. (#150-56 is recommended.)

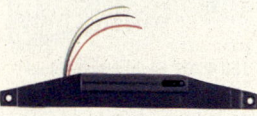

150-2715 Left Hand, Black
150-2716 Right Hand, Black

Switch Control Box

150-56 3.75
Single-pole, double-throw momentary action for control of Atlas or other twin-coil switch machines.

Snap Relay

150-200 10.25
Double-pole, double-throw electric switch.

Solderless Connectors

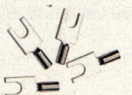

150-201 #3 Spade Tongue 4.25

Connector

150-205 7.95

Twin Connector

150-210 7.95

Selector

150-215 7.95

Controller

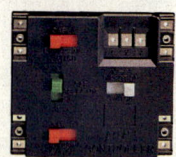

150-220 8.25

Track Nails

150-2540 2oz 3.75

FALLER

IMPORTED FROM GERMANY BY WALTHERS

Cork Roadbed

272-222555 pkg(4) 13.99
Flexible roadbed comes in double strips, each 19-5/8" long.

Daily New Product Announcements! Visit Walthers Web site at
www.walthers.com

CONTROLLERS

Lighted Switch Controllers
Will operate all switches and switch motors including Lionel®, Atlas®, and others. Light remains on after corresponding button is pressed. Instructions, red and green light bulbs, mounting screws and self-stick number sheet are included.

Each #498 and #444 comes with a contact plate. Each #894 and #888 is equipped with electro-mechanical switching circuitry controls and switches red and green light automatically. No need for contact plates or relays; unit is completely self-contained. Bulbs use the AC current from the power supply.

Surface Mount

105-444 Standard 10.75
105-888 Electro-Mechanical 17.20

Insert Mount
105-498 9.55
105-894 16.45
105-4994 GE Bulb 12-18V (red) pkg(2) .70
105-4995 GE Bulb 12-18V (blue) pkg(2) .70

PUSH-BUTTON UNITS

105-439 Double 2.95
Can be installed in any position. Dealers MUST order multiples of 12.

PANELS

Frame-Mounted
With polished aluminum mounting frame.

105-401 Operates 1 Switch 5.60
105-402 Operates 2 Switches 7.60
105-403 Operates 3 Switches 9.55
105-404 Operates 4 Switches 11.60
105-405 Operates 5 Switches 12.80
105-406 Operates 6 Switches 14.95
105-407 Operates 7 Switches 16.75
105-408 Operates 8 Switches 19.15

105-916 Operates 16 Switches 35.95

Terminal Panels

105-416 Less Switches 9.55

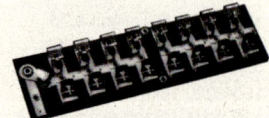

105-516 With Switches 11.60

Flush-Mounted
EXCLUSIVE FEATURE: All Acme switch controllers are equipped with crimp or solder terminals.

105-301 Operates 1 Switch 4.50
105-302 Operates 2 Switches 6.30
105-303 Operates 3 Switches 8.10
105-304 Operates 4 Switches 10.20
105-305 Operates 5 Switches 11.60
105-306 Operates 6 Switches 13.50
105-307 Operates 7 Switches 15.45
105-308 Operates 8 Switches 17.35

105-816 Operates 16 Switches 31.95

Cork Roadbed
One-piece N Scale cork roadbed sections provide a smooth transition between turnouts and track sections, and eliminate complicated nailing and cutting. Each section features realistic beveled edges, is easily ballasted and is 3mm thick.

357-1340 Right Hand Turnout pkg(2) 3.45

357-1341 Left Hand Turnout pkg(2) 3.45

357-1342 15° Crossing 2.30

357-1343 30° Crossing 2.30

357-1344 Wye or 3-Way Turnout 2.30

357-1345 Right Hand No. 8 Turnout pkg(2) 3.35

357-1346 Left Hand No. 8 Turnout pkg(2) 3.35

357-1349 Multi-Track Yard Pads pkg(2) 5.45
3-1/2 x 12" 8.7 x 30cm

TRACK & ACCESSORIES N SCALE

BK Enterprises
QUALITY TRACK PRODUCTS

Build your own custom trackwork with these turnouts and crossings. Recommended for the advanced modeler, each features accurately gauged nickel-silver rails, without ties (ties are available separately). Turnouts are offered assembled and ready for spiking, or as a kit which requires bending the outside rail and gauging the track. Frogs and point and frog sets are also available. Please visit www.walthers.com for a complete listing of all available BK Enterprises items.

NOTE: All kits are made to order and are not available for immediate delivery. A backorder is required for all track items.

Assembled Turnout

Stub Turnout

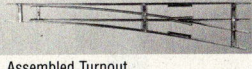
Turnout Kit

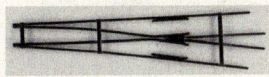
Point & Frog

CODE 40
N Turnouts

#4 Right Hand
180-4841 Assembled **24.80**
180-4843 Turnout Kit **19.60**

#4 Left Hand
180-4842 Assembled **24.80**
180-4844 Turnout Kit **19.60**

#5 Right Hand
180-4851 Assembled **21.20**
180-4853 Turnout Kit **20.00**

#5 Left Hand
180-4852 Assembled **21.20**
180-4854 Turnout Kit **20.00**

#6 Right Hand
180-4861 Assembled **25.60**
180-4863 Turnout Kit **20.40**

#6 Left Hand
180-4862 Assembled **25.60**
180-4864 Turnout Kit **19.60**

#2-1/2 Wye
180-4891 Assembled **20.80**
180-4893 Turnout Kit **19.60**

#4 Wye
180-4892 Assembled **20.80**
180-4894 Turnout Kit **19.60**

#5 Wye
180-48921 Assembled **21.20**
180-48941 Turnout Kit **20.00**

Nn3 Turnouts
Visit www.walthers.com for a complete listing of Code 40 Nn3 turnouts.

CODE 70
N Turnouts

#4 Right Hand
180-1541 Assembled **21.80**
180-1543 Turnout Kit **20.60**

#4 Left Hand
180-1542 Assembled **21.80**
180-1544 Turnout Kit **20.60**

#5 Right Hand
180-1551 Assembled **19.20**
180-1553 Turnout Kit **18.00**

#5 Left Hand
180-1552 Assembled **19.20**
180-1554 Turnout Kit **18.00**

#6 Right Hand
180-1561 Assembled **19.60**
180-1563 Turnout Kit **18.40**

#6 Left Hand
180-1562 Assembled **19.60**
180-1564 Turnout Kit **18.40**

#8 Right Hand
180-1581 Assembled **23.40**
180-1583 Turnout Kit **19.20**

#8 Left Hand
180-1582 Assembled **20.40**
180-1584 Turnout Kit **19.20**

#10 Right Hand
180-1511 Assembled **24.20**
180-1513 Turnout Kit **20.00**

#10 Left Hand
180-1512 Assembled **21.20**
180-1514 Turnout Kit **20.00**

#12 Right Hand
180-15111 Assembled **22.00**
180-15131 Turnout Kit **20.80**

#12 Left Hand
180-15121 Assembled **22.00**
180-15141 Turnout Kit **20.80**

#2-1/2 Wye
180-1591 Assembled **21.80**
180-1593 Turnout Kit **17.60**

#4 Wye
180-1592 Assembled **21.80**
180-1594 Turnout Kit **17.60**

N Curved Turnouts
#4 31.00 ea
180-15241 Right Hand
180-15242 Left Hand

#5 28.00 ea
180-15251 Right Hand
180-15252 Left Hand

#6
180-15261 Right Hand **33.00**
180-15262 Left Hand **29.00**

#8 34.00 ea
180-15281 Right Hand
180-15282 Left Hand

N Crossings 39.00 ea (Unless Noted)
180-1531 90°
180-1532 60°
180-1533 45°
180-1534 30°
180-1536 19° **49.00**

CODE 55
N Turnouts

#4 Right Hand
180-1441 Assembled **22.80**
180-1443 Turnout Kit **18.60**

#4 Left Hand
180-1442 Assembled **22.80**
180-1444 Turnout Kit **18.60**

#5 Right Hand
180-1451 Assembled **20.20**
180-1453 Turnout Kit **19.00**

#5 Left Hand
180-1452 Assembled **20.20**
180-1454 Turnout Kit **19.00**

#6 Right Hand
180-1461 Assembled **23.60**
180-1463 Turnout Kit **19.40**

#6 Left Hand
180-1462 Assembled **23.60**
180-1464 Turnout Kit **19.40**

#8 Right Hand
180-1481 Assembled **21.40**
180-1483 Turnout Kit **20.20**

#8 Left Hand
180-1482 Assembled **24.40**
180-1484 Turnout Kit **20.20**

#10 Right Hand
180-1411 Assembled **22.20**
180-1413 Turnout Kit **21.00**

#10 Left Hand
180-1412 Assembled **22.20**
180-1414 Turnout Kit **21.00**

#12 Right Hand
180-14111 Assembled **26.00**
180-14131 Turnout Kit **21.80**

#12 Left Hand
180-14121 Assembled **26.00**
180-14141 Turnout Kit **21.80**

#2-1/2 Wye
180-1491 Assembled **19.80**
180-1493 Turnout Kit **18.60**

#4 Wye
180-1492 Assembled **22.80**
180-1494 Turnout Kit **18.60**

#5 Wye
180-14921 Assembled **23.20**
180-14941 Turnout Kit **19.00**

#6 Wye
180-14922 Assembled **23.60**
180-14942 Turnout Kit **19.40**

N Curved Turnouts
#4
180-14241 Right Hand **29.00**
180-14242 Left Hand **33.00**

#5
180-14251 Right Hand **30.00**
180-14252 Left Hand **34.00**

#6 35.00 ea
180-14261 Right Hand
180-14262 Left Hand

N Crossings 41.00 ea (Unless Noted)
180-1431 90°
180-1432 60° **45.00**
180-1433 45°
180-1434 30°
180-1436 19° **47.00**
180-1438 15° **49.00**

Nn3 Turnouts
Visit www.walthers.com for a complete listing of Code 55 Nn3 turnouts.

CTT, INC.

Designing and planning your next layout will be easy with CTT track-planning templates. All items are calibrated to a 1" = 12" scale.

N Scale Templates
Templates are molded in tough, see-through plastic with outlines for curves, crossings, turnouts and other track.

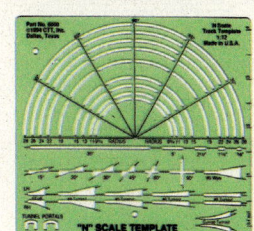

233-6000 Template **13.99**
233-6003 Template Kit w/Paper **17.99**

N Scale Flexible Ruler

233-9160 N Scale-1/160 **4.29**
12" clear plastic. Includes scale feet, inches, full-size inch, millimeter, decimal and metric conversion table.

MLR MFG CO

TRACK TOOLS

479-5001 **3.85**
Square cuts flex track on straight-aways and curves without tie separation; helps locate misaligned rail joints and straightens used flex track in seconds.

479-5002 Parallel **3.85**
Allows uniform spacing maintenance on straight-aways and curves while laying parallel tracks.

Rail Soldering Fixture
479-5004 **3.85**
Fixture will hold rail alignment for soldering rail joint.

Radius Tool
479-5007 **8.57**
Set contains two units – short unit will swing a radius from 7 to 11", long unit 1 to 23".

Ballast Spreader

479-5009 **10.05**
Easy to use. Adjustable for heavy or light flow.

Track Tool Sets
479-5011 **20.57**
Set contains one each: track tool, parallel tool, soldering tool and ballast spreader.

479-5018 Deluxe pkg(6) **35.09**
Includes one each: #5002, 5004, 5007, 5009 and 5019 in a handy 2 x 2 x 24" storage/carrying box.

Flex Track Alignment Tool

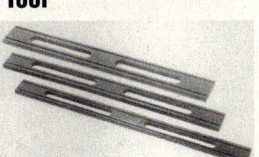

479-5015 **5.15**
8" section will keep rail straight during construction of hand-laid mainlines, sidings and yard tracks.

115

TRACK & ACCESSORIES N SCALE

UNITRACK

For track that works, without the work! With Kato N Scale Unitrack, you can have an operating layout in minutes. The modular roadbed and rail track system minimizes your set-up time so that you can get to the fun and enjoyment of operating trains. There's no need to glue down cork roadbed; tack down track sections and file rail connections smooth after soldering. Simply snap it together and you're ready to go.

This modular track system features nickel-silver rails fully integrated to a remarkably realistic-looking roadbed. The patented Unijoiners (included) lock the track sections together firmly and evenly. The frustration of derailments resulting from uneven rail joints and separating sections is eliminated.

The Feeder Track, Double Crossover and all electrical turnouts are factory-wired for "plug-and-play" operation.

Power Pack

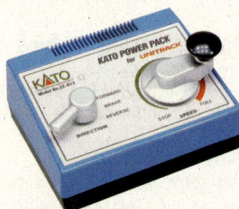

381-22014 For Unitrack 12 Volt, 1 Amp **65.00**

381-24829 Power Pack Accessory Adapter **7.95** Attaches to Kato Power Pack for plug-in connection of #381-24844 3-Color Signal Power Supply (sold separately).

Double Track Plate Girder Bridges
7-13/32" 18.6cm
21.00 ea
381-20455 Light Blue
381-20456 Light Green
381-20457 Gray

Track Sets

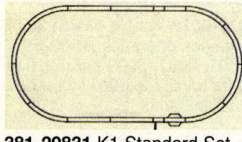

381-20831 K1 Standard Set **39.00**
This basic set makes a loop layout that is approximately 4'-2" x 2'-2". The set uses 12-3/8" radius curved track. Set includes eight 45° curved track pieces, four 9-3/4" sections of straight track, six spare rail joiners and one each of the following: 4-7/8" straight track, 2-7/16" straight track, 2-7/16" feeder track, 4-7/8" crossing track, rerailer and adapter cord.

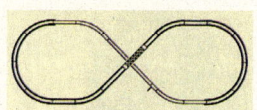

381-20833 K3 Viaduct Set **127.00**
This viaduct set can be used to construct an elaborate figure-eight layout with the use of its truss bridge and elevated pier set. The viaduct set uses 12-3/8" radius curved track. Approximately 6'-4" x 2'-2". Set includes ten 45° curved viaduct 12-3/8" radius, six spare rail joiners and 2" piers, two each of 9-3/4" straight track, 7-5/16" straight track, 45° curved track, 7-5/16" straight viaduct with track, 9/16" pier, 1" pier, 1-3/8" pier, 1-3/4" pier, stairs, and one each of 2-7/16" straight track, 2-7/16" feeder track, 9-3/4" straight viaduct with track, 4-7/8" straight viaduct with track, truss bridge and adapter cord.

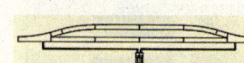

381-20832 K2 Turnout Set **82.00**
This set contains two turnouts, turnout throw switches and other track items that can expand the Standard Set. Approximately 4'-6" x 4". Set includes six each of 9-3/4" straight track and spare rail joiners, two each of 2-1/2" straight track, 28-1/4" curved track and turnout switch, one each of both right and left electric turnout, and DC converter.

Double Track Viaduct
381-20840 Complete Set **139.00**
Makes a 64-3/4 x 35" loop. Includes six 9-3/4" straights, eight 15"/16-5/16" curves, 14 piers, 14 overhead poles, two power cords and one rerailer. Separate purchase of #381-24843 Adapter Cord is recommended.

Straight Track

381-20000 9-3/4" 248mm pkg(4) **8.00**
381-20010 7-5/16" 186mm pkg(4) **7.50**
381-20020 4-7/8" 124mm pkg(4) **7.00**
381-20030 2-1/2" 64mm pkg(2) **3.00**
381-20040 2-7/16" 62mm pkg(4) **6.00**

381-20021 Crossing Track, 4-7/8" 124mm **2.50**

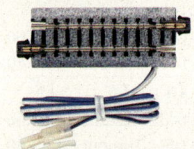

381-20032 Magnetic Uncoupler Track, 2-1/2" 64mm **5.00**

381-20041 Feeder Track, 2-7/16" 62mm **4.25**

381-20045 Snap Track Conversion Track, 2-1/2" 64mm pkg(2) **2.50**

381-20050 Expansion Track **7.00**
Expands from 3" to 4-1/4" 78 to 108mm.

381-20091 Track Assortment pkg(10) **13.00**
Includes eight 1-1/8" and two 1-3/8" straight track sections.

Track Bumpers pkg(2) 6.75 ea (Unless Noted)

381-20046 With Concrete Bumper 2-7/16" 62mm

381-20047 With Wood Bumper 2-7/16" 62mm

381-20048 With Steel Bumper 2" 50.5mm **7.00**

Curved Track

381-20100 45°, 9-3/4" 249mm Radius pkg(4) **7.50**
381-20101 15°, 9-3/4" 249mm Radius pkg(4) **6.50**
381-20110 45°, 11" 282mm Radius pkg(4) **8.00**
381-20111 15°, 11" 282mm Radius pkg(4) **6.50**
381-20120 45°, 12-3/8" 315mm Radius pkg(4) **8.00**
381-20121 15°, 12-3/8" 315mm Radius pkg(4) **6.50**
381-20130 30°, 13-3/4" 348mm Radius pkg(4) **7.50**
381-20132 45°, 13-3/4" 348mm Radius pkg(4) **9.00**
381-20140 30°, 15" 381mm Radius pkg(4) **7.50**
381-20150 15°, 28-1/4" 718mm Radius pkg(4) **7.50**
381-20160 15°, 19" 481mm Radius pkg(4) **7.00**
381-20170 45°, 8-5/8" 216mm Radius pkg(4) **7.50**
381-20171 15°, 8-5/8" 216mm Radius pkg(4) **6.50**

Electric Turnouts

No. 4 32.75 ea
Metal frog. Selectable operating modes: Power routing or nonpower routing; frog power on or off.

381-20220 Left Hand
381-20221 Right Hand

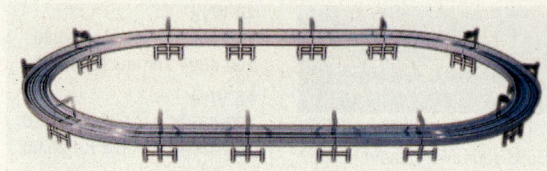

Double Track Viaduct Complete Set 381-20840

No. 6 23.50 ea
Power routing.

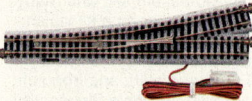

381-20202 Left Hand
381-20203 Right Hand

Crossings

381-20210 Double Crossover 12-3/4" 310mm **65.50**

381-20320 90° 4-7/8" 124mm **15.50**
Designed for single or multiple crossing use.

15°, 7-5/16" 186mm 9.50 ea

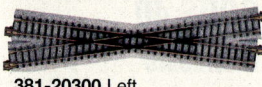

381-20300 Left

381-20301 Right

Automatic Signal

The signal changes from green to red as the engine reaches the detector position. A built-in timer then changes the signal to yellow, then back to green. (Not for use with DCC.)

381-20605 3-Color Signal **45.50**

381-24844 Signal Power Supply **23.50**
Powers up to three signals.

381-24845 Signal Extension Cord **3.25**

TRACK & ACCESSORIES N SCALE

Viaduct Sections

UNITRACK Viaduct and Bridge sections are used in conjunction with KATO's incline pier sets to create grades and overpasses. Add KATO structures along with additional track and accessory items for greater realism.

Single-Track Straight

381-20400 S248 9-3/4" 248mm pkg(2) **10.50**
381-20410 S186 7-5/16" 186mm pkg(2) **9.50**
381-20420 S124 4-7/8" 124mm pkg(2) **8.50**
381-20440 S62 2-7/8" 62mm pkg(2) **6.00**

Single-Track Curved

381-20531
Two sections of track shown

381-20505 45°, 9-3/4" 249mm pkg(2) **9.50**
381-20510 45°, 11" 282mm pkg(2) **10.50**
381-20520 45°, 12-3/8" 315mm pkg(2) **11.00**
381-20530 45°, 13-3/4" 348mm pkg(2) **11.00**
381-20531 30°, 13-3/4" 348mm pkg(2) **9.50**
381-20540 30°, 15" 381mm pkg(2) **9.50**

Signal Section

381-20421 4-7/8" 124mm Straight **2.50**
For use with N Scale 3-Color Automatic Signal #381-20605 (not included).

Double Track Sections

381-20401 Straight 9-3/4" 248mm pkg(2) **15.00**
381-20411 7-5/16" 186mm pkg(2) **14.00**

381-20541 45° R381/R414 Curve 15"/16-5/16" pkg(2) **16.00**

Piers

381-23015 Gradual Set **10.50** 9/16 - 2" 15-50mm high.
381-23016 Add-On Gradual Set **9.50** 7/16 - 1-5/8" 11-42mm high.
381-23017 2" 50mm high pkg(5) **6.00**
381-23047 Rounded Base Pier Set w/S-Joiner pkg(5) **9.00** 2" 50mm

Limited Quantity Available
381-23046 Double Track Incline Pier Set **22.50**

Double Track Viaduct Pier Set, 2" pkg(6)

381-23018 Pre-Cast **14.00**
381-23019 Poured **12.00**

Truss Bridges 13.00 ea

Comes completely assembled, measures 9-3/4 x 1-1/4" 248mm.

381-20430 Red
381-20431 Green
381-20432 Gray
381-20433 Silver
381-20434 Black

Double Track Truss Bridges 21.00 ea

Comes completely assembled, measures 9-3/4 x 3" 248mm.

381-20435 Green
381-20436 Light Blue
381-20437 Silver
381-20438 Black

Plate Girder Bridges 9.25 ea

Comes completely assembled, measures 7-5/16" 186mm.

381-20450 Red
381-20451 Green
381-20452 Gray
381-20453 Silver
381-20454 Black

Deck Plate Girder Bridge 12.00 ea

Piers sold separately (#23047 pictured in illustration). 4-7/8" 124mm.

381-20460 Red
381-20461 Green
381-20462 Gray
381-20464 Black

Ballast

381-24039 200g **9.00**
Fine-grain ballast to match UNITRACK roadbed.

Latest New Product News Daily! Visit Walthers Web site at
www.walthers.com

Unijoiners pkg(20) 5.25 ea

381-24815   381-24816
381-24815 Unijoiner
381-24816 Insulated Unijoiner

381-24817 Viaduct S-Joiner

Terminal Joiner

381-24818 **4.25**
Use in place of feeder track, provides power to rails.

Turnout Control Switch

381-24840 **7.75**

DC Converter

381-24842 **6.50**

Adapter Cord

381-24843 **3.25**

Extension Cords

All extension cords are approximately 35" long.

381-24825 DC Extension Cord **3.25**
Use to reach a distant feeder track.

381-24826 AC Extension Cord **3.25**

381-24827 3-Way **5.25**
Can be used to power multiple feeder tracks or operate multiple turnouts with a single turnout control switch.

381-24828 Double Track Power Cord pkg(2) **7.50**

381-24841 Turnout Extension Cord **3.25**

381-24845 Signal Extension Cord **3.25**

Switches

381-24830 Connector (green) **3.25**
381-24831 Selector (red) **3.75**
381-24832 Reverse (blue) **4.00**

Rerailer

381-24000 **1.30**

Overhead Poles

Can be used with ground or viaduct track.
381-23059 Single Track pkg(16) **6.00**
381-23057 Double Track, Rounded Corner pkg(6) **7.98**
381-23060 Double Track, Squared Corner pkg(8) **6.00**
381-23056 Pole Base Set **4.50**
16 each of ground and viaduct style.

117

TRACK & ACCESSORIES N SCALE

The Tortoise Switch Machine

800-6000 18.95
Easy-to-mount slow-motion switch machine features:
• Prototypical slow-motion action - three seconds to complete throw
• Precision-engineered gear drive mechanism
• Simple mounting with linkage included - no additional brackets or linkage necessary
• Convenient auxilliary contacts - two sets SPDT provided
• Easy wiring - two-wire connection possible

Tortoise Value Packs
(Dealers Note: items are not labeled for individual sale.)
800-6006 pkg(6) 110.00
800-6012 pkg(12) 210.00

NEW PRODUCTS

Switch Machine w/Internal DCC Decoder

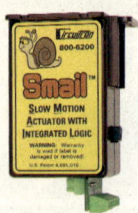

NEW 800-6200 39.95
Same size and mounting as the TORTOISE™. Compatible with all DCC systems that provide accessory address control. Two wire connection to DCC bus with no external power necessary. Easy programming. May also be controlled with panel switches or detection circuits. Adjustable throw speed. Power up position user definable or will default to last used. Other specifications same as TORTOISE.

SMAIL™ Value Packs
(Dealers Note: Items are not labeled for individual sale.)
NEW 800-6206 pkg(6) 230.00
NEW 800-6212 pkg(12) 440.00

Terminal Blocks
Set of two screw-type terminal blocks that can be soldered to the SMAIL circuit board to allow easy under-layout connections.
NEW 800-6301 Single 4.95
NEW 800-6306 pkg(6) 24.95
NEW 800-6312 pkg(12) 42.95

SMAIL w/Terminal Blocks
Includes factory installed screw-type terminal blocks for simple connections without soldering.
NEW 800-6200TB 46.95
(Dealers Note: Items below are not labeled for individual sale.)
NEW 800-6206TB pkg(6) 270.00
NEW 800-6212TB pkg(12) 520.00

Remote Tortoise Mount
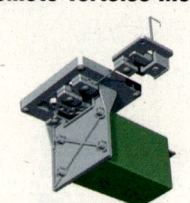
800-6100 10.95
Mounting bracket and special linkage allow you to mount the Tortoise above or below the benchwork and up to 18" from the turnout. Suitable for all scales and brands of turnouts.
800-6101 For Crossovers & Double Slip Switches 5.95
Extra cable and Actuator may be used with Remote Tortoise Mount (#800-6100, sold separately) to allow two sets of points to be thrown simultaneously by one Tortoise.

Drilling Template
800-6190 5.95
Laser-cut template of thin acrylic allows precise location of TORTOISE or SMAIL mounting holes.

AC Adapter
800-7212 12.95
110V AC wall plug adapter outputs filtered 12V DC at 500 mA, sufficient to power up to 30 Tortoise Switch Machines.

Non-Weathered Flex-Trak™
Flex-Trak™ features scale size ties, tie plates and spikes, irregular tie spacing, natural brown tie color and nickel silver rail. 3' lengths.

255-10122 Code 70 pkg(6) 31.45
255-10124 Code 55 pkg(6) 29.55
255-10125 Code 55 Concrete ties pkg (6) 29.55
255-10126 Code 40 pkg(6) 29.55

Weathered Flex-Trak™
Weathered Flex-Trak™ features realistically weathered nickel silver rail, scale size ties, tie plates and spikes, irregular tie spacing and natural brown tie color. 3' lengths.

255-12122 Code 70 pkg(6) 32.90
255-12124 Code 55 pkg(6) 30.80
255-12125 Code 55 Concrete ties pkg (6) 30.80
255-12126 Code 40 pkg(6) 30.80

Flex-Trak™ Turnouts 16.95 ea
Turnouts feature spring snap-action switch points, metal frogs, nickel silver rail and extra detail parts. Approximate length: 6".

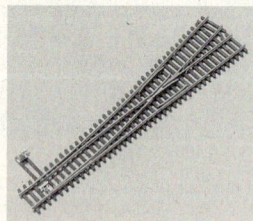

Code 70
255-15405 #6 Left Hand
255-15406 #6 Right Hand

Code 55
255-15505 #6 Left Hand
255-15506 #6 Right Hand

Bridge Flex-Trak™ 10.05 ea
Flex-Trak™ with bridge tie dimensions, ties are wider with closer spacing. This track has the same fine detail, nickel silver rail and coloring as regular Flex-Trak™, plus additional parts.

255-11110 Code 70, 3' Length Includes Code 55 guard rails, guard timbers and four barrel platforms.
255-11112 Code 55, 3' Length Includes Code 40 guard rails, guard timbers and four barrel platforms.

Weathered Rail
Pre-colored dark brown nickel silver rail. 3' lengths.
255-16070 Code 70 pkg(33) 55.15
255-16055 Code 55 pkg(33) 48.00
255-16040 Code 40 pkg(17) 27.80

Non-Weathered Rail
Nickel silver rail. 3' lengths.
255-17070 Code 70 pkg(33) 51.30
255-17055 Code 55 pkg(33) 44.20
255-17040 Code 40 pkg(17) 25.65

Track Accessories
255-80302 Switch Stand - Nonoperating pkg(2) 2.35
255-80328 Turnout Parts Code 70 #6 8.70
255-80332 Turnout Parts Code 55 #6 8.70

Weathered Ties
Scale ties, stained and weathered brown.
255-36106 Turnout Length pkg(250) 6.95

Non-Weathered Ties
Scale ties in natural wood.
255-37106 Turnout Length pkg(250) 5.95

Rail Joiners - Metal
Low profile, nickel silver, slip-on type joiners.
255-26070 Code 70 pkg(50) 8.05
255-26055 Code 55 pkg(50) 8.05
255-26040 Code 40 pkg(20) 4.20

Rail Joiners - Plastic Insulated pkg(12) 3.85 ea
255-26071 Code 70
255-26056 Code 55

Transition Rail Joiners - Plastic 4 Pair 3.85 ea
255-26004 Code 80 to 55
255-26005 Code 70 to 55

Track Gauges 4.85 ea
Three-point, diecast metal track gauges keep rail aligned when hand-laying track.

255-42108 Code 70
255-42109 Code 55
255-42110 Code 40

Spikes
Blackened metal.
255-30105 Small 1/4", Pointed pkg(15,000) 110.55
255-30106 Small 1/4", Pointed pkg(1000) 9.40
255-30108 Micro 3/16" pkg(1000) 9.40
255-30110 Small, 1/4" Chisel pkg(1000) 9.40

Track Tools

255-48101 Rail Cutter, Heavy Duty 27.70

255-48102 Rail Nipper, Light Duty 13.80

Rail Weathering Solution
This is the same solution Micro Engineering uses for weathering its Flex-Trak and rail.

255-49103 4oz 9.85
255-49104 16oz (1 pt) 25.25

118

TRACK & ACCESSORIES N SCALE

Add a finishing touch of realism to your railroad scenes with these detailed, one-piece castings. Each is hand-cast from a very strong gypsum material that picks up fine details much like dental plaster. Items are hand-painted to bring out the many realistic details. Note: all photos show HO Scale models.

Loading Ramps

506-1000 Ramp & Dock Set **10.78**
Includes one concrete End-of-Track Ramp and one Wood and Stone Loading Dock. Perfect for detailing yard scenes, small town sidings or industrial areas.

Coal Trestle

506-1010 Coal Unloading Ramp **10.78**
Trestle-style ramp with realistic coal pile detail. Great for a smalltown coal yard or as an unloading ramp for a large steam-era industry.

Track Bumpers

506-1310 End of Track Poured Concrete – Pennsylvania Prototype pkg(5) **6.46**

506-1320 Heavy Timber & Ballast Type pkg(2) **5.38**

Info, Images, Inspiration! Get It All at
www.walthers.com

NICKEL SILVER US SYSTEM

Straight Track

490-3902 5" pkg(4) **1.50**

Curved Track
490-3904 9-3/4" Radius pkg(4) **1.50**

Rerailer
490-3905 Curved, 9-3/4" **3.50**
490-3965 **1.75**

Switch Controls
490-3 Sliding w/Momentary Pushbutton **3.25**

Rail Joiners
490-5325 pkg(48) **1.75**

Curvable Track

490-4901 Flexible Track, 28-3/4" pkg(5) **10.98**

Lighted Bumper Track

490-4991 2" pkg(2) **3.50**
Compatible with Atlas or Bachmann track.

TURNOUTS

Ultra Remote Switches 10.98 ea
Fully assembled, each turnout is complete with switch machine, remote control, wiring harness and complete hook-up instructions.

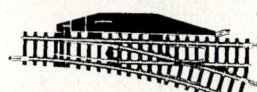

490-3962 Left Hand
490-3964 Right Hand

Crossing
490-4959 90° **10.98**

ACCESSORIES

Cork Roadbed
490-4321 36" pkg(25) **24.00**

Switch Block
490-4326 pkg(2) **3.25**

Power Pack
490-1250 Deluxe **24.98**
6 amp taper-wound rheostat. Separate forward and reverse switch.

Rail Joiners
490-6539 Insulated pkg(48) **1.75**

Track Nails
490-246 **3.25**

Track Test Light

490-16628 **8.98**

N.J. INTERNATIONAL

Switch Stands 8.99 ea
Assembled, Operating Switch Stands. All brass, painted and jeweled.

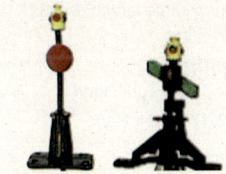

525-2911   525-2912
525-2911 Star
525-2912 Branch

525-2913   525-2914   525-2915
525-2913 Main Line
525-2914 Low Ramapo
525-2915 High Ramapo

525-2916   525-2917
525-2916 High Star Type, Standard Red Target
525-2917 High Star Type Derail w/Blue Target

Peerless Industries Inc.

Peerless Industries offers easy-to-install electronic controls for directional reversing, delayed reversing and intermediate stops. The units come completely assembled with color-coded wires and easy-to-follow instructions.

Automatic Reversing Unit

Automatically reverses train direction without the need for special switches, optical sensors, lights or magnets. Operates from a 12V DC power pack. Unit is less track. Can be used for:
- automatic single or multitrack point-to-point operation
- a wall or bookcase mini-layout or display track for your favorite locomotive
- a test or break-in track

564-525 HO Scale **74.95**
564-535 N Scale **74.95**
564-542 G Scale **82.50**
564-545 O Scale **77.95**

Automatic Train Stop Control

564-550 **77.95**
For use with the #525, 535, 542 or 545. Provides automatic delayed stops at the end points of your reversing section. Delay is adjustable up to 30 seconds. Takes only a few minutes to install and operates from your power pack accessory terminals.

Automatic Intermediate Train Stop

564-555 **77.95**
Train stops—delays up to 30 seconds—restarts automatically at preset locations such as at a train station, water tower, etc. Use with #525, 535, 542, 545 or alone in a continuous-loop layout. Operates from power pack accessory terminals.

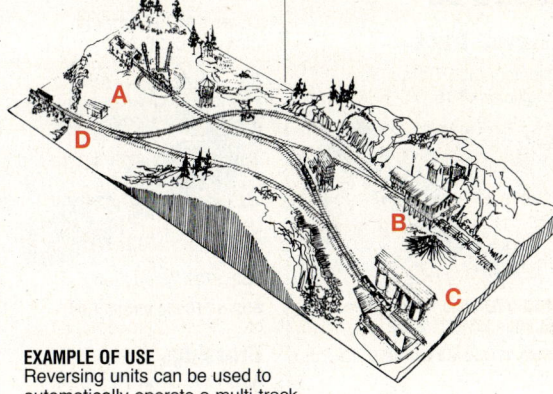

EXAMPLE OF USE
Reversing units can be used to automatically operate a multi-track logging or lumber mill, or an ore mine.

In this example, a train can start at point A, travel to point B, automatically stop and reverse to point D, then automatically stop and reverse to point C, before finally stopping and reversing automatically back to point A. Basic plans available from manufacturer.

TRACK & ACCESSORIES N SCALE

PECO

IMPORTED FROM GREAT BRITAIN BY WALTHERS
Peco offers a large selection of N and Z Scale track and accessories, including turnouts, flex track and more. All sections feature wood ties (unless noted) and nickel silver rail for best electrical performance.

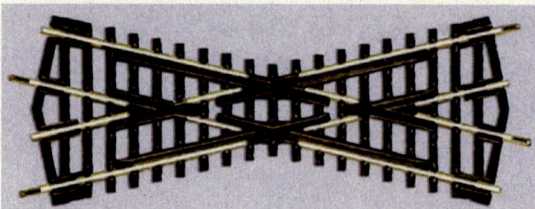
Code 80 Crossing 552-1706

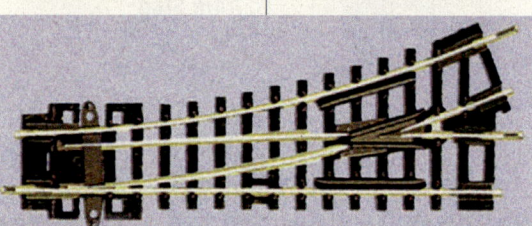
Code 80 #4 Left Hand Turnout 552-1705

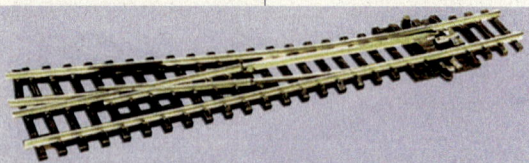
Code 55 #4 Right Hand Turnout 552-1791

CODE 80

Curved Track
Dealers MUST order in multiples of 16.

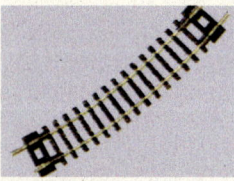

552-1702 Standard Curve, 9" Radius 22-1/2° **2.25**
552-1703 Half Curve 9" Radius 11-1/4° **1.87**
552-55 Standard Curve 10-3/8" Radius 22-1/2° **2.87**
552-56 Double Curve 10-3/8" Radius 45° **3.56**

Straight Track
Dealers MUST order in multiples of 16.

552-1700 3-7/16" 87mm **2.25**
552-1701 2-1/4" 58mm **1.87**

Flex Track 5.40 ea
Dealers MUST order in multiples of 25.
36" 91.4cm

552-1709 Wood Ties
552-1710 Concrete Ties

Crossings
552-1706 Short 25° **18.99** 3-9/16" 91mm Long
552-1740 Long 8° **19.99** 7-3/8" 187mm Long

#4 Turnouts 18.99 ea

Insulfrog, Approximate length: 3-7/16" 87mm
552-1704 Right Hand
552-1705 Left Hand

#6 Medium Radius

Approximate length: 5-3/8" 137mm
Insulfrog 18.99 ea
552-1738 Right Hand
552-1739 Left Hand
Electrofrog 19.99 ea
552-382 Right Hand
552-383 Left Hand

#8 Large Radius 21.99 ea

Approximate length: 6-9/32" 160mm
Insulfrog
552-1736 Right Hand
552-1737 Left Hand
Electrofrog
552-385 Right Hand
552-386 Left Hand

#8 Curved 21.99 ea

Approximate length: 6-3/16" 157mm
Insulfrog
552-1734 Right Hand
552-1735 Left Hand
Electrofrog
552-1386 Right Hand
552-1387 Left Hand

Wye Turnouts
Approximate length: 5" 127mm.
552-1397 #6 Medium Radius Electrofrog **19.99**

552-1741 #6 Medium Radius Insulfrog **18.99**

Derail 12.99 ea

Working model protects trains on mainline from runaway cars on sidings. Cars on siding will derail if allowed to roll through open switch.
552-1732 Right Hand
552-1733 Left Hand

CODE 55

Flex Track
36" 91.4cm. Dealers MUST order in multiples of 30.

552-5801 Wood Ties **6.43**

552-302 Concrete Ties **7.00**

Medium Radius Turnouts w/Electrofrog
#4 19.99 ea
552-1791 Right Hand
552-1792 Left Hand

#6 21.99 ea
Approximate length: 5-3/8" 137mm.
552-1795 Right Hand
552-1796 Left Hand

#8 23.99 ea
Approximate length: 6-1/4" 164mm.
552-1788 Right Hand
552-1789 Left Hand

#8 Curved 23.99 ea
Approximate length: 6-3/16" 157mm.
552-387 Right Hand
552-388 Left Hand

Wye Turnouts
552-1797 #7 **24.99**
Approximate length: 3-3/8" 86mm.

Crossings

552-54 Double Crossover w/Electrofrog **128.99**
552-74 Long Insulfrog 7-3/8" 187mm 8° **19.99**

552-1774 Long Electrofrog **23.99**
552-393 Short Crossing 20° **19.99**

Universal Slip Switches
Features live frog and fine profile rail.

Single Slip 72.99 ea

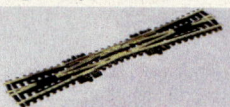

552-380 Insulfrog
552-1798 Electrofrog

Double Slip

552-3906 Insulfrog **77.99**
552-1799 Electrofrog **78.99**

Rail Joiners 3.17 ea
Dealers MUST order in multiples of 12.
552-1711 Nickel Silver
552-1712 Insulated-Nylon

CODE 60

Flex Track
Dealers MUST order in multiples of 12.

552-200 Flex Track 24" 60.9cm **8.00**
For Z or Nn3 Gauge, approximately 1/4" 6.5mm wide.

Rail Joiners
Dealers MUST order in multiples of 12.

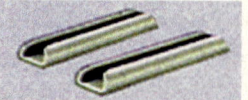

552-1307 Nickel Silver Nn3 or Z Gauge **3.33**

INSPECTION PIT
552-142566 **11.99**
This detailed, injection-molded kit contains enough parts to build one pit 6-3/4" 17.1cm long, or can also create two smaller pits. Includes Code 55 rail, but is also suitable for use with Code 80 trackwork. The pit is easily extended by using multiple kits.

TRACK & ACCESSORIES N SCALE

PECO

CROSSINGS W/GATES
552-57 14.99
A typical English level crossing, this model can be used on single or multi-track lines. Includes straight track section, four gates and two ramps.

552-58 Straight Track Add-On Section **7.99**
Build a wider crossing anywhere along your line. Simply clip as many together as needed, and install with parts from crossing #552-57 (sold separately) to finish the scene.

TURNTABLE
552-1755 Well-Type Kit **29.99**
This easy-to-build plastic kit is based on a British design, but is similar to turntables found in many parts of the world. The kit includes detailed plastic parts, plus bridge rails and electrical contacts. The bridge measures 5-15/16" 151mm, so it can handle various sizes of motive power.

UNIVERSAL

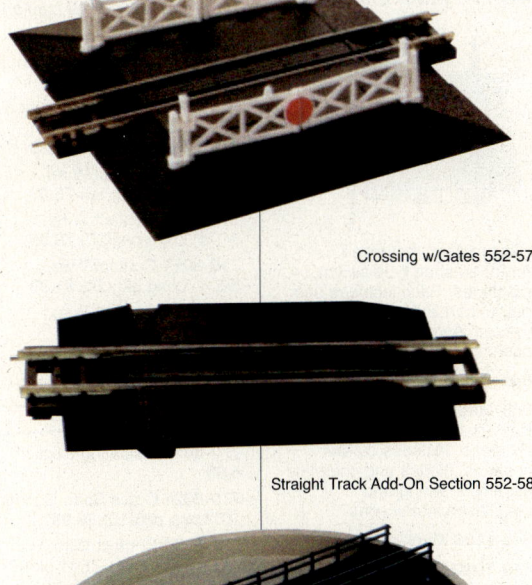

Crossing w/Gates 552-57

Straight Track Add-On Section 552-58

Turntable 552-1755

ACCESSORIES
Micro Switch

552-15 14.99
Easy-to-assemble unit provides two sets of contacts that can be used to control polarity of live frogs while simultaneously operating panel indicator lights. Other uses include signal interlocking and reverse loop switching.

Peco Catalog
552-1995 8.99
Features the complete line of Peco products, including track and much more. Loaded with color photos and helpful modeling information.

RIBBONRAIL

TRACK ALIGNMENT GAUGES
Slide between rails to correctly gauge rails. Helps in laying, spiking and joining rail. Precision machined to NMRA standards.

Straight Gauges

Item	Length	Price
170-8002	24"	8.50
170-8005	5"	3.80
170-8010	10"	4.00

Curved Radius Gauges
3.80 ea

Item	Radius
170-8015	15"
170-8016	16"
170-8017	17"
170-8018	18"
170-8019	19"
170-8020	20"
170-8021	21"
170-8022	22"
170-8023	23"
170-8024	24"
170-8025	25"
170-8026	26"
170-8027	27"
170-8028	28"
170-8029	29"
170-8030	30"
170-8031	31"
170-8032	32"
170-8033	33"
170-8034	34"
170-8035	35"
170-8036	36"
170-8037	37"
170-8038	38"
170-8039	39"
170-8040	40"
170-8041	41"
170-8042	42"
170-8043	43"
170-8044	44"
170-8045	45"
170-8046	46"
170-8047	47"
170-8048	48"

RIX
Rix Products

TRACK ACCESSORIES
N Scale switch machines and accessories.

CTC Knob Kit
628-61 8.95

Mounting Brackets
628-1 Rix-Rax Mounting Bracket **3.49**
Under layout bracket, completely adjustable. Includes nuts, bolts, screws and throw rod. For use with most twin coil switch machines.

628-5 Rix-Rax Flat Mounting Bracket Kit **3.49**
Under-layout mounting bracket works with most any switch machine for flat mounting.

Rail-It
628-3 2.99
Set on track and roll cars down ramp; automatically places wheels on track. Works with Code 70, 83 and 100 track.

Switch Machines

628-4 T-C **10.99**
Controls turnouts from above or below the layout. Includes two SPDT add-on sets of contacts and needed hardware. Operates on 6-32V.

628-15 Economy **10.25**
Same as #628-4 less contacts and mounting screws.

Rix Adjusto Pad
628-7 2.75
For mounting switch machine above or below layout. Includes wood and switch machine screws. Adjustable and interchangeable.

For Daily Product Information Click

www.walthers.com

Rix-Rax II

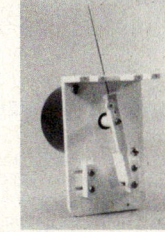

628-21 3.49
Under-layout mounting bracket complete with press-on linkage to motor shaft, adjustable limit stop blocks to limit the force on the switch points, mounting holes for most brands of adjustable limit switches and all hardware. Designed for use with the Hanscraft Display Motor. Works with all scales.

Turnout Linkage
628-6 Pivoting Turnout Linkage **2.75**
For controlling turnout from underneath layout.

NEW RAIL MODELS

NEW PRODUCTS

Blue Point™ Turnout Controllers
This innovative electrical component makes it easy to power frogs and route power on manual turnouts. Under-the-benchwork, manually thrown turnout control includes two sets of 5A electrical contacts for turnout frog or accessories such as signals. Features include locking slider tension and throw adjustment, plus dual attach points for fascia control. Also includes .032 turnout throw wire and complete instructions.

NEW 501-40018 Single **12.95**
NEW 501-400185 pkg(5) **59.95**
NEW 501-4001810 pkg(10) **99.95**

TRACK & ACCESSORIES N SCALE

TRAIN AMERICA STUDIOS

Torquemaster Switch Motors
Offers quiet, reliable operation ideal for N, HO, S, O and G Scales (working great for both standard and narrow gauges alike). Unit is powered by a 12V DC supply (provisions are made for higher voltages). A resistor is added to one lead of the input power, drawing approximately 20 milliamps. One unit has enough power to control signal aspects and panel lights. Each Torquemaster kit includes all mounting hardware required to successfully install one motor. A DPDT toggle switch is required for operation (sold separately).

703-4052 Single Unit **15.95**
703-4062 pkg(6) **89.95**
703-4054 Bulk Pack (25 Units) **358.95**

Panel Mount Kit
703-4060 **5.75**
For use with Torquemaster Switch Motors, listed above. Includes bi-polar LEDs, DPDT toggle switch and mounting hardware.

TOMAR INDUSTRIES

Hayes Wheel Stop
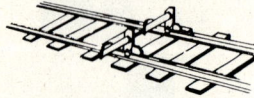

81-58080 pkg(4) **1.95**
Cast white-metal "stops" prevent cars from derailing at the end of sidings. Unpainted with instructions.

Hayes Bumping Post

81-5808 **4.50**
Assembled post mounted on track, insulated rail joiners provided.

TRACK-BED
N Scale Roadbed/Track-Bed Rolls, Strips and Sheets

- **Quieter Operation** (Sound Deadening Material)
- **Smoother Operation** (Cushions Vibrations)
- **Easier to Use** (Tack or Glue Down, Flexible, No Soaking, Compatible with Cork, Won't Dry Out or Crumble)
- **Better Value** (Higher Quality, Lower Cost)

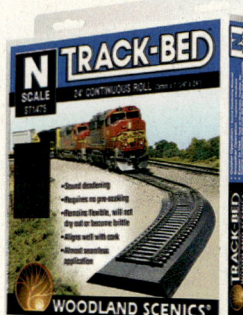

*Woodland Scenics Patented Product

Strips
Each piece is about 24" 60cm long and 1/8" 3mm thick.
785-1462 36 Pieces **18.87**
785-1472 12 Pieces **6.89**

Roll
785-1475 24' 720cm Long **6.89**
Continuous roll for almost seamless installation on your layout.

Sheets
Great for yards, station platforms, engine terminals or other areas Each measures about 1/8" 3mm thick.
785-1460 Standard 3-1/4 x 24" x 3mm pkg(6) **7.98**
785-1478 Super 12 x 24" x 3mm **3.29**
Dealers MUST order Dealer Packs of 6

SHINOHARA

Code 70 Track
Create realistic track for any part of your railroad. All items come fully assembled with Code 70 nickel silver rail for improved electrical performance, and plastic ties molded in dark brown plastic with realistic woodgrain and spike detail. Photos show HO Scale products.

#4 Turnouts 18.75 ea
669-601 Left Hand
669-602 Right Hand

#6 Turnouts 18.75 ea
669-603 Left Hand
669-604 Right Hand

Specialized Turnouts
669-607 #4 Wye **18.75**
669-608 #6 Three-Way **38.00**
669-612 #6 Double Crossover **57.25**

Double Slip Turnouts 57.25 ea
669-613 #4
669-614 #6

Flex Track
669-615 Measures 3' 90cm Long pkg(10) **48.95**

#6 Curved Turnouts 25.50 ea

669-626 Left Hand
669-627 Right Hand

Crossings 13.00 ea

669-630 30°
669-631 45°
669-632 60°
669-633 90°

SCALE SHOPS

Switch Machines
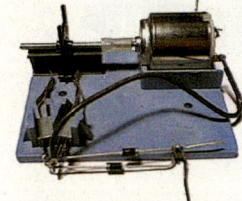

Slow motion, motorized, threaded-shaft type switch machines. Each includes one pair of contacts and switch linkage. Available fully assembled and in kit form.

649-1040 Assembled **17.98**
649-1030 Kit **10.98**
Easy-to-build kit assembles in six steps. Includes cut-out contacts, diodes and complete assembly, wiring and installation instructions.

649-1006 Kit pkg(6) **56.98**
649-1012 Kit pkg(12) **98.98**

Switch Machine Contacts
649-4080 pkg(2) **.98**
649-4082 pkg(12) **4.98**
649-4085 pkg(50) **16.98**

VOLLMER
IMPORTED FROM GERMANY BY WALTHERS

Catenary Masts

770-8001 Mast w/Long Arm pkg(20) **81.99**
770-8002 Mast Base pkg(10) **24.99**
770-8003 Feeder Mast w/Short Arm pkg(10) **80.99**

Limited Quantity Available
770-8000 Mast w/Short Arm pkg(20) **73.99**

770-8004 Wire Tensioner pkg(10) **43.99**
770-8005 Tower Mast pkg(10) **73.99**

Catenary Sets
770-8040 Catenary Set **146.99**
Includes: No. 8008 (14 pcs), No. 8001 (16 pcs), No. 8013 (4 pcs), No. 8000 (1 pc) and No. 8003 (1 pc).

770-8041 Catenary Set **164.99**
For station areas; includes: No. 8005 (8 pcs), No. 8004 (4 pcs), No. 8013 (12 pcs) and No. 8021 (4 pcs).

Catenary Wire
770-8008 Contact Wire, 3-1/2" Long pkg(20) **65.99**
770-8009 Contact Wire, 4-1/2" Long pkg(20) **75.99**
770-8010 Contact Wire, 5-1/4" Long pkg(20) **78.99**
770-8011 Contact Wire, 5-3/4" Long pkg(20) **81.99**
770-8013 Contact Wire, 8" Long pkg(20) **89.99**
770-8015 Equalizing Section pkg(2) **3.49**

770-8017 Insulating Section **4.99**
770-8021 Cross Span Support, 10" Long pkg(10) **89.99**
770-8030 Contact Wire, For Truss Bridge No. 7801 pkg(2) **10.99**
770-8032 Contact Wire, For Loco Shed No. 7801 pkg(2) **10.99**

Catenary Wire listed below is available by Special Order (see Legend Page).
770-8034 Contact Wire, For No. 7609 pkg(2) **19.99**

Models by Eric Meyer, Photo by Dan Larkee, Milwaukee, Wisconsin

Signals and signs are everywhere. Billboards tell us what we should buy, road signs give us directions, signals tell us when we should stop, go or walk and business signs tell us what's on sale and the name of the proprietor. As this Santa Fe road freight zips through town on the double track main, its route is kept clear by a variety of grade crossing signals. Circuits in the rails trigger the signals to turn on at the right moment to stop cross traffic until the train passes.

On your layout, signals and signs also have another purpose — they tell visitors what year it is. You won't find a cell phone billboard in a 50s scene, and you shouldn't see a billboard advertising 8-track tapes in the 1990s. On Eric Meyer's N Trak modules, this Kato F7 zips past a City Classics gas station sign in the midst of Design Preservation Models buildings. Traffic lights and NJ International crossing signals regulate auto traffic. They're all appropriate for 70s-era scene. Check out the products listed in the Signals, Signs & Detection Systems Section to make setting the scene on your layout easy.

SIGNALS, DETECTION UNITS & SIGNS N SCALE

LIFE-LIKE®
Div. of Wm. K. Walthers, Inc.

Spotlights

433-1628 pkg(2) 10.00

BL HOBBY PRODUCTS

Limited Quantity Available On All Items

TRAIN DETECTION SYSTEM
183-441 Block Occupancy "Regular" Unit 29.50
183-444 Automatic Block "Regular" Unit 43.00

SIGNALS
LED Lenses pkg(4) 3.95 ea
3/32" lenses.
183-250 Small, Red
183-251 Small, Green
183-252 Small, Yellow
183-253 Regular T-1, Red
183-254 Regular T-1, Green
183-255 Regular T-1, Yellow

Resistors
183-260 Drop 560 ohms pkg(5) 2.00

PANEL TRAIN CONTROL
183-462 AC Power Supply 55.00

ACCESSORIES
183-473 Wiring Harness 16.75
183-470 Blank Panel 2 x 9" 3.50
183-471 Blank Panel 4 x 9" 7.00
183-466 Train Reverse Kit 37.50

ATLAS MODEL RAILROAD CO., INC.

NEW PRODUCTS
Signals System & Accessories
The Atlas Model RR Signal System features true scale dimensions and details, and includes circuitry for North American prototype operation. These signals can be used as a stand-alone accessory, or connected to one another for complete dynamic integration. Features include easy set-up, scale signal structures that have true scale dimensions and details, prototypical operation circuitry, expandable with your railroad, modular design with telephone-style cord connections (for use with multiple signals, sold separately). Visit atlasrr.com for complete information and downloadable wiring diagrams and instructions.

Type G Signals
All signals include one jumper wire (signal plug to RJ-11 jack) and signal bungalow per signal.

NEW 150-2235 Single Target 29.95
NEW 150-2236 Single Target w/Signal Control PCB and 2-Rail (Analog) Block Detector 49.95
NEW 150-2237 Single Target pkg(4) 99.95

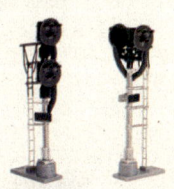
150-2238   150-2239

NEW 150-2238 Double Target 39.95
NEW 150-2239 Bi-Directional Single Target 39.95

Signal System Accessories
NEW 150-233 Analog Block Detector 12.95
NEW 150-2234 Signal Control Board 19.95

Signal Cable
NEW 150-230 7' 3.95
NEW 150-231 15' 7.25
NEW 150-232 25' 10.95

BACHMANN QUALITY SINCE 1833

Crossing Gates & Signals

160-42504 pkg(12) 5.50

160-42522 Grade Crossing w/Gates, Nonoperating 5.50

160-46720 Dual Crossing Gate Nonoperating 7.00

Signs

160-42513 Railroad & Street Signs pkg(24) 5.50

Telephone Poles

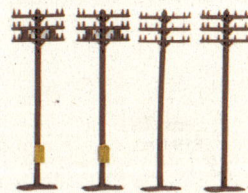

160-42506 pkg(12) 5.50

Get Daily Info, Photos and News at
www.walthers.com

Bar Mills SCALE MODEL WORKS
"THE GREAT LITTLE KIT..."
"FROM THE GREAT STATE OF MAINE"

Billboard in a Bag

171-35 Small 17.95
The kit builds at least four signs depending on size and height. Each comes with 200 etched-brass letters and some basic graphics.

Laser-Cut Wood Billboards
Though specifically made as N Scale sized billboards, these models also work well with O and HO Scales in creating a "forced perspective".

171-101 A&P Supermarket 11.95
2-3/8 x 5-1/2" 6 x 14cm

171-102 American Tool & Die 7.98
1/2 x 3-1/4" 1.3 x 8.3cm

171-104 Moxie Soda 11.95
1-1/4 x 3-1/2" 3.2 x 8.9cm

171-105 Old Dutch Cleanser 9.95
1 x 2-3/4" 2.5 x 7cm

171-111 Reddy Kilowatt Figure & Yellow Lettering 11.95

171-112 Railway Express Agency "Nationwide-Worldwide" w/Globe Symbol 9.95

171-114 Mobilgas w/Pegasus Logo (red) 10.95

171-117 Union Station 11.95

171-121 Morton Salt 10.95

171-124 Sherwin-Williams Paint 9.95
1-1/2 x 3-3/4" 3.7 x 9.3cm

Highway Signs
Feature laser-cut wood parts and full-color graphics.

171-126 Dino - Sinclair Gasoline 10.95
3 x 1-1/2" 7.5 x 3.7cm
171-127 The Star Diner 11.95
2-21/32 x 1-3/4" 6.6 x 4.3cm
171-131 Purina Mills Small 9.95
171-134 Trailways Small 8.95

124

SIGNALS, DETECTION UNITS & SIGNS N SCALE

Blair Line LLC
PRODUCTS FOR MODEL RAILROADERS

SIGNS

Laser-Cut Billboard Signs 9.95 (Unless Noted)

These laser-cut billboards are great for rooftops, or as stand-alone roadside attention-getters. Each easy-to-build kit includes four era-appropriate billboards and nonworking lamp shades. The style designation in this series refers to the frame type. Most are also suitable for HO and Z Scales.

184-1429 Deco 1930s-1960s **7.95**

184-1430 City Beautiful 1920s-1940s **7.95**

184-1431 Lattice 1900s-1960s **7.95**

184-1432 Grill 1940s-1960s **7.95**

184-1433 Pole 1950s-Present **7.95**
184-1434 Pylon 1960s-Present **7.95**

184-1435 Wall 1930s-Present **7.95**

184-1550 Do-It-Yourself Custom **11.95**
2-5/8 x 1-1/8" 6.56 x 3.28cm
184-2530 Missouri Pacific Lines "Route Of The Eagles" **11.95**
4 x 2-1/2" 10 x 6.25cm
184-2531 Ship T & P "Texas & Pacific Railway" Tall **11.95**
3 x 3" 7.5 x 7.5cm

184-1501 Western Auto **7.95**
2-1/2 x 2"

184-1503 Freight Station
2-1/2 x 1-3/8" Includes 30 different heralds.

184-1507 Jesus Saves
2-1/4 x 1-5/8"

184-1509 Union Pacific
1-1/2 x 2"

184-1510 Esso
2-1/8 x 1-7/8"

184-1511 Santa Fe
3-3/4 x 1-3/8"

184-1517 Hotel
2-1/8 x 1-1/4"

184-1519 Red Coss
1-13/16 x 1-13/16"

184-1520 Patrotic U.S. Flag (48 & 50 Stars)
1-13/16 x 1-13/16"
Includes the following slogans: In God We Trust, Buy War Bonds, United We Stand, and Support Our Troops.

Pylon 1960s-Present 184-1434

184-1526 Hollywood
4-1/2 x 13/16"

184-1528 Welcome To Your Hometown
2-3/32 x 1-1/4"
Includes custom letters to make your own town name and organization shields, such as VFW, Kiwanis, Masons, Lions Club, etc.

184-1530 Missouri Pacific Lines "Route Of The Eagles"
2-1/2 x 1-1/2" 6.25 x 3.75cm

184-1531 Ship T&P "Texas & Pacific Railway"
1-7/8 x 1-7/8" 4.67 x 4.67cm

184-1532 Eat & Business District (1 Each of 2 Signs)
2-5/32 x 1-5/16" 5.39 x 3.28cm

Storefront, Industrial & Business Sign Sets 5.00 ea

Signs printed in color on thin plastic for easy application to your commercial or scratch-built structure. Designed to duplicate porcelain and tin signs. Use for any era. Use as wall advertising and small roadside signs, too. Adds realistic detail to any layout. Many signs may be assembled back-to-back.

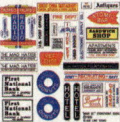
184-50 Modern Storefront Signs

184-51 "Main St." Storefront Signs I

184-52 Safety, Warning & Miscellaneous Signs

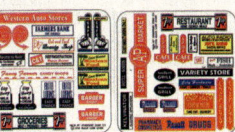
184-54 "Main St." Storefront Signs II

184-58 "Main St." Storefront Signs III

125

SIGNALS, DETECTION UNITS & SIGNS N SCALE

Blair Line LLC
PRODUCTS FOR MODEL RAILROADERS

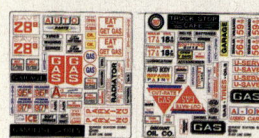
184-53 Service Station Signs

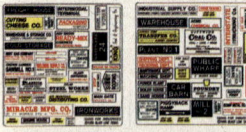
184-55 Signs for Industries

184-56 Railroad Stations & Depot Signs

184-57 Feed & Seed Store Signs

184-59 Tavern & Liquor Store Signs

Highway & Railroad Signs 4.00 ea (Unless Noted)

Scale signs, printed in color on thin plastic for easy assembly. Each set of signs includes scale posts. CAD designed to Federal Specifications for accuracy and authenticity. Great roadside, streetside and trackside details.

184-1 Railroad Right-Of-Way Signs (1900s-Present)

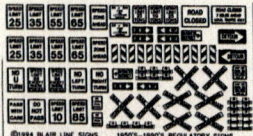
184-2 Regulatory Signs #1 (1948-Present)

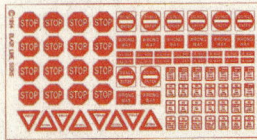
184-3 Regulatory Signs #2 (1930s-Present)

184-4 Construction Warning Signs (1950s-Present)

184-5 Warning & Symbol Signs #1 (1971-Present)

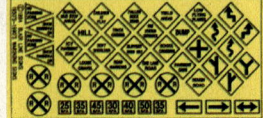
184-6 Warning Signs #2 (1948-Present)

184-7 Warning Signs #3 (1948-Present)

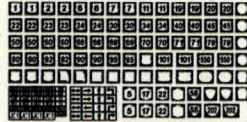
184-8 US Highway Route Markers (1950s-Present)

184-9 Street Signs, Any Era pkg(109)

184-10 Warning Signs #4 (1948-Present)

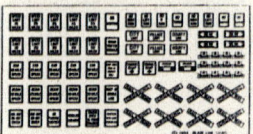
184-42 Vintage Regulatory Signs (1930s-1950s)

184-43 Vintage Warning/Stop Signs (1930s-1950s)

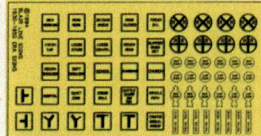
184-44 Vintage Caution Signs (1930s-1950s)

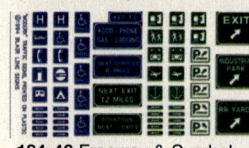
184-46 Freeway & Symbol Signs (1971-Present)

184-47 Modern Traffic & Symbol Signs

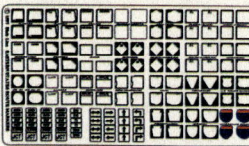
184-48 State Highway Route Signs (Eastern USA) **5.00**
Includes number decals.

184-49 State Highway Route Signs (Western USA) **5.00**
Includes number decals.

184-98 Square Wood Posts for Signs pkg(20) **2.00**
184-99 Round Plastic Posts for Signs pkg(20) **2.00**

TV Broadcast Tower

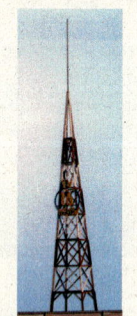
184-1516 **13.95**
1" square x 8" tall
Personalize the tower with your own station number.

Posts pkg(20) 2.00 ea
184-98 Wood
184-99 Plastic, For Highway Signs

BRAWA
LIEBE ZUM DETAIL

IMPORTED FROM GERMANY BY WALTHERS

Brawa signals are made of brass (except as noted), in exact N Scale, and come fully assembled. Each is a detailed, working model of a European prototype signal. The line features models of all signals used by the German Federal Railways (DB) and decals to identify the signal type. Signals equipped with bulbs or LEDs can be wired to transformers with a maximum output of 10 to 14V. For longer bulb life, 10 to 12V is recommended.

SIGNALS
Semaphore Signals

7840 7850

186-7840 Main Signal (red/green) **17.99**
186-7850 Starting Signal **11.99**
Tells the loco crew to start; green light; 1-1/2" high.

7942 7943

186-7942 Single Arm **47.99**
Red and green lights, 3" high.
186-7943 Switching Stop Sign **47.99**
Illuminated, 1-1/2" high.

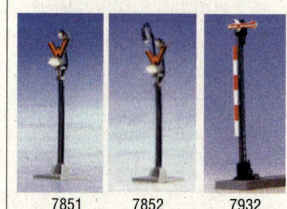
7851 7852 7932

186-7851 "Wait" Signal **27.99**
Illuminated, 2" high.
186-7852 "Wait" Signal **29.99**
Illuminated, 1-1/2" high.
186-7932 Stop/Track Closed Signal **47.99**
Bavarian Railroad prototype. Single arm, green/red lights, fixed blue light in "track closed" position. 3" high.

186-7954 2 Coupled Arms **60.99**
Red stop light, green/yellow "Proceed at restricted speed" indication, 3" high.
Limited Quantity Available

186-7554 Home Signal 2 Arm **59.99**
With memory drive; 3 positions.

186-7887 Starting Signal **68.49**
6 bulbs, 2-3/8" high.

Color Light Signals

The high intensity of the miniature LEDs makes the signals easy to see under any lighting conditions. The signals have a built-in resistor for use with any AC or DC 14-16V power supply. The low current draw (15mA from 14V supply) allows use of Brawa LED signals with transistor or integrated circuit throttles. Signals are 1-3/4" high, unless noted.

186-7811 Blinking Signal R/Y **17.99**
1-1/4" high.

Limited Quantity Available

7803 7815

186-7803 Starting Signal **64.99**
6 LEDs.
186-7815 Dwarf Track Blocked Signal **50.99**
1/4" high, 4 LEDs.

SIGNALS, DETECTION UNITS & SIGNS N SCALE

IMPORTED FROM GERMANY BY WALTHERS

CROSSINGS
Crossing Gates
Item listed below is available by Special Order (see Legend Page).

186-1144 Slow Moving Crossing Gate **295.99**

Highway Crossings
Feature red LEDs. Crossing signals can be operated automatically with relay #2760 and track contacts (sold separately).

186-4539 Crossing Signal w/Flashing Light **17.99**
Crossing signal with guard ring. Brass construction with LED and resistor for 14V power supply. Mast colored light gray. 3/4" high (19mm).

186-4541 Crossing Signal Set **91.99**
Set of four #4539 crossing signals with electronic flasher.

Highway Crossing listed below is available by Special Order (see Legend Page).
186-4542 Crossing Signal Set **68.99**
Set of four #4536 crossing signals with electronic flasher.

CLOCKS & SIGNS

4570   4571

186-4570 Platform Clock **12.99**
Illuminated. 1-1/8" high, red frame.

186-4571 Station Platform Clock **18.99**
Illuminated. Finished in dark green with four faces. 1-1/2" high.

186-4573 Clock On Lattice Mast **18.99**
2-1/16" high.

186-4574 Clock w/Advertising Cube **16.99**
Illuminated, with dry transfers for "DB" or "S-Bahn" symbols. 1-1/2" high.

186-4592 Yard Light-Masted **16.99**

NEW PRODUCTS
Signals
Kits are made of etched brass and cast parts as appropriate for great detail. Unpainted parts are simply folded together and secured with CA cement.

ATSF-Style Signal Bridge

NEW 176-1010 59.95
Kit is based on a typical 30s-40s ATSF double-track design; similar structures are used by many other railroads. Includes two signal heads (cored for the addition of LEDs, sold separately), concrete footings and relay cabinet/electrical box.

Cantilever Signal Bridge

NEW 176-1020 49.95
Based on a common prototype used by several railroads including ATSF and SP. Includes two signal heads (cored for the addition of LEDs, sold separately), footings and relay cabinet/electrical box.

NEW 176-1000 pkg(4) **7.75**
Includes four signal heads (cored for the addition of LEDs, sold separately) and mounting posts.

IMPORTED FROM GERMANY BY WALTHERS

SIGNALS

189-5850 Signals Nonworking pkg(12) **16.99**

189-5851 Block Signal **20.99**

Signals listed below are available by Special Order (see Legend Page).

189-5752 2 Crossing Signals w/Sound **91.99**
Warn motorists of oncoming trains with this crossing signal set, featuring two blinkers and warning bell sound.

189-5852   189-5853

189-5852 Main Signal **22.99**
189-5853 Block Warning Signal **28.99**

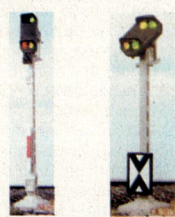

189-5949 Crossing Blinkers **27.99**

189-5951 20 Signal Expansion Set For #189-5949 **15.99**

189-5953 Crossing Signal Set, 4 Crossings w/Control **39.99**

TRAFFIC SIGNALS

189-5943 Two Traffic Lights w/Control **57.99**

189-5944 Expansion Set, Signals Only pkg(2) **32.99**

189-5945 Barricades & Control Set **35.99**

Signals listed below are available by Special Order (see Legend Page).

189-5947 Construction Sign **39.99**
Set includes seven stations (four of which blink) and control unit.

189-5952 Blinking Maintenance Trailer Set **31.99**
189-5957 Construction Sign Set pkg(15) **67.99**

SIGNAL SWITCH

189-5708 Signal Switch w/2 LEDs (red & green) **23.99**
For manual control of signals with or without train control. The red/green LEDs indicate the present position of the signal.

TOWER

189-5965 Transmitter Tower Set **46.99**

DECALS

189-6035 Graffiti Dry Transfers #2 **7.99**

Decals listed below are available by Special Order (see Legend Page).
189-8122 Guard Rail/Speed Limits **5.99**
189-8124 German Federal Railway Sign Decals w/Pen **3.99**

Daily New Arrival Updates! Visit Walthers Web site at
www.walthers.com

SIGNALS, DETECTION UNITS & SIGNS N SCALE

Circuitron Electronic Hobby Products

GRADE CROSSING DETECTION UNITS

Specifically designed for use at grade crossings, using Opto-Sensors to detect the train. Output controls flashers, gates, bells, etc. Note: DT-1, DT-2 and DT-3 Detection Units require an Alternating Flasher Unit (FL-2 or FL-3) to operate flashing lamps.

DT-1 Detection Unit
800-5201 32.95
Detects train when an Opto-Sensor is covered. Senses track polarity and activates only the Opto-Sensors for the direction of travel. Always turns off after the last piece of rolling stock clears the crossing. Includes four Opto-Sensors. Note: DT-1 cannot detect a short train or loco if it falls between Opto-Sensors. Use in any scale with DC track power. 2 x 3" printed circuit board. 10-18V AC or DC input.

DT-2 Detection Unit
800-5202 44.95
Full logic system duplicates prototype grade crossing action. Does not require sensor to stay covered to activate. Integrated memory keeps output "on" until last car clears the crossing. Activates whenever a train approaches from either direction. If train stops short then backs away, unit will detect that and turn output "off." Independent of train length – will detect a short train even if it falls between Opto-Sensors. Includes four Opto-Sensors. 3 x 3" printed circuit board. 10-18V AC or DC input.

DT-3 Single-Direction Detection Unit
800-5203 24.95
Single-direction unit for crossings where bi-directional detection is unnecessary, such as a mainline with trains traveling in only one direction. Operates with any length train. Completely independent of track power. Use in any scale. Requires 10-18V AC or DC input.

DF-1 Detector With Flasher
800-5250 39.95
Single-direction grade crossing detector with alternating flasher on one circuit board. Operates with any length train. Independent of track power. Use in any scale. Can power two 250 mA loads (five grain-of-wheat lamps or 10 LEDs per side). 10-18V AC or DC input.

BLOCK OCCUPANCY DETECTION UNITS

Tiny Opto-Sensors detect train movement. Sensors mount between the rails and activate circuitry when shaded by a passing train. Independent of track power, rolling stock requires no modifications. Sensors fit between HO Scale ties and may be ballasted over in most cases. Circuitry is extremely sensitive and will operate properly under very low levels of room light.

BD-1 Optical Detectors
Positive indication whenever a section of a layout is occupied by rolling stock. Contains all circuitry to power two-color block signals at each end of the protected block. Will give proper indications if a train leaves a block by backing out. No modifications to rolling stock needed. Completely bi-directional. No additional driver boards or relays are needed. 250 mA output can power lamp or LED-type signals. Requires 6-20V DC input. Independent of track power. Compatible with radio or carrier control systems.

800-5501 BD-1 Optical Detector **32.95**
800-5521 BD-1HD Optical Detector **35.95**
Same as #800-5501, but with 500 mA output.

BD-2 Current Sensing Detection Units
Detects current drawn by a locomotive or lighted piece of rolling stock. Unpowered equipment can be detected by using metal wheelsets with resistors connected across the insulator. Will directly drive two-color lamp or LED-type block signals. 250 mA output (500 mA for BD-2HD). Circuit boards are designed for easy daisy-chain wiring of multiple blocks and will snap into a section of Printed Circuit Mounting Track. Requires 10-18V DC. Works in any scale and with most track power, systems including most forms of carrier control.

800-5502 BD-2, 3 amp Capacity **19.95**
800-5522 BD-2HD, 6 amp Capacity **24.95**

ROLLING STOCK DETECTION UNIT

DT-4 Rolling Stock Detector

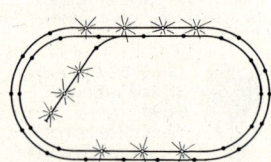

800-5204 36.95
Ideal for spotting a hidden train or piece of rolling stock. Four independent detection units combined onto one circuit board, can be used separately or together to control external devices. Supplied with four Opto-Sensors that mount between rails to detect movement. When train covers a sensor, the unit activates any connected DC accessory, such as an indicator light on a control panel. Independent sensitivity controls are provided for adjusting each Opto-Sensor to lighting conditions. Constructed on a 3 x 3" printed circuit board. Requires 10-18V DC. Independent of track power. Compatible with radio or carrier control systems.

DRIVERS

SD-1 Signal Driver
800-5510 14.95
Logic and output drivers to control any three-lamp, three-color block signal. Will power LED or lamp-type signals. LED type requires common positive (anode) connection of all LEDs. Detection circuits (such as BD-1) are needed for a minimum of three blocks to display all three aspects. 10-18V DC input.

SD-2 3-Position Semaphore Driver
800-5520 19.95
Use with the Tortoise™ Switch Machine and an upper- or lower-quadrant semaphore-style signal. Includes all the logic circuitry to drive the signal to all three positions. Works with BD-1 or BD-2 Block Occupancy Detectors. A minimum of two blocks must have detectors installed for the SD-2 to indicate all three positions. Requires 10-18V DC power. Also see the Gate/ Semaphore Activator.

SD-3 Signal Driver
800-5530 15.95
Drives any single-target tri-color LED-type signal to red, green and amber aspects. Will not drive lamp signals. Amber hue fully adjustable. May be controlled by three-position switch or automatically by detection circuits such as BD-1 (minimum of 3 blocks required). Requires 10-18V AC or DC input.

ALTERNATING FLASHERS

Use to flash signals, emergency vehicle lights, signs and more.

FL-2 Alternating Flashers
Flashes LEDs or lamps. Connects to Detection Units. Maintains constant flash rate. 1.5 x 3" printed circuit board. Requires 10-18V AC or DC input. 250 mA output.

800-5102 FL-2 **17.95**
800-5122 FL-2HD **19.95**
Same as FL-2, but with 500 mA load capability per side. Adaptable for all scales.

FL-3 Alternating Flasher
800-5103 39.95
Heavy-duty, with three control terminals and three outputs. Independent flashing at up to three locations. Outputs can control 250 mA. Can flash LEDs or lamps. 3 x 3" printed circuit board. 10-18V AC or DC input.

TRAIN CONTROL CIRCUITS

AR-1 Automatic Reversing Circuit
800-5400 44.95
Changes direction when the Opto-Sensor is covered. Use for test track, window display, mine train or automatic reverse loop operation. Pushbuttons can be connected for manual reversing. Requires 12V DC power source. Constructed on 2 x 3" printed circuit board.

AR-2 Automatic Reverse With Adjustable Display

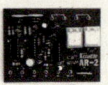

800-5401 54.95
Same as AR-1, but with adjustable delay to hold train at sensor before reversing. Adjustable delay from one second to over one minute. Can be connected to pushbutton or DT-4 to permit stops and delays without reversing. Requires 12-18V AC or DC power supply. Constructed on 3 x 3" printed circuit board.

TD-1 Time Delay Circuit
800-5602 26.95
Use with detection units for adjustable delay with self-contained relay on the output. Great for automatic stop at a station or siding. Time delay adjustable from 0 to over one minute. Requires 12V DC power supply.

GATE SEMAPHORE/ ACTUATOR

Mounting bracket and mechanism utilize the Tortoise™ (not included) and a special drive wire cable assembly to remotely actuate any crossing gate, train order or semaphore signal having a vertical control wire extending below the layout. Positive, adjustable stops are provided at both ends of travel. Can drive two cables from the one drive mechanism, if desired. Adjustable for all scales.

800-8100 Drive Mechanism w/Cable & Actuator **10.95**
800-8101 Extra Cable & Actuator **5.95**

SIGNALS, DETECTION UNITS & SIGNS N SCALE

BELL RINGER CIRCUITS

Connects to detection unit to simulate crossing bell. Rate and volume are adjustable. Use with 10-18V AC or DC.

800-5700 BR-1 w/2-1/2" Bell **45.95**
800-5702 BR-2, w/Circuit Board **29.95**
Use any dual-coil electromagnetic doorbell.

PRINTED CIRCUIT MOUNTING TRACK (PCMT)

800-9506 6" **5.95**
Plastic assembly provides simple, snap-in mounting of all Circuitron printed circuit boards.

SNAPPER SWITCH MACHINE POWER SUPPLY

800-5303 29.95
Solid state, provides positive power to dual-coil switch machines. Protects from burnout due to stuck push-buttons, short circuits, etc. Operates off accessory terminals of power pack or transformer up to 25V. 24V input can activate five to ten coils simultaneously if connected to same control. Instant recycle time. Includes a section of Printed Circuit Mounting Track (PCMT).

HIDDEN ACCESSORY SWITCHES

On-Off reed switches for strobe flashers, marker lights or other electrical accessories. Operated by holding a magnet near the loco or car. Nothing to detract from the look of the model. Kits contain a subminiature reed switch and a tiny bias magnet.

800-9101 RS-1 Kit **5.95**
Requires adjustment before mounting.
800-9102 RS-2 Kit **7.95**
Requires no adjustment.
800-9100 Magnet **1.95**
800-9103 Subminiature Slide Switch pkg(2) **2.95**

SIGN SOFTWARE

Easy-to-use software lets you print your own railside and street signs or classic advertisements in any scale. Print the signs and advertisements you need in the scale you need to add great detail to your layout. System requirements: PC running Windows 98/NT/ME/2000/XP/XP-Pro.

American Advertising Collection

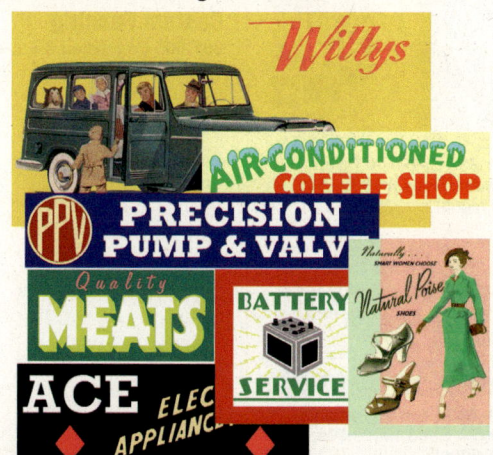

266-A03 30.00
Easy-to-use software. Over 100 classic ads for autos, food, industrial and household products from the 1940s, 50s, and 60s. The selection also includes 25 complete "Burma Shave" sign groups, along with generic signs like "Barber Shop" and "Rooms for Rent." Program lets you choose the scale and size as well as adjust sign color.

Sign Creator

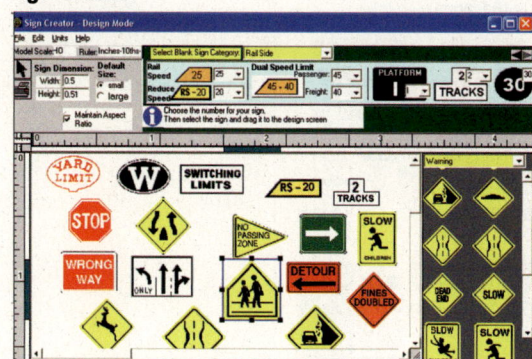

266-A22 40.00
Create and print all kinds of common railroad and street signs. Simply select the correct scale — the Design Screen resizes automatically — and select from over 200 predesigned signs. You can also make custom signs with the easy-to-use templates which are provided. Now with 100 new railroad signs and 20 blank sign templates.

FALLER

IMPORTED FROM GERMANY BY WALTHERS

Level Crossings

Kits consist of prototypically pre-colored plastic parts, and fully illustrated instructions.

272-222170 Operating **78.99**
Single-track gate crossing with signal tower features an electric motor and can be used on straight or curved track.

Crossing listed below is available by Special Order (see Legend Page).
272-222171 Nonoperating **35.99**
Same as #272-222170, less motor.

HELJAN

IMPORTED FROM DENMARK BY WALTHERS

Telephone Poles

322-701 pkg(28) **5.98**
Plastic poles molded in realistic color.

See What's New and Exciting at
www.walthers.com

Information STATION

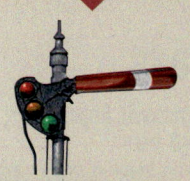

Signs of the Times

Few details place your railroad into a specific time period like signs and billboards. Logos, enameled signs, thermometers and painted ads are everywhere. The Reference Book lists printed signs and billboards from many manufacturers. Most feature graphics suitable for specific eras. With a bit of research, you can pick signs to fit very specific time periods. As for placement on your layout, here are a few obvious locations, and a few more that some modelers miss:

Roadside billboards: They advertise everything from soda to sneakers. Into the early 1970s, many had wood frames and some had streamlined decorations. Many are illuminated.
Rooftop billboards: Like roadside signs, but on top of large buildings. Some advertise the occupant, others are ads. Don't forget, some billboard were painted on rooftop water tanks.
Roadside signs: Small, handpainted direction or advertising signs for produce stands, gift shops and other businesses are either freestanding or nailed to power poles or street signs. Burma Shave signs that once lined the nation's highways are also examples.
Crop signs: You'll see plenty of colorful signs at row ends touting which company supplied the seed.
Painted signs: Large buildings often have names painted on the walls. Painted and enameled signs also appear on feed mills and grain elevators.

SIGNALS, DETECTION UNITS & SIGNS N SCALE

SIGNS

Billboard Signs pkg(10) 2.89 ea
Printed in full color on one 4 x 5-1/2" heavy paper sheet.

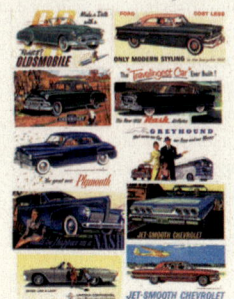

361-203 1940s-1960s Automobile Signs

361-226 Vintage Auto Signs

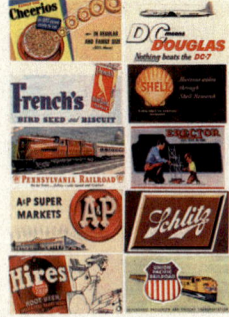

361-227 1940s-1950s Consumer Signs

Billboards

361-225 Telephone Pole Billboards pkg(2) **5.98**
Kit includes Northeastern basswood, full-color auto billboard signs and nonilluminated lamps.

361-325 Fence Base **5.98**

Sign Sets 2.89 ea

361-326 Soda Billboards pkg(6)

361-327 Railroad Billboards pkg(6)

361-328 RC Cola Billboards pkg(6)

361-606 Uncommon/Unusual Soft Drink Signs 1940s-50s (54 signs)

361-607 Railroad REA & Depot Signs 1940s-60s (122 signs)

361-622 Country Store Signs 1930s-50s (185 signs)

361-633 Saloon & Tavern Posters/Signs II 1930s-50s (62 signs)

361-683 Farm Implements Feed & Seed 1940s-50s (54 signs)

361-684 Gas Stations 1930s-60s (61 signs)

361-685 Gas & Oil Co. 1940s-50s (41 signs)

361-686 Turn of the Century Posters/Signs 1890s-1920s (40 signs)

361-696 Danger & Warning Signs (250 signs)

361-697 Vintage Soft Drink 1930s-1960s (72 signs)

Custom Fencing

361-605 Prepainted & Labeled (brown) pkg(2) **3.49**

Get the Scoop!
Get the Skinny!
Get the Score!
Check Out Walthers
Web site at
www.walthers.com

LABELLE INDUSTRIES

Burma Shave Signs pkg(6) 7.98 ea
The Burma Shave Signs were roadside staples from the mid-1920s on. Usually in sets of six, these red-and-white signs were spaced about 100 yards apart. The signs told a short but pointed story, with the last sign set always featuring the Burma Shave logo. The wording was always in full capital letters, the signs were all the same size and the type size was always the same.

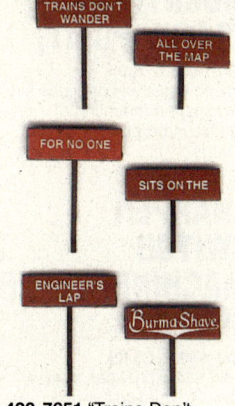

430-7651 "Trains Don't Wander..."
430-7652 "Trains Don't Whistle..."
430-7653 "Approached A Crossing..."
430-7654 "Train Wrecks Few..."
430-7655 "It's Trains, Not Girls..."
430-7656 "As Fast Train Neared..."

SIGNALS, DETECTION UNITS & SIGNS N SCALE

LIGHT WORKS USA
By Miller Engineering

ELECTROLUMINESCENT SIGN KITS

Each sign is made of special plastic that's only .008" thick for a near scale appearance. The sign is coated on one side with phosphor, which glows when current is applied. This produces a soft, neon-like light that's bright enough to be seen under regular room lights, but generates no heat. Each kit comes with an assembled 3V power supply, which requires two AAA batteries, not included. Complete instructions cover all of the steps needed for installation and operation.

NEW PRODUCTS

Animated Roadside Billboards

These new kits include an etched stainless steel support structure. Unpainted metal parts are simply folded together and glued using cyanoacrylate (CA) cement.

Gulf

NEW 502-8181 42.95
4-5/16" Wide x 5-13/16" Tall

Features illuminated letters; "Gulf" letters light up sequentially.

Amtrak

NEW 502-8281 42.95
4-5/16" Wide x 5-1/8" Tall

Features animated arrow and illuminated white and red letters.

Elephant Car Wash

NEW 502-8381 42.95
4-5/16" Wide x 6" Tall

Features illuminated letters and animated spray from elephant's trunk.

Union City Speedway

NEW 502-8481 42.95
4-5/16" Wide x 5-3/32" Tall

Features illuminated letters; car tires and road markers are animated.

Billboard Support

NEW 502-990 7.50
Designed to give that extra detail to your model. Universal design allows them to be used with any current Miller Engineering billboard.

Wall-Mount Signs

Kits are designed to mount through a slot in your structure's wall.

Amtrak 26.96 ea
1-39/64" Wide x 45/64" Tall

Features illuminated letters and animated arrow.

NEW 502-64811 Left Hand

NEW 502-64812 Right Hand

MULTI-GRAPHIC ANIMATED WALL-MOUNTED SIGN KITS

These lighted signs add realism to any storefront. Each includes colorful graphic overlays for six businesses that provide full-color lighted lettering; plug-and-play electronics, on-off switch and battery holder that uses three AAA batteries (sold separately). Signs can be used in N or HO Scales. All are available in left- or right-handed orientations and are easily mounted to the front of your storefronts. Suitable for steam or diesel eras.

Downtown Businesses Series #1

Signs features animated chase lights and arrow.

Small 1-1/2" Tall 24.95 ea

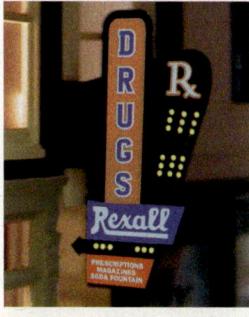

502-66821 Left
502-66822 Right

Downtown Businesses Series #2

Signs features animated rays

Small 1-1/2" Tall 24.95 ea

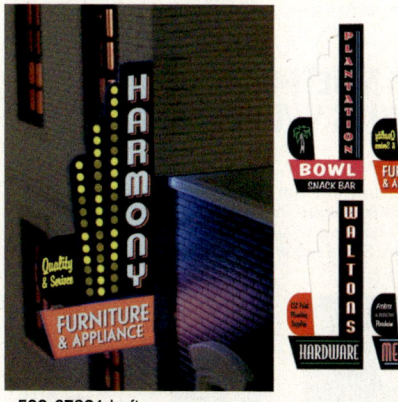

502-67821 Left
502-67822 Right

Hotel/Motel Series

Signs feature animated chase lights and arrow.

Small 1-1/2" Tall 24.95 ea

 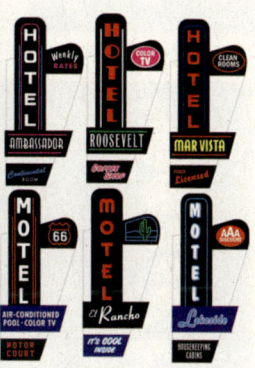

502-68821 Left
502-68822 Right

Fan Series

Signs features animated curved fan of lights.

Small 1-5/16" Tall 24.95 ea

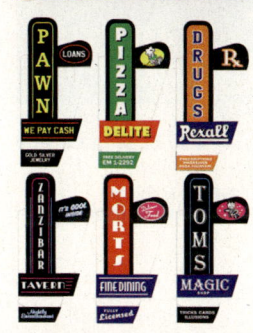 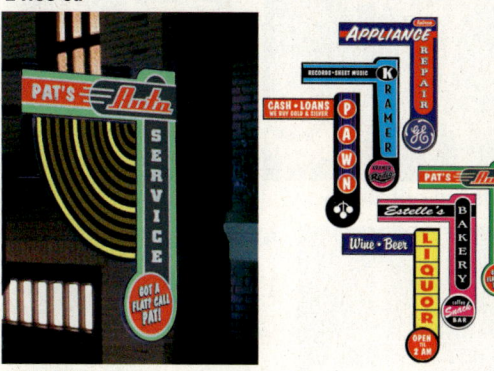

502-69821 Left
502-69822 Right

SIGNALS, DETECTION UNITS & SIGNS N SCALE

LIGHT WORKS USA™ By Miller Engineering

ANIMATED MULTI-GRAPHIC LIGHTING KITS W/OVERLAYS

28.95 ea

Animated electroluminiscent sign kits include peel-and-stick graphics that allow you to customize them for a variety of businesses. Kits include battery holder and all necessary electronics for plug-and-play installation. Signs require three AAA batteries (not included).

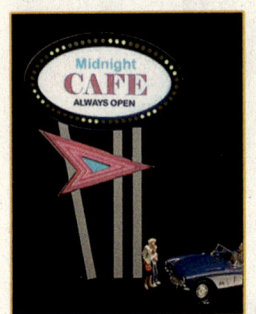

502-7182 Oval, Medium

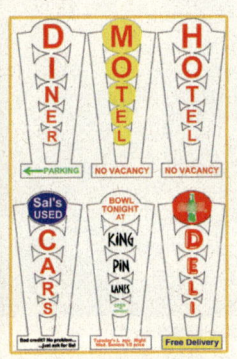

502-7282 Vertical, Medium

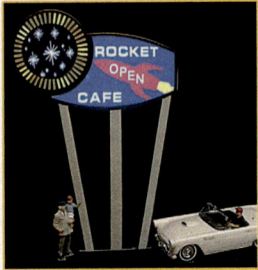

502-7382 Round, Medium

502-7482 Arrow, Medium

ANIMATED NEON BILLBOARDS

Add authenticity to your layout's skyline. These animated billboards feature lighted "neon" lettering, moving graphics and simulated black supporting structure. All are wafer thin, but rigid enough to be freestanding. Each includes plug-and-play electronics, on-off switch and battery holder that uses three AAA batteries (sold separately). Medium billboards can be used in N or HO Scales.

502-9282 City Light Medium **25.95**
2-1/2 x 1-7/8" 6.4 x 4.7cm

502-9382 I.C. Sparks Medium **25.95**
2-1/2 x 1-7/8" 6.4 x 4.7cm

Patriot Flag Co.
Features animated flag.

Building not included
502-9482 Medium 1-1/2 x 2-5/16" **26.95**

Arctic Refrigeration
Thermometer moves down as icicles grow longer.

Building not included
502-9582 Medium
2-13/16 x 1-13/16" **26.95**

Get the Scoop!
Get the Skinny!
Get the Score!
Check Out Walthers
Web site at
www.walthers.com

Polar Ice
Background features animated falling snow.

Building not included
502-9682 Medium 2-5/8 x 1-3/4" **26.95**

Noise-R-Us
Background features animated fireworks.

Building not included
502-9782 Medium 1-1/2 x 2-5/16" **26.95**

DeKays Dental Supply
Toothpaste tube squeezes out toothpaste.

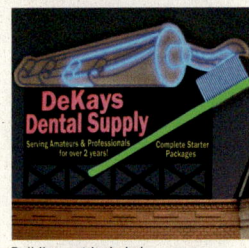

Building not included
502-9882 Medium 2-5/8 x 1-3/4" **26.95**

VERTICAL NEON SIGNS

Left and right version may be mounted together to create a sign that lights on both sides.

Bentens Bar & Grill

502-12011 Medium, Left **14.95**
502-12012 Medium, Right **14.95**
502-12021 Small, Left **13.95**
502-12022 Small, Right **13.95**

Cafe

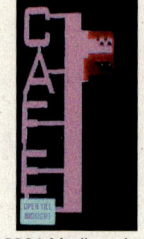

502-13021 Medium, Left **14.95**
502-13022 Medium, Right **14.95**
502-13031 Small, Left **13.95**
502-13032 Small, Right **13.95**

Hotel

502-14021 Medium, Left **14.95**
502-14022 Medium, Right **14.95**
502-14031 Small, Left **13.95**
502-14032 Small, Right **13.95**

Motel

502-15031 Small, Left **13.95**
502-15032 Small, Right **13.95**

Limited Quantity Available
502-15021 Medium, Left **14.95**
502-15022 Medium, Right **14.95**

Pizza (Square)

502-16021 Small, Left **13.95**
502-16022 Small, Right **13.95**

SIGNALS, DETECTION UNITS & SIGNS N SCALE

LIGHT WORKS USA By Miller Engineering

Star Drug
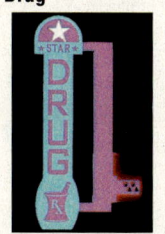
502-31021 Medium, Left **14.95**
502-31022 Medium, Right **14.95**
502-31031 Small, Left **13.95**
502-31032 Small, Right **13.95**

Mid State Bank

502-14411 Medium, Left **14.95**
502-14412 Medium, Right **14.95**
502-14421 Small, Left **13.95**
502-14422 Small, Right **13.95**

AAA Logo

502-33031 Small, Left **12.95**
502-33032 Small, Right **12.95**

Barber Shop

502-34021 Medium, Left **13.95**
502-34022 Medium, Right **13.95**
502-34031 Small, Left **12.95**
502-34032 Small, Right **12.95**

Rooms
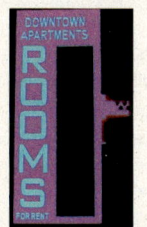
502-35021 Medium, Left **15.95**
502-35022 Medium, Right **15.95**
502-35031 Small, Left **14.95**
502-35032 Small, Right **14.95**

Open

502-36021 Medium, Left **14.95**
502-36022 Medium, Right **14.95**
502-36031 Small, Left **13.95**
502-36032 Small, Right **13.95**

Pawn Shop

502-37021 Medium, Left **14.95**
502-37022 Medium, Right **14.95**
502-37031 Small, Left **13.95**
502-37032 Small, Right **13.95**

Pizza (Round)

502-38021 Medium, Left **14.95**
502-38022 Medium, Right **14.95**

Rexall
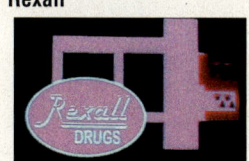
502-39031 Small, Left **12.95**
502-39032 Small, Right **12.95**

Theater

502-41021 Medium, Left **15.95**
502-41022 Medium, Right **15.95**
502-41031 Small, Left **14.95**
502-41032 Small, Right **14.95**

Bijou
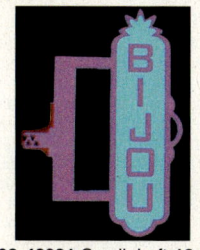
502-42031 Small, Left **13.95**
502-42032 Small, Right **13.95**

Horizontal
Horizontal signs are designed to mount on a roof or wall.

Cafe

Limited Quantity Available
502-1702 Medium **13.95**

Gilmor Hotel

502-1802 Medium **14.95**

Diner

502-1902 Medium **13.95**

Hotel

502-2102 Medium **13.95**

Motel

Limited Quantity Available
502-2202 Medium **13.95**

Union Station

502-5602 Medium **17.95**

Parkway Diner

502-2802 Medium **15.95**

Hotel Belmont

502-2902 Medium **14.95**

Clock
Left and right are the same.

502-3203 Small **11.95**
502-3202 Medium **13.95**

ANIMATED ELECTRO-LUMINESCENT SIGN KITS

These signs are created with the same EL material as the non-animated signs, with all the benefits and more. Each kit is pre-programmed with 36 different chase patterns, allowing the user to choose which pattern they want. Each pattern has its own action and will light the signs in a different way. You can have a regular flashing sign, a standard chase sign, or something more, for the businesses on your layout. And once a pattern is chosen, it is stored in memory and is remembered each time the sign is turned on again. The patterns can be changed over and over again.

Vertical
Cafe & Arrow

502-13821 Medium, Left **20.95**
502-13822 Medium, Right **20.95**

Hotel

502-14821 Medium, Left **20.95**
502-14822 Medium, Right **20.95**

MOTEL

Limited Quantity Available
502-15821 Medium, Left **20.95**
502-15822 Medium, Right **20.95**

O'Malley's Bar

502-54821 Medium, Left **21.95**
502-54822 Medium, Right **21.95**

Horizontal
Cafe

502-1782 Medium **20.95**

Diner

502-1982 Medium **20.95**

Hotel

502-2182 Medium **20.95**

133

SIGNALS, DETECTION UNITS & SIGNS N SCALE

LIGHT WORKS USA — By Miller Engineering

Motel

Limited Quantity Available
502-2282 Medium **20.95**

Blue-Star Diner

502-5582 Medium **21.95**

Shamrock Hotel

502-6182 Medium **21.95**

LIGHTING ACCESSORIES

EL Experimenter's Kits
Turn your ideas into working models with these complete accessory kits. The heart of each set is a specially designed, wafer-thin electroluminiscent (EL) lamp. It's easily cut with scissors or a sharp knife and can be used to make several lamps. The wafer-thin lamp can also be used to add even lighting to the ceilings on interior rooms in structures. Sets come with a ready-to-use power supply and an assortment of color overlays for special effects. A detailed instruction book provides tips and ideas for using EL lamps.

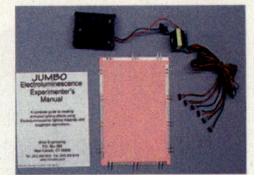

502-2501 Regular Sign Kit **22.95**
1-3/4 x 3-3/4" Makes up to six signs.

Wall Adapter
502-4801 3-Volt **7.95**
Eliminates the need for a battery pack. Will run up to five signs. For non-animated signs only.

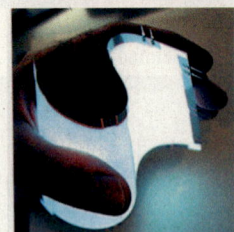

502-2504 Jumbo EL Experimenter's Kit **32.95**
4 x 6" Makes up to 14 signs.

502-2502 Animator's Kit **28.95**
Contains all the same features of non-animated kit with the addition of being able to create animation. Includes 36 pre-programmed chase patterns. Each chase pattern has five channels, meaning you can light up to five segments. By pushing the small button on the circuit board you will advance to the next chase pattern. The last chase pattern picked will be remembered when the unit is turned on again. Chase patterns can be changed over and over again.

Flasher Unit
502-4701 **5.95**
Converts any of the electro-luminescent sign kits into flashing signs. Flashes at a fixed rate of 1/2-second-on and 1/2-second-off.

Marquee Chase Light Kit

502-875052 **32.95**
Includes a special white LED and 60 fiber optic strands to simulate moving lights found on theaters everywhere. All electronics come fully assembled and are powered by a 9V battery, not included. Kit also comes with step-by-step instructions to make installation easy.

Electroluminescent Wire Kits 22.95 ea
EL wire is a very robust material that produces a soft neon-like glow, can be bent to almost any shape, with a diameter of .090". EL wire produces no heat and is perfect for illuminating the perimeter of buildings or hard-to-reach places where lighting is desired. It can also be easily cut to length. Each kit comes with a three-foot length of EL wire and driver board. Requires soldering to hook-up wire to the included driver circuit.

 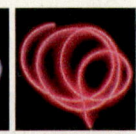
502-25031   502-25032

502-25033   502-25034

502-25031 White
502-25032 Red
502-25033 Blue
502-25034 Green

Miniature Fluorescent Lamps
Kits consist of two fluorescent lamps and one driver circuit. Lamps are extremely bright, produce very little heat, and have a life of over 15,000 hours. All lamps have a diameter of .160" and require a constant 12V DC source. Lamps should not be run with less than 12V.

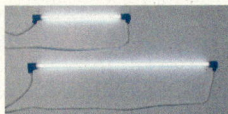

502-721 2" Lamp w/Driver Circuit **19.95**
502-722 2" Dual Lamps w/Driver Circuit **24.95**
502-741 4" Lamp w/Driver Circuit **19.95**
502-742 4" Dual Lamps w/Driver Circuit **22.95**
502-781 8" Lamp w/Driver Circuit **19.95**
502-782 8" Dual Lamps w/Driver Circuit **24.95**

Photo Etch Supports
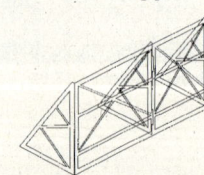

502-4502 Medium **10.95**
Support for medium, horizontal electro-luminescent signs.

502-4503 Small **6.95**
Support for small, horizontal electroluminescent signs.

MICRON ART

SIGNS

NEW 462-2055 "Railroad Crossing" Crossbucks on Box Controller Console pkg(4) **13.50**
Features brass poles, easy-to-mount arms and Swarovski crystal red stones. Does not actually light up.

462-2033 Rural Railroad Crossing Signs pkg(12) **22.00**
Make roads safer along your layout. Crossbucks feature raised brass letters for easier painting with an easy flange-type mounting. Includes 12 brass poles precut to length for sturdy mounting that won't break like other materials.

462-2051 Street Signs pkg(16) **19.95**
A neat detail for city scenes, set includes 16 common signs with raised brass letters for easier painting, and precut metal posts for easy installation.

462-2053 Telephone Poles pkg(10) **20.95**
Great track or highway detail. Set includes 10 solid brass poles with easy-to-mount cross arms. Also includes two transformer modules for added realism.

Information STATION

Pole Lines
Adding trackside pole lines to your layout is an easy way to add authenticity to your right-of-way.
At one time, most railroads had some sort of pole line along the tracks. The poles carried signal, railroad telephone and, at one time, telegraph lines. There were typically between 40 and 50 poles per mile, but this varied by terrain and railroad. Some railroads used the pole positions to describe the locations of switches and culverts in relation to the nearest milepost, and on many roads the mileposts were marked on the pole.
Pole lines vary greatly. The simplest ones consist of a wooden pole with an insulator on top and another on the side, each supporting a telegraph wire. Pole lines along single-track mainlines with ABS signals have one or two crossarms supporting as many as 10 wires each. On double-track or CTC-equipped lines, poles often have three or more crossarms and line both sides of the tracks. At interlockings and junctions five or more crossarms are typical and 10 aren't uncommon.
Most railroad pole line crossarms are of equal length and have "V" brackets to keep them from twisting. As signaling systems are modernized, pole lines are becoming less common, but up through the 90s, many still looked as they did during the steam era.

SIGNALS, DETECTION UNITS & SIGNS N SCALE

Fully assembled, painted and prewired signals, lights and accessories.

SIGNALS

Block 15.50 ea
Lighted brass signals.

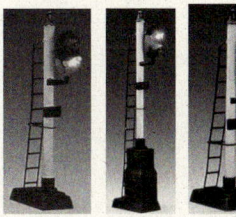

490-8568 / 490-8569 / 490-8570

490-8568 2 Indication
490-8569 2 Indication w/Relay
490-8570 3 Indication

490-8571 / 490-8572

490-8571 3 Indication w/Relay
490-8572 3 Indication

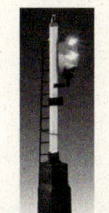
490-8575 / 490-8573

490-8575 2 Indication w/Relay
490-8573 3 Indication

CROSSINGS
490-8574 pkg(2) 18.50

LIGHTS
Lighted brass lights.

Suburban pkg(3) 8.98 ea
490-8484 Frosted
490-8486 Clear, Square Top

Traffic Lights

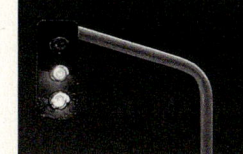
490-8560 Left 15.50

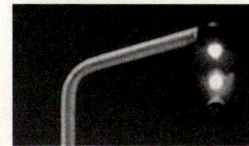
490-8561 Right 15.50
490-8566 Left & Right pkg(2) 19.50

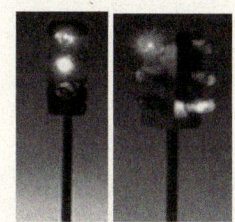
490-8562 / 490-8564

490-8562 Standard 15.50
490-8563 Standard pkg(2) 18.50
490-8564 Two-Way 16.50

Highway 8.98 ea

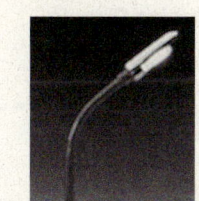
490-8480 Single pkg(3)

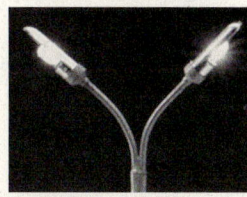
490-8481 Dual pkg(2)

Boulevard pkg(3) 8.98 ea

490-8482 / 490-8483

490-8482 Clear
490-8483 Frosted

Clock

490-8487 2-Sided Lighted pkg(2) 8.98

Goose Neck Lamp Post
490-8488 8.98

SIGNS

Movie Posters pkg(8) 8.98 ea

490-8577 1924 to 1940 Era
At the Circus, Henry V, Lost Horizon, North West Passage, Ten Commandments, The Great Dictator, The Son of the Sheik, Under Two Flags.
490-85771 1940 to 1960 Era

Lighted Signs pkg(2) 9.98 ea
490-8578 Gulf
490-8579 Exxon
490-8580 Shell

Lighted Billboard

490-8576 With Base pkg(2) 9.98

Highway & Street Set

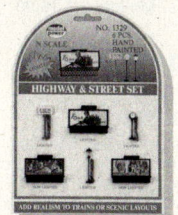

490-1329 14.50
Includes three billboards, street clock, lamp post and Exxon sign.

Tracksider Assortment
490-1331 12.98
Includes 24 telephone poles, 24 road & rail signs, and a seven-piece signal bridge.

S&S Hobby Products
"Realism in Model Railroading"

HO Scale Models Shown

E-Z Streets Kit

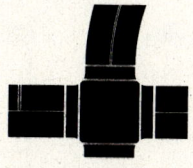

643-205 9.99
Printed on waterproof styrene, this kit includes six 12" straight sections, curves, intersection with crosswalk lines and two railroad crossing lines.

Street Stencils 4.49 ea

  (MPH 25)
643-11 / 643-12 / 643-13

643-11 Etched Brass Stop Ahead Stencil
643-12 Etched Brass RR Crossing Stencil
643-13 Etched Brass 25 MPH Stencil

Road Sign Kits
Kits include etched brass signs, steel posts and color decals.

643-200 Stop Sign Set pkg(12) 8.99
Includes four Stop signs, two Railroad Crossing signs, two Pedestrian Crossing signs, plus one each 25, 35, 45 and 55 MPH speed limit sign.

643-201 Route Sign Set pkg(10) 6.99
Includes two each: Slippery When Wet, Soft Shoulder, No Parking, Do Not Stop on Tracks and Route (with decals to select your own route numbers).

Get Your Daily Dose of Product News at
www.walthers.com

643-202 Interstate Sign Set pkg(10) 7.99
Includes two each: Train Station, Bus Stop, Yield, Do Not Enter and Interstate (with decals to select your own interstate numbers).

643-203 Street Sign Set pkg(10) 7.99
Includes two each: Fallout Shelter, No U Turn, No Passing, Truck Route and Stop Ahead.

643-204 Smokey Sign Set pkg(8) 8.99
Includes two each: Smokey Bear, Deer Crossing, National Forest and Falling Rock.

NOCH

IMPORTED FROM GERMANY BY WALTHERS
Item listed below is available by Special Order (see Legend Page).

Sign Assortment

528-32860 7.99

PASTIME HOBBIES & MINIATURES

NEW SUPPLIER

NEW PRODUCTS

Signal Bridge Kit

NEW 554-102 21.95
Animate your layout with this double track signal bridge kit. Designed for easy construction, it includes precision laser-cut wood parts for the bridge framing and signal heads, along with all the LEDs needed to complete a working model.

SIGNALS, DETECTION UNITS & SIGNS N SCALE

N.J. International

Signals are of brass construction and come assembled, painted and wired, with bulbs or LEDs.

Please visit Walthers Web site at www.walthers.com for a complete listing of all available items.

NEW PRODUCTS
Crossing Signals

Pedestal-Type Crossing Gates pkg(2) 29.99
All brass, exact scale signals feature movable gates and LEDs facing in both directions.
NEW 525-2164 Red & White Arm

NEW 525-2165 Black & White Arm

Activation System

Servo-Master Activation System

NEW 525-8000   119.99
Servo-Master activation system works with crossing gates and semaphores. Each system is capable of operating two crossing gates with flashing lights or two semaphores.

Trackside Details

Lineside Signal Cabinets

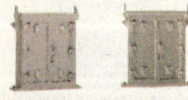

NEW 525-2359 pkg(2) 9.99
All brass, exact scale relay cabinets are ideal for detailing right-of-way scenes.

SIGNALS
Signal Disc Heads
Use brass signal disc heads on signal bridges and for making combination signals.
525-4203 3-Light **2.59**
525-4204 PRR 8-Light Position **4.99**
525-4208 2-Light **2.59**
525-4420 Signal Mounting Stem pkg(4) **2.99**

Semaphore - Upper Quadrant 3 Lite Type
29.99 ea

500-2000   500-2001

525-2000 Straight Pole w/Square Blade (yellow, red)
525-2001 Relay Cabinet Base w/Pointed Blade (white, red)

Single Board
525-2030 3-Light **16.99**
525-2080 2-Light **13.99**

Single Board w/LEDs
Exact scale.
525-2002 2-Light (black) **15.99**
525-2003 3-Light (black) **17.99**
525-2004 2-Light (silver) **15.99**
525-2005 3-Light (silver) **17.99**

Double Board
525-2038 3-Light Over 2-light **25.99**
525-2088 2-Light Over 2-Light **23.99**

Double Board w/LEDs
Multi Head D Type Signal (All Brass w/LEDs)
525-2133 3 Over 3 (black) **39.99**
525-2134 3 Over 3 (silver) **39.99**
525-2138 3 Over 2 (black) **34.99**
525-2139 3 Over 2 (silver) **34.99**
525-2188 2 Over 2 (black) **32.99**
525-2189 2 Over 2 (silver) **32.99**

Ground Signals w/LEDs
Exact scale.

2100   2110

525-2100 2-Light (black) **13.99**
525-2103 2-Light (silver) **13.99**
525-2110 3-Light (black) **14.99**
525-2111 3-Light (silver) **14.99**

SIGNAL BRIDGES
Cantilever
Injection-molded plastic kits.

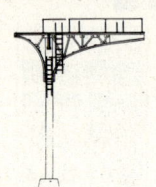

525-4211 Single Track (silver) **13.95**
525-4212 Single Track (black) **13.95**
525-4213 Double Track (silver) **14.95**
525-4214 Double Track (black) **14.95**

Standard 19.99 ea
Injection-molded plastic kit.

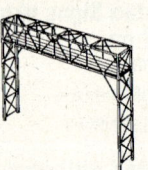

525-4209 Double Track (silver)
525-4210 Double Track (black)

Signal Head
525-2101 2-Light **12.99**
All brass with LEDs. Can be installed on signal bridges or used to construct multiple head signals.
525-2102 3 Lite Signal Head w/LEDs (For Signal Bridges & Other Mountings) **15.99**

CROSSINGS
Crossbucks
All brass, exact scale signals feature LEDs facing in both directions. Works with all flasher systems (sold separately).
525-2095 Red & White Arm pkg(2) **29.99**

Crossing Gates pkg(2) 29.99 ea
Numbers 2160-2163 are exact scale and are lighted w/LEDs.

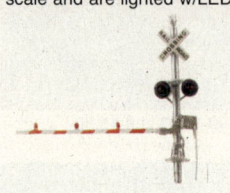

525-2160 Crossing Gate Signal, Red/White Arm pkg(2)
525-2161 Crossing Gate Signal, Black/White Arm pkg(2)
525-2162 Crossing Gate, Red/White Arm pkg(2)
525-2163 Crossing Gate, Black/White Arm pkg(2)

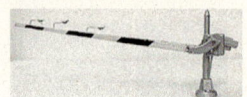

525-2170 Double Arm "A" Style Gates only (Modern red/white) pkg(2) **16.95**
525-2171 Double Arm "A" Style Gates only (Steam-Era black/white) pkg(2) **16.95**
525-2172 With Single Bar Gates (red/white) pkg(2) **16.95**
525-2173 With Single Bar Gates (black/white) pkg(2) **16.95**
525-2180 Wig Wag Crossing pkg(2) **19.95**

Crossing Signals

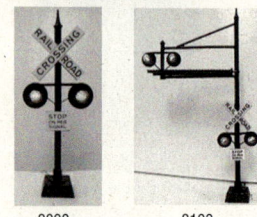
2090   2190

525-2090 Crossbuck **15.99**
525-2190 Over-Road Crossing Signal **32.99**

CROSSING SYSTEMS
Flasher Module alternately lights crossing signal lamps at a rate of 80 times per minute. Designed for 12-16V operation.
525-8020 Flasher Module **19.99**
525-8209 Flasher Module w/Crossbuck **36.99**
Crossbuck #2090 with #8020 Flasher Module.

LIGHTS
Street Lights 8.99 ea (Unless Noted)
525-5015 Boulevard Lamp
525-5017 Street Light
525-5019 Globe pkg(3)

Nonoperating lights are molded in styrene plastic.

STREET LIGHTS
570-94802 1800s Era pkg(4) **5.25**

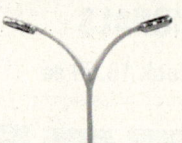

570-94808 1980s Era pkg(4) **4.95**

570-94812 1960s Era pkg(4) **4.95**

570-94816 1980s Era (metal) pkg(2) **9.95**
570-94821 3 Globe Walkway pkg(5) **14.95**
570-94826 4 Globe Walkway pkg(5) **14.95**
570-94829 Halogen Walkway pkg(5) **11.95**

570-94831 1990s Era pkg(5) **10.95**
570-94836 1990s Era Single Arm pkg(5) **10.95**
570-94842 Traffic Signal pkg(5) **5.95**
570-94852 Wood Phone Poles pkg(10) **7.00**

SIGNS
570-96052 Oil Co. Decal Set pkg(2) **2.00**
Full-color logos and warning signs are a great detail for storage tanks, fences and structures. Each sheet features nine decals.

BILLBOARDS
570-1013 pkg(4) **12.25**
Scratch model kit contains enough materials to construct four modern steel billboards. Includes posters.

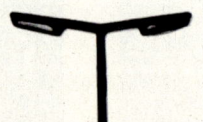

SIGNALS, DETECTION UNITS & SIGNS N SCALE

NEAL'S N GAUGING TRAINS

Signal Bridge

530-SS061 Signal Gantry Kit (Etched Brass) **16.95**

Painted Traffic Lights 8.95 ea

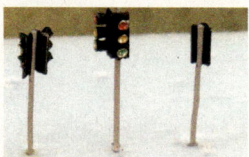

530-121 Black

530-121G Olive

530-121Y Yellow

Street Lamps

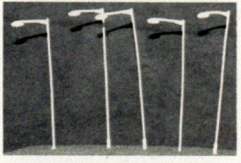

530-60 pkg(9) **8.95**
530-61 Modern Highway pkg(9) **8.95**
530-66 Swan Neck Lamp **11.95**
530-67 Ball-In-Hoop Lamp **11.95**

WINDOW GRAPHICS
8.98 ea (Unless Noted)

Transform empty storefronts with these full-color window treatments. Each includes colorful signs and curtains printed on clear acetate, that are designed for easy installation in Design Preservation Models and Walthers Cornerstone Series® structure kits (each sold separately). Basic cutting and installation instructions are provided in each set.

530-1 Paddy's Pastries Fits DPM 243-50.
530-2 Suzy's Store Fits DPM 243-502.

530-3 Dan's Diner Fits DPM 243-503.
530-4 Greze Cafe Fits DPM 243-504.
530-7 Funny Bone's Toys Fits DPM 243-507.
530-8 Shylock's Unsecured Loans Fits DPM 243-508.
530-9 Ashworth Hotel **10.98** Fits DPM 243-509.
530-10 Trackside Transfer Fits DPM 243-510.
530-11B The Boom Boom Room Fits DPM 243-511.

530-11V Val's Variety Fits DPM 243-511.

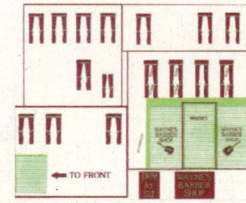

530-12 Wayne's Barber Shop Fits DPM 243-512.

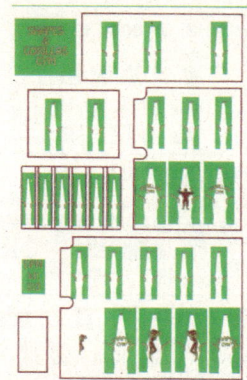

530-13 Shape's Gym Fits DPM 243-513, includes optional signs for Gorrila's Gym
530-14 David's Drugstore Fits DPM 243-514.
530-15 Bruce's Books Fits DPM 243-515.
530-16 Cuthbert's Clothing **10.98** Fits DPM 243-516.

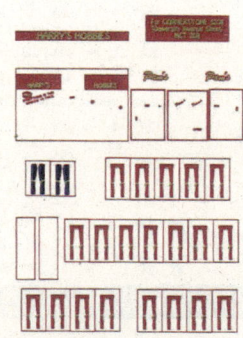

530-208 Harry's Hobbies Fits Walthers 933-3208.

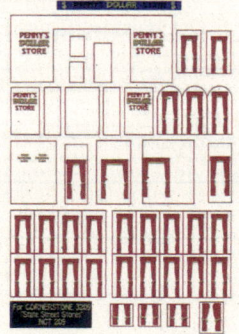

530-209 Penny's Dollar Store Fits Walthers 933-3209.

Latest New Product News Daily! Visit Walthers Web site at
www.walthers.com

Sunrise Enterprises

LAMPS

Operating Street/Parking Lamp w/Adjustable Pole
695-191000 Single Head **14.45**
695-191001 Double Head **16.45**

SIGNALS

Single Target
695-121002 Tricolor on 20' Pole **28.45**

Dual Target
695-121052 Operating Tricolor on 20' Pole **34.45**

Dwarf
695-122005 Signal "Pot" Dwarf **21.45**

Electrical Battery Box pkg(2) 4.95 ea
695-17124 Twin
695-17125 Single

Diverging Target Signals w/Bi-Color LEDs 23.45 ea
695-122001 Single Relay Box SP
695-122002 Double Relay Box SP

Crossbucks pkg(2) 2.25 ea
695-17132 Solid Pole (SP/WP)
695-17133 Split Pole (ATSF)
695-17134 Round Pipe (ATSF)

Bi-Color LED For Signal Bridges
695-122008 Single **21.45**

Items listed below are available by Special Order (see Legend Page).
695-122009 Dual **26.45**
695-122010 Triple **34.45**

Bi-Color LED On Single Relay Box-ATSF/SP/WP
695-121001 Single **28.45**
695-121051 Dual **34.45**

Tri-Color LED On Twin Electrical Box
695-121050 Dual Head, Assembled SP/ATSF **34.45**

Flasher FRED
695-1250 For Micro-Trains® Couplers **12.45**

SIGNS

Station Signs-Split Pole w/Bolts pkg(2) 2.25 ea
695-17136 8'
695-17137 10'

Limited Quantity Available
695-17135 6'

Paddle Top Warning Signs 2.25 ea
695-17138 pkg(3)
695-17139 ATSF Yard Limit Board pkg(2)
695-17140 ATSF Crossbuck 1938 to Present pkg(2)

TRAIN TRONICS

Prebuilt and tested electronics for train control, signal operation and lighting.

Automatic Reversing Circuit
723-601 **39.95**

Crossing Activator
723-502 **22.95**

Crossing Control w/Bell
723-515 **32.95**

Grade Crossing Flasher
723-501 **17.95**

Switches
723-406 Reed Switch & Magnet pkg(2) **6.95**
723-407 Pushbutton pkg(3) **6.95**

TOMAR INDUSTRIES

Two-Light Vertical Signal

81-5857 **15.95**
Assembled brass signal is painted and wired with LEDs (green on top, red on bottom). Finished in silver and black. Complete instructions included.

SIGNALS, DETECTION UNITS & SIGNS N SCALE

Dry Transfer Decals 5.98 ea (Unless Noted)

These N Scale transfers can also be used as small signs for HO Scale.

785-570 Product Logos

785-571 Railroad Signs

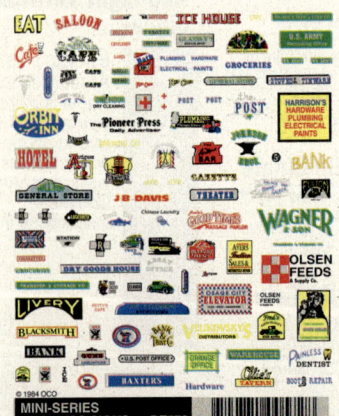

785-572 Business Signs

785-573 Signs/Posters

785-574 Service Station Signs

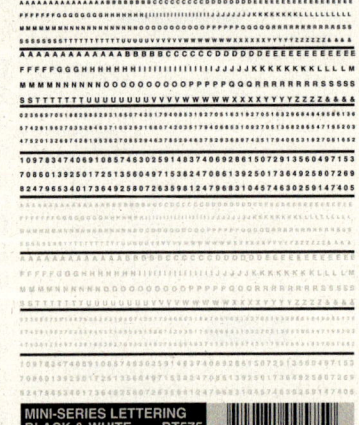

785-575 Letters and Numbers (black, white) **4.49**

SCENERY

Models & Photos by Dudley Ross, Montgomery, Alabama

Autumn is in the air as the 2pm C&O passenger train pulls out of the station in Alleghany, Virginia (spelled with an 'a'). Bright orange, yellow and red frost the surrounding forest, a sure sign that summer is at an end. But the changing leaves are just what the vacationers heading to the mineral springs resort in White Sulfur Springs have come to see.

Two tracks over the eastbound coal train has just released a string of loaded hoppers and set the brake retarders for the descent into the yard at Clifton Forge. Meanwhile the fully loaded freight train is at a halt. Just up ahead the tracks narrow so the freight must wait for the heavy coal train to pass through. In the last days of steam, H-8 Allegheny (with an 'e') 2-6-6-6 locomotives were used to pull the long coal trains to the top of Alleghany Mountain.

Dudley Ross' scenery not only helps set the place and era, it also indicates the season. Dudley constructed the scenery himself and scratch built the structures of basswood and styrene. The string wires are by Berkshire Junction and the cross arms are from Depots by John.

Look through the Scenery Section and you'll find plenty of products to help set the perfect scene on your layout.

SCENERY

INSTANT HORIZONS™

Make your layout or module look larger with Instant Horizons backgrounds. Featuring everything from vast desert scenes to forests to rural landscapes, these full-color printed scenes add visual depth that stretches for miles beyond the end of your scenery. Certain scenes can be arranged side-by-side to create an uninterrupted horizon—perfect for shelf-style and multi-module layouts. Easily added to layouts that are "finished" or under construction, complete instructions are included in each set. Each scene is 24" tall, so they're easily cut to fit NTrak standard 8" to 14" tall and similar skyboards.

BACKGROUND SCENES

Instant Horizons Scenes 7.98 ea
24 x 36"

Mountain to Desert
949-703

Drywash Desert
949-705

Saguaro Desert
949-706

Desert to Country
949-707

Desert
With little vegetation and distant foothills, these scenes capture the look of the southwestern US. For variety, several transition scenes are designed especially for use with these views.

949-705 Drywash Desert
949-706 Saguaro Desert

Transition Scenes
These special views smooth the transition between different kinds of scenery, creating a more natural and realistic change.

949-703 Mountain to Desert
949-704 Desert to Mountain
949-707 Desert to Country
949-708 Country to Desert
949-714 Country to Eastern Foothills
949-716 Country to City
949-717 City to Country

Mountain Scenes
From foothills to snow capped peaks, put your layout in a mountain setting with any of these scenes.

949-701 Sierra Boomtown (Gold Rush)
949-702 Tall Timber
949-715 Eastern Foothills

Rural Scenes
Fewer details and plenty of sky add miles of scenery and a wide, open look to any layout.

949-710 Whistle Stop

See What's Available at
www.walthers.com

SCENERY

INSTANT HORIZONS™

MANUFACTURED BY WM. K. WALTHERS, INC.

Scenes can be arranged side by side for a panoramic background. All Instant Horizons are drawn so they can easily be combined for a realistic transition between different kinds of scenery.

Country to City
949-716

Country to
Eastern Foothills
949-714

Tall Timber
949-702

Whistle Stop
949-710

Eastern Foothills
949-715

City to Country
949-717

Country to Desert
949-708

Desert to Mountain
949-704

SCENERY

Life-Like Trains
Division of Wm. K. Walthers, Inc.

TREES
Trees are assembled, self-standing, appropriately colored. Sizes are approximate.

Autumn & Spring pkg(4) 8.00 ea

- 433-1903 Autumn 3"
- 433-1922 Autumn 4"
- 433-1926 Spring 4"

Blue Spruce

433-1952 5-1/2" pkg(2) **8.00**

Deciduous 8.00 ea (Unless Noted)

- 433-1924 White Birch 4" pkg(4)
- 433-1925 Poplar 4" pkg(4)

- 433-1950 Redwood 5-1/2" pkg(2)
- 433-1971 Oak 6-1/2" pkg(2) **13.50**

Evergreens 8.00 ea (Unless Noted)

433-1941 433-1907

433-1923 433-1972

- 433-1941 Small - 2" pkg(4)
- 433-1907 3" pkg(4)
- 433-1923 4" pkg(4)
- 433-1972 6-1/2" pkg(2) **13.50**

3" Fruit pkg(4) 8.00 ea

433-1908 433-1909

- 433-1908 Apple
- 433-1909 Orange

Shade Trees 8.00 ea

433-1940 433-1902

433-1921 433-1951

- 433-1940 2" pkg(4)
- 433-1902 3" pkg(4)
- 433-1921 4" pkg(4)
- 433-1951 5-1/2" pkg(2)

Summer Shade pkg(4) 8.00 ea

433-1910 433-1927

- 433-1910 Small
- 433-1927 Large

Winter
Flocked to simulate snow on branches.

433-1901 433-1970

- 433-1901 Small 3" pkg(4) **8.00**
- 433-1970 Big 8-1/2" pkg(2) **13.50**

SCENEMASTER™ TREES (W/ BENDABLE ARMATURES)
Give outdoor scenes a burst of realism and beauty with SceneMaster trees. Each tree is individually handcrafted and finely detailed through realistic forms, colors and sizes. Each tree features bendable armatures, giving modelers a wide variety of shaping options.

433-1974

433-1975 433-1976

Elm
- 433-1974 Small pkg(4) **9.25**
- 433-1977 Medium pkg(3) **10.00**
- 433-1980 Large pkg(3) **11.00**

Maple
- 433-1975 Small pkg(4) **9.25**
- 433-1978 Medium pkg(3) **10.00**
- 433-1981 Large pkg(3) **11.00**

Oak
- 433-1976 Small pkg(4) **9.25**
- 433-1979 Medium pkg(3) **10.00**
- 433-1982 Large pkg(3) **11.00**

GROUND COVER

SceneMaster Grass Mats
Quick and easy to use, mats can be modified or removed when landscaping progresses and are completely reusable. Paper backing for easy cutting. Each features realistic textures with bright, pure colors. All flocking is nonmagnetic.

Dealers MUST order in multiples of 12.

- 433-1151 50 x 33" **5.98**
- 433-1156 50 x 99" **9.98**

Shaker Container Counter Display

433-1040   **148.50**
Includes three each #433-1041, 1942, 1043, 1044, 1045 and 1046.

Lichen
Shaker Containers 2oz **8.25 ea**

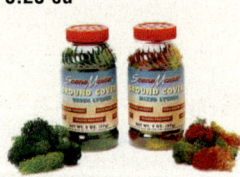

- 433-1041 Mixed Colors
- 433-1042 Green

Ground Foam
Shaker Containers 4.6oz **8.25 ea**

- 433-1043 Dark Green
- 433-1044 Light Green
- 433-1045 Dark Brown
- 433-1046 Light Brown

Ballast

1104 1105 1106

- 433-1104 Ballast/Gray 15oz **5.00**
- 433-1105 Coal 15oz **5.00**
- 433-1106 Gravel 15oz **5.00**

TUNNELS
Tunnels are lightweight durable LiFoam® and are finished in realistic colors.

433-1311 Mini Tunnel Curved **6.50**

ACCESSORIES

Mountain Paper

433-1157 **7.00**
Ready-to-use mountain paper can be used to create scenes, mountains and tunnels. Just wet, shape and install as desired. The paper is finished in a realistic color and is reusable. Measures 24 x 72".

Landscaping Cement

433-1403 **15.50**
Clean, nontoxic, non-flammable adhesive. Dries hard and clean on almost any surface. Resealable 1 pint can.

Make it Fast, Fun & Affordable with SceneMaster™ Grass Mats

EASY TO APPLY

Instant Greenery for Your Scenery!

- More Affordable – **NEW LOWER PRICES!**
- Easily Cut & Shaped
- 2 Handy Sizes
- Realistic Texture
- Perfect for Quick Scenery Projects
- Works in Any Scale
- Nonmagnetic
- Part of the Complete SceneMaster Line

SceneMaster™ Grass Mats
Small Roll 50 x 33" 0.8 x 1.27m
433-1151 Flocked Was $8.00 **NOW $5.98**

Large Roll 50 x 99" 1.27 x 2.5m – Covers Standard 4 x 8' Plywood Sheet Without Cutting!
433-1156 Flocked Was $15.00 **NOW $9.98**

Division of Wm. K. Walthers, Inc.

Get Daily Info, Photos and News at
www.walthers.com

A-West
"On target for You!"

Weathering 7.59 ea

158-1   158-2   158-4

Instructions are included with all of our weathering solutions and they are useful for a variety of effects whose exact applications are limited only by the users' imaginations.

Customers have won modeling awards with and written articles about these products. These weathering solutions have also been credited in several magazine spreads and covers. Each solution comes in a 4oz bottle.

158-1 Weather-It
Gives unpainted wood a gray, aged look. Not a paint or stain. Use for old paint effects and realistic plaster "concrete," too.

158-2 Blacken-It
Works on most metals; not a paint. Conducts electricity, can be soldered.

158-4 Patina-It
Produces shades of blue/green on copper, brass and bronze. Not a paint. Also for Corrode-It technique on white metal, producing a pewter-gray/black patina.

Using A-West Products
The following is an example of how each of the above products were used in the creation of a realistic wood trestle. To begin with, all wood parts were weathered with Weather-It, giving them the look of having endured many years of nature's hardships. The truss rods, represented by copper wire, were treated with Blacken-It. This turned the normal copper wire into the black rods that are seen on such structures. Patina-It was then used on the small details of cast white metal which were used for turnbuckles, nuts and washers on the truss rods. This allowed the parts to take on the gray/black color as seen on prototype trestles. Blacken-It could also be used in place of Patina-It, depending on the look the modeler is trying to achieve. When all is said and done, a simple kit has been transformed into a true-to-life replica by the simple use of weathering solutions.

SCENERY

ATLAS

Telephone Poles

150-2801 pkg(12) **2.35**
Parts are molded of styrene in appropriate colors.

BRAWA

IMPORTED FROM GERMANY BY WALTHERS

Platform

186-2697 Platform Side Set **7.99**
Includes four straight sides, each 5-1/2" (13cm) long, four ramp sections, each 2-3/8" (6cm) and two platform decks, each 1-1/4" (3cm) long.

Walls
Retaining walls are easy-to-build plastic kits, molded in colors. Each panel measures 5 x 2" (12.5 x 5cm) and kits can be combined to make larger structures.

186-2698 With Shops pkg(2) **11.99**
4-3/4 x 2" 12 x 5cm

Includes printed window and sign details.

186-2699 Stone w/Stairs **12.99**
4-3/4 x 2" 12 x 5cm

Includes brass handrail for lower stairway.

186-2700 Enclosed Stone Arch pkg(2) **9.99**
4-3/4 x 2" 12 x 5cm

SCENERY

AMACO

METAL SHEETS
Each sheet measures
9-1/4 x 12" 23.1 x 30cm

126-50063 Pewter Medium **10.49**

126-50064 Brass Light **7.65**

126-50065 Copper Medium **7.45**

126-50066 Copper Light **6.49**

126-50067 Aluminum Medium **5.45**

126-50068 Aluminum **4.95**

126-50114 Matte Black **5.95**

STYLUS TOOL SET
126-11107P **3.39**

MOLDING MATERIAL

Instant Paper Mache
Dry powder mixes with water, ready to use in 15 to 20 minutes. Material is nontoxic. Dries white, can be painted with any type of paint when dry.

126-41810 1lb **6.79**

126-41811 5lbs **23.99**

Sculptamold®
White, nontoxic powder material mixes with water, sets in 30 minutes without shrinking. Clings to most clean surfaces and can be applied over forms without cracking.

126-41821 3lbs **6.49**

126-41822 25lbs **42.49**

126-41823 50lbs **78.99**

Casting Compound
126-52761 5lbs **12.49**
When mixed with water and poured into a form, compound sets hard in a few minutes. Cast pieces and molds are white, fine-textured and durable.

Crea-Stone
126-53401 Natural Color 25lbs **56.49**
Dry powder mixes with water to make castings or moldings. Can be sculpted and carved for long periods if kept moist.

Plasterform™

126-50082 6.4oz **4.49**
In a few simple steps, you can have easy-to-make scenic landscapes, model train dioramas, mountains and sculptures. 4 x 180" roll

Mix-A-Mold
Nontoxic material for creating molds using 3-D objects. Picks up every detail of original. Powder mixes with water and molds are ready in two minutes.

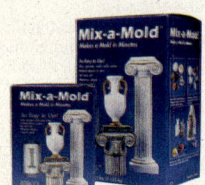

126-75541 8oz **12.49**

126-75542 2-1/2lbs **38.49**

Mountain Building Kit

126-41820 U Build The Mountain Kit **17.49**
Kit includes a 2lb bag of Sculptamold, measuring cup, craft stick, mixing bag and instructions.

Rubber Latex
126-89915 16oz **14.49**
Use to make your own custom molds for casting scenery, small parts and other hobby or craft items.

WIREFORM®
Each sheet measures 16 x 20".

Wireform Expandable Modeling Mesh
Mini-packs ideal for detailed projects on your layout.

126-50004 Contour Aluminum 1/16" Pattern **6.99**

126-50005 Sparkle Aluminum 1/8" Pattern **6.99**

126-50006 Diamond Aluminum 1/4" Pattern **6.99**

126-50007 Impression Copper 1/8" Pattern **9.49**

126-50008 CopperForm Copper 1/4" Pattern **9.49**

Wireform Woven Modeling Mesh
126-50023 Modeler's Aluminum **14.49**
The woven wires create a structural grid, assuming different textures when shaped. Includes two sheets of 16 x 20" wiremesh.

AM MODELS

Rocks

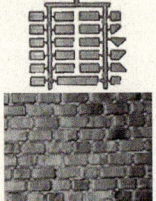

129-502 **2.80**
Molded in various shapes and colors, enough to cover 10 square inches.

Fences

129-503 pkg(4) **2.80**
Includes four sections, each eight scale feet long.

Get the Scoop!
Get the Skinny!
Get the Score!
Check Out Walthers Web site at
www.walthers.com

Blair Line LLC
PRODUCTS FOR MODEL RAILROADERS

Pre-Assembled Road Barricades pkg(2) 7.00 ea
Includes "Road Closed" sign.

184-61 Modern (orange & white)

184-612 Vintage (black & white)

Manhole Covers & Storm Drains

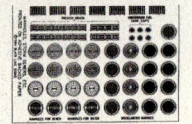

184-62 **4.00**
Printed on adhesive-backed paper. Feature cut, peel-and-stick installation.

Grade Crossings pkg(2) 6.00 ea

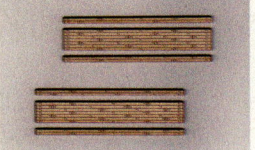

184-65 Laser-Cut Wood Grade Crossing
Each highway grade crossing is fully assembled and ready to paint/stain and install.

NEW 184-32 Angled Left

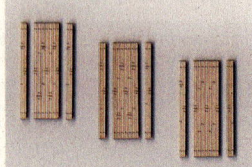

NEW 184-33 Single Lane

NEW 184-34 Angled Right

Information STATION

Litter on Your Layout
Even with no one around, clues to the presence of people are evident – a piece of paper in a bush, a can in the gutter, metal scraps along the tracks. Even in remote locations, if people have been there, they left litter. Litter is part of our everyday lives; it should also be part of your layout.

Adding realistic litter is easy. Simulate litter with small crumpled rectangles of tissue paper, foil, bits of plastic wrap, painted sprue remnants and leftover or broken parts. Bottles and other details are also available. Litter doesn't have to be perfect. Most usually ends up at the base of buildings, along fences, in gutters or on plants. Some areas have lots of debris while others may have little.

Keep in mind location and era. Populated areas are dirtier and industrial areas have large items like boxes or tires. Sanitation laws of the mid 1800s, cleared trash from the streets. Environmental awareness campaigns in the 70s brought clean up efforts that still exist today.

Other things to consider: Beverages originally came in glass bottles. Aluminum cans appeared in the mid 60s and plastic bottles showed up in the 70s. Widespread use of convenience packaging began in the 50s and foam cups were introduced in the 1960s.

A little litter may seem unsightly but adding some to your layout reflects the presence of real life.

SCENERY

A.I.M. PRODUCTS

A.I.M. Products are cast in high-density plaster to give maximum strength and stain absorption. This process is exclusive with A.I.M. Products. Includes complete installation and staining instructions.

ROCKS

110-500 1lb **12.95**
Assorted rock castings sold by the pound, about nine castings per package.

BRIDGE ABUTMENTS
pkg(2) 8.95 ea (Unless Noted)

Abutments measure: 3" high, 2-1/4" wide at base and 1/2" thick (7.5 x 5.6 x 1.2cm).

110-200 Cut Stone
110-204 Random Stone
110-600 Cut Stone - Pre-Finished **9.95**

ABUTMENT WINGS
pkg(2) 8.95 ea (Unless Noted)

Abutment wings measure: 1-7/8" tall at high end, 1-1/8" at low end, 3-1/6" wide and 5/8" thick (4.6, 2.8 x 0.4 x 1.5cm).

110-202 Cut Stone
110-205 Random Stone
110-216 Concrete
110-616 Concrete - Pre-Finished **9.95**

TUNNEL PORTALS
Single Track 8.95 ea (Unless Noted)

Tunnel portals measure: 2-3/4" high, 3-1/6" wide at base and 5/8" thick (6.8 x 7.8 x 1.5cm).

110-210 Cut Stone
110-212 Random Stone
110-214 Concrete
110-217 Granite
110-218 Modern Concrete
110-610 Cut Stone - Pre-Finished **10.95**
110-614 Concrete - Pre-Finished **8.95**
110-618 Lough Tunnel - Pre-Finished **10.95**

Double Track 7.95 ea (Unless Noted)

Tunnel portals measure: 3" high, 4" wide at base and 5/8" thick (7.5 x 10 x 1.5cm).

110-213

110-211 Random Stone
110-213 Cut Stone
110-215 Concrete
110-219 Cut Concrete
110-611 Cut Stone - Pre-Finished **10.95**
110-615 Concrete - Pre-Finished **10.95**
110-619 Clarksburg Tunnel - Pre-Finished **10.95**

RETAINING WALLS

In N Scale, walls measure: 25-1/2' tall, 40-3/4' wide and 5-3/4' thick. They can also be used as double-track bridge abutments.

110-208

110-206 Cut Stone pkg(2) **7.95**
110-207 Concrete pkg(2) **7.95**
110-208 Random Stone pkg(2) **7.95**

110-606 Cut Stone - Pre-Finished pkg(2) **8.95**
110-607 Concrete - Pre-Finished pkg(2) **10.95**

SCENERY SOLUTIONS

These easy-to-use products are compatible with one another. Using them in combination will give models a rundown rusty look.

16oz ea 7.95

110-901 Quick Age
Gives building and rolling stock an old gray look. Spray on and let dry. Add more coats until desired effect is seen.

110-902 Real Rust
Produces a rusty orange color. Great for rust streaks on tanks, tenders, etc.

110-903 Real Rust, Dark
Get the effect of older rust. Apply Real Rust over this and great multi-colored rusted model.

110-906 Grungy Grimy Black
Will make models look dirty and grimy. Great for engines, running gear, smokestacks, etc.

110-907 New Fresh Rust
Create rust streaks of that fresh orange rust color from recent scratches in metal.

SPILL & STAIN KIT

110-964 New or Used Oil, Anti-Freeze, Hydraulic & Brake Fluid **13.95**

COLORED WEATHERING POWDERS
4.95 ea (Unless Noted)

Each color approximately one ounce in volume.

110-3100 Assortment - 1ea 3101-3107, 3110 **33.95**
110-3101 White
110-3102 Grimy Black
110-3103 Medium Earth
110-3104 Dirty Yellow
110-3105 Dark Rust
110-3106 Light Rust
110-3107 Dark Earth
110-3108 Medium Rust
110-3109 New Fresh Rust
110-3110 Medium Gray
110-3111 Dark Gray
110-3112 Brick Red
110-3113 Dusty Brown

SCENIC DETAILS

110-904 Advertising Signs **6.95**
110-905 Aluminum for Scrap or Junk Piles **4.99**

DETAIL ASSOCIATES

BACKGROUND SCENES

Create a unique backdrop for your layout, module or diorama. These N Scale-sized printed backgrounds include the main scene, plus additional overlays so you can use several scenes together without repeating the same identical structures or details. Each color sheet measures 11-1/2 x 4-1/2" 29.2 x 11.4cm.

City Background Scene 229-8801

Industrial District Background Scene 229-8803

Estuary Background Scene 229-8805

Tank Farm Background Scene 229-8806

Land Background Scene 229-8809

Rail Scenes 4.98 ea

229-8801 City
229-8802 Downtown
229-8803 Industrial District
229-8804 Lumber Yard
229-8805 Estuary
229-8806 Tank Farm
229-8807 Oil Fields
229-8808 Farm Town
229-8809 Land
229-8810 Woods
229-8811 Forest
229-8812 Mountains

Instruction Manual
229-7550 **4.98**
38-page illustrated booklet contains instructions for creating backdrops, possible combinations and suggestions for details. 11 x 8-1/2".

145

SCENERY

BUSCH

IMPORTED FROM GERMANY BY WALTHERS

NEW PRODUCTS

Sunflower Field

NEW 189-8103 pkg(96) **9.99**
Create a realistic sunflower field on your pike. Each package includes parts for 96 plants and includes bases.

Industrial Fence

NEW 189-8117 **6.99**
Wire-mesh fence features super-fine aluminum mesh (1.2mm). Package includes: 23-5/8" 60cm wire mesh fence, 5/8" 1.6cm high, and 32 round fence posts.

Miniature Scenes

Create an entire scenario with these sets. Each includes figures, vehicles and accessories as shown. Background scenery not included.
NEW 189-8250 "Admiring the Scenery" **13.99**
Includes 2 figures, fence w/"FKK" sign, 1 deciduous and 1 pine tree.

NEW 189-8251 Wedding **14.99**
Bridal couple, wedding car, flowering tree and nonworking lamp.

NEW 189-8252 Parking Ticket **14.99**
Includes 2 figures, car and 2 nonworking lamps.

146

NEW 189-8253 Pumpkin Harvest **17.99**
Includes 2 figures, truck w/load, tree and pumpkin vine.

NEW 189-8254 Hitchhiker **19.99**
Includes car, figure, sunflowers, tree and guardrail.

NEW 189-8255 Campground **14.99**
Includes 2 figures, 3 tents and tree.

Aqua Model Water

NEW 189-7589 3.75oz 125ml **7.99**
Create realistic brooks and ponds with this easy-to-use plastic liquid. Simply prepare your streambed or pond bottom and pour a thin layer of Aqua Model Water. Material dries transparent. Add a second layour to build depth, if necesary. Odorless, doesn't react with other materials, does not heat while curing and provides a natural-looking water surface.

Hot New Products Announced Daily! Visit Walthers Web site at
www.walthers.com

TREES

Deciduous

Birch

189-6736 3-1/2" 9cm pkg(2) **7.99**

Beech

189-6739 3-1/2" 9cm pkg(2) **7.99**

Blooming

189-6623 pkg(2) **4.99**
Trees measure 1-3/4" 4.5cm tall.
189-6643 One Each Pink & White 3" 7.5cm **7.99**
189-6250 Small 1-5/8" 4cm pkg(2) **1.99**
189-6251 Medium 2" 5cm pkg(2) **2.99**
189-6252 Small 2-3/4" 7cm pkg(2) **2.99**

Fruit

189-6627 1-3/4" 4.5cm pkg(2) **4.99**
189-6628 Apple 1-3/4" 4.5cm pkg(2) **4.99**
189-6647 3" 7.5cm pkg(2) **7.99**
189-6584 1-5/8 to 2-3/4" 4-9mm pkg(18) **9.99**

Poplar

189-6733 3-1/2" 9cm pkg(2) **7.99**

189-6239 pkg(10) **8.99**
Includes four 3-3/4" 9.5cm and six 3" 7.5cm trees.

Forest Trees

189-6489 Mixed Assortment pkg(24) **27.99**
189-6589 Mixed Forest 2 **15.99**
Includes 18 pine trees w/roots 1-1/8 - 2-3/8" 3-6cm tall and 12 deciduous trees 1-5/8 - 2" 4-5cm tall.

Pine Trees w/Roots

189-6475 pkg(10) **9.99**
2-3/8 - 5-3/8" 6-13.5cm Tall
189-6476 pkg(20) **16.99**
2-3/8 - 5-3/8" 6-13.5cm Tall
189-6477 pkg(40) **32.99**
Includes eight each 2-1/2, 2-3/8 - 5-3/8" 6-13.5cm Tall
189-6576 1-1/8 to 2-3/8" 3-6cm Tall pkg(20) **11.99**
189-6577 1-1/8 to 2-3/8" 3-6cm Tall pkg(40) **21.99**

Pine Trees

189-6465 Winter Set **16.99**
Includes 10 white trees, snowman, aviary and snow powder.

189-6566 Snow Covered 1-1/8 to 2-3/8" 3-6cm pkg(20) **12.99**

Tree Assortments

Deciduous

189-6487 pkg(25) **24.99**
2-3/4 - 4-7/8" 7-12.5cm

Deciduous/Pine

189-6490 pkg(35) **21.99**
2 - 4-3/8" 5-11cm
NEW 189-6586 1-9/16 - 2-3/8" 4-6cm pkg(12) **11.99**
NEW 189-6587 1-3/8 - 2-5/32" 3.5 - 5.5cm pkg(25) **24.99**
189-6590 pkg(35) **11.99**
1-1/8 - 2-1/8" 3 - 5.5cm

Pine

189-6470 pkg(15) **11.99**
2-3/8 - 5-3/8" 6-13.5cm Tall
189-6471 pkg(30) **21.99**
2-3/8 - 5-3/8" 6-13.5cm Tall
189-6472 pkg(60) **41.99**
2-3/8 - 5-3/8" 6-13.5cm Tall
189-6497 pkg(50) **21.99**
2-3/8 - 4-3/8" 6-11cm
189-6498 pkg(20) **8.99**
Trees range in height from about 1-1/2 to 3-1/2" 4-9cm.

189-6499 pkg(100) **35.99**
Trees range in height from about 2-3/8 to 4-3/8" 6-11cm.
189-6571 1-1/8 to 2-3/8" 3-6cm Tall pkg(30) **12.99**

189-6572 1-1/8 to 2-3/8" 3-6cm Tall pkg(60) **24.99**
189-6599 pkg(100) **24.99**
Trees range in height from about 1-1/8 to 2" 3-5cm.

Spruce
189-6592 pkg(35) **12.99**
Trees range in height from about 1-1/8 to 2" 3-5cm.

Christmas Tree w/Lights

189-5410 2" 5cm Tall **22.99**
Includes seven miniature LEDs. 14-16V

GROUND COVER

Fall Color Flocking

189-7324   189-7325   189-7326

15oz (500ml) 2.99 ea
189-7324 Tan
189-7325 Orange-Brown
189-7326 Red-Brown

Flocking 2.99 ea
189-7331 Spring Green
189-7332 Medium Green
189-7333 Dark Green
189-7337 Light Green

SCENERY

IMPORTED FROM GERMANY BY WALTHERS

Grass Flocking 2.99 ea

189-7110 Dark Green
189-7111 Spring Green

Micro Flocking 2.99 ea

189-7321 Spring Green
189-7322 Medium Green
189-7323 Dark Green

189-7327 Light Green

Foam Scatter Material
Fine 5.99 ea

189-7311 Light Green
189-7312 Medium Green

189-7313 Dark Green
189-7314 White

189-7315 Rose

Scatter Material

189-7051 Forest Green 1.99

Medium 4.99 ea

189-7317 Light Green
189-7318 Medium Green

189-7319 Dark Green

Grass Mats
Large 13.99 ea (Unless Noted)
39-3/8 x 31-1/2" 100 x 80cm (Unless Noted)

189-7220/7221/7231
189-7220 Dark Green
189-7221 Spring
NEW 189-7224 Autumn Brown
189-7231 Spring 79 x 32" 26.99

Extra Large 25.99 ea
60 x 40" 150 x 100cm
189-7270 Dark Green
189-7271 Spring

Specialty

189-7183 Plowed Field pkg(2) 5.99

189-7256 Harrowed Field Brown 30 x 28" 75 x 70cm 8.99

Wild Grass Mats
Small 9.99 ea
Measurements: 20 x 16" 50 x 40cm.

189-7210 Light Green
189-7211 Dark Green
189-7214 Corn Field

Large 25.99 ea
Measurements: 32 x 32" 80 x 80cm.
189-7215 Light Green
189-7216 Dark Green
189-7219 Corn Field

Snow Powder
189-7171 17.5oz 500g 7.99

WATER

189-7180 Foil/Paper 8.99
18 x 14" 45 x 35cm

MODELER'S SAND

Great for modeling dirt or gravel roads with truck or tire tracks, this material retains its shape when it hardens. When dry, Modeler's Sand has a natural, sandy look and can be remoistened for reuse or modification.

500g, 6.99 ea (Unless Noted)
189-7550 Beige Sand 5.99
189-7551 Medium Brown
189-7552 Dark Brown
189-7553 Light Green
189-7554 Dark Green

GRAIN FIELD & REEDS

189-7375 125g 7.99
Ideal for modeling dried fields of grain, reeds or tall grasses. Strands are approximately 1-3/4" 4.4cm long but can be cut for use in N or Z Scales.

ROADWAY
Flexible Roadway

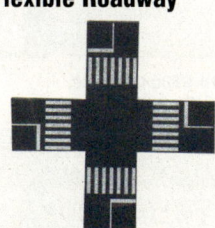

189-7075 Self Adhesive Pedestrian Crossing for 1-1/2" 4cm Street 7.99

189-7079 Cobblestone 4.79
189-7084 Flexible Field Path 1" 23mm wide 4.99
189-7085 Unmarked Asphalt Sheet 22 x 13" 56 x 33cm 8.99

189-7087 Asphalt 6.99
1-1/2 x 3/4" 4 x 2cm

NEW 189-7089 Cobblestone Sheet 22 x 13" 56 x 33cm 13.99

189-7091 Asphalt Tape - Double Faced 9.99
189-7099 Asphalt, Curved 1-5/8" 4cm 5.99 Makes a 4-3/4" 12cm diameter circle.

189-8138 Town Street 39-1/3 x 2-1/2" 100cm x 6.6cm 5.99

189-8139 Tarmac Road 39-1/3 x 1-1/2" 100cm x 4cm 3.99

4-Way Roundabout

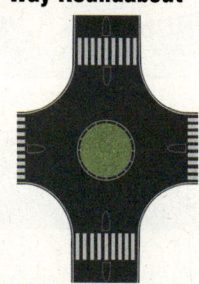

189-1102 10.99
6-3/8 x 6-3/8" 16 x 16cm

Sidewalk Sheet

189-7094 pkg(6) 4.99
8-1/2 x 6" 21 x 15cm

Parking Lot

189-7077 3.99
4-3/4 x 4" 12 x 10cm

Old Town Roadways

189-8131 Old Town Street 78-3/4 x 1-1/2" 200 x 4cm 6.99

189-8132 Old Town Square 7-3/4 x 6-1/4" 20 x 16cm 3.99

Mortar 8.99 ea
Self-adhesive putty can be used to create all kinds of scenic formations. Stays workable for up to four hours, dries completely in two days. 17-1/2oz (500g).

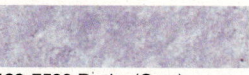

189-7590 Rocks (Gray)

189-7591 Soil (Tan)

BACKGROUND SCENES
CD-ROM Sets

Create and print your own background scenes using the images on these CDs. Features over 150 elements including structures and landscapes. Structures are photographed frontally and can be printed out in any scale and mounted on cardboard to make a variety of affordable backdrops. Images are in JPEG and PSD format for use with photo editing applications such as PhotoShop, PhotoPaint, CorelDraw and others. Requires a IBM-compatible PC running Windows 95 or higher. (German language).

189-2866 USA 2 CD Set w/180 Images 30.99

189-2867 North German Backgrounds 15.99
189-2868 Alpine Backgrounds 15.99

189-2870 Backgrounds for Model Railroads 2-CD Set 30.99

Item listed below is available by Special Order (see Legend Page).

189-2869 Dutch Backgrounds 15.99

SCENERY

IMPORTED FROM GERMANY BY WALTHERS

Day and Night Backgrounds 15.99 ea
Want to add a background scene that simulates both daylight and night lighting conditions? These unique backgrounds are printed on translucent material that allows you to use them two ways. When lit with conventional room lighting, they offer a photo-realistic background scene. To simulate a nighttime scene, simply mount the scene in a frame with a light box behind it (both sold separately) and the scene is magically transformed. The translucent base is printed with a pattern that allows bright light to shine through only in selected places such as through windows and on streetlights. The rest of the scene gets its depth from the remaining shadows. Each scene measures 77-15/16 x 13-3/8" 198 x 34cm.

189-2875 River #1

189-2876 River #2

189-2877 City #1

189-2878 City #2

New Arrivals Updated Every Day! Visit Walthers Web site at www.walthers.com

TUNNEL PORTALS

Single Track 8.99 ea
214-9720 Concrete
2-13/32 x 2-1/2"

214-9740 Cut Stone
2-1/2 x 2-1/2"   6.2 x 6.2cm

214-9760 Random Stone
3 x 2-1/2"   7.5 x 6.2cm

Double Track pkg(2) 8.99 ea

214-9730 Concrete
3-3/4 x 3-29/32"

214-9750 Cut Stone
3-1/2 x 3-29/32"

214-9770 Random Stone
3-1/2 x 2-3/4"

WALLS
All interconnect for continued walls.

Interlocking Retaining 7.99 ea

Cut Stone

214-8310 Small
6-3/4 x 3-13/32"

Random Stone

214-8300 Small
6-3/4 x 3-5/8"

Stepped pkg(2)
5-1/2 x 2-1/8"
214-9800 Cut Stone 8.99

BRIDGE ABUTMENTS

Single Track pkg(2) 8.99 ea

214-9840 Cut Stone
1-3/4 x 2-13/32"

214-9860 Cut Stone Tapered
3 x 2-13/32"

214-9800 Stepped Wall Cut Stone
3-1/2 x 2-3/4"

214-9830 Bridge Pier Cut Stone (Pointed End)

214-9831 Bridge Pier Cut Stone Rectangular (Square End)

Double Track

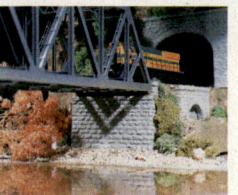

214-9850 Cut Stone pkg(2) 8.99
3 x 2-13/32"

BRIDGE PIERS

Cut Stone pkg(2) 8.99 ea
214-9830 Pointed End
2-1/2 x 5/8 x 2-1/8"

214-9831 Rectangular Square End
2-1/8 x 3/4 x 2-1/8"

MINI HIGHWAYS

DIVISION OF LEISURETIME PRODUCTS

Roadways 6.79 ea
Thin precut material with realistic black/brown color and authentic markings. Will lie flat without adhesive, but can be glued for permanent scenery.

406-101 Straight Passing Zone 9'

406-103 Curved Roadway 6'

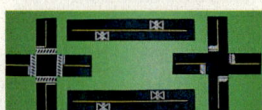

406-105 RR Crossing & Intersection 2 Each

FALLER

SCENERY

IMPORTED FROM GERMANY BY WALTHERS
Creating realistic scenery is fast and fun with the complete Faller line. No matter what kind of terrain you're creating, you'll find trees, ground cover and many other easy to use materials that produce realistic miniature scenes.

NEW PRODUCTS

Arcades

NEW 272-272645 Concrete w/Cornice Stones **13.99**
14-1/2 x 2-9/16 x 3/8"
37 x 6.5 x .9cm

NEW 272-272646 Natural Stone w/Semicircular Arch **14.99**
14-1/2 x 2-9/16 x 3/8"
37 x 6.5 x 1cm

Piers

NEW 272-222577 Viaduct Piers pkg(2) **10.99**
1-1/2 x 3/4 x 3-7/8"
3.9 x 1.9 x 10cm

Walls

NEW 272-272647 Natural Stone Retaining Walls pkg(2) **14.99**

Miniature Scenes

NEW 272-232212 Motorized Lawn Mower **75.99**
4-1/2 x 4-1/4 x 13/16"
11.5 x 10.8 x 2cm

Moving lawn mower "cuts" the grass line-by-line. Comes with powered lawn mower, figure, garden area & garage. 16V AC required for mower.

NEW 272-272568 Adventure Playground **21.99**
The whole family will have fun in this rustic-style playland. Includes tables, benches, swings, seesaws, climbing structure, adventure hut, sand pit, a wooden train and more.

Scene Details

NEW 272-272569 Park Accessories **29.99**
Finish off your village green or neighborhood park with this detail set that includes benches, a tree seat, fountains, fences and more.

TREES

Premium Trees - Conifers

272-181311 Spruces 4-3/8" 11cm pkg(2) **14.99**

Top Series Trees - Deciduous

272-181372 White Birch 5-3/16" 13cm pkg(3) **11.99**

272-181373 Holm Oaks 4-3/8" 11cm pkg(2) **13.99**

272-181374 Hornbeams 4" 10cm pkg(3) **12.99**

272-181375 Bushes 2" 5cm pkg(3) **10.99**

Deciduous

272-181405 2 Each Birch & Poplar 2-13/16" 7cm Tall **9.99**

272-181410 Large 5-1/4" pkg(3) **9.99**

272-181412 Dark Green Small 2-1/2" pkg(4) **9.99**
272-181413 Light Green Small 2-1/2" pkg(4) **9.99**
272-181416 Medium 4-1/4" pkg(4) **9.99**

272-181453 Large 5-1/2" pkg(2) **11.99**

272-181470 Trees 5" 13cm pkg(14) **29.99**
272-181471 Small 1-3/16 - 2-3/8" pkg(15) **24.99**

272-181488 Small 2-3/8" pkg(6) **9.99**

Fruit 9.99 ea (Unless Noted)
272-181400 Large 4-1/2" Without Fruit pkg(3)
272-181401 Medium 3-1/4" Without Fruit pkg(3)
272-181402 Small 2-1/2" Without Fruit pkg(4)
272-181403 Apple 3-1/4 - 4" pkg(3)
272-181406 Cherry pkg(3)
272-181407 Small 2-1/3" w/Fruit pkg(4)
272-181408 Medium 4-1/4" Rowan w/Fruit pkg(3)
272-181414 Small 1-3/16 - 2-3/8" pkg(5)
272-181445 Fruit Trees 4" 10cm pkg(4) **11.99**

Limited Quantity Available

272-181417 Green Foliage w/Fruit pkg(5) **9.99**
272-181419 Wall Fruit-Small 1-3/16 – 1-5/8" pkg(5) **9.99**

Oak

272-181450 Large 6-5/8" **11.99**
272-181483 Small 4-1/4" pkg(2) **16.99**

Weeping Willow

272-181424 Medium 3-7/8" pkg(2) **11.99**

Birch 9.99 ea (Unless Noted)

272-181423 3-1/2" pkg(4)
272-181422 Medium 4-1/4" pkg(4)

272-181456 Assorted 4-1/2" pkg(3) **8.99**
272-181420 Medium 5-1/8" pkg(3)
272-181457 6-3/4" **11.99**
272-181415 1-3/4" Mini pkg(5) **8.99**
272-181486 Small 2-3/16" pkg(5)

Beech

272-181454 7" 18cm pkg(2) **9.99**

Poplar 9.99 ea (Unless Noted)

272-181421 6" 15cm pkg(4) **15.99**
272-181425 Large 5-1/4" pkg(3)
272-181426 White 5-1/2" pkg(4) **11.99**
272-181460 Black, Medium pkg(4)
272-181487 Small 2-1/2" pkg(5)

Flowering

272-181475 Forsythia – Yellow Flowers pkg(6) **9.99**

Chestnut

272-181463 Large 6-3/4" **11.99**

SCENERY

IMPORTED FROM GERMANY BY WALTHERS

Pine Assortments

272-181440 10 each: 1-1/4, 2 & 2-3/4" pkg(30) **17.99**

272-181461 Silver Firs 2 - 3-5/8" 5-9cm pkg(30) **37.99**

272-181464 Fir, Assorted 4 - 6" 10-15cm pkg(50) **29.99**

272-181465 Fir, Assorted 4-3/4 - 6-1/2" 11.8-16.3cm pkg(25) **23.99**

Evergreens
Blue Spruce

272-181429 Tall Spruce w/Root Detail Each 7-13/64 – 8" 18-20cm Tall pkg(6) **17.99**

272-181432 One Medium 4-1/2" & 2 Large 5-1/2" pkg(3) **9.99**

Tamarack (Large) 9.99 ea
272-181437 Assorted 4-1/2" pkg(3)
272-181438 Small 3-1/2" pkg(4)

Colorado Spruce

272-181439 5 Each: 3-1/2, 4-3/4 & 6" pkg(15) **17.99**

272-181495 Mixed Forest Trees 3-5/8 – 6" 9-15cm Tall pkg(15) **28.99**

Limited Quantity Available
272-181480 pkg(6) **9.99**

Hedges 7.99 ea (Unless Noted)

272-181448 Medium 19" 47.5cm pkg(2)

272-181449 Small 19" 47.5cm pkg(2)
272-181489 Long - pkg(3) **11.99**
20 x 1" 50 x 1 x 2.7cm

Bushes (Shrubs)

272-181474 Assortment pkg(12) **15.99**
272-181476 Red Flowers pkg(6) **9.99**
272-181478 Blooming 1-1/2" 3.8cm pkg(6) **9.99**
272-181479 Green 1-1/2" 3.8cm pkg(6) **9.99**
272-181443 Large Bushes pkg(3) **7.99**

272-181468 Shrubs 1-13/16" 4.5cm Tall pkg(6) **11.99**

Pine 9.99 ea
272-181433 Large Fir 4-1/2" pkg(3)
272-181436 Medium 4" pkg(3)
272-181434 Small Fir 2" pkg(5)
272-181431 Medium Fir 3-3/4" pkg(4)
272-181430 Large Fir 5-1/2" pkg(3)
272-181441 Nordic 5-1/4" pkg(3)

272-181462 Nordic 3" 8cm pkg(4)

See What's New and Exciting at
www.walthers.com

Vines

272-181490 Vineyard w/Poles pkg(36) **17.99**
Complete vineyard with foliage and poles, each about 1-1/4" 3cm tall.

GROUND COVER

Ground Cover Material 120g 3.99 ea
272-170712 Spring Green
272-170713 Forest Green
272-170714 Flowery Meadow

Flock 2.99 ea
Fine .88oz
272-170756 Spring Green
272-170757 Dark Green
Medium .53oz
272-170758 Spring Green
272-170759 Dark Green
Coarse .53oz
272-170760 Spring Green
272-170761 Dark Green
272-170762 Multicolor

Scatter Material
1oz packages.
272-170701 Black **1.99**
272-170702 Spring Green **1.99**
272-170703 Forest Green **1.99**
272-170707 Yellow **1.99**
272-170708 Light Blue **1.99**
272-170709 Flower Red **1.99**
272-170710 Meadow Green **1.99**

272-170717 Flower Decor pkg(6) **10.99**
272-170718 Green Foam pkg(3) **12.99**
272-170727 Dark Brown **5.99**

Grass & Reeds
272-170716 Marsh Reeds pkg(20) **11.99**
272-170725 Grass Fiber **5.99**
272-170726 Grass, Dark Green **5.99**

Lichen
272-170730 5 Assorted Colors 2.8oz **10.99**

Scenery Material Assortments
272-170700 Large Material Assortment **16.99**
Contains six shades of scatter material, two shades of fibers (brown and green), green lichen and green flocks.

272-170735 Winter Scene Making Set **52.99**
Includes enough material to completely cover an area about 39-1/4 x 39-1/4" (100 x 100cm) or three to four houses and some trees. Comes with instructions, six trees, spatula and large and small icicles.

Casting Material
Colored compound for landscape formations, rock castings, etc. One each: brown, gray and ochre.

272-180502 Hydrozell Powder Assortment 3/4oz **9.99**
272-180503 Hydrozell Powder 4-1/2oz **7.99**
Uncolored.

Limited Quantity Available

272-170657 Hydrozell Powder 8-3/4oz **12.99**
Gray, 240g package.

BOOKS

272-190840 Scenic Modeling Made Easy **16.99**
English text, introduction to scenic modeling using Faller materials. Covers initial planning, tools and materials, laying track, dioramas and electrical tips. Over 120 color illustrations, softcover, 35 pages, 8-1/4 x 11-1/2".

SCENERY

FALLER
IMPORTED FROM GERMANY BY WALTHERS

GROUND MATS

Mini Ground Mats pkg(2) 3.99 ea (Unless Noted)

272-180787 Light Green

272-180788 Dark Green

272-180789 Flowery Meadow

272-180791 Wild Grass Light Green

272-180792 Wild Grass Dark Green

272-180793 Cornfield **5.99**

Light Green

272-180766 Small **13.99** 40 x 30" 100 x 75cm
272-180767 Medium **26.99** 40 x 60" 100 x 150cm
272-180769 Large **44.99** 40 x 100" 100 x 250cm

Meadow Green

272-180781 Small **13.99** 40 x 30" 100 x 75cm
272-180782 Medium **26.99** 40 x 60" 100 x 150cm
272-180783 Large **44.99** 40 x 100" 100 x 250cm

Dark Green

272-180770 Small **13.99** 40 x 30" 100 x 75cm
272-180771 Medium **26.99** 40 x 60" 100 x 150cm
272-180773 Large **44.99** 40 x 100" 100 x 250cm

Flowering Meadow

272-180774 Small **13.99** 40 x 30" 100 x 75cm
272-180775 Medium **26.99** 40 x 60" 100 x 150cm
272-180777 Large **44.99** 40 x 100" 100 x 250cm

Grass w/Shaker Applicator 12.99 ea
Makes neat, easy work of applying grass. Includes shaker. Ready for use.
272-170752 Light Green 7oz
272-170753 Dark Green 7oz
272-170754 Meadow Flowers 7oz

Grass Shaker Refills 3-1/2oz 10.99 ea
272-170736 Light Green
272-170737 Dark Green

Soil 1oz 1.99 ea
272-170704 Plowed Field
272-170705 Sand Brown

Coal
272-170723 45g **3.99**

Rocks 2.99 ea

272-170741 Natural Gray 8-3/4oz (250g)

272-170742 Dark Brown (Soil) 8-3/4oz (250g)

272-170745 Quarry Stones - Gray Granite 8-3/4oz (250g)
272-170740 Slate, Natural 8.9oz
272-170743 Slate, Gray 8.9oz
272-170744 Quartz 8.9oz
272-170747 Beach Pebble, Beige 8.9oz

Rock Walls 19.99 ea
Realistic texture and hand-painted to enhance detail. Each section is made of polyurethane foam and is easily cut to fit your layout.

272-170793 Gneiss

272-170794 Stratified Rock

Ballast
272-170706 Gray 1.58oz **1.99**
272-170720 Gravel Brown 1.6oz **3.99**
272-170721 Brown/Gray **3.99**
272-170722 Gravel, Stone Gray **3.99**
272-170731 Dark Brown 10.5oz **7.99**
272-170732 Light Brown 10.5oz **7.99**
272-170751 Track (Brown) 24oz **17.99**
272-180778 Gray Mat **11.99**
Use for yards, parking lots, etc. Measures 40 x 30" 100 x 75cm.

PLASTER CLOTH
A neat and easy way to create hills and other landscapes. Special cloth is pretreated with plaster. Dip in water and apply. Rolls include 80" of cloth.

272-170663 4" Wide **9.99**
272-170664 8" Wide **12.99**

BUILDING MATERIALS

Tunnel Wall Cards pkg (10) 20.99 ea
Cardstock panels are pre-printed in full-color, can be used to simulate rock face inside of tunnel portals.
272-222559 Red Brick
272-222561 Cobblestones
272-222562 Natural Stone
272-222563 Basalt

Stone Sheets pkg(10) 20.99 ea
Cardstock panels are pre-printed in full-color, can be used to simulate rock face.
272-222564 Cut Jura Stone
272-222565 Cut Granite
272-222566 Cut Fieldstone

Wallboards 20.99 ea

272-222567 Natural Stone Ashlars
272-222568 Red Brick

272-222569 Roman Cobblestones

Decorative Sheets 6.99 ea (Unless Noted)

272-272592 Natural Cut Stone
Measures approximately 14-3/4 x 5 x 1/6" 37 x 12.5 x .4cm.

272-272595 Tile/Wall Sill
Measures approximately 14-3/4 x 5 x 1/6" 37 x 12.5 x .4cm.

272-272610 Cobblestone Pavement Sheet pkg(2) 14-3/4 x 5 x .08" 37 x 12.5 x .2cm

272-272651 Stretching Masonry **7.99**

272-272652 Natural Stone Ashlars **7.99**

TUNNEL PORTALS

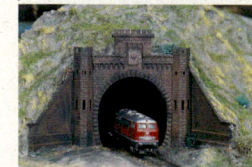
272-272581 Weathered Model **9.99**
8 x 2 x 3-5/8" 20 x 5 x 9cm
Single-track portal with 1.9" 4.8cm clearance.

272-272590 Single **8.99**
5-1/4 x 3 x 1/6" 13 x 7.5 x .4cm

272-272591 Double **10.99**
5-1/4 x 3 x 1/6" 13 x 7.5 x .4cm

272-272630 Single Track - Natural Stone Ashlars **9.99**
5-1/4 x 3 x 1/4" 13 x 7.5 x .5cm

272-272631 Double Track - Natural Stone Ashlars **10.99**
5-1/4 x 3 x 1/4" 13 x 7.5 x .5cm

272-272628 Annexed Rock Wall, Single, Painted/Weathered **19.99**
1-13/16" 4.5cm

272-272629 Annexed Rock Wall, Double, Painted/Weathered **23.99**
1-13/16" 4.5cm

272-272632 Single, Natural Stone w/Corbel Stone **9.99**
5-13/64 x 3 x 2-1/2" 13 x 7.5 x 1cm

SCENERY

FALLER
IMPORTED FROM GERMANY BY WALTHERS

ARCADES
All arcades have a natural stone finish.

272-272600 With Round Arch (gray) **13.99**
14-3/4 x 2-3/8 x 1/3"
37 x 6 x .8cm

272-272601 Ashlars w/Round Arch Right Slope (gray) **20.99**
24 x 3-1/4 x 1/3"
60 x 8 x .8cm

272-272640 Natural Stone Ashlars **14.99**
14-3/4 x 2-3/8 x 1/3"
37 x 6 x .9cm.

272-272642 Profi - Natural Stone Ashlars **20.99**
12 x 2-3/8 x 5/8"
30 x 6 x 1.5cm

272-272602 Ashlars w/Round Arch Left Slope (gray) **20.99**
24 x 3-1/4 x 1/3"
60 x 8 x .8cm

272-272644 w/Pillars, Natural Stone & Corbel Stone **16.99**
12 x 6 x 5/8"   30 x 6 x 1.5cm

GALLERY

272-272641 Profi - Natural Stone Ashlars **17.99**
12 x 2-3/8 x 5/8"
30 x 6 x 1.5cm

ARCHWAYS

272-272594 **13.99**
14-3/4 x 5 x 1/2"
37 x 12.5 x 1.3cm

TUNNEL TUBE

272-272636 Rock Structure **3.99**
7-1/4 x 5 x 1/12"
18 x 12.5 x .2cm

PILLAR

272-272643 Profi - Natural Stone Ashlars **5.99**

WIRE MESH
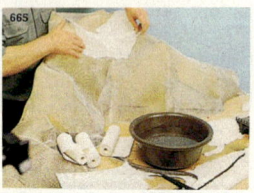
272-170665 Aluminum Screening **24.99**
Flexible and easily formed as a base for mountains, hills and other scenic formations. Measures 40 x 32"
100 x 80cm.

For Up-To-Date Information and News Bookmark Walthers Web site at
www.walthers.com

WATER

272-170791 Lake Construction Kit **13.99**
21-1/4 x 10-1/4" 53 x 26cm
Rippled plastic sheet for realistic wave surface can be painted or use the blue paper (included) for coloring. Easily cut and shaped.

272-272574 Fountain w/Statue **13.99**
1 x 1 x 1-13/16" 2.6 x 2.6 x 3cm
Add detail to any park with this impressive model. Includes fountain and statuary, plus clear plastic "water" jets and surface.

GLUE
Colofix glues are tinted and dry to the color listed. Ideal for use with various shades of ground cover, grass and ballast.

272-170660   272-170661
272-170660 Colofix-Brown 9.2oz **10.99**
272-170661 Colofix-Green 9.2oz **10.99**

272-170662 Colofix-Gray 7.5oz **9.99**
Packaged in a special applicator for use with track.

272-180501 Colofix Wood Compound-White **9.99**
Dries clear and is perfect for applying scenery material.

FILLER MATERIAL

272-170654 Terrain Filler Putty 17.5oz 500g **10.99**
Dark gray powder mixes with water for easy-to-use putty. Make rocks and other terrain, or spread smooth to model roads.

272-170655 Terrain Filler-Brown 17.5oz 500g **10.99**
Realistic brown color is perfect for rock and landscape formations. Material is self-adhesive and easy to use.

272-180500 Filler 500g **11.99**
Build realistic roads and terrain with this self-adhesive, easy-to-use material. Ideal for constructing your own road surfaces for Faller car system.

ROADWAY
Self-adhesive rub on transfers.

Parking Lot 7.99 ea
Each measures 4 x 1-5/8"
10 x 4cm.
272-222537 Straight Parking Space Markings

Roads
Each Measures 4 x 1-5/8"
10 x 4cm.

Two-Lane Highway
Self-adhesive sections are printed in full color, ready to use. Items can be mixed and matched, or easily cut to fit.

Asphalt
272-222534 Two-Lane Asphalt Highway w/White Lines **7.99**
272-222535 Two-Lane Asphalt Highway - Unmarked **6.99**

272-222552 Two-Lane 90° Curves pkg(4) **11.99**

272-222553 Two-Lane Intersection w/Sidewalks **7.99**
5-13/16 x 5-13/16"
14.5 x 14.5 cm, use with #222552 or 222554 (sold separately).

272-222554 Two-Lane Straight w/Sidewalks **8.99**
40" Long, 2-5/16" Wide 100 x 5.8 cm, matches #222553 or 222554 (sold separately).

Concrete
Each roll measures 40 x 1-5/8" 100 x 4cm.

272-222556 White Edge & Center Lines **7.99**

272-222558 Plain-No Markings **6.99**

272-222557 90° Curves w/White Edge & Center Lines pkg(4) **11.99**

SCENERY

IMPORTED FROM GERMANY BY WALTHERS

Cobblestone Pavement
Self-adhesive material with realistic color.

272-170646 Square **13.99**
Measures 19-3/16 x 9-5/8"
48 x 24cm.

272-170647 Arch **9.99**
Measures 4 x 2-13/16"
10 x 7cm.

272-222532 Small Stones-Arch **6.99**
Measures 4 x 1-1/2"
10 x 4cm.

272-222536 Roman Paving Stones **6.99**

Sidewalks

272-272540 Set Of Sidewalk Tiles w/Curbstone Strips **10.99**
Tiles: 2-13/32 x 3-1/2
6 x 8.7cm / Curbstone Strips: 66-13/32" 166cm

Markings

272-272539 Self-Adhesive Roadway Markings **5.99**

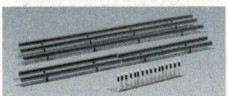

272-272541 Crash Barriers & 40 Marker Posts **12.99**
34-13/32" 86cm

TRAFFIC SIGNS

272-272538 **24.99**
Includes international traffic signs, place names, directional signs, traffic lights, parking meters and waste baskets.

Background Scene 272-180511

Background Scene 272-180512

Background Scene 272-180513

Background Scene 272-180514

Background Scene 272-180515

Background Scene 272-180516

Background Scene 272-180517

FENCES

272-272528 Rough Board Picket Style **11.99**
16" 40cm

272-272527 Fencing pkg(8) **12.99**
Each section measures 4-5/64" 10.2cm long.

272-272524 Bonanza Fence **12.99**
Fence made of rough-cut boards. Total length: 37-1/4" 93.2cm.

PAINT
Water-based acrylic paint can be thinned with water.

272-170796 Granite Rock Paint 3.5oz 118ml **13.99**

272-180507 Roadway Paint 7.5oz 250ml **10.99**
Realistic asphalt color for highways, parking lots, driveways or other paved surfaces.

Item listed below is available by Special Order (see Legend Page).
272-170797 Sand Ground Paint 3.5oz 118ml **13.99**
Perfect for country roads, beaches or other sandy areas.

SCENE DETAILS

272-232208 Dumpster Set pkg(8) **13.99**

272-232211 Recycling Containers pkg(36) **23.99**
Set includes six dumpsters and 30 bins for glass.

272-272537 **9.99**
Includes casks, barrels, planks and wooden cases.

IRON RAILING

272-272526 pkg(12) **11.99**
Total length: 39-27/32" 99.6cm.

WATER PUMP

272-180627 Water Pump & Accessories **39.99**
Pump real water anywhere on your layout. Includes 12-16V AC electric pump, 36" (90cm) PVC hose and two connecting pieces, plus detailed instructions.

BACKGROUND SCENES
Each scene is a full color photo, printed on several paper panels.

272-180511 Black Forest-Baar Extension **41.99**
Set of four panels can be used to enlarge #180514 (sold separately) to the right or left as desired. 155-3/16 x 26" (388 x 65cm) total length. Panels can be used alone.

272-180512 "Neuschwanstein" **31.99**
2 sections, totaling 10'-8" x 40" 320 x 100cm.

272-180513 "Karwendelgebirge" **31.99**
2 sections, totaling 10'-8" x 40" 320 x 100cm.

272-180514 Schwarzwald-Baar **41.99**
4 sections totaling 12'-9" x 26" 388 x 65cm.

272-180515 "Lowenstein" **31.99**
3 sections totaling 9'-8" x 17-3/4" 290 x 45cm.

272-180516 "Oberstdorf" **31.99**
3 sections totaling 9'-8" x 17-3/4" 290 x 45cm.

272-180517 Oberstdorf Expander Scene **31.99**
Three part expander scene use with #180516 to increase over-all length to about six yards (5.8 meters).

MOLDING MATERIALS

Casting Resin w/Catalyst
Water clear, shelf life of approximately nine months, (longer if stored at cool temperatures.)
207-34016 16oz **17.10**
207-34032 32oz **23.95**
207-34128 1gal **65.55**

EasyCast
Two part, low odor clear casting epoxy. Compatible with transparent dyes.
207-33008 8oz **9.49**
207-33016 16oz **15.69**
207-33032 32oz **25.69**
207-33128 1gal **78.70**

Casting Resin
Less catalyst.
207-175 16oz **13.70**
207-183 32oz **20.35**
207-191 1gal **61.80**
207-46388 Catalyst 1/2oz **4.09**
Needed to cure (harden) resin, for use with #s 175, 183 and 191.
207-46361 Catalyst 1oz **4.45**
Needed to cure (harden) resin, for use with #s 175, 183 and 191.

Envirotex Lite
Pour-on plastic material dries to a hard, clear finish.
207-2007 4oz **6.40**
207-2008 8oz **9.49**
207-2016 16oz **15.69**
207-2032 1qt **25.69**
207-2064 1/2gal **46.45**
207-2128 1gal **78.70**

Liquid Latex Rubber
207-779 Mold Builder 16oz **10.35**
For mold making.

Mixing Cup Set
207-1013 **5.95**
6 disposable cups, stirring paddles and 3 craft brushes.

Polymer Coatings
Simply mix, measure and pour these decoupage resins to create realistic water. Low odor, low heat and nonflammable. Includes resin and hardener.
207-27 Ultra-Glo 8oz **9.49**
207-35 Ultra-Glo 16oz **15.69**

Transparent Dye 1oz 4.79 ea
Add for see-through color in resin.
207-46430 Blue
207-46432 Green
207-46436 Amber
207-46440 Pearl

SCENERY

IMPRESS MOTHER NATURE WITH YOUR SCENERY SKILLS

Now, building realistic scenery for your layout is as simple as opening a box! With the complete line of assembled materials from Grand Central Gems, it's a snap to create superdetailed scenes quickly and easily.

Whether you need a city park, a new subdivision or a mountain hillside, check out this unique line of hand-made trees. Assembled from the finest natural materials with authentic colors and textures, the selection includes trees from many parts of the US. Affordably priced and offered in a wide range of sizes to fit most popular scales, the finished models are incredibly realistic, making them ideal for layouts, dioramas, seasonal or holiday displays, school projects, craft projects, dioramas and much more.

With the new selection of trestle parts, you can build custom bridges that look exactly like the real thing! Preassembled from real wood and stained with a realistic creosote color, the various parts can be arranged as needed to build virtually any size of wooden trestle.

And realistic rock formations are easily modeled with one-piece molds, available in three convenient sizes.

Check out the complete selection!

Grand Central Gems inc.

Grand Central Gems inc.

NEW PRODUCTS

Trees
Perfect for foreground scenes, dioramas and displays, these trees are hand-made from natural materials to capture the correct shape, foliage and colors of actual trees. Fully assembled and ready to install, several different types are available in a wide range of sizes, suitable for most scales.

Spruce   Pine

Pines
Medium - 5" Tall
NEW 295-T1 pkg(20) 20.00
NEW 295-T4 pkg(4) 5.00
Large - 7" Tall
NEW 295-T2 pkg(10) 15.00
NEW 295-T5 pkg(3) 5.00
Larger - 9" Tall
NEW 295-T8 pkg(7) 20.00
Small - 3" Tall
NEW 295-T3 pkg(50) 38.00
NEW 295-T6 pkg(6) 5.00
Extra Large - 11" Tall
NEW 295-T7 pkg(3) 15.00

Spruce
NEW 295-T9 Medium - 5" Tall pkg(20) 20.00

Aspens

Medium - 5-7" Tall
NEW 295-T10 pkg(4) 16.00
NEW 295-T11 pkg(10) 35.00
Small - 2-4" Tall
NEW 295-T12 pkg(15) 30.00

Fall Aspens

Medium - 5-7" Tall
NEW 295-T13 pkg(4) 16.00
NEW 295-T14 pkg(10) 35.00
Small - 2-4" Tall
NEW 295-T15 pkg(15) 30.00

Oaks

Medium - 5-7" Tall
NEW 295-T16 pkg(4) 16.00
NEW 295-T17 pkg(4) 35.00
Small - 2-4" Tall
NEW 295-T18 pkg(15) 30.00

Fall Oaks

Medium - 5-7" Tall
NEW 295-T19 pkg(4) 16.00
NEW 295-T20 pkg(10) 35.00
Small - 2-4" Tall
NEW 295-T21 pkg(15) 30.00

Fruit Trees
Small - 3-5" Tall pkg(5) 30.00 ea

95-T222   95-T23
NEW 295-T22 Orange
NEW 295-T23 Apple

NEW 295-T24 Grapefruit

Palms

Medium - 5-7" Tall pkg(2) 20.00 ea
NEW 295-T25 Mexican Palm
NEW 295-T26 Fan Palm

Juniper Pines
NEW 295-T27 Small - 2-4" Tall pkg(15) 20.00

Sage Oaks

Summer 30.00 ea
NEW 295-T28 Small - 3-4" Tall pkg(5)
NEW 295-T29 Medium - 5-7" Tall pkg(3)
NEW 295-T30 Large - 8-10" Tall pkg(2)
NEW 295-T31 Extra-Large - 11-12" Tall

Fall 30.00 ea
NEW 295-T32 Small - 3-4" Tall pkg(5)
NEW 295-T33 Medium - 5-7" Tall pkg(3)
NEW 295-T34 Large - 8-10" Tall pkg(2)
NEW 295-T35 Extra-Large - 11-12" Tall

Lodgepole Pine Trees 30.00 ea

NEW 295-T36 Small - 3-5" Tall pkg(5)
NEW 295-T37 Medium - 5-7" Tall pkg(3)
NEW 295-T38 Large - 10-12" Tall pkg(2)
NEW 295-T39 Extra-Large - 18-22" Tall

Rock Molds
Add realistic rock cliffs, walls and other formations to your scenery with these one-piece rubber molds.

NEW 295-RM1 Small 10.00
NEW 295-RM2 Medium 15.00
NEW 295-RM3 Large 20.00

SCENERY

TREES

Tree Assortments 23.99 ea

Assortments include Shade, Birch, Cedar, Oak, Ash, Maple, Evergreen, Juniper, Fir, Forest Pine and Hedgerows. Each assortment includes trees in various heights (as noted) which can be used in any scale. Trees are fully assembled, with plastic trunks and realistic foam foliage.

338-301 Small Trees 1-1/2 - 3-1/2" pkg(40)

338-302 Small Trees 2 - 3-1/2" pkg(40)

338-303 Medium Trees 2-1/2 - 4" pkg(30)

338-304 Medium Trees 3-5" pkg(24)

338-305 Medium Trees 2-1/2 - 5" pkg(12)

338-306 Small Pines 2 - 3-1/2" pkg(30)

338-307 Large Pines 4-7" pkg(12)

338-308 Large Trees 4-7" pkg(12)

338-309 Small Pines 1-1/2 - 3" pkg(100)
An entire forest in a single set! Great for use by themselves, or combine with larger trees to model a variety of scenes. Pines are fully assembled, ready for use on your layout.

HIGHBALL PRODUCTS

GROUND COVER

Ballast

N Scale 1lb 5.99 ea
330-120 Limestone
330-121 Light Gray
330-122 Dark Gray
330-123 Black
330-124 Cinder
330-125 Brown

HO Scale 1lb 5.99 ea
Genuine limestone.

330-220 Limestone
330-221 Light Gray
330-222 Dark Gray
330-223 Black
330-224 Cinder
330-225 Brown
330-226 Light Gray/Dark Gray Blend

HO Scale 5lbs 29.95 ea
330-2205 Limestone
330-2215 Light Gray
330-2225 Dark Gray
330-2235 Black
330-2245 Cinder
330-2255 Brown
330-2265 Light Gray/Dark Gray Blend

Coal 7.95 ea

330-130 Stoker 1-3" 14oz
330-131 Egg 2-5" 14oz
330-132 Lump-Over 6" 14oz
330-134 Dust 5oz

Grass 3oz 7.95 ea
Regular and electrostatic, can be used in Noch grass applicator #528-5018, sold separately.

330-160 Green - Regular - Static
330-161 Light Green - Regular - Static
330-162 Green - Fine
330-163 Light Green - Fine
330-164 Moss Green - Regular - Static

Earth 3oz 7.95 ea

330-172 Dark Brown - Regular
330-170 Light Brown - Regular
330-171 Light Brown - Fine
330-173 Dark Brown - Fine
330-174 Top Soil
330-175 Red

Scenic Rock 1lb 7.95 ea
330-150 Sand-White
330-151 Stone
330-152 Small Stone
330-153 Iron Ore
330-154 Sand-Brown

Miscellaneous
330-400 Sawdust Pack 4oz **19.95**
Six assorted packs of sawdust.
330-510 Dirt 12oz **7.95**
Real dirt, specially processed for model scenery.
330-520 Gravel 1lb **7.95**

kibri

IMPORTED FROM GERMANY BY WALTHERS

ACCESSORY PACKS

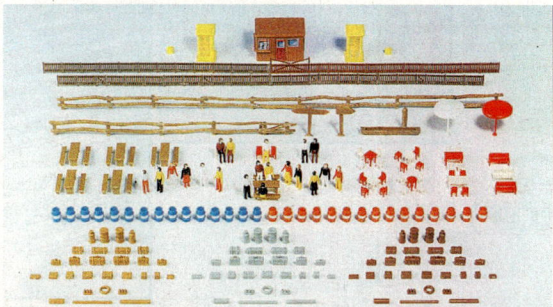

405-7490 w/Figures **23.99**
Figures are molded in color and can be converted to different poses. Set includes admission stand, picket fence, log fence, picnic tables and chairs, umbrellas, barrels and assorted freight.

405-7530 Baggage Wagon Assortment Kit **27.99**
Molded in appropriately colored plastic.

FENCES
405-7324 Fencing w/Gates **15.99**
7-1/2"
405-7480 **18.99**
405-7225 Fencing w/Gates **15.99**
92" 230cm

FLOWERS
405-7494 Assorted Flowers & Window Boxes pkg(8) **7.99**

ROCKS

405-4112 pkg(10) **26.99**
Gray molded plastic.

SIDEWALK
405-7963 **5.99**

TUNNEL PORTALS
405-7900 2-Track pkg(2) **10.99**
405-7902 1-Track pkg(2) **6.99**

WATER

405-4126 **5.99**
Sheet measures 5 x 8".

Latest New Product News Daily! Visit Walthers Web site at
www.walthers.com

SCENERY

Add a finishing touch of realism to your railroad scenes with these detailed, one-piece castings. Each is hand-cast from a very strong gypsum material that picks up fine details much like dental plaster. Items are hand-painted to bring out the many realistic details. (Note: all photos show HO Scale models.)

Coal Trestle 506-1010

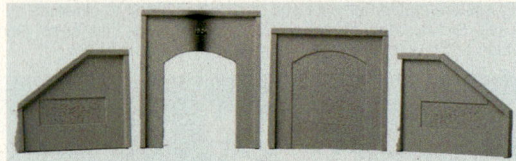
Concrete Tunnel Portal & Wing Walls 506-2100

Red Brick & Stone Culverts 506-1330

Gray Brick & Stone Culverts 506-1331

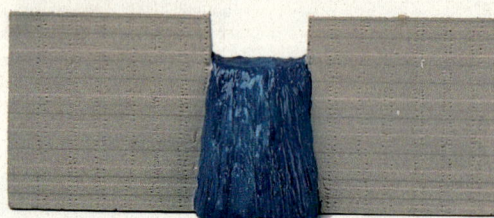
Dam 506-1370

Track Bumper 506-1320

Dam
506-1370 Concrete w/Flowing Water **6.47**

Footings

506-2150 Concrete pkg(4) **5.38**
Designed for use with Micro Engineering Viaduct kits, sold separately.

Pilings

506-1780 Dolphin (Waterfront Pole) Type **5.27**

Retaining Walls 6.47 ea

506-980

506-990

506-1350

506-980 Stone pkg(2)
506-990 Railroad Tie Type pkg(2)
506-1350 Pier Type

Track Bumpers

506-1310 End of Track Poured Concrete – Pennsylvania Prototype pkg(5) **6.46**
506-1320 Heavy Timber & Ballast Type pkg(2) **5.38**

Round Brick Industrial Chimneys 20.51 ea
One-piece casting eliminates problems of hiding seams so common with multiple-piece plastic and resin kits. Great detail for any small industry. These very thin profile chimneys are typical of designs used throughout New England on mills and other industries.
506-1460 Red
506-1470 Yellow

Oil Storage Tanks 6.47 ea
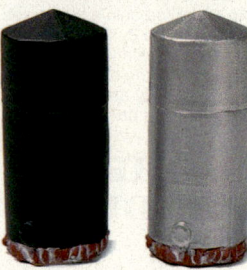
506-1730   506-1731

Vertical oil tanks are ideal for modeling smalltown oil distributors, railroad water or oil storage tanks or as a detail alongside most large industries.
506-1730 Black
506-1731 Silver

Loading Ramps
506-1000 Ramp & Dock Set **10.78**
Includes one concrete End-of-Track Ramp and one Wood and Stone Loading Dock. Perfect for detailing yard scenes, smalltown sidings or industrial areas.

Coal Trestle
506-1010 Coal Unloading Ramp **10.78**
Trestle-style ramp with realistic coal pile detail. Great for a smalltown coal yard or as an unloading ramp for a large steam-era industry.

Tree Stumps

506-1 Tiny, Assorted Sizes pkg(14) **5.39**

Matching Concrete Tunnel Portal & Wing Walls 6.47 ea
Ideal for use with Tunnel Portal (#506-2110, sold separately) and easily adapted to other portals to build a realistic structure.
506-2100 Straight
506-2120 Left, Angled
506-2130 Right, Angled
506-2110 Single Track Concrete Portal
Use by itself, or combine with Concrete Wing Walls (#506-2100, 2120 and 2130, all sold separately) to create a realistic scene.

Brick & Stone Culverts
506-1330 Red pkg(2) **16.19**
506-1331 Gray pkg(2) **16.19**

MICRO ENGINEERING

Fence
255-80145 Wooden Fence Kit pkg(2) **3.60**

NEW LONDON INDUSTRIES

Background Scene Stencils 9.98 ea
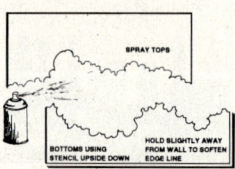

Create a unique background scene. Stencils are cut from heavy cardstock and can be used over and over. May be used for various scales. Includes instructions.
519-1 The Clouds pkg(4)
519-2 The Mountains pkg(4)
519-3 The City pkg(4)
519-4 The Details pkg(2)
Two fine-cut cloud stencils, ideal for adding extra detail to #519-1 and for smaller scales near the horizon.
519-5 The Hills pkg(4)
519-6 The Mountains II

Scenery Video
519-10 "The Sky's the Limit" **19.98**
Explains and demonstrates the techniques of making a background scene using stencils.

SCENERY

NEW PRODUCTS

Scene Accessories
15.50 ea

NEW 490-1330 Car Station Set Includes 10 automobiles, six handpainted station figures and six handpainted railroad crew figures.

NEW 490-1339 Park Scenes Includes six handpainted figures, four benches, one telephone booth, three fire hydrants, three mailboxes and three trash cans.

Trees 17.99 ea
Trees measure 1-3/4 x 3-3/4"
4.4 x 9.4cm high, unless noted.
490-1410 Medium Green, Spring pkg(18)
491-1412 Dark Green Summer pkg(18)
490-1414 Green, Pine, Winter pkg(18)
490-1416 Rust, Autumn pkg(18)
490-1425 Evergreen 5-1/2" 14cm pkg(15)

Ground Cover
490-172 Grass Mat 54 x 99" **21.98**
490-1430 Green Lichen 12oz **3.98**
490-1431 Grass & Mixed Colors 12oz **3.98**

Fences 54" 6.98 ea
490-1560 White Picket
490-1561 Iron

Tunnels
490-4370 Straight **22.00** 6-2/5 x 4"
490-4371 Curved **31.00** 10 x 10"

Monroe Models produces this series of scenery accessories made from plastic resin. Each is prepainted for faster detailing of any N Scale layout.

LOADING RAMPS

493-9105 Railroad Loading Ramps pkg(2) **10.79**
3-3/4 x 7/8 x 7/16"

These pre-painted and weathered resin loading ramps are ready to be installed on your layout. One each concrete-style and wood-style ramp included.

JUNK PILES
Designed for use in any scrap yard.

493-9101 Large **8.79**

493-9102 Medium **7.49**
493-9104 Junk Pile Set **14.99** Includes one each large and medium junk pile, along with a scrap metal gondola load.

FREIGHT CAR LOADS

493-9103 Scrap Metal pkg(2) **7.49**
Loads are 3/4 full, for use with most gondolas.

New Rail Models

Scenic Accessories
New Rail Models laser-cut wood kits make detailing your scenes quick and easy. Each includes unpainted laser-cut wood parts unless noted.

501-32001 Picnic Tables pkg(4) **6.95**

501-32002 Benches & Trash Receptacles (4 of Each) **6.95**

501-32008 Plywood Loads (Stacks) pkg(20) **12.95**

501-32009 4 x 8 Plywood Sheets pkg(40). (Truck sold separately) **4.95**

Ultra Shingles™

501-32005 Shake Shingles pkg(4) **6.95**
Peel-and-stick roofing sheets give the appearance of authentic shake shingles without having to apply separate shingle strips. Each sheet measures 24 x 53 scale feet.

Info, Images, Inspiration! Get It All at
www.walthers.com

NuComp Miniatures

NEW PRODUCTS
Vintage Campground

NEW 534-60151 **110.00**
Everyone needs a place to relax and this vintage campground provides a peaceful vacation spot for your layout. Kit includes five camping trailers, five cars, a garage, a tool shed, two pop machines, two outhouses, four pup tents, eight fire rings and two picnic tables.

Campground Details

NEW 534-60198 Fire Rings pkg(8) **5.00**
Smoke and fire not included.

NEW 534-60199 Pup Tents pkg (4) **6.00**

NEW 534-60200 Outhouse **5.00**

1950s-Era Junk Yard

534-60350 **74.95**
10 x 8"

Turn any unused area into a detailed scene with this complete kit that's typical of salvage yards in rural and big city areas. Includes Tool Shed, Garage, two lawn mowers, two pop machines, fencing with posts, and unpainted resin castings for the trailer home/office, vehicles, doghouse, tire piles, and an assortment of other junk.

Scene Details
534-60204 2 Lawn Mowers & Pop Machines **4.00**
534-60205 Tree Stumps pkg(12) **3.00**
534-60504 Lawn Mowers pkg(2) **2.00**
534-60505 Pop Machines pkg(2) **2.00**

SCENERY

IMPORTED FROM GERMANY BY WALTHERS

NEW PRODUCTS

Trees

Fruit pkg(3) 10.99 ea
NEW **528-25511** Fruit w/White Blossoms 1.7" 4.5cm
NEW **528-25513** Apple 1.7" 4.5cm

Poplar
NEW **528-25525** 2-5/32" 5.5cm pkg(3) **11.99**

Deciduous

NEW **528-32501** 2-3/8 - 3-1/2" 6-9cm pkg(25) **24.99**

Forest
NEW **528-32511** Mixed 2-3/8 - 3-1/2" 6-9cm pkg(25) **24.99**

Tree Assortments

NEW **528-32516** Spring Trees 2-3/8 - 3-1/2" 6-9cm pkg(25) **25.99**
NEW **528-32521** Fir Trees 1-9/16 - 3-15/16" 4-10cm pkg(50) **41.99**

NEW **528-32526** Spruce Trees 1-9/16 - 3-15/16" 4-10cm pkg(50) **44.99**

NEW **528-32601** Deciduous Trees 2-3/8 - 3-1/2" 6-9cm pkg(10) **10.99**
NEW **528-32606** Spring Trees 2-3/8 - 3-1/2" 6-9cm pkg(10) **10.99**

NEW **528-32611** Mixed 2-3/8 - 3-1/2" 6-9cm pkg(10) **10.99**

Ground Cover

Large Grass Mats
78-3/4 x 39-3/8" 200 x 100cm

NEW **528-10** Spring **30.99**

Reed Assortment

NEW **528-7060** Green, Beige, Brown **11.99**

Wild Grass

NEW **528-7070** Field & Wild Grass Assortment w/Glue pkg(11) **34.99**

Field Grass 1-1/2oz 42.5g 9.99 ea
Grass in approximately 3/16" .5cm tall.

NEW **528-7082** Light Green

NEW **528-7084** Mid Green

NEW **528-7086** Ochre

NEW **528-7088** Golden Brown

Flower Petals
NEW **528-7170** Heath, Poppy, Dandelion, White **11.99**

Meadow Flora
NEW **528-7172** Olive, Green, Light Brown, Reddish Brown **11.99**

Classic Flocking 20g .07oz 4.99 ea
NEW **528-7302** Light Green
NEW **528-7304** Mid Green
NEW **528-7306** Dark Green

Classic Foliage 11.99 ea
Covers approximately 9-1/2 x 5-7/8" 24 x 15cm

NEW **528-7312** Light Green

NEW **528-7314** Mild Green

NEW **528-7316** Dark Green

Styro-Flex Walls & Tunnel Portals

Sandstone Walls

NEW **528-34874** 7-13/16 x 2-29/32" 19.8 x 7.4cm **7.99**
NEW **528-34875** Extra Long 15-19/32 x 2-29/32" 39.6 x 7.4cm **15.99**

For Daily Product Updates Point Your Browser to
www.walthers.com

Nature Trees Kit 528-23100

Sandstone Retaining Walls

NEW **528-34876** 7-13/16 x 2-29/32" 19.8 x 7.4cm **8.99**
NEW **528-34877** Extra Long 15-19/32 x 2-29/32" 39.6 x 7.4cm **17.99**

Sandstone Arcade Walls

NEW **528-34878** 7-13/16 x 2-29/32" 19.8 x 7.4cm **8.99**
NEW **528-34879** Extra Long 15-19/32 x 2-29/32" 39.6 x 7.4cm **17.99**

Sandstone Tunnel Portals
Catenary compatible.

NEW **528-34871** Single Track 3-1/8 x 3" 7.9 x 7.6cm **7.99**

NEW **528-34872** Double Track 4-27/32 x 3-11/32" 12.3 x 8.5cm **8.99**

Fences
NEW **528-33095** Rural Fences 67" 170cm **15.99**
NEW **528-33096** Garden Fences 59" 150cm **15.99**

Scenic Accessories

NEW **528-35847** Park Benches pkg(6) **8.99**

Plasters
35.3oz 1000g 17.99 ea
Textured and colored spackling plaster simulates stone when used in rock castings. Cures in 15min.
NEW **528-60882** Granite
NEW **528-60892** Sandstone

Water
NEW **528-60872** Water Effects 4.2oz 125ml **10.99**

TREES

Nature Trees Kit
528-23100 Assorted Sizes **18.99**

Deciduous
Item listed below is available by Special Order (see Legend Page).

Ash

528-21650 Mountain Ash ("Bird Berry") 4-5/8" **6.99**

SCENERY

IMPORTED FROM GERMANY BY WALTHERS

Birch

528-21640 4" **6.99**
528-21690 5-3/16" **10.99**

Blossom

528-21710 Nut 5-1/2" **10.99**

Chestnut
528-21800 7-3/4" **11.99**

Spruce

528-25440 1-3/8 & 2-3/8" 3.5 & 6cm pkg(5) **10.99**

Fruit 6.99 ea (Unless Noted)

528-21550 Green 3"
528-21560 Apple w/Fruit 3"

528-21570 Blooming 3"
528-21580 Cherry 3"
528-21600 Pear - Green 4-1/2"
528-21780 Lime Tree 7-1/4" **11.99**

Oak

528-21760 6-1/4" **10.99**

Palm (Boxed)

528-21971 5-7/8" 15cm **13.99**
528-21981 7-5/8" 19cm **15.99**

Poplar
528-21680 4-3/4" **6.99**

Conifers

528-25435 Black Pine 3-3/8 & 4-3/8" 8.5 & 11cm pkg(5) **10.99**

Pine
528-32528 Assorted Winter Pines 1-3/8 to 4" 3.5-10cm pkg(25) **25.99**

Fir
528-21880 6-3/4" **11.99**
528-21890 8-3/4" **13.99**
528-32520 6-10cm pkg(25) **23.99**
528-25430 1-3/8 & 2-3/8" 3.5 & 6cm pkg(5) **10.99**

Tree Assortments
528-32525 Spruces 1-13/32 - 4" 3.5-10cm Tall pkg(25) **25.99**

528-32620 Fir Trees 1-3/8 - 3-7/8" 3.5-10cm pkg(10) **10.99**
528-32625 Spruce Trees 1-3/8 - 3-7/8" 3.5-10cm pkg(10) **10.99**

Item listed below is available by Special Order (see Legend Page).
528-32540 Long Stem Firs 3-5/8 - 6" 9-15cm Tall pkg(25) **23.99**

HEDGES
All hedges measure 19-5/8" 50cm long.

Light Green   Dark Green   Dark Red

5/8 x 3/8" 1.5 x .8cm; pkg(2) 8.99 ea
528-21512 Light Green
528-21514 Dark Green
528-21516 Dark Red

3/8 x 1/4" 1 x .6cm; pkg(2) 8.99 ea
528-21522 Light Green
528-21524 Dark Green
528-21526 Dark Red

GROUND COVER

Leaves 1-3/4oz 50g 4.99 ea

528-7142
528-7140 Olive Green
528-7142 Light Green
528-7144 Medium Green
528-7146 Dark Green
528-7148 Yellow
528-7149 Red

Palm Trees 528-21971

528-21880   528-21890

Wild Grass 1-3/4oz 50g 9.99 ea

528-7101 Beige

528-7102 Light Green

528-7106 Dark Green

Foliage
Measures 9-5/8 x 6" 24 x 15cm.

Wild Grass 11.99 ea
528-7121 Beige
528-7122 Light Green
528-7126 Dark Green

Leaf 10.99 ea
528-7160 Olive Green

528-7162 Light Green
528-7164 Medium Green
528-7166 Dark Green

Flock 10.99 ea

Limited Quantity Available
528-7280 Olive Green
528-7282 Light Green
528-7284 Medium Green
528-7286 Dark Green

159

SCENERY

IMPORTED FROM GERMANY BY WALTHERS

Flock 20g 4.99 ea

Olive Green

Light Green

528-280 Summer Meadow 24 x 48"

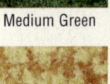
Medium Green

Dark Green

Snow

Beige

Light Brown

528-8750 Powdered 8-3/4oz 9.99

Snow Crystals

Medium

Dark Brown

Fine
528-7200 Olive Green
528-7204 Medium Green
528-7206 Dark Green
528-7221 Beige
528-7223 Light Brown
528-7225 Medium Brown
528-7227 Dark Brown

Item listed below is available by Special Order (see Legend Page).
528-7202 Light Green

528-61164 4-1/2oz 150ml 11.99

Static Grass
3/8oz 2.99 ea
528-8300 Spring Green
528-8310 Light Green
528-8320 Dark Green
528-8330 Flowering Meadow
528-8340 Brown

3-1/2oz 10.99 ea

Medium
Limited Quantity Available
528-7240 Olive Green
528-7242 Light Green
528-7244 Medium Green
528-7246 Dark Green
528-7261 Beige
528-7263 Light Brown
528-7265 Medium Brown
528-7267 Dark Brown

528-50190 Light Green
528-50200 Dark Green
528-50210 Spring Green

Terrain Mat Surfacer
528-60920 500g 8.99

Static Grass Applicators

Grass Mats 11.99 ea (Unless Noted)
Ready-to-use mats are available in many colors and textures to simulate natural ground cover. Grass mats are made with static grass, so that the blades are standing.

528-110 Spring 29 x 40"
528-120 Summer 29 x 40"

528-230 Dark Green Meadow 24 x 48"

528-240 Meadow 24 x 48"

528-8100 Dispenser Bottle 5.99
Hand-held bottle with sprinkler opening, allows for precise application in small area. Can be used with various materials.

528-61130 Cement for Grass 7-1/2oz (250ml) 9.99

528-8099 Multi-Purpose Applicator For Leaves & Grass 3.99

Prairie Grass Pads
Limited Quantity Available

528-6208 Corn-Poppy Meadow 11.99
10-5/8 x 5-1/8" 27 x 13cm

Scatter Material
Forest
528-8350 3/4oz 3.99
Combination of materials, ideal for blending with grass mats and other scenery.

Lichen

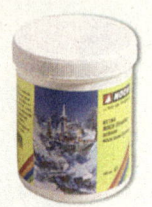

528-8630

Single Packs 1oz 3.99 ea
528-8600 Stone Gray
528-8610 Assorted Green
528-8630 Autumn Assorted

Double Packs 2-3/4oz 6.99 ea
528-8620 Autumn
528-8621 Light & Dark Green

Scatter Material
1.4oz Packs 1.99 ea
528-8400 Flower Red
528-8410 Light Green
528-8420 Dark Green
528-8440 Brown
528-8450 Mountain Grass
528-8460 Gray
528-8470 Forest

Get the Scoop!
Get the Skinny!
Get the Score!
Check Out Walthers Web site at
www.walthers.com

528-60130 Gras-Master® 129.99
For Static Grass

6.3oz Packs 5.99 ea
Each color comes in a reclosable plastic bag for easy storage.
528-8401 Summer Flowers
528-8411 Alpine Meadow (Light Green)
528-8421 Dark Green
528-8441 Brown
528-8461 Gray

Water

528-60850 Sea Mat 16-1/2 x 10-3/4" 9.99
528-60851 Sea Mat 30 x 20" 23.99

528-60855 Water-Drops® 17.99 Clear 8oz 250g

528-60856 Water-Drops 25.99 8oz clear, 1oz ea: blue, green & brown

528-60860 Wild Water Set 11.99
Includes 1-3/4oz multi-colored pebbles and 1.6 floz bottle each: blue paint and transparent blue gloss.

528-60870 2K Water Gel 2 Components, 3.3oz ea 34.99
528-60875 Riverbed Color Set 17.99
3.3oz Neutral Acrylic, .3oz Concentrated blue, green & brown

ROADS
528-34130 Parking Lot pkg(2) 9.99
8-1/8 x 4" 20.5 x 10cm
Preprinted with lines and graphics.

528-34150 Flexible Road 8.99
39 x 1-1/8" 1m x 2.8cm
With shoulder and center lines in white.

Flexible Roadways
Precolored material in a variety of authentic colors and surfaces to create custom roads. Each measures 39 x 1-1/8" 1m x 2.8cm, unless noted.

528-34070 Cobblestones 8.99
528-34072 Bike Path pkg(2) 8.99
528-34080 Country Path 6.99
528-34090 Highway 8.99
528-34100 Roadway 8.99
528-34170 Cobblestone Sheets 8 x 4" 20 x 10cm pkg(2) 9.99
528-34200 Highway Asphalt 40 x 1-5/8" 100 x 4cm 7.99
528-34201 Highway Curve Asphalt 1-5/8" 100 x 4cm pkg(2) 9.99
528-34203 Highway (gray) 40 x 1-5/8" 4cm 7.99
528-34204 Highway Curve (gray) 1-5/8" 4cm pkg(2) 9.99
528-34222 Cobblestone w/Arch Pattern 7.99
528-34224 Cobblestone w/Arch Pattern Sheets 8 x 4" 10.99

SCENERY

IMPORTED FROM GERMANY BY WALTHERS

WALLS

Arcade
528-34942 Quarrystone
7-1/2 x 3-1/2" 19 x 9cm **6.99**

528-37948 Open Arcade Wall Gray **14.99**
8-5/16 x 2-45/64" 21 x 7cm

528-37950 Arcade Wall Gray **17.99**
8-5/16 x 2-45/64" 21 x 7cm

528-37946 Arcade Wall Round Arch Gray **14.99**
8-5/16 x 2-45/64" 21 x 7cm

528-37966 Arcade Wall Round Arch Beige **14.99**
8-5/16 x 2-45/64" 21 x 7cm

528-37968 Open Arcade Wall Beige **14.99**
8-5/16 x 2-45/64" 21 x 7cm

528-37970 Arcade Wall Beige **17.99**
8-5/16 x 2-45/64" 21 x 7cm

Styro-Flex
These light-weight, ultra-thin, plastic foam walls are ideal for all types of scenery and scratchbuilding. Each panel features realistic three-dimensional surfaces, with authentic colors and textures molded in place. Easily cut to any shape or size using scissors or hobby knife, they're perfect for customizing your right-of-way. Each wall measures 9-5/8 x 5-5/8" 24 x 14cm.

528-37944 Wall (gray) **6.99**
8-13/64 x 2-45/64" 21 x 7cm

528-37964 Wall (beige) **6.99**
8-13/64 x 2-45/64" 21 x 7cm

Arcades
528-34858 Arcade Wall Gray Brick **8.99**
7-45/64 x 2-29/32"
19.8 x 7.4cm

528-34859 Arcade Wall, Extra Long Gray Brick **17.99**
15-1/2 x 2-29/32"
39.6 x 7.4cm

Profi-Plus

Walls
528-34854 Wall Gray Brick **7.99**
7-45/64 x 2-29/64"
19.8 x 7.4cm

528-34855 Wall, Extra Long Gray Brick **15.99**
15-1/2 x 2-29/64"
39.6 x 7.4cm

528-34856 Retaining Wall Gray Brick **8.99**
7-45/64 x 2-29/64"
19.8 x 7.4cm

528-34857 Retaining Wall, Extra Long Gray Brick **17.99**
15-1/2 x 2-29/32"
39.6 x 7.4cm

VIADUCTS
528-34860 Quarrystone Viaduct **69.99**

528-34861 Quarrystone Viaduct Bridge Piers **8.99**
For use with 528-34860.

FENCES

528-33010 Field Fence **11.99**
2-45/64 x 22-13/16"
6.75 x 57cm

528-33030 Field Fence Uneven **11.99**
2-25/64 x 25" 6.75 x 62.5cm

528-33060 Abandoned Fence **11.99**
2-25/64 x 19" 6.75x 47.5cm

528-33070 Garden Fence **11.99**
2-25/64 x 21" 6.75 x 52.5cm

TUNNELS
Tunnels are made of plastic.

Single Track

528-34660 Curved w/Lake **19.99**

528-34640 Straight w/Park **16.99**

528-34670 Straight **18.99**

Double Track
528-34730 Curved **15.99**

528-34710 Straight w/Walls **23.99**

Tunnel Portals

Single Track
528-34790 14 x 10.5cm **13.99**

528-34851 Single Catenary Compatible Gray Brick **7.99**
3-3/32 x 2-29/32" 7.9 x 7.6cm

528-34937 Quarrystone
6-1/4 x 3-1/2" 16 x 9cm **6.99**

528-37941 Quarrystone (gray) **8.99**
5-1/2 x 3-3/32" 14 x 8cm

528-37961 Quarrystone (beige) **8.99**
5-1/2 x 3-3/32" 14 x 8cm

Limited Quantity Available
528-37884 Gray Brick
14 x 7cm **6.99**

Double Track
528-34840 NBS Portal **13.99**

528-34852 Double Catenary Compatible Gray Brick **8.99**
7-13/16 x 3-5/16"
12.3 x 8.5cm

528-34938 Quarrystone
6-1/4 x 3-1/2" 16 x 9cm **6.99**

528-37942 Quarrystone (gray) **8.99**
5-1/2 x 3-3/32" 14 x 8cm

528-37962 Quarrystone (beige) **8.99**
5-1/2 x 3-3/32" 14 x 8cm

Limited Quantity Available
528-37885 Gray Brick
14 x 7cm **6.99**

Double Track Portals listed below are available by Special Order (see Legend Page).
528-34800 14 x 10.5cm **13.99**

SCENERY BASE MATERIALS

528-60982 Model Plaster Cloth **17.99**
4 Rolls, Assorted Widths.

Paper

528-60841 Crepe Paper **6.99**
Ideal for scenery construction.
48 x 30" 120 x 75cm roll.

Wire Landscape Form
Item listed below is available by Special Order (see Legend Page).

528-60990 Aluminum Landscape Netting 40 x 30"
100 x 75cm **23.99**
Flexible netting ideal as a base for scenery forms. Can be used with most scenery materials.

Quarrystone Tunnel Portals and Walls 528-34942

Quarrystone Viaduct w/Bridge Piers 528-34861

ROCK

Natural Stone

Limited Quantity Available
528-9180 Fine & Coarse Stone
17-1/2oz **5.99**

Cork Rock Sections
528-8820 Large 6-1/4oz - 180g **15.99**
Chunks of cork, ideal for stratified rock formations.
528-8810 Small 2-3/4oz - 80g **8.99**

Natural Stone 2.99 ea
Use this natural stone as track ballast, in freight car loads or to detail your scenery. Each package contains 8-3/4oz (250g) of material.

528-9202 Coal, Coarse

528-9204 Gray, Fine

528-9205 Gray, Coarse

528-9214 Gravel, (gray)

528-9216 Gravel, (beige)

528-9224 Rocks, Medium

528-9226 Rocks, Large

MINIATURE SCENES

528-33610 Telephone Booth Set w/Clock, Letterbox, Bench & Figures **16.99**

528-34180 Tennis Court w/Fence **11.99**

SCENERY

PERIOD MINIATURES

Color Signs/Posters
555-601 #1 pkg(2) **3.95**
555-602 #2 pkg(2) **4.95**
555-604 Nostalgia pkg(2) **4.95**

Roofing
555-603 Shingles-Brown pkg(2) **4.95**

Sidewalks
555-819 #1 w/Round Corners pkg(4) **5.45**

PIKESTUFF

Culverts

541-2 Concrete 2 x 1"
5 x 2.5cm pkg(2) **2.50**
Molded gray plastic, use as a bridge type culvert or at the base of a hill emptying into a creek, river or drainage ditch.

PREISER

IMPORTED FROM GERMANY BY WALTHERS

Fence

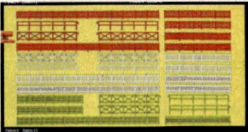

590-79551 Assortment pkg(30) **9.99**

Trees

590-18600 Palm Trees pkg(4) **16.99**
Easy-to-assemble, appropriately colored plastic. (HO Scale)

PRE-SIZE MODEL SPECIALTIES

Tunnel portals and accessories are odorless urethane castings in a natural "smoky gray" color, which can be used as-is or painted.

TUNNEL PORTALS

Single Track 8.50 ea

483-201 Timber
2-1/2 x 2-3/8" 6.2 x 5.9cm

483-203 Random Stone
2-5/8 x 2-1/2" 6.5 x 6.2cm

483-205 Cut Stone
2-3/4 x 2-3/4" 6.9 x 6.9cm

483-213 Concrete
2-3/4 x 2-1/2" 6.9 x 6.2cm

Double Track 9.25 ea

483-202 Timber
2-5/8 x 4-3/8" 6.5 x 11cm

483-204 Random Stone
2-3/4 x 3-3/4" 6.9 x 9.4cm

483-206 Cut Stone
2-3/4 x 3-7/8" 6.9 x 9.7cm

483-214 Concrete
2-3/4 x 3-5/8" 6.9 x 9cm

ABUTMENTS
pkg(2) 9.25 ea

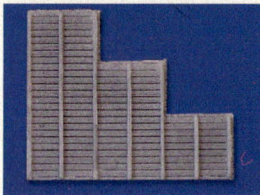
483-207 Timber
2-1/2 x 3-1/4" 6.2 x 8cm

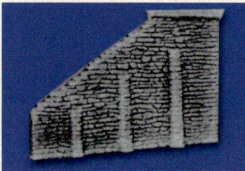
483-208 Random Stone
2-1/2 x 3-1/2" 6.2 x 9.5cm

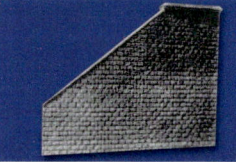
483-209 Cut Stone
2-1/2 x 3-1/2" 6.2 x 9.5cm

483-215 Concrete
2-1/2 x 3-1/2" 6.2 x 9.5cm

WALLS 9.25 ea

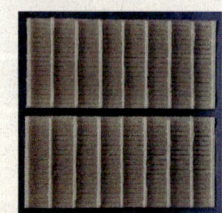
483-210 Timber pkg(2)
1-5/8 x 4-1/16" 4.7 x 10.3cm

483-211 Random Stone pkg(2)
1-3/4 x 4" 4.4 x 10cm

483-212 Cut Stone pkg(2)
1-3/4 x 4-1/4" 4.4 x 10.6cm

483-216 Concrete pkg(2)

483-219 Cut Stone
3 x 4-3/8" 7.5 x 11.1cm

FIELDS 9.25 ea
All fields measure 2-5/8 x 4"
6.5 x 10.2cm.

483-230 Plowed

483-231 Disked

PLASTRUCT

Building Sheets

570-91584 Polished Stone pkg(2) **9.75**
7 x 12" patterned sheets are vacuum-formed styrene, .020" thick.

Information STATION

Modeling Abandoned Lines

When the railroad leaves town for good, right-of-ways are subject to a variety of uses. In many cases, the use depends on the original deeds and easements negotiated with the railroad builder. But a truly abandoned line makes a great addition to any layout. An abandoned right-of-way that receives no maintenance will revert back to nature in a couple of seasons. These kinds of scenes are interesting because many of them still have telegraph poles, fencing, mileposts and sometimes even bridges left behind. In forested areas, there'll be a grassy swath through the trees. In many places where trolley/interurban lines ran, power poles or high-voltage towers will still occupy the right-of-way with a private maintenance road running where the tracks were. When modeling abandoned lines, grade and railroad crossings offer great opportunities for detailing. Many road crossings, especially on back roads, still have the rails in the pavement and the flangeways are filled in with asphalt. Sometimes grade crossing signals or their remnants are still present. At junctions and interlockings, track, signal and tie remnants are usually around for years, but the signal heads are turned to the side (if they haven't been removed from the posts).

SCENERY

Terrain For Trains
By American Plastics

Take the hard work out of layout building with these one-piece, molded plastic forms – perfect for folks with limited space, or anyone living where the mess and noise of traditional layout building could pose problems. All of the scenic forms, including rocks, streams, roads, mountains and railroad right-of-way are molded in place. Simply glue the supporting structure for the hidden track to the base unit (only required for modules having a tunnel); no major tools are required and complete instructions are provided. Then add track, trains, structures and other scenery details (all sold separately) to complete construction. The basic form weighs about 12 pounds, so it's easy to move or store between operating sessions. Forms are available prepainted to speed construction, or unpainted so you can match your favorite scenes. Layouts are designed for use with Atlas Snap-Track (sold separately), but other types can be used with some modifications. Layout forms measure 48 x 30" 120 x 75cm

LAYOUT TERRAIN FORMS

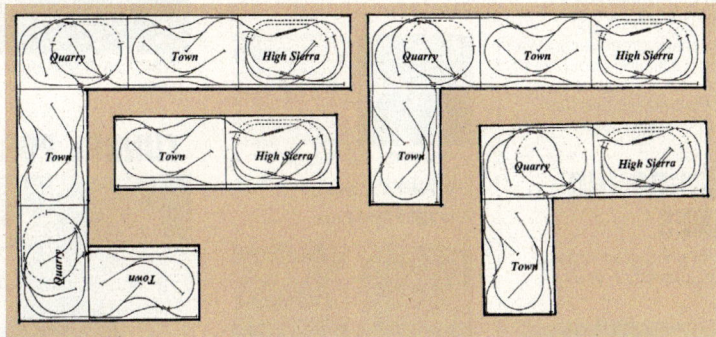

The High Sierra
Bring the flavor of mountain railroading to your layout room with this detailed base. The complete scene has hills, grades, mountains, roads, ponds a stream and a deep ravine that can be spanned with your choice of Walthers timber trestle kit or the Kato Unitrack truss bridge, both sold separately.

146-1005 Painted **349.00**
146-1000 Unpainted **279.00**

The Town of Rocky Ridge
This module extends the High Sierra layout (#146-1005 or #146-1000; both sold separately) four more feet to the left, creating a layout eight feet wide by two and half feet deep. When complete it adds another four feet of mainline operation and five more sidings for small industries.

146-1015 Painted **269.99**
146-1010 Unpainted **209.99**

The Quarry
Take your High Sierra layout (#146-1005 or #146-1000; both sold separately) to a new level with this molded plastic mountain that includes openings for two tunnels. Adds another four feet to the basic layout and can be used to create an end-loop turn or a 90° corner.

146-1025 Painted **299.99**
146-1020 Unpainted **239.99**

Smoky Hollow Junction
Enjoy plenty of railroading action on this layout that can be built so two trains can run at the same time. There's plenty of room for industry, business or residential structures (sold separately), and the scene is easily decorated to represent the eastern Smoky Mountains, the midwest or the southwest (scenery materials sold separately).

146-1055 Painted **324.99**
146-1050 Unpainted **264.99**

For Daily Product Updates Point Your Browser to
www.walthers.com

SCENERY

UNREAL DETAILS

NEW PRODUCTS

Magic Water™
NEW 754-100 **29.95**
From a mud puddle to an ocean harbor, this unique two-part resin product makes it easy to model water on any layout or diorama. Simple to use, complete instructions include project ideas and modeling tips. Each 18 ounce box covers up to 150 square inches when poured 1/8" deep, but can be poured as deep as you like without layering. You can also tint Magic Water with inks, oil based paints, enamels and more for additional realism. It cures without heat so it's safe for use on wood, foam, plastic surfaces and painted wood, and has no annoying odor or dangerous fumes. Average curing time is 24 hours, so you can easily add details without creating bubbles or tease the surface to model waves and ripples. Once set, it dries crystal clear and isn't affected by temperature, and won't yellow, shrink, bubble or crack. It has an indefinite shelf life, so left over material won't dry out or "go bad" after opening. Finished water can be cleaned with anti-static plastic cleaner (sold separately).

Get Your Daily Dose of Product News at
www.walthers.com

VOLLMER
IMPORTED FROM GERMANY BY WALTHERS
Create unique scenes along your railroad with this assortment of materials and supplies.

ARCADES

770-7815 Gray pkg(2) **6.99**
2-5/8 x 2-1/4" 6.5 x 5.3cm

Arcades make great decorative retaining walls along your lines. Each section is made of injection-molded plastic and has realistic cut-stone detail.

BACKGROUND SCENES
Full-color photographic backgrounds, printed on heavy paper.

770-6105 Sky & Clouds
112 x 32" 280 x 80cm pkg(2)
35.99

770-6110 Foothills & Mountain Scene (2 sections)
112 x 20" 280 x 50cm **34.99**

770-6111 "Alpenvorland"
120 x 24" 300 x 60cm **38.99**

770-6112 Background Clouds
108 x 20" 270 x 50cm **32.99**

ROADWAYS
Foil

770-7356   770-7357

770-7356 Road **5.99**
40 x 1-5/8" 100 x 4cm
770-7357 Street **7.99**
40 x 1-5/8" 100 x 4cm
770-7358 Cobblestone **7.99**
40 x 1-5/8" 100 x 4cm

BUILDING MATERIALS

Roofing pkg(5) 29.99 ea

770-7352   770-7353

770-7352 Slate
770-7353 Tile

Stone Pattern Embossed Paper pkg(10) 23.99 ea
Embossed paper can be used as pavement or building materials. Less adhesive. Each sheet measures 10 x 5" 25 x 12.5cm.

770-7360   770-7361

770-7360 Cobblestone
770-7361 Red Brick

770-7362   770-7363

770-7362 Brown Stone
770-7363 Sandstone

770-7365 Granite
770-7366 Gray Brick
770-7367 Lt. Gray Brick
770-7368 Brown Brick
770-7369 Porphyry

770-7371   770-7372

NEW 770-7371 Pavement
NEW 770-7372 Concrete Stones

NEW 770-7373 Design Pavement

FENCES
10.99 ea (Unless Noted)

770-7421 Diamond Pattern

770-7422 Meadow

770-7424 Factory (black)

770-7425 Roadside Railing **9.99**

TUNNEL PORTALS

770-7811 Single Track pkg(2) **6.99**

770-7812 Double Track pkg(2) **7.99**

770-7813 Double Track pkg(2) **7.99**

SCENERY

Timberline Scenery Co., LLC

Bring new realism to your railroad with this line of realistic trees, ground cover, foliage and other scenery products.

NEW PRODUCT

Rock Rite

NEW 710-8470 Rock Rite Kit pkg(4) **19.95**
This easy, four-step water-based coloring system takes the guesswork out of creating realistic scenery. Specially formulated to color plaster rock castings or carvings. Kit includes four 1 oz bottles; one each tan, red, brown, dark brown and black.

Create a realistic forest in any scale with these detailed tree replicas. Each is hand-built one at a time, to ensure the highest quality and that no two are ever identical. Pine trees (conifers) are available with real wood trunks for dioramas or foreground, or with wire forms for backgrounds and scenes requiring many trees. All leafed (deciduous) trees feature real wood trunks.

Deep Woods Green Trees

Pine Tree Assortment

ALL SCALE

TREES

Conifers w/Wire Form Trunks

Northwoods Green
710-101 1/2-2" 1.25-5cm pkg(6) **7.69**
710-102 2-4" 5-10cm pkg(3) **7.69**
710-103 4-6" 10-15cm pkg(2) **7.69**
710-104 6-9" 15-22.5cm **8.69**
710-105 9-11" 22.5-27.5cm **9.69**

Deep Woods Green
710-106 1/2-2" 1.25-5cm pkg(6) **7.69**
710-107 2-4" 5-10cm pkg(3) **7.69**
710-108 4-6" 10-15cm pkg(2) **7.69**
710-109 6-9" 15-22.5cm **8.69**
710-110 9-11" 22.5-27.5cm **9.69**

Lodge Pole Green
710-111 1/2-2" 1.25-5cm pkg(6) **7.69**
710-112 2-4" 5-10cm pkg(3) **7.69**
710-113 4-6" 10-15cm pkg(2) **7.69**
710-114 6-9" 15-22.5cm **8.69**
710-115 9-11" 22.5-27.5cm **9.69**

Deadwood Brown
710-116 1/2-2" 1.25-5cm pkg(6) **7.69**
710-117 2-4" 5-10cm pkg(3) **7.69**
710-118 4-6" 10-15cm pkg(2) **7.69**
710-119 6-9" 15-22.5cm **8.69**
710-120 9-11" 22.5-27.5cm **9.69**

Timberline Green
710-121 1/2-2" pkg(6) **7.69**
710-122 2-4" pkg(6) **7.69**
710-123 4-6" pkg(2) **7.69**
710-124 6-9" **8.69**
710-125 9-12" **9.69**

Pine Trees w/Real Wood Trunks

Northwoods Green
710-1102 2-4" 5-10cm pkg(3) **8.69**
710-1103 4-6" 10-15cm pkg(2) **8.69**
710-1104 6-9" 15-22.5cm **10.69**
710-1105 9-11" 22.5-27.5cm **11.69**

Deep Woods Green
710-1107 2-4" 5-10cm pkg(3) **8.69**
710-1108 4-6" 10-15cm pkg(2) **8.69**
710-1109 6-9" 15-22.5cm **10.69**
710-1110 9-11" 22.5-27.5cm **11.69**

Lodge Pole Green
710-1112 2-4" 5-10cm pkg(3) **8.69**
710-1113 4-6" 10-15cm pkg(2) **8.69**
710-1114 6-9" 15-22.5cm **10.69**
710-1115 9-11" 22.5-27.5cm **11.69**

Deadwood Brown
710-1117 2-4" 5-10cm pkg(3) **8.69**
710-1118 4-6" 10-15cm pkg(2) **8.69**
710-1119 6-9" 15-22.5cm **10.69**
710-1120 9-11" 22.5-27.5cm **11.69**

Timberline Green
710-1122 2-4" pkg(6) **7.69**
710-1123 4-6" pkg(2) **7.69**
710-1124 6-9" **8.69**
710-1125 9-12" **9.69**

Assortments
710-190 Without Trunks 1/2-6" 1.25-10cm pkg(17) **34.95**
710-1190 With Real Wood Trunks 1/2-6" 1.25-10cm pkg(11) **34.95**

Deciduous w/Real Wood Trunks

Summer Leaves
710-201 2-4" 5-10cm pkg(3) **8.69**
710-202 3-5" 7.5-12.5cm pkg(2) **8.69**
710-203 6-9" 15-22.5cm **11.69**

Spring Green
710-204 2-4" 5-10cm pkg(3) **8.69**
710-205 3-5" 7.5-12.5cm pkg(2) **8.69**
710-206 6-9" 15-22.5cm **11.69**

Late Autumn

710-190 Alpine Forest 1/2-6" 1.25-10cm pkg(20) **34.95**
710-207 2-4" 5-10cm pkg(3) **8.69**
710-208 3-5" 7.5-12.5cm pkg(2) **8.69**
710-209 6-9" 15-22.5cm **11.69**

Fall Splendor
710-210 2-4" 5-10cm pkg(3) **8.69**
710-211 3-5" 7.5-12.5cm pkg(2) **8.69**
710-212 6-9" 15-22.5cm **11.69**

Autumn Gold
710-213 2-4" 5-10cm pkg(3) **8.69**
710-214 3-5" 7.5-12.5cm pkg(2) **8.69**
710-215 6-9" 15-22.5cm **11.69**

Harvest Dawn
710-216 2-4" 5-10cm pkg(3) **8.69**
710-217 3-5" 7.5-12.5cm pkg(2) **8.69**
710-218 6-9" 15-22.5cm **11.69**

October Orange
710-219 2-4" 5-10cm pkg(3) **8.69**
710-220 3-5" 7.5-12.5cm pkg(2) **8.69**
710-221 6-9" 15-22.5cm **11.69**

Indian Summer
710-222 2-4" 5-10cm pkg(3) **8.69**
710-223 3-5" 7.5-12.5cm pkg(2) **8.69**
710-224 6-9" 15-22.5cm **11.69**

Fruit Trees

Lemon
710-225 2-4" 5-10cm pkg(3) **8.69**
710-226 3-5" 7.5-12.5cm pkg(2) **8.69**
710-227 6-9" 15-22.5cm **11.69**

Orange
710-228 2-4" 5-10cm pkg(3) **8.69**
710-229 3-5" 7.5-12.5cm pkg(2) **8.69**
710-230 6-9" 15-22.5cm **11.69**

Apple
710-231 2-4" 5-10cm pkg(3) **8.69**
710-232 3-5" 7.5-12.5cm pkg(2) **8.69**
710-233 6-9" 15-22.5cm **11.69**

Assortments pkg(11) 34.95 ea
Trees measure 2-5" 7.5-12.5cm in each assortment.
710-290 Summer Grove
710-291 Autumn Grove

Forest Floor / Ground Cover

SCENERY

Timberline Scenery Co., LLC

GROUND COVER

Forest Floor 3.19 ea
This special blend of fine texture foliage and real wood deadfall adds overall depth to ground cover. Each comes in a resealable bag.

20 Cubic Inch Bag 3.19 ea
710-400 Forest Floor

710-403 Deep Forest Floor

710-406 Mountain Meadow

710-409 Spring Mountain Meadow

60 Cubic Inch Bag 8.49 ea
710-60400 Forest Floor
710-60403 Deep Forest Floor
710-60406 Mountain Meadow
710-60409 Spring Mountain Meadow

Foliage-20 Cubic Inch Bag 2.99 ea
Diverse colors and textures great for scenic detailing! Comes in resealable bags.

Alpine Green
710-301 Fine
710-302 Medium
710-303 Coarse

Mid-Summer Green
710-304 Fine
710-305 Medium
710-306 Coarse

Spring Meadow Green
710-307 Fine
710-308 Medium
710-309 Coarse

Sage Brush Blue
710-310 Fine
710-311 Medium
710-312 Coarse

Bristlecone Green
710-313 Fine
710-314 Medium
710-315 Coarse

Mojave Sand
710-316 Fine
710-317 Medium
710-318 Coarse

Pine Cone Brown
710-319 Fine
710-320 Medium
710-321 Coarse

Winter Wheat
710-322 Fine
710-323 Medium
710-324 Coarse

Tumbleweed Tan
710-325 Fine
710-326 Medium
710-327 Coarse

Autumn Gold
710-328 Fine
710-329 Medium
710-330 Coarse

Santa Fe Sunburst
710-331 Fine
710-332 Medium
710-333 Coarse

October Orange
710-334 Fine
710-335 Medium
710-336 Coarse

Cherokee Sunrise
710-337 Fine
710-338 Medium
710-339 Coarse

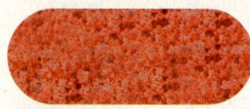
Indian Paint Brush
710-340 Fine
710-341 Medium
710-342 Coarse

Cherry Blossom Pink
710-343 Fine
710-344 Medium
710-345 Coarse

Cimarron
710-346 Fine
710-347 Medium
710-348 Coarse

Lilac
710-349 Fine
710-350 Medium
710-351 Coarse

Wild Flowers
710-352 Fine
710-353 Medium
710-354 Coarse

Forest Glen
710-355 Fine
710-356 Medium
710-357 Coarse

Lost Canyon Sage
710-358 Fine
710-359 Medium
710-360 Coarse

Foliage-60 Cubic Inch Bag 7.89 ea
All the same great colors and features of regular Ground Cover, but with three times more material for larger scenery projects.

Alpine Green
710-60301 Fine
710-60302 Medium
710-60303 Coarse

Mid-Summer Green
710-60304 Fine
710-60305 Medium
710-60306 Coarse

Spring Meadow Green
710-60307 Fine
710-60308 Medium
710-60309 Coarse

Sage Brush Blue
710-60310 Fine
710-60311 Medium
710-60312 Coarse

Bristlecone Green
710-60313 Fine
710-60314 Medium
710-60315 Coarse

Mojave Sand
710-60316 Fine
710-60317 Medium
710-60318 Coarse

Pine Cone Brown
710-60319 Fine
710-60320 Medium
710-60321 Coarse

Winter Wheat
710-60322 Fine
710-60323 Medium
710-60324 Coarse

Tumbleweed Tan
710-60325 Fine
710-60326 Medium
710-60327 Coarse

Autumn Gold
710-60328 Fine
710-60329 Medium
710-60330 Coarse

Santa Fe Sunburst
710-60331 Fine
710-60332 Medium
710-60333 Coarse

October Orange
710-60334 Fine
710-60335 Medium
710-60336 Coarse

Cherokee Sunrise
710-60337 Fine
710-60338 Medium
710-60339 Coarse

Indian Paint Brush
710-60340 Fine
710-60341 Medium
710-60342 Coarse

Cherry Blossom Pink
710-60343 Fine
710-60344 Medium
710-60345 Coarse

Cimarron
710-60346 Fine
710-60347 Medium
710-60348 Coarse

Lilac
710-60349 Fine
710-60350 Medium
710-60351 Coarse

Wild Flowers
710-60352 Fine
710-60353 Medium
710-60354 Coarse

Forest Glen
710-60355 Fine
710-60356 Medium
710-60357 Coarse

Lost Canyon Sage
710-60358 Fine
710-60359 Medium
710-60360 Coarse

TIMBERLINE BASE COAT

16oz Bottle 6.98 ea
710-8400 Forest Floor
710-8403 Deep Forest Floor
710-8406 Mountain Meadow

WEATHER-RITE

710-808 8oz **7.98**
Make your models look like they've spent years outside with this handy weathering solution. Perfect for aging ballast, wood, plaster, metal and much more. Ready to use with no thinning, it's easily applied with brush or eyedropper.

ADHESIVE

710-816 Timberline Adhesive 16oz **5.49**
Ready to use right from the bottle, this water-soluble adhesive is perfect for securing ballast or ground covers. Can be applied by brushing or spraying and dries clear.

SCENERY

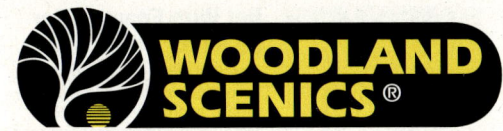

SUBTERRAIN FOAM PRODUCTS

The revolutionary SubTerrain Lightweight System® for beginners or experienced modelers.
- No Expensive Power Tools
- No Dusty Mess
- No Complicated Calculations

CREATE THE IDEAL BASE FOR REALISTIC SCENERY IN JUST FIVE EASY STEPS..............YOU CAN DO IT!

STEP 1
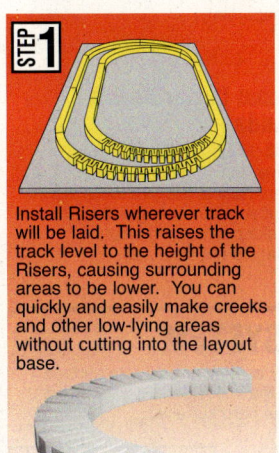
Install Risers wherever track will be laid. This raises the track level to the height of the Risers, causing surrounding areas to be lower. You can quickly and easily make creeks and other low-lying areas without cutting into the layout base.

Risers*
785-1406 1/2" pkg(4) **5.98**
785-1414 3/4" pkg(4) **6.49**
785-1407 1" pkg(4) **6.98**
785-1408 2" pkg(4) **9.29**
785-1409 4" pkg(2) **9.29**

Use at least 2" Risers* to elevate track, 4" Risers* give maximum elevation for steep relief. 1/2" and 1" Risers* are generally used with Incline Starters to create varying grades. Each piece is 2-1/2" wide x 24" long.

*Woodland Scenics Patented Product

Daily New Product Announcements! Visit Walthers Web site at
www.walthers.com

STEP 2
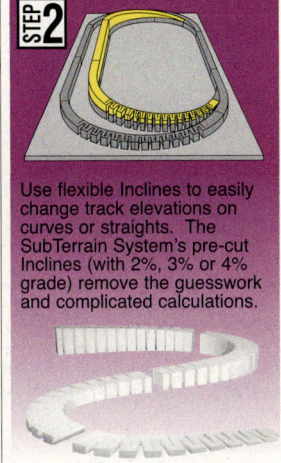
Use flexible Inclines to easily change track elevations on curves or straights. The SubTerrain System's pre-cut Inclines (with 2%, 3% or 4% grade) remove the guesswork and complicated calculations.

Incline Sets*
Stack the pre-cut Inclines on top of Risers* for quick and easy elevation changes. Each piece is 2-1/2" wide and 24" long.

785-1410 2% pkg(8) **15.98**
Elevates your track 4" in 16'.
785-1416 3% pkg(6) **13.98**
Elevates your track 4-1/2" in 12'.
785-1411 4% pkg(4) **10.98**
Elevates your track 4" in 8'.

Incline Starters*
Can be used alone or with sets to start your track on an incline. Each piece measures 2-1/2" wide x 24" long.

785-1412 2% pkg(8) **5.98**
Eight identical pieces that raise the elevation 1/2".
785-1415 3% pkg(6) **5.98**
Six identical pieces that raise the elevation 3/4".
785-1413 4% pkg(4) **5.98**
4 identical pieces that raise the elevation 1".

*Woodland Scenics Patented Product

STEP 3

Install interlocking Profile Boards with matching Connectors to make a sturdy layout perimeter that can easily be cut with the Hot Wire Foam Cutter or a hobby knife to conform to any profile desired.

Profile Boards
785-1419 (2 Connectors and 2 Boards) **7.98**
Profile Boards are used around the perimeter of your layout to define the contours. Their special interlocking design allows them to be stacked and locked together. Each board is 8" high and 24" long.

STEP 4
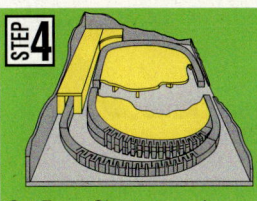
Cut Foam Sheets to enclose tunnels, create interior terrain profiles and form level, elevated areas for buildings and towns.

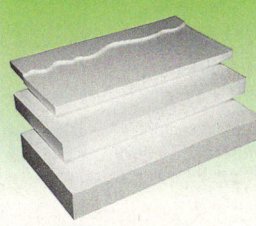

Foam Sheets
785-1422 1/4" pkg(4)* **13.96**
785-1423 1/2" pkg(4)* **15.92**
785-1424 1" pkg(4)* **19.16**
785-1425 2" **7.98**
785-1426 3" **11.98**
785-1427 4" **14.98**

Use Foam Sheets to create elevated flat areas for towns, tunnels and contour supports. The 1/4" can be bent to a tight radius. Each piece 12" x 24".
*Sold in package quantities only.

STEP 5
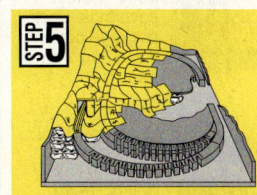
Form terrain with newspaper wads and cover with Plaster Cloth that has been dipped in water. The Plaster Cloth will dry to a hard shell without adding any plaster. Install the Track-Bed.

Plaster Cloth
785-1203 **8.79**
A simple, convenient, and lightweight way to create a durable terrain shell or base. Just wad newspaper and stack to form the desired shape. Dip Plaster Cloth in water. Lay over newspaper wads. Plaster Cloth will dry to a hard shell without adding any plaster. 8" wide x 15' long (10 sq. ft.).

SUBTERRAIN LEARNING AIDS

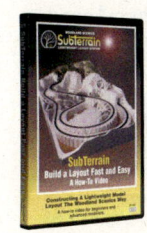
785-1400

785-1401

SubTerrain Video 24.98 ea
785-1400 DVD
785-1401 VHS
Approximately 60 minutes. A step-by-step video that shows you how to build a model railroad layout with the revolutionary SubTerrain Layout System.

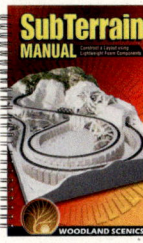

SubTerrain Manual
785-1402 **7.98**
Newly-revised, illustrated how-to manual teaches you how to create the ideal base for scenery and landscaping in five easy steps. 101 pages with 41 illustrations and 173 photos.

167

SCENERY

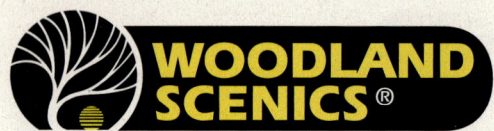

ACCESSORIES

All of these accessories are available to help you successfully build your SubTerrain Layout.

Foam Pencils
785-1431 4.79
Foam Pencils have special lead that allows you to draw on foam without causing any damage. The colors will not bleed through paint or other coverings. Each package contains 2 red and 2 black pencils.

Flex Paste
785-1205
16 fl oz 14.98
A specially formulated, non-cracking modeling paste. Use for a filler, surfacer or primer on styrofoam.

2" Foam Nails
785-1432 pkg(75) 4.98
Use Foam Nails to temporarily pin track, foam or other products to your layout.

Foam Knife
785-1433 6.98
The Foam Knife comes with a 2" replaceable blade that is ideal for cutting thick pieces of foam.

Foam Knife Blades
785-1434 pkg(4) 5.98

Foam Tack Glue
785-1444
12 fl oz 10.98
This specially formulated glue is high-tack and effective on most materials. Use as a contact cement whenever bonding two large surfaces.

Foam Putty
785-1447 1 pint
8.49
A non-shrinking, lightweight filling material that has the same characteristics as foam. Fill cracks and gaps then sand.

Low Temp Foam Glue Gun
785-1445 16.98
The Glue Gun with the Glue Sticks operates at a temperature that will not damage foam and bonds instantly.

Low Temp Foam Glue Sticks
785-1446
pkg(10) 5.98
10" Sticks.

Plaster Cloth
785-1203 8.79
A simple, convenient, and lightweight way to create a durable terrain shell or base. Just wad newspaper and stack to form the desired shape. Dip Plaster Cloth in water, lay over newspaper and allow to dry. A quick, no mess scenery base. Includes 8" wide x 15' long (10 sq. ft.) roll.

Hot Wire Foam Cutter
39.98 ea
The Hot Wire Foam Cutter has adjustable collars allowing for clean, accurate cuts in foam. Woodland Scenics recommends using this tool only with SubTerrain white foam, which has no toxic fumes. Use only special Nichrome replacement wire, listed below.
785-1435 120V - North America
785-14401 230V - Europe
785-14402 240V - United Kingdom Only
785-14403 230V or 240V - Plug for Australia/New Zealand

4' Foam Cutter Replacement Wire
785-1436 2.29
Special Nichrome wire retains an even temperature required to cut Woodland Scenics foam products. Use only with Hot Wire Foam Cutter #1435, (sold separately).

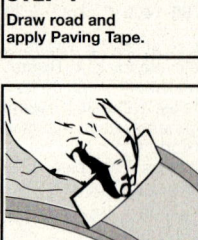

Foam Cutter Bow & Guide
785-1437 7.98
This Bow Attachment adds versatility to the Hot Wire Cutter. Attach the guide to make precise angle cuts (handle not included).

COMPLETE ROAD SYSTEM

Making roads, parking lots or any asphalt or concrete surface has never been easier than with the Woodland Scenics Road System. Use directly on any clean hard surface.

Paving Tape
785-1455 1/4" x 30' 6.98
An adhesive backed foam tape that is used to outline streets, roads and sidewalks. Fill with Smooth-It, sold separately. A spreader is included.

Smooth-It
785-1452 1 qt 5.29
Mix with water and apply directly to any hard surface. Smooth-It is a plaster material that is used to smooth rough spots, create streets, roads and parking lots.

Top Coat 4.49 ea
785-1453 Asphalt 4 oz
785-1454 Concrete 4 oz
Two realistic Top Coat colors are available: Asphalt and Concrete. Use full strength or thin with water.

STEP 1 Draw road and apply Paving Tape.

STEP 2 Fill and spread Smooth-It.

STEP 3 Remove Paving Tape.

TRACK-BED

N Scale Strips, Rolls and Sheets.

- Quieter Operation (Sound Deadening Material)
- Smoother Operation (Cushions Vibrations)
- Easier to Use (Tack or Glue Down, Flexible, No Soaking, Compatible with Cork, Won't Dry Out or Crumble)
- Better Value (Higher Quality... Lower Cost)

Track-Bed Strips
Each piece is 2' (60cm) long.
785-1462 Bulk Pack pkg(36) 18.87
785-1472 Standard Pack pkg(12) 6.89

* Woodland Scenics® Patented Product

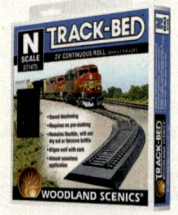

Track-Bed Roll
785-1475 24' 720cm Long 6.89
Same great material in a continuous roll for almost seamless installation.

Track-Bed Sheets
All sheets are 5mm thick; use in yards, stations or other areas.
785-1460 Standard
3-1/4" x 2' x 3mm pkg(6) 7.98
785-1478 Super
12 x 24" x 3mm 3.29

SCENERY

WOODLAND SCENICS®

TREE KITS
With Woodland Scenics Kits, no two trees need ever look alike because you design each tree! You bend the branches and shape the tree. You position the Foliage. Try using different colors of Foliage with varied placement for realism and variety.

Three Basic Steps
Bend and twist the soft metal armature to a realistic shape. Stretch out the Foliage until thin and lacy. Apply Foliage to tree and glue.

Stumps 4.29 ea

785-31 Cut Stumps pkg(14)
785-32 Broken Stumps pkg(14)

Small Tree Kits 8.98 ea
Each tree kit contains two to five bendable metal trunk castings with bark texture; pre-colored, non-metallic Foliage material; and easy to follow instructions. These are highly detailed, extremely versatile trees, designed to lend realism and variety to any layout.

785-11 Forked Tree 2-1/4" pkg(4)

785-13 Straight Trunk 2-1/2" pkg(5)

785-18 Double Forked 3-1/2" pkg(2)

785-21 Gnarled 4-1/2" pkg(2)

785-12 Ornamental 2-1/2" pkg(5)

785-14 Softwood Pine 3-1/4" pkg(5)

785-20 Columnar Pine 4-1/2" pkg(4)

785-19 Shade Tree 4" pkg(2)

785-17 Shag Bark 3-1/2" pkg(3)

785-22 Dead Trees pkg(5)

Large Tree Kits 14.98 ea
These soft white metal tree kits provide realism for the special scenes in your layout.

785-23 Pine Trees Approx. 6-9" Tall pkg(5)

785-25 Hardwood Trees Approx. 5-1/2 to 6-1/2" Tall pkg(3)

785-27 Pine Forest Approx. 2-4" Tall pkg(24)

785-24 Hedge Row Scene 24-30" long. Contains: 18 trees, 6 bushes, 3 colors Foliage, 2 colors Turf.

785-26 Big Old Trees Approx. 7 to 7-1/2" Tall pkg(2)

785-28 Hardwood Forest Approx. 2-4" Tall pkg(24)

Complete Landscape Kit

785-926 34.98
Contains: 18 trunks (2-4" tall), 3 packs Foliage, 7 stumps, 2 packs Green Blend Turf, 3 packs accent Turf.

Tree Armatures 11.98 ea
Tree armatures are bendable plastic and hold their shape once twisted into a new position. Each has a base pin for easy planting on your layout. Choose from four sets of deciduous and two sets of pine trees, which include a variety of types and sizes in each package.

Deciduous
785-1120 .75"-2" Pack of 114
785-1121 2"-3" Pack of 57
785-1122 3"-5" Pack of 28
785-1123 5"-7" Pack of 12

Pines
785-1124 2-1/2"-4" Pack of 70
785-1125 4"-6" Pack of 44

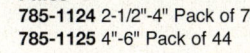

SCENERY

NEW PRODUCTS

Premium Trees

Fully assembled, Premium Trees are works of art that replicate real live trees. Each is handcrafted. The design of the branch and leaf structure easily identifies each tree type. The tree trunks are textured to look like real bark. Each tree has a planting pin so it's easy to add to new or existing scenery. Three different package sizes are available, with trees ranging from 1-3/4 (4.4cm) to 5-3/4" (14.6cm) tall. All sizes shown are approximate heights.

Birch

NEW 785-1601 4" **12.98**

Dead Elm

NEW 785-1602 One Each 3-1/4 & 2-1/4" **11.98**

Sycamore

NEW 785-1603 One Each 3 & 2-1/4" **14.98**

NEW 785-1609 4" **12.98**

Maple

NEW 785-1604 Fall - One Each 3 & 2-1/2" **14.98**

NEW 785-1610 4-1/2" **13.98**

NEW 785-1614 Dead - 4-1/4" **13.98**

Paper Birch 12.98 ea

NEW 785-1605 One Each 3, 1-1/2 & 2"

NEW 785-1616 4"

Oak

NEW 785-1606 3-1/4" **10.98**

NEW 785-1620 5" **18.98**

Locust

NEW 785-1607 One Each 3 & 2" **12.98**

Sweetgum

NEW 785-1608 4" **12.98**

Poplar

NEW 785-1611 One Each 4-3/4, 3-1/2 & 4-1/4" **15.98**

See What's Available at
www.walthers.com

Aspen

NEW 785-1612 One Each 2 & 3" **11.98**

Beech 16.98 ea

NEW 785-1613 Fall - 4"

NEW 785-1615 4"

Royal Palm

NEW 785-1617 One Each 4-1/2, 3 & 4" **19.98**

Basswood

NEW 785-1618 4" **14.98**

Juniper

NEW 785-1619 One Each 5-1/4, 2-1/2 & 3" **19.98**

Spruce

NEW 785-1621 One Each 5 & 4" **17.98**

Walnut

NEW 785-1622 4" **18.98**

Hickory

NEW 785-1623 5-3/4" **18.98**

Pine

NEW 785-1624 One Each 5-1/4 & 4" **17.98**

SCENERY

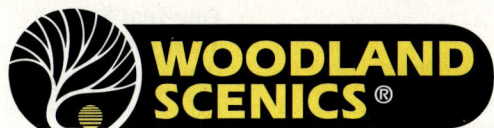

TREES

Ready Made Realistic Trees
There are 25 different packages of trees for variety. Each tree is hand-crafted, individually shaped and uniquely foliated. No two trees are exactly the same. These treees are ready to use right out of the package. Realistic Trees lend authenticity to a layout or diorama. Natural colors and realistic texture duplicate nature and blend with other Woodland Scenics landscaping products.

Deciduous Fall Trees

785-1540 Fall Mix 1.25"-3" pkg(9) **14.49**

785-1541 Fall Mix pkg(6) 3"-5" **16.49**

Pines

785-1560 Conifer Green 2.5"-4" pkg(5) **8.49**

785-1561 Conifer Green 4"-6" pkg(4) **8.49**

785-1562 Conifer Green 6"-7" pkg(3) **9.98**

785-1563 Conifer Green 7"-8" pkg(3) **11.49**

Deciduous Trees

785-1501 Medium Green .75"-1.25" pkg(8) **7.29**

785-1502 Medium Green 1.25"-2" pkg(5) **7.29**

785-1503 Light Green 2"-3" pkg(4) **7.98**
785-1504 Medium Green 2"-3" pkg(4) **7.98**
785-1505 Dark Green 2"-3" pkg (4) **7.98**

785-1506 Light Green 3"-4" pkg(3) **9.49**
785-1507 Medium Green 3"-4" pkg(3) **9.49**
785-1508 Dark Green 3"-4" pkg(3) **9.49**

785-1509 Light Green 4"-5" pkg(3) **9.98**
785-1510 Medium Green 4"-5" pkg(3) **9.98**
785-1511 Dark Green 4"-5" pkg(3) **9.98**

785-1512 Light Green 5"-6" pkg(2) **9.49**
785-1513 Medium Green 5"-6" pkg(2) **9.49**
785-1514 Dark Green 5"-6" pkg(2) **9.49**

785-1518 Medium Green 7"-8" pkg(2) **14.49**

785-1515 Light Green 6"-7" pkg(2) **10.98**
785-1516 Medium Green 6"-7" pkg(2) **10.98**
785-1517 Dark Green 6"-7" pkg(2) **10.98**

785-1519 Medium Green 8"-9" pkg(2) **16.49**

SCENERY

Ready Made Trees Value Pack 26.98 ea

Nine different Value Packs contain deciduous or pine trees ranging in size from 3/4" to 8". Quantities vary according to size. Mixed green, conifer or fall colors.

Mixed Green

Fall Colors

Conifer Green

Green Deciduous

785-1570 .75"-2" Mixed Green pkg(38)

785-1571 2"-3" Mixed Green pkg(23)

785-1572 3"-5" Mixed Green pkg(14)

Fall Deciduous

785-1575 .75"-2" Fall Colors pkg(38)

785-1576 2"-3" Fall Colors pkg(23)

785-1577 3"-5" Fall Colors pkg(14)

Pines

785-1580 2.5"-4" Conifer Green pkg(33)

785-1581 4"-6" Conifer Green pkg(24)

785-1582 6"-8" Conifer Green pkg(12)

Kit Form "Realistic Trees"
15.98 ea (Unless Noted)

Six selections of tree kits in deciduous or conifer styles ranging in size from 3/4" to 8" give you the opportunity to make easy and truly unique trees for your layout. Create the armature shape you want then add as much or as little foliage as desired. Easy for beginners.

785-1111

Green Deciduous
785-1101	.75"-3"	ABC	Mixed Green pkg(36)
785-1102	3"-5"	ABC	Mixed Green pkg(14)
785-1103	5"-7"	ABC	Mixed Green pkg(7)
785-1111	.75"-3"	B	Medium Green pkg(21) **12.49**
785-1112	3"-7"	B	Medium Green pkg(6) **12.49**

785-1105

Pines
785-1104	2.5"-4"	D	Conifer Green pkg(42)
785-1105	4"-6"	D	Conifer Green pkg(24)
785-1106	6"-8"	D	Conifer Green pkg(16)
785-1113	2.5"-6"	E	Forest Green pkg(24) **12.49**

A Light Green

B Medium Green

C Dark Green

E Forest Green

D Conifer Green

Get Daily Info, Photos and News at
www.walthers.com

Fine-Leaf Foliage*
12.98 ea

Great for modeling bushes, saplings, trees, shrubs and hedges. Fine detail is superb and adds realistic dimension. Color-fast and available in six realistic colors. 75 cu. in.

785-1130 Dark Green

785-1131 Medium Green

785-1132 Light Green

785-1133 Olive Green

785-1134 Dead Foliage

785-1135 Fall Mix

* Woodland Scenics® Patented Products

SCENERY

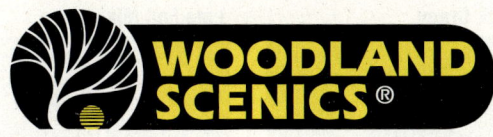

GROUND COVERS

Clump-Foliage*

Clump-Foliage is a patented foliage product available in one or three quart bags in six realistic colors. Use as Ground Cover, Bushes, shrubs, and tree foliage. Previously available in Realistic Tree Kits only.

Burnt Grass

785-181 3 Quart **14.49**

Light Green

785-182 3 Quart **14.49**
785-682 1 Quart **5.79**

Medium Green

785-183 3 Quart **14.49**
785-683 1 Quart **5.79**

Dark Green

785-184 3 Quart **14.49**
785-684 1 Quart **5.79**

Conifer Green

785-185 3 Quart **14.49**

Autumn Mix

785-186 3 Quart **14.49**
*Woodland Scenics Patented Product

Lichen

This natural product blends in a limitless variety of colors and textures when combined with Woodland Scenics Turf and Foliage lines. Two package sizes and several colors offer variety and economy.

Spring Green

785-161 1-1/2 Quart **6.98**

Light Green

785-162 1-1/2 Quart **6.98**

Medium Green

785-163 1-1/2 Quart **6.98**

Dark Green

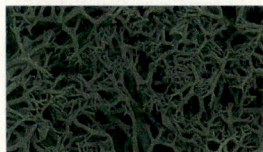

785-164 1-1/2 Quart **6.98**

Autumn Mix

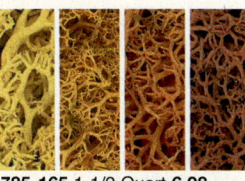

785-165 1-1/2 Quart **6.98**

Natural

785-166 1-1/2 Quart **6.98**

Light Green Mix

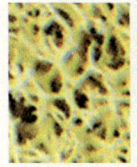

785-167 3 Quart **12.98**

Dark Green Mix

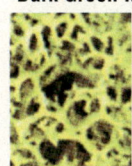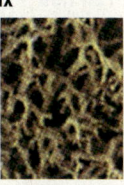

785-168 3 Quart **12.98**

Field Grass

An extremely fine natural hair product that models tall grass, field grass and weeds. Easy to follow instructions. Available in four realistic colors.

Natural Straw

785-171 8 gr. **3.49**

Harvest Gold

785-172 8 gr. **3.49**

Light Green

785-173 8 gr. **3.49**

Medium Green

785-174 8 gr. **3.49**

Static Grass Flock

Create realistic three-dimensional grass in any scene with this special material. When applied, Static Grass Flock has a tendency to stand up, so the grass looks more like the real thing. Available in six realistic colors which can be mixed and matched to create a variety of vegetation. Each comes in a 32 oz shaker with a sifter top for easy application and storage.

Wild Honey

785-631 32 oz **9.98**

Harvest Gold

785-632 32 oz **9.98**

Burnt Grass

785-633 32 oz **9.98**

Light Green

785-634 32 oz **9.98**

Medium Green

785-635 32 oz **9.98**

Dark Green

785-636 32 oz **9.98**

TURF

Blended Turf

Turf is a ground foam material for modeling grass, dead grass, and various types of plant life. Easy to apply, Turf is available in a variety of colors and sizes that allow you to create combinations and textures for any season in any scale.

Green Blend

785-49 45 cu. in. **6.98**
785-1349 32 oz Shaker **9.79**

Earth Blend

785-50 45 cu. in. **6.98**
785-1350 32 oz Shaker **9.79**

Fine Turf

Soil

785-41 18 cu. in. **3.59**
785-1341 32 oz Shaker **9.79**

Earth

785-42 18 cu. in. **3.59**
785-1342 32 oz Shaker **9.79**

SCENERY

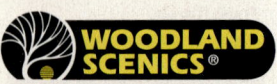

Woodland Scenics

Yellow Grass

785-43 18 cu. in. **3.59**
785-1343 32 oz Shaker **9.79**

Burnt Grass

785-44 18 cu. in. **3.59**
785-1344 32 oz Shaker **9.79**

Green Grass

785-45 18 cu. in. **3.59**
785-1345 32 oz Shaker **9.79**

Weeds

785-46 18 cu. in. **3.59**
785-1346 32 oz Shaker **9.79**

Landscape Accessories

785-47 Fruit-Apples (red) & Oranges **3.49**

785-48 Flowers (4 Colors) **3.49**

Coarse Turf
Models low grass, leaves and weeds. Provides a smooth transition from low ground cover to medium and high ground cover.

Earth

785-60 18 cu. in. **3.59**

Yellow Grass

785-61 18 cu. in. **3.59**
785-1361 32 oz Shaker **9.79**

Burnt Grass

785-62 18 cu. in. **3.59**
785-1362 32 oz Shaker **9.79**

Light Green

785-63 18 cu. in. **3.59**
785-1363 32 oz Shaker **9.79**

Medium Green

785-64 18 cu. in. **3.59**
785-1364 32 oz Shaker **9.79**

Dark Green

785-65 18 cu. in. **3.59**
785-1365 32 oz Shaker **9.79**

Conifer Green

785-1366 32 oz Shaker **9.79**

Fall Yellow

785-1353 32 oz Shaker **9.79**

Fall Orange

785-1354 32 oz Shaker **9.79**

Fall Red

785-1355 32 oz Shaker **9.79**

Fall Rust

785-1356 32 oz Shaker **9.79**

Foliage Clusters*
A specially produced ground foam cluster for bushes, undergrowth and foliage. Use as is or break into smaller clusters. Each 45 cubic inches.

Light Green

785-57 45 cu. in. **7.98**

Medium Green

785-58 45 cu. in. **7.98**

Dark Green

785-59 45 cu. in. **7.98**
*Woodland Scenics® Patented Product

FOLIAGE

Foliage can be used for trees, vines, weeds, bushes, or any other low growth. Simply stretch foliage material to desired density and apply. Each 60 sq. inches.

Light Green

785-51 60 sq. in. **3.98**

Medium Green

785-52 60 sq. in. **3.98**

Dark Green

785-53 60 sq. in. **3.98**

Conifer Green

785-54 60 sq. in. **3.98**

Early Fall Mix

785-55 60 sq. in. **3.98**

Late Fall Mix

785-56 60 sq. in. **3.98**

REALISTIC WATER
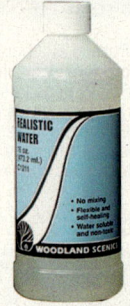
785-1211 16 fl oz **15.98**
Use for modeling various bodies of water such as lakes, rivers, ponds, creeks and streams. This ready-to-use water is flexible, self-leveling and will not dry hard or brittle. Self-healing characteristics make it an ideal choice for dioramas or modules that are handled often.

WATER EFFECTS

785-1212 8 fl oz **12.98**
Use to model impressions of moving water such as waterfalls, rapids, ripples, waves and water rings. Ready to use right from the bottle, material is flexible and easy to use. Will not dry hard or brittle, is nontoxic and water-soluble.

Get the Scoop!
Get the Skinny!
Get the Score!
Check Out Walthers
Web site at
www.walthers.com

SCENERY

UNDERBRUSH*

Available in six realistic colors, great for making bushes, shrubs and small trees.

Olive Green

785-134 12 oz **3.98**
785-1634 32 oz Shaker **11.49**

Light Green

785-135 12 oz **3.98**
785-1635 32 oz Shaker **11.49**

Medium Green

785-136 12 oz **3.98**
785-1636 32 oz Shaker **11.49**

Dark Green

785-137 12 oz **3.98**
785-1637 32 oz Shaker **11.49**

Forest Green

785-138 12 oz **3.98**
785-1638 32 oz Shaker **11.49**

Forest Blend

785-139 12 oz **3.98**
785-1639 32 oz Shaker **11.49**

BUSHES*

Available in six realistic colors and great for making hedges, bushes, shrubs and trees.

Olive Green

785-144 12 oz **3.98**
785-1644 32 oz Shaker **11.49**

Light Green

785-145 12 oz **3.98**
785-1645 32 oz Shaker **11.49**

Medium Green

785-146 12 oz **3.98**
785-1646 32 oz Shaker **11.49**

Dark Green

785-147 12 oz **3.98**
785-1647 32 oz Shaker **11.49**

Forest Green

785-148 12 oz **3.98**
785-1648 32 oz Shaker **11.49**

Forest Blend

785-149 12 oz **3.98**
785-1649 32 oz Shaker **11.49**

*Woodland Scenics® Patented Product

LEARNING AIDS . . . YOU CAN DO IT

Woodland Scenics Learning Kits 13.98 ea

Rock Faces
785-951
Teaches you how to make and color realistic rock formations.

Trees
785-953
Shows you how to make and add trees to your layout.

River/Waterfall
785-955
Learn how to create the illusion of deep water and make a river with a waterfall. Includes Earth Colors Liquid Pigments, Realistic Water, Water Effects, Talus, Plaster Cloth, Green Blend Turf, Scenic Glue and applicator.

Road System
785-952
Learn to add roads and other paved areas to any layout.

Landscaping
785-954
Teaches you how to use the complete line of Woodland Scenics ground covers and foliage products.

Scenery Details
785-956
Learn simple techniques to detail your layout. Includes Dead Fall, Fine Turf, Bushes, Underbrush, Fine-Leaf Foliage, Field Grass, Flowering Foliage, Poly Fiber and Scenic Glue.

DETAILS

Soft Flake Snow Shaker
785-140
9.98
This realistic, easy-to-use snow is available in a 32 oz Shaker with a sifter top. Perfect for adding either light dustings or heavy drifts.

Dead Fall
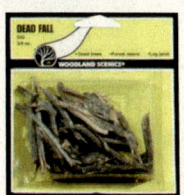
785-30 .5 oz Weight **3.98**
A natural ready-to-use product for modeling fallen or standing dead trees and stumps, as well as modeling forest floor debris.

POLY FIBER

785-178 Green **2.98**
A synthetic fiber intended for use with ground foam to create undergrowth, vines, and economical trees.

FLOWERING FOLIAGE 3.39 ea

A great way to model wildflowers or create flowering bushes and add a splash of color anywhere on your layout. Available in two colors; Purple and Yellow. Use for modeling flowerbeds along the railroad tracks, in fields, on hillsides or around buildings. Covers 100 sq. in.

785-176 Yellow

785-177 Purple

ADHESIVES

Hob-e-Tac®
785-195 2 fl oz **5.49**
Multi-purpose, water-soluble, high-tack adhesive. Perfect for making trees. Should be used as a contact adhesive.

Scenic Glue
785-190 8 fl oz **6.49**
Formulated especially for model landscaping. Dries clear with a matte (flat) finish, is flexible and leaves no residue. Use to attach various Foliage, Bushes, Underbrush and Lichen. Does not become brittle after drying.

Scenic Cement
785-191 16 fl oz **6.49**
Water-soluble, non-toxic, ready-to-use for Ballast, Turf and more. Dries to a clear, matte finish. Apply with Scenic Sprayer (sold separately) or brush on.

SCENERY

PLASTER

Plaster Cloth
785-1203 15 ft roll **8.79**
A simple, convenient, and lightweight way to create a durable terrain shell or base. Just wad newspaper and stack to form the desired shape. Dip Plaster Cloth in water, lay over newspaper and allow to dry. A quick, no mess scenery base. Includes approximately 10 square feet of cloth.

Lightweight Hydrocal*

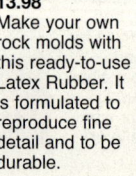

785-1201 1/2 gal **9.49**
A specially formulated new Lightweight Hydrocal for terrain model builders. Lightweight Hydrocal is nearly half the weight of Hydrocal, goes almost twice as far, and is the tough, quick setting product.

*Hydrocal is a product of U.S. Gypsum

Latex Rubber
785-1204 16 fl oz **13.98**
Make your own rock molds with this ready-to-use Latex Rubber. It is formulated to reproduce fine detail and to be durable.

Mold-A-Scene Plaster

785-1202 1/2 gal **9.49**
Mold-A-Scene is a plaster material that can be shaped without a mold like modeling clay. Its longer setting time allows a scenery modeler to add terrain contours to new or existing scenery.

Flex Paste
785-1205 16 fl oz **14.98**
Use this as a flexible, non-cracking coating over Styrofoam or as a road base for concrete or asphalt modeling.

ROCK MOLDS
7.79 ea (Unless Noted)

Highly detailed, flexible, and durable rock molds. Use to cast small boulders, rock outcroppings, top rock for fields and creeks, or make entire rock faces by combining castings produced with these molds.

5 X 7" AND 5 X 10-1/2" ROCK MOLDS

785-1230 Outcroppings

785-1235 Laced Face Rock

785-1240 Rock Mass

785-1231 Surface Rocks

785-1236 Classic Rock

785-1241 Layered Rock

785-1232 Boulders

785-1237 Wind Rock

785-1242 Washed Rock **8.79**

785-1233 Embankments

785-1238 Weathered Rock

785-1243 Base Rock **8.79**

785-1234 Random Rock

785-1239 Strata Stone

785-1244 Facet Rock **8.79**

SCENERY

MOD-U-RAIL™ SYSTEM

Build the layout of your dreams – one module at a time! This space-saving system lets you build individual modules at your own pace. There are two kits available, the Straight and Corner Module Kits.

Guidelines for creating your own track plan are provided and the system assembles without power tools or complicated calculations – and best of all, there's no dusty mess!

Even the landscape material is included to make trees, ballast track, and create beautiful ground cover using various colors and sizes of turf and foliage. Simply add your choice of track, structures and vehicles (all sold separately).

Each Kit includes bolts and two connector plates so you can bolt your modules end-to-end. You can buy the Connector Plate Set (785-4780, 10.98) which allows you to connect your modules together side-to-side or end-to-end. It includes four connector plates and hardware.

Straight Module Kit

This module is for the straight portion of your layout. It can be bolted to another straight or to a corner module.

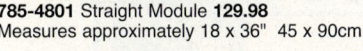

785-4801 Straight Module **129.98**
Measures approximately 18 x 36" 45 x 90cm.

Corner Module Kit

This module also makes a square and can be used as a curve for your layout. Track can be placed anywhere. This module bolts to another corner or to a straight module.

785-4802 Corner Module **149.98**
Measures approximately 36 x 36" 90 x 90cm.

Connector Plate Set
NEW 785-4780 10.98
Expand the possibilities of your Mod-U-Rail layout with this set. Special connectors allow modules to be bolted together side-by-side, so you can easily create a larger area as needed. Complete with connectors, bolts and wing nuts.

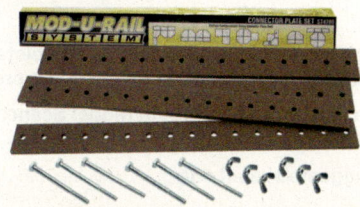

177

SCENERY

SCENIC RIDGE KIT 785-1482

Scenic Ridge includes all the SubTerrain components, Terrain products and Landscaping materials you need to build a complete 3 x 6-foot N Scale layout. It even comes with a full-size track plan printed on its base to remove all guesswork. Designed for easy expansion. You can build it as a stand-alone model or an NTRAK module.

The Woodland Scenics Road System is also included so you can add streets, roads, parking lots, sidewalks and other paved areas.

Scenic Ridge teaches you to build a layout from start to finish. When it's done, you'll not only have a great layout, but knowledge to build more.

Suggested retail only $298.00

- **No expensive power tools needed**
- **No dusty mess**
- **No complicated calculations**
- **Easy to build**

Winner! Model Railroader Readers' Choice Awards 1999 — N Scale Structure/Accessory

LEARNING AIDS...YOU CAN DO IT

The SubTerrain Scenery Kit 785-929

By building this 12 x 24-inch N Scale diorama you will learn how to:

- Build a complete layout using the revolutionary SubTerrain Lightweight Layout System®
- Add terrain features with Plaster Cloth, pre-cast Rock Faces, Talus and a Tunnel Portal.
- Apply realistic scenery with a complete selection of ground covers, ballast, trees and other landscaping products.

It's like getting a Ph.D. in Model Scenery! Great to display trains, plastic models or collectible buildings.

Suggested retail only $49.98

TOWN AND FACTORY BUILDING SET 785-1485

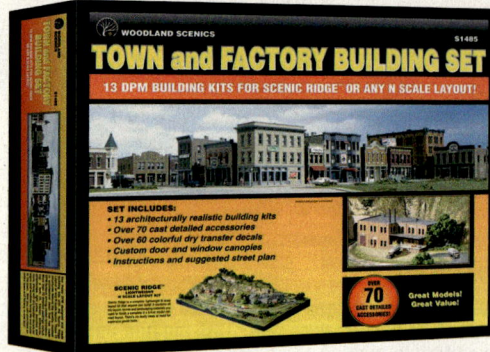

The "Town and Factory Building Set" is a complete town in a box! It includes 13 separate N Scale building kits and more than 70 white metal accessories, plus dozens of Dry Transfer decals from Woodland Scenics®. Designed especially for use with the Scenic Ridge (#785-1482, sold separately), the models will look great on any N Scale layout. All models are unassembled, unpainted kits.

Suggested retail only............................. $125.00

SCENERY

THE COMPLETE TERRAIN SYSTEM

Woodland Scenics Terrain products are a complete system for beginners and craftsmen alike. The Terrain System has all the products needed to make earth contour models that reflect any type of terrain. The system includes Lightweight Hydrocal, Mold-A-Scene, Plaster Cloth, E-Z Water, Flex Paste, Latex Rubber, Tunnel Portals, Retaining Walls, Culverts, Talus, Tunnel Liner Form, Earth Color Liquid Pigments, Scenic Sprayer, Rock Molds and The Scenery Manual. Each product has easy to follow instructions.

E-Z Water

785-1206 16 oz **10.49**
This heat activated water modeling material has been developed for the special needs of the scenery modeler. Melt on stove and pour.

Hot New Products Announced Daily! Visit Walthers Web site at
www.walthers.com

Tunnel Liner Form

785-1250 **4.79**
Easy way to cast realistic rock walls and ceilings to detail the interior of single or double track tunnels.

Pigments 5.29 ea

Earth Colors Liquid Pigments
Use the eight different colors of Earth Colors Liquid Pigment to stain rocks, terrain and plaster castings. They are water-soluble and can be diluted and blended in limitless combinations. Extremely concentrated for economical use. 4 fl oz each. (Photos show plaster rock castings, stained with color.)

785-1216 White

785-1217 Concrete

785-1218 Stone Gray

785-1219 Slate Gray

785-1220 Black

785-1221 Raw Umber

785-1222 Burnt Umber

785-1223 Yellow Ocher

Undercoat Pigments 6.98 ea

Formulated for use under Green Blend and Earth Blended Turf (785-49 and 785-50) to provide a base color. These two colors of Liquid Pigment can also be used for rocks and plaster castings. Extremely concentrated. 8 fl oz each. (Photos show plaster rock castings, stained with color.)

785-1228 Green Undercoat

785-1229 Earth Undercoat

Earth Color Kit

785-1215 Earth Color Kit **18.98**
A simple system for staining rocks, terrain and plaster castings such as portals. Beginners get quality results. The Earth Color Kits include instructions, applicator, palette and eight 1 fl oz bottles each of Earth Color Liquid Pigment (White, Concrete, Stone Gray, Slate Gray, Raw Umber, Burnt Umber, Yellow Ochre).

SCENERY

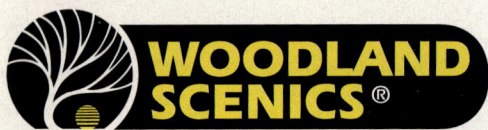

NEW PRODUCTS

ReadyGrass™ Vinyl Mat*

These high-quality grass mats can be used as-is, or mounted to plywood. They're great for model railroads, school projects, arts and crafts, gaming, military models, architectural models, collectible houses, slot cars and much more. The special vinyl back can easily be shaped with the Heat Tool (#785-5162) and newspaper wads to form hills, mountains and valleys. The turf is also removable and leaves a hard, smooth surface that's perfect for roads, sidewalks, parking lots (easily modeled with the Road Kit #785-5151) or building placement. By removing turf and using the Water Kit (#785-5153), you can add rivers, streams, lakes and ponds. Choose from three mat sizes; Large 50 x 100" (125 x 250cm), Small 33 x 50" (82.5 x 125cm) or the Project Sheet 14-1/8 x 12-1/2" (35.6 x 31.2cm) in four different colors.

Spring Grass

NEW 785-5121 Large **24.98**
NEW 785-5131 Small **9.98**
NEW 785-5141 Project Sheet **2.98**

Green Grass

NEW 785-5122 Large **24.98**
NEW 785-5132 Small **9.98**
NEW 785-5142 Project Sheet **2.98**

Forest Grass

NEW 785-5123 Large **24.98**
NEW 785-5133 Small **9.98**
NEW 785-5143 Project Sheet **2.98**

Summer Grass

NEW 785-5124 Large **24.98**
NEW 785-5134 Small **9.98**
NEW 785-5144 Project Sheet **2.98**

ReadyGrass Accessories

Road Kit

NEW 785-5151 **10.98**
Complete kit with everything needed to make roads, sidewalks and parking lots.

Landscape Kit

NEW 785-5152 **14.98**
Includes everything needed - Foliage, Bushes, Shrubs and adhesive - to enhance a 4' x 8' area.

Water Kit

NEW 785-5153 **10.98**
Everything needed to model a pond, stream, river or lake in one complete kit.

Tree Kit

NEW 785-5154 **19.98**
A complete kit with everything you'll need to make 27 deciduous and pine trees for a 4' x 8' area. Trees range in height from 2-1/2 to 6" (5 to 15.2cm).

Mat Adhesive

NEW 785-5161 **6.98**
Use for permanent or temporary mounting of ReadyGrass Mats on any surface; can also be used for mounting puzzles and posters to art board.

Heat Tool

NEW 785-5162 **24.98**
Use with ReadyGrass vinyl mats to form hills, mounds and valleys.

*Patent Pending

ReadyGrass™ Accessories

Attach Mat with Mat Adhesive

Glue to any surface with Mat Adhesive.

Form Hills with Heat Tool

Form hills over newspaper wads with Heat Tool.

Make Roads and Sidewalks with Road Kit

Wet area, scrape off turf, then paint. Detail road and parking lot with Striping Pen.

Add Water with Water Kit
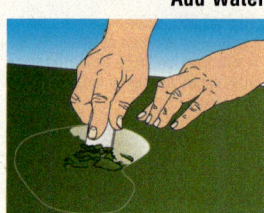

Wet area, scrape off turf, then paint. Pour water.

Add Trees with Tree Kit
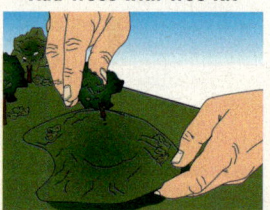
Make and plant trees.

Add Landscaping with Landscape Kit

Add bushes and highlights.

SCENERY

PORTALS AND RETAINING WALLS

Tunnel Portals and Retaining Walls are high density Hydrocal* castings that are easy to stain with Earth Color Liquid Pigments and are available in concrete, cut stone, random stone and timber styles. Retaining Walls come in three sections per package. Each section can be used alone or installed adjacent to another in an endless chain fashion. They can be cut to varying heights to accommodate the adjoining terrain.

* Hydrocal is a product of US Gypsum.

CULVERTS
pkg(2) 6.49 ea

Culverts are also high density *Hydrocal castings. There are two culverts per package.

785-1162 Concrete

785-1164 Random Stone

785-1163 Masonry Arch

785-1165 Timber

785-1152 Concrete - 2 Single 9.49

785-1155 Random Stone - 2 Single 9.49

785-1158 Concrete pkg(6) 9.98

785-1153 Cut Stone - 2 Single 9.49

785-1156 Concrete - 2 Double 10.49

785-1159 Cut Stone pkg(6) 9.98

785-1154 Timber - 2 Single 9.49

785-1157 Cut Stone - 2 Double 10.49

785-1160 Timber pkg(6) 9.98

785-1161 Random Stone 9.98 pkg(6)

New Arrivals Updated Every Day! Visit Walthers Web site at
www.walthers.com

SCENERY

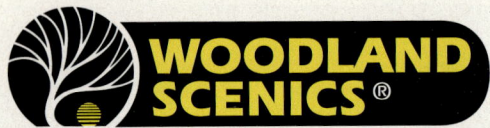

Talus 3.59 ea

Natural rock debris usually occurs near rock faces and outcroppings, near culverts and portals and in creeks and ditches. For super detailing add Talus to models in appropriate areas with white glue. Intermix grades, blend shades, and even stain your own to match rock castings with Woodland Scenics Earth Colors. 12 oz bags.

FOUR COLORS

Buff

Brown

Gray

Natural

FOUR GRADES

Fine

Medium

Coarse

Extra Coarse

COLOR	FINE	MED.	COARSE	EXTRA COARSE
Buff	785-1270	785-1271	785-1272	785-1273
Brown	785-1274	785-1275	785-1276	785-1277
Gray	785-1278	785-1279	785-1280	785-1281
Natural	785-1282	785-1283	785-1284	785-1285

Coal

Mine Run Coal

Lump Coal

785-92 Mine Run Coal 6 oz vol. Unsorted **3.79**
785-93 Lump Coal 6 oz vol. 4" or greater in diameter **3.79**

Ballast 3.79 ea (Unless Noted)
32 oz Ballast Shaker 9.98 ea

Woodland Scenics now offers its realistic colors and textures of ballast in standard Bags with 18 cubic inches, or 32 oz Shakers that hold 50 cubic inches and allow easy application and storage.

Iron Ore

Dark Brown

Brown

Buff

Light Gray / Gray

Cinders

Blended Medium Gray

COLOR		FINE	MEDIUM	COARSE
Iron Ore	Bag	785-70	785-77	785-84
Dark Brown	Bag	785-71	785-78	785-85
Brown	Bag	785-72	785-79	785-86
	32 oz Shaker	785-1372	785-1379	785-1386
Buff	Bag	785-73	785-80	785-87
	32 oz Shaker	785-1373	785-1380	785-1387
Light Gray	Bag	785-74	785-81	785-88
	32 oz Shaker	785-1374	785-1381	785-1388
Gray	Bag	785-75	785-82	785-89
	32 oz Shaker	785-1375	785-1382	785-1389
Cinders	Bag	785-76	785-83	785-90
	32 oz Shaker	785-1376	785-1383	785-1390
Blended Medium Gray				
	24 oz. Vol	785-94	7.98	
	32 oz Shaker	785-1393	785-1394	785-1395

Fine

Medium

Coarse

SCALE REFERENCE CHART: BALLAST

SCALE	FINE	MEDIUM	COARSE
Z	2.2"-7.3"	7.3"-11"	11"-18.3"
N	1.6"-5.3"	5.3"-8"	8"-13.3"
HO	.9"-2.9"	2.9"-4.3"	4.4"-7.2"
S	.6"-2.1"	2.1"-3.2"	3.2"-5.3"
O	.5"-1.6"	1.6"-2.4"	2.4"-3.9"
1	.3"-1"	1.1"-1.6"	1.6"-2.6"
G	.24"-.8"	.8"-1.2"	1.2"-1.9"

SCENIC CEMENT

785-191 16 fl oz **6.49**
Water-soluble, nontoxic, ready-to-use for Ballast, Turf and more. Dries to a clear, matte finish. Apply with Scenic Sprayer (sold separately) or brush on.

SCENIC SPRAYER

785-192 8 oz **3.98**
Nozzle is adjustable from a very fine mist to a steady stream. May be used to spray water, diluted Earth Colors Liquid Pigment.

CANISTER SHAKER

785-194 32 Ounces Volume **3.98**
A multi-purpose container used to store and organize landscape products. Comes with dual-purpose cap; one side serves as a shaker, the other is for accessing larger quantities.

785-199 Pack of Six **19.98**
Empty containers in a storage tray. Great way to organize your landscape products.

SCENERY

LEARNING AIDS... YOU CAN DO IT

THE SCENERY KIT
785-927

Whether beginner or expert, with The Scenery Kit modelers learn scenery techniques that dramatically improve their skills...in just hours! A 10" x 18" diorama displays your favorite rolling stock or engine when finished.

You Will Learn To:

Make Trees, Create Mountains, Build Rolling Terrain, Stain Rocks Realistically, Plant Grass, Weeds and Bushes, Install Track and Ballast.

- Includes a piece of HO track, but N scale can be substituted
- All scenery materials included...even paint and hardboard base (Everything!)
- **785-927** If purchased separately $61.00. Suggested retail only **$59.98**

TURN YOUR TRAIN SET INTO A MODEL RAILROAD!

MOUNTAIN VALLEY SCENERY KIT®
785-928

Once tracks are in place, use the Mountain Valley Scenery Kit to transform that basic 4' x 8' sheet of plywood into a three-dimensional sceniced layout. It includes everything needed to add trees, grass, weeds, rocks, mountains, tunnels, ballast and more to a layout. Use your HO Scale track plan or ours. Step-by-step instructions make this kit fun and easy!

785-928 $104 value if items purchased separately, only **$84.98**

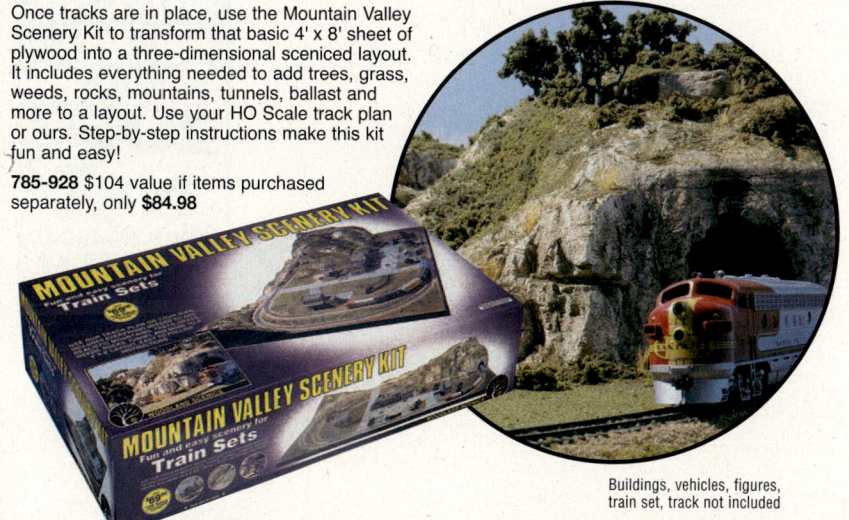

Buildings, vehicles, figures, train set, track not included

BOOKS, VIDEOS & CATALOGS

The Clinic (Video) 24.98 ea

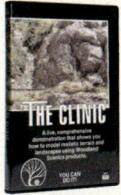 

785-970   785-990

785-970 DVD
785-990 VHS
Learn by watching the professionals demostrate landscaping and terrain modeling techiques. In this video, you'll see just how easy it is. 1 hour and 15 minutes.

Model Scenery Made Easy (Video) 24.98 ea

785-973   785-993

785-973 DVD
785-993 VHS
A comprehensive, detailed account of scenery modeling. Provides helpful information for modelers of any skill level, and shows how to do scenery the easy way. Approximately 60 minutes.

SubTerrain: Build a Layout Fast & Easy (Video) 24.98 ea

785-1400   785-1401

785-1400 DVD
785-1401 VHS
A step-by-step video that shows you how to build a model railroad layout with the revolutionary Sub Terrain Layout System. Approximately 60 minutes.

The Scenery Manual

785-1207 10.98
Fully-illustrated, with new spiral binding, teaching manual, developed by the experts on model scenery.

Catalog

785-100 2.50
Full-color, 80-page guide to Woodland Scenics products.

SubTerrain Manual

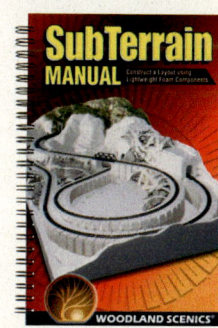

785-1402 7.98
An illustrated how-to manual that teaches you how to create the ideal base for scenery and landscaping in five easy steps.

See What's New and Exciting at
www.walthers.com

SCENERY

Models and Photo by Dennis Murphy, Girdwood, Alaska

STRUCTURES

Deep in the heart of the city's industrial district, switching leads and branches run through brick-and-mortar canyons between factories and warehouses. The lines are owned by a terminal switching railroad jointly owned by mainline roads serving the city, so switch runs from several railways compete for space on a web of track. On the line that runs past Riesen Bread, the hind end of a Chessie local rolls by as a CNW transfer run waits to get through the interlocking. Meanwhile, a CNW switcher spots a loaded covered hopper under the canopy at Riesen.

Factories and warehouses are the railroads' bread and butter. Manufacturers, warehouses and distributors ship and receive the cars that keep the railroads in business. Their buildings add interest to model railroads and give us a reason to simulate prototype operations. Whether you're modeling big cities loaded with businesses or rural towns with a team track, depot and grain elevator, you'll find buildings that will add realism to your railroad in the Structures Section.

CORNERSTONE MODULARS™

Congratulations Contest Winners!

Building unique models for your railroad has never been easier thanks to Cornerstone Modulars™! Last year, we asked you to share with other readers how you've used these parts to create totally new structures for your layout — thanks to everyone who entered — and here are the winners of our first Modular Modeling Contest! (We'd love to see your models showcased here next year — complete details on our 2007 Contest are on the following pages.)

Grand Prize Winner
Roger Holmes of Springfield, IL
Photos by John Evans of Springfield, IL
Entry: American Supply

"The American Supply complex utilizes Cornerstone Modulars parts in a unique, easy to duplicate way to create a scene that has that generic "down by the tracks" feel suitable for numerous modeling eras."

This busy trackside industry would be right at home in any big city scene and was built with Foundations & Docks (#933-3283), Wall Columns & Caps (#933-3284), along with Large Walls (#933-3282) and Small Walls (#933-3281). The actual model was completed before the release of the Roof Details set, so Roger used odds and ends from his spare parts box, including several leftover vents and a water tank from the Hardwood Furniture kit. The sign on the front was modified from the decals included with the American Hardware Supply kit.

As earlier buildings, streets and railroads competed for space many industrial areas were broken up into odd shaped parcels of land. Buildings were shoehorned in to the available area, which often resulted in large structures with slightly shorter or angled walls on one or more sides. This neat detail adds a lot of visual interest to Roger's model. This required cutting and bending corner pilasters for both structures; on the larger, they were bent outward beyond the standard 90° and for the smaller, the parts were bent inward to fit. The angled walls were then lengthened with pieces of Evergreen .80 x .125" styrene strip. The finished models were mounted on a base of 1/8" thick model airplane plywood, which matches the height of standard N Scale roadbed.

CORNERSTONE MODULARS™

First Prize Winner
Jim Tuck of Flagstaff, AZ
Entry: Ice House

"My entry is an ice house, hence the closed windows, white roofs and icing platform.

This is one of three Modular buildings (the other two will be a freight house and a farm implement warehouse) I have planned for the Timesaver section of my NTRAK module.

Thanks for creating this system — I had great fun designing and building my first building and look forward to many more."

Perishable traffic was big business for the nation's railroads. Fresh fruits and vegetables of all kinds moved cross-country from growing areas to distant markets. For many years, block ice was used in the cars to keep the loads cold in transit. Although railroads began making the transition to mechanical reefers in the 1950s, ice plants where ice was made and icehouses where it could be stored until needed, were a common site at many railroad yards into the 1970s when the last ice-cooled cars were retired.

For this unique design, Jim used Small Walls (#933-3281), Large Walls (#933-3282), Flat & Peaked Roofs (#933-

3280), Wall Columns (#933-3284), Foundations & Loading Docks (#933-3282) and Roof Details (#933-3286). Other parts used in construction include various sizes of Evergreen styrene and Plastruct Handrails. Jim made the large blocks of ice on the trackside platform by cutting down a clear plastic floral note holder obtained from a flower shop.

Second Prize Winner
Stephen D. Barker of Tuscon, AZ
Entry: Historic Industrial Building

"My model is based on an historic structure with a nearly identical floor plan located in the old Paterson, New Jersey, silk factory district. I was looking to build a multi-story structure, and found this five-floor candidate in the book "Industry, Architecture and Engineering" by Louis Bergeron and Maria Maiullari-Pontois. The design of the building fits the Walthers Modular sets nicely."

Stephen's model is constructed with Flat & Peaked Roofs (#933-3280), Wall Columns (#933-3284) plus Small Walls (#933-3281) and Large Walls (#933-3282). As the prototype had no visible foundation, Stephen used one large and two small bases. Wall sections were first assembled on a piece of plate glass to achieve the best alignment of the parts. Next, the corner pilasters were glued in place on the front and rear walls, and after these parts were dry, all four walls for each story were joined together. A paper pattern as made for the roof on the one

story section, and the final part was then cut to shape from a Small Roof. A quick coat of Zinc Chromate primer was applied for the overall brick color. Future plans include adding mortar color, signs and fire escapes.

CORNERSTONE MODULARS™

Announcing The 2008 Modeling Contest for Cornerstone Modulars™!

Build on the Power of your Imagination and Win!

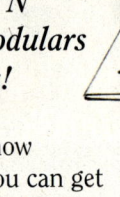

Build 'em big or small. Build 'em short or tall. We're looking for different, creative designs constructed with our N Scale Modulars products!

Show us how creative you can get and you could win:

First Prize:
$250 Walthers Gift Certificate

Second Prize:
$100 Walthers Gift Certificate

Third Prize:
One 2008 N&Z Reference Book and One Cornerstone Series® product* of your choice.

To Enter:

1) <u>Do NOT send your model!</u>

2) Typed or printed documentation of all parts used must be submitted, including manufacturer information and product numbers. Please highlight any special construction step/s that went into the building process. Please include a typed or printed description of your structure in 150 words or less – tell us what inspired your design and how you use the structure.

3) A minimum of three color photos (digital, slides or prints are fine) must accompany each entry, showing different angles or details of the finished structure. Please see the "Magic of Model Railroading" Section on walthers.com for details on image criteria.

4) If someone else takes the photographs, please include that person's name.

5) All submitted items are not returnable.

6) E-mail entries to: modularscontest@walthers.com or mail your entry to:

Attn: N Modulars Contest
Wm. K. Walthers, Inc.
P.O. Box 3039
Milwaukee, WI 53201-3039

Rules:

1. Entries will be judged on creativity, quality and ease of construction.
2. Limit one entry per person, club or group. Entry must include name(s), address, phone and e-mail information.
3. All entries must reach us by April 15, 2007.
4. Entries can be mailed or e-mailed.
5. Walthers retains all rights to use the winning designs in future promotions of Walthers products. The company retains the right to publish all submitted designs in future Reference Books and on walthers.com.
6. Winning models must be available for future photography and/or display by Walthers.
7. A list of winners and corresponding designs will be published in the 2008 N&Z Reference Book. Winners will be notified by mail upon the publication of the 2008 N&Z Reference Book.

* Applies to any in stock product valued at $30.98 or less. Walthers employees and their families are not eligible. Void where prohibited.

CORNERSTONE MODULARS™

Building on the Power of Your Imagination™

Create the N Scale Structures You've Been Dreaming of!

Custom-build them with the all-new Cornerstone Modulars™...

Each set comes with parts for a specific area of a building. Unlike traditional structure kits or assembled models, YOU choose the location of doors, loading docks, windows, roof style and more.

Whether you're just getting started or have been modeling for years, you'll achieve outstanding results with Cornerstone Modulars because each piece is engineered for perfect fit and alignment to make assembly easy. Each set also includes basic assembly instructions with loads of illustrations and modeling tips.

Just mix and match walls, doors, windows and details from the various sets – no complicated kitbashing or cutting is needed to create a one-of-a-kind industry for your layout.

Parts come molded in realistic brick, window and door, concrete or roof colors so no painting is needed. But as separate parts, it's a snap to custom-paint your project if you want to.

Best of all, you can use leftover parts with your next building and securely store them in the reclosable plastic packages until they're needed.

FROM THIS   **TO THIS**   **OR THIS**

AND MORE

All structures shown were made from Modulars parts.

An Easy, Exciting New Way to Build Unique Industries

If you can see it in your mind, you can build it on your N Scale layout with Cornerstone Modulars. Choose and combine walls, roofs, windows, doors and more to create the industries you want quickly and easily!

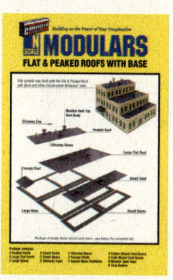 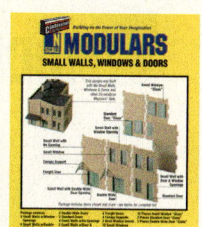

Flat & Peaked Roofs w/Base
933-3280 9.98

Small Walls, Windows & Doors
933-3281 9.98

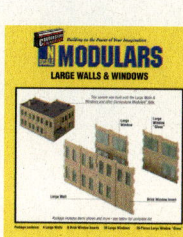 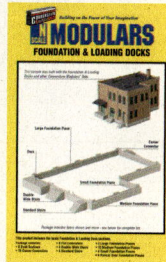

Large Walls & Windows
933-3282 9.98

Foundation & Loading Docks
933-3283 9.98

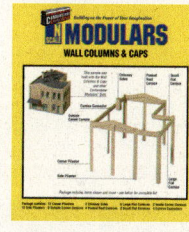

Wall Columns & Caps
933-3284 9.98

Walls w/Vehicle Doors
933-3285 9.98

Roof Details
933-3286 9.98

Large Door Wall Section
933-3287 9.98

CORNERSTONE MODULARS™

NEW PRODUCTS
- New Parts to Mix & Match
- Engineered for Perfect Fit
- Molded in Colors
- Reclosable Packages
- Basic Instructions & Modeling Tips Included

STERLING DAIRY COMPLEX
NEW 933-3298   149.98

December 2006
- Build a Complete Industry
- Several Styles of Door & Window Walls
- Easily Arranged to Fit Your Layout
- Track Bumpers, Water Tanks & Smokestack Included

3-IN-1 BUILDING #2
NEW 933-3297   39.98

December 2006
- Complete Kit - Great Value!
- Perfect Introduction to Modulars Construction
- New Building Configuration
- Builds 1 of 3 Different Structures
- Includes a Variety of Windows, Walls, Doors & Roofs

See What's Available at
www.walthers.com

CORNERSTONE MODULARS™

A Great Building Block for Your Modulars™ Adventure!

3-IN-1 BUILDING #1
933-3295 29.98

- Perfect Introduction to Cornerstone Modulars Construction
- Build One of Three Different Variations
- Walls, Doors, Windows & Roofs Included
- Complete Instructions
- Decal Lettering for Several Businesses

Discover the fun of Cornerstone Modulars construction with this complete building set!

All the parts you need to build your choice of a basic rectangular structure, two smaller structures or an "L"-shaped building are included, along with illustrated assembly tips and instructions.

And to take your finished buildings to a new level of realism, custom decal signs are included. This set makes it easy to model typical factory lettering from different eras. Just cut the backgrounds to fit — complete instructions are included — and mix and match to create one-of-a-kind signs for your new industry.

Basic Rectangle...

Small One- and Two-story...

or Expanded "L"

PARAGON HEATING (MODERNIZED FRONT BUILDING)
933-3296 29.98

- Complete Structure Kit
- Fits 1950s to Present
- "Metal" Siding on Front Upper Story
- Parts for 2 Different Front Walls
- Brick Lower Story
- New Glass Block Front Windows
- 2 Different Front Entry Doors w/Glass-Block Transoms
- 2 Front Entrance Canopies
- Use with all Cornerstone Modulars Parts

EMPIRE LEATHER TANNING (MODULAR COMPLEX)
933-3299 99.98

- Four Complete Structure Kits
- Build as Complete Complex or Individual Structures
- Customize with Cornerstone Modulars Parts
- Decal Signs for 4 Different Industries
- Smokestack & Water Tanks Included
- American Prototype
- Fits Popular Modeling Eras

STRUCTURES N SCALE

Built-ups

MORE TIME FOR FUN
- CORNERSTONE SERIES® QUALITY WITH NO ASSEMBLY NEEDED
- INSTANT FUN AND REALISM FOR YOUR RAILROAD
- MOLDED IN AUTHENTIC, MULTIPLE COLORS
- USE WITH ANY RAILROAD, ANY ERA
- MORE TIME FOR FUN

NEW PRODUCTS

SUNRISE FEED MILL
NEW 933-2615 34.98

December 2006
- Authentic Weathering
- Realistic "Wooden" Drop Siding
- Rooftop Dust Collector
- Rail & Truck Unloading Docks
- Colorful Decals
- Grain Bags, Pallets & Other Details
- Create a Scene Right Out of the Box

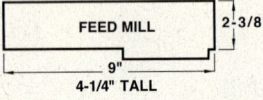

HO Model Shown

GOLDEN VALLEY DEPOT
933-2607 Yellow Ochre & Oxide Brown 29.98

933-2608 Cream & Railroad Green 29.98

933-2609 Two-Tone Gray 29.98

By the 1880s, railroads large and small were building new depots like this in smaller towns.

Fully assembled and ready to use, each includes a nonworking semaphore-style train order signal, a brick platform in the traditional "herringbone" pattern, interior walls with molded details and a working light, "wooden" interior floor, a baggage cart and decal signs.

GOLDEN VALLEY FREIGHT HOUSE
933-2610 Yellow Ochre & Oxide Brown 29.98

933-2611 Cream & Railroad Green 29.98

933-2612 Two-Tone Gray 29.98

January 2007 Delivery

While most people were familiar with their depot, just down the track was the railroad's real money-maker — the Freight House. Here, shipments of freight and packages were transferred to and from waiting rail cars and trucks for local delivery.

The fully assembled structure features detailed "wooden" siding, a loading dock and station name signs matching those included with the Golden Valley Depot.

HO Model Shown

HO Model Shown

Get Daily Info, Photos and News at
www.walthers.com

STRUCTURES N SCALE

Built-ups

DAYTON MACHINE CO.
933-2606 37.98
This detailed, layout-ready model features intricate brickwork and includes both a wood and modern roll-up door so you can customize it to fit steam or diesel-era scenes. Or, leave the door off and insert rails in the grooves on the floor so freight cars can be spotted inside. Model also comes with an interior light, and colorful printed signs for additional businesses

TRACK BUMPERS
pkg(5) 13.98 ea
Prevent accidents! Bumpers are ready to use—just place them at the ends of sidings and spurs. Each pack includes five track bumpers; available in your choice of two colors.

933-2602 Yellow
933-2605 Dark Gray

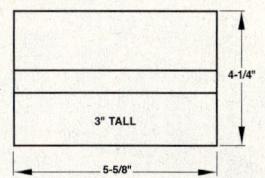

STEEL WATER TANK
933-2601 29.98
Perfect for your biggest and best steam power, this assembled model requires a small amount of layout space and comes with two standpipes and an oil column. Detailed parts are molded in color and for the finishing touch, decal signs are provided.

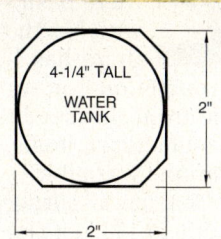

3-PIECE SET W/ ACCESSORIES
29.98 ea
Used as a group or by themselves, these buildings are typical of designs used by American railroads from the 1880s to the 1970s.

Sets include Interlocking Tower, Speeder Shed with Unpowered Speeder and Crossing Shanty with Two Positionable Crossing Gates.

933-2600 Yellow Ochre & Brown
933-2603 Cream & Railroad Green
933-2604 Two-Tone Gray

Trackside Structures Set Cream and Railroad Green 933-2603

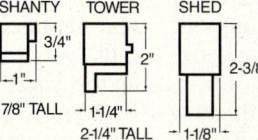

193

Building Walthers' New 130 Ft. Turntable, Modern Roundhouse, and Add-on Kit

By Keith Lyons/*photos by author*

The new Walthers turntable and roundhouse will become a focal point of your model railroad. The 130 ft. turntable accomodates an NP challenger steam locomotive.

Ever since I had started building the Northern Pacific Tacoma Division in N scale I've lamented the fact that there hasn't been a good operating large turntable with North American feel available in N scale. Yes, there has been the old Heljan kit, also marketed through Con-Cor, Walthers, and others. There has also been one from Bowser based on an H0 unit, and some custom manufactured items, but they didn't have the look and operation I was after.

That has all changed in a big way with the release of the new Walthers 130 foot Operating Turntable and the Modern Roundhouse kits. They have the look I was after, or really close to it (meaning kit-bashable!), the operation, and best of all, an affordable price. Yes, I'm happy. I even decided to make it larger by purchasing another add-on kit (total of 4) to make 12 stalls instead of 9. The turntable comes with a controller that is very easy to program and works very well. It's smooth and quiet. Just keep the gear raceway clear of any debris for best operation.

The Roundhouse kits are very cleanly molded and the initial test fit was great. I am never happy with the bare plastic color but if you don't like to paint then you could probably just weather the walls with pigments or chalks and have good results. I decided to paint all the pieces before assembly. I made some observations along the way, and had a few after-thoughts that I'll share in the captions.

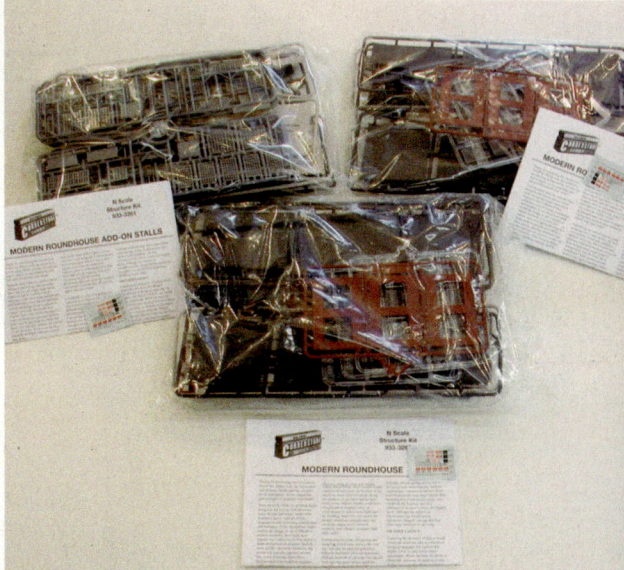

The roundhouse kits, contents, and directions are well organized and delivered nicely sealed in plastic bags.

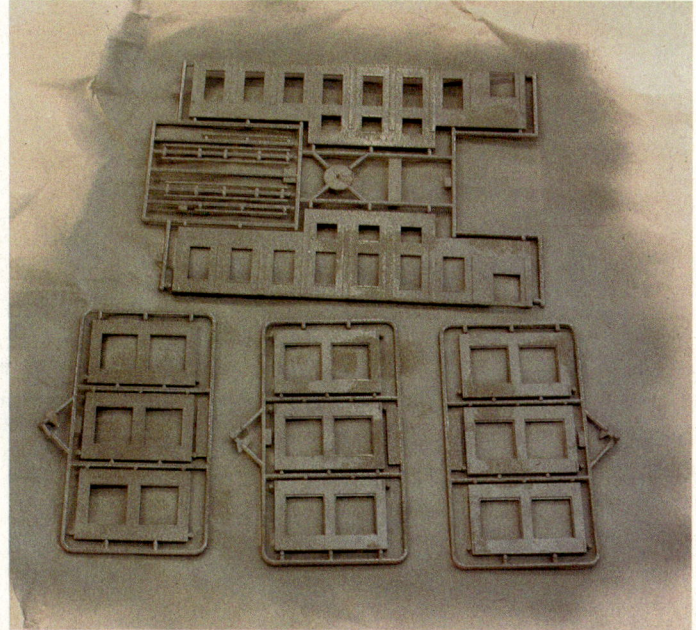

The walls are cast in a red brick with patterns on both sides. I chose to paint the walls a more earthy brown brick color, which seemed closer to the color of bricks used by Northern Pacific. This is optional, and you could simply apply some weathering to the base plastic color.

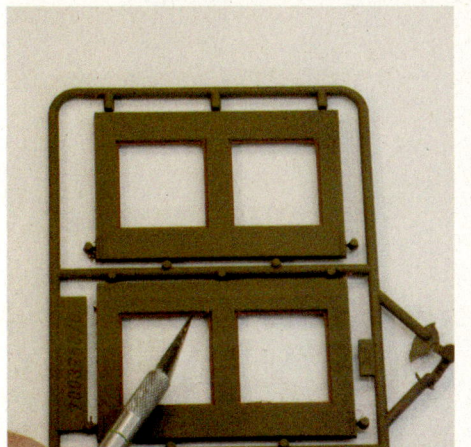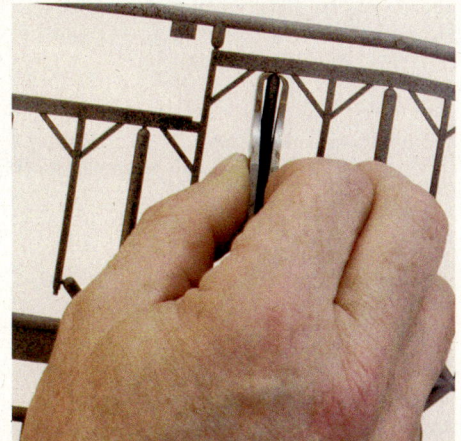

Remember to remove paint from areas where windows or other walls will be glued together (left). The middle and right views show me removing the parts at the gates with a sprue cutter. Flush cutting wire cutters, an X-acto knife, or single-edge razor blade may work as well, but I really like the sprue cutters because they do not put any unnecessary pressure on the plastic parts.

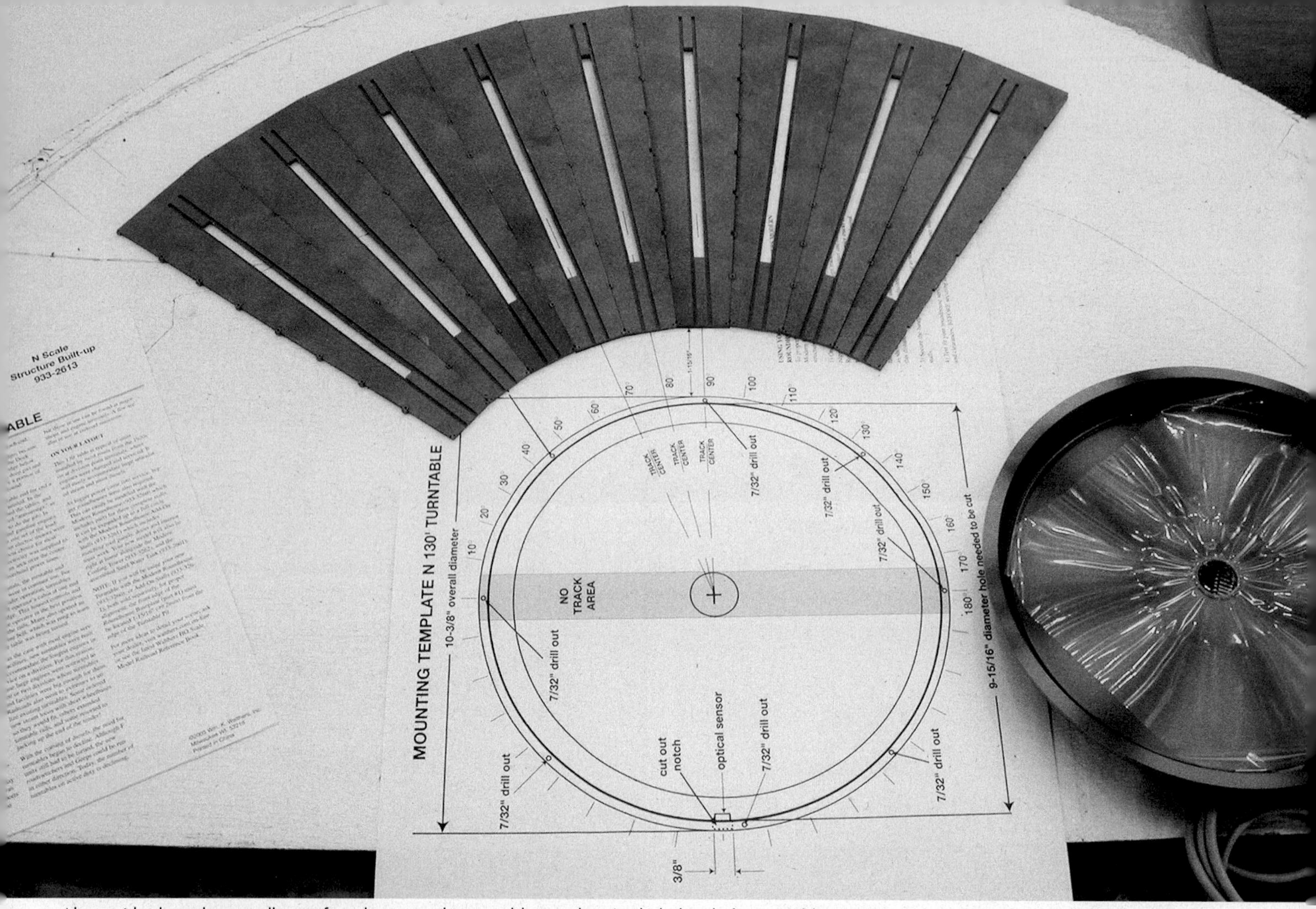

Above, I laid out the roundhouse foundation on the turntable template (included with the turntable) to get an idea of the overall size. I'm using Homasote as a base. Below, using the template, I adjusted my compass to help mark the hole. I found out later that the template circle was about 1/8" smaller than the written dimensions and I should have actually measured the opening before cutting. Use the written dimensions. (An updated template can be downloaded from: http://www.walthers.com/exec/productinfo/933-2613).

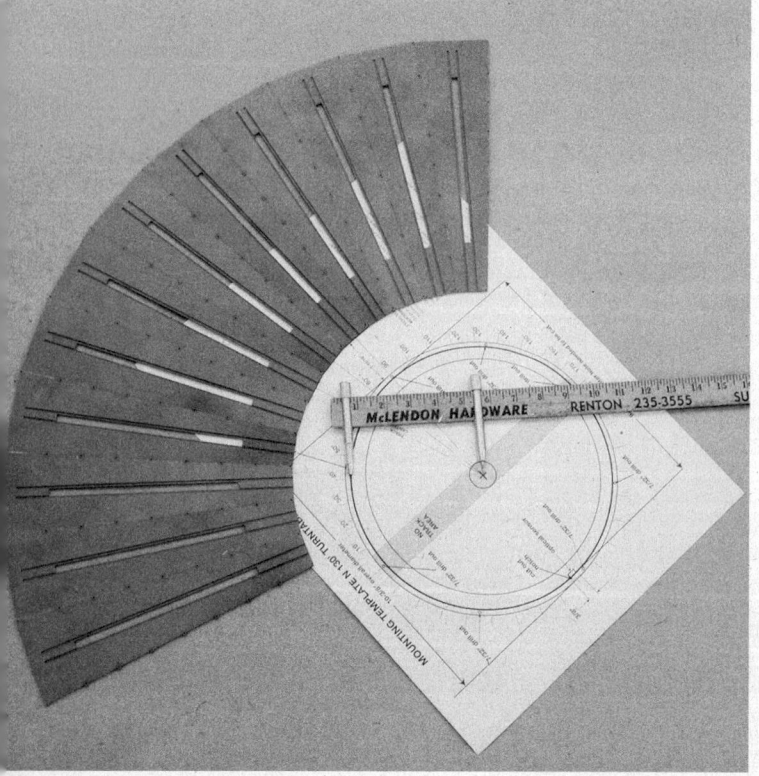

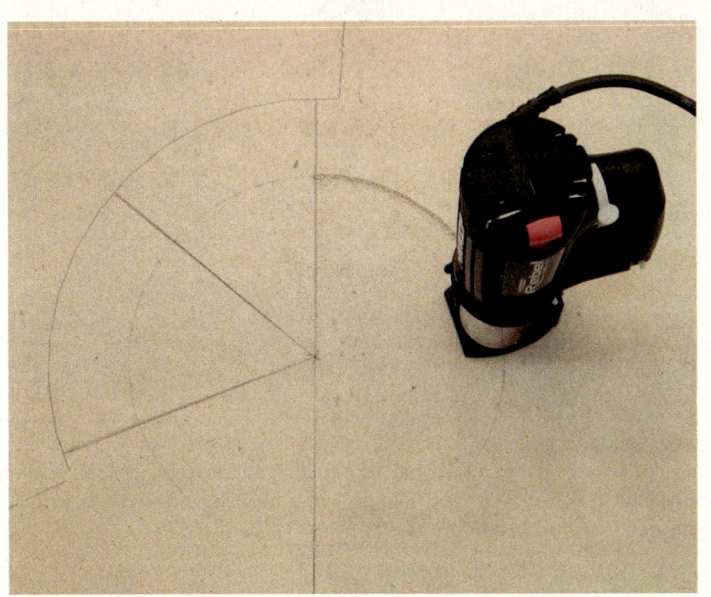 

I used a Roto-Zip tool to cut the hole. Luckily, I was easily able to make the opening a little larger with my Roto-Zip. I was also able to cut the notches for the anchor posts under the turntable pit lip, as well as for the sensor.

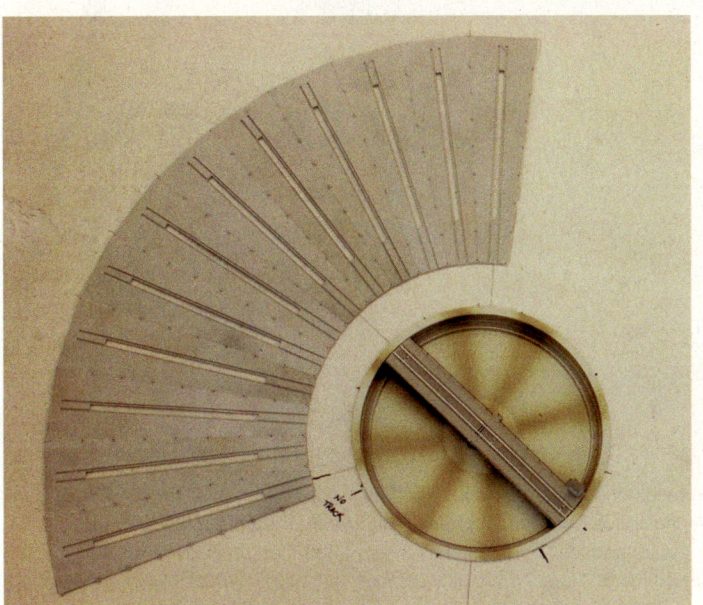 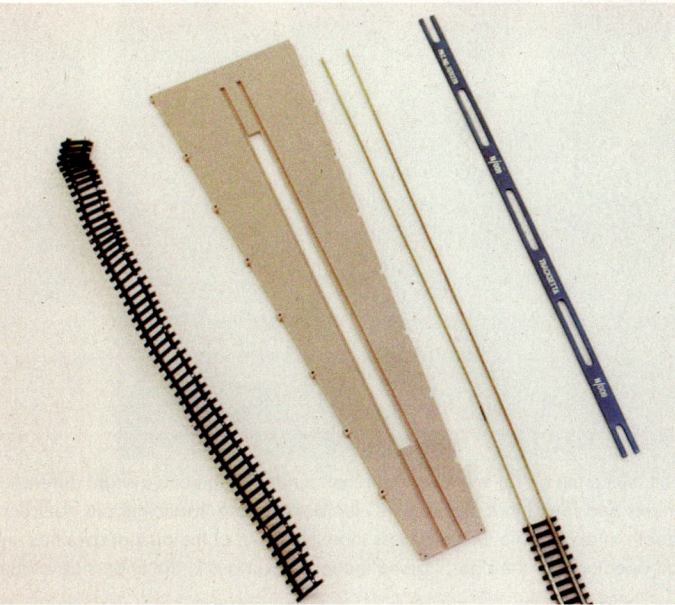

Left, after enlarging the hole just a bit I test fit the turntable to plan the alignment of the rails to the roundhouse. Right, the turntable foundations have troughs on either side of the inspection pits for rails. They appear to be able to accept code 55 rail, but I decided to use Peco code 55 as it's really code 80 with a second bottom "plate" at the code 55 level. This will match the code 80 rail height on the turntable without having to add a shim under the rails on the lip of the turntable pit. I measured and cut the length of flex track needed and removed all the ties where the rails were to go into the foundation. I left ten ties in the space between the roundhouse and the turntable pit and had the rails come up to the edge of the pit.

 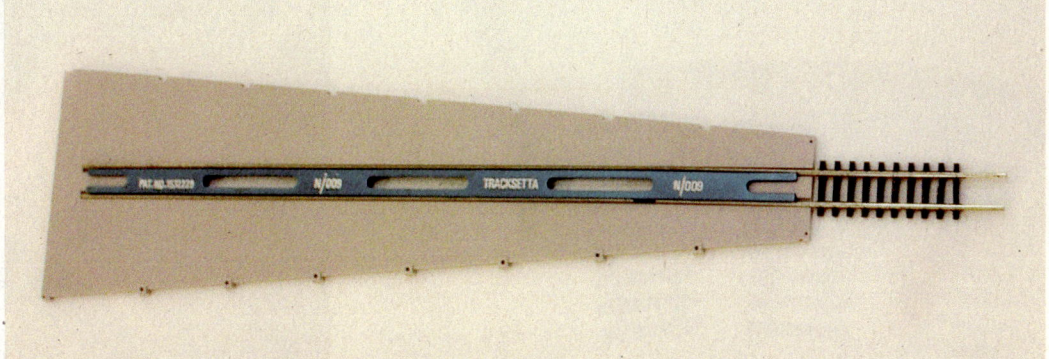

I used an adhesive called Huen's Moveable Glue to bond the rails to the foundation and I like the way it came out. It's very similar to Woodland Scenics Accent Cement. ACC or Epoxy would work as well. Above, I used a Peco straight Tracksetta tool to align the rails and a weight on top of it while the glue sets.

Left, weights hold the rails in place until the glue dries. Right, all roundhouse rails are in place and aligned with the turntable bridge to be straight. Some rails had to be gently filed for proper fit. I then marked the openings for the inspection pits. Unless you make the roof removable you may want to omit the pits and paint the area under them dark gray or black as they can't easily be seen from the open doors.

 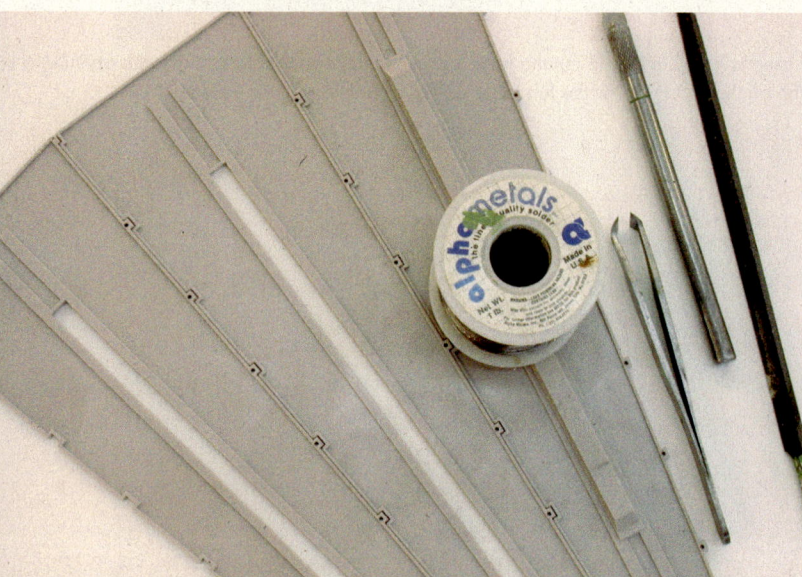

Left, since the pit lip is thicker than the foundation there is a slight difference in height that should be accounted for. I solved that by taking a few measurements and found that digging the clearance for the inspection pits could create the space I needed without needing a lot of shim stock. I set a router depth to about a tie thickness less than the depth of the pit that attaches under the foundation. I cut channels where I had marked through the inspection pit openings. At the right, I glued the inspection pits to the underside of the foundation and placed weights on them to be sure that they were fully home.

 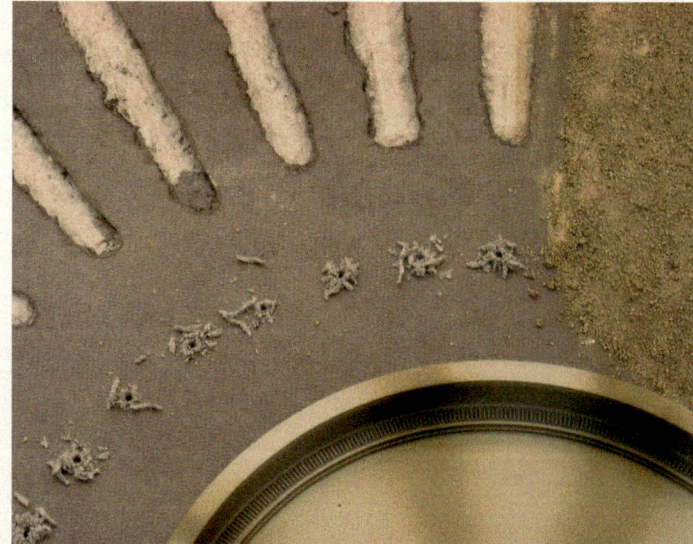

Left, power needs to be sent to the rails and I used the hidden wire method of attaching "downleads" to the bottoms of the rails. I placed them close to the foundation. I used alternating color pairs to help keep them separate as each will go to a separate momentary contact power switch. DCC users can run each pair to their bus lines. The turntable does not route power to those tracks. Right, I then drilled the holes for the roundhouse track wires.

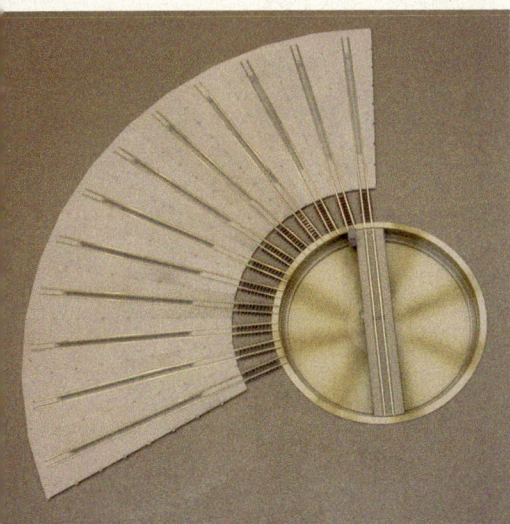

Above, the roundhouse foundation with wired tracks and turntable in place. I had painted the Homasote with brown latex paint to help avoid it soaking up water and deforming when I add scenery materials later. Right, walls are up and some roof panels set in place.

Left, I wanted to be able to remove sections of the roof and Walthers made this easy to do. I simply placed the roof windows as instructed but did not glue them to the walls or trusses. I carefully glued the roof sections to the window frames and allowed them to fully cure. The roof-window panels then rest on the structure, which allows me access to the locomotives in the stalls and permits me to detail the inside of the roundhouse if I choose.

Yes, I did this almost on the floor (left). It's elevated by the width of a 2x4 to allow for the cutting of the hole without cutting the carpet. Note the gardening kneepad.

Once completed and installed, the Walthers turntable and roundhouse complex will add many hours of operating enjoyment and viewing pleasure to your layout. ▶

N Scale Railroading Magazine

Thank you to N Scale Railroading Magazine for allowing us to provide you with the preceding article by Keith Lyons. Informative modeling tips and techniques such as this step-by-step piece about installing the Cornerstone Series® Built-ups Modern 130' Turntable and Modern Roundhouse kit on a layout is just a sampling of the useful articles you'll find in every issue of N Scale Railroading.

N Scale Railroading, the premier magazine of 1/160 Scale model railroading, is published by N Scale modelers, for N Scale modelers. It's available bimonthly at your favorite hobby shop.

Here's what you'll find in each issue:

- Informative How-To Articles
- Scenery Tips & Techniques
- Step-by-Step Kitbashing Projects
- N Scale Modeling from the Prototype
- Railfan-Style All-Color Photo Tours of Great Layouts
- Product Improvements & Upgrade Ideas
- Timely Photos of the Latest N Scale Products
- "N Horizons" — Advance Coverage of Upcoming N Scale Products
- Observations and Commentary on N Scale Subjects
- Inspiring Model Photography

Built-ups

BUILT-UP 130' TURNTABLE

933-2613   299.98

Add a turntable quickly, easily and affordably with this Built-Up model. The Modern 130' Turntable is the first fully assembled unit capable of handling locos as large as a Big Boy. A sturdy one-piece plastic pit that's preweathered, and a detailed plastic bridge with metal railings and a separate arch are included. Programmable indexing for as many as 60 different positions lets you install tracks almost anywhere you need them. And complete installation and programming instructions make set-up fast and easy on DC- or DCC-equipped layouts.

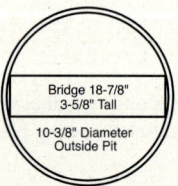

Bridge 18-7/8"
3-5/8" Tall
10-3/8" Diameter Outside Pit

STRUCTURES N SCALE

MODERN ROUNDHOUSE
933-3260 59.98

- American Prototype
- Holds Engines up to 145' Long
- Modular Design — Easily Expanded to a Full Circle with #933-3261, sold separately
- Compact 10° Stall Spacing
- Interior & Exterior Brick Detail
- Fine Window Details
- Floor Inspection Pits
- Decal Signs Included

MODERN ROUNDHOUSE- ADD ON STALLS
933-3261 49.98

- Matches #933-3260, sold separately
- Authentic American Prototype
- Holds Engines up to 145' Long
- Compact 10° Stall Spacing
- Fine Window Details
- Floor Inspection Pits
- Decal Signs Included

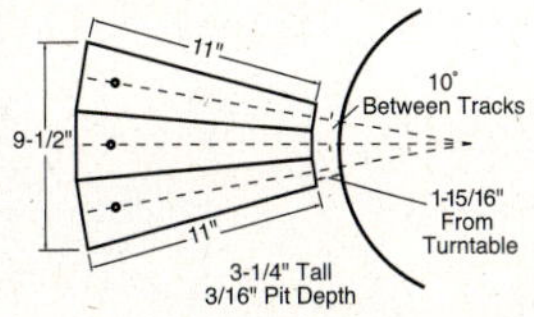

MACHINE SHOP
933-3264 44.98

- Great Accessory for Modern Roundhouse #933-3260, sold separately
- Build As Attached or Freestanding Building
- Includes Boiler House with Stack
- Doors Can Be Built Open or Closed
- Baseplate Slots Accept Popular Rail Sizes

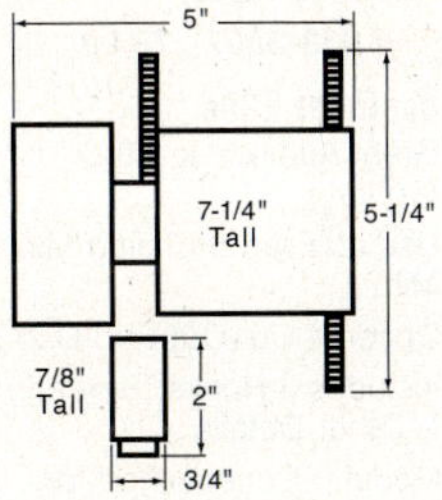

HO Model Shown

MODERN COALING TOWER
933-3262 39.98

- Authentic Concrete Design
- Serves Three Tracks
- Coal Delivery Shed
- Loaded with Separate Details
- Decal Signs Included

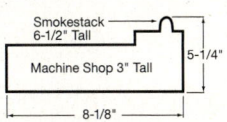

201

STRUCTURES N SCALE

NEW PRODUCTS

STATE LINE FARM SUPPLY
NEW 933-3808 29.98

November 2006
- Decorative "Brick" Façade with Barrel Roof
- Served by Rail & Road
- Separate Trackside "Wood" Loading Ramp
- Oil & Fuel Tanks
- Customize with Windows, Doors & Decals Included
- Great Addition to Agricultural Areas

3-1/4 x 4-1/4"
1-7/8" Tall

Unloading Ramp
1-3/16 x 4-7/8"

ELECTRIC FURNACE
NEW 933-3807 79.98

December 2006
- Great Addition to Steel Works
- Use as Free-Standing Mini-Mill
- Optional Cut-Out End Doors
- Includes J Hooks, Spreaders & Other Details
- Modular Construction for Easy Customizing

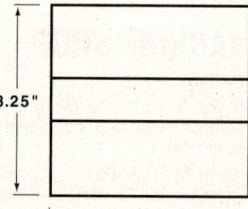

8.25"

8.875"

SANTA FE-STYLE BRICK DEPOT & FREIGHT HOUSE

December 2006
- "Brick" Exterior
- Matching Buildings
- Use Separately or Together
- Captures the Spirit of the Southwest
- Decals Included

NEW 933-3803 Depot Only 34.98

NEW 933-3804 Freight House Only 29.98

NEW 933-3805 Depot & Freight House (Combined Kit) 49.98

3-3/4 x 5-5/8"
1-1/4" High

3-7/8 x 6-3/4"
2-1/4" High

STRUCTURES N SCALE

NEW PRODUCTS

ART DECO HIGHWAY UNDERPASS
NEW 933-3800 24.98

- Detailed Deck
- Unique 30s-Era Style
- Similar Designs Still in Use Today
- Found in All Parts of the U.S.
- Fits Single or Multiple Track Lines

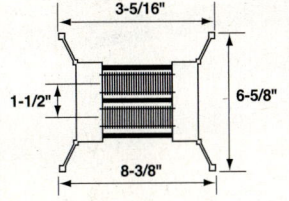

VAN DYKE FARM WINDMILL
NEW 933-3801 pkg(2) 24.98

- Common Farm Structure
- Adjustable to Four Different Heights
- "Cement" Base & "Wood" Well Cap
- Realistic 10' Fan

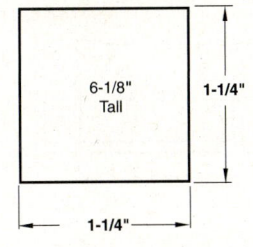

Get the Scoop!
Get the Skinny!
Get the Score!
Check Out Walthers
Web site at
www.walthers.com

COKE OVENS
NEW 933-3806 79.98

December 2006

- Features Crusher, Smokestack and Quench Tower
- Realistic "Metal" Siding
- Detailed Doors
- Safety Cages, Ladders & Walkways
- Steel Industry Must-Have

STRUCTURES N SCALE

UNION STATION
933-3257 49.98
Authentic American design, this model features simulated cut-stone architecture complete with tall columns and realistic ornamentation. Skylights allow sunlight to flood the main concourse, perfect for adding your own interior detailing. Other features include a non-operating rooftop clock, end-door canopies, a bank of railroad-side passenger doors and realistic decals with "Union Station" and "Grand Central Terminal" lettering. Complete your Union Station passenger terminal scene with trackside Butterfly-Style Platform Shelters, 933-3258 (sold separately).

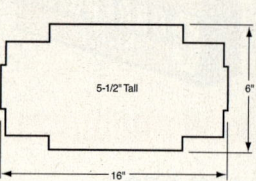

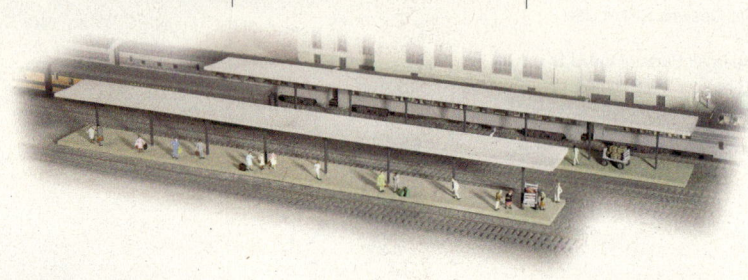

THE BRALICK BUILDING
933-3255 34.98
This kit includes modern windows, wall inserts to close off the loading dock area, a rooftop water tank support (the complete water tank is also included), plus a set of colorful signs for easy customizing. It'll look great in your post-1970s business district.

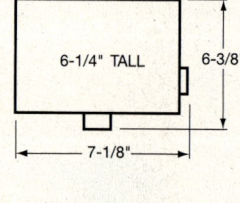

BUTTERFLY-STYLE PLATFORM SHELTERS
933-3258 19.98
Modular design makes it easy to combine kits and extend your boarding areas. Based on platforms used across the continent, each kit includes parts for eight platform sections (a total of four feet) plus signs, benches and wooden baggage cart and track crossings.

Dimensions of one section are shown. Includes parts for eight complete sections.

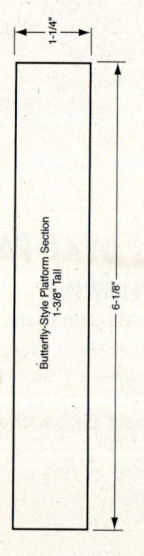

AMERICAN HARDWARE SUPPLY
933-3253 44.98
You'll find this building easy to modify! Optional loading doors, windows or solid brick panels are provided for the ground floor so you can give your model a unique appearance. Modular design makes it easy to enlarge or kitbash too.

Concrete loading dock and colorful signs round out this versatile structure.

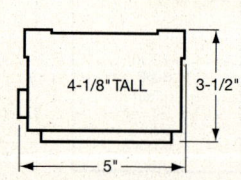

STRUCTURES N SCALE

VALLEY GROWERS ASSOCIATION
933-3251 34.98
With its tall tower with ramps, loading tunnel and positionable doors, this kit brings variety to grain-handling scenes. Includes "wooden" storage bin, clapboard scale office, segmented loading pipe and realistic decals.

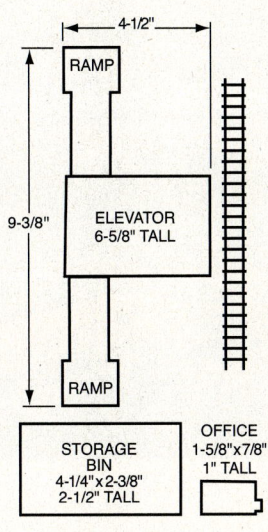

AL'S VICTORY SERVICE
933-3243 24.98
Introduced in the late 1930s, box-style stations like this sprang up from coast to coast and remained a standard well into the 1950s.

Easy-to-build kit features authentic styling that looks great on any vintage or modern street scene. Optional pumps are included to match your era from the late 30s to the 80s, along with colorful decal signs for the finishing touch. Just add vehicles, figures and interior details, available separately, to create a busy scene anywhere along your layout.

CO-OP STORAGE SHED
933-3230 17.98
Detailed plastic parts capture the look of wood construction; a rooftop vent and a set of decal signs are included.

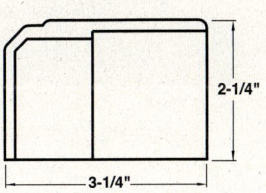

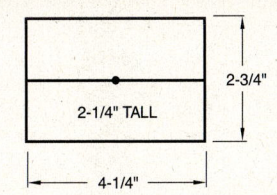

Hot New Products Announced Daily! Visit Walthers Web site at
www.walthers.com

JIM'S REPAIR SHOP
933-3229 17.98
Easy-to-build kit has parts molded in colors and includes printed signs.

205

STRUCTURES N SCALE

UNION CITY ROUNDHOUSE

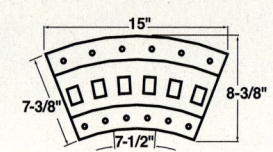

RETIRED MODEL

933-3202 39.98
This detailed six-stall building will hold engines up to 6-3/4" long, and features moveable doors, simulated brick siding, smoke jacks, windows, skylights, clerestory and window "glass." To create a larger complex, several of the kits can be combined to produce a 12-, 18-, or 24-stall roundhouse.

120' MANUAL TURNTABLE

933-3203 24.98
Ideal for use with the Union City Roundhouse, the 120' Manual Turntable measures 9" over the bridge track and 5/8" deep in the pit. Kit consists of a turntable deck and pit, plastic gears and bearing plates, a pulley assembly, a set of wipers and a nylon cord for the manual pulley drive. Pre-production model shown.

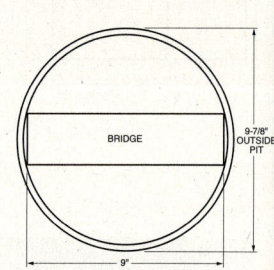

Turntable Drive
942-472 29.98
Motorize the 120' Manual Turntable (sold separately) with this drive. Features a 1 rpm motor, bracket and mounting hardware. Requires variable 0-12V DC power supply.

CAR SHOP

933-3228 34.98
Sooner or later, every car winds up at the Car Shop to be repaired, repainted and readied for service.

Ideal for steam- or diesel-era operations, this building features the longitudinal style used on most prototype designs. An authentic sawtooth roof, 22 large windows and roll-up doors are all included.

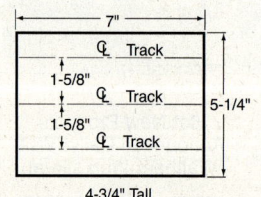

STRUCTURES N SCALE

CLARKESVILLE DEPOT
933-3240 29.98
Features a concrete platform and includes both eastern and western style gable brackets and decals.

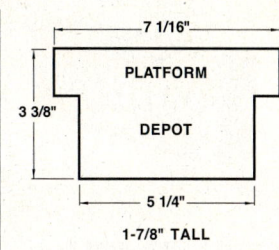

WATER STREET FREIGHT TERMINAL
933-3201 26.98
Typical of terminals found in many towns and cities, freight houses were vital to operations. Detailed structure features large office, freight house with loading docks, plus roof details and a collection of pallets, crates and drums for superdetailing.

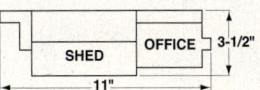

TIMBER TRESTLE
933-3217 24.98
13-3/8 x 3" 34 x 7.5cm

Perfect for main or branch-line operations. Kit features parts molded in dark brown, which can be arranged to build a straight or 20" radius curved trestle. To protect your trestle from fire, refuge platforms and water barrels are also provided. Additional kits can be combined to build a larger structure.

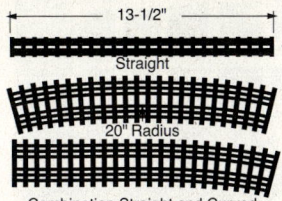

DOUBLE-TRACK TRUSS BRIDGE
933-3242 24.98
10 x 2-3/4 x 2-3/4"

Designed to handle even the most modern double stack equipment, this easy-to-build, North American bridge comes molded in realistic colors.

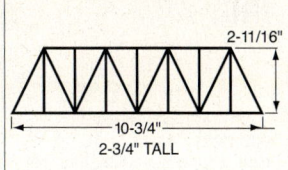

Hot New Products Announced Daily! Visit Walthers Web site at

www.walthers.com

STRUCTURES N SCALE

ROLLING MILL
933-3250 49.98

Rolling mills are some of the biggest structures in any steel works. Similar structures house continuous casters, galvanizing plants and pipe, rod or wire mills.

Big and versatile, this kit makes it easy to model a steel works and is perfect alongside the Blast Furnace (#933-3249). Its "steel" construction and size make it a natural for other types of modern manufacturing plants too.

With a modular design, plus optional cutout end doors and walls, you can easily customize it to fit your layout. The baseplate has simulated rails so you can roll cars inside. A full-length monitor-type as well as individual round vents are provided. And for the finishing touch, decal safety signs are included.

BLAST FURNACE
933-3249 129.98

At last, here's a model that captures the power of the prototype and still fits the average layout. This complete kit includes the furnace, stoves, dust collectors and cleaning system, piping, cast house, hearth, skip hoist, high line supports — over 300 parts in all. Yet, it's designed for easy construction and includes complete instructions. Your finished model can be used as the centerpiece of a layout serving the steel industry, or a super addition to any industrial area.

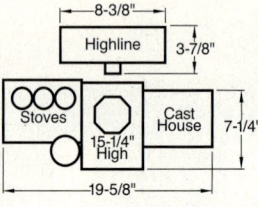

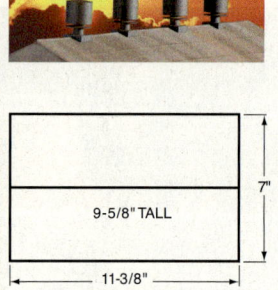

GEO. ROBERTS PRINTING CO. INC.

RETIRED MODEL

933-3231 34.98

Ready for any printing job, this is the kind of industrial building that makes any layout look right. It features authentic "brick curtain" design, which can be found in American industrial areas from the 1920s to the present. Large windows let in plenty of natural light, and lots of extras, including a roof-top water tank, 3-story fire escape and colorful decals are all provided. Plus, a covered ground-floor loading dock makes it easy to ship or receive by rail.

HO Scale Model Shown

GLACIER GRAVEL CO.
933-3241 39.98

Rock crushers like Glacier Gravel Co. load entire trains of ballast for trackwork projects. Glacier Gravel Co. Comes molded in realistic colors, includes decal.

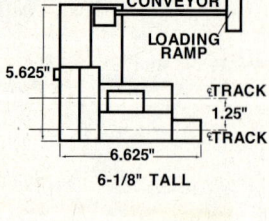

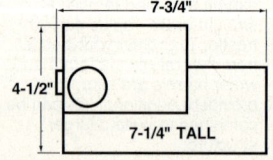

STRUCTURES N SCALE

RED WING MILLING COMPANY
933-3212 32.98
Featuring concrete construction with multi-paned windows to let in plenty of light, this three-story building is complete with dust collectors, colorful decal signs and complete instructions. Use it to add interest to your grain-handling scenes. Includes decals for several business names.

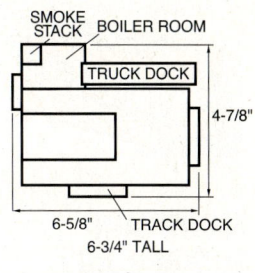

HARDWOOD FURNITURE COMPANY
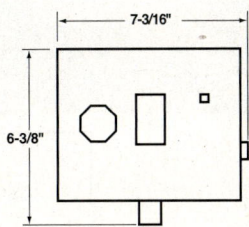
933-3232 29.98
Here's the kind of industry that brings realism to any layout or module. Walls feature authentic architectural trim and the kit includes over 50 separate easy-to-install windows! There's a covered loading dock for box cars, and roll-up doors for trucks. Up on the roof, a water tank, elevator house and chimney are included to detail this important area. Colorful decal signs complete the kit.

NORTHERN LIGHT & POWER POWERHOUSE & ACCESSORIES
933-3214 34.98
Based on a building in Milwaukee, Wisconsin, this kit is typical of plants operated by utility companies, private industries and institutions, as well as streetcar or interurban lines.

Brick walls, separate windows and doors, a smokestack and full-color signs are included. Pre-production models shown.

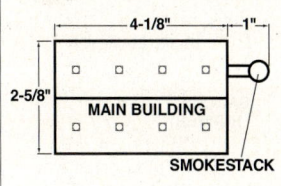

New Arrivals Updated Every Day! Visit Walthers Web site at
www.walthers.com

STRUCTURES N SCALE

MOUNTAIN LUMBER CO. SAWMILL
933-3236   49.98
This model can be the centerpiece of any logging operation. Everything you'll need is included, from the Log Conveyor to the Burner. The Mill Building is enclosed with board and batten siding and covered with a corrugated metal roof. At the back is a canopied area, where fresh-cut boards are sorted. To keep the machinery running, there's a nicely detailed Powerhouse with twin smokestacks. And for the final touch, you get a Sawdust Burner, used to dispose of scrap lumber and sawdust from the cutting operations.

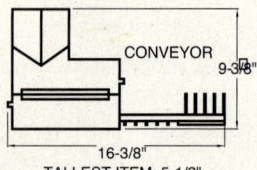

WALTON & SONS LUMBER COMPANY
933-3235   29.98
A great trackside business in any size city or town, this model builds into a typical operation that fits almost any available space. The storage buildings are designed so that you can build one large, covered building, or two free-standing, open sided buildings. There's a small office to handle the paperwork, which can also be placed along a busy street and used as a store and showroom. Lots of colorful sign decals brighten up the operation, and complete instructions make for fast and fun construction.

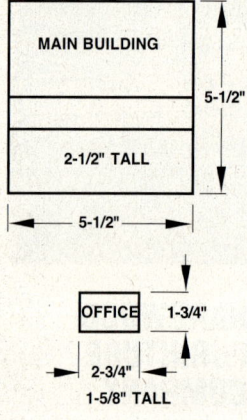

SUPERIOR PAPER COMPANY

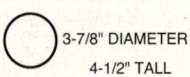

933-3237   69.98
Kit comes with two complete buildings. The kraft (German for strength) mill, where wood is transformed into pulp. is a modern steel structure complete with large smokestacks and a variety of details. Pulp is processed in the Main Building, a large brick structure complete with pulp vats, loading docks, separate windows and many other details.

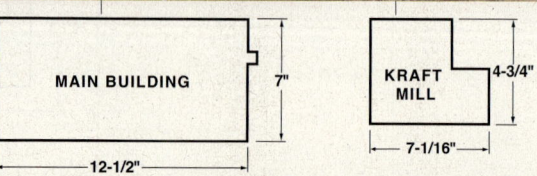

210

STRUCTURES N SCALE

FARMER'S CO-OP RURAL GRAIN ELEVATOR

RETIRED MODEL

933-3238   24.98

A perfect addition to your layout. Easy-to-build kit includes main elevator, a storage building and scale house, all molded in realistic colors. A variety of decals are included so you can add realistic signs and lettering. Preproduction Model Shown.

Elevator: 4-3/8 x 5-3/8 x 6"
11 x 13.7 x 15.2cm

Storage Building: 2-3/4 x 4-1/4 x 2-1/4"   7 x 10.5 x 5.7cm

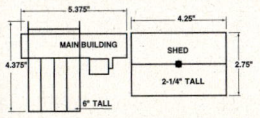

ADM® GRAIN ELEVATOR

933-3225   34.98

You'll find elevators like this wherever grain is grown, shipped or stored. This American-style building captures the massive look and feel of the prototypes, in a space that fits most layouts. Kit includes the elevator and "concrete" silos, headhouse, unloading sheds for trucks and railroad cars, and many add-on details. Full-color decals for the ADM logo and other signs are also included.

"ADM" and the ADM logo are trademarks of Archer Daniels Midland, used with permission.

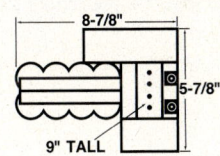

See What's New and Exciting at
www.walthers.com

STRUCTURES N SCALE

Universal Gearbox & Motor Drive Kit

933-1050 Universal Gearbox & Motor Drive Kit **19.98**
- Fully Assembled
- Drop-In Mount for Walthers Oil Pump
- Easily Adapted to other Animation Projects
- 360:1 Gear Ratio for Realistic Slow Speed

Movable Pump Can Be Positioned Up or Down or powered with optional Universal Gearbox and Motor Drive Kit #933-1050, $19.98, sold separately.

WALKING BEAM "HORSE HEAD" OIL PUMP

933-3248 21.98
Seen alone or in groups wherever oil is found, this kit is typical of American designs in use since the 1920s and includes a detailed stationary diesel power plant, walking beam, rear crank and counterweight, along with the odd-shaped "horse head" front counterweight that gives the machines their nickname.

Add the Universal Gearbox and Motor Drive Kit #933-1050, $19.98, sold separately, to power your pump.

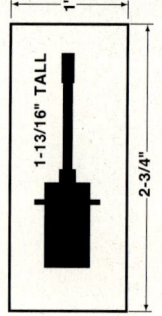

NORTH ISLAND REFINERY

933-3219 29.98
This detailed kit includes a main fractioning tower, piping group, heat exchangers, vacuum pipe still, and decal warning signs.

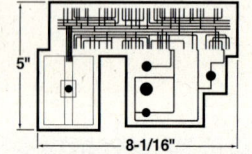

INTERSTATE FUEL & OIL

933-3200 26.98

Detailed kit includes horizontal and vertical storage tanks, piping, pump house and header stand for unloading tank cars, a truck loading rack, corrugated metal office/warehouse and more. Parts can be arranged to fit available layout space.

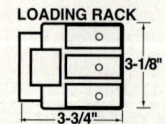

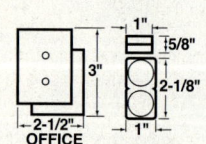

STRUCTURES N SCALE

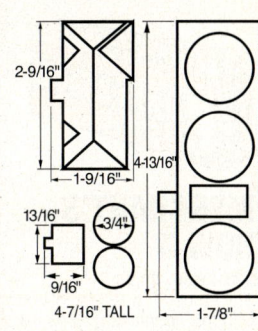

GOLDENFLAME FUEL CO.
933-3246   44.98
Typical of facilities commonly seen in the US from the 1920s to the 1960s, this kit includes detailed "concrete" storage silos, a small office with attached scale platform area, oil tanks and other details to build a complete scene. And like the prototypes, the buildings are easily arranged to fit in odd-shaped spaces.

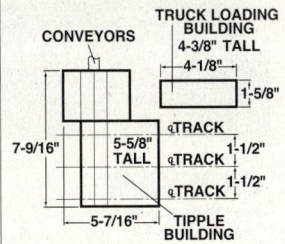

NEW RIVER MINING COMPANY
933-3221   34.98
Whether it's in the high country of Colorado, or a West Virginia "holler," the New River Mining Company can depict mine operations in any part of the country.

Kit comes with tipple building, truck loading building, enclosed conveyors, plus separate doors and windows.

WESTERN COAL FLOOD LOADER
933-3247   36.98
Put big action in a small space with this exciting industry. Used in eastern and western coal fields, these big buildings are essentially storage silos that reload unit trains. Since the actual mine operations are often miles away, this building and conveyor can be placed trackside, to imply a bigger operation located off your layout.

Kit includes a variety of rooftop machinery that puts realistic detail in this highly visible location. Modular conveyor sections can be arranged in a variety of ways, or combined with other buildings like the New River Mining Company, (933-3221) or Glacier Gravel (933-3241) to model a complete scene. And, the stackable silo sections allow you to easily build a tall or short structure that can fit where overhead clearance may be limited.

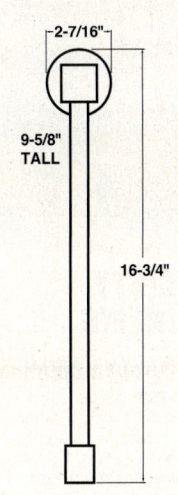

For Up-To-Date Information and News Bookmark Walthers Web site at
www.walthers.com

STRUCTURES N SCALE

MERCHANT'S ROW II
933-3224 29.98

Build a better business district with this kit that combines three stores into one space-saving structure.

Packed with realistic details including: one-piece front, side, and rear walls, corner turret, roofing, chimneys, downspouts and sidewalks, plus plastic signs and colorful decals.

VARIETY PRINTING

Background Building
933-3252 19.98

This curtain-wall front makes it easy to blend foreground scenery with your backdrop. The finished structure is typical of those used by all kinds of businesses and includes streetside facade plus decals.

7-1/2" x 1-3/4" x 4" Tall

Latest New Product News Daily! Visit Walthers Web site at
www.walthers.com

PARKVIEW TERRACE BACKGROUND BUILDINGS

933-3259 Brown w/Light Gray Trim **24.98**

933-3263 Tuscan w/Dark Green Trim **24.98**

Parkview Terrace is a great way to add detailed buildings along your city right-of-way. And the models are available in two color combinations, making it easy to create an entire trackside neighborhood.

Like the real thing, these models put the most building in the least space. The kits can be used on the edge of your benchwork, along a shelf or modular layout and in dioramas. Once installed, they provide a smooth, realistic transition between 3-D foreground scenes and printed or painted backgrounds.

STRUCTURES N SCALE

Division of Wm. K. Walthers, Inc.

Bring your layout to life with these structures, typical of those found throughout America. Each is designed for easy construction, with plastic parts molded in realistic colors.

Volunteer Fire Company
433-7483   15.25
Protect your town with this handsome fire station. Has two bays for equipment, while the upper floor provides living quarters for firefighters on duty. Also includes roof-mounted hose tower, flag pole and siren.

Rural Chapel
433-7464   12.50
Perfect for Sunday services, this church features classic architectural details such as a steeple, bell and "stained glass" windows.

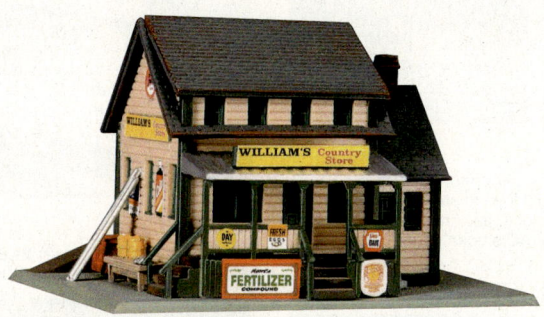

William's Country Store
433-7463   12.50
Authentic store signs bring realistic detail to this rural store.

5th Precinct Police Station
433-7481   15.25
This unique law enforcement building houses a jail and a bail bonds office.

Downtown Hotel
433-7482   15.25
Rent a room by the day, week or month. Typical of rooming houses in large cities, fits many time periods. Roof-top sign, smoke jacks and window awnings add to the realism.

Information STATION

Terminals, Stations and Depots

Your trip has come to an end. You get your luggage and step off the train into the depot. Or is it the station? Or maybe a terminal? Just what is the difference between the three buildings?

A station is the most basic of the three stops It doesn't have to have a building for people to stand; can simply be a signpost and a platform for passengers.

A depot is the simple trackside building where passengers wait for trains to arrive. The depot is often a simply constructed one- or two-story building. Common in rural communities, the depot has largely vanished from the landscape of North American railroads.

Terminals, however, are much more dynamic buildings. Terminals are, by definition, a place of convergence for multiple train lines. Terminals are often magnificent structures within a city's landscape. Their design is often were grand in scale, reflecting the architecture of the buildings around them.

Traditional terminals did face an overhaul in the mid-19th century with the development of the "union" station. The union station acted as a meeting place for multiple railroads' trains. The benefit to passengers was obvious: instead of carting your luggage between several stations to make a connection with another railroad's train, you changed trains in one facility. Centralized terminals also eliminated duplicate structures and consolidated grade crossings on lines leading in. They were also good for the railroads because the city, or shared terminal company managed the station, and costs were shared by tenant lines.

STRUCTURES N SCALE

IMPORTED FROM GERMANY BY WALTHERS
Expand your layout with these easy-to-build structures. Detailed kits feature precolored plastic parts, with printed signs and details where applicable. Complete step-by-step instructions are included. Weathered models feature hand-painted/weathered parts that give the structure an authentic, well-used look.

NEW PRODUCTS

Burning Tax Office
NEW 272-232300 w/16V AC Smoke Generator **86.99**
Here's a sight many a taxpayer would love to see. Kit features weathered facades blackened by smoke, flashing lights set and smoke oil to refill the generator. 16V AC smoke generator sends thick smoke through windows.
NEW 272-180690 Smoke Generator Kit **39.99**

Fishbellied Bridge
NEW 272-222576 **32.99**
11-1/8 x 1-1/4 x 2" 28.2 x 3.2 x 5.2cm
This unique bridge gets its descriptive name from the curved under track support trusses that resemble the rounded belly of a fish. Use w/#272-222577 Viaduct Piers (sold separately).

Block of Flats
NEW 272-232295 **26.99**
4-7/16 x 2-11/16 x 3-3/16" 11.1 x 6.9 x 8cm
Multi-story apartment building complete with balconies.

Coaling Station
NEW 272-222154 **27.99**
4-11/16 x 1-3/4 x 2-5/8" 11.9 x 4.4 x 6.6cm
Great for small service areas. Features manually moveable loading crane and tender.

Platforms
NEW 272-222126 pkg(2) **21.99**
Build several in a row for a busy station scene.

Trackside Shanties
NEW 272-222177 pkg(3) **21.99**
1-3/8 x 1 x 1" 3.4 x 2.4 x 2.4cm
1-9/16 x 1-3/8 x 7/8" 4 x 3.5 x 2.2cm
13/16 x 3/4 x 3/4" 2.1 x 2 x 2cm

Factory Halls
NEW 272-222203 pkg(2) **26.99**
Great addition to the Kolb & Co. building #272-22201 (sold separately).

Hochdorf Station
NEW 272-212106 **39.99**
9-7/8 x 4-3/4 x 3"
25.1 x 12 x 7.4cm
Classic station for a rural area. Features covered platform and adjoining goods shelter. Use with platforms #272-222120 & #272-222125 (sold separately).

Brugge Signal Box
NEW 272-222160 **25.99**
4-13/16 x 3-3/8 x 3-13/16"
12.3 x 8.5 x 9.5cm
This gantry signal box sprawls three tracks and will enhance any station approach. Clearance: 1-11/16".

One-Family Houses w/Garages
NEW 272-232226 pkg(2) **21.99**
3-7/8 x 2-1/4 x 2"
10 x 5.7 x 5cm

Development House
NEW 272-232301 **25.99**
3 x 1-9/16 x 3-1/16"
7.7 x 4 x 7.8cm
This narrow one-family house comes with front garden fencing.

Terrace Development House
NEW 272-232302 **29.99**
This pair of semi-detached houses features dormer windows and a front porch. Matches nicely with #272-232301 (sold separately).

STRUCTURES N SCALE

IMPORTED FROM GERMANY BY WALTHERS

Lodge w/Raised Hide
NEW 272-272532   15.99
Create an ideal place for hunting on your layout. Kit features hunting lodge, raised deer stand (hide), a fountain and fir trees.

BP Gas Station
NEW 272-232219   29.99
4-1/8 x 3 x 1-3/8"
10.5 x 7.7 x 3.5cm

Gas prices are still reasonable at this 50s-style station. Features rounded pump covering and cashier's office.

St. Joseph's Hospital
NEW 272-232296 w/Roofed Casualty Entrance   61.99
8-7/8 x 4-1/16 x 4-3/8"
22 x 10.3 x 11.2cm

Every city needs a hospital and this one is complete with an emergency entrance.

Nordex Wind Generator
NEW 272-232251 w/Motor & 3-Propeller Rotor   37.99
2 x 2 x 16-3/8"   5 x 5 x 41.5cm

Free wind from Mother Nature provides an inexpensive power source. Kit features three-propellor rotor and 12-16V AC motor.

Kolb & Co.
NEW 272-222201 Machine Factory   26.99
3-1/2 x 3-3/8 x 5"   9.2 x 8.7 x 12.8cm

Highly detailed brickwork accents this typical factory building. Combine several kits to extend building in height and/or length.

Boiler House
NEW 272-222202   26.99
Complete with a brick chimney, this kit adds a finishing touch to buildings #272-22201 & #272-22203 (each sold separately).

Sawmill
NEW 272-232248   77.99
9-1/16 x 5-1/8 x 3-5/8"
23 x 13 x 9.2cm

Features built-on sawdust tower and small railroad crane.

Footbridge w/Roofed Stairways - Weathered Model
272-222152   27.99
6-7/8 x 3-1/8 x 4-15/16"
17.5 x 12 x 7.5cm

St. Bernhard Chapel - Weathered Model
272-232239   31.99
2-1/16 x 1-3/8 x 2-5/8"
5.3 x 3.5 x 6.6cm

Half-Timbered Black Forest House - Weathered Model
272-232259   72.99
5-13/16 x 6 x 3-1/2"
14.8 x 15.3 x 9cm

Townhall w/Arcades & Small Belfry
272-232297   31.99
4-1/4 x 4-7/16 x 4"
10.7 x 11.2 x 10.2cm

Bus Stop Shelter
272-272534 pkg(2)   17.99
1-3/8 x 3/4 x 3/4"
3.5 x 1.9 x 2cm
1-5/8 x 1/2 x 7/8"
4.1 x 1.3 x 2.2cm

Bicycle Stands
272-272535 pkg(2)   15.99
1-1/2 x 11/16 x 1/2"
3.8 x 1.8 x 1.4cm
1-15/16 x 5/8 x 5/8"
3.3 x 1.5 x 1.6cm

Fleckenstein Castle Ruin
272-272660   37.99
7-7/8 x 3-15/16 x 5-7/8"
20 x 10 x 15cm

Features two assembled and decorated pieces — perfect for backgrounds or mountaintops.

Two Town Houses - Weathered Model
272-232307   44.99
Each house measures:
4 x 3-1/2 x 5"
10.1 x 8.8 x 12.8cm

Urban Post Office/ Corner House - Weathered Model
272-232305   38.99
5 x 3-15/16 x 4-1/2"
12.7 x 10 x 11.5cm

Town House w/Small Shop On Ground Floor - Weathered Model
272-232306   34.99
3-9/16 x 2-3/4 x 5-1/2"
9 x 7 x 14cm

Two Apartment Houses - Weathered Model
272-232308   44.99
Each house measures:
4 x 3-1/2 x 5"
10.1 x 8.8 x 12.8cm

Schwarzach Platform
272-222125   19.99
23 x 1-7/16 x 1-5/8"
58.4 x 3.7 x 4.1cm

With its wooden shelter and benches, this platform is ideal for use with any North American or European-style station. It features modular design so you can combine multiple kits to fit your scene.

See What's Available at
www.walthers.com

STRUCTURES N SCALE

FALLER
IMPORTED FROM GERMANY BY WALTHERS

Glass-Roofed Train Shed
272-222127 29.99
14-3/8 x 8-11/16 x 3-3/8"
36.5 x 22 x 8.5cm

Perfect for any big-city depot, this model features realistic see-through panels and "steel" framework. Its modular construction allows it to be lengthened with parts from additional kits.

Warehouse w/Annexed Goods Shed - Weathered Model
272-222192 27.99
6-1/2 x 3-1/8 x 4-5/16"
16.5 x 8 x 11cm

Use this model anywhere freight must be transferred between trucks and trains. Also makes a great addition to grain handling scenes.

Rural Half-Timbered House - Weathered Model
272-232340 38.99
2-7/8 x 2-1/16 x 2"
7.3 x 5.3 x 5cm

Cattle Loading
272-222129 24.99
8-3/8 x 2-1/4 x 1"
21 x 5.6 x 2.4cm

Cows can wait on the loading ramp before they are moved onto railway wagons. Includes a series of holding pens to keep the cows corralled.

Gatekeeper's Lodge
272-222155 22.99
2-9/16 x 2-1/6 x 1-3/4"
6.4 x 5.4 x 4.4cm

Exterior details include an attached shed and rooftop board cladding.

Inspection Pits
272-222147 With 2 Molded Rails pkg(2) 22.99
8-3/8 x 2 x 5/16"
20.9 x 5.1 x .8cm

Two Steel-Girder Bridges - Weathered Model
272-222579 With Attached Walkways 28.99
13-1/4 x 2-1/16 x 2-9/16"
33.6 x 5.3 x 6.5cm

Kit includes two brickwork abutments and a center pier.

Bad Durkheim Station
272-212101 95.99
15-1/8 x 6-5/8 x 3-5/8"
27.8 x 16.5 x 9cm

This 2004 exclusive station building includes a roofed platform, large stairs, movable doors, window fanlights and an electronic voice announcer.

Engine Shed
272-222141 24.99
7 x 2-1/16 x 2-1/2"
17.5 x 5.2 x 6.2cm

For storing one engine, the overall length (6.1") can be shortened.

Sussenbrunn Water Tower
272-222145 22.99
2-5/16 x 2-5/16 x 5-7/16"
5.8 x 5.8 x 13.5cm

Harmony Old-Time Cinema
272-232264 31.99
4 x 3-1/2 x 6" 10 x 8.8 x 15cm

Includes a large marquee with advertising signs.

Old-Town Corner House
272-232260 24.99
3-3/4 x 3-1/4 x 3-1/4"
9.3 x 8 x 8.1cm

Includes a small shop on the ground floor.

Old-Town House
272-232261 24.99
2-7/16 x 3 x 3-1/2"
7 x 7.6 x 8.8cm

Coal-Tipping Platform
272-222148 29.99
8-3/8 x 3-1/4 x 2-1/2"
21 x 8.1 x 6.2cm

Coal is delivered to the loading track, then transferred to awaiting engines through chutes.

Sawmill - Weathered Model
272-232255 89.99
7-1/16 x 4-1/2 x 3-1/8" 18 x 11.4 x 8cm

This non-powered model is patterned after one used in the Black Forest. Its water wheel and saw frame are easily powered using motor 272-180629 (sold separately).

Old Stone Crushing Plant - Weathered Model
272-222197 23.99
4-1/2 x 3-7/8 x 3-15/16" 11.5 x 9.8 x 10cm

Here's the plant that feeds carloads of gravel to plants like the concrete mixing plant. Modeled after an early 1900s facility, this plant features a wooden tipple housing and rests on a stone and concrete base.

1950s Shell Gas Station w/Garage - Weathered Model
272-232218 21.99
3-3/8 x 2-15/16 x 1-11/16" 8.5 x 7.5 x 4.2cm

Perfect for any roadside scene, this 50s-era stucco gas station includes two pumps under its corrugated-metal canopy. It'll look at home on any North American or European layout.

Branchline-Style Railroad Stop w/Roofed Loading Ramp - Weathered Model
272-212105 29.99
3-1/2 x 2-3/8 x 1-11/16" 8.9 x 6 x 4.2cm

This small utilitarian wooden freight house is perfect for any branch line or small town stop. It will also be at home when used as part of a larger industrial complex.

STRUCTURES N SCALE

IMPORTED FROM GERMANY BY WALTHERS

Townhouse Under Demolition
272-232265 27.99
6-1/8 x 3-5/16 x 4-1/2"
15.3 x 8.3 x 11.2cm

The front of this building looks like it's being torn down, and the roof frame is partially exposed. The base frame features a realistic rubbish heap.

Bridge Parapet Set
272-222594 With Two Bridge Piers pkg(2) 24.99
3-7/16 x 1-7/16 x 2-15/16"
8.5 x 3.5 x 7.3cm

Viaduct Piers
272-222595 pkg(2) 12.99
2 x 3/4 x 3-15/16"
5.9 x 1.8 x 9.8cm

Approach/Exit Set
272-222591 46.99
Includes five straight and eight curved track beds, along with a 32-piece pier set.

Bonn Passenger Station
272-212113 139.99
20-1/2 x 5 x 4-5/16"
52 x 12.7 x 11cm

Concrete Mixing Plant - Weathered Model
272-222195 62.99
Build concrete and stone traffic along your railroad with this detailed model. Includes cement silos, rotary sorter with divided bins and bucket crane, office and machinery/truck loading shed and appropriate sand and gravel (vehicles sold separately).

Six Relief Houses

272-232380 69.99
This row of six half-depth houses is perfect for adding depth to your background scenes. Each is detailed only on the front side so they're easily placed against your painted or printed background. The six houses measure:

3-1/2 x 1-1/8 x 3-9/16"   8.9 x 2.8 x 9cm
3-1/2 x 1-1/4 x 3-9/16"   8.9 x 3.2 x 9cm
1-3/4 x 1-1/8 x 3-5/8"   4.5 x 2.8 x 9.2cm
1-3/4 x 1-1/4 x 3-5/8"   4.5 x 3.2 x 9.2cm
1-3/4 x 1-1/8 x 3-1/4"   4.5 x 2.8 x 8.2cm
1-3/4 x 1-1/8 x 3-1/4"   4.5 x 2.8 x 8.2cm

Two Box-Girder Bridges - Weathered Model
272-222578 With Attached Walkways 31.99
16-7/16 x 2-1/16 x 3-1/4" 41.8 x 5.3 x 8.2cm
Kit includes two brickwork abutments and a center pier.

Intercity Express (ICE) Station Platforms
272-222121 38.99
20 x 2-1/8 x 1-13/32"
50 x 5.3 x 3.5cm

Platforms are crafted from a modern design, and feature a glazed waiting area for your passenger's protection. Includes accessories such as benches, baskets and information boards.

ICE Platform Extension
272-222122 pkg(2) 17.99
7-1/8 x 2 x 1/4"
17.9 x 5.2 x .6cm

These platform parts are for use with ICE station platform #272-222121 (sold separately).

Overhead Signal Tower
272-222159 41.99
5-3/32 x 4-17/32 x 3-23/32"
12.7 x 11.3 x 9.3cm

This classically designed tower spans two lanes of track. Catenary operation possible. Clearance: 1-23/32" 4.3cm (without track).

Alpine Boarding House w/Accessories
272-232234 25.99
3-13/64 x 3-13/64 x 2"
8 x 8 x 5cm

Visitors to the Alpine foothills will love spending the nights in this glorious boarding house, whose design (featuring paintings on exterior walls) is typical of the area's landscape. The house also features an open-air terrace for relaxing afternoons. Also comes with tables, benches and parasols.

Main Post Office
272-232203 38.99
6-1/2 x 4 x 3-1/2"
16.4 x 10 x 8.7cm

Factory Wall
272-272525 12.99
27-3/8" 68.4cm

Bietschtal Bridge
272-222580 79.99
23-3/4 x 2-3/4 x 5-1/4"
59.4 x 6.9 x 13.1cm

Two-Stall Engine Shed
272-222136 53.99
8-1/2 x 4-1/4 x 3-3/4"
21.5 x 10.5 x 9.5cm

Designed to store engines up to 5-1/2" 13.8cm length over buffers. Gate length: 1-1/2" 3.7cm. Distances between centers: 1-1/2" 3.7cm.

Bielefeld Water Tower
272-222144 52.99
2 x 2 x 5-1/3"
5.1 x 4.9 x 13.3cm

Features a masonry entrance, clinker tower and spherical water holder.

Modern Service Boards
272-222123 pkg(3) 12.99
Used today in European railroad stations, these information boards are designed to look like railroad passengers, and are painted in red, yellow and blue.

Three-Stall Duderstadt Engine House
272-222135 68.99
9 x 5 x 3-3/4"
23 x 12.5 x 9.5cm

Designed to store engines up to 6-1/2" 16.2cm length over buffers. Gate length: 1-1/2" 3.7cm. Distances between centers: 1-1/2" 3.7cm

219

STRUCTURES N SCALE

FALLER
IMPORTED FROM GERMANY BY WALTHERS

Factory Premises
272-222188 **69.99**
10-3/4 x 7-1/2 x 5-1/4"
24 x 19 x 13cm

Create an industry in seconds! The factory premise contains a main building, a factory building and a boiler house. The facility is surrounded by a wall with gates.

Large Town Church
272-232271 **82.99**
6-1/4 x 3-1/4 x 8-5/8"
15.6 x 8.2 x 21.5cm

This twin-spire church features a variety of interesting architectural elements: an extended nape, a semicircular apse, and a laterally annexed vestry entrance. Choose from different spires and tower elements to customize the church.

Arcades w/Shops
272-272577 pkg(2) **21.99**
1-7/8 x 13/64 x 8-11/64"
4.7 x .5 x 20.4cm

Sawmill
272-222181 **41.99**
6-13/16 x 5 x 6"
17 x 10 x 15cm

Includes wood storage area, exhaust chamber and loading ramp.

Mercedes-Benz Car Dealership
272-222189 **99.99**
13 x 10.7 x 12.8"
9.1 x 5.6 x 3.5cm

This four-story automobile dealership features sales and office rooms and two separate workshop buildings. The workshops feature a sliding door and interior equipment.

Builder's Yard
272-232183 **57.99**
Garage: 8-1/16 x 4-1/2 x 2"
20.2 x 11.3 x 5cm;
Office: 4-3/8 x 2-3/8 x 1-15/16"
11 x 6 x 4.8cm

The main building features a three-stall garage with movable rolling shutter doors. Also includes an office building and a three-stall parking area.

Alpine Wood Carver's Shop
272-232231 **28.99**
3-13/64 x 2-13/16 x 2-13/32"
8 x 7 x 6cm

From ornate chairs to simpler wares, the wood carver in your village will always have something to keep him busy. This beautiful building features many unique architectural details, including a window display, an attached bay window and detailed printings on exterior walls.

Summer Houses
272-232209 pkg(3) **13.99**
Houses measure:
1-1/4 x 1-13/32 x 3/4"
27/32 x 13/16 x 11/16"
1 x 27/32 x 11/16"

Party Tents & Garden Furniture
272-232207 pkg(34) **8.99**
Includes four tents, 24 garden chairs and six tables.

Town Dwelling House
272-232272 **41.99**
3-13/64 x 3-13/64 x 5"
8 x 8 x 12.5cm

A perfect compliment to town houses (#272-232266), House of Fashion store and apartments (#272-232267), Manhattan Club city bar (#272-232268) and People's Bank & Offices/Apartments (#272-232269), each sold separately.

Garden Grills, Pools & Flowers
272-232210 pkg(17) **7.99**
Set contains four bricked-up garden grills, seven garden pool trays and six flower boxes.

Alpine Hotel
272-232230 **36.99**
7-1/8 x 6-5/16 x 4"
18 x 16 x 10cm

Old-Town Wall Set
272-232350 **104.99**
Surround your city perimeter in a variety of ideal wall combinations.

Lichtenfels Castle
272-232243 **53.99**
7-31/32 x 6-13/16 x 8-13/32"
19.9 x 17 x 21cm

Castle features thick exterior walls and an annexed dwelling wing. A perfect background building for HO Scale layouts as well!

Old-Town Wall
272-232351 **18.99**
Perfect for use with the Old-Town Wall Set (#272-232350) or the Old-Town Bell Tower (#272-232352), each sold separately.

Schwarzburg Station
272-212111 **122.99**
12-13/32 x 4-1/4 x 4-13/16"
31 x 10.7 x 12cm

Villa
272-232298 **38.99**
6-5/8 x 5-13/16 x 6"
16.5 x 14.5 x 15cm

Turn-of-the-century architectural detailing, like a roofed entrance and a rooftop terrace, make this palatial two-story manor a glorious setting for elegant countrysides.

Drugstore
272-232236 **27.99**
3-1/4 x 2-3/4 x 2-3/8"
8 x 7 x 6cm

Freight Depot w/Crane
272-222180 **41.99**
6-1/2 x 4 x 2-5.8"
16.2 x 9.8 x 6.5cm

A large turntable crane is located at the end of the loading ramp. Additional details include movable gates and roofed ramps on both sides of the depot.

Co-Operative Warehouse
272-222182 **72.99**
Main Building:
6-7/16 x 4-7/16 x 3-7/8"
16.1 x 11.1 x 9.7cm;
Silo: 3-7/8 x 3 x 6-5/8"
9.7 x 7.5 x 16.7cm

Features loading ramps on both sides, attached silo and accessories.

Corner House
272-232262 **48.99**
3-13/16 x 3-13/16 x 5"
9.5 x 9.5 x 12.5cm
3-1/10 x 3-1/16 x 5"
8 x 7.7 x 12.5cm

Includes two buildings, with a drugstore on the ground floor of the corner house.

Gantry Crane
272-222133 **16.99**
3-7/16 x 1-5/8 x 2-7/8"
8.6 x 4 x 7.2cm

STRUCTURES N SCALE

FALLER

IMPORTED FROM GERMANY BY WALTHERS

Lindau Town Hall
272-232299   96.99
4-3/8 x 3-15/16 x 5-3/8"
10.9 x 9.8 x 13.4cm
This eye-catching model features elaborate designs on the front and back sides of this majestic structure.

Black Forest Farmyard
272-232258   72.99
4-3/8 x 3-15/16 x 5-3/8"
10.9 x 9.8 x 13.4cm

Beer Benches & Tables
272-272570 pkg(72) 11.99
Set contains 24 tables and 48 benches.

Manhattan Club City Bar
272-232268   41.99
3-31/32 x 3-1/2 x 5-41/64"
9.9 x 8.8 x 14.1cm

Get Daily Info, Photos and News at
www.walthers.com

Two-Track Viaduct Bridges
Features track bed and high piers. Several bridges can be joined together for larger areas.

272-222592 Straight 46.99
8-13/16 2-15/16 x 5-7/16"   22 x 7.3 x 13.6cm

272-222593 Bent 48.99
Inside Radius: 6-7/8" 17.2cm; Outside Radius: 9-13/16" 24.5cm.
Also includes two bridge heads.

Mine Head & Winch House
272-222190   65.99
6-3/4 x 4-1/2" 17.4 x 11.8cm

Guglingen Rural Station
272-212107   56.99
6-1/2 x 3" 16.5 x 7.8cm

Roofed Platform
272-222120 pkg(2) 18.99
6-3/4 x 1-1/8" 16.7 x 4.3cm

Reichenbach Station
272-212104   29.99
6-1/2 x 2-3/4" 16.3 x 7.1cm

Signal Tower
272-222158   21.99
2-1/2 x 1-1/2" 6.4 x 3.8cm

Rail/Road Bridge
272-222587   37.99
7-11/16 x 3 x 5-3/8"
19.2 x 7.4 x 2-15/16cm
Clearance: 1.3-2" 3.3-5cm

Old-Town Bell Tower
272-232352 pkg(2) 27.99
Towers are designed as links and ends for other old-town wall pieces. One 45° and one 90° tower included.

Farm
272-232360   99.99
5 x 7-13/64 x 2-41/64"
12.5 x 18 x 6.6cm
Turn any empty rural area into a detailed scene with this kit. Includes detached farmhouse, barn, hog barn with pen and rough board fence, manure wagon, dog kennel, stork's nest for the roof and much more.

Mittelstadt Passenger Station
272-212115   83.99
12-5/8 x 5 x 4-5/16"
32 x 12.7 x 11cm

One Open & Two Roofed Platforms
272-222119 pkg(3) 24.99
6-1/2 x 1-1/4" 16.7 x 2.9cm

Post Inn
272-232278   25.99
2-13/16 x 3-13/16 x 3-13/16"
7 x 8 x 9.5cm

Oil Storage Tanks
272-222131 pkg(2) 19.99
5 x 3-1/4" 13 x 8.5cm

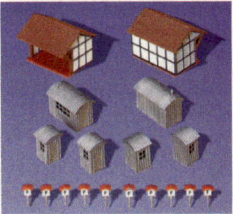

Trackside Accessories
272-222178   17.99
Contains two waiting points, two worker's huts, four corrugated sheds and 10 line-side telephones.

Drug Store
272-232279   25.99
2-3/8 x 3-3/16 x 4"
6 x 8 x 10cm

Haltingen Water Tower
272-222143   22.99
2-1/2 x 1-1/2" 6.5 x 3.8cm

STRUCTURES N SCALE

FALLER

IMPORTED FROM GERMANY BY WALTHERS

Black Forest House
272-232256 46.99
3-5/8 x 2-1/4 x 2-1/2"
9 x 5.5 x 6.2cm

50 Years Malteser Emergency Service
272-232393 106.99
Garage: 8-1/16 x 4-1/2 x 2"
20.2 x 11.3 x 5cm;
Office: 4-3/8 x 2-3/8 x 1-15/16"
11 x 6 x 4.8cm

This exclusive kit consists of a three-stall garage with movable rolling shutter doors, an office building, a three-stall vehicle shelter and three emergency vehicles with special detailing.

Heating & Power Plant
272-222140 54.99
6-3/4 x 5-3/8 x 7-3/8"
17 x 13.4 x 18.4cm

Level Crossing
272-222174 33.99
8-1/8 x 5-3/8 x 1-7/8"
20.4 x 13.4 x 4.6cm

This crossing can be used with one- or multi-track routes. Includes a gatekeeper's lodge.

Freight Shed
272-222134 53.99
6-3/4 x 3-1/4" 17.3 x 8.2cm

Vine Growing Estate w/Winegrower's Tavern
272-232362 89.99
5-1/2 x 7-1/2 x 2-5/8" 14 x 19 x 6.6cm

A great addition to any coastal community or European village where vineyards are a part of local design. The estate is surrounded by a high wall. Can also be used on a farmer's estate.

Factory On Fire
272-232202 149.99
15-1/4 x 12-1/2 x 7-5/8" 38.2 x 31.1 x 19cm

This exclusive seven-story factory simulates the look of a burning building, thanks to the dense smoke produced by the 16V smoke generator and 16V flash lamp set to represent flickering light. The burning building features annexes, production bays, and a heating station with chimney. Five firemen and a firefighting vehicle fight to put out the blaze.

Garden Center
272-232206 54.99
4-3/4 x 4-1/2 x 2-3/8"
12 x 11.3 5.8cm

Landscaping options have never been easier! This great garden center comes with complete interior finish and full garden supply. Metal fencing surrounds the store.

Coaling Station
272-222137 69.99
7-3/8 x 6-3/8" 18.9 x 16.2cm

Water Cranes
272-222139 pkg(4) 10.99

Blumenfeld Station
272-212102 38.99
5-1/4 x 3" 13.5 x 7.8cm

Motorized Rolling Lift Bridge
272-222584 49.99
11-5/8 x 6 x 3-3/4"
29.2 x 15 x 9.5cm

The 12-16V AC drive motor controls the lifting and lowering of the bridge section.

Town House "Schwabentor"
272-232374 43.99
3-3/8 x 2-1/16" 8.6 x 5.3cm

Sandhouse
272-222146 31.99
Tower: 1 x 1 x 3-1/8"
2.4 x 2.4 x 7.8cm
Sandhouse:
3-13/32 x 1-13/64 x 3/4"
8.6 x 3 x 1.8cm

Wooden Hut w/Shutters & Tar Paper Roof
272-222187 18.99
2-7/16 x 1-9/16" 6.2 x 4cm

Cinder Removal Facility
272-222149 49.99
3-13/32 x 8-5/16 x 2-9/32"
8.5 x 20.9 x 5.7cm

2-Stall Stone Engine Shed
272-222116 33.99
7-1/2 x 4-1/4" 19 x 11cm

Engine Repair Shed
272-222142 57.99
6 x 4-1/4" 15.4 x 10.9cm

See What's New and Exciting at
www.walthers.com

Castle w/Moat
272-232242 37.99
5-1/4 x 3" 13.5 x 7.5cm

Row Of Town Houses
272-232266 99.99
11-3/8 x 5-3/32 x 5-41/64"
28.4 x 12.7 x 14.1cm

Create a complete city block quickly and easily with this kit. Set includes two each House of Fashion store and apartments (#272-232267) for the corners and one People's Bank & Office Apartments (#272-232269) for the middle of the block.

Natural Gas Storage Tank
272-222130 19.99
4-1/4 x 2-3/4" 11 x 7.2cm

Alpine Farm House
272-232232 28.99
5-1/8 x 5-1/8 x 4"
13 x 13 x 10cm

Accessories For Service Area
272-222138 16.99

222

STRUCTURES N SCALE

FALLER
IMPORTED FROM GERMANY BY WALTHERS

Brilliant Model Home
272-232344   21.99
3-1/4 x 3-13/32 x 2"
8.1 x 8.5 x 5cm

Water Tower
272-222150   19.99
3 x 2-3/4"   7.5 x 7cm

Gardening Premises
272-232253   37.99
3 x 3 x 2-1/4"
7.3 x 7.2 x 5.5cm
4 x 1-7/8 x 1-3/16"
9.8 x 4.6 x 3.0cm
2-11/16 x 1/2 x 5/16"
6.7 x 1.2 x 0.8cm

With house, two glass hothouses, three hot-beds, straw mats and accessories. Can be enlarged with Greenhouse Set #272-232225 (sold separately).

Lower Saxon Farmhouse
272-232361   49.99
4-7/8 x 2-5/8 x 2-41/64"
12.2 x 6.5 x 6.6cm

A typical European design, with first-floor stables and living quarters upstairs. Put your imagination to work and this versatile design could easily be converted into a small town business such as a tavern or hotel.

Karlsberg Station
272-212114   69.99
14-3/4 x 6-1/4"   37.5 x 16cm

Station Set
272-212109 pkg(4)   66.99
Includes Blumenfeld Station (#272-212102), Roofed Platform (#272-222120), Water Tower (#272-222150), and Signal Tower (#272-222158). Note: Each building also sold separately.

2-Stall Roundhouse
272-222118   56.99
8-11/16 x 8-1/4" x 3-15/16"   22 x 21 x 10cm
Holds locos up to 7" 18cm long. Individual kits can be combined to build a larger roundhouse.

Four Haycocks & Accessories
272-272531   18.99
1-5/8 x 1-7/16"   4.2 x 3.8cm

Greenhouse Set
272-232225   21.99
4-5/16 x 2-5/16"   9.8 x 4.6cm

Homes Under Construction
272-232223 pkg(2)   16.99
1-3/4 x 2-1/2"   2 x 6.1cm

Village Set
272-232220   34.99
3-3/8 x 2-1/8"   7.2 x 4.2cm

Alpine Ingeborg House
272-232235   17.99
3-3/4 x 3-3/8 x 2"
9.5 x 8.5 x 5cm

Alpine Barn
272-232233   24.99
5-1/8 x 5-1/8 x 2-3/4"
13 x 13 x 7cm

Mill w/Waterwheel
272-232254   28.99
5-1/2 x 3-1/8"   14 x 8.3cm
Kit is less motor, can be powered with electric motor #272-180629 (sold separately).

Glass Train Shed
272-222128   31.99
6-1/2 x 4-1/2"   16.7 x 10.8 cm

Edeka Local Mini Market
272-232205   51.99
4-13/16 x 4-1/2 x 2-5/16"
12 x 11.3 x 5.8cm
Complete interior. Can be lighted with grain-of-wheat bulb #272-180671 (sold separately).

Electric Motor
272-180629   31.99
18RPM, 16V, AC, Revolves clockwise or counterclockwise. Will operate the Sawmill, Windmill, Watermill or Oil Pump.

Ferris Wheel
272-242312   94.99
8 x 5-13/16 x 8-13/16"   20 x 13 x 22cm

As exciting as the real thing, the detailed model is complete with 24 colorful gondolas, a ticket booth/entryway and lots of details. For more fun, you can build a working model using the 18 RPM Electric Motor (#272-180629), sold separately.

Service Station
272-232217   28.99
4-1/4 x 3-1/8"   11 x 9.3cm

Alpine House & Barn Silo
272-232237   15.99
2-9/16 x 2-9/16 x 2"
6.5 x 6.5 x 5cm

Windmill
272-232250   29.99
3-1/8 x 2-5/8"   8.1 x 6.5cm
Kit is less motor, can be powered with electric motor #272-180629 (sold separately).

Condominiums
272-232227 pkg(2)   21.99
1-11/16 x 2-3/16"   4.3 x 6.2cm

Gantry Crane
272-222199   17.99
3-13/32 x 6 x 2-9/32"
8.5 x 15 x 5.7cm

Modern House w/Pool
272-232229   23.99
3-1/8 x 2-1/8"   8.2 x 5.4cm
Includes two pools and garden furniture.

STRUCTURES N SCALE

IMPORTED FROM GERMANY BY WALTHERS

Old City Gate
272-232284   41.99
3-15/16 x 1-3/4 x 6-11/16"
10 x 4.5 x 17cm

Curved Viaduct
272-222586   pkg(2)   24.99
7-1/2"   19.2cm

Meadowland Mill w/Wheel
272-232289   33.99
5-3/8 x 4-3/8 x 4-5/8"
13.5 x 11 x 11.5cm

Whether grinding grain to make flour or animal feed, the local mill was one of the most important buildings in town. Powered by a fast-flowing stream, the rhythmic turning of the wheel drove the machinery inside. This detailed model is complete with water wheel and a wooden shed.

Black Forest Mill
272-232257   65.99
4-3/4 x 3-5/8 x 2-7/8"
12 x 9.2 x 7.1cm

The water wheel drives the grain mill inside!

Drug Store
272-232375   34.99
2-1/2 x 2-1/4 x 3-3/8"
6.4 x 6 x 8.3cm

Forester's House
272-232281   21.99
2-5/8 x 2-13/16 x 3-3/8"
6.5 x 7 x 8.5cm

This home makes a great hunting lodge or ranger station. It features the typical style of construction and has a large front balcony.

Two Suburban Homes w/Garage
272-232222   16.99
1-3/4 x 3-1/8"   2 x 7.8cm

Urban Dwelling House
272-232377   29.99
1-1/16 x 2-1/16"   4.3 x 5.3cm

Concrete Footbridge
272-222151   18.99
8-1/2 x 4-3/4"   21.5 x 12cm

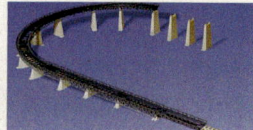

Access Ramp
272-222539   39.99
Includes four straight and four curved track beds, along with 16 piers.

Chairoplane w/Motor
272-242315   65.99
Diameter: 2-3/4"   6.8cm
Height: 2-3/4"   6.8cm

With a swirl of motion and bright lights, this operating ride will animate any midway! This colorful kit is perfect for any fair midway, carnival or amusement park scene. It's complete with motor #272-180629 and can be illuminated with light set #272-180671 (sold separately).

Grade Crossing w/Guardhouse
272-222173   21.99
4-1/4 x 5-3/4 x 4"
10.7 x 14.3 x 9.8cm

Timbered House w/Garage
272-232215   21.99
3 x 3 x 2-7/32"
7.3 x 7.2 x 5.5cm

Platform
272-222124   19.99
23-3/8 x 1-1/2 x 1-5/8"
58.4 x 3.7 x 4cm

A great companion piece to the Schwarzbach Station #272-212108 (sold separately), this platform features decorative parts for further detailing.

Franken Half-Timbered House
272-232280   31.99
3-1/2 x 2-5/8 x 4"
8.8 x 6.8 x 1cm

St. Martin's City Gate
272-232270   59.99
3-1/8 x 1-3/4 x 10-5/8"
8 x 4.6 x 27cm

Old Time Sawmill
272-232249   41.99
8-5/8 x 5"   22 x 13cm

Two 2-Story Stucco Homes
272-232224   21.99
2-3/4 x 2-5/8"   7 x 6.5cm
2-1/4 x 1-3/4"   5.5 x 4.5cm

Single-Family House
272-232214   21.99
3 x 3 x 2-7/32"
7.3 x 7.2 x 5.5cm

City Optic Town House
272-232376   34.99
1-11/16 x 1-13/16"
4.3 x 4.6cm

Three Modern Houses
272-232221   pkg(3)   21.99
3 x 1-7/8"   7.5 x 4.8cm
3-1/4 x 2-1/4"   8.3 x 5.8cm
3-1/2 x 2-1/4"   9.3 x 5.6cm

Town Accessory Kit
272-272573   pkg(67)   19.99
Includes phone booths, billboards, mail boxes, clocks, planters, benches and flags.

Chapel Sils-Maria
272-232263   16.99
3-1/8 x 2-1/2"   7.9 x 6.1cm

St. Bernard's Church
272-232240   24.99
5 x 4-1/2"   12.8 x 11.5cm

224

STRUCTURES N SCALE

IMPORTED FROM GERMANY BY WALTHERS

Krone Inn
272-232370 34.99
2-7/8 x 2-1/2 x 3-3/8"
7.4 x 6.4 x 8.3cm

Freight House
272-222117 29.99
5-1/8 x 2-1/4" 13 x 5.5cm

Schwarzbach Station
272-212108 39.99
12-3/8 x 3-3/4 x 3"
31 x 9.5 x 7.5cm
Features an annexed freight shed and platform roofing.

Schwarzbach Signal Tower
272-222157 17.99
2-15/16 x 1-5/8 x 2-3/4"
7.3 x 4 x 6.8cm

Steel Arch Deck Bridge
272-222581 31.99
Single Track: 16" 40cm;
Double Track: 8" 20cm
Kit includes piers and mounting posts for catenary masts. Requires Straight Steel Bridge, #272-222540, (sold separately).

Grade Crossing w/Tower
272-222170 Operating w/Motor 78.99
5-15/16 x 5-7/8" 15.1 x 15cm
272-222171 Dummy, Less Motor 35.99

Iron Foundry
272-222185 97.99
13-1/2 x 4-5/8" 34.4 x 11.8cm
Includes three separate structures that can be built together or separately.

Market Stands & Cart
272-272533 26.99

Rothenburg Inn
272-232282 34.99
4-5/8 x 3-1/4 x 3-5/16"
11.7 x 8.3 x 10cm

Arcades w/Wall Arches
272-272580 pkg(2) 9.99
1-7/8 x 13/64 x 8-11/64"
4.7 x .5 x 20.4cm

Steel Arch Bridge w/2 Girder Bridges & Piers
272-222583 28.99
16" 40cm

Concession Booths
272-242321 pkg(2) 16.99
Each: 2-1/8 x 3/4 x 1-1/2"
5.3 x 1.8 x 3.8cm
Includes Cookie and Fried Chicken food stands.

Garage Workshop
272-222186 28.99
3-5/8 x 2-7/16 x 1-13/64"
9 x 6.1 x 3cm

Straight Viaducts
272-222585 pkg(2) 24.99
This versatile viaduct set will get your trains across the toughest N Scale terrain! The set includes two 4" (10cm) simulated brick viaducts with a clearance of 2-1/4" (5.7cm).

Merry-Go-Round
272-242316 36.99
Diameter: 2-3/4" 6.8cm;
Height: 2-5/8" 6.5cm
Motorize this kit with electric motor #272-180629 (sold separately).

Get the Scoop!
Get the Skinny!
Get the Score!
Check Out Walthers Web site at
www.walthers.com

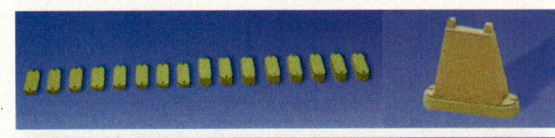

Pier Set For Approach Ramp
272-222547 21.99
1/8 x 2-1/4" 0.5 x 6.0cm

Assorted Concrete Bridge Piers
272-222548 15.99
3-1/8 x 1/2" 8 x 1cm
3-1/8 x 3/4" 8 x 2cm

Straight Steel Bridge
272-222540 pkg(4) 24.99
3-1/8 x 4" 8 x 10cm

Curved Steel Bridge
272-222542 pkg(4) 25.99
7-1/2" 19.3cm radius

Curved Steel Bridge
272-222543 pkg(4) 34.99
8-7/8" 22.5cm radius

Limited Quantity Available

House Of Fashion Store & Apartments
272-232267 46.99
3-31/32 x 5-3/32 x 5-1/4"
9.9 x 12.7 x 13.1cm

Limited Quantity Available

Concrete Bridge Head Set
272-222590 pkg(2) 14.99
For use with Steel Arch Deck Bridge (#272-222581), Steel Arch Bridge with two girder bridges and piers (#272-222583), or Straight Steel Bridge (#272-222540), each sold separately.

Limited Quantity Available

Town Dwelling House/Shop
272-232273 40.99
3-13/64 x 3-13/64 x 5"
8 x 8 x 12.5cm

Limited Quantity Available

Stone Arch Bridge
272-222588 20.99
8" 20cm

225

STRUCTURES N SCALE

BUILDING KITS

Designed for ease of construction, all Laserkit structures feature precision laser-cut basswood and plywood parts that assemble much like plastic kits. Unless noted, all kits feature peel-and-stick assembly windows with positionable sashes, doors, trim and roofing material. All walls and major assemblies have tab-and-slot construction. Kits may also include white metal and acrylic detail parts.

Alton Elevator Laser-Cut Kit
152-651   34.95
3-1/2 x 3 x 6"   8.75 X 7.5 X 15cm

Hinkle Mill Laser-Cut Kit
152-653   74.95
7 x 10"   17.5 x 30cm

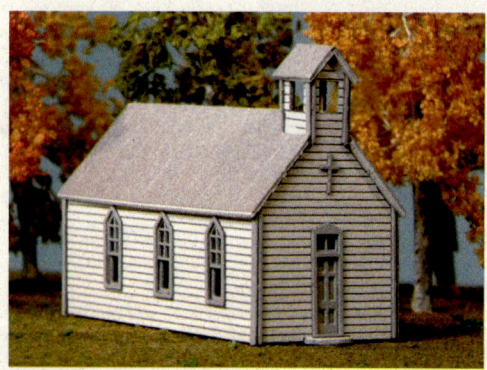

Crossroads Church
152-691   15.95
2-1/2 x 1-1/8 x 2"   6.4 x 2.9 x 5.1cm

McCormac's Dry Goods
152-693   15.95
3 x 1-3/8 x 1-3/4"   7.6 x 3.5 x 4.5cm

Santa Fe #3 One-Story Depot
152-607   49.95
5 x 1-3/4 x 1-1/2"   12.7 x 4.5 x 3.8cm

Two-Story Farmhouse w/Front Porch
152-640   34.95
2-1/2 x 1-3/4 x 2-1/4"   6.2 x 4.3 x 25.6cm

A.C. Brown Manufacturing Company
152-615   62.95
6-1/4 x 3-1/2 x 3-1/2"   15.9 x 8.9 x 8.9cm

General Service Building
152-601   24.95
4-1/2 x 2-1/4 x 1-1/2"
11.2 x 5.6 x 3.7cm

Farmer's Grain & Stock Company
152-606   32.95
5 x 3 x 4"   12.7 x 7.6 x 10.2cm

Interlocking Tower
152-602   27.95
1-1/4 x 1 x 2-1/4"
3.1 x 2.5 x 5.6cm

Country Barn
152-619   42.95
4-1/2 x 3 x 3-1/2"
11.2 x 7.5 x 8.7cm

Springfield Depot
152-638   29.95
3 x 1-1/4 x 1-1/4"
7.5 x 3.1 x 3.1cm

Transfer Building
152-604   64.95
6-1/2 x 4-3/4 x 3"
16.3 x 11.9 x 7.5cm

STRUCTURES N SCALE

Sonny's Shack
152-605 pkg(2) **22.95**
2-3/8 x 1-3/8 x 1"
5.9 x 3.4 x 2.5cm

Single-Stall Engine House
152-608 29.95
4-1/2 x 2-1/2 x 2"
11.3 x 6.3 x 5cm

Yard Office
152-609 19.95
2 x 1 x 2"   5 x 2.5 x 5cm

Grain Elevator
152-610 32.95
3-3/4 x 2-1/4 x 5"
9.4 x 5.6 x 12.5cm

Hitzeman Feed Mill
152-611 32.95
4-1/4 x 2-1/2 x 3-3/4"
10.6 x 6.3 x 9.4cm

Corydon General Store & Post Office
152-623 24.95
3-3/4 x 2-3/4 x 1-3/4"   9.3 x 6.8 x 4.3cm

Nine Mile House & Tavern
152-645 39.95
2-3/4 x 2-1/4 x 2-3/4"   7 x 5.7 x 7cm

Railroad Rooming House
152-613 32.95
6-1/4 x 1-1/4 x 2"   15.9 x 3.8 x 5cm

Feeder & Livestock Barn
152-617 19.95
4 x 2-1/2 x 2"   10 x 6.2 x 5cm

Dill's Market
152-622 15.95
2-1/4 x 1-1/2 x 1-1/2"
5.6 x 3.7 x 3.7cm

Hot New Products Announced Daily! Visit Walthers Web site at
www.walthers.com

Silex Elevator
152-621 32.95
3 x 2-1/2 x 4"
7.5 x 6.2 x 10cm

Springfield Cafe
152-636 19.95
1-1/4 x 2-1/2 x 1-3/4"
3.1 x 6.2 x 4.3cm

UP Style One-Story Depot
152-627 32.95
6 x 2-1/2 x 2-3/4"
15 x 6.2 x 6.8cm

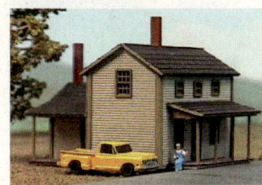

Two-Story Section House
152-628 24.95
2 x 2-1/2 x 1-1/2"
5 x 6.2 x 3.7cm

One-Story Section House
152-629 18.95
3 x 1-1/4 x 1-1/2"
7.5 x 3.1 x 3.7cm

Ellington Mercantile
152-635 29.95
3-1/2 x 3-1/4 x 2"
8.7 x 9.3 x 5cm

Windsor Hotel
152-643 34.95
2 x 4 x 2-1/2" 5 x 10 x 6.3cm

SP Combination-Type 23 Depot w/Dock
152-650 59.95
6-1/4 x 2 x 1-3/4"
15.6 x 5 x 4.4cm

Hillview Volunteer Fire Co.
152-647 24.95
1-3/4 x 2-1/4 x 2-1/2"
4.4 x 5.6 x 6.3cm

Northern Pacific Depot
152-649 49.95
5-3/4 x 2 x 1-3/4"
14.4 x 5 x 4.4cm

Company Houses
152-698 pkg(3) **24.95**
1-1/2 x 1-1/2 x 1"
3.8 x 3.8 x 2.5cm

STRUCTURES N SCALE

Detail your right-of-way with these easy-to-build kits which fit any era. Models feature plastic parts molded in colors and assemble with plastic-compatible cements, sold separately.

LOVELY LADIES HOME SERIES™

Build authentic residential neighborhoods with this model, the first in a new series based on popular designs sold by a major catalog retailer in the 1920s. Available as a kit or fully assembled, all parts are molded in appropriate colors, so no painting is needed.

Barb's Bungalow
Modeled after popular catalog homes from the 1920s, Barb's Bungalow features realistic clapboard siding, shingles, rain gutters and downspouts, Bilco® cellar doors and more. Parts come molded in appropriate colors and the model is available as an easy-to-build plastic kit or completely assembled.

150-2846 Kit **19.95**
150-2847 Assembled **29.95**

Kate's Colonial Home
This charming home is perfect for any family in a city or country scene. The structure features clapboard siding on the lower half and shingle detail on the upper half. A brick chimney, rain gutter and downspout detail, window glazing and an authentic Bilco® cellar door are all included.

150-2844 Kit **18.95**
150-2845 Assembled (Colors Vary) **26.95**

Signal Tower
150-2840 **18.95**
Protect a junction, yard or other busy trackage along your line. This handsome American building is packed with details, including intricate inlaid bricks, drain pipes and eave supports. For the area around the tower, a tool shed, oil tank and barrels are included.

Manual Turntable
150-2790 **21.75**
A great detail for any roundhouse or engine service area. Model comes fully assembled with a 7-1/2" diameter deck. Serves up to 24 tracks, with 15° spacing.

Turntable Drive
150-2791 **18.95**
Motor drive for manual turntable (#150-2790), sold separately. Easy to install and wire.

New Arrivals Updated Every Day! Visit Walthers Web site at
www.walthers.com

Passenger Station w/Platform
150-2841 **25.25**
Any small town or suburb would be proud of this depot. Classic American styling and lots of details make this a real eye-catcher! Check out the inlaid brick chimney, shingled roof, downspouts, a heating oil tank, benches, a baggage cart with luggage and freight, a hand truck and a freight scale, which are all included to add the finishing touch. A single platform section is also included, which is easily expanded with the matching Station Platform kit (#150-2842), sold separately.

Station Platform
150-2842 pkg(2) **13.95**
Passengers will appreciate this covered waiting area in any kind of weather. Identical to the platform parts included with the Passenger Station (#150-2841), sold separately, this versatile kit can be used to build a longer attached platform. It can also be assembled as a free-standing structure for use across or between tracks. Several can also be combined to build a longer structure. Perfect for steam- or diesel-era scenes.

Roundhouse
150-2843 **28.50**
Longest Section: 10-3/8" 26.4cm
Widest Section: 11" 27.9cm
Tallest Section: 3" 7.6cm

The basic three-stall kit features brick detail, opening doors, stalls spaced at 15°, an office and two styles of ventilators. Molded in appropriate colors, it is designed to work with Atlas N Scale Turntable (#150-2790) and Turntable Motor Drive (#150-2791), each sold separately.

STRUCTURES N SCALE

BRIDGES

These realistic bridge kits are based on some of the most common American railroad designs. Each easy-to-build kit is molded in black or gray plastic, and includes complete assembly instructions, where appropriate. All bridges measure 5" long, and several can be combined to build a larger structure.

Straight Bridge Girders
150-2542 pkg(4) 2.95

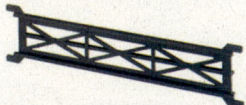

Pier Set
150-2541 pkg(25) 8.75
Use to raise tracks on approach to bridge. Snap-fit mounting for Atlas track.

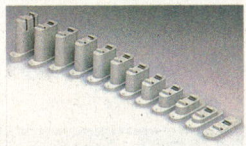

Viaduct
150-2826 5.25
Realistic cut stone detail.

Bridge Piers
150-2543 pkg(3) 2.95

Deck Girder Bridge
150-2547 4.75

Warren Truss Bridge
150-2546 4.75

Plate Girder Bridge
150-2548 4.75

BLMA

NEW PRODUCT
Antenna Tower

Radio Tower
NEW 176-602 10.75
This 70 scale foot tall lattice tower is based on those located near yards and along the mainline. Includes tower and common antennae.

Trackside Structures

176-89 Trackside Signal/Grade Crossing Electronics Box pkg(2) 5.75

Towers

176-600 Cell Phone Antenna Tower 12.50

Outhouses

176-601 Outhouses pkg(2) 5.50

BRAWA
LIEBE ZUM DETAIL

IMPORTED FROM GERMANY BY WALTHERS
Brawa Structures include metal and plastic parts, requiring only minor assembly and installation. Cableways do not include station buildings which are required to finish scenes as shown.

Funicular Set
186-6410 312.99
Set includes two passenger cars, four straight track sections with built-in rollers, one passing loop (Abt system), a drive motor with automatic stop action, one electronic relay with color-coded wiring, two (#3530) reed switches, 13 feet (4m) of drive cable and cable stations. Car length is 2-1/2". Track section is 4-3/4" long, passing loop is 10-1/2" long. Includes instructions (English text).

Item listed below is available by Special Order (see Legend Page).

Funicular Shed
186-6411 198.99
Kit builds a covered passenger platform for use with #6410 (sold separately).

Straight Track
186-6412 pkg(2) 9.99
Molded in dark brown plastic.

Platform Side Set
186-2697 7.99
Set includes four straight sections, each approximately 5-1/8" long, four ramps, each approximately 1-3/16" long.

Cableways
The Brawa cableway is a working model, complete with drive cable stations and "cars," less speed control and structures. Systems can be expanded to any length using additional pylons and cable, available separately. Speed can be adjusted using Brawa #6150 controller. All sets comply with VDE standards for radio and TV interference. The set is designed for use with 14-16V DC systems, use with AC requires rectifier (#2185) (sold separately).

"Seilschwebebahn" Cableway Set
186-6560 174.99
Set includes valley and summit cable stations (less structures), four cars, center pylon 3-3/4" high, drive cables and complete instructions (English text).

Extra Car For "Seilschwebebahn" Set
186-6561 12.99

Station Buildings
186-6570 41.99
Set of two structure kits for use with #6560 cableway set. Summit and Valley station are both 6 x 5-3/16".

Replacement Motor
186-9713 27.99
For cableways made after September, 1992.

Operating Container Terminal
186-1151 339.99
Presentation Pack with motors and drives for lifting and lowering containers onto trucks or freight cars and moving the gantry left or right. Fully automatic grippers. Includes travel gear, crane, control unit and four containers. Dimensions 16 x 8 x 4". For use with DC power supply or AC with Brawa #2185 bridge rectifier (sold separately).

Lighted Telephone Booths

186-4561 Swisscom 14.99

186-4562 FH32 13.99

186-4563 FeH 78 10.99
186-4568 FH 32 13.99

Telephone Booth
186-4566 10.99
Illuminated, includes resistor for use with 16V power supply. Measures 1/4 x 1/4 x 1/2".

Replacement Bulb
186-3268 3.99

STRUCTURES N SCALE

These structures are fully assembled (unless noted), meaning no assembly is necessary! Just pull these great buildings out of the box and place them on your N Scale layout for immediate fun!

Station w/Steam Whistle
160-46709 23.00
5-3/4 x 6" 14.6 x 15.3cm
Realistic sounding whistle is hidden inside the station. Model is fully assembled and easy to install on your layout.

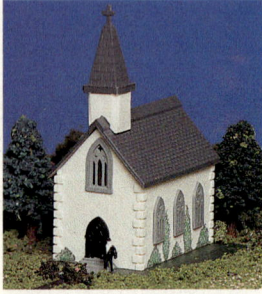

Country Church
160-45815 10.50
3-1/4 x 2-1/2" 8.3 x 6.4cm
Includes a figure.

Station Platform w/Roof
160-45906 11.50
1-3/16 x 3-7/8" 3 x 9.9cm
Includes a figure.

18-Piece Blinking Bridge Set
160-46721 11.50

Factory w/Accessories
160-45902 11.50
Includes figures.

For Up-To-Date Information and News Bookmark Walthers Web site at
www.walthers.com

Water Tank
160-45810 10.50
Includes a figure.

Coaling Station
160-45811 10.50
1-5/8 x 2-1/8" 4.1 x 5.4cm
Includes a figure.

Two-Story House w/Garage
160-45813 10.50
3 x 4-3/4" 7.6 x 12.1cm

31-Piece Up & Over Bridge Set
160-46723 11.50

New England Ranch House
160-45814 10.50
2-3/4 x 3-1/2" 7 x 9cm

Farm House
160-45812 10.50
2-1/4 x 2-1/2" 13.5 x 6.4cm
Includes figures.

Auto Body Shop
160-45708 10.50
3-3/8 x 4-7/8" 8.1 x 12.4cm
Includes figures.

Drive-In Bank
160-45804 10.50
3 x 4-3/4" 7.7 x 12.1cm
Includes figures.

Oil Tank w/Diesel Horn
160-46708 Kit 23.00
2-3/4" 7cm diameter
Built-in horn with push button.

Shell Gas Station
160-45904 11.50
3-1/2 x 5-1/2" 8.9 x 14cm

Modern Home
160-45909 11.50
3-3/4 x 4-3/4" 9.5 x 12.1cm

Freight Station
160-45907 11.50

Passenger Station
160-45908 11.50
2-7/8 x 5-1/8" 7.3 x 13cm
Includes figures.

Drive-In Hamburger Stand
160-45709 10.50
4-3/4 x 3" 12.1 x 7.7cm

New Car Showroom
160-45903 11.50
3-1/2 x 5-1/2" 8.9 x 14cm
Includes automobile.

Oil Tank w/Light
160-46712 Kit 14.00
2-3/4" 7cm diameter
ARCO tank has flashing light on top.

Schoolhouse w/Playground Equipment
160-45807 10.50
3-1/4 x 4-1/2" 8.3 x 11.4cm

STRUCTURES N SCALE

"THE GREAT LITTLE KIT..."
Bar Mills
SCALE MODEL WORKS
"FROM THE GREAT STATE OF MAINE"

Create detailed scenes along your right-of-way with this selection of structure kits. Each model features wood parts that are precision-cut and/or etched with a laser. The result is a highly detailed building that assembles much like a plastic kit. Complete instructions are included to make construction quick and easy. Kits also include signs and metal details where appropriate.

Whistle Stop Junction 171-912

Earl's Oil 171-801

Mooney's Plumbing Emporium 171-821

Waterfront Willy's/Trackside Jack's 171-921

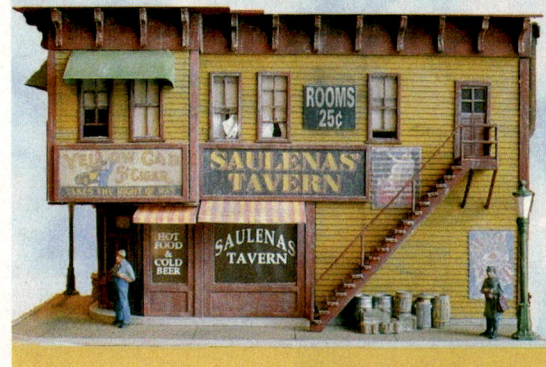
Saulena's Tavern 171-931

Majestic Hardware 171-941

Swanson's Lunch Stand w/Billboard 171-951

The Shack Pack 171-991

Low Boy Trestle Kit 171-304

STATIONS

Whistle Stop Junction
171-912 37.95
The kit features siding that shows individual nail holes and includes white metal details.

BUSINESSES

Earl's Oil
171-801 34.95
Includes "Insta-Fence," three detailed resin tanks, billboards, signs, lampheads and instructions.

Mooney's Plumbing Emporium
171-821 47.95
Includes a billboard, detailed castings and the "Insta-Fence," which adds 160 scale feet of fencing around the building.

Waterfront Willy's/Trackside Jack's
171-921 44.95
Includes a set of pilings to support the structure over water. Laser-cut "cedar shake" shingles, windows (which can be built open or closed), optional doors and shutters and white metal detail parts are included.

Saulena's Tavern
171-931 44.95
Kit comes complete with metal details, awnings, signs, and a corner sidewalk.

Majestic Hardware
171-941 67.95
Based on an actual structure, kit features laser-cut lumber, double laminated roofing, 30 white-metal castings, laser-cut precision fitting windows, and roof-lettering stencils.

Swanson's Lunch Stand w/Billboard
171-951 19.95
This Thumbnail Series™ kit is complete with interior framing and appliances, fencing, metal details and a colorful billboard.

The Shack Pack
171-991 34.95
Includes three different and separate shacks, white metal detail castings, signs, fencing and a dry transfer.

BRIDGES

Low Boy Trestle Kit
171-304 8.95
When assembled, thhis modular kit is about 4" 10cm long, but each section is slotted so you can easily combine several kits to build a longer structure. All parts are laser-cut and notched to speed assembly.

STRUCTURES N SCALE

"THE GREAT LITTLE KIT..."
Bar Mills SCALE MODEL WORKS
"FROM THE GREAT STATE OF MAINE"

STREET ELEVATORS

171-301 Two Complete Elevators & Door Sets **8.95**
Kit includes etched-brass parts for two complete elevators with doors that can be modeled in the open or closed position.

THE "1-KIT"

171-31 27.95
The "1-Kit" takes you beyond the limits of traditional kits that only model a specific building. It provides you with a set of basic basswood parts that can be assembled and modified in a variety of ways to make unique wooden structures.

The basic two-story clapboard wall sections (kit includes four) feature partially laser-cut window and door openings on the rear. Wall sections are easily cut to size or combined and door and window spaces, already partially cut, are easily opened. Separate laser-cut windows can be assembled in a variety of sizes and modeled opened or closed. Five entry doors and two styles of freight doors are also included. Layered design and assembly make multi-colored paint jobs a snap. Each "1-Kit" also includes printed paper signs, stripwood interior bracing and acetate window glazing. Add your favorite roof and roofing (sold separately) to complete your model. Includes a 15-page manual with 1-Kit instructions and tips.

INSTA-FENCE

171-41 Approximately 160 Scale Feet **7.95**

COVERED STAIRWELLS

171-305 pkg(2) **11.95**
This detail can be used to quickly improve and detail almost any structure.

EVAN DESIGNS

Create great detail for your layout in any scale with these easy to use software titles. Choose from a large variety of ready to print designs to make your layout unique. Never have your model buildings all look the same, or look like someone else's. System requirements: PC running Windows 98/NT/ME/2000/XP/XP-Pro.

BUILDING SOFTWARE

Brickyard

266-A31 15.00
This program allows you to print full sheets of bricks and stones in any scale for modeling walls, foundations, bridge abutments and more. Program includes 20 different brick and stone patterns.

Modeler's Toolkit

266-A100 125.00
A compilation of Evan designs software titles, set includes American Advertising Collection, Window Designer, Sign Creator, Brickyard and Stained Glass software. Also comes with a Printer Variety Pack with inkjet paper, transparencies, printable vinyl and decal paper for various modeling applications.

Model Builder

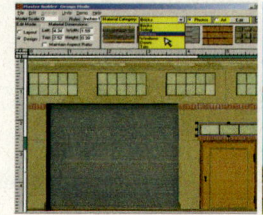 

Building constructed using printouts from Model Builder software

266-A51 Version 1 **45.00**
With this revolutionary program, you are in charge. Print all the materials you need in your scale, for your layout, from our designs! All with an ordinary inkjet printer! Create your building your way. Model Builder is loaded with nineteen different material categories, 230 high quality images in all. "Building Materials" such as brick, stone, cement, stucco, metal sheeting, wood, siding, roofing, trim, factory windows and doors, residential windows and doors, storehouse doors, lattice and grills. Any of these images can be seamlessly tiled to fill a full size sheet, or any wall or roof size. There is also a custom Brick Designer and Siding Editor. You get fast, fun and easy to use complete software and a user's manual.

Window Designer

266-A12 40.00
End the vacant building look. Print window treatments, text, silhouettes and artwork for every building window on your layout. Window templates provided for many popular manufacturer's N Scale and larger buildings, or you can lay out your own custom arrangements. Simply print out your finished designs on transparency or vellum (one sheet of each included to get you started) and install.

Stained Glass

266-A41 15.00
Add color and variety to all types of structures with this unique software program that allows you to scale, arrange and print over 25 different stained glass images. Shapes include rectangle, round and half-round.

STRUCTURES N SCALE

BRANCHLINE TRAINS

Branchline's Laser-Art structures are designed to be built with a minimum of fuss. The kits include precision laser cut wood parts engineered with tab and slot construction and utilize peel and stick trim for maximum ease of assembly. Detailed instructions with clear diagrams are included in every kit. Also included are cast resin details for that finishing touch.

NEW PRODUCTS

Catalog Homes

The Avon House
NEW 181-836 28.50
5 x 5 x 3" 12.7 x 12.7 x 7.6cm

Commercial Buildings

The Roscoe Store
NEW 181-843 46.99
3 x 3-1/2 x 3" 7.6 x 8.9 x 7.6cm

Based on a New York prototype that stood near the O&W station in its namesake, the structure also housed a barber shop, confectionary store and bakery over its life.

The Majestic Theater
NEW 181-854 31.50
3-1/2 x 3 x 1-1/2" 8.9 x 7.6 x 3.8cm

This small-town theater includes vintage movie posters and marquee signs.

Stations & Platforms

Cannondale Station
NEW 181-861 32.50
2 x 1 x 1" 5.1 x 2.5 x 2.5cm

Based on an NH prototype on the famed Danbury branch, this detailed combination station is typical of those found on many railroads. The prototype is still in service, making it an ideal addition to any steam- or diesel-era layout. Includes a resin chimney and signs.

Center Hall Depot
NEW 181-863 57.50

An 1884-built prototype built by a Pennsy predecessor, this depot now houses a restaurant. This kit is based on the structure's 1940 appearance and includes appropriate signs.

Santa Fe #4 Standard Station
NEW 181-865 44.98
6 x 2-1/2 x 1-1/2" 15.2 x 6.4 x 3.8cm

Based on an ATSF system design, this style of depot was used across the railroad. Includes combination depot and freight platform.

Laura Station
NEW 181-868 23.29
3-1/2 x 2-1/2 x 1-1/2" 8.9 x 6.4 x 3.8cm

Another ATSF system standard design, this style of depot was used in many small towns.

Trackside Structures

Flour Mill
NEW 181-886 28.99

This small structure is ideal for any steam- or diesel-era railroad.

Grain Elevator
NEW 181-889 43.98
2 x 2-1/2 x 3-1/2" 5.1 x 6.4 x 8.9cm

A staple along all railroads in rural areas, this wooden elevator includes the main silo and a small office.

YARD EQUIPMENT & FACILITIES

Engine House
181-883 51.98

This classic single stall engine house will be at home on most layouts. While typical of designs throughout the country, the prototype was built for the Central Vermont. It can provide protection for a variety of locomotives from moderate sized steam locos to almost any diesel. This building includes a machine shop addition allowing light repairs to be made on the locomotives.

For Daily Product Updates Point Your Browser to

www.walthers.com

STRUCTURES N SCALE

BRANCHLINE TRAINS

VICTORIAN CLASSICS

Dubois House
181-800   82.48
The Dubois House prototype in Livingston Manor, NY was built in 1884 for A.P. Dubois, a successful merchant. The house sat adjacent to the railroad tracks and still stands, beautifully restored.

Thelma & Stanley Houses
181-819   19.98
These compact wood-frame houses are typical of those built in the early 1900s. Each kit includes one of each house.

Church
181-842   36.98
Perfect for any denomination, this compact church will fit on any layout.

CATALOG HOMES

Throughout the later half of the 19th century and well into the 20th century many architectural firms offered stock house plans that could be purchased for use in constructing homes.

The Albion
181-821   24.99

The Drayton House
181-824   14.98
The Drayton house is based on a plan in the 1917 Aladdin catalog. The compact Drayton was one of Aladdin's smaller designs.

The Finley House
181-825   25.99
Based on a plan from the 1917 Aladdin catalog, the Finley will fit very nicely on a narrow lot and still leave ample space for a walk on either side.

Beverly 2 Family House
181-827   32.98
Based on a design from the 1917 Aladdin catalog, the Beverly offered two complete apartments, each with its own entrance.

Tucson House w/Garage
181-839   26.50
The Tucson is a compact design that can fit on almost any layout.

Suburban House & Hudson Garage Combo
181-873   29.98
Based on a plan shown in the 1917 Aladdin catalog, this kit contains 2 individual structures.

COMMERCIAL BUILDINGS

Dubois Store
181-840   79.98
The prototype was located in Livingston Manor, NY and is typical of small town general mercantile stores. Originally built in the 1880s as a general merchandise store, over the years it housed a barbershop, drug store, offices, even a hobby shop! Set alongside the railroad tracks, side doors allowed access to railroad cars. The building stood until destroyed by a fire in the 1970s. Kit includes resin interior details.

Gas Station
181-887   38.24
For many years the local service station was a fixture in towns. Attendants would pump your gas, check your oil, wash your windshield and trade stories. This canopy style station was a common design used by many companies. Includes 1930s Gas Pumps & 1940s-50s Gas Pumps.

STRUCTURES N SCALE

BRANCHLINE TRAINS

RURAL BUILDINGS

Barn & Out Buildings
181-850 36.99
This set contains all the buildings you need to make your farm complete. Includes a small barn, chicken coop, shed, smokehouse and outhouse.

The Farm House
181-853 33.98
This simple farmhouse is typical of those found on many farms.

TRACKSIDE STRUCTURES

Creamery
181-880 42.98
The prototype was built at Clark's, near Campbell Hall, NY on the New York, Ontario & Western. Similar designs could be found throughout the Northeast. The O&W was unique in that in built many of its own creameries. As a result they were most likely painted in the railroad's colors - a cream/buff wall color with green trim and red window sashes. Kit includes loading docks and a delivery shed.

Ice House
181-881 19.98
Ice houses were kept near to dairy creameries to keep milk products cool. This kit features loading docks, large vertical loading doors and a rooftop ventilator.

Meat Packing Plant
181-882 45.98
Based on a prototype built by Swift in Burlington, VT, similar buildings could be seen in the Northeast and other areas. This classic Greek Revival design was not unique to Swift. The garage annex is most likely an addition built when trucks became more common. Such a plant would get in whole carcasses in meat reefers to be cut up by butchers and shipped out.

County Feed
181-884 36.98
This typical small trackside industrial building could be used for a number of different applications. Kit comes with printed signs for County Feed.

Caldwell Tool & Die
181-885 34.98
Another typical trackside industry, this kit is patterned after a shop owned by an eccentric machinist.

Weimer's Mill
181-888 37.98
This mill was built by and owned by Jacob Weimer, a feisty immigrant who located the mill in the most prominent spot on his property.

Nickels Feed Mill
181-892 35.98
Nickels Feed is a classic trackside industry perfect for any layout. It can be used as a feed mill or other light industries. Features laser cut wood siding, peel-and-stick trim, laser-cut shingles, appropriate signs and complete instructions including weathering tips.

Valley Fuel
181-893 63.98
Valley Fuel is a typical trackside business that serves local farmers and residents by keeping them supplied with fuel. This kit features a canopied trackside loading dock and two coal silos on one end. It'll add interest to any siding and is an ideal destination for coal hoppers, box cars and tank cars. Kit includes laser cut wood siding, peel-and-stick trim, laser-cut shingles, appropriate signs and complete instructions including weathering tips.

STRUCTURES N SCALE

Blair Line
PRODUCTS FOR MODEL RAILROADERS

CAD design and laser cutting produce a kit with all the precision of a plastic kit, but with all the advantages of wood. Walls, roofing, doors, windows and trim are laser-cut and ready to assemble. Models are highly detailed, easy to build and look great too!

NEW PRODUCT

Gerald Depot
NEW 184-95   39.95
1-3/4 x 3-3/4"   4.5 x 9.5cm
Combination depot features a "pagoda-style" roof. Includes signs and a cast-metal chimney.

Fred & Red's Cafe
184-90   27.95
1-3/32 x 2-1/2"   2.75 x 6.25cm
Long before look-alike fast food chains, small roadside cafes like these catered to travelers and truck drivers along the nations major two-lane highways. Here and there, a few still survive today. packed with details, the kit includes a laser-cur floor, aged sidewalks, and exterior walls feature laser-etched nail holes. Plastic windows are included, along with signs, burglar bars, lampshades, a cast metal smokejack and laser-cut OPEN and EAT signs.

Warehouse Backdrop Building
184-92   79.95
7-1/8 x 1-1/8 x 3-7/8"   17.8 X 2.8 x 9.69cm
Includes laser-etched nail holes on aged clapboard siding, positionable windows, lampshades, exhaust fans, crates, pallets and a do-it-yourself rooftop sign to make a custom factory name.

Boston Depot
184-93   37.95
A small combination depot based on a Missouri Pacific prototype found in Boston, Missouri.

Tom's Corn Crib
184-91   19.95
1-1/2 Diameter x 1-5/8" Tall
3.75 x 4.0cm
Used to air-dry corn for animal feed, corn cribs are a common sight on farms large and small. This model captures all the intricate detail of the eight-sided original which still stands in Kansas, in an easy-to-build kit.

Leeton Depot
184-88   39.95
Structure (including optional ramp): 1-3/4 x 3-1/2"
4.5 x 8.9cm
Structure only: 1-13/16 x 3"
4.6 x 7.6cm
Based on depots used by the Rock Island (their standard design) and several other railroads, this 24 x 40' wood combination station is at home on any layout or module.

Clark Oil Gas Station
184-87   32.95
1-1/2 x 2-1/2"   3.8 x 6.3cm
Based on the popular station design from the 1950s (which can still be seen today), this kit features laser-cut exterior and interior walls along with many other details.

Chesapeake & Ohio Depot
184-85   39.95
1-1/2 x 3-3/4"   3.7 x 9.3cm
Designed from plans for a standard No. 1 combination bay window depot. Includes peel-n-stick trim and interior walls.

Dari-King Drive-In Restaurant
184-82   26.95
2-1/4 x 3"   5.6 x 7.5cm
Bring retro styling and a touch of nostalgia to your layout with this eatery. Attract customers with a laser-cut roadside sign that will catch any motorist's eye.

Cash Mine Works Ore House
184-86   74.95
4 x 4-1/2 x 5"
10 x 11.2 x 12.5cm
Based on the Silver King Ore House in Park City, Utah, this kit creates a mine works with varied roof lines, exposed structural frames, and covered loading areas for trucks and rail cars. Includes over 270 parts, includes laser-cut walls with tab and slot connections and Grandt Line windows.

Ernie's Gas Station
184-81   34.95
2-3/4 x 1-3/4"   6.8 x 4.3cm
Based on a gas station on Route 66 in Carthage, Missouri, this kit includes laser-cut walls, doors, window frames, trim, floor, roofing and sign frames. Also comes with gas pumps and island, chimney, tire display, soda machine, a billboard and a variety of decals and signs.

Wood Frame Church
184-69   32.95
3 x 1-7/8 x 4"   7.5 x 4.7 x 10cm
Based on churches found throughout North America. May be used with any era modeled. Great church for small town, country or city scenes.

Company House
184-76   17.95
2-1/4 x 1-1/2"   5.6 x 3.8cm
Employers provided housing of a standard design for workers, and company towns would consist of several of these housing units.

Truck Dump
184-77   17.95
2 x 1"   5 x 2.5cm
Found in coal mining areas of Appalachia and anywhere coal, stone and other minerals were mined and delivered by truck or wagon to be transported by rail.

Blairstown 2-Story Depot
184-78   39.95
4-1/2 x 1-1/2"   11.3 x 3.8cm
Great depot for your community. The second floor was often used as a living quarters for the station agent, while the one-story addition served as the freight and baggage room.

STRUCTURES N SCALE

Blair Line™
PRODUCTS FOR MODEL RAILROADERS

Shotgun House
184-79   18.95
1 x 3"   2.5 x 7.5cm
The "row house" of the South and Appalachia but found through the United States. May be built with or without the back porch addition.

One-Car Garage
184-73   11.95
1-1/2 x 1"   3.8 x 2.5cm

Laser-Cut Pile & Frame Trestle
184-71   24.95
5-5/8" long x 1-1/4" tall
14.1cm long x 3.1cm tall
This bridge has square post piers that sit on a horizontal bottom support. Trestle may be built straight or curved and includes bulkheads and Bridge Flex Trak.

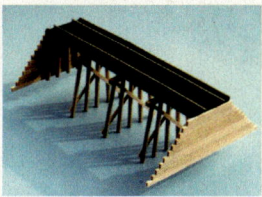
Common Pile Trestle
184-67   21.95
5-5/8" long x 1-1/4" tall
14.1cm long x 3.1cm tall
Common wood pile (with round piers. May be built straight or curved. Includes a section of Bridge Flex Trak.

Blairstown General Store
184-80   29.95
2 x 3"   6 x 7.5cm
Nearly every town had one of these common structures, which were found through the United States not too many years ago. Includes full color signs.

Coal Storage House
184-83   11.95
3/4 x 3/4"   1.9 x 1.9cm
Coal houses were used for coal used as heating fuel.

Scale House
184-84   11.95
1/2 x 1"   1.3 x 2.5cm

Drive-In Theatre
184-68   21.95
Kit includes screen tower, ticket booth, signs and fences. Components are precolored plastic, ready for assembly. Includes three different marquee signs and 17 movie signs from the 1930s-90s.

Roadside Tourist Trap
184-70   26.95
2-3/4 x 1-3/4"   6.9 x 4.4cm
Includes one laser-cut wood structure, and full-color signs for: Fireworks Stand, Totem Pole Trading Post, Reptile Ranch and Hollywood Wax Museum. Also includes advertising signs.

Section Car Toolhouse
184-75   11.95
1-1/8 x 1"   2.8 x 2.5cm
This structure was a common trackside storage building in every railroad town in the United States and Canada.

Wood Loading Ramp
184-74   11.95
3 x 3/4"   7.5cm x 1.875cm

CITY CLASSICS

Crafton Avenue Service Station
195-401   17.98
3-1/4 x 2 x 1-1/4"
8.1 x 5 x 3.1cm
Fill up an empty corner with this classy kit! A must-have detail for street scenes from the late 1940s to the present. Includes the station building, two pump islands with nonworking lamps, two different sign posts and heads, soda and ice machines, oil and tire displays, plus an array of full color decals.

Concrete Retaining Walls
Hold back those hillsides with City Classics modular retaining walls. Based on poured-concrete walls used along railroads and highways, these walls feature injection-molded styrene plastic parts molded in a realistic concrete gray color. Each package includes two three-panel sections plus an additional concrete pilaster. Wall sections are easily combined for additional length, or easily cut using a razor saw.

195-601 pkg(2)   **9.98**
8-9/16 x 3-1/4"   21.5 x 8.1cm

Campbell Scale Models
Craft Train Kits feature all-wood construction, with many parts pre-cut to size. Template drawings and instructions are included with all kits.

HO Scale Version Shown
Grain Elevator
200-445   44.30
6-1/4 x 3-3/4"   16 x 9.7cm

HO Scale Version Shown
Idaho Springs Mine
200-448   43.64
2 x 7-1/8"   5.2 x 18.2cm

Tall Straight Timber Trestle
200-752   61.87
11" (27.5cm) span, 3-3/8" (8.1cm) high.

Low Curved Timber Trestle
200-753   45.02
5-1/2" (13.7cm) span, 1-3/8" (3cm) tall.

High Curved Trestle
200-754   64.00
8-1/2" (21.2cm) span, 3-1/4" (8.1cm) tall.

Thru Timber Bridge
200-760   58.19
Span measures 5-1/4" (13.1cm, 70 scale feet), overall length 7-5/8" (19cm, 101 scale feet).

CAL-FREIGHT

Steel Shed
201-2370   4.75

Boat Dock Set
201-2375   29.95

Well Pump House
201-2380   4.75

Latest New Product News Daily! Visit Walthers Web site at
www.walthers.com

237

STRUCTURES N SCALE

N Scale Modular System
UNLIMITED BUILDING OPTIONS
Interchangeable plastic wall sections to create buildings of any size, shape, or height. Use plastic model cement or solvent.

BUILD AS MANY STORIES AS YOU NEED:
• One-story building - use street or dock level wall sections and cornice.
• Two-story building - use street or dock level wall sections, top with one-story wall sections and cornice.
• Three-story building - use street or dock level sections, top with two-story wall sections and cornice.
• More stories - add additional wall sections to create as many stories as desired.

Packages include three identical double-bay wall sections with pilasters, doors, windows, and clear window material where needed. All sections are the same color and width (3-1/2" 8.7 cm). Cornice packages include nine pieces of Cornice with Cornice pilasters, and Dock Riser Wall packages include six Dock Riser Wall sections with dock pilasters.

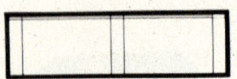

One Story Blank Wall
243-60111 pkg(3) **3.98**
3-1/2" x 15/16"
8.7 x 2.5cm

One Story Window
243-60112 pkg(3) **4.98**
3-1/2" x 15/16"
8.7 x 2.5cm

Cornice
243-60132 pkg(9) **3.98**

Two Story Wall Sections

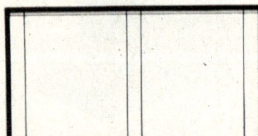

Two Story Blank Wall
243-60121 pkg(3) **3.98**
3-1/2" x 1-15/16"
8.7 x 4.8cm

Two Story 12 Windows
243-60122 pkg(3) **4.98**
3-1/2" x 1-15/16"
8.7 x 4.8cm

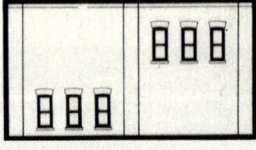

Two Story 6 Windows
243-60123 pkg(3) **4.98**
3-1/2" x 1-15/16"
8.7 x 4.8cm

Street Level Wall Sections

Street Level Window
243-60103 pkg(3) **4.98**
3-1/2" x 1-13/32"
8.7 x 3.5cm

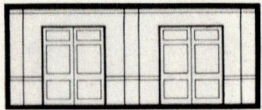

Street Level Freight Door
243-60106 pkg(3) **4.98**
3-1/2" x 1-13/32"
8.7 x 3.5cm

Street/Dock Level Wall Sections

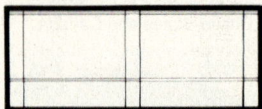

Street/Dock Level Blank Wall
243-60101 pkg(3) **3.98**
3-1/2" x 1-13/32"
8.7 x 3.5cm

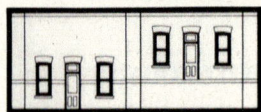

Street/Dock Level Entry Doors
243-60104 pkg(3) **4.98**
3-1/2" x 1-13/32"
8.7 x 3.5cm

Dock Level Wall Sections

Dock Level Window
243-60102 pkg(3) **4.98**
3-1/2" x 1-13/32"
8.7 x 3.5cm

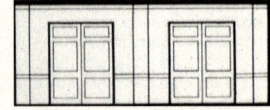

Dock Level Freight Door
243-60105 pkg(3) **4.98**
3-1/2" x 1-13/32"
8.7 x 3.5cm

Dock Riser Wall
243-60131 pkg(6) **3.98**
3-1/2" x 13/32"
8.7 x 1cm

Daily New Product Announcements! Visit Walthers Web site at
www.walthers.com

N Scale Planning Packet
243-60191 **.98**
Pre-plan buildings with paper mock-ups. The N Scale Planning Packet contains full-size drawings of wall sections. To use, make photocopies of drawings, cut out the wall section copies you want and arrange into paper walls. Tape walls on cardboard, cut out cardboard and tape together to form a three-dimensional paper mock-up. Modify mock-up until it is satisfactory, then purchase the required wall sections to construct your building.

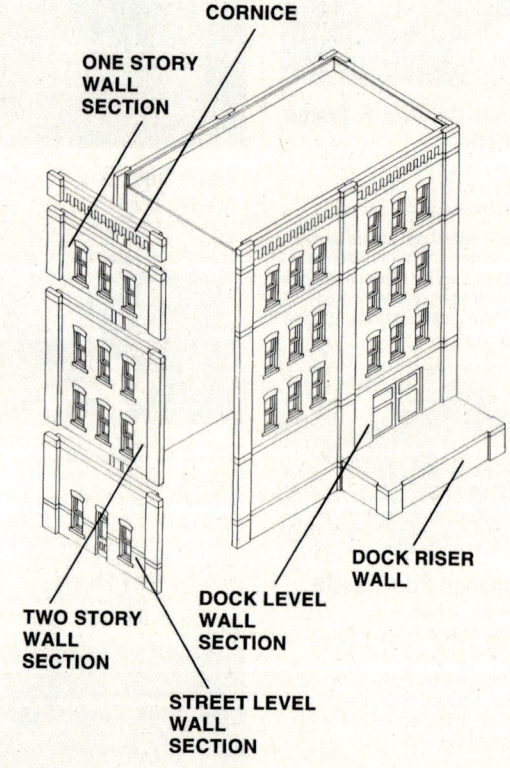

STRUCTURES N SCALE

DESIGN PRESERVATION MODELS

Finely detailed plastic N scale building kits. Architectural components are molded in place for assembly in minutes. Use any plastic model cement or solvent. These realistic kits include authentically designed walls plus roof and clear window material and complete instructions with painting tips. Figures, vehicles and decals not included.

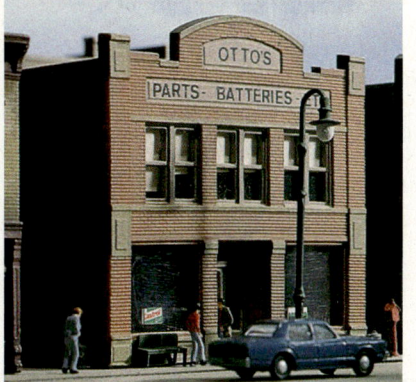

Otto's Parts
243-503 11.98
2-3/4 x 3"

Roadkill Cafe
243-512 11.98
2-1/4 x 2-3/4"

Trackside Transfer
243-510 14.98
11-1/2 x 4-1/4"

Gripp's Luggage Mfg.
243-506 15.98
7-3/4 x 4"

Hilltowne Hotel
243-509 17.98
5-1/4 x 2-5/8"

Char's Soda Shoppe
243-504 11.98
2-5/8 x 3-1/4"

Goodnight Mattress Co.
243-505 15.98
6-1/4 x 4-3/4 x 3-3/4"

Crestone Credit Union
243-508 11.98
2-7/8 x 3-1/4"

STRUCTURES N SCALE

Cricket's Saloon
243-511   11.98
1-3/8 x 2-3/4"

Wilhelmi's Mercantile
243-516   15.98
5-1/4 x 2-5/8"

Reed's Books
243-515   13.98
3-1/4 x 3"

Corner Turret Building
243-513   12.98
2 x 2-7/8" deep

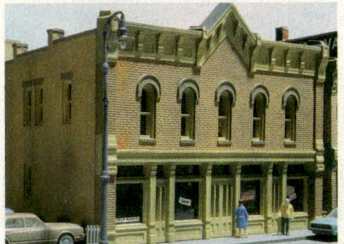

Erik's Emporium
243-514   12.98
3-1/4 x 3"

Hayes Hardware
243-502   11.98
2-1/2 x 3-1/4"

Corner Apothecary
243-507   11.98
3-3/8 x 1-3/8"

Bruce's Bakery
243-501   11.98
1-3/4 x 3"

DPM GOLD KITS

Night Life
243-663   54.98
9 x 4-1/8"

Night Life consists of three separate DPM plastic buildings with molded-in architectural details. Over 60 white metal castings including a searchlight, benches, swamp cooler, lampposts, plus Dry Transfer Decals and more.

Jerry Riggs Quick Service
243-662   46.98
13-1/2 x 9"

This styrene gas station comes to life with over 130 white metal castings, including tow truck, gas pumps, lift, garage doors, billboard, tires, signs, soda machine, utility poles, Dry Transfer Decals and more.

Olsen Feeds & Larsen's Implement
243-661   46.98
16 x 9"

Two separate DPM styrene buildings with over 70 white metal castings including tractors, combines, farm wagon, gas pump Dry Transfer Decals and more.

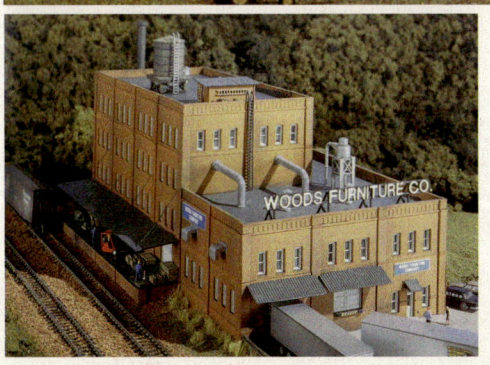

Woods Furniture Co.
243-660   59.98
11 x 7"

This plastic DPM Gold Kit comes with rooftop maintenance building, water tank, awnings, Dry Transfer Decals and over 90 detailed white metal castings such as fuel stand, forklift, sign, roof vents, cyclone and more... making Woods Furniture Co. come to life.

STRUCTURES N SCALE

DELUXE INNOVATIONS

NEW PRODUCTS
Assembled Buildings

Food Market
NEW 238-201 TBA

Sportsman Firearms
NEW 238-202 TBA

Premium Pool & Patio
NEW 238-203 TBA

INSTANT SCENES

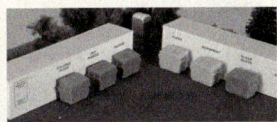

Community Recycling Center
238-103 14.95

Tom & Bobbi's Tru-Weld
238-106 22.95
Includes two-color flashing light unit.

Tru-Weld Accessories
238-993001 Power Adapter
9.95

Get Your Daily Dose of Product News at
www.walthers.com

DEPOTS BY JOHN
DETAILED REPLICAS IN SCALE

Typical of trackside buildings on most American railroads, these craft train structures consist of highly detailed resin castings. Window openings are molded into each wall, so "glass" and the separate window castings can be installed for a more realistic look. Styrene roofs, add-on signs and other details are included with most kits. All parts are unpainted. For more information on Depots By John structures and parts, visit Walthers web site at www.walthers.com.

Class D1 Station
87-6001 9.95
12 x 28'

Class D3 Station
87-6002 9.95
10-1/2 x 34'

Freight House
87-6003 18.95

Country Station
87-6004 23.95
18 x 36'

Garage/M-O-W Building
87-6007 8.95

JL INNOVATIVE DESIGN
SCALE MODELS

Add detail to your city or country scenes with this line of Craft Train kits. Each features Laser-cut Northeastern basswood siding and stripwood, plus Grandt Line doors and windows. Illustrated instructions include multi-view drawings. Models are less vehicles and figures.

NEW PRODUCT

McSoreley's Old Ale House
NEW 361-330 33.95
Includes pre-cut basswood siding, Grandt Line windows and doors, metal and plastic details, plus custom-designed full-color signs.

Saw Pit Store
361-320 21.95
Kit features signage and a complete set of parts to build an authentic Socony Vacuum shield sign, 185 country store poster signs and over a dozen cast-metal detail and accessory parts.

Hubermill Warehouse
361-120 24.95
This large trackside warehouse fits any era. Includes both clapboard and scribed siding, over 20 Grandt Line doors and windows, plus crimped aluminum for the roof.

Labosky's Auto Repair
361-140 19.95
Based on a 1950s vintage dealership/repair facility, a board style fence is also included.

Brookside Ice House
361-190 24.95
Includes large ice storage house and trackside loading platform.

Avon Street Elevated Gate Tower
361-240 16.95
Make busy city streets safer with these gate towers installed along your line. Based on a Milwaukee Road prototype, the model can also be used as a switch tower.

East Junction Section House
361-260 16.95
A perfect trackside structure, typical of smaller buildings found in yards and out along the right-of-way.

McLeod Super Service
361-310 23.95
Each kit includes over 60 new full-color signs, a fence-base billboard, precut siding, Grandt Line windows and doors, pumps and station details.

Front

Back

Woody's
361-210 27.95
A unique city tavern scene. Kit features Plastruct steps/railing, cast detail parts, plastic board fencing and 72 full-color soft drink/tavern signs.

Bagwell Junction Tower
361-290 21.95
Includes separate storage shed, precut basswood siding, laser-cut shingles, plastic doors, windows, steps and railings.

STRUCTURES N SCALE

GCLaser

Take your layout, module or diorama to a new level of realism with these laser-cut structure kits. Every detail of the prototype is carefully captured and all parts are laser-cut to ensure accuracy and ease of assembly. Interlocking walls and bases keep parts aligned. Doors and windows are separate pieces and can be positioned open or closed. All kits include complete instructions; larger structures include full elevation drawings.

NEW PRODUCTS

Elmhurst Depot
NEW 292-332 49.99
3-7/16 x 2-9/16 x 1-9/16"

This finely detailed structure is based on a Chicago Great Western prototype located along the mainline in Elmhurst, Illinois. It's typical of other wood depots found throughout the Midwest.

Barns 89.99 ea

NEW 292-4282 Partially Built
3-7/8 x 2-1/2 x 2-15/16"

Bring back the days of old-fashioned barn raisings when everyone in the community pitched in to help new settlers get started. The tradition of these one or two day events continues on in some parts of the U.S. and rural Canada.

NEW 292-4283 Completed
3-7/8 x 2-1/2 x 2-15/16"

This large barn is typical of those found on farms throughout the country. It's the finished version of #292-4282 (sold separately).

Passenger Shelter
NEW 292-250 Pennsylvania Railroad Circa 1911 10.99
7/8 x 1-1/8 x 1-3/16"

This simple shelter protected passengers from the rain, wind and elements while they waited for their train to arrive. These small structures were placed at whistle or flag stops on lightly used routes where there weren't enough passengers to build a full-size depot.

Stock Loading Ramp
NEW 292-225 14.99
1-15/16 x 1/2 x 1-1/8"

Herd those cattle and other livestock into waiting stock cars with this wooden ramp.

Storage Shed
NEW 292-1391 7.99
1 x 1-1/8 x 7/8"

This basic structure can serve a variety of purposes on the farm, in a back yard or trackside. Features board and batten vertical siding.

Tower B12 Circa 2000
292-108 Circa 2000 27.99
2-11/16 x 1-5/8 x 2-3/8"

A great trackside structure for a busy junction or crossing! Kit includes floor sections, rolled roof sheathing, siding, chimney assembly with decorative cap, etched entry doors, windows, corner trim, stair with railings and acetate glazing.

Tool Shed
292-201 7.99
1-9/32 x 1 x 15/16"

Great for use down on the farm or trackside as a railroad shanty. Kit includes a small outside tool/coal box.

Ellis' Barn & Silo
292-304 59.99
Barn: 6-5/8 x 5-1/8 x 4-7/16"
Silo: 2 x 1-11/16 x 4-7/16"

Dress-up any rural area with this set of structures! Kit includes parts to build both the barn and silo.

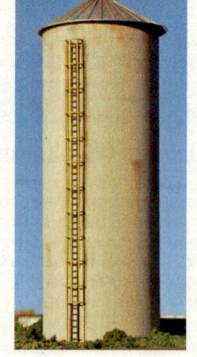

Silo
292-312 pkg(2) 25.99
Each: 2 x 1-11/16 x 4-7/16"

Keep your livestock fed year 'round with this neat structure on your scale farm. A dryer house, ladder with enclosure, assembly jig and one-piece conical roof are all included.

M&J Service Station
292-305 36.99
5-3/8 x 4-3/16 x 1-15/16"

With appropriate vehicles and figures (sold separately) it will make a great used car dealership, body shop, trucking terminal garage and more. Walls and chimney are laser-etched to simulate cinder block construction.

Country Market
292-309 13.99
1-3/4 x 2-1/32 x 15/16"

A great detail for modern layouts, you'll find all kinds of fresh fruit, honey, vegetables and more sold in roadside stands like this. The kit includes display table, lattice work and more.

Lou's Drive-In
292-311 34.99
2-3/16 x 6-1/2 x 1-3/8"

An American classic! Typical of drive-ins from the late 50s and early 60s, some of these buildings are still used by other types of businesses. Kit features printed signs, roof vent assembly, two seating assemblies and roof jig system with precut holes for lighting and interior walls.

Tony's Lumber Warehouse
292-316 124.99
13-7/8 x 7-5/8 x 3-11/16"

Kit includes rolled roofing and cap pieces, etched chimney assemblies with caps, working entry doors, working double freight doors, platforms with cross-buck framing, stair assemblies, a billboard, gable vents, cupolas, corner trim, printed peel-n-stick signs, pallets and ladders.

Covered Bridge
292-418 29.99
8-3/4 x 2-1/8 x 1-1/2"

A reminder of long-ago days, this handsome model adds a neat detail to rural scenes. Perfect for period layouts or as a restored structure in a modern setting, the kit is fully detailed inside and out. Laser-etched decking, railings, walls and roof sections, along with joists with phosphor-bronze guy wires are included.

Brennon Seed Company
292-507 51.99
7-1/2 x 4-1/4 x 3-7/16"

Neat addition to any industrial area, this kit includes an etched chimney assembly with cap, working sliding service doors, working entry/service doors, windows and laser-cut corner trim.

Sturtevant, Wisconsin, Depot
292-514 58.99
6-5/8 x 6-5/8 x 2-11/16"

One of the most handsome of all Milwaukee Road depots, this elaborate structure was built at the intersection of two routes at Sturtevant, Wisconsin, where it still stands today. Includes: shingle and cap pieces, notched interlocking wall sections, foundation, floor sections, roof alignment grid and jig system, etched siding, chimney assembly with cap, working entry doors, working freight doors, windows, wall trim sections with window, door, frieze and corner trim, eight columns, decorative eave corbels and clear acetate glazing.

Ice House w/Platform
292-526 89.99
9-25/32 x 11-15/16 x 3-7/16"

Great for steam- and early diesel-era scenes, this structure provides convenient storage for ice and a delivery platform to service reefers.

242

STRUCTURES N SCALE

GCLaser

Icing Platform
292-3061 29.99
11-7/8 x 1-7/16 x 1-7/16"

In the days of ice-cooled reefers, large docks like these were often seen at the edges of yards and along the mainline. Kit includes bent assemblies with sway braces, a laser-etched deck with wheel tracks for ice carts, plus three ladders, railings, stairs, braces and spacers. Can be enlarged with Icing Platform Add-On (#292-3062), sold separately.

Icing Platform Add-On
292-3062 26.99
10-3/4 x 1-7/16 x 1-7/16"

Use with Icing Platform (#929-3061, sold separately) to build a longer structure. Kit includes bent assemblies with easy assembly sway detailing, etched deck with ice cart wheel tracks, three laser-cut ladders and end railing detail.

Freight Depot
292-3021 31.99
6-15/16 x 2-13/16 x 2-1/8"

This structure packs a lot of detail in a compact space. Kit includes notched interlocking walls, floor sections for squaring structure, etched horizontal siding, four each freight and entry doors, windows, roof sheathing pieces with decorative trusses at the roof line, chimney assemblies and laser-cut shingles.

Freight Depot – Trussed Walls
292-3022 54.99
7-21/32 x 2-11/16 x 2-5/16"

This fancy structure features decorative trussed walls. The kit includes three sets of stairs, a ramp, roof trusses, four each freight and entry doors, windows, one-piece wall trim sections with corner, door and window trim etched in place, roof sheathing parts with decorative sheathing on the roofline, chimney assemblies and shingles.

International Hobby Corp.

Easy-to-build kits feature pre-colored molded plastic construction and include base and concrete sidewalks, trim details and clear plastic windows unless noted.

2007 2008 2009 20010 20011

Colonial Houses
12.98 ea (Unless Noted)

Huntington
348-2007

Vanderbilt
348-2008

Stevenson
348-2009

Pullman
348-20010

Baldwin
348-20011

Gift Pack
348-20089 pkg(5) 64.90
Includes one each of the following: #2007, 2008, 2009, 20010 and 20011.

20014 20015 20016 20017 20018

Store Fronts 13.98 ea (Unless Noted)
Extras include fire hydrants, brick sidewalks, mailboxes, delivery elevators, signs, sheets of printed scenes for large first-floor windows, and curtains for upstairs windows.

Second Hand Rose Store
348-20014

Rita's Antiques Shop
348-20016

O'Weeds Greenery
348-20017

Grant Cary's Apothecary
348-20018

Limited Quantity Available
South Street Smoke Shop
348-20015

Ferris Wheel
348-5410 17.98

Carousel
348-5411 28.98

GRANDT LINE

HO Scale Version Shown

Reese Street Row Houses
300-8023 pkg(3) 21.95
Great for kitbashing, this easy-to-build styrene kit creates three separate buildings with lean-tos and outhouses. Windows, doors and trim are molded separately.

Outhouses
300-8026 pkg(2) 3.75

Hot New Products Announced Daily! Visit Walthers Web site at
www.walthers.com

JV MODELS
Scale Kits for the Discerning Modeler

For a complete listing of available JV Models products, please visit www.walthers.com. Wood Craft Train kits, less figures.

Double Track Sand Tower & Drying House
345-1008 27.98
Scale 45 x 46 x 40' high.

Bunk Houses
345-1011 pkg(2) 19.98
Scale 10 x 20'.

Branchline Water Tower
345-1012 19.98
Approximately 60,000-gallon capacity. Scale 22 x 42'.

Mainline Water Tower
345-1013 23.98
Approximately 120,000-gallon capacity. Scale 28 x 56'.

Timber Trestle
345-1014 24.98
Up to 12" long x 8" high. Includes N.B.W. castings.

Curved Trestle
345-1016 30.98
Up to 24" long x 8" high. Includes N.B.W. castings.

Boyd Logging Camp
345-1018 30.98
Includes eight structures.

Burnt River Mining Co.
345-1019 26.98
Scale 15 x 23'. Includes N.B.W. castings.

Watson's Siding (Backwoods Ghost)
345-1020 26.98
Scale 30 x 40'.

Lucas Sawmill
345-1021 26.98
Scale 50 x 95'.

Ward's Salvage Co.
345-1022 26.98
Scale 50 x 60'.

Haliburton Single-Stall Engine House
345-1024 24.98
Scale 23 x 79'.

Victoria Station
345-1025 26.98
Scale 23 x 56'.

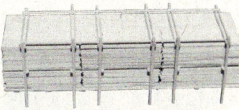

Lumber Loads
345-1010 pkg(3) 18.98
This kit includes enough material for three wood loads for 40-60' cars, plus braces and stake posts. Suitable for flat cars or gondolas. Removable design for more operating possibilities.

Ponty-Pool Farm Supply
345-1023 24.98

STRUCTURES N SCALE

IMPORTED FROM DENMARK BY WALTHERS
Create detailed scenes for your layout with these easy-to-build, N Scale kits. Based on American and European prototypes (which are easily modified for use on US layouts), each kit includes precolored plastic parts and instructions.

Restaurant
322-601 16.98
6 x 6 x 2-3/16"
15 x 15 x 5.5cm

Bank Block
322-603 16.98
6 x 6 x 2-3/16"
15 x 15 x 5.5cm

Fire Station
322-605 18.98
6 x 6 x 2-3/16"
15 x 15 x 5.5cm

Sand & Coaling Complex
322-606 16.98
6-1/4 x 2-3/4 x 5-1/8"
15.6 x 6.8 x 12.8cm

Diesel Fueling & Sanding Complex
322-607 16.98

Movie Theatre
322-609 18.98
5 x 4 x 2-13/16"
12.5 x 10 x 7cm

Coal Yard
322-610 18.98
8-5/16 x 6 x 1-7/8"
20.7 x 15 x 4.7cm

Drug Store
322-611 18.98
3-15/16 x 3-3/4 x 2-13/16"
9.8 x 9.3 x 7cm

Railroad Wash Facility
322-612 26.98
7-1/2 x 4-5/16 x 3-1/4"
18.9 x 10.8 x 8.1cm

Car Repair Shop
322-613 28.98
7-1/2 x 4-7/8 x 2-5/8"
18.9 x 12.1 x 6.7cm

Railway Station
322-639 18.98
12-3/8 x 4 x 2-5/8"
31 x 10 x 6.5cm

Passenger Station
322-640 12.98
8-3/4 x 3" 22 x 7.5cm

Small Freight Station
322-641 10.98
5-7/16 x 2-5/8 x 1-13/16"
13.5 x 6.5 x 4.5cm

Freight & Passenger Platform
322-645 11.98
16-13/16 x 1-5/8 x 1-13/16"
42 x 4 x 4.5cm

Engine House
322-650 18.98
6 x 3-3/8 x 3-3/16"
15 x 8.5 x 8cm

Sand & Gravel Silo
322-652 10.98
3-3/16 x 3" 8 x 7.5cm

Coaling Tower
322-653 10.98
4-13/16 x 2 x 4-5/8"
10.5 x 5 x 11.5cm

Bakery
322-654 16.98
6-5/8 x 4-13/16 x 4-3/16"
16.5 x 12 x 10.5cm

Weekly Herald Print Shop
322-655 16.98
7 x 4-4/5 x 2-4/5"
17.5 x 12 x 7cm

Arch Bridge w/Piers
322-661 13.98
10-3/8 x 1-13/16 x 3-7/16"
26 x 4.5 x 8.5cm

Girder Bridge
322-662 6.98
6-5/8 x 1-1/2 x 5"
17 x 4 x 12.5cm

Truss Bridge
322-663 6.98
6-5/8 x 1-1/2 x 5"
17 x 4 x 12.5cm

Stone Bridge Pier
322-664 2 Pair 7.98
1-5/8 x 3/4" 4 x 2cm

Container Transfer Crane
322-665 10.98
5-1/4 x 2-1/8" 13 x 5.5cm

Timber Trestle Bridge
322-666 18.98
13-5/8 x 3 x 6-5/8"
34 x 7.5 x 16.6cm

Feed Mill
322-670 12.98
6-3/8 x 3 x 3-5/8"
16 x 7.5 x 9cm

Warehouse
322-671 10.98
6-3/8 x 4 x 2-13/16"
16 x 10 x 7cm

Meat Packing Plant
322-673 10.98
3-3/16 x 3-3/16 x 4-3/16"
8 x 8 x 10.5cm

Cold Storage Plant
322-674 11.98
8 x 4 x 4-3/8"
20 x 10 x 11cm

Appliance Warehouse
322-675 13.98
3 x 4-3/8 x 3-3/16"
7.5 x 11 x 8cm

Machine Works
322-676 15.98
7-7/8 x 4-1/2" 20 x 11.5cm

244

STRUCTURES N SCALE

IMPORTED FROM DENMARK BY WALTHERS

Grain Elevator
322-677 21.98
8 x 4-5/8 x 5"
20 x 11.5 x 12.5cm

Brewery
322-678 41.98
16-13/16 x 4-3/8 x 10"
42 x 11 x 25cm

Brewery Bottling Plant
322-679 39.98
16 x 8-13/16 x 7-5/8"
40 x 22 x 19cm

Slaughterhouse w/Cattle Pen
322-681 38.98
16-13/16 x 12 x 12-7/16"
42 x 30 x 31cm

Farmer's Supply House
322-682 15.98
11 x 3-13/16 x 3-5/8"
27.5 x 9.5 x 9cm

Farm House
322-702 pkg(2) 15.98
1-5/8 x 1-5/8" 4 x 4cm

Gothic Church & Farm
322-704 pkg(3) 15.98
6-5/16 x 3-9/16" 16 x 9cm
4-3/8 x 3-9/16" 11 x 9cm
Church, farmhouse and wooden out building ideal for country scene.

N.J. INTERNATIONAL

Elevated Gate Tower
525-4215 7.95

525-4217 Ladders Only.
1" 2.5cm long. pkg(4) **1.99**

Maintenance Platforms
Includes photo-etched, stainless steel, see through platform walkway and steps.
525-4220 68' pkg(2) **17.95**
525-4221 102' pkg(2) **21.95**
525-4222 136' pkg(2) **25.95**

Platform Accessories
525-4223 Handrail Kit 68' **3.99**
525-4224 Walkway 68' **5.99**

Get the Scoop!
Get the Skinny!
Get the Score!
Check Out Walthers
Web site at
www.walthers.com

These injection-molded, styrene kits are designed for the builder with some experience. Modern metal buildings feature pre-scored lines for optional door and window placement on all exterior walls. These kits also include prototypical aluminized, seamed roofs. Kits can be combined to model larger buildings.

Murphy Manufacturing
255-55001 16.80

Trans World Truck Terminal
255-55002 18.20
3 x 7-1/2"
Includes steps, sidewalk, sign, pallets and ventilators.

Petroff Plumbing Supply
255-55003 18.20
Includes mansard roof, pallets, steps and ventilators.

Doyle Distributing
255-55007 18.20

Section House
255-60149 18.20

Poor Boy Mine
255-60002 16.80

Modern Engine House
255-60001 16.80

1940s Gas Station w/Tow Truck
255-65139 19.60
Kit includes many white metal details, with tow truck, gas pumps, oil racks, oil drums, hoist, torch cart, compressor, acetylene tanks, tires and V-8 engines.

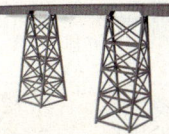

Outhouse
255-80151 White Metal pkg(2)
9.10

Plate Girders
255-80170 80' Long pkg(4)
5.45
255-80171 40' Long pkg(4)
5.20

Deck Girder Bridges
Kits include highly detailed plate girders and bracing. Open deck bridges include Bridge Flex-Trak™. Ballasted deck bridges include a simulated concrete deck for regular track.

80' Open Deck
255-75150 6" Girder 9.90

40' Open Deck
255-75151 3" Girder 9.10

80' Ballasted Deck
255-75152 6" Long 10.40

40' Ballasted Deck
255-75153 3" Long 9.60

Tall Steel Viaducts

Tall Steel Viaducts are one of the most spectacular and interesting types of bridge. The N Scale Tall Steel Viaducts are available in two base kits, three length extension kits and a tower kit. The various kits allow you to design and build your own custom bridges of any length with full towers or bents, straight or curved.

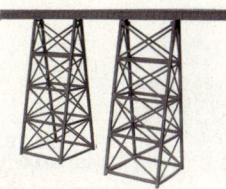

320' Tall Steel Viaduct, Standard Bridge
255-75519 38.45
Three 80' spans, two 40' spans and two 4 story towers, 24 x 8-1/8" 60 x 20.2cm

200' Tall Steel Viaduct, Standard Bridge
255-75518 35.15
Five 40' spans, and two 4 story towers 15 x 8-1/8" 37.7 x 20.2cm

Tall Steel Viaduct Length Extension Kits
NEW 255-75542 120' Extension **19.75**
One 80' span, one 40' span & one tower.

NEW 255-75543 80' Extension **17.55**
Two 40' spans & one tower.

NEW 255-75544 40' Connector **13.15**
One 40' span and one tower.

Tall Steel Viaduct Tower or Two 4 Story Bents
255-75176 10.95
3-1/8 x 3-1/4 x 7-3/4"
7.8 x 8.1 x 19.4cm

STRUCTURES N SCALE

NEW PRODUCTS
Trestle Parts

Creating realistic wooden trestles is easy with this assortment of parts made from real wood. Each piece comes fully assembled and stained in a realistic weathered creosote color, ready to install in new or existing scenery.

Bents pkg(5)

NEW 295-TB7
Small 15.00

NEW 295-TB8
Medium 20.00

NEW 295-TB9
Large 20.00

NEW 295-TB10
Extra-Large 25.00

6" Bridge Deck

NEW 295-TB11 With Backheads 25.00
Use for short trestles or as the end pieces of longer structures.

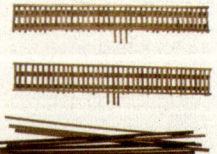

NEW 295-TB12 With Stringers pkg(2) 30.00
Use as intermediate sections on long trestles.

NEW PRODUCT
Structure
NEW 346-N1112 Estate House 12.50

STRUCTURES

346-N1000 Tavern 8.50
346-N1001 Farmhouse 8.50
346-N1002 Barn 8.50
346-N1003 Stone House 8.50
346-N1004 Three-Story Gabled House 8.50
346-N1005 Mayor's House 9.50
346-N1008 Condemned House 10.50
346-N1009 Town Church 12.50
346-N1012 Gate House 8.50
346-N1100 Country Church w/Steeple (2 Sections) 16.75
346-N1104 Carriage Shed 8.50
346-N1106 Country Inn 12.50
346-N1107 City Hall Building 23.00
346-N1109 Alpine Hotel 23.00
346-N1200 City Museum 9.50
346-N1201 Townhouse w/Arch Walkway 8.50
346-N1203 Freight House 8.50
346-N1204 Church Bell Tower 9.50
346-N1205 Town Clock 8.50
346-N1206 Tool Shed 6.25
346-N1207 City Arch 8.50
346-N1208 Railway Inn 16.75
346-N1209 Townhouse 8.50
346-N1210 Artist Studio 8.50
346-N1211 Hotel 9.50
346-N1212 Apartment Building 9.50
346-N1213 Arched Market Place (2 Sections) 9.50
346-N1214 Small Bridge 8.50
346-N1215 City Block w/Courtyard 23.00
346-N1300 Pennsylvania Stone House 13.50

MICRON ART

Add a new level of realism to your railroad with these detailed craft train kits. Perfect for period layouts, they also add a touch of nostalgia to modern scenes. Designed for modelers with some experience, each kit consists of photo-etched metal parts that capture many fine details and are near-scale thickness. Some also include white metal castings and/or pre-cut metal parts. All are designed for assembly with simple hobby tools and CA or fast epoxy type adhesives so no soldering is needed. Complete step-by-step instructions guide you through assembly, and painting tips are provided to help finish your models.

50,000 Gallon Water Station
462-2001 75.95
2-3/16 x 2 x 3"
5.6 x 5 x 7.6cm

Super detail features in this photo-etched brass kit include fully defined barrel, moveable water spout, ladder, moveable roof access hatch, .025 thick supporting timbers and floor joists. Two different style roof peaks are available to kit builders.

Mechanical Interlocking Switch Tower
462-2009 35.95
1-3/8 x 1-1/2 x 2"
3.4 x 3.7 x 5cm

Designed for easy assembly, this model is complete with second floor interior details, including switch levers and a stove. The staircase is a white metal casting.

Yard Facilities
462-2049 pkg(3) 25.00

Dress-up your freight yards or engine terminals with these tiny buildings, typical of the small sheds in every railroad yard. The kit includes three complete buildings: an Engineering Office and two Storage Buildings, all with stovepipe tubes. A photo-etched three-man survey crew, including a "rod man" with a range pole, engineer with transit and an apprentice, are also included.

Rocky Mountain Branch Line Water Station
462-2005 37.95
1-1/2 x 1-3/16 x 3"
3.7 x 3 x 7.5cm

Based on towers used in Colorado, similar water tanks were used throughout the American west. The roof is based on those used in the Rocky Mountain area, where a steeper pitch was needed to hold heavy snow. Two different roof peaks are included; a finial as used from 1850-1890, and a simpler version, typical of new roofs applied during the 20th century. With careful assembly, the water spout can be moved up and down and the frost box door opened and closed. The kit also includes a baggage cart, often used at these facilities by repair crews to move tools and supplies.

Watchman's Tower
462-2047 23.50

Elevated crossing shanties like this were commonly installed at busy stations and streets where the watchman needed a better view of approaching trains and traffic. Kit is complete with staircase, handrails and stovepipe stack.

Capitol Station 1888
462-2015 169.95
11-11/16 x 4-3/8 x 4"
29.2 x 11 x 10cm

Based on a prototype built in 1888 by the International Great Northern in Austin, Texas, this station makes a superb addition to a layout, or a fine stand-alone diorama as well. The kit comes with complete easy-to-follow instructions, stained glass windows, cast metal roof finials, detailed friezes, wrought iron ornamentation, 17 figures in 19th-Century fashions, plus a baggage cart and buckboard with horse and driver.

Rooftop Water Tank

Transform empty skylines with this neat detail, perfect for city apartments, offices or industries.
462-2041 Single Kit 18.00
462-20412 Set of 2 Kits 32.00

Info, Images, Inspiration! Get It All at
www.walthers.com

STRUCTURES N SCALE

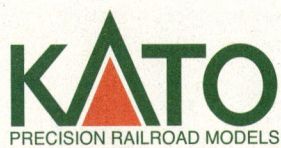

Designed to complement the Kato Unitrack system, these structures also fit in easily on layouts using other brands of track. All are well-detailed and feature colored pieces. Most are pre-assembled; some are snap-together kits.

RURAL STRUCTURES SERIES

Rural Platform Set
Limited Quantity Available
381-23130 78.00

Rural Station Set
Limited Quantity Available
381-23220 57.60

RESTAURANTS

Denny's® Restaurant
381-23407 32.00
Does not include interior light.

WOODEN-STYLE STRUCTURE SERIES

Viaduct Station Shops
Limited Quantity Available
381-23231 43.20

Viaduct Platform Extension Kit
Limited Quantity Available
381-23232 27.60

URBAN PLATFORM SERIES

Island Platform- Complete Set
381-20806 21.60
Contains one each of Island Platforms 23100, 23101, 23103 and 23104. Excellent to use as a siding platform with the K2 track set.

One Side Platform Complete Set
381-20815 21.60
Contains one each of 23110, 23111, 23112 and 23113.

Island Platform Type A
Limited Quantity Available
381-23100 8.40

Island Platform Type B
Limited Quantity Available
381-23101 8.40

Island Platform End Type #1
Limited Quantity Available
381-23102 4.80

Island Platform End Type #2
Limited Quantity Available
381-23103 4.80

DOUBLE TRACK STRUCTURE SERIES

Viaduct Station Set
Limited Quantity Available
381-23125 99.98
This modern bi-level station is the hub of activity when used with Kato's Double-Track Viaduct Track. In five 9-3/4" 24.8cm modular sections (48-13/16" 124cm when used full length), the station is wide enough to accommodate two tracks and an island platform. Expand the length and width using #381-23230 Station Entrance, #381-23231 Station Shops and 381-23232 Extension Kit to accommodate additional tracks and platforms. Railroad equipment, vehicles and figures sold separately.

Viaduct Station Entrance
Limited Quantity Available
381-23230 45.60

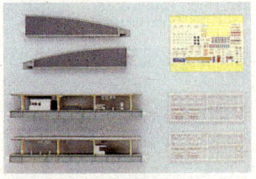

Island Platform Type D
Limited Quantity Available
381-23106 4.80

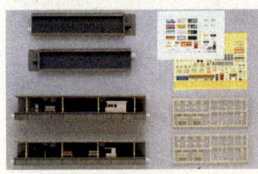

One Side Platform Type A
Limited Quantity Available
381-23110 8.40

One Side Platform Type B
Limited Quantity Available
381-23111 8.40

One Side Platform End Type #1
Limited Quantity Available
381-23112 4.80

One Side Platform End Type #2
Limited Quantity Available
381-23113 4.80

SUBURBAN SERIES

Suburban Station
Limited Quantity Available
381-23211 60.75
Same building style as Double-Track Plate Suburban Station House (#381-23126, sold separately), without track, track plate or opposite platform. Features a green roof.

Double-Track Plate Suburban Platform Set
Limited Quantity Available
381-23127 101.89
Includes one left end section, one right end section and two center sections. 248mm each.

OVERHEAD POLES & TOWERS

Catenary Poles

381-23059 Single Track pkg(16) 6.00
381-23057 Double Track, Rounded Corner pkg(6) 7.98

381-23060 Double Track, Squared Corner pkg(8) 6.00
381-23056 Pole Base Set 4.50 16 each of ground and viaduct style.

STRUCTURAL DETAILS

Ballast
381-24039 200g 9.00
Fine-grain ballast to match roadbed.

Fence Sections
Limited Quantity Available
381-23223 6.85
Four sprues of three different lengths, same fence as provided with Double Track Plates. Also good for scenery use.

STRUCTURES N SCALE

kibri®

IMPORTED FROM GERMANY BY WALTHERS
Make a scene with Kibri easy-to-build structure kits! Consisting of a large range of European prototypes, the kits feature realistically colored, molded plastic parts, so no painting is required. Many can be easily Americanized by leaving off trim or by adding signs and other details. Complete step-by-step instructions are included for easy assembly.

NEW PRODUCTS

Railroad Structures

Osterburken Train Station
NEW 405-7706 79.99
21-11/16 x 4-5/16 x 4-5/16" 55 x 11 x 11cm

Unterlenningen Station
NEW 405-7704 44.99
10-5/8 x 3-3/16 x 3/13/16"
27 x 8 x 9.5cm

Schonried Station
NEW 405-7705 36.99
12-316 x 2-9/16 x 2-3/8"
31 x 6.5 x 6cm

Railway Station
NEW 405-7758 39.99
9-1/4 x 5 x 3-3/16"
23.5 x 12.5 x 8cm

Railway House w/Outhouse
NEW 405-7158 34.99
Main House: 3-3/8 x 2-3/16 x 3"
8.5 x 5.5 x 7.5cm
Outhouse: 2-9/16 x 1-3/16 x 1-9/16" 6.5 x 3 x 4cm

Signal Tower in Stuttgart-Feuerbach
NEW 405-7805 26.99
3-1/2 x 2 x 2-3/4" 9 x 5 x 7cm

Signal Tower in Backnang
NEW 405-7807 27.99
4-3/4 x 2 x 3-3/16"
12 x 5 x 8cm

Water Tower
NEW 405-7303 23.99
1-13/16 x 1-9/16 x 4-3/4"
4.5 x 4 x 12cm

Locomotive Shed
NEW 405-7806 39.99
7-5/16 x 5 x 2-9/16"
18.5 x 12.5 x 6.5cm

Box Car Shed
NEW 405-7809 39.99
10-13/16 x 3 x 2-3/16"
27.5 x 7.5 x 5.5cm

Guardhouse
NEW 405-7808 19.99
2-9/16 x 2 x 2" 6.5 x 5 x 5cm

Rural Buildings

Farm
NEW 405-7026 44.90

Barns
NEW 405-7028 w/Wooden Fence pkg(2) 15.99
1-13/16 x 1-9/16 x 1-3/16"
4.5 x 4 x 3cm

Tradehouse
NEW 405-7157 22.99
3-7/8 x 3-3/8 x 3-3/16"
10 x 8.5 x 8cm

Windmill
NEW 405-7301 31.99
2-3/4 x 3 x 6" 7 x 7.5 x 15cm

Church
NEW 405-7025 63.99
11-1/4 x 6-11/16 x 10-1/4" 28.5 x 17 x 26cm

Village Church in Sertig
NEW 405-7031 17.99
3-13/16 x 3 x 5-1/8" 9.5 x 7.5 x 13cm

Rustic Houses in Sertig
NEW 405-7030 pkg(2) 26.99
3-3/8 x 2-9/16 x 2-3/16"
8.5 x 6.5 x 5.5cm
3-3/8 x3-3/8 x 2-3/16"
8.5 x 8.5 x 5.5cm

Churches

Schanbach Church
NEW 405-7027 31.99
5-1/2 x 3-3/16 x 5-1/8"
14 x 8 x 13cm

For Daily Product Updates Point Your Browser to
www.walthers.com

City Buildings

Row of Brick Houses in Schwabisch Hall
NEW 405-7110 44.99
11-13/16 x 4-3/8 x 5-1/2"
30 x 11 x 14cm

Town House in Hamein
NEW 405-7151 31.99
2-1/2 x 3-3/16 x 5"
6.4 x 8 x 12.5cm

Period Houses
NEW 405-7100 pkg(2) 33.99
2-3/8 x 2-3/8 x 3-1/2"
6 x 6 x 9cm
2 x 2 x 3-7/8" 5 x 5 x10cm

Period Houses
NEW 405-7101 pkg(2) 39.99
2-9/16 x 2 x 4-3/4"
6.5 x 5 x 12cm
2-3/4 x 2-9/16 x 3-13/16"
7 x 6.5 x 9.5cm

Double-Fronted Town House
NEW 405-7153 w/Covered Passage 31.99
3-5/16 x 4-1/8 x 4-3/4"
8.3 x 10.5 x 12cm

City Residence in Schleswig
NEW 405-7155 23.99
5-5/16 x 3-1/2 x 3-1/2"
13.5 x 9 x 9cm

STRUCTURES N SCALE

kibri®
IMPORTED FROM GERMANY BY WALTHERS

Bietlgheim City Entrance
NEW 405-7103 28.99
2-3/4 x 2-3/8 x 7-1/8"
7 x 6 x 18cm

Rodertor Tower in Rothenburg
NEW 405-7107 44.99
9-7/8 x 5-11/16 x 8-1/4"
25 x 14.5 x 21cm

Round Tower w/Wall in Markbreit
NEW 405-7109 30.99
6-11/16 x 5-1/2 x 7-7/8"
17 x 14 x 20cm

1871 Boiler House w/Chimney
NEW 405-7224 31.99
4-3/8 x 3-3/8 x 8-13/16"
11 x 8.5 x 22cm

Industrial

1871 Factory Building
NEW 405-7223 68.99
8-3/16 x 4 x 5-31/16" 20.5 x 10 x 13cm

Gravel Works & Loading Silo
NEW 405-7226 44.99
6 x 4-3/16 x 4-5/8" 15 x 10.5 x 11.5cm

Brick Tower in Rothenburg
NEW 405-7108 30.99
9 x 2-3/8 x 5-1/2" 23 x 6 x 14cm

RAILROAD STRUCTURES

Freidrichsdorf Station Covered Passenger Platform
405-7751 42.99
17-13/16 x 1-1/2 x 3/8"
44.5 x 3.7 x 1cm

Freidrichsdorf Station Covered Passenger Platform Extension
405-7753 30.99
8-3/16 x 1-1/2 x 3/8"
22 x 3.7 x 1cm
Matches parts from #7751 (sold separately).

Goldberg Station Platform w/Pedestrian Overpass
405-7756 149.99

Freiburg Station Platform
405-7503 36.99
26-13/32 x 1 x 1-7/16"
66 x 2.5 x 3.6cm
Includes platform and ramp sections, signs, simulated stairway, newsstand, schedule board, nonworking lamps and more.

Lichtenau Modern Signal Tower
405-7800 w/Diesel Refueling Equipment 47.99

Single Track Loco Shed
405-7802 21.99
5-5/8 x 2-3/8 x 2-3/8"
14 x 6 x 6cm

Sanding & Fuel Tower
405-7444 Two Track 27.99

Sondernau Goods Depot
405-7804 26.99
5-13/16 x 3-5/8 x 2-3/16"
14.5 x 9 x 5.5cm

Items listed below are available by Special Order (see Legend Page).

Sondernau Gantry Mounted Signal Tower
405-7803 31.99
6-5/8 x 2-3/8 x 4"
16.5 x 6 x 10cm

Sulzbach Station w/Platform
405-7702 214.99

Sulzbach Station
405-7703 79.99

Modern Open Station Platform
405-7752 39.99
17-13/16 x 1-1/2 x 3/8"
44.5 x 3.7 x 1cm

Station Platform Accessories
405-7755 30.99

Rauenstein Station w/Goods Shed
405-7396 34.99

249

STRUCTURES N SCALE

IMPORTED FROM GERMANY BY WALTHERS

HOUSES

Am Ostweg Single Family Houses
405-7022 pkg(2) 26.99
3-13/32 x 2-13/16 x 2-13/16"
8.5 x 7 x 7cm
2-13/16 x 2-13/16 x 2-38/64"
7 x 7 x 6.5cm

Kirchsteig Single Family Houses
405-7023 pkg(2) 26.99
3-3/8 x 2-13/16 x 2-13/16"
9.5 x 7 x 6cm
3 x 2-13/16 x 2-3/8"
7.5 x 7 x 6cm

Rosenhof Villa
405-7021 71.99

CITY BUILDINGS

Inn Zur Eisenbahn
405-7114 39.99
5 x 3-3/4" 13 x 9.5cm

Schiller Junior High School
405-7106 36.99
5 x 2-21/64 x 3-5/8"
12.5 x 5.8 x 9cm

Volksbank
405-7116 36.99
5 x 3-1/8" 13 x 8cm
Here's a kit you can bank on. Featuring simple construction, the modern building "lends" itself to any downtown scene.

CHURCHES

St. Hochstadt Church
405-7024 26.99
5-3/16 x 3-3/16 x 6-3/8"
13 x 8 x 16cm

INDUSTRIAL

Trucking Office w/Loading Platform
405-7221 31.99

Suix Shoe Factory
405-7222 159.99

Oil Distributor Office w/Truck Filling Rack & Loading Dock
405-7469 28.99

Items listed below are available by Special Order (see Legend Page).

Industrial Park w/Forum Café
405-7020 76.99

Distribution Fuel Depot Set
405-7465 55.99
Includes one each of #s 7467, 7469, 7480 and fencing.

Twin Fuel Tanks w/Loading Facility
405-7467 28.99

Grain Silo & Office
405-7220 74.99

BRIDGES & VIADUCTS

Double-Track Pedestrian Overpass
405-7801 41.99

Box Girder Bridge
405-7667 w/Piers (blue) 23.99
12-23/32 x 1-23/64"
31.8 x 3.4cm

Bridge w/End Supports
405-7668 Single or Double Track 17.99
7 x 2" 17.5 x 5cm

Bridge w/End Supports
405-7669 31.99
13-15/16 x 2" 34.8 x 5cm

Straight Stone Viaduct
405-7660 Gray 14.99
7-1/2 x 1-1/2" 18.7 x 3.8cm

Single Track Curved Stone Viaduct
405-7664 w/Ice Breaker Piers 36.99
10-3/8 x 1-1/2" 26 x 3.8cm

Single Track Curved Stone Viaduct
405-7665 w/Ice Breaker Piers 36.99
12-3/8 x 1-1/2" 31 x 3.8cm

Items listed below are available by Special Order (see Legend Page).

Curved Stone Viaduct
405-7661 Gray 14.99
Radius 8", 45 Degrees

Curved Stone Viaduct
405-7662 Gray 14.99
7-1/4 x 1-1/2" 18.1 x 3.8cm,
Radius 8", 45 Degrees

River Valley Single Track Viaduct
405-7663 w/Ice Breaker Piers 36.99
14 x 1-1/2" 34.8 x 3.8cm

Stone Arch Viaduct Bridge
405-7666 20.99
8-3/8 x 1-1/2" 20.9 x 3.8cm

LIGHTHOUSES

Lighthouse w/Living Quarters
405-7300 45.99
Easily adapted to any era, the kit includes a lighthouse, living quarters and baseplate.

Blinking Light
405-7302 26.99
Shining from your lighthouse, this blinking light will be a comforting sight to passing ships.

STRUCTURES N SCALE

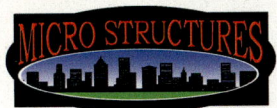

By *Miller Engineering*

Re-create detailed buildings for your favorite era or display with this series of residential and commercial structure kits. Each consists of thin, photo-etched stainless steel or brass parts which are assembled in layers to create 3-D structures with extremely fine details.

Assembly is fast and easy, as pieces are simply cut out (each kit includes from one to four sheets of parts), folded to shape, then glued together. Most parts are slotted and tab-aligned for a perfect fit. Comprehensive, step-by-step instructions take you easily from start to finish. A list of recommended tools and glues, along with suggested colors and brands of paint, are also provided to simplify construction. And since the parts are not harmed by solvents, glues and paints can easily be stripped off if you do need to start over. (Photos show assembled and painted models; figures and other accessories are sold separately.)

VICTORIAN HOME KITS

All the splendor of the Victorian age, captured in miniature! Ideal for vintage or modern layouts, each is from a unique period, ranging from the 1850s to the 1890s. Models are designed for easy construction using photo-etched brass parts to capture every intricate detail.

The Empire
502-601014   54.95
2-1/2 x 2-3/8 x 4-1/4"   6.2 x 6.1 x 10.8cm
A stunning example of these ornate buildings that dates from the 1860s.

The Eastlake
502-602023   48.95
2-3/4 x 3-1/4 x 3-5/8"   7 x 8.3 x 9.1cm
Complete with a second-story sleeping porch, used as a bedroom on hot summer nights before air conditioning.

The Marlet House
502-607011   48.95
2-5/8 x 2-1/8 x 3-3/8"   6.7 x 5.5 x 8.5cm
An all-brick structure, typical of period homes built in the midwest.

The Victoria
502-606061   47.95
2-1/8 x 2-3/8 x 3-1/8"   5.5 x 6.1 x 7.9cm
Copy of a prototype built in Seattle, Washington, in 1900.

The Seaside Cottage
502-608011   46.95
2-5/8 x 1-7/8 x 3-1/4"   6.7 x 4.8 x 8.1cm
A popular style of home, built in many seaside areas during the 1850s.

Daily New Product Announcements! Visit Walthers Web site at
www.walthers.com

The Queen Anne
502-603031   47.95
2-7/8 x 3 x 3-3/8"   7.2 x 7.5 x 8.7cm
Features a square tower, typical of many grand Victorian homes of the 1890s.

The Seattle
502-604041   46.95
1-5/8 x 2-5/8 x 3-1/4"   4 x 6.7 x 8.4cm
Based on a prototype built in Seattle, Washington, in 1900. (Shown with optional one-car garage #502-221003, sold separately.)

Gothic Revival
502-605051   46.95
2-3/4 x 1-3/4 x 3"   7.1 x 4.6 x 7.7cm

251

STRUCTURES N SCALE

By Miller Engineering

One-Car Garage
502-601003   15.95
3/4 x 1-3/8 x 1-1/4"
1.9 x 3.5 x 3.2cm

The perfect place for the family sedan. A common sight from the 1930s on, many can still be found in the older residential areas of most American towns.

DOWNTOWN BUILDINGS

Turn empty lots into detailed downtown settings with this series of commercial building kits.

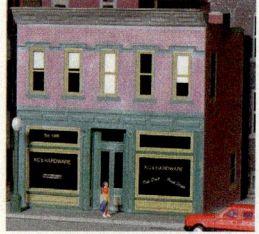

K.C.'s Hardware
502-603030   36.95
2-1/4 x 1-1/2 x 2-1/4"
53.7 x 3.8 x 5.6cm

The local hardware store remains an important business along main street, and this classic looks great in any era. Includes colorful printed signs.

Fire Engine Company #2
502-609010   42.95
2-5/8 x 2-5/8 x 2-1/8"
6.7 x 6.7 x 5.4cm

Built in the days of horse-drawn engines and iron men, these charming buildings can still be found in big cities today. Many have been restored and are now used as offices or upscale apartments. This model features large apparatus doors, plus an elegant facade and highly realistic brick walls which are assembled in layers for added depth.

Logan Savings & Loan
502-602021   39.95
2-1/2 x 1-3/4 x 2-5/8"
6.4 x 4.3 x 6.6cm

Add interest to any city scene with this handsome three-story building. Ideal for offices, too. (Can be combined with the Mid State Bank, #502-602020 sold separately, to create a six-story building.)

Pitman's Deli
502-606060   36.95
1-3/8 x 2 x 2-1/8"
3.5 x 5.2 x 5.3cm

Enjoy your favorite snacks and savor those specialty foods when you shop at this delightful store. Looks great in any commercial district. Comes with a classy awning for the front sidewalk and printed signs.

Theater Marquee Chase Light Kit
502-605052   32.95

Transform the Crestline Theater (#502-605050, sold separately) into a masterpiece after dark with this accessory. Includes a special white LED and 60 fiber optic strands to simulate the "moving" lights found on theaters everywhere. All electronics come fully assembled and are powered by a 9V battery, not included. Kit comes with step-by-step instructions to make installation fast and fun.

Get the Scoop!
Get the Skinny!
Get the Score!
Check Out Walthers
Web site at

www.walthers.com

Pink Elephant Car Wash
502-60960   42.95
4-3/8 x 2-3/8 x 2-1/2"   11 x 6 x 6.2cm

This 1950s-era car wash is produced from etched stainless steel and is complete with decals and painting tips.

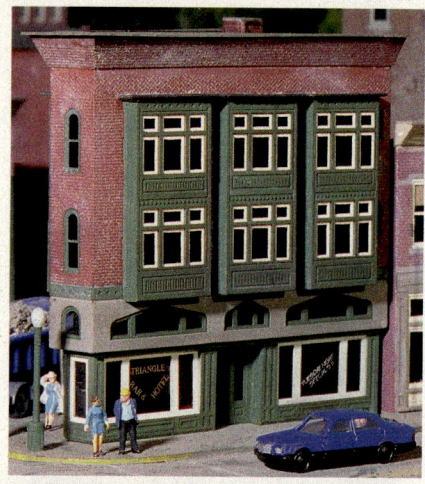

Triangle Hotel & Bar
502-604040   42.95
2-3/4 x 1-3/4 x 2-7/8"   6.9 x 4.3 x 7.3cm

Put an odd-shaped city lot to use with this detailed building. Colorful printed signs are provided to complete your new business venture.

Crestline Theater
502-605050   41.95
2-1/4 x 3 x 2-1/2"   5.8 x 7.5 x 6.3cm

All that's missing from this detailed kit is the smell of popcorn! Includes ticket booth and front entrance marquee with signs for a variety of period movies and additional printed signs. (Marquee can be illuminated with Chase Lights #502-605052, sold separately.)

Gazebo
502-601004   15.95
1 x 1 x 1-7/8"   2.4 x 2.4 x 4.8cm

A shady spot for any backyard, perfect for use with any of the Victorian Home Kits (sold separately). Includes turned brass posts for more realism.

STRUCTURES N SCALE

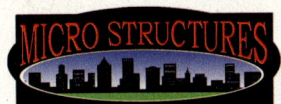
By Miller Engineering

Parkway Diner
502-601001 39.95
3-1/8 x 2 x 1-5/8" 7.9 x 5.1 x 4.1cm

A great detail for busy streets from the 1940s to the present. Made of real stainless steel with art deco style, just like the prototypes!

Parkway Diner Interior & Lighting
502-601015 26.95
Transform the Parkway Diner (#502-601001, sold separately) with this exciting accessory. Includes a full interior complete with counter, tables, benches, stools and more, right down to the plates and silverware! Includes custom electroluminescent lamps and ready-to-run power supply to showcase the interior day or night.

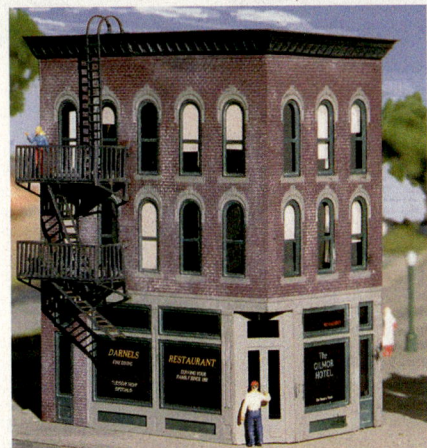

The Gilmor Hotel
502-601010 39.95
2-1/4 x 1-1/2 x 2-7/8" 5.7 x 3.7 x 7.4cm

Perfect place for travelers to spend a restful night, hotels like this were often found a block or two from the depot. Many are still standing, though weather-beaten and neglected, and used as apartments. Includes colorful, printed signs. (Photo shows model equipped with Fire Escape #502-602022, sold separately.)

Mile Stone Gravel Co.
529-609200 109.95
7-3/4 Wide x 6-1/4" Deep x 2-3/4 Tall 19.6 x 15.9 x 7cm

Add industrial action to your N Scale empire with this complete kit. Includes several large sheets of photo-etched brass parts with loads of detail, and can be built to accommodate two or three rail sidings.

Gulf Gas Station
502-609300 42.95
3-1/2 x 2-1/8 x 2-3/8" 8.7 x 5.3 x 6.2cm

Turn any empty corner into a superdetailed scene with this art deco style station. Licensed scale replica of the original Gulf design, reproduced in photo-etched brass. Complete with authentic decals.

Gulf Gas Station Lighting Kit

502-609310 35.95
esigned for the N Scale Gulf Gas Station (#502609300, sold separately), this kit includes interior and exterior lighting, the rooftop sign and ready-to-run electronics.

STRUCTURE DETAILS

502-60970 Rooftop Modular Duct System **16.95**
Kit consists of several different components that allow you to construct a variety of duct configurations. Parts are made of photo-etched stainless steel and the kit includes enough parts for several buildings. The photo above is just one possible configuration.

Photo-Etched Fencing
Ideal for use with the Victorian Home kits (sold separately), around city parks, cemeteries and other models.

502-60985 10' High Chain Link Security Fence **13.95**
Approximately 186 scale feet per package. Produced from photo etched stainless steel.

502-603032 Victorian Style **11.95**

502-604042 Gothic Style **15.05**

STRUCTURES N SCALE

By Miller Engineering

Air Conditioners

502-601016 Window Style **3.50**
Modernize any smaller window in minutes, perfect for homes and apartments.

502-602000 Roof Top Style **4.95**
Larger style often found on the roof of commercial and industrial buildings.

Picnic Tables

502-609440 pkg(4) **8.95**
The perfect detail for a backyard or a park scene. Includes parts for four picnic tables.

Garbage Cans

502-601400 pkg(4) **5.95**
These kits are produced in photo-etched brass for easy construction. Contains parts to build four garbage cans.

Fire Escapes
Make any model building safer when you add these detailed accessories. A great addition to downtown buildings of every kind, they can be adapted to most structures. Both kits include a drill template for correct placement over windows and enough photo-etched parts to add a fire escape to a building up to three stories tall.

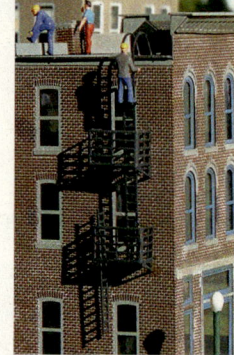

502-601011 Single Window **7.95**

502-602022 Double Window **9.60**

CATALOG

502-1 **3.00**
This 32-page full-color Miller Engineering catalog. Showcases over 300 unique model railroad products including photo-etched structures, lighting kits and Lightworks neon signs. Covers Z through O Scales.

Add a finishing touch of realism to your railroad scenes with these detailed, one-piece castings. Each is hand-cast from a very strong gypsum material that picks up fine details much like dental plaster. Items are hand-painted to bring out the many realistic details. (Note: all photos show HO Scale models.)

Coke Ovens
Beehive (Bell) Style 32.39 ea
506-860 Intact
506-870 Collapsed

Oven Front Only

506-1360 Open Doors **9.71**
Molded as a four-oven battery, with alternate doors open and closed (two open and two closed). Several castings can be combined side-by-side to model an early battery style coke oven.

Round Brick Industrial Chimneys
One-piece casting eliminates problems of hiding seams so common with multiple-piece plastic and resin kits. Great detail for any small industry.

New England Style 20.51 ea
These very thin profile chimneys are typical of designs used throughout New England on mills and other industries.
506-1460 Red
506-1470 Yellow

Large Diameter Style 19.42 ea

506-1020   506-1030

This larger diameter design is perfect for customizing any kit or scratchbuilt industry.
506-1020 Red
506-1030 Yellow

Intact Coke Oven 506-860

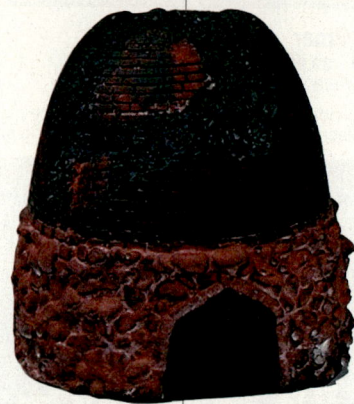
Collapsed Coke Oven 506-870

Coal Trestle

506-1010 Coal Unloading Ramp **10.78**
Trestle-style ramp with realistic coal pile detail. Great for a small town coal yard or as an unloading ramp for a large steam-era industry.

Oil Storage Tanks
6.47 ea

506-1730   506-1731

Vertical oil tanks are ideal for modeling smalltown oil distributors, railroad water or oil storage tanks, or as a detail alongside most large industries.
506-1730 Black
506-1731 Silver

Loading Ramps

506-1000 Ramp & Dock Set **10.78**
Includes one concrete End-of-Track Ramp and one Wood and Stone Loading Dock. Perfect for detailing yard scenes, smalltown sidings or industrial areas.

For Daily Product Updates Point Your Browser to
www.walthers.com

STRUCTURES N SCALE

NEW PRODUCTS

Micro-Seasons

Micro-Seasons™ No matter the season, family and friends are sure to enjoy a visit to these charming holiday communities. Each series includes a variety of resin structures, which are fully assembled and painted (PLEASE NOTE: buildings are not actual N Scale and sizes vary). To complete your display, special base sections and N Scale car and loco sets are available separately, or choose a complete starter set with everything included.

North Pole Village
Come home for Christmas to this winter wonderland!

Claus' House
NEW 489-96007001 12.95
3 x 2-3/4 1-1/2"

Reindeer Barn
NEW 489-96007002 14.95
4-3/8 x 4-3/8 x 3-1/8"

Elf Lodge
NEW 489-96007003 14.95
4-3/4 x 4-1/2 x 3-1/4"

North Pole Train Station
NEW 489-96007004 14.95
4-1/4 x 2-3/8 x 2-1/2"

Candy Cane Kitchen
NEW 489-96007005 12.95
4-1/4 x 3-3/4 x 3-1/8"

Mrs. Claus' Cookies
NEW 489-96007006 12.95
4-1/2 x 2-1/2 x 2"

North Pole Post Office
NEW 489-96007007 12.95
3-3/4 x 3 x 2-3/8"

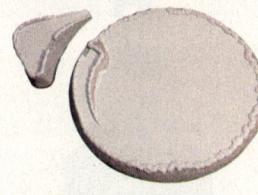

Sleigh Repair Shop
NEW 489-96007008 12.95
3-7/8 x 3-1/2 x 2"

Toy Factory
NEW 489-96007009 15.95
5-1/2 x 3-3/4 x 4-1/2"

Village Square Christmas Trees
3-1/4 x 3-1/4"
NEW 489-96009050 With Working Lights 11.95
Includes battery-powered lights in changing colors.
NEW 489-96009051 Standard 9.95

Covered Bridge
NEW 489-96009052 9.95
3-1/2 x 1-1/8 x 1-1/2"

6-Pack of North Pole Trees
NEW 489-96009057 9.95
Trees range in size from 1-3/4 to 2-1/4" Tall.

Village Set Only
NEW 489-96000101 139.95
Include one each #96007001 through 9609057.

Complete Platform
NEW 489-9600003 26.95
18 x 18 x 1-3/4"

The perfect setting for the North Pole Village. Raised ramp allows use of Covered Bridge (sold separately) to connect both pieces. Includes center and corner base pieces.

North Pole Central Train Set
NEW 489-99321731 149.95
Finished in festive holiday colors, this set includes a powered Life-Like GP20 Diesel, Toy Factory Transfer Car, Egg Nog Delivery Tank Car, Sugar & Spice Cookie Car and a Letters to Santa Mail Car.

PREMIUM PACKS

North Pole Village
Packs include all village pieces, basic tabletop with track, center base and train set.
NEW 489-96000100 #1 Without Legs 399.95
NEW 489-96000102 #2 With Legs 479.95

Haunted Hamlet
NEW 489-96000110 449.95
Includes all village pieces, basic tabletop & track without legs, center base and train set.

Liberty Town USA
NEW 489-96000120 399.95
Includes all village pieces, basic tabletop & track without legs, center base and train set.

Haunted Hamlet
A hauntingly good time awaits visitors to this whimsical Autumn-themed community that's populated with glowing ghosts and goblins.

Brimstone Manor
NEW 489-96007011 18.95
.5 x 4-1/4 x 4-3/4"

Cider Shack Café
NEW 489-96007012 14.95
4 x 3-3/8 x 2-1/4"

Creepy Critters Pet Shop
NEW 489-96007013 14.95
3-7/8 x 2-3/8 x 2-5/8"

STRUCTURES N SCALE

Ghostly Spirits Tavern
NEW 489-96007014   16.95
4-1/2 x 4-1/4 x 3"

Booville Train Station - Lighted
NEW 489-96007015   20.95
5 x 3-1/2 x 3-1/8"

Misery Mansion
NEW 489-96007016   18.95
4-1/4 x 4 x 5-1/8"

Nightmare Factory
NEW 489-96007017   18.95
5 x 3-3/4 x 5"

Spooky's Costume Shop
NEW 489-96007018   14.95
3-3/8 x 3-1/4 x 2-1/2"

Witches Brew Spell Shop
NEW 489-96007019   16.95
4 x 3-3/4 x 4"

Pumpkin Patch
NEW 489-96009061   14.95
6-1/4 x 4-1/4 x 2-1/2"

Booville Cemetery
NEW 489-96009062   14.95
5 x 4-1/4 1-7/8"

Spooky Hollow Tree
NEW 489-96009063   9.95
3-1/2 x 3-3/8 x 3-7/8"

Autumn Mix Trees
NEW 489-96009064 pkg(9)   14.95
Set of nine ready-to-use trees in two sizes and three fall colors.

Bare Mix Trees
NEW 489-96009065 pkg(4)   5.95

Centerpiece Platform
NEW 489-96005004   24.95
Display your Haunted Hamlet in style on this base with its brown surface and low brimstone wall.

Town Set
NEW 489-96000111   199.95
Includes one each of all town pieces #96007011 through 96005004.

Starter Set
NEW 489-96000113 Set of 5   76.95
Includes Spooky's Costume Shop, Misery Mansion, Cider Shack Café, Booville Train Station and Cemetery.

Booville & Beyond Railroad
NEW 489-99321040   149.95
This spooky set adds to the fun with its glow-in-the-dark cars and gleaming blue ghosts, plus a load of ghosts in one of the cars! Comes complete with powered Micro-Trains FT Diesel, B&BRR "Moving Freight for the Afterworld" car with ghost load, B&BRR Flying Banshee Box Car and B&BRR Phantom Caboose.

Liberty Town USA
Patriotic pride fills this small American community!

Liberty Town Church
NEW 489-96007021   17.95
5-3/4 x 3-1/4 x 6-1/8"

Freedom Hall
NEW 489-96007022   18.95
5-1/4 x 4 x 4-1/2"

Liberty Train Station
NEW 489-96007023   17.95
5 x 3-1/4 x 3-5/8"

Main Street #1
NEW 489-96007024   18.95
5-3/4 x 3-1/2 x 3-1/2"
One-piece structure with Soda Shop, Flower Shop and Liberty Book Store.

Main Street #2
NEW 489-96007025   18.95
5-3/4 x 3-1/2 x 3-1/2"
One-piece structure with Emporium, Barber & Toy Shoppe.

Mayor's House
NEW 489-96007026   14.95
4-1/4 x 3-1/8 x 3-1/4"

Banker's House
NEW 489-96007027   14.95
3-1/2 x 3-1/2 x 3-3/4"

Info, Images, Inspiration! Get It All at
www.walthers.com

Town Square Fountain
NEW 489-96009071   9.95
3-1/8 x 3-1/8 x 3"

Patriot Park
NEW 489-96009072   14.95
6 x 4 x 2-5/8"

Liberty Town Trees
NEW 489-96009073 pkg(9)   13.95
Set includes nine trees in two sizes and two different shades of green.

Centerpiece Platform
NEW 489-96005005   24.95
This grassy knoll is an ideal way to display your village.

Town Set
NEW 489-96000121   154.95
Includes one each of village items #96007021 through 96005005.

Starter Set
NEW 489-96000123   69.95
Includes Freedom Hall, Liberty Train Station, Banker's House, Mayor's House and Fountain.

Liberty Railroad
NEW 489-99321030   149.95
Decorated in red, white and blue this patriotic passenger train features two Liberty Railroad Sleepers and a Liberty Railroad Kitchen Car (all former troop cars) pulled by a Micro-Trains FT Diesel.

Table-Top n' Track
Solid wood tables are complete with pre-installed track, and a built-in power pack so you can start running trains right away! Choose from two versions: with legs for a freestanding display, or without legs for use on your own table.

NEW 489-96001100 N Scale w/Legs 199.95

NEW 489-96001110 N Scale, No Legs 129.95

NEW 489-96002110 Z Scale No Legs 119.95

STRUCTURES N SCALE

NEW PRODUCTS

Building Kits

Freight Station
NEW 490-1576 16.98

Railroad Water Tower
NEW 490-1577 15.98

Motorized Windmill
NEW 490-1578 37.98

Built-Up Buildings

Wine & Cheese Shop
NEW 490-2576 20.98

Podiatrist Office
NEW 490-2578 22.98

Post Office & Bank
NEW 490-2587 26.98

Joe's Fruit & Vegetables & Al's Deli
NEW 490-2609 31.98
Includes two lighted buildings and two figures.

BUILDING KITS

These easy-to-build kits feature colored plastic parts, preprinted signs and complete instructions. Deluxe versions are assembled and lighted buildings with two handpainted figures, unless noted.

Gift Shop & Boutique
490-2605 Deluxe Built-Up, Limited-Run 31.98

Wayside Station
490-1551 17.98
490-2562 Deluxe Built-Up 20.98

Twin Oil Tanks
490-1569 18.98

Freight Depot
490-2580 Deluxe Built-Up 22.98
7 x 3-1/2" 17.5 x 8.8cm

Malden Station
490-1524 20.98

Farm House
490-1513 19.98
5 x 3-3/4" 12.5 x 9.3cm
490-2603 Deluxe Built-Up 23.98

Tank Filling Station
490-1570 17.98
490-2591 Deluxe Built-Up 28.98
5-1/2 x 5/8 x 1-1/2"
14.1 x 1.8 x 3.8cm

Fire House w/Fire Engine
490-1511 19.98
490-2565 Deluxe Built-Up 23.98
3-1/2 x 3-1/2" 8.8 x 8.8cm

Loco Maintenance Building
490-1516 17.98
490-2564 Deluxe Built-Up w/Dummy Loco 23.98

Coverall Paints
490-1566 19.98
490-2589 Deluxe Built-Up 37.98
5-1/2 x 4-13/16 x 7-5/16"
14 x 12.2 x 18.4cm

National Casket
490-1573 20.98
490-2594 Deluxe Built-Up 37.98
5-5/8 x 3-13/16 x 7-3/16"
14 x 9.4 x 18.2cm

Jackson Meat Packing
490-1572 22.98
490-2593 Deluxe Built-Up 37.98
6-3/8 x 6-5/16 x 7-3/16"
16.2 x 16 x 18.2cm

Arlee Railroad Station
490-1501 18.98
490-2561 Deluxe Built-Up 23.98
6-1/2 x 2-1/2" 16.3 x 6.3cm

Barn, Silo & Chicken Coop
490-1517 21.98
490-2581 Deluxe Built-Up 28.98
Figures and lights not included.

Blue Coal Depot
490-1506 20.98
490-2563 Deluxe Built-Up 23.98
3-1/2 x 3" 8.8 x 7.5cm

Saw Mill
490-1523 19.98
490-2567 Deluxe Built-Up 26.98

Exxon Service Station
490-1503 18.98
490-2586 Deluxe Built-Up 21.98
5-3/4 x 4-1/2" 14.4 x 11.3cm

Remco Cleaning Building
490-2573 Deluxe Built-Up 22.98

Hotel & YMCA
490-2606 Deluxe Built-Up, Limited-Run 31.98

257

STRUCTURES N SCALE

Twin Loco Shed
490-1550 23.98
11 x 5-5/16" 27.9 x 13.5cm
14-1/4 x 1-1/2" 35.6 x 3.8cm

Lumber Yard
490-1565 20.98
490-2566 Deluxe Built-Up
23.98

The Grabitski's
490-1554 18.98
5-1/2 x 6-1/4" 14 x 15.9 cm

Mr. Rodger's House
490-2555 Deluxe Built-Up
21.98

Two-Story House
490-1514 20.98
6-1/2 x 6" 16.3 x 15cm
490-2604 Deluxe Built-Up
26.98

Church w/Fence & Grass Mat
490-1575 18.98
490-2553 Deluxe Built-Up
21.98

Brewery
490-1509 20.98
8-1/2 x 5-1/2" 21.3 x 13.8cm

Building Under Demolition
490-2584 Deluxe Built-Up
21.98
3-1/4 x 6" 8.2 x 15.2cm

Mr. & Mrs. Diggers
490-1558 18.98
5-1/2 x 6-1/4" 14 x 15.9cm

Simpson's House
490-2559 Deluxe Built-Up
21.98

Victoria House
490-1526 24.98
5-3/4 x 6-1/2" 14.1 x 16.5cm

Post Office & Bank Building
490-1539 22.98
490-2587 Deluxe Built-Up
26.98
7-1/2 x 3-5/8" 18.8 x 9cm

Bella's Farm House
490-1559 With Fence & Grass Mat 18.98

Jordan's House
490-2560 Deluxe Built-Up
21.98
1-3/4 x 3-1/4" 4.5 x 8.2cm

Sinatra's House
490-2554 Deluxe Built-Up
21.98
2 x 3" 5 x 7.6cm

Stone & Gravel Depot
490-2568 Deluxe Built-Up
23.98

US Army Munitions Depot
490-1574 19.98
490-2595 Deluxe Built-Up w/Tanks 28.98
4-7/8 x 3-11/16 x 2-5/16"
12.4 x 9.4 x 4.3cm

Apartment House
490-1540 18.98
3-5/8 x 3-1/2" 9 x 8.8 cm

Hardware & Supermarket
490-1534 22.98
6-1/2 x 3" 16.3 x 7.5cm

Shell Gas Tank
490-1567 19.98
490-2590 Deluxe Built-Up
37.98
4-3/16 x 4-3/16 x 4-5/8"
11.1 x 11.1 x 11.6cm

Suburban Houses
490-1502 pkg(3) 20.98
490-2588 Deluxe Built-Up
23.98
4 x 2-3/4" 10 x 6.9 cm

Police Station
409-1504 20.98

Truck Depot
490-1549 Modern 18.98
3-5/8 x 2-1/8" 9 x 5.3 cm

CF Truck Depot
490-2583 Deluxe Built-Up
21.98

Gantry Crane
490-1522 16.98
1-3/4 x 1-3/4" 4.4 x 4.4cm

Crane
490-2582 Deluxe Built-up
19.98

US Customs Warehouse
490-1547 18.98
7-1/2 x 3-5/8" 18.8 x 9cm

STRUCTURES N SCALE

model power

Holland Iron & Steel
490-1546 18.98
6 x 3" 15 x 7.5cm

Moving In
490-1553 16.98
5-1/2 x 6-1/4" 14 x 15.9cm

Star-Journal Building
490-1510 18.98
3-5/8 x 2-1/2" 9 x 6.3cm

490-2598 Deluxe Built-Up
22.98

Haunted House
490-1555 With Base, Fence & Grass 18.98
5-1/2 x 6-1/4" 14 x 15.9cm

490-2556 Deluxe Built-Up
21.98
2 x 2-1/6" 5 x 5.2cm

Built-Up Searchlight Tower
490-2631 13.98

Built-Up Water Tower
490-2630 13.98

Double Tunnel Portal
490-1521 13.98

St. Mary's Hospital
490-1505 20.98

Coal Mine
490-1552 21.98
7-5/16 x 7-1/2" 18.6 x 19cm

Grandma's House
490-1556 18.98
5-1/2 x 6-1/4" 14 x 15.9cm

Grandma Moses' House
490-2557 Deluxe Built-Up
21.98

Oil Facility Office
490-1571 16.98
3-5/16 x 1-5/16 x 1"
8.8 x 3.6 x 2.5cm

New Arrivals Updated Every Day! Visit Walthers Web site at
www.walthers.com

Movie Theater & Restaurant
490-2607 Deluxe Built-Up, Limited-Run 31.98

The Sullivan's
490-1557 18.98
5-1/2 x 6-1/4" 14 x 15.9cm

Kennedy's House
490-2558 Deluxe Built-Up
21.98

General Electric Co.
490-2608 Deluxe Built-Up
23.98
3-5/8 x 3-1/2" 9 x 8.8cm

Railroad Hotel
490-1512 18.98
490-2597 Deluxe Built-Up
22.98
4-1/2 x 2-3/4" 11.3 x 6.9cm

Oscar Mayer
490-2574 20.98

Eastern Chemical
490-2575 2 Buildings 22.98

BUILT-UP BRIDGES

Decorated bridges are fully assembled and painted. Each bridge features wood detail, and comes with 5" nickel-silver track and handpainted figures. Bridges can be ganged together.

Truss Bridge
490-1102 6.50

High Truss Bridge
490-1112 7.50

Girder Bridges 6.50 ea (Unless Noted)

490-1120 ATSF
490-1121 PRR
490-1123 Amtrak 7.50
490-1119 Unlettered

Information STATION

Milk Stations

One of the more common trackside "industries" in the steam- and transition-eras, milk stations are an ideal addition to your railroad right of way.

In some regions, milk stations were found every mile or so, usually next to a rural road crossing for easy access by farmers. They were also used in smaller towns where they were built near the depot. While the station might be alongside a passing siding in town, it was right next to the mainline in the country. This meant that the milk train had to keep a tight schedule and transfer cans very quickly to avoid delaying other trains.

For convenience and to speed the loading/unloading work, a timber platform about 4' (120cm) tall formed the basis of the structure. This height made it easy to back a wagon into place and slide the full and heavy 10 gallon cans directly onto the platform. This also made it easy to slide cans aboard milk cars or into the baggage compartment of a combine or motorcar.

Most also included a small shed-like structure at one end of the platform, which was enclosed on three sides and open facing the tracks. This provided a shady spot where loaded cans would stay cool on hot days.

STRUCTURES N SCALE

MOUNTAINEER PRECISION PRODUCTS
Makers of Craftsman Quality Laser Cut Structures & More

Add a slice of authentic American flavor to any scene with this line of laser-cut kits. The selection includes five different types of barns, plus colorful billboard signs designed especially for them, pre-1950s houses, and a wide selection of historic railroad structures based on prototype plans. Each kit consists of laser-cut wood parts and includes complete instructions.

NEW PRODUCTS

ATSF Building

San Bernardino Sandhouse
NEW 511-990N 54.98
As diesels began to replace steam engines, sandhouses and other structures needed to be adapted to fit the new locomotives. This unique kit is based on Santa Fe's San Bernardino sandhouse as appeared in the late 40s and 50s after it was expanded to accommodate both steam and diesel locos. Similar sandhouses were used throughout the system and by other roads. This detailed structure is perfect for a transition-era engine terminal. Kit includes materials for the main building, sand bin and trestle leading to the bin. Walls are thin, durable plywood that resists warping. Ladders, windows, glazing and a door are cut specifically for the kit. Wire is included for modeling the sanders (requires some soldering). Tichy nut-bolt-washer castings, light fixtures, a track bumper and a custom fire extinguisher casting are also included.

Barns
12.98 Each
Add color and charm to rural scenes with these models, typical of various styles of barns found on farms everywhere.

Type #1
511-101N
1-1/2 x 2-1/4"

Type #2
511-102N
2-1/4 x 2-1/4"

Type #3
511-103N
2-1/4 x 2-1/4"

Type #4 with Small Addition
511-104N
1-3/4 x 1-3/4"

Type #5
511-105N
1-1/2 x 1-3/4"

Barn Decals
Classic, full-color re-creations of actual billboards seen on barns across the Southern states for decades. Sized to fit Barn kits 1-5, (sold separately), adaptable to other models.

Mail Pouch Tobacco
1.00 ea
511-MPD1N Straight Name (white & yellow)
511-MPD2N Stacked Name (white & yellow)
511-MPD3N Straight Name (red, yellow, white)

Rock City 1.00 ea
511-RCD1N See Beautiful Rock City
511-RCD2N … You See the Best
511-RCD3N … Atop Lookout Mountain
511-RCD4N … See 7 States
511-RCD5N See Beautiful Rock City To-Day

Kentucky Club Pipe Tobacco
511-KCD1N It Never Tires Your Taste **1.00**

Eat More Possum!
511-EPD1N At Joe's Diner **1.00**

Old Loyalty Cigarette Tobacco
511-OLD1N Big Bag & Papers 5 Cents **1.00**

Baltimore & Ohio Office Building

511-201N 8.98
Designed from actual B&O plans, this small structure is perfect as a yard office or flag stop station, but can easily be adapted for other uses. Finished model is at home on layouts from the late 1800s to the present.

Universal Building
511-202N 19.98
Measures 24 x 32 scale feet
This building is a natural on any layout in any era. Use it as a local business, a railroad structure, or whatever your heart desires. The two-sided dock can be installed along any wall or converted to a double-length dock.

Rabbit Hash General Store

511-203N 27.98
Based on an actual store founded in 1831 and still in use today, this little retail establishment serves the tiny hamlet of Rabbit Hash, Kentucky. Kit consists of laser-cut plywood, basswood, roofing and injection-molded chimney parts. Two laser-cut benches and stair sets with railings are also included. Two front signs from different eras that are accurate for the building are provided, along with extra advertising signs. The model can be built on stilts like the prototype or flat on the ground. A six-page instruction manual is included along with several reference photos of the prototype.

Pre-1950s Houses

White Residence
511-301N 22.98
This two-story house features laser-cut, three-tab shingles, windows that can be positioned open or closed, and dormers that can be positioned where you'd like, or left off if desired.

Greene Residence
511-302N 22.98
Perfect addition to any subdivision, many homes of this type are still standing today.

Central of Georgia Standard Station

511-910N 23.98
This standard Class C style depot was found throughout the south, but is typical of small town depots everywhere. Kit was produced from actual company architectural drawings.

Chesapeake & Ohio Standard Stations
To reduce costs, many railroads designed standard station buildings. To meet local needs, the basic structure could easily be modified as needed, but common elements (such as doors, trim, window style etc.) were retained to give each a "family" appearance that instantly identified the owner. These authentic replicas of C&O stations present three variations of the same design.

511-941N Standard #1 **29.98**
This medium sized combination station is typical of those built for bigger towns, where more space was needed to handle freight and/or passenger traffic.

511-942N Standard #2 **34.98**
This larger version of the Standard #1 depot features a larger area to handle freight or baggage.

511-943N Standard #3 **24.98**
This small town station has a tiny waiting room, office and freight/baggage room under one roof.

C&O Small Buildings
511-944N pkg(3) 17.98
Great details to complete any station or yard scene; based on C&O prototypes.

Pennsylvania Railroad Buildings

Class A Station
511-961N 29.98
Measures 16 x 40 Scale Feet
The Class A passenger and freight station, built between 1887 and 1906, was found in scores of towns served by the Pennsy. Laser-cut slate shingles and injection molded chimney are included, and the kit is engineered with tab and slot construction, along with many other time-saving features.

Section House

511-962N 10.98
Measures 12'-4" x 16'-4" Scale Feet & Inches
The 1st class section house was found almost everywhere along Pennsy rails from 1899 to the end of the railroad. They were used by section gangs to house handcars, track tools, and the foreman's office. Laser-cut plywood model faithfully follows the prototype and is based on tracing #8140.

Watch Box 3-Pack

511-963N 12.98
Each Measures 6 x 6 Scale Feet
Watch boxes were found at street crossings and railroad yards (as shelters from the elements for switchmen and brakemen) from 1887 onward. These very accurate models capture the known variations. Kits contain laser-cut plywood walls, trim and windows, plus injection-molded smoke jacks and laser-cut tarpaper roofing material. Each kit contains enough parts to make three watch boxes; walls are interchangeable so you can model variations.

STRUCTURES N SCALE

New Rail Models

New Rail Models laser-cut wood kits offer the detail of a craftsman kit combined with easy assembly of laser-cut, wood parts featuring tab-in-slot assembly. Kits also include peel-and-stick roofing sheets and complete instructions.

NEW PRODUCTS
Structures

Bungalow
NEW 501-12017 TBA
Perfect for city or country, houses like this have been in use across the continent since they were constructed in the 1920s. Easy-to-assemble kit includes peel-and-stick Ultra Shingles and full-color instructions.

Bunk House
NEW 501-12019 TBA
Modest shacks like this are used as crew bunk houses, cabins, fishing shacks and anywhere else where quick, affordable shelter is needed. They're also used in multiples as company housing. Easy-to-assemble kit includes see-through porch screens and full-color instructions.

Log Scaling Platform
501-12010 25.95
5 x 1"
Log scaling platforms are an important part of the logging industry wherever logs are transported by truck on their way from the logging site to the lumber mill; they're used to put a value on a load of lumber. This model is patterned after the facility at the Hull-Oakes Lumber Co. in Dawson, Oregon, but is a design found at sawmills across the continent.

Bingen Loading Warehouse
501-12007 49.95
7-3/8 x 4-1/2"
This model is based on a 1946-built plywood loading warehouse located in Bingen, WA at the SDS Lumber Co. This barrel-roofed building features a sheltered loading dock and plenty of staging space for outbound lumber and plywood. Kit includes the structure, peel-and-stick tarpaper roofing and instructions. Plywood stacks are sold separately as part #501-32008 (see listing in the Scenery Section).

A-Frame Cabin
501-12003 24.95
Looking for a weekend getaway? Add realism to any forest scene with this unique kit. Includes a realistic cabin structure, deck with railing and peel-and-stick Ultra Shingles™ shake shingle roofing.

Classic 1920s Garage
501-12006 15.95
Patterned after an actual 1920s catalog design, this building is perfect for keeping cars out of the elements in any neighborhood. Simply place this building near houses or along alleys in residential neighborhoods for extra realism. Includes details like trellises, carry-through beams on the ends and rafters and peel-and-stick Ultra Shingles shake shingle roofing.

Passenger and Freight Shelter
501-12013 19.95
This small passenger and freight shelter is typical of those used along branches and interurban lines at stops that didn't warrant a full-blown depot. This diminutive wooden building features a small passenger bench and tiny LCL storage room under a single roof. Features Ultra Asphalt Shingle™ roofing.

NEAL'S N GAUGING TRAINS

NEW PRODUCTS
Branchline Single-Stall Engine House

NEW 530-SS604 54.95

STRUCTURES

530-SS029 Victorian Gents Lavoratory 15.95

530-SS051 Bandstand w/Chairs and Music Stands 22.95

530-SS052 Extra Chairs & Different Music Stands 11.95

530-SS603 US 2 Story Shop 49.95
Includes Details f/The Window Displays & 3 Dimension Window Sashes

SMALL INDUSTRIAL WORKSHOP

530-SS606 Small Industrial Workshop w/fronts for manufacturing facility 54.95

This etched-metal structure is a typical small business seen in any commercial district. It features board and batten walls and a metal roof. Other details include two fronts, one with a roll-up door, plus etched signboards for two business names, so customers can customize them to fit their scenes.

Daily New Product Announcements! Visit Walthers Web site at
www.walthers.com

STRUCTURES N SCALE

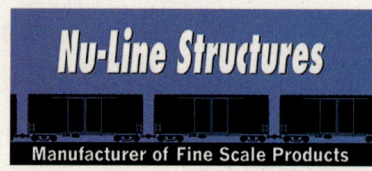

Add realism to your railroad with this line of easy-to-build, affordably priced, plastic structure kits.

Modern Concrete Warehouse Style #1 533-161001

Modern Concrete Warehouse Style #2 533-161002
Beige Building Not Included

Azusa Style Station 533-161003

NEW PRODUCT
Modern Concrete Bridge

NEW 533-164000 54.95
15 x 2 x 2" 38.1 x 5.1 x 5.1cm

Designed as a double-track or two-lane highway bridge that is able to cross up to eight lanes of traffic or four railroad lines.

"L" SHAPED WOOD LOADING DOCK
533-161503 7.98
Measures: 2-3/4 x 5-1/2"
6.9 x 13.8cm.

AZUSA STYLE STATION
533-161003 38.95
With simple, clean lines, this building is typical of many stations built in the years following World War II. The prototype, which is mostly concrete, was built in 1946 by the Santa Fe in Azusa, California, and is still standing along the former ATSF Pasadena sub, which is now owned by Metrolink.

This detailed model captures the look of the original including the rounded edges on the west wall of the structure, grooved walls and a separate loading dock. The model is complete with separate "wooden" cargo doors, drain pipes, doors, wall bumpers and windows which make it easy to paint in your favorite color scheme.

MODERN CONCRETE WAREHOUSE
39.95 ea
A great addition to any industrial park, structures like these are found all across America and in some foreign countries. Each kit features parts made from high-density styrene to reduce warping and simplify construction. The kits also include two types of stairwells, three different sizes of freight doors, 28 roof skylights molded in white, darkened window "glass," roof access hatches, two sizes of sidewalks and more.

Both buildings measure 12-1/2 x 9-1/4 x 3" 31.2 x 23.1 x 7.5cm, but they can easily be cut in half for use alongside a backdrop or at the edge of a layout or module.

533-161001 Style #1
The perfect home for any modern industrial operation served by road and rail.

533-161002 Style #2
Distinctively different from #161001, this building features a centered front entryway with freight doors to the right and left. A round planter is included for the porch in front of the windows. And attractive grooves extend the length of the building to add eye-appeal.

Plastruct

Welded Steel Water Tank
570-2009 15.60
1-3/4" 4.5cm diameter
100,000 gallon, used during the last days of steam.

Water Tanks
570-94881 1-3/4" .06cm Outside Diameter **4.65**
570-94882 1" 2.5cm Outside Diameter pkg(2) **4.65**
570-94883 1/2" 1.2cm pkg(4) **3.65**
570-94884 1/4" .6cm Outside Diameter pkg(8) **3.30**

Cone Roof Elevated Water Tank
570-2028 22.35
1-1/2 x 8-1/2" 3.8 x 22cm

Probably the most common style of water tower found in industrial settings.

Towers
570-94893 3-1/2" **6.60**
570-94892 5-1/2" **7.30**
570-94891 8" **8.30**

1" Oil Tanks
570-94877 pkg(4) **3.65**
23/64" 0.9cm tall,
1" 2.5cm diameter.

Twin Bulk Oil Storage Tanks
570-2014 15.60
3/4 x 3" 1.9 x 7.6cm

Oil Storage Tank
570-2015 15.60
2 x 3" 5 x 7.5cm
For expanding your refinery, tank farm or bulk oil distribution center.

Truss Bridge
570-2002 15.60
Authentic steel construction bridge with 120' span.

Old Time Moving Bridge
570-2007 13.40
Opens horizontally using a central pivoting system.

Twin LP Gas Storage Tanks
570-2019 17.85
3/4" 1.9cm diameter,
5" 12.7cm long.

Petro/Chemical Refinery

570-2008 67.95
12 x 15" 30 x 37cm
Includes all of the piping, angles, valves, tanks and other details to model a storage and rail car loading facility.

Steel Mill Fakefront

570-1030 49.95
12" high x 22" wide x 3" deep
30 x 56 x 75cm
Designed for HO Scale, but may also be used in N Scale with slight modifications.

STRUCTURES N SCALE

NuComp Miniatures

Seen all over North America, these mobile home kits and accessories offer great detail for any modern layout. The cast polyurethane resin kits are available in a set to build a complete trailer park, or as individual kits. Kits can be painted using water based acrylic paints. Figures, details and accessories shown in pictures are not included. Detail and assembly required.

1950s Era House Trailer/Mobile Home Kits 534-610

1950s Era House Trailer/Mobile Home Kits 534-611

1950s Era House Trailer/Mobile Home Kits 534-612

1950s Era House Trailer/Mobile Home Kits 534-613

Mobile Home #1 w/Porch 534-602

1950s Era Trailer Park Kit
534-60150 115.00
Includes six different 50s style trailers, one tool shed, two lawn mowers, two pop machines, six assorted cars, one garage, one work shed and twelve tree stumps.

1950s Era House Trailer/Mobile Home Kits
534-601 Office/Utility Trailer **13.00**

534-610 Super **16.00**
3-1/4 x 1/2" 8.1 x 1.3cm

534-611 Deluxe **16.00**
3-1/8 x 9/16" 7.8 x 1.41cm

534-612 Large **15.00**
2-1/4 x 5/8" 5.6 x 1.6cm

534-613 Midsized **14.00**
1-7/8 x 9/16" 4.62 x 1.41cm

Mobile Home #1 w/Porch
534-602 **16.00**
5-1/8 x 1" 13 x 2.5cm
Early 1970s style mobile home kit.

Mobile Home #1
534-603 **16.00**
4-1/2 x 1-1/8" 11.4 x 2.9cm
Late 1970s style mobile home kit.

Single Wide Mobile Home
534-604 **12.00**
4-1/2 x 3/4" 11.4 x 1.9cm

Trailer Park Kit
534-60101 **115.00**
Creating a trailer park scene has never been easier! Now you can build a complete trailer park with a single, convenient kit. Set includes one each of trailer kits #601-603 and 605-607, as well as a Tool Shed (#60201), a One Car Garage (#60202), two lawn mowers, two pop machines, tree stumps and a 4-pack of cars from the late 1940s/50s. Includes 601, 602, 603, 605, 606 and 607.

For Up-To-Date Information and News Bookmark Walthers Web site at
www.walthers.com

1950s Era Trailer Park Kit 534-60150

Mobile Home #1 534-603

Trailer Park Kit 534-60101

Single Wide Mobile Home 534-604

Office/Utility Trailer 534-601

263

STRUCTURES N SCALE

NuComp Miniatures

Mobile Home #2 534-605

Mobile Home #2 w/Porch 534-606

Tool Shed 534-60201

One-Car Garage 534-60202

Work Shed 534-60203

Double Wide Mobile Home 534-6041

Mobile Home #3 534-607

Mobile Home #2
534-605 16.00
3-3/4 x 3/4" 9.5 x 1.9cm
Tip Out: 1-5/8 x 5/8"
4.1 x 1.6cm
Mid 1970s style mobile home with a tip out.

Mobile Home #2 w/Porch
534-606 16.00
4 x 3/4" 10.2 x 1.9cm

Mobile Home #3
534-607 16.00
3-5/8 x 3/4" 9.2 x 1.9cm
Late 60s style mobile home kit.

1950s Era Mobile Home #1
534-608 14.00
2 x 3/4" 5 x 1.87cm

1950s Era Mobile Home #2
534-609 14.00
2 x 3/4" 5 x 1.87cm

Double Wide Mobile Home
534-6041 16.00
4-5/8 x 1-5/8" 11.7 x 4.1cm

Tool Shed
534-60201 6.00
1-1/4 x 5/8" 3.2 x 1.6cm

One-Car Garage
534-60202 9.00
1-7/8 x 1-1/2" 4.8 x 3.8cm

Work Shed
534-60203 9.00
1-7/8 x 1-1/2" 4.8 x 3.8cm

1950s Era Mobile Home #2 534-609

1950s Era Mobile Home #1 534-608

STRUCTURES N SCALE

Create superbly detailed trackside scenes along your railroad with this line of laser-cut wood kits. Two series are available. For modelers just starting out, the Journeyman Series offers a complete line of smaller buildings with fewer parts and easier construction. For more experienced modelers, there are Master Craftsman Series kits of larger and more complex structures. All kits include laser-cut micro-plywood pieces, numerous details and comprehensive illustrated instructions to make assembly fast and fun.

NEW PRODUCTS
Structures

Waterville Freight House
NEW 716-10007 59.95
5 x 2-1/2 x 2-1/2"
12.5 x 6.25 x 6.25cm

This complete trackside operation includes scenic details, an interior loading platform, full-color roofing, window glazing and numerous castings.

MASTER CRAFTSMAN SERIES LASER-CUT WOOD KITS

Kits include laser-cut parts and easy-to-follow instructions. Components are cut from warp-resistant, durable micro-plywood sheets. Also feature window and door castings from Tichy, custom designed detail parts from P. D. Marsh and Fine N Scale, and corrugated aluminum siding from Builders in Scale.

Somerville Junction
716-10103 68.95
Keep your steam power ready for the road with this complete service facility kit. Includes a 850- to 1000-ton Conveyor Coal Station, 65,000 Gallon Water Storage Tank with two Standpipes, a Two-Track Sand Column and a Skip-Hoist Cinder Plant with Pit.

Ogden Creek Viaduct
39.95 ea
716-10200 Base Kit
8 x 2 x 4-1/2" 20 x 5 x 11.2cm
Includes left and right side supports with partial arch and supports, plus complete central arch.
716-10300 Expansion Kit
9 x 2 x 4-1/2" 22.5 x 5 x 11.2cm
Adds two central arches and columns.

Greendel Station & Tower
716-10101 59.95
3-1/2 x 6" & 2-1/2 x 3"
8.7 x 15cm & 6.2 x 7.5cm
A complete station and tower in one kit! Great detail for any small town scene. Matching towers are available separately in kit #716-10102.

Sheffield Farms Creamery
716-10502 69.95
4 x 6" 10 x 15cm
For decades, railroads moved milk from country collection points like this to bottling plants in big cities. This charming building makes a great trackside industry in a small town and some were freestanding operations alongside the tracks as well. Includes covered pull-through can unloading/loading area, smokestacks, roof vents and more.

Rode-A-Way Transfer Company
716-10503 59.95
4-1/2 x 7" 11.2 x 17.5cm
Ideal as a trackside freight house, road-to-rail transfer or trailer-to-trailer reload facility, this kit has lots of versatility and is based on a prototype built in the 1950s. Two rail loading platforms are included that can be placed as needed alongside the structure, or use the modern "rubber bumpers" that are provided for a modern truck terminal.

Lackawanna Coal Company
716-10504 149.95
10 x 11 x 6-1/2"
25 x 27.5 x 16.2cm

The prototypes that inspired this kit were located in the anthracite coal region of northeastern Pennsylvania. In these immense structures know as "breakers" or "collieries," anthracite was washed & broken into sizes usable for home heating and industrial processes. Breakers of the size and type represented by this kit were typically built in the 1930s to consolidate several smaller, older processing plants and many were still operational into the 1970s.

Quality Meat Packers
716-10603 133.95
12 x 5 x 5" 30 x 12.5 x 12.5cm
A superb trackside industry for any era, this kit includes window glazing with mullion detail and numerous custom castings, including the large brick chimney and feeding troughs.

Waterville Freight House 716-10007

Greendel Station & Tower 716-10101

Quality Meats Stockyard
716-10703 49.95
10 x 5" 25 x 12.5cm

Everything you need to model a modern stockyard. Includes hay barns, shelters, unloading chutes, holding pens and feed troughs. Includes positionable gates and modular construction allows several kits to be easily combined. (Cows and additional details are available separately, see the complete listing in the Super Detailing Parts Section.)

Shue Cement Company
716-10702 75.95
Standard Version: 5 x 7-1/2"
13.7 x 18.7cm
Backdrop Version: 4-1/2 x 10"
11.2 x 25cm

Model can be built as a freestanding building, or as a partial structure for use along your scenic backdrop.

Union City Station
716-10900 85.95
10-1/2 x 7" 26.2 x 17.5cm

This building looks right along any railroad and fits all popular modeling eras. Complete your scene with the Union City Station Expansion Platform kit #716-10901, sold separately.

Eagle River Mine
716-10902 72.95
8 x 3-1/2" 20 x 8.7cm

Based on a prototype alongside the Eagle River at Gilman, Colorado, this impressive kit includes most of the major structures of the prototype and is ideal for any kind of mining operation along your railroad.

Get Daily Info, Photos and News at
www.walthers.com

STRUCTURES N SCALE

Racquette Lake Navigation Company
716-10999   59.95
4-1/2 x 4-1/2"   11.2 x 11.2cm

Wherever rails meet water, you'll find impressive docking facilities like this where freight cars can be moved to or from ferries or carfloats.

RAILWAY HERITAGE MODELS™ LASER-CUT WOOD KITS

Alto Tower
716-10001   69.95
3 x 2 x 3"   7.5 x 5 x 7.5cm

The ALTO Tower kit is based on the ALTO interlocking tower that still stands along the Norfolk & Southern mainline in Altoona, Pennsylvania. It was originally built in the 1880s by the Pennsylvania Railroad as part of their sprawling yard complex. Through the Penn Central and Conrail years this tower underwent several "modernization" efforts. We have restored this tower close to its original condition for the purposes of preserving it in kit form.

Branchville Station
716-10002   69.95
5-1/2 x 2-3/4 x 1-3/4"
13.75 x 6.8 x 4.38cm

This kit is based on the station that once stood at the terminus of the Delaware Lackawanna & Western's Sussex Branch in Branchville, New Jersey. It was originally built by the Sussex Railroad in 1869 and was unfortunately razed in 1994 after a heavy snow collapsed its roof.

Williamstown Coal
716-10003   99.95
5 x 3-1/2 x 4"
12.5 x 8.75 x 10cm

This kit is based on a pair of retail coal structures that still stand in Williamstown, MA. Though the exact date of their construction is unknown, we estimate that they were originally built in the late 1800s or early 1900s when coal was the primary source of fuel.

Long Valley Lumber Mill
716-10004   145.95
10" x 6" x 6"   25 x 15 x 15cm

This kit represents the lumber mills that existed in California, Idaho, Minnesota, Oregon, and West Virginia from the 1890s to today. This kit takes the most interesting elements from each of the prototypes and blends them into one solid kit.

"Cal Fame Packing"
716-10006   89.95
12-1/2 x 9 x 3"
31.25 x 22.5 x 7.5cm

This kit is based on a citrus packing plant that once stood in Escondido, California. The prototype, designed by William W. Achet was first opened in 1935 by the Escondido Orange Association and continued until 1987 when it was closed by the Paramount Citrus Association.

New Haven Tower
716-10005   45.95
1-1/2 x 1-3/4 x 3"
3.75 x 4.37 x 7.5cm

The New Haven Tower kit is based on actual drawings of the New York & New Haven Railroad's "standard" reinforced concrete interlocking tower. This design was created in the early 1900s (drawings are dated 11/16/1915) and replicated at dozens of locations along the New Haven's busy Northeast Corridor mainline.

JOURNEYMAN SERIES LASER-CUT WOOD KITS

This series of smaller laser-cut wood kits features complete instructions with actual-size elevation and floor plan drawings, complemented by step-by-step text, tips and techniques, and assembly photos. Kits use micro-plywood for its superior durability and resistance to warping. A system of tabs and slots reduces errors in construction and produces a sturdier model. Self-stick adhesive is applied to allow for quick and easy installation of windows, doors, glazing and trim pieces. For more realism, kits features laser-etched siding grooves, individual planking, nail holes and low-relief carving details as appropriate; laser-etched lines are also provided as a guide to position overlaid architectural details.

Waterville Switchman's Shanty
NEW 716-10008   10.95
1 x 3/4 x 1"   2.5 x 1.9 x 2.5cm

The perfect kit for your first kit building experience! It's designed to be built in about an hour and is an excellent introduction to the design approach and materials used in our larger laser-cut micro-plywood kits.

Long Valley Lumber Mill 716-10004

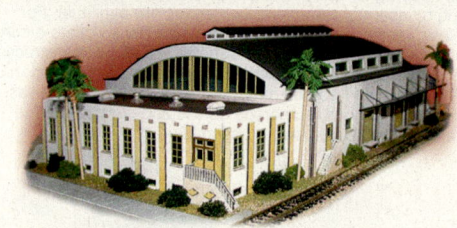

"Cal Fame Packing" 716-10006

Lehigh Valley Standard Tower
NEW 716-10009   49.95
1 x 1-3/4 x 1-1/4"
2.5 x 4.4 x 3.1cm

Based on actual system standard drawings, several of these towers were built along LV lines beginnign in 1900.

Greendel Tower
716-10102 pkg(2) 39.95
2-1/2 x 3"   6.2 x 7.5cm

Controlling important junctions, freight yards, passenger terminals, drawbridges and more, interlocking towers like this were used all along American railroads. Matches the tower included with #716-10101 so it's easy to give your line's structures a family look.

Grover Cleveland Mine
716-10204   45.95
6 x 7-1/2"   15 x 18.7cm

A composite of several small mines, this kit includes Head Frame, Hoist House and Load-Out Platform that can be placed in two different layout configurations. Figures and vehicles shown are included.

East Stroudsburg Tower
716-10304   39.95
1-1/2 x 3"   3.7 x 7.5cm

Based on a Delaware, Lackawanna & Western prototype and also includes a "concrete" mechanical relay building. Built in 1908, it still stands today as the last DL&W wooden interlocking tower.

Andrew's Auto & Gas
716-10404   45.95
3 x 3"   7.5 x 7.5cm

Includes a variety of signs from different eras and plenty of castings to add junk to the scene.

Union City Station Expansion Platform
716-10901 pkg(2) 24.95
11"   27.5cm

Complete your big city station scene with these "butterfly" style shelters alongside the tracks. Kit includes two 11" platforms with canopies. Looks great with the Union City Station Kit #716-10901, sold separately.

STRUCTURES N SCALE

NORTHEASTERN SCALE MODELS INC.

Create a complete small town on your layout with this line of easy-to-build wood kits. The parts of these structures are made from the finest quality basswood, which has been laser-cut and engraved. This produces detail that rivals most plastic models, and re-creates the look of stone or wood construction. The models can be assembled in about the same time as a plastic kit, but since wood parts are used, no toxic glues are needed. The kits are also easy to paint and have a true-to-life look when finished.

NEW PRODUCTS

Old-Fashioned General Store
NEW 520-30024   39.95
3 x 4-29/32" 7.6 x 12.5cm

25-Ton Coaling Station
NEW 520-10105   30.75
1-3/4 x 1-1/4 x 4" 4.3 x 3.1 x 10cm

SMALL TRACKSIDE STRUCTURE SERIES

Passenger Shelter
520-30001   6.35

Storage Shed
520-30002   8.75

Freight Depot
520-30003   20.15

Motor Car Shed
520-30004   7.65

Watch Tower
520-30006   7.65

Yard Storage
520-30008   13.15
Kit was created from plans originally published in *Railroad Model Craftsman*, used with permission of Carstens Publications, Inc.

Dairy Barn
520-30009   14.25
Perfect for that farmyard scene, this kit builds into a traditional American barn with sliding end doors and a cupola for ventilation.

Tool & Die Shop
520-30013   29.65
This tool and die shop will look great in any industrial area on your layout.

Railroad Covered Bridge
520-30014   30.75
Covered bridges such as this one used to be a commonplace sight throughout North America. With this decorative structure you can now cross waterways with style!

Box & Crate Factory
520-30015   32.95
Ideal for any layout that needs a small manufacturing plant, this laser-cut kit includes instructions, all-wood parts including doors and windows, and finishing suggestions.

"SIGNATURE SERIES" BUILDINGS

Create exact replicas of famous model railroad buildings for your layout with this series of craft train kits. The models feature laser-cut and engraved wood parts for ease of assembly with professional results.

Tenement Row
520-10108   66.95
This model is based on Earl Smallshaw's original, which stands beside the right-of-way on his Middletown & Mystic Mines. A terrific detail for a big city scene, it fits well in steam- or diesel-era settings. The kit includes parts for three complete buildings with laser-cut windows. Complete assembly instructions also provide information on building a diorama scene for the finished model.

Sam Cahoon's Fish Pier
520-10109   66.98
This detailed model is based on a Dave Frary original and adds a neat touch to any waterfront area.

Feed & Grain Storage
520-30016   43.95

Valley Hardware & Plumbing Supply
520-30017   32.95

Farm & Garden Supply
520-30018   43.95
Features all-wood laser-cut parts, plastic windows and doors, paper roof shingles, chimneys and a choice of signs. Painting and weathering suggestions are also included.

Sheet Metal Shop
520-30019   32.95

267

STRUCTURES N SCALE

NORTHEASTERN SCALE MODELS INC.

Cobble Creek Transfer Station
520-30020 20.15

First National Bank & Trust Co.
520-30021 20.15
1-3/4 x 4" 4.3 x 10cm

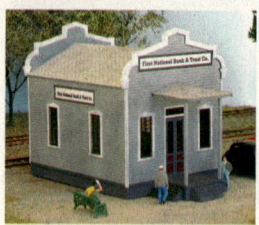

Barnsboro Depot
520-30022 41.95
2-1/4 x 5-1/2" 5.6 x 13.7cm

Springfield Fire Station
520-30023 39.95
3 x 3-3/16" 7.5 x 7.65cm

For Up-To-Date Information and News Bookmark Walthers Web site at
www.walthers.com

MONROE MODELS

NEW PRODUCT
Bridge

Branch Line Trestle
NEW 493-9008 29.95
10 x 1-1/16 x 2-1/8" 25.4 x 2.7 x 5.4cm
Underpass opening:
1-15/16 x 2-3/16" 4.9 x 5.6cm

Kit features laser-cut basswood, plywood parts and includes cast-metal girders and warning signs.

BUSINESSES

Jurgens Junk Yard
493-9204 29.95
3-1/2 x 2-1/2 x 1-3/4" 8.9 x 6.3 x 4.4cm

Kit features laser-cut wood corrugated siding, white metal detail parts, resin junk pile, fencing and vintage signs.

BRIDGES

Bridge kits #9001 and 9002 contain unpainted parts made of high-density gypsum; kits #9003 and 9004 contain six to ten lead-free white metal castings, plus parts made of high-density gypsum. Some kits also include printed signs for the roadway underpasses where applicable.

Stone Arch Bridge
493-9001 19.99

Concrete Bridge
493-9002 19.99

Art Deco Bridge
493-9003 Double Track 26.95

Trestle & Girder Bridge
493-9004 24.95

Concrete & Girder Bridge
493-9005 23.99
1-7/8 x 6" 4.8 x 15.2cm

Modular design; easily expanded from single to double or triple track with expansion kit #493-9006 (sold separately). Includes two abutments, four girders and four wingwalls. Spans 36 scale feet.

Expansion Bridge Kit
493-9006 10.99
Includes four girders and two abutments. Use to expand Concrete and Girder Bridge #493-9005 (sold separately).

Country Road Bridge
493-9007 29.95
9-1/4 x 2 x 2-1/4"
23.5 x 5 x 5.7cm

All parts made of laser-cut wood with easy to follow photo instructions.

TRACKSIDE STRUCTURES

Trackside Freight House
493-9201 29.95
4-1/2 x 2-1/4 x 1-1/2"
11.4 x 5.7 x 3.8cm

Features laser-cut wood walls, tab and slot construction, corrugated metal roofing, vintage signs, 10 white metal shed doors with number decals, two empty pallets and two pallets with loads.

Trackside Freight House w/Dock
493-9202 25.95
2-15/16 x 1-13/16 x 1-13/16"
7.5 x 4.4 x 4.4cm

Precision tab and slot wood walls, simulated tar paper roof, white metal details, vintage signs and a laser-cut wood loading dock with ramp.

Railroad Loading Dock
493-9203 pkg(2) 10.49
3-1/2 x 3/4 x 3/8"
8.9 x 1.9 x 1.3cm
Laser-cut wood kit builds two pier-style railroad loading docks.

Information STATION

Oil Dealer Freight Traffic

Small-town oil dealers and distributors supplied heating oil for residential use, gasoline for local dealerships, kerosene, diesel fuel and other bulk petroleum. Bulk liquid products arriving in tank cars were stored in tanks on the property. Underground piping led to a pumphouse that supplied delivery truck loading booms.

Many dealers also handled lubricants for industrial machinery, as well as motor oils. These materials arrived in box cars, usually in large metal drums or as cases of cans. Lubricants are stored in an on-site warehouse.

Small oil dealer/distributors are a great source of traffic for your railroad. In your operating scheme, way freights will typically deliver a loaded car one day and pick up the empty on the next. Smaller dealers might only receive a couple of cars per week. In the steam and classic diesel eras, an occasional box car of lubricants can also be spotted next to the warehouse for unloading, which might take a couple of days (or operating cycles).

STRUCTURES N SCALE

Period Miniatures

Expand your traffic on your pike with these commercial buildings. All kits are easy to build and are resin, unless noted. A typical structure has three or four major parts, which you just glue together and personalize with paint.

Stan's Hardware Supply
555-206   29.95
Wood kit.

Brick Two-Stall Engine House
555-518   52.95

Merchant's Row
555-535   42.95

Steel Water Tank
555-408   11.95
2 x 2"   5.1 x 5.1cm

Reggie's Veggies
555-421   14.95
This farmer's market features an old refrigerator car, loading dock and shed.

Mel's Produce
555-204   29.95
2-3/4 x 3"   6.8 x 7.5cm
Wood kit.

Storage Tank Facility
555-402   14.95

Purina Chow Loader
555-425   18.95

Weston's Warehouse
555-426   14.95
3/4 x 3-1/2"   1.9 x 8.9cm

40' Concrete Loading Dock w/Ramp
555-430   7.95

Automobile Junk Yard
555-803   12.95

Broken Back Mine
555-829   16.95

Old Freight Depot
555-205   29.95
1-3/4 x 3-3/4"   4.5 x 9.5cm

Track Gang Baggage House
555-405   13.95
3 x 6"   7.5 x 15.2cm
A retired baggage car, converted to a storage shed.

Trackside Shanties
555-406 pkg(6) 11.95
Set of six different buildings.

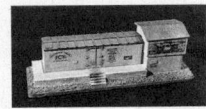

Meltnick's Ice Station
555-407   16.95
Many old reefers were converted to small ice storage sheds. Kit includes reefer body, loading dock and storage building.

Steel Tanks
555-459 pkg(6) 14.95
Great for almost any industry, realistic rivet detail.
Three large tanks: 1-1/2 x 3/4"   3.8 x 1.9cm; three small tanks: 1 x 1"   2.5 x 2.5cm.

Industrial Warehouse
555-207   34.95
Wood kit.

1880 Union Hotel
555-201   34.95
3-1/4 x 5"   8.2 x 12.5cm
Wood kit.

Branchline Water Tank
555-427   14.95
2 x 2"   5.1 x 5.1cm

Country Garage
555-445   16.95

Halloway's Plumbing Supply
555-447   19.95

Berghoff Brewery
555-203   34.95
3-1/2 x 6"   9 x 15.3cm

40' Wooden Loading Dock w/Ramp
555-431   6.95

J.E. Works' Gravel Yard
555-433   19.95

Triangle Corner Drug Store
555-441   19.95

McHugh's Hardware Store
555-450   19.95

STRUCTURES N SCALE

Period Miniatures

Dixie's Diner
555-442 11.95
2 x 4-1/4" 5.1 x 10.8cm

Yard Master's Office
555-429 TBA
Base approximately 1" x 3"
2.5 x 7.5cm
This old caboose has reached the end of the line, but it's still in service as an office building. Kit includes resin base, plastic caboose body, cast metal details and instructions.

Victoria Falls Hotel
555-514 42.95

Engine Crew Shed
555-428 16.95

Birthplace Of Model Railroader
555-544 19.95

Combination Town Depot
555-202 34.95
2-3/8 x 9" 6 x 23cm
Wood kit includes milk can and barrels.

Maple Valley Coal & Ice
555-443 16.95
3 x 6" 7.5 x 15.2cm

Tickner's Watch Works
555-526 31.95

Structure Detail Sets
555-701 Union Hotel 8.95
555-702 Combination Station 12.95
555-703 Berghoff Brewery 10.95
555-704 Mel's Produce 10.95
555-705 Old Freight Depot 8.95
555-706 Stan's Hardware Supply 8.95
555-707 Industrial Warehouse #1 8.95
555-708 Bachmann Coaling Station 10.95
555-709 Bachmann Coaling & Sandhouse Complex 12.95
555-710 Martha's Country Market 8.95
555-712 Toadsuck Canning Company 19.95
555-718 Brick 2-Stall Engine House 15.95
555-744 Bachmann's Sears House Exterior 10.95
555-745 Country Garage 10.95
555-750 McHugh's Hardware Store 12.95

Period Miniatures Catalog #10
555-9999 TBA

Pikestuff
Division of Rix Products

These craft train kits feature molded plastic parts with separate doors and windows. Easily kitbashed or combined with more kits to build a larger structure. Measurements are N Scale feet.

Yard Office
541-8001 Blue 10.95
30 x 40'

Small Engine House
541-8002 Blue 13.95
30 x 60'

Pre-Fabricated Warehouse
541-8003 Blue 15.95
30 x 80'

Truck Terminal
541-8004 Blue 17.95
30 x 80'

Multi-Purpose Building
541-8005 Blue 13.95
40 x 60'

Contractors Building
541-8006 Blue 14.95
40 x 60'

Two-Stall Enginehouse
541-8007 Blue 17.95
40 x 80'

Atkinson Engine Facility
541-8008 Blue 21.95
40 x 80'

Fire Station
541-8009 Blue 13.95
50 x 40'

Two-Story Modern Office Building
541-8010 Blue 13.95
50 x 40'

Diamond Tool & Engine Building
541-8011 Blue 14.95
60 x 40'

Distribution Center
541-8012 Blue 15.95
70 x 40'

Tri-Star Industries
541-8013 Blue 17.95
70 x 60'

The Shops
541-8014 Blue 22.95
70 x 80'

U&K Plastics
541-8015 Blue 22.95
70 x 100'

Milton A. Corporation
541-8016 Blue 34.95
80 x 130'

Office & Warehouse
541-8017 Blue 13.95
30 x 60'

For Up-To-Date Information and News Bookmark Walthers Web site at
www.walthers.com

STRUCTURES N SCALE

Rix Products

QUONSET HUT

628-710 11.95

GRAIN BINS
These popular storage bins can be found on farms, ranches, feedlots and alongside many grain elevators. Each easy-to-build kit consists of several bands (each made up of six segments) which are stacked to the desired height. Plastic parts are molded in a galvanized metal color. Each bin measures 24' diameter, with door and peaked roof.

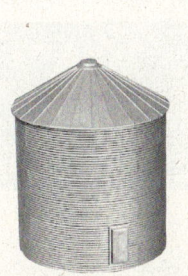
628-703   628-704

30' Corrugated Grain Bin
628-703 9.95

40' Corrugated Grain Bin
628-704 13.95

Grain Bin Extension
628-705 3.49
Three additional bands to extend #703 or 704 up to 11 scale feet.

30° Peaked Grain Bin Roof
628-706 2.49

Guthrie Grain Elevator
628-707 11.95
Comes equipped with ladders, platforms and distribution box; and can be built up in increments of 30 feet. The color matches galvanized steel.

Guthrie Grain Set
628-708 23.95
Includes a 60' tall grain elevator, two 30' tall grain bins and grain chute tubes.

MODERN HIGHWAY OVERPASS
All parts are molded in realistic concrete color. Each overpass section is 25 scale feet wide. Modular design and interlocking parts make it easy to construct a longer overpass.

50' Deck w/Pier
628-162 11.95

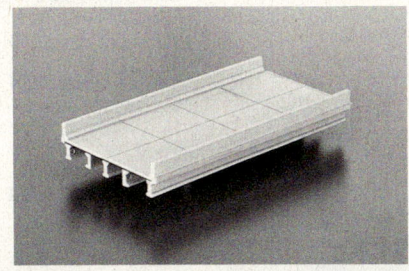
50' Deck Only
628-161 6.99

150' Deck w/4 Piers
628-163 34.95

1930s HIGHWAY OVERPASS
These kits model concrete overpasses, typical of those built in the 1930s and 1940s, which are still in use today.

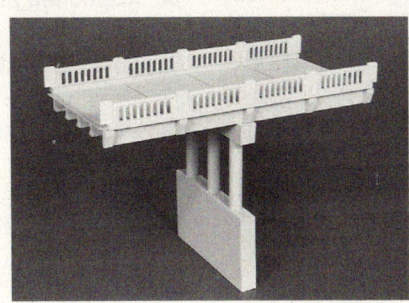
50' Deck w/Pier
628-152 11.95

50' Deck Only
628-151 6.99

150' Deck w/4 Piers
628-153 34.95

OVERPASS PARTS
Ideal for kitbashing or scratchbuilding, the following are 50' sections to match those used in the overpass kits.

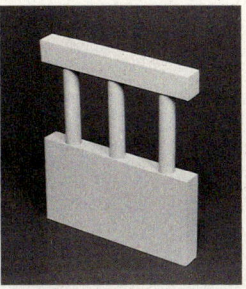

Modern Highway Pier
628-150 4.99

1930s Railing
628-154 pkg(4) 4.99

Beams
628-155 pkg(10) 4.99

Roadway
628-156 pkg(4) 4.99

Modern Railings
628-164 pkg(4) 4.99

SUNRISE ENTERPRISES

These structures are laser-cut wood buildings, which are assembled, painted and decorated.

Rural House
695-NB01 49.95

Casper's Electric
695-NB02 49.95

STRUCTURES N SCALE

These laser-engraved wood kits feature great attention to detail to give the appearance of a well-built structure.

Goodnite Moon Motel
654-122   39.95
Motel Office 1-1/4 x 3/4"
3.1 x 1.9cm
Guest Complex 1-3/4 x 3"
3.1 x 7.6cm

This roadside respite resembles many of the motels commonly found across America. The kit consists of two structures – a motel office and 4-room guest complex. It includes the road sign, signage graphics decal, shrubs, brick planter, ice machine and cola vending machine – all that you need to create a complete scene.

99 Desert Café
654-123   34.95
1 x 3"   2.5 x 7.6cm

A favorite stop of regulars and the local railroad crew, the 99 Desert Café features distinctive mission revival/art deco-style architecture. This kit features ice cube style bricks to enhance interior lighting, a swamp cooler and attached utility shed. Building signage decal graphics and numerous fine details are included. It's ideal for southwestern scenes.

The Black Butte
654-119   29.95
1-1/2 x 2"   3.8 x 5.1cm

This small train order office/depot is perfect for any trackside scene. The structure also makes a great office/security headquarters for your large industrial complexes.

Deloney's Barn
654-115   44.95
A perfectly weathered exterior makes this a great kit for people who want a rustic look to their layout.

Section Foreman's House
654-118   44.95
3-3/8 x 1-7/8" 8.6 x 4.8cm

At one time, railroads supplied housing for section foremen, signal maintainers and other important field personnel. This detailed model is based on a mission revival style home typical of those in the southwestern U.S.

The Kickin' Donkey
654-120   29.95
7/8 x 2-1/8" 2.2 x 5.4cm

Add a little bit of the "Old West" to your layout. Many hard-working men have awakened the morning after patronizing this period saloon only to find out how it got its name. The model features a realistic false front, wood siding and a plank sidewalk.

Radio Transmission Tower
654-111   19.95
Typical of modern radio towers seen everywhere, this etched brass tower includes two antennas.

Get Your Daily Dose of Product News at
www.walthers.com

Craft Train Kits are composed of unpainted cast metal parts.

Fuel Column
683-1100   4.95

Water Column
683-1101   4.95

Sand Tower
683-1102   5.95

Sand Tower, Fuel & Water Column
683-1103   12.95
Sand Tower: 3/8 x 1-1/4"
Fuel Column: 5-1/16 x 3/4"
Water Column: 5-1/16 x 1/2"

Car Washer Kits
683-1105 Four Brush 9.95
1/2 x 1/2" on both sides of track.

Oil Storage Tank & Pumping House
683-1107   12.95
1-3/8 x 2"

Double Track Diesel Sanding Tower
683-1114   6.95

Double Track Diesel Service Facility
683-1115   18.95
One sand, two fuel and three water facilities.

Trackside Shanty
683-1116   5.95

Yard Diesel Maintenance Facility
683-1211   31.95
Includes Inspection Pit, Oil Storage Tank and Pumphouse, Heavy-Duty Steam Cleaner and I-Beam Crane Hoist.

Portable Heavy-Duty Steam Cleaner
683-1212   5.95

60' Inspection Pit
683-1213   9.95

"I" Beam Crane Hoist
683-1214   6.95

Refinery Type Pressure Tank
683-1216   5.95

Diesel Oil Storage Tank
683-1218   6.95

Vertical Storage Tank
683-1219   5.95

VOLLMER

IMPORTED FROM GERMANY BY WALTHERS
These easy-to-build structures feature injection molded, styrene parts. Parts are molded in color, so no painting is needed. For easier assembly, all parts are numbered and coordinate with the instruction sheets. Construction time varies with size of the kit.

NEW PRODUCTS
Structures

Eichenreid Station
NEW 770-7515   35.99
6-7/8 x 2-9/16 x 4-1/2"   17.5 x 6.5 x 11.5cm

Shanty
NEW 770-7560   26.99
3-11/32 x 2-9/16 x 1-1/2" 8.5 x 6.5 x 3.8cm

A perfect addition to any any scene, it can be used as a maintenance shack, utility shed and more.

House w/Stork's Nest
NEW 770-7643   33.90
3-7/32 x 2-9/16 x 4-1/8"
8.2 x 6.5 x 10.5cm

House
NEW 770-7644   29.99
3-7/32 x 2-9/16 x 4-1/8"
8.2 x 6.5 x 10.5cm

Station "Neustadt"
770-7510   35.99
7-5/16 x 3-13/64 x 2"
18.3 x 8 x 5cm

Boat Rental "Max Ziegler"
770-7744   26.99
4-5/64 x 2-7/8 x 1-27/64"
10.2 x 7.2 x 4.6cm

STRUCTURES N SCALE

VOLLMER
IMPORTED FROM GERMANY BY WALTHERS

Grain Mill
770-7750 48.99
5-5/8 x 4-13/16 x 4-13/32"
14 x 12 x 11cm

House "Edelweiss" w/Car Port
770-7754 31.99
3-5/8 x 3 x 2" 9 x 7.5 x 5cm

Police Station
770-7779 30.99
3 x 3 x 1-13/16"
7.5 x 7.5 x 4.5cm

Fire Station
770-7785 31.99
4 x 3-5/8 x 2-13/32"
10 x 9 x 6cm

Stable
770-7716 17.99

Auto Repair Shop
770-7555 25.99
3-3/8 x 2-1/8 x 1-5/16"
8.5 x 5.3 x 3.3cm

"Rebmann" Winery
770-7685 35.99
5-13/16 x 4-3/16 x 3-7/16"
14.5 x 10.5 x 8.6cm

Shepherd's Carriage w/Sheep
770-7717 17.99
5-13/16 x 4-3/16 x 3-7/16"
14.5 x 10.5 x 8.6cm

Engine Repair Platform
770-7548 7.99
2-5/8 x 5/8 x 1"
6.5 x 1.6 x 2.4cm

Coaling Station w/Crane
770-7549 28.99
3-3/16 x 1-7/8 x 2-3/8"
8 x 4.7 x 6cm

Country Inn w/Beergarden
770-7698 47.99

Contractor's Yard
770-7915 60.99

Signal Box Nurnberg
770-7601 28.99
3-1/4 x 1-1/4 x 3-1/16"
8.1 x 3.1 x 7.7cm

Butcher's Shop
770-7656 35.99
3-3/16 x 2-5/8 x 4-13/16"
8 x 6.6 x 12cm

Wine Tavern
770-7657 35.99
3-3/16 x 2-5/8 x 4-13/16"
8 x 6.6 x 12cm

Drug Store
770-7658 35.99
3-3/16 x 2-5/8 x 4-13/16"
8 x 6.6 x 12cm

Country Inn, Restaurant w/Patio
770-7747 34.99
5-5/8 x 3-13/32 x 2-13/32" 14 x 8.5 x 6cm

Main Street Buildings
770-7659 136.99
Includes one each #'s 7655, 7656, 7657 & 7658.

Corner Building/Shop
770-7655 41.99
3-7/8 x 3-7/8 x 4-7/8" 9.7 x 9.7 x 12.2cm

Village Fire Station
770-7781 48.99

Farmhouse w/Barn
770-7715 45.99

273

STRUCTURES N SCALE

VOLLMER
IMPORTED FROM GERMANY BY WALTHERS

Police Station w/3-Stall Garage
770-7776 42.99

Round Water Tower
770-7546 41.99
Diameter: 3-1/8" 7.8cm
Height: 6-5/8" 16.5cm

Spherical Gas Tank
770-7547 27.99
Diameter: 3" 7.5cm
Height: 3-13/32" 8.5cm

Neuffen Passenger Station
770-7522 78.99
10-5/8 x 4" 27 x 10cm

City Station "Altstadt"
770-7506 63.99
13-1/8 x 4-1/2 x 5-1/2"
33 x 11.5 x 13.5cm

Station Platform
770-7503 13.99
18-1/8 x 5/8" 46 x 1.5cm

Freight Platform
770-7541 24.99
6-1/8 x 5" 15.3 x 12.5cm

Main Railroad Station: Baden-Baden, Germany
770-7505 107.99
20-1/2 x 4-1/2 x 5-1/2"
51 x 11.5 x 13.5cm

Farm Yard w/House & Barn
770-7714 89.99

Baden Station Platform
770-7501 58.99
31-27/32 x 1-5/8 x 1-5/8"
79.6 x 4 x 4cm

Karlsbad Steam-Era Station Platform Hall
770-7531 53.99
18-13/16 x 3-3/4 x 2-5/8"
47 x 9.3 x 7cm

Overhead Crane
770-7901 23.99

Market Street House
770-7630 45.99
4 x 4 x 4-5/16"
10.2 x 10.2 x 10.8cm

Barn
770-7707 31.99
3-7/8 x 2-15/16" 9.8 x 7.5cm

Farmyard Accessories
770-7708 16.99

Alpine Restaurant
770-7742 50.99
4-1/2 x 3-3/4 x 3-1/8"
11.5 x 9.5 x 8cm

Alpine Lodge
770-7743 21.99
2 x 2-11/16" 5 x 6.8cm

Market Street Value Set
770-7634 105.99
Includes one each #7630, 7632 and 7633.

A Walthers U.S. Exclusive
Vampire Villa Haunted Mansion w/Flickering Light
770-7679 58.99
5 x 4 x 4-3/4" 12.5 x 10 x 11.8cm

So realistic, it's downright scary! Creepy old house is complete with blinking red lights. And for more fun, add a Smoke Generator (#770-4113 or 4114) and Smoke Fluid (#770-4115), all sold separately, to create an eerie fog in or around the finished model.

Viaduct
770-7318 44.99
17-3/5 x 1-1/5 x 4-3/4" 44 x 3.3 x 11.8cm

Half-Timbered House
770-7730 35.99
3-7/8 x 2-5/8" 9.8 x 6.8cm

Highland Station Platform
770-7528 15.99
13-3/8 x 1" 34 x 2.5cm

STRUCTURES N SCALE

VOLLMER
IMPORTED FROM GERMANY BY WALTHERS

Freight Station
770-7540 49.99
9-1/4 x 3-3/4" 23.5 x 9.5cm

"Waldbronn" Station
770-7523 65.99
8-5/8 x 4-3/4" 22 x 12cm

Hunting Tower
770-7749 12.99
13/16 x 1-3/8 x 2-1/2"
2 x 3.4 x 6.6cm

Small Covered Platform For ICE Trains
770-7524 27.99
6-3/8 x 1-3/4" 16 x 4.5cm

Double Track Engine Shed
770-7608 53.99
7-1/2 x 4-5/8 x 3-1/8"
18.7 x 11.6 x 7.6cm

KOF Engine Shed
770-7610 21.99
2-3/4 x 1-1/2" 6.7 x 4 x 4.2cm

Signal Tower
770-7600 21.99
2-3/8 x 1-3/8" 6 x 3.5cm

Mountain Cabin
770-7746 24.99
3-3/4 x 3-1/2" 9.5 x 9cm

Ranch House
770-7718 25.99
4-3/8 x 4-1/8" 11 x 10.5cm

Double Track Switch Tower
770-7603 41.99
8 x 2-1/2" 20 x 6cm

Container Crane
770-7905 28.99
6-1/2 x 2-1/2 x 3-1/8"
16.5 x 6.3 x 8cm

Cinder Conveyor
770-7551 26.99
1-3/8 x 1" 3.5 x 2.5cm

Country Chalet
770-7745 35.99
4-7/8 x 4-1/4 x 2-3/4"
12.5 x 11 x 7cm

Sand Tower
770-7550 30.99
2 x 1-9/16" 4.1 x 8.5cm

Post Office w/Bus Station
770-7724 41.99
6-1/4 x 4-1/2" 15.8 x 11.5cm

Fire Station
770-7780 78.99
9-5/8 x 3-5/8" 24.6 x 9.3cm

Circus Tent
770-7792 30.99
4-5/8 x 3-1/4 x 2"
12 x 8 x 5cm

Station Road Shops
770-7648 pkg(3) 102.99
Includes one each #7645, 7646 and 7647.

Freight Shed
770-7539 43.99
6-13/16 x 4 x 2-5/8" 17 x 10 x 7cm

Delicatessen w/Awnings
770-7672 60.99
3-13/16 x 3-11/16"
9.9 x 9.3cm

Trackside Details
770-7542 34.99
3-1/4 x 1-1/4" 8.2 x 3.3cm
Includes water spout, coal bin with small crane and clearance gauge.

3-Car Garage
770-7778 20.99
3 x 1-3/4" 7.5 x 4.5cm

Signal Box Brick
770-7604 39.99
3-1/2 x 1-3/4" 9 x 4.4cm

Bungalow
770-7700 16.99
2-1/2 x 1-1/2" 6.5 x 4cm

City House
770-7702 16.99
2-3/4 x 3" 7 x 7.5cm

275

STRUCTURES N SCALE

VOLLMER
IMPORTED FROM GERMANY BY WALTHERS

2-Story House
770-7701   16.99
2 x 2"   5 x 5cm

The Mayor's House
770-7753   33.99
3 x 2-7/8"   7.5 x 7.3cm

Cathedral
770-7760   103.99
8 x 4 x 10-1/2"
20 x 10 x 26cm

For extra realism, full-color stained glass "windows", printed on translucent paper, are included. For a slightly larger and more detailed scene, the Cathedral Steps (#770-7759), which measure 10-1/4 x 5-1/8", can be added.

Cathedral Foundation/ Steps
770-7759   21.99
10-1/4 x 5-1/8"   26 x 13cm

2-Story Parson's House
770-7732   35.99
3-7/8 x 2-5/8"   9.8 x 6.8cm

Guild House
770-7752   33.99
3 x 2-7/8"   7.5 x 7.3cm

Church
770-7704   28.99
4-1/8 x 2-1/8"   10.5 x 5.5cm

Church
770-7740   35.99
5-1/4 x 3"   13.5 x 7.5cm

Gift Store
770-7728   24.99
3-5/8 x 1-3/4"   9.2 x 4.3cm

Ditzingen Church
770-7736   60.99
6-1/4 x 3-13/16"   16 x 9.8cm

Beer Hall
770-7756   41.99
3-1/2 x 2-3/8"   9 x 6cm

Department Store
770-7751   28.99
3 x 2-7/8"   7.5 x 7.3cm

Get the Scoop!
Get the Skinny!
Get the Score!
Check Out Walthers Web site at
www.walthers.com

Box Girder Bridge
770-7801   28.99
8-7/8 x 1-5/8"   22.5 x 4cm

Moritzburg Station
770-7502   98.99
16-4/5 x 4-4/5 x 5-1/5"   42 x 12 x 12.8cm

Shoe Shop
770-7646   30.99
3-1/8 x 2-5/8 x 3-3/8"   7.8 x 6.5 x 8.4cm

Half-Timber Gasthaus Inn
770-7711   53.99
6-1/2 x 4-1/4"   16 x 10.6cm

Half-Timbered Inn
770-7731   35.99
3-1/4 x 2-7/8"   8.3 x 7.2cm

STRUCTURES N SCALE

VOLLMER
IMPORTED FROM GERMANY BY WALTHERS

Department Store
770-7726 28.99
4-3/8 x 1-3/4" 11 x 4.5cm

Coffee House
770-7650 49.99
3-13/16 x 2-1/8" 9.8 x 7.6cm

Truss Bridge
770-7800 22.99
5-7/8 x 1-7/8" 15 x 4cm

Liquor Store
770-7687 57.99
5-5/8 x 4" 14.4 x 10.2cm

Hotel
770-7652 49.99
3-5/16 x 3" 8.4 x 7.6cm

Village Inn
770-7772 40.99
3-1/2 x 2-7/8" 9 x 7.2cm

House Under Construction
770-7739 45.99
4 x 2-3/4" 10 x 7cm

Bank
770-7651 49.99
3-1/2 x 3" 8.8 x 7.6cm

Public Archives
770-7654 49.99
3-5/8 x 3-5/16" 9.2 x 8.4cm

Pizza Restaurant w/Terrace
770-7681 45.99
4-1/2 x 3-3/8" 11.3 x 8.5cm

Truss Bridge w/Arched Sides
770-7302 15.99
6-1/4 x 1-3/8" 16 x 3.5cm

Viaduct
770-7313 35.99
6-13/16 x 1-3/8 x 2-13/16"
17 x 3.4 x 7cm

Fire Station w/Hose Tower
770-7775 42.99
4-1/2 x 3-5/8" 11.6 x 9.3cm

770-7810   770-7820

Bridge Pier Kit
770-7810 7.99
1-3/4 x 3/4" 4.5 x 2cm

Abutment Kit
770-7820 12.99
1-1/4 x 2" 3.2 x 5cm

8" Bridge - Curved
770-7831 16.99
7-11/16" radius with two piers (5/8" high each) and two supports.

Village
770-7710 pkg(5) 69.99
Includes one each: #7700, 7701, 7702, 7703 and 7704.

Log Mountain Lodge
770-7741 28.99
6-11/16 x 4-1/8" 17 x 10.5cm

Super Market
770-7660 44.99
4-1/8 x 3-1/4" 10.7 x 8.3cm

Lamm Gasthaus Restaurant
770-7645 45.99
3-3/4 x 3-3/4 x 3-3/8"
9.5 x 9.5 x 8.4cm

House On Fire
770-7738 46.99
4 x 2-3/4" 9.8 x 6.8cm

For extra action, add a smoke generator (#770-4113 or 4114 sold separately), emergency vehicles, figures and other details.

Half-Timbered Ratskeller Inn
770-7712 49.99
5 x 3-7/8" 12.5 x 9.8cm

City Hall
770-7761 103.99
5-5/8 x 3-5/8" 14 x 9cm

Items listed below are available by Special Order (see Legend Page).

Boutique
770-7693 44.99
4-1/2 x 4-5/16" 11.3 x 11cm

Sawmill
770-7713 67.99

STRUCTURES N SCALE

MAGIC OF MODEL RAILROADING

Models and Photo by Jim Younkins, Olympia, Washington

Medium-sized towns like Mud Bay can be hotbeds of activity for the railroads serving them. Even for a road dedicated to serving the logging and lumber industry, there's enough traffic from other businesses to warrant a daily switch job. Back in the 70s, bulk grain was still shipped in 40' box cars; this load just in off the Milwaukee Road connection is being eased into place by a venerable VO-1000, a favorite of local railfans. This scene on the Mud Bay & Southern features structures from Walthers and Rix, kitbashed vehicles from GHQ, Athearn and Atlas and Signals from NJ International. The loco is by Atlas and the cars are by Walthers and Micro-Trains®.

The true magic of model railroading is that you can create a realistic-looking scene in a make-believe land or build an authentic replica of a past or present railroad. Although the yard depicted in this photo never existed, it seems very real. Dudley chose actual prototypes as the models for his structures, applied appropriate weathering and paid close attention to all the details, down to the weeds growing between the tracks.

Whether you model the glory days of steam, modern diesels or are CEO of your very own railroad, we invite you to share the scenes on your layout in next year's Magic of Model Railroading Photo Contest. Cash prizes are awarded for first, second and third places as well as honorable mentions.

Be sure to include a short typed or printed description of each photo and the names of the modeler and photographer. Print your name clearly on each slide, photo or CD you submit. Deadlines will be announced at walthers.com and in Walthers publications. Color slides, high-resolution electronic images or glossy color photos can be mailed to:

ATTN: SLIDES FOR CATALOG

C/O Wm. K. Walthers Inc.
PO Box 3039
Milwaukee, WI
53201-3039

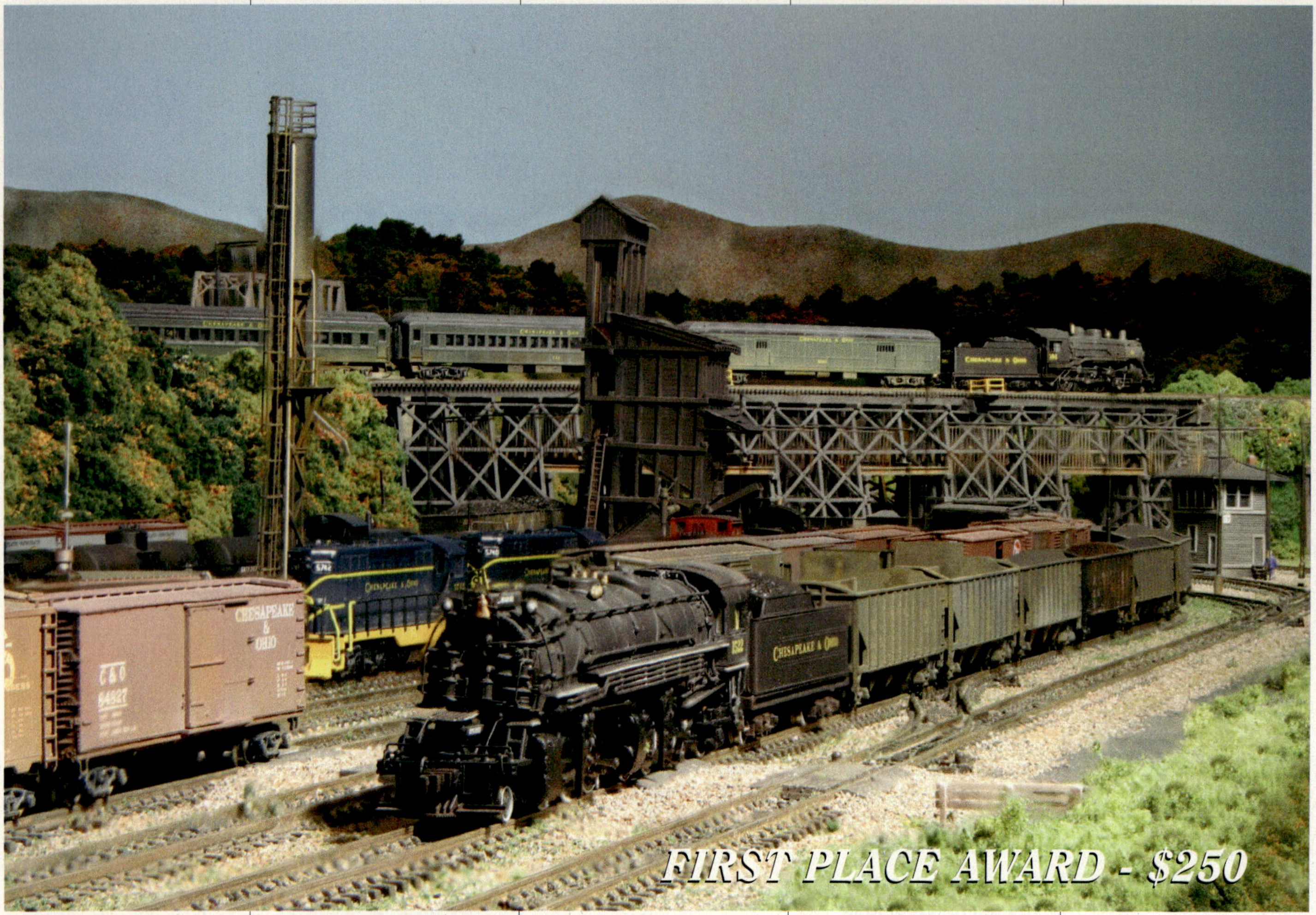

FIRST PLACE AWARD - $250

Models and Photo by Dudley Ross, Montgomery, Alabama

H-5 #1522 is leaving Charlestown Yard with a string of empty hoppers headed to the mines. While a mythical yard, Charlestown is full of scratch-built C&O structures. All of the structures except the coaling tower are constructed from C&O plans and photographs. The coaling tower is a model of the tower at Chama, New Mexico and is built of styrene from plans that appeared in two 1960 issues of Model Railroader magazine. The interlocking tower is the prototype for a kit offered by Showcase Miniatures. It was given to Dudley by Walter Vail, the man who designed and built the kit. The tower is a model of a C&O standard tower.

SECOND PLACE AWARD - $100

Models and Photo by Marc Pitanza, Old Bridge, New Jersey

An important part of the Baltimore & Ohio system's eastern end, the Staten Island Rapid Transit handled a great deal of traffic heading to New York City by carfloat, as well as on-line industries. The unique railroad also handled passengers as part of New York's subway system. In the 50s, the SIRT operated its network of freight lines with a small fleet of switchers like this Alco S-2 #488 trundling under Meredith Avenue in Chelsea, Staten Island with a cut of Western Maryland hoppers. The Travis branch was the most scenic of the Staten Island branches; it weaved its way through swampy land and remote industry to reach a few important customers. Marc Pitanza customized his Rivarossi locomotive with Microscale alphabet decals. The hopper cars are from Atlas.

THIRD PLACE AWARD - $75

Models and Photo by Lee Edgar, Wye Mills, Maryland

First you hear an airhorn, then another, the high-pitched thunder of diesels at speed, the pounding of wheels on rail joints jars you to the core as a silver-blue blur of stainless steel whooshes by, and suddenly there's silence, save for the occasional screech of a red-tailed hawk high overhead. Two "Zephyrs" just met at speed somewhere north of Onalaska, Wisconsin, on the Burlington's La Crosse Subdivision. Known for it's scenic beauty with tracks running at the base of high bluffs, this stretch of high iron was featured heavily in company passenger train ads.

Lee Edgar has captured the charm of this scenic, high speed mainline on his portable photo diorama. Lee built the scene with Woodland Scenics materials, the speeder shed is from Blair Line and the trackside details are from Period Miniatures. The locos and cars are by Kato.

281

Models and Photo by Jim Berling, University Place, Washington

The rumbling of EMD 645s and GE FDLs at full throttle reverberates off the canyon walls as an SP auto rack train grinds its way upgrade. The reverberation is one reason why SP's Cascade Line passes through snowsheds along the route. In the winter, snow and steep hillsides conspire to send avalanches roaring down the cliffs and onto the mainline. The spring thaw and summer rains have their own set of problems — mud and rock slides. Today, trains have an easy trip ahead, but wait until the snows come! Snowsheds are just one unique feature of Jim Berling's Cascade Line. The sheds are scratchbuilt, the locos are Intermountain and Kato and cars are from Con-Cor and Athearn.

Models and Photo by Charles Devine, Philadelphia, Pennsylvania

It's a sunny Friday afternoon as Reading GP7 #625 leads a northbound freight from Newberry Junction into St. Anne's, Pennsylvania, with local and interchange traffic. The RDG has haulage rights on the Tioga & Great Lakes' Williamsport secondary track as far north as this central Pennsylvania town. The loco is a repainted Atlas Classic, the cars are from Micro-Trains, with a homemade load of telephone poles in the gondola directly behind the loco.

Models and Photo by Marc Pitanza, Old Bridge, New Jersey

A Staten Island Rapid Transit Alco S-2 thunders across Neck Creek in Travis, Staten Island. The loaded hoppers are heading towards the Con Ed power plant with a fresh delivery of coal. This is just one of many coal trains that arrive each day to keep the power plant operating and the lights on in New York City. The Alco is a Rivarossi model and the hoppers are from Atlas. The wood pine trestle model is from Blair Line.

Models and Photo by Richard Bailey, Cartersville, Georgia

There's never a dull day at the St. Jude yards. The sun has barely risen above the horizon when this big diesel pulls out with its consist to begin a long journey north. In another hour or so the gravel-filled ore cars will be picked up and taken to their final destination. The track is Kato Unitrack and the locomotive is also by Kato. Rolling stock is from Micro-Trains, Atlas, Bachmann and others. Scenery is by Woodland Scenics and the telephone/telegraph poles are Bachmann. The gravel loads in the ore cars are ballast glued in with watered-down Elmer's white glue.

283

Scenery by Ron Freeman. Models and Photo by Mike Reardon and B.J. Davis, Elk Grove, Illinois

It's such a busy day with today's run-through power on the tracks behind the Republic Steel Mill that it's difficult to know whose railroad we're watching. The Amtrak Lake Shore Limited has been rerouted as it passes the CP Autorack train and BNSF grain train. Two Bluebird lease locomotives are waiting to be added as helper units to the grain train while a CP-acquired UP SD40-2 is switching at the mill. This action-packed scene was shot on the Midwest N Pioneer Model Railroad Club layout near Chicago, Illinois.

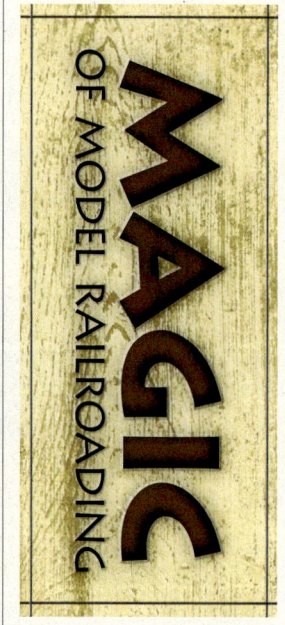

Models and Photo by Lee Edgar, Wye Mills, Maryland

Premier streamliners meet "Where nature smiles for 300 miles," along the mighty Mississippi. High-speed high-iron gives the diesels on the head end a place to reach full gallop as the "Empire Builder" and a detouring "Olympian Hiawatha" zip by one another in a blur of orange, Pullman Green and maroon. The high speed meet takes place on Lee's photo diorama. The stunning scenery is a mix of natural materials and Woodland Scenics products. Track is from Atlas and the cars from Bachmann and brass imports.

MAGIC OF MODEL RAILROADING

Models and Photo by Bernard Kempinski, Alexandria, Virginia

With a blast on the airhorn and a loud rumble, a C&O mail train bolts out of Brookville tunnel. On this hilly line over the Virginia Blue Ridge you can hear trains coming for miles before they actually appear, and this mail train was no exception — that is until just before it entered the other portal of the bore. For a few minutes all was quiet, and then the shiny E8 burst into daylight. This hilly line is part of Bernard's N Trak module group. The locomotive is by Life-Like and the cars are Con-Cor.

Models and Photo by Charles Devine, Philadelphia, Pennsylvania

Blasting out of the eastern portal of the Green Mountain tunnel, a pair of Tioga & Great Lakes' GP7s send out a deafening roar that reaches all the way to the top of the Mountain. They're about to lead an eastbound freight across the diamond crossing with the Pennsylvania Railroad. The consist of Micro-Trains cars is pulled by two Atlas Classic GP7s that Charles painted for his freelance road. The scenery is a combination of Woodland Scenics and natural materials.

285

Models and Photo by Richard Bailey, Cartersville, Georgia

This small industrial area is strategically located halfway between St. Jude and Trackmore. It's easily reachable by workers from both towns and is a hub of activity during the week. Today, two locomotives have just pulled in with consists to unload before going the rest of the way to their respective destinations. It's just another busy day on Richard Bailey's St. Jude and Trackmore layout. The F3 unit is from Kato and the GP unit is Atlas. The track is also from Atlas and the scenery is from Woodland Scenics. The structures are a combination of DPM and scratch-built buildings.

Models and Photo by Jim Younkins, Olympia, Washington

Even though the Mud Bay & Southern is mainly a logging road serving a few industries, its daily roadfreight runs over a twisting line with steep grades requiring locos with plenty of traction. EMD's SD35 was an ideal choice for this line, so when one came up on the used loco market, the MB&S snapped it up. Today, #2525 heads the afternoon train of loaded lumber flats and box cars over to the connection with the BN. Jim scratchbuilt the wooden bridge, the loco is by Atlas and the car is from Micro-Trains.

Scenery by members of the Midwest N Pioneer MRRC, Models and Photo by Ryan Schmitz, Lodi Wisconsin and Mike Reardon, Addison, Illinois

The flags are flying as this Union Pacific coal drag pounds the high iron with a set of newly delivered coalporters. The train is on its way east with a load of black diamonds from the Power River Basin. It is passing through hilly countryside as evidenced by the far embankment. UP started displaying the flag on their new locomotives in 2002 as part of their new "Building America" campaign. This scene is just a small portion of the Midwest N Pioneer Model Railroad Club layout that is currently in storage while awaiting a new home.

Models and Photo by Marc Pitanza, Old Bridge, New Jersey

A cut of cars remain on the North Shore subdivision mainline as Staten Island Rapid Transit S-2 pulls a single box car out of the Wallerstein Corporation siding. The car was dropped off yesterday loaded with sacks of barley hops. The Roadway truck driver has stepped out of his cab to wave at the engineer. As soon as the train has passed, the truck will be able to maneuver into loading bay 2 to pick up a load of hops for the local brewery. Wallerstein is a major distributor in the area transferring tons of goods from train to truck and vice versa. The cars are from Micro-Trains and the loco is a custom-decorated Rivarossi model. The Wallerstein building is a Walthers kit, the truck is from Classic Metal Works and the figures are by Preiser.

MAGIC OF MODEL RAILROADING

Models by Tim Wickerham and Dennis Pehoski, Photo by Tim Wickerham, Milwaukee, Wisconsin

Talk about a success story! When the Soo Line sold off its original mainlines between Duluth, Sault Ste. Marie, St. Paul and Chicago, newcomer Wisconsin Central stepped in and more than tripled traffic. By the mid 90s, even its local freights rated road power and sometimes ran with over 50 cars — a far cry from the single GP7 and a dozen cars in the Soo era. This wayfreight, led by GP40 #3026, a unit commemorating Wisconsin's sesquicentennial, scurries through the state's northern forests south of Superior. Today's consist includes a custom decorated Atlas loco and cars from Atlas, Precision Masters, Delaware Valley and Roundhouse. Vehicles in this diorama scene are from Atlas and Athearn and scenery is made from Woodland Scenics products.

Models and Photo by Dudley Ross, Montgomery, Alabama

Deep in the heart of coal country, yards send out "mine shifters" every day. Several of these runs leave the yard daily, each toting a string of empties up a branch to a mine. Now, these are no three-car locals! It takes muscle to handle trains on the steep twisting lines up the hollers to the coal tipples. On the C&O, these important trains rated H-5 Class 2-6-6-2 locomotives whose articulated drivers gave excellent traction on tight curves. Today's run is behind a mighty H-5 — a fine offering of Broadway Limited Import and Rivarossi. The woodland surrounding adds to the charming scene. Other rolling stock is by Roundhouse, Mantua Metal Works, Athearn and Wiking. The structures are Model Power and Micro-Engineering.

Models and Photo by Charles Devine, Philadelphia, Pennsylvania

Reading GP7 #625 spots a hopper of "Famous Reading Anthracite" coal at the George F. Burnwell Fuel Company's dump track in St. Anne's, Pennsylvania. Over the next few weeks, the fuel company will be delivering truckloads of coal to local businesses and residents to fill up their bins. They'll need plenty of coal to stay warm throughout the long cold Pennsylvania winter. The loco is an Atlas Classic painted and decorated for the RDG as is the Micro-Trains hopper that sports Microscale decals. The buildings are from DPM and Heljan.

Models by Ron Freeman, Photo by Mike Reardon, Addison, Illinois

Wherever there's a large rail-served manufacturing plant there's a yard dedicated to serving it. Conrail's ADM yard is no exception; it's assigned switcher shuffles back and forth through a sea of corn syrup tank cars, readying them for loading or transfer to roadfreights. This yard was on the Midwest N Pioneer layout in Chicago.

Scenery by Mike Gazda, Models and Photo by Ryan Schmitz and B.J. Davis, Elk Grove, Illinois

Amtrak P42s pull the Lake Shore Limited towards the tunnel on the water level route. The smoke stain above the portal entrance shows evidence of a past era when steam engines plied the high iron. Nowadays diesel-powered locos roar through the tunnel several times a day. The scene was shot on Midwest N Pioneer Model Railroad Club's Western Division.

Models and Photo by Marc Pianza, Old Bridge, New Jersey

Staten Island Rapid Transit #488 is pulling a Lehigh Valley gondola through Elm Park in Staten Island. The gondola, loaded with telephone poles, is heading for a siding at Wentworth Avenue on the South Beach Branch. A hurricane in the summer of 1953 knocked out many of the telephone poles on Staten Island's eastern shore. This is a priority shipment for the island. As soon as it arrives, dozens of Con Ed workers will be working overtime to put up the poles and restore phone service to all of the residents. The car is from Micro-Trains.

Models and Photo by Eric Meyer, West Bend, Wisconsin

The Western Pacific served a number of smaller northern California towns. Typically, its tracks skirted the edges of business districts that grew up around the train station. In the 60s, it was common for the afternoon local to be led by a colorful pair of EMD switchers tugging on cars bound for local businesses. This workaday scene is on one of Eric's N Trak modules. He created it with Design Preservation Models and City Classics structures detailed with Bar Mills and other signs and vehicles from Classic Metal Works and Wiking. A pair of customized Life-Like PROTO N locos are toting Walthers, Micro-Trains and Atlas freight cars.

MAGIC OF MODEL RAILROADING

Models and Photo by Jim Younkins, Olympia, Washington

As logging lines retrenched or abandoned their operations in the 50s and 60s, quite a few locos were available to the highest bidder. Even though Weyerhaeuser operated steam over many of its lines, it had a sizeable fleet of Fairbanks-Morse switchers. As operations were reduced, many were sold off to other lines in the area; #45 was one example. Mud Bay Terminal simply painted the cab black and added its own lettering to the long hood — a quick and cheap conversion typical of a shortline! Ten years later, #45 is still kept busy shuttling cars in Mud Bay. This scene was captured on Jim Younkins' Mud Bay Southern. Jim scratchbuilt the oil distributor; the structure in the background is from Walthers. The loco is a heavily reworked Minitrix model and the cars are from Micro-Trains.

Models and Photo by Richard Bailey, Cartersville, Georgia

This railfan has found a perfect place for train watching – a waterside bench outside the old tire plant. Not only can he see the train, he gets a waterfront view. On today's agenda is taking a long look at an old GP unit as it rolls its consist around the bend at the edge of the Trackmore industrial complex. The engineer gives a wave as he passes by, making the railfan's day complete. The engine and track are both Atlas products. Rolling stock is Atlas and Micro-Trains. Figures are hand-painted Preiser and vehicles are Classic Metal Works, GHQ and Busch. The factory is a Kibri kit and the scenery is from Woodland Scenics.

Models and Photo by Lee Edgar, Wye Mills, Maryland

Controlled by the NP and GN, the Burlington Route gave its owners a fast route to Chicago and connections with eastern lines. While the route was revered by Zephyr passengers and "Q" fans, it was, and still is, a major freight artery. Long roadfreights carried cars from GN and NP lines to the Windy City. In the early 60s, this meant shiny red SD7s, SD9s and SD24s, plus "grayback" F7s like these skirting the shores of the Mississippi near East Winona. Lee built the scene using Woodland Scenics materials, cars are from Micro-Trains and locos are from several makers.

Models and Photo by Charles Devine, Philadelphia, Pennsylvania

A Pennsy SW9 pulls a cut of cars from the interchange track and across the diamond of the Tioga & Great Lakes crossing. In the distance we see a T&GL RS-1 working the Green Mountain Coal Company tipple. The large PRR depot behind the train is a reminder of the glory days of passenger rail travel that have since passed. The PRR loco is a stock Life-Like SW9 while the RS-1 is a repainted Atlas/Kato unit. The box cars are a combination of stock and repainted Micro-Trains cars. The depot is from Model Power and the tower is from Dimi Trains, both painted to resemble PRR structures. The vehicle is from Classic Metal Works. The two-lane road was made with HO Scale AMI Instant Roadbed painted with Polly Scale paints.

Models and photo by Dennis Pehoski, Milwaukee, Wisconsin

When railfans think of western Wisconsin, visions of the old CB&Q double-track mainline along the Mississippi river come to mind. On this line the Burlington's "Zephyrs" flew like the wind on a smooth, water-level route. By the 1990s, the "Zephyrs" had blown away and the "Q" had become part of the Burlington Northern. Freight was (and still is) the big business. Another change found Canadian National using the BN as a bridge line to connect its Duluth, Winnipeg & Pacific and Grand Trunk Western subsidiaries between Duluth and Chicago. This loaded potash train lumbering south shares the "Way of the Zephyrs" with a unit coal train north of La Crosse, Wisconsin. The locos are customized Kato units and the cars are from Atlas and CS Models.

Scenery by Phil Keller and Mike Reardon
Models and Photo by Ryan Schmitz and Mike Reardon, Addison, Illinois

The vehicles on the road are unaware of the heavy weight that is about to pass overhead as the CP Autorack train cruises past the outcropping and over the girder bridge above them. The first cars in the consist are the new high-capacity articulated version from Trailer Train. Today's train is employing a CEFX-leased AC4400 as the lead unit because CP is short of power while awaiting the delivery of new locomotives from GE. This photograph was taken on the Midwest N Pioneer Model Railroad Club layout.

Models and Photo by Bernard Kempinski, Alexandria, Virginia

Jake's Gas is a favorite hiding spot for the local police. The wooded area next to the station screens the police car from oncoming vehicles as they round the bend into town. The locals all know that if they take the downhill turn too fast, deputy Dan will be there to greet them and he's not very forgiving when it comes to giving out tickets. But on this sunny day in late June, Dan is more interested in out-of-towners. School's been out for a few weeks and vacationers have been tearing down the bend at high speeds. Some of them keep their speed up all the way through town, endangering the safety of the residents.

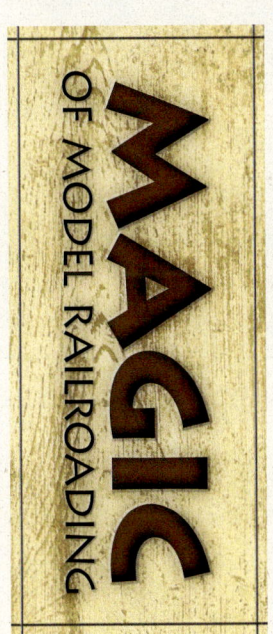

MAGIC OF MODEL RAILROADING

Models and Photo by Richard Bailey, Cartersville, Georgia

Some mornings you just have to have that second cup of coffee. After being held up in the yard, the mid-day freight is running late as it roars past the Trackmore Tire Plant. It's a good day for the Mustang though. Had the train been on time, the Mustang would have had to wait on the other side of the tracks before continuing on its journey home. Something is always happening on Richard Bailey's St. Jude and Trackmore layout. The SD45 locomotive and Unitrack are by Kato and the box car is from Micro-Trains. The Mustang is by Classic Metal Works. Scenery is from Woodland Scenics and the background is Walthers Instant Horizons.

Models and Photo by Dudley Ross, Montgomery, Alabama

Autumn is a beautiful time of year in Alleghany, Virginia. Rich hues of dark red, brilliant orange, deep burgundy and bright yellow cover the mountainside. The air is cool and dry and, with the kids back at school, the main action during the day is at the railyard. Alleghany is an important stop along the C&O. After negotiating their way along a steep grade to the top, it's here where eastbound coal trains set off some of their cars to lighten the load before beginning the long descent into Clifton Forge. Passenger trains heading west stop at the station then head down the other side of the mountain to the resort town of White Sulfur Springs. Dudley scratch-built all of the structures of basswood or styrene. The strung wires are by Berkshire Junction and the cross arms are from Depots by John.

295

Models by Mike Reardon and Fred Kaiser, Photo by Mike Reardon, Addison, Illinois

Container yards are incredibly important to modern railroads. Trains come and go 'round the clock, keeping cranes like this Mi-Jack busy. At the bustling yard on the Midwest N Pioneer railroad three trains are on the "ramp" tracks against a background of stacked containers waiting for shipment or loading. The Mi-Jack Crane is a Walthers model, well cars are from Walthers and containers are by Walthers, deLuxe Innovations and Con-Cor.

MAGIC OF MODEL RAILROADING

Models and Photo by Eric Meyer, West Bend, Wisconsin

Sunday, Sunday, Sunday at the motor speedway, watch the action as racers reach death-defying speeds up to 200 miles per hour! Colorful cars and fast action are the order of the day at the West Bend Speedway. Fans have filled the stands as the cars zoom past, all anxious to see who wins. The action is on Eric Meyer's N Trak module. Those racers are actually moving thanks to an ingenious magnetic drive system. The racers are modified Racing Champions cars and the vehicles in the pit are Wiking, Atlas and Busch.

Models and Photo by Jim Berling, University Place, Washington

Intermodal traffic is big business in the Pacific Northwest. In several places, containers are trucked from dockside to inland container yards like this. The crane driver has his work cut out for him today as he positions the boom to lift another container for placement in a well car. Jim Berling captured the action on his large Cascade Line layout. The containers are from Walthers and deLuxe Innovations, the trailers by Micro-Trains and Atlas and structures are by New Rail Models and Blair Line. Freight cars are by Micro-Trains and LBF.

Scenery and Models by Ron Freeman Photo by BJ Davis, Elk Grove, Illinois

The patrons at Lucy's Diner are getting an extra treat for free today. They're enjoying the spectacle of two trains passing simultaneously on either side of the building. There's even stereo sound when the RDC blows its horn and the light Mikado responds with its whistle. The RDC is heading for the street running down Main Street while the Mikado is pulling into the station with a local. Traffic is being alerted to all the action by the swinging wig-wag sign. BJ took this photo on the Midwest N Pioneer Model Railroad Club layout in Illinois.

Models and Photo by Charles Devine, Philadelphia, Pennsylvania

It's late afternoon and the sky is starting to look a little threatening. The brewing storm will soon arrive with its blowing winds and heavy rains. The car drivers wait anxiously for the Tioga & Great Lakes RS-1 to complete its task of pushing the tank car and box car onto Ajax Chemical's siding. Both drivers want to get home before the storm hits and the train crew is working fast so they can be back at the yard when the rain falls. The loco is a repainted Atlas/Kato unit pushing a deluxe Innovations tank car and a Micro-Trains box car. The chemical company is a combination of kit-bashed Model Power kits and scratch-built additions and details. The autos are from Classic Metal Works.

Models and Photo by Keith Kohlmann, Racine, Wisconsin

Back when every train had a caboose, a friendly wave from the conductor or rear brakeman could make a kid's day. Life was more relaxed, people were friendlier and the pace of railroading was a bit slower. Railroaders had assigned runs, and many even had assigned cabooses — and they all knew the kids and neighbors along their route. Chances are the hind-end crew in this wayfreight at Berryville, Wisconsin, recognizes the driver of the car stopped at the crossing. Keith Kohlmann took this image of his modified Micro-Trains caboose outdoors on a photo diorama. The vehicle is by Classic Metal Works and the crewmember is a modified Preiser figure.

Models by Ron Johns and Keith Lyons, Photo by Kirk Reddie, Seattle, Washington

"What ifs" are always fun to contemplate. The "North Coast Limited" was Northern Pacific's premier train between Chicago and the west coast. Equipped with dome cars so passengers could have a great view of the scenery along the Mississippi and in the mountains of the Northwest, the train reached Chicago over subsidiary CB&Q, and Portland, Oregon, over subsidiary Spokane, Portland & Seattle. CB&Q's fleet of "Zephyrs" featured Budd stainless steel cars with full skirting. Unlike its owners, the SP&S was fiercely devoted to Alco locomotives. So, what if the SP&S loco choices and the CB&Q carbuilder choices had affected the streamlined North Coast Limited. Would it have looked like this custom decorated streamliner (which is also patterned after a 60s-era American Flyer set)? Those Kato Alco PAs and Budd corrugated cars sure look good in two-tone green as they soar across this Micro-Engineering viaduct! Luckily, in model railroading it's easy to model "what ifs!"

MAGIC OF MODEL RAILROADING

Models and Photo by Gary Seymour, West Bend, Wisconsin

Keeping diesels ready for service is a big job. Fueling racks, inspection pads, sanding towers and associated structures are necessary to perform the job properly. The Great Northern was known for keeping its diesels in tip-top shape. Even smaller facilities like this could handle several locos at once and offered car repair shops as well. Today finds several Con-Cor and Bachmann units being prepared for the next few trains, plus a few Con-Cor passenger cars and Atlas freight cars are being held for repair. This scene on Gary's N Trak modules also features Walthers, Bachmann and Pola buildings, and Peco track.

299

Models by Jim Kelly, Photo by Tim Wickerham, Milwaukee, Wisconsin

On an afternoon in the 80s, a herd of beef cattle gets stirred up as two Santa Fe trains meet at Bena, at the extreme south end of the San Joaquin Valley. The power is working hard; what looks like flatland running is the start of the climb over the legendary Tehachapi mountains. Peering over the orange orchard from high on the bluffs, the photographer caught the instant the cattle got startled and began to bolt.

MAGIC OF MODEL RAILROADING

Models and Photo by Jim Younkins, Olympia, Washington

Paper mills are incredible sources of traffic for many railroads including the Mud Bay & Southern. The large Cascade Papers mill keeps a switch crew busy 24 hours per day. Wood chips, chemicals and clay arrive by rail and huge paper rolls are shipped out in box cars. The MB&S F-M switcher drifting past the tank car spur is rolling toward the wood chip yard to grab another cut of loads for dumping. Cascade Papers is a big customer on Jim Younkins' Mud Bay & Southern. It's kitbashed from several Walthers kits and has scratchbuilt additions. The loco is a heavily reworked Minitrix model and the cars are from deLuxe Innovations, Atlas and Roundhouse.

Models and Photo by Marc Pitanza, Old Bridge, New Jersey

A cut of cars remain on the North Shore subdivision mainline as Staten Island Rapid Transit S-2 pulls a single box car out of the Wallerstein Corporation siding. The Seaboard Air Line was dropped off yesterday loaded with sacks of barley hops. The Roadway truck driver has stepped out of his cab to wave at the engineer. As soon as the train has passed, the truck will be able to maneuver into loading bay 2 to pick up a load hops for the local brewery. Wallerstein is a major distributor in the area transferring tons of goods from train to truck and vice versa. The cars are from Micro-Trains® and the loco is a custom-decorated Rivarossi model. The building is a Walthers kit and the truck is from Classic Metal Works.

What really adds life to this scene are the Preiser figures working "out back" in the alley. One pauses to wave at the passing train as the other keeps working on a company truck. The Figures Section is loaded with people, aimals and details like this to add realism to your layout scenes.

FIGURES N SCALE

IMPORTED FROM GERMANY BY WALTHERS

NEW Painters & Workers 272-155312

NEW Guys at the Station 272-155313

NEW Shop Assistants 272-155314

NEW Forest Hands, Forester, Deer 272-155511

Seated Persons pkg(36) 272-155252

Street Cleaning Crew pkg(6) 272-155311

Recreation & Sports - Bathers II 272-155408

Shepherd w/Dog & Flock of Sheep 272-155510

Stair Climbing 272-155004

Travelers 272-155250

At The Blacksmith 272-155308

Firemen 272-155405

Farm 272-155406

Horses 272-155501

Washing Day 272-155404

Transport Workers 272-155305

Craftsmen I 272-155306

NEW PRODUCTS
NEW 272-155312 Painters & Workers **13.99**
NEW 272-155313 Guys at the Station **13.99**
NEW 272-155314 Shop Assistants **13.99**
NEW 272-155511 Forest Hands, Forester, Deer **23.99**

Animals
272-155501 Horses (brown & white) **13.99**

Pedestrians 13.99 ea (Unless Noted)

272-155001 Travelers Set I

272-155002 Travelers Set II

272-155003 Travelers Set III

272-155004 Passers-By Stair Climbing

272-155101 Sitting Travelers Set I

272-155102 Sitting Travelers Set II

272-155103 Sitting Persons III

272-155104 Playing Children III

272-155201 Passengers Set I

272-155202 Passengers Set II

272-155250 Travelers pkg(36) **46.99**
272-155402 Wedding Guests
272-155252 Seated Persons pkg(36) **46.99**

Working People 13.99 ea

272-155301 Train Crew pkg(8)
272-155302 Shunters/Dispatch Crew pkg(8)

272-155303 Enginemen pkg(8)
272-155304 Track Layers pkg(8)
272-155305 Transport Workers
272-155306 Craftsmen I

272-155307 Craftsmen II
272-155308 At The Blacksmith

272-155401 Fair Operators pkg(7)

272-155403 Policemen
272-155404 Washing Day
272-155405 Firemen
272-155406 Farm
272-155311 Street Cleaning Crew pkg(6) **13.99**
272-155408 Bathers II pkg(9) **13.99**

272-155409 German Policemen w/Dog (7 Policemen, 1 Dog) **13.99**
272-155510 Shepherd w/Dog & Flock of Sheep **13.99**

FIGURES N SCALE

Handpainted, ready-to-use plastic figures.

Figures

160-42502 Assortment pkg(12) **5.50**

Animals

160-42505 Cows & Horses pkg(12) **5.50**

Manufactured by Preiser of Germany to KATO specifications. Finely proportioned figures with dress and personal characteristics typical of Japanese persons. Suitable for all scenes.

Railroad Personnel pkg(6) 12.50 ea

381-24201 Train Crew

381-24202 Station Attendants w/Red Flags

381-24203 Maintenance Workers

Pedestrians pkg(6) 12.50 ea

381-24204 Standing Passengers

381-24205 Seated Passengers

381-24207 Walking Passengers

381-24209 Elementary School Children

381-24210 High School Students

381-24211 Young People

381-24216 Joggers & Dogs

NEW PRODUCTS

Pedestrians 7.98 ea
NEW 490-1371 Sitting Figures w/Benches (unpainted)

NEW 490-1375 Women on the Move
NEW 490-1378 People Eating
NEW 490-1380 City Park People
NEW 490-1381 Homeless People
NEW 490-1382 Crime Scene Figures

Travelers 7.98 ea

NEW 490-1374 Travelers

Working People 7.98 ea

NEW 490-1372 Farmer's Market

NEW 490-1373 County Road Workers

NEW 490-1376 Prisoners (black & white stripes)
NEW 490-1377 Prisoners (orange)
NEW 490-1379 Postal Workers

Travelers pkg(12) 7.98 ea
490-1333 Fat People
490-1334 Sitting
490-1335 Station

490-1336 Sitting
490-1341 Work People
490-1342 Work People
490-1343 Steam People

Railroad Personnel pkg(12) 7.98 ea

490-1337 Work Crew
490-1338 Station Crew

Pedestrians pkg(9) 7.98 ea
490-1369 People Waving
490-1344 Street People
490-1349 Tourists

Working People pkg(9) 7.98 ea

490-1367 Utility Workers
490-1368 Masons & Bricklayers

Religious Figures pkg(9) 7.98 ea
490-1347 Deacon & His Flock
490-1352 Pastor & Congregants w/Pulpit

Animals pkg(9) 7.98 ea
490-1348 Deer
490-1350 Cows & Calves (black & white)
490-1351 Cows & Calves (brown)
490-1353 Cows (brown & white)

Get the Scoop!
Get the Skinny!
Get the Score!
Check Out Walthers
Web site at

www.walthers.com

FIGURES N SCALE

NEAL'S N GAUGING TRAINS

Add life to layout scenes in seconds with this series of cast metal figures, which are fully painted and ready to use.

FIGURES

Railroad Personnel

530-62 Locomotive Crew **11.95**

Animals

530-55 Cats & Dogs pkg(5) **10.95**

530-71 Moose (1 male with antlers, 1 female) **11.95**

Pedestrians 11.95 ea

530-50 Mother w/Baby in Baby Carriage pkg(2)

530-51 Cyclists (2 Men, 2 Bikes)
530-56C Children

530-63 Seated People
530-65 Children

530-65A Children w/ Crossing Guard

Working People

530-54 Gardeners (2 Men, Wheelbarrow, Mower) **11.95**

Miscellaneous

530-74 Scarecrow **5.49**

LABELLE INDUSTRIES

Steam/Early Diesel Era Engineer & Fireman Sets

Figures are molded in plastic, fully painted and include one engineer and one fireman per set.

430-7501 Slouching & Leaning **6.49**

430-7502 Waving & Sitting **6.49**
430-7504 All Four Unpainted **4.98**

Contemporary Diesel Engineer & Fireman Sets 6.49 ea

430-7505 Slouching & Leaning

430-7506 Waving & Sitting

NOCH

IMPORTED FROM GERMANY BY WALTHERS
All figures and scenic details are appropriately colored in hand-painted plastic.

Working People

528-33390 Horse Pulling Logs w/Figure & Acessories **16.99**

528-33620 Construction Workers **18.99**

Miniature Scenes

NEW 528-33362 Lumberjacks (3 figures & accessories) **13.99**

528-33542 Flower Stand Figure Set **18.99**
Includes 2 Figures, Bicycle, Umbrella, 1 Flower Pot, Sales Stand, Bus Stop

NEW 528-33682 Foal Pasture (5 animals, 1 tree & accessories) **16.99**

528-33713 Ice Cream Stand Figure Set **18.99**
Includes 5 Figures, Umbrella, Bench, Ice Cream Cart

528-33711 Rendezvous In The Park **18.99**

See What's Available at
www.walthers.com

528-33780 Graveyard Scene **16.99**
Includes two figures, two graves and one statue.

528-33911 Lighted Tree w/Couple on Bench **29.99**

Recreation & Sports

528-33260 With Rowboat **11.99**

528-33280 With Outdoor Furniture **16.99**

528-33700 Campers w/Tent **16.99**

Animals 18.99 ea

528-33740 Cows & Calves w/Milkmaid

528-33750 Horses & Fence

528-33760 Deer & Hunter

Scenic Accessories 15.99 ea

528-35846 Pallets

528-35873 Tombstones

PLASTRUCT

Family Figures pkg(9)
570-93358 Painted (N) **7.00**
570-93354 Unpainted (N) **5.85**

City Figures pkg(12)
570-93393 Painted Style A (N) **20.95**
570-93335 Unpainted Style A (N) **5.95**
570-93394 Painted Style B (N) **20.95**
570-93342 Unpainted Style B (N) **5.95**
570-93397 Painted (Z) **26.95**
570-93337 Unpainted (Z) **5.95**
570-93398 Painted Style B (Z) **26.95**
570-93344 Unpainted Style B (Z) **5.95**
570-93395 Painted (1:200) **26.95**
570-93336 Unpainted (1:200) **5.95**
570-93396 Painted (1:200) **26.95**
570-93343 Unpainted (1:200) **5:95**
570-93345 Unpainted (1:500) **5.95**

VOLLMER

IMPORTED FROM GERMANY BY WALTHERS

Animals pkg(4) 8.99 ea
770-2289 Horses (3 brown, 1 white)

Passengers pkg(5) 10.99 ea
770-2285 Passengers
770-2287 Sitting Persons
770-2288 Travelers w/Luggage

Railroad Personnel
770-2286 pkg(5) **10.99**

FIGURES N SCALE

ORIGINAL Preiser
IMPORTED FROM GERMANY BY WALTHERS

NEW PRODUCTS

Pedestrians

NEW 590-79193 Protestant Funeral **15.99**

NEW 590-79194 Catholic Funeral **15.99**

NEW 590-79195 Funeral **12.99**

Working People

NEW 590-79196 Paramedics **13.99**

Travelers

NEW 590-79197 People Waiting on the Platform **12.99**

NEW 590-79198 Walking Passengers **12.99**

NEW 590-79199 Seated Passengers pkg(14) **20.99**

Animals

590-79093 Set of Small Animals **12.99**

590-79122 Hounds **12.99**

590-79150 Horses, Assorted **8.99**

590-79155 Cows, Assorted **8.99**

590-79160 Shepherd & Flock w/Dog **8.99**

590-79252 Shepherd's Flock **22.99**

590-79179 Deer pkg(6) **8.99**

590-79710 Elephants **11.99**

590-79711 Camels **11.99**

590-79712 Show Horses **11.99**

590-79713 Lions **15.99**

590-79714 Tigers **15.99**
590-79715 Giraffes **19.99**

590-79716 Polar Bears **11.99**

590-79717 Brown Bears **11.99**

Pedestrians

590-75011 Shopping Promenade 1:120 **12.99**

590-79013 Sitting People #1 pkg(6) **8.99**

590-79014 Sitting People #2 pkg(6) **8.99**

590-79019 Standing **11.99**

590-79022 Townspeople **8.99**

590-79024 Women **8.99**

590-79026 Walking **11.99**
590-79032 Passers-By **11.99**

590-79037 Teenagers **11.99**

590-79043 School Children **11.99**

590-79044 Children **11.99**

590-79045 Franciscan Friars **11.99**

590-79047 Passers-By **8.99**

590-79057 Wedding Group, Protestant **11.99**

590-79058 Wedding Group, Catholic **11.99**

590-79068 Family in the City **11.99**

590-79075 Girls **11.99**

590-79078 Young Persons **11.99**

590-79083 Youth Sitting **11.99**

590-79094 Passers-By Hurrying **12.99**
590-79095 Shopping Promenade **12.99**

590-79106 Dangerous Way Home **12.99**

590-79108 Passers-By **12.99**

590-79109 School Crossing Patrol **12.99**

590-79111 Pedestrians w/Policeman **12.99**

FIGURES N SCALE

Original Preiser
IMPORTED FROM GERMANY BY WALTHERS

590-79113 Businessmen Standing **12.99**

590-79114 Businessmen Walking **12.99**

590-79125 Seated Industrial Workers pkg(6) **12.99**

590-79126 Standing Commuters pkg(7) **12.99**

590-79127 Nun w/Children pkg(7) **12.99**

590-79146 Passers-By w/Children pkg(6) **12.99**

590-79148 Pedestrians At Bus Stop pkg(6) **17.99**

590-79152 Bus Drivers & Passengers pkg(7) **12.99**

590-79156 Seated Passengers pkg(6) **12.99**

590-79157 Passers-By #1 pkg(5) **12.99**

590-79158 Passers-By #2 pkg(6) **12.99**

590-79163 Guide w/Tourists pkg(7) **12.99**

590-79164 American City People pkg(5) **12.99**

590-79165 Street Scene pkg(6) **11.99**

590-79166 Villagers pkg(6) **11.99**

590-79167 Fieldtrip pkg(6) **11.99**

590-79173 School Children pkg(6) **12.99**

590-79174 People Sitting On Stairs pkg(6) **12.99**

590-79175 Street Scene/Fight pkg(5) **12.99**

590-79178 Formal Guests pkg(6) **12.99**

590-79182 Family Krause Taking A Walk **11.99**

590-79190 Walking Couples **12.99**

590-79206 Standing Japanese **8.99**

Police & Firefighters

590-79011 Crossing Guards **8.99**

590-79031 German Police & Dog **11.99**

590-79048 Emergency Team **8.99**

590-79115 Firefighters Set #1 **11.99**

590-79116 Firefighters Set #2 **11.99**

590-79117 Firefighters Set #3 **11.99**

590-79118 Firefighters Set #4 **11.99**

590-79138 German Mounted Police In Summer Uniform pkg(2) **15.99**

590-79139 German Mounted Police pkg(2) **15.99**

590-79149 Mounted Police U.S.A. pkg(2) **15.99**

590-79151 Guards On Horseback, Italian pkg(2) **15.99**

590-79172 Seated Firemen **12.99**

Railroad Personnel

590-75008 1:120 Railway Personnel **12.99**

590-79010 Railroad Workers **8.99**

590-79012 German, DB **8.99**

590-79016 Freight Loaders pkg(6) **11.99**

590-79034 Track Gang w/Tires **11.99**

590-79035 Track Maintenance **11.99**

590-79056 Engine Driver & Stoker **8.99**

590-79060 1989 Railway Personnel **11.99**

590-79061 1989 Train Personnel **11.99**

590-79062 1989 Shunters **11.99**

590-79096 Track Maintenance Workers **8.99**

590-79100 1:60 Railway Personnel **12.99**

590-79144 Railroad Personnel w/Passenger pkg(6) **12.99**

590-79147 Railway Workers pkg(7) **12.99**

590-79200 US Railroad Workers **12.99**

590-79201 US Railroad Workers/Travelers **12.99**

590-79207 Japanese **8.99**

Sports & Recreation

590-75013 Bikers 1:120 **12.99**

590-79027 Hikers **11.99**

FIGURES N SCALE

ORIGINAL Preiser

IMPORTED FROM GERMANY BY WALTHERS

590-79038 Party Guests & Waiters **11.99**

590-79041 Tennis Players pkg(6) **8.99**

590-79054 Couples Sitting On Benches **8.99**

590-79059 Photographers **11.99**

590-79063 Figures For Round-A-Bout **8.99**

590-79065 Figures For Chair-O-Plane **8.99**

590-79066 Figures On Beach **8.99**

590-79069 Family In Allgan **11.99**

590-79070 Family At Beach **8.99**

590-79071 Bathers Standing **8.99**

590-79072 Golfers **11.99**

590-79073 People At Grill Party **11.99**

590-79074 Wanderers/Hikers **11.99**

590-79076 Joggers, Badminton Players **8.99**

590-79077 Fishermen **11.99**

590-79085 Spectators **11.99**

590-79086 Spectators **11.99**

590-79087 Cyclists **11.99**

590-79088 Divers **11.99**

590-79089 Cyclists **11.99**

590-79091 Children At Pool **11.99**

590-79092 Seated Couples **12.99**

590-79079 At Sweets Stand **11.99**

590-79107 Self Service Restaurant **12.99**

590-79129 Ludwig II Bavarian Suite **27.99**

590-79159 Resting Wanderers pkg(6) **12.99**

590-79161 People Resting By Village Fountain pkg(6) **15.99**

590-79162 Wanderers At Water Pump pkg(6) **15.99**

590-79183 Horse Riders Set #1 **15.99**

590-79184 Horse Riders Set #2 **15.99**

590-79185 At The Riding School #1 **15.99**

590-79186 At The Riding School #2 **15.99**

590-79700 Clowns **15.99**

Travelers

590-75012 Hurrying 1:120 **12.99**

590-79015 Walking People #1 **11.99**

590-79017 Waiting pkg(6) **11.99**

590-79018 Walking pkg(6) **11.99**

590-79020 Standing pkg(6) **8.99**

590-79021 Walking pkg(6) **8.99**

590-79023 Teenage **8.99**

590-79025 Large Family pkg(6) **11.99**

590-79028 Arriving **8.99**

590-79029 Departing **8.99**

590-79084 Seated Passengers **11.99**

590-79090 Hurrying **11.99**

590-79098 Female Commuters **12.99**

590-79099 Male Commuters **12.99**

590-79103 Seated **8.99**

590-79112 Travelers Waiting **12.99**

590-79123 Seated Passengers Set #1 pkg(8) **12.99**

590-79124 Seated Passengers Set #2 pkg(9) **12.99**

590-79128 Nuns w/Luggage pkg(6) **12.99**

590-79140 With Bags, Waiting pkg(6) **12.99**

590-79141 Streetcar Driver & Passengers pkg(7) **12.99**

590-79143 Travelers w/Luggage pkg(6) **12.99**

590-79145 Checking Schedule pkg(7) **12.99**

590-79153 SBB Personnel pkg(7) **12.99**

590-79187 Standing Travelers **12.99**

590-79188 Walking Travelers #1 **13.99**

FIGURES N SCALE

Original Preiser
IMPORTED FROM GERMANY BY WALTHERS

590-79189 Seated Travelers **12.99**

590-79191 Walking Travelers #2 **12.99**

590-79192 Walking Travelers #3 **12.99**

590-79251 Passengers **61.99**

Working People

590-75009 Workers 1:120 **12.99**

590-75010 Hay Harvest 1:120 **12.99**

590-79030 Road Construction Workers **8.99**

590-79036 Truckers Standing **11.99**

590-79039 Farm People w//Cow **11.99**

590-79040 Farm Workers **11.99**

590-79046 Gardeners **8.99**

590-79050 Women Hanging Wash **11.99**

590-79051 Housewives **11.99**

590-79052 Food Vendors & Stands **11.99**

590-79055 Hay Harvest **11.99**

590-79080 At Market/Cow/Figures **11.99**

590-79081 Delivery Men w/Loads **11.99**

590-79082 Warehouse Men **11.99**

590-79097 Baker Krause **12.99**

590-79101 Workers **12.99**

590-79102 Workers **12.99**

590-79104 Mechanics **11.99**

590-79105 Steeplejacks **8.99**

590-79110 Industrial Workers **12.99**

590-79137 Ship Crewmen pkg(6) **12.99**

590-79142 Workers in Protective Clothing pkg(6) **12.99**

590-79154 City Workers pkg(6) **12.99**

590-79176 Painters pkg(5) **13.99**

590-79177 Painters w/Accessories pkg(6) **15.99**

590-79180 THW Federal Technical Emergency Service Workers #1 **13.99**

Firefighters 590-79004

Seated 590-79007

Passengers 590-79008

Firefighters 590-79005

Assorted Figures 590-79000

Walking People 590-79006

590-79181 THW Federal Technical Emergency Service Workers #2 **13.99**

Musicians

590-79120 Bavarian Musicians #1 **11.99**

590-79121 Bavarian Musicians #2 **11.99**

See What's New and Exciting at
www.walthers.com

Unpainted Sets

590-79004 Firefighters pkg(20) **13.99**

590-79000 Assorted Figures pkg(120) **27.99**

590-79005 Firefighters pkg(40) **12.99**

590-79006 Walking People pkg(125) **27.99**

590-79007 Seated pkg(120) **27.99**

590-79008 Passengers pkg(120) **27.99**

Catalog

590-93029 **14.99**

FIGURES N SCALE

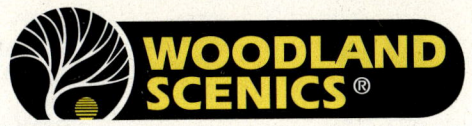

WOODLAND SCENICS

Scenic Accents

Scenic Accents are colorful, action-packed N scale people, animals, details, and accessories that are superbly sculpted and painted to capture the finest details. Human figures include professionals, travelers, shoppers, workers, and people walking, talking, and relaxing. The animal sets include cats, dogs, horses, pigs, cows, deer and many more animal species. Their fine features add the realism needed to bring any layout to life. Scenic Accents set the scene.

Scenic Accents Glue

For temporary or permanent placement of figures. Stays tacky. Removes easily. Non-toxic.

785-198 1 fl oz **4.29**
Specially formulated to attach Scenic Accents or any type of figure or detail to a layout or diorama. Figures can be positioned without waiting for glue to dry. And since it stays tacky, they can be placed in one position, picked up and moved to another without regluing at any time. Scenic Accents Glue leaves no puddles or residue. It's water-soluble and a small brush applicator is included.

Gentle Grips

785-200 Tweezers w/Cushion Tips **5.98**
These unique tweezers are perfect for handling Scenic Accents or any type of figure or detail. Protective tips prevent damage while curved ends and special non-slip thumb and forefinger grips help you hang on to small items. Longer length lets you reach into any area without damaging nearby details.

NEW PRODUCTS

Economy Packs

99.98 ea
Populate your layout at an affordable price with these little works of art! Each package contains more than 100 themed figures, animals and accessories to create multiple scenes on layout. (Contents may vary and include duplicates.)

NEW Assorted Farm Set **785-2061**
NEW Assorted Worker Set **785-2062**
NEW Assorted Figure Set **785-2063**

Figure Sets

NEW Farmer's Market 785-2170 **13.98**

NEW Masonry Workers 785-2173 **11.98**

NEW Rail Workers 785-2177 **11.98**

NEW Jug Band 785-2180 **12.98**

NEW Park Benches 785-2181 **8.98**

NEW Snowball Fight 785-2183 **11.98**

NEW Ice Skaters 785-2184 **11.98**

NEW Couples in Coats 785-2189 **10.98**

Pedestrians 785-2121 **9.49**

Policemen 785-2122 **9.49**

Dock Workers 785-2123 **10.49**

Ordinary People 785-2124 **9.49**

Window Shoppers 785-2125 **9.49**

FIGURES N SCALE

WOODLAND SCENICS

City Workers 785-2126 **10.49**

Graveside Service 785-2127 **10.49**

Roofers 785-2128 **10.49**

People Sitting 785-2129 **9.49**

Full Figured Folks 785-2130 **10.49**

Train Personnel 785-2131 **10.49**

Checker Players 785-2132 **10.49**

Lovers 785-2133 **9.49**

Bus Stop People 785-2134 **9.49**

Professionals 785-2135 **9.49**

Rebels 785-2136 **9.49**

Road Crew 785-2137 **9.49**

Hobos 785-2138 **10.49**

Hampshire Pigs 785-2139 **10.49**

Dogs & Cats pkg(10) 785-2140 **10.49**

Farm Horses pkg(6) 785-2141 **9.49**

Farm Animals pkg(7) 785-2142 **9.49**

People & Pets (3 People, 4 Dogs) 785-2143 **9.49**

Hereford Cows pkg(6) 785-2144 **9.49**

Baseball Players I 785-2145 **10.49**

Baseball Players II 785-2146 **10.49**

Train Mechanics 785-2147 **10.49**

General Public 785-2149 **9.49**

Commuters 785-2150 **9.49**

Firemen to the Rescue 785-2151 **11.49**

Farm People 785-2152 **11.49**

Engineers 785-2153 **10.49**

Factory Workers 785-2154 **10.49**

FIGURES N SCALE

Travelers 785-2155 **10.49**

Bystanders 785-2156 **9.49**

Welders & Accessories 785-2157 **12.49**

People & Pesky Raccoons 785-2158 **11.49**

Horseback Riders 785-2159 **11.49**

Lumberjacks 785-2160 **11.49**

Game of Horseshoes 785-2165 **10.49**

Dairy Farmers 785-2166 **11.49**

Chain Gang 785-2167 **11.98**

Casual People 785-2168 **10.49**

Youth Football Players 785-2169 **16.49**

Accident Waiting to Happen 785-2171 **12.49**

Spectators 785-2172 **12.49**

Painters 785-2174 **11.98**

Surveyors 785-2175 **11.98**

Shoe Shiners 785-2176 **11.49**

Beekeepers 785-2178 **11.98**

Gone Fishing 785-2179 **11.98**

Children 785-2182 **10.49**

Deer 785-2185 **10.98**

Black Bears 785-2186 **10.49**

Holstein Cows 785-2187 **10.49**

2nd Shift Workers 785-2188 **10.98**

Passengers 785-2190 **10.49**

Scenic Accents® Details

Assorted Skids 785-2161 **11.98**

Assorted Crates 785-2162 **11.49**

Assorted Junk 785-2163 **12.98**

Tombstones 785-2164 **11.49**

FIGURES N SCALE

Models and Photo by Keith Kohlmann, Racine, Wisconsin

When the wayfreight arrives around noon, you have to get up awfully early to fill a reefer full of sacked onions — especially if you're doing it on your own! By the time the sun rises you'd better be on the second truck or you won't be done in time. At a hundred pounds per sack, that's a lot of backbreaking work. From the 30s into the 60s, the scene was common on many rural team tracks and loading spurs. In the fields between Milwaukee and Chicago, small producers of onions, cabbage and potatoes loaded reefers for the long haul to major markets. Farmers would drive their flatbeds right up to the reefer door and start transferring stacks of sacks into the waiting car. Here, a worker heaves onion sacks from the back of a Classic Metal Works stakebed into a modified Micro-Trains wood reefer. With only a couple more truckloads to go, he'll be done by the time the local arrives.

Scenes like this are easy to add to your layout. A truck next to the team track, or backed up to a freight house door goes a long way toward adding implied action to any scene. Vehicles from every era are listed in the Vehicles Section.

VEHICLES N SCALE

TRUCKS

Ford F-150 Pickup Trucks

With Standard Sides pkg(2) 12.95 ea (Unless Noted)
150-2941 Black

150-2942 Moonlight Blue
150-2943 Pacific Green
150-2944 Dark Red
150-2945 Tan
150-2946 White
150-2940 Undecorated 8.95

Two-Tone Paint, Standard Sides pkg(2) 13.95 ea

150-2947 Green & Tan

150-2948 Red & Tan

150-2949 White & Tan

150-2950 Black & Silver

Railroad Maintenance-of-Way Schemes, Standard Sides pkg(2) 15.95 ea
150-2987 BNSF (white)
150-2988 CR (yellow)
150-2989 CSX (white)
150-2990 NS (yellow)

150-2991 New York, Susquehanna & Western (yellow)
150-2992 UP (white)

With Flared Sides pkg(2) 12.95 ea (Unless Noted)

150-2983
150-2981 Black
150-2982 Moonlight Blue
150-2983 Pacific Green
150-2984 Dark Red
150-2985 Tan
150-2986 White
150-2980 Undecorated 8.95

Limited Quantity Available

1984 Ford LNT 9000 Tractor Cab 10.95 ea (Unless Noted)

150-2924
150-2921 Black
150-2922 Dark Blue
150-2923 Green
150-2924 Red
150-2925 White
150-2926 Yellow
150-2920 Undecorated 8.95

AUTOMOBILES

Limited Quantity Available

1996 Ford Taurus Four-Door Sedans pkg(2) 12.50 ea (Unless Noted)

150-2910
150-2902 Medium Willow Green
150-2903 Charcoal Gray
150-2904 Rose Mist
150-2905 Toreador Red
150-2907 Ebony
150-2908 Iris Frost
150-2909 Light Saddle
150-2910 Midnight Red
150-2911 Pacific Green
150-2912 Silver Frost
150-2900 Undecorated 8.50

IMPORTED FROM GERMANY BY WALTHERS
Add life to highways and city streets with these detailed models. Each is fully assembled from plastic parts.

AUTOMOBILES

Automobile Sets 10.99 ea (Unless Noted)

189-8300 Volkswagen Passat & Taxi Station Wagons pkg(2)

189-8306 German Post Office/Telecom Set - 1 Each VW Passat & Mercedes Sprinter 12.99

189-8309 Mercedes Sprinter Vans pkg(2) 12.99 Includes 1 hearse (black) and 1 garden center van (green).

189-8310 A-Klasse & M-Klasse Set

189-8311 Mercedes 2-Pack A-Class 4-Door Compact (silver) & M-Class 4-Door SUV (dark green) 13.99

189-8315 Mercedes-Benz C-Class 4-Door Sedan Set pkg(2) One each red and blue.

189-8320 Chevrolet 1950 Pick-Up & 1950 Buick

189-8330 Opel Rekord 4-Door Sedan 1 each (light blue) & Taxi (black)

189-8340 Audi A4 Limousine Set

189-8346 Audi A4 Avant Sedan (dark green) & Mercedes C-Class Station Wagon (light metallic blue) 13.99

189-8350 Smart 2-Door Subcompact City Coupe (one each red & yellow) 11.99

With Working Headlights

Mercedes

189-5690 Sprinter Van w/Extended Roof 16.99

189-5692 M-Klasse SUV 16.99

VW

189-5691 Passat w/Headlights & Taillights 15.99

MILITARY VEHICLES

189-8307 Staff Car/Light Truck Set – VW Passat & Mercedes Sprinter Van pkg(2) 12.99

EMERGENCY VEHICLES

13.99 ea (Unless Noted)

189-5685 VW Passat Set Police (green) and Fire Department (red) w/Flashing Blue Light 33.99

189-8308 Mercedes Sprinter Vans - Fire & Ambulance pkg(2) 12.99

189-8312 Mercedes A Class & M Class Notarzt (Emergency Doctor, German)

189-8316 Mercedes Benz C-Klasse/Sprinter Police Set (green, white) pkg(2)

189-8321 US Fire Dept. Set - 1 Each Chevrolet Pick-Up & Buick (red)

189-8322 Buick Police Car (black) & Chevrolet Pick-Up DPW (yellow) 12.99

189-8331 Opel Rekord 4-Door Sedan 1 each Police (green) & Fire (red) 12.99

189-8342 Audi A4/Mercedes Benz M-Klasse Fire Set (red) pkg(2) 11.99

189-8347 Audi A4 Avant Police & Mercedes A-Class Fire

189-8351 Smart City Coupe 2-Door Subcompact Set - Police & Fire pkg(2)

189-8352 Mercedes Smart Car & C Class Police (German)

TAXIS

189-8341 Mercedes C-Klasse/Audi A4 Set pkg(2) 11.99

See What's Available at
www.walthers.com

314

VEHICLES N SCALE

Street scenes come to life in seconds with these fully assembled, licensed replicas of American autos and trucks! Great for steam-, transition- and diesel-era layouts, the selection includes popular models from the 1940s to the 70s, which also look great as restored collector cars in modern scenes. Off the layout, the small size is ideal for collecting and display. The highly detailed diecast bodies are painstakingly finished in official factory paint colors. Next, they're pad printed to capture other details like chrome trim and graphics. The models also feature plated parts to simulate chrome hubcaps, wheels, grilles and bumpers. Each set includes two identical vehicles finished in different colors.

NEW PRODUCTS

Trucks

White WC Delivery Vans, pkg(2) 13.00

NEW 221-50266 Falstaff Beer

NEW 221-50267 CP

White WC Tractor/Trailer Sets, pkg(2) 19.00

NEW 221-51142 Tractor w/Covered Wagon Trailer Ralston Purina

NEW 221-51143 Tractor w/AeroVan Trailer Kroger

NEW 221-51144 Tractor w/AeroVan Trailer REA

NEW 221-51145 Tractor w/AeroVan Trailer Coles Express

AUTOMOBILES

Chevrolet

1978 Impala 4-Door pkg(2) 10.00 ea

221-50239 Dark Brown
221-50246 Dark Blue
221-50259 Carmine Red
221-50260 Light Blue Metallic w/Black Vinyl Roof

Ford pkg(2) 10.00 ea

Limited Quantity Available

221-50201 1948 2-Door Convertible
221-50202 1953 Victoria 2-Door Hardtop
221-50207 1948 "Woody" Station Wagon

1967 Ford Custom 500 4-Door pkg(2) 12.25 ea
221-50235 Burgundy

221-50245 Lime Mist
221-50257 Dark Green
221-50258 Pebble Beige w/Black Vinyl Roof

1951 Hudson Hornet pkg(2) 10.00 ea

Limited Quantity Available

221-50221 Bali Blue & Northern Gray Metallic

1949 Mercury

Limited Quantity Available
221-50217 Black & Calabash Yellow pkg(2) 10.00

Plymouth

Limited Quantity Available

221-50208 1941 2-Door Hardtop Coupe pkg(2) 10.00

EMERGENCY VEHICLES

221-50234 1967 Ford Custom 500 4-Door Police pkg(2) 12.25
221-50237 1978 Chevrolet Impala 4-Door Police pkg(2) 12.25

221-50244 1967 Ford Custom 500 Fire Chief 12.25

221-50247 1978 Chevy Impala Fire Chief 12.25

TAXIS

221-50233 1967 Ford Custom 500 4-Door pkg(2) 12.25
221-50236 1978 Chevrolet Impala 4-Door pkg(2) 12.25

TRUCKS

Ford

1948 Delivery Truck pkg(2) 10.00 ea

221-50219 1948 Panel Delivery Truck (Cream White & Sheridan Blue)

221-50220 Green & Birch Gray

International Harvester

R-190 Express Van pkg(2) 12.25 ea

Single Axle

221-50240 NYC

221-50241 PRR
221-50242 ATSF
221-50243 Ice Delivery
221-50248 A&P Grocer

221-50249 U.S. Mail

221-50250 B&O
221-50251 CB&Q

221-50252 NKP

NEW 221-50262 Sears
221-50253 Undecorated (red cab, white van)
221-50254 Undecorated (dark green cab, silver cab)
221-50256 Undecorated (yellow cab, silver van)

Double Axle Refrigerator

221-50230 Swift's
NEW 221-50261 Armour Star

Flatbed
NEW 221-50256 Builder's Supply

221-50232 Undecorated

Metro Delivery Truck

221-50210 Gray & Red pkg(2) 10.00

1953 3000 Cabover pkg(2) 10.00 ea

Limited Quantity Available

221-50203 Box Style Delivery Van
221-50204 Local Fuel Delivery Tank Truck

221-50205 Single-Axle Semi Tractor

Single-Axle Dump Truck pkg(2) 10.00 ea

Limited Quantity Available

221-50224 Gray & Black

Tractor/Trailers

1954 International R-190 Tractor w/Fruehauf 32' Aerovan Trailers 17.99 ea

221-51101 Hennis
221-51102 Roadway

221-51103 P-I-E

Tractor 12.25 ea

221-51108 Chicago Express

315

VEHICLES N SCALE

221-51109 Mid-States

221-51110 Cooper-Jarrett
221-51111 Undecorated (red)
221-51112 Undecorated (green)
221-51113 Undecorated (white)

Trailers
32' Fruehauf Aerovan Trailers pkg(2) 11.00 ea
221-51104 Chicago Express
221-51105 Mid-States
221-51106 Cooper-Jarrett
221-51107 Undecorated

White WC-22 pkg(2) 12.25

Delivery Vans

221-50263 Kraft Refrigerated

221-50264 NABISCO

Flat-Bed
221-50265 Flat-Bed (red)

International Harvester R-190 Semi Tractor pkg(2)
These detailed models feature an all-new 136" single-tandem fifth-wheel cab.

With 32' Fruehauf® Aerovan Reefer 17.99 ea
Features early 50s Thermo-King® refrigeration unit.

221-51120 Swift's Premium

221-51121 Sealtest
With 32' Fruehauf Aerovan Trailer 17.99
Features curbside trailer door.

221-51114 Eastern Motor Express

221-51115 Illinois California Express

221-51133 Navajo

221-51135 Consolidated Freightways

With 32' Flatbed Trailer pkg(2) 17.99
221-51122 Roadway
221-51123 P-I-E
221-51124 ICX

221-51125 US Steel National Tube Co.
221-51126 Undecorated (red)
221-51127 Undecorated (green)

With 32' "Covered Wagon" Trailer

221-51129 P-I-E pkg(2) 17.99
Semi Tractor Only pkg(2) 12.25
221-51118 Pennsylvania Railroad Merchandise Service

221-51119 Santa Fe Railroad Express Service

White WC-22 Tractor/Trailer Sets
With 32' Aerovan Reefer pkg(2) 17.99

221-51139 Carnation

221-51140 A&P Grocers

With 32' Aerovan Trailer pkg(2) 17.99

221-51134 Spector

221-51136 Yale Transport

With 32' "Covered Wagon" Trailer pkg(2) 17.99
221-51130 Wayne Feeds
221-51141 US Steel American Sheet Steel Co.

White WC22 Semi-Tractors pkg(2) 12.25

221-51137 Undecorated (red)
221-51138 Undecorated (green)

TRAILER SETS
32' Fruehauf Aerovan Trailer Only pkg(2) 12.25

221-51116 Pennsylvania Railroad Merchandise Service

221-51117 Santa Fe Railroad Express Service
32' "Covered Wagon" Trailers Only pkg(2) 12.25
221-51131 Undecorated (red)
221-51132 Undecorated (green)

CAL-FREIGHT

Buses

201-3000 30' Metro Bus **12.20**
201-3005 40' Metro Bus **14.20**

Boats
201-2350 Row Boats pkg(3) **4.95**

201-2360 Pleasure Boat #1, Enclosed Cabin **4.95**

201-2365 Pleasure Boat #2, Open Seating **4.95**

Trailers
4 x 8' Utility 3.25 ea
201-2330 Empty
201-2335 With Open Load
201-2340 With Tarp-Covered Load

DETAIL ASSOCIATES
Craft Train Kits consist of unpainted metal castings.

Automobiles
Ford Model A 3.50 ea
229-8431 Coupe
229-8432 Pick-Up Truck
229-8433 Panel/Delivery Truck

Trailers
229-8706 Sand-Bottom Dump **4.85**
229-8708 Truck Bogie w/Extra Wheels **2.00**
229-8709 Tank **4.85**

Trucks
229-8705 White Cabover **4.85**

DELUXE INNOVATIONS

AMERICAN HIGHWAY TRAILERS
14.95 ea (Unless Noted)

48'
Quantum ATSF/JB Hunt

238-711301 #1
238-711311 #2

CSL Intermodal

NEW 238-711601 #1 **15.95**
NEW 238-711611 #2 **15.95**

53'
Vermont Railway

NEW 238-711501 #1
NEW 238-711511 #2

53' Duraplate
Interstate Distribution
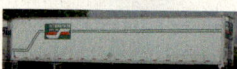
NEW 238-711401 #1
NEW 238-711411 #2

Schneider National
NEW 238-711701 #1
NEW 238-711711 #2

US Xpress Enterprises
NEW 238-711301 #1
NEW 238-711311 #2

Get Daily Info, Photos and News at
www.walthers.com

VEHICLES N SCALE

Pewter kits feature high quality castings.

NEW PRODUCT
Automobiles
NEW 284-57009 1935 Chevrolet Master DeLuxe **5.95**

AUTOMOBILES

284-51011 Taxi Cab - Checker **5.95**
Kit comes with a set of decals to help you create one of the most recognizable vehicles in a big city — the Checker Cab.
284-51015 Sports Car Variety Pack pkg(4) **12.95**

284-57003 Buick Coupe 1936 **7.95**

284-57004 Ford Model A Tudor Coupe **7.95**
284-57005 Model A Deluxe Phaeton **7.95**

CONSTRUCTION EQUIPMENT
284-50007 Fairmont Speeder **TBA**

284-53001 Caterpillar D8H Bulldozer **14.95**

284-53005 Road Grader/Scraper **19.95**

284-53007 Bobcat Skid Steer Loader On Trailer **17.95**

284-53009 CB-534 Compactor **12.95**

284-53010 C 631 E Scraper **24.95**

284-53011 Bucyrus Erie 30-B Crane **24.95**

284-53012 Komatsu Log Loader w/Heel Bottom **21.95**

284-53013 Ford 9000 Dump Truck **17.95**

HO Model Shown
284-53014 IT18F Log Loader **17.95**

284-53015 Ford 9000 Cement Truck **21.95**
284-53016 Forklift **9.95**
284-53017 Snow Plow Dump Truck **TBA**

EMERGENCY VEHICLES

284-51012 Ambulance **5.95**

284-51013 Highway Patrol/Police Car **5.95**

284-51014 Fire Chief Truck **5.95**

American Lafrance 1000 Series

284-52008 Pumper Truck **21.95**

284-52009 Ladder Truck **24.95**

FARM MACHINERY

HO Model Shown; Figure Shown Not Included
284-54005 1954 "Red" Super M-TA **7.95**

284-54006 Bin Wagon **9.95**

284-54007 "Green" 7800 Farm Tractor **12.95**

284-54008 1940 "Green" 12-A Combine **14.95**

284-54009 "Green" 9500 Combine w/Wheat Head **21.95**

TRUCKS

284-51004 Ford F-150 Pick-Up w/Topper **5.95**

284-51006 Dodge Grand Caravan Mini-Van **5.95**

284-51008 Chevrolet Crew-Cab Pick-Up w/Accessories **9.95**

284-51009 Chevrolet Panel Van **5.95**

284-51010 Ford Tow Truck **9.95**

284-52001 Peterbilt 359 Semi Tractor **14.95**

284-52005 1975 Freightliner Cabover Tractor **14.95**

284-52007 Peterbilt 359 Tractor w/Skeleton Logging Trailer **21.95**

284-52010 Ford 9000 Semi Tractor **14.95**

284-56003 1939 Peterbilt 334 Stake Body **17.95**

284-56004 1953 Kenworth Bullnose Tractor **14.95**

284-56005 White Refrigerated Delivery Truck **17.95**

284-56006 1941 Peterbilt Model 344 Tractor Only **14.95**
284-56007 White 1950 6x2 Truck w/Low Sided Box **17.95**
284-56008 1941 Peterbilt 344 Logging Truck w/Trailer **21.95**
284-56009 1930 Ford Model AA 1-Ton w/Stake Body **14.95**

284-56010 1941 Chevy 1-Ton w/Stake-Body **17.95**
284-56011 1950s Fuel Truck **14.95**
284-56012 1930s Fuel Truck **14.95**

284-57006 1930 Ford Model A Pickup **7.95**
284-57007 1941 Chevrolet Pick-Up **7.95**

284-57008 1950 Ford F-1 Pick-Up **7.95**

TRAILERS

284-52002 50-Ton Lowboy Trailer **11.95**

VEHICLES N SCALE

FALLER

IMPORTED FROM GERMANY BY WALTHERS

Items listed below are available by Special Order (see Legend Page).

Bring a new dimension of realism to your railroad with this moving car system. Vehicles move along streets and highways under their own power. Starter sets include battery charger, special guide wire, crash barriers and marker posts as well as roadway filler, markings and paint. Detailed assembly instructions help you create a car system to fit your layout.

NEW PRODUCTS
Car System Vehicles

NEW 272-162042 Mercedes Benz Actros LH Articulated Truck, DHL **134.99**

NEW 272-162043 Mercedes Benz SK **124.99**

Car System Accessories

NEW 272-162055 Traffic Lights w/Switch **91.99**

NEW 272-162056 Traffic Lights w/no Switch **39.99**

NEW 272-162057 Bus Stop **136.99**

Car System
Starter Sets

272-162000 Bus (Wiking) **154.99**
Includes a Wiking Post Office bus, charging unit, 10m of special contact wire, road compound and color, and detailed instructions.

272-162001 Starter Set w/MB O 302 Railway Bus **134.99**

272-162002 Starter Set w/MB Truck **134.99**

Vehicles

272-162031 Bus (Reitze) Wide **124.99**

272-162032 MB O 305 Bus **124.99**

272-162041 MB Actros LH Articulated Truck **133.99**

Get the Scoop!
Get the Skinny!
Get the Score!
Check Out Walthers Web site at
www.walthers.com

kibri

IMPORTED FROM GERMANY BY WALTHERS

CONSTRUCTION EQUIPMENT

Cranes

405-19600 GOTTWALD GS 100.06-Ton Railroad Crane **114.99**

Excavators 39.99 ea
Plastic Kits

405-19100 Menck Excavator w/Shovel **56.99**

405-19101 Menck Tracked Excavator (yellow)

405-19102 Menck Tracked Excavator w/Deep Bucket (blue)

Farm Machinery
Combine

405-19000 CLAAS Lexion 480 w/Small Grain Head **56.99**

405-19001 CLAAS Lexion w/Corn Head & Head Transport Trailer **56.99**

KATO

Automobiles
Toyota
Assembled, pre-colored plastic autos.

381-23500 pkg(6) **8.00**

381-23505 1990s Body Styles pkg(6) **13.98**

Metal Miniatures

One-piece, unpainted cast metal vehicles.

Automobiles
340-28 Ford Mustang & Station Wagon pkg(4) **5.00**
340-30 Vintage Ford/Maxwell pkg(4) **4.00**

Farm Machinery
340-45 Farmall Tractor pkg(6) **5.00**

Construction Equipment pkg(6) 5.00 ea
340-27 Bulldozer
340-46 Caterpillar Tractor

Assortments
340-47 Cars & Trucks pkg(10) **9.00**
Includes pick-up truck, antique truck, VW "Beetle," three sports cars and four assorted sedans.

340-48 Truck Assortment pkg(3) **4.00**
Includes a fire truck, dump truck and camper.

VEHICLES N SCALE

MICRON ART

Superdetail your streets or add unique models to your collection with these vehicle kits. Each includes a variety of fine details such as spoked wheels, tires, horn, steering wheel, seat and side lamps. Designed for modelers with some experience, each kit consists of photo-etched metal parts that capture many fine details and are near-scale thickness. All kits include parts for two complete vehicles.

NEW PRODUCTS
Horse-Drawn Vehicles

NEW 462-2069 1889 Four-Passenger Sleigh **19.95**
Photo-etched easybrass® kit includes horse, driver, two passengers, wire reins and thrill harness.

NEW 462-2073 1905 Express Delivery Wagon w/Upright Piano Load **26.95**
Features fifth-wheel design for the front "cut-under" wheels. Photo-etched brass kit includes two wagons, two drivers (one can play the piano), two horses (one trotting, one standing), one piano, two thrill harnesses, wire for reins and color instructions.

1937-57 Tractor Trailer

462-2065 10-Wheel Conventional Tractor w/30' Trailer **50.95**
Models feature cast wheels with detailed hubs, Swarovski crystal headlamps and saffire color rear lights. Tractor has diesel horn, side mirrors, seat, steering wheel, stack, air filter unit, two fuel tanks, trailer tongue and running boards. Three grilles are included: Kenworth, AutoCar and a generic grille to make Peterbilt, Whites or other tractors. Trailer comes with trailer stand and box loads and can be modeled with rear doors open or closed. A complete set of period decals for four different lines is included.

AUTOMOBILES
Ford Model T

462-2021 1911-15 Touring Car pkg(2) **25.95**
Completely revised design features Swarovski crystal headlights, windshield with support stays, provision for a crank on front radiator, easily installed top-down piece, real cloth top with prototypical support frame, attached horn etched to body side and stronger, more easily formed fenders. Kit includes enough materials to build two "top-down" or "top-up" vehicles.

462-2025 1915 Center-Door Sedan pkg(2) **25.50**

Oldsmobile

462-2029 1904 Runabout pkg(2) **24.00**
Introduced in 1897, these tiny Runabouts were America's first popular priced car. Kit includes top made of real cloth and white jewel stones for headlights.

BAGGAGE CARTS

462-2007 pkg(4) **13.50**
Now includes 8 pieces of luggage per kit.

HAND CARS

462-2013 Crew Type pkg(2) **22.95**
This model represents the larger "crew" type handcar often seen in old photographs. They were commonly used on many western railroads from the 1860s through the 1900s. Kits consist of .010" photo-etched brass sheet, .020" brass rod and four lathe-turned, nickel-silver wheels with bronze finish.

EMERGENCY VEHICLES

462-2039 1914 Knox Chemical Fire Engine **42.00**
Sure to be the pride of any department, this exquisite model is perfect for period scenes or as a restored rig in the present day. Incredible detail includes spoked wheels, steering wheel, seat, side lamps, ladders, bell, folded hose load, chemical tank, extinguishers, horn, siren, headlamps and a spotlight. The kit also comes with full-color, illustrated instructions.

HORSE-DRAWN VEHICLES

462-2023 1880s Buckboard w/Horse & Driver pkg(2) **17.00**
Includes parts for two complete rigs with horses in different poses.

TRUCKS
Ford Model T

462-2017 1913 Delivery Van pkg(2) **18.95**

462-2019 1923 Stake Bed pkg(2) **19.95**

462-2035 1923 Open Cab Steel Bed pkg(2) **24.00**
Includes two crates for a load.

NuComp Miniatures

NEW PRODUCTS
Camping Trailers w/Cars
14.95 ea (Unless Noted)

NEW 534-614 Extended Top Trailer   1 x 9/16"

NEW 534-615 End Extension Trailer   15/16 x 9/16"

NEW 534-616 Large Trailer   1 x 9/16"

NEW 534-617 Small Trailer   11/16 x 1/2"

NEW 534-618 Teardrop Trailer **13.95**   9/16 x 5/16"

Automobiles
Each kit includes cars, wheels and positionable parts. Individual cars will vary. Cars must be assembled and painted.

534-60302 2-Pack **6.00**

534-60303 3-Pack **8.00**

534-60304 4-Pack **10.00**

Rowboat

534-60206 With Oars **4.00**
Kit includes parts for one rowboat and two oars (figure not included.)

NOCH

IMPORTED FROM GERMANY BY WALTHERS

Easy-to-build kits feature appropriately colored plastic parts.

BOATS
Barges

528-35720 Coal Barge Kit **28.99**

528-35730 Assembled Motor Barge **31.99**

528-35740 Motor Tank Kit **33.99**

Boat Kits

528-35710 Tug Boat **37.99**

528-35750 Pilot Boat **37.99**

VEHICLES N SCALE

NEAL'S N GAUGING TRAINS

Add instant detail to streets, highways, parking lots or driveways with this line of cast metal models. Each comes fully assembled and painted, ready to add to your layout.

AUTOMOBILES

Cadillac
530-109 2-Door Limousine 9.95

530-109P 1950s Style (pink) 9.95

530-111 1950s Style Hearse 13.95

Chevrolet

530-105 1957 Impala w/Continental Spare Tire Kit 9.95

Ford

530-104 1949 Sedan (Assorted Colors) 9.95

Volkswagen
530-24 1958 Beetle 9.95

BICYCLES

530-52 pkg(4) 11.95
530-SS040 Bicycles 10.95

BOATS

530-69 Row Boats - Painted 10.95

530-70 Sailing Dinghy - Painted 8.95

BUSES

530-99 American Style School Bus 22.95

EMERGENCY VEHICLES

Cadillac

530-112 1950s Style Ambulance (white w/red cross) 13.95

Ford
1949 Ford Sedan 9.95 ea
530-101 Police (black, white roof & doors)

530-102 (white roof & doors, with black fenders)

530-103 Police (blue, gray)

530-106 1949 Ford Fire Chief's Car 9.95

FARM MACHINERY

530-38 Open Trailer 8.95
530-39 Tank Trailer 8.95
530-40 1947 Ferguson TE 20 (Ford 9N) Tractor 11.95

Old Time Tractors w/Metal Wheels
Etched Brass Kits 11.95 ea
530-72 New
530-72R Rusty, Weathered

Modern Tractors
11.95 ea

530-73B Blue

530-73C Cream Red

530-73G Farm Green

530-73R Flat Red
530-73Y Yellow

FORKLIFT

530-68 With Operator 11.95

MILITARY VEHICLES

1949 Ford 9.95 ea

530-107 Military Police

530-108 Staff Car

MOTORCYCLES

530-75 With Rider 9.95

530-76 With Sidecar & Rider 9.95
530-76O With Open-Top Side Car & Rider 10.95

SPORT UTILITY VEHICLES

Land Rover 8.95 ea
530-35 1971 Series III

530-36 1948 Series I – Top Up
530-37 1948 Series I – Top Down

WAGONS

14.95 ea
530-SS023 Pony And Trap
530-SS053 Farm Cart
530-SS054 Farmers Market Cart

530-SS058 Amish Buggy
530-SS017 Horse Drawn Single Axle Delivery Van
530-SS022 Coal Merchant's Cart
530-SS057 Victorian Carriage w/ Horse
530-SS060 Hansom Cab

TRAILERS/ CAMPERS

530-110 1950s Single-Axle Camper 11.95
530-113 1950s Airstream Trailer 13.95

TRUCKS

Chevrolet Independence Series Flatbed 15.95 ea (Unless Noted)

530-27 Flatbed
530-28 Coal Delivery
530-114 1940s Style Pick-Up 11.95

N SCALE ARCHITECT

NEW PRODUCT
Motorcycles

NEW 716-20047 Motor Bikes pkg(3) 8.95
Unpainted metal castings.

VEHICLES

1929 Chevrolet Truck

716-20027 Flatbed 11.95

716-20028 Coal Delivery Truck w/Figure 12.95

VEHICLES N SCALE

PERIOD MINIATURES

NEW PRODUCTS
Construction Equipment
NEW 555-3000 3000LB Clark Forklift **3.65**
NEW 555-3001 7000LB Champ Forklift **3.65**

Automobiles
Kits feature multiple pieces, unpainted metal castings.

555-3004 1957 Chevrolet Bel-Air **6.95**

555-3005 Jeep CJ **4.95**

PIRATE MODELS, LTD.

IMPORTED FROM GREAT BRITAIN BY WALTHERS
Craft Train kits feature unpainted metal castings. Models are less seats, window glazing and decals.

Bluebird

559-2009 School Bus-1975 **35.99**

GMC Buses
RTS Series 35.99 ea

559-201 RTS-1 Slope Back

559-202 RTS-4 Square Back

40' "Fishbowl"
559-2004 Standard-1959 **35.99**

Grumman/Flxible

559-2012 870 Series-1981 **35.99**

PLASTRUCT

Airplanes
570-93554 pkg(6) **6.55**

Automobiles pkg(5) 9.95 ea
570-93665 Shadow
570-93666 Mini Pickup
570-93667 Falcon
570-93668 Station Wagon
570-93669 Mustang

Bicycles
570-93417 pkg(4) **12.25**

Pleasure Boats
570-93542 pkg(4) **3.50**

Buses
570-93468 City Bus pkg(2) **11.15**
570-93497 Trolley Bus pkg(2) **7.50**

Truck Kits 11.15 ea
570-93461 Dump Truck
570-93462 Short Oil Tanker
570-93463 Delivery Truck
570-93464 18 Wheeler
570-96465 Tank Truck
570-93466 Long Oil Tanker
570-93467 Fork Lift

New Arrivals Updated Every Day! Visit Walthers Web site at
www.walthers.com

Original Preiser

IMPORTED FROM GERMANY BY WALTHERS
Handpainted plastic figures and accessories.

Hanomag w/Wagon 590-79502

Hanomag w/Log Trailer 590-79504

Deutz D w/Side Mower 590-79506

Ore Wagon 590-79475

Log Wagon 590-79477

Brewery Beer Wagon 590-79478

Open Carriage-White 590-79479

Farm Machinery 29.99 ea
590-79502 Hanomag Tractor w/Wagon
590-79504 Hanomag w/Log Trailer
590-79506 Deutz D 6206 w/Side-Mount Sickle Mower pkg(2)

Horse-Drawn Wagons 23.99 ea (Unless Noted)
Includes team, wagon and figures as shown.
590-79475 Ore
590-79476 Delivery

590-79477 Log
590-79478 Brewery Beer Wagon
590-79479 Open Carriage-White **25.99**

Pallet Jacks
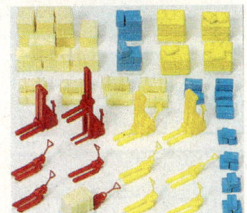
590-79567 Pallet Jacks & Cargo Kit **12.99**

SHOWCASE Miniatures

These accurately detailed vehicles feature a minimal number of parts to ensure quick and easy assembly.

EMERGENCY VEHICLES

654-34 1957 International Fire Truck **17.95**

MOTORCYCLES

654-28 1950s Hawg pkg(2) **9.95**

INTERMODAL

654-21 Kalmar Container Loader Kit **35.95**

TRACTOR/TRAILER

654-20 Kenworth T-600 w/Sleeper (Long Haul) **14.95**

TRUCKS
654-11 F-800 MOW w/Knuckle Boom **14.95**
654-17 Divco '50s Model V Delivery Van **10.95** Perfect for moving, dairy, bakery and linen.

VEHICLES N SCALE

RAILWAY EXPRESS MINIATURES

MAINTENANCE-OF-WAY-VEHICLES

Perfect for small repairs or major renovation projects, these kits feature cast pewter parts.

623-2001 Heavy Duty Speeder & Crew Car **9.95**

623-2008 Crawler w/Side Boom - Railroad Wreck Crane **12.95**

623-2009 Generator/Compressor Trailer w/Hy-Rail Wheels pkg(2) **5.95**

623-2010 Etched Brass Crane Boom pkg(2) **6.95**

623-2011 Kershaw Tie Crane & Tie Cart **10.95**

623-2012 Fairmont Tie Cart pkg(2) **5.95**

623-2013 Fairmont Derrick Crane **4.95**

623-2014 Velocipede pkg(2) **5.95**

623-2021 Pyke Utility Crane **9.95**

623-2031 Box Van High-Rail Inspection Vehicle **12.95**

623-2041 Burro Crane **17.95**

623-2042 Bucket, Hook & Magnet (Cranes) **4.95**

623-2043 Dragline Bucket/Wrecking Ball/Grapple **5.95**

623-2051 Swingmaster w/Loading Bucket **13.95**

623-2061 Bantam Excavator Truck **10.95**

623-2071 American High Cab Dragline Crane **17.95**

623-2081 MOW Gondola Crane **11.95** Gondola not included.

623-2091 Bantam Dragline Crane **15.95**

623-2101 100-Ton Lectra Haul Mine Truck **19.95**

623-2111 Euclid Mine/Dump Truck **11.95**

623-2121 Bucyrus Excavator Shovel **16.95**

623-2131 Hydraulic High Rail Crane **9.95**

623-2161 Bantam Backhoe Excavator **10.95**

623-2171 Euclid Tank Truck **11.95**

DETAIL SETS

623-2141 Railroad Yard Detail Set **8.95**

623-2151 Railroad Mainline Detail Set **7.95**

623-2181 Deluxe Gas Station Detail Set **10.95**

Sea Port Model Works

Complement any marine display on your layout with these kits, made of polyurethane resin or metal. See the line of Seaport Model Works detail parts in the Super Detailing Parts section of this Reference Book.

Boats
Barge Kits

663-H1101N 79' Square Bow w/12-1/2 x 16' Cabin SA6N **22.95**

663-H1102N 79' Square Bow w/10-1/2 x 16-1/2' Cabin SA5N **22.95**

663-H1131N 79' Pointed Bow w/12-1/2 x 16' Cabin SA6N **22.95**

663-H1132N 79' Pointed Bow w/10-1/2 x 16-1/2' Cabin SA5N **22.95**

663-M44N 79' Long Square Bow Type Kit **16.95**

663-M47N 80' Long Pointed Bow Type **16.95**

Coasters/Fishing Vessels

663-H114N 83' Sardine Carrier **29.95**

663-M46N 75' Coaster/Fishing Boat **6.95**

Hulls For Scratchbuilding

663-M45N 85' Schooner/Sloop **16.95**

663-M48N 115' Coastal Freighter Hull **25.95**

Accessory Boats

663-P49N Small Row Boat pkg(4) **3.95**

VEHICLES N SCALE

TRACKSIDE TREASURES

Re-create exciting battles or home-front production lines with this series of kits based on equipment used throughout World War II. Each cast metal kit requires only minor assembly and painting. Ideal for flat car loads or war gaming, they can also be used as park monuments or veteran's memorials in modern scenes.

NEW PRODUCTS

US & Allies - World War II

Light Tanks
NEW 726-2102 M3A3 "Stuart" pkg(2) 7.99

Medium Tanks pkg(2) 7.99 ea

NEW 726-2103 M3 "Lee"

NEW 726-2104 M4 "Sherman"

Armored Vehicles pkg(2) 7.99 ea

NEW 726-2105 M18 "Hellcat" Tank Destroyer
NEW 726-2106 M3 White Scout Car

Half-Tracks
NEW 726-2107 M3 pkg(2) 7.99

Light Trucks

NEW 726-2101 1/4-Ton "Jeep" pkg(4) 7.99

Medium Trucks pkg(2) 7.99 ea

3/4-Ton Dodge Weapons Carrier

NEW 726-2108 Standard

NEW 726-2109 With Tilts (Separate Windshield & Canvas Cover)

Heavy Trucks pkg(2) 7.99

1-1/2-Ton Dodge Cargo/Personnel Carrier
NEW 726-2110 Standard

NEW 726-2111 With Tilts (Separate Windshield & Canvas Cover)

GMC 2-1/2-Ton
NEW 726-2114 Fuel/Water Tank Truck
NEW 726-2115 Field Command Unit

Cargo/Personnel Carrier

NEW 726-2112 Standard
NEW 726-2113 With Tilts (Separate Windshield & Canvas Cover)

Studebaker 2-1/2-Ton

NEW 726-2118 Fuel/Water Tank Truck
NEW 726-2119 Field Command Unit

Cargo/Personnel Carrier

NEW 726-2116 Standard

NEW 726-2117 With Tilts (Separate Windshield & Canvas Cover)

Germany - World War II

Medium Tanks pkg(2) 7.99
NEW 726-2301 PzKfw IV F2
NEW 726-2302 PzKfw IV H
NEW 726-2303 PzKfw V

Heavy Tanks

NEW 726-2304 PzKfw VI "Tiger" pkg(2) 7.99

Light Trucks
NEW 726-2305 "Kubelwagen" (Bucket Car) Light Staff Car pkg(4) 7.99

United Kingdom & Allies - World War II

Trucks

AEC
NEW 726-2201 "Matador" pkg(2) 7.99

Bedford pkg(2) 7.99 ea
OY
NEW 726-2202 Cargo Carrier

NEW 726-2203 Fuel/Water Tank Truck
OX
NEW 726-2204 Cargo Carrier

QLD

NEW 726-2209 With Tilts (Separate Windshield & Canvas Cover)
NEW 726-2210 Standard

CMP 3-Ton pkg(2) 7.99 ea
NEW 726-2207 Fuel/Water Tank Truck

Cargo Carrier
NEW 726-2205 Loaded
NEW 726-2206 Empty
NEW 726-2208 With Tilts (Separate Windshield & Canvas Cover)

See What's New and Exciting at
www.walthers.com

Information STATION

Weathering Vehicles

Next time you're out and about, check out the cars on the road. They're not usually all that clean, many are dull and faded, and unless you live in areas without a lot of snow or rain, many have rusted parts showing.

For added realism, weather your automobiles. Add dust effects by brushing on powdered chalks or drybrushing some light paint streaks along the bottom of the doors and rear fenders to simulate road grime and dust. Older cars may appear more weatherbeaten; for these cover the entire vehicle with a light coat of dusty colored chalk, along with a small amount of chalk which roughly matches the vehicle color to simulate oxidized paint. Mask off the windows and spray on a dulling coat which is compatible with the materials and paint on the vehicle.

Another easy way to make autos on your pike more realistic is to add battle scars. Accidents, weather and flat tires take their toll on cars and trucks. Try repainting an occasional door or fender in primer gray or another vehicle color. If your car has whitewall tires, paint one all black. And, don't forget rusty body rot around the wheel wells, easily added by drybrushing on some dark oxide paint.

VEHICLES N SCALE

IMPORTED FROM GERMANY BY WALTHERS
Assembled, appropriately colored plastic vehicles. Markings and colors may vary from photos.

NEW PRODUCTS

Automobiles
European Auto Assortments pkg(3)
NEW 781-91805 15.99
Includes Mercedes-Benz A 160, New Beetle & Porsche Boxter.
NEW 781-91905 12.99
Includes VW Passat Variant, Mercedes-Benz E 230 & Audi A6.

Construction Equipment

NEW 781-94506 3-Axle Cabover Cement Mixer & Dump Truck (red) 9.99

Emergency Vehicles
Technical Rescue Service (THW) Equipment

NEW 781-93802 Magirus Truck (blue) 13.99

Farm Machinery

NEW 781-95301 Hanomag R16 Tractor w/Trailer 15.99

Trucks
Mercedes-Benz

NEW 781-94305 Covered 3-axle L10000 & 2-axle L2500 Flatbeds 12.99
NEW 781-95406 Actros 12.99
NEW 781-94405 L2500 Delivery Van, Chocolade Hanner & Stiebel Eutron pkg(2) 15.99

Magirus

NEW 781-94901 Round-Hood Covered Flatbed & Low-Floor Delivery Van 16.99

AUTOMOBILES

Auto Assortments
781-91605 European Modern pkg(3) 9.99
Includes van, automobile and jeep.

Volkswagen

781-93701 Passat Variant 4-Door Station Wagon - German Customs (green) 9.99

EMERGENCY VEHICLES

Ambulances

781-93301 Mercedes Benz A-Class 160 4-Door Compact Ambulance 9.99

Fire Department 12.99 ea

781-96140 Magirus TLF 16 Sedan Cab Pumper

781-96240 Magirus DL 25 H Rear-Mount Aerial Ladder

Mercedes

781-93401 E-Class 4-Door Sedan Chief's Car 9.99

Volkswagen

781-93503 Passat Variant Brandenbug Police 13.99

Emergency Equipment Sets pkg(3) 8.99 ea
Includes one each: Volkswagen 1300, van and ambulance.

781-934 Fire Department (red)

781-935 Police (green)

Technical Rescue Service (THW) Equipment

781-93801 Command Car 10.99

FARM MACHINERY

Massey Ferguson MF 8280 Tractors 12.99 ea
781-95739 w/Front Fork (red)
781-95740 w/Front Loader (red/gray)

Pottinger
781-95601 "Jumbo Jet" Hay Wagon w/Front Power Rake 10.99

TRUCKS

Flatbeds

781-94304 European Classic Flatbeds pkg(2) 13.99
Includes one each Wandt and Herforder Bier.

Mercedes-Benz

781-95405 MB Actros John Deere Container Lorry 13.99

NEW European Auto Assortments Includes Mercedes-Benz A 160, New Beetle & Porsche Boxter. 781-91805

NEW European Auto Assortments Includes VW Passat Variant, Mercedes-Benz E 230 & Audi A6 781-91905

NEW Mercedes-Benz L2500 Delivery Van Chocolade Hanner & Stiebel Eutron pkg(2) 781-94405

Massey Ferguson MF 8280 Tractors w/Front Fork 781-95739

Massey Ferguson MF 8280 Tractors w/Front Loader 781-95740

European Modern Automobile Assortment 781-91605

WALTHERS 75TH ANNIVERSARY EDITION 2007 N&Z MODEL RAILROAD REFERENCE BOOK

Models and Photo by Lars Ringqvist, Upplands Vasby, Sweden

UP SD45 #48 and SD40-2 #3798 haul a container consist through a mountain valley on Lars Ringqvist's Z Scale layout. Lars modeled this scene with American Z-Lines locomotives, Micro-Trains Gunderson Husky-Stack cars and decals from Nansen Street.

It's been more than 50 years since White Pass & Yukon Route's Clifford J. Rogers, the first dedicated container ship, went into service in November 1955 between Vancouver and Skagway, Alaska. Some months later, in April 1956, the converted tanker, Ideal-X, left Newark, New Jersey with a load of 58 containers bound for Houston, Texas.

The advent of an integrated container system made it easy to transfer cargo from truck to ship to train. Cargo was sealed into a container at its origin and remained intact until reaching its destination. Unloading took much less time, reducing freight handling costs and increasing trade flows. Container shipping became more efficient when standard sizes were designated in the mid 1960s. Stacktrain service introduced in the 1980s allowed containers to be double stacked onto railroad cars, making container shipping even more cost-effective, productive and secure.

The earliest ships carried less than 60 containers but today's ships carry several thousand and the trend is toward even larger capacities. Millions of containers are now shipped throughout the world so you'll want to include at least one container consist on your post mid-1950s layout.

Whether you're modeling railroads in the intermodal era or classic steam trains, you'll find a great selection of products in our Z Scale section.

Z SCALE

IMPORTED FROM GERMANY BY WALTHERS

NEW PRODUCTS
Figures

NEW 272-158034 Policemen **13.99**

NEW 272-158051 Shepherd & Sheep **13.99**

Structures

Engineering Works
NEW 272-282741 **69.99**
5-3/16 x 3-3/8 x 4" 13.2 x 8.6 x 10.2cm

This impressive building complex makes a great addition to any industrial scene. Features administrative wing, production hall and storehouse with covered loading platform.

Village Set
NEW 272-282777 **82.99**
Church: 4-5/16 x 2-3/8 x 6-3/16" 11 x 6 x 15.8cm
Houses: 2-5/16 x 1-9/16 x 1-1/2" 5.8 x 4 x 3.9cm
Restaurant: 2-5/16 x 1-13/16 x 1-11/16" 5.6 x 4.5 x 4.2cm
Includes church, two houses, restaurant and village square details.

Scenery

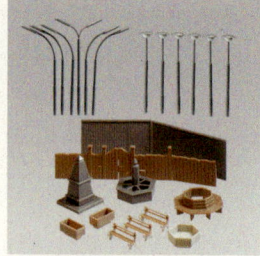

NEW 272-282791 Park Accessories **22.99**
Decorate your neighborhood park or village green with this detail set.

STRUCTURES

Expand your layout with structures from Faller! These detailed easy-to-build kits feature prototypically precolored plastic parts and preprinted signs and details where applicable.

Development Houses

272-282761 **16.99**
1-1/2 x 1-1/2 x 1-1/2"
3.9 x 3.7 x 3.6cm

272-282762 With Attached Garage **16.99**
2-1/4 x 1-1/2 x 1-1/2"
5.5 x 3.7 x 3.6cm

272-282763 Plastering & Half-Timbered Construction **17.99**
1-9/10 x 1-5/8 x 1-1/2"
4.8 x 4.1 x 3.8cm

272-282764 Clinker & Half-Timbered Construction **17.99**
1-9/10 x 1-5/8 x 1-1/2"
4.8 x 4.1 x 3.8cm

Village Church
272-282775 **32.99**
3-5/8 x 2 x 4-3/8"
9 x 5 x 11cm

Half-Timbered House
272-282760 **17.99**
2-1/4 x 1-1/2 x 1-1/2"
5.5 x 3.7 x 3.6cm

One-Family House
272-282765 **16.99**
1-9/10 x 1-5/8 x 1-1/2"
4.8 x 4.1 x 3.8cm.

Dwelling House
272-282770 **29.99**
2-1/4 x 1-3/4 x 1-1/2"
5.5 x 4.3 x 4cm

Neustadt Town Station
272-282710 **69.99**
8-1/8 x 3-5/32 x 2-15/16"
20.3 x 7.9 x 7.3cm

Engine Repair Shed
272-282733 **42.99**
4-3/4 x 3-5/16 x 4-15/16"
11.8 x 8.3 x 12.3cm

Gatekeeper's Lodge w/Shed
272-282738 **17.99**
2-1/32 x 1-5/16"
5.2 x 3.9 x 3.1cm

Goods Shed
272-282740 With Loading & Unloading Ramps **38.99**
5-5/16 x 2-33/64 x 2-1/4"
13.3 x 6.3 x 5.6cm

Guglingen Station
272-282707 **38.99**
4-3/4 x 2-1/4 x 2-1/2"
11.9 x 5.6 x 6cm
Includes an attached shed.

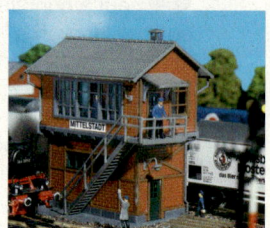

Yard Tower "Mittelstadt"
272-282717 **31.99**
1-5/8 x 1-1/8 x 1-5/8"
4 x 2.8 x 4.2cm
Features an open staircase and a half-timbered exterior.

Bridge w/Lookout Towers
272-282922 **26.99**
8-5/8 x 2-1/2" 22 x 6.2cm
This single-track steel bridge includes four lookout towers that offer a beautiful view of the Z Scale landscape to visiting sightseers.

Z SCALE

IMPORTED FROM GERMANY BY WALTHERS

Wayside Station
272-282706   19.99

Two Covered & One Open Platform
272-282718   19.99
6-1/2"   16.7cm

Glass Train Shed
272-282726   32.99
6-1/2 x 3-5/8"   16.7 x 9cm

Engine House
272-282732   32.99
6-5/8 x 4-1/8 x 2-3/4"   16.8 x 10.5 x 6.9cm

This engine house is perfect for loco servicing repairs! The brick and stone structure is suitable for catenary operation and features two stalls, working doors and roof vents.

Station House
272-282703   46.99
9 x 2-1/2"   22.9 x 6.5cm

Model a complete mainline station scene with this distinctive depot! The kit includes a station, passenger platform, freight shed and signal tower.

Girder Bridge
272-282912   18.99
1/8 x 4-3/8"   .2 x 11cm

Deck Arch Bridge
272-282915   24.99
8-5/8"   22cm long

Stone Arch Bridge
272-282924   27.99
8-5/8 x 7/8"   22 x 2.5cm

Natural Gas Tank
272-282745   19.99
4-1/4 x 2-5/8"   10.7 x 6.6cm

Up & Down Pier Set
272-282909   pkg(22) 18.99
3/8 x 1-1/2"   1 x 4cm

Curved Steel Bridges
272-282903   pkg(4) 25.99
5-3/4" R145, 45°

Curved Steel Bridges
272-282905   pkg(4) 25.99
1/8 x 7-5/8"R   .2 x R19.5cm
1/8 x 8-1/2"R   .2 x R22cm

Straight Steel Bridges
272-282901   pkg(4) 24.99
1/8 x 4-3/8"   .4 x 11cm

Z SCALE

IMPORTED FROM GERMANY BY WALTHERS

SCENERY

Assorted Goods

272-282790 7.99
Includes casks, barrels and wooden cases.

Arcades
All arcades feature a natural stone facade.

272-282947 With Round Arch (gray) 9.99
8-3/4 x 1-3/4 x 1/3"
22 x 4.5 x .8cm

272-282948 With Round Arch Right Slope (gray) 13.99
16-1/2 x 1-3/4 x 1/3"
41 x 4.5 x .8cm

272-282949 With Round Arch Left Slope (gray) 13.99
16-1/2 x 1-3/4 x 1/3"
41 x 4.5 x .8cm

Tunnel Portal Set

272-282934 14.99
Two double and two single tunnel portals, made of precolored plastic, suitable for electric and steam engines.

Tunnel Portals

272-282940 Single Track 7.99
3-1/4 x 2-3/8 x 1-5/8"
8 x 6 x 4cm

FIGURES
Pedestrians pkg(8) 13.99 ea

272-158001 Travelers w/Bags

272-158002 Travelers

272-158003 Passers-by

272-158021 Sitting Persons

Working People

272-158031 Railway Personnel pkg(8)

272-282941 Double Track 7.99
4-3/8 x 2-3/8 x 1-5/8"
11 x 6 x 4cm

Archways

272-282943 Tile/Wall Sill 4.99

Decorative Sheets

272-282942 Natural Cut Stone 4.99
8-3/4 x 2-3/8 x .16"
22 x 6 x 2/5cm

272-282944 9.99
8-3/4 x 1-3/4 x .16"
22 x 4-1/2 x 2/5cm

SIGNALS, DETECTION UNITS & SIGNS

Grade Crossing
272-282730 27.99
For use with single- or multi-track routes. Includes a gatekeeper's lodge. NOTE: Unit does not include drive unit. Gates measure
4-3/8 x 2-3/4 x 3/8"
11 x 7 x 1cm; lodge measures
2 x 1-1/4 x 1-1/4"
5.2 x 3.9 x 3.1cm.

IMPORTED FROM GERMANY BY WALTHERS

SIGNALS
Item listed below is available by Special Order (see Legend Page).

Crossing Signal Set

189-5954 2 Crossings w/Control 29.99

SCENERY

Highway

189-7081 Asphalt 1-1/4 x 39" 32mm x 1m 5.99

Deciduous Trees
1-3/8" 3.5cm pkg(2)
4.99 ea (Unless Noted)

189-6613 Blooming

Tunnel

189-6617 Fruit
189-6817 Fruit 3.99

2-3/4" 7cm pkg(2)
5.99 ea

189-6723 Poplars
189-6726 Birches

189-6729 Beeches

2" 5cm
189-6719 Beeches pkg(3) 7.99
NEW 189-6919 Beeches pkg(3) 5.99

189-8541 Over/Under Crossover Tunnel 34.99
13-3/8 x 10-1/4 x 6-3/4" 34 x 26 x 17cm

Add a realistic mountain outcropping to your railroad with this layout-ready tunnel. Completely decorated and ready for placement on your pike, it includes space for two tracks or roads to cross over one another.

Z SCALE

Add realism to your Z Scale railroad with these etched-metal details. Unpainted brass parts simply fold together and are cemented with CA glue — no soldering necessary.

NEW PRODUCTS
Signals

ATSF-Style Signal Bridge
NEW 176-8010 **44.95**
Kit is based on a typical early ATSF design; similar structures are used by many other railroads. Includes two signal heads (cored for the addition of LEDs, sold separately), concrete footings and relay cabinet/electrical box.

Trackside Electrical Box
NEW 176-8104 pkg(2) **4.25**
These relay boxes house signal wiring at crossings and block signals.

Antenna Towers

Radio Tower
NEW 176-8100 **9.75**
This 70 scale foot tall lattice tower is based on those located near yards and along the mainline. Includes tower and typical antennae.

Cell Phone Antenna Tower
NEW 176-8101 **11.75**
These towers are familiar sights all across the continent and look right at home on any modern layout. Kit includes support pole and etched-metal antennae and platforms.

Super Detailing Parts
Locomotive Details
NEW 176-8500 Locomotive Detail Set #1 **TBA**
Includes common diesel locomotive parts for detailing your favorite Z Scale diesels. Includes 15" and 18" grab irons, cab sunshades, 3 styles of rear-view mirrors, lift rings and windshield wipers.

NEW 176-8501 Locomotive Cut Levers **TBA**
Includes four each of the Early, Modern EMD and GE-style cut levers.

HIGHBALL PRODUCTS

Ballast pkg(1lb) 5.99 ea
330-20 Limestone

330-21 Light Gray
330-22 Dark Gray
330-23 Black
330-24 Cinder
330-25 Brown

BRAWA

IMPORTED FROM GERMANY BY WALTHERS
All Brawa lights are made of brass (with plastic parts where appropriate), fully-assembled and ready to install. Lamps can be powered from any AC or DC transformer with a maximum output of 10V.

SIGNALS & LIGHTS

Lamps For Catenary Towers
Add-on lamps are designed for Marklin's #8914 Catenary Mast (sold separately).

186-4808 Twin Arm **11.99**
Dual bulbs, black.

Lattice Mast Lights

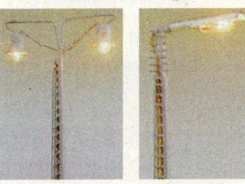

186-4801   186-4802

186-4801 Two Arm Lamp **16.99**
Light gray, 1-1/2" height.
186-4802 Single Arm w/Festoon Bulb **11.99**
Light gray, 1-1/2" height.

186-4804   186-4805

186-4804 Ring Lamp **11.99**
Light gray, 1-1/2" height.
186-4805 Single Arm Lamp **11.99**
Light gray, 1-1/2" height.

Signals
Brawa signals are made of brass and feature operating LEDs. Maximum voltage 10V AC-DC unless noted.

186-4806 Crossing Signal w/Guard Ring **24.99**
German prototype, all brass construction with LED. Includes resistor for use with 10-14V power supply. 1/2" height.

186-4807 Crossing Signal Set **122.99**
Set of four #4806 crossing flashers with electronic flashing module.

186-4901   186-4905   186-4907

186-4901 Home Signal **58.99**
4 LEDs, 1-1/4" height.
186-4905 Block Signal **53.99**
2 LEDs, 1-1/4" height.

Spotlight

186-4812 **10.99**
With mirror, reflector, approximate length 7/16", height w/base 3/8", diameter approximately 1/4".

For Up-To-Date Information and News Bookmark Walthers Web site at
www.walthers.com

Streetlamps
Lamps are made of brass and finished in appropriate colors. Maximum voltage 10V AC-DC unless noted.

186-4820   186-4821   186-4822

186-4820 "Berlin-Charlottenburg" Lamp **16.99**
Black, 1-7/8" height.
186-4821 "Waiblingen" Single Arm **11.99**
Black, 1-3/16" height.
186-4822 "Waiblingen" Double Arm **20.99**
Black, 1-3/16" height.

186-4823   186-4824

186-4823 "Baden-Baden" Double Arm **18.99**
Includes 1.5V bulb and resistor, green, 1-3/16" height.
186-4824 "Baden-Baden" Historic Gas **13.99**
Includes 1.5V bulb and resistor, dark green, 1-1/8" height.

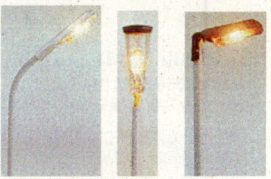

186-4800   186-4803   186-4830

186-4800 Curved Arm Streetlight **9.99**
Light gray, 1-3/4" height.
186-4803 Street Lamp **9.99**
Light gray, 3/4" height.
186-4830 Street Lamp-Rectangular Head **10.99**
Light gray, 1-1/2" height.

186-4815   186-4840

186-4815 Platform Light **7.99**
Black, for station platform roofs.

186-4840 Station Clock **10.99**
Includes 1.5V bulb and resistor. Red frame, light gray post, diameter approximately 1/4", 7/8" height.

Z SCALE

IMPORTED FROM GERMANY BY WALTHERS
Make a scene with Kibri easy-to-build structure kits! Consisting of a large range of European prototypes, the kits feature realistically colored, molded plastic parts, so no painting is required.

NEW PRODUCTS
Structures

Rodach/Coburg Station
NEW 405-6702 44.99
13 x 3-1/2 x 2-9/16" 33 x 9 x 6.5cm

Chateau d'Oex Station
NEW 405-6703 44.99
10-1/4 x 2-9/16 x 2-3/8" 26 x 6.5 x 6cm

Timber-Framed Houses
NEW 405-6406 pkg(2) 26.99
2-3/4 x 2-3/8 x 2" 7 x 6 x 5cm
3 x 2-9/16 x 2-3/16" 7.5 x 6.5 x 5.5cm

Chalet Le Diablerets
NEW 405-6807 26.99
3-3/16 x 2-3/4 x 2" 8 x 7 x 5cm

Gsteig Chalet
NEW 405-6809 26.99
3-3/8 x 2-3/4 x 2" 8.5 x 7 x 5cm

Alsfeld City Hall
NEW 405-6403 39.99
2-3/8 x 2-3/8 x 4-15/16"
6 x 6 x 12.5cm

Weincastell Hotel/Restaurant
NEW 405-6405 26.99
2-9/16 x 2-3/7 x 2-9/16"
6.5 x 6 x 6.5cm

Biel Townhouses
NEW 405-6801 pkg(3) 33.99
3-3/16 x 2-3/8 x 3-/12"
8 x 6 x 9cm

Biel School of Music
NEW 405-6803 33.99
3-3/8 x 2-3/8 x 3-7/8"
8.5 x 6 x 10cm

Murten City Gate
NEW 405-6805 w/Pharmacy
33.99
3-3/16 x 2-3/8 x 6-1/8"
8 x 6 15.5cm

House on the Square
NEW 405-6407 26.99
1-9/16 x 2-9/16 x 3-3/8"
4 x 6.5 x 8.5cm

See What's New and Exciting at
www.walthers.com

Timber-Framed Townhouses
NEW 405-6404 pkg(2) 33.99
3 x 3 x 3-3/16" 7.5 x 6.5 x 8cm

Timber-Framed Town Building
NEW 405-6408 26.99
2-3/32 x 2-9/16 x 3-7/8"
5.3 x 6.5 x 10cm

Church w/Red Roof
NEW 405-6815 25.99
3 x 2-3/8 x 3-1/2"
7.5 x 6 x 9cm

STRUCTURES

Sonnenbuhl Hotel & Riding Stable
405-6400 109.99

Item listed below is available by Special Order (see Legend Page).

Monastary Ruin/Garden & Open Air Stage
405-6401 77.99

Farm Supply/Grain Elevator
405-6602 88.99

Z SCALE

kibri
IMPORTED FROM GERMANY BY WALTHERS

Steiner Gravel Works
405-6603 85.99

Castle w/Open Air Theatre
405-6402 Includes #6679 Theatre 47.99
10-13/16 x 8 x 6-13/16"
27 x 20 x 17cm

Open Air Theatre w/Bleachers
405-6679 34.99

Worker's Living Quarters
405-6784 pkg(2) 29.99
2-1/2 x 1-1/2" 6.5 x 4cm
1-3/8 x 3/4" 3.5 x 2cm

Settler House-20 Years
405-6782 pkg(2) 26.99
2 x 2-1/8" 5.2 x 5.5cm
1-3/4 x 1-3/4" 4.5 x 4.5cm

Settler House-30 Years
405-6780 pkg(2) 26.99
1-5/8 x 2" 4 x 5cm
1-5/8 x 1-3/4" 4 x 4.5cm

Factory Building
405-6762 105.99
5 x 3-13/16 x 3-13/16"
12.5 x 9.5 x 9.5cm
Includes two trucks, fencing, and overhead crane.

Freight Yard Accessory Set
405-6696 With Crane, Shed & Details 47.99

Alpine House Set
405-6892 79.99
3-3/16 x 2-13/16 x 2"
8 x 7 x 5cm
Includes "Enzian" and "Almgrund" houses, fence details and two trucks.

St. Christopher's Church w/Fountain & Accessories
405-6894 62.99
3 x 2-3/8 x 3-5/8"
7.5 x 6 x 9cm

Warehouse Building
405-6764 61.99
3-13/16 x 2 x 1-5/8"
9.5 x 5 x 4cm
Includes smokestack and storage tanks.

Seebruck Station
405-6701 84.99

Goppingen Church
405-6818 49.99
9 x 5-1/2" 23 x 14cm

Large Fuel Tanks
405-6726 26.99
6-2/5 x 4 x 2-2/5"
16 x 10 x 6cm

Factory Buildings
405-6770 56.99
4-7/8 x 3-3/4" 12.5 x 9.5cm

Modern Station Platform
405-6720 31.99
26 x 1-1/4" 66 x 3.2cm

Dreichen Station
405-6714 35.99
9 x 2-5/8 x 3-3/16"
22.5 x 6.5 x 8cm
Perfect for European or American layouts, lots of decorative trim and signs included.

PARTS

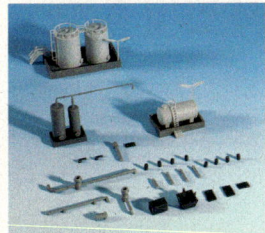

405-6690 Industrial Building Accessories 26.99

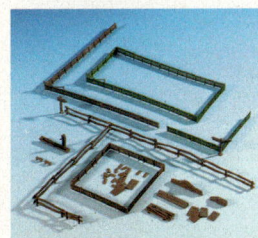

405-6692 Fence (3 Styles) & Accessories 35.99

405-6694 Fountain & Park Accessories Set (Benches, Tables, Wall) 44.99

BUILDING MATERIALS
All sheets are 5-7/8", 15 x 10cm, appropriately colored plastic.

405-6910   405-6912

405-6910 Brick Wall 5.99
405-6912 Stone Wall 5.99

405-6920   405-6921

405-6920 Round Roof Tile 6.99
405-6921 Lap Roof Tile 6.99

TUNNEL PORTALS
Molded in appropriately colored plastic.

405-6900 Single Track pkg(2) 6.99

405-6902 Double Track pkg(2) 10.99
4" 4 x 4.5cm

VEHICLES

Emergency Vehicles
405-6932 THW, DRK, Malteser (2 blue, 2 yellow) 26.99
Emergency Services Tractor-Trailer Set (Plastic Kits)

Construction Vehicles
405-6933 Set of 4 Tipper Trucks/Trailers Red 31.99

Brewery Trucks
26.99 ea
405-6934 Malteser (blue)

405-6936 Paulaner (red/blue)

Item listed below is available by Special Order (see Legend Page).

405-6935 Erdinger (white)

405-6981 Tractor/Trailer Set pkg(6) 31.99

Trucks w/Open Trailers
405-6931 pkg(4) 31.99

Z SCALE

PRR GG-1 Electric Locomotive
441-88490

Conrail "Stars And Stripes" GG-1 Electric Locomotive 441-88491

NEW Class G 12 2-10-0 Royal Prussian Railroad Administration (KPEV) Steam Locomotive 441-88122

NEW Class 482 Swiss Federal Railways (SBB) Electric Locomotive 441-88482

DB Class V 200.1 Heavy General-Purpose Loco 441-88201

NEW PRODUCTS

Locomotives

Steam
NEW 441-88122 Class G 12 2-10-0 Royal Prussian Railroad Administration (KPEV) **313.15**

NEW 441-88291 Class 96 0-8-8-0T German State Railroad (DRG) **362.75**

German Federal Railroad (DB)

NEW 441-88272 Class 042 2-8-2 w/Oil Tender **331.60**

Electric

NEW 441-88411 Class E 10.3 German Federal Railroad (DB) **252.25**

NEW 441-88481 Class 185 German Railroad, Inc. (DB-AG) **284.80**

NEW 441-88482 Class 482 Swiss Federal Railways (SBB) **284.80**

NEW IC "Diamond Special" Set 441-81438

NEW "Metronom" Commuter Set 441-81481

DRG Class SVT 137.2 Diesel Rail Car Diesel Locomotive 441-88871

Train Sets
Sets are less track and power pack.

IC "Diamond Special" Set
NEW 441-81438 **483.20**
Includes newly tooled 4-6-0 loco, old-time combine and three old-time coaches.

"Metronom" Commuter Set
NEW 441-81481 **447.75**
Model of private commuter trains from Uelzen, Germany. Includes Class 146.1 electric, DBz 751 bi-level second-class coach, DBAz 756 bi-level first/second-class coach and DBbzf 761 cab control car.

Publications
NEW 441-19872 Catalog — Märklin Z **13.95**

LOCOMOTIVES
Marklin steam locomotives feature all-axle power, illuminated triple headlights and metal bodies on most models. Diesel locomotives and railcars feature all-axle power and illuminated triple headlights on both ends of most models. Electric locomotives feature powered trucks, triple headlights at both ends which change over with the direction of travel, and the ability to be operated from track or catenary.

Items are available by Special Order (see Legend Page).

Electric Locomotives

American Locomotives
America's most famous electric loco, GG-1s served the Pennsylvania and its successors for decades. This authentic model features a five-pole motor powering both sets of driving wheels, large pantographs with increased extension and maintenance-free LED headlights. Because of its length, a minimum radius of 7-11/16" 19.5cm is required.

441-88491 Conrail "Stars And Stripes" GG1 for 25th Anniversary of Märklin Inc. (E) (L) **337.20**

Limited Quantity Available
441-88490 PRR GG-1 **326.10**

German Federal Railways-DB

441-88080 Class E 18 **306.05**

441-88081 Class 118 **306.05**

United German Railways - DB-AG

441-88581 DB-AG Class 182 General-Purpose Loco **282.00**

Swiss Federal Railway-SBB
441-8856 "Crocodile" Class Be 6/8 **331.55**

441-88501 Lucern City Class Ae 6/6 **259.30**

Austrian Federal Railways

441-88584 ÖBB ES 64 U2 022 Electric Loco (E) **276.30**

National Railways of Belgium

441-88630 SNCB cl 54 Diesel Locomotive (E) **225.25**

Railcars & Railcar Trains
441-8817 German Federal Railways-DB Railbus Trailer Class 998 **51.70**

Diesel Locomotives

German Federal Railways-DB
441-8878 Class 218 (cream, brown, blue) **208.25**
441-88201 DB Class V 200.1 Heavy General-Purpose Loco **215.35**

441-88690 Class 212 Hydraulic **255.00**

United German Railways - DB-AG

441-88641 Class 361 Switcher Era V **160.10**
Finished in current Traffic Red/DB Cargo scheme.

American Railroads

441-88606 ATSF A-B EMD F7 **286.20**

American Locomotives

441-88604 EMD F7 A-B Unit – Atlantic Coast Line (purple, silver) **220.65**

441-88605 EMD F7 A/B Unit PRR "Broadway Limited" **248.75**

See What's Available at
www.walthers.com

Z SCALE

märklin

Steam Locomotives

American Locomotives
441-88035 DRGW 2-6-0 #268 (Bumble Bee Scheme) **354.20**
This steamer is finished in the Grande Gold and black stripe scheme. A powerful five-pole motor powers all three driver sets. Tender is cast metal for better performance. Put your loco to work with the matching four-car passenger set #441-87910, sold separately.

German Federal Railways-DB
441-8895 2-6-0 Loco Class 74 **144.50**

441-8889 4-6-2 Loco & Tender Class 10 **264.95**

441-88836 Class 52 w/Condensation Tender (gray) **359.85**

441-88041 DB cl 42.90 "Franco Crosti" Steam Loco w/Tender **313.10**

441-88092 DB cl 39 Steam Loco w/Tender **260.70**

441-88121 DB cl 58 Steam Loco w/Tender **313.10**

German State Railroad-DRG

441-88051 Class 89 Powered **149.95**

441-88090 Passenger Class 39 w/Tender **260.70**
441-88181 4-6-2 Express Loco w/Tender Era II **283.35**
Perfect motive power for the Express Train Set (#441-87945, sold separately).

TRAIN SETS

DB-AG Electric Freight Train Set
441-81432 **436.35**
This modern freight is pulled by a Class ES 64 U2 loco that pulls four flat cars loaded with six 20' & two 40' containers.

Steam Passenger Train Set
441-81426 **602.10**
Includes DRG class S 3/6 express locomotive with tender, two baggage cars and four salon cars.

Christmas Fun Starter Set
441-81522 **126.40**
Includes battery controller & music CD. Battery Not Included

Limited Quantity Available

American Mikado
441-88812 **311.70**
Features a C&O 2-8-2 steam locomotive with tender and a matching caboose in a red paint scheme.

Starter Sets

American Steam Freight Starter Set
441-81535 **266.80**
This starter set includes one NP steam locomotive with tender, one GN gondola, one Spokane, Portland & Seattle gondola, and one NP caboose.

American Super Starter Set
441-81835 **658.75**
Includes SP Mikado locomotive with tender, Tennessee Central gondola, Burlington Route hopper, Seaboard Air Line box car, SP caboose, Southern Railway F7 A unit, four Southern Railway Streamliner Cars, two track ovals and two power packs.

Deluxe Freight Starter Set
441-81865 **470.35**
Includes German Federal Railroad class 50 freight locomotive, two reefers, low-side car, hopper, tank car with brakeman's platform, 42 x 16" track layout and power pack.

DB-AG Electric Freight Train Set 441-81432

Steam Passenger Train Set 441-81426

American Mikado 441-88812

DRGW 2-6-0 Steam Locomotive 441-88035

4-6-2 Express Loco w/Tender Era II 441-88181

Christmas Fun Starter Train Set 441-81522

Freight Starter Set 441-81535

American Super Starter Set 441-81835; Southern Railway Passenger Train Not Shown

Deluxe Freight Starter Set 441-81865

333

Z SCALE

Train Sets

German Federal Railroad Passenger Car Set (no loco)
441-87670   108.65
Includes one each Bie second class coach, ABie first/second class coach and PwPosti-34a baggage/mail car.

German State Railways (DRG) Passenger Train
441-81430   481.70
Includes Class V 120 diesel-pneumatic compressed-air locomotive, 1st/2nd/3rd class Wurttemberg-design express train car, two 3rd class Bavarian-design express train cars, and express train baggage car.

Bavarian Briefcase Layout
Item listed below is available by Special Order (see Legend Page).

441-4051   986.00
Highly detailed, richly colored and features picturesque scenery and buildings. Also includes a steam loco and three freight cars. Power is supplied by a 9V battery controller (battery not included). Briefcase measures 14 x 19"   35 x 47.5cm.

US Style Z Layout
Item listed below is available by Special Order (see Legend Page).
441-510   1,182.95
This special layout board has two train operation ability and is mounted on a sturdy wood frame. (Rolling stock and transformer not included). Layout measures 28 x 21".

FREIGHT CARS
These sets include a variety of models with colorful schemes.

Tarp-Covered Cars

441-82421 DB-AG 44.35

Dump Cars

441-82432 DB-AG 75.95

Wood Transport Cars
Limited Quantity Available
441-82516 pkg(4) 161.50
Two stake cars and two gondolas designed for wood transport.

Auto Transport Cars
441-86222 DB pkg(2) 36.40

Grain Silo Cars
441-82620 NMBS/SNCB pkg(4) 174.40

Freight Car Sets
441-82203 Tank Car Set SBB Lebensmitteltransporte (dark blue) pkg(2) 72.70
441-82400 Gas Car Freight Set pkg(3) 115.05 Royal Bavarian State Railroad (K.Bay.Sts.B.).
441-82420 DB Cargo Type Rils 652 Flat Car Set w/Retractable Tarp Covers (Traffic Red) pkg(2) 133.60
441-82514 American Four-Car Freight Set 164.35 Includes L&N box car, ATSF gondola, Gulf Oil tank car and UP flat car with scrap tank.
441-88126 Auto Companies-France 62.35
441-881261 Special Edition International Cars pkg(3) 84.80 Cars for Hungary, Czech Republic and Poland.

Box Cars
German Federal Railways-DB

441-8609 Freight Train Baggage Car 24.50

Reefers
441-82550 DRG Type GK "See Fische" Reefer 2-Pack 74.95

Hoppers
German Federal Railways - DB
441-8630 Self-Unloading Open Hopper 34.30
441-86331 DB Coal 2-Car Set with Truck Model 76.35

United German Railways - DB-AG
441-82373 Cargo Side Dump Car 37.85
441-82377 DB-AG Type TD w/Hinged Roof pkg(3) 113.05

441-82391 Coal Hopper K.Bay.St.B. 38.10

441-82433 DB-AG/Kümmel Type Fas 126 Pneumatic Side Dump Hoppers pkg(2) 75.95

American
441-82590 C&O (black w/white lettering) pkg(4) 154.45
441-82591 PRR pkg(5) 194.60

US Style Z Layout 441-510 (Track Plan & Scenery May Vary From Photo Shown)

DRG Passenger Train 441-81430

Wood Transport Cars 441-82516

Grain Silo Cars 441-82620

Tank Car Set SBB Lebensmitteltransporte 441-82203

Gas Car Freight Set 441-82400

DB Cargo Type Rils 652 Flat Car Set 441-82420

American Four-Car Freight Set 441-82514

DB-AG Type TD w/Hinged Roof 441-82377

DB Coal 2-Car Set w/Truck Model 441-86331

Z SCALE

märklin

Covered Hoppers

441-82621 High-Capacity Covered Hopper 2-Pack **87.70**
Privately owned by the firm Millet, these cars transport foodstuffs. Set includes one car with SNCF markings, and one with SBB markings.
441-82622 Silo 3-Car Set for Grain Transport (E) **130.90**
441-86661 Clubmast-Clubcraft Cement Co. **38.95**

Gondolas

German Federal Railways-DB
441-8622 Side Unloading Door **17.00**

Flat Cars

Bavarian State Railways
441-82571 K.Bay.St.E Flat Car w/Real Sandstone Blocks **42.80**

German Federal Railways - DB
441-82271 Type Sdgkms 707 Piggyback Flat Car - DB Cargo (Traffic Red) **46.05**

441-82352 Heavy-Duty Flat Car **37.85**
441-86221 Auto Transport Car Set w/VW Beetle Load Era III pkg(2) **55.40**
Open auto racks loaded with 1960s Beetles.

Class Ssym 46 Heavy-Duty Flat Car 2-Pack 84.30 ea

441-82357 DB w/Thermal Hoods
441-82358 DB w/Steel Slabs

German State Railways-DRG

441-82570 4-Axle w/Brakeman pkg(3) **127.80**

United German Railways – DB-AG

441-82660 With 40' & 20' Containers **41.50**

441-82661 4-Axle Container Car w/2 20' Containers **41.50**

441-82580 Type Res 687 4-Axle Set w/Shop Crane Load pkg(2) **86.30**

441-82581 With Steel Beams **42.95**

441-82582 DB-AG Firma AWILOG Type Res 687 Flat Car w/7 Tarped System Containers **42.95**
441-82584 DB-AG Flat Car With Load (E) **42.95**

German Federal Railways 4-Axle Log Cars
441-8226 Stake Car w/Logs **42.40**

Intermodal Equipment

441-86172 Congratulations Container Car **31.20**
A great gift for any modeler, this car has a built in sound module with speaker and microphone so you can record a special message lasting up to 10 seconds! Simply open the package to begin playback; can be recorded over if desired.

441-82283 Piggyback Deep Well Flat Car & Flat Car Set **83.30**
DB-AG with four 20' Tank Containers; two Bertschi AG Durrenasch, and two Hoyer.

Tank Cars

441-82070 DRG Shell, With Brakeman's Cab pkg(2) **80.05**

441-82072 "Minera" Tank Car DB **40.10**

441-82171 KPEV Wine Barrel Car w/Brakeman's Cab **37.85**

441-82173 Robert Metzger & Co Wine Barrel Car w/Brakeman's Cab **38.55**

441-82182 Pressurized Gas Tank Car SKW PiaNOx **36.40**

Carbide Container Car 441-82090

441-82204 SBB Wascosa.com (aluminum) **36.30**
441-86281 DB Tank 3-Car Set **104.55**

Oil Company Tank Cars
441-8611 Shell 2-Axle **21.80**

Work Train Cars

German Federal Railways - DB

441-8624 Ballast Car **32.30**
Unloading hatches can be opened.

441-8657 Crane Car Set **58.50**
Crane features positionable cab, boom and boom support. Hook can be raised and lowered with hand crank.

Carbide Container Cars

German Federal Railways – DB
441-82090 pkg(3) **116.05**
Two come with brakeman's platforms, and one comes with a brakeman's cab.

Track Cleaning Car

441-86501 Type Eaos Gondola – Jorger System **79.65**
Comes with two replacement pads.

441-88021 DB Rail Detector-Powered Era V **165.75**
Clean tracks as you run trains. Powered model has special ridged wheels that break up and remove grime as car moves along the track. Great for cleaning your Z Scale layout without damaging scenery.

Steel Mill Cars

441-86200 DB Hot Metal "Torpedo" 18-Axle Ladle Car **90.95**
441-86210 Steel Plant 4-Car Set **117.30**

Silo 3-Car Set for Grain Transport (E) 441-82622

Steel Plant 4-Car Set 441-86210

DB Tank 3-Car Set 441-86281

Piggyback Flat Car DB Cargo 441-82271

Auto Tranport Car w/VW Beetle Load 441-86221

Tank Car 441-82070

PASSENGER CARS

Royal Württemberg State Railways

Local Coaches 22.25 ea

441-8700 Green

441-8701 Red

Express Set

441-87945 Three Car Set Rr **132.60**

German Federal Railways

Express Train Cars 33.15 ea (Unless Noted)
441-8710 Coach 1st Class
441-8711 Coach 2nd Class
441-8712 Baggage Car **32.60**
441-8713 Dining Car

"Thunderbox" Coaches 36.15 ea
Nicknamed for their very noisy ride, these cars originally had wood roofs and interior walls.

441-8750 1st/2nd Class

441-8751 2nd Class

441-8752 DB Local Baggage Car

Z SCALE

Four-Axle Rebuilt Local Coaches 43.10 ea

441-8753 1st/2nd Class

441-8754 2nd Class

441-8755 Coach/Baggage 2 Class

DB Passenger Cars 45.05 ea

441-87561 DB Passenger Car 1st and 2nd Class

441-87562 DB Passenger Car 2nd Class

441-87563 DB Passenger Car 2nd Class

441-87581 DB Baggage Car

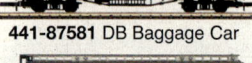
441-87582 DB Mail Car

United German Railways DB-AG

"Regionalbahn" Commuter Cars
All cars painted in "Traffic Red" paint scheme.

441-87161 Type Bnz 2nd Class 36.55

441-87171 Type Abn 1st & 2nd Class 36.55

441-87181 Type BDnrzf 2nd Class w/Engineer's Cab 77.50

Bi-Level Cars
All these Destination: "Regional Express Kassel Hbf" cars are painted "Traffic Red."

441-87291 2nd Class Type DBz 751 48.75

441-87292 1st/2nd Class Type DABz 756 48.75

441-87293 Cab Control 2nd Class Type DBbzf 761 96.65

Interegio Express Cars

441-8743 1st Class Coach 33.60

441-8744 2nd Class Coach 33.60

441-87751 DB-AG 2-Car Passenger Train Set 126.95 Includes one 1st class Bistro Café car and one 2nd class cab control car.

ICE 3 Passenger Trains
Latest Inter-City Express (ICE) equipment, based on Class 406 trainsets used in international service.

441-87713 2nd Class Type 406.2 98.05

441-87711 Class 406 Car 98.05
Unpowered version, includes LED interior lighting and special ICE 3 close-coupling, for use only with #88712, sold separately.

Express Train Passenger Cars
441-87251 1st Class 35.45 Type Apmz 121.2.

441-87732 2nd Class 42.95 Type Bpmz 291.2.

441-87752 1st Class & 2nd Class pkg(2) 124.40 Type ARkimbz 262.4.

Center Entry Coaches 34.45 ea

441-87330 1st/2nd Class

441-87335 2nd Class

DB-AG 2-Car Passenger Train Set 441-87751

4-Axle Passenger Car Set 441-87560

Three Coaches & Combine 441-87910

BLS Push/Pull Train Set 441-87457

Streamliner Passenger Car Set 441-87847

ATSF Streamliner Set 441-87848

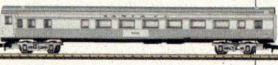
Mail Car & Baggage Car Set 441-87580

SBB Passenger Cars 441-87456

French State Railways – SNCF Passenger Train 441-87505

DRG Prussian Design Cars
These authentic models include truss rod underframes, complete underbody details and separately applied details.
441-87560 4-Axle Passenger Car Set 179.95 Includes one Type BC4pr04 for Second/Third Class and three Type C4pr04 cars for Third Class passengers.
441-87580 Mail Car & Baggage Car Set 90.95 Includes one type Pw4pr04 Baggage Car with center cupola and one type Post4b17 Mail Car with brakeman's cabin.

Denver & Rio Grande Western
441-87910 Three Coaches & Combine 145.95
Western adventures begin aboard this old-time set that includes three coaches and a combine. Complete your train with the DRGW 2-6-0 steamer #441-88035, sold separately.

Bern-Lotschberg-Simplon Railroad - BLS

Push/Pull Express Train
441-87457 pkg(4) 205.45
Set includes one 1st class type A express train passenger car, two 2nd class type B express train passenger cars, and one 2nd class express train cab control car with engineers' cab for push/pull operation.

Swiss Federal Railways – SBB
441-87456 208.25
Dressed in the current SBB paint scheme, this set includes four different express train passenger cars: one Mark IV type A standard design car, two Mark IV type B standard design cars, and one EuroCity design 2nd class control car with headlight and marker lights.

American Streamliners
441-87846 Atlantic Coast Line/Richmond, Fredericksburg & Potomac Limited-Edition 6-Car Set 182.60
Includes one each baggage car, diner, sleeper and observation car in Atlantic Coast line paint scheme, and one each coach and duplex roomette in Richmond, Fredericksburg & Potomac paint scheme.

441-87847 Streamliner Passenger Car Set pkg(6) 213.70
Includes six different streamliner cars, all decorated in the Pennsylvania Railroad "Broadway Limited" paint scheme: baggage car, dining car, duplex sleeping car, chair observation car and two type 10-6 sleeping cars.
441-87848 ATSF pkg(6) 245.10
Includes one each baggage car, sleeping car, dining car, duplex sleeping car, vista dome car and observation car.

French State Railways - SNCF
441-87505 pkg(3) 107.25
Includes two passenger cars and one baggage car.

American Steamliner 441-87846

Z SCALE

märklin

TRACK

Mini-Club track comes fully assembled, ready to install and enjoy on your layout. Rail joiners connect each section, and an additional lug/socket built into the tie strip reinforces the track joint. A wide range of sizes and accessories are available so you can build virtually any track plan. Each section features nickel silver rail and black plastic ties with woodgrain detail.

441-8997 Turntable Extension Set **58.50**
Each extension set adds eight additional fan tracks to the Turntable for a larger terminal scene. (Turntable serves up to 24 tracks, requires two sets.)

441-212 Track Planning Stencil **23.70**
One-piece, clear plastic stencil. Includes instructions. All track sections are at 1:5 scale.

441-232 Track Planning Game **32.60**
Color-coded pieces replicate actual track sections on a scale of 1:2. Just connect the sections to plan your Z Scale layout. Additional sets can be combined for larger layouts.

Track Extension Sets

Designed to expand the basic oval of the starter train sets, each is complete with curves, straights, turnouts and more.

441-8190 E Manual Turnouts Track Extension Set **86.15**
Increases overall size from 21 x 16" to 42 x 16". Includes one each right and left hand turnouts, 10 straight tracks, two curves and instructions.

441-8191 E Electric Turnouts Track Extension Set **143.10**
Expands basic track oval to 42 x 16" and includes a pair of remote controlled turnouts. Comes with one each right-and left-hand turnouts, 10 straight tracks, two curves, control box, distribution strip, wire, plugs, sockets and instructions.

441-8192 T1 Double Track Set **151.60**
Combine this set with your starter oval and set #8190 or 8191 (sold separately) to build a 44 x 17" double track line. Includes six straights, six curves, left hand remote curved turnout, right hand remote curved turnout, control box, distribution strip, wire, plugs, sockets and instructions.

441-8193 T2 Station Track Set **144.50**
Combine this set with your starter oval, set #8190 or 8191 and 8192 (sold separately). Includes eight straight tracks, two curves, two remote curved turnouts (one each left and right hand),control box, distribution strip, wire, plugs, sockets and instructions.

441-8194 T3 Yard Track Set **218.20**
Set comes with 10 straight tracks, one double slip switch, two electric turnouts (one each left and right hand), four track bumpers, control box, distribution strip, wire, plugs, sockets and instructions.

Track Accessories
441-8974 Rerailer **2.85**

Track Bumpers

441-8991 European Steel Type **4.70**

441-8931 With Working Light **13.45**

Track Nails
441-8999 pkg(100) **3.00**

Rail Joiners
441-8954 20 Standard, 10 Insulating **6.80**

Grade Crossing Set
441-8992 With One Lane Gates **92.10**
3-3/4 x 1-1/2" 96 x 37mm
Set includes 1/2" gates and working red lights to stop oncoming motorists. Manual operation requires one Manual Signal Controller #8946 (sold separately). Automatic operation by passing trains requires one Universal Relay #8945 and two circuit tracks (#8529, 8539 or 8589 to fit your layout) for each track. Each sold separately.

Reverse Loop Kit
441-8993 **25.80**
Insulates loop so trains can operate in either direction. Includes three special track sections and short filler section.

Individual Track Sections

Straight Track
441-8500 4-3/8" pkg(10) **27.80**

441-8503 2-3/16" pkg(10) **26.05**

441-8504 1" pkg(10) **26.05**

441-8505 8-13/16" pkg(10) **35.85**

441-8506 4-5/16" pkg(10) **27.80**

441-8507 4-7/16" pkg(10) **27.80**

441-8587 Electric Uncoupler **25.50**

441-8588 Isolating Track **7.95**

441-8589 Circuit Track **12.90**
441-8590 4-3/8" Circuit Track **9.05**

Flex Track

441-8592 Adjustable pkg(10) **86.45**
Can be adjusted in length from 3-15/16 to 4-3/4" 10 to 12cm for situations where a standard length of track will not fit.

441-8594 Flex Track pkg(10) **99.45**
Each section measures 26" 66 cm, can be cut to fit smaller lengths. By cutting the tie strip, the sections can also be made flexible.

Curved Track

5-3/4" Radius

441-8510 45° pkg(10) **31.05**

7-11/16" Radius
441-8520 45° pkg(10) **32.60**
441-8521 30° pkg(10) **31.05**

441-8529 30° Circuit Track **14.60**

8-11/16" Radius

441-8530 45° pkg(10) **32.60**
441-8531 30° pkg(10) **32.60**
441-8539 30° Circuit Track **14.60**

Turnout Curve

441-8591 19-1/4" Radius, 13° pkg(10) **31.05**
Matches the curvature of the diverging route on Mini-Club Turnouts.

13° Crossing

441-8559 **20.40**
Matches angle of Mini-Club turnouts. 4-7/16" 112.8mm long.

Turnouts
Remote Turnouts

441-8562 Left Hand **43.80**
441-8563 Right Hand **43.80**
441-8560 Double Slip **63.90**

Manual Turnouts
27.05 ea

441-8565 Left Hand
441-8566 Right Hand

Curved Remote Turnouts
47.05 ea

441-8568 Left Hand
441-8569 Right Hand

CATENARY

Experience the thrill of operating your locomotives from overhead lines with Marklin catenary sets, which function just like the real thing.

Catenary Sets

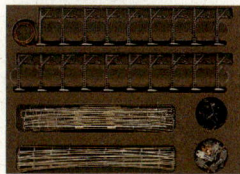

441-8198 For S&E **131.75**
19 masts, 20 wire sections, eight separator clips, six connecting springs and instructions.

441-8199 For T1, T2 & T3 **281.95**
Supplements for #8198 including four catenary masts, 16 tower masts, 39 sections of catenary wire, eight cross spans, 30 catenary wire insulators, eight insulators, six connecting springs, five catenary terminal clips and instructions.

441-8995 Catenary Set for Transfer Table #8994 **46.20**
Includes two gantry masts, wire and 10 short wire sections.

Grade Crossing Set 441-8992

Catenary Parts

441-8911   441-8912

441-8911 Catenary Mast pkg(10) **27.80**
With base plate.

441-8912 Feeder Mast **8.25**
For supplying power. Includes base plate and wires.

441-8913 Bridge Mast pkg(10) **27.80**
Can be clipped to the sides of bridges and ramps.

441-8914 Tower Mast pkg(10) **45.65**
With notches for attaching #8924 and 8925 cross spans.

441-8921 Insulators pkg(10) **7.25**

441-8922 Wire 6-1/2" pkg(10) **24.50**

441-8923 Wire 7-1/8" Adjustable pkg(10) **45.65**

441-8924 Cross Span 4-7/8" pkg(10) **86.45**

441-8925 Cross Span 2-7/8" pkg(10) **74.95**

441-8926 Hardware Kit **6.25**

441-8927 Catenary Terminal Clips **5.25**

SIGNALS, DETECTION UNITS & SIGNS

441-8945 Universal Relay **39.55**

441-8946 Manual Signal Controller **21.00**

Color Light Signals
441-89391 Block **19.85**
441-89392 Entry **24.40**
441-89393 Exit **36.40**

Block Signals
441-89394 Track Low **23.40**
441-89395 Track High **27.50**
441-89403 **39.40**

Z SCALE

märklin

Home Signals
441-89401 Single **47.60**
441-89402 Double **55.25**

Semaphore Signals
441-89390 Distant **26.35**

LIGHTING-ELECTRICAL

Street Lights
441-601223 Park Light **16.10**
441-601224 Historic Street Light **18.95**
441-601225 Light w/Wooden Mast **18.95**
441-601226 Curved Street Light **16.10**
441-601227 Curved Light **16.10**
441-601228 Station Platform Light **16.10**
441-601229 Station Light On Tower Mast **18.95**
441-601231 Station Light On Catenary Mast **18.95**
441-8950 Building Illumination Kit **8.30**

441-8953 10V Bulb **4.86**
Replacement bulb for building light #8950, signals #8939 and #8940, crossing gate #8892, all illuminated engines and ICE intermediate car (all sold separately).

441-72090 Distribution Strip **2.30**
For 11 plugs and 1 socket. All 12 connections are electrically connected.

Control Boxes
Each measures 3-1/8 x 1-9/16" 80 x 40mm

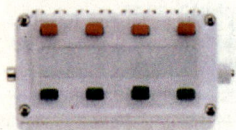

441-72720 Solenoid Controller **17.45**
Controls up to four solenoid accessories. Position of button shows the setting. Use with turnouts, signals and more.

441-72730 On-Off Controller **18.00**
Turns up to four different tracks or accessories on and off. Use to control power to sidings, engine shed tracks and most electrical accessories.

441-72740 Dividing Control Box **18.00**
For dividing or switching up to four track or accessory circuits. For example, four building lighting circuits can be turned on or switched over.

Single Conductor Wire 33' **2.85 ea**
441-7100 Gray
441-7101 Blue
441-7102 Brown
441-7103 Yellow
441-7105 Red

Plugs & Sockets
NEW 441-71400 Plug & Socket Set **22.80**
Includes 66 plugs and 34 sockets in a color assortment based on average needs.

Plugs pkg(10) **2.15 ea**
NEW 441-71411 Brown
NEW 441-71412 Yellow
NEW 441-71413 Green
NEW 441-71414 Orange
NEW 441-71415 Red
NEW 441-71416 Gray

Sockets pkg(10) **2.15 ea**
NEW 441-71421 Brown
NEW 441-71422 Yellow
NEW 441-71423 Green
NEW 441-71424 Orange
NEW 441-71425 Red
NEW 441-71426 Gray

Motor Brushes
NEW 441-89871 1 Pair **4.10**
For locomotives 8803, 88035, 88051, 88052, 88641, 8895, 88951 and 88952

NEW 441-89881 1 Pair **4.10**
For locomotives 88021 and 8831

NEW 441-89891 1 Pair **4.10**
For locomotives 88040, 88062, 88063, 88080-88082, 88090, 88091, 88120, 88121, 88181, 8820, 88201, 88223, 88290, 88321, 88410, 88433, 88463, 88464, 88490, 88491, 88501, 88520, 88523, 88524, 88536, 88541, 8856, 88580, 88583, 88584, 88606, 88630, 88670, 88671, 88690, 88691, 88693-88695, 88712, 8878, 8879, 88812, 88836, 88841, 88851-88853, 88871, 88885-88887, 8889, 88893, 8896 and 88991.

STRUCTURES

Plastic Kits
Easy-to-build kits are molded in color.

Rural Station
441-8970 **24.50**
2-7/8 x 4-3/8 x 2-1/8"
72 x 112 x 54mm

Rural Freight Shed
441-8971 **20.00**
2-1/8 x 5-1/8 x 1-1/2"
53 x 130 x 38mm

3-Stall Roundhouse Kit
441-8983 **113.80**
5-29/32 x 9-7/8"
Includes electric controls to open doors and special track sections to bring engines to a stop.

Arched Bridge
441-8975 **15.45**
8-13/16" 220mm long

Bridge Ramps 12.05 ea

441-8976 Straight 4-3/8" pkg(2)

441-8977 Curved 5-3/4" Radius 45°

PILLAR SETS

441-8978 Approach Ramp Set **15.00**
Graduated pillars gently lift your tracks upward. Set includes 10 pillars, ranging in height from 5/32 to 1-5/8" 4 to 40mm.

441-8979 Bridge Pillar Set pkg(5) **8.10**
Includes five pillars, each 1-5/8" 40mm tall.

Wood Screws
441-7599 pkg(200) **8.00**
For mounting bridge sections on bridge pillars.

Anhalter Station Kit
441-89200 **313.10**
34 x 18" 87 x 46cm; Height: 7" 18cm (approximate)
Based on the famous Berlin concourse, this station features three entry portals, a main building with lobby, waiting room, and service and administration buildings built on the side.

High-Rise Apartments
441-89690 pkg(2) **60.95**
3-3/8 x 3-5/16" 86 x 84mm

Blast Furnace
441-89700 Kit **242.25**
19-5/16 x 7-3/16 x 14-3/4" 49 x 18.2 x 37.5cm
Sure to be the focal point of a layout or diorama, this impressive structure captures all the lines of these fascinating structures. Designed for modelers with some experience, this plastic kit is complete with stoves, piping, cast house, skip hoist, dust collection equipment and builds into a super replica of the prototype. Complete instructions are provided to make assembly easier.

Z SCALE

Transfer Table
441-89941 415.10
Features two approach and eight stall tracks, a controller for remote control of the transfer table deck, and a five-pole electric motor for drive mechanism. Modelers note: requires sunken installation.

Turntable
441-89981 498.70
Eight spoke tracks surround the outer edge of the turntable pit. A remote controller operates the turntable. Includes a five-pole electric motor for drive mechanism. Modelers note: requires sunken installation.

Water Tower Kit
441-8996 16.30
2 x 2-1/2 x 3"
52 x 52 x 75mm
Includes separate water column.

Right-Of-Way Detail Set
441-8986 22.10
Pedestrian bridge, two turnout levers, four grade crossing signs, 12 crossing warning signs and phone shanty.

Station Platform
441-8961 pkg(2) **18.85**
17-1/4 x 1-1/2 x 29/32"
440 x 38 x 23mm

Engine Sheds
Each includes electric controls to open doors, and special track sections to bring engines to a stop.

441-8980 Modern 2-Stall **66.75**
6 x 2-7/8 x 2" 152 x 74 x 51mm
Simulated glass and steel construction, perfect for use with the Transfer Table (#441-8994, sold separately.)

441-8981 Steam-Era 1-Stall **54.80**
5-29/32 x 2" 150 x 50mm
A handsome brick building that fits most eras.

Coaling Station Kit
441-8982 23.65
6-9/16 x 1-3/4" 167 x 45mm
Includes coal bunker with crane, water tank and standpipe, plus a sand tower.

American Buildings
Re-create a bit of your hometown on any Z Scale layout with these American prototype structures. Each is a one-piece casting that's highly detailed. Add your personal touch with paint to create unique structures for your railroad.

Passenger Depot
441-2630 11.00

Two-Story House
441-2631 8.10

Factory
441-2632 12.75

Feed Mill
441-2633 10.65

Freight Terminal
441-2634 13.00

Mine Head
441-2635 12.20

Country Church
441-2637 11.20

Modern Ranch House
441-2638 8.45

Barn
441-2639 8.50

Store Fronts
441-2640 12.35

VEHICLES
Add life to your Z Scale highways with these vehicles. Parts are molded in color and designed for easy construction.

441-8903 Truck Set Kit **28.35**
Includes cement truck, dump truck, two Mercedes closed vans and two Mercedes vans with side and rear windows.

441-8904 Automobile Set Kit **21.85**
Includes parts for three each Mercedes Benz 500 SE, Opel Station Wagons, BMW 735i and VW Passats.

441-8917 Fire Truck Set pkg(3) **48.20**
Includes fire truck with ladder, ambulance and equipment truck.

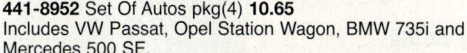

441-8952 Set Of Autos pkg(4) **10.65**
Includes VW Passat, Opel Station Wagon, BMW 735i and Mercedes 500 SE.

441-89010 Container Set w/Truck Transport **39.10**
You'll get six 20' and six 40' containers (two each of three schemes), plus parts for three truck tractors. There are also three 40' trailer frames to move your new containers by road.

441-89021 Model Cars from Economic Miracle Era Set of 10 **40.80**

POWER PACK
441-67271 Mini Club Power Pack **148.75**
Designed for use with standard US household current (110V), the unit is UL and CSA tested.

BOOKS
441-296 Track Plan Book **23.80**
Illustrated instruction book for extending track layouts, signals, catenary, accessories and tips on layout construction. In four languages; English, German, French and Dutch. Hardcover, 94 pages.

Latest New Product News Daily! Visit Walthers Web site at
www.walthers.com

339

Z SCALE

GCLaser

NEW PRODUCTS

Structures

Passenger Shelter
NEW 292-5250 Pennsylvania Railroad Circa 1911 **9.99**
11/16 x 7/8 x 7/8"

This simple shelter protected passengers from the rain, wind and elements while they waited for the train to arrive. These small structures were placed at whistle or flag stops on lightly used routes where there weren't enough passengers to build a full-size depot.

County Co-op
The perfect trackside business for any small town, this big elevator/feed mill is typical of designs found all over the United States. Kit features rolled roofing, chimney, vents, etched floor with grate detail, platforms, loading ramps, door and window awnings and more.

NEW 292-5320 w/Office **49.99**
3-1/4 x 4-1/16 x 3-3/4"

NEW 292-53202 Mirror Image Grain Elevator w/o Office **34.99**
2-5/16 x 3-3/8 x 3-3/4"

NEW 292-53203 Elevator w/o Office **34.99**
2-5/16 x 3-3/8 x 3-3/4"

Storage Shed
NEW 292-51391 pkg(2) **12.99**
23/32 x 7/8 x 9/16"

This basic structure can serve a variety of purposes. Features board & batten vertical siding.

Tool Shed
NEW 292-5201 pkg(2) **14.99**
13/16 x 15/16 x 5/8"

Great detail for back yards and rural settings.

Parts

Cable Reel 6-Packs
1/4 x 7/16" Diameter Each **9.99 ea**

292-5119   292-51191

292-51192

NEW 292-5119 Empty
NEW 292-51191 Loaded
NEW 292-51192 Covered

Miniature Tool Set

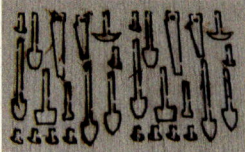

NEW 292-5154 **2.99**
Includes ten shovels, four saws, two picks and fourteen hammers.

Pergola Set

NEW 292-5234 Pergola Set w/2 Trellises **9.99**
Includes one large pergola, one small pergola, one arbor and two trellises.

MICRO-TRAINS LINE

Prepainted and lettered injection molded styrene bodies, free-rolling trucks and diecast metal underframe.

Important Note: This listing includes items which are available by special order only. Please see the Legend Page for information, and visit www.walthers.com for a complete listing of in-stock and special order products.

EMD GP35 UP #753 489-98101020

DIESEL LOCOMOTIVES

EMD GP35
Models feature powerful, flywheel equipped mechanism realistic painting and printing, plus working headlights and Magne-Matic® Couplers.

489-98101010 PRR #2365 **165.95**
NEW 489-98101020 UP #753 **195.95**

NEW 489-98101030 CP #5016 **175.95**

NEW 489-98101040 ATSF #2893 **185.95**

489-98101050 Chessie/C&O #3562 **195.95**
489-98101520 Smokey Bear **165.95**

NEW 489-98101060 BN #2504 **185.95**
NEW 489-98101062 BN #2507 **185.95**

NEW 489-98101070 SOO #727 **185.95**
NEW 489-98101072 SOO #731 **185.95**

F7A
Items listed below are available by special order (see Legend Page).
489-98001010 UP **108.50**

489-98001080 GN **99.55**
489-98001090 PRR (Brunswick Green) **100.60**
489-98001120 CP (tuscan, gray) **111.85**
489-98001130 B&O (Bando Blue) **108.85**

489-98001140 MILW **102.30**

489-98001150 Atlantic Coast Line (black, yellow) **100.95**

489-98001510 12 Days of Christmas **95.85**

F7B
Items listed below are available by special order (see Legend Page).
489-98012070 ATSF (Passenger) **43.65**
NEW 489-98012080 GN **43.65**
489-98012090 PRR **44.45**

489-98012100 ATSF (Freight) **48.20**
489-98012120 CP #4459 **56.60**

TRAIN SETS
All sets are complete with powered loco and matching MOW caboose, four assorted Micro-Trains freight cars, an oval of track measuring about 17 x 20" and a rerailer.

Items listed below are available by special order (see Legend Page).

With F7 239.95 ea (Unless Noted)
489-99403010 UP **229.95**
489-99403020 PRR (Tuscan) **229.95**
NEW 489-99403070 ATSF (Passenger Warbonnet)
489-99403080 GN
NEW 489-99403090 PRR (Brunswick Green) **229.95**
489-99403110 ATSF (Freight Warbonnet)
NEW 489-99403120 B&O
NEW 489-99403130 CP
NEW 489-99403140 MILW
NEW 489-99403150 Atlantic Coast Line **23**

With GP35
NEW 489-99403210 PRR **279.95**
NEW 489-99403220 UP **299.95**
NEW 489-99403230 CP **289.95**
NEW 489-99403240 ATSF **289.95**
NEW 489-99403250 Chessie/C&O **299.95**
NEW 489-99403260 BN **289.95**

FREIGHT CARS
All models are fully assembled and feature prepainted, detailed plastic bodies, free-rolling trucks, a diecast metal underframe and Magne-Matic® knuckle couplers.

12 Days of Christmas Series

50' Plug Door Box Car 23.75 ea
489-149312 #1 "A Partridge in a Pear Tree"
489-149322 #2 "Two Turtle Doves"
489-149332 #3 "Three French Hens"
NEW 489-50200340 #4 "Four Calling Birds"

NEW 489-50200350 #5 "Five Golden Rings"

NEW 489-50200360 #6 "Six Geese a'Laying"

Z SCALE

MICRO-TRAINS® LINE

NEW 489-50200370 #7 "Seven Swans a'Swimming"
NEW 489-50200380 #8 "Eight Maids a'Milking"
NEW 489-50200390 #9 "Nine Ladies Dancing"

Steel Caboose

489-53500230 **21.40**

Ornaments 9.99 ea
Full-size holiday decorations for display on your tree.

489-96060001 #1 "A Partridge in a Pear Tree"
489-96060002 #2 "Two Turtle Doves"
489-96060003 #3 "Three French Hens"

489-96060004 #4 "Four Calling Birds"

489-96060005 #5 "Five Golden Rings"

489-96060006 #6 "Six Geese a'Laying"
NEW 489-96060007 #7 "Seven Swans a'Swimming"
NEW 489-96060008 #8 "Eight Maids a'Milking"
NEW 489-96060009 #9 "Nine Ladies Dancing"

50' Standard Double-Door Box Car

NEW 489-50600090 B&O #471415 **19.55**

50' Plug-Door Box Car w/Roofwalk
489-136272 Pacific Great Eastern #4521 **21.30**

50' Rib Side Box Car
NEW 489-51000150 Norfolk Southern Railway **24.30**

Smokey Bear Forest Fire Prevention Series
This series salutes Smokey Bear and his tireless efforts to protect America's woodlands for over 40 years.

50' Plug Door Box Cars 23.70 ea
Cars are finished in Charcoal Gray and feature a full-color reproduction of an historic fire prevention poster, plus the "Remember - Only You can Prevent Forest Fires" slogan.

489-50700310 #1; 1953 "Please... help people be more careful!"
489-50700320 #2; 1959 "Why?"
489-50700330 #3; 1953 "This Shameful Waste Weakens America!"
NEW 489-50700340 #4; 1980 "Remember, You're Among Friends"

NEW 489-50700350 #5; 1983 "Think Before You Strike"

NEW 489-50700360 1982 "Think, Think, Thanks!"

Steel Caboose

NEW 489-53500260 "Please Prevent Forest Fires" **22.20**

PS-2 70-TON TWO-BAY COVERED HOPPER
NEW 489-53100020 PRR #257128 **17.15**
NEW 489-53100022 PRR #257235 **17.15**

STEEL CABOOSE

NEW 489-53500180 UP #25457 **19.25**

NEW 489-53500250 Happy Birthday **17.35**

40' MODERN LOG CAR
NEW 489-53800040 w/New Log Load **16.95**

FREIGHT CAR LOADS
NEW 489-79943901 Scrap Iron for 50' Gondolas pkg(3) **11.95**

MICRO-TRACK™
This realistic, trouble-free track features molded gray roadbed with Code 55 nickel-silver rail and the DJS™ Dual Joining System that ensures positive electrical contact. Its integral roadbed allows setup on most surfaces and the roadbed is easily blended into layout scenery for a realistic appearance.

489-99040101 12-Piece Starter Set Oval **20.95**
489-99040902 4-11/32" 110mm Straight Track pkg(12) **20.95**

489-99040903 7-11/16" 195mm Radius 30 Degree Curved Track pkg(12) **23.05**
489-99040904 7-11/16" 195mm Radius 45 Degree Curved Track pkg(12) **23.05**
489-99040905 4-11/32" 110mm Straight Terminal Track w/Electrical Clips & Wire **4.15**

489-99040906 4-11/32" 110mm Straight Track w/Uncoupler **4.15**

50' Plug Door Box Car #4 "Four Calling Birds" 489-50200340

50' Rib Side Box Car Norfolk Southern Railway 489-51000150

50' Plug Door Box Car #4; 1980 "Remember, You're Among Friends" 489-50700340

PS-2 70-Ton Two-Bay Covered Hopper PRR #257128 489-53100020

40' Modern Log Car w/New Log Load 489-53800040

Flex Track
NEW 489-99040901 10 Sections & 24 Rail Joiners **47.15**

Joiners pkg(24) 4.15 ea
NEW 489-99040000 Nickel Silver Rail Joiners

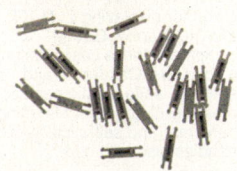

NEW 489-99040908 Roadbed Joiners

NEW 489-99040909 Rail Joiners

Manual Turnouts - 490mm 13 Degree 24.95 ea
NEW 489-99040910 Left Hand
NEW 489-99040911 Right Hand

See What's Available at
www.walthers.com

Z SCALE

HEICO MODELL

Freight Car Loads
Transform empty cars into detailed models in seconds. Fully assembled, one-piece loads are complete with real wood bracing and are ideal for use with various flat cars and gondolas. Simply set in place for loads-in/empties out operation or glue down for permanent detail. Can be used to model finished products stacked for loading or unloading alongside industries, too. Short loads may be kitbashed for use with trucks. All photos shown are HO Scale loads. Freight cars shown in photos are not included.

335-22125 Large Drive Gears 2" 5cm **18.99**

335-22311 Concrete Sewer Pipe 2" 5cm **19.99**

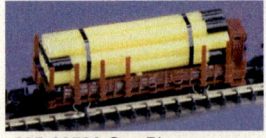

335-22506 Gas Pipe w/Mounting Flange, Short 1-5/8" 4cm **18.99**

335-22833 Air Conditioner w/Air Duct Piping 1-5/8" 4cm **20.99**

Item listed below is available by Special Order (see Legend Page).

335-22507 Gas Pipe w/Mounting Flange, Long 3-1/8" 8cm **19.99**

Get Daily Info, Photos and News at
www.walthers.com

342

Itty Bitty Lines

Display Case 357-1330

TRACK

Cork Roadbed
Precut sections fit Marklin® track. Made of fine grained cork material that's easy to install. Sections feature beveled edges and are easily ballasted.

357-1005 Single Track 18" pkg(5) **3.95**

357-1010 Catenary Mast Pads pkg(10) **3.95**
357-2002 Double Track 18" pkg(2) **3.35**
357-3001 Straight Turnout (right & left hand) **3.75**
357-4001 Curved Turnout (right & left hand) **3.95**
357-5001 Double Slip Turnout **2.85**
357-6002 Cork Base 5 x 7" pkg(2) **2.95**

357-7002 Multi-Track Yard Pads pkg(2) **4.95**

MISCELLANEOUS

Display Cases
Great for displaying Z, N, TT and HO Narrow Gauge equipment, these cases feature a solid Red Oak frame and shelves, white plastic back and plastic sliding doors. Mounting hardware and self-sticking door handles also included.

30 x 13 x 2-1/2"
357-1330 124.95

47 x 17 x 2-1/2"
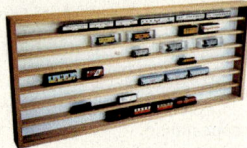
357-1740 199.95

Riser Blocks
Items listed below are available by Special Order (see Legend Page). Riser blocks double shelf capacity.

357-1335 pkg(10) **23.95** For use with #1330 wood display case, Z Scale rolling stock only.
357-1745 pkg(14) **46.95** For use with #1740 wood display case, Z Scale rolling stock only.

Plastic Polishing Kit
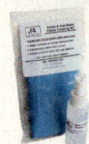
357-1339 Plastic Polish/Anti-Static Cleaning Solution 2oz **6.95** Kit contains a pump spray and polishing cloth. Cleaned surface resists dust and fingerprints. Kit comes in re-sealable poly bag with hang hole for easy storage.

Radius Ruler
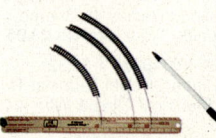

357-180 Radius Ruler **10.50** Make accurate measurements of Z Scale models with this ruler. Measures from 0 to 180 scale feet, with graduated 6" measurements through 5 scale feet. Radius template includes pivot hole and 3 holes matching Marklin curved track; corresponding holes help locate cork roadbed. The ruler is transparent and is made of lightweight, durable plastic.

MOUNTAINEER PRECISION PRODUCTS
Makers of Craftsman Quality Laser Cut Structures & More

Add a slice of authentic American flavor to any scene with this line of laser-cut kits. The selection includes five different types of barns, plus colorful billboard signs designed especially for them, pre-1950s houses, and a wide selection of historic railroad structures based on prototype plans. Each kit consists of laser-cut wood parts and includes complete instructions.

BARNS
9.98 Each

Add color and charm to rural scenes with these models, typical of various styles of barns found on farms everywhere.

Type #1
511-101Z
1-1/2 x 2-1/4"

Type #2
511-102Z
1-3/4 x 1-3/4"

Type #3
511-103Z
1-3/4 x 1-3/4"

Type #4 with Small Addition
511-104Z
1-3/8 x 1-3/8"

Type #5
511-105Z
1-1/8 x 1-3/8"

BARN DECALS
Classic, full-color re-creations of actual billboards seen on barns across the Southern states for decades. Sized to fit Barn kits 1-5, sold separately, adaptable to other models.

Mail Pouch Tobacco 1.00 ea
511-MPD1Z Straight Name – White & Yellow
511-MPD2Z Stacked Name – White & Yellow
511-MPD3Z Straight Name – Red, Yellow, White

Rock City 1.00 ea
511-RCD1Z See Beautiful Rock City
511-RCD2Z … You See the Best
511-RCD3Z … Atop Lookout Mountain
511-RCD4Z … See 7 States
511-RCD5Z See Beautiful Rock City To-Day

Kentucky Club Pipe Tobacco
511-KCD1Z It Never Tires Your Taste **1.00**

Eat More Possum!
511-EPD1Z At Joe's Diner **1.00**

Old Loyalty Cigarette Tobacco
511-OLD1Z Big Bag & Papers 5 Cents **1.00**

BALTIMORE & OHIO OFFICE BUILDING

511-201Z 7.98
Designed from actual B&O plans, this small structure is perfect as a yard office or flag stop station, but can easily be adapted for other uses. Finished model is at home on layouts from the late 1800s to the present.

PRE-1950s HOUSES

White Residence
511-301Z **19.98**
This two-story house features laser-cut, three-tab shingles, windows that can be positioned open or closed, and dormers that can be positioned where you'd like, or left off if desired.

Greene Residence
511-302Z **19.98**
Perfect addition to any subdivision, many homes of this type are still standing today.

Z SCALE

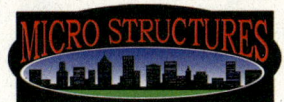

By Miller Engineering

Re-create detailed buildings for your favorite era or display with this series of residential and commercial structure kits. Each consists of thin, photo-etched stainless steel or brass parts which are assembled in layers to create 3-D structures with extremely fine details.

Assembly is fast and easy, as pieces are simply cut out (each kit includes from one to four sheets of parts), folded to shape, then glued together. Most parts are slotted and tab-aligned for a perfect fit. Comprehensive, step-by-step instructions take you easily from start to finish. A list of recommended tools and glues, along with suggested colors and brands of paint, are also provided to simplify construction. And since the parts are not harmed by solvents, glues and paints can easily be stripped off if you do need to start over. (Photos show assembled and painted models; figures and other accessories are sold separately unless noted.)

CHURCH

St. Mary's Church
502-229700   39.95
1-3/16 x 2-5/8 x 4-3/16"   2.9 x 6.5 x 10.4cm

Tucked into a busy city neighborhood or in a quiet country scene, this classic church is a perfect addition to any layout or display. The kits is complete with the church building along with a cemetery, that includes headstones and fencing.

RURAL BUILDING

Adam's Dairy Farm
502-229800   39.95
2 x 2-3/16 x 2-3/16"   5 x 5.4 x 5.4cm

Set up your own farm along the line with this complete kit. A classic barn, 23 dairy cows, six horses and over 400 scale feet of fencing are all included.

VICTORIAN HOME KITS

All the splendor of the Victorian age, captured in miniature! Ideal for vintage or modern layouts, each is from a unique period, ranging from the 1850s to the 1890s. Models are designed for easy construction using photo-etched brass parts to capture every intricate detail.

The Empire
502-221014   39.95
1-3/4 x 1-3/4 x 3-1/8"
4.5 x 4.4 x 7.8cm

A stunning example of these ornate buildings that dates from the 1860s.

Gothic Revival
502-225051   34.95
2 x 1-1/4 x 2-1/4"
5.2 x 3.3 x 5.6cm

The Eastlake
502-222023   36.95
2 x 2-3/8 x 2-5/8"
5.1 x 6 x 6.6cm

Complete with a second story sleeping porch, used as a bedroom on hot summer nights before air conditioning.

The Queen Anne
502-223031   35.95
1-1/2 x 2-1/8 x 2-1/4"
3.7 x 5.5 x 5.8cm

Features a square tower, typical of many grand Victorian homes of the 1890s.

Gazebo
502-221004   13.95
3/4 x 3/4 x 1-3/8"
1.8 x 1.8 x 3.6cm

Perfect for use with any of the Victorian Home Kits (sold separately). Includes turned brass posts for added realism.

The Seattle
502-224041   34.95
1-1/8 x 1-7/8 x 2-3/8"
2.9 x 4.9 x 6.1cm

Based on a prototype built in Seattle, Washington, in 1900.

The Victoria
502-226061   35.95
1-5/8 x 1-3/4 x 2-1/4"
4 x 4.5 x 5.7cm

Copy of a prototype built in Seattle, Washington, in 1900.

The Marlet House
502-227011   36.95
1-7/8 x 1-5/8 x 2-1/2"
4.9 x 4 x 4.6cm

An all-brick structure, typical of period homes built in the midwest.

The Seaside Cottage
502-228011   34.95
1-7/8 x 1-3/8 x 2-3/8"
4.9 x 3.5 x 5.9cm

A popular style of home, built in many seaside areas during the 1850s.

One-Car Garage
502-221003   12.95
1/2 x 1 x 7/8"   1.4 x 2.5 x 2.2cm

A common sight from the 1930s on, many can still be found in older residential areas.

DOWNTOWN BUILDINGS

Turn empty lots into detailed settings with these commercial building kits.

Parkway Diner
502-221001   29.95
2-1/4 x 1-1/2 x 1-1/8"
5.7 x 3.7 x 2.9cm

Made of stainless steel with art deco style, just like the prototypes!

Z SCALE

By *Miller Engineering*

Pink Elephant Car Wash
502-22960   36.95
3-1/8 x 1-3/4 x 1-3/4"   8 x 4.4 x 4.5cm

This 1950s-era car wash is produced from etched stainless steel and is complete with decals and painting tips.

Mile Stone Gravel Co.
502-229200   89.95
5-5/8 x 4-1/2 x 2"   14.2 x 11.5 x 5.1cm

Add industrial action to your Z Scale empire with this complete kit. Includes several large sheets of photo-etched brass parts with loads of detail, and can be built to accommodate two or three rail sidings.

Gulf Gas Station
502-229300   32.95
2-1/2 x 1-1/2 x 1-3/4"   6.4 x 3.8 x 4.5cm

Turn any empty corner into a superdetailed scene with this art deco style station. Licensed scale replica of the original Gulf design, reproduced in photo-etched brass. Complete with authentic decals.

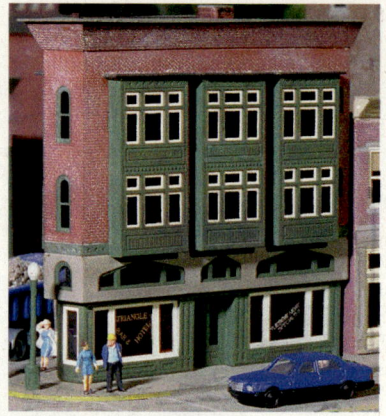

Triangle Hotel & Bar
502-224040   32.95
2 x 1-1/4 x 2-1/8"   5 x 3.1 x 5.3cm

Put an odd-shaped city lot to use with this detailed building. Colorful printed signs are provided to complete your new business venture.

Parkway Diner Interior & Lighting
502-221015   24.95

Transform the Parkway Diner (#502-221001, sold separately) with a full interior with counter, tables, benches, stools and more, right down to the plates and silverware! Includes custom electro-luminescent lamps and ready-to-run power supply.

City Scoop Drive-In
502-221002   27.95
1-1/4 x 1-5/8 x 1-3/8"
3.3 x 4.2 x 3.6cm

Photo-etched stainless steel construction provides super realism. Colorful sign decals are included.

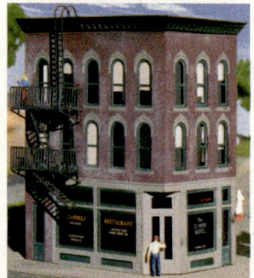

The Gilmor Hotel
502-221010   28.95
1-5/8 x 1-1/8 x 2-1/8"
4.1 x 2.7 x 5.4cm

Hotels like this were often found a block or two from the depot. Includes colorful, printed signs. (Shown with Fire Escape #502-222022, sold separately.)

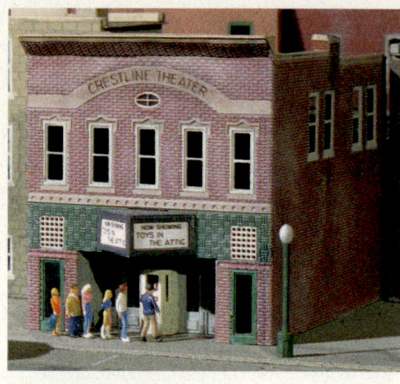

Crestline Theater
502-225050   29.95
1-5/8 x 2-1/8 x 1-3/4"   4.2 x 5.5 x 4.6cm

All that's missing is the smell of popcorn! Includes ticket booth and front entrance marquee with signs for a variety of period movies and additional printed signs. (Marquee can be illuminated with Chase Lights #502-605052, sold separately.)

Train Station
502-221012   32.95
1-3/8 x 3-5/8 x 1-3/8"   3.6 x 9.3 x 3.6cm

Serve a small town in style with this handsome trackside structure. Fits perfectly in steam- or diesel-era scenes and includes a covered platform that can be used with the main building, or as a free-standing structure across the tracks.

Fire Engine Company #2
502-229010   29.95
1-7/8 x 1-7/8 x 1-1/2"
4.9 x 4.9 x 4cm

Built in the days of horse-drawn engines and iron men, these charming buildings can still be found in big cities today. Many have been restored and are now used as offices or upscale apartments. This model features large apparatus doors, plus an elegant facade and highly realistic brick walls which are assembled in layers for added depth.

Z SCALE

By Miller Engineering

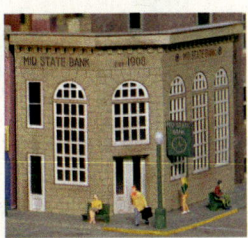

Mid State Bank
502-222020 28.95
1-3/4 x 1-1/8 x 1-1/2"
4.6 x 3 x 3.8cm

This sturdy building will inspire confidence. Detailed parts capture the look of cut stone. (Combine with Logan Savings & Loan, #502-222021 sold separately, to create a six-story building.)

Phone Booth
502-221000 pkg(2) 4.95
A must for 1960s scenes! Includes parts for two booths.

Telephone Poles
502-229500 pkg(16) 13.95

Theater Marquee Chase Light Kit
502-605052 32.95
Transform the Crestline Theater (#502-225050, sold separately) into a masterpiece after dark with this accessory. Includes a special white LED and 60 fiber optic strands to simulate the "moving" lights found on theaters everywhere. All electronics come fully assembled and are powered by a 9V battery, not included. Kit comes with step-by-step instructions to make installation fast and fun.

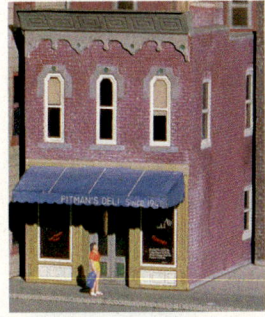

Pitman's Deli
502-226060 27.95
1 x 1-1/2 x 1-1/2"
2.5 x 3.8 x 3.9cm

Enjoy your favorite snacks and savor those specialty foods when you shop at this delightful store. Looks great in any commercial district. Comes with a classy awning for the front sidewalk and printed signs.

K.C.'s Hardware
502-223030 26.95
1-1/8 x 1-5/8 x 1-5/8"
2.7 x 4.1 x 4.1cm

The local hardware store remains an important business along main street, and this classic looks great in any era. Includes colorful printed signs.

Town House #1
502-227010 26.95
Elegant living for big city residents. Built as single family homes in the late 1880s, many survive as apartments, or have been restored to their former glory. (Build a complete block of town houses with kit #502-228010, sold separately.)

Town House #2
502-228010 26.95
Featuring all-brick construction and fancy windows, this building makes a handsome home for city residents of any era. (It will look great next door to kit #502-227010, sold separately.)

SUPER DETAILING PARTS

Air Conditioners
502-221016 Window Style
3.50
Modernize any smaller window in minutes, perfect for homes and apartments.

502-222000 Roof Top Style
4.95
Larger style often found on the roof of commercial and industrial buildings.

FIRE ESCAPES

Make any model building safer when you add these detailed accessories. A great addition to downtown buildings of every kind, they can be adapted to most structures. Both kits come with a drill template for correct placement over windows and enough photo-etched parts to add a fire escape to a building up to three stories tall.

502-221013 Single Window
5.95

502-222022 Double Window
6.95

SCENERY

Photo-Etched Fencing
Ideal for use with the Victorian Home kits (sold separately), around city parks, cemeteries and other models.

502-22985 10' High Chain Link Security Fence 10.95
Approximately 260 scale feet per package. Produced from photo etched stainless steel.

502-223032 Victorian Style
8.95
Approximately 260 scale feet per package.

502-224042 Gothic Style 10.95
Approximately 270 scale feet per package.

Get the Scoop!
Get the Skinny!
Get the Score!
Check Out Walthers
Web site at
www.walthers.com

Information STATION

Parts From Other Scales

As you build your Z Scale model railroad, don't forget that similar parts of different sizes are often available in other scales.

Parts that can be used in several scales include detail parts such as machinery, wheels, gears, pulleys, ventilators, fans and ductwork. Small etched-metal numbers, plaques and building details, as well as small metal castings that may be considered small in N Scale may be average suitable for use in Z Scale scenes. N (and even a few HO) Scale locomotive details and components make great building and industrial details. Locomotive fans look great on cooling towers or on mills, passenger car vents look great as vents on buildings.

Decals and dry transfer building signs are also usable in Z. Good examples include small posters for N Scale building walls that can be used as billboards, and small alphabet lettering sets that can be used to make your own custom signs. Even some HO sets have usable logos and lettering for your buildings and cars.

By using your imagination, you might just find that perfect part or detail made and sold in a different scale. If you're looking for just the right part, check out the listings in the Walthers HO and N&Z Reference Books.

345

Z SCALE

MICRON ART

These detailed craft train kits add a touch of nostalgia to modern scenes. Designed for modelers with some experience, each kit consists of photo-etched metal parts that capture many fine details and are near-scale thickness. Some also include white metal castings and/or pre-cut metal parts. All are designed for assembly with simple hobby tools and CA or fast epoxy type adhesives so no soldering is needed. Complete step-by-step instructions guide you through assembly, and painting tips are provided to help finish your models.

NEW PRODUCTS

Signals & Signs
NEW 462-1055 "Railroad Crossing" Crossbucks on Box Controller Console pkg(4) **12.50**
Features brass poles, easy-to-mount arms and Swarovski crystal red stones. Does not actually light up.

Vehicles

Horse-Drawn

NEW 462-1069 1889 Four-Passenger Sleigh **17.50**
Includes horse, driver, two passengers, wire reins and thrill harness.

NEW 462-1073 1905 Express Delivery Wagon w/Upright Piano Load **23.95**
Features fifth-wheel design for the front "cut-under" wheels. Includes two wagons, two drivers, two horses (one trotting, one standing), one piano, two thrill harnesses, wire for reins and color instructions.

Trucks

Ten-Wheel Conventional Tractors
Tractors feature cast wheels, detailed wheel hubs, diesel horn, side mirrors, seat, steering wheel, stack, two fuel tanks, trailer tongue, running boards, Swarovski crystal headlamps and saffire-color brake lights. Three different style grills. Trailers have cast wheels, detailed wheel hubs, trailer stand, new refrigeration units, Swarovski crystal saffire rear tail lights and rear doors that can be opened and closed. A full set of decals for four different lines is included.

NEW 462-1075 w/30' Ribbed Trailer **34.95**

NEW 462-1077 w/30' Panel Trailer **34.95**

NEW 462-1079 w/40' Panel Trailer **40.95**

Scratch Building Supplies

Modulscratch® Walls **15.50 ea**
Over 17-1/2 square inches of material. Cut at any angle.

NEW 462-91216 Modern Brick
NEW 462-91217 Corrugated Steel
NEW 462-91218 Wood Siding (horizontal or vertical)
NEW 462-91219 Z Scale Cinder Block or N Scale Modern Brick
NEW 462-91220 Stone

Woggle_fret® Brass Wall Connectors
NEW 462-91902 Economy Pack **5.20**
Includes 20 large, 22 medium, 5 square and 24 beveled small connector.

Ladders & Fences

NEW 462-91405 Six Foot High Chain Link Security Fencing w/Double Gate **14.00**
Inside posts feature a "split finial" so you can make 90 degree bends anywhere without disturbing the top barbed wire. Measures 6' High x 180' Long.

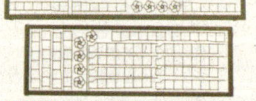

NEW 462-91406 Freight Car Ladders & Brake Wheels **5.50**
Ladders are fitted for the sides and ends of box cars; 9 brake wheels with one spare. Top rung can be removed and filed smooth for ore cars. Includes parts for 2 cars.

Iron Ornamentation
Balcony Rails 10.50 ea (Unless Noted)
These kits are ideal for adding that finishing touch to balconies and porches on your scratch-built buildings.

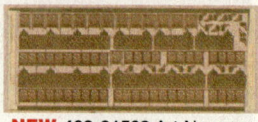

NEW 462-91503 Art Nouveau Edgar Brandt **12.00**
NEW 462-91504 Deco Aztec
NEW 462-91505 Mondrian Reel
NEW 462-91506 Frame Reel
NEW 462-91507 Helix Full
NEW 462-91508 Southwest Corral
NEW 462-91509 Straight Corral

Building Details
Frame edges come off easily and woggle_fret parts simply woggle off.

NEW 462-91510 Weather Vanes & Lightning Rods Set **5.50**
NEW 462-91703 Modern Chimney w/TV Antenna **15.50**
Includes 19 chimneys and three antennas.

TRACK

Archimedean Ground Throw
Item listed below is available by Special Order (see Legend Page).
462-1045 pkg(2) **11.95**
Includes precut metal pins, axles, tall and short flag indicators and clear, easy-to-follow instructions. Suitable for use with Nn3 layouts too.

SIGNALS & SIGNS

462-1033 Rural Railroad Crossing Signs pkg(12) **21.00**
Crossbucks feature raised brass letters for easier painting with an easy flange-type mounting. Includes 12 brass poles precut to length for sturdy mounting.

462-1051 Street Signs pkg(16) **16.50**
Set includes 16 common signs with raised brass letters for easier painting, and precut metal posts for easy installation.

462-1053 Telephone Poles pkg(10) **18.95**
Set includes 10 solid brass poles with easy-to-mount cross arms. Also includes two transformer modules for added realism.

STRUCTURES

Water Station
462-1001 **47.95**
1-3/16 x 1-1/2 x 3"
3 x 3.7 x 7.5cm

Kit includes a full tank, moveable water spouts (two sets of spouts are included to model a double-track operation), ladder, roof access hatch, frost box and five different roof finials. Support timbers and floor joists are just .040" thick for more realism.

Rocky Mountain Coal Tipple
462-1003 **58.95**
1-5/8 x 1-3/8 x 2-5/16"
4 x 3.5 x 5.7cm

Model includes a flexible coal chute, chute and coal door lift wheels, pulley and cable details, under-track coal bunker grating, coal lift buckets, ladders and platforms, plus .040" thick outer structure timbers. Will not actually handle model coal.

Mechanical Interlocking Switch Tower
462-1009 **26.95**
1 x 1-13/64 x 1-1/2"
2.5 x 3 x 3.7cm

Designed for easy assembly, this model is complete with second-floor interior details, including switch levers and a stove. The staircase is a white metal casting.

Rooftop Water Tanks

462-10412 Set of 2 Kits **30.00**

Item listed below is available by Special Order (see Legend Page).
462-1041 Single Kit **17.50**

Watchman's Tower
462-1047 **20.95**
Kit is complete with staircase, handrails and stovepipe stack.

Yard Facilities
462-1049 pkg(3) **22.95**
Kit includes three complete buildings: an Engineering Office and two Storage Buildings, all with stovepipe tubes. A photo-etched three-man survey crew, including a "rod man" with a range pole, engineer with transit and an apprentice, are also included.

Early 20th Century Metal Foundry
462-1011 **129.95**
5-1/2 x 3-5/16 x 2-15/16"
13.7 x 8.2 x 7.2cm

Based on a Burlington facility, this kit includes large upper-case windows that rotate, sliding doors that slide, plus large freight car doors that are hinged and swing open and closed. There are eye-cleats for the smokestack stay wires. Ventilation duct hoods are cast metal. Brass telescoping tubing comes pre-cut to length to make the smokestacks very easy to assemble. Also includes parts for a handcar.

Z SCALE

MICRON ART

Capitol Station 1888
462-1015   144.95
Based on a prototype built in 1888 by the International Great Northern in Austin, Texas, this kit comes with complete easy-to-follow instructions, stained glass windows, cast metal roof finials, detailed friezes, wrought iron ornamentation, 17 figures in 19th Century fashions, plus a baggage cart and buckboard with horse and driver.

Bridge
462-1043 Pedestrian Crossover & Signal Bridge **41.00**
Bridges like this allowed people to cross tracks safely. Many also doubled as signal bridges. Kit is complete with staircases, crystal signal light jewels and metal steps.

VEHICLES
Each features a variety of fine details such as spoked wheels, tires, horn, steering wheel, seat and side lamps. All kits include parts for two complete vehicles.

Automobiles
Ford Model T

462-1021 1911-15 Touring Car pkg(2) **23.95**
Features Swarovski crystal headlights, windshield with suppport stays, provision for a crank on front radiator, easily installed top-down piece, real cloth top with prototypical support frame, attached horn etched to body side and stronger, more easily formed fenders. Kit includes enough materials to build two "top-down" or "top-up" vehicles.

462-1025 1915 Center-Door Sedan pkg(2) **25.00**

Oldsmobile
462-1029 1904 Runabout pkg(2) **24.00**
Introduced in 1897, these tiny Runabouts were America's first popular priced car.

Baggage Carts

462-1007 pkg(4) **13.00**
Kits are complete with spoked wheels, two types of handles.

Emergency Vehicles

462-1039 1914 Knox Chemical Fire Engine **36.00**
Incredible detail includes spoked wheels, rubber tires, steering wheel, seat, side lamps, ladders, bell, folded hose load, chemical tank, extinguishers, horn, siren, headlamps and a spotlight. The kit also comes with full-color, illustrated instructions.

Horse-Drawn Vehicles

462-1023 1880s Buckboard w/Horse & Driver pkg(2) **17.00**
Includes parts for two complete rigs with horses in different poses.

Trucks
Ford Model T

462-1017 1913 Delivery Van pkg(2) **17.95**
These delivery vans mounted a roomy body on the popular and affordable Model T chassis. Owners used them as rolling billboards, painting elaborate advertising on the sides.

462-1019 1923 Stake Bed pkg(2) **18.95**
Perfect for hauling chores at the factory or down on the farm. Includes parts to build a load of boxes.

462-1035 1923 Open Cab Steel Bed pkg(2) **24.00**
Includes two crates for a load.

SCRATCH BUILDING SUPPLIES – Z SCALE BRASS SCRATCH©
Create custom metal structures for any Z Scale scene with this line of photo-etched parts.

Simply combine walls, windows, roofs, doors and details as needed to bring your designs to life.

Window & Door Sets 12.00 ea (Unless Noted)

462-91101 Medium-Sized Windows & Doors **11.50**

462-91102 Tall, Arched & Square **11.50**

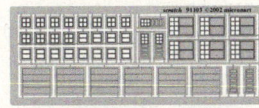

462-91103 Loading Dock Doors, Double Doors, Medium Doors & Square Windows **11.50**

462-91107 Pilasters & Doors, Deco & Modern

462-91109 Modern Wide Windows - Square Height

462-91113 Large Tilt Windows & Big Doors, Small Pane

Items listed below are available by Special Order (see Legend Page).
462-91104 Big Arch Windows

462-91105 Large Arch Pilasters & Headers – Classical

462-91106 French Doors, Grand Entrances, Doors

462-91108 Modern Wide Windows - Medium Height

Walls
Wood – Horizontal Boards
462-91202 Fits Square Windows & All Doors **10.00**

462-91206 30 & 45° End Wall Roof Peaks **7.50**

462-91212 15° End Wall Roof Peaks (Multiple Sizes) **11.00**

Item listed below is available by Special Order (see Legend Page).
462-91201 Fits Medium Height Windows & All Doors **10.00**

Wood – Vertical Boards
462-91208 Fits Medium Windows & Doors (Transitions Included) **9.00**

462-91209 Fits Square Windows & Doors (Transitions Included) **9.00**

462-91210 30 & 45° End Wall Roof Peaks **7.50**

462-91213 15° End Walls (Multiple Sizes) **11.00**

Fine Brick
462-91203 Fits Medium Height Windows & All Doors **9.00**

462-91211 Modern Brick 15° End Wall Roof Peaks (Multiple Sizes) **11.00**

Items listed below are available by Special Order (see Legend Page).
462-91204 Fits Square Windows & All Doors **9.50**

462-91205 30 & 45° End Wall Roof Peaks **7.50**

462-91207 High Wall w/Big Arched Windows **9.50**

Corrugated Steel
462-91214 High Industrial Type **10.50**

Roofs
462-91301 Composition Shingle **15.50**

462-91302 Slate pkg(2) **14.00**

462-91303 Standing Seam Steel, Modern pkg(2) **9.00**

462-91304 Corrugated pkg(2) **14.00**

462-91305 Simulated Barrel Tile (Spanish Tile) pkg(2) **15.00**

Balcony Rails, Platforms & Supports 12.00 ea
462-91501 Art Nouveau Orleans

462-91502 Art Nouveau Rainbow

Building Details
462-91401 Photo-Etched Brass Ladders **3.50**

462-91402 Fire Escape Ladder & Hoist Tackle **3.50**

See What's Available at
www.walthers.com

462-91601 Sills, Lintels, Transoms & Basement Foundations **11.00**

462-91602 Multi-Story Transitions or Stylized Foundations **11.00**

Loading Docks 14.00 ea
Kits include steps, entry porches and handrails.

462-91603 Concrete

462-91604 Lath

462-91605 Masonry

Brick Chimneys
462-91701 Standard Style **12.00**

462-91702 Large Industrial Type; Fits 15, 30 & 45° & Flat Roofs **8.50**

Commercial Building Cornices 11.00 ea
Designed to fit PennZee kits, not included.

462-91704 Art Deco Aztec

462-91705 Main Street

SUPER DETAILING PARTS
These items are unpainted white metal castings and can be used with kits or scratchbuilt structures.

Finials

462-10155 Small Spire Type **1.50**

Funnels

462-10013 Water Station Funnel .060" Long **1.50**

Ventilators

462-10114   462-10156

462-10114 Small, for Factory Roof **1.25**

462-10156 Victorian, Small **1.50**

Steps

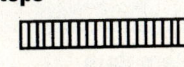

462-10093 1.30" Long, .20" Wide **2.25**

462-16011 1.30" Long, .40" Wide **3.50**

Z SCALE

Nansen Street Models
Z SCALE — From The N Scale Architect

Customize your layout or diorama scenes with this line of Z Scale kits, which feature resin castings unless noted.

NEW PRODUCTS

ABC Recycling
NEW 716-30031 **35.95**
5-1/2 x 2 x 2-1/4"
A great addition to any business district. Kit is a single-piece unpainted resin casting with separate roof details.

Garbage Trucks
NEW 716-30032 pkg(2) **16.95**

Modern Barn Shown Not Included

Grain Silos
716-30002 Set of 3 w/Vacuum Pipe System **18.95**
Modernize a farm or grain elevator with this set that includes three large metal grain bins, a pneumatic elevator and piping system.

Modern Barn
716-30003 **12.95**
3-5/16 x 1-5/16 x 3/4"
8.2 x 3.2 x 1.8cm
Typical of contemporary farm buildings seen everywhere, this kit can be used for any kind of outbuilding.

Farm House
716-30005 Laser-Cut Wood Kit **19.95**
1-1/2 x 7/8 x 1-9/16"
3.7 x 2.1 x 3.9cm
This charming structure looks great in a country scene or older city neighborhood. Kit consists of laser-cut wood parts for easier assembly.

Barn Silos
716-30008 pkg(2) **18.95**
2-9/16" Tall x 7/8" Diameter
6.4 x 2.1cm
A must-have detail for rural areas, these resin castings include the later style rounded "metal" roof.

Low-Relief Warehouses
These partial buildings put big detail in small spaces and are perfect for use in front of a printed or painted backdrop scene, sold separately. Models include a variety of rooftop details for added realism.

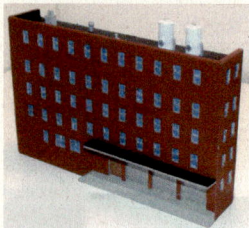

716-30009 5-Story **39.95**

716-30010 3-Story **39.95**

Get Daily Info, Photos and News at
www.walthers.com

Corrugated Storage Building
716-30012 With Rooftop Details **14.95**
A great facility for a small industry or business, this model will also be right at home as part of a larger industrial complex on a modern layout. Includes rooftop vents.

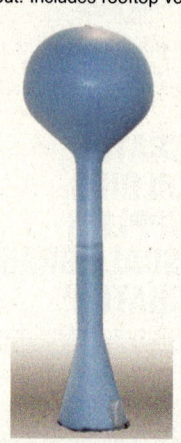

Pedestal Water Tower
716-30011 **24.95**
Modern water tower looks great in residential or industrial settings. Kit is ready to accept an LED (available separately) to simulate the red warning lamp on top.

SCENIC ACCESSORIES

716-30023 Three Stacks of 11 Wooden Barrels **10.95**

716-30024 Four Stacks of 8 55-Gallon Drums **10.95**

716-30025 Three Stacks of 20 Closed Sacks **10.95**

716-30026 Three Clusters of Barrels, Sacks, Crate and Wire Reel **10.95**

716-30027 Freight Assortment: Barrels, Sacks, Drums & Clusters **10.95**

716-30030 Wrapped Rolled Hay Bales pkg(6) **10.95**

Farm House, Carriage Shed & Windmill
716-30007 Boxed Set **41.95**
Perfect for any popular modeling era, this set includes three complete kits. Farm House and Carriage House consist of laser-cut wood parts, while the Windmill is photo-etched brass.

Modern Barn & Grain Silo
716-30004 Boxed Set **26.95**
Includes all of the structures and accessories from kits #30002 and 30003 in one money-saving set!

Wiliamstown Coal
716-30022 Laser-Cut Wood Kit **89.95**
3-3/4 x 2-1/2 x 3"
9.4 x 6.25 x 7.5cm
The "Williamstown Coal" kit is based on a pair of retail coal structures that still stand in Williamstown, MA. Though the exact date of their construction is unknown, we estimate that they were originally built in the late 1800s or early 1900s when coal was the primary source of fuel for heating homes and powering businesses.

Z SCALE

FARM ACCESSORIES

716-30001 Farm Detail Set **10.95**
Includes tractor, wagon and two stacks of hay bales.

716-30006 Windmill (Etched Brass Kit) **16.95**
1-5/8" Tall x 3/8" Wide
4 x .9cm
A neat touch that's perfect for period scenes, many are still standing today.

ANIMAL FIGURES

Farm Animals 9.95 ea
Unpainted Metal Castings.

Farm Animal Assortment
716-30018 Beef Cows pkg(10)
716-30019 Horses pkg(10)
716-30020 Hogs pkg(10)
716-30021 Farm Animal Assortment-Beef Cows, Hogs, Horses

VEHICLES

Trailers/Containers
Detail your intermodal terminals, industrial loading docks or highways with these resin kits. Each includes parts to build five trailers/containers and decals for five different companies are also included.

716-30013 40' w/Decals pkg(5) **19.95**

716-30014 20' w/Decals pkg(5) **16.95**

Truck Tractor & Container Chassis
Keep freight moving on your modern layout with these tractor-trailer rigs. Each kit is complete with parts for two vehicles.

716-30015 w/40' Chassis pkg(2) **13.95**
716-30016 w/20' Chassis & Tandem Bogies pkg(2) **13.95**

Piggy Stacker

716-30017 pkg(2) **13.95**
Modern intermodal facilities will need several of these versatile machines. Kit is complete with spreader bars that can be used with 20 or 40' trailers/containers, sold separately.

Delivery Trucks

716-30028 1940 Ford Flat Bed Delivery Truck **10.95**

716-30029 1940s Ford Coal Delivery Truck **11.95**

NEAL'S N-GAUGING TRAINS

NEW PRODUCTS

Bandstand & Accessories
NEW 530-SZ051 With Chairs & Music Stands **24.95**
NEW 530-SZ052 Extra Chairs & Different Music Stands **11.95**

Horse-Drawn Wagons 14.95 ea
530-SZ017 Horse Drawn Single Axle Delivery Van

530-SZ023 Trap
530-SZ053 Farm Cart
530-SZ057 Victorian Carriage

530-SZ058 Amish Buggy
530-SZ060 Hansom Cab

Platform Details
530-SZ601 US Style Baggage Carts **14.95**
530-SZ01V Benches, Carts & Handtrucks **15.95**
530-SZ605 US Style Benches **11.95**

Scenic Accessories
530-SZ038 Gravestones Some w/Legible Epitaphs **11.95**
530-SZ040 Bicycles **10.95**

530-SZ042 Picnic Tables w/Benches, Sun Umbrellas & Sandwich Boards (2 Each) **10.95**
530-SZ098 Ladders **11.95**

Structures
530-SZ603 US 2 Story Shop — Includes Details for Window Displays & 3-D Window Sashes **49.95**

530-SZ604 Single Stall Engine Shed — Branchline **54.95**
530-SZ606 Small Industrial Workshop — With Fronts for Manufacturing Facility **54.95**

Signals

530-SZ061 Signal Gantry Kit (Etched Brass) **16.95**

PLASTRUCT

Street Lights

570-94814 1960s Era pkg(4) **3.65**

570-94819 1980s Metal pkg(2) **5.95**

City Figures

570-93337 Unpainted pkg(12) **5.95**
570-93397 Painted pkg(12) **26.95**

570-93398 Painted Style B pkg(12) **26.95**
570-93344 Unpainted Style B pkg(12) **5.95**
570-93345 Unpainted (1:500) pkg(12) **5.95**

Information STATION

Station Agents

Station agents were supervisors, retail sales agents, travel agents, movement coordinators, dispatchers' assistants, telegraph operators, accountants, building inspectors, express clerks and trainers for new employees all rolled into one.

At most depots, the station agent was the "eye of the needle". Everything involving the operation of the depot was his domain. At larger stations, this included keeping track of clerks, baggage handlers, ticket sellers and other employees; at small depots he performed all these functions. Agents also kept the books and handled the money.

Agents at smaller depots also controlled train traffic with directions from the train dispatcher. They copied and handed up train orders and operated interlocking plants. They also worked as freight clerks, filling out waybills and handling express shipments as contractors for Railway Express Agency.

Agents also trained new hires. In the old days, this included teaching local teenagers Morse code and railroad practices in preparation for a job with the railroad.

Finally, some agents were responsible for structure upkeep including housekeeping, purchasing supplies, light maintenance and inspecting the structure for major defects.

Thanks to technology, consolidations and fewer passenger trains, there are far fewer depots and even fewer agents. Remaining station agents handle passenger train-related duties such as ticket sales, baggage handling and general housekeeping. In many places, there are no agents on duty, simply a caretaker who opens the waiting room near train time and keeps the place clean.

Z SCALE

Original Preiser

IMPORTED FROM GERMANY BY WALTHERS
Handpainted, plastic figures in lifelike poses.

NEW PRODUCTS

Travelers

NEW 590-88553 Seated Passengers **12.99**

NEW 590-88554 Seated Passengers #2 **12.99**

Animals 12.99 ea

590-88575 Cows pkg(6)

590-88577 Shepherd w/Flock & Dog pkg(8)

590-88578 Horses

Pedestrians 13.99 ea (Unless Noted)

590-80900 People Standing (1:200)

590-80901 People Walking (1:200)

590-80902 Foreign Visitors (1:200)

590-80905 Pedestrians (1:200)

590-80906 Seated Persons (1:200) pkg(6)

590-80907 Passers-By (1:200) pkg(6)
590-80910 Businessmen Standing (1:200)

590-88515 People Shopping **12.99**

590-88516 Passers-By pkg(6) **12.99**

590-88517 Passers-By pkg(6) **12.99**

590-88527 Shopping Promenade **12.99**

590-88531 Female Pedestrians Walking **12.99**

590-88532 Male Pedestrians Walking **12.99**

590-88542 Passers-By #1 pkg(6) **12.99**

590-88543 Passers-By #2 pkg(6) **12.99**

Railroad Personnel 12.99 ea

590-88510 Railroad Workers pkg(6)

590-88511 Railroad Track Workers #1

590-88512 Railroad Track Workers #2

590-88513 Railroad Track Workers #3

590-88514 Workers/ Surveyors pkg(6)

590-88528 Railroad Personnel

590-88529 Railroad Personnel

590-88536 Railway Personnel w/Passenger pkg(6)

590-88539 Rail Yard Workers DB pkg(7)

Sports & Recreation

590-80911 People Riding Bicycles pkg(3) **13.99**

590-88524 Family at the Beach pkg(6) **12.99**

Travelers 12.99 ea (Unless Noted)

590-80903 Mecca Pilgrims (1:200) **15.99**

590-88518 Passengers Waiting pkg(6)

590-88519 Traveling Family

590-88520 Passengers Walking

590-88521 Passengers Seated pkg(6)

590-88522 Teenage Travelers

590-88525 Seated Passengers

590-88526 Hurrying Passengers

590-88534 Seated Passengers pkg(8)

590-88535 Passengers w/Bags, Waiting pkg(6)

590-88538 Standing Passengers pkg(7)

590-88540 Travelers w/Luggage pkg(6)

590-88541 Passengers w/Handbags

590-88545 Seated Passengers

590-88546 Walking Passengers w/Luggage pkg(6)

590-88547 Travelers

590-88548 Walking Travelers #1

590-88549 Walking Travelers #2

Working People 12.99 ea (Unless Noted)

590-80908 Workers **13.99**

590-80909 Mechanics (1:200) pkg(6) **13.99**

590-88530 Industrial Workers

590-88533 Seated Industrial Workers pkg(6)

590-88537 Workers w/Protective Clothing pkg(6)

590-88544 Cattle at Market

Unpainted Figures

590-88500 Assortment pkg(160) **27.99**
590-80990 Assorted Figures (1:200) pkg(190) **40.99**

Z SCALE

IMPORTED FROM GERMANY BY WALTHERS

NEW PRODUCTS

Trees

Assortments pkg(25)
1-3/8 - 2-5/8" 3.5 - 6.5cm Tall

NEW **528-42501** Deciduous **23.99**

NEW **528-42511** Mixed Forest (Deciduous & Firs) **21.99**

NEW **528-42516** Spring (light green, white and red blossoms) **23.99**

Pines pkg(50)
1-9/16 - 2-3/8" 4 - 6cm Tall

NEW **528-42521** Fir **34.99**
NEW **528-42526** Spruce **37.99**

Assortments pkg(10) 9.99 ea
1-3/8 - 2-5/8" 3.5 - 6.5cm Tall
NEW **528-42601** Deciduous
NEW **528-42606** Spring (light green, white and red blossoms)
NEW **528-42611** Mixed Forest (Deciduous & Firs)

TRACK

528-50140 Track Cleaning Block **8.99**
Keep your Z Scale track clean with this Track Cleaning Block! The block slides across the top of the rails to clean your track quickly and easily.

SCENERY

Tree Assortments
Trees are assembled and appropriately colored.

528-42520 Model Firs pkg(25) **19.99**
528-42620 Fir Trees pkg(10) **9.99**
Trees measure 1-3/8 to 2-3/8" 35-60mm tall.

528-42525 Spruces pkg(25) **21.99**
528-42625 Spruce Trees pkg(10) **9.99**
Trees measure 1-3/8 to 2-1/2" 35-65mm.

Static Grass
Static grass is appropriately colored flocking material and may be used in various scales.

528-8310 Light Green pkg(3/8oz) **2.99**
528-50190 Light Green pkg(100g) **10.99**
528-8320 Dark Green pkg(3/8oz) **2.99**
528-50200 Dark Green pkg(100g) **10.99**
528-8340 Brown pkg(3/8oz) **2.99**
528-8100 Dispenser Only **4.99**

Grass Mats 11.99 ea (Unless Noted)
Grass mats are made of appropriately colored flocking material and may be used in various scales.

528-110 Spring Meadow 29 x 40"
528-120 Autumn Meadow 29 x 40"

528-230 Dark Green Meadow 24 x 48"

528-240 Meadow 24 x 48"
528-280 Autumn Meadow 24 x 48"

Large Grass Mats
78-3/4 x 39-3/8" 200 x 100cm
528-10 Spring **30.99**
528-11 Flowering **32.99**
528-12 Summer **32.99**

Water

528-60860 Wildwater River Set **11.99**
Includes one bottle of blue paint, one bottle of transparent blue gloss and multi-colored pebbles.

Roads 6.99 ea

528-44070 Cobblestone Street (39")

528-44100 Flexible Roadway (39")

528-44150 Flexible Road Roll (39")

Walls & Arcades 6.99 ea
Assembled, pre-colored plastic.

528-44920 Wall w/Arches 5 x 2-13/16"

528-44960 Natural Stone Wall

528-44970 Natural Stone Arcade

Tunnels & Portals
Molded plastic finished in appropriate colors, covered with static grass.

528-44420 Single Track Portal pkg(2) **4.99**
528-44430 Double Track Portal pkg(2) **4.99**

Latest New Product News Daily! Visit Walthers Web site at

www.walthers.com

528-44670 Single Track, Curved w/Pond **15.99**

528-44710 Double Track, Straight w/Arch **24.99**

528-44810 Single Track-Stone **7.99**
2-5/8 x 2-13/32" 6.5 x 6cm

528-44820 Double Track-Stone **7.99**
3-13/32 x 2-5/8" 8.5 x 6.5cm

Miniature Scenes 17.99 ea

528-43400 Outdoor Garden Scene
Includes two figures & accessories.

528-43610 Platform Details & People

528-43780 Alps Farm Scene
Includes one figure, two cows, well, outhouse and accessories.

528-43680 Memorial Set w/Figures

Z SCALE

IMPORTED FROM GERMANY BY WALTHERS

FIGURES
Handpainted figures.

Sports

528-43700 Camp Tents & 4 Campers **17.99**

Animals

528-43390 Horse Pulling Lumber **17.99**
Includes figure and accessories.

528-43750 Horses & Fence **18.99**

Outdoor Scenes

528-43811 Lighted Tree w/Couple On Bench **26.99**

VEHICLES

Volkswagen pkg(2) 12.99 ea
Ready-to-run vehicles are made of appropriately colored plastic and feature clear windows and painted details.

528-43902 Golf Sedan
528-43903 Beetles
528-43904 Delivery Van

PRE-SIZE

Tunnel Portals 8.00 ea
Each portal measures 2-3/8 x 1-3/4" 5.94 x 4.37cm. Note: engines shown in photos below not included.

483-901 Cut Stone

483-902 Concrete

S&S HOBBY PRODUCTS

E-Z Streets Kit
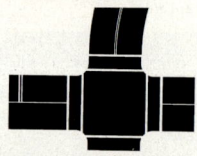

643-105 **9.99**
Printed on waterproof styrene, this kit includes six 12" straight sections, curves, intersection with crosswalk lines and two railroad crossing lines.

Road Sign Kits
Kits include etched brass signs, steel posts and color decals.

643-100 Stop Sign Set pkg(12) **8.99**
Includes four Stop signs, two Railroad Crossing signs, two Pedestrian Crossing signs, plus one each 25, 35, 45 and 55 MPH speed limit signs.

643-101 Route Sign Set pkg(10) **6.99**
Includes two each: Slippery When Wet, Soft Shoulder, No Parking, Do Not Stop on Tracks and Route (with decals to select your own route numbers).

VOLLMER

IMPORTED FROM GERMANY BY WALTHERS
These easy-to-build, detailed structures are molded in a realistic color, so no painting is needed.

Station Zavelstein
770-9511 **42.99**
3-7/8 x 3 x 1-7/8" 10 x 7.7 x 4.9cm

Village Set w/Church
770-9555 **133.99**
Includes a church and #s 9552, 9553 and 9554.

House Set
770-9575 **109.99**
Includes one each #'s 9571, 9572, 9573 & 9574.

Travel Agency
770-9548 **35.99**
2-5/8 x 2" 6.6 x 5cm

Mayor's House
770-9542 **35.99**
2 x 1-1/2" 5 x 3.8cm

Gray House w/Red Roof
770-9572 **31.99**
2-3/8 x 2-1/4 x 2"
6 x 5.8 x 5.2cm

House w/Gray Roof
770-9573 **31.99**
2-3/8 x 2-1/4 x 2"
6 x 5.8 x 5.2cm

White House w/Red Roof
770-9574 **31.99**
2-3/8 x 2-1/4 x 2"
6 x 5.8 x 5.2cm

Small House
770-9552 **31.99**
2 x 1-1/2 x 2-1/8"
5 x 3.8 x 5.3cm

Cottage
770-9553 **31.99**
2 x 1-1/2 x 2-1/8"
5 x 3.8 x 5.3cm

Z SCALE

VOLLMER
IMPORTED FROM GERMANY BY WALTHERS

Family House
770-9554 31.99
2 x 1-1/2 x 2-1/8"
5 x 3.8 x 5.3cm

Haunted Mansion
770-9679 43.99
3-3/32 x 2 x 2-21/64"
7.7 x 5 x 5.8cm

House On Fire
770-9538 39.99
2 x 1-1/2" 5 x 3.8cm

Farmhouse w/Barn
770-9540 40.99
2 x 1-1/2" 5 x 3.8cm
2 x 1-5/8" 5 x 4.2cm

Barn Only
770-9541 21.99
2 x 1-5/8" 5 x 4.2cm

Vicarage
770-9544 35.99
2 x 1-1/2" 5 x 3.8cm

Highland Station
770-9510 82.99
8-1/4 x 2-3/4" 22 x 7cm

Platform Only
770-9525 pkg(2) 15.99
9-1/2 x 3/4" 22 x 7cm

Country House
770-9570 35.99
3-1/8 x 2 x 1-7/8"
8 x 5.2 x 4.9cm

House w/Shop
770-9571 31.99
2-7/8 x 3 x 1-7/8"
7.2 x 7.7 x 4.7cm

Half-Timber House
770-9530 35.99
2 x 1-1/2" 5 x 3.8cm

Farmhouse
770-9531 35.99
3-1/8 x 2-1/4" 8 x 5.8cm

Small City Hall
770-9532 35.99
2 x 1-1/2" 5 x 3.8cm

Half-Timber Inn
770-9533 35.99
2-5/8 x 2" 6.6 x 5cm

Village Inn
770-9545 35.99
2-5/8 x 2" 6.6 x 5cm

Bakery
770-9546 35.99
1-3/16 x 2-5/16" 3 x 5.8cm

Get Your Daily Dose of Product News at
www.walthers.com

Manufacturing Plant
770-9610 42.99
7-1/2 x 3-1/2" 19 x 9cm

German Village
770-9535 pkg(4) 115.99
Includes one each: #9530, 9531, 9532 and 9533.

Wine Store
770-9547 35.99
1-3/16 x 2-5/16" 3 x 5.8cm

Fire Station
770-9550 44.99
2-15/16 x 1-7/8" 7.5 x 4.8cm

Village Church
770-9560 45.99
4-9/16 x 3" 11.6 x 7.7cm

Z SCALE

Models by Pamela Young, Photo by Bob Gallegos, Milwaukee, WI

On a hazy morning the white sky signals that it's going to be a hot, muggy day. Only a couple of commuters are making their way to work as a motel guest gets a breath of fresh air in the sidewalk. In the older part of town, old buildings like the hotel are undergoing revitalization; the lobby is in the midst of being remodeled. The windows of adjacent businesses are still dark, illuminated only by streetlamps. In a few minutes, they'll be extinguished, along with the flickering neon sign and the lights in the windows of the apartments in the distance. Lighting plays a big part in adding realism to any layout. Streetlights, building lights, lights inside autos and other lighting effects add implied action. In this scene, lighting inside the Design Preservation Models buildings makes them look occupied, and in combination with the hazy sky, helps build an atmosphere. Check out the Lighting, Electrical & Motors section for ideas on how to add atmosphere to your layout.

LIGHTING - ELECTRICAL - MOTORS

WALTHERS

BULBS

16V, .100 Amp Mini-Bulb pkg(3) 4.98 ea
For longer bulb life, our 16V bulbs can be operated from a 12V power supply.

942-3491 Amber
942-3493 Clear
942-3495 Green
942-3496 Red

1.5V, .083 Amp Micro Bulb

942-433 Clear **5.98**

1.5V, .083 Amp Grain-O-Rice pkg(3) 4.98 ea
942-435 Clear
942-436 12V Clear

6V Grain-O-Wheat
942-441 Clear pkg(2) **2.98**

16V, .100 Amp Grain-O-Wheat pkg(3) 4.98 ea (Unless Noted)

942-3451 Amber
942-3453 Clear
942-3455 Green
942-3456 Red
942-13453 Clear pkg(50) **59.98**

16V, .100 Amp Sub-Miniature Bulb
942-365 Clear pkg(3) **6.98**

Cornerstone Series® Building Replacement Bulb
942-473 pkg(5) **4.98**
Replacement bulb fits lighting unit in Walthers O Scale structures kits, and HO Gold Ribbon Series™ buildings, adaptable to other uses.

Sockets

942-350 pkg(6) **4.98**

Hook-Up Wire
942-414 6', 4 Colors **2.49**

LIFE-LIKE TRAINS
Division of Wm.K.Walthers, Inc.

Bulbs 4.75 ea

433-1213 Lamp Bulb pkg(3)
For use with #433-1808 (sold separately.) Screw-in style, 14V AC or DC.

433-1215   433-1217

433-1215 With Wired Socket pkg(2)
14V AC or DC.

433-1217 Grain Of Wheat pkg(2)
For use with Gas Light #433-1257 and Highway Light #433-1705, (each sold separately.) Clear, 14V AC or DC.

House Lighting Kit

433-1205 With Base **4.75**
All-purpose house light is pre-wired for easy operation. Use lamp bulb #433-1213, (sold separately,) as replacement.

ATLAS

Layout Wire 6.95 ea

20 gauge standard copper, 50' spool.
150-315 Black
150-316 Red
150-317 Green
150-318 Yellow
150-319 Blue

5 Conductor Ribbon Wire

150-312 pkg(50') **18.95**
Wire matches what is included in all Atlas HO and N Scale switches. Can be used for any scale.

BACHMANN

Electrical Accessories
Water Pump Electric, Mini

160-42219 **12.75**

Interior Lighting Kit w/Wire

160-42240 pkg(2) **6.50**

ARNOLD/RIVAROSSI
Limited Quantity Available On All Items.

Lighting
Panel Lights 6.99 ea
For interior illumination of buildings, tunnels or as control panel switch indicator lights. 12-16V, 30mA. Includes 3-9/16" 90cm wire.

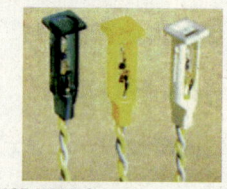

125-7317 Green
125-7318 Yellow
125-7319 White

Switches

125-7230 Double Slip Controller **18.99**
125-7252 Simplex **27.49**

Wires
125-7120 Two Strand Conductor Wire **1.99**
Red and black, 19" 50cm long with plug-in connectors.

For Daily Product Updates Point Your Browser to
www.walthers.com

BL HOBBY PRODUCTS
Limited Quantity Available On All Items

ELECTRICAL ACCESSORIES

LEDs pkg(4) 3.95 ea
Small, 3/32" Lens
183-250 Red
183-251 Green
183-252 Yellow

Regular T-1
183-253 Red
183-254 Green
183-255 Yellow

Resistors
183-260 Drop 560 ohms pkg(5) **2.00**

FIBER OPTICS

Light Kits
Stars In Your Sky
183-532 HO Scale **45.00**

Moon In Your Sky
183-535 **12.00**

Auto
183-720 **7.95**

Fibers
183-701 100', .010" Fiber **7.50**
183-702 30', .020" Fiber **6.25**

Fiber w/Light Source
Includes two each of .020" and .030" optic fiber.
183-711 Clear **6.75**
183-713 Red **6.75**
183-714 Yellow **6.50**
183-715 Multiple Light Source **11.95**

LIGHTING - ELECTRICAL - MOTORS

BRAWA
LIEBE ZUM DETAIL

IMPORTED FROM GERMANY BY WALTHERS
Brawa offers a comprehensive line of electrical accessories, lighting equipment and wire suitable for use with all model railroad systems.

NEW PRODUCTS

Pin-Socket System Lights
Easy to add system features interchangeable lights and spring-loaded sockets.

Street Lamps
NEW **186-4000** Single Curved Arm Light 1-7/8" 4.8cm **10.99**
NEW **186-4001** Double Curved Arm Light 2-5/32" 5.5cm **17.99**
NEW **186-4020** Rectangular Light 1-13/32" 3.6cm **10.99**

Railroad Yard Lamps
NEW **186-4010** Single Extended Headlight 2-3/4" 7cm **14.99**
NEW **186-4011** Double Extended Headlight 2-3/4" 7cm **18.99**
NEW **186-4040** Wooden Mast Light 2" 5cm **13.99**

LIGHTS

Station Lights

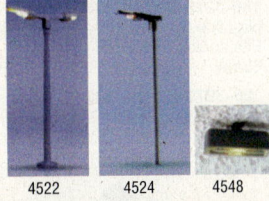

4522   4524   4548

186-4522 Double Arm **14.99**
Finished in light gray, 2-1/2" high.
186-4524 Single Arm **10.99**
Finished in light gray, 2-1/2" high.
186-4548 Platform Light-Modern **7.99**
Measures 5/32 x 5/32 x 1/2", finished in gray.

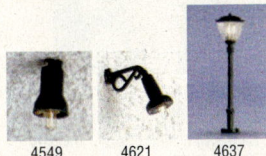

4549   4621   4637

186-4549 Platform Light **7.99**
Roof mounting, finished in black.
186-4621 Wall-Mounted Light **12.99**
186-4637 Bavarian Station Platform Light **10.99**

4638   4598

186-4638 Platform Light **12.99**
186-4598 Station Light with Festoon Bulb **12.99**
Rectangular section mast, 3" high.

4640   4641   4643

186-4640 Tall **12.99**
3-5/8" high.
186-4641 Tall, Old-Time **13.99**
3-5/8" high.
186-4643 Station Light **11.99**

Limited Quantity Available

186-4639 Angular Post Platform Light **11.99**
Station Light listed below is available by Special Order (see Legend Page).

186-4591 Station Light **12.99**

Lattice Mast Lights

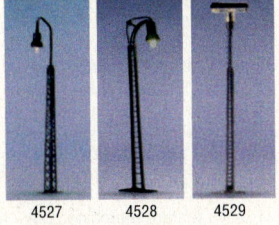

4527   4528   4529

186-4527 Lattice Mast Light **14.99**
Square tower; 3" high.
186-4528 Modern Lattice Mast Light **13.99**
Modern flat pattern; 3" high.
186-4529 Modern w/Festoon Bulb **16.99**
Rectangular section mast, 3" high.
186-4592 Yard Light-Masted **16.99**

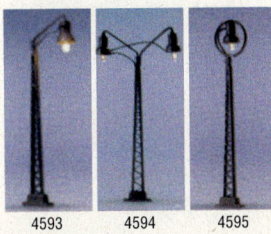

4593   4594   4595

186-4593 Single Arm **13.99**
2-3/4" high.
186-4594 Double Arm **17.99**
2-3/4" high.
186-4595 Lattice Mast w/Ring **13.99**
2-3/4" high.

Wooden Post Lights
Used in rural areas, stations or villages. 2" high.

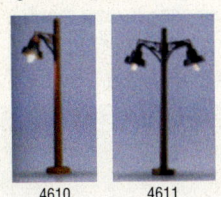

4610   4611

186-4610 Single Arm Lamp **15.99**
186-4611 Double Arm Lamp **21.99**
186-4612 Wooden Post Lamp **16.99**

Catenary Tower Lights
Add-on lights for N Scale overhead catenary towers.

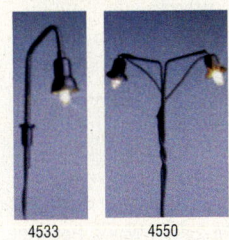

4533   4550

186-4533 Single Bulb **8.99**
Single add-on light fits Arnold, Vollmer and Sommerfeld towers.
186-4550 Double Bulb **11.99**
Twin add-on light fits Arnold, Vollmer and Sommerfeld towers.

Street Lights
Based on German prototypes, these modern street lights are typical of lights used around the world. For use with 16V power supply.

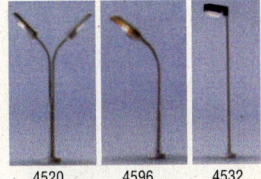

4520   4596   4532

186-4520 Double Curved Arm Light **16.99**
1-1/4" high.
186-4596 Single Curved Arm Light **9.99**
2" high.
186-4532 Single Rectangular Head **8.99**
3" high.

4601   4620   4628

186-4601 "Waiblingen" Street Lamp **16.99**
With two modern rectangular lamps. 2-3/4" high.
186-4620 "Waiblingen" Wall-Mounted Lamp **10.99**
With Shade. 5/8" high, diameter 1/4".
186-4628 Park Light **9.99**

4534   4525   4526

186-4534 "Baden-Baden" Park Light-Dual Lamp **19.99**
2" high.
186-4525 "Baden-Baden" Park Light-Triple Lamp **31.99**
2" high.
186-4526 "Berlin" Gas Lamp **10.99**
1-1/2" high.

4531   4535   4597

186-4531 Modern Park Light **8.99**
1-1/2" high.
186-4535 Modern Street Light **8.99**
Rectangular, 1-1/2" high.
186-4597 Street Light **8.99**
1-1/2" high.

4605   4606   4631

186-4605 "Waiblingen" Lamp **13.99**
With shade. 1-5/8" high.
186-4606 "Baden-Baden" Gas Lamp **14.99**
1-1/2" high.
186-4631 "Stuttgart" Gas Lamp **14.99**
2" high.
186-4642 Street Light **10.99**
2" high.
186-4644 Modern Street Light **10.99**

Old-Fashioned Street Lamps

186-4604 "Berlin-Charlottenburg" Lamp **15.99**
2-1/2" high.

357

LIGHTING - ELECTRICAL - MOTORS

IMPORTED FROM GERMANY BY WALTHERS

Floodlights & Spotlights

4551   4552

186-4551 Floodlight-Single **11.99**
With one #4538 spotlight. 2" high.

186-4552 Floodlight-Double **18.99**
Includes two #4538 spotlights, 2-1/2" high.

186-4538 Spotlight **8.99**
Mirror reflector. Measures 3/8" square, diameter 1/4".

ELECTRICAL ACCESSORIES

Adjustable Resistor

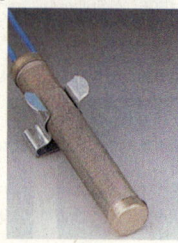

186-6154 **18.99**
Adjustable output clip. Reduces train speed for slow-running train blocks. 0-100 ohms; 1/4 x 2".

Bridge Rectifier

186-2185 **11.99**
3/4 x 1/2 x 1/4", 10-16V, 1A.

Distributor
Several distributors can be connected to supply more accessories.

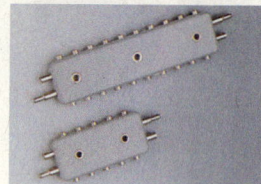

186-2591 5-Way, 2-Pole **7.99**
186-2592 10-Way, 2-Pole **10.99**

Illuminated Push-Button 10.99 ea

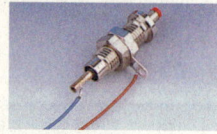

186-3511 Yellow
186-3512 Red
186-3513 Green
186-3519 White

Magnetic Reed Switch

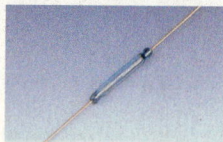

186-3530 Inert Gas-Filled Tube Contact **3.99**
Contact load is 0.5A capacity, 3/4 x .1".

Magnets
186-3543 Bar Magnet **2.99**
For use with #3530; 1/4 x 1/2" (6 x 12 x 4mm).

Momentary Contact Push-Button pkg(2) 8.99 ea

186-3501 Yellow
186-3502 Red
186-3505 Blue
186-3508 Black
186-3509 White

Non-Illuminated Push-Button 7.99 ea
1/4" diameter.
186-3471 Yellow
186-3472 Red
186-3473 Green
186-3475 Blue
186-3478 Black
186-3479 White

Push-Buttons
186-3573 Push-Button 3/4" pkg(4) **6.99**

Limited Quantity Available
186-3500 Panel, Nickel-Plated **5.99**
Multi-purpose on/off switch with retaining clip. 1/4 x 1-1/2".

Relays
Relays feature matching color-coded wiring for Brawa signals and accessories. Units may be operated manually or automatically with reed switches.
186-2760 Double 10-20V AC **66.99**
186-2761 Triple 10-24V AC **87.99**

Screw Terminal Strip

186-3094 **3.99**
12-way, 4" long.

SPST Panel Push-Button Switch w/Nut
186-3524 **2.99**
Base approximately 1 x 1/2"; threaded neck length is approximately 1/2".

Toggle Switch - On/Off
220 V/2A.
186-3520 Single-Pole **10.99**
186-3574 Tumbler Toggle Switch 3/4" pkg(4) **6.99**

Wire Holder

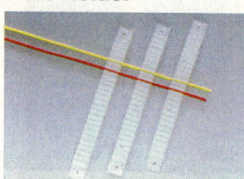

186-3910 pkg(10) **5.99**
Holds up to 25 wires or leads securely.

PLUG & SOCKET

30 Piece Set
186-3071 **9.99**
15 plugs, 15 sockets in five colors.

Battery Cap Socket 6-Pole

186-3572 **1.99**

For Marklin
186-3070 **5.99**
Eight crosshole plugs, eight sleeves.

Panel Sockets pkg(10) 30.99
For use on control panels.

186-3083 Green
186-3085 Blue
186-3086 Orange
186-3087 Gray
186-3088 Black
186-3089 White

Single Sockets 3.49 ea
186-3081 Yellow
186-3082 Red
186-3084 Brown

Plug 2-Pole

186-3571 pkg(5) **9.99**
1/3" centers.

Round Plugs pkg(10) 3.99 ea
With crossover hole.
186-3051 Yellow
186-3052 Red
186-3053 Green
186-3054 Brown
186-3055 Blue
186-3056 Orange
186-3057 Gray
186-3058 Black
186-3059 White

Round Socket pkg(10) 3.99 ea
186-3041 Yellow
186-3042 Red
186-3043 Green
186-3044 Brown
186-3045 Blue
186-3046 Orange
186-3047 Gray
186-3048 Black
186-3049 White

Socket 2-Pole

186-3570 pkg(5) **9.99**

LIGHTING

Bulb Accessories

186-3400 Building Light **1.99**
Plastic with brass socket (male) and 16" brown and yellow leads 16V. Two (female) plastic plugs for simple hook up.

186-3422 Screw Metal Base w/2 Connectors Size E5.5 pkg(10) **7.99**

186-3423 Recessed Base w/Bracket Size E5.5 pkg(10) **10.99**
186-3424 E5 Screw Base, Raised pkg(10) **9.99**
186-3433 E10 Screw Base, Raised pkg(10) **9.99**

Festoon Bulb
186-3250 Frosted 16V 30mA pkg(2) **6.99**
186-3276 Candle Bulb, Amber pkg(4) **6.99**
Fits socket size E5.5, 19V, 65mA.
186-3277 Candle Bulb, Clear pkg(4) **5.99**
Fits socket size E5.5, 19V, 65mA.

186-3278 Reflector Bulb, Clear pkg(2) **7.99**
80mA, 1 watt, approximate total length is 3/4", 16V.

Fits E10 Size Sockets

186-3330 3.5V Clear, 200mA pkg(4) **5.99**
186-3331 19V Clear, 100mA pkg(4) **6.99**
186-3332 3.5V Red, 200mA pkg(4) **5.99**
186-3333 19V Red, 100mA pkg(4) **7.99**
186-3334 3.5V Green, 200mA pkg(4) **5.99**
186-3335 3.5V Green, 100mA pkg(4) **7.99**

LIGHTING - ELECTRICAL - MOTORS

IMPORTED FROM GERMANY BY WALTHERS

Grain-O-Wheat Bulb
16V, 30mA, unless otherwise noted.

186-3254 Clear pkg(2) **4.99**
Two exposed electrodes, 16V, 35mA.

186-3286 Short, Green pkg(2) **6.99**

186-3287 2-Wire, Clear **3.99**

186-3288 Clear for 5760, 14V, 40mA **3.99**

186-3291 Clear For Z Lights, 10V, 30mA pkg(2) **3.99**

186-3293 Clear, 1 Black Wire **3.99**

186-3290 Spare Bulb For Z Lights pkg(2) **5.99**
Two exposed electrodes, clear, 10V, 30mA.

186-3292 Miniature Bulb **3.99**
Two electrodes for #7942; 1.5V, 15mA; connect only through resistor.

186-3267 Micro Bulb, Clear, 3V pkg(2) **6.99**

LED Panel Light
6.99 ea
Each LED features a built-in ballast resistor. Each 1/4" diameter, installed depth 1". 14-16V.

186-3481 Yellow
186-3482 Red
186-3483 Green

LEDs
Connect only through 1000 Ohm resistor.

186-3295 Yellow, 2mm pkg(2) **2.99**
186-3296 Red, 2mm pkg(2) **2.99**
186-3297 Red, 1mm pkg(2) **5.99**
186-3298 Red, 3mm pkg(2) **1.99**
Miniature type for #4806. Approximate size 1/4 x 5/32".

186-3339 For Marklin Loco pkg(4) **5.99**

Lilliput Bulb
186-3263 24V, Clear pkg(2) **8.99**

16V, 35mA pkg(2) 4.99 ea
186-3271 Clear
186-3272 Red
186-3273 Green
186-3274 Yellow

Miniature Bulb pkg(2) 6.99 ea
14V, 30mA; for Brawa metal signals.
186-3259 Clear
186-3260 Yellow
186-3261 Red

Item listed below is available by Special Order (see Legend Page).
186-3262 Green

Mini Pin Terminal Strip
186-3091 **6.99**
20 contacts that can be separated at any point; for use as pin and tubular socket. Spacing 1" 2.54mm, for all systems.

Push-In Bulb
186-3251 Clear pkg(2) **6.99**
3 x 2.55, 16V, 30mA.

186-3340 Clear pkg(4) **4.99**
For Marklin, 19V, 50mA.

186-3341 Red pkg(4) **5.99**
For Marklin, 19V, 50mA.

186-3342 Green pkg(4) **5.99**
For Marklin, 19V, 50mA.

186-3343 Clear pkg(4) **5.99**
Marklin, new pattern with locating lugs; 19V, 50mA.

186-3345 Clear pkg(4) **5.99**
For Trix, 14V, 50mA.

Push-In Panel Lights
12.99 ea
For control panels and other installations where small diameter indicator lamps are needed. Units feature heat-resistant black plastic body with colored cap, nickel plated mounting ring, long life bulb and 6" leads. Fits mounting hole of 3/16". 12-14V, 60mA.

186-3461 Amber
186-3462 Red
186-3463 Green
186-3465 Blue
186-3469 White

Replacement Bulb For Telephone Booth
186-3268 Clear, 3V **3.99**

Screw Panel Light pkg(2) 8.99

Limited Quantity Available
186-3449 White
Size E5.5 for use on control panel. Current draw 50mA at 14-16V.

Special Bulbs pkg(2) 4.99 ea
With two electrodes. Replacement bulb for Brawa HO and N plastic signals made before 1981. 16V, 30mA.

Limited Quantity Available
186-3257 Green
186-3258 Yellow

Thread Spherical Bulb pkg(4) 4.99 ea (Unless Noted)
Fits E5.5 size sockets.

186-3300 1.5V Clear, 100mA, 5mm
186-3301 3.5V Clear, 200mA, 5mm
186-3302 6V Clear, 100mA, 5mm
186-3303 14V Clear, 50mA, 5mm
186-3304 19V Clear, 60mA, 5mm
186-3307 19V Clear, 50mA, 5mm **5.99**
186-3310 19V Red, 50mA, 5mm **5.99**
186-3311 19V Yellow, 50mA, 5mm **5.99**
186-3275 19V Clear, 50mA, 5mm
186-3316 3.5V Clear, 200mA, 8mm **5.99**
186-3318 14V Clear, 50mA, 8mm **5.99**
186-3319 19V Clear, 50mA, 8mm
186-3322 19V Green, 50mA, 8mm **5.99**
186-3325 1.5V Clear, 100mA, 8mm **5.99**

Miscellaneous Bulbs
186-3264 Screw-In Bulb For #4621 & 4591 pkg(2) **6.99**

186-3289 For Z Spotlight, 6V pkg(2) **2.99**

186-3279 Valve Base 16V Clear pkg(2) **5.99**

186-3337 Flat Top 19V Red pkg(4) **7.99**

186-3338 Replacement Bulb For Marklin #60008 pkg(4) **7.99**

186-3348 Mini Bayonet Bulb, 14V **1.99**

186-3380 Replacement Bulb, (clear) **2.49**
Mini 16V 30mA w/Plug Base

186-3381 Replacement Bulb, 6V 30mA (clear) **1.99**

19V Tubular Bulb
186-3282 32mm pkg(2) **4.99**
186-3283 42mm pkg(2) **6.99**

Get Your Daily Dose of Product News at
www.walthers.com

WIRE

Fine Strand
Fine stranded copper wire, approximately .036" diameter. Maximum load 2.5A.

#28 33' Roll 1.69 ea
Dealers MUST order in multiples of 10.
186-3160 Purple
186-3161 Yellow
186-3162 Red
186-3163 Green
186-3164 Brown
186-3165 Blue
186-3168 Black

#18 133' Roll 19.99 ea
186-3222 Red
186-3228 Black

Multi-Conductor Flat Cable Hook-Up Wire
#24 solid copper wires in assorted colors, maximum load, 6A per wire.

186-3139 2-Conductor, pkg(164") White **17.99**

186-3170 Brown/Yellow pkg(16') **3.49**
186-3171 Brown/Yellow pkg(164') **20.99**

186-3172 Blue/Yellow/Blue pkg(16') **4.99**
For use with Marklin.

186-3173 Blue/Yellow/Blue pkg(164') **34.99**
For use with Marklin.

186-3174 Yellow/Red/Blue pkg(16') **4.99**
For use with Marklin.

186-3175 Yellow/Red/Blue pkg(164') **34.99**
For use with Marklin.

186-3176 Gray/Violet/Blue pkg(16') **4.99**
For use with Arnold.

186-3177 Gray/Violet/Blue pkg(164') **34.99**
For use with Arnold.

186-3182 Blue/Yellow/Red/Green pkg(16') **5.99**

186-3184 Five Conductor pkg(16') **6.99**

186-3186 Blue/Brown/Yellow/Red/Green/Black pkg(16') **7.99**

186-3188 Yellow/Brown/Red/Green/Blue/Gray/Black/White pkg(16') **10.99**

186-3189 Same as #3188 pkg(164') **107.99**

186-3230 #18 2-Conductor, Orange, White pkg(65') **24.99**

186-3235 #18 3-Conductor, Yellow, white and green. pkg(65') **34.99**

Solid Strand
Solid Strand #24 copper wire with PVC insulation. Max load 6A; length, 11 yards per coil, approximate diameter, .048".

33' Roll 1.80 ea
Dealers MUST order multiples of 10.

186-3100 Purple
186-3101 Yellow
186-3102 Red
186-3103 Green
186-3104 Brown
186-3105 Blue
186-3107 Gray
186-3108 Black
186-3109 White

Limited Quantity Available
186-3197 Brown **7.49**

328' Roll 17.99 ea
186-3111 Yellow
186-3112 Red
186-3113 Green
186-3114 Brown
186-3115 Blue
186-3117 Gray
186-3118 Black
186-3119 White

Item listed below is available by Special Order (see Legend Page).
186-3110 Purple

Wire Accessories
186-3091 29/0 Pin Miniature Connector **6.99**

186-3914 Terminal Strip, 30 Position **12.99**

186-3913 Resistor 1000 Ohm pkg(10) **2.99**

186-3915 Soldering Plates 10 Terminal **8.99**

186-3916 Soldering Plates 20 Terminal **15.99**

#24 2 Conductor pkg(16') 1.80 ea
Dealers MUST order multiples of 10.

186-3122 Red
186-3123 Green
186-3128 Black
186-3129 White

LIGHTING - ELECTRICAL - MOTORS

IMPORTED FROM GERMANY BY WALTHERS

Add electronic animation to your layout with these accessories. Each unit comes fully assembled, with bulbs and/or LEDs. Small component size is adaptable to most any N Scale building or vehicle.

LEDs

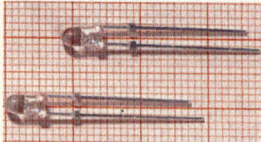

189-5987 Standard LEDs (white) pkg(2) **11.99**
White LEDs produce light approximating the glow of Xenon/Neon lamps. Great for replacing or adding headlights on locomotives, rolling stock, automobiles and building interiors. 1/8" 3mm Diameter, 14-16V.

Random Electronic Switch

189-5749 61.99
Activates sound and other accessories at random intervals. Includes hookup instructions. 12-16V.

Blinker Sets

Item listed below is available by Special Order (see Legend Page).
189-5936 2 Alternating w/Blinker Control Blue **22.99**

Structure Lights

189-4280 Building Lights w/Sockets & Bulbs pkg(2) **2.49**
Fully assembled sockets with wire leads and replaceable bulbs. Ideal for interior lighting in most structures.

Light & Sound

Items listed below are available by Special Order (see Legend Page).

189-5750 Blue Blinker Set w/Sound **89.99**
Light and sound control unit with speaker and two bulbs.
189-49965 Vehicle Accessory Warning Set **6.99**

Timers

189-5961 With Infra Red Unit **36.99**
189-5963 Without Infra Red Unit **28.99**

189-5962 Standard Infra Red Switch Unit **13.99**
For use with timers #189-5961 and 189-5963, each sold separately.

Cable Lamp w/250mm of Cable 5.99 ea (Unless Noted)

189-4290 Clear 16V/30mA **4.99**
189-4291 Red 5V/60mA
189-4292 Amber 5V/60mA

Items listed below are available by Special Order (see Legend Page).
189-4293 Blue 5V/60mA
189-4294 Turquoise 5V/60mA

Conductive Paint

189-5900 Silver **12.99**
With the stroke of a brush you have a painted line which will conduct electricity on plastic, wood, glass, etc. It can be painted over and still conduct electricity.

Scenes

189-5400 Luminous Advertising **25.99**
Includes eight LEDs and extra letters (dry decals). Perfect for advertising restaurants, clubs and more.

189-5405 Flexible Light Band **27.99**
Features a string of 12 yellow LEDs. A nice addition to campsites, restaurants or as Christmas lights.

189-5920 Advertising Signs **67.99**

189-5921 Electronic Flames **27.99**

189-5931 Electronic Welder **24.99**

Item listed below is available by Special Order (see Legend Page).

189-5956 Construction Zone **29.99**
When it's time to repair city streets and sewers, keep motorists alert with construction zone blinkers. Set includes seven barricades (four blinking) and control unit.

KATO

Lighting Kits
Interior w/White LED
Recommended for DCC operation. Includes filter to change light from white flourescent to yellowish incandescent tint.
381-11209 1-car **10.00**
381-11210 6-cars **50.00**

Daily New Arrival Updates! Visit Walthers Web site at
www.walthers.com

Information STATION

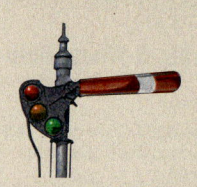

Lights are Everywhere

What would a city street be without lampposts? Besides dark, it would also look a little bare and not quite detailed. In scenery, lights are important elements; they add detail and imply activity. Many styles of small lights and bulbs are available, making them easy and fun to add. Most work off the accessory terminals of your power packs. Here are a few typical, and very visible, kinds of lights you can add to your scenes:

Streetlights are found in many places. While in older and smaller villages, there weren't many, today even small towns have them. Lighted gaslamps and ornate lampposts with electric lights were common during the steam- and transisition-era. In some areas, streetlights with shades were mounted on wood power poles with brackets. Today, simple metal or concrete vapor lamps keep streets bright at night.

Floodlights illuminate railroad yards and industrial facilities. Many older installations feature large positionable lights on latticework supports, modern floodlights are on tall, modular steel poles. Exterior building lights keep sidewalks and doorways safely lit at industrial sites. In the steam- and classic diesel-eras, the familiar "gooseneck" lamp with a metal shade was common, today, more modern vapor lamps mounted on walls suffice.

Billboards and signs painted on buildings are also illuminated. Many billboards up through the 1970s had gooseneck lamps mounted on top of the frames. Modern billboards have fluorescent tubes on top and bottom or several vapor lamps mounted on the frame.

360

LIGHTING - ELECTRICAL - MOTORS

Relative intensity of mitey lites:

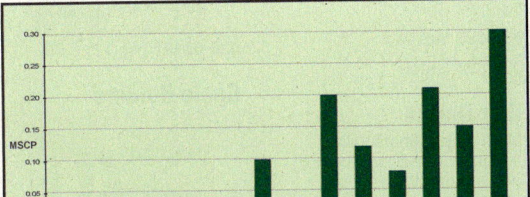

Lamps

7400 Sub-Micro
0.75mm diameter axial lead. 1.5V, 18 mA with 1" bare wire leads. Use for marker lights, number boards, step lights, etc.

800-740002 pkg(2) **3.95**
800-740006 pkg(6) **9.95**
800-740012 pkg(12) **16.95**
800-940012 Dropping Resistor For 12V pkg(10) **2.49**
800-940016 Dropping Resistor For 16V pkg(10) **2.49**

7411 Standard Output
1.40mm diameter lens end, with 8" black stranded wires. 1.5V, 13mA.

800-741102 pkg(2) **3.50**
800-741106 pkg(6) **7.75**
800-741112 pkg(12) **12.95**
800-741125 pkg(25) **24.95**
800-941112 Dropping Resistor For 12V pkg(10) **2.49**
800-941116 Dropping Resistor For 16V pkg(10) **2.49**

7414 Medium Output
1.40mm diameter lens end, with 8" black wire leads. 1.5V, 30mA. Ideal for headlights, mars lights, ditch lights, etc, to minimize total current draw.

800-741402 pkg(2) **4.95**
800-741406 pkg(6) **11.95**
800-741412 pkg(12) **16.95**
800-941612 Dropping Resistor For 12V pkg(6) **2.49**

7416 High Output
1.40mm diameter lens end, with 8" black wire leads. 1.5V, 60mA. Very bright! Use for headlights, etc.

800-741602 pkg(2) **4.95**
800-741606 pkg(6) **11.95**
800-741612 pkg(12) **16.95**
800-941412 Dropping Resistor For 12V pkg(6) **2.49**
800-941416 Dropping Resistor For 16V pkg(6) **2.49**
800-941612 Dropping Resistor For 12V pkg(6) **2.49**
800-941616 Dropping Resistor For 16V pkg(6) **2.49**

Colored Lamps
Same specifications as #7416 lamps. Use same dropping resistors as #7416. Ideal for warning lights, signals, signs and more.

Set of 2 4.95 ea
800-7416202 Red
800-7416302 Amber
800-7416402 Green
800-7416502 Blue
800-7416702 Yellow

Set of 6 11.95 ea
800-7416206 Red
800-7416306 Amber
800-7416406 Green
800-7416506 Blue
800-7416706 Yellow

7418 Very High Output
1.40mm diameter lens end, with 8" black wire leads. 3.0V, 26mA. Ideal for headlight, mars light, etc.

800-741802 pkg(2) **4.95**
800-741806 pkg(6) **11.95**
800-741812 pkg(12) **16.95**
800-941812 Dropping Resistor for 12V pkg(6) **2.49**
800-941816 Dropping Resistor For 16V pkg(6) **2.49**

7421 Very High Output
1.70mm diameter lens end, with 8" black wire leads. 1.5V, 75mA. Extremely bright! Ideal for headlights, mars lights or ditch lights.

800-742102 pkg(2) **4.95**
800-742106 pkg(6) **11.95**
800-942112 Dropping Resistor For 12V pkg(4) **2.49**
800-942116 Dropping Resistor For 16V pkg(4) **2.49**

7426 Very High Output
2.4mm diameter lens end, with 8" black wire leads. 1.5V, 90mA. Extremely bright! Use for headlights, etc.

800-742602 pkg(2) **4.95**
800-742606 pkg(6) **11.95**
800-942612 Dropping Resistor For 12V pkg(4) **2.49**
800-942616 Dropping Resistor For 16V pkg (4) **2.49**

7424 Extra High Output
1.70mm diameter lens end, with 8" black wire leads. 3.0V, 105mA. Extremely bright! Ideal for headlights, mars lights or ditch lights.

800-742402 pkg(2) **4.95**
800-742406 pkg(6) **11.95**
800-942412 Dropping Resistor For 12V pkg(4) **2.49**
800-942416 Dropping Resistor For 16V pkg(4) **2.49**

7431 Very High Output
2.4mm diameter lens end, with 8" black wire leads. 12-14V, 50mA. Ideal for headlights in locomotives not equipped with constant lighting and for structure lighting.

800-743102 pkg(2) **4.95**
800-743106 pkg(6) **11.95**

7428 Maximum Output
2.4mm diameter lens end, with 8" black wire leads. 3.0V, 120mA. Extremely bright! Ideal for headlights, mars lights or ditch lights, etc.

800-742802 pkg(2) **4.95**
800-742806 pkg(6) **11.95**
800-942812 Dropping Resistor For 12V pkg(4) **2.49**
800-942816 Dropping Resistor For 16V pkg(4) **2.49**

7440 General Purpose
Long-life miniature lamp. 3.0mm diameter lens end, with 8" wire leads. 14-16V, 30mA. Use for equipment and structure lighting.

800-744006 pkg(6) **3.95**
800-744012 pkg(12) **5.95**
800-744025 pkg(25) **10.95**

7452 Bi-Pin Style
3.0mm diameter with plug-in style, short, stiff leads. 5.0V, 60mA. Ideal replacement lamp for LGB™ in-car and locomotive lighting applications.

800-745202 pkg(2) **4.95**
800-745206 pkg(6) **11.95**
800-745212 pkg(12) **16.95**

7458 Bi-Pin Style
3.0mm diameter with plug-in style, short, stiff leads. 18-22V, 45mA. Ideal replacement lamp for in-car and locomotive DCC lighting applications.

800-745802 pkg(2) **4.95**
800-745806 pkg(6) **11.95**
800-745812 pkg(12) **16.95**

LIGHTING SYSTEMS

FL1 Strobe Flashers 14.95 ea
Bright flash, small package, battery operation. Long battery life; six months continuous operation from one AA alkaline cell. Will operate off hearing aid or watch cell. 1/2 x 3/4" high. N 1.5V.

800-1021 Orange LED
800-1022 Red LED
800-1023 Yellow LED

FLW White Strobes
Bright white flash from small incandescent lamp (included). Battery or track power adapter powered. Same size as FL-1.

800-1031 Bright 1.4mm Lamp, 1.5V **14.95**
800-1032 Very Bright 1.7mm Lamp, 3.0V **14.95**
800-1033 Extra Bright 2.4mm Lamp, 3.0V **14.95**

Opto-Sensors
.185" diameter. For use with all Circuitron Detection Circuits.

800-9201 Single **3.95**
800-9202 Set of 2 **7.50**
800-9206 Set of 6 **19.95**

Basic Flashers
Simple, inexpensive circuits for flashing LEDs or lamps (sold separately).

800-1601 Fixed Rate LED Flasher **9.95**
800-1602 Fixed Rate Lamp (<250 mA) Flasher **12.95**
800-1603 Adjustable Rate & Duty Cycle Flasher for Lamp or LED (<250 mA) **15.95**

SQ-8 Sequencing Strobe
800-5838 **39.95**
Provides a rapid sequencing of eight high-intensity white strobe lights (included). When the lamps are aligned, the effect is one of a light sweep from one end to the other. This type of lighting effect is commonly used near airports on the approaches, but can also be very effective on signs and other applications. Both the sweep speed and the delay between the sweeps are independently adjustable. Requires a 10-18V AC or DC input. For use with HO and larger scales.

Diodes
800-9350 3 Amp pkg(2) **1.95**
800-9351 1 Amp pkg(6) **1.95**
800-9352 6 Amp pkg(2) **2.95**
800-935012 3 Amp pkg(12) **6.95**
800-935212 6 Amp pkg(12) **12.95**

TL-1 Traffic Light Controller

800-5820 **36.95**
Timing circuitry for standard traffic light. Outputs drive LED or lamp signals (not included). If LEDs are used, they must be common anode design. All four times are adjustable. Requires 10-18V AC or DC input. Red, yellow and green outputs provided for each direction (six total) and each can drive a 250mA maximum load. Adaptable for all scales.

LIGHTING - ELECTRICAL - MOTORS

AW-1, AW-2 Arc Welder Circuits 19.95 ea
The AW-1 and AW-2 circuits utilize two lamps, one yellow and one blue, along with a circuit that provides a random flickering effect of the lamps. The result is a very convincing representation of an arc welder in operation. Requires a 10-18V AC or DC input for proper operation. Adaptable for all scales.

800-5841 AW-1
Includes micro-bulbs and is designed for direct viewing in all scales. A small wisp of cotton placed over the lamps will serve to diffuse the light and produce a very realistic smoke effect.

800-5842 AW-2
Includes larger lamps and is designed to illuminate a window from within a structure. If the window is frosted to represent years of grime, the flickering effect is very realistic.

LIGHTING ACCESSORIES

Track Power Adapters

TP-1
800-2001 12.95
Miniature voltage regulator can power any Circuitron LED-type Strobe Flasher or EOT flasher from track power. Can be used as a constant lighting unit in unpowered rolling stock. 35 mA output will power two to three Strobes or EOT Flashers, LEDs with a 47 ohm resistor, one #7418 or two #7414 Mitey Lites™ wired in series. Bi-Directional, output will be present whether train is moving forward or backward. Can be used with DC, AC or Carrier Control systems. 0.3 x 0.3 x 0.8".

TP-2

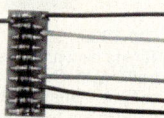

800-2002 12.95
Will power the ML-1 Mars Light and Strobe Flashers, and also has outputs that will provide constant directional lighting. Fits most HO locos, can be used with motors drawing up to 1 amp.

TP-3
800-2003 15.95
Adjustable output (1.5 or 3.0V DC). Ideal for constant lighting source in unpowered rolling stock. No ballast lamps or motors required. Will power Mars flasher in models driven by low-current can motors. Works with all forms of track power. Max current output is 1/2 amp.

PS-3 Power Supply
800-5304 12.95
Designed to power the EF-1 Emergency Flasher in situations where battery operation is undesirable. Accepts AC or DC input of 10-18V and converts it to 9V DC.

Battery Holders
For use with HO and O Scale Strobe Flashers.

800-9611 AA, 1 Cell, 1.5V **2.95**
800-9612 AA, 2 Cell, 3V **3.49**
800-9613 AAA, 1 Cell, 1.5V **2.95**
800-9614 AAA, 2 Cell, 3V **3.49**
800-9615 N, 1 Cell, 1.5V **2.95**
800-9616 N, 2 Cell, 3V **3.49**

Hidden Accessory Switch Kits
A completely hidden switch for controlling strobe flashers, marker lights or other rolling stock electrical accessories. Reed switch kits are turned on and off simply by bringing an external magnet up to the outside of the locomotive or car body. No external projections detract from the appearance of the model. Kits contain a subminiature reed switch and a tiny bias magnet.

800-9101 RS-1 **5.95**
Requires adjustment before mounting.

800-9102 RS-2 **7.95**
Requires no adjustment.

800-9100 External Magnet for Actuating Reed Switches **1.95**

800-9103 Sub-Miniature Slide Switches SPDT pkg(2) **2.95**

Miniature Switches

Sub-miniature toggle switches for panel mounting. 6 amp rating. Solder lug terminals. Chrome handle. 1/4" panel hole.

SPDT
800-911002 On-On pkg(2) **5.95**
800-911006 On-On pkg(6) **15.95**
800-911102 On-Off-On pkg(2) **6.95**
800-911106 On-Off-On pkg(6) **18.95**
800-911202 On-Off-On Momentary pkg(2) **7.49**
800-911206 On-Off-On Momentary pkg(6) **19.95**

DPDT
800-912002 On-On pkg(2) **6.95**
800-912006 On-On pkg(6) **18.95**
800-912102 On-Off-On pkg(2) **7.49**
800-912106 On-Off-On pkg(6) **19.95**
800-912202 On-Off-On Momentary pkg(2) **7.95**
800-912206 On-Off-On Momentary pkg(6) **20.95**

Plastic Sleeve for Handle pkg(6) 2.50 ea
800-9128 Red
800-9129 Black

Solderless Connectors 2.95 ea
Female .110" solderless connectors for all Circuitron printed circuit boards.

800-9602 Non-Insulated pkg(8)
800-9603 Insulated pkg(6)

Heat Shrink Tubing 3.49 ea
Use to insulate and protect wire connections quickly and easily. Shrinks to half the listed diameter when heated with a match, soldering iron or heat gun.

800-8703 3/64" 1.191mm Diameter - 36" 0.9m Long
800-8704 1/16" 1.588mm Diameter - 36" 0.9m Long
800-8706 3/32" 2.381mm Diameter - 36" 0.9m Long
800-8708 1/8" 3.175mm Diameter - 30" 75cm Long
800-8712 3/16" 4.763mm Diameter - 30" 75cm Long

800-8700 Assortment
Includes 6" 15cm of each diameter from 3/64 to 3/16".

Ultrafine Hook-Up Wire 2.95 ea
Ultrafine stranded wire measures just 0.015" 0.397mm outside diameter. Vinyl insulation is easily stripped. Ideal for wiring locomotive lights, signals, signs and other small models. Each pack includes 10' 2.9m.

800-8610 Black
800-8612 Red
800-8619 White

LEDS

.125" Diameter pkg(2) 2.95 ea
Super-bright, diffused lens, ideal for strobe flashers, signs, signals and more.

800-9301 Orange
800-9302 Red
800-9303 Yellow
800-9304 Green
800-9306 Red/Green, Bi-Color

.200" Diameter pkg(2) 2.95 ea
800-9311 Orange
800-9312 Red
800-9313 Yellow
800-9314 Green
800-9316 Red/Green, Bi-Color

.75" Diameter pkg(2) 2.95 ea
800-9321 Orange
800-9322 Red
800-9323 Yellow
800-9324 Green

Fiber Optics
PMMA plastic fibers with a special fluoro-polymer coating. Light entering the end is transmitted along the length by internal reflection and exits the far end with very little loss in intensity. Use for signals, signs and special effects.

800-8020 0.020" dia 30' **6.95**
800-8030 0.030" dia 20' **6.95**
800-8040 0.040" dia 15' **7.95**
800-8060 0.060" dia 10' **7.95**

Circuitron Catalog & Application Book

800-9999 52 pages **7.00**

See What's New and Exciting at
www.walthers.com

INTERNATIONAL HOBBY CORP.

Deluxe Motorizing Kit
348-5190 For Circus Rides **7.98**

NOCH
IMPORTED FROM GERMANY BY WALTHERS

Cable Clamps
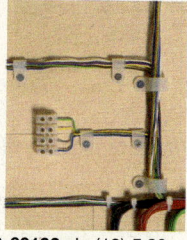
528-60192 pkg(12) **5.99**

Cable Holders
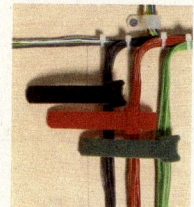
528-60194 pkg(6) **5.99**
With Velcro fastening. Two each red, black and green.

Cable Ties

528-60196 Plastic pkg(50) **3.99**

LIGHTING - ELECTRICAL - MOTORS

IMPORTED FROM GERMANY BY WALTHERS

LIGHTING

Structure Light

272-180670 **1.99**
Set comes with lighting socket, bulb, cables and plugs.

Flashing Lights

272-180689 16V AC (red) pkg(2) **9.99**

12-16V Grain Of Wheat Bulbs 2.99 ea
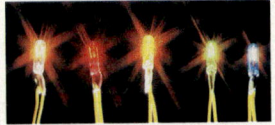
272-180671 Clear
272-180672 Red
272-180673 Yellow
272-180674 Green
272-180676 Blue

Micro Bulbs

272-180677 White, 12-16V AC 35mA w/Wire Leads **5.99**

ELECTRICAL ACCESSORIES

Synchronous Motors

272-180629 **31.99**
Speed of 4/15 RPM. Revolves clockwise or counter-clockwise. 16V AC.

272-180628 Extra Power **36.99**
Provides 35% more power than #180629 for a variety of applications. Speed of 4/15 RPM, with reversible rotation. 12-16V AC, 60mA.

Bell Chimes
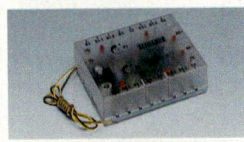
272-180642 **82.99**
Features five different bell chime sounds. 12-16V AC. For use with Faller and Pola churches in HO, N and TT Scales.

Warning Crossbucks w/Bells

272-180643 pkg(2) **71.99**
As soon as the signal flashes, the bell sounds. Comes with loudspeaker. 12-16V AC.

Plug Strip

272-180686 **4.99**
Features 10 pairs of sockets.

NORTHWEST SHORT LINE

Flatcan Miniature Motors 34.95 ea
Double 1.2 x 15mm shafts.
53-102039 10 x 20mm
53-102539 10 x 25mm

Mini Gearboxes 50-1 Ratio 29.95 ea (Unless Noted)
60" minimum driver diameter.
53-1706 2.4mm Axle Fit
53-1716 2.0mm Axle Fit
53-1726 1.5mm Axle Fit
53-1756 Input Shaft 1.2mm Conversion **7.95**

Itty Bitty Lines

WIRE MANAGEMENT PRODUCTS

Cable Clamps
Feature natural nylon.
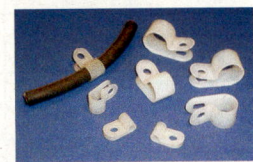
357-1214 1/8" Inside Diameter pkg(15) **1.85**
357-1215 1/4" Inside Diameter pkg(15) **1.85**
357-1216 3/8" Inside Diameter pkg(15) **2.15**
357-1217 1/2" Inside Diameter pkg(15) **2.95**

Cable Tie Mounts pkg(15) 2.85 ea
These adhesive-backed cable tie mounts will secure cable ties to any clean, flat surface. Cable ties slide into any of the four sides for easy application. Feature natural nylon.
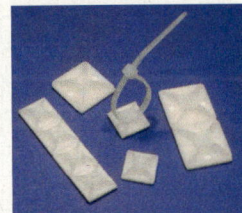
357-1210 1/2" Square
357-1211 3/4" Square

Cable Ties
Nylon cable ties for wire organization and many other uses. Bent tip design for ease of insertion.
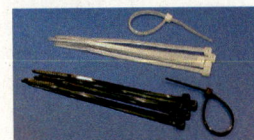
357-1200 4" Long, Natural Nylon, pkg(100) **2.95**
357-1201 4" Long, Black Nylon, pkg(100) **3.25**

357-1203 5-1/2" Long, Mixed Colors Nylon pkg(100) **3.95**

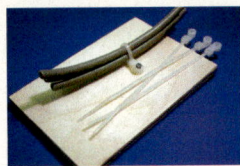
357-1204 Screw Mount Cable Ties pkg(20) **4.95** 4" 10cm

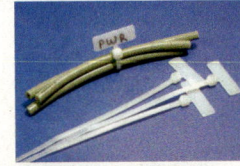
357-1205 Flag Cable Ties pkg(20) **4.95** 4" 10cm

Spiral Wire Wrap
Spiral polyethylene wrap organizes wires and cables. Simple to apply and very flexible, it also protects wire bundles from sharp edges and repeated handling. Solvent and abrasion resistant. Each package includes three three-foot sections of varying diameters for a total of nine linear feet. Bundling range 1/16 to 3". Multiple colors allow easy color coding of wire bundles.

357-1225 Natural Color, Mixed Diameters 1/8", 1/4" and 3/8" **5.95**

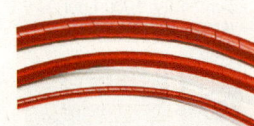
357-1226 Red, Mixed Diameters 1/4", 3/8" and 1/2" **6.25**

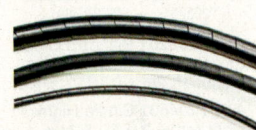
357-1227 Black, Mixed Diameters 1/8", 1/4" and 3/8" **6.75**

Terminal Block
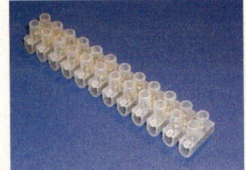
357-1209 3-1/2" Long, 12-Position, 3 Amp **2.75**

Wire Twist Locks
A simple and easy way to organize groups of wires or small cables. Can be untwisted and used again. Feature natural nylon.
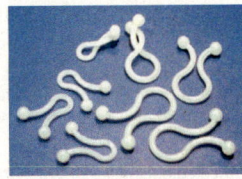
357-1220 1/4" Inside Diameter pkg(15) **1.85**
357-1221 1/2" Inside Diameter pkg(15) **2.45**

Test Lead Set

NEW 357-1208 5-Color Test Lead Set pkg(10) **9.95** 24" 60cm

LABELLE INDUSTRIES

Light Bulbs
Angel Hair
430-6451 Clear 1.5V pkg(3) **4.29**

Grain-Of-Rice
430-6551 Clear 12-14V pkg(3) **3.79**

Hook-Up Wire
Multi-strand, 33', 23 gauge.

430-6001 Single-Conductor Black, Red, Green **3.99**
430-6002 Two-Conductor Brown, Yellow **4.49**
430-6003 Three-Conductor Red, Green, Yellow **5.69**
430-6004 Four-Conductor Green, Yellow, Red, Blue **6.89**

LIGHTING - ELECTRICAL - MOTORS

Miniatronics
"electronics for the hobbyist"

Miniatronics offers an extensive variety of electrical components, lamps, LEDs and special effects lighting units to add realism to your layout. Most products are usable in any scale. Check out Walthers Web-site at www.walthers.com for a complete list of Miniatronics products.

NEW PRODUCTS
Interior Lighting Kits
For N and HO Scales, DC or DCC. Pick-up shoes included.
NEW 475-100ICL01
Passenger Car **25.95**
Seven LEDs, 42mA. 1/2 x 10"
NEW 475-100CB201
Caboose **22.95**
Six LEDs, 36mA. 1/2 x 5"

Outdoor Building/Billboard Lights

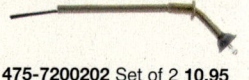

475-7200202 Set of 2 **10.95**
Easy way to model security lights on the exterior of any factory, warehouse, or railroad building. Or install it facing up or down to light a billboard sign for a neat diorama scene.

Ultra Bright Headlight
475-10030201 White LED **17.55**
Operate from track power or 4-16V DC. Board measures 5/16 x 5/8".

Two Directional Light

475-100NL201 12" Leads **18.65**
Great for modern industrial smokestacks, water towers, radio/TV/telecommunications towers and other large structures as well as buoys and bridges. Red lamp slowly brightens and dims automatically. Requires 12V filtered DC power source, sold separately. See the #475-WT412 transformer.

Tower
475-TW00101 Brass Tower (Communications, Transmission or High Voltage Type) 2-5/8" 6.5cm High **11.80**
Use this etched brass tower as a tall industrial lamppost, as an antenna tower or as an electrical transmission tower.

Rail Yard Spotlights
Detail modern yard scenes in minutes. Unique mounting foot makes installation fast and easy and lamps can be adjusted up or down. Run from 14-16V AC/DC power source. Each lamp stands 3" 7.5cm tall.

475-7261801 475-7262801

475-7261801 Single Searchlight **21.45**
475-7262801 Double Searchlight **29.45**

Lamp Posts
Fully assembled with brass poles in a variety of styles suitable for layouts from the 1920s to the present and feature 16V 30mA, 5000-hour average life bulbs unless noted.

475-7201002 475-7201601

475-7201002 Full Globe Style-Black pkg(2) **10.95**
Each 1" 2.5cm tall. 1.5V, 1000-hour average bulb life.
475-7201601 Park Lamppost (Brass) w/Decorative Globe 1" 2.5cm 1.5V, 1000-hour average bulb life **8.75**

475-7203201 475-7204801

475-7203201 Bishop's Crook Street Lamp (black) 1-7/8" 4.6cm **15.25**
475-7204601 Single Highway Light (gray) 2-1/8" 5.3cm **13.25**
475-7204801 Double Highway Light (gray) 2-1/8" 5.3cm **19.25**

For Up-To-Date Information and News Bookmark Walthers Web site at
www.walthers.com

Incandescent Lamps
All lamps have 8" insulated leads unless noted by an asterisk (*).

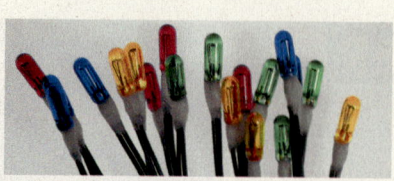

COLOR	VOLTAGE	mA	mm Diameter	HOURS	PKG	PRICE	Item #
Clear-axial**	1.5	20	0.75	1,000	10	14.95	1807510
Clear	1.5	15	1.2	500	10	9.75	1800110
Clear	1.5	15	1.2	500	20	16.95	1800120
Assorted (4 of each)*	1.5	30	1.2	1,000	20	19.45	18A0320
Blue*	1.5	30	1.2	1,000	10	10.95	18B0310
Clear*	1.5	30	1.2	1,000	10	10.95	18C0310
Green*	1.5	30	1.2	1,000	10	10.95	18G0310
Red*	1.5	30	1.2	1,000	10	10.95	18R0310
Yellow*	1.5	30	1.2	1,000	10	10.95	18Y0310
Clear	1.5	40	1.7	5,000	10	13.25	1870110
Clear	1.5	40	1.7	5,000	20	23.95	1870120
Clear	1.5	40	2.4	1,000	10	9.75	1820110
Clear	1.5	40	2.4	1,000	20	16.95	1820120
Clear	12	30	1.7	5,000	10	13.25	1871210
Clear	12	30	1.7	5,000	20	23.95	1871220
Clear	12	50	2.4	10,000	10	9.75	1801210
Clear	12	50	2.4	10,000	20	16.95	1801220
Assorted (5 of each)	12	50	2.4	10,000	20	19.45	18A1220
Blue	12	50	2.4	10,000	10	10.95	18B1210
Green	12	50	2.4	10,000	10	10.95	18G1210
Red	12	50	2.4	10,000	10	10.95	18R1210
Yellow	12	50	2.4	10,000	10	10.95	18Y1210
Clear	14	30	2.4	16,000	10	10.45	1801410
Clear	14	30	2.4	16,000	20	17.55	1801420
Clear	16	30	2.4	10,000	10	10.45	1801610
Clear	16	30	2.4	10,000	20	17.55	1801620
Clear	6	40	5.5	10,000	10	9.85	1801810
Clear	6	40	5.5	10,000	20	17.45	1801820
Clear	12	50	5.5	10,000	10	9.85	1802410
Clear	12	50	5.5	10,000	20	17.45	1802420
Clear	14	80	5.5	10,000	10	9.85	1802810
Clear	14	80	5.5	10,000	20	17.45	1802820

** Bare wire leads   *12" Insulated wire leads

Park Lights

7204201 7204401 7204501

475-7204201 Single Globe (green) 1-3/8" 3.4cm **13.95**
475-7204401 Double Globe (green) 1-1/2" 3.7cm **18.55**
475-7204501 Triple Globe (green) 1-5/8" 4cm **23.25**

Lamp Shades w/Bulbs pkg(5) 10.95 ea

Versatile lamps with metal shades can be used to model outdoor or indoor lighting. Bulbs have an average life of 1,000 hours.
475-7200105 1.5V 30mA w/Small Shades pkg(5)
475-7211505 1.5V 40mA pkg(5) w/Large Shades

Spotlights

475-7200801 N Scale **14.80**
Great for exterior lighting of homes, factories and more, or as a garden light. Fixture is adjustable. Use with 14-16V power source.

LIGHTING - ELECTRICAL - MOTORS

Miniatronics
"electronics for the hobbyist"

Fire and Flame Effects
Great for realistic fire and blaze effects. Adds character to many scenes. Requires a 12 volt DC power source

475-100101 Simulated Fire and Flame Effects **23.95**
475-7200801 Arc Welding Light **29.95**

Strobe Lights
Will operate on 9-14V AC/DC.

Single Simulated 13.95 ea

475-100BS101 Blue
475-100NS101 White
475-100RS101 Red
475-100YS101 Yellow

Dual Sychronized Simulated 15.95 ea

475-100BS201 Blue
475-100NS201 White
475-100RS201 Red

475-100YS201 Yellow

Alternating 19.95 ea
475-100ABS01 Blue
475-100ANS01 White
475-100ARS01 Red
475-100AYS01 Yellow

Adjustable 21.95 ea
Flash rate can easily be adjusted for a variety of effects. Choose from units which flash alternately or in unison. Requires 1.50 bulb. Operates on 9-14V AC/DC.

Alternating Strobe

475-100AAB01 Blue
475-100AAN01 White
475-100AAR01 Red
475-100AAY01 Yellow

Dual Synchronized Strobe
475-100ADB01 Blue
475-100ADN01 White
475-100ADR01 Red
475-100ADY01 Yellow

Adjustable 8-Position 34.95 ea
Simulate the rapid sequencing of pulsing strobe lights for emergency vehicles, road barricade lights or circus attractions. Operate on 9-14V AC/DC.

475-1008CS01 Red & Yellow
475-1008NS01 White
475-1008RS01 Red
475-1008YS01 Yellow

Diodes
White LEDs

475-1230002 3mm Diameter pkg(2) **8.95**
Must be used with a 560 ohm resistor, which is included with each package.

YELOGLO White LEDs
These LEDs feature a clear lens and combine the super-bright intensity of a white LED with the warm yellow glow of an incandescent lamp to make engine headlights more realistic.

5-Pieces 7.95 ea
475-1231005 3mm
475-1251005 5mm

10-Pieces 14.95 ea
475-1231010 3mm Diameter
475-1251010 5mm Diameter

ELECTRICAL ACCESSORIES

Switches
Magnetic Reed Switches

475-32N5805 Set of 5 Matched Switches & Magnets **8.95**
Use these versatile switches to activate signals, turnouts or train detection systems. Simply place switches between rails as needed and install magnet on bottom of loco or car.

Micro Leaf Switches
SPDT, 3A, 120V.

475-3401004 pkg(4) **6.75**
475-3401008 pkg(8) **11.40**

Sub-Miniature Latching Push Button Switch
475-3301806 pkg(6) **6.95**
Single pole, single throw; rated 1 Amp 24V DC; 5/16" Diameter

Push Buttons
SPST momentary, normally open.

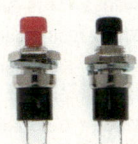

475-3302502 1/4" (1 red, 1 black) pkg(2) **4.95**
475-3310004 1/2" (2 red, 2 green) pkg(4) **7.45**

Six Position Rotary Switch

475-3562001 **11.95**
Enclosed, 2-pole with non-shorting contacts. 2.5 Amps, includes knob. Good for switching blocks and throttles.

Toggle Switches
Sub Miniature
DPDT, 3A, 120V, with solder lugs, 3/16" diameter threaded bushing mount.

475-3610002 pkg(2) **5.50**
475-3610005 pkg(5) **12.50**

Miniature
SPST
Single pole, single throw on/off switches; 5 amps, 120V.
475-3620004 pkg(4) **6.00**
475-3620008 pkg(8) **10.40**
5A, 120V, with solder lugs, 1/4" diameter threaded bushing mount.

SPDT
475-3621004 pkg(4) **6.95**
475-3621008 pkg(8) **11.95**
475-3622002 Center Off, Momentary/Spring Return pkg(2) **5.50**
475-3622005 Center Off Momentary/Spring Return pkg(5) **12.50**
475-3623004 Center Off pkg(4) **10.95**
475-3623008 Center Off pkg(8) **18.95**

DPDT

3625008　3626008　3627005

475-3625004 pkg(4) **9.50**
475-3625008 pkg(8) **16.90**
475-3626004 Center Off pkg(4) **10.95**
475-3626008 Center Off pkg(8) **18.95**
475-3627002 Center Off, Momentary/Spring Return pkg(2) **6.00**
475-3627005 Center Off, Momentary/Spring Return pkg(5) **13.75**

Slide Switches

3805004　3810005　3820005

475-3805004 Micro Miniature SPDT pkg(4) **3.95**
475-3810005 Sub Miniature SPDT pkg(5) **3.75**
475-3820005 Sub Miniature DPDT pkg(4) **3.95**

Micro Mini Connectors
Fully assembled with mated interlock assembly. Great for lighting, wiring, command control applications and special effects wiring. Connectors and attached wires have polarity markings for use as an indicator. Not recommended for powering rolling stock or other high-current applications. Rated at 1 Amp.

475-5000102 2 Pin, 12" Flexible Leads 2 Sets **9.95**
475-5000301 3 Pin, 12" Flexible Leads 1 Set **8.95**
475-5000401 4 Pin, 12" Flexible Leads 1 Set **9.95**
475-5050201 2 Pin Waterproof 1 Set **10.95**

Terminal Block

475-TB10 10 Screw, Double Row pkg(3) **8.95**
4-1/2 x 7/8"　11.2 x 2.1cm.
475-TB4 2-3/16 x 7/8", 4-Screw Double Row pkg(3) **4.50**

Heat Shrink Tubing
Shrinks to half its diameter to fit many irregular shapes.
475-HST36410 3/64" Size, 10' Long **6.95**
475-HST10 10' **6.95**
Includes five sizes: 3/64, 1/16, 3/32, 1/8 and 3/16".

Capacitive Discharge Unit

475-PDC1 **31.95**
Fully assembled unit operates up to ten switch machines simultaneously. Easy to connect.

Opto Sensors
475-3900104 pkg(4) **8.95**
Light-sensitive Opto Sensors can be used wherever you need a detection device. Strategically placed sensor activates when light is blocked from the face. Requires an electronic circuit for activation.

Power Distribution Blocks

475-PDB1 12 Position **18.95**
Hook up two wires from a power source to the binding posts on a heavy-duty PC board. Can use either AC or DC power source. Prewired, rated @ 15 amps. Comes with mounting feet.

475-PDB2 24 Position **31.95**
Designed for maximum 24 accessories AC/DC. Rated at 15 amps.

Automatic Reversing Unit

475-RU11 **45.95**
Automatically reverses from one point to another. Value-added package includes sensing device, push-button switches, mounting feet, heat shrink tubing, transformer and screwdriver. 3 amps.

475-RU21 **99.95**
Easy way to automate trolleys, displays or other layouts. This unit will handle from two to five stops and stop time is adjustable. Unit operates under varied lighting conditions and includes self-adjusting sensors, which can be installed where needed. Value-added package is complete with 12-Volt transformer, 50' of 28 gauge, two-conductor wire, heat shrink tubing, and wood screws.

ELECTRAK CLEAN

475-PEC31 Electrak Clean **99.95**
Don't let grime or dirt slow down your trains. Great for those hard-to-reach places. Works without abrasives, chemicals, rollers or pads. Safe for engines, wheels and DCC. Completely assembled and housed in a box that sits trackside. Simply place an engine on the tracks, hook up the wires to the track and the included transformer. When your engine is moving, Electrak does its work. Unit uses high-energy impulses between the wheels and track. Not effective on pitted, rusted or warped tracks.

365

LIGHTING - ELECTRICAL - MOTORS

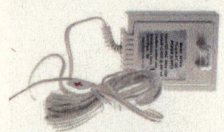

Miniatronics
"electronics for the hobbyist"

Transformers
475-WT12 Regulated, 12V DC @ 1 Amp **16.95**
Good for any application that requires a regulated power source.

475-WT412 Filtered 12V DC, 400mA **8.95**
Use with Miniatronics two directional lights, light house warning beacon and other lighting effects. Can power from one to four units.

475-WT816 8 or 16VAC, 800mA **6.95**
This plug-in wall transformer can run up to 25 Miniatronics 16V lampposts.

475-WT1515 1.5V DC @ 1.5 Amp **24.95**
Includes free 10 1.5V 15mA bulbs, will handle up to 100 1.5V 15mA bulbs

8 OHM Speakers

475-6007501   475-6007801

475-6007501 3/4" Round x 3/16" High (Fits N & HO scale) **4.95**

475-6007801 7/8" Round x 5/16" High (Fits N & HO Scales) **4.95**

475-6011501 15mm x 25mm 1 Watt **9.95**

WIRE

4812401 4818301 4816101

16 Gauge, Stranded, Single Conductor, 100' 30m 17.95 ea
Good for DCC hook-up.
475-4816001 Black
475-4816101 Blue
475-4816301 Green
475-4816501 Red
475-4816701 White
475-4816801 Yellow

18 Gauge, Stranded, Single Conductor, 100' 30m 12.95 ea
475-4818001 Black
475-4818301 Green
475-4818401 Orange
475-4818501 Red
475-4818601 White
475-4818701 Yellow

22 Gauge, Stranded, Single Conductor, 100' 30m 8.25 ea
475-4812001 Black
475-4812201 Gray
475-4812301 Green
475-4812401 Orange
475-4812501 Red
475-4812601 Violet
475-4812701 White
475-4812801 Yellow

28 Gauge Flat, Stranded, 25' 7.5m

475-4822825 Black 2 Conductor **6.95**
475-4842825 Black 4 Conductor **10.95**

16 Gauge Standard, Two Conductor, 50'
475-4826050 Black/Red **23.95**

30 Gauge Ultra Flexible, Stranded, Single Conductor, 10' 3m 5.95 ea

475-4813001 Black
475-4813004 2-1/2' Sections (1 each black, green, red, white)
475-48G3001 Green
475-48R3001 Red
475-48W3001 White

Work Bench Aids
Mini-Magnifying Clip-On Lamp

475-10051801 34.95
Magnifying lamp features a three-diopeter lens, swivel gooseneck and heavy-duty mounting clip.

Catalog
475-2006 2006 Catalog of Premiere Lighting Accessories **4.00**

model power

WIRE
All purpose, color-coded, flexible pre-tinned wire.

490-5201 1 Conductor Red pkg(400') **24.25**
490-5202 2 Conductor Red, Black pkg(200') **27.50**
490-5203 3 Conductor Red, White, Black pkg(100') **24.25**
490-5204 4 Conductor Red, White, Yellow, Black pkg(100') **26.50**
490-2301 1 Conductor cd **2.25**
490-2302 2 Conductor cd **2.25**
490-2303 3 Conductor cd **2.25**
490-2304 4 Conductor cd **2.25**
490-2310 18 Gauge Wire 1 Conductor pkg(25') **3.29**
490-2311 18 Gauge Wire 2 Conductor pkg(12.5') **3.29**
490-2299 2 Spools #1 Conductor Wire, Extra Fine- 2 Colors pkg(50') **2.25**

Limited Quantity Available
490-2403 3 Conductor Blue, White, Black pkg(11.5') **1.89**
490-2404 4 Conductor Green, Red, White, Black pkg(8.5') **1.89**

BULBS

14V Grain-O-Sand pkg(3) 5.49 ea
490-146 Clear, 1.2mm
490-147 Red, 1.2mm
490-148 Green, 1.2mm
490-149 Amber, 1.2mm

Grain-O-Rice pkg(3) 4.39 ea
1.5V
490-152 Clear, 2.2mm
490-153 Red, 2.2mm
490-154 Green, 2.2mm
490-155 Amber, 2.2mm
3V
490-345 Clear, 150mA
14V
490-252 Clear, 2.2mm
490-253 Red, 2.2mm
490-254 Green, 2.2mm
490-255 Amber, 2.2mm

Grain-O-Wheat
1.5V
490-344 Pointed, 150mA pkg(3) **4.39**

3V pkg(3) 3.29 ea
490-391 Clear, 3.2mm
490-392 Red, 3.2mm
490-393 Green, 3.2mm
490-394 Amber, 3.2mm

14V pkg(3) 3.29 ea
490-381 Clear, 3.2mm
490-382 Red, 3.2mm
490-383 Green, 3.2mm
490-384 Amber, 3.2mm

14V Gas Pea Lamps pkg(2) 3.89 ea
490-395 Clear, 6mm
490-396 White, 6mm

Headlights pkg(3) 4.39 ea
490-340 16V 70mA Wired Flat Head
490-341 14V 70mA Flat Head Screw
490-342 14V Oval Screw
490-343 14V Oval Bayonet

Bayonet Base 3.29 ea (Unless Noted)
6V
490-51960 #51 Clear pkg(2)
14V
490-398 Pointed, N Scale w/14V G-O-W Bulbs pkg(3) **4.39**
490-53961 #53 Clear pkg(2)
490-53962 #53 Red pkg(2)
490-257961 Red pkg(2)
490-257962 #257 Red pkg(2)
490-363960 #363 Clear pkg(2)
18V
490-1445960 #1445 Clear pkg(2)

Building Lights
490-491 Socket Stand & Bulb pkg(2) **3.89**
490-492 12V w/Screw Base pkg(6) **6.59**
490-9898 Fire Lighting **6.50**
490-10096 With Screw Base pkg(2) **3.89**

Screw Base pkg(2) 3.29 ea
14V
490-1449960 #1449 Clear
490-1449961 #1449 Red
490-1449962 #1449 Green
490-258960 #258 Clear
490-430960 #430 Clear
490-432960 #432 Red
490-432962 #432 Green
490-461960 #461 Clear

18V
490-144790 #1447 Clear

1.5V Sub Mini
490-145 Clear, 12.5mA pkg(3) **5.49**
Angel Hair 1.2mm.

3V Brite
490-397 Clear, G-O-W pkg(3) **4.39**

14V Blinker pkg(2) 3.89 ea
Blinks after 20-second warm-up.
490-10097 Clear, 250mA
490-10098 Red, 250mA
490-10099 Amber, 250mA

Lamp Post Bulbs
490-10095 pkg(2) **3.89**

LIGHTING ACCESSORIES

Track Test Light

490-16628 **8.98**

Get Daily Info, Photos and News at
www.walthers.com

LIGHTING - ELECTRICAL - MOTORS

Create a wide rage of special lighting effects for your motive power and other models with this line of LEDs and accessories.

2x3   Typical 3mm   Micro   Nano

NEW PRODUCTS

Ultra-Miniature Lighting Effects Modules

Utilizing the industry's smallest microcontroller, these modules are smaller than any decoder, just .31 x .31 x .118". Designed specifically to provide realistic lighting effects using LEDs. Input voltage range 6-18VDC. Ideal for DCC applications. Extra input wires included. LEDs sold separately.

NEW 514-N8031 Mars Light Simulator **12.95**
Provides a dazzling variable intensity output that represents the reflective bursts of a Mars Light. Truly eye catching.

NEW 514-N8032 Beacon Simulator **12.95**
Provides a single repeating burst, increasing and decreasing in intensity to accurately represent roof beacons like those made by Prime and Federal used by most railroads.

NEW 514-N8033 Gyralight Simulator **12.95**
Generates a varying (bell curve like) intensity to accurately represent Gyralight motion.

NEW 514-N8034 Ditch Light Module **13.95**
Provides output for two LEDs, both on, then switches to alternating with realistic ramping of intensity when input is momentarily grounded (or activated by DCC function control). Momentarily ground input again and Ditch lights return to continuous on.

Super Flashers

Flashers automatically support all colors of 20ma LEDs with no additional resistors required. Colors can be mixed on the same circuit. Will drive multiple LEDs in series depending on power supply voltage. resistors can be added to on-board solder pads for LED brghtness control. 7-16V DC Less than 1" square. LEDs sold separately.

NEW 514-N8011 Emergency Flasher **12.95**
Provides flashes in short bursts similar to lights used on emergency vehicles. Multiple LEDs can be wired in series.

NEW 514-N8012 Signal Flasher **12.95**
Flashes like a typical stop/caution signal.

NEW 514-N8013 Alternating Flasher **13.65**
Alternately flashes a pair of LEDs (or up to 4 pair depending on power source). Each light is on for 3/4 second, typical of grade crossings, school zones etc.

NEW 514-N8014 Variable-Rate Flasher **15.25**
Adjustable flash rate from 30 times per second to once every three seconds. On time and off time are equal (50% duty cycle).

NEW 514-N8015 Variable-Rate Alternating Flasher **15.95**
Alternately flashes a pair of LEDs (or up to 4 pair depending on power source). Adjustable flash rate from 30 times per second to once every three seconds. On time and off time are equal (50% duty cycle).

LED Tester

NEW 514-N8021 **8.95**
Design allows any color LED to be tested. No need to worry about choosing the proper resistor for protect the LED. simply snap the tester on a 9V battery and start testing. Includes spring-loaded contact block to hold wired LEDs.

Power Supply

NEW 514-N3512 **15.95**
This power supply is fully filtered and regulated to within 3% over the full range with no load to full load. It's protected against accidental shorting of the outputs and includes a EMI/RFI shield on the output cable. It's ideal for projects where highly regulated voltage is important. Includes a 6' 12V output cord.

Micro Clips w/Smooth Jaws

NEW 514-N440010 pkg(10) **2.75**
Handy copper-plated clips are ideal for holding small parts like LEDs during soldering. 5A current rating.

LEDS

Super-White LEDs - 2 x 3mm

Much smaller than the typical 3mm LED, this surface-mounted device (SMD) has a ceramic case with gold-plated solder pads on the back. Produces a very bright, pure white light output. Requires appropriate current limiting resistor, sold separately. Device Voltage: 3.6V DC, Current: 20 Ma, Average Life: 50-80,000 hours.

514-N10212 pkg(2) **7.50**
514-N102110 pkg(10) **35.00**

Super-Incandescent LEDs - 2 x 3mm

Identical to the 2 x 3 Super-White LED, except the warm light output color simulates an incandescent (filament) light source.
514-N10222 pkg(2) **7.50**
514-N102210 pkg(10) **35.00**

Micro Super-White LEDs - 030 x .060"

Extremely small size of just .030 x .060 and very bright, pure white light output. Device Voltage: 3.3V DC, Current: 20 ma, Average Life: 50-80,000 hours.
514-N10112 pkg(2) **4.95**
514-N101110 pkg(10) **22.50**

Micro Super Yellow-White LEDs

Identical to the Micro Super-White LED, except the color output is a very warm, bright yellow-white that simulates the color of early incandescent or gas lighting; ideal for steam-era modelers.
514-N10152 pkg(2) **4.95**
514-N101510 pkg(10) **22.50**

Micro LEDs in Colors - .030 x .060"

Pure colors to simulate signal and marker lights. Intensity can be adjusted by adding the appropriate resistor, sold separately.

Red
514-N10125 pkg(5) **3.50**
514-N101215 pkg(15) **9.45**

Yellow
514-N10135 pkg(5) **3.50**
514-N101315 pkg(15) **9.45**

Green
514-N10145 pkg(5) **3.50**
514-N101415 pkg(15) **9.45**

Blue
NEW 514-N10165 pkg(5) **6.95**
NEW 514-N101615 pkg(15) **19.45**

Nano Super-White LEDs - .020 x .040"

Officially the smallest LED in the world! Though just .020 x .040" this tiny device is extremely bright. It produces a cool white color that can easily be tinted to a warmer hue if desired. Device Voltage: 3.6V DC, Current: 20 Ma, Average Life: 50-80,000 hours.
514-N10312 pkg(2) **6.75**
514-N103110 pkg(10) **29.75**

Nano LEDs in Colors .020 x .040"

Identical spectral hues to the Micro LEDs in colors and the same physical size as the Nano Super-white LED.

Red
514-N10325 pkg(5) **3.95**
514-N103215 pkg(15) **10.65**

Yellow

514-N10335 pkg(5) **3.95**
514-N103315 pkg(15) **10.65**

Green
514-N10345 pkg(5) **3.95**
514-N103415 pkg(15) **10.65**

LIGHTING ACCESSORIES

Wire

#38 Magnet Wire

514-N5038 Red & Green; Each 100' **4.95**
Includes 100 feet each of red and green - the durable insulation is easily stripped as part of the tinning process.

Super-Flexible Insulated Electrical Wire - 5'

514-N5029 #29 **4.50**
Contains 51 strands of #46 wire, will carry 600 ma.
514-N5030 #32 **4.00**
Contains 18 strands of #44 wire, will carry 250 ma.

Ultra-Miniature SPST Electrical Switch

This tiny switch measures just 1/4" in its longest dimension. It will carry 150 Ma at 12 volts and is ideal for controlling lighting in rolling stock.

514-N32002 pkg(2) **2.85**
514-N320010 pkg(10) **13.25**

367

LIGHTING - ELECTRICAL - MOTORS

Surface Mount (SMD) Resistors
These precision SMD resistors fit in the smallest spaces due to their flat shape and miniature size. Solder pads on each end are pre-tinned.

1/8 Watt pkg(20) 1.65 ea

514-NA60R4 61 Ohm
514-NA80R6 81 Ohm
514-NA1000 100 Ohm
514-NA1001 1K Ohm
514-NA1210 121 Ohm
514-NA1500 150 Ohm
514-NA1501 1.5K Ohm
514-NA1780 178 Ohm
514-NA2000 200 Ohm
514-NA2320 230 Ohm
514-NA2740 274 Ohm
514-NA3010 301 Ohm
514-NA3011 3K Ohm
514-NA5100 510 Ohm
514-NA5111 5.11K Ohm

1/4 Watt 20-Pack 1.65 ea
514-NB1001 100 Ohm
514-NB3010 301 Ohm
514-NB3011 3K Ohm
514-NB3400 340 Ohm
514-NB3570 357 Ohm
514-NB4020 402 Ohm
514-NB4530 453 Ohm
514-NB5111 5.11K Ohm
514-NB5230 523 Ohm

Assortments
514-NX9V 9 Volt pkg(150; 15 10-Packs) **9.85**
514-NX12V 12 Volt pkg(170; 17 10-Packs) **11.50**

Tiny Bridge Rectifier – 1/2 Amp
Less than 1/4" square, this full-wave bridge will carry a full 1/2 Amp. It can easily drive 20 LEDs!

514-N301S2 pkg(2) **1.85**
514-N301S10 pkg(10) **8.40**

100uf Tantalum Capacitor
These tiny 16V DC capacitors can be "ganged" in parallel. Perfect for rolling stock lighting flicker control.

514-N31006 pkg(6) **4.95**
514-N310024 pkg(24) **17.80**

N Scale Lampshades & Escutcheons
These aluminum lampshades and escutcheons have a very thin (.005") cross-section for prototypical appearance. The concave shape easily accepts many lighting products. Mounting holes are easily added.

514-N70088 12" Lampshades pkg(8) **2.50**
514-N70018 18" Lampshades pkg(8) **2.50**
514-N70028 24" Lampshades pkg(8) **2.50**
514-N70078 Escutcheons pkg(8) **1.85**

Precision Scale Co

BULBS

Micro-Mini

585-410 1.5V pkg(8) **10.75**

12V Small Screw pkg(2) 2.75 ea

585-48300 Amber
585-48301 Green
585-48302 Red

12V Brass Base pkg(2) 2.75 ea

585-48303 Clear
585-48304 Amber
585-48305 Green
585-48306 Red

For Caboose
585-48307 12V pkg(2) **3.75**
In special case, red and green light.

12V Tubular Clip-In 2.75 ea

585-48308 Amber
585-48309 Green
585-48310 Blue
585-48311 Red

Dual Filament pkg(2) 3.50 ea
585-48315 1.5V, Clear
585-48316 2.5V, Clear
585-48317 3.0V, Clear

Grain-O-Wheat pkg(2) 2.75 ea
2.5V
Item listed below is available by Special Order (see Legend Page).
585-48297 Red

4.5V
585-48314 Red

6V
Items listed below are available by Special Order (see Legend Page).
585-48302 Red
585-48298 Green

12V

585-48294 Clear
Item listed below is available by Special Order (see Legend Page).
585-48295 Amber

Elongated 12V pkg(4) 3.75 ea
Designed for trackside signals of all types.

585-400 Clear
585-401 Red
585-402 Green
585-403 Amber

STATE TOOL & DIE CO.

Wire Ties - Reusable

661-26519 3-1/2" 8.75cm pkg(30) **3.50**

661-26512 4-1/2" 11.25cm pkg(30) **4.50**

Daily New Arrival Updates! Visit Walthers Web site at
www.walthers.com

SOUNDTRAXX

MICROBULBS
Bright, long-lasting 1.5 Volt bulbs are an easy way to upgrade or replace existing lighting in locos when converting to DCC. Choose from two sizes to fit most applications.

.053 1.3mm Diameter x .125" Long
678-810022 Single **2.50**
678-810023 6-Pack **13.50**

.094" 2.5mm Diameter x .186" Long
Items listed below are available by Special Order (see Legend Page).
678-810024 Single **2.50**
678-810025 6-Pack **13.50**

INSULATIVE TUBING
678-810036 24" Package **3.00**
24 gauge tubing for covering exposed component leads and wires.

SHRINK TUBING
678-810037 Assortment **6.00**
Provides 6" each of 1/16", 3/32", 1/8" and 1/4" diameter tubing, perfect for insulating solder connections.

EXHAUST CAM SET
678-810038 **10.00**
An assortment of exhaust synchronization cams that can be mounted quickly and easily to the inside face of driver wheels, often without disassembly of the loco. Includes cams for 2-cylinder, shays and articulated engines. For N-Scale and larger. For use with Steam Sound Decoders and the S220-IR Steam Sound System only.

CONNECTORS
678-810012 2-Pin Microconnector Set **3.50**
These 2-pin microconnectors allow locomotive wiring to be quickly disconnected for easier painting and servicing.

678-810058 Micro-Mini Connectors pkg(10) **9.00**
Use these tiny connectors between loco and tender to make them easier to disconnect. Includes ten .025" diameter pins and mating receptacles.

LIGHTING - ELECTRICAL - MOTORS

Make your models more realistic with this assortment of miniature electronic supplies.

CONNECTORS

Miniature size multi-pin connectors feature gold-plated contacts for reliable operation.

Miniature
649-3020 2-Pin **1.98**
649-3030 3-Pin **2.49**
649-3040 4-Pin **3.49**
649-3200 20-Pin **15.98**

Sub-Miniature
649-3420 2-Pin **2.49**
649-3430 3-Pin **3.49**
649-3440 4-Pin **4.49**
649-3442 20-Pin **20.98**

DIODES

50 PIV

649-4009 3 amp pkg(3) **1.98**
649-4010 1 amp pkg(10) **1.49**

Constant/Directional Lighting Diodes Kit
649-7051 **2.98**

LEDs

.085" dia x .115 High
.98 ea
649-5030 Red
649-5031 Green

R-Y-G
649-5049 5mm Diameter **1.39**
649-5110 Right Angle **.98**

3mm dia pkg(2)
649-5080 Red **.80**
649-5090 Green **.80**
649-5100 Yellow **.80**
649-5105 Orange **.98**

5mm dia pkg(2) .98 ea
649-5106 Red
649-5107 Green
649-5108 Yellow
649-5109 Orange

PHOSPHOR BRONZE SHEETS

Sheets measure 1-5/8 x 6". Measurement indicates sheet thickness.
649-8003 .003" **2.98**
649-8008 .088" **3.98**

SWITCHES

Miniature Toggle
649-4050 SPDT **2.79**

SPDT Slides .98 ea
649-4052 Miniature
649-4053 Sub-Miniature

Miniature Toggles
649-4060 DPDT/CO **2.98**
649-4070 DPDT **2.89**

HEAT SHRINK TUBING

pkg(12") Black
649-4501 3/64" Diameter **1.39**
649-4502 1/16" Diameter **1.49**
649-4503 1/8" Diameter **1.69**
649-4504 3/16" Diameter **1.89**
649-4505 3/32" Diameter **1.59**
649-4600 Assortment **2.98**
4" of each listed above.

pkg(12") Red
649-4601 3/64" Diameter **1.69**
649-4602 1/16" Diameter **1.49**
649-4603 1/8" Diameter **1.69**
649-4604 3/16" Diameter **1.89**
649-4605 3/32" Diameter **1.59**
649-4700 Assortment **2.98**
4" of 3/64", 1/16", 1/8" and 3/16".

TRAIN TRONICS

LIGHTING

Chase Light
723-201 **34.95**

Constant Light Kits
723-101 One Bulb **4.25**
723-102 Two Bulb **4.50**
723-103 Two Bulb, Reversing **4.95**
May be used for cab light and one headlight or dual headlight engines.

Fiber Optics
723-401 .020" Diameter pkg(25') **8.95**
723-413 .030" Diameter pkg(25') **8.95**
723-414 .040" Diameter pkg(25') **12.95**

Light Emitting Diodes pkg(4) 3.50 ea
No heat, low current drain, low voltage, .120" diameter.
723-402 Red
723-403 Green
723-404 Yellow

Progressive Light Kit
723-205 **39.95**

Replacement Bulbs
723-104 1.5V For Constant Light Kits #101 & 102, and Reversing Constant Light Kit #103 **3.95**
723-107 12V G-O-W Red pkg(3) **3.95**
723-108 12V-.080 Amps .2 Diameter 6" Leads pkg(3) **3.40**
723-109 12V-.27 Amps Bulbs Flasher Type, Min. Bayonet Base pkg(2) **4.40**
723-110 12V-.2 Amps Bulbs Min. Bayonet Base, Clear pkg(3) **3.30**

SWITCHES

Push-Button
723-407 SPST pkg(4) **6.95**

Reed Switch & Magnet
723-406 **6.95**

TOMAR INDUSTRIES

End-Of-Train Device 16.50 ea

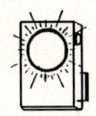

Includes red face metal casing and lens, 1.5V lamp installed in casting, electronic flasher unit and N cell battery holder.
81-5806 Amber Lens
81-5822 Red Lens

Flasher Unit
81-5823 **9.95**
Includes electronic flash and N cell battery holder.

UTAH PACIFIC

Constant Lighting Kits
Reversing headlight and back-up light. Constant light for numberboards, cab lights, etc. Kit includes diodes and polarity board. Less light bulbs.

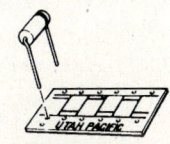

755-96 Locomotive **7.30**

755-66 Non-Directional **4.75**

VOLLMER

IMPORTED FROM GERMANY BY WALTHERS

Lighting Accessories

770-6550 Lighting Strip 2-Socket **12.99**

Western Rail Products

Lighting Kits 10.95 ea

757-102 End of Train Flasher w/Batteries
Flashing red LED, electronic circuit, on/off switch and batteries included.

757-104 Diesel Engine Strobe Flasher w/Batteries
Includes flashing yellow strobe LED, electronic control circuit, switch and batteries.

757-106 Caboose Flashing, Warning Lights
Flashing red LED, electronic circuit, on/off switch and batteries included. Kit comes completely wired and ready for installation.

Switches

757-401 SPDT pkg(2) **4.95**
Single-pole double-throw miniature toggle switch. On-Off-On positions. Rated 6 amps at 125V.

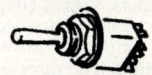

757-402 DPDT pkg(2) **5.95**
Double-pole double-throw miniature toggle switch. On-Off-On positions. Rated 6 amps at 125V.

757-403 Push Button pkg(2) **1.95**
Miniature push-button switches. Momentary-on push buttons.

Batteries

757-902 pkg(2) **1.95**
Small "watch type" batteries are replacements for original batteries sold with EOT flasher (#101) Diesel Engine Strobe Light (#104) and the Caboose Flasher (#106).

LIGHTING - ELECTRICAL - MOTORS

WIRE WORKS

Wire

One Conductor - #24 Gauge - 60' 5.50 ea
851-124070600 Black
851-124070602 Red
851-124070609 White
Item listed below is available by Special Order (see Legend Page).
851-124070605 Green

One Conductor - #22 Gauge - 50' 5.50 ea
851-122070500 Black
851-122070501 Brown
851-122070502 Red
851-122070503 Orange
851-122070504 Yellow
851-122070505 Green
851-122070506 Blue
851-122070509 White

One Conductor - #22 Gauge - 90' 9.00 ea
851-122070900 Black
851-122070902 Red
851-122070905 Green
851-122070909 White

Two Conductor - #22 Gauge - 30' 9.00 ea
851-222070300 Black/Red
851-222070304 Yellow/Blue
851-222070305 Green/Brown

Three Conductor - #22 Gauge - 23' 9.00 ea
851-322070230 Black/Red/Green
851-322070234 Yellow/Blue/White

Heat Shrink Tubing 4.00 ea

Add extra protection around splices, exposed wires and connectors. Shrinks 50% Packaged in 6" pieces, total length per package shown.
851-21062 1/16" (30")
851-21093 3/32" (30")
851-21125 1/8" (30")
851-21187 3/16" (24")
851-21250 1/4" (18")

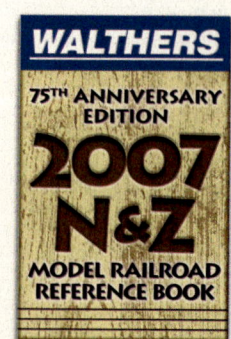

Models and Photo by Keith Kohlmann, Racine, Wisconsin

POWER

"Bigger is better." At least that's what the man from Fairbanks-Morse told the heads of railroad motive power departments as he tried to convince them to order his company's 2,400-horsepower Train Master locomotives. He also mentioned a lower-horsepower unit designed for slow-speed service on heavy trains. The folks at the Chicago & North Western asked a few questions about that one with ore trains and huge local freights in mind — after all, horsepower really only matters at higher speeds anyway.

H16-66 #1696 was one of those 1,600-horsepower units. With its huge size and six-axle trucks, this burly machine could develop the tractive effort to move long trains at low speeds. One misty morning, the quiet berg of Berryville, Wisconsin, was awakened by the throaty grumble of #1696 as it lugged a hundred-car wayfreight toward Chicago. A blast on the airhorn warned motorists that the big engine meant business and wasn't going to stop for anything.

From the rumbling of a diesel at work to the sound of a dog barking in the night, sound adds a new dimension to your railroad's atmosphere. In this scene with Keith's modified Atlas loco, you can almost feel the ground quaking under your feet as the train pounds across the crossing. Fortunately, adding the dimension of sound is easy with systems listed in the Power, Sound & Smoke Section.

POWER SUPPLIES - SOUND - SMOKE SYSTEMS

LIFE-LIKE®
Div. of Wm. K. Walthers, Inc.

Smoke Fluid

433-1414 1oz **9.00**
Can be used in any smoke generator designed for petroleum-based smoke fluid.

ATLAS

NEW PRODUCT
Right Track™ Power Pack

NEW 150-311 44.95
Features upgraded electronics for smooth operation, separate power and direction switches, overload indicator lamp, no pulse power to damage precision motors, UL/C-UL listed.

BACHMANN

POWER PACKS
Power Pack with Speed Controller

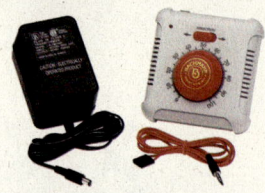

160-44212 38.50
This easy-to-use power pack includes a wall transformer, speed controller and plug-in wiring for E-Z Track®.

Spectrum® Magnum Power Pack

160-44281 .9 Amp **50.00**
The perfect beginner's power pack. Features include precision throttle control, master on-off switch, direction control, AC output for accessories and shockproof casing. Covered by a lifetime warranty.

Smoke Fluid

160-99993 2-1/4oz **6.25**

CREST

THE TRAIN ENGINEER

Revolutionize your model railroad with this wireless walkaround throttle system. You'll be able to run trains and accessories from up to 300' away - with your current power pack and wiring!

The Original Train Engineer (#227-55470) includes a special receiver which operates with your current power pack. Simply connect the receiver into the existing wiring between the pack and the track. No modifications to locos or cars are needed!

Now you're ready to run a train with the hand-held transmitter, which controls speed and direction by broadcasting a multi-directional, low-power FM signal (27 megahertz) to the receiver. Built-in Pulse-Code-Modulation (PCM) eliminates outside signal interference.

For more fun and easy remote control operations, add the Remote Accessory Unit (#227-55474, sold separately) to run trackside turnouts, signals and lights with your transmitter. Connect additional units to run up to 50 different accessories!

For club or show layouts, or just running trains with another person, additional receivers (#227-55471) and Transmitters (#227-55473) are available separately.

227-55470 Original Train Engineer Walkaround Control 2-Piece Set **182.00**
Includes Receiver and Hand-Held Transmitter.

227-55471 Original Train Engineer Additional Receiver Only **121.00**

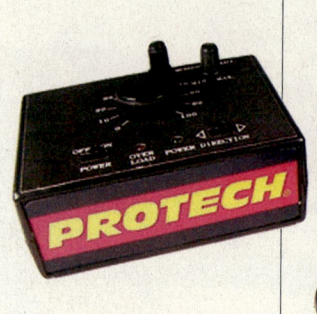

ProTech Ultra Power Pack 227-5

227-55473 Original Train Engineer Transmitter (27 Megahertz) **91.00**

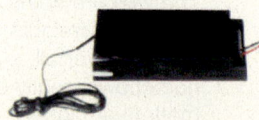

227-55474 Original Train Engineer Remote Accessory Controller **61.00**
Operates up to five lights, turnouts or accessories; additional units can be combined to control up to 50 accessories.

227-55475 Original Train Engineer Accessory Receiver **66.00**
Designed for remote control of turnouts only. Operates up to five turnouts; additional units can be combined to control up to 50 turnouts.

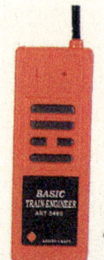

227-55480 Basic DC/Train Engineer 2 Amp w/100' Range **83.00**
Simplified version of Train Engineer. A wireless radio control system for all DC electric trains. Includes one transmitter and one receiver.

227-55499 Cooling Fan For Receiver **17.00**
Increases airflow to keep interior components of Receiver (#227-55471; also included with #55470, both sold separately) cooler.

POWER PACKS

227-5 ProTech Ultra HO 16V 2 Amp w/Switching Power Supply **20.00**

227-55400 1.8 Amp w/Pulse Width Control **55.50**
Perfect for those just starting out in the hobby. Features include 1.8 amp and directional control, auto electronic circuit protection, power and over current indicator lights, constant voltage pulse width speed control, plus automatic electronic momentum circuit for smooth operation.

372

POWER SUPPLIES - SOUND - SMOKE SYSTEMS

BUSCH

IMPORTED FROM GERMANY BY WALTHERS

SOUND SYSTEMS
Items listed below are available by Special Order (see Legend Page).

131.99 ea

Railway Station

189-5768 American Railway Station
Realistic sounds, stored on a chip, create the atmosphere of a busy railway station. Sounds include Western bell, steam whistle, crossing bell, station voice announcement and "Tickets, please" voice announcement. Includes separate speaker; operates on 10-16V AC or DC.

City Sounds
189-5764 Street Traffic
189-5765 Church Bells

FALLER

IMPORTED FROM GERMANY BY WALTHERS

Station Voice Announcer (German)

272-180645 54.99
This self-contained unit produces various station announcements (in German) for a 90-second duration when triggered by trains tripping a photoelectric sensor. Simply place it under your layout or inside your station building. Easy hookup to your power packs 12-16V AC accessory terminal.

KATO

Power Pack

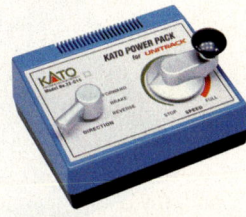

381-22014 65.00
The best choice to use with Kato Unitrack and locomotives! This easy-to-use power pack features UL-approved power unit, separate tabletop control unit with variable speed control and direction control, direct plug-in of the Kato Feeder Track Cord and direct snap-on connection of the Kato Turnout Control Switch. The control unit is also equipped with automatic shut-off/reset switch for protection against short circuit damage. Includes an adapter cord to connect with track by other manufacturers. 12V DC, 1 AMP output.

Daily New Arrival Updates! Visit Walthers Web site at
www.walthers.com

MODEL POWER

Power Packs

490-1250 Deluxe Electric Power Pack **24.98**
.6 amp taper-wound rheostat. Separate forward and reverse switch.

490-3800 Electropak **43.98**
This reliable, ultra-smooth power pack features circuit breaker protection, individually tested circuit breakers, overload indicator, separate "on-off" switch, separate detection switch, quick clip wire connectors and a power indicator. 1.3 amps.

Smoke Fluid

490-12 4oz **6.59**
For any scale of trains. Use only a few drops at a time. Nontoxic and non-flammable.

SEUTHE

IMPORTED FROM GERMANY BY WALTHERS
A quality line of smoke/steam generators for various foreign and domestic locomotives. Generators for structures and ships are also available.

SMOKE & STEAM

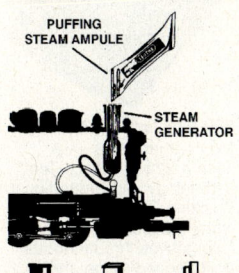

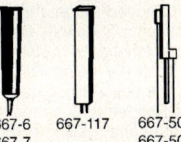
667-6 667-117 667-501
667-7   667-503

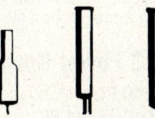
667-20 667-99   667-9
667-21 667-100 667-10
667-22

Accessories
667-101 Loco Smoke 10ml **4.99**
Bottle with filling tool.

667-105 Neutral Steam Distillate, 50ml **8.99**

667-106 Neutral Steam Distillate, 250ml **17.99**

667-200 Steam Pipes pkg(6) **5.99**
For use with Steam Generator #667-10 (sold separately).

Smoke Generators
667-5 Smoke Generator, Ships, 4-6V **23.99**
Smoke generator for ships and similar models.

667-27 10-16V **23.99**

667-28 16-22V **23.99**

667-117 Smoke Chimney 16V **12.99**
Smoke generator for house or building.

667-117E Chimney - Ready for Model Buildings **7.99**
No accessories included.

Steam Generators
23.99 ea

667-6 Operating Voltage 14V
For model structures and factory chimneys, as well as all O Gauge locomotives.

667-7 Operating Voltage 16V
For model structures and factory chimneys, as well as all O Gauge locomotives. Especially for Marklin 5700.

667-9 Operating Voltage 14V
For Fleischmann 4170, 4175, 4177 and 4178; also, Marklin-Hamo DC (8335).

667-10 Maximum 16V AC/DC
For Marklin 3046, 3047, 3048, 3084, 3085 and 3102 locomotives, as well as Fleischmann and Liliput locomotives.

667-11 Maximum 16V AC/DC
Same as #10 except for Marklin digital.

667-12 Operating Voltage 16V
Same as #100 except for Marklin digital.

667-20 Maximum 16V AC/DC
For Marklin 3083, 3091 and 3093; also, Hamo 8391, 8392 and 8393.

667-21 Maximum 16V AC/DC
Universal type for all locomotives with metal bodies and extremely slim chimneys.

667-22 Maximum 16V AC/DC
Universal type for all locomotives with plastic bodies and extremely slim chimneys.

667-23 Maximum 16V AC/DC
Same as #22 except for Marklin digital.

667-24 Maximum 16V AC/DC
Same as #20 except for Marklin digital.

667-99 Operating Voltage 14V
For all types of locomotives with plastic bodies.

667-100 Operating Voltage 16V
For all types of locomotives with plastic bodies.

Supersteam Generator
667-490 With Hose Connector **35.99**

667-491 For Storage Vessels **29.99**

Super Smoke Units
667-500 Ship Models/Large Chimneys **35.99**

667-501 12V w/Smoke Fluid **29.99**

667-503 16V w/Smoke Fluid **29.99**

POWER SUPPLIES - SOUND - SMOKE SYSTEMS

POWER PACKS

Tech 4 Series
Introducing the Tech 4 Series with Accu-Tec technology, which provides the smoothest control available today. Most Tech 4 packs have nearly 25% more power than a comparable Tech II. In addition to the power, these durable packs are feature-rich and provide precise control.

500-200 Tech 4 200 w/17VA **54.98**
This Tech 4 is perfect for upgrading any train set. Complete with sleek new design, improved features and powerful performance.

500-260 Tech 4 260 w/20VA & Momentum **79.98**
The Tech 4 260 is packed with power and all the features you need for realistic operation, including Accu-Tec technology, PTC, precise momentum circuitry and braking with 25% more power than the comparable Tech II.

500-280 Tech 4 280 Dual Power **79.98**
This Tech 4 has two units in one housing, controlling two trains in different blocks with common rail. With dual controls, Accu-Tec technology and Proportional Tracking Control, this Tech 4 provides power and precision in one convenient unit.

500-220 Tech 4 220 w/16VA & Momentum **68.98**
Tech 4 220 with Accu-Tec technology and Proportional Tracking Control provides instant response from locomotives throughout their entire speed range and automatically adjusts pulse characteristics to match the locomotive's motor. This Tech 4 has the power to upgrade train sets and features momentum circuitry and braking control to make you feel as if you're running a real locomotive.

Tech 3 Power Command
500-9500 Power Command 9500 (30VA) **114.98**
Here is the power pack for the serious modeler! Get maximum control: Ammeter and voltmeter let you monitor loco operation and identify problems before damage occurs. Achieve maximum realism: Advanced Proportional Tracking Control, momentum circuitry, plus braking and acceleration control make you feel like you're running a real locomotive. Available with 30VA of power, pack can run HO, N, G and other DC trains. Comes with Throttle Master control knob, 300° of control, thermostat protection, AC terminals for accessories and much more.

Standard Power Packs
Maximum realism at an economical price. Check out the features on these durable power packs: extended range control throttle, master on-off switch, mainline direction switch and much more.

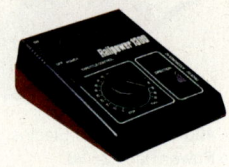

500-1300 Railpower 1300 **34.50**
For use with HO, N and Z Scale trains. Total output 7VA on solid state circuitry, designed to deliver superior slow-speed acceleration for increased realism. Features a mainline direction switch, 300° speed control, circuit protection to guard against overload and more.

500-1370 Railpower 1370 **39.98**
Power for up to five average HO trains! Solid state circuitry delivers 18VA output and superior slow-speed acceleration. Mainline direction switch, on-off switch, red LED pilot light, 300° speed control and circuit protection.

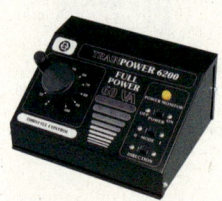

500-6200 Trainpower 6200 **134.98**
Maximum power for G Scale, but also runs HO and N gauge. Unit provides 60VA output power, plus 0-18.5V DC track voltage. Includes AC output for accessories, mode switch to select HO and N Scale or Large Scale, 300° throttle control and power monitor lamp. Delivers 3.6 amps of power to trains.

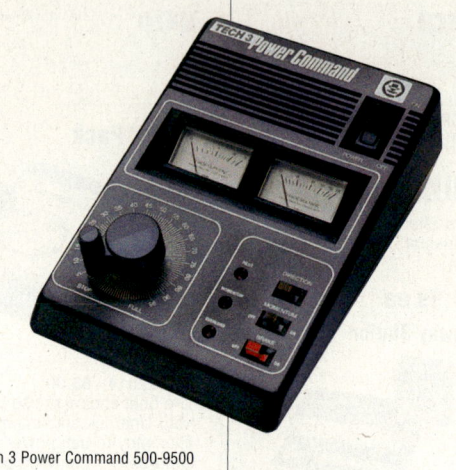

Tech 3 Power Command 500-9500

Control Master 20 500-444

Slow Motion Switch Machine Power Supply
500-AH362 35.98
Designed to power all slow-motion (latching) switch machines where the power output must be +12V and –12VDC. Built to handle multiple switch machines. Good for all types of layout control.

Walkaround Control
500-444 Control Master 20 **199.98**
Hand-held control with memory function. HO/N Scale. Terminals for ammeter and voltmeter hookup, filtered and regulated DC output, momentum circuitry, nudge switch control and a mode switch. 5.0 amps plus reserve power.

PART NUMBER	DESCRIPTION	5 YEAR LIMITED WARRANTY	OVERLOAD LIGHT INDICATOR	ACCU-TEC TECHNOLOGY	MOMENTUM EQUIPPED	POWER FOR AVERAGE TRAINS	PROPORTIONAL TRACKING CONTROL (PTC)	PILOT LAMP	FIXED AC TERMINALS FOR ACCESSORIES
500-200	TECH 4 200	•		•		4-5	•	•	•
500-220	TECH 4 220	•		•	•	4-5	•	•	•
500-260	TECH 4 260	•	•	•	•	6-8	•	•	•
500-280	TECH 4 280	•		•		4-6	•	•	•
500-1300	RAILPOWER 1300					2		•	•
500-1370	RAILPOWER 1370					4-5		•	•

POWER SUPPLIES - SOUND - SMOKE SYSTEMS

SOUND SYSTEMS

Symphony 77
NEW 500-AA555 82.98
Do you want the sights and sounds of a real railroad on your layout? You provide the sights, M.R.C. provides the sounds. The Symphony 77 provides many high-quality digital railroad sounds to bring your layout to life. There are two modes of operation for the era that you model - steam or diesel. Sounds include: choice of horns and whistles, steam or diesel bell, rail clack, crossing gate and many more. Also features user controllable speed rate, high power amplifier, two-way speaker system and a handheld controller.

Handheld Synchro Sound 75.98 ea
Provides realistic synchronized sounds, plus 12 buttons for 12 different associated sounds. Adjustable volume. Includes speaker for under-layout mounting. Easy hook-up to your current power pack and layout. Works with DC and DCC systems.

500-1022 Steam
Adjustable chuff rate.
500-1023 Diesel

Symphony 77 500-AA555

Adjustable exhaust rate.

City-Country Sound Station 552
500-AA552 75.98
Eighteen high-quality sounds make your layout more realistic than ever. Place one speaker in a country setting and the other in an urban setting; then select the sounds that correspond with the speaker locations (rain, thunder, crickets, sirens, jackhammers, etc.). Add sound on sound for added realism. Includes a two-way speaker system, handheld controller, and hefty five-watt amplifier.

ACCESSORIES

500-2040 Terminal Strip-Plain 6.98

500-2041 Terminal Strip-Wired 7.98

500-AT880 Universal Voltage Reducer 9.98
Can be used with any power control (AC, DC or DCC), scale or gauge (but is especially useful in N Scale applications where top speeds are an issue). It lowers top voltage by approximately four volts. Installs in series between your power source and track.

SWITCHES

500-2001 SPST Slide 1.98
500-2003 DPDT Slide 2.98

See What's New and Exciting at
www.walthers.com

NEW PRODUCTS
Wireless Color Camera Systems

2.4gHz Camera System

NEW 655-10008 CCS-811T1 2.4 gHz w/Audio **149.95**
Perfect for adding a second camera-equipped train to your layout! This system has the same features as 655-10002, plus it includes two AC power supplies - one for the receiver and another for stationary camera operation. Also comes with a camera mounting bracket, 9V battery clip and 9V battery for mobile camera operation. This system operates on 2.4 gHz and will not receive or interfere with 1.2 gHz cameras.

Night Vision Camera System

NEW 655-10009 CCS-812T **199.95**
Now you can see and hear in total darkness—perfect for nighttime operations on your layout! It's also ideal for checking inside tunnel clearances on your layout. Designed for indoor or outdoor use, the camera/transmitter is completely weather proof and has an unobstructed effective range of 100 meters or more between the camera and the receiver! Built in infrared LEDs illuminate up to 23 feet from camera. The camera view angle is 62°. The camera can be Operated from 9 volt battery, also incldes 9 volt AC power supply.

WIRELESS COLOR CAMERA SYSTEMS
Now you can get the thrill of seeing what it's like to "ride" inside your trains. The WirelessMicroColorCam produces a full-color image and is available with or without sound. The wireless signal range is 300 to 1000'—perfect for most home or club layouts. Tiny enough to be mounted on an N or HOn3 flat car or inside an unpowered HO locomotive (and it'll fit in a few powered units too). Each system includes the camera, wireless receiver, AC power supplies for the camera and receiver, TV/VCR hookup cables, nine volt battery clip for the camera, one nine volt battery and complete instructions. 2.4 gHz receivers cannot receive 1.2 gHz signals and vice-versa.

655-10001 No Audio 1.2 gHz **79.95**
655-10002 With Audio 1.2 gHz **99.95**

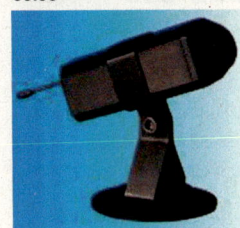

655-10003 Rechargeable Single Camera With Audio 2.4 gHz **169.95**
Features built-in battery with five-hour recharge life. Also can operate on one of four channels so you can operate four systems at once. Includes recharger.

655-10004 Two Camera System With Audio 2.4 gHz **199.95**
Double your fun with a two camera system. Switch between the two cameras with the button on the receiver or use the hand held TV-style remote. You can also program the receiver to automatically switch between the two cameras at a 7-8 second interval. The cameras have built-in microphones and mounting brackets so you can position them in your desired location.

655-10005 9V Battery Eliminator For DCC & BEC Control **29.95**
Use in place of battery for operation on DCC, TMCC and DCS layouts. Operates off track current or connection to function outputs on a DCC decoder.

655-10006 Super Bright White LED Light Board **29.95**
Light the way for your camera with this bright light board. Operates off a 9V battery or from any 5-18V AC or DC power source.

655-10007 9V AC Power Supply For Receivers or Cameras **12.95**

375

POWER SUPPLIES - SOUND - SMOKE SYSTEMS

SOUNDTRAXX

Bring new dimensions of operation to your models with this line of digital sound decoders compatible with all DCC systems. Choose from a wide range of assembled, drop-in units for steam and diesel locos, along with numerous accessories for custom conversion.

OWNER'S MANUALS
678-140067 For DSX Digital Sound Decoders **Free**
678-140068 For "LC" Version 2.0 Digital Sound Decoders **Free**

BIPOLAR CAPACITOR
678-810067 Bipolar Capacitor 33uF, 16V For DSXs, LC Decoders **0.75**

SPEAKERS
8 Ohm
678-810053 3/4" Diameter **9.95**
678-810054 1" Diameter **9.95**
678-810055 1-1/2" Diameter **8.95**
678-810056 2" Diameter **8.95**
678-810057 3" Diameter **8.95**
678-810059 4" Diameter **12.50**
678-810078 Oval 1-1/8 x 1-9/16" **13.50**
678-810083 3/8" Diameter **9.95**
678-810084 Oval 1-1/2 x 2-1/2" **15.25**
678-810087 2-1/2" Diameter **8.95**
678-810089 1/2" Diameter **9.95**
678-810090 Oval 2 x 3-1/2" **16.50**
678-810103 Oval 13/16 x 1-9/16" **13.50**
678-810112 Oval 9/16 x 1" **13.50**

678-810113 8 Oval 5/8 x 1-3/8" **13.50**

WIRING HARNESSES
DSX
678-810092 Steam **10.00**
678-810093 Diesel **10.00**
DSD
678-810069 Power Wiring Harness **10.00**
678-810097 DSD-100LC **6.00**

SPEAKER ENCLOSURES
3.00 ea
678-810107 3/8"
678-810108 1/2"
678-810109 3/4"
678-810110 1"

SPEAKER GASKET KITS
1.50 ea
678-810118 3/4"
678-810119 1"
678-810120 20 x 40mm
678-810121 14 x 25mm

DSD-100LC 1 AMP DIGITAL SOUND DECODERS
45.00 ea
678-820001 Steam
678-820002 Diesel

MICRO DIGITAL SOUND DECODERS DSD-090
75.00 ea
Steam Locomotives
678-821101 Light Engines
678-821102 Medium Engines
678-821103 Heavy Engines
Diesel Locomotives
678-821200 EMD 1st Generation
678-821210 ALCO
678-821220 EMD 2nd Generation
678-821230 General Electric
678-821250 Goose/Railbus

DSX DIGITAL SOUND DECODERS
75.00 ea
Steam Engines
678-824208 DRGW 2-8-2, K-27 Class No.463
678-824210 UP 4-6-6-4 Challenger #3985
678-824212 N&W 2-6-6-4 Class A
678-824215 Westside Lumber Co. Three-Truck Shay
678-824216 C-16
678-824218 Santa Fe 3751

Items listed below are available by Special Order (see Legend Page).
678-824203 DRGW 2-8-2, K-36 Class No.484
678-824206 DRGW 2-8-2, K-37 Class No.497
678-824207 DRGW 2-8-2, K-28 Class No.473
678-824209 East Broad Top 2-8-2
678-824211 SP 4-8-4 "Daylight" GS-4
678-824214 British L-1 Class Tank
678-824224 SLSF #1522 4-8-2 Mountain

Diesel
678-825202 EMD 1st Generation w/Leslie S3 Airhorn
678-825214 ALCO w/Wabco E2 Airhorn
678-825222 EMD 2nd Generation w/Leslie S3 Airhorn
678-825227 EMD 2nd Generation w/Nathan M3 Airhorn
678-825250 Rio Grande Southern Galloping Goose

Items listed below are available by Special Order (see Legend Page).
678-825201 EMD 1st Generation w/Wabco Airhorn
678-825203 EMD 1st Generation w/Nathan K3 Airhorn
678-825204 EMD 1st Generation w/Wabco E2 Airhorn
678-825205 EMD 1st Generation w/Nathan M5 Airhorn
678-825208 EMD 1st Generation w/Nathan P3 Airhorn
678-825211 ALCO w/Wabco Airhorn
678-825212 ALCO w/Leslie S3 Airhorn
678-825213 ALCO w/Nathan K3 Airhorn
678-825215 ALCO w/Nathan M5 Airhorn
678-825218 ALCO w/Nathan P3 Airhorn
678-825220 EMD 2nd Generation w/Leslie S5 Airhorn
678-825223 EMD 2nd Generation w/Nathan K3 Airhorn
678-825226 EMD 2nd Generation w/Nathan K5 Airhorn
678-825228 EMD 2nd Generation w/Nathan P3 Airhorn
678-825230 GE w/Leslie S5 Airhorn
678-825231 GE w/Wabco Airhorn
678-825232 GE w/Leslie S3 Airhorn
678-825234 GE w/Wabco E2 Airhorn
678-825236 GE w/Nathan K5 Airhorn
678-825238 GE w/Nathan P3 Airhorn

TEST KIT
678-829001 Decoder Test Kit **3.00**

TRAIN TRONICS

SOUND SYSTEMS
Diesel Horn
723-301 3-Toned Diesel Horn Kit **27.95**
Kit includes push button speaker mounting clips and 3" speaker. To expand system add #723-415 speakers at various points around your layout. 6 to 16V AC/DC.

Steam Whistle w/Diesel Horn
723-305 **89.95**
Provides both three-toned steam whistle with background steam hiss and three-chimed diesel horn. Kit contains solid-state prebuilt and tested circuit, push button, slide control, speaker and mounting clips.

Speaker
723-415 **5.95**
8 ohm, 3" in diameter.

SWITCH POWER
Switch Machine Power Unit
Capable of operating up to 20 turnouts simultaneously, with "positive snap-action." Operates any type of dual coil switch machine.
723-603 Switchman Capacitive Discharge Unit **39.95**
723-1801 AC Converter for Zero-1 **7.95**
723-1804 Conductive Paint for Zero-1 **2.50**

Item listed below is available by Special Order (see Legend Page).
723-1805 Power Booster for Zero-1 **99.95**

SCALE SHOPS

Voltrollers

1.5 Amp
649-1315 Walk-Around Throttle Kit **39.98**
649-1316 Walk-Around Throttle, Assembled **69.98**
649-1319 Panel Throttle Kit **19.98**

3 Amp
649-1339 Panel Throttle Kit **29.98**
Items listed below are available by Special Order (see Legend Page).
649-1335 Walk-Around Throttle Kit **49.98**
649-1336 Walk-Around Throttle, Assembled **79.98**
649-1338 Cabinet Throttle, Assembled **69.98**

VOLLMER

IMPORTED FROM GERMANY BY WALTHERS

Smoke Unit
770-4112 Smoke Generator, Large, HO Scale **42.99**

770-4114 Smoke Generator **41.99**
Features a large tank for smoke-making. Includes enough fluid for 70 minutes of smoke.

770-4116 Smoke Fluid Refill, 7-1/2oz 250ml **20.99**
770-4120 Smoke Distillate Fragrant 7-1/2oz 250ml **22.99**

Scenery by Ron Freeman, Models and Photo by Mike Reardon, Addison, Illinois

It's a hectic day on the mainline behind the Republic Steel Mill. Everyone wants to leave town at once as three freights with a variety of loads scurry east along the triple track. And just when the CSX needed it most, they've had to send out a Maintenance-of-Way GP40 to drag an SD40-2 "Bluebird" home to the shops. The Bluebird is sidelined with a failed generator and, with business booming at nearly every industry along the route, it needs to get back in service — and soon! This busy scene was shot on the Midwest N Pioneer MRRC layout in Illinois.

Today's command control systems offer a wide range of ways to make your layout more fun, with independent control of engines, sound and lighting effects, signals and more. Check out the complete selection of starter sets, accessories, decoders and much more in the Command Control section!

COMMAND CONTROL

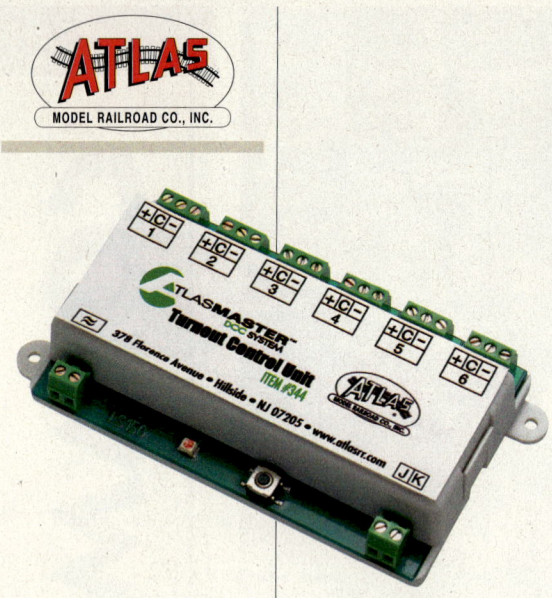

Turnout Control Unit 150-344

ATLAS MASTER™ DCC SYSTEM

150-344 Turnout Control Unit **49.95**
Featuring two sets of outputs, this unit can control up to two Atlas Snap-Switch motors per output. Designed specifically for use with the Atlas Master DCC Commander and Atlas twin-coil/snap-switch motors. 8-18V AC or DC, 4.5A maximum output current.

Atlas Generator

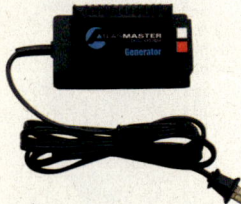

150-335   42.95
Power up with the Atlas Generator! This compact component provides power to the Commander. It is a UL Recognized Component with a thermal fuse for overload protection. Easy access terminals hold wires in place. Output: 15V, 3.0 Amps.

Accessories

150-331 Hand Command **144.95**
Includes throttle, universal panel connector 6' coiled cord and 7' cable wire. Add complete walk-around capability to the Atlas Commander, or any other system that supports XpressNet technology. Some features include stack function for simple recall of up to eight locomotives and more.

150-343 15' Cable Wire **6.50**
Includes a 15' cable wire with a six pin modular connector.

150-322 Universal Panel Connector **26.95**
This high-quality UPC has an LED track status indicator, two DIN jacks and one modular jack that will allow you to convert up to three Hand Commands, slave commander or other XpressNet devices.

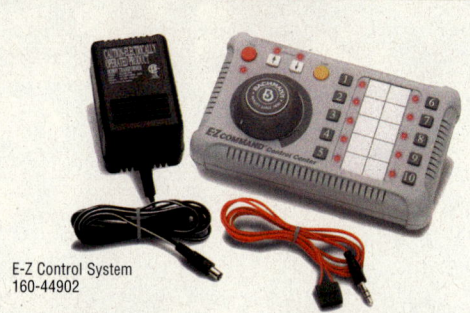

E-Z Control System
160-44902

E-Z COMMAND® SYSTEM

Control System
160-44902   106.00
This DCC system, developed in conjunction with Lenz, allows modelers to digitally control speed, lighting and direction of multiple locomotives with simplified, one-button, main-track programming. The system features plug-and-play compatibility with all DC and DCC systems.

E-Z COMMAND ACCESSORIES

Walk-Around Companion

160-44907   94.00
Control multiple trains from convenient locations around your layout or coordinate independent operations between a primary and a secondary user. Features a plug-and-play connection to E-Z Command Control Center. It duplicates all locomotive addresses set on E-Z Command Control Center and allows simultaneous throttle control of several locomotives. Includes connector wires.

Walk-Around Companion Connector Panel
160-44908   35.50
Used in conjunction with the Walk-Around Companion, multiple connector panels let you establish a series of control points virtually anywhere on the perimeter of your layout. Features plug-in ports and simple connections to all brands of track. Includes connector wires.

Five-Amp Power Booster
160-44910   149.95
This device provides extra current to the track for the control of an increased number of DCC locomotives on your HO, N, or On30 layout. Also appropriate for DCC decoder-equipped large scale locomotives.

Automatic Reversing Loop Module
160-44912   64.95
Eliminates the complicated wiring previously needed to operate analog reverse-loop track layouts. The module senses train as it moves along the loop, automatically switching polarity to allow reverse loop control.

E-Z Command DCC Decoders

Turnout & Accessory Decoder
160-44911   69.95
Assume digital command of your entire layout with on/off control of turnouts, operating accessories, and scenery elements.

Information STATION

Adding Decoders To Older Locomotives

While many locomotives now come with factory-installed decoders or simple connections to add one, older locomotives can also be converted to DCC.

Decoders are typically identified to scale (such as HO, N, etc.) to show which size models they fit and the current rating. You must make sure there's space inside the model for the decoder. The motor MUST be electrically isolated from the frame to electrical pickups - the motor must only receive power from the decoder.

Today, there are plenty of micro decoders, so finding one to fit shouldn't be a problem.

To prevent damaging the decoder, you must know the operating current, which is the amount of current needed to drive the motor and any accessories. Any mechanical problems (binding, lack of lubrication, etc.) should be corrected before installing a decoder, as they can raise the operating current.

You also need to determine the stall current, which is the amount of current drawn by the motor if stalled. Whenever you start an engine from a dead stop, the motor will pull almost as much current as it would if stalled. If the decoder isn't rated to handle this, the potential is there for damage.

COMMAND CONTROL

Run your trains, not your track with the complete line of Digitrax Command Control Sets and components.

NEW PRODUCTS

Decoders

Plug N' Play Decoders
NEW 245-DN163I1B 34.99
For Intermountain FT-B Units 1.0/1.5 Amp w/6 FX3 Functions Rated At 1/2 Amp
NEW 245-DN163I1C 34.99
For Intermountain F3A&B and F7A&B Units 1.0/1.5 Amp w/6 FX3 Functions
NEW 245-DN163K1C 35.99
For Kato SD40-2 2006+ Production

Computer Interface

Sound Decoder Programmer

NEW 245-PR2 99.95
Includes Soundloader™ software. The PR2 lets SoundFX users download new Project sound files and even reflash the decoder's firmware for latest updates.

Plug 'N Play Signaling

Digitrax Plug 'N Play Signaling

The Digitrax Plug 'N Play Signal system is the perfect way to add signaling to your layout. And whether you use DC or DCC controls, it will add a new dimension of realism to operations.

The SE8C Signal Decoder is the heart of the system, and can drive up to 32 signal heads using most popular signal types like bi-color LED searchlight types with two or three leads, or 3-LED heads with common anode or cathode. It can even drive B&O or Pennsy type heads with multiple indicators. Current resistors are built-in for setting LED brightness. The SE8C can also be used to drive 8 slow-motion turnout machines, such as Circuitron's Tortoise™ or eight semaphore signals driven by slow-motion turnout machines. The SE8C provides 16 inputs, eight control lines for local turnout control and eight occupancy sensor inputs.

A full line of accessory products let you use modular plug 'n play wiring and components to install a fully customizable signaling system on your railroad. The Signal Driver Cable Kits take the hassle out of running wires for your signal system. Signal Mast Base Kits, Terminal Mounting Strip Kits and Signal Hardware Mounting Kits make it easy to use either inexpensive circuit board type signals, or your own finely detailed signals with the system.

If you're using a computer to control your layout, the Digitrax Plug 'N Play Signaling System is a great way to add prototypical signaling to your railroad. If you're not using a computer, the SE8C Signal Decoder lets you manually operate signals on the layout from your throttle. With a computer and compatible software, you'll be able to realize the full potential of the Digitrax Plug 'N Play Signaling System.

245-SE8C Signal Decoder **125.00**
245-SDCK Signal Driver Cable Kit **19.99**
245-SMHK Signal Mounting Hardware Kit **19.99**
245-TSMK Terminal Strip Mounting Kit (2 Boards) **14.99**
245-SMBK Signal Mast Base Kit pkg(3) **14.99**

STARTER SETS

Zephyr Basic Digitrax Command Control Starter Set

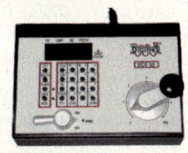

245-ZEP 199.99
An affordable entry into the world of DCC, this set is designed with the small layout in mind, but can easily grow if your railroad expands. Ideal for single or multiple operators, up to 10 additional throttles/operators can be accommodated. All-in-one unit incorporates throttle, command station and booster into an easy-to-use DCC controller. The Zephyr provides 128-step speed control, easy access to 10 functions that can be used for a multitude of special effects including sound (functions 0 through 8), constant brightness headlight on/off, direction control, access to four-digit addresses and turnout control. Set includes Zephyr DCS50 and power supply, decoder test kit, Zephyr Users Manual and Digitrax Decoder Users Manual. No decoder is included with this set, giving you the freedom to choose from Digitrax' wide variety of DCC decoders to fit your needs (decoders sold separately).

Super Empire Builder Advanced Digitrax Command Control Starter Set

Advanced features provide easier, more prototypical operation. You spend lots of time making your locos look like the real thing, now make them run like the real thing, too!

Super Empire Builder delivers access to all Digitrax LocoMotion® System and FX³ System features including 128-step speed control and consist control, as well as access to four-digit addressing, turnout control, consisting, adjustable network synchronized fast clock and much more. The DT400 handheld walk-around dual throttle with full numeric keypad gives you control of two locos—you can run more than one train, control helpers, or handle multiple-unit operation on the head end. Backlit LCD display shows you train speed, direction, function status and more. The DT400 throttle even has a built in flashlight so you can read your paperwork in darkened layout rooms. Run up to 22 addresses with up to 22 operators with Super Empire Builder.

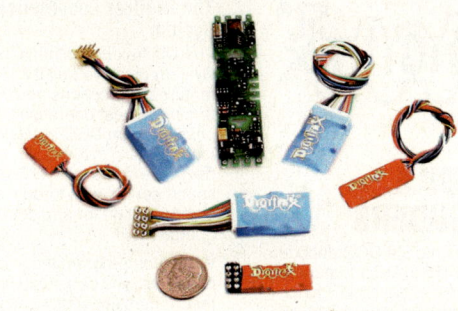

Various decoders shown.

Super Empire Builder comes with a simple and intuitive Infra-Ready DT400 throttle that makes converting to wireless infrared operation as easy as adding IR Receiver UR90 or UR91 (sold separately). Also included is a DB150 Command Station/Booster with Intelligent Auto Reversing, UP5 LocoNet Panel, LT1 LocoNet Cable & Decoder Test Kit and easy-to-understand Super Empire Builder and Digitrax Decoder Users Manuals. Decoders not included.

The radio equipped version comes with the DT400R Radio Throttle and UR91 radio receiver. Approximate signal range is a 300' circle. Operates approximately 6-8 hours on fully charged NiCad batteries, 10-20 hours on alkaline batteries or can be run as a plug-in throttle with no batteries. (Please Note: Radio-equipped sets are available only in the US and Canada.)

245-SEB Super Empire Builder Advanced Starter Set **349.99**
245-SEBRE Radio-Equipped Super Empire Builder Advanced Starter Set **549.99**

Daily New Product Announcements! Visit Walthers Web site at
www.walthers.com

Super Chief Premium Digitrax Command Control Starter Sets

Designed for the needs of any size home or club layout where operations are the key, the Super Chief Starter Set has more features than any other DCC set on the market. Large system command station has capacity for handling up to 120 addresses with up to 120 operators at a time. Super Chief gives you access to all Digitrax LocoMotion System and FX³ System features including four digit addressing, 128-step speed control, consist control, programming "on the fly," turnout control, adjustable network synchronized fast clock, and much, much more.

Your Super Chief has a separate programming output that allows for read back of programming information. Super Chief sets come with a DT400 Infra-Ready throttle that makes converting to wireless operation as easy as adding the Infra-Red Receiver UR90 or UR91 (sold separately). The radio-equipped version comes with the DT400R Radio Throttle and UR91 radio receiver. (Please Note: Radio-equipped sets are available only in the US and Canada.)

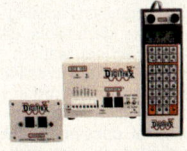

245-SCF Super Chief Premium Starter Set 5 Amps **449.99**
245-SCF200 Super Chief Premium Starter Set 8 Amps **469.99**
245-SCFRE Radio-Equipped Super Chief Premium Starter Set 5 Amps **639.99**
245-SCFRE200 Radio-Equipped Super Chief Premium Starter Set 8 Amps **659.99**

COMMAND CONTROL

MOBILE DECODERS

Digitrax mobile DCC decoders offer exciting DCC features at great low prices! All Digitrax decoders are rated for at least 1 amp for robust operation and long-term reliability. Available in a variety of shapes and sizes to fit in almost any locomotive, Digitrax offers both traditional wired decoders as well as plug n' play decoders that make installation a snap. Visit Digitrax on the internet to determine which Digitrax decoder fits in your loco!

Digitrax decoders feature variable frequency Supersonic™ motor drive for quiet motor operation. They support all DCC standard programming methods. One-step decoder factory reset makes it easy to troubleshoot decoders. Motor isolation protection protects your investment in locos and decoders. Digitrax decoders support both two and four digit addressing and basic, advanced and universal consisting. They also have operations mode read-back capability so you can read back programming information while the decoder is on the main line.

Digitrax decoders are DCC compatible and can be used with any DCC compatible system.

Digitrax FX and FX³ Function Systems

Digitrax decoders offer standard FX or enhanced FX³ features. FX makes it easy to install prototypical lighting effects, like Mars lights, ditch lights and others, without having to buy and install an additional circuit board in your loco. All Digitrax decoders offer directional, constant-brightness headlights that can also be programmed for independent operation by the user. All Digitrax decoders offer full function re-mapping so you can choose which function (F0-F12) controls each function lead.

The Digitrax LocoMotion® System

The Digitrax LocoMotion System gives you all the features and options you need to get the best operation possible from DCC equipped locos. All Digitrax mobile decoders come with 128-step speed control with torque compensation for smooth operation.

When you program the decoders, you can customize the momentum with acceleration and deceleration settings, set the normal direction of travel for your loco — long hood or short hood forward — just like the prototype. The switching speed feature gives you convenient, quick access to low speeds for switching operations.

With easy-to-set-up 3-step speed tables, you can determine the throttle response curve of each individual loco on the railroad. Your switchers run like switchers and your road engines run like road engines. Advanced 28-step speed table with 256 level resolution gives you even more precise control over how each loco responds to the throttle.

Premium decoders also include the Digitrax smooth, scaleable speed stabilization feature. You can further enhance your LocoMotion system by setting up this feature to compensate for the load on the loco to smooth out operation at very slow speeds and speed changes caused by track grade.

These Tiny Decoders Handle One Full Amp!

245-DZ143 Wired Decoder **34.95**

245-DZ143PS Decoder w/Medium DCC Plug on Short Harness **37.95**

This premium decoder will fit in those tiny spaces where nothing else will! Rated at one full amp for reliability in HO scale operation, these decoders are small enough to fit in N or Z scale engines. Measures .36 x .55 x .13" 9.1 x 13.9 x 3.2mm. Decoders are equipped for the Digitrax LocoMotion System with Scaleable Speed Stabilization, full FX³ features with four functions available, and transponding.

245-DZ123 Wired Decoder **19.99**

245-DZ123PS Decoder w/Medium DCC Plug on Short Harness **22.99**

This full-featured, economy-priced decoder is the same size as DZ143. Includes the Digitrax LocoMotion System and standard FX features with two functions available.

Mobile Decoders – Non Locomotive Specific

245-DN143IP 29.99
With integrated eight pin medium plug; 1.0/1.5 Amp, four functions, rated at 1/2 Amp. Measures 0.36" x 0.55 x 0.13".

245-DN163 34.99
1.0/1.5 Amp, six functions, rated at 1/2 Amp.

245-DN163PS 37.99
Features eight pin medium plug, 1.0/1.5 Amp, six 6 functions, rated at 1/2 Amp.

Plug-N-Play Decoders for N Scale Locos 34.99 ea (Unless Noted)

These premium Digitrax N Scale Plug-N-Play decoders are made to fit specific locomotives so you don't have to do any soldering or frame modifications, just a simple replacement of the factory-installed light board. Decoders are rated at 1.0 amp for reliable operation. All have the Digitrax LocoMotion™ System with momentum, simple three-step speed tables, high resolution 28-step speed tables, simplified scaleable speed stabilization, SuperSonic™, torque compensation, transponding and much more. Decoders are also equipped for full FX3 features with six functions available and more ways to make your lighting realistic. Units may also be adapted to fit other N Scale locos but additional work may be required.

245-DN122K2 For Kato RDC **44.99**
This is a three-part decoder made specifically for the RDC with the main body installed in the loco frame and two lamp boards for each end of the car. Lighting effects are set up to automatically reverse with white in the forward direction and red in the reverse direction. Includes white LEDs on light boards.

245-DN163A0 For Atlas B23-7, B30-7, B36-7, Dash 8-40B, GP38, GP40, GP40-2, H15-44, H16-44, SD35, Trainmaster, U25B and others FX3 features and white LEDs

245-DN163A1 For Atlas SD50, SD60, SD60M FX3 features and white LEDs

245-DN163I0 For Intermountain SD40T-2 Tunnel Motor; w/golden-white LEDs

245-DN163I1A For Intermountain FT-A Units 1.0/1.5 Amp with six functions, rated At 1/2 Amp.

245-DN163K0A For Kato P42 Genesis, E8 & PA-1 FX3 features and white LEDs

245-DN163K0B For Kato F3A & B Units

245-DN163K1B For Kato AC4400, C44-9, SD70MAC, SD40-2

245-DN163K2 For Kato SD80-90MAC, RS-2, RSD-2 FX3 features and white LEDs

245-DN163M0 For Micro-Trains® FT FX3 features and white LEDs

Function Decoders with Transponding

Various function decoders shown

Put more fun in your DCC operations with these tiny, function-only decoders. Use them to control lighting effects aboard your locomotives and other rolling stock. Approximate size is 0.461 x 0.31 x 0.161". Function decoders support two- and four-digit addressing and feature on/off functions or configurable strobe operation to simulate special lighting effects. TL1 supports F0 forward and reverse, it's great for adding a FRED at the end of the train. TF4 supports F0-F12, expanding the functions available for making loco lighting more realistic.

Programmable from DCC compatible programmers which can handle Digitrax transponding.

245-TL1 Single Function Decoder w/Transponding **18.95**

245-TF4 Quad Function Decoder w/Transponding **20.95**

STATIONARY DECODERS

Designed to control turnouts and other accessories.

245-DS44 Quad Stationary Decoder **39.99**
Control four slow-motion turnout machines. Quick set up for sequential addresses or set up for four independent addresses.

245-DS51K1 For Kato Unitrack Turnouts **14.99**
Easy to use, cost-effective control for a sngle Kato Unitrack turnout or similar device. Rated at 1/2 amp. Great for HO and N Scale turnouts. Small size .319 x .509 x .152" 8.11 x 12.94 x 3.88mm.

245-DS52 Dual Stationary Decoder **24.95**
Screw terminals make installation and set-up easy. Control two solenoid type turnout machines: two-wire bi-polar (Kato Unitrack Switches, etc.) and/or three-wire (Peco, Atlas Snap Switches etc.). Addresses can be independent or sequential. For all scales up to 22V track power.

245-DS54 Quad Turnout Decoder **79.99**
Measures About: 2-1/2 x 4 x 3/4" 6.2 x 10 x 1.8cm
DCC control of turnouts and a variety of other accessories, such as lights, signals or crossing gates. Works with most DCC systems and can be used to run turnouts right out of the box without additional programming. Each unit operates up to four turnout motors (slow-motion or solenoid). Programmable features allow you to automate functions for more fun with less work.

245-DM1 Motor Adapter for DS54 **9.99**
In-line adapter modifies DS54 output to provide bi-polar drive current to run reversible DC motors, solenoid switches (like Kato & LGB turnouts), lamps and similar devices that draw up to 1/12 amp.

THROTTLES

Utility Throttles

These new throttles provide the optimum features requested for model railroad operation. The UT4 family integrates intuitive operation with rock solid design and low cost into a single, hand-held throttle featuring:
• 4-Digit Addressing
• Affordable Price
• Standard InfraReady
• UT4 upgradable to UT4R radio version
• Functions F0-F12 for sound decoder operation
• Direction switch with center brake position
• Improved battery life
• Large knob for precise throttle control
• Automatic Selection and Speed matching features

245-UT4 Standard **79.95**
245-UT4R Radio **129.99**

Get Your Daily Dose of Product News at
www.walthers.com

COMMAND CONTROL

Advanced Throttles

Digitrax user-friendly advanced throttles are designed for use with all LocoNet based systems; these dual control throttles offer tethered operation or wireless remote control with your choice of radio or infra-red signals.

With two sets of controls for locos, you can easily run two separate trains, multiple-unit lash-ups or mid- and end of train helpers. The dual controls make setting up and breaking up consists simple! Each throttle knob is a click encoder that rotates several times from zero to full speed. This gives you very fine speed control. Because it's an encoder, when you select a loco to run, the throttle knob will pick up the loco at its actual speed. You won't have to adjust the throttle knob to the speed of the loco on the track and if the loco is sitting still, it won't move until you turn the throttle knob. With the click encoder feature, single click the knob to recall locos previously in use and double click to reverse the loco you're running.

The multi-line, backlit LCD gives you all the information you need to run the railroad including controlling locos and turnouts, handling consist operations, programming locos and turnouts, controlling loco functions and setting up system parameters to customize your operation.

Units do not require batteries for tethered operation. For radio or infra-red operation, units use a 9V battery. When a battery is in use, they will operate for approximately 6-8 hours on fully-charged NiCad batteries or 10-20 hours on alkaline batteries. For radio operation, a UR91 Radio Receiver (sold separately) is available. For infra-red operation, one or more UR90 IR Receivers (sold separately) are needed.

245-DT300 Advanced Throttle Walk-Around IR **154.99**

245-DT300R Advance Throttle Radio **204.99**

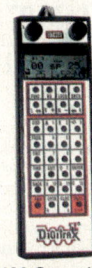

245-DT400 Super Walk-Around IR **179.99**
245-DT400R Super Throttle Radio **229.99**
Full numeric keypad, single key controls for function control, MU operations, programming, editing and more. Controls functions 0-12.

Radio throttles have an approximate circular signal range of 300' 7.5m and operate in the 900Mhz band. The antenna is located inside the case. Radio throttles have short cords to allow user to plug-in in case of emergency. Safety selection feature prevents more than one user from running the same loco. (Note: Radio control throttles are available only in the US and Canada.)

WIRELESS SYSTEM RECEIVERS

UR90 and UR91 wireless receivers let you use your Digitrax Infra-Red or Radio Equipped Throttles (sold separately) as wireless throttles. You won't have to be plugged in to the layout to run your trains! Receivers look like other Digitrax Universal Panels and mount in the fascia of your layout. They connect quickly and simply to your existing LocoNet wiring. Each receiver supports approximately 10 throttles. Both types of receivers can be used at the same time on the layout. Normal tethered operation can also be used at the same time. UR90 and UR91 support all Digitrax IR or Radio equipped throttles including DT300, DT400, DT300R, DT400R, DT100IR and DT100R.

245-UR90 Infra-Red Receiver **45.95**
Most layouts will need more than one receiver, as infra-red operation requires a line of sight signal. UR90 also includes one regular throttle jack for plugging in any Digitrax throttle. Digitrax IR throttles have a wide coverage area because they use dual LED emitters for better coverage. Requires 12V DC external power supply, use a single Digitrax PS12 power supply (sold separately) to power up to 10 UP and/or UR panels.

245-UR91 Radio/Infra-Red Receiver **149.99**
Radio antenna is concealed under the layout. Most layouts need only one UR91, but some large areas may require a second unit to compensate for "dead" spots. UR91 also has an infra-red receiver and a regular throttle jack for plugging in any Digitrax throttle. PS12 power supply is included.

AUTOMATIC REVERSING & POWER MANAGEMENT EQUIPMENT

AR1 Single Automatic Reversing Section Controller
245-AR1 29.99
Easy to use, works with any DCC layout. Use one or more AR1s to to make reverse loops and wyes work like the real thing. Each AR1 gives you cost-effective automatic control of one reversing section without any manual switch operation — "Look Ma, no hands!"

Smart Booster w/Intelligent Autoreverse
Use to expand your Digitrax or other DCC systems. Additional units provide more power to run more trains, automate reverse loops and simplify electrical isolation of portions of your layout so a short circuit stops only one area. Automatically shuts down if command control drive signal is lost - layout will not convert to DC operation if a cable or connection is broken so trains won't "take-off" if they suddenly lose the DCC signal. Accepts 50/60Hz AC or DC from your current transformer, minimum input 12V AC or DC, maximum input 22V AC or 28V DC. Auto reset for overheating and short circuit protection, with unique "smart" protection that won't "weld" derailed locos to the track. Uses LocoNet Expansion Network for easy, reliable hook up and future system expansion. All connections are made with 6 conductor telephone jacks and wire.

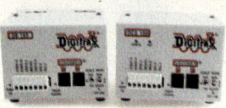

245-DB150 5 Amp/80 Watts **179.99**
245-DB200 8 Amp Booster **199.99**

Command Station/Booster
Operates as the command station (generates DCC packets that tell decoders what to do) and main system booster (receives the DCC signal from the Command Station, amplifies it and puts it on the track as the power that runs the locos) on a Digitrax LocoNet system, and accepts input from any Digitrax throttle, sold separately. Can also be used in conjunction with your computer if desired.

245-DCS100 5 Amp **285.00**
245-DCS200 8 Amp **305.00**

Loconet Universal Interconnect Panels

245-UP5 Universal Panel **16.95**
The UP5 has two RJ12 six-pin throttle jacks in the front for plugging in Digitrax walk-around throttles and two RJ12 six-pin expansion jacks on the back for hook up and expansion of LocoNet. An additional dual purpose RJ12 six-pin male connector is included on the side of the UP5 to allow for additional throttle jacks to be added or for branching the LocoNet network. Using six conductor telephone cable with RJ12 six-pin male connectors on each end, it's easy to daisy chain your network around the layout without hooking up a lot of wires. An indicator LED displays the power state of a local track section. In addition, the UP5 has a 2mm power supply jack. The UP5 gives your layout a professional look and provides a simple, cost effective way to add throttle jacks and expand your LocoNet wiring. Use a single PS12 power supply (sold separately) to power up to 10 UP and/or UR panels on your layout.

Computer Interfaces
Items listed below are available by Special Order (see Legend Page).

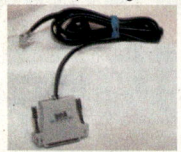

245-MS100 RS232 Computer Interface **45.00**
Allows computers with an IBM-compatible COM, or RS232 communications port, monitor Digitrax LocoNet. Application software running in the computer can then interpret the activity on the LocoNet and report via a monitor. The MS100 is a signal-level translator between LocoNet and a 25 pin DB25 style RS232 port. As an example, you can set up a CTC-type panel which will respond to LocoNet messages. For IBM compatibles with 9-pin male DB9 type COM port connector.

Power Supplies

245-PS515 Ready to Run 15V AC, 5 Amps, 75VA Output **49.99**
Recommended for powering all Digitrax starter sets and accessories. Works for DC too!

Simply plug your PS515 into an appropriate wall outlet (AC120V 60Hz), attach the two output leads to your DCC Booster or other device that accepts up to 5 amps 15V AC.

Unit is overload protected.

245-PS12 12V AC Adapter **8.50**
Recommended for use with Digitrax accessories like UP3, BD46, UR90 and UR91.

245-PS2012 20 Amp **179.99**
Regulated power supply delivers more power with less heat for more efficient booster operation. Operate up to four five-amp boosters with the PS2012 supply. Scale selectable for use with N, HO or large scale. DC Ammeter. On/Off Switch. Integral cooling fan. Design coordinated for use with Digitrax products.

COMMAND CONTROL

Quad Power Manager

245-PM42 Quad Power Manager with Auto Reversing **79.95**
Get the benefits of sectioning your layout and auto reversing without additional boosters. PM42 has 4 levels of short circuit detection sensitivity settings so you can use it with a wide range of DCC equipment.

The PM42 lets you divide the output of a single booster into four sections for auto reversing, or to isolate areas of your layout so only an affected area shuts down if a short circuit occurs. Each unit can run four sections from a single booster, in any combination of regular sections and auto reversing sections.

OCCUPANCY DETECTORS

245-BD4 Quad Occupancy Detector **29.95**
This unit provides cost-effective occupancy detection for four sections. Unit features outputs for panel-mounted LEDs (sold separately) to display occupancy. It will detect any powered loco, and unpowered rolling stock equipped with resistor wheelsets. Requires DS54 or SE8C, both sold separately, to transmit occupancy information to the LocoNet System.

245-BDL168 For 16 Detection Sections **149.99**
Cost-effective occupancy detection for 16 detection sections. Add one or two RX4 Transponder Receivers (sold separately) and you can have Transponding in 8 zones. This means that you'll know when a detection section is occupied and the unique ID of all transponders in that section. Ops Mode Read Back lets you read back CV Values on any section of track that is set up for transponding with BDL168 and one or more RX4s. Unit also includes outputs for panel-mounted LEDs to display local occupancy and power zone status. Detects any powered loco, and unpowered rolling stock equipped with resistor wheelsets. Simply connect to LocoNet to transmit occupancy information to your LocoNet System.

TRANSPONDING

Proven technology for bi-directional layout control! Does not require expensive modifications to your existing DCC system investment.

Track multiple locomotives and rolling stock as they move around your layout. Know the detection section and/or zone location and address of any specific locomotive or other rolling stock equipped with a trasnponding device. Yes, now your dispatcher will be able to know "who you are and where you are!"

Location and address information are updated constantly on LocoNet and can be displayed on a track diagram.

Transponding adds operations mode readback to your layout capabilities. This means you can read an CVs from your decoders while on the layout.

Data received by the system from mobile decoders can be used for display, automation, aosund processing and much more.

Transponding allows you to automate staging yards and other operations.

You can use transponding devices in rolling stock in conjunction with transponding detectors on industry tracks to display the location of your freight cars. Transponding will bring you an under layout system that will allow you to follow the locomotives around the layout based on transponding information received by the system.

You'll even be able to put transponders in other rolling stock and generate sounds like couplers, flat wheels etc. Wow!

The possibilites are endless! One person even said "It's like LoJack for your Locomotives!"

Transponders are incorporated into many Digitrax Premium Decoders. If you already have a DCC decoder (Digitrax or non-Digitrax) installed in a loco and you want to add a transponder, use TL1 or TF4 described above. These can also be used in nonpowered equipment like freight cars to provide transponding. Transponder equipped locos and rolling stock will not affect the operation of other command control systems that do not support transponding.

Transponder receivers are the track level component that you use to set up the track sections where you want transponding to be active. You won't need to equip every track section to have adequate coverage in most cases. Visit the Digitrax Web site at www.digitrax.com for some ideas on equipping your layout with transponding.

245-TL1 Single Function Decoder w/Transponding **16.95**
245-TF4 Quad Function Decoder w/Transponding **20.95**

ACCESSORIES

Decoder Wire
245-DCDRWIRE 9-Conductor 30 AWG pkg(10') **14.99**
The same fine wire Digitrax uses on its N and Z Scale decoders. Great for installing extra lamps and other accessories in your locomotives.

 MODEL RAILROAD NETWORK PRODUCTS

Simplify wiring and operating accessories along your Digitrax DCC-equipped layout with this family of ready-to-use stationary decoders. Each is designed for fast installation and includes an easy to use instruction sheet.

DUAL SIGNAL DECODER

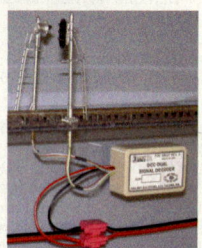

621-64627 **34.95**
Adding working signals to a Digitrax DCC-equipped layout will be fun and easy with this accessory unit. The decoder operates by "listening" to the rails, and lights each signal head corresponding to the patterns of block occupancy and turnout position messages it receives. Each Signal Decoder drives two signal heads (three LEDs each) and is compatible with most LED-type signals (sold separately). Fully assembled, the unit mounts under your benchwork using a self-adhesive patch (included). Simply connect two wires to your DCC cables and two 4-pin connectors to signal wires. Unit is adjusted by simply throwing turnouts and occupying blocks during an initial session and signals can be operating in half an hour. Other features include:

• Conforms to NMRA Standards.

• ABS (Automatic Block Signal) and CTC (Centralized Traffic Control) modes supported.

• Auto-detects Common Anode or Common Cathode LEDs.

• Wide Addressable Range: 0001 to 9983.

• Service-Mode and Ops-Mode Programming supported.

• Compatible with RR&Co, WinLok and other control software.

• Works great with #621 64802 Integrated Block Detector (sold separately.)

• Requires use of Railnet Translator (#621-646249 sold separately), one per layout.

Got a Mouse? Click Walthers Web Site at

www.walthers.com

INTEGRATED BLOCK DETECTOR

621-64802 **19.95**
Simplifies installation and operation of block detection on your Digitrax™ equipped DCC layout. Detector actually monitors a block for occupancy and generates a LocoNet message in response. When locos, lighted cars, or wheels equipped with resistors are detected, the "Block Occupied" LED turns on, and a LocoNet "Occupied" message is sent out. When the block clears, the LED turns off, and a "Clear" message is sent. Unit mounts under your benchwork and is easily added to new or existing layouts without complex wiring or soldering. Other features include:

• LocoNet Certified.
• Block Occupancy LED.
• Address Pushbutton.
• Wide Addressable Range: 0001 to 4096.
• Supports both Service-Mode and Ops-Mode Programming.
• Compatible with MS100, LocoBuffer, as well as RR&Co, WinLok and other train control software.
• Works great with #621-64627 Dual Signal Decoder sold separately.

TRANSLATOR

NEW **621-64629** Railnet Translator **16.95**

The Translator listens for LocoNet feedback messages from block detectors and switch machine decoders, and translates them for signal decoder operation. One required per layout. For use with Dual Signal Decoder (#612-64627 sold separately).

COMMAND CONTROL

BOOSTER

246-PPX PowerPax DCC Programming Booster **59.95**
Overcome programming problems with BLI, Soundtraxx and multiple decoder/loco combinations. Microprocessor controlled unit safely boosts and controls programming power to about 200 mA. When hooked up for programming, unit initially powers programming track to charge-up decoder components like capacitors that would otherwise reduce programming energy and cause a programming failure. Built-in circuit protection, with LED indicator, shuts down instantly in the event of an overload or short to protect the decoder and system programming circuits. Compatible with Broadway Limited locos, Digitrax, Lenz, MRC, NCE, TCS and Soundtraxx decoders in both single and dual decoder configurations and also works with programming software, RR&Co (Train Programmer) and JMRI (Decoder Pro), all sold separately.

ONGUARD ACCESSORIES

Protect your system and accessories with these easy-to-use components. Each is rated at four amps and works without relays or a power supply. Simple screw terminals make them easy to add to existing wiring. Both are compatible with most DCC systems, however the Digitrax Zephyr and Atlas Commander do not have enough power to operate these units. Units are not for use with direct current (DC) applications.

246-OGAR Auto Reverser-Breaker **39.95**

POWER SUPPLY

246-MF615 Magna Force **44.95**
This advanced and affordable power supply was developed especially for DCC and can be used with Digitrax, Lenz, NCE and other systems. Features include grounded 16-gauge fail-safe, three wire input and output, illuminated rocker power switch, circuit breaker protection on output, and a sealed, impact-resistant enclosure. Input: 120V AC 60HZ; Output 15V AC 6 AMP.

STATIONARY DECODERS

The "Hare"

Designed to drive the Tortoise Switch Machine (sold separately), this accessory decoder plugs directly on to the Tortoise – simply connect to track power using the two handy screw terminals and the unit is ready to use. The Hare is compatible with all DCC systems that support accessory operations. And, many advanced features are provided to enhance operation including:

- Auto Throw™ automatically throws points when train approaches against the points. Eliminates derailments, layout shorts, loco and scenery damage, and is ideal for difficult to reach turnouts and hidden staging. Works with both insul-frog and electro frog turnouts for Versions I and II.
- Smart Route™ sets up to 13 routes by simple address programming in addition to the primary decoder address. Each Smart Route can control an unlimited number of turnouts. Eliminates complicated programming, the need for computer operation or system macros.
- Smart Default Ops™ allows all Hare-controlled turnouts to move to a predetermined position when layout is powered up or to remain as last thrown. Eliminates possibly fouling the mainline when you power-up your layout.
- Operates LED turnout signals or remote panel LED indicators.
- Manual push button option for control panel operations.
- System reset by simple CV programming. Resets to factory defaults.
- Digitrax LocoNet, NCE Cab Bus and Lenz Express Net feedback and position reporting options are supported by Version II (246-DSPHARE2).
- Automates reverse loop turnouts using Smart Throw.

246-DSPHARE1 No Feedback **29.95**

246-DSPHARE2 With Feedback **34.95**

PowerPax DCC Programming Booster 246-PPX

Circuit Breaker 246-OGCB

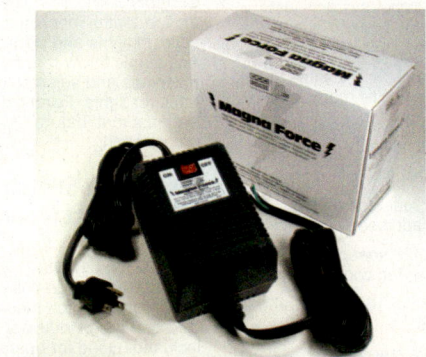

Magna Force 246-MF615

Hare

No Feedback 246-DSPHARE1

No Enclosure 246-RAMPMETER1

RAMPMETER DIGITAL METER

Get accurate measurements of DCC, DC and AC volts and amps on your layout with these meters. Units are rated at 10 Amps and measure true RMS Volts/Amps, ± 2%. Compatible with all scales, adjustable contacts permit direct track voltage measurements; no batteries are needed for use with DCC systems. Use as a portable troubleshooting tool, or mount on control panel or fascia; rear screw terminals allow for easy connection to layout wiring.

246-RAMPMETER1 No Enclosure **59.95**

246-RAMPMETER2 Enclosed w/Clip Leads **89.95**

246-RAMPMETER3 Enclosed w/Clip Leads & Battery Backup **99.95**

NEW RAIL MODELS

THROTTLE POCKETS

Protect your electronics investment with the Universal Throttle Pocket which holds DCC Throttles from Atlas, CVP, Digitrax, Lenz and NCE. Includes matching black mounting scres. These pockets are molded from durable ABS plastic. Simply screw them to the fascia of any layout and they're ready for use.

NEW PRODUCTS

Universal Throttle Pocket

Universal throttle pocket holds Atlas, CVP, Digitrax, Lenz and NCE throttles.

NEW 501-40016 Single **11.95**
NEW 501-400163 3-Pack **29.95**
NEW 501-4001610 10-Pack **79.95**

PRECISION CRAFT

NEW PRODUCT

NEW 588-1001 DC Master Analog Control Module **39.99** Four-button, multi-function control/programming module for DC analog sound operation.

COMMAND CONTROL

DIGITAL COMMAND CONTROL (DCC)

Prodigy Advance DCC System
500-1406   329.98
A DCC system that's easy to use and has all the advance features you desire. No thick manuals, no need for programming experience to get started. The design is so brilliant we were able to put basic operating instructions right on the back of the handheld. Prodigy Advance features a handheld with an easy-to-read LCD, console, power supply and basic operating instructions on the back of the handheld.

- Two or four digit addressing (0-9999 addresses available)
- 14, 28/128 speed steps for precise speed control
- Run up to 99 throttles using plug'n play technology
- Program on the main or the program track without affecting active locos
- Capable of 20 accessory functions
- Easily upgradeable to any future NRMA protocols
- Advance consisting
- Fast clock with adjustable ratios for running on an accurate timetable
- Program all CVs with ease

Prodigy Express System
500-1408   184.98
So easy to use model railroaders can operate it without the need of instructions. Just enter in the loco number (address) you wish to operate and move the throttle. It's intuitive. Programming is easy as well. Select the address you wish to assign and push the Enter button! Prodigy Express is loaded with advanced features most beginner systems just don't have. An excellent way to get started in DCC!

- Easy hook up – 2 wires to the track and you're ready to go
- Large LCD screen is easy to read and navigate
- Emergency stop button
- Two or four digit addressing (0-9999 addresses available)
- 14, 28/128 speed steps for precise speed control
- Capable of 16 accessory functions
- Advance consisting
- Program all CVs with ease

Prodigy Accessories
Prodigy Advance DCC LCD Walkaround

500-1407   98.98
Allows the Prodigy Advance user to add up to 99 more additional walkaround handhelds to the Prodigy Advance DCC system network.

500-1501 Extension Plate **33.98**
Fascia-mounted plate for two cabs, 12' cord included. For Prodigy Advance only.

500-AD492 Prodigy Extension Plate for 2 Handhelds **32.98**
Allows modelers access to the entire track. Simply install the pre-assembled plate around the layout and plug in the handheld into the extension plate. Can control two handhelds. Equipped with 12' extension cables. For Prodigy only.

500-AD493 Y-Harness for Extension Plates **8.98**
Allows for use of multiple extension plates (#500-AD492, sold separately) around your layout. For Prodigy only.

Accessory Decoder
500-1628   56.98
This decoder is like having four accessory decoders in one. Controls twin-coil or slow-motion switch machines, building lights and signals. Adjustable throw rate for switch machines and adjustable flash rates for lights. For most DCC systems that feature CV programming.

Dispatcher Switch Machine/Accessory Decoder
500-AD360   17.98
Operates both twin-coil and slow-motion switch machine. Red and green indicator LEDs included. Good for operating accessory lighting. Uses mobile decoder addresses. Good for all types of DCC systems.

Power Station 8

500-AD501   179.98
You can boost your DCC system up to eight powerful amperes with an easy hookup to run more trains or engines with bigger motors. Includes Built-in power supply and has adjustable output voltage capability. Compatible with other brand DCC systems.

DCC Auto Reverse

500-AD520   39.98
Automatically controls reverse loop circuits. Simple hook-up with two input and two output wires, 2 amp rating. Works with all DCC layouts.

Prodigy Advance DCC System 500-1406

Prodigy Express System 500-1408

Decoders

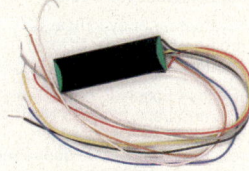

500-AD332   34.98
Good for small, low current draw locomotives. Two or four digit addressing, six functions with MRC Light Effects, advanced consisting, (CV19), programming on the main and 14, 28/128 speed steps.

Build a complete operating system for your layout with this line of Digital Command Control (DCC) starter sets and accessories.

NEW 500-1636 N Gauge Diesel Sound Decoder **84.98**
Replaces stock decoder in most Atlas diesel locos. Milling of frame needed to install speaker. Multiple bells and horns, two or four digit addressing. Speaker included.

NEW 500-1637 N Gauge Steam Sound Decoder **84.98**
Fits in most steam locomotive tenders. Multiple bells and whistles, two or four digit addressing. Speaker included.

COMMAND CONTROL

NCE — The Power of DCC

NEW PRODUCTS

Power Cab Accessories
For #524-25 (sold separately)
NEW 524-26 SB3 Smart Booster **99.95**
Adds a 3 Amp booster to your Power Cab and support for additional cab. Wireless compatible.

NEW 524-221 Power Supply **29.95**

NEW 524-222 Power Panel **19.95**

NEW 524-223 USB Interface **TBA**

Signal Decoder
NEW 524-135 For 4 Signal Heads **59.95**

Switch Machine Decoder
NEW 524-136 **59.95**
Controls 8 Tortoise™ Switch Machines (sold separately).

Silent Running™ Plug & Play Decoders **29.95 ea**

NEW 524-137 NAVO for Atlas VO-1000 (sold separately)

NEW 524-138 NMP15 for Atlas MP15DC (sold separately)

Power Supplies
NEW 524-28 DB3 3 Amp Generic DCC Booster **79.95**

NEW 524-224 P1018 10 Amp 18V Transformer **89.95**
For 10 Amp DCC systems.

Circuit Breaker
NEW 524-225 Single Output Electronic Circuit Breaker **29.95**
EB1, 3-10 Amps per output w/status LEDs & block detection.

Wire
NEW 524-220 6-Wire Straight Cab Bus Cable **22.95**
RJ12-40 40' RJ12 cable for RPT1 wiring.

POWER PRO STARTER SETS

User-friendly sets include everything to get two DCC controlled trains running (except power transformer). Choose standard plug-in or wireless radio cab. ProCab™ throttles walk you through operation with clearly labeled buttons and menu prompts in plain English on backlit LCD displays. Sets include ProCab throttle, Command Station with integral 5 Amp power unit and two locomotive decoders, plus system reference manual with quick start guide.

5 Amp System

524-1 PH-PRO Standard **499.95**

524-2 PH-PRO-R Wireless w/916 MHz Radio & RB01 Base Station **699.99**

Power Boosters
524-3 PB105 5 Amp **159.95**
Delivers five full amps of voltage stabilized power; output is adjustable from 10 to 18 volts. Requires 14-16V transformer of 5 Amps or more.

Power Pro Command Stations
524-8 CS02 Command Station Only (No Cab, Booster or Decoders) **219.95**

For Daily Product Updates Point Your Browser to
www.walthers.com

Wireless System Accessories
524-23 RB02 Wireless Base Station **159.95**
Improved transmitter for NCE wireless radio-controlled systems; includes expansion ports for two RPT1 signal repeaters (sold separately.)
524-24 RPT1 Repeater (Use with 524-23, sold separately) **129.95**

Power Supplies
524-215 P515 15V AC 5 Amp **34.95**
Five Amp power transformer for use with Power Pro Command Station/starter sets, (sold separately)

Power Cab
524-25 **179.95**
A complete DCC starter system in the palm of your hand! Includes all the features of the NCE Powerhouse PH-PRO, but at a lower price. Operates up to 6 trains plus extra cabs. Wireless compatible. Includes 120/230V power supply.

THROTTLES

Deluxe Master ProCab
Deluxe cabs provide user-friendly access to advanced system features. Backlit LCD displays guide you through operations easily. Both a thumb wheel knob and repeating push buttons for speed control are provided. Control of single or multiple turnouts, animated accessories and lights is a snap. Recall button allows control of one to six trains per cab. The ProCab supports all DCC-compatible sound units. All wireless (radio-control) systems operate at 916 MHz.

524-10 ProCab Standard **159.95**

524-11 ProCab-R Wireless **249.95**

Engineer Cabs
These handheld cabs are ideal for operating sessions. Each provides easy selection of locos/consists, single-button operation of decoder functions, momentary HORN button, selection and control of individual turnouts or entire routes (via the MACRO key) and the unique OPTION button which can be programmed to act as any button you wish.

Potentiometer Speed Control
Large control knob (300° rotation) provides smooth speed control. Can also be set to "Yard" mode so the speed knob acts as a "center off" speed control. Ideal for one-handed switching in the yard.

524-12 CAB04p Standard Model **89.95**

524-13 CAB04pr Wireless **179.95**

Digital Encoder Speed Control
All the features of the CAB04 series plus the ability to control two trains. A large knob provides speed control through a digital encoder with adjustable "ballistic tracking;" the faster you turn the knob, the faster speed will increase, or decrease.

524-14 CAB04e Standard w/2-Train Control **119.95**

524-15 CAB04er Wireless w/2-Train Control **199.95**

Speed Buttons Control
Push buttons feature adjustable automatic repeat rate from once every 4 seconds to as fast as 4 times per second. Just hold the button down and the speed changes smoothly from one speed step to the next as long as you hold the button.

Items listed below are available by Special Order (see Legend Page).
524-16 CAB05 Standard **89.95**

524-17 CAB05r Wireless **179.95**

7' Coiled Cords for Cabs
524-209 CoilcordRJ w/RJ12 (Telephone Type) Plug **8.95**

524-210 CoilcrdDIN w/Molded Right Angle DIN Plug **9.95**

SILENT RUNNING™ DECODERS

29.95 (Unless Noted)
Sized to fit N Scale models, these smaller decoders can be adapted to some small HO Scale locos too.

524-117 NIMFT-A - For Intermountain FT-A

524-118 NIMFT-B - For Intermountain FT-B

524-119 N12SR 1 Amp, 2-Function

524-120 N12A0 - For Atlas Fits GP40-2, U25B, B23-7, 30-7, 36-7, GP38, SD25 and Train Master.

524-122 N12A1 - For Atlas EMD SD50, SD60, SD60M & More

524-123 N12SRP 1 Amp, 2 Function w/NMRA 8 Pin Plug **34.95**

524-127 N12A0e - For Intermountain Tunnel Motors; White LEDs

524-128 N14IP Plug In For Con-Cor PA-1, 4-8-4; 1 Amp, 4 Function

524-129 Z14SR 1 Amp, 4 Function .57 x .34 x .125" w/Harness **34.95**

524-130 Z14SRP 1 Amp, 4 Function w/8 Pin NMRA Plug **39.95**

524-131 N14SR Narrow; 1 Amp, 4 Function, 4" Wire Harness

524-132 N14SRP Thin, 1 Amp. 4 Function w/8 Pin NMRA Plug **34.95**

SWITCH MACHINE DECODERS

524-114 SWITCH-IT Stall Motor Type Machines **24.95**
Controls two Tortoise™, SwitchMaster™ or similar stall motor switch machines. Unit also remembers position of switches during a power failure. Supports accessory addresses from one to 2044. Each output of the decoder can have a completely different accessory address for easier operation.

524-115 SNAP-IT For Twin Coil Type **19.95**

524-116 Switch/Kat For Kato Unitrack Remote Switch **24.95**

COMMAND CONTROL

CAB BUS FASCIA PANELS
19.95 ea
524-207 UTP Panel w/RJ12 (Telephone Type) Connectors
524-208 DIN Panel w/DIN Connectors

SIGNAL DECODERS
Built-in occupancy detector, drives two signal heads (searchlight or two and three color types, includes built-in yellow balance adjustment for LED signals). Use in one of three modes: DCC, Stand Alone or Stand Alone with DCC Override. Decoders provide logic to operate Automatic Block Signals (run as two, three or four block with overlap or permissive), CTC with manual or automatic interlocking and approach lighting, or Manual Block Control signaling. Easy to install with no soldering.

524-203 SIG-12 w/Occupancy Detector **29.95**

BLOCK DETECTOR MODULE
524-205 BD20 - .01 to 20 Amps **14.95**
Detects presence of train in block by the current it draws in a range from 0.01 to 20 Amps. No electrical connection to track, simply route track feeder wire through holes in "tombstone" current transformer. Unit does not reduce track voltage or get hot. Easily connects to Auxiliary Input Unit (#524-200, sold separately) or most commercial signal systems.

524-200 AIU01 Auxiliary Input Unit (For Block Detection) **49.95**

524-201 MACROPANEL For Turnout, or CTC Signal Control **59.95**
Issues Macro and CTC panel commands to signal, accessory (turnout) and auxiliary (lighting) decoders. 29 pushbutton inputs.

524-202 INDICATOR Track Occupancy Status Indicator **39.95**

CIRCUIT BREAKER
524-217 EB3 Triple-Output Circuit Breaker **54.95**

6 WIRE STRAIGHT CAB BUS CABLE
524-213 RJ/12-7 - 7" **5.95**
524-214 RJ/12-12 - 12' **6.95**

LEDS
524-218 LED PACK 3mm Golden Glow LEDs pkg(10) **16.95**

DECODER TEST KIT
524-219 DTK **24.95**
A perfect companion for any DCC operation and layout. Self-contained unit allows you to program and test any decoder before it's installed in your loco. Can be used to test track power as well as accessory decoders and functions OF, OR, F1 and F2. Built-in indicator lights show Motor Forward or Reverse; add an optional motor (sold separately) for under-load testing.

NEW PRODUCTS
LokSound V3.5 Decoders
139.00 ea
These decoders combine DCC operation with a programmable sound module and speaker.

A large 8 MBit memory allows for a wide range of sound with four channels for realistic mixing and playback, with up to three sounds running simultaneously with exhaust. Load-dependent sound (easily switched off if desired) lets you hear your engine working, and the sound can be synchronized with speed steps or external sensors (sold separately). Sound can be operated on DC or DCC layouts running most popular systems.

Suitable for most engines, each decoder has a pulse frequency of 32 KHz for super-quiet operation. Load compensation provides smooth operation uphill or down, while Dynamic Drive Control (back EMF) improves low speed performance. Helper mode mutes bell and whistle, and Switcher mode sets half-speed for yard operations. Includes four auxiliary inputs for special effects. Light brightness can be adjusted independently, or to add firebox flicker, Mars or Gyra-Lights, ditch lights, strobes and more. Function mapping can be allocated to any of 20 buttons, and functions can be combined for one-touch operation. Units feature integrated function keys F13-F20 to meet current NMRA DCC standards. Built-in short circuit protection guards motors and decoders from potential problems.

Steam Sound Decoders
American
NEW **397-82854** Big Boy 4-8-8-4

European
NEW **397-52801** 2 Cylinder Narrow Gauge - BR99
NEW **397-52802** 3 Cylinder - BR 44, Belgian 25.021
NEW **397-52803** 2/4 Cylinder - BR 01

Diesel Sound Decoders
ALCO 244 16 Cylinder w/Turbocharger
NEW **307-72811** With Leslie S3 Airhorn

EMD 567 12-Cylinder
NEW **397-72837** Single-Chime

NEW **397-72838** Single-Chime w/Dynamic Brakes

EMD 16-645E 16-Cylinder w/Dynamic Brakes
NEW **397-72882** Non-Turbocharged, Nathan 3-Chime

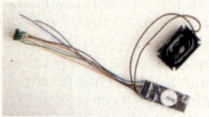

NEW **397-72885** Non-Turbocharged, Leslie 5-Chime
NEW **397-72886** Turbocharged, Nathan 3-Chime

EMD 12-710GB Turbocharged

NEW **397-82800** 12-Cylinder, Nathan 3-Chime, Dynamic Brakes

EMD 16-710GB 16-Cylinder w/Dynamic Brakes

NEW **397-82808** Turbocharged, Nathan 3-Chime

GE 7FDL16 16-Cylinder - Turbocharged
NEW **397-72866** Nathan 3-Chime Air Horn, Dynamic Brakes

European
NEW **397-52433** BR 218

European Electrics
NEW **397-52861** E40

LokPilot V2.0 DCC Standard Decoders

NEW **397-52680** NMRA 6-Pin Plug & Cable **29.99**
For modelers using DCC without sound, this versatile decoder is ideal for most motive power. Unit automatically detects if used on DC or DCC. On DCC, decoder will determine the number of speed steps and you can select any address up to 9999. A programmable speed curve allows precise adjustment. Function mapping can be assigned to any of 12 buttons in any combination, The unit also supports Mars lights, ditch lights, Gyra-Lights, strobes and more, and lamp brightness is adjustable. Dynamic. Drive Control (back EMF) improves low speed performance. Overload protection is provided for motor output and the four function outputs. 40KHz high frequency motor control provides smooth and quiet operation; output handles a maximum current of 1.1 Amps, functions are designed to handle .180mA each.

LokSound Programmer

NEW **397-53452** **159.00**
Add or change sounds and fine-tune performance using this unit with any PC with an audio card and a Windows® operating system. Just connect the programmer to the serial port or the USB adapter (included). Start the software then place a loco with a LokSound decoder on your programming track. The software automatically detects which type of decoder is installed and provides specific information; easy to follow on-screen graphics let you change loco address, speed steps, acceleration and deceleration, load control, speed curve and analog functions, assign function buttons for lighting effects and brightness, and all special settings. Plus, you can change or completely replace the current sounds with additional selections included on the software. You can also use your own recordings or choose from a wide range of downloads available on the LokSound Web-site. Unit is complete with power supply, serial cable, USB adapter, manual and CD.

ECoS Central Unit Digital Command Station

NEW **397-50001** **699.00**

Models by Ron Freeman, Photo by Mike Reardon, Addison, Illinois

Steel mills are busy railroad-served industries. Tall blast furnaces consume many carloads of coke, taconite ore and limestone. Lengthy rolling mills take steel and roll it into sheet, slabs or wire. Even where the mill is served by ship, raw materials arrive by rail, and much of the mill's output moves out in coil cars, slab flats and gondolas. The in-plant railroad rolls 24 hours per day, shuttling molten steel, finished products and slag around the plant. At Republic Steel, an SW1200 shoves a slag car toward the dump as the "George W. Hanna" positions for unloading.

With their huge structures and network of track, steel mills are fascinating modeling subjects. This scene on the Midwest N Pioneer club in Chicago features several Cornerstone Series® kits modified with details made from plastic, resin and metal. As modelers, we're lucky that it's possible to mix modeling materials thanks to the many types of cements like those listed in the Adhesives, Cleaners & Lubricants Section.

ADHESIVES

ADHESIVES - CLEANERS - LUBRICANTS

WALTHERS

Goo® 904-299

ADHESIVES

GOO®
904-299 1oz **2.98**

- **ALL PURPOSE ADHESIVE**
GOO is the permanent rubber base adhesive that grips most anything. It never lets go.

- **FAST-SETTING JOINTS**
Easy contact action opens new possibilities for fast-setting joints with any material.

Walthers GOO is the perfect adhesive for building or repairing jobs on your layout and around the house!

The easy contact action of GOO produces fast-setting joints with any material. GOO works with all types of metals (including steel, brass, aluminum, copper and others) plus items like wood, plastic, cardboard, china, leather, vinyl, ceramics, paper, concrete and many more, on any smooth or porous surface.

GOO is a permanent rubber-base adhesive that's shockproof, waterproof and crackproof—it's as flexible as rubber. Joints won't crack when flexed back and forth, won't break loose when the temperature changes and won't weaken when wet or damp. It sticks forever!

Dealers: MUST order in multiples of 6.

Mikro Tip

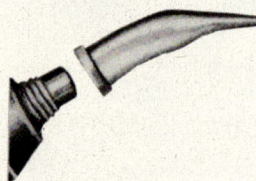

904-302 pkg(10) **2.98**

For Precision Gluing Fits Most Any Glue Tube
- Easily added to GOO Adhesive Tube
- Helps eliminate waste and mess
- Allows more precise application of glue
- Mounts on 3/16" diameter glue nozzle

CLEANERS

Bright Boy Abrasive Track Cleaner

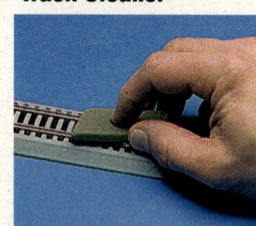

949-521 **5.98**
Improve the conductivity of your tracks by keeping them clean with easy-to-use Bright Boy!

LIFE-LIKE®
Div. of Wm. K. Walthers, Inc.

Maintenance Kit

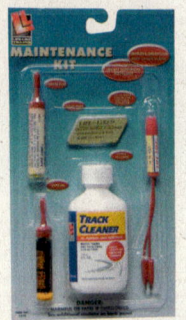

433-1418 **19.98**
Includes Grease Gun, Oil Gun, Track Cleaner, Track Brite and Trouble Shooter Circuit Tester.

Track Cleaner

433-1415 8oz **9.50**

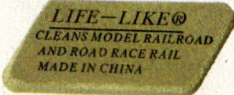

433-1416 Track Brite **5.00**

ATLAS

Gear Lubricant
150-190 **8.25**

Heavy-Duty Motor Bearing Lubricant
150-191 **10.95**

Conducta Lube Cleaner
150-192 **10.95**

Loco & Track Maintenance 3-Pack

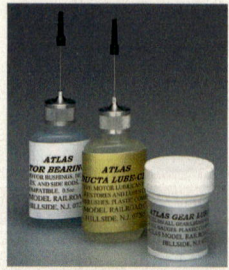

150-193 **27.50**
Contains one each of items #190, 191 and 192.

AMBROID

ADHESIVES

Clear Vinyl Cement

130-1611 5/8oz Tube **2.00**
Crystal-clear cement for joining or mending rigid or flexible vinyl. Made for joining vinyl figure models. Waterproof.

EZ Mask

130-154 1oz Bottle **2.15**
Eliminate the use of messy tape with this brush-on, peel-off, water soluble masking liquid.

Fas'N-All Adhesive/Sealant

130-157 1oz **2.45**
Rubber-based general purpose adhesive and sealant. Cured material remains flexible, waterproof and shock absorbent.

Liquid Cement
Waterproof cement mainly for use on wood but binds well to leather, canvas, metal, most fabrics and glass.

Dealers: MUST order Dealer Pack of 12.

130-101 Regular Cement 1.8oz Tube **2.45**
130-102 Regular Cement 3.2oz Tube **4.29**
130-1511 Regular Cement 1oz Tube **2.15**

Plastic Welder

130-110 Pro Weld 2oz **3.10**
A clear, super fast plastic fusing adhesive. Bonds styrene, butyrate, ABS and acrylic.

Dealers: MUST order Dealer Pack of 12.

Resin Glue

130-126 Se•Cur•It 4oz **2.45**
Great for porous materials. Sandable resin glue will not stain and is nonflammable.

Safe Bond

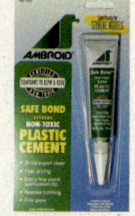

130-1701 5/8oz Tube **2.00**
This fast-drying, nontoxic adhesive for styrene plastics is designed for filling gaps in plastic joints. Tube has an extra-fine-point application tip.

Safe Weld

130-160 1oz Bottle **3.10**
Used for fusing styrene plastic, this nontoxic solution includes an applicator brush.

Styrene Plastic Cement

130-1521 5/8oz Tube **1.95**
Improved, fast-drying, more aggressive formula with super gap-filling qualities. Dries clear. Resistant to running.

Tac-N-Place Adhesive

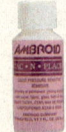

130-158 1oz **2.15**
Nontoxic, brush-on, pressure sensitive adhesive. For temporary or permanent joining of plastic, wood, paper, fabric, glass, foam and metal. Remains tacky. Items may be removed and repositioned again and again.

ADHESIVES - CLEANERS - LUBRICANTS

A-West

"On target for You!"

STAINLESS NEEDLEPOINT APPLICATOR BOTTLES

Precision application of solvent, flux, paint, oil, glue, ink, cement, contact cleaner, fuel, ACC accelerators, ceramic decor, etc., etc. Length 1" or 4" snaps into bottle neck. Includes 1oz bottle, cap and cleaning wire.
o = outer diameter
i = inner diameter
f = relative flow rate

1" Needle 2.99 ea (Unless Noted)
158-16 Blue .016o .008i 1f
158-20 Yellow .020o .010i 2f
158-25 Red .025o .013i 3f
158-35 White .035o .023i 8f
158-50 Black .050o .033i 17f
158-65 Clear .065o .047i 35f
158-73 Set #1 **6.59**
Includes tips for kit #s 16, 25, 50 and 1 bottle.
158-76 Set #2 **12.19**
Includes tips for kit #s 16, 20, 25, 35, 50, 65 and 1 bottle.

4" Needle 3.99 ea
158-164 Blue .016o .008i 1f
158-204 Yellow .020o .010i 2f
158-254 Red .025o .013i 3f
158-354 White .035o .023i 8f
158-504 Black .050o .033i 17f
158-654 Clear .065o .047i 35f

G-GUN
Makes applying grease, glue, putty, or latex/plaster molding material to delicate or hard-to-reach places easy.

158-900 1/2oz **1.98**
158-901 Jr. G-Gun pkg(2) **1.98**

A.J. FRICKO COMPANY

Track & Wheel Cleaner

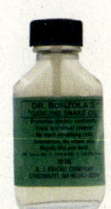

274-10 Dr. Bonzola's Genuine Snake Oil 30ml **34.95**
The end of scrubbing rails! Keep electricity running to your cars with this greaseless track and wheel cleaner.

Track & Motor Cleaner

274-8 Cleano 30ml **34.95**
Universal track and motor cleaner for layouts and locomotives. Just one drop per rail per 4 x 8' area remains effective for one year. Cleano will protect against rust even in the dampest basements.

Get the Scoop!
Get the Skinny!
Get the Score!
Check Out Walthers
Web site at
www.walthers.com

BACHMANN

Keep your track, rolling stock and motive power running in top condition with this line of high-grade lubricants.

Lubrication
160-99981 Conductive Contact Lube **13.00**
Designed for use with electric motor maintenance and track cleaning.

Grease
160-99982 **13.00**
Heavy-duty grease is best used for applications requiring heavier viscosity materials.

Oil 13.00 ea

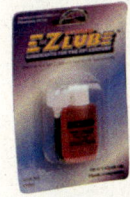 
160-99983   160-99984

160-99983 Heavy Gear
Designed for longer periods of time, for use on bearings, draft gear boxes, motor bushings, side rods and valve gear.
160-99984 Light Gear
Perfect for any shafts, gears, bolsters and bushings.

DR. MIKE'S MODEL-N' CRAFTER'S GLUE

GLUE
Handle all types of hobby and household gluing chores with this line of Cyanoacrylate (CA) adhesives and accessories.

352-200 Dr. Mike's Model-n' Crafter's Glue® 1/2 oz **12.95**
Make easy work of any project with this CA adhesive designed especially for models and crafts. It produces fast, strong bonds between all types of woods, plastics (including styrene, Delrin and ABS), metals, ceramics, rubber, glass and much more. It can also be used to glue dissimilar materials together such as Delrin to wood. And, the special formula doesn't evaporate in the container or clog the delivery tube — average shelf life after opening is 8 months or more at 70° or lower.

CREST

Lubricants
Lubricants inhibit rust as well as prevent friction, heat and wear.

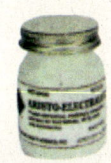

227-29602 Lubricant-Conductive **6.00**
Add extra conductivity and smooth operation to locomotives by adding to axle bearings and bushings.

227-29603 Crest Lube Oil 1.125oz **4.00**
227-29604 Crest Grease For Gears 1oz **4.00**

Smoke Fluid & Track Cleaner

227-29601 **3.50**
For improved conductivity and engine performance, keep your track and wheels clean with Crest Track Cleaner. It also doubles as smoke fluid for the cleanest smoke around without the build-up.

FALLER
IMPORTED FROM GERMANY BY WALTHERS

Plastic Cements

272-170490 Super EXPERT Cement **6.04**
With special hollow needle and protective cap. Quicker, stronger bond. Dealers MUST order multiples of 24.

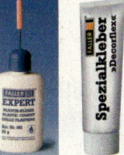  
170492   170493   170495

272-170492 EXPERT Liquid **6.04**
With needle applicator. 25ml. Dealers MUST order multiples of 24.
272-170493 Decroflex **8.99**
An ideal adhesive for use with solvent-sensitive materials. 60g.
272-170495 Model Maker's Cement-17g Tube **4.99**
Made especially for styrene models, this quick-drying cement is gap-filling and can also be used with wood, cardstock or paper.

Lubricants

272-170488   272-170489

272-170488 Synthetic Gear Lube 25ml **9.99**
Specially formulated for use on plastics, this long-lasting lubricant is acid-free to protect parts.
272-170489 Special Oiler 25g **9.99**
All-around oiler for small motors and gears. Resin and acid free.

Limited Quantity Available
272-170487 Teflon Lubricant 50ml **17.99**
Acid-free, non-gumming, cleans and protects from corrosion. Comes in a spray bottle with mechanical pump.

ADHESIVES - CLEANERS - LUBRICANTS

For almost 50 years Labelle Lubricants have been the preferred choice by model railroaders and model train repairman.

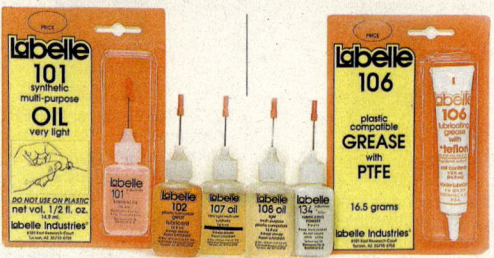

Lubricants 5.89 ea

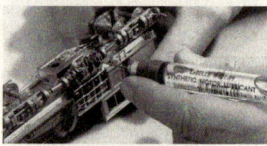

430-101 Synthetic Multi-Purpose Oil 1/2oz
Very light oil for motors, bearings, etc. Natural penetrating action will usually free a "frozen" motor, will damage paints and some plastics.

430-102 Plastic Compatible Gear Lubricant 1/2oz
A true gear oil. Should NOT be used on bushings, bearings, etc. Can be used on plastic.

430-104 Synthetic Multi-Purpose Oil 1/2oz
Medium weight, non-gumming, long lasting. For small power tools, major appliances, etc. Will damage paints and some plastics.

430-106 Plastic Compatible Grease w/PTFE (a close relative to Teflon™) 1/2oz
Compatible with other lubricants and can be applied over them if necessary. Non-staining, non-toxic.

430-107 Plastic Compatible Motor Oil 1/2oz
Medium-weight lubricant for large-scale models with high-torque motors.

430-108 Plastic Compatible Motor Oil 1/2oz
Lightweight lubricant for small locomotives with low- and medium-torque motors, precision instruments, sewing machines, etc. Will not harm plastics, painted surfaces. Non-staining.

430-111 Racing Oil 1/2oz
For road race cars.

430-134 Micro-Fine Powdered w/PTFE (a close relative to Teflon™)
A clean, white, dry, non-staining powdered lubricant. Will not harm plastics or paints. Use dry or add to oils or greases to make them "slipperier."

Lube Kits 17.49 ea
Sets include extension needle adapter for those hard to reach places.

430-1001 Kit #1
Includes one each of #s 101, 107 and 134.

430-1002 Kit #2
Includes one each of #s 102, 106 and 108.

MICRO ENGINEERING CO.

Pliobond® Adhesive
For gluing Delrin® track or hand-laid rail to ties.

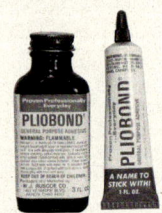

255-49101 With Brush Top 3oz **8.05**
255-49102 With Fine Tip Tube 1oz **5.35**

MASCOT® PRECISION TOOLS

Instant Adhesive

230-752 3 Gram Tube .10 fl oz Gel **3.15**
High-performance, extended-range adhesive that bonds metal, plastic, rubber, ceramics and glass in seconds. Bonds colorless, eliminating the "white frosting" effect of other adhesives. No-drip formula fills gaps and is ideal for use on vertical surfaces.

MODEL POWER

Track Cleaner
490-14 4oz **6.59**

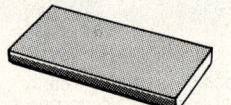

490-250 Cleaning Block **3.25**
Blue ceramic stone.

NGINEERING

Low-Temp Silver-Bearing Solder

514-N4200 **1.95**
A unique blend of 62% tin, 36% lead and 2% silver alloy with a rosin flux core. The .020" diameter is well-suited for reaching tight spaces. Low melting point of 354-372°F 179-189°C makes it ideal for temperature-sensitive components. Includes dispenser tube.

NOCH
IMPORTED FROM GERMANY BY WALTHERS

528-60157 Snap on Track Cleaners pkg(5) **8.99**
528-60158 Track Cleaning Pads **8.99**

PECO
IMPORTED FROM GREAT BRITAIN BY WALTHERS

Lubricant

552-640 Electro Lube Cleaner & Oil **15.99**
Use to lube motors, gears, commutators and bearings. Pen-type applicator for reaching small parts. Safe for most plastics.

RIBBONRAIL

Track Cleaning Block
Manual cleaning block for rail and wheels consists of an abrasive stone block (1 x 3 x 1/4").

170-11 Less Handle **4.15**
170-12 With Handle **5.25**

Information STATION

Loco Care & Maintenance

It is important to remember that model railroad equipment are not toys and should not be exposed to rough handling, especially locomotives. Yes, it is true that they will stand up to considerable abuse, but as with all things, they will last longer and work better if they are treated well.

Cleanliness, or lack thereof, is probably the most common problem. This is easily addressed by keeping your track clean. Regularly wipe down your track with a cloth dampened with some type of cleaning fluid. Keep your engines away from dust and dirt as much as possible. Avoid using cloth, whether as a cleaning device or storage device, that sheds lint.

Proper lubrication is also a necessity to avoid performance dilemmas. Read your locomotive manuals carefully. Never use too much oil. Getting oil in the motor or on the driving wheels will cause difficulties. Do not be afraid of disassembling the locos when necessary; just do so gently and with care.

When treated properly, there is no reason that your locomotives, and all railroad equipment, should not last a lifetime.

ADHESIVES - CLEANERS - LUBRICANTS

ADHESIVES

Plasti-Zap CA++ Instant Plastic Glue

547-442 1/3oz **3.99**
Will not attack painted surfaces, tacking cures in 10-20 seconds, full cure in 1-3 minutes. Nonflammable, non-sniffable.

Slo-Zap CA
547-443 1oz **7.59**
High viscosity, slow-cure adhesive. 30-40 second positioning time, cures in 1-2 minutes. Permits use on poorly fitting surfaces and large bond areas. Also a surface-sealing agent for cloth and porous surfaces. Bonds oily surfaces.

Zap-A-Gap/CA + Filling Adhesive
Bonds woods, veneers, cork, vinyl, fabrics, rubber, leather, plastics, metals, stone, porcelain and oily surfaces.

547-425 4oz **23.99**
547-429 2oz **12.99**
547-431 1oz **7.39**
547-433 1/2oz **4.39**
547-435 1/4oz **3.49**

Zap/CA Super-Thin Instant Adhesive
Very thin, penetrating, instant-curing cyanoacrylate adhesive. Cures in 1-5 seconds. Bonds close-fitting surfaces.

547-426 4oz **23.99**
547-428 2oz **12.99**
547-430 1oz **7.39**
547-432 1/2oz **4.39**
547-434 1/4oz **3.49**

Zip-Kicker Glue Accelerator
Accelerator for super glues forces immediate cure for all cyanoacrylates. Also expands gap filling ability, permits structural fillet forming and solves tough-to-bond combinations of materials.

547-438 2oz **6.39**

CLEANERS

Z-7 Debonder Debonding Agent

547-439 1oz **4.29**
Waterbased material softens and removes cured cyanoacrylates, paint and hobby decals. Safe for most plastics.

Rail Zip

547-452 1oz **5.39**
Liquid track cleaner, corrosion inhibitor and conductivity restorer. Retards corrosion. Nontoxic; safe for all metals and plastics.

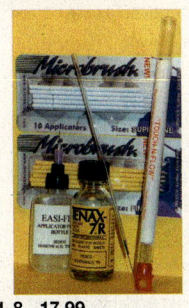

The Space Age Plastic Welder.

Space Age Construction Kit

731-8 **17.99**
This new kit includes one bottle of Tenax-7R, one "Touch-N-Flow" liquid applicator, one "Easi-Fill" applicator filling bottle, one 10 unit packet of fine and one 10 unit packet of superfine "Microbrushes" and instructions.

Plastic Welder

731-7 **3.99**
Tenax-7R causes plastic to become its own bonding agent. Works on styrene, butyrate, ABS and acrylic plastics. Apply Tenax-7R with a fine-hair bristled brush, a microbrush (#731-9, 10, 11 & 12), or a Touch-N-Flow applicator (#232-711). Nonflammable, non-sniffable, non-sticky and leaves no residue. Tenax-7R bonds in seconds and dries in minutes.
Dealers MUST Order Dealer Pack of 12.

Microbrush Cement Applicator Brushes pkg(10) **1.59 ea**
Designed for use with liquid cement, the Microbrushes allow for precise control of cement application. Available in several sizes, they are perfect for touchup, polishing, working in limited space and for pinpoint cementing.

731-9 Regular
731-10 Fine
731-11 Superfine
731-12 Ultra Brush

ADHESIVES
Fast drying, non-yellowing cements.

Plastic Cement
704-3501 Tube 5/8oz **1.69**
Dealers MUST order Dealer Pack of 48.

704-3502 Liquid–Bottle 1oz **2.99**
For clean, transparent plastic-to-plastic joints.
Dealers MUST order Dealer Pack of 12.

704-3507 Liquid Cement w/Precision Applicator **4.49**
Dealers MUST order Dealer Pack of 6.

704-3515 Clear Parts Cement 1oz **4.79**

704-3521 Non-Toxic Tube 5/8oz **1.69**
For use by children.
Dealers MUST order Dealer Pack of 48.

Wood Cement
704-3503 Extra-Fast Drying 5/8oz **1.99**
Hot fuel proof.
Dealers MUST order Dealer Pack of 24.

Plastic Putty
704-3511 5/8oz **2.19**
Can be used to fill, sculpture or redesign a surface.
Dealers MUST order Dealer Pack of 24.

Cement Pen
704-3532 1/3oz **4.25**
Fast-drying, high-strength cement for plastic.

Decal Setting Solution
704-8804 1/4oz Bottle **1.49**

Gluing Tips
704-8805 pkg(5) **1.99**
Fits most tubes of glue for precise glue application.
Dealers MUST order Dealer Pack of 12.

Model Master Adhesives

704-8872   **704-8874**

704-8872 Liquid **6.29**
704-8874 Instant Glue **5.59**

SCALE SCENICS

DIVISION OF CIRCUITRON

Solder
652-1502 pkg(10') **3.95**
Ultra-fine rosin core solder (.014" diameter), is electronics grade (60% tin, 40% lead). Ideal for soldering miniature circuits, detailing for brass models or to simulate scale size hose or piping.

For Up-To-Date Information and News Bookmark Walthers Web site at
www.walthers.com

ADHESIVES - CLEANERS - LUBRICANTS

Hob-E-Lube®
by Woodland Scenics®

OILS & GREASE

Complete line of oils, greases and dry lubricants for model railroad equipment of any scale. All seven are paint and plastic compatible.

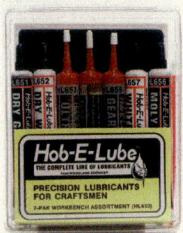

785-650 7-Pak Workbench Assortment **24.98**
Get all seven in one pack and save yourself more than seven dollars!

785-651 Dry Graphite **4.49**
With Molybdenum. Does not attract dust or dirt. Ideal for metal, wood, plastic and rubber.

785-652 Dry White Lube w/Teflon* **4.49**
White, non-staining lube doesn't conduct electricity. Use on electrical switches, N & Z worm and gears.

785-653 Ultra-Lite Oil **4.49**
Use with close tolerance precision parts.

785-654 Lite Oil **4.49**
General purpose hobby lube, rust preventative.

785-655 Gear Lube **4.49**
Tough, long-lasting lube with high adhesion to prevent dripping.

785-656 Moly Grease **4.49**
With Molybdenum, covers entire surface and maintains high viscosity. Ideal for parts exposed to water.

785-657 White Grease w/Teflon* **4.49**
Non-staining lube with corrosion protection and waterproof lubrication. Good for use outside.

* "Teflon" is a registered trademark of DuPont.

Premium Oils

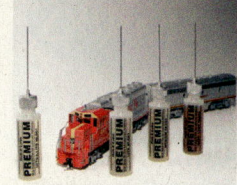

Premium Oils from Woodland Scenics are specially formulated for specific uses. All are paint and plastic compatible, and come in a needle applicator bottle for precise lubrication of small parts.

785-661 Ultra-Lite Oil **7.49**
Contains proven anti-wear additives. Use on HO or smaller scales of model trains, precision instruments or where a light oil is needed.

785-662 Lite Oil **7.49**
Multi-viscosity additives for trouble-free operation, even at extreme temperatures. Great for home and workshop applications.

785-663 Medium Oil **7.49**
Prevents metal contact and surface scuffing. Specially formulated for use on R/C cars, airplanes, boats and HO Scale and larger model trains.

785-664 Gear Lube **7.49**
A true gear lubricant, where tough, lasting gear oil is needed.

ADHESIVES

Mat Adhesive

NEW 785-5161 7 fl oz **6.98**
Use for permanently or temporarily attaching Grass Mats to any surface. Great for mounting puzzles or posters to mat board.

Scenic Accents Glue

Scenic Accents Glue
- For temporary or permanent placement of figures
- Stays tacky
- Removes easily
- Non-toxic

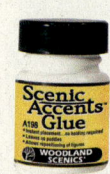

785-198 1 fl oz **4.29**
Created especially for use with Scenic Accents. Accent Glue is water-soluble, high-tack and easy to apply. Objects can easily be repositioned and removed. Simply brush on bottom of figure and allow glue to become tacky and clear (about 15 minutes). Position figure and press gently into place. To reposition the figure, simply lift and press into a different place. To remove adhesive, rub and pull off.

Scenic Glue

785-190 8 fl oz **6.49**
Formulated especially for model landscaping. Dries clear with a matte (flat) finish and is flexible. Use to attach various medium to large foliage, Bushes, Underbrush and Lichen. Does not become brittle after drying.

Scenic Cement

785-191 16 fl oz **6.49**
New and improved water-soluble, non-toxic, ready-to-use for Ballast, Turf and more. Dries to a clear, matte finish. Apply with Scenic Sprayer (sold separately) or brush on.

Hob-e-Tac® Adhesive

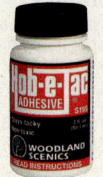

785-195 2 fl oz **5.49**
All purpose non-flammable, high-tack adhesive. For making trees and for attaching Field Grass. Can also be used as a contact adhesive.

Foam Tack Glue

785-1444 12 fl oz **10.98**
This specially formulated glue is high-tack and effective on most materials. Use as a contact cement whenever bonding two large surfaces.

Low Temp Foam Glue Sticks

785-1446 pkg(10) **5.98**
Low Temp Foam Glue Sticks melt at a temperature that will not damage foam. Use with Low Temp Foam Glue Gun #785-1445, sold separately.

Scenery by Ron Freeman. Models and Photo by Mike Reardon, Addison, Illinois

Suburban sprawl will soon encroach on this pastoral scene, but for now the farmer is enjoying a clear, calm afternoon of fishing. Summer is coming to an end and the corn is almost ready for picking, so he's decided to play hooky for a day.

The lake's mirror finish reflects the nearby signal tower and the wispy clouds in the sky. Breaking the afternoon stillness is the roar of the Southwest Chief as it rounds the curve heading south to Texas. An FP40 rides behind the brace of P42s pulling the passenger train.

This peaceful scene was shot on the Midwest N Pioneer club layout. Envirotex was used to create the glossy finish of the water.

From the dark details at the bottom of the lake to the smudge of red on the barn, paint helps tell the story. Painting the center of the lake bottom a deeper color creates depth and the not-quite-matching paint on the side of the barn shows that a section was recently repainted. Flat, dull colors chosen for the silo and bridge give the effect of metal and the translucent white clouds in the sky are a good indication that the weather is calm and sunny.

You can easily customize your trains, structures, scenery and other details with the variety of products available in the Paint Section.

PAINT & PAINT SUPPLIES

BADGER AIR-BRUSH CO.

Airbrushes, parts and accessories ideal for finishing all types of models, home, craft and art projects or professional painting and illustration. Brushes are equipped with spray head assembly and needle to produce one of three adjustable spray patterns.

CAUTION: For your safety, the use of a properly vented spray booth and a respirator which is paint mist and vapor compatible is strongly recommended when painting with an airbrush.

NEW PRODUCTS

Hybrid Air Brush

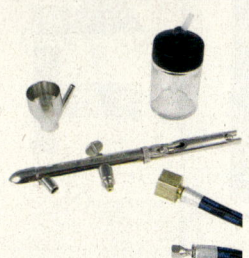

NEW 165-31553 126.00
Quality precision-crafted airbrush features a single-size paint tip, spray regulator, and needle that work with any properly reduced medium including acrylics, inks, enamels, stains and more. Suitable for many applications requiring a finer spray pattern. Includes one 1/4 oz color cup, 3/4 oz jar with adaptor and 6" braided hose.

Whirlwind 10 Air Compressor

NEW 165-18010 185.00
Diaphragm compressor never needs oil or lubrication. 1/10 HP, 2cfm, 30 PSI with on/off switch. Portable unit weighs just 9 pounds. Suction cup feet reduce compressor movement. Operates one airbrush.

Model 100 Airbrush
Dual action, internal mix for fine detail work, each features: color cup or cavity, counter-balanced handle, self-lubricating Teflon® needle bearing, and head seal, plus a non-slip, one-piece trigger that can be used in either hand.

Items listed below are available by Special Order (see Legend Page).

165-100 Fine **104.00**
Model 100 Airbrush with Fine needle and head, 1/16oz (2cc) color cup, protective cap, spare needle, wrench for head, hanger, instruction book and storage case.

165-101 Medium **104.00**
Same as #165-100, with Medium needle and head.

165-102 Gravity Feed - Fine **111.00**
Same as #165-100, but with gravity-feed color cup which holds 1/16oz (2cc).

Model 100 LG Gravity Feed Airbrush Basic Sets 117.00 ea
For use with thinned artist acrylics and vinyls, and lighter viscosity materials.

Model 100 LG series airbrush with permanent top-mounted color cup and fitted cover (holds 1/3oz (10.5cc) of color), hanger, extra needle, wrench, protective cap and padded case.

165-1005 Fine

Items listed below are available by Special Order (see Legend Page).
165-1006 Medium
165-1007 Heavy

Model 100 SG Airbrush
Item listed below is available by Special Order (see Legend Page).
165-1008 Extra Fine **104.00**

Model 150 Airbrush
Identical to Model 100, but uses jars or a removable color cup to hold paint.

Basic Sets 111.00 ea
Model 150 airbrush, attachable 3/4oz (22cc) and 2oz (60cc) paint jars with covers for big jobs, or force-fit color cup for smaller work, case, hanger, wrench, protective cap, self-lubricating Teflon needle bearing, head seal and siphon tube, plus non-slip, one-piece trigger.

165-150 Fine
165-153 Heavy

Item listed below is available by Special Order (see Legend Page).
165-1501 Medium

Deluxe Sets

165-152 Fine **149.00**
Fine head assembly and needle, 8' (2.45m) braided air hose, 1/4" pipe thread adapter (for use with compressor or CO2 tank), wrench for head, hanger, instruction booklet and wooden case.

165-1507 Fine & Heavy **138.00**
Same as #165-152, but with Fine and Heavy head assemblies and needles, plus cardboard storage box.

Crescendo Model 175 Airbrush
Bottom-feed, dual action, internal mix design.

Airbrush Only 97.00 ea
Items listed below are available by Special Order (see Legend Page).
165-1754 Fine
165-1755 Medium
165-1756 Heavy

Basic Sets 117.00 ea
Items listed below are available by Special Order (see Legend Page).
Includes Model 175 airbrush, 1/4oz (7cc) metal color cup, 3/4oz (22cc) jar with adapter, 2oz (60cc) jar, spare needle, instruction book, protective cap, hanger and plastic case.

165-1751 Fine
165-1752 Medium
165-1753 Large

Deluxe Set
165-1757 139.00
Crescendo 175 Airbrush with all three tips (Fine, Medium and Heavy), spray regulators and needles, 8' (2.45m) braided air hose, 3/4oz (22cc) jar with adapter, two 2oz (60cc) paint jars, one 1/4oz metal paint cup, hanger, protective cap and instruction book.

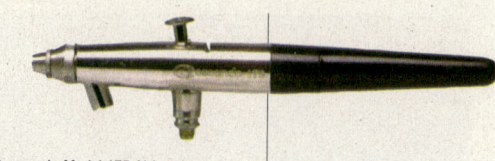
Crescendo Model 175 Airbrush 165-1754

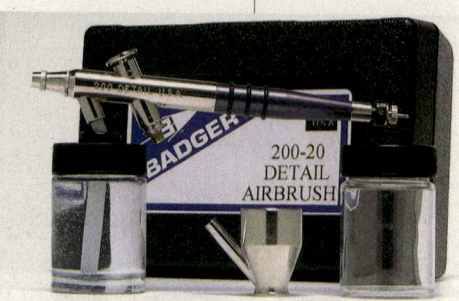
Model 200 Airbrush 165-20020

Model 200 Airbrush Sets
Single action delivers a pre-set amount of fluid.

Basic Set
165-2001 Medium **74.00**
Model 200 airbrush, attachable 3/4oz (22cc) jar and 2oz (60cc) jar with cover, protective cap and wrench.

Deluxe Sets
165-2003 Fine **90.00**
6' (1.83m) vinyl hose, Propel regulator, attachable 3/4oz jar, spare 3/4oz jar with cover and can of Propel.

165-2005 Medium Only **85.00**
Includes: 6' (1.83m) vinyl airhose, Propel regulator, attachable and spare 3/4oz jars, one 2oz jar with cover and protective cap.

Item listed below is available by Special Order (see Legend Page).
165-2004 Medium w/Compressor **251.00**
Model 18010 portable diaphragm compressor, 10' (3.05m) braided air hose, 1/4" pipe thread fitting (adapts brush to compressor or CO2 tank), attachable and spare 3/4oz jar, one 2oz jar with cover and protective cap.

Badger Detail Airbrush
165-20020 Fine **82.00**
Set includes color cup, two mixing jars, Fast Blast adapter cap, wrench, instructions and black Badger airbrush case.

Gravity Feed Basic Set 72.00 ea (Unless Noted)
Identical to Model 200, but with permanently attached 1/16oz (2cc) color cup, ideal for smaller jobs. All sets include protective cap, wrench for head and storage case.

Items listed below are available by Special Order (see Legend Page).
165-2009 Fine
165-20010 Medium
165-20011 Fine w/Built-in Cavity **67.00**
Built-in color cavity holds enough color for small jobs.

Model 200 Airbrush Accessories
Items listed below are available by Special Order (see Legend Page).
165-41043 Guarded Regulator **6.95**

165-51071 Replacement Head **11.60**

Model 250 Airbrush Sets
Single action, external mix, bottom feed design. Spray pattern adjusts from 3/4" (18.9mm) to 2" (50.8mm).

Basic Sets
Model 250 airbrush with 3/4oz (22cc) jars and cover, 6' (1.83m) vinyl air hose and Propel regulator.

165-2501 Boxed Set **26.00**

165-2502 Carded Set **23.00**

165-2503 Boxed Set w/Propel Can **33.00**

165-2504 Large Capacity Set **35.00**
Same as #165-2503, with larger Model 250 Airbrush and attached 4oz (120cc) jar.

165-2507 Basic Spray Gun Hobby Set **49.00**
Includes Model 250 airbrush with attached and spare 3/4oz (22cc) jars and cover, 6' (1.83m) vinyl air hose and Propel regulator, three hobby colors, mixing pipette, how-to book and instructions.

Model 250 Accessories
NEW 165-500012 8' Vinyl Air Hose **7.20**

NEW 165-500242 Cork Gasket **1.45**

PAINT & PAINT SUPPLIES

Model 350 Airbrush Sets

Single action, external mix, bottom feed design. Makes a larger dot spray pattern.

Basic Sets 53.00 ea
Include: Model 350 airbrush, 2oz (60cc) jar with cover, attachable 3/4oz (22cc) jar, wrench for head and instruction booklet, plus storage box.
165-3501 Fine

165-3504 Medium

Basic Sets w/Accessories
Both sets include 6' (1.83m) vinyl air hose and Propel regulator.
165-3502 Medium **60.00**
165-3503 Medium **67.00**
1/4oz (7cc) self-standing color cup and can of Propel.

Deluxe Sets
165-35004 Model 350 Airbrush Set **93.00**
Includes three tips (Fine, Medium and Heavy) and needles, attached 3/4oz (22cc) jar, 2oz (60cc) jar with cover, plus 8' (2.45m) braided air hose and 1/4" pipe thread fitting (converts airbrush for use with compressor or CO2 tank).

Item listed below is available by Special Order (see Legend Page).
165-3506 Complete Craft Set **96.00**
Model 350 medium tip with attachable 3/4oz (22cc) jar, 6' (1.83m) vinyl air hose, Propel can and regulator, 3/4oz jar with cover, three reusable Mylar stencils, two sheets BriteWhite airbrush paper, five Air-Tex textile colors, one 1oz Air Tex cleaner, hanger and how-to booklet.

Model 360 Universal Airbrush

This unique dual-action design has a rotating front which allows a quick conversion from gravity to syphon feed or vice versa. Needle can be removed without taking the handle off. No additional tips are required to change spray patterns.
165-3601 Airbrush w/Two 3/4oz Jars **176.00**

165-3602 Airbrush Only **169.00**

Model 400 Touch-Up Gun 148.00 ea

Fan control needle adjusts spray pattern from round to fan-shape.
165-4001 Fine
165-4002 Medium

165-4003 Heavy

Anthem Series

Design features a thinner diameter needle; spray material without having to change spray heads. Body is a streamlined, lightweight design that provides exacting balance for easy operation and maximum user comfort.

165-1551 Anthem Airbrush Starter Set **118.00**
Includes 1/4oz cup, 3/4oz jar/adapter and 2oz jar.
165-1557 Anthem Airbrush Complete Set **131.00**
Includes brush, hose, three jars with adapter, color cup, hanger and display box.

Item listed below is available by Special Order (see Legend Page).
165-1552 Anthem Airbrush Only **97.00**
165-1559 Anthem Airbrush w/Classic Wooden Storage Gift Case **152.00**

SPRAY BOOTH

165-1352 Hobby Spray Booth **295.00**
No more paint overspray or odors. Expanded design is easy to clean and features sturdy metal body, replaceable air filter, 165 cfm motor w/ 4' output adaptor. Measures: 17-1/2" wide x 14-1/2" tall x 9" deep.

165-1362 Replacement Filter for #165-1352 **14.95**

AIR COMPRESSORS

Thayer & Chandler Air Star V

165-909 **309.00**
Lightweight, quiet, 1/8-horsepower, automatic shut-off piston compressor with an adjustable air regulator and pressure gauge. Features include a built-in moisture filter and airbrush holder; on-off switch; and a maximum running pressure of 40 PSI. Maintenance and oil free. Measures 12 x 6 x 6".

Silent Compressors

Powered by a highly efficient, oil-reciprocating piston motor, silent compressors feature automatic on/off pressure switch, thermal overload protection, adjustable air regulator, moisture trap, gauge for line pressure, pressure release safety valve, manual on/off valve and intake air filter.

Items listed below are available by Special Order (see Legend Page).

Million-Air
165-4801 **719.00**
1/6th HP motor with .45 gallon (1.70l) tank which develops .70 CFM at 116 P.S.I. Operates up to two airbrushes.

Billion-Air
165-4802 **857.00**
1/4 HP motor with 1.06 gallon (4.08l) tank which develops .90 CFM at 116 P.S.I. Operates up to three airbrushes.

Trillion-Air
165-4803 **1009.00**
1/2 HP piston motor with 1.06 gallon (4.08l) tank which develops 1.75 CFM at 116 P.S.I. Operates up to five airbrushes.

Cyclone I Air Compressor
NEW 165-18012 Automatic Shut-Off **260.00**
1/12 HP, .80CFM, 25PSI

Compressor Accessories

165-50023 1/4" Pipe Thread Fitting Adapter **4.00**
Adapts airhose to compressor or CO_2 tank.

165-50051 Moisture Trap **48.70**
Air filter and water trap for air compressors.

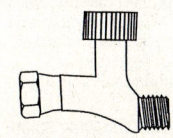

165-50054 Air Regulator Filter & Gauge Set **68.85**
For use with compressors. Allows easy adjustment of maximum air pressure, built-in filter traps moisture.

165-502035 Mini Air Flow Regulator **11.70**
Chrome-plated regulator easily attaches to Badger diaphragm compressors. Easy to operate: the top adjustment screw increases and/or decreases air flow. Gauge not included.

Item listed below is available by Special Order (see Legend Page).
165-50057 CO_2 Regulator & Gauge **105.00**
For use with CO_2 tanks only.

AIRBRUSH ACCESSORIES

165-121 Paint Mixer **11.55**
Requires two AA batteries, sold separately.

165-126 Color Mixing Kit **.45**
Includes three mixing cups and stirring sticks.

165-127 Spot Touch-up Prep Pen **8.20**

Oil & Lubricant
165-122 REGDAB™ Airbrush Lubricant 1oz (30cc) **4.90**
Maintains smooth trigger action and eliminates needle friction caused by dried paint.

165-502019 Replacement Oil 22oz (.75l) **17.35**
Special lightweight oil for use in all silent compressors.

Airbrush Holders
165-125 Model 125 **25.70**
Heavy-duty unit holds two airbrushes; rotates, swivels and clamps on any surface up to 2" thick.

165-50021 Airbrush Hanger **3.60**
Metal holder included with sets.

Paint Filter
165-502016 **6.25**
For all airbrushes using jars or bottles. Micro screen mesh filter passes only particles which will flow through the airbrush.

Daily New Arrival Updates! Visit Walthers Web site at
www.walthers.com

Color Cups 8.15 ea (Unless Noted)

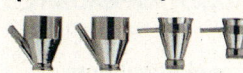

165-50047 1/6oz (2cc) **8.05**
165-50048 1/8oz (3.5cc)
Self-standing, for Model 100 side-feed airbrushes. Screw-off bottom for easy cleaning.
165-500482 1/4oz (7cc)
Self-standing, fits 150 and 200 only.
165-500483 1/4oz (7cc)
Self-standing, fits 350 only.

Cleaning Reamers
165-50060 For Heads 100-200 **4.90**
165-50061 3-Cornered for Models 100 & 200 **6.20**

Jars & Covers
Fast Blast Airbrush Caps 3.10 ea
Easy-to-clean Fast Blast jar adapter caps can be used in place of existing jar adapter caps and match those now included in complete airbrush sets.
165-50208 1-5/16" 33mm
165-51017 25/32" 20mm
For 150/200 series airbrushes w/tube for 1oz jars
165-51019 25/32" 20mm
For 150/200 series airbrushes w/tube for 4oz jars
165-51228 1-1/8" 28mm
Fits Floquil jars.

Jar Adaptors For 350 Series Airbrushes 3.10 ea
These jar adapters are direct replacements for metal jar adaptors and feature the correct 60° siphon tube angle.
165-50308 1-5/16" 33mm
165-51018 Fits 1oz Air Opaque Jars
165-51020 Fits 4oz Air Opaque Jars

Jar Adaptors For Models 200, 250, 350 and 150
165-500052 3/4oz (22cc) **1.45**
165-500053 2oz (60cc) **1.95**

Badger Propel
165-50002 11oz (33ml) **9.35**
165-50202 17oz (51ml) **13.40**
Works with all types of airbrushes, requires regulator #165-50200 (sold separately).

395

PAINT & PAINT SUPPLIES

BADGER AIR-BRUSH CO.

Propel Regulators
165-50029 Tire Adapter **5.20**
Convert any spare tire into an air supply. Special fitting modifies Propel regulator #165-50200 (sold separately) to fit standard valve stem.

165-50200 Complete Regulator **8.00**
Makes Propel last longer, regulates air pressure from can at 10-50 P.S.I.

165-50118 O-Ring Only **1.30**

Items listed below are available by Special Order (see Legend Page).
165-50117 Stem w/O-Ring **4.00**

165-50119 Washer **1.30**

Air Hoses
165-502011 Braided w/Swivel Connections **17.90**
10' (3.05m) of heavy duty hose for use with compressors.

Vinyl Airhoses
165-50001 5' **6.75**

165-500011 8' **9.70**
Flexible, lightweight, sturdy hose. With connectors at each end. Not recommended for use with compressors.

10' Re-Coil™ Hoses 20.15 ea
165-504011 For Badger

Item listed below is available by Special Order (see Legend Page).
165-504012 For Binks

In-Line Moisture Filters
165-502014 Filter Only **18.20**
For use with #165-50205 Air Hose Only.

165-502025 With Hose **31.80**
Complete assembly with 10' (3.05m) braided air hose.

Foto-Frisket Film
165-600 pkg(10) **15.20**
Low tack, easy lift-off masking film.

Respirators
165-1902 Replacement Cartridge for #165-1901 **18.25**

165-1903 Replacement Pre-Filter for #165-1901 **9.20**

Item listed below is available by Special Order (see Legend Page).

165-1901 Double Cartridge Type **86.75**
Protects against paint mists and vapors.

AIR ABRASIVE GUNS
Removes rust or paint from metal, and roughs the surface for improved paint adhesion.
NOTE: Use of wraparound safety goggles and a dust mask or respirator is recommended. Not for use by children.

165-2601 Gun Only **33.00**
165-2603 Starter Set **46.00**
Set includes: gun with attached 4oz (120cc) jar, 8' (240cm) hose and 12oz (336kg) net weight of aluminum oxide, face mask, Propel® and regulator.

BOOKS

How-To
165-500 Hobby & Craft Guide to Airbrushing **7.60**
Includes instructions on preparation for painting, mixing paint, cleaning and maintenance. Softcover, 32 pages, over 130 full color illustrations, 8-1/2 x 11".

165-505 Step by Step Modelers Guide to Airbrushing **11.20**
Painting models, figures and dioramas. Includes techniques from shadowing to mixing paint. Softcover, over 180 color photos, 32 pages, 8-1/2 x 11".

MODELFLEX™ PAINT
Specially formulated for models, goes on super thin (.25 to .50 thousands) to color without hiding fine details. Non-toxic and with no foul odor, Modelflex cleans up with water and can be sprayed or brushed.

Modelflex Sets 23.70 ea
165-1701 Railroad Rolling Stock
One each: Engine Black, Reefer White, Reefer Gray, Reefer Yellow, Reefer Orange, Dark Tuscan Red, Light Tuscan Red.

165-1702 Weathering & Railroad Off-Line
One each: Weathered Black, Antique White, Primer Gray, Concrete Gray, Sand, Signal Red, Light Green.

165-1703 Railroad Private Colors
One each: Caboose Red, Rail Box Yellow, Mopac Blue, Pullman Green, Super Gloss Black, Maroon, Tuscan Red, ATSF Silver.

165-1704 Military Colors
One each: Forest Green, Olive Drab, European Dark Green, Armor Sand, Field Drab, Medium Green, Camouflage Gray.

165-1705 Gloss Auto Colors
One each: Black, White, Red, Blue, Brown, Yellow, Green.

Individual Paints 1oz (30cc) 3.50 ea
165-1601 Engine Black
165-1602 Reefer White
165-1603 Grimy Black
166-1604 Reefer Gray
165-1605 Weathered Black
165-1606 Antique White
165-1607 Signal Red
165-1608 Caboose Red
165-1609 Reefer Orange
165-1610 Reefer Yellow
165-1611 Concrete Gray
165-1612 Primer Gray
165-1613 Dark Tuscan Oxide Red
165-1614 Light Tuscan Oxide Red
165-1615 Maroon Tuscan Oxide Red
165-1616 Brunswick Green
165-1617 Pullman Green
165-1618 SOO Maroon
165-1619 SOO Dulux Gold
165-1620 Super Gloss Black
165-1621 PRR Green
165-1622 PRR Maroon
165-1623 CNW Dark Green
165-1624 UP Armor Yellow
165-1625 UP Harbor Mist Gray
165-1626 BN Green
165-1627 NYC Gray Dark 1
165-1628 NYC Gray Light 1
165-1629 CR Blue
165-1630 Sand
165-1631 ATSF Red
165-1632 ATSF Silver
165-1633 ATSF Yellow
165-1634 ATSF Blue
165-1635 SP Lark Light Gray
165-1636 SP Daylight Red
165-1637 SP Scarlet Red
165-1638 SP Daylight Orange
165-1639 SP Letter Gray
165-1640 SP Lark Dark Gray
165-1641 SP Armor Yellow
165-1642 MILW Orange
165-1643 MILW Maroon
165-1644 MILW Gray
165-1645 MILW Brown
165-1646 SOU Sylvan Green
165-1647 Light Green
165-1648 Weyerhauser Yellow Green
165-1649 CSX Blue
165-1650 Insignia Yellow
165-1651 EL Gray
165-1652 EL Yellow
165-1653 EL Maroon
165-1654 Rail Box Yellow
165-1655 CNW Old Yellow
165-1656 CNW Zeto Yellow
165-1657 SOO Red
165-1658 Amtrak Red
165-1659 Amtrak Blue
165-1660 B&M Blue
165-1661 DRGW Orange
165-1662 DRGW Gold
165-1663 GN Big Sky Blue
165-1664 GN Orange
165-1665 GN Green
165-1666 GTW Blue
165-1667 C&O Enchantment Blue
165-1668 C&O Yellow
165-1669 B&O Royal Blue
165-1670 CSX Gray
165-1671 WC Maroon
165-1672 WC Cream
165-1673 IC Orange
165-1674 IC Brown
165-1675 GM&O Red
165-1676 D&H Blue
165-1677 NP Light Green
165-1678 NP Yellow
165-1679 Rock Island Blue
165-1680 MKT Green
165-1681 MKT Yellow
165-1682 L&N Blue
165-1683 L&N Gray
165-1684 L&N Yellow
165-1685 RDG Green
165-1686 MP Blue
165-1687 Missabe Road Maroon
165-1688 Missabe Road Yellow
165-1689 WP Orange
165-1690 Penn Central Green
165-16151 BNSF Green
165-16152 BNSF Orange
165-16153 CB&Q Chinese Red
165-16154 CB&Q Gray
165-16155 Wabash Blue
165-16156 Wabash Gray
165-16157 Frisco Orange
165-16158 CP Action Yellow
165-16159 CP Action Red
165-16160 CP Tuscan Red
165-16161 CP Yellow
165-16162 CP Gray
165-16163 CN Red #11
165-16164 CN Green #11
165-16165 CN Orange #10
165-16166 CN Yellow #11
165-16167 CN Gray #11
165-16168 Trailer Train Yellow
165-16169 MP Eagle Blue
165-16170 MP Eagle Roof Gray
165-16171 MP Eagle Gray
165-16172 Rust
165-16173 Mud
165-16174 Earth
165-16175 Rail Brown
165-16176 Roof Brown
165-16177 NH Hunter Green
165-16178 NH Warm Orange
165-16179 NH Imitation Silver
165-16180 NH Pullman Green
165-16181 NH Imitation Gold
165-16182 NH Red-Orange
165-16183 NH Socony Red
165-16184 LV Cornell Red
165-16185 SAL Pullman Green
165-16186 ACL Imitation Aluminum
165-16187 CNW Red
165-16188 D&H Gray
165-16189 B&M Maroon
165-16190 B&O Dulux Gold
165-16191 Pullman Harbor Mist Gray
165-16192 WP Green
165-16193 CB&Q Imitation Aluminum
165-16194 CB&Q Red
165-16195 BNSF Silver
165-16196 BNSF Yellow
165-16197 SP/ATSF Overland Light Gray
165-16198 SP/ATSF Overland Dark Gray
165-16199 Rock Maroon
165-16200 Rock Red
165-16201 Rock Aluminum White
165-16202 John Deere Yellow
165-16203 John Deere Green
165-16204 Light Flesh
165-16205 Medium Flesh
165-16206 Dark Flesh
165-16208 Metallic Gold

Military Colors
165-1691 Bomber Green
165-1692 SAC Bomber Green
165-1693 Bomber Blue
165-1694 Field Drab
165-1695 Green Drab
165-1696 Olive Drab
165-1697 Camouflage Gray
165-1698 Camouflage Brown
165-1699 Flat Gull Gray
165-16100 Euro Dark Green
165-16101 Medium Field Green
165-16102 Forest Green
165-16103 Armor Sand
165-16104 Dark Green
165-16105 Medium Green

Gloss Colors
165-16106 Black
165-16107 White
165-16108 Red
165-16109 Orange
165-16110 Blue
165-16111 Green
165-16112 Yellow
165-16113 Brown
165-16114 Silver
165-16115 Midnight Blue
165-16116 Deep Red
165-16117 Bright Orange
165-16118 Sunset Yellow

PAINT & PAINT SUPPLIES

Flat Colors
165-16119 Flat Black
165-16120 Flat White

Clear Finish
165-16601 Flat
165-16602 Satin
165-16603 Gloss

Extender
165-16600 Extender

Marine Paints 1oz Bottles 3.50 ea

165-16401 Anti-Fouling Red Oxide
165-16402 Navy Red
165-16403 Coast Guard Red
165-16404 Coast Guard Orange
165-16405 Deck Tan
165-16406 Navy Brown
165-16407 Quartermaster Brown
165-16408 Navy Buff
165-16409 Panama Buff
165-16410 Navy White
165-16411 Deck Green
165-16412 Hull Black
165-16413 Wrought Iron Black
165-16414 Bulwarks Red
165-16415 Caprail Green
165-16416 Midship Blue
165-16417 White
165-16418 Slate Gray
165-16419 Umber
165-16420 Yellow Ochre
165-16421 Hull Cream
165-16422 Windjammer White
165-16423 Windjammer Yellow
165-16424 Windjammer Red
165-16425 Windjammer Green
165-16426 Windjammer Blue
165-16427 Salmon Buff
165-16428 Orange Ochre
165-16429 Shipyard Rust
165-16430 Shipyard Grimy Gray
165-16431 Deck Red
165-16432 Dark Deck Gray
165-16433 Tug Light Blue
165-16434 Tug Medium Blue
165-16435 Tug Deep Blue
165-16436 Tug Light Green
165-16437 Tug Olive Green
165-16438 Tug Orange
165-16439 Tug Yellow
165-16440 Tug Light Gray
165-16441 Army Corps Engineer Buff
165-16442 Golden Yellow
165-16443 Bright Silver
165-16444 #5 Standard Navy Gray
165-16445 #20 Standard Deck Gray
165-16446 5-L Light Gray (Early 1941)
165-16447 5-O Ocean Gray (Early 1941)
165-16448 5-D Dark Gray (Early 1941)
165-16449 5-H Haze Gray (Late 1941)
165-16450 5-O Ocean Gray (Late 1941)
165-16451 5-S Sea Blue A (Late 1941)
165-16452 5-N Navy Blue (Late 1941)
165-16453 Deck Blue 20B (Late 1941)
165-16454 #82 Black (1943)
165-16455 5-P Pale Gray (1943)
165-16456 5-L Light Gray (1946)
165-16457 Dull Coat
165-16458 Matte Coat
165-16459 Gloss Coat
165-16460 Retarder

Cleaner
165-16606 16oz **9.75**

DECAL ACCESSORIES

Decal Solutions 2.40 ea
Use these handy solutions to make decals adhere to your models like paint.

165-16801 Setting Solution
165-16802 Softening Solution
165-16803 Liquid Decal Film Allows you to create your own decals by brushing it on a flat clean surface, allow to dry, and draw or paint on your image. Also allows you to save old decals when brushed over an old decal, film seals and provides a new surface.

ACCESSORIES

Just-a-Dab Applicators
Flexible plastic applicators with textured shaft and micro-fibre heads for applying paints with accuracy. Washable and reusable.

165-50560 Fine pkg(12) **2.05**
165-50570 Regular pkg(12) **2.05**
165-50580 Combo (9 Fine & 9 Regular) **3.05**

CATALOGS

165-BA2000 Catalog 2005 **N/C**
165-BA200 Retail Price Guide 2005 **N/C**

WALTHERS

Decal Setting Solution

904-470 Solvaset 2oz 60ml **2.98**
Dealers MUST Order Multiples of 6.

Make decals snuggle down on any surface. Softens decal film so it stretches over surface details like rivets, seams and hinges. Eliminates air bubbles, white spots and draping without hiding detail.

Masking Liquid

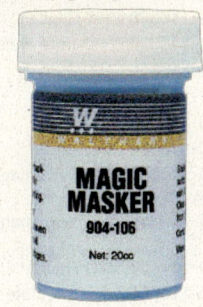

904-106 Magic Masker 20cc **2.98**
Dealers MUST Order Multiples of 12.

An easy way to mask off small areas or odd shaped parts where tape won't work. Just brush it on and allow to dry. Then spray your color, let dry and peel off. Works on plastic, wood, metal, paint, doped surfaces, chrome and silver.

See What's New and Exciting at
www.walthers.com

FALLER

IMPORTED FROM GERMANY BY WALTHERS

Paint Marker Pens

272-170690 Modeler's Color Pens pkg(6) **35.99**
Ideal for painting any kind of models. Water-based paints are opaque, economic and quick drying. Set includes red, yellow, orange, lavender, blue and green.

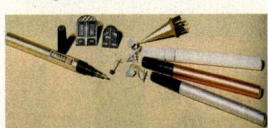

272-170691 Metallic Paint Pens pkg(4) **31.99**
A fast and easy way to simulate a variety of natural metal finishes on your models. Includes white for base coat, plus gold, silver and copper. Colors are durable, permanent and quick drying.

Patina Set

272-170697 55.99
Give any building exterior or scenery detail an aged appearance with this series of patina paints. This set includes six water-soluble acrylic paints, thinner and an applicator brush. Comes with instructions.

Information STATION

The Benefits of an Airbrush

When you look at a prototype locomotive roaring down the tracks, you don't see the brush strokes where the design team applied color to the engines or rolling stock. You see just a uniform application of color. This process of adding color to the cars is most likely done with the use of a spray gun. And an airbrush in model railroading closely duplicates this process. Prototype realism is just one reason why an airbrush is one of the best ways to apply color to your models.

The finish that an airbrush provides is a smooth, even finish across the entire surface. In addition, many of the fine details on metals or plastics will not be hidden. You're also able to control the width of the spray pattern, so it's the perfect tool for any job, be it painting fine lines or covering large surfaces on a structure. It's also a great applicator for weathering, so the appearance of dust or outdoor exposure is simpler to apply.

Search through the Paint & Paint Supplies section of this Reference Book to get a better idea of what is the best airbrush for you. You can choose from different styles (internal and external mix, referring to how the paint and air are mixed to create the spray pattern) and accessories to add this useful tool to your modeling time.

PAINT & PAINT SUPPLIES

FLOQUIL

Made especially for painting miniatures, Floquil colors cover without hiding detail. Floquil is solvent based, while Polly Scale™ colors are water-reducible acrylics. Dealers: Ask about merchandising display racks.

NEW PRODUCTS

Polly Scale Acrylic Weathering Markers

These new three-marker sets are ideal for quick, neat weathering applications.

Pkg(3) 7.49
NEW **270-3801** Rail Brown, Railroad Tie Brown, Rust
NEW **270-3802** Aged Concrete, Weathered Black, Roof Brown
NEW **270-3803** Earth, Mud, Grime

RAILROAD COLORS

1oz 4.49 ea

270-110001 Thinner-Brush Cleaner
Only chemical compatible solvent for Floquil colors, can be used for thinning, mixing and cleaning equipment.

270-110002 Retarder
Slows drying time of solvent-based colors, for airbrushing and covering large areas.

270-110003 Hi-Gloss
Light amber-colored coating for indoor use. Heat, water and alcohol resistant. Dries in about four hours with an extremely high-gloss finish.

270-110004 Crystal Cote
Water-clear, quick-drying gloss and fixative. Use indoors or out; does not yellow. Durable, resists abrasion and most common chemicals except alcohol.

270-110005 Glaze
Amber-colored, semi-gloss coating. Use indoors or out. Dries in about 15-20 minutes and resists water, alcohol and most common chemicals. Can be used for priming, or mix with solvent-based colors for an eggshell finish.

Railroad Colors 1oz (30ml) 4.49 ea

- 270-110006 Dust
- 270-110007 Rail Brown
- 270-110009 Primer
- 270-110010 Engine Black
- 270-110011 Reefer White
- 270-110012 Reefer Gray
- 270-110013 Grimy Black
- 270-110014 Railroad Tie Brown
- 270-110015 Flat Finish
- 270-110016 Aged Concrete
- 270-110017 Weathered Black
- 270-110020 Caboose Red
- 270-110023 Flesh Tone Base
- 270-110025 Tuscan Red
- 270-110030 Reefer Orange
- 270-110031 Reefer Yellow
- 270-110033 Railbox Yellow
- 270-110034 Brunswick Green
- 270-110035 BN Green
- 270-110040 Dark Green
- 270-110041 Light Green
- 270-110044 Depot Olive
- 270-110045 Pullman Green
- 270-110048 Coach Green
- 270-110050 Dark Blue
- 270-110051 Light Blue
- 270-110056 GN Big Sky Blue
- 270-110058 CR Blue
- 270-110065 Signal Red
- 270-110070 Roof Brown
- 270-110073 Rust
- 270-110074 Box Car Red
- 270-110081 Earth
- 270-110082 Concrete
- 270-110083 Mud
- 270-110084 Foundation
- 270-110085 Antique White
- 270-110086 Grime
- 270-110087 Depot Buff
- 270-110088 D&H Caboose Red
- 270-110100 Old Silver (metallic)
- 270-110101 Bright Silver (metallic)
- 270-110103 Bright Gold (metallic)
- 270-110104 Brass (metallic)
- 270-110105 Copper (metallic)
- 270-110108 Gun Metal (metallic)
- 270-110119 Graphite (metallic)
- 270-110130 SP Lettering Gray
- 270-110131 SP Lark Light Gray
- 270-110132 SP Lark Dark Gray
- 270-110133 SP Armour Yellow
- 270-110134 SP Daylight Orange
- 270-110135 SP Daylight Red
- 270-110136 SP Scarlet
- 270-110144 Platinum Mist (metallic)
- 270-110166 UP Armour Yellow
- 270-110167 UP Harbor Mist Gray
- 270-110168 UP Light Orange
- 270-110174 SOU Green
- 270-110175 SOU Freight Car Brown
- 270-110176 ATSF Red
- 270-110177 ATSF Blue
- 270-110178 ATSF Yellow
- 270-110179 ATSF Mineral Brown
- 270-110180 BNSF Orange
- 270-110181 BNSF Green
- 270-110182 BNSF Yellow
- 270-110183 RDG Green
- 270-110184 Tuscan Red #2
- 270-110186 Railroad Oxide Red
- 270-110250 CN Orange #11
- 270-110252 CN Gray #17
- 270-110254 CN Yellow #12
- 270-110256 CN Green #12
- 270-110260 CNW Yellow
- 270-110262 CNW Green
- 270-110280 WC Gold
- 270-110282 WC Maroon
- 270-110310 TTX Yellow
- 270-110320 MKT Green
- 270-110330 NYC Jade Green
- 270-110350 CSX Gray
- 270-110352 CSX Blue
- 270-110354 CSX Black
- 270-110356 CSX Yellow
- 270-110357 CSX New Image Blue
- 270-110358 CSX New Image Gold
- 270-110450 SOO Red
- 270-110601 Zinc Chromate Primer

Thinner - Brush Cleaner

Only chemically compatible solvent for Floquil colors. Use for thinning, mixing, correcting, cleaning brushes, air brushes and solvent-resistant surfaces. Dealers must order packs of three.

- **270-120001** Bottle - 2oz (60ml) **3.49**
- **270-140001** Can - 8oz (240ml) **8.99**
- **270-150001** Pint (0.24l) **10.49**
- **270-160001** Quart (0.95l) **14.99**
- **270-151611** Airbrush Thinner 16oz (0.24l) **9.99**

Railroad Aerosols 3oz (150ml) 5.49 ea

Same colors, but in spray cans for covering large areas, or quick paint jobs.

- 270-130004 Crystal Cote
- 270-130007 Rail Brown
- 270-130009 Primer
- 270-130010 Engine Black
- 270-130011 Reefer White
- 270-130012 Reefer Gray
- 270-130013 Grimy Black
- 270-130015 Flat Finish
- 270-130016 Instant Weathering
- 270-130020 Caboose Red
- 270-130025 Tuscan Red
- 270-130030 Reefer Orange
- 270-130031 Reefer Yellow
- 270-130040 Dark Green
- 270-130045 Pullman Green
- 270-130048 Coach Green
- 270-130050 Dark Blue
- 270-130070 Roof Brown
- 270-130074 Box Car Red
- 270-130081 Earth
- 270-130082 Concrete
- 270-130101 Bright Silver (metallic)
- 270-130601 Zinc Chromate Primer

Aerosol Figure Primer 3oz 5.49 ea

Permanent, high-adherence primers resist chipping. Made especially for metal figures and miniatures, works well on most models. Fine pigments cover completely without filling in or hiding fine details. Can be used as a base under water- or solvent-based paints. Available in four colors to highlight detail and simplify application of finish coats. Dealers must order packs of three.

- **270-330022** Figure Flat
- **270-330009** Light Gray
- **270-330010** Base Black
- **270-330021** Base White

POLLY SCALE™

A comprehensive line of user-friendly acrylics, Polly Scale colors are water-reducible, odor-free and environmentally safe. A wide selection of railroad and military colors are available, excellent for plastics, metals and brass. Fine ground pigments cover without hiding surface details and the formula is self leveling. Easily brushed, drybrushed and airbrushed. Can be sprayed at low pressure. Use plain water for clean-up or thinning. All colors are intermixable with older Polly S paints.

Railroad Colors 1/2oz (15ml) 3.99 ea

- 270-404046 Atlantic Coast Line Purple
- 270-404049 Maine Central Harvest Gold
- 270-404052 Maine Central Pine Green
- 270-404055 Toronto, Hamilton & Buffalo Cream
- 270-404058 CP Yellow
- 270-404061 CP Red
- 270-404064 PRR Buff
- 270-404067 TTX Yellow
- 270-404070 Depot Olive
- 270-404073 MOW Gray
- 270-404076 Coach Green
- 270-404079 Oxide Red
- 270-404082 Roof Red
- 270-404085 Signal Yellow
- 270-404088 Signal Green
- 270-404091 Signal Red
- 270-404094 Utility Orange
- 270-404097 Prussian Blue

Railroad Colors 1oz (30ml) 4.99 ea

- 270-414110 Steam Power Black
- 270-414113 Reefer White
- 270-414116 Reefer Gray
- 270-414119 Reefer Orange
- 270-414122 Reefer Yellow
- 270-414125 Railbox Yellow
- 270-414128 Caboose Red
- 270-414131 Aged White
- 270-414134 Undercoat Light Gray
- 270-414137 Grimy Black
- 270-414140 Tarnished Black
- 270-414143 ATSF Silver
- 270-414146 ATSF Catwhisker Yellow
- 270-414149 ATSF Red
- 270-414150 ATSF Blue
- 270-414152 MILW Orange
- 270-414155 MILW Maroon
- 270-414158 MILW Gray
- 270-414161 PRR Maroon
- 270-414164 PRR Brunswick Green
- 270-414167 PRR Tuscan
- 270-414170 UP Armor Yellow
- 270-414173 UP Dark Gray
- 270-414176 UP Harbor Gray
- 270-414179 SP Letter Gray
- 270-414182 SP Lark Dark Gray
- 270-414183 SP Scarlet
- 270-414185 SP Daylight Orange
- 270-414186 SP Daylight Red
- 270-414188 CNW Green
- 270-414191 CNW Yellow
- 270-414194 D&H Avon Blue
- 270-414197 D&H Gray
- 270-414200 WC Maroon
- 270-414203 GN Big Sky Blue
- 270-414206 CR Blue
- 270-414209 BN Green
- 270-414212 SOO Red
- 270-414215 CSX Yellow
- 270-414218 CSX Gray
- 270-414221 CSX Blue
- 270-414222 CSX Tan
- 270-414224 GN Orange

PAINT & PAINT SUPPLIES

FLOQUIL

- 270-414227 GN Empire Green
- 270-414228 GN Glacier Green
- 270-414230 Bangor & Aroostook Blue
- 270-414233 Bangor & Aroostook Gray
- 270-414236 EL Yellow
- 270-414239 EL Gray
- 270-414242 EL Maroon
- 270-414245 Boston & Maine Blue
- 270-414248 Rock Island Maroon
- 270-414251 CP Gray
- 270-414254 DRGW Orange
- 270-414255 DRGW Cream
- 270-414256 DRGW Brown
- 270-414257 DRGW Yellow
- 270-414258 DRGW Freight Red
- 270-414260 C&O Enchantment Blue
- 270-414263 Pacemaker Red
- 270-414266 Pacemaker Gray
- 270-414269 B&O Royal Blue
- 270-414272 Dark Green
- 270-414275 Roof Brown
- 270-414278 Depot Buff
- 270-414281 Box Car Red
- 270-414284 Pullman Green
- 270-414287 Vermont Green
- 270-414290 Engine Black
- 270-414293 Zinc Chromate Primer
- 270-414296 Stainless Steel
- 270-414299 Flat Aluminum
- 270-414302 Sand
- 270-414305 Dust
- 270-414308 Dirt
- 270-414311 Earth
- 270-414314 Mud
- 270-414317 Concrete
- 270-414320 Aged Concrete
- 270-414323 Rust
- 270-414326 Oily Black
- 270-414329 Railroad Tie Brown
- 270-414332 New Gravel Gray
- 270-414350 Mineral Red
- 270-414352 Light Freight Oxide Red
- 270-414354 Special Oxide Red
- 270-414356 Grand Trunk Western Morency Orange
- 270-414358 Grand Trunk Western Blue
- 270-414360 LV Cornell Red
- 270-414362 Detroit, Toledo & Ironton Cherry Red
- 270-414364 St. Lawrence Blue
- 270-414366 Weyerhauser Green
- 270-414368 Penn Central Green
- 270-414370 NYC Jade Green
- 270-414372 Guilford Gray
- 270-414374 SOU Sylvan Green
- 270-414376 RDG Green
- 270-414378 RDG Yellow
- 270-414380 L&N Gray
- 270-414382 Seaboard Air Line Chinese Red
- 270-414384 Seaboard Air Line Yellow
- 270-414386 Seaboard Air Line Orange
- 270-414388 Seaboard Coast Line Hopper Car Beige
- 270-414390 Seaboard Coast Line Hopper Car Yellow
- 270-414392 Seaboard Coast Line Caboose Orange
- **NEW** 270-414393 CSX New Image Blue YN3
- **NEW** 270-414394 CSX New Image Gold YN3
- **NEW** 270-414396 BNSF Heritage Orange
- **NEW** 270-414397 BNSF Heritage Green
- **NEW** 270-414398 BNSF Yellow

Polly Scale Air/Armor Colors 1/2oz (15ml) 3.99 ea

Recreate equipment from World War I to the present. Matched to Army/Navy (A/N), Federal Standard 595 (FS) and German WWII (RLM orders) as noted. Colors marked * indicate an approximate match to the Federal Standard color listed.

- 270-505011 White (RLM 21 *37886)
- 270-505014 Scale Black (RLM 66 *36081)
- 270-505017 Yellow (RLM 04 *33538)
- 270-505020 Red (RLM 23 FS 31302)
- 270-505023 Dark Blue (RLM 24 *25053)
- 270-505026 Green (RLM 25 *34108)
- 270-505029 Doped Linen (*33727)
- 270-505032 Brown Drab PC-10 (FS 34098)
- 270-505035 German Mauve (FS 37144)
- 270-505038 FR/FOK Dark Green (FS 34096)
- 270-505041 FR Chestnut Brown (FS 20140)
- 270-505044 FR Beige (FS 33546)
- 270-505051 Light Blue (RLM 65 *35352)
- 270-505055 Black Green (RLM 70 *34050)
- 270-505056 Dark Green (RLM 71 *34083)
- 270-505059 Dark Gray (RLM 74 *36081)
- 270-505060 Gray Violet (RLM 75 *36152)
- 270-505061 Light Gray (RLM 76 *36473)
- 270-505070 Brown Violet (RLM 81 *34079)
- 270-505071 Dark Green (RLM 82 *34083)
- 270-505072 Light Green (RLM 83 *34138)
- 270-505075 Gray (RLM 02 *16165)
- 270-505080 US Olive Drab (A/N613 *33070)
- 270-505082 US Medium Green (A/N612 *34092)
- 270-505084 US Sand (A/N616 *30279)
- 270-505086 US Neutral Gray (A/N603 *36118)
- 270-505088 USN Blue Gray (*35189)
- 270-505090 USN Light Gray (A/N602 *36440)
- 270-505092 USN Sea Blue (A/N607 *35045)
- 270-505094 USN Intermediate Blue (A/N608 *35164)
- 270-505096 US Interior Green (A/N611 *34089)
- 270-505098 US Olive Drab (*34088)
- 270-505110 Panzer Dark Gray (*36152)
- 270-505111 Panzer Dark Yellow (*33440)
- 270-505112 Panzer Red Brown (*30111)
- 270-505113 Panzer Olive Green (*34092)

Polly Scale Model & Hobby Colors 1/2oz (15ml) 3.99 ea

Matched to Federal Standard 595 (FS) and German WWII (RLM orders) as noted. Colors marked * indicate an approximate match to the Federal Standard color listed.

- 270-505200 Rust (FS 30215)
- 270-505202 Dust (FS 37778)
- 270-505204 Grimy Black (FS 36081)
- 270-505205 Dirty White
- 270-505206 Mud (FS 33440)
- 270-505208 Dirt (FS 30095)
- 270-505210 Old Concrete (FS 30318)
- 270-505212 Flesh (*32648)
- 270-505214 Night Black (22) (FS 37038)

U.S. Army Air Corps
- 270-505216 Blue (23) (*15102)
- 270-505218 Olive Drab (22) (FS 10118)
- 270-505220 Orange Yellow (4) (FS 13432)

U.S. Army
- 270-505222 Khaki (*30219)
- 270-505224 Olive Drab (FS 34087)

Get the Scoop!
Get the Skinny!
Get the Score!
Check Out Walthers
Web site at
www.walthers.com

Soviet Union (USSR)
- 270-505226 Underside Blue (FS 12500)
- 270-505228 Light Earth Brown (FS 33434)
- 270-505230 Topside Green (FS 34201)
- 270-505232 Dark Topside Gray (FS 36176)
- 270-505234 Light Topside Gray (FS 36270)

France
- 270-505236 Dark Blue Gray (FS 35164)
- 270-505238 Khaki (FS 34127)
- 270-505240 Earth Brown (*30140)
- 270-505242 Light Blue Gray (FS 36238)

Royal Australian Air Force
- 270-505244 Earth Brown (FS 30099)
- 270-505246 Foliage Green (FS 34092)
- 270-505248 Sky Blue (FS 35550)

Royal Air Force - Britain
- 270-505250 Dark Green (*34079)
- 270-505252 Dark Earth (*30118)
- 270-505254 Sky (Type "S" *34504)
- 270-505256 Ocean Grey (*35237)
- 270-505258 Sea Grey Med (FS 36293)
- 270-505260 Middlestone (*30266)
- 270-505262 Azure Blue (*35231)
- 270-505264 Extra Dark Sea Grey (*36118)
- 270-505266 Dark Slate Grey (*34096)
- 270-505268 P.R.U. Blue (*35189)
- 270-505270 Interior Grey Green (*34226)

Imperial Japanese Army
- 270-505272 Green (*34098)
- 270-505274 Light Gray (*36628)
- 270-505276 Brown (FS 30108)

Imperial Japanese Navy
- 270-505278 Green (*34058)
- 270-505280 Sky Gray (*36495)
- 270-505282 Deep Yellow (*33538)

Italian
- 270-505284 Hazel Tan (*30219)
- 270-505286 Camo Brown 2 (FS 10076)
- 270-505288 Camo Green (FS 34227)
- 270-505290 Light Blue Gray 1 (FS 36307)
- 270-505292 Camo Yellow 2 (FS 33481)
- 270-505294 Camo Yellow 3 (FS 33434)
- 270-505296 Dark Olive Green 2 (FS 34052)

Germany
- 270-505298 Uniform Gray (*34158)
- 270-505300 Dark Brown (RLM 61 - *30040)
- 270-505302 Green (RLM 62 *34128)
- 270-505304 Light Gray (RLM 63 - *36375)
- 270-505306 Light Blue (RLM 64 - *25414)
- 270-505308 Dark Olive Green (RLM 67 - *34151)
- 270-505310 Light Olive Green (RLM 68 - *34258)
- 270-505312 Light Tan (RLM 69 - *33695)
- 270-505314 72 Green (RLM 72 - *36081)
- 270-505316 73 Green (RLM 73 - *34064)
- 270-505318 78 Light Blue (RLM 78 - *35414)
- 270-505320 Sand Yellow (RLM 79 - *30215)
- 270-505322 Olive Green (RLM 80 *34083)
- 270-505324 Sky Green (RLM 84 *34554)

U.S. Navy
- 270-505326 Pale Blue Gray 5P (*36440)
- 270-505328 Light Gray 5L (*36373)
- 270-505330 Haze Gray 5H (*36251)
- 270-505332 Ocean Gray 50 (*36173)
- 270-505334 Navy Blue 5N (*36081)
- 270-505336 Deck Tan (FS 1735)
- 270-505338 Weathered Deck Blue 20-B (*36076)

Israel - Early
- 270-505340 Camo Blue (*35053)
- 270-505342 Tan (*31433)
- 270-505344 Light Gray (*37722)

Israel
- 270-505346 Gray (*36300)
- 270-505348 Khaki (*30277)

NATO Tricolor
- 270-505350 Black (FS 37038)
- 270-505352 Brown (FS 30051)
- 270-505354 Green (FS 34094)

Soviet
- 270-505356 Brown #2 (*32473)
- 270-505358 Green (*34226)
- 270-505360 Khaki #2 (*34088)
- 270-505362 Sand (*33798)
- 270-505368 Warsaw Pact Gray Green (*34258)

PAINT & PAINT SUPPLIES

FLOQUIL

U.S. - Modern
270-505364 Desert Storm Sand (FS 33446)
270-505366 Earth Red (FS 30117)
270-505370 Olive Drab (FS 34087)
270-505372 Brown Special (FS 30140)
270-505374 Dark Ghost Gray (FS 36320)
270-505376 Light Ghost Gray (FS 36375)
270-505378 Dark Gull Gray (FS 36231)
270-505380 Light Gull Gray (FS 36440)
270-505382 Gunship Gray (FS 36118)
270-505384 Neutral Gray (FS 36270)
270-505386 Tan Special (FS 10400)
270-505388 Tac Dark Green (FS 34079)
270-505390 Tac Mid-Green (FS 34102)
270-505392 USTAC Tan
270-505394 Tac Light Gray (FS 36622)
270-505396 Light Blue (FS 35622)

POLLY SCALE™ ACCESSORIES

Clear Finishes 3.49 ea
270-404100 Gloss 1/2oz

Decal Setting Solutions 3.15 ea
270-505401 Decal Softening Solution
A stronger solution, makes decals snuggle down in problem areas where surface detail is more pronounced.
270-505403 Decal Solution Set
Softens decal film to hug surface details. Works fast.

Plastic Cement
270-505408 Liquid 1/2oz (15ml) 4.75

Paint & Decal Remover
Slow acting, safe for plastics. Removes both paint and decals.
270-522142 2oz (60ml) 4.49
270-542143 8oz (240ml) 10.49

Plastic Prep
A pre-painting cleaner for use on plastics. Removes mold release, silicones, grease, etc. Leaves plastic clean, static-free and dust-free.

270-546007 8oz (240ml) 6.85
270-556007 16oz (0.47l) 9.99

Airbrush Thinner
Made for airbrush application of colors. For smoother mixing, better flow and faster drying.

270-546008 8oz (240ml) 8.99
270-556008 16oz (0.47l) 12.59

Mixing Bottles
Empty glass bottle with seals and lids. Ideal for mixing and storing custom colors or thinned paints for airbrushing.
270-190231 1/2oz (15ml) pkg(6) 5.94

270-190232 1oz (30ml) pkg(6) 7.14

BRUSHES
Manufactured and designed especially for the demands of hobby painting, all brushes are hand-made from the finest materials. Natural hairs or synthetic fibers are set in seamless nickel ferrules.

Red Sable
Prized for its ability to hold a needle point, found in detail and specific-use brushes.

Round 6.89 ea (Unless Noted)
270-201 #3 8.49
270-202 #2
270-203 #1
270-204 #0
270-205 3/0
270-206 5/0
270-207 10/0
270-208 15/0

Flat 8.49 ea (Unless Noted)
270-209 #4 8.99
270-210 #3
270-211 #2
270-212 #1

Kolinsky Premium 8.49 ea
270-101 #3
270-102 #0
270-103 3/0
270-104 5/0

Camel Hair
A blend of natural hairs obtained from various animals. Brushes are versatile and can be used with all types of colors.

Lacquering Series
270-501 1" 8.49
270-502 3/4" 6.89
270-503 1/2" 5.25
270-504 3/8" 5.25
270-505 1/4" 5.25

Round Detailing Series
270-506 #6 5.25
270-507 #5 5.25
270-508 #4 5.25
270-509 #3 5.25
270-510 #2 2.49
270-511 #1 2.49
270-512 #0 2.49
270-513 3/0 2.49
270-514 5/0 2.49

Silver Fox 8.49 ea
Brushes feature synthetic fibers, designed to provide excellent performance and longer life, with performance qualities like red sable.

Flat
270-401 1/4"
270-402 #4
270-403 #3
270-404 #2
270-405 #1

Round
270-406 #2
270-407 #0
270-408 3/0
270-409 5/0

Golden Fox
270-301 #1 Round 6.89
270-302 #0 Round 6.89
270-303 3/0 Round 6.89
270-304 5/0 6.89
270-305 10/0 8.49
270-306 20/0 8.49
270-307 25/0 8.49
270-308 #4 Flat 8.49
270-309 #2 Flat 8.49

Recommended Air Pressures & Thinning Ratios For Airbrushing
All measurements are approximate. Thinning ratio and pressure needed may vary, depending upon the type of finish required or brand of compressor.

Always Test First!
Floquil solvent-based Model Railroad.
Thinning Ratio: 75% color, 5% glaze, 20% Thinner-Brush Cleaner. Approximate Pressure: 12-20lbs.

Clear Coatings
Crystal-Cote Thinning Ratio: Usually none required, if needed use Airbrush Thinner. Approximate Pressure: 12-20 lbs.

Polly Scale Colors
Thinning Ratio: 10-15% distilled water. Approximate Pressure: 15-20lbs.

IMPORTANT: For best results, it's imperative that your airbrush be cleaned thoroughly when you are done spraying to keep paint from drying inside and clogging the spray tip. This should be done immediately, especially when using acrylics, which set up faster than enamels and lacquers.

GB ENGINEERING

Work Holder

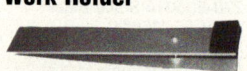

298-600 Painting Handle **7.50**
Hold models securely and keep your hands clean while you paint. Works well with all types of models. "V"-shaped aluminum handle has foam pads on ends to prevent damage. Spring-loaded legs are adjusted with screw and nut to provide constant holding force. Secure grip lets you safely turn model to any position while airbrushing or spray painting.

NOCH

IMPORTED FROM GERMANY BY WALTHERS

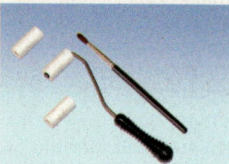

528-60142 Micro Paint Roller **28.99** 29/32" wide 2.25cm
528-60143 Replacement Rollers for Micro Paint Roller pkg(3) **7.99**

ROBART

Paint Shaker

547-411 Electrically Powered **37.95**
Keep your hobby paints mixed and ready to use. Great for mixing thinner and paint when airbrushing or blending custom colors. Eliminates messy stirring sticks and paint spills. Paint is shaken at 5,000 cycles/minute. Adjustable rubber strap holds all 1/4, 1/3, 1/2, 5/8 and 1oz bottles. Assembled and ready for use. Complete with transformer, plugs into any U.S. standard outlet (110V AC).

547-415 Replacement Straps pkg(5) **5.45**
Adjustable replacement straps for shaker.

For Up-To-Date Information and News Bookmark Walthers Web site at
www.walthers.com

PAINT & PAINT SUPPLIES

iwata
Professional Airbrushes

AIRBRUSHES

Iwata Revolution

Manufactured with the same high-quality materials as the rest of the Iwata line. These general-purpose, high-flow airbrushes are able to spray detail and background work, as well as a variety of different paint types. They feature a siphon feed assembly, a larger needle chucking nut for easy assembly, a trigger with an attached auxiliary lever to the needle chuck guide, and easy-to-replace internal Teflon needle packing for use with any types of solvent-based paints.

385-R2001 Dual Action w/Hose **115.00**

Item listed below is available by Special Order (see Legend Page).
358-R1000 Single Action **95.00**

Eclipse Airbrush

358-2001 Eclipse Bottle Feed Airbrush Set **157.00**
The Eclipse airbrush is a dual-action, internal-mix, bottom-feed airbrush designed for fine artists, wall muralists, students and hobbyists. The .5mm needle and nozzle combination allows for a spray pattern from fine lines to large backgrounds, thin to heavy paints and stippling patterns. Set includes airbrush, paint jar and braided hose. High-paint flow, high-detail airbrush covers a wide range of uses. This Eclipse airbrush is both easy to maintain and highly durable. Commonly used to spray premixed or heavier paints, it is well-suited for uses demanding precise control of spray when applying moderate to large amounts of paint to a variety of surfaces and to various-sized areas.

AIRBRUSH ADAPTERS

Airhose Adapters 8.50 ea

Allows conversion of most other manufacturers' airbrush hoses to be used with Iwata airbrushes.

358-1001 Adapts Iwata Airbrushes to Paasche Airhoses

358-1002 Adapts Iwata Airbrushes to Badger or Thayer & Chandler Airhoses

Quick Disconnect Set

Item listed below is available by Special Order (see Legend Page).
358-11601 Fits Iwata Airhose **52.50**
Allows use of multiple airbrushes with one air source and hose. This miniature quick disconnect completely shuts off air flow when disconnected and fits all Iwata airhoses and airbrushes. With its quick-release action, changing airbrushes is fast and easy. Iwata quick disconnects are rated for air pressures up to 120 P.S.I.

Quick Disconnect Adapter

Item listed below is available by Special Order (see Legend Page).
358-11602 **11.50**
For adapting Iwata airbrushes to a quick disconnect airhose. The adapters screw onto each airbrush and are used in conjunction with the quick disconnect set on the airhose.

AIRBRUSH ACCESSORIES

Braided Nylon Covered PVC Airhose

358-10 For Iwata (10') **25.50**

Caps

Items listed below are available by Special Order (see Legend Page).

Head
358-16031 For Eclipse Airbrushes **11.50**

Needle
358-16011 For Eclipse Airbrushes **5.25**

Nozzle
358-16021 For Eclipse Bottom Feed & Revolution Single Action Airbrushes **8.50**

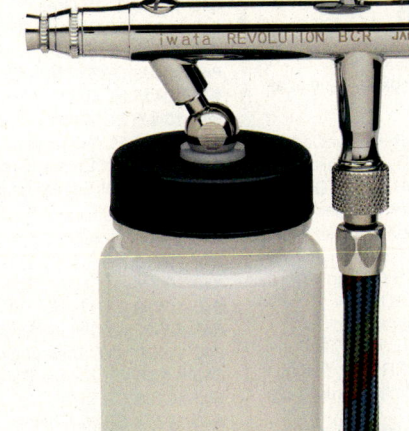

Revolution Airbrush Set 358-R2001

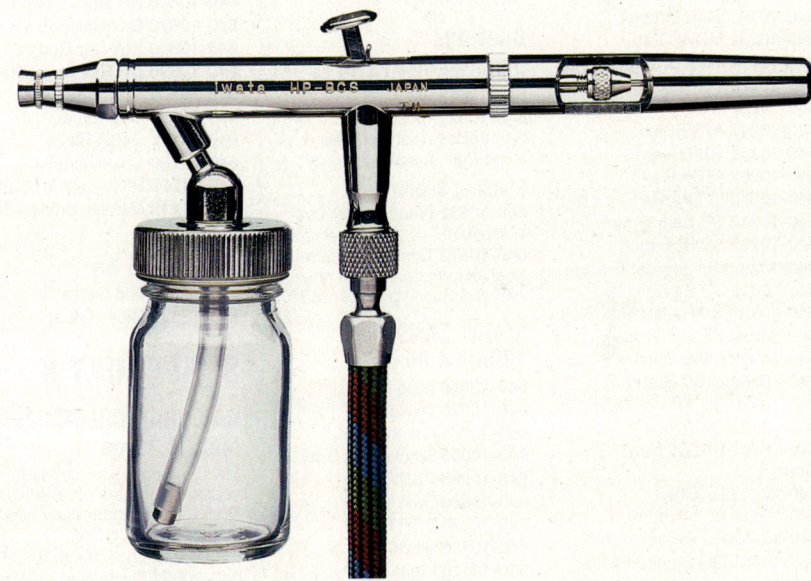

Eclipse Bottle Feed Airbrush Set 358-2001

- **Precision Made**
- **One Needle/One Tip Does It All**
- **Get A Fine Line Up To A 2" Spray Pattern**
- **Easy To Use & Easy To Clean**

Handles

Item listed below is available by Special Order (see Legend Page).

Single Cut
358-16191 For Eclipse Bottom Feed, Side Feed & Gravity Feed Airbrushes **23.00**

Jars 6.00 ea

Items listed below are available by Special Order (see Legend Page). Jars are made of high-strength translucent plastic.

358-14802 2oz 56ml
358-14803 3oz 84ml

Needles 8.50 ea

358-16172 .35mm For Eclipse Side Feed & Gravity Feed Airbrushes

Items listed below are available by Special Order (see Legend Page).
358-17171 For Revolution Single- or Dual-Action Airbrushes

358-16171 .55mm For Eclipse Bottom Feed & Revolution Single Action Airbrushes

Needle Chucking Nut

358-11202 For Eclipse Airbrushes **5.25**

Nozzles

Items listed below are available by Special Order (see Legend Page).
358-17041 For Revolution Single- or Dual-Action Airbrushes **23.00**

358-16041 .50mm For Eclipse Bottom Feed & Revolution Single Action Airbrushes **11.50**

358-16042 .35mm For Eclipse Side Feed & Gravity Feed Airbrushes **23.00**

Packing Head (O-Ring)

Item listed below is available by Special Order (see Legend Page).
358-16051 For Eclipse Airbrushes **5.25**

PAINT & PAINT SUPPLIES

SCALECOAT

Scalecoat I and II also available in 1oz bottles. Please visit Walthers web site at www.walthers.com for a complete listing of all available products.

SCALECOAT I

RAILROAD COLORS 2oz 60ml 4.19 ea

- 640-10012 Locomotive Black (Low Gloss Finish)
- 640-10022 Oxide Red (Low Gloss Finish)
- 640-10032 Graphite & Oil (Low Gloss Finish)
- 640-10052 Smoke Box Gray
- 640-10062 Brunswick Green
- 640-10082 D&H Yellow
- 640-10092 D&H Blue
- 640-10102 Black
- 640-10112 White
- 640-10122 Tuscan Red
- 640-10132 Box Car Red
- 640-10142 Caboose Red
- 640-10152 Reefer Yellow
- 640-10162 Reefer Orange
- 640-10172 Pullman Green
- 640-10182 Coach Olive
- 640-10192 SOU Green
- 640-10202 MOW Gray
- 640-10212 Roof Brown
- 640-10222 UP Yellow
- 640-10232 Silver
- 640-10242 ATSF Blue
- 640-10252 GN Green
- 640-10262 ATSF Red
- 640-10272 IC Orange
- 640-10282 SP Dark Gray
- 640-10292 SP Scarlet
- 640-10302 SP Daylight Orange
- 640-10312 SP Daylight Red
- 640-10322 UP Harbor Mist Gray
- 640-10332 UP Dark Gray
- 640-10352 CNW Canary Yellow
- 640-10362 CNW Green
- 640-10372 B&O Royal Blue
- 640-10382 BN Green
- 640-10402 DRGW New Orange
- 640-10412 EL Gray
- 640-10422 EL Maroon
- 640-10432 EL Yellow
- 640-10452 GN Empire Builder Green
- 640-10462 GN Empire Builder Orange
- 640-10472 Aluminum
- 640-10602 NP Light Green
- 640-10612 NP Dark Green
- 640-10622 LV Cornell Red
- 640-10632 D&H Gray
- 640-10652 NYC Light Gray
- 640-10662 NYC Dark Gray
- 640-10692 CP Tuscan Red
- 640-10752 CR Blue
- 640-10762 CB&Q Chinese Red
- 640-10772 RDG Green
- 640-10782 BNSF Orange
- 640-10792 BNSF Green
- 640-10802 BNSF White
- 640-10812 PRR Freight Car Red
- 640-10822 N&W Red
- 640-10832 MILW Orange
- 640-10842 UP Hopper Car Gray
- 640-10852 New UP Yellow
- 640-10862 NH Hunter Green
- 640-10872 Box Car Red #2
- 640-10882 Box Car Red #3
- 640-10892 CP Rail Bright Red
- 640-10902 NH Orange
- 640-10912 C&O Blue
- 640-11122 Detail Black
- 640-11192 Chessie Yellow
- 640-11202 PRR Dark Tuscan
- 640-11212 Metallic Smoke Box Gray

Scalecoat Thinner

- 640-10487 Can 8oz .24L 4.75
- 640-10499 Can 1qt .95L 9.95
- 640-10502 Bottle 2oz 60mL 2.79

Strippers

- 640-10568 Paint Remover 16oz .47L 8.95
- 640-10599 Metal Stripper 32oz .48L Can 10.95

Coatings

Glaze 2oz 60ml 4.19 ea
- 640-10512 Flat
- 640-10522 Gloss Semi-gloss finish, with less shine than actual paint finish.

Sanding Sealer
- 640-10532 Wood Sealer 2oz 60mL 4.19
- 640-10572 Thinner 2oz 60mL Special formula, for use only with #53 Sanding Sealer. 2.79

SPRAY CANS 6oz 180ML 6.95 ea

- 640-10016 Loco Black
- 640-10026 Oxide Red
- 640-10036 Graphite & Oil
- 640-10056 Smoke Box Gray
- 640-10066 PRR Green
- 640-10086 D&H Yellow
- 640-10096 D&H Blue
- 640-10106 Black
- 640-10116 White
- 640-10126 Tuscan Red
- 640-10136 Box Car Red
- 640-10146 Caboose Red
- 640-10156 Reefer Yellow
- 640-10166 Reefer Orange
- 640-10176 Pullman Green
- 640-10186 Coach Olive
- 640-10196 SOU Green
- 640-10206 MOW Gray
- 640-10216 Roof Brown
- 640-10226 UP Yellow
- 640-10236 Silver
- 640-10246 ATSF Blue
- 640-10256 GN Green
- 640-10266 ATSF Red
- 640-10276 IC Orange
- 640-10286 SP Dark Gray
- 640-10296 SP Scarlet
- 640-10306 SP Daylight Orange
- 640-10316 SP Daylight Red
- 640-10326 UP Harbor Gray
- 640-10336 UP Dark Gray
- 640-10356 CNW Yellow
- 640-10366 CNW Green
- 640-10376 B&O Royal Blue
- 640-10386 BN Green
- 640-10406 DRGW New Orange
- 640-10416 EL Gray
- 640-10426 EL Maroon
- 640-10436 EL Yellow
- 640-10456 GN Empire Green
- 640-10466 GN Empire Orange
- 640-10476 Aluminum
- 640-10606 NP Light Green
- 640-10616 NP Dark Green
- 640-10626 LV Cornell Red
- 640-10636 D&H Gray
- 640-10656 NYC Light Gray
- 640-10666 NYC Dark Gray
- 640-10696 CP Tuscan Red
- 640-10756 CR Blue
- 640-10766 CB&Q Chinese Red
- 640-10776 RDG Green
- 640-10786 BNSF Orange
- 640-10796 BNSF Green
- 640-10806 BNSF White
- 640-10816 PRR Freight Car Red
- 640-10826 N&W Red
- 640-10836 MILW Orange
- 640-10846 UP Hopper Gray
- 640-10856 New UP Yellow
- 640-10866 NH Hunter Green
- 640-10876 Box Car Red #2
- 640-10886 Box Car Red #3
- 640-10896 CP Rail Bright Red
- 640-10906 NH Orange
- 640-10916 C&O Blue
- 640-11126 Detail Black
- 640-11196 Chessie Yellow
- 640-11206 PRR Dark Tuscan
- 640-11216 Metallic Smoke Box Gray

Glaze 6.95 ea
- 640-10516 Flat Glaze
- 640-10526 Gloss Glaze

SCALECOAT II

RAILROAD COLORS 2oz 60ml 4.19 ea

Matching colors formulated especially for use on plastics. Drying time can be decreased by adding Quick-Dry.

- 640-20012 Locomotive Black
- 640-20022 Oxide Red
- 640-20032 Graphite & Oil
- 640-20052 Smoke Box Gray
- 640-20062 PRR Brunswick Green
- 640-20082 D&H Yellow
- 640-20092 D&H Blue
- 640-20102 Black
- 640-20112 White
- 640-20122 Tuscan Red
- 640-20132 Box Car Red
- 640-20142 Caboose Red
- 640-20152 Reefer Yellow
- 640-20162 Reefer Orange
- 640-20172 Pullman Green
- 640-20182 Coach Olive
- 640-20192 SOU Green
- 640-20202 MOW Gray
- 640-20212 Roof Brown
- 640-20222 UP Yellow
- 640-20232 Silver
- 640-20242 ATSF Blue
- 640-20252 GN Green
- 640-20262 ATSF Red
- 640-20272 IC Orange
- 640-20282 SP Dark Gray
- 640-20292 SP Scarlet
- 640-20302 SP Daylight Orange
- 640-20312 SP Daylight Red
- 640-20322 UP Harbor Mist Gray
- 640-20332 UP Dark Gray
- 640-20352 CNW Yellow
- 640-20362 CNW Green
- 640-20372 B&O Royal Blue
- 640-20382 BN Green
- 640-20402 DRGW New Orange
- 640-20412 EL Gray
- 640-20422 EL Maroon
- 640-20432 EL Yellow
- 640-20452 GN Empire Builder Green
- 640-20462 GN Empire Builder Orange
- 640-20472 Aluminum
- 640-20602 NP Light Green
- 640-20612 NP Dark Green
- 640-20622 LV Cornell Red
- 640-20632 D&H Gray
- 640-20652 NYC Light Gray
- 640-20662 NYC Dark Gray
- 640-20692 CP Tuscan Red
- 640-20752 CR Blue
- 640-20762 CB&Q Chinese Red
- 640-20772 RDG Green
- 640-20782 BNSF Orange
- 640-20792 BNSF Green
- 640-20802 BNSF White
- 640-20812 PRR Freight Car Red
- 640-20822 N&W Red
- 640-20832 MILW Orange
- 640-20842 UP Hopper Car Gray
- 640-20852 New UP Yellow
- 640-20862 NH Hunter Green
- 640-20872 Box Car Red #2
- 640-20882 Box Car Red #3
- 640-20892 CP Rail Bright Red
- 640-20902 NH Orange
- 640-20912 C&O Blue
- 640-21122 Detail Black
- 640-21192 Chessie Yellow
- 640-21202 PRR Dark Tuscan
- 640-21212 Metallic Smoke Box Gray

Scalecoat II Thinner
- 640-20487 Can 8oz .24L 4.75
- 640-20499 Can 1qt .97L 9.95
- 640-20502 Bottle 2oz 60mL 2.79

Quick Dry
- 640-10542 Quick-Dry 2oz 60mL 4.19
Speeds drying time of Scalecoat colors on plastic and wood. Drying times varies.

SPRAY CANS 6oz 180ML 6.95 ea
- 640-20016 Loco Black
- 640-20026 Oxide Red
- 640-20036 Graphite & Oil
- 640-20056 Smoke Box Gray
- 640-20066 PRR Green
- 640-20086 D&H Yellow
- 640-20096 D&H Blue
- 640-20106 Black
- 640-20116 White
- 640-20126 Tuscan Red
- 640-20136 Box Car Red
- 640-20146 Caboose Red
- 640-20156 Reefer Yellow
- 640-20166 Reefer Orange
- 640-20176 Pullman Green
- 640-20186 Coach Olive
- 640-20196 SOU Green
- 640-20206 MOW Gray
- 640-20216 Roof Brown
- 640-20226 UP Yellow
- 640-20236 Silver
- 640-20246 ATSF Blue
- 640-20256 GN Green
- 640-20266 ATSF Red
- 640-20276 IC Orange
- 640-20286 SP Dark Gray
- 640-20296 SP Scarlet
- 640-20306 SP Daylight Orange
- 640-20316 SP Daylight Red
- 640-20326 UP Harbor Gray
- 640-20336 UP Dark Gray
- 640-20356 CNW Yellow
- 640-20366 CNW Green
- 640-20376 B&O Royal Blue
- 640-20386 BN Green
- 640-20406 DRGW New Orange
- 640-20416 EL Gray
- 640-20426 EL Maroon
- 640-20436 EL Yellow
- 640-20456 GN Empire Builder Green
- 640-20466 GN Empire Builder Orange
- 640-20476 Aluminum
- 640-20606 NP Light Green
- 640-20616 NP Dark Green
- 640-20626 LV Cornell Red
- 640-20636 D&H Gray
- 640-20656 NYC Light Gray
- 640-20666 NYC Dark Gray
- 640-20696 CP Tuscan Red
- 640-20756 CR Blue
- 640-20766 CB&Q Chinese Red
- 640-20776 RDG Green
- 640-20786 BNSF Orange
- 640-20796 BNSF Green
- 640-20806 BNSF White
- 640-20816 PRR Freight Car Red
- 640-20826 N&W Red
- 640-20836 MILW Orange
- 640-20846 UP Hopper Gray
- 640-20856 New UP Yellow
- 640-20866 NH Hunter Green
- 640-20876 Box Car Red #2
- 640-20886 Box Car Red #3
- 640-20896 CP Rail Bright Red
- 640-20906 NH Orange
- 640-20916 C&O Blue
- 640-21126 Detail Black
- 640-21196 Chessie Yellow
- 640-21206 PRR Dark Tuscan
- 640-21216 Metallic Smoke Box Gray

PAINT & PAINT SUPPLIES

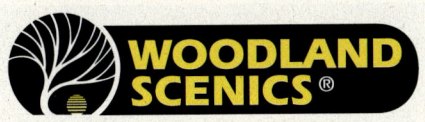

MINI-SCENE™ PAINT SET

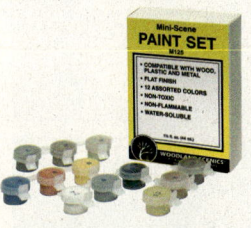

785-125 Set of 12 **6.98**
For metal details. Set includes 12 assorted colors each 1-1/2 fluid ounces (44ml): red, yellow, blue, black, gray, white, cream, tan, rust, yellow ocher, brown and pewter. Paint is nontoxic, nonflammable and water-soluble.

TOP COAT

4.49 ea
Use full-strength or dilute with water. Color highways, streets and sidewalks with Concrete Top Coat. For blacktop surfaces use Asphalt Top Coat.

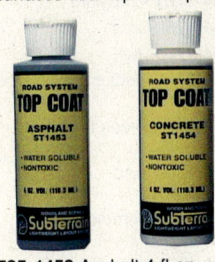

785-1453 Asphalt 4 fl oz
785-1454 Concrete 4 fl oz

PEWTER PATINA FINISH

785-126 7/8 fl oz (30ml) Bottle **2.29**
Gives any metal the look of a fine pewter casting. Great for figures or special effects. Dealers MUST order multiples of 5.

EARTH COLOR KIT

785-1215 18.98
A simple system for staining rocks, terrain, and plaster castings such as portals. Beginners get quality results. The Earth Color kit includes instructions, applicator, palette and eight one Fluid ounce bottles each of Earth Color, Liquid Pigment (White, Black, Concrete, Stone Gray, Slate Gray, Raw Umber, Burnt Umber and Yellow Ocher).

UNDERCOAT

8 Fluid Ounce Bottle 6.98 ea
Formulated for use under Blended Turf to provide a base color for terrain. Extremely concentrated.

785-1228 Green

785-1229 Earth

MINI-SCENE™ GLASS DISPLAY DOME

785-127 with Plastic Base **11.49**
Perfect for protecting and displaying small scenes, figures and keepsakes. Features plastic base with separate clear glass dome; measures 3" 7.5cm in diameter.

EARTH COLORS LIQUID PIGMENTS

4 Fluid Ounce Bottle 5.29 ea
Use these eight different pigments to stain rocks, terrain and other plaster castings. They are water-soluble and can be diluted and blended in endless combinations. Extremely concentrated for economical usage.

785-1216 White

785-1220 Black

785-1217 Concrete

785-1221 Raw Umber

785-1218 Stone Gray

785-1222 Burnt Umber

785-1219 Slate Gray

785-1223 Yellow Ocher

For Daily Product Updates Point Your Browser to
www.walthers.com

PAINT & PAINT SUPPLIES

A complete line of colors for railroad, automobile and military modelers. Enamel, acrylic and lacquer formulas are available to meet your painting needs.

ENAMELS

Bottles - 1/4oz (7.5ml) 1.49 ea

All-purpose paints are fast drying, easy to apply, and can be used on many different surfaces. Colors are carefully controlled from batch to batch so that each bottle exactly matches the corresponding spray. Use on styrene, ABS plastic, wood, metal, leather, glass, wax and other materials. Colors dry fast to a hard gloss finish (unless noted).

Dealers MUST order multiples of 12.

704-1103 Red
704-1104 Dark Red
704-1108 Light Blue
704-1110 Medium Blue
704-1111 Dark Blue
704-1112 Pale Yellow
704-1114 Yellow
704-1116 Cream
704-1124 Green
704-1127 Orange
704-1133 Light Brown
704-1134 Purple
704-1138 Gray
704-1140 Brown
704-1141 Wood
704-1144 Gold
704-1145 White Gloss
704-1146 Silver
704-1147 Black Gloss
704-1149 Flat Black
704-1150 Flat Red
704-1151 Copper
704-1152 Metallic Red

Brush-On Metal Flake
704-1529 Ruby Red
704-1530 Jade Green
704-1531 Burgundy Purple
704-1539 Sapphire Blue
704-1542 Lime Gold

Military Flat Colors
704-1162 Sky Blue
704-1163 Battle Gray
704-1164 Olive Drab Green
704-1165 Army Olive
704-1166 Military Brown
704-1167 Desert Tan
704-1168 White
704-1169 Yellow
704-1170 Light Tan
704-1171 Beret Green
704-1172 Sea Blue
704-1180 Steel

704-1181 Aluminum
704-1182 Brass
704-1183 Rubber
704-1184 Zinc Chromate
704-1185 Rust

SPRAY ENAMELS

3oz (90ml) 4.49 ea

Matching colors for bottled colors in a handy spray can. Dries to hard gloss finish unless noted.

Dealers MUST order multiples of 3.

704-1203 Red
704-1204 Dark Red
704-1208 Light Blue
704-1210 Bright Blue
704-1211 Dark Blue
704-1214 Yellow
704-1224 Green
704-1226 Aircraft Gray
704-1231 Bright Red
704-1233 Flat Light Gray
704-1234 Purple
704-1237 Primer
704-1238 Gray
704-1240 Brown
704-1241 Wood
704-1244 Gold
704-1245 White Gloss
704-1246 Silver
704-1247 Black Gloss
704-1249 Flat Black
704-1250 Flat Red
704-1251 Copper
704-1257 Transparent Blue
704-1258 Flat White
704-1261 Glosscote
704-1265 Flat Olive Drab

Spray Custom Colors
704-1601 Candy Emerald Green
704-1605 Candy Apple Red
704-1607 Candy Hot Rod Red
704-1617 Candy Grape
704-1628 Competition Orange

Spray Metal Flake
704-1629 Ruby Red
704-1630 Jade Green
704-1631 Burgundy Purple
704-1639 Sapphire Blue
704-1642 Lime Gold

Chrome Spray
704-1290 Chrome Silver

Automotive Enamels
704-1801 Cherry Red
704-1804 Blue Pearl Metallic
704-1813 Black Pearl

MODEL MASTER

FS Enamels 1/2oz (15ml) Bottles 2.99 ea (Unless Noted)

FS Series colors match Federal Standard number indicated. Bottled paints are specially formulated for airbrushing, with popular colors also offered in spray cans.

Dealers MUST order in multiples of 6.

704-1701 Military Brown (FS 30117)
704-1702 Field Drab (FS 30118)
704-1704 Armor Sand (FS 30277)
704-1705 Insignia Red (FS 31136)
704-1706 Sand (FS 33531)
704-1707 Chrome Yellow (FS 13538)
704-1708 Insignia Yellow (FS 33538)
704-1709 Radome Tan (FS 33613)
704-1710 Dark Green (FS 34079)
704-1711 Olive Drab (FS 34087)
704-1712 Field Green (FS 34097)
704-1713 Medium Green (FS 34102)
704-1714 Forest Green (FS 34127)
704-1715 Interior Green (FS 34151)
704-1716 Pale Green (FS 34227)
704-1717 Dark Sea Blue (FS 15042)
704-1718 Flat Sea Blue (FS 35042)
704-1719 Insignia Blue (FS 35044)
704-1720 Intermediate Blue (FS 35164)
704-1721 Medium Gray (FS 35237)
704-1722 Duck Egg Blue (FS 35622)
704-1723 Gunship Gray (FS 36118)
704-1725 Neutral Gray (FS 36270)
704-1726 Light Sea Gray (FS 36307)
704-1728 Light Ghost Gray (FS 36375)
704-1729 Gloss Gull Gray (FS 16440)
704-1730 Flat Gull Gray (FS 36440)
704-1731 Aircraft Gray (FS 16473)
704-1732 Light Gray (FS 36495)
704-1733 Camouflage Gray (FS 36622)
704-1734 Green Zinc Chromate
704-1735 Wood
704-1736 Leather
704-1740 Dark Gull Gray (FS 36231)
704-1741 Dark Ghost Gray (FS 36320)
704-1742 Dark Tan (FS 30219)
704-1744 Gold
704-1745 Insignia White (FS 17875)
704-1747 Gloss Black (FS 17038)
704-1749 Flat Black (FS 37038)
704-1764 Euro Dark Green (FS 34092)
704-1768 Flat White (FS 37875)
704-1772 Blue Angel Blue (FS 15050)
704-1775 Fluorescent Red (FS 28915)
704-1780 Steel
704-1781 Aluminum
704-1782 Brass
704-1785 Rust
704-1786 Medium Field Green (FS 34095)
704-1787 Green Drab (FS 34086)
704-1788 Euro 1 Gray (FS 36081)
704-1790 Chrome Silver (FS 17178)
704-1791 Navy Gloss Gray (FS 16081)
704-1792 SAC Bomber Tan (FS 34201)
704-1793 SAC Bomber Green (FS 34159)
704-1794 Navy Aggressor Gray (FS 36251)
704-1795 Gunmetal
704-1796 Jet Exhaust
704-2021 Tan (FS 20400)
704-2022 International Orange (FS 12197 - Gloss)
704-2023 Blue Angels Yellow (FS 13655 - Gloss)
704-2024 US Army Helo Drab (FS 34031)
704-2025 Marine Corps Green (FS 34052)
704-2026 Dark Drab (B-52 FS 24091- Semi-Gloss)
704-2027 Dark Green (B-52 FS 34096)
704-2028 Willow Green (FS 14187 - Gloss)
704-2029 Green (FS 34258)

PAINT & PAINT SUPPLIES

704-2030 True Blue (FS 15102 - Gloss)
704-2031 Blue (FS 35109)
704-2032 Bright Blue (FS 35183)
704-2033 Blue (FS 35414)
704-2034 Engine Gray (FS 36076)
704-2035 Air Mobility Command Gray (FS 36173)
704-2036 Dark Gray (F-15 FS 36176)
704-2037 Flint Gray (FS 36314)
704-2038 Light Gray (FS 36492)
704-2039 Canadian Voodoo Gray (FS 16515)
704-2040 Aircraft Interior Black (FS 37031)
704-2041 Fluorescent Red-Orange (FS 28913-Semi Gloss)

Figure Colors
Special flat colors for skin tones and uniforms.
704-2001 Skin Tone-Light Base
704-2002 Skin Tone-Dark Base
704-2003 Skin Tone-Warm Tint
704-2004 Skin Tone-Shadow Tint
704-2005 Burnt Umber
704-2006 Raw Umber
704-2007 Burnt Sienna
704-2008 Raw Sienna
704-2009 British Crimson
704-2010 Piping Pink
704-2011 Cadmium Yellow Light
704-2012 Cobalt Blue
704-2013 Napoleonic Violet
704-2014 German Uniform Feldgrau
704-2015 Flat Clear Lacquer **3.29**
704-2016 Semi-Gloss Clear Lacquer **3.29**
704-2017 Gloss Clear Lacquer **3.29**
704-2018 Thinner **3.29**

Decal Solutions
704-2145 Solvent
704-2146 Setting

World War II United States & Royal Air Force
704-2048 RAF Azure Blue (ANA 609)
704-2049 RAF Sky Type "S" (ANA 610)
704-2050 Olive Drab (ANA 613)
704-2051 Faded Olive Drab
704-2052 RAF Middlestone (ANA 615)
704-2053 Sand (ANA 616)
704-2054 Dark Earth (ANA 617)
704-2055 Navy Blue Gray
704-2056 RAF Dark Slate Grey
704-2057 RAF Ocean Gray
704-2058 RAF Medium Sea Grey
704-2059 RAF Dark Sea Gray
704-2060 RAF Dark Green
704-2061 RAF P.R.U. Blue
704-2062 RAF Interior Green
704-2063 RAF Trainer Yellow

World War II Italian Colors
704-2110 Sand
704-2111 Dark Brown
704-2112 Olive Green
704-2113 Blue Gray

World War II German Luftwaffe
These semi-gloss colors match the RLM specifications for camouflage colors used on German Aircraft during World War II.
704-2071 Grun (RLM 02)
704-2072 Gelb (RLM 04)
704-2073 Rot (RLM 23)
704-2074 Dunkelblau (RLM 24)
704-2075 Dunkelbraun (RLM 61)
704-2076 Grun (RLM 62)
704-2077 Lichtgrau (RLM 63)
704-2078 Hellblau (RLM 65)
704-2079 Schwarzgrau (RLM 66)
704-2080 Schwarzgrun (RLM 70)
704-2081 Dunkelgrun (RLM 71)
704-2082 Grun (RLM 72)
704-2083 Grun (RLM 73)
704-2084 Graugrun (RLM 74)
704-2085 Grauviolett (RLM 75)
704-2086 Lichtblau (RLM 76)
704-2087 Hellblau (RLM 78)
704-2088 Sandgelb (RLM 79)
704-2089 Olivgrun (RLM 80)
704-2090 Braunviolett (RLM 81)
704-2091 Dunkelgrun (RLM 82)
704-2092 Lichtgrun (RLM 83)

World War II German Panzer Colors
704-2094 Schwarzgrau (1939-43 RAL 7021)
704-2095 Panzer Dunkelgelb
704-2096 Schokololaden-braun (1943 RAL 8017)
704-2097 Panzer Olivgrun 1943
704-2098 Afrika Khakibraun 1941 (RAL 7008)
704-2099 Afrika Grunbraun 1941 (RAL 8000)
704-2100 Signalbraun (RAL 8002)
704-2101 Anthracitgrau (RAL 7016)
704-2102 Afrika Braun 1942 (RAL 8020)
704-2103 Afrika Dunkelgrau 1942 (RAL 7027)
704-2104 Panzer Interior Buff-Semi-Gloss

World War II French Colors
704-2105 Dark Blue Gray
704-2106 Khaki
704-2107 Chestnut
704-2108 Earth Brown
704-2109 Light Blue Gray

World War II Japanese Colors
704-2114 Imperial Japanese Army Green
704-2115 Imperial Japanese Army Light Gray
704-2116 Imperial Japanese Navy Green
704-2117 Imperial Japanese Navy Gray
704-2118 Deep Yellow
704-2119 Interior Metallic Blue

World War II Russian Colors
704-2120 Topside Gray
704-2121 Underside Gray
704-2122 Topside Green
704-2123 Underside Blue
704-2124 Earth Brown
704-2125 Earth Gray
704-2126 Topside Blue
704-2127 Marker Red
704-2128 Marker Yellow
704-2129 Russian Armor Green

Modern Russian Colors
All colors have a semi-gloss finish.
704-2130 Flanker Pale Blue
704-2131 Flanker Medium Blue
704-2132 Flanker Blue/Gray
704-2133 Fulcrum Gray
704-2134 Fulcrum Gray/Green
704-2135 Interior Blue/Green

Modern Armor (Gulf War) Colors
704-2136 US Army/Marines Gulf Armor Sand
704-2137 British Gulf Armor Light Stone
704-2138 Israeli Armor Sand/Gray

Tint Whites
704-2142 Flat White (FS 37295)
704-2143 Semi-Gloss White (RLM 21)
704-2144 Gloss White (FS 17295)

Automotive Enamels
704-2702 Arctic Blue Metallic
704-2709 Light Ivory
704-2710 Sand Beige
704-2711 Anthracite Gray Metallic
704-2712 Graphite Metallic
704-2713 Black Metallic
704-2714 German Silver Metallic
704-2715 French Blue
704-2716 British Green Metallic
704-2717 Bright Yellow
704-2718 Guards Red
704-2719 Italian Red
704-2720 Classic White
704-2721 Classic Black
704-2723 Turn Signal Amber
704-2724 Stop Light Red
704-2725 Header Flat White
704-2726 Ford Engine Light Blue
704-2727 Ford/GM Engine Blue
704-2728 Pontiac Engine Blue
704-2729 Oldsmobile Engine Blue
704-2730 Chrysler Engine Blue
704-2731 Chevy Engine Red
704-2732 Chrysler Engine Red
704-2733 Ford Engine Red
704-2734 Silver Chrome Trim
704-2735 Black Chrome Trim
704-2736 Clear Top Coat
704-2737 Gray Primer
704-2738 Flat Interior Tan
704-2739 Flat Interior Gray
704-2740 Semi-Gloss Black
704-2750 Plum Crazy
704-2755 Hot Magenta
704-2757 Panther Pink
704-2764 Grabber Blue
704-2765 Turquoise
704-2767 Sublime Green
704-2770 Go Mango

Limited Quantity Available
704-2703 Copenhagen Blue Metallic **2.69**
704-2704 Kiln Red Metallic **2.69**

Spray Enamels 3oz (90ml) 4.99 ea
Dealers MUST order multiples of 3.
704-1910 Dark Green (FS 34079)
704-1911 Olive Drab (FS 34087)
704-1913 Medium Green (FS 34102)
704-1917 Dark Sea Blue (FS 15042)
704-1920 Intermediate Blue (FS 35164)
704-1923 Gunship Gray (FS 36118)
704-1926 Light Sea Gray (FS 37307)
704-1929 Gloss Gull Gray (FS 16440)
704-1930 Flat Gull Gray (FS 36440)
704-1933 Camouflage Gray (FS 36622)
704-1942 Dark Tan (FS 30219)

See What's Available at
www.walthers.com

704-1947 Gloss Black (FS 17038)
704-1949 Flat Black (FS 37038)
704-1950 Panzer Gray (FS 36076)
704-1954 Light Earth (FS 30140)
704-1955 Afrika Mustard (FS 30266)
704-1972 Blue Angel Blue (FS 15050)
704-1988 Euro 1 Gray (FS 36081)
704-1992 SAC Bomber Tan (FS 34201)
704-1993 SAC Bomber Green (FS 34159)
704-1994 Navy Aggressor Gray (FS 36251)

Automotive Colors
704-2901 Silver Blue Metallic
704-2902 Arctic Blue Metallic
704-2905 Burgundy Red Metallic
704-2909 Light Ivory
704-2910 Sand Beige
704-2913 Black Metallic
704-2914 German Silver Metallic
704-2915 French Blue
704-2916 British Green Metallic
704-2917 Bright Yellow
704-2918 Guards Red
704-2919 Italian Red
704-2920 Classic White
704-2921 Classic Black
704-2922 Champagne Gold Metallic
704-2936 Clear Top Coat
704-2937 Gray Primer
704-2938 Racing Orange
704-2939 Racing Red
704-2940 Racing Blue
704-2942 1950s Aqua
704-2943 Bright White
704-2944 Gloss Pearl Clear Coat
704-2945 Turquoise Metallic
704-2947 Deep Pearl Purple
704-2948 White Primer
704-2949 Transparent Black Window Tint
704-2950 Plum Crazy
704-2955 Hot Magenta
704-2957 Panther Pink
704-2964 Grabber Blue
704-2965 Turquoise
704-2967 Sublime Green
704-2970 Go Mango

Clear Finish - Enamel
704-1959 Semi-Glosst
704-1960 Flat
704-1961 Gloss

Thinner - Enamel
Dealers MUST order multiples of 12.
704-1148 1/4oz (7.5ml) Bottle **1.49**
704-1156 1-3/4oz (52.5ml) Bottle **2.89**

405

PAINT & PAINT SUPPLIES

Paint Marker Sets
pkg(3) 10.49 ea

Enamel
These easy-to-use, fast-drying markers provide a glossy appearance and are highly pigmented for superior coverage.

704-25001 Gloss Black, Gloss White, Gloss Red
704-25002 Flat Black, Gloss Blue, Gloss Yellow

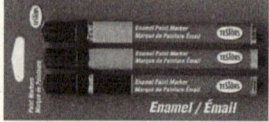

704-25003 Gloss Black, Gold, Silver

Paint Markers 3.99 ea
Perfect for painting small parts, doing touch-up and more. Colors match PLA Enamels and sprays. Fast drying, with double chisel tip for fine lines or bold strokes. 1/3oz.
Dealers MUST order multiples of 6.

Enamel
704-2503 Gloss Red
704-2508 Gloss Light Blue
704-2511 Gloss Dark Blue
704-2514 Gloss Yellow
704-2524 Gloss Green
704-2527 Gloss Orange
704-2538 Gloss Gray
704-2540 Gloss Brown
704-2544 Metallic Gold
704-2545 Gloss White
704-2546 Metallic Silver
704-2547 Gloss Black
704-2549 Flat Black
704-2575 Fluorescent Red

Model Master Metalizer Lacquer
Recreate virtually any natural metal finish on plastic models using these special lacquer colors. Designed for airbrush application only, colors are premixed in Buffing (which can be polished to various degrees of sheen) or Nonbuffing types.

Buffing 1/2oz (15ml) Bottle 3.49 ea
Dealers MUST order multiples of 6.

704-1401 Aluminum Plate
704-1402 Stainless Steel
704-1403 Magnesium
704-1404 Titanium
704-1405 Gunmetal
704-1406 Exhaust

704-1412 Dark Anodonic Gray
704-1415 Burnt Metal

Buffing Spray 30oz (90ml) 5.25 ea
Same great colors in easy to use spray cans.
Dealers MUST order multiples of 3.

704-1451 Aluminum Plate
704-1452 Stainless Steel
704-1453 Magnesium
704-1454 Titanium
704-1455 Gunmetal
704-1459 Metalizer Sealer

Nonbuffing 1/2oz (15ml) Bottle 3.49 ea
Dealers MUST order multiples of 6.

704-1417 Brass
704-1418 Aluminum
704-1420 Steel
704-1423 Gunmetal
704-1424 Burnt Iron

Metalizer Thinner & Sealer 3.99 ea
Special formulas for use with Metalizer colors. 1-3/4oz (52.5ml) bottle.
Dealers MUST order multiples of 12.

704-1409 Sealer
704-1419 Thinner

Model Master Airbrush Thinner
704-1799 8oz 8.49
Dealers MUST order in quantities of 12.
704-1789 1-3/4oz 4.99

PAINT SETS

704-9120 Auto Detail 12.49
Get a new model builder revved up for his or her first project with this set. Complete with six 1/4oz bottles of paint, 1/4oz bottle of thinner, paint brush, cement pen for clean and easy application of model glue and a handy storage tray.

704-9121 Aircraft 12.49
Make ready on the flight deck with this starter set! Comes with six 1/4oz bottles of paint, 1/4oz bottle of thinner, paint brush, cement pen to make gluing easier and a storage tray.

704-9131 Military Flats 12.49
Black, blue, gray, green, brown, tan, white and blue.
704-9132 Fluorescent 10.49

704-9146 Promotional Paint Set 10.49

704-9116 Standard Finishing - Model Building 12.49

Acrylic Spray Sets
Sets include five 1/4oz nontoxic colors, 1/2oz primer, propellant and spray cap.

704-9215 Model Car 19.99

704-9216 Military Aircraft 19.99

704-9135 Model Car Refill Set 12.99

704-9136 Model Aircraft Refill Set 12.99

Acrylic Pot Sets
Each includes a paint brush and mixing tray.

Hobby Craft

704-9184 12 Colors 6.85

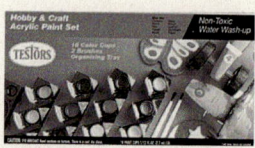

704-9186 18 Colors 7.99

Model Car

704-9185 12 Colors 6.85

Supplies Kit
704-9111 Model Building Supplies Kit 10.49
Drop cloth, three brushes, hobby knife, five gluing tips and five sanding films.

Plastic Model Finishing Kits 23.99 ea (Unless Noted)
11 bottles of enamel, bottle thinner, tube plastic cement, putty, broad tip brush, fine tip brush, 1/4" (.6cm) brush, hobby knife, drop cloth, three gluing tips, five sanding films and plastic tray.

704-9160 Flat
704-9161 Gloss
704-9115 Enamel Set - Small 10.49
Red, yellow, blue, silver, white and black, plus brush.

Clear Finish

Dullcote
A protective, transparent lacquer that dries dead flat without altering the color.

704-1160 1-3/4oz 52.5ml 2.89
Dealers MUST order Dealer Pack of 12.

704-1260 Spray 3oz 90ml 4.49
Dealers MUST order multiples of 3.

Glosscote
Clear lacquer dries to a transparent, high-gloss protective finish that does not alter the color.

704-1161 Bottle 1-3/4oz 52.5ml 2.89
Dealers MUST order multiples of 12.

704-1261 Spray 3oz 90ml 4.49
Dealers MUST order multiples of 3.

Lacquer Brush Cleaner
704-1159 1oz 30ml Bottle 2.89
Use with Clear and Dull Coat.
Dealers MUST order multiples of 6.

Decal Setting Solution
Softens decal film to conform to surface details.

704-8804 1/4oz 7.5ml 1.49
Dealers MUST order Dealer pack of 12.

704-1737 1/2oz 15ml 2.99
Dealers MUST order Dealer pack of 6

PAINT BRUSHES
Applying colors, highlighting fine details, weathering, washes, drybrushing and many other painting jobs are easy with this complete selection of brushes. Choose from natural and synthetic hairs in various shapes and sizes.

Round 4.79 ea

704-8731 #3
704-8732 #0
704-8733 #2

Flat

704-8734 5/16" 5.39

Model Master
These top quality brushes help insure professional results. All Model Master brushes are made with solid birch handles and seamless nickel-plated ferrules.
Dealers MUST order multiples of 12.

Sable

704-8841 #2 Red Sable Round 5.79
For fine detail work and pinpoint washes.

704-8842 #3/0 Red Sable Round 5.25
For precise, small scale work.

704-8861 1/2" Black Sable Flat 8.39
For broad color applications and washes.

Camel

704-8851 3/8" Camel Hair Flat 7.89
Soft, fine bristles designed for high-gloss finishes.

Synthetic

704-8831 #2 Round 5.25
Fine tip and good body, for painting small assemblies.

704-8832 #0 Round 5.49
Durable bristles and fine point are ideal for applying liquid cement.

PAINT & PAINT SUPPLIES

704-8833 1/4" Chisel **7.39**
Use for blending, such as secondary camouflage patterns.

Shed Proof Synthetic
Unique brushes feature nylon bristles stapled in the tip to keep them from falling out.

Dealers MUST order multiples of 12.

Individual Brushes

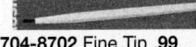

704-8701 Broad Tip **.99**

704-8702 Fine Tip **.99**

704-8705 1/4" Tip **1.69**

Sets

704-8703 1 Flat Tip & 1 Pointed pkg(2) **1.49**

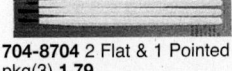

704-8704 2 Flat & 1 Pointed pkg(3) **1.79**

704-8706 Flat, Pointed 1-1/4" Tips pkg(3) **1.99**

AIRBRUSHES

CAUTION:
For your safety, the use of a properly vented spray booth and a respirator which is paint mist and vapor compatible is strongly recommended when painting with an airbrush.

Testors Airbrush Sets
Use standard paint bottles to supply color and speed color changes. Spray width is adjusted by turning nozzle. Volume can be changed by raising or lowering bottle.

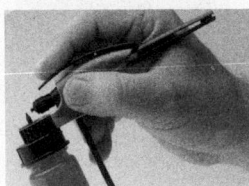

704-8814 Multi-Purpose Paint Sprayer **17.99**
Perfect for covering large areas with almost any paint or stain. This external-mix, single-action sprayer comes with a 2oz bottle.

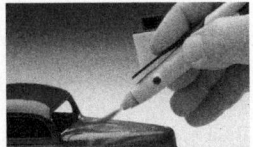

Limited Quantity Available
704-8826 Detailing Airbrush Set **29.99**
Airbrush is an internal-mix, single-action airbrush with great accuracy and control capabilities, thanks to a low trigger that precisely directs air flow. Paint volume regulates with adjustment flange.

Aztek Airbrushes
Easy to use and maintain. Available in both single- and dual-action, as well as internal or external mix. Bodies are acetal resin, which is impervious to solvents, lightweight and nearly unbreakable.

Double Action Airbrush

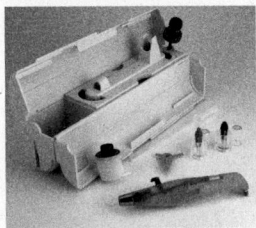

704-4704 With Case **99.99**
Comes with two nozzles and a mixing cup.

External Mix
Fully assembled, single-action, with 6' air hose.

Model 1220
704-2203 Set **29.99**
704-2206 Set w/6oz Can Ozone-Safe Propellant **39.99**
Includes airbrush, two 1/2oz (15cc) bottles, 28mm quick change cap, compressor adapter and instructions.

Model A270

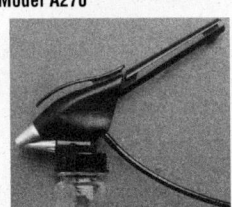

704-2705 Set **49.99**
704-2706 Set w/6oz Can Ozone-Safe Propellant **52.99**
Includes airbrush, 28 and 33mm bottle/cap assemblies, compressor adapter, instruction book and video.

Model A320

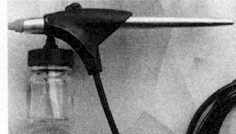

704-3205 Set **64.99**

704-3208 Set w/6oz Can Ozone-Safe Propellant **74.99**
Includes airbrush, general detail nozzle (.53mm), 28 and 33mm siphon caps and bottles, compressor adapter, video and instruction book.

Internal Mix
Superb control, with interchangeable nozzles. Paint travels through the nozzle, not the body, so only the nozzles need to be cleaned. Gravity feed color cup can be positioned for right or left hand. Dual-action brushes are fully assembled and include air hose.

Model A470
704-4702 Set w/Plastic Storage Case **119.99**

704-4709 Set w/Wooden Storage Case **199.99**
Includes airbrush with 15' air hose, fine, medium and large nozzles, 2.5, 3 and 7.5cc gravity feed color cups, 28 and 33mm siphon bottles and caps, aircan hose adapter, instruction manual and video, plus storage case.

Model A430
704-4305 Set w/Plastic Storage Case **99.99**

704-4308 Set w/Wooden Storage Case **129.99**
Includes airbrush with 10' hose, general detail, medium coverage and large coverage nozzles, 7.5cc gravity feed color cup, 28 and 33mm siphon bottles and caps, instruction manual and video, plus storage case.

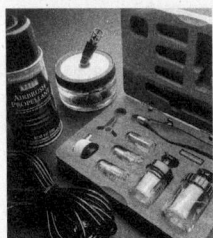

704-4309 Professional Set w/Wooden Storage Case **149.99**
Set includes airbrush with 6' hose, three nozzles, gravity feed color cup, two siphon caps and bottles, airbrush cleaning station and 6oz ozone-safe propellant, all stored in a wooden storage case.

Hot New Products Announced Daily! Visit Walthers Web site at

www.walthers.com

Metal Airbrush Set

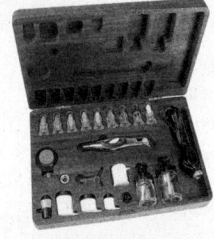

Limited Quantity Available
704-7778 **269.99**
Includes airbrush and hose, eight nozzles, 2.5cc side-feed paint cup, three gravity-feed paint cups, 12cc top-feed paint cups, 28mm and 33mm siphon caps and bottles, compressor and propellant can adapters, instruction manual and wooden case.

Metal-Body Airbrush Kits

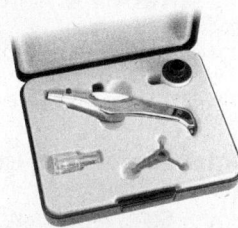

704-4802 With Plastic Case **199.99**
Includes airbrush, hose, general-purpose nozzle, 7.5cc gravity-feed paint cup, cleaning tool, nozzle wrench and video.

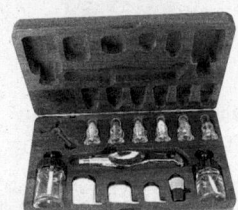

704-4809 With Wooden Storage Case **249.99**
Includes airbrush, hose, six nozzles, four paint cups, 28 and 33mm siphon cap and jars, cleaning tool, nozzle wrench and detailed instructional video.

Complete Airbrush System

704-50654 **229.99**
Includes double-action airbush and hose, general purpose nozzle, high flow nozzle, acrylic general nozzle, acrylic high-flow nozzle, 12cc gravity feed cup, 28mm siphon cap, four 1/2oz bottles, pipette, cleaning station, compressor adapter, blue-mini compressor, and instruction manual.

AIR COMPRESSORS

Aztek

704-50201 AC100 **299.99**
Features 1/8 horsepower, 1.58 CFM, 35 P.S.I. maximum pressure, oil-less diaphragm, 1/4 NPS air hose fitting and an on/off switch. 110V, .8 amps.

704-50202 AC200 **349.99**
Delivers up to 25lbs of air. Built-in moisture trap and pressure gauge. Rubber feet minimize vibration and noise with oil-less operation, fan cooling and built-in thermal protection switch. Two-year guarantee and 10,000 hour service life.

704-50205 AC500 **399.99**
Features a pressure holding tank with an automatic pressure switch, allowing the unit to maintain constant pressure while reducing pulsing. Features 1/8 horsepower, 1.58 CFM, 32 psi maximum pressure, an air pressure auto-shutoff switch, air pressure gauge and a pressure holding tank with a water drain valve. 110V, .08 amps; weight: 16-1/2lbs.

PAINT & PAINT SUPPLIES

Blue Mini Compressor

704-50204 129.99
Styled in an "ice blue" transparent case, this UL-approved, 110V mini compressor features oil-less operation, 0.18 CFM, approximately 20psi, 6' power cord, and a fan-cooled motor.

COMPRESSOR ACCESSORIES

Regulator & Moisture Trap
704-50680 99.99
Built-in regulator to increase or decrease pressure. Moisture trap dries air. Fully assembled.

Pressure Gauge
704-50681 29.99
Large, easy-to-read black and white markings. Assembled, fits most compressors.

Spray Booth

704-50210 599.99
20W x 15D x 14H"
50 x 37.5 x 35cm
Powered fan collects overspray in three-stage filter system and vents vapors. Mounting brackets provided for additional lighting (sold separately).

HOBBY TOOLS

704-50628 Sprue Cutters 16.99

AIRBRUSH ACCESSORIES

Air Hose 10'
704-9311 Straight 16.99
704-9312 Coiled 25.99

Adapter
704-9313 Air Can Hose Adapter 10.49

Siphon Caps & Bottles

704-9314 33mm 7.39
704-9319 28mm 6.99
704-9326 Bottles 1/2oz pkg(2) 6.99
704-9327 Bottles 2/3ozpkg(2) 6.99

Aztek Nozzles 11.99 ea (Unless Noted)

704-9304 Fineline (.30mm)
704-9305 General Coverage (.40mm)
704-9306 High Flow (.50mm)
704-9342 General (.53mm)
704-9343 Medium (.70mm)
704-9344 Large (1.02mm)
704-9302 Nozzle Set 4 Assorted 44.99

Acrylic Paint Nozzles 11.99 ea
704-9307 .40mm Spatter
704-9340 General (.30mm)
704-9341 High Flow (.40mm)

Cleaning Station

704-9315 Airbrush Cleaning Station 34.99
Convenient, environmentally sound way to clean your airbrush. Simply insert in the adjustable neck and spray. Solvent passes through the nozzle, then through a filter and is trapped in the jar.

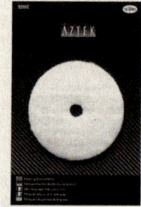
704-9316 Replacement Filters for #9315 13.99

Color Cups
704-9308 1.0cc Side Feed 3.69
704-9309 2.5cc Side Cup 3.69
704-9310 8.0cc Side Cup 4.75
704-9303 Color Cup Set 11.99
704-9346 12cc Top Feed 4.75

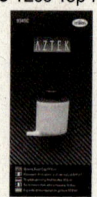
704-9347 3.0cc 3.69
704-9348 7.5cc 3.69
704-9349 12.0cc 4.75

Model Master
Pipettes
704-50642 pkg(6) 4.75
Transfer color or thinner for mixing custom colors. Plastic, easy to clean and reusable.

Masking
704-50622 Modeling Tape 7.35
1/2" x 20' 1.25cm x 6m
For sharp separations between colors. Light adhesive will not lift paint under normal use.

Propellant
704-8822 15oz 450ml 14.99
Ozone-safe air supply with fittings. For any airbrush designed to accept propellant cans.

Cleaners
Limited Quantity Available
704-65160 4oz 5.25

T-Connector
704-50682 19.99

Models and Photo by Keith Kohlmann, Racine, Wisconsin

Railroads are the best way to move something from where it's made, mined or grown to where it will be used or sold. Grain or green hides, autos or artichokes, coal or construction cranes, they all move by rail. Freight cars of all kinds are supplied by the railroads to handle the loads — they're the tools the lines use to get the job done. Hoppers haul coal coke, aggregates, grain and more, tank cars handle liquids and box cars carry manufactured or canned goods. Flat cars and gondolas are especially interesting because we can see what they're carrying.

In South Milwaukee, Wisconsin, the huge Bucyrus-Erie plant generates countless carloads of heavy-duty construction machinery. Cranes, draglines and more are essentially powered tools used for mining and more. Chicago & North Western's switchers regularly drilled the sidings leading into the plant to fetch flats loaded with components of mining machines; the parts of these cranes and draglines were too big to ship assembled. Today's crew shoves an empty flat car past the boom and bucket of a mining shovel being shipped out. The switch move underscores how common tools are in industry; freight cars and locomotives are the tools used to ship tools of the mining industry.

Keith photographed this scene on a diorama (a tool used for his photography), the locomotive is a PROTO N from Life-Like, the freight cars are from Micro-Trains® and the loads are modified Boley HO models. As you can imagine, many modeling tools were used to create this scene; you'll find most of them listed in the Tools Section.

TOOLS

A.J. FRICKO COMPANY

Pinhole Lens For 35mm SLR Camera* 189.95 ea
Focusing pinhole lens with colens to overcome fuzziness.

*Must have a camera with removable lens. Pinhole lens fits onto a camera body.

Lens features:
- 0.018" diameter aperture
- 105 f/stop
- etched in stainless steel
- a much sharper image
- a brighter viewing screen
- a shorter exposure time
- depth of field from 1" to infinity

All items listed below are available by Special Order (see Legend Page).

274-842 Canon Manual focus camera body.
274-843 Konica
274-844 Minolta Manual focus camera body.
274-845 Nikon Either manual or auto focus camera body.

274-846 Olympus
274-847 Pentax K Bayonet mount, also works for Ricoh.
274-848 Pentax S Universal screw mount for all screw mount body types.
274-849 Yashica/Contax
274-851 Minolta Maxxum
274-852 Canon EOS

ATLAS

Snap Saw

150-400 **3.25**
Long-lasting, all-purpose saw.

CREATIONS UNLIMITED HOBBY PRODUCTS

TOOLS

FLEX-I-FILE™

Tough, flexible, polyester tapes, for wet or dry sanding, on lightweight, high-strength, anodized aluminum frames.

232-700 Starter Set **10.95** Includes frame and two each of polyester fine, medium and coarse tapes.

232-123 Combo Set **16.95** Includes frame with eight each fine, medium and coarse polyester tapes, plus one bonus tape on frame.

232-301 3-in-1 Set **24.95** Includes three frames plus seven each fine, medium and coarse polyester tapes.

Tool-Tender Plus

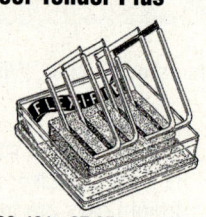

232-401 **37.95**
Five-place tool stand with four complete sets and room for five. Includes clear plastic storage case.

232-400 Tool Stand Only **19.95**

Replacement Polyester Sanding Tapes pkg(6) 2.59 ea
232-150 Coarse
232-280 Medium
232-320 Fine
232-600 X-Fine

ABRASIVE SHEETS 4.29 ea

232-801 Polyester Abrasive Includes two sheets each of #150, 280, 320 and 600 grit.

232-802 Ultra-Fine Finishing/Polishing Includes two sheets each of polyester abrasive #1000, 1500, 6000 and 10,000 grit.

POLISHER
232-3210 Triple Grit **5.49** Three-in-one polisher/finisher.

SCRIBES

Scribe-N-Cut
232-6087 Folding Knife **5.49** Large blade is ideal for cutting big sheets of styrene and small vacuum-formed parts.

Needle Point Scriber
232-6114 Ultra-Fine w/2 Needle Points **5.49**
232-6115 Replacement Needles for #6114 pkg(3) **2.75**

FLEX-PAD
Flexible polyester sanders with angled end. Available in handy 1/2 x 6" sizes.

Sets

232-525 Intro Set **16.49** One each of above, plus triple-grit polisher.

232-550 Flex Set **24.95** Includes Flex-I-File with an assortment of polyester tapes and all 5 Flex-Pads.

Individual Flex-Pad Files 2.98 ea
232-1500 Coarse
232-2800 Medium
232-3200 Fine
232-6000 X-Fine

ADHESIVES

A+B Epoxy
Hand-moldable epoxy ribbon. Easily carved and worked before curing; easy to sand, file and paint when dry.

232-1 Putty Regular Gray 1lb **16.79**

232-2 Fast Set Putty 8oz **16.29**
232-5 Fast Set Paste 5oz **16.79**

APPLICATORS

Touch-N-Flow

232-711 **6.49**
Touch-N-Flow applies liquid plastic cements with pinpoint accuracy.

Touch-N-Flow shown with Filler Bottle (232-715), sold separately.

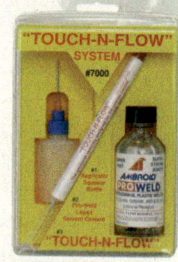

232-7000 Touch-N-Flow System **16.79** Bottle of ProWeld Cement, a Filler Bottle and the Touch-N-Flow. All in one package.

232-715 Filler Bottle **6.49**

Applicator Tool

232-805 Cyanoacrylate Adhesive (CA) Applicator Tool **6.29**

Applicator Bottles 6.49 ea
One-drop applicators for precise use of thin liquids.

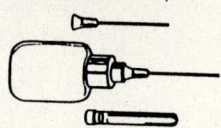

232-6003 With 2 Tubes

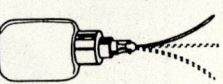

232-6051 With "Flex" Tube Good for filling Touch-N-Flow applicator.

AIRBRUSH CLEANING KIT

NEW 232-7011 14.95
Everything you need to keep your airbrush clean and working properly, in one handy package. Includes one each #7012 - 7020; also available separately.

Cleaning Kit Accessories

Cotton Swabs
NEW **232-7012** pkg(20) **1.50**

Plastic Eye Droppers
NEW **232-7013** for Mixing Paint pkg(6) **2.99**

Pipe Cleaners
NEW **232-7014** pkg(20) **2.49**

Mixing Cups
NEW **232-7015** pkg(5) **1.29**

Rubber Gloves
NEW **232-7016** One Size fits All **1.10**

Small Funnel
NEW **232-7017** **1.99**

Squeeze Bottle
NEW **232-7018** For Thinner **4.99**

Cleaning Brushes
NEW **232-7019** For Air-Brush pkg(6) **2.49**

Wiping Cloths
NEW **232-7020** pkg(3) **1.99**

MODEL DUSTING BRUSH

232-8050 Brush Duster **4.99**

TOOLS

 **DONEGAN OPTICAL COMPANY**

NEW PRODUCT

OptiVISOR® Professional Set

NEW 240-400 OptiVISOR Professional Series Set **247.00** Includes an OptiVISOR, six lenses, OptiLOUPE®, VisorLIGHT® and carrying case.

Optivisor

The Optivisor is a precision-made binocular magnifier that is worn on the head, leaving both hands free. Can be instantly tilted downward when needed and upward when not in use. Can be worn over regular prescription or safety glasses. Comes with dial, adjustable, conforming headband, high impact visor, genuine leather padded comfort band and optical glass lenses mounted in an interchangeable frame. Six lens powers available, plus an attachable auxiliary OptiLOUPE lens for additional magnification.

240-402 1-1/2x, 20" Focal Length **40.39**
240-403 1-3/4x, 14" Focal Length **40.39**
240-404 2x, 10" Focal Length **40.39**
240-405 2-1/2x, 8" Focal Length **40.39**
240-407 2-3/4x, 6" Focal Length **41.79**
240-410 3-1/2x, 4" Focal Length **41.79** For extremely fine work.

Optivisor LX 30.45 ea
Includes all the same great features of the regular OptiVISOR, except it has acrylic lenses instead of glass.

240-15 1-3/4x, 14" Focal Length
240-16 2x, 10" Focal Length
240-17 2-1/2x, 8" Focal Length
240-18 2-3/4x, 6" Focal Length

Accessories For Optivisor
Optiloupe

240-300 **7.99** Adds 2-1/2x to all other lenses.

Optivisor Lens Plate 24.59 ea (Unless Noted)
240-2 Lens Plate 2 For #402
240-3 Lens Plate 3 For #403
240-4 Lens Plate 4 For #404
240-5 Lens Plate 5 For #405
240-7 Lens Plate 7 For #407 **25.85**
240-10 Lens Plate 10 For #410 **25.89**

Replacement Lens Plate For Accursite/Optivisor LX Magnifiers 11.19 ea
240-213 1-3/4x, 14" Focal Length
240-214 2x, 10" Focal Length
240-215 2-1/2x, 8" Focal Length

Visorlight

240-6 With Battery Pack & 10" Cord. **22.49**
240-42 With Battery Pack & 42" Cord **22.49**
240-2204 Replacement Bulb **7.15**

Flex Arm Magnifiers
With Acrylic Lens

240-204 Flex-A-Mag **28.79** Features optical grade acrylic material which has been selected for its hard surface qualities as well as its refractive index. Weighted base.

With Optical Glass Lens
91.35 ea

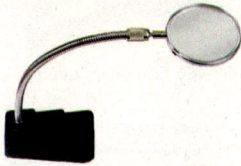

Items listed below are available by Special Order (see Legend Page).
240-1043 4" Round w/Clamp
240-1044 4" Round w/Base

Optisight Magnifying Visor

240-600 **27.69** Visor tilts up for normal viewing, or down for magnification. Constructed of a high-strength plastic, the visor can be worn over prescription or safety glasses. Its state-of-the-art design shields out unwanted glare, so modelers can focus on the project in hand! Features a precision optical grade acrylic prismatic lens, and three interchangeable lens plates (3, 4 and 5).

ULTRA-LIGHT EYEGLASS LOUPE

Single 24.69 ea
240-28 10 Power
240-29 7 Power
240-30 5 Power
240-31 4 Power
240-32 3 Power

Double 30.79 ea

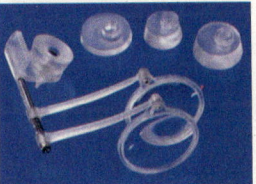

240-33 5 Power & 10 Power/15 Power Combined
240-34 4 Power & 10 Power/14 Power Combined
240-35 5 Power & 7 Power/12 Power Combined

Items listed below are available by Special Order (see Legend Page).
240-36 4 Power & 7 Power/11 Power Combined
240-37 3 Power & 7 Power/10 Power Combined
240-38 3 Power & 5 Power/8 Power Combined

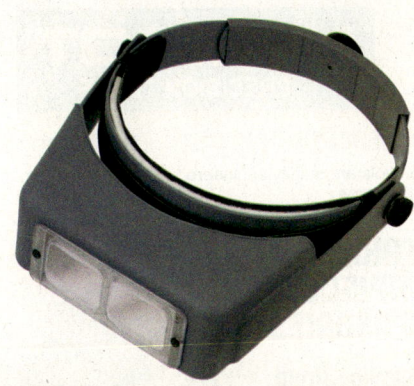

Optivisor LX 240-15

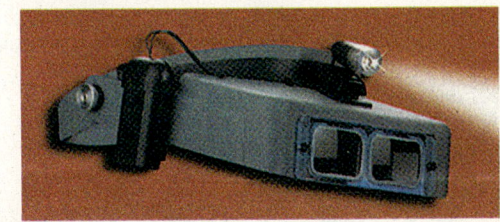

VisorLight 240-6 Shown With Optivisor, Sold Separately

Clip-On Binocular Magnifier 27.69 ea

Hands free magnification for detailed tasks. Lightweight frame can be used with frame included, or easily clipped onto most eyeglass frames. Pivots up when magnification is not needed. Relieves eye strain and increases accuracy.

240-503 1-3/4x, 14" Focal Length
240-504 2x, 10" Focal Length
240-505 2-1/2x, 8" Focal Length
240-507 2-3/4x, 6" Focal Length

Pocket Magnifiers
6.69 ea (Unless Noted)

240-703 3x
240-704 4x
240-705 5x

240-903 Single Fold 3x
240-904 Single Fold 4x
240-905 Single Fold 5x

240-937 Double Fold 3/4/7x **7.79**
240-949 Double Fold 4/5/9x **7.79**

Classic Series Magnifiers
These lightweight, handheld magnifiers feature ABS plastic handles and acrylic lenses that are produced to high opthalmic standards.

240-602 Round, 2-1/2" Lens, 6" Focal Length **9.79**
240-603 Round, 3-1/4" Lens, 8" Focal Length **10.89**
240-604 Round, 4" Lens, 9" Focal Length **12.25**

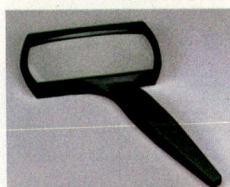

240-624 Rectangular, 2 x 4" Lens, 9" Focal Length **12.25**
240-625 Rectangular w/Bifocal, 2 x 4" Lens, 9" Focal Length **12.25**

Daily New Arrival Updates! Visit Walthers Web site at
www.walthers.com

TOOLS

MASCOT® PRECISION TOOLS

Mascot tools are quality engineered to give top performance and satisfaction.

MOTORIZED HANDPIECE ACCESSORIES

1/4" Sanding Drum Assortment

Limited Quantity Available

230-81031 5.99
Includes four each fine, medium and coarse; with 1/8" mandrel.

1/2" Sanding Drum Assortment

Limited Quantity Available
230-81041 6.50
Includes four each fine, medium and coarse; with 1/8" mandrel.

Adapter Chuck

230-982 8.15
The 3/32" shaft fits all portable electric rotary tools. Holds miniature drills from #80 (.014") to #43 (.089").

Bur & Wheel Stand

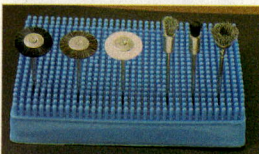

230-81049 For 3/32" Shank Burs **5.99**
Holds all your shaft tools upright and ready for quick access.

Cut Off Disks

230-81030 7/8" pkg(50) **10.50**
These high-speed resin-bonded, aluminum-oxide disks offer fast, cool and smooth cutting on all metal.

Sander Set

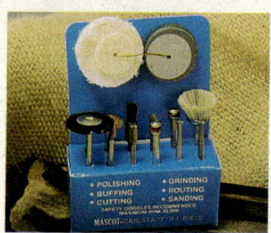

230-980 41.95
Rotary Tool Accessory Kit (18 pieces) 1/8" and 1/32" shanks. Fits all electric portable rotary tools.

PLIERS

Joint Pliers 12.60 ea

230-480 Flat Nose
230-481 Chain Nose
230-483 Diagonal Cutters
230-485 Bent Nose
230-488 Round Nose

Long Ranger Pliers 11.55 ea

These unique pliers have an extra long body that gets the user closer to the work than regular pliers. The hinged joint of the plier jaws is closer to the working end of the tool, giving the maximum possible holding power. Each has matte finish with closed-cell handle covers and leaf spring return.

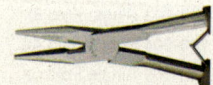

230-495 Lineman's w/Cutter

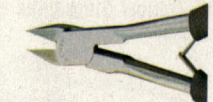

230-496 Diagonal Cutters

230-498 Serrated Jawed Needle Nose

Miniature Electronic Pliers 8.40 ea

Features double-leaf spring return for extra-smooth and quiet, nonbinding opening and closure.

230-380 Flat Nose

230-383 Diagonal

230-384 End Nippers

230-385 Bent Needle Nose

230-387 Needle Nose

Miniature Pliers 5.25 ea (Unless Noted)

Each pliers offers a brushed satin finish and spring action return with a solid feel.

230-370 Flat Nose

230-371 Needle Nose

See What's New and Exciting at

www.walthers.com

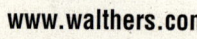

230-373 Diagonal **10.80**

230-374 End Nippers **10.80**

230-376 Long Nose

Premier Pliers

230-400 Flat Nose **24.15**
230-402 Needle Nose **26.25**
230-403 Wire Cutter **31.50**

Sprue & Fine Wire Cutting Pliers

230-450 11.30
Features hardened, slim-line, razor-sharp jaws, cushion grips and is perfect for cutting sprue cleanly. Can also cut wire up to .40" 1mm.

TWEEZERS

230-500 Cross-Locking 6-3/8" **5.25**
Tips serrated for sure grip.

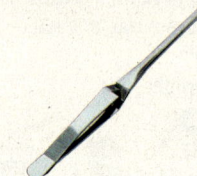

230-501 Fine-Pointed 4-1/4" **19.95**
Sharp tips and light tension for fine work. Nickel-plated steel. Magnetic.

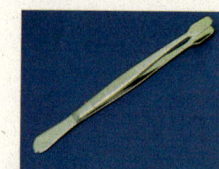

230-503 Stamp 4-1/2" **3.70**
Smooth, wafer-thin points. Nickel-plated steel.

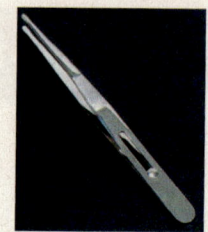

230-504 Slide Lock 5-7/8" **8.15**
Thin serrated tips for firm grip, thin flat back permits holding tweezer vise. Chrome plated.

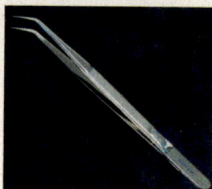

230-505 Curved 6" **6.60**
Nickel-plated steel with slender tips, serrated for positive grip.

230-506 Sharp Pointed 4-3/4" **5.80**

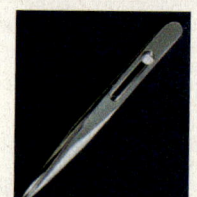

230-507 Slide Lock 4-3/4" **6.50**

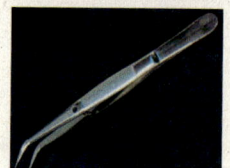

230-508 Curved 4-1/2" **6.50**

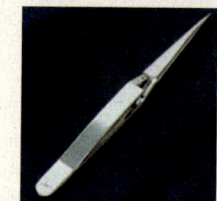

230-509 Cross Lock 4-1/2" **5.80**

230-510 Curved 6-7/8" **5.80**

TOOLS

MASCOT PRECISION TOOLS

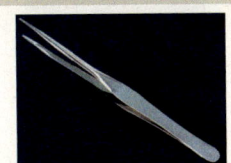
230-511 Straight 7" **5.25**

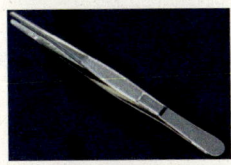
230-512 Round Point 6" **5.25**

230-515 Glass Filled Tweezer Non-Conductive/Anti-Magnetic **2.10**

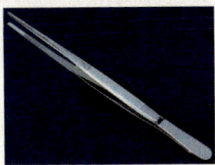
230-520 Retrieving 8" **8.35**

230-521 All Purpose Tweezer Set **23.95**
4-3/4" stamp, 4-1/2" sharp pointed, 6" retrieving, 6" curved, 6-1/2" curved and 6-1/2" self-closing.

230-530 Magnifying Tweezers **8.40**

230-531 Decal Tweezers 4-1/2" **7.35**
Nickel-plated steel tweezers with thin, smooth spade points, angled to allow perfect placement of decals.

230-532 Utility Solder Tweezer 4" **5.80**

230-533 Slotted Tweezers 4" **7.35**

230-534 Soft Tipped Decal Tweezer 5" **4.20**
Ultra-lightweight flexible plastic tweezers feature round, smooth, spatula-like tips.

KNIVES

Knife Blades w/Safe Vial

Blades for #230-1 Knife Handle

230-11 #11 pkg(5) **2.10**

230-16 #16 pkg(5) **1.95**

Blades For #230-2, 230-5, 230-9 Knife Handles

230-19 #19 pkg(5) **2.45**

230-22 #22 pkg(5) **3.50**

230-23 #23 pkg(5) **5.60**

230-24 #24 pkg(5) **2.30**

Mini Blades For #230-110 Knife Handles
230-1101 pkg(5) **5.05**

Knife Sets

Deluxe Hobby-Craft Modelers Knife & Tool Set

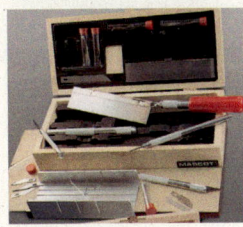
230-866 **41.90**
Contains one each lightweight, medium weight, heavy-duty knife, hobby awl, miter box, razor saw, sander, screwdriver and 20 assorted blades.

Precision Knife Set

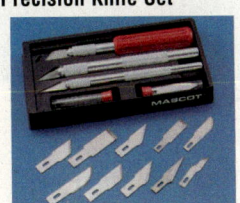
230-182 **15.75**
Includes a lightweight, medium weight and heavy-duty knife plus a plastic storage tray.

Deluxe Knife Set

230-865 **19.70**
Same knives as #182 plus 10 assorted blades and wooden storage box.

Modeling Knives

#1 Lightweight w/Blade
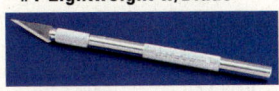
230-1 **2.55**
230-111 With 3 Blades **5.05**

#2 Medium Weight w/Blade

230-2 **3.80**

#5 Heavy-Duty w/Blade

230-5 **4.40**

Scalpel w/Blades

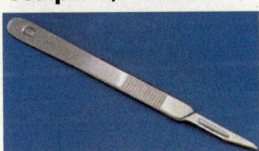
230-30 **5.25**
True medical-surgical instrument with slim-line, stainless-steel scalpel handle. Includes two German-engineered scalpel blades.
230-3011 Replacement Blades pkg(5) **3.45**

SAWS

Hobby Saw w/Blades

230-99 **10.50**
Holds blades securely. Offers rigidity for accurate cut. Includes 12 Swiss-made jeweler's saw blades.

Jeweler's Saws
Includes 12 blades.

230-100 2" Throat **21.00**

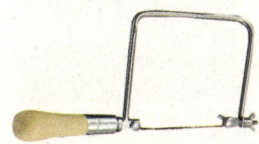
230-103 4" Throat **24.15**

Jeweler's Saw Blades, Bulk Packs pkg(144) 27.25 ea
230-120 Blade #3
230-121 Blade #2
230-122 Blade #1
230-123 Blade #0
230-124 Blade #2/0
230-125 Blade #4/0

Pocket Hacksaw

230-105 7-1/2" Folded **17.95**
230-1051 Blades For Pocket Hacksaw pkg(3) **2.70**

Razor Saw Blade

230-102 1-1/4" **4.35**
Fits #2 and #5 handles.

MITER BOXES

Aluminum Miter Box

230-206 **8.40**
Just 5-1/2 x 2". Uses 1-1/4" blade, has two 45° slots and one 90° slot.

Mini Miter Box

230-208 **5.25**

Portable Bench Double Miter Box

230-209 **6.95**

FILES

Double End Scriber

230-300 7" **10.50**

Individual Files 4.10 ea

230-770 Flat
230-771 Half Round
230-772 Round
230-773 Square
230-774 Equaling
230-775 Three-Square

Reamers

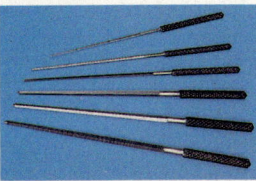
230-311 Set pkg(6) **17.85**

Swiss Single Cut Set

230-777 3 Pieces **11.55**
Includes three-square, round and half-round. 5-1/2" long.

230-778 6 Pieces **22.60**
Includes round, half-round, square, flat, three-square and equaling. 5-1/2" long.

Utility File Set

230-780 6 Pieces **17.80**

WOODWORKING TOOLS

Burnishers 10.95 ea

230-296 Curved Blade

Scraper

230-297 **11.95**

TOOLS

MASCOT PRECISION TOOLS

Woodcarving Knife Set
230-860 4 Pieces **64.95**
Finely balanced knives with alloy blades and wooden handles. Designed for carving, incising, shaving, splicing and notching.

Wood Rasp Set
230-779 59.95
Equaling, flat, half-round, round and three-square. Overall 5-1/2" in length.

Woodworking Tool Sets Miniature
Both sets include one each of the following: a bent square chisel (7/32"), straight skew chisel (1/4"), straight small gouge (3/32"), bent large gouge (7/32") and a "V" parting tool (3/32").

230-863 Mini Mushroom **75.10**
230-864 Mini Straight **69.95**

Woodworking Tool Sets Standard
Each set has five basic shapes and you have a choice of palm-grip mushroom-shape handles (#862) or the conventional straight handle styling (#861). Both sets include one each of the following: a bent square chisel (5/16"), straight skew chisel (5/16"), straight small gouge (5/32"), bent large gouge (5/16") and a "V" parting tool (5/32").

230-861 Mushroom **69.95**
230-862 Straight **72.95**

Get the Scoop!
Get the Skinny!
Get the Score!
Check Out Walthers
Web site at
www.walthers.com

JEWELER'S TOOLS
Model Making

230-463 Chamois Buff Set pkg(6) **10.50**

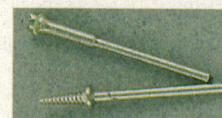
230-465 Mandrel Set - 3/32" **4.20**

230-470 Jeweler's Wax Set **18.95**

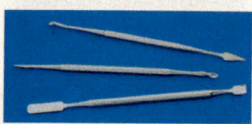
230-475 Wax Carver/Spatula Set pkg(3) **10.50**

DRILLS

230-840 Mini Hand Drill **9.75**

230-841 Spiral Drill **17.85**

12 Carbon Twist Drills
230-178 11.05
Includes one dozen assorted drills from #50 to 80.

Carbon Twist Drill Assortments
230-86 6 Carbon Twist Drills **6.30**
Assortment of the top six drill sizes preferred by hobbyists; 50, 56, 60, 65, 70 and 76.

Carbon Twist Drills
Carbon twist drills are only available in packages of 12.

pkg(12) 9.45 ea	pkg(12) 12.60 ea
230-50 #50	230-68 #68
230-51 #51	230-69 #69
230-52 #52	230-70 #70
230-53 #53	230-71 #71
230-54 #54	230-72 #72
230-55 #55	230-73 #73
230-56 #56	230-74 #74
230-57 #57	230-75 #75
230-58 #58	
230-59 #59	
230-60 #60	

pkg(12) 11.55 ea	pkg(12) 13.15 ea
230-61 #61	230-76 #76
230-62 #62	230-77 #77
230-63 #63	230-78 #78
230-64 #64	pkg(12) 13.40 ea
230-65 #65	230-79 #79
230-66 #66	230-80 #80
230-67 #67	

Pin Vises

230-810 Double End **8.95**

230-811 Swivel Head **7.80**

230-815 Slide Lock **9.95**

230-812 Wood Head Pin Vise Drill Set **19.95**

230-822 Pin Vise & Drill Set **13.55**

Precision Drill Set

230-177 30.20
#61-80 set (20 pieces) carbon drills with plastic case.

CLAMPS
File Block & Clamp
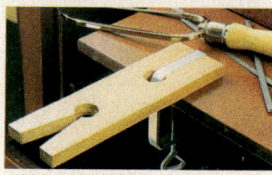
230-150 7.90

Mini Clamps pkg(2)
Made of rigid, high-impact, nylon-filled plastic, these clamps are lightweight and virtually indestructible.

230-213 1" **5.25**
230-214 2" **6.30**

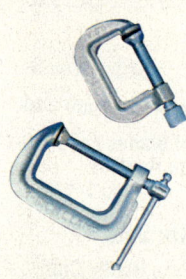
230-210 9.95
Includes 1" and 3/4".

Non-Mar Wedge Clamp

230-202 12.60
Leather-lined jaws grip securely without marring. Resin body.

The Third Hand

230-200 14.65
Tweezer-mounted work positioner.

Twin Grip Positioner
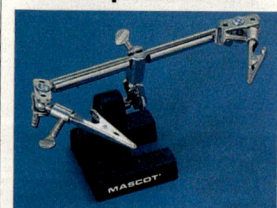
230-201 19.95

Twin Grip w/Magnifier
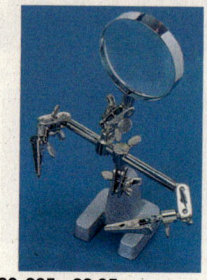
230-205 22.05

Wood Handle Hand Vise
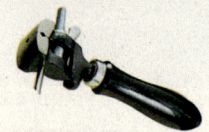
230-199 12.60

MAGNIFIERS

230-899 Spectacle Loupe (2x) **5.25**
Loupe fits securely to right or left lens. Flips out of way for convenience. Scratch-proof plastic-coated clip. Lightweight.

230-900 Eyepiece (2.5x) **7.90**

230-901 Pocket (10x) **11.55**

230-903 With Case (4x & 5x) **13.65**
230-904 Dual Focus Magnifier **7.95**

230-909 Bench Magnifier (3x) **24.15**

TOOLS

230-910 Binocular (2.5x) **19.45**

230-999 Lighted Head Band Magnifier **39.99**

MALLETS & HAMMERS

230-600 Mascot Multi Hammer w/6 Heads **13.65**

230-601 Swiss Style Watchmakers Hammer **8.40** Double-faced head is only 2-1/4" long with flat and chisel faces. Forged head mounted on a hardwood handle. Overall length 8".

230-602 Brass Mallet **10.50** Overall length is 9" with 2" head.

230-603 Mallet w/Interchangeable Face **18.40** Includes brass, fiber and nylon faces. Overall length is 9" with 2" head. Comes with wrench for changing faces.

Hammer/Screwdrivers Set

230-604 5 Pieces **16.75**

SCREWDRIVERS

Eyeglass Screwdriver

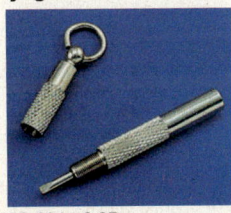

230-804 **2.25**

Metric Screwdriver Set w/2 Phillips

230-853 6 Pieces **5.95**

Precision Screwdriver Set

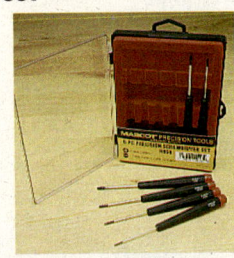

230-850 6 Pieces **18.90** This one-of-a-kind set features non-rolling handles with contoured swivel heads, shafts made of molybdenum steel (hardened and chrome plated for strength and torque) and precision ground tips for sure fit and absolute control. Includes four slotted heads (1.5 x 50mm, 2 x 50mm, 3 x 50mm) and two Phillips head sizes (00 x 50mm, 0 x 50mm) and a handy hard-plastic carrying case.

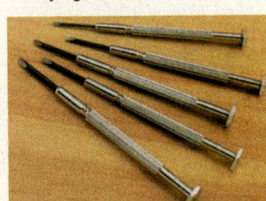

230-855 5 Pieces **14.95** Nickel plated, with swivel heads. 3" to 3-5/8" length, sizes .048" to .085". Blades permanently fixed in handles.

Reversible Blade Screwdrivers

230-800 Flat Head **7.50** Blade has 1/16" and 3/32" ends with swivel head.

Screwdriver Sharpener

230-847 **10.50** Spring-action device holds screwdriver firmly in place while rolled over sharpening stone (stone not included)

MISCELLANEOUS

Blower

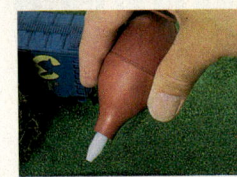

230-915 **7.35**

Dental Probes

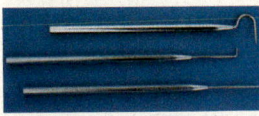

230-303 Set(3) **7.60**

Electrician Scissors

230-163 **13.15** Double-plate, chrome-over-nickel with notches for stripping wire. 5" long.

Gear Pullers

230-220 Stationary **17.95**
230-221 Adjustable **24.95**

Hemostats 8.30 ea

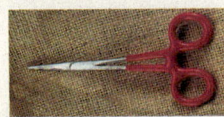

230-340 Straight Blade

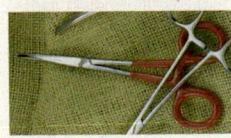

230-341 Curved Blade

Inspection Mirrors
1" diameter, stainless-steel mirrors mounted in 8" long handle.

230-905 Plain Mirror **8.95**

Metric Nut Driver Set
230-858 **6.10** Sizes 3.0mm, 3.5mm, 4.0mm, 4.5mm and 5.0mm.

Micro Cleaner Set

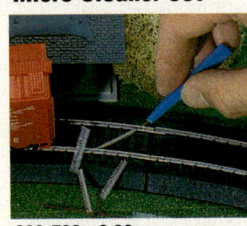

230-700 **6.30** Assortment of five micro-cleaning wire brushes in sizes .09", .12", .15", .18" and .30". Includes a separate handle that will accommodate all but the largest brush. Packed in a reusable plastic vial.

Miniature Open-End Wrench Set

230-856 **17.60** Sizes include 3/32", 1/8", 5/32", 3/16", 1/4" and 5/16".

Mini-Automatic Punch

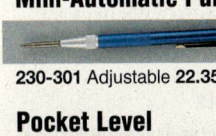

230-301 Adjustable **22.35**

Pocket Level

230-805 **2.19**

Prong Holders

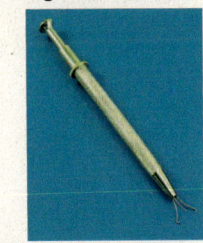

230-203 3 Prongs **6.30**

230-204 4 Prongs **6.85**

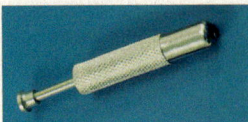

230-2031 Mini 3 Prong **5.99**

Rulers
6" Metric/English

230-710 **2.85**

12" Model Railroad Scale

230-711 **9.45** Scale conversions for HO, O and S Gauges.

Steel Scratch Brush

230-916 **3.70** Hundreds of applications. Features straight steel wire tightly packed in vinyl sleeve that can be peeled away as brush wears.

Titanium Solder Pick

230-917 **10.95** Use to move solder to and from desired spot.

Track Cleaners

230-971 Tunnel Tablet Track Cleaner **21.95**

230-970 Track & Tool Cleaning Tablet **7.95**

Mascot Hobby Tool Catalog

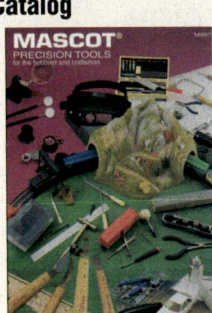

230-997 N/C

TOOLS

FALLER
IMPORTED FROM GERMANY BY WALTHERS

Abrasive Files

272-170689 pkg(5) 9.99
Five different grits from #80 to 120. Small size makes sanding and shaping metal, wood or plastic parts easy.

Dust Brush

272-170686 13.99
This brush is great for removing dust from structures, vehicles figures, or any other detail work on your layout. Removes even the finest dust particles.

Professional Tool Set
Item listed below is available by Special Order (see Legend Page).
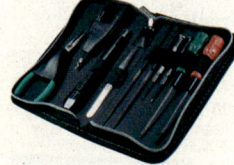
272-170685 81.99
This set contains one side cutter, one pair of pliers, one cutter knife, one pair of tweezers, two files and four screwdrivers, all in a handy storage case.

MÄRKLIN

NEW PRODUCT
Automatic Wire Stripper

NEW 441-603026 34.75
Strips insulation from single-conductor wire .019 to 6mm dia. Self adjusting for wire diameter, can be adjusted to cut 5 to 12mm of insulation. Also features built-in side cutter.

MICRO-TRAINS®

Accessories
Coupler Height Gauge

489-98800031 N Scale Standards Gauge 7.75
For adjusting and mounting couplers and uncouplers. Five tools in one - wheel gauge, track width gauge, coupler mounting platform height gauge, coupler height gauge and uncoupler gluing jig.

Coupler Trip Pin Height Gauge
489-98800034 1.65
For N, Nn3 and Z Scales.

Height Gauge
489-98800032 Z & Nn3 9.10

Micrometer Height Gauge
489-98800033 18.85
Adjustable micrometer accurately measures car underbody height, wheel width, track width and trip pin height for N, Nn3 and Z Scales. Great for body mount and pilot applications.

Rerailer Ramp
489-98800132N Rerailer Ramp straight or curved track 2.05

Tools
Coupler Assembly Fixture
489-98800191 For N & Z Scales 9.40
Fixture holds parts in place for easier assembly.

Coupler Tweezers
489-98800061 4.15

Speedi Driver Cleaner
489-98800151 For N & Z Scale Locos 11.75

Tap & Drill Set
489-98800121 6.60

For Up-To-Date Information and News Bookmark Walthers Web site at
www.walthers.com

MISSION MODELS

NEW SUPPLIER

NEW PRODUCTS
Take on tough modeling tasks with this line of tools. Ideal for all kinds of modeling, these unique items are precision engineered and manufactured to provide years of service.

The Grabhandler™

NEW 466-MM06 69.00
Make custom grab irons and handrails from 1/16 to 1-1/2" long quickly, easily and accurately with this handy tool. Unlike pliers, the Grab Handler provides exact spacing for perfect results every time, and a simple screw handle can be tightened to hold material securely. The unit will handle rods, tubes, flat stock and wire made of soft or hard metals without damage. Made of carbon steel, the tool has a black oxide finish to prevent corrosion and is fully indexed with English and Metric dimensions.

Multi Tool™
30.00 ea
Designed to bend photo-etched parts, this handy tool lets you create accurate and efficient radii up to 360 degrees for a wide range of small details. Made of machined aluminum and tool steel, with laser-marked sizing index in both English and Metric sizes.

NEW 466-MM07 Small
For use with smaller parts, handles the following sizes: .375"/9.53mm, .325"/8.26mm, .275"/6.99mm, .225"/5.72mm, .175"/4.45mm, .100"/2.54mm, .047"/1.20mm.

NEW 466-MM08 Large
For use with larger parts, handles the following sizes: .500"/12.70mm, .350"/8.89mm, .300"/7.62mm, .250"/6.35mm, .200"/5.08mm, .125"/3.18mm, .063"/1.60mm.

Micro Chisel
Perfect for removing molded on details, cleaning seam lines, sculpting and much more, the Micro Chisel is designed to get into hard to reach areas and remove as much or as little material as needed. Available in two sizes, each features a stainless steel handle with rubber grip. The chisel tip is produced from hardened spring steel and honed to a fine razor-sharp cutting surface; tips are removable and replaceable using the built-in set screw.
The Micro Chisel will cut through, both hard and soft plastics, resins, plaster, all putties, epoxy putties, wood, soft white metal and similar materials. NOTE: Tips are extremely sharp and safety glasses should always be worn when using these tools.

NEW 466-MM09 2mm Tip 14.99
NEW 466-MM10 1mm Tip 11.50

NEW 466-MM11 2mm Tip Set; Flat & Angled Blades, Allen Wrench 8.50

Etch Mate™

NEW 466-EM001 Photo Etch Bending Tool 75.00
Now it's easy to bend photo-etched details quickly and accurately using the Etch Mate. Measuring just 6.5" x 3.5" (16.2 x 8.7cm), this state-of-the-art bending tool is CAD designed and CNC produced to the finest aerospace specs. Both the folding head and base are matched sets. Each Folding head is put through a hand-leveling process that allows the folding head to sit flat against the fixture base resulting in superior clamping strength. With the hand-leveling process, the tool head requires less force when tightening the photo-etch into the Etch Mate.
The unit also includes a fine triangular folding channel, which produces accurate square bends. The folding channel also acts as an alignment guide, which will assure you that your photo etch is properly aligned with the folding fingers before bending your valuable photo etch.
Five guide pins eliminate any play between the tool head and base, yet assure trouble-free movement of the tool head.
The front side of the tool head is duplicated on the backside in the form of a straight edge. This feature allows you to remove the tool head, flip it around and bend larger pieces such as fenders, railings, side skirts and much more.
Using chemical etching, media blast and a final khaki drab anodizing process, the tool has a tough non-reflective work surface that allows you to spend more time working with greater visibility between the work surface and any type of photo etch.

Extended Folding Blades for Etch Mate

NEW 466-EM002 8.50
Custom made for the Etch Mate (#466-EM001, sold separately), these folding blades feature a .009" double beveled edge. Designed to slide effortlessly underneath the photo etch, use these blades to bend longer pieces such as fenders, ship railings, side skirts, railroad parts, structures and much more. NOTE: These are actual razor blades and extremely sharp! A protective case is included.

TL MARSHALL CO.

FOAM CUTTERS
A must-have for every modeler's toolbox, these knives allow you to cut high density foam with ease, speed and accuracy. The rigid blade can plunge into the foam without bending or warping to cut concave terrain like riverbeds, caves and tunnels. Use the edge of the blade to cut fine lines and the flat of the blade to smooth foam corners. Cutting foam with heat leaves a finished foam edge without messy airborne particles to clean up.

715-12050 Crafter's 69.95
Has an operational time of 5-10 minutes before shutting down to cool. The "Deadman's switch" shuts the knife off automatically when set down.

NEW 715-12051 PRO-1 89.95
Will operate continuously for up to five hours.

TOOLS

NGINEERING

NEW PRODUCT
Micro Clips w/Smooth Jaws

NEW 514-N440010 pkg(10) **2.75**
These handy copper-plated clips are ideal for holding small parts like Ngineering LEDs during soldering, but have hundreds of uses in model making. 5-Amp current rating.

EASY-REACH CURVED TIP SYRINGE

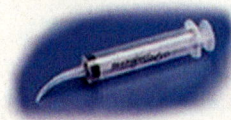

514-N4310 **1.85**
This is the Monoject® #412, with a long, curved tip that allows easy access in tight places. The small tip opening of just .028" diameter provides precise dispensing control. It can be used with a wide variety of materials including glues, caulking, oils, grease, cleaners, soldering flux and more. Holds up to .4 ounces 12cc of material to handle big jobs or for more work time between refills.

NorthWest Short Line

The Puller

53-454 **9.95**
A rigid, precision tool for removing wheels, drivers and gears from axles and shafts. Made for HO Scale modeling, but handles larger and smaller scales. Capacity: axles 1/16" to 1/8"; drivers, wheels and gears up to 1-5/8" O.D. Maximum press depth 1". See Professional Press Tool Set (#53-45394, sold separately) to handle N Scale axles.

Press Screws
Optional for #454 with thumb screw head (will not accept Allen wrench).
53-45314 1/16" Tip **2.25**
53-45324 3/32" Tip **2.25**
53-45334 Cone Tip **1.95**
53-45344 Flat Tip **1.95**
53-45074 V-Plate For Puller **.95**

The Puller II
53-554 **9.95**
This Puller can remove gears from a shaft with a distance of 1-5/8" 4cm from the face of the gear to the shaft end. Great for repairs or rebuilding in smaller scales.

Puller Accessories
Individual Press Tools pkg(2) 9.95 ea
53-45404 1mm
53-45424 1.2mm
53-45444 1.5mm
53-45464 2.4mm

The Chopper

53-494 **29.95**
Heavy-duty stripwood length cutter. Also can do miter cuts (guides for 30, 45 and 60° included). Adjustable stop piece permits setting any cut length up to 3-1/4". Four blades and operating suggestions included. Also cuts styrene and other model making plastics. Safety top keeps handle from slipping or raising dangerously high.

53-49154 Extra Blades pkg(8) **1.25**

The Chopper II

53-694 **44.95**
Precision cutting tool includes replaceable cutting mat. It also features rigid aluminum handle and base, miter guides for 30, 45, 60 and 90° angles and a safety stop. Cut wood and styrene strip material up to 1/8".

53-69054 Replacement Cutting Mat For Chopper II **3.95**

The Chopper III
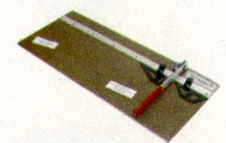

53-594 **39.95**
Heavy-duty wide-base version of the Chopper allows easier handling of long pieces of material. Chopper III provides for installation of up to 3 handles, permitting multiple setups. Includes one handle only, additional are available. The 18" wide base is a sturdier work area and the safety top keeps handle from slipping or raising dangerously high.

Professional Press Tool Sets
53-45394 Complete Set pkg(4) **29.95**
Includes one each #53-45404, 45424, 45444 and 45464. Use with the Puller (#53-454) and the Puller II (#53-554), both sold separately. Allows pullers to work N Scale shafts. Each set consists of a short, hardened steel pin mounted in a mandrel press to "break" the shaft free of the gear and a long pin to press the loosened shaft out of the gear or wheel. The tools can also help in the accurate assembly of short, small shafts with gears and wheels.

Sanding Sticks 3.75 ea
53-25019 120 Grit (red)
53-25029 240 Grit (blue)
53-25039 320 Grit (green)
53-25049 400 Grit (yellow)
53-25059 600 Grit (black)

Replacement Belts For Sanding Sticks 1.75 ea
53-28069 For #25019
53-28079 For #25029
53-28089 For #25039
53-28099 For #25049
53-28109 For #25059

TESTORS

Decal Applicator System
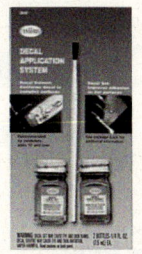

704-8809 **3.69**
System helps decals conform to difficult shapes through improved adhesion. System includes two bottles of decal solution and one brush.

Drop Cloth

704-8803 **4.49**
24 x 36" sheet is impervious to most solvents.

Hobby Knives
Specially designed for building plastic kits. Blade can be resharpened.

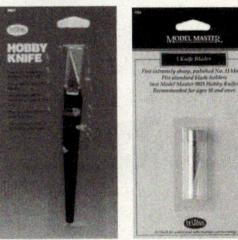

704-8801   704-8816

704-8801 Hobby Knife **1.99**
Dealers MUST Order Packs of 12.
704-8816 Knife Blades pkg(5) **4.75**
704-8830 Hobby Knife w/5 Blades pkg(5) **4.75**

Needle File Set
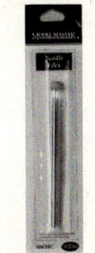

704-50630 **5.39**

Pin Vise

704-50629 **13.79**
With six drill bits.

Sandpaper

704-8802 **2.99**
These hobby sanding films are washable, flexible, reusable and tough. Five grades: coarse, medium, fine, extra-fine and ultra-fine.

Sprue Cutters

704-50628 **14.99**

Tweezers
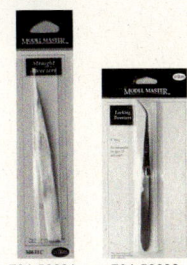

704-50631   704-50632

704-50631 Straight **4.29**
704-50632 Lock **5.39**

417

TOOLS

NMRA

Standards Gauge 10.00 ea

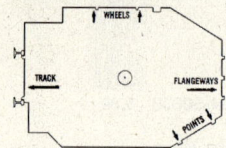

Designed and developed by the NMRA (National Model Railroad Association) Engineering Committee, this pocket-sized gauge enables you to check all important dimensions on your track and rolling stock as follows:

- Gauge of track and turnouts
- Flangeway depth and "check gauge"
- Clearance
- Height of loading platform and coupler

If cars do not run correctly, this gauge will pinpoint the trouble for you. Complete instructions come with each gauge.

98-1 HO Standard Gauge
98-2 HOn3 Standard Gauge
98-5 O Standard Gauge
98-6 On3/00 Standard Gauge
98-7 Sn3 Standard Gauge
98-8 N Standard Gauge

XURON CORP.

NEW PRODUCT
Pliers

NEW 791-90140 Bent Nose **19.49**

SHEARS

These high-precision shears have a special ultra-tapered shape that provides a simple way to quickly and cleanly cut in hard-to-reach areas. Perfect for cutting sprue and wire.

791-90001 Premium Quality Shear - Oval Head **20.49**

791-90005 Premium Quality Shear - Tapered Head **20.49**

791-90026 Crafter's Shear **14.49**

791-90028 Track Cutter **14.49**

791-90033 Hard Wire & Cable Cutter **17.49**

791-90036 Ultraflush Cutting Shear **11.49**

791-90039 High Precision Shear **11.49**

791-90043 Angled High Precision Shear **17.49**

791-90046 Photo Etch Shear **16.49**

791-90137 Track Cutter for MarklinTrack **18.49**

Item listed below is available by Special Order (see Legend Page).
791-90006 Shear - Tapered Head with Wire Retainer **22.49**

SCISSORS

791-90118 Modeler's **18.99**
This handy stainless-steel scissors easily cuts mylar, fabric, styrene, soft aluminum or brass sheet stock.

791-90128 High Durability **22.99**
These user-friendly scissors are designed to cut through tough Kevlar fibers, but can be used to trim photo-etched parts. Feature high carbon steel blades, ultra-durable plasma spray coating and serrations on one edge.

PLIERS

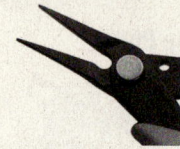

791-90065 Tweezernose™, Smooth **18.99**
791-90066 Tweezernose, Serrated **18.99**

791-90075 Longnose, Smooth **11.99**

791-90122 Round Nose **15.49**

791-90123 Combination Tip **15.99**

791-90124 Split Ring **13.99**

791-90125 Micro Former **16.99**

STAINLESS STEEL TWEEZERS
25.99 ea

High-quality, Swiss-manufactured, electronic-grade tweezers manufactured from anti-magnetic, anti-acid stainless steel.

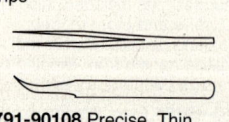

791-90107 Tapered, Extra Fine Tips

791-90108 Precise, Thin, Curved Tips

TOOL KITS

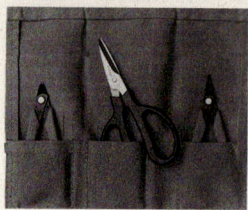

791-90119 Modeler's **49.99**
Includes #90039 high-precision shear, #90065 Tweezernose pliers and #90118 modeler's scissors in a durable tri-fold pouch.

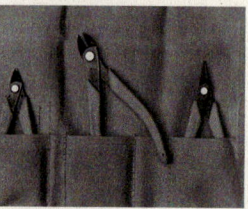

791-90120 Railroader's **47.00**
Features the #90028 Xuron track cutter, #90039 high-precision shear and #90066 serrated Tweezernose pliers in a tri-fold fabric pouch.

791-90121 Pouch Only **13.99**

DISPENSING BOTTLES
4.49 ea (Unless Noted)

Polyethylene bottles with stainless-steel dispensing tubes for controlled dispensing of a wide variety of liquids, including solvents. 2oz.

791-90115 0.010" ID Needle
791-90116 0.020" ID Needle
791-90117 0.040" ID Needle
791-90114 2oz Dispensing Bottle Nozzle Spout **2.49**

WIRE STRIPPERS

791-90134 Adjustable **13.99**

791-90136 Solid Wire Adjustable w/Gauge Markings **15.49**

TOOLS

RIBBONRAIL

Work Cradle

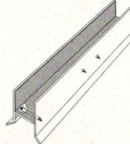

170-1055 7.50
Hold your favorite models safely and securely while detail painting, decaling or making repairs. Made of Alclad aluminum, this easy-to-assemble holder is adjustable and padded to protect the finish of your work.

STATE TOOL & DIE CO.

Glue & Mixing Dishes

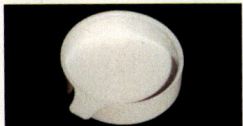

661-800 pkg(6) **2.00**
Reusable glue and mixing dishes.

WOODLAND SCENICS®

Low Temp Foam Glue Gun

785-1445 16.98
The Glue Gun with the Low Temp Glue Sticks operates at a temperature that will not damage foam.

785-1446 pkg(10) **5.98**
10" glue sticks.

Hot Wire Foam Cutter

785-1435 39.98
The Hot Wire Foam Cutter has adjustable collars allowing for clean, accurate cuts in foam. Attach the Guide for more precise cutting. The Bow attachment adds versatility to the Hot Wire Foam Cutter. Woodland Scenics® recommends using only on SubTerrain white foam which emits no toxic fumes. Use only special Nichrome replacement wire.

Foam Cutter Replacement Wire
785-1436 4' **2.29**

Foam Cutter Bow & Guide

785-1437 7.98
This accessory increases the versatility of the Hot Wire Foam Cutter (785-1435, sold separately), allowing cuts in material from 1/4 to 5" thick, or cuts at precise angles.

Foam Knife

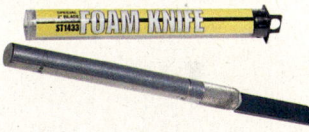

785-1433 6.98
The Foam Knife comes with a 2" replaceable blade that is ideal for cutting thick pieces of foam.

Foam Knife Blades

785-1434 pkg(4) **5.98**

Get Your Daily Dose of Product News at
www.walthers.com

TOOLS

Models by Jim Kelly, Photo by Tim Wickerham, Milwaukee, Wisconsin

SCRATCH BUILDING

If it weren't for the big fertilizer plant along the tracks, Bena, California, would have no industries at all — just grazing cattle and a couple of oil wells. But the big plant receives materials by rail and ships fertilizer products by rail and truck. Serviced by a siding off the busy SP/ATSF mainline, the distinctive complex features various tanks, elevators and a long, angular bulk storage shelter with truck loading apparatus. It's sandwiched between the road and tracks, so it's a bit cramped — perfect for a layout scene! On a typical weekday, a Santa Fe wayfreight has just dropped a couple of cars in the siding and is getting back on the train.

Sometimes a kit just won't do — especially when a key scene on your layout or module has unique buildings like the plant at Bena on Jim Kelly's N Trak module. Jim built the complex with styrene and other structural parts from a variety of manufacturers, all of which you'll find in the Scratch Building Supplies Section.

SCRATCH BUILDING SUPPLIES

WALTHERS

A complete range of miniature. Wood, machine and nylon screws, plus hex nuts and washers in assorted sizes are available. (Machine and wood screws may be brass or brass plated.)

SIZE INFORMATION

Size	00-90	0-80	1-72	2-56
Screw Body Diameter	.047	.060	.073	.086
Clearance Drill Number	55	52	48	43
Tap Drill Number	61	55	53	50
Hex Head Across Flat	.078	.097	.109	.123
Height	.042	.042	.055	.064
Round Head Diameter	.089	.108	.136	.164
Height	.041	.047	.055	.065
Flat Head Diameter	.089	.108	.136	.164
Height	.024	.035	.043	.051

HARDWARE

Brass Washers pkg(16) 2.98 ea

947-1270 #00 (O.D.=105" I.D.=060" .020" Thick)
947-1271 #0 (O.D.=125" I.D.=068" .020" Thick)
947-1272 #1 (O.D.=156" I.D.=084" .025" Thick)
947-1273 #2 (O.D.=188" I.D.=094" .025" Thick)

Flat-Head Brass Machine Screws 2.98 ea

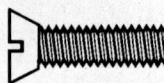

00-90
947-1042 3/16 x .047" pkg(12)
947-1043 1/4 x .047" pkg(12)
947-1045 3/8 x .047" pkg(12)
947-1046 1/2 x .047" pkg(10)

0-80
947-1052 3/16 x .060" pkg(16)
947-1053 1/4 x .060" pkg(16)
947-1055 3/8 x .060" pkg(12)
947-1056 1/2 x .060" pkg(10)

1-72
947-1062 3/16 x .073" pkg(16)
947-1063 1/4 x .073" pkg(16)
947-1065 3/8 x .073" pkg(12)
947-1066 1/2 x .073" pkg(10)

2-56
947-1072 3/16 x .086" pkg(16)
947-1073 1/4 x .086" pkg(16)
947-1075 3/8 x .086" pkg(12)
947-1076 1/2 x .086" pkg(10)

Hex-Head Brass Machine Screws 2.98 ea

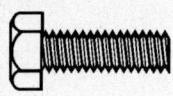

00-90
947-1122 3/16 x .047" pkg(12)
947-1123 1/4 x .047" pkg(12)
947-1125 3/8 x .047" pkg(12)
947-1126 1/2 x .047" pkg(10)

0-80
947-1132 3/16 x .060" pkg(12)
947-1133 1/4 x .060" pkg(12)
947-1135 3/8 x .060" pkg(12)
947-1136 1/2 x .060" pkg(10)

1-72
947-1142 3/16 x .073" pkg(12)
947-1143 1/4 x .073" pkg(12)
947-1145 3/8 x .073" pkg(12)
947-1146 1/2 x .073" pkg(10)

2-56
947-1152 3/16 x .086" pkg(12)
947-1153 1/4 x .086" pkg(12)
947-1155 3/8 x .086" pkg(12)
947-1156 1/2 x .086" pkg(10)

Hex Nuts pkg(12) 2.98 ea

Brass
947-1250 00-90 (.040 x 5/64")
947-1251 0-80 (.050 x 5/32")
947-1252 1-72 (.062 x 7/64")
947-1253 2-56 (.072 x 1/8")

Nylon
947-1255 2-56 (.075 x 3/16")
947-1256 4-40 (.100 x 1/4")

Round-Head Brass Machine Screws 2.98 ea

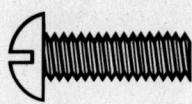

00-90
947-1002 3/16 x .047" pkg(12)
947-1003 1/4 x .047" pkg(12)
947-1005 3/8 x .047" pkg(12)
947-1006 1/2 x .047" pkg(10)

0-80
947-1012 3/16 x .060" pkg(16)
947-1013 1/4 x .060" pkg(16)
947-1015 3/8 x .060" pkg(12)
947-1016 1/2 x .060" pkg(10)

1-72
947-1022 3/16 x .073" pkg(16)
947-1023 1/4 x .073" pkg(16)
947-1025 3/8 x .073" pkg(12)
947-1026 1/2 x .073" pkg(10)

2-56
947-1032 3/16 x .086" pkg(16)
947-1033 1/4 x .086" pkg(16)
947-1035 3/8 x .086" pkg(12)
947-1036 1/2 x .086" pkg(10)

Round-Head Nylon Machine Screws pkg(12) 2.98 ea

947-1163 1-72 1/4 x .073"
947-1177 2-56 5/8 x .086"
947-1188 4-40 3/4 x .112"

Self-Tapping #2 Sheet Metal Screws pkg(24) 2.98 ea

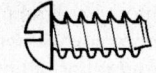

947-1189 3/16 x .088"
947-1190 1/4 x .088"
947-1191 1/2 x .088"

Wood Screws - Brass or Brass-Plated pkg(24) 2.98 ea

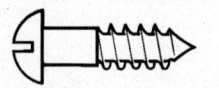

#0
947-1195 3/8 x .060"

#1
947-1196 3/8 x .073"
947-1197 1/2 x .073"

#2
947-1198 #2 3/8 x .086"
947-1199 #2 1/2 x .086"

TOOLS

Drill Bits

pkg(2) 1.98 ea
947-43 .089"
947-48 .076"
947-50 .070"
947-52 .064"
947-53 .060"
947-55 .052"
947-56 .047"
947-57 .043"
947-58 .042"
947-60 .040"

pkg(2) 2.29 ea
947-61 .039"
947-62 .038"
947-63 .037"
947-64 .036"
947-65 .035"
947-66 .033"
947-67 .032"
947-68 .031"
947-69 .0292"
947-70 .028"
947-71 .026"
947-72 .025"
947-73 .024"
947-74 .0225"
947-75 .021"
947-76 .020"
947-77 .018"
947-78 .016"
947-79 .0145"
947-80 .0135"

Drill Set & Accessories

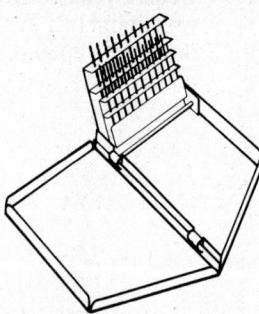

949-659 Set of 20 Bits w/Case **18.98** in a metal case.

949-660 Drill Case Only **4.98**

Pin Vise

949-664 Double Ended **9.98** Includes two single end collets. Holds bits from #42 to #70.

Tap & Die Holder

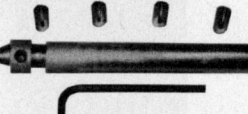

949-663 Tap Holder **17.98** Includes storage case, holder, Allen wrench and collets for 00-90, 0-80, 1-72 and 2-56 taps.

Taps 3.98 ea

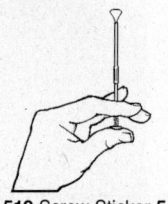

947-1301 00-90
947-1302 0-80
947-1303 1-72
947-1304 2-56

Work Holder

949-519 Screw Sticker **5.98** Get a firm grip on tiny screws, parts and more. One-handed operation makes the miniature fingers an extension of your own.

Wrenches 3.98 ea

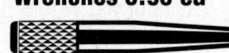

Will fit brass hex nuts and hex head screws.
947-1321 #00
947-1322 #0
947-1323 #1
947-1324 #2

949-662 Wrench Set pkg(4) **15.98** Includes one each #1321-1324.

POURABLE METAL

Temp-Low™

949-525 3oz (84g) **4.98** Melt in hot water (158° to 190° F). Pour in without fear of unsoldering detail. Make custom castings in cardboard, rubber or plaster molds. Makes a great filler to support tubing while bending.

SCRATCH BUILDING SUPPLIES

WALTHERS

ADHESIVE

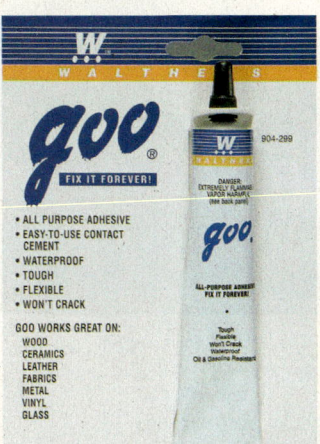

Fix It Forever with GOO®!
904-299 GOO Adhesive, Large Tube 1oz **2.98**

- **All Purpose Adhesive**
GOO is the permanent rubber base adhesive that grips most anything. It never lets go.

- **Fast Setting Joints**
Easy contact action opens new possibilities for fast-setting joints with any material.

GOO is the perfect adhesive for building or repairing jobs on your layout and around the house!

The easy contact action of GOO produces fast-setting joints with any material. GOO works with all types of metals (including steel, brass, aluminum, copper and others.) plus items like wood, plastic, cardboard, china, leather, vinyl, ceramics, paper, concrete and many more, on any smooth or porous surface.

GOO is a permanent rubber base adhesive that's shockproof, waterproof and crack proof—it's as flexible as rubber. Joints won't crack when flexed back and forth, won't break loose when the temperature changes and won't weaken when wet or damp. It sticks forever!

Dealers MUST order multiples of 6.

PAINTING ACCESSORIES

Masking Liquid

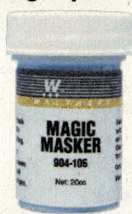

904-106 Magic Masker (20cc) **2.98**
Get professional results when covering odd shaped or small areas, such as windows, without the time and trouble of cutting and fitting tape. Brush it on and allow to dry. Then spray your color, let dry and peel off. Works on plastic, wood, metal, paint, chrome and silver.

Dealers MUST order multiples of 12.

Decal Setting Solution

904-470 Solvaset 2oz **2.98**
Softens decal film so it snuggles down on surface, details Eliminates air bubbles, white spots and draping.

Dealers MUST order multiples of 6.

BRAWA
LIEBE ZUM DETAIL

IMPORTED FROM GERMANY BY WALTHERS

PLASTIC SHEETS
4.99 ea
Ideal for all kinds of scratchbuilding projects, each pack includes two sheets measuring 4 x 6". Thickness varies from 1/32 to .039".

186-2800   186-2801

186-2800 Wood Flooring (Dark Brown)
186-2801 Wood Flooring (Natural Finish)

186-2805   186-2806

186-2805 Cobblestones
186-2806 Historic Cobblestones (gray)

186-2810   186-2815

186-2810 Curved Cobblestones
186-2815 Random Stone Paving

186-2825   186-2826

186-2825 Masonry Slabs (Sandstone)
186-2826 Masonry Slabs (Brick Red)

186-2827   186-2830

186-2827 Brick Wall Sheet
186-2830 Sidewalk Paving

186-2835   186-2840

186-2835 Ribbed Metal Sheet (silver)
186-2836 Ribbed Metal Sheet (black)
186-2840 Window Glazing

186-2845   186-2850

186-2845 Artificial Paving Stone
186-2850 Sheet Piling

186-2855   186-2856

186-2855 Corrugated Metal Sheet (gray)
186-2856 Corrugated Sheet (translucent)

186-2867

186-2867 Wall Tiles (Brick Red)

TUBING/RODS
Brass tube and angles are 12" long unless noted; dimensions shown are external diameter x wall thickness in millimeters.

Dealers MUST order multiples of 10.

Limited Quantity Available On All Items

Angle
186-3764 4.0 x 4.0 x 0.50 **5.45**
186-3767 3.5 x 3.5 x 0.30 **3.85**

Hexagon Tube
186-3750 3.0 x 0.30 **2.45**

Square Tube
186-3722 4.0 x 4.0 x 0.30 **2.90**

ALPINE DIVISION SCALE MODELS

Aluminum Paper
700-1001 Corrugated, 4 x 11-1/2" pkg(6) **4.02**

Tin Siding Sheets
.010" Corrugated
700-100 4 x 12" pkg(6) **8.25**
700-101 2 x 12" pkg(6) **5.50**

.010" Plain
700-102 4 x 12" pkg(6) **6.05**

90° Angle
700-104 1/8 x 12" pkg(6) **4.13**

GC LASER

ROOF SHINGLES
Put a new roof on any model. Each package includes six matching laser-cut sheets plus instructions and drawings. Includes enough material to cover 32 square inches.

3-Tab 7-1/4" Long
10.99 ea
292-1131 Black

292-1132 Brown
292-1133 Green
292-1134 White

Diamond 7-1/4" Long
10.99 ea
NEW 292-1135 Black
NEW 292-1136 Brown

NEW 292-1137 Green
NEW 292-1138 White

Scalloped 7-1/4" Long
16.99 ea
NEW 292-1139 Black
NEW 292-11310 Brown

NEW 292-11311 Green
NEW 292-11312 White

For Daily Product Updates Point Your Browser to
www.walthers.com

SCRATCH BUILDING SUPPLIES

Styrene is one of the most common modeling plastics. It can be used to simulate concrete, metal or wooden surfaces, and is easily cut and sanded to virtually any shape. When cutting sheets, simply score with a sharp knife, then "break" on the scored line. Small strips and very thin sheets can be cut through. Parts can be joined with plastic solvents, while epoxies and CA adhesives can be used to join painted parts or other materials. Before brush painting with Floquil, Scalecoat or other lacquers, a primer coat of Floquil Barrier or Scalecoat Shieldcoat should be applied to prevent the paint from "attacking" the plastic.

SIDING SHEETS

Duplicate many common types of building siding with these opaque white sheets. Each is pre-scribed to match different widths of lumber. Sheets measures 6 x 12".

V-Groove 4.59 ea

Used on freight and passenger cars, railroad, commercial and residential buildings. Many 19th- and early 20th-century structures had panels of v-groove siding applied in horizontal, vertical and diagonal patterns, or in combination with clapboard and novelty siding for decorative effects. Part dimension indicates spacing.

.020" Thick
269-2025 .025"
269-2030 .030"
269-2040 .040"
269-2050 .050"
269-2060 .060"
269-2080 .080"
269-2100 .100"
269-2125 .125"

.040" Thick
269-4030 .030"
269-4040 .040"
269-4050 .050"
269-4060 .060"
269-4080 .080"
269-4100 .100"
269-4125 .125"
269-4188 .188"
269-4250 .250"

Novelty .040" 4.59 ea

Many buildings of the mid-19th to early-20th century used novelty siding, also known as shiplap or drop siding. It consisted of overlapping boards, with a rabbet in the bottom of each board, overlapping in the round cove on the top of the board below. Part dimension indicates spacing.

269-4062 .060"
5-1/4 HO Scale inches, 9-1/2 N Scale inches.
269-4083 .083"
7-1/4 HO Scale inches.
269-4109 .109"
9-1/4 HO Scale inches.
269-4150 .150"

Board & Batten Sheets 4.59 ea

Part dimension indicates spacing. Sheets are .040" thick.

269-4542 .075"
269-4543 .100"
269-4544 .125"

Latest New Product News Daily! Visit Walthers Web site at
www.walthers.com

Clapboard 4.59 ea

One of the most common sidings (often called lap siding) is a prominent feature of many wooden railroad buildings as well as city, town and farm structures of all kinds. Sheets are .040" thick. Part dimension indicates spacing.

269-4031 .030"
269-4041 .040"
269-4051 .050"
269-4061 .060"
269-4081 .080"
269-4101 .100"

Corrugated Metal 4.59 ea

Part dimension indicates spacing. Sheets are .040" thick.

269-4525 .030"
269-4526 .040"
269-4527 .060"
269-4528 .080"
269-4529 .100"
269-4530 .125"

STRIPS

Square 2.59 ea
269-196 3/16 x 3/16" pkg(4)
269-199 1/4 x 1/4" pkg(3)

Dimensional
Opaque white strips.

14" long 2.19 ea

.010" Thick pkg(10)
269-100 .020"
269-101 .030"
269-102 .040"
269-103 .060"
269-104 .080"
269-105 .100"
269-106 .125"
269-107 .156"
269-108 .188"
269-109 .250"

.015" Thick pkg(10)
269-110 .020"
269-111 .030"
269-112 .040"
269-113 .060"
269-114 .080"
269-115 .100"
269-116 .125"
269-117 .156"
269-118 .188"
269-119 .250"

.020" Thick pkg(10)
269-120 .020"
269-121 .030"
269-122 .040"
269-123 .060"
269-124 .080"
269-125 .100"
269-126 .125"
269-127 .156"
269-128 .188"
269-129 .250"

.030" Thick pkg(10)
269-131 .030"
269-132 .040"
269-133 .060"
269-134 .080"
269-135 .100"
269-136 .125"
269-137 .156"
269-138 .188"
269-139 .250"

.040" Thick pkg(10)
269-142 .040"
269-143 .060"
269-144 .080"
269-145 .100"
269-146 .125"
269-147 .156"
269-148 .188"
269-149 .250"

SCRATCH BUILDING SUPPLIES

evergreen scale models

.060" Thick
269-153 .060" pkg(10)
269-154 .080" pkg(10)
269-155 .100" pkg(10)
269-156 .125" pkg(10)
269-157 .156" pkg(9)
269-158 .188" pkg(9)
269-159 .250" pkg(8)

.080" Thick
269-164 .080" pkg(9)
269-165 .100" pkg(8)
269-166 .125" pkg(8)
269-167 .156" pkg(8)
269-168 .188" pkg(8)
269-169 .250" pkg(7)

.100" Thick
269-175 .100" pkg(8)
269-176 .125" pkg(7)
269-177 .156" pkg(7)
269-178 .188" pkg(7)
269-179 .250" pkg(6)

.125" Thick
269-186 .125" pkg(6)
269-187 .156" pkg(6)
269-188 .188" pkg(6)
269-189 .250" pkg(5)

STRUCTURAL SHAPES
14" actual length, molded in opaque white styrene.

Channels 2.59 ea
269-261 .060" pkg(4)
269-262 .080" pkg(4)
269-263 .100" pkg(4)
269-264 .125" pkg(4)
269-265 .156" pkg(4)
269-266 .188" pkg(3)
269-267 .250" pkg(3)
269-268 .312" pkg(3)

I-Beams 2.59 ea
269-271 .060" pkg(4)
269-272 .080" pkg(4)
269-273 .100" pkg(4)
269-274 .125" pkg(4)
269-275 .156" pkg(3)
269-276 .188" pkg(3)
269-277 .250" pkg(3)
269-278 .312" pkg(2)
269-279 .375" pkg(2)

H-Columns 2.59 ea
269-281 .060" pkg(4)
269-282 .080" pkg(4)
269-283 .100" pkg(4)
269-284 .125" pkg(3)
269-285 .156" pkg(3)
269-286 .188" pkg(3)
269-287 .250" pkg(2)

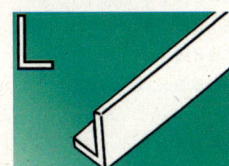

Angles 2.59 ea
269-291 .060" pkg(4)
269-292 .080" pkg(4)
269-293 .100" pkg(4)
269-294 .125" pkg(3)
269-295 .156" pkg(3)
269-296 .188" pkg(3)
269-297 .250" pkg(2)

ROD & TUBING
Each piece molded in white styrene.

14" Long 2.59 ea
269-217 Rod & Tube Assortment pkg(7)

Round
269-210 .030" pkg(10)
269-211 .040" pkg(10)
269-212 .080" pkg(6)
269-213 .100" pkg(5)
269-214 .125" pkg(4)
269-218 .020" pkg(10)
269-219 .025" pkg(10)
269-220 .035" pkg(10)
269-221 .047" pkg(10)
269-222 .062" pkg(8)

Round Tubing
269-223 .093" pkg(6)
269-224 .125" pkg(5)
269-225 .156" pkg(4)
269-226 .187" pkg(4)
269-227 .219" pkg(3)
269-228 .250" pkg(3)
269-229 .281" pkg(3)
269-230 .312" pkg(3)
269-231 .344" pkg(2)
269-232 .375" pkg(2)
269-234 .438" pkg(2)
269-236 .500" pkg(2)

Half Round
269-240 .040" pkg(5)
269-241 .060" pkg(5)
269-242 .080" pkg(4)
269-243 .100" pkg(3)
269-244 .125" pkg(3)

Quarter Rounds
269-246 .030" pkg(5)
269-247 .040" pkg(5)
269-248 .060" pkg(4)
269-249 .080" pkg(3)
269-250 .100" pkg(3)

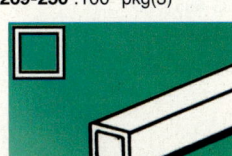

Square Tubing
269-252 .125" pkg(3)
269-253 .187" pkg(3)
269-254 .250" pkg(2)
269-255 .312" pkg(2)
269-256 .375" pkg(2)

Rectangular Tubing
269-257 .125 x .250" pkg(3)
269-258 .187 x .312" pkg(2)
269-259 .250 x .375" pkg(2)

STYRENE SHEETS
Part dimension indicates thickness.

White 6 x 12" 2.99 ea
269-9008 Assortment Includes one each .010, .020 and .040"
269-9009 .005" pkg(3)
269-9010 .010" pkg(4)
269-9015 .015" pkg(3)
269-9020 .020" pkg(3)
269-9030 .030" pkg(2)
269-9040 .040" pkg(2)
269-9060 .060"
269-9080 .080"

White 8 x 21" 9.60 ea (Unless Noted)
269-9101 .010" pkg(8)
269-9102 .015" pkg(6)
269-9103 .020" pkg(6)
269-9104 .030" pkg(4)
269-9105 .040" pkg(3)
269-9106 .060" pkg(2)
269-9107 .080" pkg(2) 12.00
269-9108 .125"

11 x 14" 21.60 ea
269-9210 .010" pkg(15)
269-9215 .015" pkg(12)
269-9220 .020" pkg(12)
269-9230 .030" pkg(8)
269-9240 .040" pkg(6)
269-9260 .060" pkg(4)
269-9280 .080" pkg(3)

12 x 24"
Individual Sheets
269-19010 .010" 2.16
269-19015 .015" 2.70
269-19020 .020" 2.70
269-19030 .030" 4.05
269-19040 .040" 5.40
269-19060 .060" 8.10
269-19080 .080" 10.80
269-19100 .100" 13.50
269-19125 .125" 16.20

Multi-Packs 32.40 ea (Unless Noted)
Dealers MUST order in these quantities.
269-19010 .010" pkg(15)
269-19015 .015" pkg(12)
269-19020 .020" pkg(12)
269-19030 .030" pkg(8)
269-19040 .040" pkg(6)
269-19060 .060" pkg(4)
269-19080 .080" pkg(3)
269-19100 .100" pkg(2) 27.00
269-19125 .125" pkg(2)

Sheet Assortment
269-9002 Odds & Ends 6.59
A scratchbuilder's delight—a 1/2lb (8oz) of sheet plastic in various thicknesses and lengths.

Clear 6 x 12" 3.59 ea
269-9005 .005" pkg(3)
269-9006 .010" pkg(2)
269-9007 .015" pkg(2)

TILES
Scribed in squares to represent flooring. Opaque white sheets are .040" thick.

6 x 12" 4.59 ea
269-4501 1/16" Square
269-4502 1/12" Square
269-4503 1/8" Square
269-4504 1/6" Square
269-4505 1/4" Square
269-4506 1/3" Square
269-4507 1/2" Square

SIDEWALKS
Opaque white sheets are .040" thick, scribed in squares, just paint and cut to model sidewalks.

6 x 12" Sheet 4.59 ea
269-4514 1/8" Square
269-4515 3/16" Square
269-4516 1/4" Square
269-4517 3/8" Square
269-4518 1/2" Square

STANDING SEAM ROOFING

6 x 12" Sheet 6.59 ea
With seam strips, measures .040" thick.
269-4521 3/16"
269-4522 1/4"
269-4523 3/8"
269-4524 1/2"

BOOKS

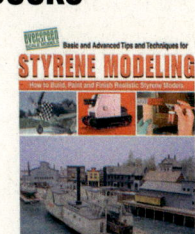

269-14 Styrene Modeling 14.95
88 pages.

FALLER

IMPORTED FROM GERMANY BY WALTHERS

Sidewalk Tiles

272-180597 13.99
Two large sidewalk tiles that can be divided into eight footway tiles, four footway sheets. 16 separate edging strips are included.

425

SCRATCH BUILDING SUPPLIES

Hob-Bits® by Woodland Scenics®

Hob-Bits® – High quality brass machine screws, nuts and washers in four different sizes and four different styles. Hob-Bits tools include wrenches, taps and dies for all four sizes.

Fillister Head Screws

00-90 pkg(5) 2.19 ea
785-821 1/8 x .046"
785-822 1/4 x .046"
785-823 3/8 x .046"
785-824 1/2 x .046"

0-80 pkg(5) 2.19 ea
785-825 1/8 x .058"
785-826 1/4 x .058"
785-827 3/8 x .058"
785-828 1/2 x .058"

1-72 pkg(5) 2.19 ea
785-829 1/8 x .072"
785-830 1/4 x .072"
785-831 3/8 x .072"
785-832 1/2 x .072"

2-56 pkg(5) 2.19 ea
785-833 1/8 x .085"
785-834 1/4 x .085"
785-835 3/8 x .085"
785-836 1/2 x .085"

Flat Head Screws

00-90 pkg(5) 2.19 ea
785-841 1/8 x .046"
785-842 1/4 x .046"
785-843 3/8 x .046"
785-844 1/2 x .046"

0-80 pkg(5) 2.19 ea
785-845 1/8 x .058"
785-846 1/4 x .058"
785-847 3/8 x .058"
785-848 1/2 x .058"

1-72 pkg(5) 2.19 ea
785-849 1/8 x .072"
785-850 1/4 x .072"
785-851 3/8 x .072"
785-852 1/2 x .072"

2-56 pkg(5) 2.19 ea
785-853 1/8 x .085"
785-854 1/4 x .085"
785-855 3/8 x .085"
785-856 1/2 x .085"

Hex Head Screws
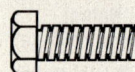

00-90 pkg(5) 2.19 ea
785-861 1/8 x .046"
785-862 1/4 x .046"
785-863 3/8 x .046"
785-864 1/2 x .046"

0-80 pkg(5) 2.19 ea
785-865 1/8 x .058"
785-866 1/4 x .058"
785-867 3/8 x .058"
785-868 1/2 x .058"

1-72 pkg(5) 2.19 ea
785-869 1/8 x .072"
785-870 1/4 x .072"
785-871 3/8 x .072"
785-872 1/2 x .072"

2-56 pkg(5) 2.19 ea
785-873 1/8 x .085"
785-874 1/4 x .085"
785-875 3/8 x .085"
785-876 1/2 x .085"

Round Head Screws

00-90 pkg(5) 2.19 ea
785-801 1/8 x .046"
785-802 1/4 x .046"
785-803 3/8 x .046"
785-804 1/2 x .046"

0-80 pkg(5) 2.19 ea
785-805 1/8 x .058"
785-806 1/4 x .058"
785-807 3/8 x .058"
785-808 1/2 x .058"

1-72 pkg(5) 2.19 ea
785-809 1/8 x .072"
785-810 1/4 x .072"
785-811 3/8 x .072"
785-812 1/2 x .072"

2-56 pkg(5) 2.19 ea
785-813 1/8 x .085"
785-814 1/4 x .085"
785-815 3/8 x .085"
785-816 1/2 x .085"

Hex Nuts

pkg(5) 2.19 ea
785-881 00-90
785-882 0-80
785-883 1-72
785-884 2-56

Washers

pkg(5) 2.19 ea
785-891 00-90
785-892 0-80
785-893 1-72
785-894 2-56

TOOLS

Dies 49.98 ea
785-877 00-90
785-878 0-80
785-879 1-72
785-880 2-56

Taps 6.98 ea
785-895 00-90
785-896 0-80
785-897 1-72
785-898 2-56

Wrenches 6.98 ea
785-885 00-90
785-886 0-80
785-887 1-72
785-888 2-56

Kappler Mill & Lumber Co.

A complete selection of stripwood and scale lumber, cut to match common construction sizes. Please visit Walthers Web site at www.walthers.com for a complete listing of all available items.

Scale Lumber 2.75 ea

Dimensions shown in N Scale inches, each piece is 12" long

2"
385-515 x 4" pkg(11)
385-516 x 6" pkg(11)
385-517 x 8" pkg(10)
385-518 x 10" pkg(10)
385-519 x 12" pkg(10)

4"
385-538 x 4" pkg(12)
385-539 x 6" pkg(12)
385-540 x 8" pkg(12)
385-541 x 10" pkg(12)
385-542 x 12" pkg(10)

6"
385-549 x 6" pkg(12)
385-550 x 8" pkg(12)
385-551 x 10" pkg(12)
385-552 x 12" pkg(10)

8"
385-559 x 8" pkg(12)
385-560 x 10" pkg(10)
385-561 x 12" pkg(10)

10"
385-568 x 10" pkg(12)
385-569 x 12" pkg(12)

12"
385-576 x 12" pkg(12)

Fuzz 3.00 ea
Fuzz is a prepackaged, multi-scale wood material for use in scratchbuilding and railroad scenery.

385-621 Fine 6 x 6" Bag
385-622 Medium 6 x 6" Bag
385-623 Coarse 6 x 6" Bag

See What's Available at
www.walthers.com

kibri®

IMPORTED FROM GERMANY BY WALTHERS

BUILDING MATERIALS

Simplify scratchbuilding and kitbashing with these items which are made in exact N Scale. Each injection-molded plastic sheet is highly detailed and easily cut to fit. All sheets measure 4-5/8 x 7-13/16" 11.9 x 19.8cm.

Wall Sections 5.99 ea
405-7960 Random Cut Stone
405-7961 Cut Stone
405-7962 Brick (yellow)

405-7964 Brick, Clinker (brown)

Roofing 5.99 ea

405-7965 Rough Cut Slate

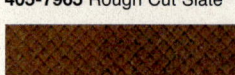
405-7967 Shingles, 1/2 Square, 1/2 Diamond
405-7970 Tile

405-7971 Slate Tile

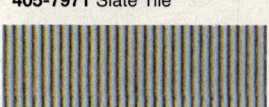
405-7972 Corrugated & Tin

SCRATCH BUILDING SUPPLIES

NEW PRODUCTS

Customize your scratch-built projects with these highly detailed, photo-etched brass parts. Combine windows, doors and other details to bring your designs to life.

Window & Door Sets 15.00 ea (Unless Noted)
NEW 462-92101 Bungalow Windows & Doors
NEW 462-92102 Tall Narrow, Arch & Square Windows
NEW 462-92103 Loading Dock Doors, Medium & Square Windows
NEW 462-92110 Window Pane Combo
NEW 462-92111 Western Windows & Sills, Durango Style 15.50
NEW 462-92112 Western Doors & Portals, Durango Style & Others 15.50
NEW 462-92113 Industrial Windows & Operational Railroad Door 15.50

Ladders 8.50 ea
NEW 462-92401 Long Ladders
NEW 462-92402 Roof or Caboose Tapered & Step Ladders

Fences 15.00 ea
NEW 462-92404 4' High Chain Link Fence w/Two Gates
NEW 462-92405 6' High Chain Link Security Fence w/Gate

Building Details 15.50 ea
NEW 462-92501 Art Nouveau Orleans Balcony Railing
NEW 462-92701 Brick Chimneys

Photo-Etched Brass Mesh 28.50 ea
Ideal for all types of scratchbuilding projects, these etched mesh screens feature fine square hatches at 45°. Sheet measures 5 x 8" 12.5 x 20cm.

462-90801 1/8" Separation - 15 mil Lines

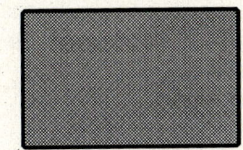
462-90802 3/32" Separation - 12 mil Lines

462-90803 1/16" Separation - 10 mil Lines

462-90804 3/64" Separation - 8 mil Lines

STAINLESS STEEL TUBING

Laser-welded stainless steel, plug-drawn for increased density, smoothness and straightness, with no visible seams. Easily formed and cut, all sizes are supplied in 9" lengths.

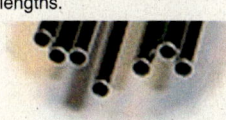

.018" Outside Diameter — .002" Thick Wall
514-N20182 pkg(2) 3.95
514-N20184 pkg(4) 7.25

.032" Outside Diameter — .006" Thick Wall
514-N20322 pkg(2) 3.40
514-N20324 pkg(4) 6.35

.042" Outside Diameter — .0035" Thick Wall
514-N20422 pkg(2) 5.35
514-N20424 pkg(4) 9.95

.050" Outside Diameter — .004" Thick Wall
514-N20502 pkg(2) 5.35
514-N20504 pkg(4) 9.75

.065" Outside Diameter — .005" Thick Wall
514-N20652 pkg(2) 5.65
514-N20654 pkg(4) 10.50

.095" Outside Diameter — .005" Thick Wall
514-N20952 pkg(2) 5.95
514-N20954 pkg(4) 10.95

STRAIGHTENED STAINLESS STEEL WIRE

.004" Diameter
514-N210410 pkg(10) 3.65
Straight within .002" over total 9" length — ultra thin!

.012" Diameter
514-N210410 pkg(10) 3.65
Straight within .010" over total 9" length

.005" Thick Plate Glass 2.75 ea
This super-flat borosilicate glass has superior strength and is ideal for any model windows where a realistic appearance is desired. Simply scribe and snap to size, glue in place with any adhesive.
514-N70038 .85 x .85" pkg(8)

Truck Shown Not Included
514-N70044 .85 x 1.70" pkg(4)

MODEL BUILDER'S SUPPLY LINE™

Styrene Building Sheets HO/N pkg(2) 19.95 ea
11 x 14 x .020"
27.5 x 35 x .005cm
These crisp and well defined, textured sheets are available in many different surfaces. The large sheet size helps the modeler avoid unsightly seams on large projects and, because it's styrene, it is easy to apply. These sheets are produced in a neutral white.

716-50001 Modern Brick

716-50002 1900's Alternate Row On-End

716-50003 1900's Alternate Brick On-End
716-50004 Brick Arches & Columns

716-50005 Concrete Block
716-50006 Cermaic Tile/Paving Stones

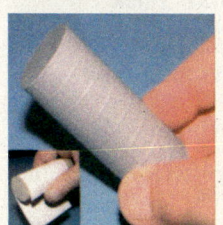
716-50007 Small Welded Plate
716-50008 Large Welded Plate

Information STATION

Railroad Talk

Just like in any profession, there's an inside language used among those familiar with the job. That can be said of railroading. There are many pseudonyms and nicknames used for a variety of railroading terms. Check out the following and see if any sound familiar. The section boss was also referred to as brains, gaffer, gang pusher, herder, king swipe, push, pusher, snipe king or warden.
A telegraph operator was sometimes called brass pounder, buzzer, lightning, slinger, op, puncher, sparks or wire tapper.
A small station or town could be referred to as a falling-off place, filling station, fresh-water town, jerkwater town, jumping-off place, mudhole, stopping-off place, tank, tank station, tool box or whistle stop.
A brakeman was known as air giver, braker, brakie, car catcher, club winder, deadhead, donegan, donniker, fielder, hook, juggler, mule, nipper, pin, pinhead, scissorbill, shack, shack stinger, shag, stringer or stinger.
Passenger coaches were labeled cushions, steam cars or varnished cars. Tank cars also went by the names of cans, oil cans, oilers, tanks or tankers. The switchman was also called cherry picker, cinder cruncher, clown, goose, lever jerker, reptile, snake or yard goose.

SCRATCH BUILDING SUPPLIES

All items are prepackaged and available only in the quantities shown.

HO SCALE LUMBER

For N and Z Scale use make appropriate conversions.

11" Long 2.35 ea
Large dimension is height, small dimension is thickness. Decimals are actual size.

1 Scale Inch
(Actual size .012")
521-3001 x 2 (x .024) pkg(14)
521-3002 x 3 (x .036) pkg(14)
521-3003 x 4 (x .048) pkg(14)
521-3004 x 6 (x .072) pkg(12)
521-3005 x 8 (x .096) pkg(12)
521-3006 x 10 (x .120) pkg(12)

2 Scale Inches
(Actual size .024")
521-3010 x 2 (x .024) pkg(14)
521-3011 x 3 (x .036) pkg(14)
521-3012 x 4 (x .048) pkg(14)
521-3013 x 6 (x .072) pkg(12)
521-3014 x 8 (x .096) pkg(12)
521-3015 x 10 (x .120) pkg(12)
521-3016 x 12 (x .144) pkg(10)

3 Scale Inches
(Actual size .036")
521-3020 x 3 (x .036) pkg(14)
521-3021 x 4 (x .048) pkg(14)
521-3022 x 6 (x .072) pkg(12)
521-3023 x 8 (x .096) pkg(12)
521-3024 x 10 (x .120) pkg(12)
521-3025 x 12 (x .144) pkg(10)

4 Scale Inches
(Actual size .048")
521-3030 x 4 (x .048) pkg(12)
521-3031 x 6 (x .072) pkg(12)
521-3032 x 8 (x .096) pkg(12)
521-3033 x 10 (x .120) pkg(12)
521-3034 x 12 (x .144) pkg(12)

6 Scale Inches
(Actual size .072")
521-3040 x 6 (x .072) pkg(12)
521-3041 x 8 (x .096) pkg(10)
521-3042 x 10 (x .120) pkg(10)
521-3043 x 12 (x .144) pkg(10)

8 Scale Inches
(Actual size .096")
521-3050 x 8 (x .096) pkg(10)
521-3051 x 10 (x .120) pkg(10)
521-3052 x 12 (x .144) pkg(10)

10 Scale Inches
(Actual size .120")
521-3060 x 10 (x .120) pkg(10)
521-3061 x 12 (x .144) pkg(8)

12 Scale Inches
(Actual size .144")
521-3070 x 12 (x .144) pkg(8)

STRIPWOOD

Basswood. Each piece is 24" 60cm long. Large dimension indicates thickness, small dimension indicates width.

1/32" Thick
521-70120 x 1/32" pkg(10) 2.50
521-70122 x 3/64" pkg(10) 2.50
521-70123 x 1/16" pkg(10) 2.50
521-70124 x 5/64" pkg(10) 2.90
521-70125 x 3/32" pkg(10) 2.90
521-70126 x 1/8" pkg(10) 2.90
521-70127 x 5/32" pkg(10) 3.30
521-70128 x 3/16" pkg(10) 3.30
521-70130 x 1/4" pkg(10) 3.10
521-70131 x 5/16" pkg(10) 4.30
521-70132 x 3/8" spkg(10) 5.90
521-70134 x 1/2" pkg(10) 6.90
521-70135 x 3/4" pkg(10) 6.95
521-70136 x 1" pkg(5) 4.35
521-70137 x 2" pkg(5) 7.20
521-70138 x 3" pkg(2) 3.95
521-70139 x 4" pkg(2) 5.27

3/64" Thick
521-70161 x 3/64" pkg(10) 3.20
521-70162 x 1/16" pkg(10) 3.20
521-70163 x 5/64" pkg(10) 3.20
521-70164 x 3/32" pkg(10) 3.20
521-70165 x 1/8" pkg(10) 3.20
521-70166 x 5/32" pkg(10) 3.85
521-70167 x 3/16" pkg(10) 3.85
521-70169 x 1/4" pkg(10) 4.90
521-70170 x 5/16" pkg(10) 5.90
521-70171 x 3/8" pkg(10) 6.00
521-70173 x 1/2" pkg(10) 6.99
521-70174 x 3/4" pkg(10) 7.10
521-70175 x 1" pkg(5) 4.35
521-70176 x 2" pkg(5) 8.56
521-70177 x 3" pkg(2) 5.59
521-70178 x 4" pkg(2) 5.77

1/16" Thick
521-70180 x 1/16" pkg(10) 3.20
521-70181 x 5/64" pkg(10) 3.20
521-70182 x 3/32" pkg(10) 3.20
521-70183 x 1/8" pkg(10) 3.68
521-70184 x 5/32" pkg(10) 3.90
521-70185 x 3/16" pkg(10) 4.10
521-70187 x 1/4" pkg(10) 5.20
521-70188 x 5/16" pkg(10) 5.40
521-70189 x 3/8" pkg(10) 6.90
521-70191 x 1/2" pkg(10) 7.85
521-70192 x 3/4" pkg(10) 9.65
521-70193 x 1" pkg(5) 6.15
521-70194 x 2" pkg(5) 8.75
521-70195 x 3" pkg(2) 4.65
521-70196 x 4" pkg(2) 5.95

5/64" Thick
521-70198 x 5/64" pkg(10) 3.30
521-70199 x 3/32" pkg(10) 3.75
521-70200 x 1/8" pkg(10) 3.75
521-70201 x 5/32" pkg(10) 4.00
521-70202 x 3/16" pkg(10) 4.25
521-70204 x 1/4" pkg(10) 5.45
521-70205 x 5/16" pkg(10) 5.75
521-70206 x 3/8" pkg(10) 7.25
521-70208 x 1/2" pkg(10) 7.90
521-70211 x 2" pkg(5) 8.95
521-70212 x 3" pkg(2) 4.95
521-70213 x 4" pkg(2) 6.75

Items listed below are available by Special Order (see Legend Page).
521-70209 x 3/4" pkg(10) 9.50
521-70210 x 1" pkg(5) 6.20

3/32" Thick
521-70215 x 3/32" pkg(10) 3.75
521-70216 x 1/8" pkg(10) 3.75
521-70217 x 5/32" pkg(10) 3.75
521-70218 x 3/16" pkg(10) 4.35
521-70220 x 1/4" pkg(10) 5.15
521-70221 x 5/16" pkg(10) 6.25
521-70222 x 3/8" pkg(10) 7.65
521-70224 x 1/2" pkg(10) 8.50
521-70225 x 3/4" pkg(10) 9.65
521-70226 x 1" pkg(5) 6.45
521-70227 x 2" pkg(5) 9.15
521-70228 x 3" pkg(2) 4.95
521-70229 x 4" pkg(1) 3.75

1/8" Thick
521-70231 x 1/8" pkg(10) 3.80
521-70232 x 5/32" pkg(10) 4.70
521-70233 x 3/16" pkg(10) 4.95
521-70235 x 1/4" pkg(10) 5.80
521-70236 x 5/16" pkg(10) 6.30
521-70237 x 3/8" pkg(10) 7.90
521-70239 x 1/2" pkg(10) 10.10
521-70240 x 3/4" pkg(10) 12.50
521-70241 x 1" pkg(5) 6.85
521-70242 x 2" pkg(5) 9.95
521-70243 x 3" pkg(2) 5.50
521-70244 x 4" pkg(1) 4.10

5/32" Thick
521-70246 x 5/32" pkg(5) 2.50
521-70247 x 3/16" pkg(5) 2.75
521-70249 x 1/4" pkg(5) 3.15
521-70250 x 5/16" pkg(5) 3.85
521-70251 x 3/8" pkg(5) 3.95
521-70253 x 1/2" pkg(5) 5.30
521-70254 x 3/4" pkg(5) 6.55
521-70255 x 1" pkg(2) 3.05
521-70256 x 2" pkg(2) 4.85
521-70257 x 3" pkg(2) 5.60
521-70258 x 4" pkg(1) 4.10

3/16" Thick
521-70260 x 3/16" pkg(5) 3.14
521-70262 x 1/4" pkg(5) 3.45
521-70263 x 5/16" pkg(5) 3.95
521-70264 x 3/8" pkg(5) 4.95
521-70266 x 1/2" pkg(5) 5.70
521-70267 x 3/4" pkg(5) 6.65
521-70268 x 1" pkg(2) 3.20
521-70269 x 2" pkg(2) 4.80
521-70270 x 3" pkg(2) 6.00
521-70271 x 4" pkg(1) 4.50

1/4" Thick
521-70285 x 1/4" pkg(5) 4.10
521-70286 x 5/16" pkg(5) 4.30
521-70287 x 3/8" pkg(5) 5.30
521-70289 x 1/2" pkg(5) 6.70
521-70290 x 3/4" pkg(5) 6.80
521-70291 x 1" pkg(2) 4.10
521-70293 x 3" pkg(2) 6.75
521-70294 x 4" pkg(1) 5.15

Item listed below is available by Special Order (see Legend Page).
521-70292 x 2" pkg(2) 5.40

5/16" Thick
521-70296 x 5/16" pkg(5) 5.40
521-70297 x 3/8" pkg(5) 6.60
521-70299 x 1/2" pkg(5) 7.10
521-70300 x 3/4" pkg(5) 8.35
521-70301 x 1" pkg(2) 3.75
521-70303 x 3" pkg(2) 8.15

Item listed below is available by Special Order (see Legend Page).
521-70302 x 2" pkg(2) 5.95

3/8" Thick
521-70306 x 3/8" pkg(5) 6.55
521-70308 x 1/2" pkg(5) 6.95
521-70309 x 3/4" pkg(5) 8.50
521-70310 x 1" pkg(2) 4.10
521-70311 x 2" pkg(2) 6.65
521-70312 x 3" pkg(2) 8.10

1/2" Thick
521-70323 x 1/2" pkg(2) 3.70
521-70324 x 3/4" pkg(2) 4.00
521-70325 x 1" pkg(2) 4.65
521-70326 x 2" pkg(2) 9.10
521-70327 x 3" pkg(2) 12.75

3/4" Thick
521-70330 x 3/4" pkg(2) 4.40
521-70331 x 1" pkg(2) 5.75
521-70332 x 2" pkg(1) 5.20
521-70333 x 3" pkg(1) 8.05

Bulk Packs-50 Pieces
Each piece is 24" 60cm long.
521-120 1/32 x 1/32" 10.50
521-123 1/32 x 1/16" 10.50
521-125 1/32 x 3/32" 12.50
521-126 1/32 x 1/8" 12.50
521-161 3/64 x 3/64" 13.00
521-180 1/16 x 1/16" 13.00
521-183 1/16 x 1/8" 15.00
521-231 1/8 x 1/8" 16.50

SCRATCH BUILDING SUPPLIES

SCRIBED SHEATHING

pkg(2) 6.95 ea (Unless Noted)

First dimension indicates scribe spacing, second is thickness. Each item is 24" long and 3-1/2" wide.

521-70350 .025 x 1/32"
521-70351 1/32 x 1/32"
521-70353 3/64 x 1/32" **6.98**
521-70354 1/16 x 1/32"
521-70355 3/32 x 1/32"
521-70356 1/8 x 1/32"
521-70357 3/16 x 1/32"
521-70358 1/4 x 1/32"
521-70359 3/8 x 1/32"
521-70360 1/2 x 1/32"
521-70361 Random x 1/32"
521-70362 .025 x 1/16"
521-70363 1/32 x 1/16"
521-70365 3/64 x 1/16"
521-70366 1/16 x 1/16"
521-70367 3/32 x 1/16"
521-70368 1/8 x 1/16"
521-70369 3/16 x 1/16"
521-70370 1/4 x 1/16"
521-70371 3/8 x 1/16"
521-70372 1/2 x 1/16"
521-70373 Random x 1/16"

SIDING

Each sheet measures 24" long, 6" wide and 1/8" thick.

Conventional Clapboard 7.25 ea
521-6510 1/16" Spacing
521-6512 3/32" Spacing
521-6511 1/8" Spacing

Aged Clapboard 7.25 ea
521-6504 1/16" Spacing
521-6505 3/32" Spacing
521-6507 1/8" Spacing

Scribed Sheathing 7.25 ea
521-6506 1/16" Spacing
521-6509 3/32" Spacing
521-6508 1/8" Spacing

Clapboard pkg(2) 6.95 ea
Dimension indicates lap spacing. Each item is 24" long and 3-1/2" wide.
521-70375 1/32"
521-70377 3/64"
521-70378 1/16"
521-70379 3/32"
521-70380 1/8"
521-70381 3/16"
521-70382 1/4"
521-70383 3/8"
521-70384 1/2"

Board & Batten pkg(2) 6.95 ea
Dimension indicates cap spacing.
521-70402 1/16"
521-70403 3/32"
521-70404 1/8"
521-70405 3/16"
521-70406 1/4"
521-70407 3/8"
521-70408 1/2"
521-70409 3/4"

Imprinted Concrete pkg(2) 6.95 ea
521-70415 1/16"
521-70417 1/8"
521-70418 3/16"

Corrugated pkg(2) 6.95 ea
Dimension indicates corrugation spacing.
521-70424 .40"
521-70426 1/16"
521-70436 3/32"
521-70437 1/8"

Steel pkg(2) 6.95 ea
521-70347 HO Steel Siding
521-70349 O Steel Siding

Siding Packs pkg(2) 3.79 ea
Each pack includes two pieces of scale lumber 3 x 11".

Board & Batten
521-6006 3/32"
521-6007 1/8"
521-6008 3/16"

Clapboard
521-6001 1/16"
521-6002 3/32"
521-6003 1/8"

Corrugated
521-6020 1/16"
521-6021 3/32"
521-6022 1/8"

Scribed
Dimensions show distance between scribes and material thickness.
521-6010 1/32-1/32"
521-6011 1/16-1/32"
521-6012 3/32-1/32"
521-6013 1/8-1/32"
521-6015 1/16-1/16"
521-6016 3/32-1/16"
521-6017 1/8-1/16"

STRUCTURAL SHAPES

Angles

22" Multi-Packs
521-70499 1/32" pkg(5) **4.70**
521-70500 3/64" pkg(5) **4.70**
521-70501 1/16" pkg(5) **5.10**
521-70502 5/64" pkg(5) **5.10**
521-70503 3/32" pkg(5) **5.10**
521-70504 1/8" pkg(5) **5.65**
521-70505 5/32" pkg(5) **6.20**
521-70506 3/16" pkg(5) **6.20**
521-70507 1/4" pkg(5) **6.45**
521-70508 5/16" pkg(2) **3.10**
521-70509 3/8" pkg(2) **4.35**
521-70527 1/2" pkg(2) **5.15**

Channels

22" Multi-Packs
521-70540 1/16" pkg(5) **5.10**
521-70541 5/64" pkg(5) **5.10**
521-70542 3/32" pkg(5) **5.10**
521-70543 1/8" pkg(5) **5.65**
521-70544 5/32" pkg(5) **6.20**
521-70545 3/16" pkg(5) **6.20**
521-70546 1/4" pkg(5) **6.45**
521-70547 5/16" pkg(2) **3.20**
521-70548 3/8" pkg(2) **4.35**
521-70549 1/2" pkg(2) **5.30**

Hot New Products Announced Daily! Visit Walthers Web site at www.walthers.com

Corner Posts

521-593 1/8" **1.07**
521-595 3/16" **1.18**

H Columns

22" Multi-Packs
521-70550 1/16" pkg(5) **5.10**
521-70551 5/64" pkg(5) **5.10**
521-70552 3/32" pkg(5) **5.10**
521-70553 1/8" pkg(5) **5.65**
521-70554 5/32" pkg(5) **6.20**
521-70555 3/16" pkg(5) **6.20**
521-70556 1/4" pkg(5) **6.45**
521-70557 5/16" pkg(2) **3.20**
521-70558 3/8" pkg(2) **4.35**
521-70559 1/2" pkg(2) **5.30**

I Beams

22" Multi-Packs
521-70560 1/16" pkg(5) **5.10**
521-70561 5/64" pkg(5) **5.10**
521-70562 3/32" pkg(5) **5.10**
521-70563 1/8" pkg(5) **5.65**
521-70564 5/32" pkg(5) **6.20**
521-70565 3/16" pkg(5) **6.20**
521-70566 1/4" pkg(5) **6.45**
521-70567 5/16" pkg(2) **3.20**
521-70568 3/8" pkg(2) **4.35**
521-70569 1/2" pkg(2) **5.30**

Tees

521-70510 3/64" pkg(5) **4.70**
521-70511 1/16" pkg(5) **5.10**
521-70512 5/64" pkg(5) **5.10**
521-70513 3/32" pkg(5) **5.10**
521-70514 1/8" pkg(5) **5.65**
521-70515 5/32" pkg(5) **6.20**
521-70516 3/16" pkg(5) **6.20**
521-70517 1/4" pkg(5) **6.45**
521-70518 5/16" pkg(2) **3.20**
521-70519 3/8" pkg(2) **4.35**
521-70525 1/32" pkg(5) **4.70**

Zees

22" Multi-packs
521-70520 3/64" pkg(5) **4.70**
521-70521 1/16" pkg(5) **5.10**
521-70523 3/32" pkg(5) **5.10**

MOULDINGS

All items are 24" 60cm long unless noted.

Cove

521-91 1/16" **.91**
521-92 5/64" **.91**
521-93 3/32" **.91**
521-94 1/8" **.95**
521-95 5/32" **1.00**
521-96 3/16" **1.00**
521-98 1/4" **1.16**

Double Bead

521-871 1/8" **1.04**
521-872 3/32" **.91**
521-873 5/64" **.91**
521-874 1/16" **.91**
521-875 3/64" **.84**

Half Round

521-490 3/64" **.93**
521-491 1/16" **.93**
521-492 5/64" **.93**
521-493 3/32" **.93**
521-494 1/8" **1.04**
521-495 5/32" **1.16**
521-496 3/16" **1.16**
521-498 1/4" **1.26**

Quarter Round

521-570 3/64" **.84**
521-571 1/16" **.84**
521-572 5/64" **.84**
521-573 3/32" **.84**
521-574 1/8" **.94**

Round

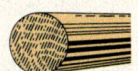

521-485 3/64" **.84**
521-486 1/16" **.91**
521-487 5/64" **.91**
521-488 3/32" **.91**
521-489 1/8" **1.01**

SCRATCH BUILDING SUPPLIES

ABS PLASTIC

Stronger than styrene, ABS is ideal for all types of model building, especially architectural models, or items subject to frequent handling. For easy identification, Plastruct ABS products are molded in gray. Measurement indicates N Scale length.

Structural Shapes
pkg(2) 2.25 ea

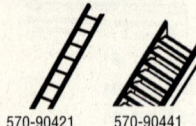

Ladder
570-90421 3"

Stairs
570-90441 3" **3.25**

Handrails
570-90471 3-5/8"

Stair Rails
570-90481 3-5/8"

STYRENE PLASTIC

The most common modeling plastic, available in sheets, strips and special shapes, as well as vacuum-formed parts. For ease of identification, Plastruct styrene products are molded in white, unless noted. Easily cut, drilled, sanded or scored and snapped. Bonds with most Styrene cements. Accepts most acrylic paints; a primer coat is recommended. Measurement indicates N Scale length.

Structural Shapes

Balcony Railings
570-90901 6-1/2" pkg(2) **6.40**
Molded in brown.

Ladders
570-90671 3" pkg(2) **1.95**

Handrails
570-90681 3-5/8" pkg(2) **2.00**

Stairs
570-90661 3-5/8" pkg(2) **1.95**

Stair Rails
570-90691 3-5/8" pkg(2) **1.95**

Steps/Louvers
Vacuum-formed or injection-molded. 3-7/8 x 2-1/8".

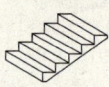

570-90951 34° **4.65**
570-90956 17° **3.00**

PATTERNED SHEETS

Vacuum formed from .020" styrene. Scales shown indicate relative size; most items can be used for larger or smaller models. Sheets measure 12 x 7" unless noted; dimension shown is the size of an individual object in the pattern.

Brick
570-91608 .062" (N) pkg(2) **9.75**

Flooring
570-91530 Planking .039" (N) pkg(2) **9.75**

Spanish Tile Roofing
570-91640 .048" (N) pkg(2) **9.75**

Corrugated Siding
570-91510 .030" (N) pkg(2) **9.75**

Stone pkg(2) **9.75 ea**
570-91562 Coursed 100" (N)
570-91584 Polished 125" (N)

Safety Tread Plate
pkg(2) **6.25 ea**
570-91701 .035" (Z)
3-7/8 x 2-1/4"
570-91702 .055" (N)
3-7/8 x 2-1/4"

Pikestuff
Division of Rix Products

BUILDING MATERIAL

Cap Tiles

541-1008 For Concrete Sheets **2.25**

Concrete Block Walls **2.75 ea**
Molded in gray plastic, use to create warehouses, gas stations, garages and other concrete structures. Measurement in HO scale feet.

541-1004 14-1/2 x 28' pkg(4)
541-1005 14-1/2 x 18-1/2' pkg(4)
541-1006 14-1/2 x 9-1/4' pkg(8)

Prefab Steel Warehouse Walls

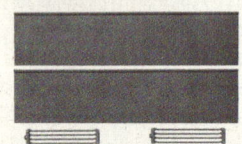

541-1011 Two Wall Panels & Downspouts (18 x 80' Scale Feet) **4.75**

541-1012 Peaked End Panels pkg(2) **4.25**

541-1013 Two Roof Panels & Supports (15 x 80' Scale Feet) **4.75**

Shingles

541-1007 Panels (7-3/16 x 2-1/32") pkg(2) **3.00**
541-1015 Roof (5 x 8") **4.25**

Siding

541-1014 Board & Batten (5 x 8') **4.25**

PRECISION SCALE CO.

Brass Wire Screen **7.00 ea**
Fine mesh screen is ideal for all types of air intakes, spark arrestors, window screens, etc. Each sheet measures 4 x 6".

585-48117   585-48262

585-48117 60 Mesh
585-48262 70 Mesh

585-48118   585-48119

585-48118 80 Mesh
585-48119 100 Mesh

SCALE SCENICS

DIVISION OF CIRCUITRON

Flat Wire
652-1504 Nickel Silver **2.95**
Used for simulating strapping. Measures .010 x .030". Package contains 5' (150cm) of wire.

Gears
652-2001 Gear Assortment **5.95**

Micro-Mesh
Lightweight, non-woven, raised diamond pattern mesh. Measures just .005" thick. 3 x 6" 7.5 x 15cm.

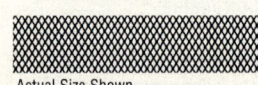

Actual Size Shown

652-3500 Aluminum **4.95**
652-3501 Brass **5.95**
May be soldered.

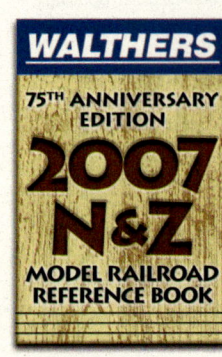

Models and Photo by Richard Bailey, Cartersville, Georgia

The morning may have gotten off to a slow start in the Trackmore industrial district but things are going to change very soon. An SD45 has just arrived with a long line of cars that need to be unloaded today. The next few hours are going to be very busy for all the workers on the docks.

Richard Bailey created this scene on his St. Jude and Trackmore Railroad. The SD45 and Unitrack are by Kato. One of the buildings is scratch-built and the other structures are from DPM, Faller, Kibri and Vollmer. Vehicles are Classic Metal Works and the scenery is from Woodland Scenics.

Details tell the story here. Empty pallets waiting to be filled, barrels and boxes on the docks, figures standing in wait for the train, vehicles parked alongside the buildings and the bits of gravel and debris scattered about are all indications that this is an active industrial area. Without those finishing touches, the scene would have no life. Whether you're adding details to a locomotive, utility poles in a city or crates on a dock, it's easy to create a more realistic railroad using items found in the Super Detailing Parts Section.

SUPER DETAILING PARTS N SCALE

ADAIR SHOPS
Weight Upgrade Kits for Contemporary Model Railroad Car Kits

Improve the operation of your freight and passenger car fleet with Rite-Wey™ weight kits. Most can be installed so the weights are virtually invisible, so they're perfect for assembled models or kits, including many open cars or models with lights and interiors. Each weight kit consists of precut and finished segments made of a nontoxic industrial lead alloy. Each piece fits a specific location in or under the car with no cutting or sanding needed. Simply glue the pieces in place to bring the car up to or beyond NMRA weight standards quickly and easily without disturbing any details. Kits are available in two versions: Standard for normal applications, or the heavier Heavy Weight series — cars equipped with Heavy Weight kits should be coupled next to your motive power. For best results on wood, metal or plastic models, nontoxic, water-based Weight Bond™ Glue is recommended for a strong, permanent installation.

NEW PRODUCTS

Rite-Wey™ Weight Upgrade Kits

Atlas Cars 2.95 ea
NEW **143-6201** 90-Ton Hopper
NEW **143-6207** 55-Ton Hopper
NEW **143-6213** Coalveyor
NEW **143-6219** Piggyback Flat

deLuxe Innovations Cars 2.95 ea
NEW **143-6351** Twin Tub Coal Gondola

Red Caboose Cars 2.95 ea
NEW **143-2404** Fish Belly Flat Car
NEW **143-2407** Ortner Gondola

Trainworx Cars
NEW **143-6101** 4-Bay Hopper pkg (3) **5.80**

RITE-WEY™ WEIGHT UPGRADE KITS

Intermountain Cars
143-2000 Composite Gondola **2.95**

Roundhouse Cars
Regular Weight 2.95 ea
143-3300 Old Time Stock Car
143-3303 Old Time Reefer; Ready-to-Run
143-3307 Old Time Box Car; Ready-to-Run
143-3311 Thrall Hi-Side Gondola; Ready-to-Run
143-3316 40' 3-Bay Offset Side Hopper; Ready-to-Run
143-3320 67' Gunderson Husky Stack
NEW **143-3324** 34' Overton Passenger Car

Heavy Weight 3.45 ea
143-3306 Old Time Reefer
143-3310 Old Time Box Car
143-3315 Thrall Hi-Side Gondola

Con-Cor 2.95 ea
143-3701 Budd Bi-Level Commuter
143-3707 75-Ton 4-Bay Coal Hopper
143-3713 Longitudial Hopper
143-3719 Hi-Cube Box Car
143-3723 50' Mill Gondola
143-3727 50' Flat Car
143-3731 Twin Stack Container

Bowser
143-4601 4-Bay Hopper **2.95**
NEW **143-4607** GLA 2-Bay Hopper

LBF & E&C Cars
Regular Weights 2.95 ea
143-4651 Boeing Skybox
143-4655 Mill Gondola
143-4659 Woodchip Car
143-4663 Johnstown America Bethgon Coal Gondola
143-4669 Trinity Aluminator Coal Gondola
143-4675 Johnstown Aeroflo Coal Gondola

Heavy Weights 3.45 ea
143-4654 Boeing Skybox
143-4658 Mill Gondola
143-4662 Woodchip Car

Micro-Trains Cars
143-6001 33' Twin Bay Hopper
143-6007 100-Ton 3-Bay Hopper
143-6013 2-Bay ACF Center Flow Covered Hopper
143-6016 89' Tri-Level Open Auto Rack
143-6020 Despatch Stock Car

ADHESIVES

Weight Bond™ Glue
143-7000 Single **3.95**
143-7001 2-Pack **7.00**

Pink Sound Bond™ Glue
143-7002 General Electronic Uses (1oz Dries Pink) **3.95**
143-7003 2-Pack (Dries Pink) **7.00**

AMERICAN MODEL BUILDERS, INC.

Car Floors pkg(2) 4.95 ea (Unless Noted)
Laser-cut in one piece from ultra-thin plywood, easy to install.
152-520 Walthers 40' Gondola
152-521 Atlas 50' Flat Cars **5.95**
152-523 Atlas 40' Flat Car
152-524 Con-Cor 50' Flat Car

Chimneys 3.95 ea
Cast metal parts.
152-513 Single pkg(4)
152-514 Double pkg(3)
152-515 Smoke Jacks pkg(6)
152-516 Victorian Chimney pkg(3)

Freight Car Load

152-522 Crankshaft Load For Flat Car **10.95**
Laser-cut plastic and wood parts.

152-525 Large Wooden Crate **7.95**
Laser-cut wood parts and dunnage (bracing).

Roofing
152-510 Tabbed Shingles **14.95**
152-511 Hexagonal Shingles **11.95**
152-512 Rolled Roofing Strips **5.95**
152-517 Diamond Shingles **8.95**

ALEXANDER SCALE

120-2597 Transom pkg(4) **2.80**
120-2598 Single Window pkg(4) **2.80**
120-2599 Double Window pkg(4) **2.80**
120-2799 Chimney pkg(2) **1.50**

ATLAS

Mill Lumber

150-791 **4.25**
Molded plastic parts in realistic tan color.

CREATIVE MODEL ASSOCIATES

Phosphor Bronze Wire 2.50 ea
Make handrails, grab irons, plumbing and more. Harder than brass and easier to work, each piece is 8" long and perfectly straight. Packed in a rigid plastic tube for protection and storage.
363-1100 .008" pkg(10)
363-1101 .010" pkg(12)
363-1106 .0125" pkg(12)
363-1102 .015" pkg(12)
363-1103 .020" pkg(12)
363-1104 .025" pkg(12)
363-1105 .032" pkg(12)

Wood Crate Kit
363-1020 Plastic Wood Crate Kit pkg(8) **4.95**

CAMPBELL SCALE MODELS

Wooden Barrels
200-247 Unpainted pkg(12) **4.60**
200-248 Red pkg(12) **5.18**

DELUXE INNOVATIONS

Baldwin RF-16 "Shark" Body Shell
238-50001 With Accessories **14.45**

Rotary Beacons pkg(2) 1.95 ea
238-991102 Clear
238-991202 Amber

Miscellaneous
238-990101 Container Glue **3.95**
238-990304 Roof Top Turbines pkg(4) **2.49**
238-990612 Brass Stirrups pkg(12) **7.55**

Get the Scoop!
Get the Skinny!
Get the Score!
Check Out Walthers Web site at
www.walthers.com

SUPER DETAILING PARTS N SCALE

Transform your motive power into showstoppers with this line of detail parts! Ideal for upgrading plastic or brass locos, the line includes an assortment of precisely scaled etched metal, formed wire and injection molded parts.

NEW PRODUCTS

Diesel Details

Cut Levers
.009" machine-bent wire.

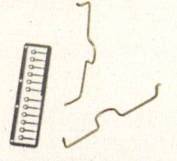

NEW 176-11 Early EMD & GE Locos 1 Pair **4.25**

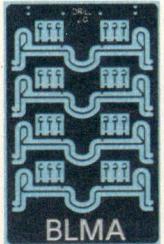

NEW 176-14 Modern GE Locos 2 Pair **4.50**

E/F Unit Ultimate Detail Set

NEW 176-99 **14.75**
Includes parts etched in .005" stainless steel for detailing three units. Details include cab sunshades, three-styles of rear-view mirrors, cut levers, four styles of ladder grab irons, windshield wipers, curved grabs for above windshield, MU hoses and cable receptacles, tall grab irons, cab side-mounted walkway and curved grab irons.

Grab Irons
.007" machine-bent stainless steel wire unless noted.

NEW 176-58 18" Straight pkg(20) **5.75**

NEW 176-60 18" Drop pkg(20) **5.75**
NEW 176-61 18" Drop pkg(60) **15.50**

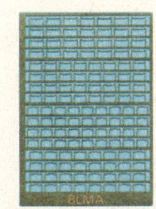

NEW 176-98 E/F Units & Passenger Cars, Etched, 4 Styes **8.75**

Grab Iron Drilling Template

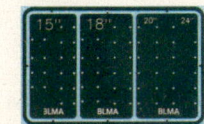

NEW 176-57 4 Sizes **3.50**

MU Hoses

NEW 176-100 7 Sets **5.95**
MU hoses are found on all diesel and electric locomotives. Prototype hoses allow simultaneous operation of multiple locos in a consist.

Freight Car Details

Coupler Platforms

NEW 176-403 pkg(20) **6.50**
Included ten each Apex- and Morton-style platforms. Highly visible detail adds realism to cars quickly and easily.

Ladders

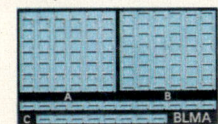

NEW 176-400 For Transition-Era Box Cars **7.75**
Includes two styles of ladders and the most common style of freight car side grab iron. Also included are three complete sets of transition era box car ladder and grab iron upgrades.

NEW 176-401 Modern Freight Cars **TBA**

Stirrups

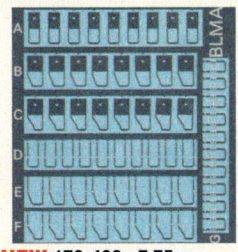

NEW 176-402 **7.75**
This set includes the four most common styles of freight car stirrups with multiple ways of mounting. This set can retro-fit up to fourteen cars!

DIESEL DETAILS

Air Conditioners

176-70 Vapor Air Conditioner **3.50**

176-71 Prime Air Conditioner **3.50**

176-91 Air Conditioner Cover Plate for Removed Units pkg(2) **3.75**

Antenna Stands
176-92 Diesel Locomotive Short & Regular Styles pkg(4) **5.75**
Includes Sinclair antenna.

Bells

176-75 Frame Mounted Etched Metal pkg(6) **4.25**

Cab Doors

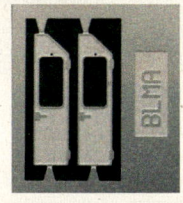

176-17 Spartan Type pkg(2) **3.25**
Used on most models from GP35 to Standard Cab SD70. Etched-metal parts include small mounting hole to add windshield wipers (not included) if desired.

Cab Sunshades

176-16 Modern Style pkg(4) **3.25**
Fits EMD wide cab diesels from the SD60 on. Includes four sunshades, enough for two locos, and drilling jig to simplify installation.

176-74 Angled 4 Pair **5.50**

Cut Levers – Modern Style
These modern loco cut levers fit most EMD diesels produced or rebuilt after the early 70s. Includes two cut levers and mounting pins; assembly requires minor bending.

176-13 Set of Two **3.00**
176-62 Set of Ten **10.00**

Grab Irons

15" Drop Style Grab Irons
Preformed of machine-bent wire and measuring just .009" thick, these grabs are ideal for detailing locos, and passenger and freight cars.

176-59 Set of 20 **5.75**
176-67 Set of 60 **15.50**

176-76 Etched-metal Straight pkg(20) **5.75**

176-93 Rear Fan Round Style pkg(3) **4.75**

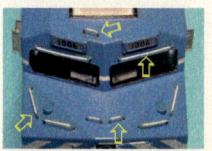

176-94 Rear Fan Grab Iron "V" Style pkg(3) **4.75**

176-95 Modern Wide Cab GE Diesel Set 2 Sets **6.00**

EMD Locomotive Fans
48" 8.75 ea

Without Center Plate pkg(5)

176-81 8 Blade

176-82 10 Blade

With Center Plate pkg(8)

176-83 8 Blade

176-84 10 Blade

"Q" Fan Grilles pkg(5)

176-85 8 Blade

SUPER DETAILING PARTS N SCALE

176-86 10 Blade
36" pkg(2) 4.00 ea

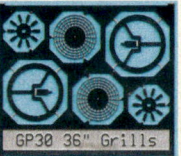
176-87 With Center Plate for EMD GP30 & others

176-88 No Center Plate for EMD GP35 & others

Fan Package

176-66 Modern Style (4 Piece Set) **7.00**
Fits most late EMD locos including SD60, SD70 and SD90MAC. Includes three 53" radiator fans and one 60" dynamic brake fan to convert one loco.

Lift Rings

176-90 GE & EMD pkg(4) **4.25**

Lighting

176-72 Removed Headlight Covers 5 Styles pkg(10) **4.50**

176-73 Beacon Stands pkg(4) **4.25**

176-97 Diesel Locomotive Safety Step Lights pkg(40) **4.50**

Rear-View Loco Mirrors

176-65 Modern Short & Standard Styles **3.25**
Used on modern locos by most American railroads; includes four each of standard and short styles.

Windshield Wipers

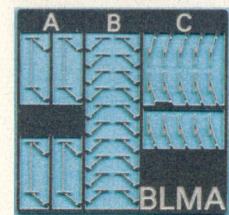
176-96 3 Styles **4.50**

TRAINLINE AIRHOSES

176-69 Injection Molded Plastic pkg(24) **4.75**
Great detail for locos, freight or passenger cars. One-piece with detailed angle cock and glad hand.

MODERN GRADE CROSSINGS

176-77 Rubber **7.00**

176-78 Expander Set, Rubber **6.75**

176-79 Concrete **7.00**

176-80 Expander Set, Concrete **6.75**

CAL-FREIGHT
CALIFORNIA FREIGHT AND DETAIL COMPANY

Unpainted, hand-made resin castings.

Air Conditioners
201-1055 Roof Top Small #1 pkg(2) **3.30**
201-1060 Roof Top Small #2 pkg(2) **3.30**
201-1065 Roof Top Small #3 pkg(2) **3.30**
201-1070 Roof Top Small #4 pkg(2) **3.30**
201-1075 Roof Top Small #5 pkg(2) **3.30**
201-1080 Roof Top Air Conditioning Vents pkg(4) **3.05**
201-2035 Roof Top Industrial-Large #1 **3.50**
201-2040 Roof Top Industrial-Large #2 **3.50**
201-2045 Roof Top Industrial-Large #3 **3.50**
201-2090 Air Conditioning Duct Set #1 pkg(6) **4.50**
201-2095 Air Conditioning Duct Work Set #2 pkg(8) **4.50**
201-2100 Air Conditioning Unit & Duct Work Set #1 **3.50**
201-2105 Air Conditioning Unit & Duct Work Set #2 **3.50**
201-2175 Window Unit pkg(4) **3.05**

Boxes pkg(3) 2.80 ea (Unless Noted)
201-1005 Boxed Appliances pkg(4) **2.50**
201-1010 Pallet Stack-Large
201-1015 Pallet Stack-Medium
201-1020 Pallet Stack-Small
201-1025 Floor Stack-Large
201-1030 Floor Stack-Medium
201-1035 Floor Stack-Small

Cement Blocks pkg(3) 2.80 ea
201-1085 Pallet Stack
201-1090 Floor Stack

City Details
201-2385 36" Round Urban Planters Concrete **2.80**

Crates pkg(4) 3.30 ea (Unless Noted)
201-1040 Plywood Crates 4 x 4 x 8' pkg(3)
201-1045 Medium-Long
201-1050 Medium-Short
201-2150 Produce Crates **3.05**

Drainage Culverts
201-2155 Wooden **3.05**
201-2160 Concrete-Small **2.80**
201-2165 Concrete-Large **3.05**

Dumpsters
201-1150 Open w/Load **2.80**
201-1155 Closed Lid **2.80**
201-2010 Roll-Off Garbage Bin w/Load **4.15**
201-2345 Low Boy Roll-Off Bin w/Load **4.15**

Flat Car Loads 4.50 ea
201-2080 Turbine Generator
201-2085 Transformer

Gas Station Details
201-2185 Retail Propane Tank **3.05**
201-2190 Tire Display Rack **2.50**
201-2195 Office Details Set **4.50**
201-2200 Heavy Duty Sink & Solvent Tank (1 Each) **2.50**
201-2205 Work Benches pkg(3) **5.10**
201-2210 Fire Extinguisher pkg(2) **2.50**

Hay Bales
201-2115 Stacked pkg(4) **3.05**

Interior Details
201-2065 Interior Open Shelving pkg(2) **2.50**
201-2070 Work Bench **2.00**
201-2075 Cabinets-Small Free Standing pkg(2) **2.50**

Light Bulb Holder
Limited Quantity Available
201-2805 Double pkg(2) **2.80**

Lighted Interior Sets 7.95 ea
201-2810 Office
201-2815 Store
201-2820 Diner

Orchard Details pkg(3) 2.80 ea
201-2400 Bee Hives On Pallets
201-2405 Smudge Pots

Road Details
201-2355 Highway Guard Rail Rock & Cable (24" 60cm) **13.20**

Roll-Up Doors pkg(2) 3.05 ea
201-2130 7'-8" x 10'
201-2135 10' x 12'

Roof Details
201-1000 Access Stair Cover **2.25**
201-1165 Access Hatch pkg(2) **2.50**
201-1170 Chimney Pots pkg(2) **2.50**
201-2030 Sky Lite 2 x 4' White pkg(3) **2.80**

Sacks
201-1095 Pallet Stack pkg(4) **3.05**
201-1100 Floor Stack pkg(4) **3.05**
201-1115 Piled In Corner pkg(2) **2.80**

Steel Drums pkg(3) 2.80 ea
201-2390 3-, 5- & 7- Piece Castings
201-2395 On Pallets

Structure Details
201-2120 Halogen Building Lights pkg(3) **2.80**
201-2125 Trash Bin Enclosure **2.50**
201-2140 Industrial Step-Concrete & Block **2.25**

Stumps pkg(7) 2.80 ea
201-1120 Small
201-1125 Medium
201-2410 Small, For Slopes
201-2415 Large, For Slopes

Tarp-Covered Loads pkg(3) 2.80 ea
201-1135 Freight Sacks
201-1140 Boxes
201-1145 Small Machinery

Trackside Details
201-1185 Wood Plank Grade Crossing **3.50**
201-1190 Relay Cabinet-Small pkg(2) **2.50**
201-1195 Relay Shed pkg(2) **2.80**
201-2000 Tool Shed 9 x 9 x 10' **4.75**
201-2005 Horizontal Storage Tank-Small pkg(2) **2.80**
201-2110 Relay Cabinet-Large pkg(2) **2.50**
201-2145 Trash Piles pkg(3) **2.80**
201-2170 Steel Utility Shed **5.00**

Vents
Cyclone pkg(3) **2.80 ea**
201-2015 Small
201-2020 Large
Industrial Roof Type
201-1175 Small pkg(4) **2.00**
201-1180 Large pkg(3) **2.80**

Wood Stacks
201-1105 Firewood-Cord pkg(2) **2.50**
201-1130 Plywood pkg(3) **2.80**
201-1160 Lumber pkg(3) **2.80**

See What's New and Exciting at

www.walthers.com

DETAIL ASSOCIATES

All detail parts are cast metal unless noted.

Items listed in blue ink may not be available at all times (see Legend Page).

Air Conditioners 1.25 ea

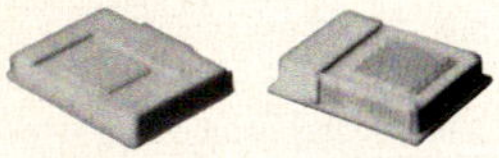

229-8220 229-8221

229-8220 Prime Type (plastic)
229-8221 Vapor Type (plastic)

Air Pumps

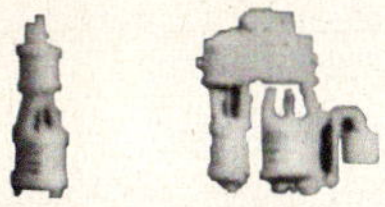

229-8012 229-8013

229-8012 Single Phase pkg(2) **1.00**
229-8013 Cross Compound pkg(2) **1.25**

Bells

229-8005 Locomotive pkg(2) **1.25**
229-8203 Roof Mount pkg(2) **1.00**

Brake Cylinders

229-8025 For Locomotive pkg(2) **1.25**
229-8401 Freight Car K Type pkg(2) **1.00**

Domes

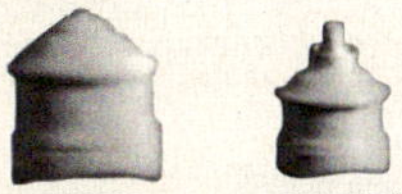

229-8003 229-8004

229-8003 Sand, Fluted pkg(2) **1.00**
229-8004 Steam, Fluted pkg(2) **1.00**

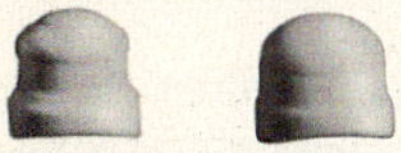

229-8021 229-8022

229-8021 Sand, Baldwin pkg(2) **1.25**
229-8022 Steam, Baldwin pkg(2) **1.25**

Feedwater Heaters

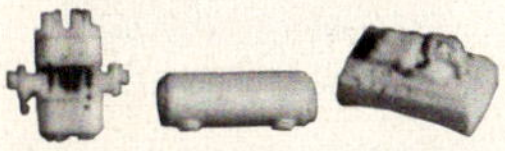

229-8014 229-8015 229-8024

229-8014 Elesco Feedwater Pump pkg(2) **1.25**
229-8015 Elesco Feedwater Tank pkg(2) **1.25**
229-8024 Feedwater Heater-Recessed Worthington pkg(2) **1.00**

Headlights & Marker Lamps

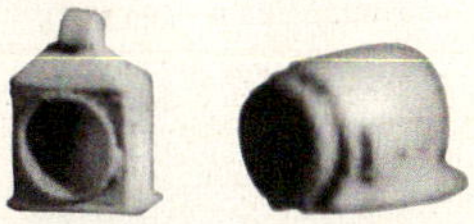

229-8006 229-8009

229-8006 Square, Oil Type pkg(2) **1.25**
229-8007 Pyle Type pkg(2) **1.00**
229-8009 Sunbeam pkg(2) **1.00**
229-8202 Dual Oscillating pkg(2) **1.00**
229-8209 Large, Switcher pkg(2) **1.00**
229-8016 Round Marker Lamp pkg(2) **1.00**
229-8216 Dual, Early (plastic) pkg(4) **1.25**
229-8217 Dual, Late (plastic) pkg(4) **1.25**
229-8218 Dual Oscillating, Pyle (plastic) pkg(4) **1.25**
229-8219 Oscillating, Pyle (plastic) pkg(4) **1.25**
229-8222 Flashers (plastic) pkg(3) **1.25**

Horizontal Boilers

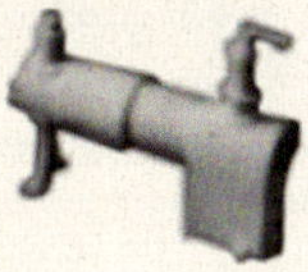

229-8444 Small Steam Engine **1.50**
229-8445 Mill/Factory Engine **1.75**

Interior Details

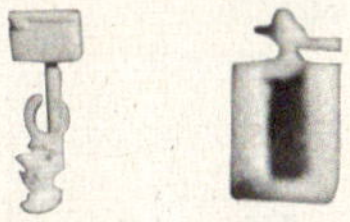

229-8421 229-8422

229-8421 Toilet Bowl & Tank **1.00**
229-8422 Urinal pkg(2) **1.00**
229-8423 Small Sink pkg(2) **1.00**
229-8424 Large Sink pkg(2) **1.00**
229-8427 Paper Waste Bin pkg(2) **1.00**
229-8428 Lockers pkg(2) **1.25**
229-8429 Pot Belly Stove pkg(2) **1.25**

Miniature Tools

229-8405 Assorted Etched Brass Hand Tools 35 Pieces **2.50**
229-8414 Air Compressor w/Tank **1.85**
229-8415 Welding Cart & Two Tanks **1.85**
229-8416 Drill/Press Stand **1.50**
229-8417 Grinder & Stand **1.00**
229-8418 Anvil w/Stand pkg(2) **1.00**
229-8425 Steam Hammer **2.50**
229-8426 Large Lathe **2.25**

Pilot & Plows 1.25 ea (Unless Noted)

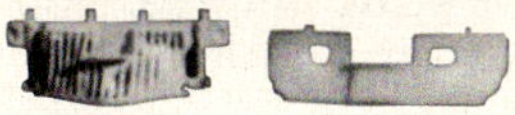

229-8008 229-8210

229-8008 Tube Type **1.50**
229-8210 High, Early

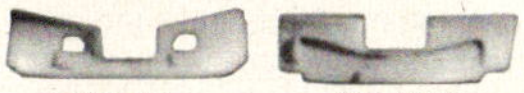

229-8211 229-8212

229-8211 Low, Late
229-8212 "E" & "F" Unit Type

Scale Flat Wire pkg(6) 3.00 ea

229-2522 .015 x .018"
229-2524 .015 x .030"
229-2526 .015 x .024"
229-2528 .015 x .042"
229-2530 .015 x .060"

Scale Wire & Pipe 3.00 ea

Brass wire is ideal for modeling pipes, railings, etc., and is easily bent to fit. Size shown is approximate N Scale inches, followed by actual dimensions.

Number Qty.	N Scale Pipe Outside Dia.	Wire Dia.
229-2501 pkg(5)	1"	.006
229-2502 pkg(5)	1-1/4"	.008
229-2503 pkg(5)	1-5/8"	.010
229-2504 pkg(10)	1-7/8"	.012
229-2505 pkg(10)	2-3/8"	.015
229-2506 pkg(10)	3"	.019
229-2507 pkg(10)	3-1/2"	.022
229-2508 pkg(10)	4-1/2"	.028
229-2509 pkg(10)	5"	.033
229-2510 pkg(6)	6-3/8"	.040
229-2511 pkg(6)	7-3/8"	.046
229-2512 pkg(6)	8-3/8"	.052
229-2513 pkg(6)	10"	.0625

Steps

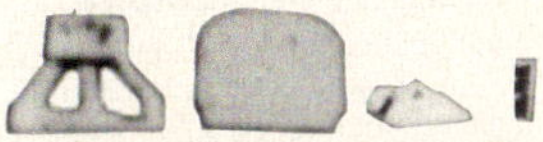

229-8019 229-8206 229-8420

229-8019 Tender pkg(2) **1.00**
229-8206 Drop pkg(2) **1.00**
229-8420 Passenger Car pkg(4) **2.85**

Spark Arrestors/ Exhaust Stacks

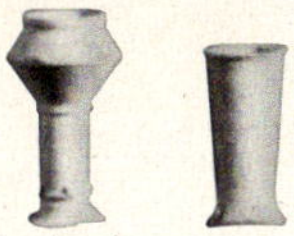

229-8001 229-8002

229-8001 Diamond Stack pkg(2) **1.25**
229-8002 Flared Stack pkg(2) **1.00**

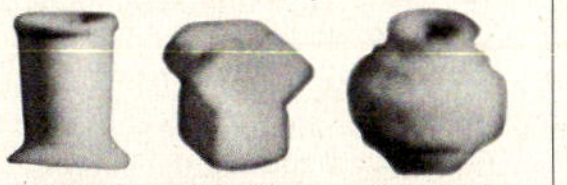

229-8023 229-8207 229-8208

229-8023 Baldwin Stack pkg(2) **1.25**
229-8207 Flared pkg(2) **1.00**
229-8208 Round pkg(2) **1.00**

Steam Donkey Engine Kit

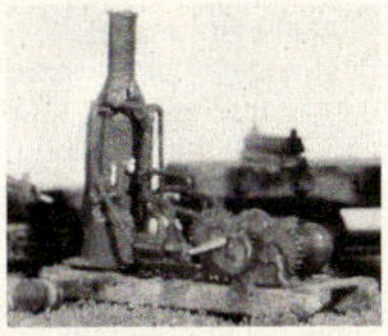

229-8701 7.95
Kit includes metal castings, brass etching detail and wood strips for skidder frame.

Street Details

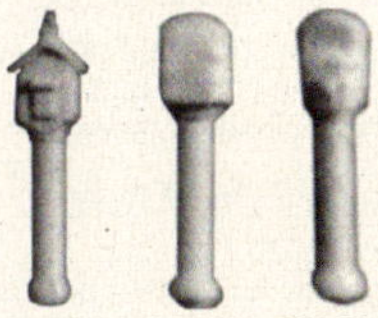

229-8409 229-8410 229-8411

229-8409 Fire Call Box pkg(2) **1.00**
229-8410 Police/Taxi Call Box pkg(2) **1.00**
229-8411 Parking Meter pkg(2) **1.00**

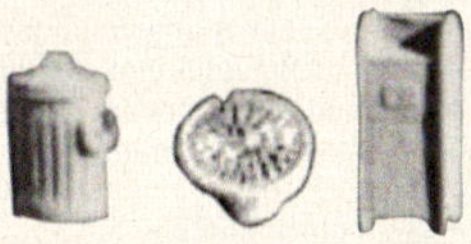

229-8412 229-8413 229-8419

229-8412 Garbage Can pkg(2) **1.00**
229-8413 Manhole Cover pkg(2) **1.00**
229-8419 Curb Deposit Mailbox pkg(2) **1.25**
229-8430 Waiting Bench **1.00**

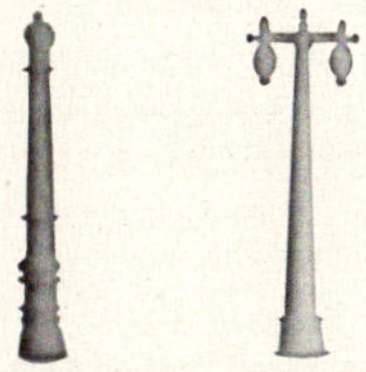

229-8434 229-8435

229-8434 Single Union Square Street Lamp **1.25**
229-8435 Double-Arm "Post Street" Lamp **1.50**
229-8436 Flagpole w/Mounting Bracket **1.50**
229-8437 Freestanding Flag Pole **1.25**

Sunshades pkg(4) 1.25 ea

229-8201 Cab (plastic)
229-8214 F & E Units (plastic)

Miscellaneous

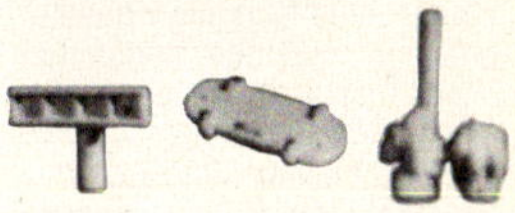

229-8010 229-8011 229-8017

229-8010 Number Board Steam pkg(2) **2.00**
229-8011 Tender Water Hatch pkg(2) **1.00**
229-8017 Pyle Generator pkg(2) **1.00**

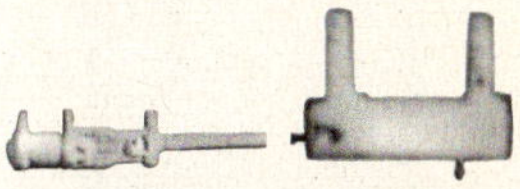

229-8018 229-8020

229-8018 Power Reverse **1.00**
229-8020 Rerailing Frog pkg(2) **1.00**
229-8026 Stream Turret pkg(2) **1.25**
229-8027 Injector pkg(2) **1.25**
229-8028 Lubricator pkg(2) **1.25**
229-8204 3-Chime Air Horn **2.75**

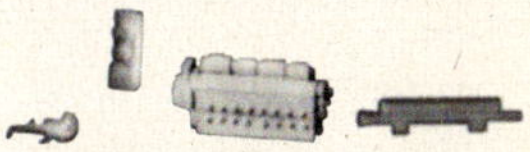

229-8205 229-8213 229-8215

229-8205 MU Stand pkg(2) **1.00**
229-8213 Engine Block EMD 645 **7.00**
229-8215 Cab Armrest (plastic) pkg(4) **1.25**

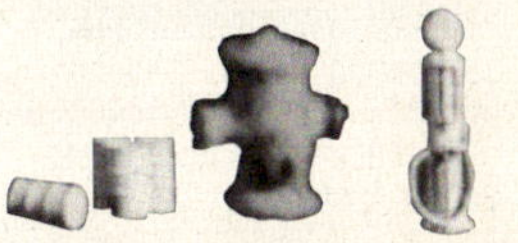

229-8402 229-8403 229-8404

229-8402 Oil Drum pkg(8) **1.50**
229-8403 Fire Hydrant pkg(2) **1.00**
229-8404 Old Time Gas Pump **2.00**
229-8406 Brake Wheel Etched Brass, Assorted 35 Pieces **2.00**
229-8407 Harp Switch Stand pkg(2) **1.00**
229-8408 High Target pkg(2) **2.25**
229-8438 Roof Vent, Small pkg(2) **1.25**
229-8439 Five Stamp Mill **3.85**
229-8440 Ore-Rock Crusher **1.25**
229-8441 Ore Slurry Pump **1.25**
229-8442 Wilfley Mine Table **1.50**
229-8443 Ore Car Argo Mine Type **1.25**

SUPER DETAILING PARTS N SCALE

Loren Perry's GOLD MEDAL MODELS *for that professional look*

These accessory sets are constructed from high-quality, photo-etched materials (either brass or stainless steel). These easy-to-construct sets require only simple hand tools and ordinary CA-type glue or epoxy to put together. All sets include instructions.

Bracing 16.00 ea
X-Shaped

304-16058 Over 800 Scale Feet.
304-16063 Over 1000 Scale Feet

W-Shaped
304-16064 Over 800 Scale Feet
304-16065 Over 1000 Scale Feet

Bicycles

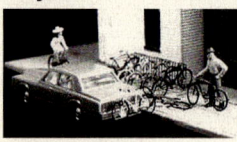

304-16028 7.00
Includes ten bicycles and three bike racks, made from photo-etched metal.

Brake Wheels
304-16055 pkg(90) 8.00
Photo-etched metal brakewheels include six each of fifteen different styles.

Bulkheads
304-16050 UP/BN Style 18.00
Parts for two Micro-Trains 51' flat cars.

Burglar Bars
304-16020 8 Pieces (2 Sizes) 9.00
For use in storefront windows. Brass, relief-etched.

Chairs
304-16057 pkg(16) 8.00
Includes four each of four different styles of chairs.

Detailing Sets
For Locomotives
304-1607 Diesel 7.00
Parts for over 12 locomotives! Includes 36 windshield wipers, 76 lift rings, eight cab sunshades and eight rearview mirrors. All parts constructed from .005" stainless steel.

304-16040 For EMD GP7, GP9 & GP18 12.00
For Life-Like models. .008" brass parts include 16 intake grilles, 16 fan grilles, two pairs of lower side skirts and 32 sets of louvers. Parts to add to two locomotives.

304-16042 Steam 16.00
.010" brass details includes 18 sets of brake hangers, 200 handrail stanchions, four pairs of pilot ladders, four tender ladders, over two dozen headlight number boards, and eight uncoupling lever lift bars for pilot couplers.

304-16049 For Con-Cor Diesel PA/PB 16.00
Equips a three-unit A-B-A set of locomotives with .010" brass details. Includes fan grilles with fans, SP-style snowplows, roof catwalks, icicle breakers, cab sun-shades and four sets of wagon wheel antennae.

For Passenger Cars
304-16026 For Kato Smoothside Passenger Cars 7.00
Includes antenna mounts and stirrups for eight cars. Etched in .005" stainless steel.

304-16044 For Heavyweight Passenger Cars 16.00
Each set includes 12 fold-to-step vestibule steps, 20 stirrups in two sizes and four sets of observation/lounge car railings in four different styles. Made from .010" brass.

For Freight Cars
Each set outfits two freight cars with see-through roofwalks, stirrup steps and brakewheels. Parts are constructed from .010" brass. Includes spare parts.

For Tank Cars
304-16023 Model Die Casting 50' & Shorty 9.00
304-16024 Atlas Beer 8.00
304-16045 Con-Cor Funnel Flow 9.00
304-16051 Atlas & Con-Cor Jumbo 22.00

For Box Cars
304-16047 Modern 9.00

For Well Cars
304-16046 Walthers Thrall Stand-Alone 12.00
304-16052 Walthers 5-Unit Thrall 16.00
304-16053 Con-Cor Gunderson 12.00
304-16054 Model Die Casting Gunderson 12.00

Fences 16.00 ea
All fences include a drilling jig for installation.

Chain Link
Sturdy .006" stainless-steel fences topped with three strands of etched barbed. Includes approximately 240 scale feet of ready-to-use fencing (four 60' sections, standing six scale feet tall).

304-1601 With Gates
Can be positioned open or closed
304-1602 No Gates

Spike-Tipped Wrought Iron
304-16029
240 scale feet of fences, along with two styles of gates and six interchangeable signs.

304-16030 Extender Set for Spike-Tipped Wrought-Iron Fences
Includes additional 300 scale feet of matching fencing.

Fire Escapes 10.00 ea
Basic Sets
Designed for a three-story building, complete with roof and sidewalk access ladders.

304-1603   304-1605

304-1603 Standard
Fire escapes are styled for use on industrial buildings.

304-1605 Fancy
For use with apartment buildings and hotels. Features three-dimensional relief-etched railing.

Add-On Sets
Add three additional stories to basic sets.
304-1604 Standard
304-1606 Fancy

Grab Irons
304-16056 pkg(165) 8.00
Includes five different styles. Comes with drilling jigs.

Handrail Stanchions
304-16032 pkg(150) 7.00
Five different styles of handrail stanchions constructed from photo-etched metal. Designed for use on diesel locomotives.

Highway Guard Rails & Reflectors
304-16039 16.00
Stainless-steel guardrails reach over 200 scale feet. Also includes 20 safety reflectors.

Industrial Railings & Walkways 16.00 ea
304-16034 Railings
Photo-etched metal railings include over 300 scale feet of three scale foot tall railings. Also includes a drilling jig.

304-16059 Walkways
192 scale feet of 4' wide perforated walkways with two handrails for both sides. For use in petrochemical plants, grain elevators, tank farms and locomotive servicing facilities. Etched in .013" brass.

Ladders
304-16025 9.00
3-1/4" vertical ladders (approximately 495 scale feet) in two styles: one style designed for Micro-Trains 40 and 50' steel box cars, the other for Micro-Trains wooden reefers. Brass design.

304-16038 Industrial Safety Cage 16.00
Brass ladders stretch over 200 scale feet.

Radio Antenna Mounts
304-16033 pkg(116) 7.00
Six types of PRR induction phone/radio antenna mounts are included in each package, made from photo-etched brass. For use with cab units, hood units and cabooses. Also includes two transmitter units.

Roadkill

304-16060 8.00
Great for use on country roads and city intersections! Etched tire tracks across a number of flattened figures, including armadillos, rabbits and opossums.

Roofwalks
Each set outfits two freight cars with see-through roofwalks, stirrup steps and brakewheels. Parts are constructed from .010" brass. Includes spare parts.

For Hoppers
304-1608 Atlas 2-Bay Centerflow 8.00
304-1609 Model Power 55' Cylindrical 9.00
304-16011 Con-Cor 3-Bay Covered 9.00
304-16012 Delaware Valley 50' Airslide 9.00
304-16013 Con-Cor Four-Bay Covered 9.00
304-16016 Locomotives Two-Bay Covered 8.00
304-16022 Atlas GATX Airslide 8.00
304-16027 CS Models Cylindrical 13.00
304-16041 Atlas PS2 Two-Bay Cylindrical 8.00

For Box Cars
304-16010 Con-Cor 50' 9.00
304-16014 Atlas 50' 9.00
304-16015 Atlas 40' 8.00

For Reefers
304-16017 Con-Cor Mechanical 9.00

For Cabooses
304-16018 Model Power Bay Window 9.00

Shopping Carts
304-16037 pkg(8) 7.00
Carts fold into shapes. Made from .005" stainless steel.

Signs (Decals)
304-16031 6.00
Set includes over 60 full-color downtown business signs from the 1930s to the present.

Stairways
304-16035 pkg(12) 16.00
Three sizes of ladders for 4' loading docks, 8' platforms and 10' platforms, four of each size. Stairways fold into shape, so no assembly is needed.

Steel Plating

304-16062 Diamond Pattern 14.00
Simulated non-skid steel plate for industrial usage. Four 32' sections in widths of 16', 8' and two 4' sections.

SUPER DETAILING PARTS N SCALE

Loren Perry's GOLD MEDAL MODELS
for that professional look

Stirrups
304-16048 pkg(76) **9.00**
Designed for use on cab-type diesel locomotives. Includes 32 stirrups for EMD E and F units, 16 stirrups for Alco PA and FA units, 16 stirrups for Fairbanks-Morse "Erie Built" units, and 12 stirrups for Baldwin Shark-Nose Units. Made of stainless steel.

Telephone Booths
304-16043 pkg(2) **7.00**
Made of stainless steel, these booths fold into shape. Includes telephones and two-position doors.

Tell Tales
304-16036 pkg(8) **12.00**
Low-clearance warning devices circa 1900 to 1960s for use at tunnel portals, etc. Offered in two styles. Etched in .006" stainless steel.

TV Antennas
304-16021 pkg(20) **9.00**
Rooftop additions to houses, hotels, taverns and other structures. Designed to be mounted on thin wire masts (not included). Stainless steel. Features five different styles of antennae.

Venetian Blinds

304-16019 32 Pieces (4 Sizes) **9.00**
Designed for structures and passenger cars.

Windows
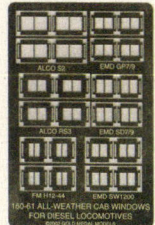
304-16061 Locomotive Cab Windows **12.00**
Etched-brass, fold-to-shape windows for up to 12 locomotives of six types. For first-generation hood and switcher units.

GRANDT LINE
These detailed castings are injection-molded, black styrene plastic.

STRUCTURAL DETAILS

Doors 3.00 ea
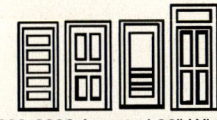
300-8006 Assorted 36" Wide pkg(6)

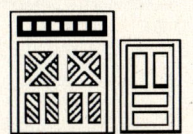
300-8011 Baggage Assortment, 2 Sets

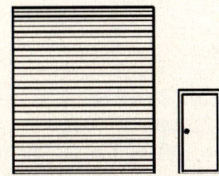
300-8015 Roll Up, 12 x 14', 2 Sets

300-8017 **300-8018**
300-8017 Victorian Depot w/Transom, 32" Wide pkg(8)
300-8018 Victorian Baggage, 80" Wide pkg(4)

Windows 3.00 ea (Unless Noted)

300-8001 Window (36 x 56") & Door (36") pkg(16)
Includes four doors and 12 windows.

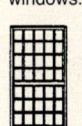 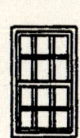 
300-8002 **300-8004** **300-8005**
300-8002 Double Hung 40-Pane (8 x 16") pkg(8)
300-8004 Double Hung 12-Pane (60 x 96") pkg(8)
300-8005 Double Hung 8-Pane (27 x 48") pkg(16)

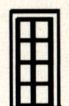 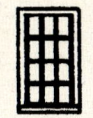
300-8007 **300-8008**
300-8007 8-Pane (27 x 64") pkg(12)
300-8008 Double Hung 12-Pane (36 x 64") pkg(12)

300-8009 **300-8010**
300-8009 8-Pane (52 x 33") pkg(12)
300-8010 Double Hung 16-Pane (36 x 56") pkg(12)

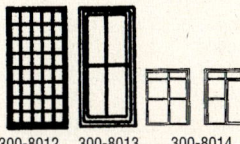
300-8012 **300-8013** **300-8014**
300-8012 40-Pane Engine House Window (64 x 127") pkg(8)
300-8013 Factory Window Double Hung 4-Pane (44 x 92") pkg(8)
300-8014 Warehouse/Factory Office Door & Window Set (115 x 97") 2 Sets

300-8019 **300-8020**
300-8019 4-Pane Station (30 x 69") pkg(12)
300-8020 Victorian Set 4 Sets

300-8021 **300-8022**
300-8021 Window/Door Grab Bag pkg(90) **19.95**
300-8022 Victorian Picture Window pkg(8)

Miscellaneous 3.00 ea
 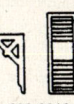
300-8003 **300-8016**
300-8003 Cable Sheave, 38" Diameter pkg(3)
300-8016 Eave Bracket & Louver Vent pkg(4)

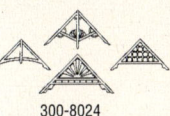 
300-8024 **300-8025**
300-8024 Gable Trim Assortment
300-8025 Brick Chimney pkg(2)

GCLaser

NEW PRODUCTS
Laser-Cut Wood Details

Lumber Loads
3 x 12" 9.99 ea

NEW 292-13311 One Each 8 & 20'
NEW 292-13312 One Each 10 & 18'
NEW 292-13313 One Each 12 & 16'
NEW 292-13314 Two 14' Loads

Miniature Tool Set

NEW 292-154 2.99
Includes 10 shovels, four saws, two picks and 14 hammers.

Pergola Set

NEW 292-234 w/2 Trellises **12.99**
Dress up the back yards of your houses with this delightful kit. Measures 6 x 1-1/16 x 5/8"

Billboard Supports
Kits include 13 laser-cut pieces including five trussed main supports, five sway braces, main grid with optional sheathing panel, cat-walk and illustrated instructions. Model measures 2-15/32 x 1/2 x 1-1/2".

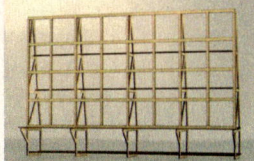
292-1031 Single **7.99**
292-1032 3-Pack **22.99**

Get Your Daily Dose of Product News at
www.walthers.com

Cable Reel 6-Packs
13.99 ea
Great flat car or truck loads. Kits come with seven laser-cut pieces and laser-etched end boards and complete instructions. Measure 3/8 x 9/16" diameter.
292-119 Empty
NEW 292-1191 Loaded
NEW 292-1192 Covered

Grade Crossings pkg(2) 6.99 ea
Each kit includes six laser-cut pieces; instructions with isometric drawings, plus laser-etched planks and bolt heads with shim stock. Easy to install; use with Code 83 track.

292-1271 Straight
292-1272 9-3/4" Radius Curve
292-1273 11" Radius Curve
292-1274 15" Radius Curve
292-1276 19" Radius Curve

Ladders

292-1101 9.99
Includes 75 laser-cut pieces to assemble four 20' ladders, four 10' ladders, three 8' step ladders, three 6' step ladders, four 4' step ladders and four saw horses.

Pallets

292-1102 11.99
Parts to build 36 wood pallets with notched fork lift supports.

Tables & Chairs

292-1103 9.99
Parts to build three round tables, two rectangular tables, two picnic tables, four benches, four back rest benches and four chairs.

SUPER DETAILING PARTS N SCALE

For a complete listing of JnJ Trains products visit Walthers Web site at www.walthers.com.

Air Tanks
344-245 Roof Air Tanks pkg(4) **3.25**
Used on GP7s and GP9s in passenger service.

Bells
344-102 Low Hood pkg(4) **3.50**

Brake Wheels pkg(8) 3.00 ea
344-350 Style Ajax
344-351 Style Equipco
344-352 Style Universal
344-353 Style Assorted

Cab Window
344-21 All Weather Cab Window pkg(2)
344-22 All-Weather Type w/Angled Top **3.00**
344-37 Cab Window 3 Pane All Weather pkg(4)

Catwalks
Photo-etched stainless steel walkways.
344-370 Atlas 47' Covered Hoppers **3.25**
344-371 Con-Cor 52' 4-Bay Covered Hoppers **3.40**
344-372 Atlas 2-Bay ACF Covered Hoppers **3.25**
344-374 LM 2-Bay Covered Hoppers **2.75**
344-375 Atlas 54' ACF Covered Hoppers **4.25**
344-376 Delaware Valley 50' 2-Bay Airslide® Covered Hoppers **3.25**
344-377 50' Box Cars **3.25**
344-378 40' Box Cars **3.00**
344-379 C&S 100-Ton Cylindrical Hoppers **4.00**
344-381 For Atlas 35' 2-Bay Covered Hopper **3.25**
344-385 Con-Cor 4-Bay to Trough Style **6.00**
344-387 Atlas/Con-Cor 47' to Trough Style **5.25**

Detail Kits 7.00 ea
344-3102 ATSF 6 Car Hi-Level Fits #344-3002
Items listed below are available by Special Order (see Legend Page).
344-3100 Stirrup/Antenna Fits #344-3000
344-3101 51 Super Chief Fits #344-3001
344-3103 1939 "Hiawatha" 9 Car

Doors 3.00 ea
344-7 Superior 5 Panel pkg(3)
344-9 ATSF Corrugated 5-5-5 pkg(3)

Drop Steps pkg(4) 3.00 ea
344-11 EMD
344-12 ALCO
344-13 GE

Fans For GP Diesels pkg(2) 3.00
344-78 36" Modern Raised Hub
344-79 48" Modern Raised Hub
344-80 Modern Flat Hub
344-104 36" Fan
344-105 48" Fan

Fan Upgrade
344-552 For #344-4481 pkg(2) **3.00**

Gates
344-36 Passenger Car Safety pkg(4) **3.00**

Grab Irons 3.00 ea
344-390 15" Regular w/Drill Template pkg(18)
344-391 18" Style B w/Drill Template pkg(18)
344-392 24" Style C pkg(18)
344-393 24" Style D w/Drill Template pkg(18)
344-394 30" Style E w/Drill Template pkg(18)
344-395 15" Drop Type w/Drill Template; pkg(18)

Handrail/Stantion Kit 10.95 ea
344-602 EMD 2nd Generation SW/SD
344-604 ALCO MLW Lite RD
344-607 GE Late RD Unit Etched Brass
Handrail/Stantion Kit listed below is available by Special Order (see Legend Page).
344-606 GE SW/Early RD Unit

Horns 3.50 ea (Unless Noted)
344-112 2-Chime GP pkg(4)
344-114 RS-3 w/Bracket pkg(4) **3.25**
344-115 5-Chime GP pkg(2)
344-116 5-Chime Nathan Forward pkg(2)
344-138 5-Chime Forward Leslie
344-144 E&F Single Chime pkg(4)
344-171 Single Chime Westinghouse pkg(4) **3.00**
344-266 3-Chime Forward - Amtrak pkg(4)

Lift Rings 3.00 ea
344-15 E&F Units Etched Brass
344-16 EMD Etched Brass pkg(16)
344-17 GE Etched Brass pkg(16)

Miscellaneous 3.00 ea (Unless Noted)
Realistic parts to upgrade cars and locos.
344-3 Freight Car Tack Boards pkg(12)
344-14 MU Hoses 4 Wide pkg(12)
344-18 Freight Car Ladder pkg(4)
344-26 Icicle Breaker 3 Piece Kit For Cab
344-34 Mail Catcher pkg(2)
344-88 Boston & Maine Light Generator Box
344-93 Sunshade For GPs pkg(4)
344-97 Grain Outlet Detail (fits Precision Models) pkg(6)
344-123 Weight, 90-Ton Sill Cover, Fits Atlas pkg(2)
344-141 Frame Mount Coupler Adapter For Hoppers pkg(4)
344-188 Snow Shields for UP E-Units pkg(2) **3.50**
344-264 Exhaust Manifold For GE pkg(2)

344-388 Autorack Upgrade Panels pkg(8) **16.00**
344-501 Brake Cylinder Clevis Rod Etched Brass pkg(16)
344-553 Service Ladder PRR pkg(4)
344-608 Safety Chain pkg(3)

Number Boards pkg(4) 3.00 ea
344-175 RS-3 Three Digit Mounted Over Headlight
Number Board listed below is available by Special Order (see Legend Page).
344-211 ATSF Type

Placard Holder
344-4 Tank Car pkg(16) **3.00**

Radio Antenna pkg(4) 3.00 ea
344-28 Caboose Dish Style
344-253 Sinclair Antenna w/No Base
344-555 PRR Diesel RF16 & BP20 Etched Brass

Snow Plows
344-197 For F Units pkg(2) **3.00**

Spark Arrestors 3.00 ea
344-119 CN Style For SW1200 pkg(2)
344-139 18" Cabbage Style For SWs pkg(4)
344-172 ATSF pkg(4)
344-173 Round Wire Screen For EMD Switchers pkg(4)
344-174 CN Style For GP9 pkg(2)

Stainless Steel Grilles
344-360 Farr Type For Fairbanks-Morse C-Liner Diesels **5.50**
344-361 Horizontal Type F7A **3.00**
344-362 Horizontal Type **3.25**
344-363 Farr Type F7A **3.00**
344-364 Farr Type F7B **3.25**
344-365 Horizontal Type E8A **3.75**
344-367 Farr Type E8A **3.75**
344-368 Farr Type E8B **4.00**
Grille listed below is available by Special Order (see Legend Page).
344-366 Horizontal Type E8B **4.00**

Steel Coils pkg(3) 3.00 ea
344-267 60" Diameter
344-269 84" Diameter

Stirrup Steps pkg(6) 3.00 ea
344-82 FA/PA
344-83 E&F
344-84 Sharknose pkg(8)
344-85 C-Liner
344-86 Erie Built
344-87 F/FP45 pkg(8)

Sunshades pkg(4) 3.00 ea
344-91 E&F Units
344-92 FA & PA Units
344-93 Hood Unit-Wide
344-94 Hood Unit-Narrow
344-95 Hood Unit-Wide/Long
344-96 72" Square Sunshade
344-100 SD60M 72"

Tank Car Details
344-369 Stainless Steel Ladders, Platforms & Rails **4.00**
Fits Atlas beercan tank cars.

Trackside Details
344-5 B&O Communication Shacks pkg(2) **3.25**

Wind Deflector
344-25 Locomotive/Caboose pkg(16) **3.00**

Windshield Wipers 3.00 ea
344-31 EMD pkg(9)
344-32 GE pkg(9)

Winterization Hatches 3.00 ea
344-108 RS-3
344-109 GP20
344-124 EMD SD45
344-127 FA
Hatch listed below is available by Special Order (see Legend Page).
344-209 FA-2 CP (2 pieces)

SUPER DETAILING PARTS N SCALE

MICRON ART

These items are unpainted white metal castings and can be used with kits or scratchbuilt structures.

Finials

462-20054 462-20155

462-20054 Post Type **1.25**
462-20155 Medium Spire Type **2.00**

Ventilators

462-20114 462-20156

462-20114 Medium for Factory Roof **1.25**
462-20156 Victorian, Medium **2.00**

Miscellaneous

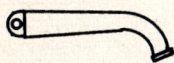

462-20053 Water Station Funnel .082" Long **1.80**

462-20093 Steps 1.87" Long **2.50**

PIKESTUFF

Dome Window

541-1001 Dome Window Insert **4.25**
One-piece, clear green plastic dome for Oriental Limited "California Zephyr," can also be used with other manufacturers' brass Budd dome cars.

Micro Engineering Company

Parts are white metal castings, unless noted.

Plate Girders

255-80170 80' Girder pkg(4) **5.45**
255-80171 40' Girder pkg(4) **5.20**

Doors

Plastic doors and windows.

255-80200 Warehouse Overhead pkg(4) **2.95**
255-80201 Office Doors & Windows pkg(10) **2.95**
255-80204 Warehouse Roll-Up Doors pkg(4) **3.20**

Mine Car 3.20 ea

255-80157 Car pkg(2)
255-80158 Mine Track 2" lengths, plastic pkg(4)

Miniature Tools pkg(2) 3.20 ea

255-80142 255-80143

255-80142 Acetylene Torch & Cart
255-80143 Air Compressor

Tanks & Drums

255-80146 255-80148

255-80146 Oil Drums pkg(7) **3.60**

255-80148 Acetylene Tanks pkg(21) **3.20**

255-80156 Oil Drum Platform pkg(2) **3.20**

Trackside Details pkg(2) 3.20 ea

255-80152 255-80153

255-80152 Telephone Box
255-80153 Relay Box

Miscellaneous

255-80140 255-80144

255-80140 Tires, Assorted **3.20**
255-80141 Gas Pump (1940s Era) pkg(2) **3.20**
255-80144 Pallets, Plastic pkg(24) **3.60**

255-80147 255-80154

255-80147 V-8 Engine pkg(4) **3.20**
255-80154 Push Cart pkg(2) **3.20**

255-80155 Coal Boxes pkg(2) **3.20**

255-80202 255-80203

255-80202 Roofs, Vents & Fans pkg(6) **3.20**
255-80203 Step & Stoops plastic pkg(4) **2.95**

Daily New Product Announcements! Visit Walthers Web site at
www.walthers.com

MICRO-TRAINS LINE

Freight Car Loads

489-49943902 Log Loads pkg(3) **11.95**

489-49943904 Stone Load pkg(3) **12.95** Fits 50' Gondola (sold separately).

Caboose Window Kits

489-49988905 Fits 50000 Series Cars **10.45**
489-49988906 Fits 51000 Series Cars **10.45**

Box Car Doors pkg(12) 7.05 ea

489-49920935 Youngstown Style-40' Cars
489-49920937 Youngstown Style-50' Cars
489-49920940 Double-Doors For 40 or 50' Cars pkg(6)
489-49920942 For 50' Rib Side Car
489-49920915 Superior Style-40' Cars
489-49920925 1-1/2 Doors For 40 or 50' Cars pkg(6)
489-49920920 Wood, For Single or Double Sheathed Cars
489-49920922 For Stock Cars

Brake Wheels pkg(12) 5.20 ea

489-49905901 Horizontal Type
489-49905905 Miner Horizontal-Mount Type
489-49905910 For Tank Car
489-49905911 Vertical Type

Caboose Parts

489-49950905 End Rails pkg(12) **7.80**
489-49957905 Smokestacks pkg(12) **5.20**

Car Stirrups pkg(12) 5.20 ea

489-49965905 #3001
489-49965910 For Gondola
489-49965915 For Reefers Includes eight end and four center stirrups.
489-49965920 For Stock Car
489-49965925 For Flat Car
480-49965930 For Rib Side Car

Freight Car Parts pkg(12) 5.20 ea (Unless Noted)

489-312032 Truck Bolster Pins **3.30**
489-49910915 Reefer Hatches & Latches
489-49920950 Bay Doors For Hoppers
489-49925905 Gondola Drop Ends **7.05**
489-49925910 Bridge Plates (6 Each Small & Large) For 89' Flat Cars
489-49940905 Tank Car Ladders
489-49948905 Tank Car Placard Boards
489-49959905 Stakes For Flat Cars (4 Sets)
489-49965935 Hopper Stirrup Braces & Brake Hardware (black)
489-49975905 TOFC Trailer Hitches (6 Each Retracted & Raised) **7.05**
489-49965936 Hopper Stirrup Braces & Brake Hardware (brown)

Roofwalks pkg(12) 5.20 ea

489-49955905 40' PS-1 Box Cars
489-49955910 50' PS-1 Box Car
489-49955915 Short, For Caboose
489-49955920 40' Box Cars
489-49955921 Reefers

Screws

489-112020 Multi-Purpose 00-90 - 5/16" pkg(24) **2.95**

Storage Container

489-98409000 Clear Plastic Container pkg(30) **27.00** For all items that need a special place of their own. Perfect for keeping track of parts during construction or for storage.

439

SUPER DETAILING PARTS N SCALE

MODEL POWER

Prepainted plastic parts are ready for use on your layout.

Detail Sets
490-1330 Station Set pkg(22) **15.50**
Includes 10 automobiles, six station figures and six railroad crew figures.

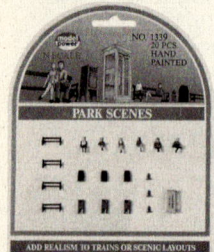

490-1339 Street Accessories pkg(20) **15.50**
Includes six handpainted figures, four benches, one telephone booth, three fire hydrants, three mail boxes and three trash cans.

490-1340 Park Benches Only pkg(8) **7.98**
One-piece green plastic.

For Up-To-Date Information and News Bookmark Walthers Web site at
www.walthers.com

NEAL'S N GAUGING TRAINS

SCENIC ACCESORIES
530-120RB Road Cones pkg(15) — Red/Black **7.50**
530-SS01V Benches, Carts & Handtruck **15.95**
530-SS026 Rubbish Tips/Dumpster **10.95**
530-SS027 Platform Trolleys/Carts (Mail, Parcels, etc.) **12.95**
530-SS038 Gravestones, Some w/Legible Epitaphs **11.95**
530-SS041 Knife Grinder w/Cart **10.95**
530-SS042 (2) Each Picnic Tables w/Benches, Sun Umbrellas & Sandwich Boards **11.95**
530-SS098 Ladders **11.95**
530-SS601 US Style Baggage Carts **14.95**
530-SS602 Wind Pump **12.95**
530-SS604 Single Stall Engine Shed - Branchline **54.95**
530-SS605 US Style Benches **11.95**

METAL DETAILS

Barrels

530-41 Stacked **8.25**
530-47 Picnic (green/rust & green/black) pkg(5) **8.50**
530-48 Circus (red, blue & white) **9.50**

Benches

530-59 Assorted Painted **9.95**

Chairs
530-25 Etched Metal Folding Chairs pkg(132) **19.95**

Construction Zone Accessories

530-43 Barrels (orange & white) pkg(9) **11.95**

Gravestones

530-56 pkg(8) **10.95**

Handtrucks 6.95 ea (Unless Noted)
530-57 With 2 Red Caps/Porters **11.95**
530-49B Brown pkg(3)

530-49G Green pkg(3)
530-49R Red pkg(3)
530-49Y Yellow pkg(3)

Ladders

530-45 Painted **9.95**

Milk Cans
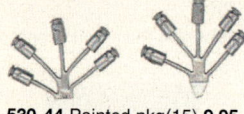

530-44 Painted pkg(15) **9.95**

Oil Drums
530-42 Stacked **8.25**

Parking Meters
530-20 **8.95**

Road Cones

530-120 Bright Orange pkg(15) **9.95**

Wheel Barrow & Lawn Mower
530-54A **11.95**
Includes 2 wheel barrows and 2 lawn mowers.

ETCHED BRASS DETAILS

Detail Parts 14.95 ea
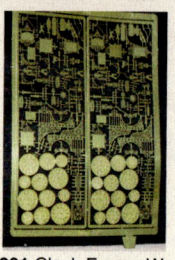

530-301 Clock Faces, Weather Vanes & Hanging Sign
530-302 Ornamental Tables, Chairs & Benches
530-303 Industrial Staircases & Railings

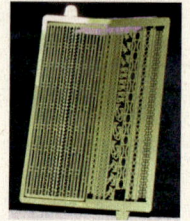

530-304 Assorted Valance Boards, Trim, Etc.
530-305 Windmills pkg(2)
530-306 Wrought & Cast Iron Gates
530-307 Cast Iron Railings

530-308 Ornate Estate Gates
530-309 Iron Balustrades
530-312 Ladders, Steps & Painters' Scaffold

Foliage 20.95 ea

530-331 Bracken Fronds

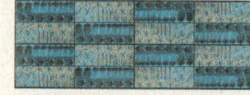

530-332 Pond & Canal Plants

530-333 Oak Leaves/Branches

530-334 Ash Leaves/Branches

530-335 Maple

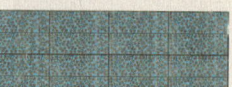

530-336 Horse Chestnut

530-337 Weeping Willow

Diamond Tread 14.95 ea
530-310 Solid w/Raised Diamond Pattern
530-311 Solid w/Depressed Diamond Pattern

Fences 8.95 ea (Unless Noted)
530-E1 Pedestrian Walkway Fence - Approx. 20" Long
530-E3 Wood Plank Fence (Wavey) - Approx. 21.5" Long
530-E4 Iron Rail Fence - Approx. 16.5" Long
530-E5 5-Rail Pasture Fence w/Gate - Approx. 21.5" Long
530-E7 Picket Fence w/Gate - Approx. 22" Long **9.95**
530-E8 Corral Fence w/1 Gate & 2/Style - Approx. 19" Long **9.95**
530-E37 5-Rail Fence - Approx. 46" Long **19.95**

ETCHED STAINLESS STEEL DETAIL PARTS

Mesh 18.95 ea
Measures 2-1/2 x 3-3/4" 6.2 x 9.3cm.

Square
530-313 .22mm Spacing
530-314 .35mm Spacing
530-315 .50mm Spacing

Diamond
530-316 .20mm Spacing
530-317 .35mm Spacing
530-318 .50mm Spacing

Hexagonal
530-319 .25mm Spacing

Octagonal
530-320 .25mm Spacing

SUPER DETAILING PARTS N SCALE

NEW PRODUCTS

Cargo Stacks
Add interest to loading docks and open truck beds with these cargo stacks. Unpainted metal castings.

NEW 716-20039 Wooden Crate Stacks pkg(4) **11.95**

NEW 716-20040 Hops & Barley Sack Stacks pkg(4) **11.95**

NEW 716-20041 Cotton Bales pkg(4) **12.95**

716-20032 Critter Locomotive & Driver **12.95**
Includes 5 Lumber Bogies

MAKING A SCENE™ DETAIL PARTS

Add more realism to any layout scene with this selection of unique details. Each includes instructions for preparing, painting and weathering, and color photos are provided to show how the parts are used in the real world.

Barrel Assortments
9 stacked, 3 rows
716-20025 Small Barrels **9.95**
716-20026 Large Barrels **10.95**

Beef Cows

716-20001 pkg(8) **7.95**

Chimneys
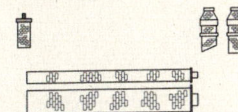
716-20004 **8.95**
Includes two each of three different styles of brick chimneys.

Chutes & Ladders
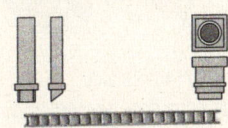
716-20005 **7.95**
Includes two each of Slide and Box chutes, along with 2" long ladder.

Detail Assortments

716-20007 Stockyard **8.95**
Includes five beef cows, a rolled hay bale and a feed trough.

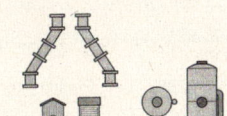
716-20009 Industrial **8.95**
Includes two each of tank pipes and peak vents, plus a single chemical tank.

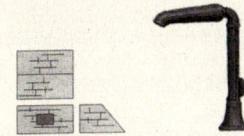
716-20010 Railyard **9.95**
Includes two water standpipes and a Lackawanna-style concrete track bumper.

716-20011 Creamery **6.95**
Includes two figures and ten milk cans.

716-20022 55-Gallon Drums **8.95**
Includes a stack of 12 drums and six single drums.

Dormers & Vents

716-20006 **7.95**
Includes two each of roof vents with flat or angled base, two dormers and four station roof brackets.

Hay Bales
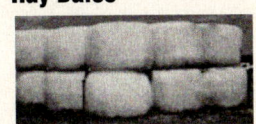
716-20002 Modern Plastic-Wrapped Round pkg(5) **7.95**
716-20021 Rectangular pkg(4) **8.95**
Includes four stacks of 12.

Sack Assortments
9.95 ea
716-20023 Open Sacks
30 stacked sacks, 5 sacks, 2 figures & dolly.
716-20024 Closed Sacks
24 stacked sacks, 5 sacks, 2 figures & dolly.

Steps
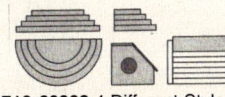
716-20003 4 Different Styles **8.95**

Vents & Blowers
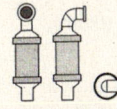
716-20008 pkg(6) **8.95**
Includes two each of three different styles.

LUMBER
14.95 ea (Unless Noted)
Self-stick adhesive on these laser-cut lumber stacks, tie bundles and pallets allow you to add them to your layout in minutes with no gluing and minimal cutting.

716-20033 Timber Stacks 8 x 8 w/Separator Webs pkg(4)
716-20034 Plank Stacks 2 x 12 w/Separator Webs pkg(4)
716-20035 Stud Stacks 2 x 4 w/Separator Webs pkg(4)
716-20036 Tie Bundles w/Base Webs pkg(6)

716-20037 Random Tie Stacks w/Separator Webs pkg(6)

716-20038 Wooden Pallets w/2 Layers pkg(15)

M-TRAK™ SYSTEM
Transform mining operations along your layout with this new series of models. Typical of the small, narrow gauge equipment used under and above ground, the M-Trak system provides a complete assortment of 2' 6" gauge track and equipment that can be used to detail any mine complex.

Loco & Cars
These unpainted metal castings are typical of the equipment used at all types of mines.

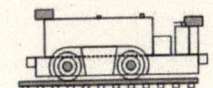
716-20012 Mine Loco (Nonpowered), Driver, & Two 4-Ton Cars **14.95**

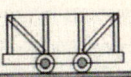
716-20013 4-Ton Cars pkg(3) **12.95**

Track
Easy to use, each section features metal rails and laser-cut wood ties. Each package also includes a measuring tool, track gauge and bending jig specifically developed for each type of track section.

Straight Sections
10.95 ea

716-20014 1-1/2" Straight pkg(6)
Includes six pieces of straight track, each measuring 1-1/2" long for a total of 9" and 24" of rail per package.

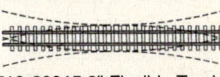
716-20015 3" Flexible Track pkg(3)
Each section measures about 40' scale feet long (about 3") and builds up to 9" of track; 24" of rail per package. Sections can be bent up to 15°.

Turnouts pkg(4)
10.95 ea
Each includes 4 turnout sections and 24" of rail per package.

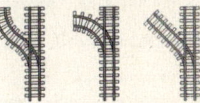
716-20016   716-20017   716-20018
716-20016 Siding
716-20017 90°
716-20018 45°

Curved Sections
Each includes 6 track sections and 24" of rail per package.

716-20019   716-20020
716-20019 90°
716-20020 45°

441

SUPER DETAILING PARTS N SCALE

NEW PRODUCTS
Super Detailing Parts

Vents
NEW 533-161501 pkg(5) **1.75**
4-1/2 x 2-1/2 scale feet each.

Control/Access Panels
NEW 533-161601 pkg(10) **2.25**
Various sizes.

Barricades
533-162100 Street Barricades pkg(18) **5.95**
Includes 10 folding types and eight sawhorse style barricades.

Drainage Ditches

533-160301 Concrete pkg(4) **5.75**
A quick and easy way to add this important detail to almost any layout location. Simply remove the folded ditch from the package, run a bead of glue down the grooves, then fold to the desired width. Includes four 9" long sections,

Chain-Link Fencing
533-161500 Residential Style **TBA**
Scale 4' high fence includes large double gates for autos.
533-162300 Commercial Style **TBA**
Scale 6' high fence used at businesses and parking lots. Features barbed wire on top of fence which can be easily removed if desired. Large double gates for autos are included along with a small personnel gate.
533-162400 Industrial Style **TBA**
Scale 8' high fence like that used around warehouses, industrial buildings and parking lots. Features barbed wire on top of fence which can be easily removed if desired. Includes large double gates for autos and a small gate for personnel.

Doors 2.25 ea
(Unless Noted)
533-160601 8 x 10' Truck Cargo pkg(6)
533-160701 10 x 10' Rail Cargo pkg(4)
533-161703 8 x 8' Wood Cargo pkg(4)
533-160801 12 x 15' Vehicle Entry pkg(2)
533-161803 8 x 8' Wood Cargo pkg(4)
533-161903 Personnel Doors - 2 Each of 2 Styles **1.75**

Exit Stairway pkg(2) 2.25 ea
533-160901 Type 1 Narrow profile, ideal for use where space is limited.
533-161101 Type 2 Wider profile fits most applications where space is available.

Fence
533-160501 Steel Rod Type **10.50**
Includes three 8" lengths of fencing material measuring a scale 8' tall and 14' wide.

Gates
533-160101 Steel pkg(4) **4.95**
Each measures a scale 8' tall and 25' long.
533-162000 Swing Type pkg(8) **6.25**
Includes eight different gates ranging in size from 15 to 21 scale feet long.

Garbage Bin Storage
533-161301 pkg(2) **2.25**
Prototypes secure trashcans and prevent them from blowing around.

Loading Ramp
533-161201 pkg(2) **3.25**
Includes enough material to build two ramps that rise from ground level to .300"

Sidewalks
533-161401 pkg(3) **2.25**
Includes two 3" long sections each measuring a scale 53' long by 3' wide and one 3" long section measuring a scale 40' long by 6' wide.

Skylights
533-160401 Low Profile pkg(10) **3.25**
Molded in white.

Tunnel Motor Air Intake Screens
533-162200 Rear Screens pkg(4) **6.25**
Give your Tunnel Motor diesels a more realistic look with these see-through screens that replace molded details on most locos. Includes four screens, enough to detail two locos.

Walls
533-160201 Concrete **7.95**
Includes approximately 1440 scale feet of wall material including 6, 10 and 12' tall walls.

Windows
533-161603 3 x 6' pkg(8) **1.75**

Wood Loading Dock

533-161503 **7.98**
This kit matches the loading dock included with the Azusa Station kit. When placed along the tracks it makes rail-to-truck transfer a snap.

PRECISION SCALE CO.

One-piece brass castings, or molded plastic parts as noted.

Air Hose 2.75 ea

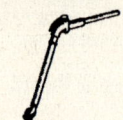

585-6704 Brass pkg(6)
585-6705 Plastic pkg(24)

Air Reservoir, Wabco AB

585-6706 Brass pkg(5) **3.00**
585-6707 Plastic pkg(5) **2.00**

Brake Cylinder, Wabco For Cars

585-6708 Brass pkg(5) **3.50**
585-6709 Plastic pkg(5) **2.25**

Wabco AB
585-6712 Plastic Kit **3.00**
585-6713 Brass Kit **6.50**
Includes air reservoirs, distributing valves, brake cylinders and air hoses for four cars.

585-6732 Brake Cylinder, Brass **2.00**

Catalog
585-9738 Complete N Scale Catalog **4.00**

Distributing Valve, Wabco AB

585-6710 Brass pkg(5) **3.50**
585-6711 Plastic pkg(5) **2.25**

Check Valves pkg(2) 2.00 ea

585-6719 Pipe, Nathan
585-6724 Nathan

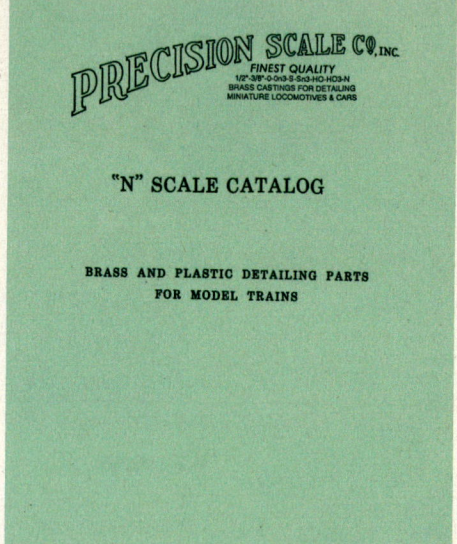

N Scale Catalog 585-9738

Generators

585-6714   585-6727

585-6714 Pyle **2.50**
585-6727 Pyle, Modern **2.25**

Marker Lights

585-6739 Small, #M-10000 Style pkg(2) **2.25**
585-6740 Plastic pkg(4) **1.75**

Vents
585-6721 Small, Brass 1 Pair **1.75**

585-6737   585-6741   585-6743

585-6737 Small #M-1000 Style **3.25**
585-6738 Small, Plastic pkg(4) **2.25**
585-6741 Large, M-1000 Style for Car Body pkg(4) **3.50**
585-6742 Large, Plastic pkg(4) **2.25**
585-6743 Medium, M-1000 Style for Car Body pkg(4) **3.25**

Miscellaneous

585-6715   585-6716   585-6717

585-6715 Boiler Front, N&W Class J, 4-8-4 **5.00**
585-6716 Marker Lamps, N&W Class J, One-Piece, Front Shroud. **2.75**
585-6717 Pilot, N&W Class J, Steel **3.00**

585-6718   585-6720   585-6722

585-6718 Cylinder Block, N&W Class J One-Piece w/Heads & Pistons **6.00**
585-6720 Bell & Bracket **2.50**
585-6722 Dupont Duplex Stoker Engine **2.50**

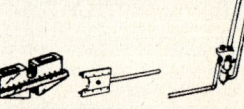

585-6723   585-6726   585-6728

585-6723 Nathan NV7 Lubricator **1.50**
585-6726 Alligator Crosshead, Metal pkg(2) **2.50**
585-6728 Injector, Non-Lift 1 Pair **2.25**

585-6729   585-6733

585-6729 Power Reverse, Alco **2.75**
585-6733 Tender Steps, Cast Steel pkg(4) **2.50**

585-6734   585-6736

585-6734 Headlight UP **2.25**
585-6736 Power Car Exhaust Stacks **2.75**
585-6744 8-1/2" Westinghouse Cross Compound Air Pump **3.25**

SUPER DETAILING PARTS N SCALE

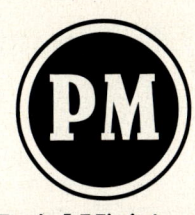

Period Miniatures

NEW PRODUCTS

Roof Details

NEW 555-1000 Rooftop Entryways pkg(2) **TBA**

NEW 555-1001 Rooftop Skylights pkg(2) **TBA**

Smokestacks

NEW 555-1002 Tall Industrial Brick **TBA**

NEW 555-1003 Tall Industrial **TBA**

Staircases

NEW 555-1004 Narrow Concrete pkg(2) **TBA**
For single door access.

Air Conditioners

555-2127 Window pkg(3) **2.45**

555-2130 20-Ton Roof Kit **3.65**

Barrels, Drums, Cans & Crates 2.45 ea (Unless Noted)

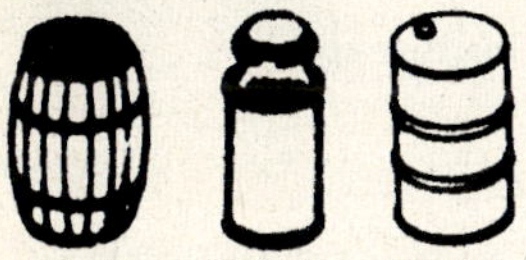

555-2011 555-2012 555-2034

555-2011 Barrels pkg(10)

555-2012 Milk Cans pkg(8)

555-2034 Oil Barrels pkg(8)

555-2052 Large Open Top Barrel pkg(4)

555-2054 55-Gallon Oil Drum w/Rack (2 Sets)

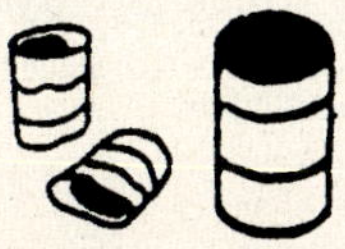

555-2119 555-2120

555-2119 Open Used/Abused 55-Gallon Drum pkg(7) **3.65**

555-2120 Open 55-Gallon Drums pkg(7) **3.65**

555-2124 Barrel Racks w/Barrel Kit **4.45**

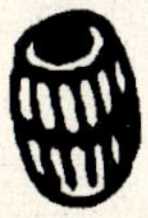

555-2135 Small Open Top Barrels pkg(4)

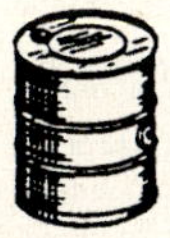

Limited Quantity Available

555-2096 75-Gallon Oil Drums pkg(8)

Chimneys 2.45 ea

555-2010 Brick pkg(2)

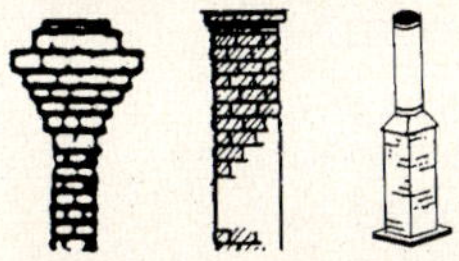

555-2043 555-2061 555-2097

555-2043 Short Brick pkg(2)

555-2061 Small Brick pkg(3)

555-2157 Fat Brick pkg(2)

555-2158 Standard pkg(2)

Limited Quantity Available

555-2097 Brick w/Taper Flue

555-2159 Brick pkg(2)

555-2162 Brick Chimney Stone pkg(2)

555-2163 Brick w/Taper pkg(2)

Corbels 2.45 ea

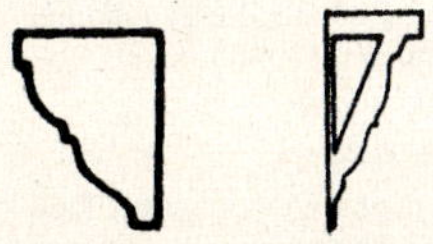

555-2013 555-2032

555-2013 Corbels pkg(8)

555-2032 Corbels pkg(8)

555-2033 Angle Corbels pkg(8)

555-2035 Corbels Style #2 pkg(8)

555-2036 Ornate Post w/Corbel pkg(4)

555-2039 Ornate Square Post w/Corbel pkg(4)

555-2042 Ornate Square Post w/Double Corbel pkg(4)

Cornices, Gables & Finials 2.45 ea (Unless Noted)

555-2038 Cornice Trims pkg(6)

555-2060 Medium Ball Finial pkg(8)

Limited Quantity Available

555-2165 Storefront Cornice #1 **3.15**

Doors 2.45 ea

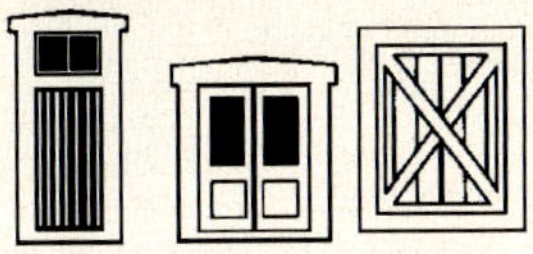

555-2003 555-2004 555-2005

555-2003 Single pkg(4)

555-2004 Double pkg(8)

555-2005 Braced pkg(3)

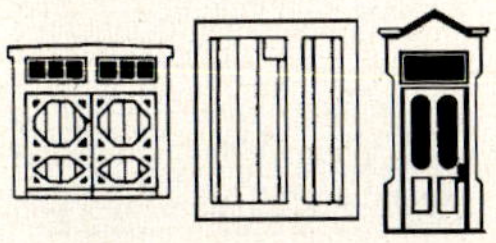

555-2006 555-2007 555-2014

555-2006 6-Pane Freight pkg(2)

555-2007 Solid Freight pkg(2)

555-2014 Victorian pkg(4)

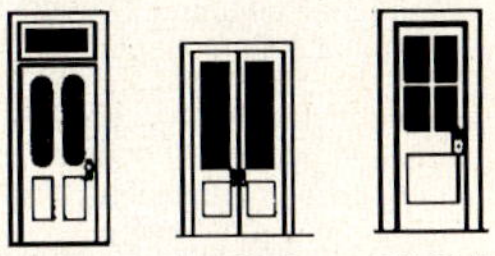

555-2016 555-2018 555-2019

555-2016 pkg(4)

555-2018 Double pkg(3)

555-2019 Single pkg(4)

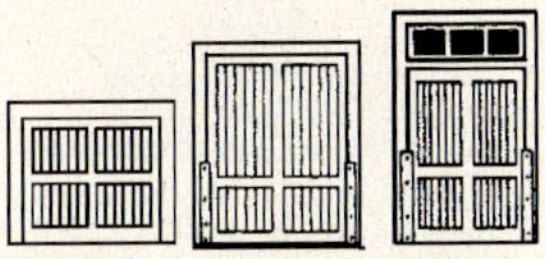

555-2023 555-2024 555-2025

555-2023 Freight pkg(2)

555-2024 Freight pkg(2)

555-2025 3-Pane Freight pkg(2)

555-2026 4-Pane Single pkg(3)

555-2149 Engine House Doors

Electric Power Services 2.45 ea

555-2069 pkg(3)

Fences

555-818 Chain Link Fence w/Gates (brass) 200' **16.95**

555-820 Corrugated Iron Fence (metal) 200' **12.95**

Forklift Kits 3.65 ea

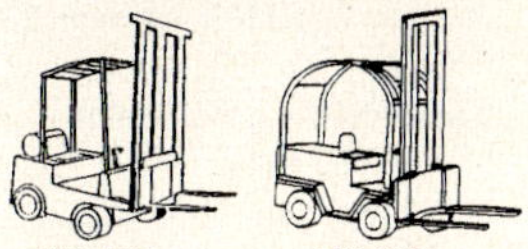

555-3000 555-3001

555-3000 3,000lb Capacity

555-3001 7,000lb Capacity

Lamps

555-2065 With Shade pkg(8) **2.45**

See What's Available at **www.walthers.com**

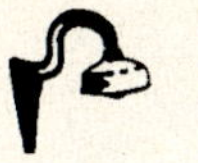

555-2070 Wall w/Shade (brass) pkg(6) **4.95**

Railings pkg(2) 2.45 ea

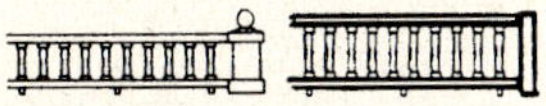

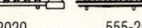

555-2020 555-2021

555-2020 Western w/Post

555-2021 Porch w/Post

555-2037 Porch Railings Less Post

Scuppers pkg(8) 2.45 ea

555-2154 Drain Scuppers

Limited Quantity Available

555-2160 Industrial Drain Scuppers

Smokestacks & Smokejacks pkg(4) 2.45 ea

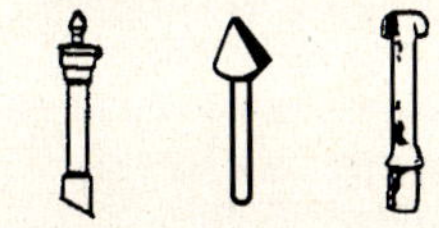

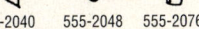

555-2040 555-2048 555-2076

555-2040 Ornate Smoke Stack

555-2048 Cone Top Smokejack

555-2049 "T" Smokejack

Limited Quantity Available

555-2076 Tall Smokestack

Tanks 2.45 ea (Unless Noted)

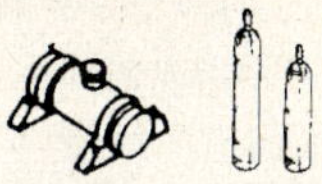

555-2083 555-2114

555-2053 Bulk Heating Oil Storage w/Rack (2 Sets)

555-2063 Water Tank Spout Kit **3.15**

555-2114 Oxygen pkg(10)

Limited Quantity Available

555-2083 Propane pkg(3)

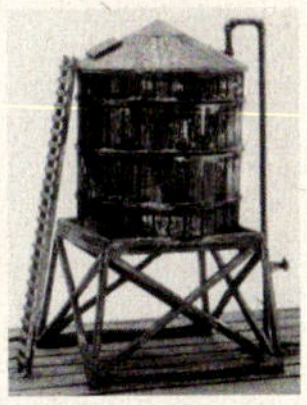

555-2136 Roof Top Water Tank Kit **6.15**

Vents

555-2044 Stove pkg(4) **2.45**

555-2152 Engine House Roof **3.15**

Limited Quantity Available

555-2153 Round Industrial Roof pkg(2) **2.45**

Windows 2.45 ea

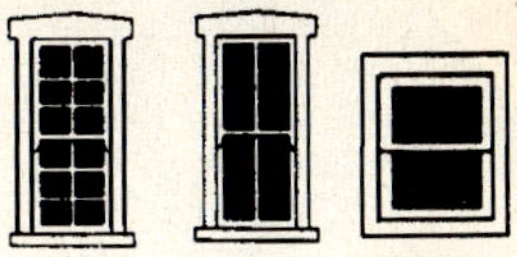

555-2000 555-2001 555-2002

555-2000 12-Pane pkg(4)

555-2001 4-Pane pkg(4)

555-2002 2-Pane pkg(6)

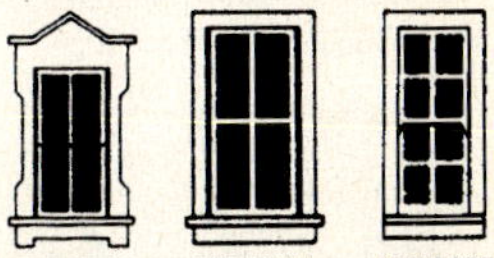

555-2015 555-2017 555-2027

555-2015 Victorian pkg(4)

555-2017 4-Pane pkg(4)

555-2027 8-Pane pkg(4)

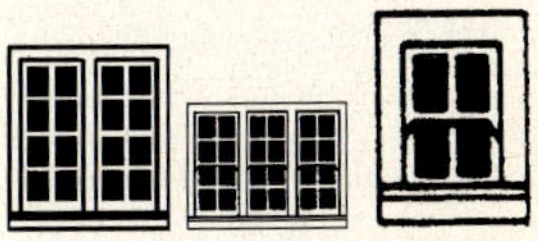

555-2028 555-2029 555-2030

555-2028 8-Pane Double pkg(2)

555-2029 8-Pane Triple pkg(2)

555-2030 4-Pane Wash Room pkg(5)

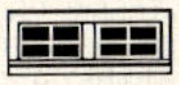

555-2031 Horizontal Double pkg(3)

Limited Quantity Available

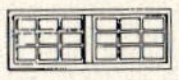

555-2086 Tall Engine House pkg(2)

Miscellaneous 2.45 ea (Unless Noted)

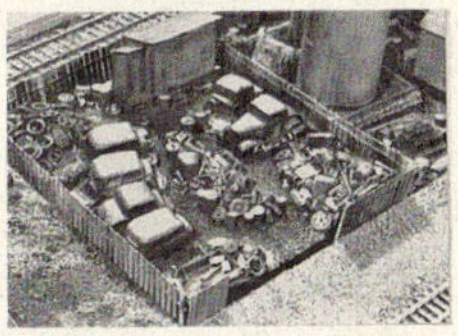

555-827 Assorted Junk Piles **11.95**

555-860 Earth Bumper pkg(2) **5.45**

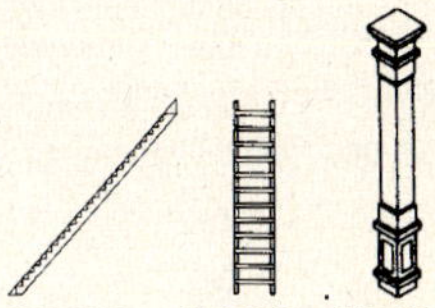

555-2008 555-2009 555-2022

555-2008 Stairway pkg(2)

555-2009 Ladder pkg(4)

555-2022 Ornate Square Posts pkg(4)

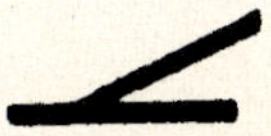

555-2041 Roof Eave Supports pkg(4)

ER DETAILING PARTS N SCALE

Period Miniatures

555-2045 Ornate Roof Sign

555-2046 555-2050 555-2051
555-2046 Outhouse pkg(2)
555-2050 Shovel pkg(6)
555-2051 Broom pkg(6)

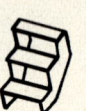
555-2055 Open Frame Stairs (3 Pieces)

555-2056 555-2057
555-2056 Coal Bin pkg(2)
555-2057 Junk Tire pkg(6)

555-2058 555-2059
555-2058 Coke Machine Upright
555-2059 Coke Machine Open Top

555-2064 555-2066 555-2067
555-2064 Wash Tub pkg(4)
555-2066 Water Spigot pkg(8)
555-2067 Coal Hod pkg(6)

555-2068 Gas Pump pkg(2)

555-2112 555-2113
555-2112 Wooden Benches pkg(3)
555-2113 Assorted Skids w/Junk & Empty pkg(6) **3.65**

555-2115 555-2118
555-2115 Platform Scale pkg(3)
555-2118 Trash Dumpster pkg(2)

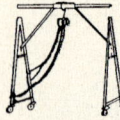 
555-2121 555-2122
555-2121 A-Frame Hoist w/Chain Fall Kit **3.65**
555-2122 Saw Horses pkg(3)
555-2123 Diamond Plate Sheets 4 x 8' pkg(3)

555-2125 Work Tables, 3 Types pkg(3) **4.45**

555-2126 Pallet Jack

555-3002 D-6 Caterpillar Bulldozer Kit **4.95**

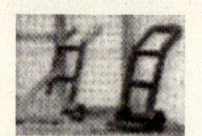
555-2129 2-Wheel Hand Truck pkg(2)

Limited Quantity Available

555-2131 Cable Reels Small, Medium & Large 3 Each pkg(9) **3.65**
555-2150 Industrial Electric Insulators pkg(8) **3.15**
555-2164 Large Safe pkg(2)

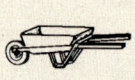 
555-2133 555-2134
555-2133 Wheelbarrow pkg(2)
555-2134 Exhaust Blower 30" Kit **3.65**

555-2137 Billboards w/Signs Kit **4.95**

555-2138 Roll-On/Off Trash Body Kit **4.95**

555-2139 Station Baggage Cart **3.65**

555-3003 Brass Gandy Dancer Track Hand Car **3.65**
555-2141 Commercial Building Roof Details **4.75**
555-2145 Metal Column pkg(4)
555-2146 Hoist Pulley & Beam pkg(4)
555-2147 Hand Water Pump pkg(2)
555-2148 Sidewalks pkg(2)
555-2151 Engine House Cupola
555-2155 Industrial Lampshades pkg(8)
555-2156 Open Stairs pkg(3)

555-2132 Wooden Step Ladder (6 Feet)

PLANO

Make your equipment more realistic with these photo-etched brass and stainless steel parts. Designed to replace molded plastic parts in kits or ready-to-run models, new parts are closer to scale thickness and have realistic see-through appearance.

Intake Grilles
F7A 3.00 ea
565-280 Horizontal
565-281 Farr
F7B 3.25 ea
565-282 Horizontal
565-283 Farr
E8A 3.75 ea
565-284 Horizontal
565-285 Farr
E8B 4.00 ea
565-286 Horizontal
565-287 Farr

Tank Cars
565-235 Beer Can Tank Platform & Ladder **3.95**

Walkways
All walkways are made of photo-etched stainless steel which is .006" thick. This produces a very strong part, with realistic detail. All walkways feature a slotted pattern which represents the prototype "Tri-Loc" running boards made by Apex Railway Products.

Covered Hoppers
565-234 PS 2-Bay LM Slot **2.50**
565-236 36' 2-Bay ACF - Atlas Car **3.25**
565-247 47' 3-Bay PS Con-Cor Car **3.25**
565-255 55' 3-Bay ACF - Atlas Car **4.25**
565-256 100T Canadian Grain **4.00**
565-258 58' 4-Bay PS Con-Cor Car **3.40**

Airslide® Hoppers
565-243 40' Atlas **2.75**
565-249 50' Delaware Valley **3.25**

Box Cars
565-240 40' Car **3.00**
565-250 50' Car **3.25**
565-2404 40' - Apex Pattern pkg(4) **9.00**
565-2504 50' - Apex Pattern pkg(4) **9.75**

PLASTRUCT

Fountains
570-94733 1" Square **6.95**
570-94732 1-1/2" Square **8.30**
570-94735 1" Hexagon **6.95**

Georgian Column
570-90993 1-31/32" **6.55**

Lattices/Trellis
570-90911 2-1/8 x 15/16" **4.95**
570-90912 1-1/4 x 4" pkg(2) **6.35**
570-90913 4-1/8 x 2" pkg(2) **6.35**
570-90914 2-7/16 x 4" pkg(2) **6.35**
570-90915 1-7/16 x 1-7/8" **4.95**
570-90916 5-7/8 x 2-7/8 x 1/8" **8.95**

Outdoor Furniture
570-94703 Playground Set **10.95**
570-94709 Diving Board **2.95**
570-94753 Umbrella Tables pkg(3) **5.95**
570-94773 Park Bench Set pkg(5) **2.95**

Swimming Pool
570-94710 4-5/8 x 4" **7.85**

PREISER

IMPORTED FROM GERMANY BY WALTHERS

One-piece plastic parts are molded in color.

Accessories

590-79554 Tables, Chairs, Umbrellas **9.99**

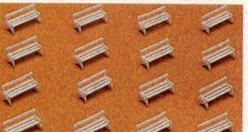
590-79565 Park Benches pkg(24) **12.99**

590-79566 Assorted Cargo **12.99**

SUPER DETAILING PARTS N SCALE

RED CABOOSE

Clear Plastic Freight Car Boxes
629-51401 1.95
629-51402 pkg(12) 14.95

Plastic Freight Car Parts

Bulkhead Ends 1 Pair 3.00 ea
629-51210 For Con-Cor Flat Cars (10' tall)
629-51220 For Micro-Trains® Flat Cars (10' tall)
629-51230 For Con-Cor Flat Cars (8' tall)
629-51240 For Micro-Trains Flat Cars (8' tall)

Steel Coils pkg(6) 3.30 ea
629-51502 24"
629-51503 36"
629-51504 48"

Miscellaneous
629-51300 Coal Load for Ortner Hopper (black) pkg(2) 2.50
629-51505 Angled Coil Car Cover w/Details, Undecorated pkg(2) 3.50
629-51506 Round Coil Car Cover w/Details, Undecorated pkg(2) 3.50

STEWART PRODUCTS

Unpainted metal castings.

Rural Utility Poles pkg(12) 6.95 ea
683-1126 With Single Insulator
683-1127 With Brackets

Miscellaneous 2.95 ea
683-1800 Signal Relay Box, pkg(4)
683-1804 Fire Extinguisher, pkg(12)

Hot New Products Announced Daily! Visit Walthers Web site at www.walthers.com

Sea Port Model Works

Seaport Model Works creates a line of marine components for model railroads. They specialize in products such as fishing boats, ferries and generic boat parts. Customize any kit or scratchbuilt marine model with this line of highly detailed parts, made of polyurethane resin, wood or metal. See the complete line of Seaport Model Works boat kits in the Vehicles section.

Boat Fittings

Bitts 3.95 ea
Unpainted white metal castings
663-P36N Single Bitt
663-P35N Double Bitt

Bollards pkg(4) 2.95 ea

663-P13N 663-P19N 663-P48N

663-P13N Double Bollard
663-P19N Bollard w/Crossbar 9/32" pkg(3)
663-P48N Bollard w/Crossbar 7/32" .55cm Tall

Cabins
Unpainted Resin Castings

663-SA2N Pilot House Cabin & Deck Furniture for Sardine Carrier 12.00

663-SA5N Cabin, Without Clutter; Measures 10-1/2 x 16-1/2' 6.95

663-SA6N Cabin, w/Clutter; Measures 12-1/2 x 16' 6.95

663-SA8N Cabin 14.95

663-SA17N Pilot House Cabin 8.95

Capstan
Unpainted white metal casting
663-P77N Capstan 3.00

Cleats

663-P15N 663-P45N

663-P15N 9/32 x 3/32" .71 x .23cm pkg(8) 3.50
663-P30N 3/8 x 1/8" 3.95
663-P45N 5/32 x 3/32" .39 x .23cm pkg(8) 3.95

Hatches & Companions

663-M38N Cargo Hatch w/Cover pkg(4) 5.95

663-M39N Companion 1/2 x 1/2 x 9/16" 1.25 x 1.25 x 1.42cm 3.95

663-M40N Deck Hatch pkg(5) 3.95

663-M41N Companion/Hatch pkg(4) 3.95

663-M49N Deck Hatch w/Cover pkg(4) 4.95

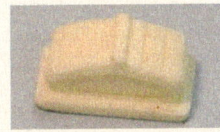

663-M51N Deck Hatch pkg(4) 3.95

663-M52N Companion Hatch 17/64 x 15/64" .67 x .59cm 3.95

663-P57N Manhole cover/Car Float Hatch pkg(8) 3.95

Lights

663-P43N Searchlights pkg(3) 2.95

Masts

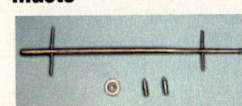

663-P18N Main Mast w/Spreaders, Lights & Base 3.50
663-P23N Cabin Top Mast w/Lights 2.95

Smokestacks pkg(4) 3.00 ea

663-P39N 663-P46N 663-P50N

663-P39N Single Flue
663-P46N "Tee"-Shaped 1-1/2" 3.87cm
663-P50N Straight Galley Stack

Ventilators & Accessories

663-P24N 663-P32N

663-P24N Ventilator Long Cowl Type pkg(3) 3.50
663-P32N Ventilator Stubby Cowl Type 11/32" Tall pkg(4) 3.00

663-P47N Cowls 3/8" Tall pkg(4) 2.95

Miscellaneous
663-P63N Life Ring 3.50
663-P70N Steps 3/8 x 5/8" 3.50
663-P80N Ship's Wheel 3.50

663-SA7N Deck Fittings for Sardine Carrier 8.95

663-SA11N Car Float Fitting Kit (11 pieces) 27.95

663-P44N Winch pkg(4) 3.00

663-P52N 3-Step Stairway pkg(4) 3.00
663-P65N Rail Fasteners pkg(12) 6.95

SUPER DETAILING PARTS N SCALE

Sunrise Enterprises

Upgrade your motive power and more with these finely detailed metal castings. For a complete listing of products, visit Walthers web site at www.walthers.com.

Air Chime
695-15642 Hancock SCL, MILW & Others pkg(3) **2.25**

Air Horns 2.25 ea
695-15700 3-Chime
695-15701 3-Chime w/Bracket
695-15702 Single Chime pkg(4)
695-15704 5-Chime
695-15705 Blat Type GP7/9, F7/9

Air Intakes
695-15629 Central Air Filter Box pkg(2) **2.25**
695-15650 All Weather Shield pkg(4) **2.45**

Bells 2.25 ea
695-15350 Roof Mount pkg(2)
695-15351 Frame Mount pkg(3)
695-15352 Body Mount w/Bracket pkg(3)
695-15353 Body Mount - Covered pkg(3)
695-15356 Gong w/Square Base pkg(3)
695-15358 Hood Mount for GPs of BN/GN/NW pkg(2)
695-15359 Nose Mount for NS/SOU pkg(2)

Brackets 2.25 ea
695-15370 For Horn-Bell pkg(4)
695-15371 For Spare Coupler Knuckles pkg(3)

Brake Gear 2.25 ea (Unless Noted)
695-15632 Truck Brake Cylinder Pod pkg(8) **3.25**
695-15697 Stand w/Wheel - Porch Mount - Modern pkg(2)
695-15698 Brake Wheel pkg(3)
695-15699 Stand w/Wheel - Porch Mount 2 Pieces

Cab Sunshades
695-15311 E&F Units pkg(4) **2.25**

Caboose Parts 2.25 ea
695-151000 Smoke Stack - Tall pkg(3)
695-151001 Smoke Stack - Short pkg(3)

Coils pkg(4) 2.45 ea
695-17101 Large
695-17102 Small

Detail Parts 2.25 ea
695-152007 Rural Route Mailbox
695-151011 Old Style Milk Cans pkg(4)

Diesel Parts
695-15309 Drain Pipe Engine Compartment pkg(4) **2.25**
695-15425 Steam Generator Vent/Exhaust (4 Pieces) **2.25**
695-15800 Rerail Frog pkg(3) **2.25**
695-153001 Photo-Etched Sunshades pkg(6) **6.25**

Ditch Lights 2.25 ea
695-15602 pkg(4)
695-15613 Porch Mount - Low/SP pkg(4)
695-15614 Porch Mount - Tall/SP pkg(4)
695-15626 With Bracket EMD/GE pkg(4)
695-156261 With Bracket

Electrical Box
695-15502 Electrical Box - Front Porch pkg(3) **2.25**

Exhaust Stacks pkg(2) 2.25 ea
695-15325 SD7/9
695-15326 GP/SD38

Hopper Dress-Up Kit
695-17145 Detail & Weight for Walthers PS-2 **4.99**

Headlights 2.25 ea (Unless Noted)
695-15600 WP/CP GP7/9/20 pkg(3)
695-15601 WP GP35/40 pkg(3)
695-15603 Nose Light-SP pkg(2)
695-15606 Rear Light Cluster Bracket pkg(3)
695-15608 Rear Light Cluster Assembled pkg(2)
695-15615 Cluster Bracket SP GP9/20 pkg(4)
695-15616 Cluster Assembly GP9-SP pkg(2) **2.95**
695-15617 Dual Pyle - Early All Roads pkg(2)
695-15621 GE Nose Light w/Bracket pkg(2)
695-15622 Cluster Assembly SD7 BN/UP/CB&Q pkg(2)
695-15630 Barrel Type - SP Style
695-15636 Dual Beam Pyle Type pkg(3)
695-15639 Barrel WP/Sacramento Northern/Spokane International Style - Fits Life-Like SW9 pkg(2)

Lift Rings
695-153000 Photo-Etched pkg(36) **5.25**

Light Cluster Package
695-15640 For Life Like SP GP9/20 **4.10**

Light Housing Cover Plates pkg(4) 2.25 ea
695-15627 Square
695-15628 Round

Marker Lamps
695-15652 Caboose **2.25**

MU Hoses
695-15550 Pilot Mount pkg(4) **4.10**
695-15850 Cables w/Receptacle pkg(3) **2.25**

MU Housing pkg(4) 2.25 ea
695-15801 EMD Early GP/SD
695-15802 Single Receptacle, Right Angle Horizontal Porch Mount

Nose Light Parts 2.25 ea
SP/SSW Style.
695-15637 Cluster Assembly - No Gyralite w/Blank Plate pkg(3)
695-15641 Nose Light w/Bracket CB&Q GP20 pkg(2)

Numberboard Roof Mount pkg(3) 2.25 ea
695-15675 PA
695-17675 ATSF Alco PA

Oscillating Type Lights pkg(2) 2.25 ea
695-15611 Dual Mars - DRGW
695-15612 Dual Pyle w/Base
695-15619 Oscillating Gyralight Bracket

Radio Antennas 2.25 ea
695-15453 Firecracker Type pkg(4)
695-15454 Can Type pkg(3)

Roof Flashers 2.25 ea
695-15300 Beacon - Late
695-15301 Beacon - Rotary
695-15302 Strobe

Snow Plows
Pilot Mount - Single 2.25 ea (Unless Noted)
695-15101 ATSF Style
695-15202 SP/UP/ATSF
695-15203 GN/BN/SP
695-15204 All Roads - Late
695-15206 Debris Kicker Penn Central/MILW
695-15207 All Roads w/Grab Iron **2.25**
695-15208 E&F Units SP, WP, GN, Others **2.45**

Pilot Mount - pkg(3) 5.75 ea
695-15226 ATSF
695-15227 Large - SP
695-15228 Short - UP
695-15229 SP/UP/ATSF
695-15230 GN/BN/SP
695-15231 All Roads - Late
695-15232 All Roads Without Doors
695-15233 Debris Kicker
695-15234 All Roads w/Grab Iron
695-15236 E&F Units SP, WP, GN, Others

Spark Arrestors pkg(2) 2.25 ea
695-15401 Screen Type
695-15402 CN
695-15403 MILW

Speed Recorders 2.25 ea
695-15499 With Adapter pkg(3)
695-15500 Cone Type pkg(2)

Trackside Details
695-17100 Poage Water Column w/Fenner Spout Assembled **22.00**
695-17103 Wig-Wag Pole w/Guardrail **7.95**
695-17104 Wig-Wag for Street Island WP **7.95**
695-17106 200-Gallon Propane Tank pkg(2) **2.25**

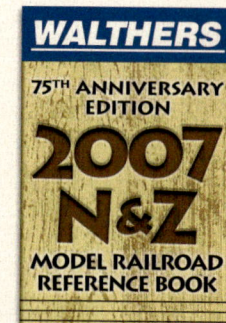

Models & Photo by Tony Koester

An Allegheny Midland steam locomotive switches cars at a two-track tipple on Tony Koester's former HO Scale layout.

"The Model Railroader's Guide to Coal Railroading," Tony Koester's latest project for Kalmbach Books examines the critically intertwined histories of the railroad and coal industries. This mutually dependent relationship continues today, as railroads currently haul more coal than any other commodity. The best part of the story for model railroaders is that coal makes an excellent subject to model, whether the setting is the steam era or a modern layout.

Railroads themselves were once major coal customers, as their fleets of steam locomotives burned more than 100 million tons a year of the flammable rock. Homeowners also relied on coal for heating and cooking into the 1940s.

The use of coal declined through the 1950s and 1960s as diesels replaced steam locomotives and natural gas and propane replaced coal for home use. However, the development of large electrical generating plants, coupled with increased oil prices and the oil crises of the 1970s lead to a dramatic resurgence in coal use that continues. Today, hundreds of underground surface mines from the Appalachians, Midwest and West yield more than a billion tons of coal each year – most of it bound for power plants.

Most of this coal travels by rail. The 55-ton bottom-dump hopper car of the steam era has given way to 110-ton capacity gondola unloaded a train at a time by rotary dumpers. Instead of single-car shipments to local coal dealers, railroads now haul 100-car unit trains directly from mines to power plants.

Whether you want to re-create a small Appalachian coal tipple or a large Western surface mine, or even if you want to model a unit coal train passing through your layout, "The Model Railroader's Guide to Coal Railroading" will be a great reference for getting the details of coal operations just right.

Check out the many books, DVDs, videos and software in this section and you'll discover a wide variety of topics that will help you accurately model different industries, sharpen your modeling skills, learn more about your favorite railroad and more.

BOOKS - VIDEOS - RAILROADIANA

LIFE-LIKE®
Div. of Wm. K. Walthers, Inc.

Books
Basics For Beginners 13th Edition

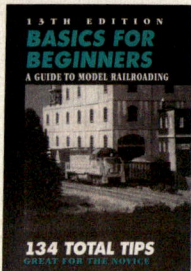

433-8003 1.00
Useful tips on detailing, building and landscaping your layout.

BRAWA

IMPORTED FROM GERMANY BY WALTHERS

Catalog
NEW **186-1061** 2006 English-Language Catalog **15.99**

ATLAS MODEL RAILROAD CO., INC.

NEW PRODUCT
Atlas' Fantastic Layouts Booklet

NEW **150-4** 1.00
This booklet makes it easy to choose your favorite layout. Features all 54 classic HO and N Scale layouts, plus twelve HO True-Track® layouts and 5 N Code 5.5 layouts. Also provides required space, instruction book that includes specific plans and more.

BOOKS
The Complete Atlas Wiring Book

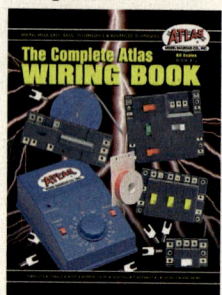

150-12 6.50
Learn how to install and use Atlas' quality components on any layout. Starts beginners with the basics of wiring, and takes advanced modelers through some complex wiring situations. Complemented by more than 100 diagrams and complete glossary. For all scales and skill levels.

Introduction to N Scale Model Railroading

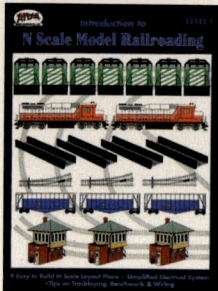

150-6 5.50
Complete information for beginners on building a layout – tips on benchwork, wiring and track layout. Includes Atlas Master™ DCC wiring instructions.

Nine N Scale Railroads

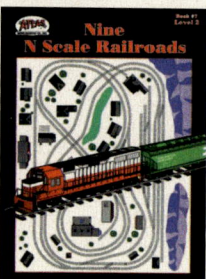

150-7 6.50
Nine different layouts with tips on construction, control panel wiring, scenery, etc. Photos, diagrams, softcover, 56 pages, 8-1/2 x 11".

BACHMANN

NEW PRODUCT
Catalogs
2006 Bachmann Catalog

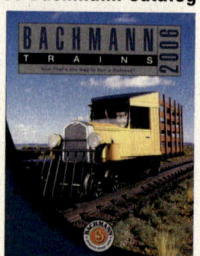

NEW **160-99906** 10.00
This full-color, 216-page catalog shows the top-of-the-line products included in the Bachmann and Spectrum lines.

BADGER AIR-BRUSH CO.

BOOKS
Air Brushing
Hobby & Craft Guide To Air-Brushing

165-500 7.60
Preparation for painting, mixing paint, cleaning and maintenance.

Step By Step Modelers Guide to Air-Brushing
165-505 11.20
Covers painting models, figures and dioramas. Techniques from shadowing to properly mixing paint. 32 pages, 8-1/2 x 11".

Introduction to Airbrushes, Accessories & Airbrushing Mediums
165-222001 25.70

Items listed below are available by Special Order (see Legend Page).

The Fundamentals of Airbrush Technique: Basic Exercises
165-222002 Volume I **25.70**

Intermediate Airbrush Technique: Working In Color
165-222003 Volume II **25.70**

VIDEO
Aging and Weathering Models (and Stuff) with an Airbrush

165-11 25.70
With a few basic colors and a little ingenuity you'll learn the techniques necessary to weather your own models for a truly realistic look. 60 minutes.

BL HOBBY PRODUCTS

Limited Quantity Available
Flasher Lapel Pin

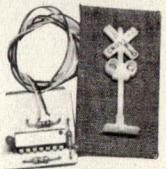

183-580 21.25
Pin is a plastic HO Scale operating railroad crossing flasher that uses a 9V battery. Includes 10" wires and printed circuit board, less battery.

BUSCH

IMPORTED FROM GERMANY BY WALTHERS

NEW PRODUCTS
Catalogs
Discover the entire line of Busch models in these catalogs. Each features full-color images of products, descriptions (mostly in German) and appropriate measurements.

NEW **189-999895** 2006 Catalog w/CD ROM **12.99**

NEW **189-999904** 2006 New Products Flyer **No Charge**

BOOKS - VIDEOS - RAILROADIANA

C M SHOPS, INC.

MUGS
Full-color, baked enamel ceramic mugs. Dishwasher safe.

12-9095   12-8012

Railroad Heralds
5.95 ea

12-9001 EL
12-9002 CNJ
12-9004 Lehigh & Hudson River
12-9005 B&O
12-9006 Family Lines
12-9007 BN
12-9008 Illinois Central Gulf
12-9009 Lehigh & New England
12-9010 CNW (Employee Owned)
12-9011 PRR (Keystone)
12-9012 PC
12-9013 RDG
12-9014 Erie
12-9015 Lackawanna Railroad
12-9016 ATSF
12-9017 Rio Grande
12-9018 Chessie
12-9020 CNW
12-9021 The Rock
12-9023 LV
12-9024 SOU
12-9025 UP
12-9026 Erie Western
12-9027 CB&Q
12-9028 WP
12-9031 WM
12-9032 Seaboard Air Line
12-9033 Providence & Worchester
12-9034 Richmond, Fredericksburg & Potomac
12-9035 MP
12-9036 Boston & Maine
12-9037 SP
12-9038 New York, Susquehanna & Western
12-9039 Frisco
12-9040 NP
12-9041 Pennsylvania - Reading Seashore Lines
12-9042 New York, Ontario & Western
12-9043 Kansas City Southern
12-9044 Ann Arbor
12-9045 MKT
12-9046 C&O
12-9047 Maine Central
12-9048 Detroit, Toledo & Ironton
12-9049 CR

12-9050 N&W
12-9051 SOO
12-9052 Rock Island
12-9053 Green Bay & Western
12-9054 Rutland
12-9055 Raritan River
12-9056 Wabash
12-9057 Vermont Railway
12-9058 Gulf, Mobile & Ohio
12-9059 IC
12-9060 Long Island-Dashing Dan
12-9061 Bangor & Aroostook
12-9062 Duluth, Missabe & Iron Range
12-9063 NKP
12-9064 L&N
12-9065 SOO-Modern
12-9067 SSW-Blue Streak
12-9068 Clinchfield
12-9069 NH (McGinnis)
12-9070 Pittsburgh & Lake Erie
12-9072 Florida East Coast
12-9073 New York, Susquehanna & Western - Susie Q
12-9074 Chicago Great Western
12-9075 Chattahoochee Industrial
12-9076 Spokane, Portland & Seattle
12-9077 Minneapolis, Northfield & Southern
12-9078 Atlantic Coast Line
12-9079 CV-Old
12-9080 Grand Trunk Western
12-9081 CP-Old
12-9082 Delaware Otsego
12-9083 Seaboard
12-9084 Model Railroader 50th Anniversary
12-9085 Morristown & Erie
12-9086 Chicago & Illinois Midland
12-9087 Texas & Pacific
12-9088 NMRA 50th Anniversary
12-9089 Appalachicola Northern
12-9090 Central of Georgia
12-9091 Seaboard Coast Line
12-9092 MON
12-9093 Bessemer & Lake Erie
12-9094 Amtrak®
12-9095 Colorado Midland
12-9096 NS
12-9097 Alaska
12-9098 Virginian
12-9099 Texas-Mexican Railway
12-9100 NJ Transit
12-9101 Mexican National Railways
12-9102 CNW System
12-9103 C&O Kitten

12-9104 Boston & Maine (McGinnis)
12-9105 CP Rail
12-9106 Erie Centennial
12-9107 GN (Big Sky Blue)
12-9108 Minneapolis & St. Louis
12-9109 Montana Rail Link
12-9110 WC
12-9111 UP "Overland"
12-9112 Trona
12-9113 Toronto, Hamilton & Buffalo
12-9114 Reading Anthracite
12-9115 British Columbia
12-9116 Belt Railway of Chicago
12-9117 Bangor & Aroostook (shield)
12-9118 Monongahela
12-9119 Connecticut Central
12-9120 Ashley, Drew & Northern
12-9121 BNSF
12-9122 Chicago & Eastern Illinois
12-9123 Housatonic
12-9124 Detroit, Toledo & Ironton - Compass Herald
12-9125 CSX
12-9126 Rio Grande Thru the Rockies

F Units 5.95 ea

12-8001 Ontario & Western
12-8002 LV
12-8003 GN
12-8004 DRGW
12-8005 CNW
12-8006 Gulf, Mobile & Ohio
12-8007 SP
12-8008 L&N
12-8009 CN
12-8010 EL
12-8011 ATSF
12-8012 NYC
12-8013 PRR
12-8014 Wabash
12-8016 PRR (Passenger)
12-8017 Southern
12-8018 ATSF
12-8019 Erie
12-8020 Clinchfield
12-8021 Burlington Route
12-8022 NP
12-8023 Frisco
12-8024 WP
12-8025 CP
12-8026 B&O

DPA-LTA ENTERPRISES INC

NEW PRODUCTS

BOOKS

Official Locomotive Rosters & News

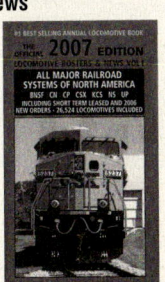

NEW 237-16 2007 Edition, Volumes I & II 39.90
800 current listings (in alphabetical order) of all North American railroads, listing all their locomotives, plus all new orders for 2007, as well as rented locomotives seen on the trains. Includes Volume I (major Class I roads) and II (shortlines and regionals). This book is used by the railroad industry as a valuable operations tool.

Illustrated Modern Freight Cars of North America
NEW 237-102 (120 Pages, 240 Photos) 19.95
A great modeler's reference, this book includes 240 large builder's photos of all kinds of cars. Perfect bound, softcover, 120 pages.

DESIGN PRESERVATION MODELS

Structure Catalog

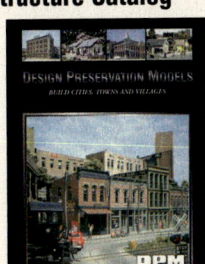

243-13 1.95
A complete listing of all N (plus O and HO Scale) kits, shown in full color.

EVERGREEN SCALE MODELS

Books
Styrene Modeling

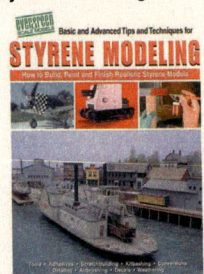

269-14 14.95
The first complete and informative text on styrene modeling. Some of the top authors in modeling use projects called "Case Studies In Styrene" to describe their tips and techniques for building and finishing styrene models. Along with easy-to-follow text, there are 174 color and 106 B&W photos. 88 pages, 8-1/2 x 11".

Daily New Arrival Updates! Visit Walthers Web site at

www.walthers.com

BOOKS - VIDEOS - RAILROADIANA

FALLER

IMPORTED FROM GERMANY BY WALTHERS

NEW PRODUCTS
NEW 272-190886 2006/2007 Catalog **13.99**
Complete listing of structures, car system products, accessories and more. English, French & German text.

Books
Scenic Modeling Made Easy

272-190840 **16.99**
English text, covers tools, materials and techniques. Over 120 color illustrations, softcover, 35 pages, 8-1/4 x 11-1/2".

Model Making Made Easy

272-190846 **23.99**
Designed to show modelers how to use Faller's Car System II. Text in German only.

INTERNATIONAL HOBBY CORP.

Books
All books are hardcover.

Steam Locomotive 3-D Pop-Up Book
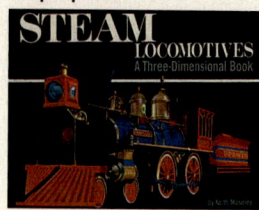
348-51795 **2.98**
A pop-up guide to the history and use of steam engines. Seven intricate dimensional spreads show famous steam locomotives, and the accompanying text is full of facts.

Stations
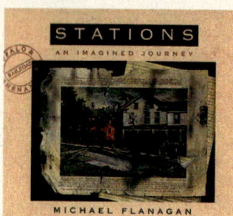
348-52100 **3.98**
The fictional journey we each take along the tracks of memory, where time and place intersect the lost world of home.

KIBRI

IMPORTED FROM GERMANY BY WALTHERS

Catalog
NEW 405-99902 2006/2007 Catalog **15.99**
Check out all the latest model railroad releases in N and HO Scales.

NEW 405-2006 Kibri New Items Flyer **NC**

For Up-To-Date Information and News Bookmark Walthers Web site at
www.walthers.com

krause publications

NEW PRODUCTS

Books

Warman's Lionel Train Field Guide 1945-1969
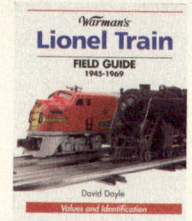
NEW 213-2999 **12.99**
A great reference for collectors. Offers tips on identifying specific pieces and determining values.

O'Brien's Collecting Toy Trains

NEW 213-7690 Sixth Edition **29.99**
Covers pre- and post-war Lionel as well as American Flyer, Buddy L, Marx, Ives, Kusan and AMT.

BOOKS

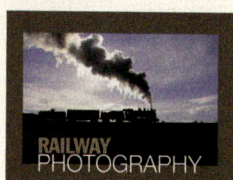
Railway Photography
213-7 **19.99**
Full of inspiration and how-tos, this tribute to railroading contains images from well-known contemporary photographers. Covers history, equipment, film, planning photo journeys, working with light, photo storage and presentation, publishing and more.

Classic Railroad Advertising
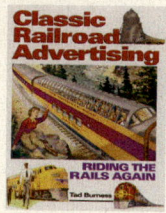
213-1201 **19.99**
Collection spans from 1917 through the present. Hardcover, 224 pages, 212 color photos, 8-1/4 x 10-7/8".

Getting Started With Lionel Trains: Your Introduction To Model Railroading Fun
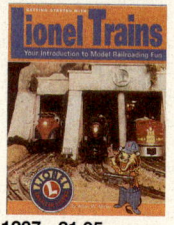
213-1207 **21.95**
Softcover, 128 pages, 100+ color photos, 8-1/4 x 10-7/8".

Model Railroading With M.T.H. Trains
213-1208 **24.95**
Softcover, 144 pages, 200 color photos, 8-1/4 x 10-7/8".

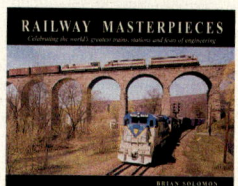
Railway Masterpieces
213-1209 **19.99**
This pictorial captures some of the most impressive, significant and interesting elements of railroading from today and yesterday. Hardcover, 160 pages, 100 color and 100+ B&W photos, 10-7/8 x 8-1/4".

Standard Catalog of Lionel® Trains 29.99 ea
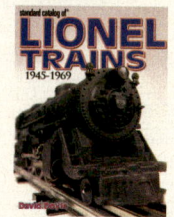
213-8909 1945-1969 Revised Edition

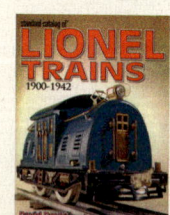
213-8910 1900-1942

Information STATION

The Big Hook

"WK, WK, WK. . . ." those letters coming over the telegraph meant big trouble as they urgently requested the wreck crane or "big hook."

Heavy steam-powered cranes appeared in the 1880s and were a big improvement. Early cranes used simple hand-cranked winches and a boom mounted on a flat car. Using reduction gears, they could lift lighter engines and any wooden cars that survived.

Most roads bought one steam crane, while larger roads owned several. They were stationed at a major terminal, where the boiler that powered the winches was kept hot and ready to go. Cranes were not self-propelled but were moved to a wreck by any available locomotive.

Cranes were top-heavy and moved at low speeds with an idler flat or boom car under the hook. Spreader bars, tools and trucks, plus fuel and water for the crane were often carried on boom cars.

Though associated with wreck trains, cranes were often put to work on major construction projects, such as new railroad bridges. In the days before truck cranes, they sometimes helped local industries that needed machinery lifted.

Many railroad cranes led long lives and were later converted to diesel-electric power.

BOOKS - VIDEOS - RAILROADIANA

KALMBACH PUBLISHING CO.

NEW PRODUCTS

Booklets

Easy Model Railroading Series

Get Started in N Scale

NEW 400-12414 7.95
Make the most of your train space with N Scale trains and track. Explains advantages of N Scale and offers a variety of ideas on getting started. Ideal for beginners with limited space. Softcover, 8-1/4 x 10-3/4", 16 pages, 45 color photos.

Basic Buildings

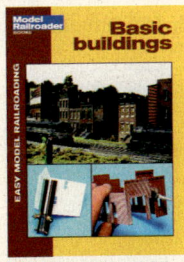

NEW 400-12413 7.95
Learn the basic skills to build realistic models. Step-by-step photos and instructions cover the basic building methods, kitbashing unique structures and finishing with paint, signs and details. Perfect for beginners. Softcover, 8-1/4 x 10-3/4", 16 pages, 45 color photos.

Books

DCC Projects & Applications

NEW 400-12407 17.95
This book takes the reader through a series of DCC projects, including setting up a DCC layout, decoder installation, lighting effects, sound effects, layout wiring projects, advanced decoder programming and tips and ideas for advanced DCC projects. Also includes a list of important considerations for choosing a DCC system. More technical than DCC Made Easy but still comprehensible to the average modeler. Softcover, 8-1/4 x 10-3/4", 96 pages, 150 color photos, 30 illustrations.

The Model Railroader's Guide to Junctions

NEW 400-12408 18.95
Get the scoop on railroad junctions - where tracks meet and cross. Photos show how junctions work and the details that surround them. Softcover, 8-1/4 x 10-3/4", 88 pages, 150 color photos, 20 illustrations.

The Model Railroader's Guide to Industries Along the Tracks 2

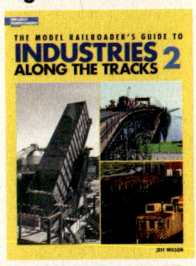

NEW 400-12409 19.95
Provides insights, photos, and guidelines for modeling several rail-served industries. Includes overviews of creameries and milk traffic, the paper industry, breweries, iron ore mining and transloading, coal customers, freight houses and less-than-carload traffic. Softcover, 8-1/4 x 10-3/4", 88 pages, 120 color photos, 70 b&w photos, 12 illustrations.

Mountain to Desert

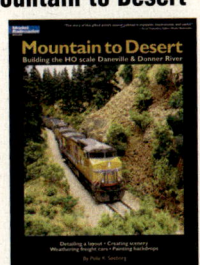

NEW 400-12416 Building the HO Scale Daneville & Donner River **19.95**
Pelle Soeborg's practical guide is packed with how-to information. Learn innovative ways to scratchbuild modern businesses, replicate scenery, paint backdrops and weather cars. Softcover, 8 1/4 x 10 3/4", 96 pages, 200 color photos, 15 illustrations.

The Model Railroader's Guide to Passenger Equipment & Operations

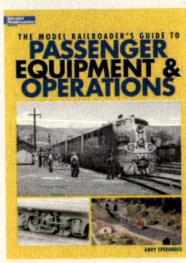

NEW 400-12244 19.95
Helps modelers integrate realistic passenger trains and operations into any layout. Learn about passenger train history, types, equipment and terminals. Softcover, 8-1/4 x 10-3/4", 96 pages, 130 color photos, 70 b&w photos, 20 illustrations.

The Model Railroader's Guide to Coal Railroading

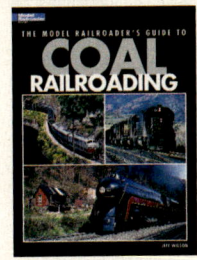

NEW 400-12453 19.95
Handy reference for modeling a coal-hauling prototype-based or freelance railroad. Includes information on modeling coal trains, company towns and coal customers, plus operating tips. Softcover, 8-1/4 x 10-3/4", 96 pages, 130 color photos, 70 b&w photos, 20 illustrations.

FineScale Modeler

Airbrushing Basics

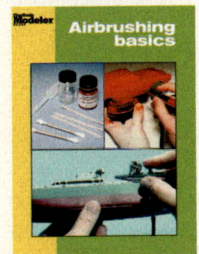

NEW 400-12430 7.95
Learn airbrushing tips and techniques from the experts. This booklet provides a clear guide on getting the most out of your airbrush, including proper cleaning and maintenance techniques. Softcover, 8-1/4 x 10-3/4", 16 pages, 45 color photos, 5 illustrations.

Modeler's Guide to Realistic Painting & Finishing

NEW 400-12257 16.95
Perfect for the beginning plastic modeler who wants to learn more advanced techniques, this photo-driven guide includes an introduction to airbrushing and sections on brush painting, dry-brushing, applying washes and pastel chalk weathering. Softcover, 8-1/4 x 10-3/4", 80 pages, 200 color photos, 10 illustrations.

TRAINS
BOOKS AND VIDEOS

Books

Tourist Trains 2006

NEW 400-1206 18.95
Photographs, locomotive rosters, ticket prices, directions and even trip times are included in this guide to more than 6000 preserved and restored railroads and train museums. Includes discount coupons and maps to some of the railroad and museum sites. Softcover, 5-1/4 x 8", 512 pages, 560 b&w photos.

Calendars

The Art of Model Railroading 2007 Calendar

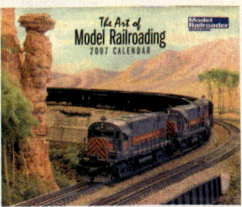

NEW 400-68146 12.95
Stunning, full-color pictures portray lifelike scenes of model railroading. Layouts include Lance Mindheim's N scale layout, Gary Hoover's HO scale layout and Frank Miller's O scale layout. 13 x 10-1/2".

Railroads at Work 2007 Calendar

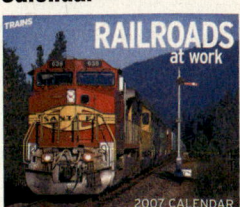

NEW 400-68147 12.95
Dramatic contemporary images of Amtrak, BNSF, CP, U, and more show North America's favorite railroads hard at work moving people and freight. 13 x 10-1/2".

BOOKS - VIDEOS - RAILROADIANA

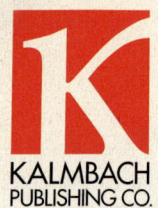

N Scale Model Railroad That Grows

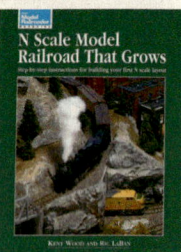

400-12145 18.95
Shows how to build an N scale railroad in a few easy steps. Includes instructions on constructing framework, laying track, building scenery and assembling structures that result in an outstanding layout.

N Scale Model Railroading: Getting Started In The Hobby

400-12205 19.95
Learn about N Scale modeling and everything that makes it unique: from benchwork to realistic scenery. Colorful photos and illustrations are provided to guide the reader in everything that is N Scale. Softcover, 96 pages, 100 color and 50 B&W photos, 50 illustrations, 8-1/4 x 10-3/4".

The Model Railroader's Guide To Freight Cars

400-12450 19.95
Freight cars are the backbone of any railroad — in the real world or on your operating layout. Get a brief history of each type of North American freight car, then learn how car designs have changed from WWI to the present. Includes techniques for modeling realistic rolling stock in any scale. Contains 180 photos, 15 illustrations. Softcover, 96 Pages.

The Model Railroader's Guide To Bridges, Trestles & Tunnels

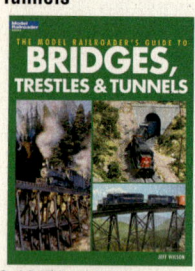

400-12452 19.95
Prolific Kalmbach author Jeff Wilson shows modelers how to re-create numerous types of railroad and highway bridges based on prototype designs. Divided into chapters by bridge type, each chapter shows several prototype examples and demonstrates techniques for modeling, painting, weathering and installing the models on a layout. Covers the history of railroad bridges, trestles and tunnels. Includes specific details for modeling iron and steel truss bridges, plate girder bridges, concrete bridges, lift bridges, tunnels and more. Lists currently available models. Ideal for intermediate and advanced hobbyists. Contains 175 photos, 15 illustrations. Softcover, 88 pages.

Realistic Model Railroad Operation

400-12231 19.95
Covers the history, practice, terminology and benefits of operating realistically. Guides the reader through the steps leading to realistic operation, and includes pictorial examples of working model railroads and operating sessions. Softcover, 96 pages, 125 color and 25 B&W photos, 40 illustrations, 8-1/4 x 10-3/4".

Basic Model Railroad Benchwork: The Complete Photo Guide

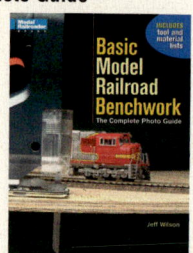

400-12241 18.95
A concise, illustrated teaching method takes the mystery out of model railroad benchwork. Covers the materials, tools and basic skills required to make sturdy benchwork for any size or scale layout. Softcover, 96 pages, 300 B&W photos, 25 illustrations, 8-1/4 x 10-3/4".

DCC Made Easy

400-12242 14.95
Explains DCC methods and techniques in a straightforward way. Covers the history of Command Control, dissects the components of a DCC system and addresses the full range of commercially available systems. Softcover, 48 pages, 100 color photos, 10 illustrations, 8-1/4 x 10-3/4".

The New Scenery Tips And Techniques

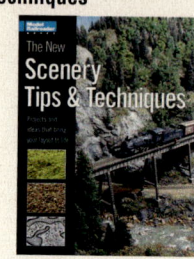

400-12243 18.95
Compiled from the pages of Model Railroader, this completely revised edition includes intriguing ideas on how to create realistic ground cover, trees, bushes, rocks, water and more, for your model railroad. Softcover, 104 pages, 225 color and 25 B&W photos, 8-1/4 x 10-3/4".

Basic Painting & Weathering For Model Railroaders

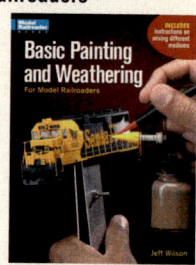

400-12247 19.95
Presents step-by-step techniques to finish, paint, decal and weather railroad models. Introduces the tools, products and techniques while guiding hobbyists through several basic projects. Softcover, 80 pages, 250 color photos, 8-1/4 x 10-3/4".

The Model Railroader's Guide To Freight Yards

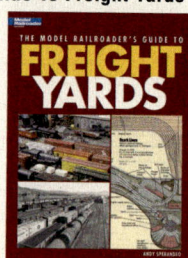

400-12248 18.95
Learn the basic techniques and facilities needed for building a freight yard on a layout of any size, scale or era! A great book for skilled beginners or intermediate-level modelers. Softcover, 80 pages, 180 color and B&W photos, 8-1/4 x 10-3/4".

Basic Scenery For Model Railroaders

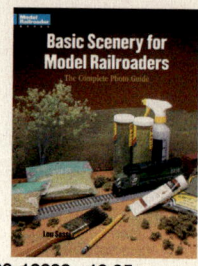

400-12233 19.95
Covers simple techniques for making realistic scenery (including ground cover, trees, water, rocks, roads and trackside details) for any size or scale layout. Includes color photos and diagrams that demonstrate basic steps to adding prototypical scenery to a model railroad. Softcover, 96 pages, 200 color photos, 8-1/4 x 10-3/4".

The Model Railroader's Guide To Locomotive Servicing Terminals

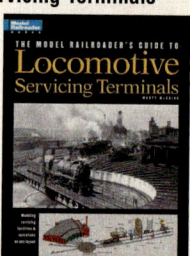

400-12228 18.95
Includes tips and techniques for modeling trackage, structures and terminal details appropriate for the steam or diesel era. Softcover, 80 pages, 125 color and 50 B&W photos, 8-1/4 x 10-3/4".

Basic Model Railroad Track Plans

400-12237 16.95
Includes simple, ideal layout designs for beginning model railroaders. Features plans for a variety of HO and N Scale starter layouts. Also includes general construction techniques that are useful in building any layout. Softcover, 64 pages, 15 color and B&W photos, 60 illustrations, 8-1/4 x 10-3/4".

BOOKS - VIDEOS - RAILROADIANA

KALMBACH PUBLISHING CO.

Classic Railroads You Can Model
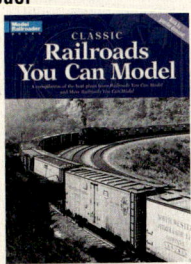
400-12238 15.95
A compilation of the best plans from two popular model railroading books. Includes realistic, prototype-oriented track plans. Features U.S. prototype railroads condensed to HO and N Scale track plans, extensive descriptions of operations, modeling suggestions, representative photos, a railroad system map and more. Softcover, 104 pages, 280 B&W photos, 8-1/4 x 10-3/4".

The Classic Layout Designs Of John Armstrong
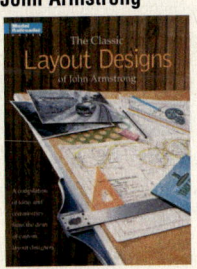
400-12230 18.95
A compilation of ideas and commentary from the dean of custom layout designers. This notable designer has contributed to *Model Railroader* since the 1950s. Book features easy-to-follow layout designs for sophisticated layouts. Ideal for intermediate and advanced model railroaders. Softcover, 96 pages, 25 B&W and 50 color photos, 100 illustrations, 8-1/4 x 10-3/4".

How To Build Realistic Model Railroad Scenery

400-12216 24.95
One of model railroading's best-known scenery modelers offers new techniques for adding realism to a layout of any size or scale. Featuring today's newest products and equipment, this third edition of one of Kalmbach's top-sellers will attract modelers with contemporary images of diesel locomotives and urban settings, plus updates to Dave's trademark scenery "recipes." Hundreds of photographs bring the techniques to life and make it easy for modelers to get started quickly. Includes new chapters on Western scenery and desert modeling, and city scenery and urban settings. Ideal for beginning, intermediate and advanced modelers planning a layout. 450 photos, 20 illustrations. 3rd Edition, Softcover, 144 pages.

How To Build and Detail Model Railroad Scenes
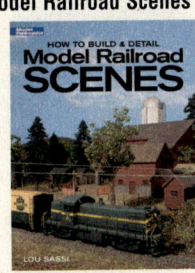
400-12249 21.95
This practical, photo-driven guide covers the principles and techniques of designing and constructing detailed, realistic model railroad scenes. The various projects include structure, scenery and detailing techniques for both urban and rural settings. It's the essential information modelers need to make a good layout look great! Softcover, 88 Pages, 225 photos, 20 illustrations.

Get Your Daily Dose of Product News at
www.walthers.com

Project Railroads You Can Build
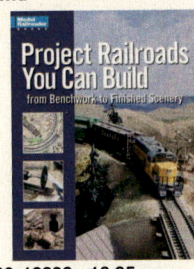
400-12236 16.95
Includes easy-to-follow instructions for constructing moderately sized N or HO Scale model railroads from benchwork through finished scenery. Ideal for novice model railroaders or experienced hobbyists interested in exploring other scales. Softcover, 80 pages, 180 B&W photos, 8-1/4 x 10-3/4".

Building City Scenery For Your Model Railroad
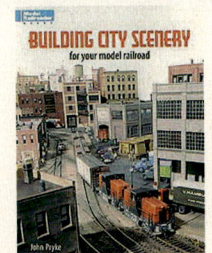
400-12204 19.95
Learn how to model realistic city structures and objects. Softcover, 96 pages, 120 color and 40 B&W photos, 25 illustrations, 8-1/4 x 10-3/4".

Scenery For Your Model Railroad

400-12194 18.95
Teaches you everything you need to know about scenery from ground cover and rockwork, to trees, water and more. Includes photos of models and prototype scenes for inspiration. Softcover, 8-1/4 x 10-3/4".

Scenery & Airbrushing Made Easy
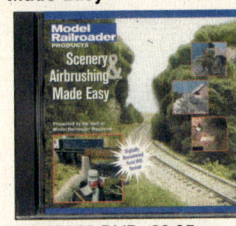
400-15060 DVD 29.95
Covers everything you need to build layout scenery, as well as use an airbrush to apply scenery paint. Covers tools, applications and special techniques. 120 minutes; stereo sound; color.

Model Railroader Cyclopedia Vol. 1: Steam Locomotives
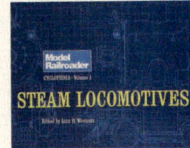
400-1001 49.95
Tells what all the piping, springs and pumps are for. 272 pages, 127 HO Scale drawings, 700 photos, 14 x 11".

Basic Wiring For Model Railroaders
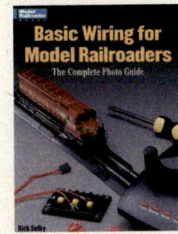
400-12212 18.95
Teaches basic electrical connections for a two-rail DC powered layout of any size or complexity. Basic layout wiring techniques are presented simply, with numerous photos, illustrations and diagrams. Softcover, 8-1/4 x 10-3/4".

Track Planning For Realistic Operations
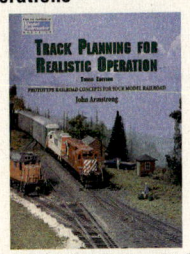
400-12148 3rd Edition 21.95
Must-have for track planning. Includes design tips and techniques. 144 pages, 45 B&W and 120 illustrations, 8-1/4 x 10-3/4".

Basic Trackwork For Model Railroaders
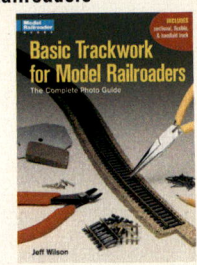
400-12254 19.95
Using a step-by-step photographic approach, this book offers proven, easy-to-follow techniques for the installing of sturdy trackwork, including fitting the roadbed, laying sectional or flexible track and finishing the track with lineside details. Also covers installing turnouts, cleaning and maintaining trackwork, and other special techniques suitable for a layout of any size or scale.

The Model Railroader's Guide To Industries Along The Tracks
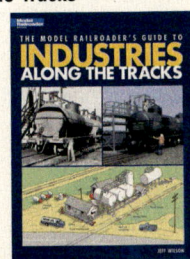
400-12256 19.95
Learn how to add great industries like mining, refining and agriculture to your layout. Detailed descriptions and illustrations make expanding these operations easier than ever. Softcover, 80 pages, 180 color and B&W photos, 8-1/4 x 10-3/4".

Realistic Model Railroad Design

400-12250 19.95
Learn creative and do-able options for building your next model railroad. From choosing a theme to selecting a scale to bringing in creative design, it's all covered! Softcover, 96 pages, 150 color and B&W photos, 20 illustrations, 8-1/4 x 10-3/4".

BOOKS - VIDEOS - RAILROADIANA

KALMBACH PUBLISHING CO.

Basic Model Railroading: Getting Started In The Hobby

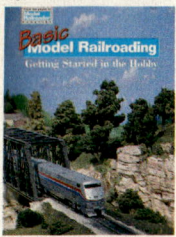

400-12197 17.95
Packed with simple tips and techniques, detailed photos, diagrams and drawings. Basics of tracklaying, wiring, maintaining locomotives, scenery, painting, weathering and more. 80 pages, 150 color photos, 8-1/4 x 10-3/4".

Trackwork & Lineside Detail For Your Model Railroad

400-12235 18.95
An introduction to the basics of tracklaying and lineside detailing. Includes tips, techniques and ideas for working with track and the details immediately alongside it. Softcover, 96 pages, 150 color photos, 50 Illustrations, 8-1/4 x 10-3/4".

Basic Structure Modeling For Model Railroaders

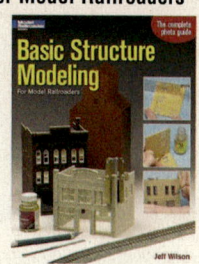

400-12258 19.95
Learn the reasons for including structures on your layout, then select and build your own! Photo-driven projects demonstrate the tools, materials and techniques used when modeling plastic or wood structures. Offers techniques for realistic finishing, including painting, weathering, sign making, interior detailing and more. Contains 225 color photos, 12 illustrations. Softcover, 88 Pages.

Realistic Model Railroad Building Blocks

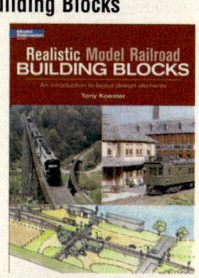

400-12405 19.95
Long-time Model Railroader magazine contributor Tony Koester offers techniques for incorporating Layout Design Elements into a larger layout, a sectional or modular approach to model railroading that he invented. Various LDEs based on actual railroad scenes - towns, yards, terminals, industries and more - are offered as track plans suitable for N to large scale layouts. Applies the "kit building" concept to track planning. Features new material compatible with Koester's previous books, Realistic Model Railroad Operations and Realistic Model Railroad Design. Contains 135 photos, 75 illustrations. Softcover, 96 Pages.

Steam Locomotive Projects And Ideas

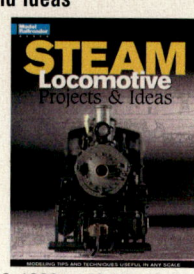

400-12221 18.95
Learn to detail, kitbash, paint and maintain a steam locomotive of any scale. Includes information about the history of steam motive power and components of the prototype. Compiled from the pages of Model Railroader, with additional new material from John Pryke. Softcover, 80 pages, 100 color and 50 B&W photos, 40 illustrations, 8-1/4 x 10-3/4".

Easy Model Railroad Wiring

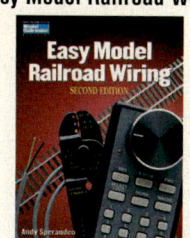

400-12207 2nd Edition **21.95**
Provides easy and reliable layout wiring techniques that every level of modeler needs to know. Each chapter includes photos, illustrations and detailed schematics. Softcover, 128 pages, 80 B&W photos, 160 illustrations, 8-1/4 x 10-3/4".

Maintaining & Repairing Your Scale Model Trains

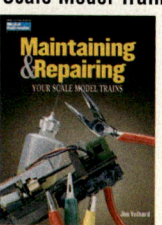

400-12210 17.95
With simple, instructional information, this book covers the basic techniques needed to maintain and repair DC-powered scale model locos, rolling stock and layouts. 80 pages, 150 B&W photos, 8-1/4 x 10-3/4".

Get Daily Info, Photos and News at
www.walthers.com

Trackside Scenes You Can Model

400-12234 18.95
Historic color and black-and-white photographs capture intriguing prototype railroad settings from all over the U.S. The author details how you can realistically model each prototype scene on your own layout. Each chapter features a description of the scene including trackage, structures, and operating environment, and a suggested track plan. Softcover, 80 pages, 80 color and 20 B&W photos, 25 illustrations, 8-1/4 x 10-3/4".

Model Railroad Bridges And Trestles

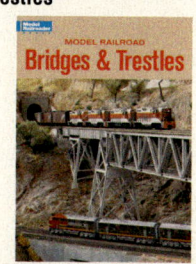

400-12101 21.95
Includes 12 construction plans, prototype photos and over 20 sets of scale drawings. 152 pages, 8-1/2 x 11".

How To Build Model Railroad Benchwork

400-12175 2nd Edition **16.95**
New tools, materials and techniques that make benchwork construction easy. 80 pages, 115 B&W photos and 120 illustrations.

48 Top-Notch Track Plans From Model Railroader

400-12132 18.95
You'll find a layout to fit any space limit or scale preference including HO (HOn2-1/2 and HOn3), O, S, N and Z scales. 120 pages, 100 color and 220 B&W photos, 8-1/4 x 10-3/4".

101 Track Plans For Model Railroaders

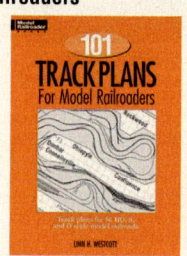

400-12012 14.95
Easy-to-use plans in every size, shape and scale — from tiny card-table layouts to giant garage-size railroads. Demonstrates how to design a railroad to fit any space and shows how to convert plans to N, HO, S and O Scales. 8-1/4 x 11-1/4", 72 pages.

Building Your First Model Railroad

400-10002 VHS **12.95**
400-10003 DVD **12.95**
Exciting instructional video teaches you everything you need to know to build a model railroad layout. Narrated by Michael Gross, actor and model railroad enthusiast. 60 minutes, VHS, all-digital format, stereo sound, color.

BOOKS - VIDEOS - RAILROADIANA

KALMBACH PUBLISHING CO.

Easy Model Railroading Booklets

Tables for Your Trains

400-12401 7.95
This full-color booklet will help new model railroaders build a simple, semi-permanent tabletop for displaying and running model trains. Softcover, 16 pages.

Tips on Track

400-12402 7.95
Perfect for new hobbyists, this booklet features an overview of the various types of track and how to use them to set up a basic model railroad with semi-permanent trackwork. Softcover, 16 pages.

Wiring Basics
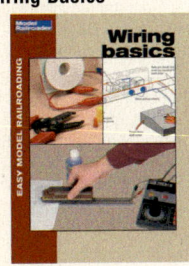
400-12403 7.95
Featuring information about how model trains work, this booklet will help beginners properly install wiring and maintain their trackwork. Softcover, 16 pages.

Simple Scenery
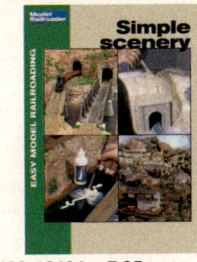
400-12404 7.95
This simple booklet takes the guesswork out of adding scenery to a model railroad, offering new hobbyists various ways to make simple trees, construct landscapes and build basic structures. Softcover; 8-1/4 x 10-3/4" format; 16 pages.

FineScale Modeler

Easy Scale Modeling

400-12259 7.95
The ideal introduction to scale modeling. Simple tips and techniques, detailed photos, and easy-to-follow diagrams get new scale modelers started on the right track. The editors and writers of Fine Scale Modeler magazine offer basic information on assembling, painting, finishing and displaying car, plane and ship modelers.

The Basics of Scale Modeling
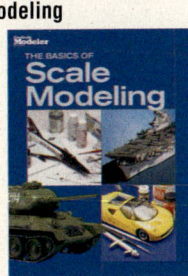
400-12251 16.95
A how-to for modelers who want the best tips and techniques from the pages of Fine Scale Modeler magazine. Covering the basics of painting, decaling and model assembly, it's packed with information that's relevant to model railroading as well as plastic model building and detailing. 230 color photos, 10 illustrations. Softcover, 80 pages.

How To Build Armor Dioramas
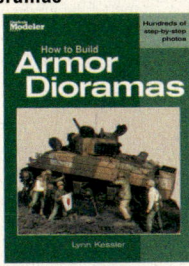
400-12239 22.95
Learn the steps to building detailed armor vehicles. Then get tips on the best ways to display your new models. Also includes great tips on figure modeling, kit assembly and finishing details. Softcover, 112 pages, 300 color photos, 8-1/4 x 10-3/4".

How To Paint Realistic Military Figures

400-12240 2nd Edition **21.95**
Covers military figures and horses from medieval times to Desert Storm. This revised edition includes more tips for resin models and oil paints, plus new chapters on camouflage and black-and-white uniforms. Softcover, 96 pages, 120 color and 75 B&W photos, 8-1/4 x 10-3/4".

How To Model World War II German Armor
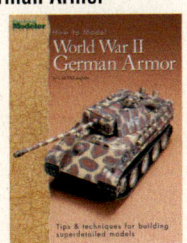
400-12232 22.95
Offers techniques for creating most types of German armored vehicles. Covers weathering, special battle effects, airbrushing camouflage and German armor paint schemes, working with flexible track, working with resin, creating accessories, using photo-etched brass, creating figures and dioramas, and more. Softcover, 104 pages, 230 color photos, 8-1/4 x 10-3/4".

How To Use An Airbrush
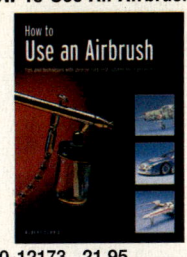
400-12173 21.95
Learn how to achieve special airbrushing effects on a variety of plastic models. Eleven projects teach the basics of realistic finishes, camouflage, weathering and other special effects for scale plastic modeling. Softcover, 96 pages, 196 color photos, 8-1/4 x 10-3/4".

Basics Of Ship Modeling

400-12220 19.95
Step-by-step photos guide you from basic assembly techniques to painting and weathering, detailing, masking and displaying your model ships. Softcover, 112 pages, 25 color and 400 B&W photos, 8-1/4 x 10-3/4".

Modeling Classic Combat Aircraft
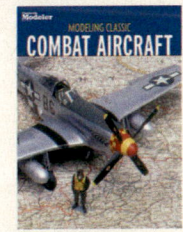
400-12255 21.95
Learn to build, paint and finish military aircraft models from WWII to today. Over 15 projects are featured, including the P-51 Mustang F-18 Sabre, the A-7D Corsair, the B-17 Flying Fortress and more. Compiled from the pages of *FineScale Modeler* magazine and edited by Mark Thompson. Softcover, 96 pages, 300 color photos, 8-1/4 x 10-3/4".

Building And Displaying Scale Model Aircraft With Paul Boyer
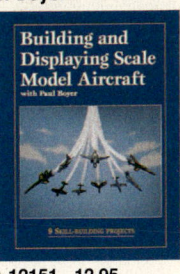
400-12151 12.95
Teaches basic aircraft modeling preparation and assembly techniques. Includes suggestions for painting and decaling with special attention to creative displays and mounting tips for finished projects. 88 pages, 50 color and 110 B&W photos, 8-1/4 x 10-3/4".

Armor Conversion And Detailing Projects From Finescale Modeler

400-12166 15.95
Shows how to convert commercial kits into dramatically detailed armored and tactical vehicles. 104 pages, 44 color and 160 B&W photos, 8-1/4 x 10-3/4".

How To Build Dioramas
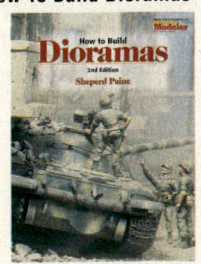
400-12136 2nd Edition **24.95**
With this newly updated book, making realistic dioramas has never been easier. Includes new projects and photos, along with tips on weathering, painting, detailing and more. Softcover, 144 pages, 290+ photos, 41 illustrations, 8-1/4 x 10-3/4".

BOOKS - VIDEOS - RAILROADIANA

KALMBACH PUBLISHING CO.

Books

Field Guide To Modern Diesel Locos

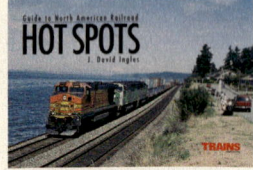

400-1113 28.95
Covers EMD diesels manufactured after 1972 and GE diesels manufactured after 1977, and includes all the major spotting and roster information. Ideal for beginning and intermediate railfans, as well as modelers looking for inspiration. Softcover, 208 pages, 300 color photos, 30 illustrations, 8-1/4 x 5-1/2".

Guide To North American Hot Spots

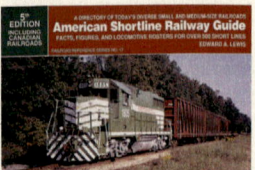

400-1097 24.95
This guide takes you to 100 of the busiest, most interesting train-watching sites across the U.S. and Canada. Each spread includes a color photo and authoritative text about the site written by train-watching experts. Softcover, 208 pages, 200 color photos, 8-1/2 x 5-1/2".

American Shortline Railway Guide

400-1073 5th Edition **24.95**
A ready reference for nearly 600 shortline and regional railroads in the United States and Canada. 320 pages, 100 B&W photos, 8-1/4 x 5-1/2".

Guide To North American Steam Locomotives

400-1051 29.95
The development of steam locomotives on all North American railroads since 1900. 400 pages, 400+ B&W photos, 8-1/4 x 5-1/2".

KROMER CAP CO.

Railroad Cap

407-775 Adjustable Cap **9.69**
Blue-and-white striped cotton cap. Fully washable. Pleated one-piece top.

Info, Images, Inspiration! Get It All at
www.walthers.com

MICROSCALE

NEW PRODUCTS
Die Cut Vinyl Stickers

2.50 ea
NEW 460-20001 PRR
NEW 460-20009 SOU
NEW 460-20010 CP

8" Metal Signs

10.95 ea
NEW 460-10032 Pacific Electric
NEW 460-10033 Northwestern Pacific
NEW 460-10034 N&W - Late

DIECUT VINYL STICKERS
460-20002 UP **2.50**
460-20004 GN **2.50**
460-20005 SP **2.50**

RAILROAD SIGNS
High-quality and lightweight, these metal signs are diecut to retain the shape of the original railroad logos. They're also embossed to give them a slight 3-D effect. Signs have pre-drilled holes for mounting.

8" 10.95 ea (Unless Noted)
460-10001 PRR
460-10002 UP
460-10003 ATSF
460-10004 GN
460-10005 SP
460-10006 NYC
460-10007 NH
460-10008 Western Pacific
460-10009 SOU
460-10010 CP
460-10011 CNW
460-10012 Atlantic Coast Line
460-10013 NP
460-10014 Kansas City Southern
460-10015 IC
460-10016 Florida East Coast
460-10017 Rock Island
460-10018 RDG
460-10019 Seaboard Air Line
460-10020 B&O
460-10021 Erie
460-10022 DRGW
460-10023 CB&Q
460-10024 LV
460-10025 Boston & Maine
460-10026 CR
460-10027 BN
460-10028 Frisco
460-10029 MKT
460-10030 Penn Central
460-10031 Microscale Logo (blue, black, white)
460-10501 SP "Daylight" **14.95**
460-10502 ATSF Indian Head **14.95**

18"
460-10201 Railroad Crossing Advance Warning (round; yellow & black) **29.95**

24"
460-10200 Railroad Crossing (Crossbuck) **34.95**

Information STATION

What DID Those Look Like Back Then?

So, how did the railroad you model paint its trackside structures back in the early 1960s? Were they cream and green, or had they switched to two-tone gray? Were they generally run down? Was the mainline weedgrown?

Can't remember? As always, books and videos are your best source of information.

Even if there's no book on your specific prototype, you can still glean plenty of information from books and videos about similar railroads in the region you model.

When you look at photos, check the background for details like billboards, signs, logos, lettering fonts and building styles and color schemes. If you're a steam-era modeler, old photos also show lineside details and industries. You'll also find plenty of visual information about weathering, faded paint, ballast color, tree mix and other scenery features.

Photographic information will also help you create one of the most important elements of all for your pike: ambiance. Steam railroads weren't always pristine with carefully manicured rights-of-way as shown in heavily retouched publicity photos. And during the 1960s, few railroads mainlines looked as good as they did in the 50s or the 80s; railroads were on hard times and the weeds on the tracks, slow orders and ties sinking into the mud helped tell the story. Those old photos will help you set the scene just by inspiring the feeling your railroad conveys to others.

BOOKS - VIDEOS - RAILROADIANA

Morning Sun Books Inc.

Each full-color, hardcover book contains hundreds of images and most volumes are 128 pages long.

NEW PRODUCTS
Books 59.95 ea

Color Series
Rio Grande Narrow Gauge in Color
NEW **484-1153** Vol. 1 1947-1959

Refrigerator Car Color Guide

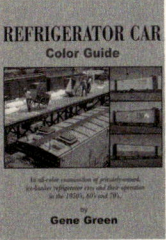
NEW **484-1156**

Southern Railway Through Passenger Service in Color
NEW **484-1161**

Canadian Pacific Steam in Color
NEW **484-1162** Vol. 1

Chicago, North Shore & Milwaukee Railway in Color

NEW **484-1166** Vol. 1

Erie Lackawanna Through Passenger Service
NEW **484-1168** Vol. 1: 1960-1965

Western Pacific in Color
NEW **484-1171**

Canadian Pacific Steam in Color
NEW **484-1172** Vol. 2: Montreal & West

Erie Lackawanna in Color
NEW **484-1173** Vol. 6

Canadian Trolleys in Color
NEW **484-1177** Vol. 1: Eastern Canada

Trackside Series
Appalachia
NEW **484-1176** w/Gene Huddleston

Around British Columbia
NEW **484-1167** w/Matt Herson

Around Charlottesville, VA
NEW **484-1170** 1967-1984

Around Duluth
NEW **484-1154** 1957-1960

Around Kansas
NEW **484-1175** 1950-1975 w/Lloyd Stagner

Around New Jersey
NEW **484-1164** 1968-1983 w/Robert Yanosey

Milwaukee Road East
NEW **484-1157**

Milwaukee Road West
NEW **484-1165** w/Jim Boyd

Northern New England Steam
NEW **484-1174** w/John Morrison

Reading Anthracite Country
NEW **484-1160**

Atchison, Topeka & Santa Fe
Santa Fe In Color 1940-1971
49.95 ea
484-30 Volume 1: Chicago to KC
484-130 Volume 2: KC to Albuquerque
484-224 Volume 3: Albuquerque to L.A.
484-232 Volume 4: Texas and the El Capitan

Color Guide To Freight And Passenger Equipment
484-958 49.95

Santa Fe All The Way
484-1011 Volume 1 49.95

Santa Fe Facilities in Color
59.95 ea
484-1141 Volume 1
NEW **484-1163** Volume 2 59.95

Santa Fe Trackside
484-1021 54.95

Atlantic Coast Line
Color Guide To Freight And Passenger Equipment
484-1034 54.95

Baltimore & Ohio
B&O Steam In Color
484-1050 54.95

Color Guide To Freight And Passenger Equipment
484-969 49.95

Trackside with Willis McCaleb
484-1005 49.95

Trackside Along The B&O 1957-1958
484-1033 54.95

484-1097 Baltimore & Ohio In Color Volume 1 59.95

Bangor & Aroostook
Bangor & Aroostook in Color
484-1133 59.95

Boston & Maine
B&M In Color

484-991 49.95

Trackside With Arthur E. Mitchell
484-1025 54.95

Buffalo, Rochester & Pittsburgh Railway
484-1114 Buffalo, Rochester & Pittsburgh Railway in Color Volume 1: New York 59.95

Burlington Northern
Color Guide To Freight And Passenger Equipment
484-1068 59.95

Canadian National
Color Guide To Freight And Passenger Equipment
484-1035 Volume 1 54.95
484-1054 Volume 2 54.95

Canadian National Steam in Color
484-1145 Volume 1: Ontario & East 59.95
NEW **484-1159** Volume 2: Ontario & West 59.95

Canadian Pacific
Color Guide To Freight And Passenger Equipment
484-947 49.95

Canadian Pacific In Color
484-1092 Volume 1: Eastern Lines 59.95

Central RR Of New Jersey
CNJ In Color
484-19 Volume 2 49.95
484-1091 Volume 3 59.95

CNJ Steam In Color
484-1048 54.95

CNJ/Lehigh Valley Color Guide To Freight And Passenger Equipment
484-954 49.95

Central Vermont
CV In Color
484-1044 54.95

Chesapeake & Ohio
Color Guide To Freight And Passenger Equipment
484-944 49.95

Chesapeake & Ohio In Color
59.95 ea
484-1083 Volume 1
484-1101 Volume 2
84-1130 Volume 3

Chessie System
484-1094 Color Guide To Freight Equipment 59.95

Chicago, Burlington & Quincy
CB&Q In Color
484-229 Volume 1 49.95
484-959 Volume 2 49.95
484-1031 Volume 3 54.95
484-1084 Volume 4 59.95

Color Guide To Freight And Passenger Equipment
484-953 49.95

Chicago & Eastern Illinois
C&EI In Color
484-1051 54.95

Chicago Great Western
Chicago Great Western In Color
484-987 49.95

Color Guide To Freight And Passenger Equipment

484-1009 49.95

Chicago, Milwaukee, St. Paul & Pacific/Milwaukee Road
Milwaukee Road In Color
49.95 ea (Unless Noted)
484-962 Volume 1: The East End
484-970 Volume 2: The Milwaukee Area
484-971 Volume 3: Wisconsin & Michigan
484-972 Volume 4: Iowa, Missouri, Minnesota & the Dakotas 54.95

Color Guide To Freight And Passenger Equipment
484-974 Volume 1 49.95
484-1036 Volume 2 54.95

Under Milwaukee Wires
484-985 49.95

Chicago & North Western
CNW In Color
484-997 Volume 1: 1941-53 49.95
484-1029 Volume 2: 1954-58 54.95
484-1142 Volume 3: 1959-1964 59.95

CNW Official Color Photography
484-1020 54.95

Chicago, Rock Island & Pacific
Rock Island In Color
49.95 ea

484-234 Volume 1: 1948-64
484-951 Volume 2: 1965-80

Color Guide To Freight and Passenger Equipment
484-981 49.95

Chicago, South Shore & South Bend in Color
484-1137 Volume 1: 60 Years of the South Shore 59.95

Clinchfield
484-1113 Clinchfield in Color 59.95

Conrail
Color Guide To Freight Equipment
484-1042 54.95

Delaware & Hudson
D&H Steam In Color
484-1053 54.95

484-1124 Volume 3: D&H in the Diesel Years 59.95

Delaware, Lackawanna & Western
Lackawanna Railroad Trackside
484-1017 54.95

Erie/DL&W Color Guide To Freight And Passenger Equipment
484-1059 54.95

Lackawanna Railroad In Color
59.95 ea
484-1098 Lackawanna Railroad In Color Volume 2
484-1138 Volume 3: The Transition Years

Denver & Rio Grande Western
DRGW In Color
484-114 Volume 1: Colorado 45.00

BOOKS - VIDEOS - RAILROADIANA

484-946 Volume 2: Utah 49.95

484-1061 Volume 3 59.95

Color Guide To Freight And Passenger Equipment
484-982 Volume 1 49.95

Rio Grande Trackside
484-1019 54.95

Deroit, Toledo & Ironton
DT&I In Color
484-1057 54.95

Duluth, Missabe & Iron Range
484-1088 Duluth, Missabe & Iron Range In Color 59.95

484-1120 Erie Lackawana in Color Volume 5: Merger and Memories 59.95

Grand Trunk Western 59.95 ea
484-1106 Grand Trunk Western In Color Volume 1: Steam & Green 1941-61

484-1118 Volume 2: Visual Redesign

Great Northern
GN Steam & Electric In Color
484-1016 54.95

Color Guide To Freight And Passenger Equipment
484-952 49.95

Illinois Central
IC In Color
484-975 49.95

IC/GM&O Color Guide To Freight And Passenger Equipment
484-1073 59.95

Illinois Terminal
Illinois Terminal In Color
484-1003 Volume 1 49.95
484-1058 Volume 2 54.95

Kansas City Southern

484-1102 Kansas City Southern In Color 59.95

Lehigh & Hudson River In Color
484-1064 59.95

Locomotive & Car Builders
Pullman-Standard Color Guide To Freight Equipment
484-955 49.95

Fairbanks-Morse In Color
484-978 49.95

Alco Official Color Photographs
484-1008 49.95

Passenger Alcos In Color

484-1043 54.95

Baldwin Diesels In Color 59.95 ea
484-1070 Volume 1: A-G
484-1079 Volume 2: H-P
484-1085 Volume 3: Q-Z

Louisville & Nashville
Color Guide To Freight And Passenger Equipment
484-1046 Volume 1 54.95
484-1132 Volume 2 59.95

Louisville & Nashville In Color Volume 1
484-1111 59.95

Maine Central
Maine Central In Color
484-1007 Volume 1 49.95
484-1028 Volume 2 54.95

Minneapolis & St. Louis
M&St.L In Color
484-984 49.95

Missouri-Kansas-Texas
MKT In Color
484-225 49.95

Missouri Pacific 59.95 ea
484-1115 Color Guide to freight and passenger equipment 59.95

Missouri Pacific in Color

484-1129 Volume 1: The Era of the Eagles
484-1150 Volume 2: Screamin' Eagles

Monon
484-1089 Monon In Color 59.95

National Railways Of Mexico
NdeM In Color
484-1047 54.95

New Haven
NH Trackside
484-1010 49.95

484-1086 Trackside Along The New Haven 59.95

New Haven In Color 59.95 ea

484-1107 Volume 1: The Battle For Profits 1945-61 59.95
484-1126 Volume 2: The Struggle for Survival
484-1149 Volume 3: 1961-1968

New York Central
New York Central Lightning Stripes
484-67 Volume 1 45.00
484-165 Volume 2 49.95

NYC Color Guide To Freight And Passenger Equipment
484-228 49.95
484-1151 Volume 2 59.95

New York Central Trackside w/Eugene Van Dusen
484-950 49.95

Michigan Central Trackside w/Emery Gulash
484-1055 54.95

New York Central In Color Volume 1
484-1066 59.95
484-1082 Volume 2 59.95
484-1087 New York Central Facilities In Color 59.95

Trackside along New York Central's Western Division 1949-55
484-1099 59.95

New York, Ontario & Western
NYO&W In Color
484-990 49.95

New York, Susquehanna & Western In Color
484-1072 59.95

Norfolk & Western
N&W In Color
484-988 Volume 1 49.95

Color Guide To Freight And Passenger Equipment
484-1039 54.95

Northern Pacific
Color Guide To Freight And Passenger Equipment
484-963 49.95

Northern Pacific In Color Volume 1: 1949-1959
484-1074 59.95

Pacific Electric
Pacific Electric In Color
484-999 Volume I 49.95

484-1024 Volume II 54.95

Penn Central
Color Guide To Freight And Passenger Equipment
484-948 49.95

Pennsylvania Railroad
Color Guide To Freight And Passenger Equipment
484-968 Volume 2 49.95
484-1071 Volume 3 59.95

Pennsy, Standard Railroad Of The World
484-1018 Volume 1 54.95
484-1045 Series Books Under Pennsy Wires w/James P. Shuman 54.95
484-1052 Trackside On The PRR North Of Washington, DC 54.95
484-1127 Central Pennsylvania 59.95

Pennsy Steam Years
484-1060 Volume 3 54.95

New York Harbor Railroads In Color
484-1049 Volume 1 54.95
484-1082 Volume 2 59.95

Pennsy Electric Years

484-1069 Volume 2 59.95
A photographic journey along Pennsy's electrified lines.

NEW 484-1158 Volume 3 59.95

Pittsburgh & Lake Erie In Color
484-1076 Volume 1: 1976-1992 59.95
484-1136 Volume 2: 1956-1976

Reading
Reading Company In Color
484-1078 Volume 2 59.95

Richmond, Fredericksburg & Potomac
484-1093 Richmond, Fredericksburg & Potomac In Color 59.95

Rutland
484-1103 Rutland In Color 59.95

St. Louis-San Francisco
Frisco In Color
484-961 49.95

Seaboard Air Line
Color Guide To Freight And Passenger Equipment
484-1004 49.95

Soo Line
Soo Line In Color
484-993 49.95

Southern Railway
Southern Railway In Color
484-1013 Volume 2 49.95

Color Guide To Freight And Passenger Equipment
484-977 49.95

Southern Pacific
Southern Pacific In Color
484-1096 Volume 3: Classic Scarlet 59.95

484-1109 Volume 4: The Tunnel Motor Era 59.95

484-1121 Volume 5: Merger and Memories 59.95

Color Guide To Freight And Passenger Equipment
484-1015 Volume 1 49.95
484-1148 Volume 2 59.95

NEW 484-1169 Volume 3 59.95

Official Color Photography
484-1038 54.95

Spokane, Portland & Seattle
Color Guide To Freight And Passenger Equipment
484-945 49.95

458

BOOKS - VIDEOS - RAILROADIANA

Morning Sun Books Inc.

Traction

Pennsylvania Trolleys In Color

484-1022 Volume III: The Pittsburgh Region **54.95**
484-1108 Volume IV **59.95**

Street Car Scenes Of The 1950s In Color
484-1032 **54.95**

New Jersey Trolleys In Color
484-1077 **59.95**

New York City Trolleys In Color
484-1080 **59.95**

California Trolleys In Color Volume 1: San Diego & Los Angeles
484-1081 **59.95**

Boston Trolleys in Color 59.95 ea
484-1117 Volume 1: The North Side
484-1128 Volume 2: The South Side

Great Lakes Trolleys in Color
484-1119 **59.95**

Union Pacific

UP Steam In Color
484-957 **49.95**

UP Trackside
484-1006 **49.95**

Union Pacific Official Photography
484-254 Volume I **49.95**
484-1023 Volume II **54.95**

Color Guide To Freight And Passenger Equipment
484-262 Volume 1 **49.95**
484-986 Volume 2 **49.95**

Union Pacific Diesels In Color Volume 1: 1934-59

484-1105 **59.95**

Union Railroad
URR In Color
484-1056 **54.95**

484-1140 Virginian Railway in Color **59.95**

Wabash
Wabash In Color
484-41 **45.00**

Wabash Trackside With Emery Gulash 1954-74
484-1112 **59.95**

Western Maryland
Trackside with George M. Leilich
484-1075 **59.95**

Western Pacific
Trackside w/Bob Larson
484-1027 **54.95**

Color Guide To Freight and Passenger Equipment
484-1063 **59.95**

Regional Interest
Southern States Trolleys in Color
484-1134 **59.95**

Northern New England Color Guide To Freight And Passenger Equipment
484-233 **49.95**

East Of The Hudson: 1941-1953 w/Bill McChesney
484-949 **49.95**

Chicago 1957-1965
484-1026 **54.95**

Scranton, PA 1952-1976
484-1030 **54.95**

Philadelphia 1945-1969
484-1037 **54.95**

St. Louis 1952-59 w/Jim Ozment
484-1040 **54.95**

Boston 1942-62 w/Lawson Hill
484-1041 **54.95**

Buffalo 1953-1976
484-1062 **59.95**

New York City 1953-1968
484-1065 **59.95**

Allentown, PA 1947-68
484-1067 **59.95**

Sayre-Towanda-Waverly Pa. With Lloyd Hall
484-1095 **59.95**

Frisco/Katy Color Guide To Freight Equipment
484-1100 **59.95**

Pennsylvania Shortlines In Color
484-1104 Volume 1 **59.95**
484-1147 Volume 2 **59.95**

Trackside Series 59.95 ea

Trackside Around Ontario 1955-60
484-1110

Trackside Around Massachusetts 1950-1970
484-1116

Trackside Around the Niagara Peninsula 1953-1976
484-1122

Trackside Around Illinois 1960-1973

484-1123   **59.95**

Trackside Around Atlanta 1955-1975
484-1125   **59.95**

Trackside Detroit Downriver 1946-1976
484-1135 With Emery Gulash

Trackside Along the Boston & Maine 1945-1975
484-1139

Trackside Around Granger Country 1952-1955
484-1131

Trackside Around Cleveland 1965-1979
484-1143

Trackside with EMD Field Representative Casey Cavanaugh 1960-1962
484-1144

Trackside Along the Erie-Lackawanna New Jersey Commuter Zone
484-1146

Trackside in Louisville (East) 1948-1958
484-1152

NOCH

IMPORTED FROM GERMANY BY WALTHERS

NEW PRODUCTS

Catalog
NEW 528-71070 2007 Noch Catalog **TBA**

DVD
NEW 528-71071 2007 Noch DVD **14.99**

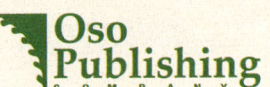

Please visit Walthers Web site at www.walthers.com for a complete listing of all available items.

BOOKS

Railroads

Logging Railroads of Weyerhaeuser's Vail-McDonald Operation

537-1931064059   **49.95**
Logging Railroads of Weyerhaeuser's Vail-McDonald Operation covers the fascinating history of northwest railroad logging. Authors Frank Telewski and Scott Barrett capture the story through research and interviews with Weyerhaeuser employees who share their work in the woods. You'll find a host of imagery inside, including Shay, Climax, Heisler, and rod locomotives—featuring the second largest logging mallet ever built. Also depicted are the powerful steam donkeys and imposing tower skidders Weyerhaeuser used to harvest the massive timbers. 446 Images. Hardbound. 376 Pages.

The MODOC: Southern Pacific's Back Door to Oregon

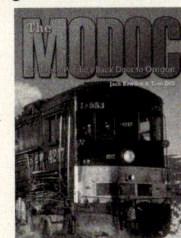

537-1931064091   **49.95**
Noted authors Tom Dill and Jack Bowden give a historical look at SP's shortcut from the Overland line to Oregon: the Modoc Line. This tortuous route was a favorite with railfans, but its remote northeast California location made it difficult to visit. Hardbound, 352 pages.

Railroad Camp Picture Book
537-920698433   **14.95**
Visit logging camps from the past in the woods of the Pacific Northwest. 80 pages of black-and-white photos illustrate the role the railroad played in their success.

Logging Railroads in the Klamath Country

537-1931064113   **49.95**
See great photos and learn lots of information about the logging railroads that run through Southern Oregon's Klamath area. 336 pages.

Vista-Dome North Coast Limited

537-1931064067   **74.95**
Bill Keubler's carefully researched work on the Northern Pacific's luxurious named train.

New Arrivals Updated Every Day! Visit Walthers Web site at

www.walthers.com

BOOKS - VIDEOS - RAILROADIANA

BOOKS

Styrene Fabrication

585-9784 6.00
Fully illustrated handbook by Al Armitage explains simple techniques of building with styrene. Loose-leaf form, 8-1/2 x 11".

CATALOGS

Detailing Parts

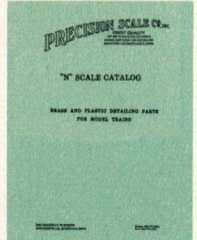

585-9738 N Scale **4.00**
Fully illustrated, includes complete listing of Precision Scale detail parts in each category.

General Use

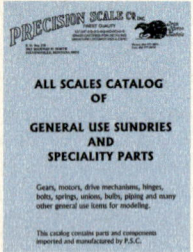

585-9748 **5.00**
Includes all sundries, pipe, wire, bulbs, nuts, bolts, screen, springs, gears, etc.

RailDriver

NEW PRODUCTS

Trailer Hitch Cover

Item listed below is available by Special Order (see Legend Page).

NEW 560-270 Knuckle Coupler Decorative Hitch Cover (rusty dark brown) **39.95**
Now it's easy to pretend you're driving a train. This solid cast aluminum hitch cover looks like a knuckle coupler. Fits either 1-1/4 or 2" receiver. Use for decorative purposes only.

DESKTOP TRAIN CAB CONTROLLER FOR PERSONAL COMPUTER

560-120 RailDriver Desktop Cab Controller **149.95**.
Ever want to sit behind the controls of a real locomotive? The RailDriver Desktop Train Cab Controller lets you run your train simulation games on your personal computer. Features realistic throttle, brake, reverser, and switch controls, plus 34 programmable buttons. The RailDriver supports Microsoft® Train Simulator, TrainMaster™ and Auran Trainz Virtual Railroad Simulator. The control stand measures 13.5 x 7 x 4"
4 x 18 x 10cm—about 1/3 the size of the real thing. The controller requires a USB connection to the PC running your train simulator.
Coming Soon: Add-on control modules for DCC and analog control of model trains.

SOFTWARE

RailDriver reference software brings you hard-to-find books on easy-to-use CD-ROMs. Each book has been scanned, so they are easily navigated like a Web site. While optimized for Microsoft Internet Explorer, the CDs can also be read on other systems including Macintosh.

Cyclopedias 29.95 ea

Railway cyclopedias were used by railroaders for maintenance and modifications. Because the information was supplied by the railroads or their suppliers, everything is accurate, making this information a must for modelers wanting to recreate railroading as it was in the steam era. Also included on each CD is the RailDriver Scale Print Utility (PC only) that makes it easy to enlarge or reduce the drawings and photos to any size.

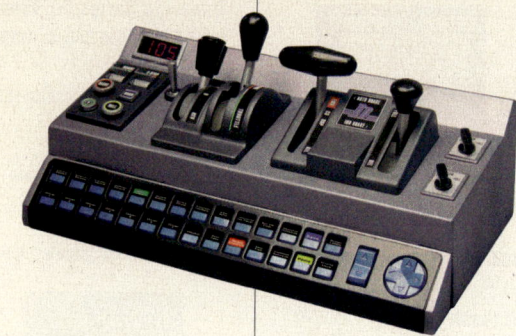

Desktop Train Cab Controller for Personal Computer 560-120

560-90 1922 Locomotive Cyclopedia
560-91 1922 Car Builders Cyclopedia
560-92 1921 Maintenance of Way Cyclopedia
560-93 1911 Electric Railroad (Traction) Cyclopedia

NEW 560-269 1906 Locomotive Dictionary First Edition **29.95**

Train Simulator Expansion Packs

These CD-ROM sets add new routes, features and tools to the Microsoft Train Simulator.

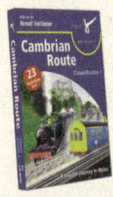

560-135 Cambrian Route **29.99**

560-136   560-137

560-136 Tools 2 Design Your Own Routes **29.99**
560-137 Black Forest Route **29.99**
560-138 Glacier Express **35.99**

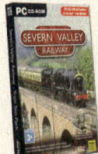 

560-146   560-147

560-146 Severn Valley Route **34.95**
560-147 American Classics **22.95**

BOOKS

Operating Manuals 19.95 ea

Railroaders and mechanics use operating manuals for maintenance and troubleshooting. These reproductions feature interesting information and component photos of the locomotives. They make great gifts for railroaders or great reference for railroad museum operations.

560-194GP38 EMD GP38
560-195SD45 EMD SD45

560-196RS3 Alco RS-3

560-197SF Steam Locomotive Firing

PREISER

Catalog

590-93029 Preiser Catalog **14.99**

VOLLMER

IMPORTED FROM GERMANY BY WALTHERS

Catalog

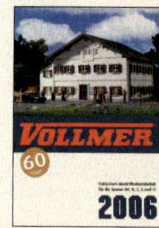

NEW 770-2006 2006 **10.99**
Separate sections for G, HO, N & Z Scale, with measurements for all buildings. Full-color, 8-1/4 x 11-3/4".

WHISTLES UNLIMITED

Wood Train Whistles

753-30 Mini **4.00**
753-20 Junior **4.50**
753-10 Regular **4.95**

RAILROAD AVENUE ENTERPRISES

All books are softcover.

Railroad Stations Of New England

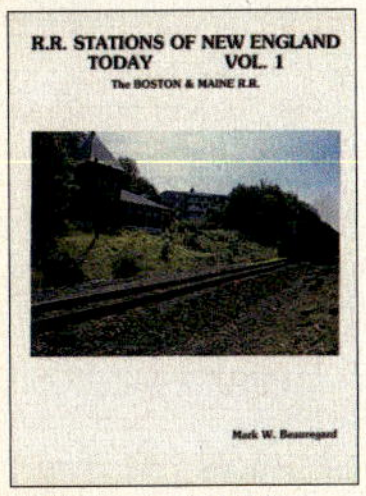

615-5 Volume 1 **4.00**
At the turn of the century, stations were radiant, better kept than many private homes. They were the yardstick by which the public measured and valued individual railroads. 190 B&W photos, 72 pages, 8-1/2 x 11".

Lehigh Valley Passenger Cars

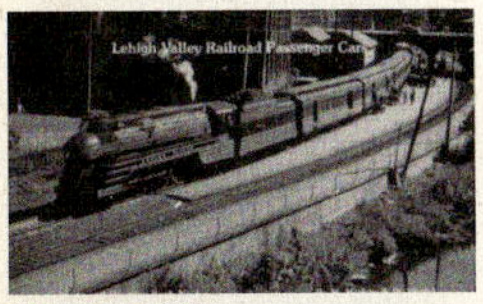

615-6 7.00
Features blueprints redrawn from original LV shop prints. Follows the changes particular cars went through over the years. 64 pages, B&W photos and illustrations.

26 Miles To Jersey City

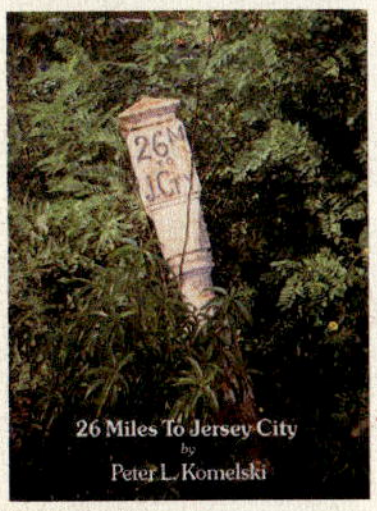

615-7 8.95
Pictorial documents the conditions of stations existing in New Jersey during the early 1970s and early 80s. Focuses on CNJ stations. 62 pages, B&W photos.

The Morristown & Erie Railway

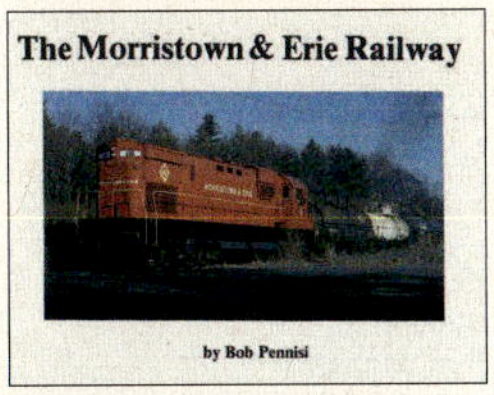

615-9 8.95
Features 48 pages of B&W photography depicting the railroad after its 1982 reorganization which brought it out of bankruptcy.

A Colorful Look At The Chicago & North Western

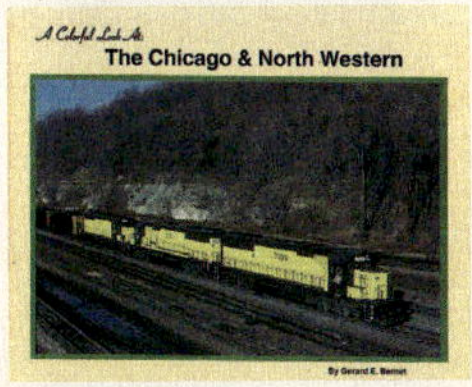

615-19 19.95
Looks at the line from the mid 60s to the UP merger. Includes 80 color photos showcasing a wide range of diesels across the system. 48 pages, full-color.

The Hard Coal Carriers

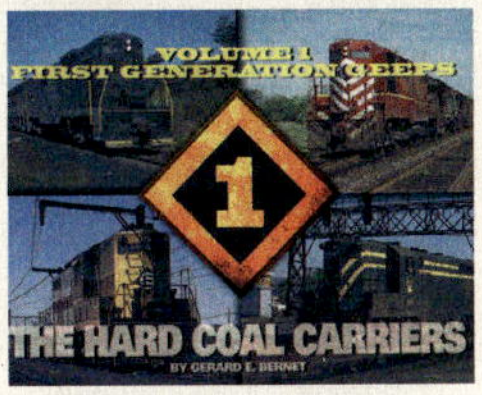

615-14 Volume 1: First Generation Geeps **19.95**
Covers the CNJ, Lackawanna, Erie, EL, LV and RDG.130 photos, 80 pages.

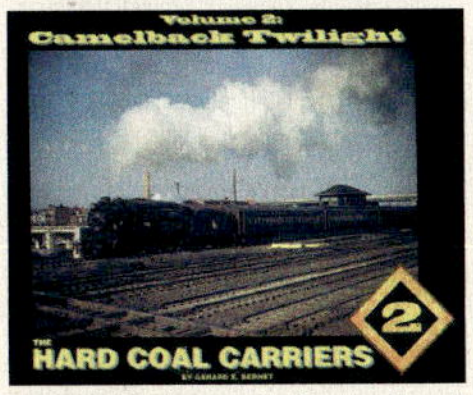

615-16 Volume 2: Camelback Twilight **19.95**
Covers the CNJ, Lackawanna, Erie, Erie Lackawanna, LV and RDG with complete roster information and detail data. 11 color and 119 B&W photos, 80 pages.

Conrail's SD40 & SD40-2

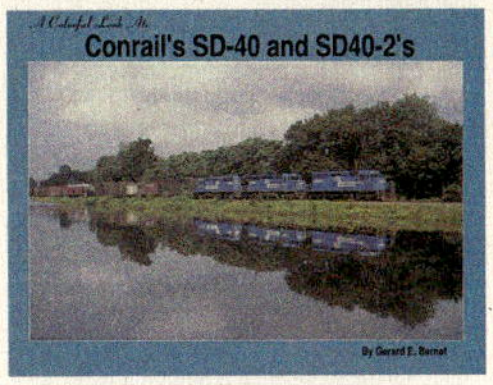

615-17 19.95
Complete roster and specifications. 66 color photos.

Anthracite Country Color

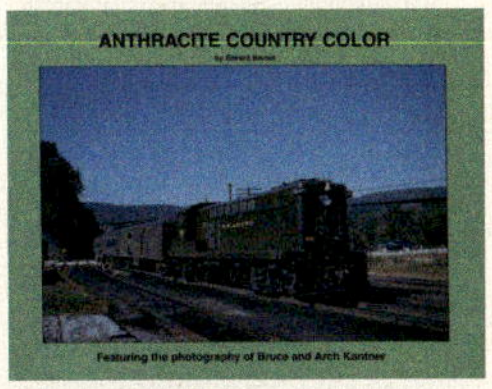

615-20 19.95
Pennsylvania's central coal region during the 1950s. Includes 64 photos from the RDG, CNJ, Pennsy and LV operating in Schuylkill and Carbon County. Lots of steam and early diesels from a by-gone era. 48 pages, full-color.

Diamondbugs

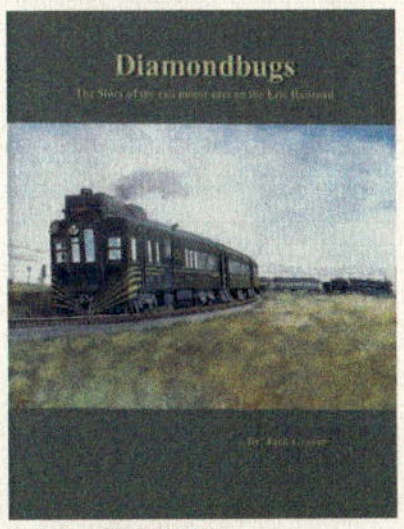

615-21 14.95
Over 80 black and white photos illustrate the evolution of the gas-electrics on the Erie. Also included are diagrams and charts giving a comprehensive look at these cars. 64 pages.

Colorful Memories Of Reading's Shamokin Division

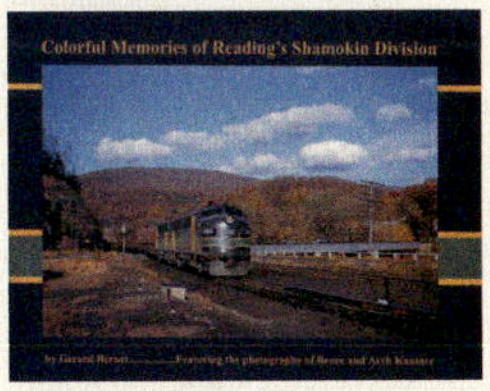

615-22 19.95
Covers the Reading Co. during the steam-to-diesel transition-era with 48 pages of full color.

Latest New Product News Daily! Visit Walthers Web site at
www.walthers.com

Memories Of Eastern Pennsylvania Railroading

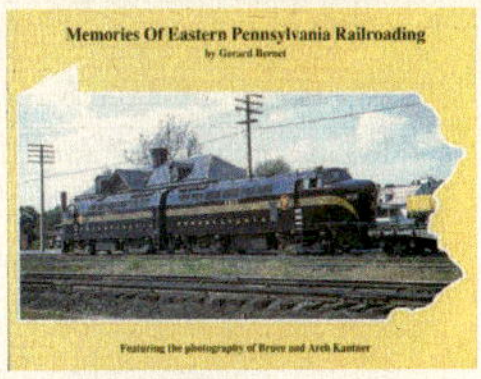

615-23 24.95
Contains photos from the 1950s and 1960s of PRR, LV, CNJ, RDG, EL, Erie and Delaware, Lackawanna & Western. Full-color, 64 pages.

Dutch Country Trolleys

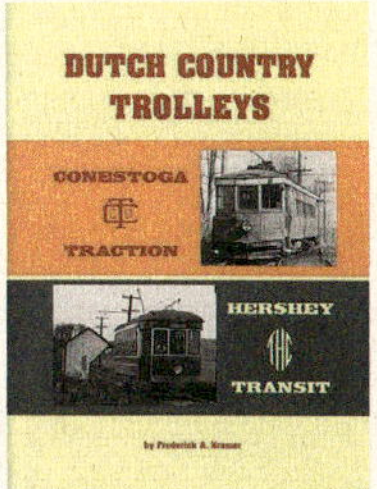

615-24 15.95
Covers the Conestoga Traction Company and the Hershey Transit Company. 64 pages.

Third Avenue Railway: A Cityscape Of Manhattan & The Bronx

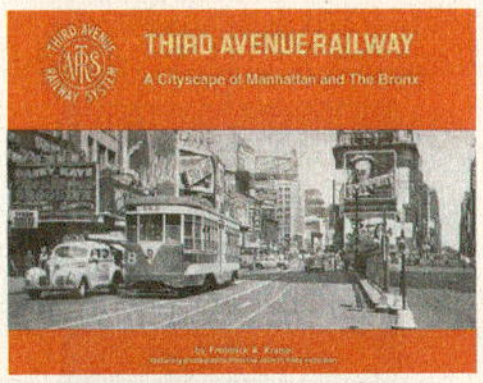

615-25 18.95
Pictorial review of the Third Avenue Railway during the 1940s. Full of nostalgic B&W photos of Manhattan and the Bronx street scenes. 80 pages.

Unifying The Subways

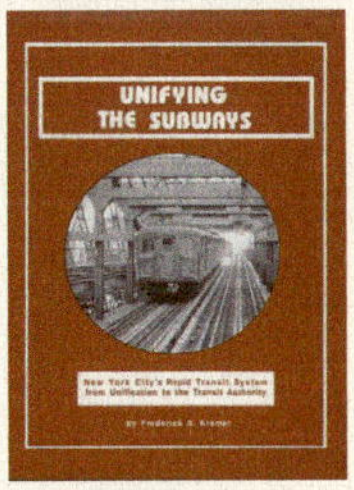

615-26 17.95
Covers New York City Subway System from its unification through the Transit Authority's control. 72 pages, B&W photos. Written by Frederick A. Kramer.

A Colorful Look At The Erie Lackawanna

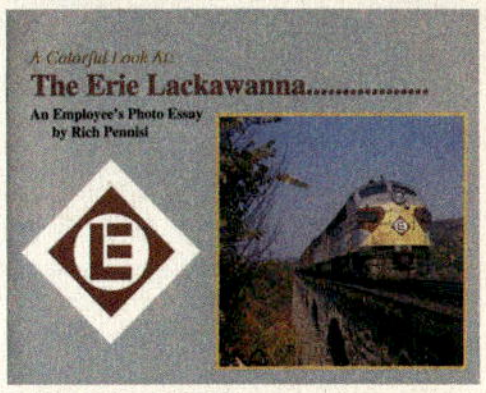

615-27 24.95
A full-color photo essay by an employee of the EL; Rich Pennisi. 64 pages, 8-1/2 x 11".

BQT: The Brooklyn & Queens Transit

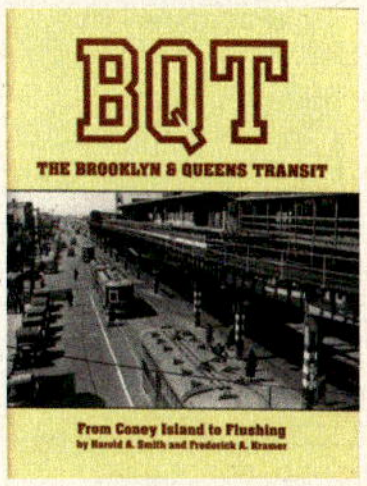

615-28 19.95
Historic review through 1960 featuring numerous, nostalgic B&W photos. 80 pages.

A Colorful Look At Selected Pennsylvania Shortlines

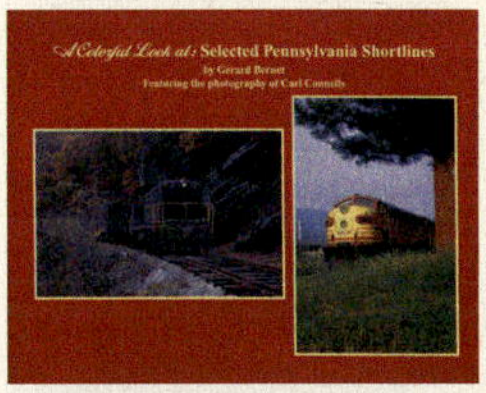

615-29 19.95
Take a look at the work of Carl Connelly as he traveled across the state in pursuit of his hobby during the 1960s and 70s. 48 pages, 90 color photos.

Operation CUT...The First 30 Years (Cleveland Union Terminal)

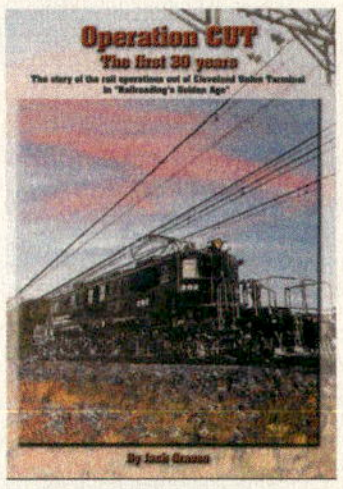

615-30 18.95
Depicts rail operations, both railroad and transit, that ran out of the Cleveland Union Terminal from 1930 to 1960. 72 pages, B&W photography.

BOOKS - VIDEOS - RAILROADIANA

THE RAILROAD PRESS

NEW PRODUCTS

Books

Railroading in Downtown Chicago

NEW 52-38 18.95
Vintage photography featuring Chicago freight and passenger action by Robert P. Olmsted. Includes Monon, PRR, C&NW, EL, CB&Q, C&EI, NYC, B&O, C&O and more!

New York Central Steam on the Harlem and Putnam Divisions

NEW 52-39 19.95
NYC steam photography from 1917 thru 1952 from the collection of Edward L. May, with commentary by Richard Stoving. Most of the images are pre-WWII.

BOOKS

Prototype Railroading

ALCO Reference #1

52-15 29.95
200 black-and-white photos show the locomotives built at the ALCO plant in Schenectady, New York.

Altoona Action

52-18 44.95
Railroading around Horseshoe Curve! Color and black-and-white photos show PRR, Penn Central and CR in the area between the mid-1960s and the mid-1990s.

Anthracite Classics

52-23 19.95
This all-color book covers steam and diesel engines from PRR, RDG, LV and CNJ from the early 1950s to the mid-1960s. 48 pages.

Delaware & Hudson: Thunder & Lightning Stripes

52-21 19.95
All-color look at the D&H, famous for its Alcos and brilliant paint schemes. 48 pages.

Canadian Steam in the Prairies, Towns and Cities

52-33 16.95
Features beautiful black-and-white steam photography, mainly from the 1930s and 1940s, with many surprises— great for modelers of that era! 40 pages, 60 photos, softbound.

Railroaders in the Lehigh River Valley

52-34 24.95
This beautiful book features brilliant photography that gives readers a first-hand look at railroading in this region. It's packed with plenty of images of Alcos, GE's and cabooses.

Hawaiian Railway Album WWII Photos

Volume 1: The Oahu Railway and Land Company in Honolulu

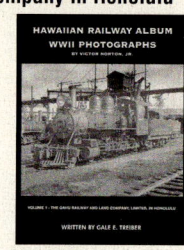

52-20 15.95
Classic black-and-white photographs taken by a WWII serviceman show nearly all the railroad's steam engines and center-cab diesels. 56 pages.

Volume 2: Along the Main Lines of the Oahu Railway & Land Co. and The Hawaii Consolidated Railway

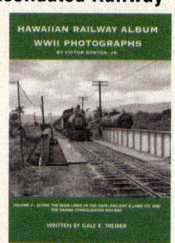

52-35 21.95
This book features plenty of freight and passenger equipment, structure and trackside photos. Includes 13 maps, plus schedules, rosters and more.

Daily New Product Announcements! Visit Walthers Web site at

www.walthers.com

Illinois Central: North of the Ohio River

52-2 59.95
All-color hardcover book covering the IC in depth, with maps, freight schedules and nearly 200 photos of trains, towers and structures. 136 pages.

Chessie System: Cumberland Action

52-16 39.95
All-color book covering the B&O, WM and Chessie in the Allegheny Mountains. Includes roster, track charts. 112 pages.

Freight Equipment of the New York Central, Volume 1: Box Cars, Stock Cars & Reefers

52-24 13.95
Covers from turn-of-the-century wood cars to the modern steel cars of the 1950s and 1960s. 48 pages.

CF7 Locomotives: From Cleburne to Everywhere

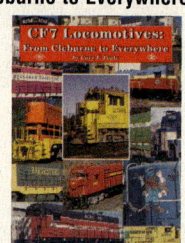

52-12 24.99
Details their conversion from ATSF F-Units. Includes complete roster and dispositions for entire fleet. Hundreds of photos and diagrams. 112 pages.

Wellsboro's Own Railroad
52-31 11.95
An all-encompassing history of the railroad from its humble beginnings in 1859 through its different incarnations. 40 pages.

New England 1930s Steam Action - Worcester

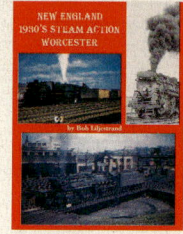

52-17 11.95
Discover the impact of steam power in Massachusetts during the 1930s, from railroads like Boston & Albany, NH, Boston & Maine and Maine Central. 48 pages.

New England Classics, Volume 1
52-22 19.95
An all-color tribute to Boston & Maine, Central Vermont, Maine Central, Bangor & Aroostook and more. 48 pages.

Passenger Cars of New England 13.95 ea
Featuring wooden coaches, milk cars and more. 48 pages.

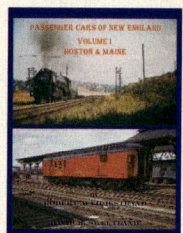

52-28 Volume 1: Boston & Maine

52-29 Volume 2: Bangor & Aroostook/Maine Central

52-30 Volume 3: Central Vermont/Rutland

New York Central Power Along the Hudson 18.95 ea
Packed with plenty of black-and-white photos taken before WWII by noted photographer Ed May, these volumes capture the essence of NYC steam, electric and diesel railroading along the mighty Hudson.

52-36 Volume 1: Harmon

52-37 Volume 2: Oscawana to Albany

BOOKS - VIDEOS - RAILROADIANA

PRR Lines West, Volume 1: Pittsburgh to St. Louis 1960-1999

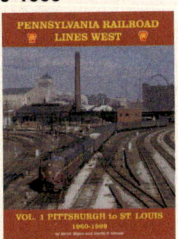

52-19 59.95
Features over 190 color photos of stations, towers and trains from the latter half of the 20th century. Hardcover 136 pages.

Coloring Books

The Alphabet Train Coloring Book
52-26 5.00
Ages 2 through 8.

Railroads in 50 States Coloring Book

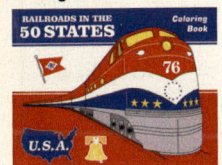

52-25 5.00
Also teaches state capitals, mottos, nicknames and symbols. Ages 6 through 12.

Railroad Learning & Activity Book

52-27 5.95
Features fun activities like word games, connect-the-dots, and matching exercises. Ages 2 through 8.

RK PUBLISHING

NEW PRODUCT
DVDs

NEW 611-20059 Dome Car Magic: A History of Dome Cars DVD **19.95**
From Burlington's 1945 Silver Dome to present-day full-length domes operating in Canada and Alaska, this program chronicles the history of those glamorous sightseeing dome cars. Includes archival footage of the Empire Builder, Super Chief, California Zephyr and more. Produced by award-winner Richard Luckin and hosted by Michael Gross. 26 minutes.

DVDs

Super Chief: Speed, Style, Service

611-20029 24.95
Tells the story of Santa Fe's legendary Super Chief as told through interviews and vintage footage. Long regarded as an icon of America's southwest, this silver speedster was THE way for movie stars and VIPs to travel between Chicago and Los Angeles. Narrated by Michael Gross.

Silver Thread Through The West: The California Zephyr

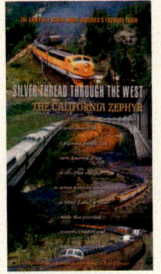

611-20039 24.95
Touted as "America's most talked-about train" the California Zephyr took travelers from Chicago to Oakland/San Francisco in style. It was the flagship of the CB&Q, DRGW and Western Pacific and was known for the spectacular scenery of the Rockies as seen through its domes.

Daylight: The Most Beautiful Train In The World

611-20049 24.95
Flagship of the SP, these colorful speedsters were the preferred way for travelers to get from Los Angeles to San Francisco.

S&S HOBBY PRODUCTS

My Train Coloring Book

643-700 4.49
Fun for kids of all ages. Twenty pages of the many faces of North America's Railroads.

Sandia Software

NEW PRODUCT
DVD

Denver & Rio Grande Multimedia Adventure Kit

NEW 645-11 99.95
The largest collection of Rio Grande information ever assembled into one product. This multimedia product covers D&RG, D&RGW, RGW, RGS, and Moffat lines. Narrow and standard gauge (emphasis on the narrow gauge circle) from 1871 to present. Over 200 Town descriptions with history, USGS maps, yard drawings. Over 3000 images of rolling stock, bridges, buildings, towns, mines, etc. Includes interactive software browser that is fully searchable by keyword, index, or contents. CAD drawings of buildings, bridges, etc. you can view and print to any scale. Hours of high quality MPEG2 video, Slide Shows, Walk Throughs, Sounds, Clip Art, Track Profiles. Complete ebooks: 1922 DRG USGS summary, 1930s travel book, 1925 employee magazines, 1930s rule book, 1950s MOW standard drawings, locomotive catalog, time tables, equipment rosters and more. A must for any modeler or fan of the Rio Grande. System requires a PC running Windows 98 or higher, 1078 x 768 monitor, MPEG2 capability (for videos), DVD player and mouse.

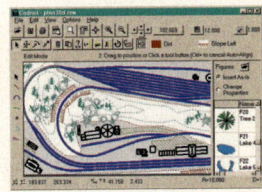 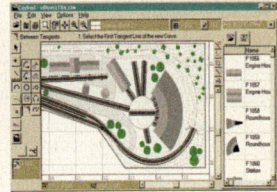

Cadrail
645-3 Version 8 for MS Windows 95 or Higher **99.95**
This powerful CAD program lets you create track plans of any size and shape. Easy-to-use, flexible CAD tools allow you to create complex shapes, snap track sections together, add turnouts, create complex combinations of yard ladders, sidings and crossovers, add your walls and benchwork to the drawing, make a detailed building elevation or trestle template, and make wiring diagrams and track schematics. Auto-alignment tools make it easy to put these items together—just drop one object onto another and the ends automatically come together. Plan, Profile and 3D views let you add elevations to your drawing so you can see things from any angle. You can also run a train on your drawing to get a feel for how your trains will operate. Program allows you to make printouts to any scale, in any unit of measurement and in any device supported by Windows.

Software comes with a 200-page printed manual, interactive computerized help file and extensive libraries with thousands of shapes you can use for things like layouts, buildings, bridges, scenery, track and more. Requires VGA, Mouse, CD-ROM.

BOOKS - VIDEOS - RAILROADIANA

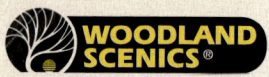

Build a Display For Collectible Houses Video 19.98 ea

Create the magic through this step-by-step, detailed video that teaches you how to build a 31 x 44" 77.5 x 110cm display for your collectible houses. This enchanted scenery display can be shown year-round and modified to fit any table, buffet, TV, dresser, fireplace opening or mantel. You'll learn how to: build a base including different levels using lightweight foam components, install street and house lights into the base and out of sight, learn how to make rocks, hillsides, roads, bushes, trees, streams and a waterfall and complete your masterpiece, landscaping it with Turf and Snow. A pamphlet listing all of the products needed is included, and the one hour video also provides various tips, techniques, ideas and instructions for each product.

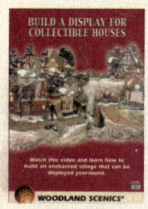 

785-1055 DVD
785-1056 VHS

Model Scenery Made Easy (Video) 24.98 ea

785-973 DVD
785-993 VHS

A comprehensive, detailed account of scenery modeling. Provides helpful information for modelers of any skill level and shows how to do scenery the easy way. Approximately 60 minutes.

SubTerrain: Build A Layout Fast And Easy (Video) 24.98 ea

785-1400 DVD
785-1401 VHS

A step-by-step video that shows you how to build a model railroad layout with the revolutionary SubTerrain Layout System. Approximately 60 minutes.

The Clinic (Video) 24.98 ea

 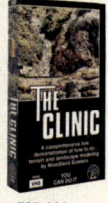

785-970 DVD
785-990 VHS

Learn by watching the professionals demostrate landscaping and terrain modeling techiques. In this video, you'll see just how easy it is. 1 hour and 15 minutes.

SubTerrain Manual

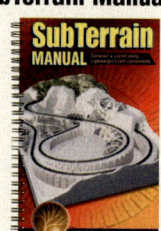

785-1402 7.98
An illustrated how-to manual that teaches you how to create the ideal base for scenery and landscaping from start to finish. Spiral-bound

The Scenery Manual

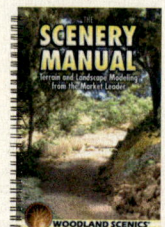

785-1207 10.98
An illustrated start-to-finish guide, with new spiral binding, to terrain construction and landscaping. It is full of basics for beginners and secrets of skilled scenery modelers.

JOIN THE NATIONAL MODEL RAILROAD ASSOCIATION

You may know that the NMRA developed interchange standards for model railroad products. Maybe you've been to a club open house, or heard about regional and national conventions. But there are many other benefits for members.

Whether you invest in a brass loco, a bag of detail parts or a complete kit, you expect to get your money's worth of fun and relaxation from your purchase. A one-year membership is just $45.00, far less than most craft train kits, a brass model or a hardcover book. And the return on your investment, in the form of new friends, knowledge and modeling skills, is priceless.

In today's fast-changing world, the NMRA can help you keep up with your favorite hobby. The monthly "Scale Rails" provides the latest news, along with how-to articles and much more. The Kalmbach Memorial Library, located near the National Headquarters in Chattanooga, Tennessee, houses thousands of articles, books and other reference materials on model and prototype railroading. And, the NMRA is also publishing prototype reference books, in addition to the Data Sheets covering recommended practices.

Whether on a local, regional or national level, you'll be able to meet fellow modelers.

We think you'll agree that it makes good sense to belong to an organization that's doing so much for so many people—and doing it all for fun! Use the application blank below (or make a photocopy) and join today.

Phil Walthers

MEMBERSHIP APPLICATION
NMRA, INC. • 4121 CROMWELL RD. • CHATTANOOGA, TN 37421-2119
Telephone (423) 892-2846 • Fax (423) 899-4869

❑ Regular, One Year $45.00
❑ Regular, Five Year $215.00
❑ Sustaining, One Year $90.00
❑ Student, One Year $30.00
 (Under 25 Years)

❑ Affiliate, One Year . . .(No Scale Rails) .$23.00
❑ Family Member, One Year $9.00
 (Available to Spouse or Minor Child of Member)
❑ Life Membership, Apply to Headquarters Office with date of birth for a quotation.

enclose . . . ❑ Check ❑ Money Order ❑ Charge

Occupation _____
Scale & Gauge _____
Special Interests (include prototype) _____
(U.S. FUNDS ONLY) ❑ NEW ❑ RENEWAL
Name _____
Street _____
City _____
State & Zip _____
Telephone _____

Date of Birth _____
NMRA # (renewals only) _____

Charge to:
❑ American Express
❑ VISA ❑ Master Card ❑ Discover
Expiration Date _____
CARD NUMBER

JW/Revised 3/95

Recommended by **WALTHERS**

Signature _____